SEXUALITY NOW
embracing diversity 3e

JANELL L. CARROLL
University of Hartford

WADSWORTH
CENGAGE Learning

Australia • Brazil • Japan • Korea • Mexico • Singapore • Spain • United Kingdom • United States

WADSWORTH
CENGAGE Learning

Sexuality Now: Embracing Diversity,
Third Edition
Janell L. Carroll

Senior Publisher: Linda Schreiber

Senior Acquisitions Editor: Jaime Perkins

Senior Development Editor:
Kristin Makarewycz

Assistant Editor: Trina Tom

Editorial Assistant: Sarah Worrell

Media Editor: Mary Noel

Marketing Manager: Elisabeth Rhoden

Marketing Assistant: Molly Felz

Marketing Communications Manager:
Talia Wise

Senior Project Manager, Editorial Production:
Pat Waldo

Creative Director: Rob Hugel

Senior Art Director: Vernon T. Boes

Print Buyer: Judy Inouye

Permissions Editors: Audrey Pettengill,
Tim Sisler

Production Service: Dan Fitzgerald, Graphic
World Publishing Services

Text Designer: Terri Wright

Photo Researcher: Roman Barnes

Copy Editor: Graphic World Inc.

Cover Designer: Terri Wright

Cover Images: Scott Kleinman/Digital Vision
RF/Getty Images; insets from top to bottom:
Queerstock RF/Getty Images; Image Source
Pink/Alamy; Derek Blanks/Getty Images;
Thinkstock Images RF/Jupiterimages; Ariel
Skelley/Blend Images RF/Getty Images

Compositor: Graphic World Inc.

For product information and technology assistance, contact us at
Cengage Learning Customer & Sales Support, 1-800-354-9706.
For permission to use material from this text or product,
submit all requests online at **www.cengage.com/permissions.**
Further permissions questions can be e-mailed to
permissionrequest@cengage.com.

Library of Congress Control Number: 2008942749

Student Edition:

ISBN-13: 978-0-495-60274-3

ISBN-10: 0-495-60274-4

Loose-leaf Edition:

ISBN-13: 978-0-495-60499-0

ISBN-10: 0-495-60499-2

Wadsworth
10 Davis Drive
Belmont, CA 94002-3098
USA

Cengage Learning is a leading provider of customized learning solutions
with office locations around the globe, including Singapore, the United
Kingdom, Australia, Mexico, Brazil, and Japan. Locate your local office at
www.cengage.com/international.

Cengage Learning products are represented in Canada by
Nelson Education, Ltd.

To learn more about Wadsworth, visit **www.cengage.com/wadsworth**

Purchase any of our products at your local college store or at our preferred
online store **www.ichapters.com.**

Printed in the United States of America
1 2 3 4 5 6 7 12 11 10 09 08

This book is dedicated to my husband Greg,
who teaches me
new ways to look
at the world every day;
and to Reagan, Kenzie, and Sam,
who reflect the promise of a more
sexually informed tomorrow.

About the Author

A certified sexuality educator with the American Association of Sexuality Educators, Counselors, and Therapists, Dr. Janell L. Carroll received her Ph.D. in human sexuality education in 1989 from the University of Pennsylvania. A dynamic educator, speaker, and author, she has published many articles, authored a syndicated sexuality column, and written two college-level textbooks on human sexuality. Dr. Carroll has traveled throughout the world exploring sexuality—from Egypt's sex clinics, to Tokyo's "love hotels," and Amsterdam's red-light district—and has been instrumental in the development of a television pilot exploring cross-cultural sex. She has lectured extensively, hosted radio talk shows, appeared on numerous television talk shows, and has been quoted in several national publications, Internet news media outlets, and cyber-press articles. Dr. Carroll has also published a popular press book for young girls about menstruation titled *The Day Aunt Flo Comes to Visit.*

On a personal level, Dr. Carroll feels it is her mission to educate students and the public at large about sexuality—to help people think and feel through the issues for themselves. Dr. Carroll's success as a teacher comes from the fact that she loves her students as much as she loves what she teaches. She sees students' questions about sex as the foundation for her course and has brought that attitude—along with her enthusiasm for helping them find answers—to the third edition of *Sexuality Now.*

Dr. Carroll has won several teaching awards, including University of Hartford's Gordon Clark Ramsey Award for Creative Excellence, for sustained excellence and creativity in the classroom, and Planned Parenthood's Sexuality Educator of the Year. Before teaching at University of Hartford, Dr. Carroll was a tenured psychology professor at Baker University, where she was honored with awards for Professor of the Year and Most Outstanding Person on Campus. Dr. Carroll's website (http://www.drjanellcarroll.com) is a popular site for people to learn about sexuality and ask questions.

BRIEF contents

contents

2
 in Video

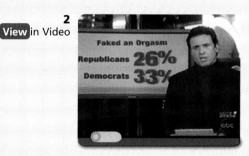

49
View in Video

CHAPTER 3

Communication:
Enriching Your Sexuality 60

© Radius Images/Alamy

62
View in Video

CHAPTER 4

Gender Development, Gender Roles, and Gender Identity 82

98
View in Video

CHAPTER 5

Female Sexual Anatomy and Physiology 114

CHAPTER **6**

Male Sexual Anatomy and Physiology   144

CHAPTER **7**

Love and Intimacy   166

168
View in Video

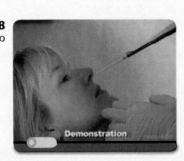

Demonstration

CHAPTER **8**

Childhood and Adolescent Sexuality   190

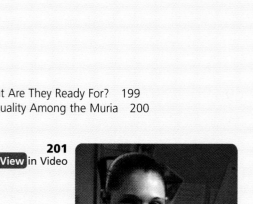

201
View in Video

CHAPTER **11**

Sexual Orientation   278

295
View in Video

Phill Snel/Getty Images

CHAPTER **12**

Pregnancy and Birth 310

313
View in Video

CHAPTER **13**

Contraception and Abortion 344

347
View in Video

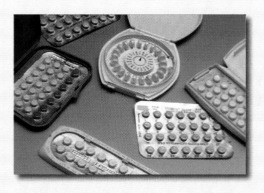

CHAPTER **14**

Challenges to Sexual Functioning   388

© Masterfile

400
View in Video

CHAPTER **15**

Sexually Transmitted Infections and HIV/AIDS   418

© SGO/Image Point FR/Corbis

CHAPTER **16**

Varieties of Sexual Expression   450

© Roger Cracknell 19/Shambhala/Alamy

CHAPTER **17**

Power and Sexual Coercion   478

© Masterfile

489

View in Video

© Atlantide Phototravel/Corbis

CHAPTER **18**

Sexual Images and Selling Sex 508

523

View in Video

preface

Out of all the courses I teach, the human sexuality course is my favorite. Students come to this class with so much interest and enthusiasm—it's hard not to be as excited as they are! My approach to teaching has always been built on the belief that students and teachers have a unique relationship—we teach and learn together. Although it's true that students have much to learn about sexuality, they also are wonderful teachers. I learn a lot in class just by listening to my students open up and share their own experiences, beliefs, and attitudes about sexuality. It is through these conversations with students that I've learned to appreciate where students are today and what their experiences in college are like. I've had many conversations about what they want to know and what causes problems in their relationships. All that I have learned throughout my many years of teaching I bring to you in the third edition of *Sexuality Now: Embracing Diversity*.

For me, the decision to write this book was an easy one. After teaching this course for more than 20 years, I was aware that many textbooks didn't address the experience of today's students. Although I realize that authors include information they think students *need* to know, they often miss teaching what the students *want* to know. I feel strongly that we need to teach students both what they need and want to know. For this reason, I have incorporated a feature called "What Do You Want to Know?" that allows students to find answers to the common questions they have about human sexuality.

Students who come to this course often have high levels of interest, but their experience and knowledge levels vary tremendously. Teaching a course with such varied student experience and knowledge levels can be tricky at best. But that's why it's important to have a textbook that is inclusive and speaks to every student, regardless of his or her experience, family background, knowledge levels, age, race, ethnicity, sexual orientation, or religion. Students have always been the foundation of *Sexuality Now*, and this is even more evident in the third edition of the text.

This new edition of *Sexuality Now: Embracing Diversity* builds on the successes of prior editions and maintains many of the original features. Large-scale changes include a new design and photo program, an increased multicultural and multiethnic focus, and completely updated research with hundreds of new reference citations. There are comprehensive changes in the major areas of sexuality, such as gender, contraception, sexually transmitted infections, sexual orientation, and pornography. You will also find this edition to be more inclusive of gay, lesbian, bisexual, and transgendered students.

New to This Edition

There are many new and exciting changes to the third edition. We have totally reworked the design of the text, updated the majority of figures, and added many new photos throughout the textbook.

In this new edition, each chapter opens with a story, the majority of which are written by college students. These stories specifically pertain to the chapter in which they appear, and each helps draw the reader in to the material. For example, in Chapter 3 ("Communication: Enriching Your Sexuality"), a student writes about the idea that a relationship isn't "real" unless it's on Facebook; in Chapter 4 ("Gender Development, Gender Roles, and Gender Identity"), a man explores his transgenderism and sex change; and in Chapter 15 ("Sexually Transmitted Infections and HIV/AIDS"), a student describes finding out her partner is infected with both genital warts and herpes. All of these changes give the third edition a wonderfully engaging, fresh, and contemporary feel.

As I look over the many changes made to the third edition, I think that one of the most important changes is the increased coverage of cultural, ethnic, gender, and sexual orientation research. This is reflected throughout the textbook in new research studies, figures, features, and photos. New and revised features include the following:

REAL RESEARCH

The third edition continues to explore cutting-edge research in sexuality by including a redesigned feature called "Real Research." Students consistently rate this feature a favorite. It developed out of my experiences in the classroom. I noticed that students loved to learn "fun facts" about sexuality, and they would talk to their friends after class about them. I loved this! My students had become teachers and were taking the facts they had learned outside the classroom. Many long discussions were born out of these fun facts. The majority of "Real Research" features in the third edition include new and cutting-edge research, and they are placed where appropriate throughout the book. Following are some examples of *Real Research* features:

- botanical labial modification; breast pain and sports bras; caffeine, osteoporosis, and fertility problems (Chapter 5, "Female Sexual Anatomy and Physiology")

- birth order and love styles; male height and jealousy (Chapter 7, "Love and Intimacy")

- relationship satisfaction and marijuana use; long-distance relationships; hormones and physical sexual satisfaction; ethnicity and sexual behavior; benefits of male ejaculation (Chapter 10, "Sexual Expression: Arousal and Response")

- gaydar; brain physiology; spatial abilities; handedness and sexual orientation (Chapter 11, "Sexual Orientation")

- morning sickness and breast cancer risk; embryo donation and stem cell research; carbohydrate intake and infertility; ovarian reserve screening tests; marijuana use and fertility; and caffeine and miscarriage (Chapter 12, "Pregnancy and Birth")

- oral contraceptives and sexual desire (Chapter 13, "Contraception and Abortion")

- PTSD and sexual dysfunction; aging and sexual dysfunction (Chapter 14, "Challenges to Sexual Functioning")

- STIs and obesity; STIs and alcohol use, HIV and infectivty (Chapter 15, "Sexually Transmitted Infections and HIV/AIDS")

TIMELINES

Visual representations can often make difficult material easier for students to conceptualize and understand, and for this reason, you will find three new and visually compelling timelines added to this edition. In this edition, there are timelines on the following topics:

- The History of Sexuality
- The Changing Role of Sex on Television
- Important Developments in the History of Sex Research
- Same-Sex Relationships Around the Globe
- The History of Assisted Reproduction
- The History of Contraception

WHAT DO YOU WANT TO KNOW?

Throughout my many years of teaching this course, I have collected thousands of questions about sexuality from students. I have visited colleges and universities all over the world to better understand the questions that college students have today and how these questions might vary within the United States and abroad. My search for these student questions has taken me as far away as Japan, New Zealand, Australia, Egypt, and Europe. I also receive questions about sexuality on my website—http://www.drjanellcarroll.com. Student questions are helpful in understanding what information students need. Examples include, "Can I get HPV from the HPV vaccine?" "Can a woman breastfeed if her nipples are pierced?" and "Can you have an epidural if you have a lower back tattoo?" These types of questions are the backbone of *Sexuality Now*, because they reflect what students want to know.

SEX IN REAL LIFE

In these features, I present information about sexuality that is relevant to everyday life. "Sex in Real Life" explores such concepts as the use of vibrators, sex on television, cell phone usage and sperm production, heterosexual female same-sex behavior on college campuses, and the safety of spermicides, including nonoxynol-9. Many features contain personal voices from students discussing real-life experiences or events.

HUMAN SEXUALITY IN A DIVERSE WORLD

One way students can challenge their assumptions about sexuality is by understanding how attitudes and practices vary across and among cultures, both within the United States and abroad. In addi-

tion to cross-cultural and multicultural information integrated into chapter material, "Human Sexuality in a Diverse World" features present in-depth accounts of topics such as female genital mutilation, ethnicity, religion and circumcision, arranged marriages, same-sex couples, paraphilias, and cultural expressions of sexuality.

CULTURE, GENDER, AND SEXUAL ORIENTATION THEME INDEXES

The third edition contains a multitude of new references and information on issues related to culture, gender, and sexual orientation. The theme indexes on gender and culture are updated in the third edition, and an index on sexual orientation is also a new addition. Look for all of these theme indexes directly following the preface.

OTHER IMPORTANT FEATURES

Throughout each chapter, you will find pronunciation guides to help students understand how to pronounce difficult words—helping to improve student communication about sexuality. Review Questions conclude each major section so that students can test their retention of the material. In addition, a Chapter Summary appears at the end of each chapter to help review important information.

Distinctive Content and Changes by Chapter

CHAPTER 1
Exploring Human Sexuality: Past and Present

This chapter presents an in-depth look at the early evolution of human sexuality, including how sexuality was viewed by ancient Hebrews, Greeks, Romans, and throughout ancient Asian cultures. It also traces sexuality throughout history and examines how Christianity, the Middle Ages, Islam, the Renaissance, the Reformation, and the Victorian era all have affected our views of sexuality. Chapter 1 also explores the impact of slavery, the free love movement, the social hygiene movement, feminism, and queer theory. Chapter 1 includes:

- Two timelines, a newly revised timeline of historical events that helps students understand the changing attitudes and cultural acceptance of sexuality throughout history and a timeline of sex on television, which provides students with an historical overview of how sexuality has been portrayed on television

- An updated section on African American sexuality explores myths about Black sexuality

- A new section reviewing beauty standards, which explores the practice of Chinese foot binding

- A new section on female hysteria and the history of vibrators and another looking at the practice of honor crimes throughout the world

CHAPTER 2
Understanding Human Sexuality: Theory and Research

This chapter contains comprehensive coverage of theories, research methods and issues, and landmark sexuality studies, providing students with the necessary background for understanding the theoretical basis of sexuality research, for evaluating that research, and for sorting out the "pop psychology" that is so prevalent in our society. It contains discussions of changing societal attitudes and how these attitudes have affected sexuality research; classic early researchers and theorists as well as less widely known contributors—particularly female researchers; and modern trends, including Internet-based sexuality research. Chapter 2 includes:

- A review of major research studies, both in the United States and worldwide, from age-specific studies such as the National Survey of Adolescent Males (NSAM) and more recent, broader studies, particularly the Pfizer Global Study of Sexual Attitudes and Behavior and the Durex Sexual Wellbeing Global Study 2007/2008, two of the most comprehensive global studies of sexuality ever done with responses from men and women from all over the globe

- A newly revised visual timeline that reviews important developments in the history of sex research to provide students with an overview of major developments, a summary table of the major theories, and a list of questions that each theorist would ask to help students conceptualize theoretical differences

- Updated section on the popularity of Internet-based sexuality research

- A comprehensive exploration of the future of sexuality research, including a review of problem-driven research and current setbacks by governmental and religious institutions

CHAPTER 3
Communication: Enriching Your Sexuality

In the third edition of *Sexuality Now*, this chapter was moved up to come earlier in the book to emphasize the importance of communication in sexuality. It covers learning to communicate, theories of communication, gender differences in communication, and nonverbal and computer-mediated communication. In addition, at the request of students, an in-depth section on enriching personal sexuality is included. Chapter 3 also includes:

- Streamlined information on gender and communication, including newer research on gender similarities in communication

- Two new comprehensive sections exploring the effects of sexual orientation and communication and culture and communication

- A new section on culture and the self, which explores the impact of individualistic and collectivistic cultures on communication patterns

- An expanded section on computer-mediated communication, including e-mailing, IMing, texting, and chatrooms and the impact of this technology on communication patterns; also explores impact of social networks, such as Facebook and MySpace, on communication

CHAPTER 4
Gender Development, Gender Roles, and Gender Identity

This chapter begins with prenatal sexual development and theories of gender development, which provides a springboard for the nature–nurture debate, including discussion of intersexuality. In addition, this chapter offers a comprehensive look at gender development, gender roles, and gender identity and contains a full review of important psychological theories and a newly designed summary table of the major theories. Chapter 4 includes:

- A newly updated and revised section on varieties of gender and transgenderism

- Updated information on transexualism and sex reassignment surgery, including metoidioplasty, and includes male-to-female and female-to-male reassignment surgery photos

- Revised tables on sex hormones and prenatal sex differentiation syndromes to help simplify and clarify material

- A review of current debate about the use of puberty-delaying drugs in trans-children and explores the use of these drugs both in the United States and abroad

- A review of new research that explores rising U.S. panic about sexual offenders and a growing fear of men and boys

- A new section on gender variations, which explores the various transgendered groupings

CHAPTER 5
Female Sexual Anatomy and Physiology

This chapter contains comprehensive coverage of the female sexual and reproductive system and includes information on diseases and conditions that affect the female reproductive organs—endometriosis, toxic shock syndrome, urinary tract infections, uterine fibroids, vulvodynia, vaginal infections, and the various cancers that affect the female reproductive organs. Chapter 5 includes:

- Full female body nudes to illustrate variation in the female anatomy

- A completely revised section on clitoral anatomy and physiology, including a new review of all the clitoral structures and research on clitoral magnetic resonance imaging

- Updated research on the BRCA1 and BRCA2 genes from the *American Cancer Society: Facts and Figures* (2008)

- Updated information about menstrual suppression through long-term birth control pills, including Lybrel; also explores safety issues related to menstrual suppression

- Up-to-date information on menopause and the use of hormone-replacement therapy

- New figure on obesity and mother's age at menarche

- Information on "green" alternatives to tampons and menstrual pads, including the Diva cup

CHAPTER 6
Male Sexual Anatomy and Physiology

This chapter contains comprehensive coverage of the male sexual and reproductive system and includes information on diseases and conditions that affect the male reproductive organs—testicular torsion, cryptorchidism, priapism, Peyronie's disease, and the various cancers that affect the male reproductive organs. Chapter 6 includes:

- Full male body nudes to illustrate variation in the male anatomy

- Updated circumcision research and statistics

- A new section exploring environmental and dietary causes of decreasing sperm counts and the impact of cell phones, laptops, toxins, and certain foods

- Research on phthalates and the effects on sperm production and male reproductive health

- Updated information on BRCA genes and breast cancer in men

CHAPTER 7
Love and Intimacy

This chapter contains a review of theories of attraction and love, including life-span coverage and cross-cultural ideas of love and attraction. The chapter also addresses the relationship between love and sex, as well as trust, intimacy, respect, jealousy, compulsiveness, and possessiveness. Chapter 7 also includes:

- Expanded information on neuroscience, the major histocompatibility complex, pheromones, and brain imaging and their roles in the development of love

- An updated cross-cultural exploration of intimacy

- Updated information on pheromones and sexual attraction

CHAPTER 8
Childhood and Adolescent Sexuality

This chapter explores physical and psychosexual development and sexual behavior from birth through early and middle childhood, preteen, and adolescent years. The discussion of adolescence also addresses the influence of family, peers, and religion. The second part of the chapter is devoted to sexuality education in the United States and elsewhere, describing various approaches and reviewing social and political influences, heterosexual bias, government mandates, and research measuring the effectiveness of sexuality education programs. Chapter 8 includes:

- Current ongoing governmental research into childhood sexuality, including the National Survey of Family Growth, National Longitudinal Study of Adolescent Males, National Longitudinal Study of Adolescent Health, and the Youth Risk Behavior Surveillance System, with a summary table that shows students the target populations and data methods these four studies used

- An exploration of the impact of ethnicity and race on adolescent sexual behavior

- Current information on adolescents and oral sex

- Updated research on sex education from National Campaign to Prevent Teen and Unplanned Pregnancy's 2007 report titled *Emerging Answers: Research Findings on Programs to Reduce Teen Pregnancy and STDs*

- New figures on sex in high school students, contraceptive use, and pregnancy, birth, and abortion rates by ethnicity and race

CHAPTER 9
Adult Sexual Relationships

This chapter explores dating, cohabitation, marriage, domestic partnerships, same-sex marriage, and divorce, as well as adult sexual relationships such as arranged marriages. It contains up-to-date material on same-sex marriage, including information on recent laws and changes in domestic partnerships and civil unions across the United States, as well as same-sex marriage policies in other countries and recent changes in the legalization of same-sex marriage. Chapter 9 includes:

- Updated information on college hooking up, buddy sex, and casual dating

- Updated information on dating, cohabitation, and swinging

- A completely updated section on same-sex relationships with information on cohabitation, civil unions, domestic partnerships, and same-sex marriage both in the United States and abroad

- A review of the 2008 University of California–Los Angeles report, *Economic Impact of California Same-Sex Marriage Ruling*

- A new timeline illustrating legality of same-sex relationship worldwide, including the new rulings from various U.S. states

- A comprehensive review of research on same-sex divorce

CHAPTER 10
Sexual Expression: Arousal and Response

Beginning with an in-depth look at the importance of hormones in sexual arousal and response, this chapter explores the factors that have been found to affect sexual expression and challenges assumptions about sexual behavior and attitudes. This chapter contains information on the sexual response cycle and research by Masters and Johnson, Helen Singer Kaplan, David Reed, Beverly Whipple, Rosemary Basson, and Leonore Tiefer. A variety of sexual behaviors are reviewed, including foreplay, manual sex, oral sex, masturbation, sexual intercourse, anal sex, and sexual fantasy. Information on physiological changes that occur with age and how these changes affect the sexual response cycle, and thus sexual functioning, is also presented. Chapter 10 includes:

- Updated information on ethnicity/race and sexual behavior

- An updated section on the influence of hormones and neurotransmitters

- A critique of Masters and Johnson's sexual response cycle with research from Beverly Whipple, Rosemary Basson, and Leonore Tiefer

CHAPTER 11
Sexual Orientation

This chapter includes discussions of same-sex parents, transgenderism, and related issues, including our society's tendency toward heterocentrism. This chapter evaluates the biological research (genetics, hormones, birth order, and physiology), developmental theories (Freud, gender-role nonconformity, peer group interaction, and behaviorist theories), sociological theories, and interactional theories. Taking an essentialist and constructivist approach, the chapter provides a comprehensive review and comparison of theories. Chapter 11 includes:

■ A streamlined section on sexual orientation theory, including biological, developmental, sociological, and interactional theories

■ Updated research on the biological theories of sexual orientation, including finger length, brain, and hormone research; inclusion of new research on sexual orientation and magnetic resonance brain imaging and spatial ability

■ Revised and updated information on the ex-gay movements and conversion and reparative therapy

■ Updated research on same-sex parenting and adoption

■ Updated research on homosexual workplace discrimination and hate-crime law

■ Updated research on religion and sexual orientation

CHAPTER 12
Pregnancy and Birth
This chapter reviews conception, sex selection, pregnancy signs, pregnancy testing, problems during pregnancy, and fetal development throughout the trimesters, with information on delivery and problems during the birth process. Chapter 12 includes:

■ A newly revised Timeline of Assisted Reproduction

■ Updated research on pregnancy rates and medical errors involving assisted fertility procedures

■ Updated research on ova cryopreservation and preimplantation genetic diagnosis

■ Updated research on fertility treatments and assisted reproduction for gay, lesbian, and unmarried persons from the American Society for Reproductive Medicine Ethics Committee Report, *Access to Fertility Treatments for GBS and Unmarried Persons*

■ Updated research on same-sex pregnancy, prenatal classes, birth, postpartum depression, and miscarriage

CHAPTER 13
Contraception and Abortion
Contraception and abortion are covered after pregnancy and birth so that students have a clear understanding of hormonal and developmental physiological processes. Information on historical development in contraceptive research and a review of barrier, hormonal, chemical, natural, permanent, emergency, and ineffective methods are included. A review of the abortion debate and surgical and medical procedures is also included. Chapter 13 includes:

■ Research from *Contraceptive Technology* (2007 edition) and a completely updated and revised section on contraceptive options

■ A newly revised Timeline of Contraceptive Methods

■ Updated research on extended birth control use

■ A newly updated section on the safety of nonoxynol-9 spermicide

■ A new at-a-glance comparison of contraceptive methods table providing students with a quick contraceptive comparison

■ Information on the debate to overturn *Humanae Vitae* and lift the Catholic church's ban on contraception

■ New data and figures from Alan Guttmacher Institute's (2008) longitudinal analysis of trends in characteristics of women obtaining abortion

■ Completely updated and revised section on surgical and medical abortion procedures

CHAPTER 14
Challenges to Sexual Functioning
Chapter 14 includes a thorough review of sexual dysfunction, including *Diagnostic and Statistical Manual of Mental Disorders* (4th edition, text revision; *DSM-IV-TR*) information with details on symptoms, causes, and treatment options, as well as a completely revised sexual response cycle section, including critiques by Leonore Tiefer, and includes alternative female models by Rosemary Basson. Also includes a full review of illness, disability, and sexual functioning. Chapter 14 includes:

■ An updated review of sexual dysfunctions with current research and statistics

■ Data from a 2008 nationally representative study of U.S. women on sexual dysfunction and personal distress

■ A consolidation of ejaculatory disorders, including a discussion of retrograde ejaculation

■ A newly designed table summarizing the various sexual dysfunctions

CHAPTER 15
Sexually Transmitted Infections and HIV/AIDS
This chapter contains information on attitudes about sexually transmitted infections and reviews the various infections. A complete review of HIV and AIDS is also included, and a section on the global aspects of AIDS looks at global issues. Chapter 15 includes:

■ Completely revised and updated research on sexually transmitted infections and HIV with statistics from the Centers for Disease Control and Prevention's (CDC) *Sexually Transmitted Disease Surveillance* and the UNAIDS Report on the *Global AIDS Epidemic*

■ Updated recommendations for partners of persons with HIV, syphilis, gonorrhea, and chlamydia from the CDC

■ Revised and updated section on the Gardasil vaccine, including new CDC recommendations, side effects, warning, and controversial vaccine requirements for immigrants

■ Global coverage of the AIDS epidemic, including current information on AIDS vaccines and one-pill-a-day AIDS treatments

■ New cross-cultural feature on AIDS orphans in Africa

Chapter 16
Varieties of Sexual Expression

This chapter explores how sexual behaviors are classified, beginning with a review of typical and atypical sexual behaviors that includes an extensive theoretical explanation of paraphilias, including biological, psychoanalytic, developmental, behavioral, and sociological theories. Chapter 16 includes:

- Updated and revised section on *DSM-IV-TR* diagnoses for paraphilias and sexual addiction

- Revised and updated paraphilia psychopathology, theory, assessment, and treatment section with research from *Sexual Deviance: Theory, Assessment and Treatment* (2nd edition, 2008)

Chapter 17
Power and Sexual Coercion

Beginning with definitions and an overview of rape and sexual assault, this chapter reviews theories of rape. It also examines gender differences in attitudes about rape, rape on campus, date-rape drugs, and the rape of men; offers guidance on reporting and avoiding rape; explores partner reaction to rape; and describes various treatments for rapists. This chapter also reviews the research on the sexual abuse of children, intimate partner violence, and sexual harassment. Chapter 17 includes:

- A new age of consent table with information that includes U.S. and global ages of consent

- Updated research on date-rape drugs, the incidence and effects of rape and sexual abuse, and posttraumatic stress disorder

- A comprehensive discussion of rape on college campuses, using data from the *U.S. Criminal Victimization Statistical Tables,* published by the U.S. Bureau of Justice Statistics

- Current research on the relationship between rape and alcohol use, fraternity membership, and athletics

- Updated research on increases in postrape alcohol consumption and risky sexual behavior

- Updated and revised section on the sexual abuse of children

- Updated research on intimate partner violence in both heterosexual and same-sex relationships, stalking, sexual harassment, and cyber-harassment on college campuses

Chapter 18
Sexual Images and Selling Sex

Chapter 18 presents full historical coverage of erotic representations and the invention of pornography, erotic literature, television and films, advertising, and the sex industry. This chapter reviews the portrayal of minority and gay-lesbian-bisexual sexuality in the media and contains full coverage of prostitution, including definitions, types of prostitution, predisposing factors, and prostitution and the law. Cross-cultural and global coverage reviews prostitution both inside and outside the United States. Chapter 18 includes:

- Research from the most current Henry J. Kaiser Family Foundation study *Sex on TV4,* which identifies and analyzes sex on television

- Updated research on online and portable pornography and pornography on cell phones, iPods, and other devices

- Updated research on adolescents, Internet filters, and exposure to pornography

- Updated research on gender differences in pornography exposure and usage

- Increased coverage of global prostitution and trafficking

Supplements to Help Teach the Course

CENGAGENOW™

www.cengage.com/login

CengageNOW™ for Carroll's *Sexuality Now: Embracing Diversity* offers teaching and learning resources in one intuitive program organized around the essential activities that instructors perform for class—lecturing, creating assignments, grading, quizzing, and tracking student performance. For students, **CengageNOW** *Personalized Study* is a diagnostic tool consisting of chapter-specific resources, including a personalized study plan. Because students focus on what they don't know, they learn more in less time to get a better grade. Students work through learning modules featuring animations, videos, and pages from the **Cengage Learning eBook,** an interactive online version of the text.

Special Resources in CengageNOW for *Sexuality Now:*

- **The Cengage Learning eBook**—an interactive version of the text

- **The Virtual Safer-Sex Kit,** featuring information about contraception, how to avoid sexually transmitted infections (STIs), and the pros and cons of many devices

- **Animations** of the sexual response cycle

- **Videos** on a variety of human sexuality topics

- **"What Do You Want to Know?"** questions with audio student responses

Learn more at **http://www.cengage.com/tlc/.**

WEBTUTOR™

Jumpstart your course with customizable, rich, text-specific content within your Course Management System. Save time building or Web-enhancing your course, posting course materials, incorporating multimedia, tracking progress, and more with this customizable, engaging course management tool. WebTutor saves you time and enhances your students' learning—pairing advanced course management capabilities with text-specific learning tools. View a demo at **http://www.cengage.com/tlc/.**

POWERLECTURE™

With ExamView® and JoinIn™ Student Response System
0-495-80504-1

The fastest and easiest way to build powerful, customized media-rich lectures, PowerLecture assets include chapter-specific Power-Point presentations written by Aaron Goetz of California State University of Fullerton, animations and videos, instructor manual, test bank, and more. Included in this edition of the PowerLecture:

■ Images of various types of sex toys

■ Animations and panel-discussion videos

■ Centers for Disease Control and Prevention STD Clinical Slides to supplement your lectures on sexually transmitted infections

■ Animations of the sexual response cycle for lectures of biological processes

Also included on the PowerLecture is the ability to quickly create customized tests that can be delivered in print or online with Exam-View® Computerized Testing. ExamView's simple "what you see is what you get" interface allows you to generate tests of up to 250 items easily. All test bank questions are electronically preloaded.

Turn your lecture into an interactive experience for your students, using "clickers." The JoinIn™ Student Response System allows you to transform your classroom and assess your students' progress with instant in-class quizzes and polls. Pose book-specific questions and display students' answers seamlessly within the Microsoft® PowerPoint® slides of your own lecture, in conjunction with the "clicker" hardware of your choice. Enhance your students' interactions with you, your lecture, and each other. The "JoinIn content for Carroll" includes questions specifically written to accompany the Virtual Safer-Sex kit and Centers for Disease Control and Prevention STD Clinical Slides. Students can also "participate" in polls and surveys from the text. Contact your local Cengage Learning representative to learn more.

STUDY GUIDE

0-495-80506-8

Written by Shirley Ogletree of University of Texas–San Marcos, the Study Guide chapters contain a chapter summary, a list of learning objectives, a detailed chapter outline, personal assessments and activities, writing assignments, 15 fill-in-the-blank and 5 short-answer questions per main subhead, labeling of anatomic art in appropriate chapters, and a post-test consisting of 10 true/false, 30 multiple-choice, and 10 matching quiz questions covering the entire chapter. The answers, rejoinders, and main text page references for all quiz items will be included at the end of each chapter.

BOOK COMPANION WEBSITE

www.cengage.com/psychology/carroll

There is a substantial collection of online resources, featuring:

■ A Practice Quiz with online scoring for each chapter, including multiple-choice, true-false, and short essay questions, as well as a final exam

■ Chapter outlines and objectives

■ An online Pronunciation Glossary of all margin terms from the main text

■ Web links, flash cards, and InfoTrac® College Edition activities

INSTRUCTOR'S MANUAL WITH TEST BANK

0-495-80505-X

This comprehensive, easy-to-customize three-ring binder gives you all the support you need to run an effective course, including the *Instructor's Manual* written by Teri Tomatich of Highland Community College and Pierce College, which contains:

■ A comprehensive film and video guide that provides extensive listings of what Wadsworth provides as well as descriptions of suggested videos with their running times and suppliers

■ A resource integration guide that shows, at a glance, how all of this text's supplements can be used with each chapter of the text

■ A detailed outline for each chapter of the text

■ Two to four classroom activities or demonstrations per text chapter, some of which use websites and other resources

■ Two questions designed for online discussions and two to five additional annotated Web links per text chapter

■ Opposing Viewpoints Resource Center activities and writing assignments

■ Lecture and discussion tie-ins for "Real Research" and "What Do You Want to Know?" topics that get students to think critically about sexuality.

Test Bank, written by Tori Bovard of American River College, features 50 multiple-choice questions, 15 true/false items, and 8–15 short-answer/essay questions for every chapter of the text. Answers, with text page references and cognitive level, are provided for all items.

Note to the Student

Campus life is different today from what it was when I was in college. For one thing, you have cell phones and the Internet. Instant messaging, chatrooms, cyber-relationships, and text messaging weren't around when I was in college. Both cell phones and the Internet have had an impact on your views and attitudes about sexuality. I often overhear my students deciphering and explaining their IMs from various friends and lovers. We also didn't have VCRs, DVDs, iPods, or iPhones, so, unlike the majority of students today who tell me they've seen at least one pornographic tape, we never watched any in college. Times were different—we communicated in person or via telephone, and we didn't have emergency contraception, watch reality television, or know what a Brazilian wax was!

College *is* different today and college textbooks need to reflect these changes. The book you are holding in your hands is contemporary and fun. I think you'll find it easy to keep up with the reading in this class because I've really worked hard to keep the material fresh and thought-provoking. I've included lots of personal stories from students just like you to help in your exploration and understanding of human sexuality. The result is a book that talks to students like yourself, answering questions *you* have about sexuality.

As you read through the book, if you have any questions, thoughts, or opinions you'd like to share with me, I'd love to hear from you. Many students e-mail me and suggest additions, changes, or just share their thoughts about this book. You can e-mail me at jcarroll@hartford.edu, or contact me through my website, http://www.drjanellcarroll.com. You can also send snail mail to Dr. Janell L. Carroll, University of Hartford, Department of Psychology, 200 Bloomfield Avenue, West Hartford, CT 06117.

Acknowledgments

Undertaking a book such as this is a huge task and one that I could never have done without the help of many smart, creative, and fun people. Recognition should first go to all my students who, over the years, have opened themselves up to me and felt comfortable enough to share intimate, and sometimes painful, details of their lives. I know that their voices throughout this book will help students truly understand the complexity of human sexuality.

Second, and of equal importance, a big thank you goes to my family, who helped me pull off this new edition. I couldn't have done it without their support and encouragement. They understood my crazy schedule and worked hard to help make life manageable in our household. My husband was an endless support who allowed me to constantly interrupt him for statistical and mathematical clarifications. My children also helped me pull this together and through the process have continued to learn—I am certain they will all grow up with a true understanding of the importance of sexuality in their lives. As in all projects of such magnitude, there are hundreds of others who supported me with friendship, advice, information, laughter, and a focus on the "big picture."

The third edition of *Sexuality Now* is truly the result of a team effort—and the team was fantastic. Jaime Perkins, my senior editor on this third edition, deserves a big thank you for his determination to help make *Sexuality Now* all it could be. Kristin Makarewycz, my developmental editor, was the backbone of this project and her name could legitimately appear on the cover. She was relentless in her pursuit of research and was invested in making the third edition of *Sexuality Now* the best one yet. She made it (almost) painless! I will truly look forward to many years of revision work with Jaime and Kristin. My original senior editor, Marianne Taflinger, who left Cengage Learning to pursue her own dreams, was an integral piece of both the first and second editions. Her fingerprints will always remain a part of *Sexuality Now*. I also thank Kim Russell, executive marketing manager, who was always

thinking of ways to get *Sexuality Now* out there and ahead of the pack. Dan Fitzgerald, editorial production manager at Graphic World, and Mary Noel, content project manager at Wadsworth/Cengage Learning, did a superb job of managing all the production details calmly and creatively. I also appreciate the efforts of Roman Barnes, our awesome photo researcher, who made an art of finding just the right images with very little direction, and Elizabeth Budd for her detailed eye during copyedit. Vernon Boes (senior art director) and Terri Wright (designer) were instrumental in creating the book's inviting design. I also thank Amy Cohen (media editor), Trina Tom (assistant editor), Sarah Worrell (editorial assistant), and Liz Rhoden and Molly Felz in marketing for all their hard work. You guys are the best. I will look forward to a long and productive relationship with everyone at Wadsworth/Cengage Learning.

A special thanks to Karen Hicks, Robin McHaelen, and Regan Gurung for their expert reviews and suggestions to this new edition, and to all the professors using this textbook who shared feedback and offered suggestions. Also, a big thank you to my research assistant, Lisa Belval, who was an enormous support throughout the revision process. I am so grateful to many others who so willingly gave their time or support (or both), especially students Danielle Antolini, Greg Betz, Amanda Dillman, Sarah Donihe, Rachel Gearhart, Jillian Goldberg, Kayleigh Ingraham, Alan Kelley, Jason Kobelski, Fred Langford, Caitlin Massey, Kris Rochette, Amanda Sais, Kyle Simmons, Julia Weston, and Christianne Wolfson. Also thank you to my colleagues and friends, without whom this would not have been possible, including Kim Acquaviva, Genevieve Ankeny, Audrey Conrad, Barbara Curry, Keith D'Angelo, Teo Drake, Angela Hanlon, David Holmes, Peg Horne, Will Hosler, Petra Lambert, Lisa Lepito, Carole Mackenzie, Megan Mahoney, Laura Saunders, Maryann Schuppe, Bill Stayton, Toby, Peterson Toscano, and the Tsacoyeanes family.

Finally, I also want to thank Maxine Effensen Chuck and Paul Root Wolpe whose early work helped lay some of the groundwork for this textbook. I am grateful to both for their past contributions and continued support of this textbook.

Reviewers

It is important to acknowledge the contributions of the reviewers who have carefully read my manuscript and offered many helpful suggestions. I would like to thank them all for their time and dedication to this project.

THIRD EDITION
REVIEWERS

Kristin Anderson, Houston Community College; Sheryl Attig, University of Arizona; Janice Bass, Plymouth State University; Dorothy Berglund, Mississippi University for Women; Rebecca L. Bosek, University of Alaska, Anchorage; Glenn Carter, Austin Peay State University; Jane Cirillo, Houston Community College–Southeast; Kristen Cole, San Diego City College; Lorry Cology, Owens Community College; Randolf Cornelius, Vassar College; Nancy P. Daley, University of Texas at Austin; Christine deNeveu, National Louis University–Chicago; Edward Fliss, Saint Louis Community College; Joyce Frey, Pratt Community College; Irene Frieze, University of

Pittsburgh; George Gaither, Ball State University; Debra L. Golden, Grossmont College; Shelley Hamill, Winthrop University; Michelle Haney, Berry College; Helen Hoch, New Jersey City University; Jean Hoth, Rochester Community and Technical College; Jennifer Hughes, Agnes Scott College; Bobby Hutchison, Modesto College; Ethel Jones, South Carolina State University; Michael Kelly, Henderson State University; Gloria Lawrence, Wayne State College; Genevieve Martinez Garcia, George Washington University; Jennifer McDonald, Washington State University; Robert Morgan, University of Alaska, Fairbanks; Jennifer Musick, Long Beach City College; Shirley Ogletree, Texas State–San Marcos; Peggy Skinner, South Plains College; Cassandra George Sturges, Washtenaw Community College; Silvea Thomas, Kingsborough Community College; Karen Vail-Smith, East Carolina University; Laurie M. Wagner, Kent State University; Glenda Walden, University of Colorado–Boulder; Michael Walraven, Jackson Community College; Andrew Walters, Northern Arizona University; Tanya Whipple, Missouri State University; Julie Wilgen, University of Delaware; Amanda Woods, Georgia State University; Patty Woodward, Sacramento State University; Lester Wright, Western Michigan University; Susan Wycoff, California State University, Sacramento; Lynn Yankowski, Maui Community College

THIRD EDITION
SPECIALIST REVIEWERS

Regan A. R. Gurung, University of Washington; Karen M. Hicks, Lehigh University; Robin P. McHaelen, University of Connecticut

SECOND EDITION
REVIEWERS

Katherine Allen, Virginia Polytechnic Institute and State University; Glenn Carter, Austin Peay State University; Cindi Ceglian, South Dakota State; Nancy Daley, University of Texas; Joe Fanelli, Syracuse University; Jorge Figueroa, University of North Carolina, Wilmington; Anne Fisher, New College of Florida; Lois Goldblatt, Arizona State University; Helen Hoch, New Jersey City University; Susan Horton, Mesa Community College; Alicia Huntoon, Washington State University; Bobby Hutchison, Modesto Junior College; Ingrid Johnston-Robledo, SUNY at Fredonia; Jody Martin de Camilo, St. Louis Community College, Meramec; Laura Miller, Edinboro University; Jennifer Musick, Long Beach City College; Robin Musselman, Lehigh Carbon Community College; Shirley Ogletree, Texas State University, San Marcos; Lisabeth Searing, University of Illinois, Urbana–Champaign; Kandy Stahl, Stephen F. Austin State University; Dana Stone, Virginia Polytechnic Institute and State University; Karen Vail-Smith, East Carolina University; Mary Ann Watson, Metropolitan State College of Denver; Tanya Whipple Missouri State University; Susan Wycoff, California State University, Sacramento

SECOND EDITION
SPECIALIST REVIEWERS

Talia Ben-Zeev, University of California, San Francisco; Leah Millheiser Ettinger, Stanford University; Vicki Mays, University of California, Los Angeles; Cheryl Walker, University of California, Davis

FIRST EDITION
REVIEWERS

Michael Agopian, Los Angeles Harbor College; Veanne Anderson, Indiana State University; Amy Baldwin, Los Angeles City College; Sharon Ballard, East Carolina University; Jim Backlund, Kirtland Community College; Sally Conklin, Northern Illinois University; David Corbin, University of Nebraska, Omaha; Michael Devoley, Northern Arizona University; Jim Elias, California State University, Northridge; Sussie Eshun, East Stroudsburg University; Linda Evinger, University of Southern Indiana; Randy Fisher, University of Central Florida; Sue Frantz, Highline Community College; David Gershaw, Arizona Western College; Lois Goldblatt, Arizona State University; Anne Goshen, California Polytechnic State University, San Luis Obispo; Kevin Gross, East Carolina University; Gary Gute, University of Northern Iowa; Shelley Hamill, Winthrop University; Robert Hensley, Iowa State University; Roger Herring, University of Arkansas, Little Rock; Karen Hicks, CAPE; Karen Howard, Endicott College; Lisa Hoffman-Konn, The University of Arizona; Kathleen Hunter, SUNY College at Brockport; Shelli Kane, Nassau Community College; Joanne Karpinen, Hope College; Chrystyna Kosarchyn, Longwood College; Holly Lewis, University of Houston–Downtown; Kenneth Locke, University of Idaho; Betsy Lucal, Indiana University, South Bend; Laura Madson, New Mexico State University; Sue McKenzie, Dawson College; Mikki Meadows, Eastern Illinois University; Corey Miller, Wright State University; Carol Mukhopadhyay, San Jose State University; Jennifer Musick, Long Beach Community College; Missi Patterson, Austin Community College; Julie Penley, El Paso Community College; Robert Pettit, Manchester College; Judy Reitan, University of California, Davis; William Robinson, Purdue University Calumet; Jeff Wachsmuth, Napa Valley College; Mary Ann Watson, Metropolitan State College of Denver; Kelly Wilson, Texas A&M University; Midge Wilson, DePaul University

FIRST EDITION
SPECIALIST REVIEWERS

In-depth reviewers of Chapter 15, "Sexually Transmitted Infections and HIV/AIDS": Thomas Coates, University of California San Francisco AIDS Research Institute; and Linda Koenig, Centers for Disease Control and Prevention

In-depth reviewer of Chapter 12, "Pregnancy and Birth," and Chapter 13, "Contraception and Abortion": Valerie Wiseman, University of Connecticut Medical Center, Department of Obstetrics and Gynecology

FIRST EDITION
FOCUS GROUP PARTICIPANTS

Also thanks to all the Focus Group participants, including Jonathan Karpf, San Jose State University; Jennifer Musick, Long Beach City College; Lisa Schwartz, St. Joseph's College; Beverly Whipple, Rutgers University; Kathie Zaretsky, San Jose State University.

CULTURE index

GENDER index

SEXUAL ORIENTATION index

Exploring Human Sexuality: Past and Present

I magine you're a young woman in the late 1800s getting ready for your wedding day. What would you be thinking as you prepare for the big day? Following are some excerpts from an 1894 booklet for young brides.

To the sensitive young woman who has had the benefits of proper upbringing, the wedding day is, ironically, both the happiest and most terrifying day of her life. On the positive side, there is the wedding itself, in which the bride is the central attraction in a beautiful and inspiring ceremony, symbolizing her triumph in securing a male to provide for all her needs for the rest of her life. On the negative side, there is the wedding night, during which the bride must pay the piper, so to speak, by facing for the first time the terrible experience of sex.

At this point, dear reader, let me concede one shocking truth. Some young women actually anticipate the wedding night ordeal with curiosity and pleasure! Beware such an attitude! A selfish and sensual husband can easily take advantage of such a bride. One cardinal rule of marriage should never be forgotten: GIVE LITTLE, GIVE SELDOM, AND ABOVE ALL, GIVE GRUDGINGLY. Otherwise what could have been a proper marriage could become an orgy of sexual lust.

Most men, if not denied, would demand sex almost every day. The wise bride will permit a maximum of two brief sexual experiences weekly during the first months of marriage. As time goes by she should make every effort to reduce this frequency. Feigned illness, sleepiness, and headaches are among the wife's best friends in this matter. Arguments, nagging, scolding, and bickering also prove very effective if used in the late evening about an hour before the husband would normally commence his seduction. A good wife should expect to have reduced sexual contacts to once a week by the end of the first year of marriage and to once a month by the end of the fifth year of marriage (Smythers, 1894).

◁ Opposite: amana productions inc./Getty Images

s a young bride, are you nervous about your wedding night? As a young groom, what do you think your future wife might be thinking? Do you think couples enjoyed a healthy sex life during the Victorian age? Welcome to the study of human sexuality! Many students come to this class believing they already know everything they need to know about human sexuality. The truth is, we all come to this class with differing levels of knowledge. Some students have parents who provided open and honest conversation about **sexuality,** whereas others had parents who never spoke a word about sex. Some students had various levels of sex education in school, whereas others bring knowledge gained from years of watching scrambled porn on cable television. In the end, it doesn't really matter what knowledge level you bring into this class. I guarantee that you will leave with plenty more.

Many people believe that we don't need to be taught about human sexuality—we just know everything we need to know. It might surprise you to know that most of sexuality is learned. We learn from culture and society, our family, friends, romantic partners, religion, and many other sources. Our exposure is augmented by the fact that we live in a sex-saturated society that uses sexuality to sell everything from cologne to cars. However, we also live in a time when there is a taboo against good, honest informa-

tion about human sexuality. Some people believe that providing sexuality information can cause problems—including increased teenage sexual activity and adolescent pregnancy rates. Others believe that learning about sexuality can empower people to make healthy decisions both today and in the future.

Many recent events have profoundly affected the way we view sexuality. From the advent of birth control pills that eliminate menstrual periods to ongoing debates about the legality of same-sex marriage, newspapers are full of stories relating to our sexuality and relationships with others. These stories tell us much about how our culture understands, expresses, and limits our sexuality. The continuing controversy over whether young girls should have mandatory vaccines for **sexually transmitted infections (STIs)** or whether children should be allowed to obtain birth control pills from the school nurse in middle school, along with ever-increasing chlamydia rates on college campuses, all influence and shape our sexuality.

sexuality
A general term for the feelings and behaviors of human beings concerning sex.

sexually transmitted infection (STI)
Infection that is transmitted from one person to another through sexual contact. This used to be called sexually transmitted disease (STD) or venereal disease (VD).

Exploring Human Sexuality: Past and Present ■ **1**

REALResearch > Virginity was of little value before the Middle Ages, but it became very important between the 4th and the 15th centuries when dowries and family integrity became increasingly important (CHERULLI, 2004).

If a vaccine offered protection from future sexually transmitted infections but you had to have it by age 11, would you want your daughters (or sons) to have it? Why do you think some parents might say no?

In this opening chapter, we define sexuality, examine sexual images in our culture, and explore the effect of the media's preoccupation with sex. A historical exploration of sexuality follows, in which we review the early evolution of human sexuality beginning with the impact of walking erect to ancient civilizations. Following that, we look at religion's role in sexuality and examine some of the early sexual reform movements. Finally, we take a look at modern developments and influences that continue to shape our sexuality today.

Human Sexuality in a Diverse World

Human sexuality is grounded in biological functioning, emerges in each of us as we develop, and is expressed by cultures through rules about sexual contact, attitudes about moral and immoral sexuality, habits of sexual behavior, patterns of relations between the sexes, and more. In this section, let's look at how we define sexuality and discuss how our sexuality is affected by the media and changing technologies.

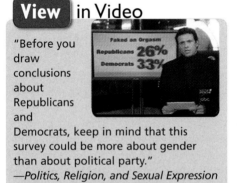

View in Video

"Before you draw conclusions about Republicans and Democrats, keep in mind that this survey could be more about gender than about political party."
—*Politics, Religion, and Sexual Expression*
To view go to CengageNOW at www. cengage.com/login

ONLY HUMAN:
WHAT IS SEXUALITY?

The sexual nature of human beings is unique in the animal kingdom. Although many of our fellow creatures also display complex sexual behaviors, only human beings have gone beyond instinc-

tual mating rituals to create ideas, laws, customs, fantasies, and art around the sexual act. In other words, although sexual intercourse is common in the animal kingdom, sexuality is a uniquely human trait.

Sexuality is studied by **sexologists,** who specialize in understanding our sexuality, but also by biologists, psychologists, physicians, anthropologists, historians, sociologists, political scientists, those concerned with public health, and many other people in scholarly disciplines. For example, political scientists may study how sexuality reflects social power; powerful groups may have more access to sexual partners or use their legislative power to restrict the sexual behaviors of less powerful groups.

Few areas of human life seem as contradictory and confusing as sexuality. We come from a society that is often called sexually "repressed," yet images of sexuality are all around us. We tend to think that everyone else is "doing it"; still, we are often uncomfortable talking about sex. Some feel that we should all be free to explore our sexuality; others believe that there should be strong moral restrictions around sexual behavior. To some, only sex between a man and a woman is natural and acceptable; others believe that all kinds of sexual expression are equally "natural" and valid. Many people find it puzzling that others find sexual excitement by being humiliated or spanked, exposing themselves in public, or wearing rubber. Although parents teach their children about safe driving, fire safety, and safety around strangers, many are profoundly uncomfortable instructing their children on safe sexual practices.

SEX SELLS:
THE IMPACT OF THE MEDIA

Modern life is full of visual media. Magazines, newspapers, book covers, CD and DVD packaging, cereal boxes, and food products are adorned with pictures of people, scenes, or products. Advertisements peer at us from billboards, buses, cell phones, iPods, and anywhere else that advertisers can buy space. Television, movies, computers, and other moving visual images surround us almost everywhere we go, and we will only depend on them more as information technology continues to develop. We live in a visual culture with images we simply cannot escape.

Many of these images are subtly or explicitly sexual. Barely clothed females and shirtless, athletic males are so common in ads that we scarcely notice them anymore. The majority of movies today, even some of those directed at children, have sexual scenes that would not have been permitted in movie theaters 50 years ago. The humor in television situation comedies has become

sexologist
A person who engages in the scientific study of sexual behavior. Sexologists can be scientists, researchers, or clinicians and can hold a variety of different graduate degrees.

more and more sexual, and nudity has begun to appear on prime-time network television shows. American media are the most sexually suggestive in the Western hemisphere (Kunkel et al., 2005).

Sex is all over television today—from *Desperate Housewives* or *Grey's Anatomy* to *Dirty Sexy Money.* Shows use sex to lure viewers. Talk show hosts such as Jerry Springer and Tyra Banks seek out unconventional guests, many of whom have sexual issues. Other shows, such as *Real Sex, Taxicab Confessions,* and even *Sex in the City* reruns, don't beat around the bush—they talk about graphic sexual issues. Other shows, such as *America's Top Model, Girls Next Door,* or *Gossip Girls* show us the importance of beauty and perfection. Shows like these, along with a push for perfection in the youth-obsessed beauty industry, have resulted in increasing rates of plastic surgery, dieting, tanning, teeth whitening, hair coloring, and body waxing. The images that inundate us on television and other forms of media are of youthful, slim, and attractive people. High-definition media has raised the bar even higher for the beauty industry to address what were previously imperceptible blemishes.

Sexuality is an important component of each of us, but it is also one of the most difficult aspects for us to express and explore (McKenna et al., 2001). Social norms, embarrassment, and fear hold us back from expressing many of our sexual needs and desires. However, the Internet is changing patterns of social communication and relationships (Frieden, 2007; M. Griffiths, 2001).

Social networking sites, such as MySpace and FaceBook, along with e-mail, cell phones, and text and instant messaging, have changed the way people communicate with one another. Now you can communicate by "poking" someone, tagging them in a photo, or writing on their superwall. You can text a breakup message and let the world know you're dating someone with the click of a button. We talk more about these social networks in Chapter 3 (Communication).

Countless websites are also available, offering information and advice and providing visitors with answers to their most personal questions. Vibrators and other sex toys, pornographic pictures and videos, and access to a variety of personal webcam sites can be purchased online, and a variety of blogs cater to just about any conceivable fantasy. The Internet allows for anonymity and provides the freedom to ask questions, seek answers, and talk to others about sexual issues.

All of this information has not been lost on today's teenagers. Today's teens rate the media as one of their leading sources of sex information (behind school sex education programs; Kunkel et al., 2005), yet much of this information is not very educational. Each year the average American adolescent is exposed to nearly 14,000 sexual references in the media, but few of these have anything to do with contraception, STIs, or pregnancy risk. Even though sexual information in the media is often inaccurate, unrealistic, and misleading, many young people accept it as fact. As you read about various aspects of sexuality covered in this text, keep this media saturation in mind.

We now turn our attention to the history of human sexuality, from prehistoric times to the present. Of course, in the space of one chapter, we cannot begin to cover the variety and richness of human sexual experience. It is hoped that this overview will give you an idea of how varied human cultures are, while also showing that human beings throughout history have had to grapple with the same sexual issues that confront us in American society today. As we begin our review of this material, pay attention to the way that at some points in history, attitudes about sexuality were very conservative, whereas at other times, attitudes became more liberal. The pendulum continues to swing back and forth today as our society debates issues related to human sexuality, such as sex education, birth control, or same-sex marriage.

REALResearch > Despite what we hear about tanning and increased skin cancer risks, women with tans are often viewed as healthier and more attractive than women without tans (K. L. SMITH ET AL., 2007). In fact, tan skin has been found to be an important determinant in judgments of attractiveness.

review questions

1 Explain how sexuality can be both contradictory and confusing, and provide one example of how this might be so.

2 Identify some of the ways we learn about sexuality, and give two reasons for questioning the accuracy of these sources.

3 Explain how today's teenagers get messages about sexuality through various media.

How Do You Decide What Type of Sex You'll Engage In?

There are few areas of life in which moral principles are so clearly and commonly debated. Why is it that sexuality evokes so strong a moral response in us?

All sexually active people make decisions about when, where, and with whom they will engage in sexual activity. For most people, at least part of that decision is based on their views of what behaviors are morally acceptable, which may be derived from their religious beliefs, upbringing, family of origin, or personal decisions about the kind of person they want to be. For example, some people would not have sex with a partner whom they did not love, perhaps because they feel it is meaningless, immoral, or against God's wishes; others find it acceptable if both partners are willing and go into the encounter openly and freely. There are few areas of life in which moral principles are so clearly and commonly debated. Why is it that sexuality evokes so strong a moral response in us?

Human sexual behavior differs from that of all other animals, in part because of our moral, religious, legal, and interpersonal values. How simple it seems for animals, who mate without caring about marriage, pregnancy, or hurting their partner's feelings! Human beings are not (typically) so casual about mating; every culture has developed elaborate rituals, rules, laws, and moral principles that structure sexual relations. The very earliest legal and moral codes archaeologists have uncovered discuss sexual behavior at great length, and rules about sexual behavior make up a great part of the legal and ethical codes of the world's great civilizations and religions.

Sexuality is a basic drive, and it is one of the few that involves intimate, one-on-one interaction with another person's basic needs. Conflicts may arise when our own needs, feelings, fears, and concerns are not the same as our partner's. People can be hurt, used, and taken advantage of sexually, or they can be victims of honest miscommunication, especially because sex is so difficult for many people to discuss.

Sexuality is also closely related to the formation of love bonds and to procreation. Every society has a stake in procreation, for without adequate numbers of people a society can languish, and with too many people, a society can be overwhelmed. Most societies create rules to prevent accidental births and births that do not fit conventional family structures (such as teenage births). Societies also formulate sexual rules to control the size of their population (such as the outlawing of contraception or abortion in cultures that want to encourage childbirth, or distributing free contraception and free abortions, as they do in modern China, when the population gets too high).

There are certainly other possible explanations for the moral and ethical standards that have developed around sexual behavior. Why do you think morality and sexuality are so closely bound?

The Early Evolution of Human Sexuality

Our ancestors began walking upright more than 3 million years ago, according to recent fossil records. Before that, our ancestors were mostly **quadrupeds** (KWA-drew-peds) who stood only for brief moments—as baboons do now—to survey the terrain. The evolution of an upright posture changed forever the way the human species engaged in sexual intercourse.

quadruped
Any animal that walks on four legs.

timeline Television

1927	1930	1939	1946	1947
Philo T. Fransworth **develops** the first black-and-white television set.	*The Association of Motion Pictures* **devises** a rating code to govern events portrayed in motion pictures.	**Television makes** its debut when the Radio Corporation of America (RCA) brings it to the World's Fair in New York City. Here the first televised presidential debate with Franklin D. Roosevelt is shown.	**First color television set is presented** to the Federal Communications Commissions (FCC).	Sitcom *Mary Kay and Johnny* **shows** first married couple in bed together.

© Bettmann/Corbis

I can't believe how blatantly sexual advertising is today. Sometimes when I look at ads with sex and nudity, I can't even tell what the ad is for. Some ads for jeans don't even have any jeans in the picture! How does an ad like this sell jeans?

Ahhh, you ask a very important question. Advertisers know that consumers are emotional beings. When half-naked men or women are flaunting their sexuality in ads, it arouses us and helps us to associate our arousal with whatever the product is that they are trying to sell. Then we want the jeans because we want to be sexy—just like the model in the ad. So even when the advertised item isn't in the ad, we associate the feeling the ad generates with a particular item or brand name.

STAND UP AND LOOK AROUND:
WALKING ERECT

In an upright posture, the male genitals are rotated to the front of the body, so merely approaching someone involves displaying the genitals. Because male confrontation often involved acts of aggression, the **phallus**—the male symbol of sex and potency—became associated with displays of aggression. In other words, upright posture may have also contributed to a new tie between sexuality and aggression (Rancour-Laferriere, 1985).

The upright posture of the female also emphasized her breasts and hips, and the rotation of the female pelvis forward (the vagina faces the rear in most quadrupeds) also resulted in the possibility of face-to-face intercourse. Because more body area is in contact in face-to-face intercourse than in rear entry, the entire sensual aspect of intercourse was enhanced, manipulation of the breasts became possible (the breasts are sexual organs only in humans), and the female clitoris was much more easily stimulated. Only in human females does orgasm seem to be a common part of sexual contact.

About 200,000 years ago, **homo sapiens** appeared on the scene. We do not know much about how these early ancestors behaved or what they believed. However, anthropological evidence suggests that they developed monogamous relationships and lived in fairly stable sexual pairings (Margulis & Sagan, 1991).

Do female primates experience orgasm?
Yes, some do, although it is relatively rare compared with human females. Female primates rarely masturbate, although occasionally they stimulate themselves manually during intercourse. Bonobos (pygmy chimpanzees) do have face-to-face intercourse on occasion and may reach orgasm. However, most chimpanzees engage in rear-entry intercourse, a position that does not favor female orgasm (Margulis & Sagan, 1991).

SEXUALITY IN
THE ANCIENT MEDITERRANEAN

From writings and art, we know a bit about ancient accounts of sexually transmitted infections (some ancient medical texts discuss cures), menstruation (there were a variety of laws surrounding menstruation), circumcision (which was first performed in Egypt and possibly other parts of Africa), and contraception (heterosexual Egyptian women inserted sponges or other objects in the vagina). Because a great value was put on having as many children as possible—especially sons, for inheritance purposes—abortion was usually forbidden. Prostitution was common, and **temple prostitutes** often greeted worshippers.

It is important to remember that throughout history, men dominated public life and women's voices were effectively silenced; we know far more about what men thought, how men lived, and even how men loved than we do about the lives and thoughts of women. In fact, it was only relatively recently in human history that women's voices have begun to be heard on a par with men's in literature, politics, art, and other parts of public life.

It may seem that ancient civilizations were very different from ours, yet some societies had surprisingly modern attitudes about sex. Although the Egyptians condemned adultery, especially

---

phallus
Term used to refer to the penis as a symbol of power and aggression.

homo sapiens
The technical name for the species to which all human beings belong.

temple prostitutes
Women in ancient cultures who would have sex with worshippers at pagan temples to provide money for the temple or as a form of worshipping the gods.

1950	1953	1953	1956	1957
Sitcom *I Love Lucy* **shows** married couples in separate beds.	**First network children's show,** *Captain Kangaroo*, debuts.	Color broadcasting on television **begins** after FCC approves modified version of RCA system.	Elvis Presley **appears** on the *Ed Sullivan Show* and is broadcast from the waist up because his dance moves are thought to be too suggestive.	First remote control for television **is introduced.**

© Bettmann/Corbis	© John Springer Collection/Corbis		© Bettmann/Corbis	

among women, it may still have been fairly common. A woman in Egypt had the right to divorce her husband, a privilege, as we will see, that was not allowed to Hebrew women. Egyptians seem to have invented male circumcision, and Egyptian workers left behind thousands of pictures, carvings, and even cartoons of erotic scenes (Doyle, 2005). All told, ancient Egyptians had sexual lives that do not seem all that different from the way humans engage in sex throughout the world today.

Of all the ancient civilizations, modern Western society owes the most to the interaction of three ancient cultures: Hebraic (Hebrews), Hellenistic (Greek), and Roman. Each made a contribution to our views of sexuality, so it is worthwhile to examine each culture briefly. At the beginning of each section, we give a date as to when these effects began.

The Hebrews (1000–200 B.C.)

The Hebrew Bible, which was put into written form some time between 800 and 200 B.C., contains explicit rules about sexual behavior, such as forbidding adultery, male homosexual intercourse, and sex with various family members and their spouses. The Bible includes tales of sexual misconduct—ranging from incest, to sexual betrayal, to sex outside of marriage, to sexual jealousy—even by its most admired figures. Yet the Bible also contains tales of marital love and acknowledges the importance of sexuality in marital relations.

The legacy of the Hebrew attitude toward sexuality has been profound. The focus on marital sexuality and procreation and the prohibition against such things as homosexuality were adopted by Christianity and formed the basis of sexual attitudes in the West for centuries thereafter. On the other hand, as opposed to the Greeks, the Hebrew Bible sees the marital union and its sexual nature as an expression of love and affection, as a man and woman "become one flesh."

The Greeks (1000–200 B.C.)

The Greeks were more sexually permissive than the Hebrews. Their stories and myths are full of sexual exploits, incest, rape, and even **bestiality** (beest-ee-AL-i-tee; as when Zeus, the chief god, takes the form of a swan to rape Leda). The Greeks clearly distinguished between love and sex in their tales, even giving each a separate god: Aphrodite was the goddess of sexual intercourse; Eros (her son) was the god of love.

Greece was one of the few major civilizations in Western history to institutionalize homosexuality successfully. In Greek **pederasty** (ped-er-AST-ee), an older man would befriend a postpubescent boy who had finished his orthodox education and aid in the boy's continuing intellectual, physical, and sexual development. In return, the boy would have sex with his mentor. The mentor was always the active partner, the penetrator; the student was the passive partner. Socrates, for example, was supposed to

Greek cups, plates, and other pottery often depicted erotic scenes, such as this one from the fifth century B.C.

Scala/Art Resource, NY

WHAT DO YOU WANT TO KNOW?

I've heard that the Greeks believed that sex between men and boys was a "natural" form of human sexuality. Couldn't they see that it was perverted?

One society's perversion is another society's normal sexual practice. Every culture sees its own forms of sexuality as natural and obvious—including ours. Not too long ago in our own society, it seemed "obvious" to most people that things such as oral sex and anal sex were perversions (they are still technically illegal in many states) and that masturbation was a serious disease that could lead to mental illness. Today many people see these acts as part of a healthy sexual life. Sexual beliefs and practices change over time and are different in various cultures.

bestiality
The act of having intercourse with an animal.

pederasty
Sexual contact between adult men and (usually) postpubescent boys.

timeline Television

Hulton Archive/Getty Images

CBS-TV/The Kobal Collection

have enjoyed the sexual attentions of his students (all male), and his students expressed jealousy when he paid too much physical attention to one or another.

In Greece, men and the male form were idealized. When the ancient Greek philosophers spoke of love, they did so almost exclusively in **homoerotic** terms. Man's nonsexual love for another man was seen as the ideal love, superior to the sexual love for women. Plato discussed such an ideal love, and so we have come to call friendships without a sexual element **platonic.**

The Romans (500 B.C.–A.D. 700)

In Rome, marriage and sexual relations were viewed as a means to improve one's economic and social standing; passionate love almost never appears in the written accounts handed down to us. Bride and groom need not love each other, for that kind of relationship would grow over the life of the marriage; more important was fair treatment, respect, and mutual consideration. Wives even encouraged their husbands to have slaves (of either gender) for the purposes of sexual release. Rome had few restrictions about sexuality until late in the history of the empire, so early Romans had very permissive attitudes toward homosexual and bisexual behaviors, which were entirely legal until the sixth century A.D. (Boswell, 1980).

In Rome, as in Greece, adult males who took the passive sexual position in homosexual encounters were viewed with scorn, whereas the same behavior by youth, foreigners, slaves, or women was seen as an acceptable means to try to please a person who could improve one's place in society. Still, long-term homosexual unions did exist.

*In early Rome, **love grew** over the course of the marriage.*

carnations. The goal, then, is to live a just life now to avoid suffering in the future. One of the responsibilities in this life is to marry and procreate, and because sex is an important part of those responsibilities, it was generally viewed as a positive pursuit, and even a source of power and magic.

There are legends about great women rulers early in India's history, and women had important roles in ceremonies and sacrifices. Still, India's social system, like others we have mentioned, was basically **patriarchal** (PAY-tree-arc-al), and Indian writers (again, mostly male) shared many of the negative views of women that were characteristic of other civilizations. Being born a woman was seen as a punishment for sins committed in previous lives. In fact, murdering a woman was not seen as a particularly serious crime, and **female infanticide** (in-FAN-teh-side) was not uncommon (V. L. Bullough, 1973).

By about 400 B.C., the first and most famous of India's sex manuals, the **Kama Sutra** (CAH-mah SUH-trah), appeared. India is justifiably famous for this amazing book. The Kama Sutra discusses not just sex but also the nature of love, how to make a good home and family, and moral guidance in sex and love. The Kama Sutra is obsessive about naming and classifying things. In fact, it categorizes men by the size of their penis (hare, bull, or horse man) and women by the size of their vagina (deer, mare, or cow-elephant woman). A good match in genital size was preferred between heterosexual partners, but barring that, a tight fit was better than a loose one (Tannahill, 1980). The Kama Sutra recommends that women learn how to please their husbands, and it provides instructions on sexual techniques and illustrations of

SEXUALITY IN ANCIENT ASIA

Chinese and Indian civilizations also had unique views of sexuality. In Indian culture, Hinduism and rebirth give life direction. In Chinese culture, people work to live in harmony with the Tao, which is made up of **yin and yang.**

India (Beginning About 400 B.C.)

Hinduism, the religion of India for most of its history, concentrates on an individual's cycle of birth and rebirth, or **karma.** Karma involves a belief that a person's unjust deeds in this life are punished by suffering in a future life, and suffering in this life is undoubtedly punishment for wrongs committed in previous in-

homoerotic
The representation of same-sex love or desire.

platonic
Named after Plato's description, a deep, loving friendship that is devoid of sexual contact or desire.

yin and yang
According to a Chinese belief, the universe is run by the interaction of two fundamental principles: yin, which is negative, passive, weak, yielding, and female, and yang, which is positive, assertive, active, strong, and male.

karma
The idea that there is a cycle of birth, death, and rebirth and that deeds in one's life affect one's status in a future life.

patriarchal
A society ruled by the male as the figure of authority, symbolized by the father's absolute authority in the home.

female infanticide
The killing of female infants; practiced in some countries that value males more than females.

Kama Sutra
Famous ancient Indian sex manual.

1983	1987	1987	1991	1992
Bay City Blues **is** the first television series to show bare buttocks in locker room scene.	*Playtex* **shows** first television commercials with live models wearing bras and underwear.	*StarTrek* **introduces** alien race named "Ferengi" who require females to be naked and subservient to males.	*LA Law* **shows** lesbian kiss by characters C.J. Lamb and Abby Perkins.	**Mariel Hemingway bares** her breasts in an episode of *Civil Wars* on *ABC*.

Beauty, Status, and Chinese Foot Binding

Foot binding originated out of men's desire for women with small, feminine feet. In fact, many men would refuse to marry women without bound feet.

It is often difficult to imagine how sexuality and gender are viewed outside the United States. We become accustomed to norms, practices, and behaviors where we live and may not understand how other cultures view the same practices differently. In this chapter, we've looked at images of beauty in U.S. culture. It may seem strange that some men and women undergo nose jobs, breast implants, liposuction, tattooing, piercing, waxing, or other procedures to look and feel more beautiful. Throughout history cultures have searched for unique ways to achieve beauty, especially for women. At one point in U.S. history, exceptionally small waists on women were considered beautiful, and many women wore tight-fitting corsets. Women who did so often underwent tremendous pain and broke ribs or damaged internal organs. More disturbing than corsets, however, was the Chinese practice of foot binding, which began in the 10th century and lasted for 1,000 years (Ko, 2007).

Foot binding originated out of men's desire for women with small, feminine feet. In fact, many men would refuse to marry women without bound feet. One woman, Zhang Ru-lain, who is now in her late 70s said:

> *Men would choose or reject you as a prospective wife based on the size of your feet. There was a well-known saying, "If you don't bind, you don't marry". . . . When a girl became eligible for marriage, a matchmaker would find a man for whom the young girl might be suitable. Then she would arrange a foot viewing. The man would come to the girl's house just to look at her feet. If he thought they were too large he would turn her down. This was a very embarrassing affair, should it happen, since the whole village would surely hear about it (Rupp, 2007).*

Foot binding was also sexual in nature—women with bound feet had a sway in their walk that was often viewed as erotic. However, they couldn't walk far, which is why

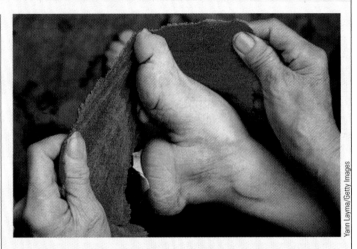

Yann Layma/Getty Images

many believe foot binding literally kept women in their place.

The ideal foot length was three inches, which was referred to as a Golden Lotus (Golden Lotus feet were often adorned with beautiful silk shoes). Feet that were 3 to 4 inches long were called Silver Lotuses. It is estimated that 40% to 50% of Chinese women had their feet bound in the 19th century, although in the upper classes the percentages were closer to 100% (W. Rossi, 1993).

Foot binding was typically done on girls as young as 4 or 5 years because this is when the bones are still flexible. To bind feet, the mother or grandmother would first soak a girl's feet in warm water. She would then cut the toenails very short, massage the feet, and break the four small toes on each foot. These toes would be folded under, leaving the big toe intact. Silk bandages were wrapped tightly around the toes, and the bandages pulled each broken toe

continued

timeline Television

1993	1994	1995	1996	1997
David Caruso and Sherry Stringfield are shown nude while making love in a scene from *NYPD Blue*.	**Rosanne Barr and Mariel Hemingway kiss** on *Roseanne*.	**Drew Barrymore bares** her breasts on David Letterman.	*Friends* **airs** episode of lesbian wedding, even though vows are not sealed with a kiss.	**Ellen DeGeneres comes out** on the air, making *Ellen* the first openly gay sitcom. Several advertisers withdraw all commercials from this episode.

© Reuters/Corbis

continued

closer to the heel. These bandages were changed and tightened every couple of days so that the foot would not be allowed to grow normally. Typically this process went on for ten or more years. It was immensely painful, and most girls could not walk for long distances with their feet bound. Most mothers would start the foot-binding process in the winter months so that the cold would help to numb the pain.

In the beginning, only wealthy families bound their daughters' feet because they could afford not to have their children work in the fields. In the 17th and 18th centuries, peasants and women from the countryside began foot binding when they realized that doing so might attract more wealthy suitors for marriage.

There were long-term consequences to foot binding. Many women had difficulties balancing, walking, standing, and squatting (using the toilet was especially difficult). Muscular atrophy and infections were common, and many girls developed a terrible foot smell from the practice. Older women typically developed severe hip and spinal problems.

The practice of foot binding was outlawed in the latter part of the Qing Dynasty (1644–1911). At that time, women were told to unwrap their feet or face heavy fines. Even so, the practice continued for years, and it wasn't until the formation of the People's Republic of China in 1949 that a strict prohibition was placed on foot binding. This prohibition continues today.

Although it's disturbing to read about this practice, it is interesting to look at how far societies will go for beauty. Foot binding became an integral part of the culture and was much more than a beauty statement. Women whose feet were bound were viewed as more desirable and of a higher social status, making it more likely they would find a husband to provide for them.

SOURCE: The material in this feature was taken from several texts, including *Splendid Slippers: A Thousand Years of an Erotic Tradition* (Jackson, 1998), *In Every Step a Lotus: Shoes for Bound Feet* (Ko, 2001), *Cinderella's Sisters: A Revisionist History of Footbinding* (Ko, 2007), *Aching for Beauty: Footbinding in China* (Ping, 2002), and *The Sex Life of the Foot and Shoe* (W. Rossi, 1993).

---

many sexual positions, some of which are virtually impossible for anyone who cannot twist his or her body like a pretzel. The Kama Sutra proposes that intercourse should be a passionate activity that includes scratching, biting, and blows to the back, accompanied by a variety of animal noises.

In India, marriage was an economic and religious obligation; families tried to arrange good marriages by betrothing their children at younger and younger ages, although they did not live with or have sex with their future spouses until after puberty. Because childbearing began so young, Indian women were still in the prime of their lives when their children were grown, and they were often able to assert themselves in the household over elderly husbands. However, when a husband died, his wife was forbidden to remarry, and she had to live simply, wear plain clothes, and sleep on the ground. She was to devote her days to prayer and rituals that ensured her remarriage to the same husband in a future life. Many women chose (or were forced) to end their lives as widows by the ritual act of *sati*, which consisted of a woman throwing herself on her husband's burning funeral pyre to die (Jamanadas, 2008).

China (Beginning About 200 B.C.)

Chinese civilization emphasizes the interdependence of all things, unified in the Tao, which represents the basic unity of the universe. The Tao itself is made up of two principles, yin and yang, which represent the opposites of the world: yin is feminine, passive, and receptive; yang is masculine, active, and assertive. Sexuality in Chinese thought is not a matter of moral or allowable behavior but, rather, is a natural procreative process, a joining of the yin and yang, the masculine and feminine principles.

1998	**1998**	**1998**	**1999**	**1999**
Network and broadcast executives design a rating system to help parents monitor what their children watch on television.	*Sex and the City* **debuts** on HBO, and covers sex and relationships in unprecedented candor from the point of view of the four female lead characters.	**First episode of NBC hit show** *Will & Grace,* wherein a gay male lives with his female friend.	*Naked News,* a Toronto-based internet show, **features** anchors who strip completely while reporting the news. Billed as the program with "nothing to hide."	**FCC passes** law that all television sets 13 inches or larger must have a V-chip installed.

© HBO/Courtesy: Everett Collection

Jim Watson/AFP/Getty Images

Because sex itself was part of the basic process of following the Tao, sexual instruction and sex manuals were common and openly available in early Chinese society. These texts were explicit, with pictures of sexual positions and instructions on how to stimulate partners, and were often given to brides before their weddings.

Because women's essence, yin, is inexhaustible, whereas man's essence, yang (embodied in semen), is limited, man should feed his yang through prolonged contact with yin. In other words, heterosexual intercourse should be prolonged as long as possible, without the man ejaculating, to release all the woman's accumulated yin energy. (The man may experience orgasm without ejaculation, however, and techniques were developed to teach men how to do so.) Heterosexual men should try to have sex with many women to prevent the yin energy of any single woman from becoming depleted. It was also important for the man to experience the woman's orgasm, when yin is at its peak, to maximize his contact with yin energy. The Chinese were unique in stressing the importance of female orgasm (Margolis, 2004).

Same-sex relations were not discouraged, but because semen was seen as precious and primarily for impregnation (we discuss Chinese views of homosexuality more in Chapter 11), male homosexuality was viewed as a wasteful use of sperm. Aphrodisiacs were developed, as were drugs for all kinds of sexual problems. Also common were sexual devices to increase pleasure, such as penis rings to maintain erection, balls and bells that were grafted under the skin of the head of the penis to increase its size, and ben-wa balls (usually two or three) containing mercury and other substances that were inserted in the vagina and bounced against each other to bring sexual pleasure.

Taoists believed that yin and yang were equally necessary complements of all existence, so one might guess that men and women were treated more equally in China than in the West. Yet because yin is the passive, inferior principle, women were seen as subservient to men throughout their lives: first to their fathers, then to their husbands, and finally to their sons when their husbands died. **Polygamy** (pah-LIG-ah-mee) was practiced until late in Chinese history, and the average middle-class male had between three and a dozen wives and concubines, with those in nobility having thirty or more.

polygamy
The practice of men or women marrying more than one partner.

WHAT DO YOU WANT TO KNOW?

Wasn't the original Kama Sutra pretty sexist? I don't understand how it could still be popular today when we work so hard for equality.
Although the original Kama Sutra has been criticized for its heterosexist and oppositional male and female power imbalances, there have been several translations over time. Today we understand that the Kama Sutra may have a more balanced power structure than originally thought and that it also provides women more power to say no (Kong, 2004). Perhaps these new understandings account for the Kama Sutra's continued popularity today.

REALResearch > Research on the practice of Hindu tantric sexual practices has found that there is more to sex than just the act—many sexual practices are performed to provide strength and even magical powers. Consumption of semen, for example, is thought to be one such practice (J. C. GOLD, 2004).

review questions

1 How did prehistoric changes in our posture influence human sexuality?

2 What sources provide information on sexuality in early cultures?

3 Explain how the moral standards of past civilizations influence our own judgments about modern events today.

timeline Television

1999	2000	2000	2000	2001
Debut of *Queer as Folk,* which follows the lives of five gay men and two lesbians.	**Popular teen drama *Dawson's Creek* discusses** gay character coming out of the closet.	***All My Children* features** character coming out of the closet, the first major homosexual role in a soap opera.	**Inquiry into former White House intern Monica Lewinsky's** relationship with President Bill Clinton finally concludes.	***Naked News* begins** airing on television. An all-nude cast of females delivers both the serious and lighter side of the news on cable.

Getty Images

Indian sculptors followed the tradition of tantric art, which is famous for its depictions of eroticism. Of the 85 temples with tantric art originally built, 22 still stand today.

Sexuality from St. Paul
to Martin Luther

Throughout my many years of teaching this course, it has become apparent to me how one's religion influences his or her values and attitudes about sexuality. I've talked with many students about their religions and the impact of their religious beliefs on their attitudes and values concerning sexuality. Religion has influenced many of our views about sexuality throughout history. Perhaps no single system of thought had as much impact on the Western world as Christianity, and nowhere more so than in its views on sexuality (Stark, 1996). We explore early Christianity and the Middle Ages, look at the influence of Islam and Islamic law, and consider the views of sexuality that developed during the Renaissance.

CHASTITY BECOMES A VIRTUE (BEGINNING ABOUT 50 A.D.)

Christianity began as a small sect following the teachings of Jesus. It was formalized into a religious philosophy by St. Paul and other early leaders who were influenced by the Roman legal structure. Within a few hundred years, this little sect would become the predominant religion of the Western world, and it has influenced the attitudes of people toward sexuality until the present day.

Jesus himself was mostly silent on sexual issues such as homosexuality or premarital sex. Jesus was born a Jew and was knowledgeable in Jewish tradition, and many of his attitudes were compatible with mainstream Jewish thought of the time. However, he was liberal in his thinking about sexuality, preaching, for example, that men should be held to the same standards as women on issues of adultery, divorce, and remarriage (V. L. Bullough, 1973). The Gospels also show that Jesus was liberal in his recommendations for punishing sexual misadventurers. When confronted with a woman who had committed adultery, a sin for which the Hebrew Bible had mandated stoning, Jesus replied with one of his more famous comments, "Let he who is without sin cast the first stone."

It was St. Paul and later followers, however, such as St. Jerome and St. Augustine, who established the Christian view of sexuality that was to dominate Western thought for the next 2,000 years. St. Paul condemned sexuality in a way found in neither Hebrew nor Greek thought—nor anywhere in the teachings of Jesus. Paul suggested that the highest love was love of God and that the ideal was not to allow sexual or human love to compete with that love. Therefore, although sexuality itself was not sinful when performed as part of the marital union, the ideal situation was **celibacy** (SEH-luh-buh-see). **Chastity,** for the first time in history, became a virtue; abstaining from sexual intercourse became a sign of holiness (Bergmann, 1987). Paul suggested that those unable to make a commitment to chastity could engage in marital sex, occasionally abstaining for periods of prayer and devotion.

The legacy of early Christianity was a general association of sexuality with sin. All nonprocreative sex was strictly forbidden, as

celibacy
The state of remaining unmarried; often used today to refer to abstaining from sex.

chastity
The quality of being sexually pure, either through abstaining from intercourse or by adhering to strict rules of sexuality.

2002	2003	2004	2004	2004
Reality show *American Idol,* a competition to find the best U.S. singer, debuts on FOX.	**Bravo network begins** airing the popular show *Queer Eye for the Straight Guy.*	**Reality shows such as** *The Bachelor, Survivor, Blind Date,* and *Extreme Makeover* flood the market.	**Janet Jackson exposes** her breast during halftime Super Bowl show. The Federal Communications Commission fines CBS over $500,000.	**During ABC's** *Monday Night Football,* Nicollette Sheridan (*Desperate Housewives*) attempts to lure Philadelphia Eagles Terrell Owens into sex by dropping her towel and appearing nude in the locker room.

SGranitz/WireImage/Getty Images

© Steve Azzara/Corbis

Giulio Marcocchi/Getty Images

© Pierre Ducharme/Reuters/Corbis

were contraception, masturbation, and sex for pleasure's sake. The result was that the average Christian associated the pleasure of sexuality with guilt (Stark, 1996). Christianity's view of sex has been one of the harshest of any major religious or cultural tradition. You can see how religious views such as these could certainly influence your views on sexuality. It is not uncommon for students to experience **cognitive dissonance** over their disparate views about sexuality and religion.

Early Christians associated sexuality with guilt.

THE MIDDLE AGES: EVE THE TEMPTRESS, **MARY THE VIRGIN (500 A.D.—1400 A.D.)**

In the early Middle Ages, the church's influence slowly began to increase. Christianity had become the state religion of Rome, and although the church did not have much formal power, its teachings had an influence on law. For example, homosexual relations (even homosexual marriage) had been legal for the first 200 years that Christianity was the state religion of Rome, and the church was very tolerant of homosexuality. Eventually, however, church teachings changed and became much stricter.

Between about 1050 and 1150 (the High Middle Ages) sexuality once again became liberalized. For example, a gay subculture was established in Europe that produced a body of gay literature that had not been seen since the Roman Empire and would not emerge again until the 19th century (Boswell, 1980).

However, the homosexual subculture disappeared in the 13th century when the church cracked down on a variety of groups—including Jews, Muslims, and homosexuals (Boswell, 1980). In 1215, the church instituted **confession,** and soon guides appeared to teach priests about the various sins **penitents** (PENN-it-tents) might have committed. The guides seem preoccupied with sexual transgressions and used sexual sins more than any other kind to illustrate their points (Payer, 1991). All sex outside of marriage was considered sinful, and even certain marital acts were forbidden.

European women in the early Middle Ages were only slightly better off than they had been under the ancient Greeks or Romans. By the late Middle Ages, however, new ideas about women were brought back by the Crusaders from Islamic lands (see the section on Islam that follows). Women were elevated to a place of purity and were considered almost perfect (Tannahill, 1980). Woman was no longer a temptress but a model of virtue. The idea of romantic love was first created at this time, and it spread through popular culture as balladeers and troubadours traveled from place to place, singing songs of pure, spiritual love, untroubled by sex.

At the same time that women were seen to be virtuous, however, they were also said to be the holder of the secrets of sexuality (Thomasset, 1992). Before marriage, men would employ the services of an **entremetteuse** (on-TRAY-meh-toose) to teach them the ways of love. These old women procured young women (prostitutes) for the men and were said to know the secrets of restoring potency, restoring virginity, and concocting potions. It was a small step from the scary accounts of these old women's powers to the belief in witches. By the late 15th century, the church began a campaign against witchcraft, which it said was inspired by women's insatiable "carnal lust" (Covey, 1989).

Perhaps no person from the Middle Ages had a stronger impact on subsequent attitudes toward sexuality than Thomas Aquinas (1225–1274). Aquinas established the views of morality and correct sexual behavior that form the basis of the Catholic Church's attitudes toward sexuality even today (Halsall, 1996). Aquinas drew from the idea of "natural law" to suggest that there were "natural" and "unnatural" sex acts. He argued that the sex organs were "naturally" intended for procreation, and other use of them was unnatural and immoral; in fact, he argued that semen and ejaculation were intended only to impregnate, and any other use of them was immoral. Aquinas's strong condemnation of sexuality—and especially homosexuality, which he called the worst of all sexual sins—set the tone for Christian attitudes toward sexuality for many centuries.

ISLAM: A NEW RELIGION **(ABOUT 500 A.D.)**

In the sixth century, a man named Muhammad began to preach a religion that drew from Jewish and Christian roots and added Arab tribal beliefs. Islam became a powerful force that conquered the entire Middle East and Persian lands; swept across Asia, and so touched China in the East; spread through Northern Africa and, from there, north into Christian Europe, particularly Spain. Between about the 8th and 12th centuries, Islamic society was the most advanced in the world, with a newly developed system of

cognitive dissonance
Uncomfortable tension that comes from holding two conflicting thoughts at the same time.

confession
A Catholic practice of revealing one's sins to a priest.

penitents
Those who come to confess sins (from the word *penance,* meaning "to repent").

entremetteuse
Historically, a woman who procures sexual partners for men or one who taught men about lovemaking.

timeline Exploring Human Sexuality: Past and Present

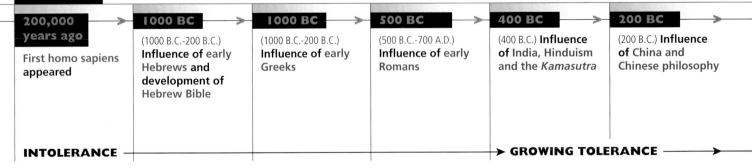

200,000 years ago	**1000 BC**	**1000 BC**	**500 BC**	**400 BC**	**200 BC**
First homo sapiens appeared	(1000 B.C.-200 B.C.) **Influence of early Hebrews and development of Hebrew Bible**	(1000 B.C.-200 B.C.) **Influence of early Greeks**	(500 B.C.-700 A.D.) **Influence of early Romans**	(400 B.C.) **Influence of India, Hinduism and the *Kamasutra***	(200 B.C.) **Influence of China and Chinese philosophy**

INTOLERANCE ————————————————————————▶ **GROWING TOLERANCE** ————▶

Honor Crimes

Honor crimes target women whose actions—actual or suspected—violate the honor of her family.

Honor crimes target women whose actions—actual or suspected—violate the honor of her family. Crimes might include speaking to someone with whom you should not speak, loss of virginity, wearing inappropriate clothing, extramarital affairs, or speaking out about various issues. Some women and girls have been raped or murdered to reestablish the family honor. Honor crimes occur most frequently in places where female chastity is of utmost importance, including the Middle East and South Asia.

Birgul Isik, a mother of five, was gunned down by her 14-year-old son in Turkey for appearing on a television talk show to discuss her abusive marriage (BBC News, 2006). She had left her abusive husband several times and had agreed to talk about it on television so that other women would know they have choices about staying in abusive marriages. Domestic violence is not spoken of in many parts of conservative Turkey, and to discuss it publicly was seen as a shame on her family's honor. Honor crimes are often carried out by a son or a younger brother, because the younger family members are less likely to get stiff sentences or penalties (BBC News, 2006; Goodwin, 2007).

A more recent development, honor suicide, occurs when a woman is pressured into killing herself (or ordered to do so) to restore family honor. This way, the family will avoid any penalties for killing her. Derya, a 17-year-old Turkish girl, began receiving text messages on her cell phone from her family that said, "You have shamed our honor. You must kill yourself. If you don't, we will." Her family had been shamed because Derya had spoken to a male classmate on her cell phone. In strict Islamic societies, dating, hanging out, or even talking to a boy on a cell phone is strictly forbidden. Derya was torn between what her family had taught her and the feelings she was having for the boy. Soon she realized she had fallen in love with him, even though she had always been taught that love came after marriage (Goodwin, 2007). After numerous threats and pressure from her family, Derya took her own life.

Honor crimes and suicides have been reported in places such as Pakistan, Afghanistan, India, Turkey, Saudi Arabia, Bangladesh, Brazil, Ecuador, Egypt, Israel, Jordan, Morocco, and Uganda. In Chapter 17, we explore other forms of gender-based violence, including domestic violence and sex trafficking.

---

mathematics (Arabic numbers) to replace the clumsy Roman system and having the world's most sophisticated techniques of medicine, warfare, and science (Wuthnow, 1998).

Many Muslim societies have strong rules of *satr al-'awra*, or modesty, that involve covering the private parts of the body (which for women means almost the entire body). Muhammad had tried to preserve the rights of women. There are examples in the **Koran** (koe-RAN), the Muslim bible, of female saints and intellectuals, and powerful women often hold strong informal powers over their husbands and male children. Still, women in many Islamic lands are subjugated to men, segregated and not permitted to venture out of their homes, and forbidden to interact with men who are not family members.

In Islamic law, as in Christian law, sexuality between a man and a woman is legal only when the couple is married (Coulson, 1979). Sexual intercourse in marriage is a good religious deed for the Muslim male, and the Koran likens wives to fields that men should cultivate as frequently as they want. Islam restricts sex to the marital union exclusively (Shafaat, 2004).

In traditional Islamic communities, women who were married to wealthy men usually lived in secluded areas in their husbands' homes, called **harems.** Harems were not the dens of sex and sensuality that are sometimes portrayed but were self-

Koran
The holy book of Islam. Also spelled Quran or Qur'an.

harem
Abbreviation of the Turkish word *harêmlik* (*harâm* in Arabic), meaning "women's quarters" or "sanctuary."

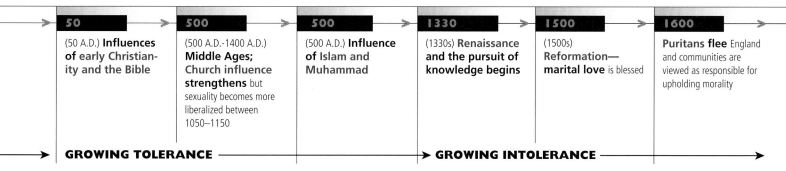

50	500	500	1330	1500	1600
(50 A.D.) **Influences of early Christianity and the Bible**	(500 A.D.-1400 A.D.) **Middle Ages; Church influence strengthens** but sexuality becomes more liberalized between 1050–1150	(500 A.D.) **Influence of Islam and Muhammad**	(1330s) **Renaissance and the pursuit of knowledge begins**	(1500s) **Reformation— marital love** is blessed	**Puritans flee** England and communities are viewed as responsible for upholding morality

GROWING TOLERANCE ———→ **GROWING INTOLERANCE** ————→

contained communities where women learned to become self-sufficient in the absence of men. Among the middle and lower classes, men had less wealth to offer potential wives, which gave women more power.

The sultans of the Ottoman Empire, which ruled most of the Islamic world from the 15th to the 20th century, had between 300 and 1,200 concubines, mostly captured or bought slaves. The sultan's mother ruled the harem and even sometimes ruled the empire itself if she was strong and her son was weak willed (Tannahill, 1980). Because each woman might sleep with the sultan once or twice a year at most, **eunuchs** (YOU-niks) were employed to guard the women. Eunuchs would not have sex with the women, because they often had their testicles or penises (or both) removed. Some eunuchs had their testicles crushed to eliminate testosterone production. Many died under the surgeon's knife.

THE RENAISSANCE: THE PURSUIT OF KNOWLEDGE (BEGINNING ABOUT 1300 A.D.)

The Renaissance, which began in Italy in the late 1300s, may be summed up as a time when intellectual and artistic thought turned from a focus on God to a focus on human beings and their place in the world; from the sober and serious theology of the Middle Ages to a renewed sense of joy in life; from **asceticism** (ah-SET-ah-siz-um) to sensuality (New, 1969). Part of the cultural shift of the Renaissance was new views of sexuality and, to some degree, the roles of women in society.

During the Renaissance, women made great strides in education and began to become more prominent in political affairs (Bornstein, 1979). Lively debates about the worth and value of women took place, and in 1532 it was argued that each of God's creations in the biblical book of Genesis is superior to the one before. Because the human female is the last thing God created, she must be his most perfect creation. In the Bible, a male is the first sinner; men introduce polygamy, drunkenness, and murder into the world; and men are aggressive and tyrannical. Women, on the other hand, are more peaceful, chaste, refined, and faithful.

However, as seems to happen so often in history when women make modest gains, there was a backlash. By the 17th century, witchcraft trials appeared once again in Europe and the New World, symbols of the fears that men still held of women's sexuality. Thousands of women were killed, and the image of the evil witch became the symbol of man's fear of women for centuries to come (see the accompanying Human Sexuality in a Diverse World for more information about witch hunts).

THE REFORMATION: THE PROTESTANT MARITAL PARTNERSHIP (BEGINNING ABOUT 1500)

In western Europe in the early 16th century, Martin Luther challenged papal power and founded a movement known as Protestantism. Instead of valuing celibacy, Luther saw in the Bible the obligation to reproduce, saw marital love as blessed, and considered sexuality a natural function. John Calvin, the other great Protestant reformer, suggested that women were not just reproductive vessels but men's partners in all things.

To Luther, marriage was a state blessed by God, and sexual contact was sinful primarily when it occurred out of wedlock, just as any indulgence was sinful. Marriage was inherent in human nature, had been instituted in paradise, and was confirmed in the fifth commandment and safeguarded by the seventh (V. L. Bullough, 1973). Because marriage was so important, a bad marriage should not continue, and so Luther broke away from the belief of the Catholic Church and allowed divorce.

Sexuality was permissible only in the marital union, but it had other justifications besides reproduction, such as to reduce stress, avoid cheating, and increase intimacy—a very different perspective on sex than that preached by the Catholic Church. Calvin, in fact, saw the marital union as primarily a social and sexual relationship. Although procreation was important, companionship was the main goal of marriage.

Luther did accept the general subjugation of women to men in household affairs and felt that women were weaker than men and should humble themselves before their fathers and husbands. He excluded women from the clergy because of standards of "decency" and because of women's inferior aptitudes for ministry. Although Calvin and Luther tried to remove from Protestantism the overt disdain of women that they found in some older Christian theologians, they did not firmly establish women's equal place with men.

eunuch
Castrated male (or less often, a man with his penis removed) who guarded a harem. At times, children were also made eunuchs in childhood to sing soprano in church choirs.

asceticism
The practice of a lifestyle that rejects sensual pleasures such as drinking alcohol, eating rich food, or engaging in sex.

timeline Exploring Human Sexuality: Past and Present

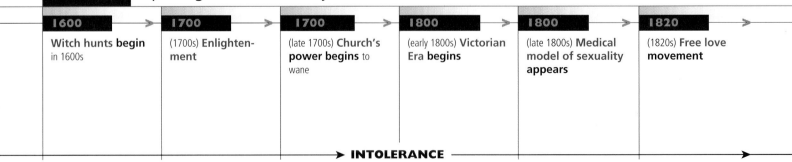

1600	1700	1700	1800	1800	1820
Witch hunts begin in 1600s	(1700s) **Enlighten-ment**	(late 1700s) **Church's power begins** to wane	(early 1800s) **Victorian Era begins**	(late 1800s) **Medical model of sexuality appears**	(1820s) **Free love movement**

→ INTOLERANCE

The Fear of Female Sexuality

Many images of women have been created by men throughout history, some of which have expressed heterosexual male fears of female sexuality and helped to keep women subjugated.

Men have created many images of women throughout history, and some of these have expressed male fears of female sexuality and helped to keep women subjugated. The woman as whore, temptress, shrew, simple-minded, virtuous, and the image of perfection—all have prevented men from seeing women as simply the other half of the human species. Yet perhaps none has been so dangerous to women's lives as the image of the witch.

Although the idea of witchcraft has been around at least since the Bible (which mandates killing witches), the Catholic Church did not take witches seriously until the 13th century, when Thomas Aquinas suggested they still existed (Halsall, 1996). Witch-hunting became an obsession in Europe when Pope Innocent VIII decreed in 1486 that witches should be wiped out. A pamphlet released that year claimed that witches were more likely to be female because women were the source of all evil, had defective intelligence, tried to dominate men, and "[knew] no moderation whether in goodness or vice" (V. L. Bullough, 1973).

From the 1500s through the 1700s over 100,000 people (mostly women) in Germany were executed for witchcraft (Roach, 2004). In England, where most of the accused women were married, executions for witchcraft continued until 1712. Witchcraft trials seemed to happen at times of social disruption, religious change, or economic troubles. Such was the case in Salem, Massachusetts, in 1692, where three young girls began acting strangely, running around, falling to the ground in convulsions, and barking like dogs (Norton, 2002). Soon the other girls of Salem began to follow suit, and the doctors decided that the girls had been bewitched. Forced to identify the witches who had put spells on them, the girls began to name the adults they did not particularly like. Not one suspect dragged before the courts was acquitted, and 22 women were executed or died in prison. When the tide finally turned, 150 people were in prison awaiting trial, and another 200 stood accused. All were finally released (Roach, 2002).

Accusations of witchcraft were often used as a way to punish women who did not conform to social expectations of appropriate female behavior. It was also a means to reaffirm men's dominance over women. Even in many contemporary tribal cultures in which witchcraft is very much a part of the cultural beliefs, women are seen as potentially more evil than men (Janeway, 1971).

review questions

1 Explain Christianity's impact on our views of human sexuality. Were Islamic views of sexuality more or less conservative than Christianity?

2 Explain how views of sexuality changed from the Reformation through the Renaissance.

3 Explain the changes in the church's view of sexuality from St. Paul to Luther.

4 Explain how religious beliefs can lead to cognitive dissonance in college students.

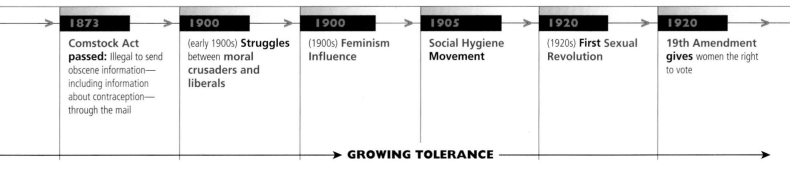

1873	**1900**	**1900**	**1905**	**1920**	**1920**
Comstock Act passed: Illegal to send obscene information—including information about contraception—through the mail	(early 1900s) **Struggles** between **moral crusaders and liberals**	(1900s) **Feminism Influence**	**Social Hygiene Movement**	(1920s) **First Sexual Revolution**	**19th Amendment gives** women the right to vote

→ GROWING TOLERANCE

The Enlightenment and the Victorian Era

The Enlightenment, an intellectual movement of the 18th century, influenced most of Europe; it prized rational thought over traditional authority and suggested that human nature was to be understood through a study of human psychology. Enlightenment writers argued that human drives and instincts are part of nature's design, so one must realize the basic wisdom of human urges and not fight them (Porter, 1982).

THE ENLIGHTENMENT
(BEGINNING ABOUT 1700)

During the Enlightenment, sexual pleasure was considered natural and desirable. In fact, of all the earthly pleasures, enlightenment thinkers praised sexuality as supreme. Sexuality had become so free that there was an unprecedented rise in premarital pregnancy and illegitimate births; up to one fifth of all brides in the late 17th century were pregnant when they got married (Trumbach, 1990).

As liberal as the Enlightenment was, many sexual activities, such as homosexuality, were condemned and persecuted. For example, starting in 1730, there was a 2-year "sodomite panic" in the Netherlands; hundreds of men accused of homosexual acts were executed, and hundreds more fled the country. France burned homosexuals long after it stopped burning witches. Yet there were also times of relative tolerance. Napoleon so eased laws against homosexuality that by 1860 it was tolerated, and male prostitutes were common in France (Tannahill, 1980).

THE VICTORIAN ERA
(EARLY 1800s)

The Victorian era, refers to Queen Victoria's rule, which began in 1837 and lasted until early 1901. It was a time of great prosperity in England. Propriety and public behavior became more important, especially to the upper class, and sexual attitudes became more conservative. Sex was not to be spoken of in polite company and was to be restricted to the marital bed, in the belief that preoccupation with sex interfered with higher achievements. Privately, Victorian England was not as conservative as it has been portrayed, and pornography, extramarital affairs, and prostitution were common. Still, the most important aspect of Victorian society was public propriety, and conservative values were often preached, if not always practiced.

During this period, the idea of male chivalry returned, and women were considered to be virtuous, refined, delicate, fragile, vulnerable, and remote; certainly, no respectable Victorian woman would ever admit to a sexual urge. The prudery of the Victorian era sometimes went to extremes. Victorian women were too embarrassed to talk to a doctor about their "female problems" and so would point out areas of discomfort on dolls (Hellerstein et al., 1981; see Sex in Real Life in this section for more information on women who shared their gynecological concerns with their physicians). Women were supposed to be interested in music but were not supposed to play the flute because pursing the lips was unladylike; the cello was unacceptable because it had to be held between the legs; the brass instruments were too difficult for the delicate wind of the female; the violin forced the woman's neck into an uncomfortable position. Therefore, only keyboard instruments were considered "ladylike" (V. L. Bullough, 1973).

Sexuality was repressed in many ways. Physicians and writers of the time often argued that semen was precious and should be conserved; Sylvester Graham, a Presbyterian minister and founder of the American Vegetarian Society, recommended sex only 12 times a year. He argued that sexual indulgence led to all sorts of ailments and infirmities, such as depression, faintness, headaches, blindness—the list is almost endless.

The Victorian era had great influence on sexuality in England and the United States. Many of the conservative attitudes that still exist today are holdovers from Victorian standards.

timeline Exploring Human Sexuality: Past and Present

1939	1948	1953	1960	1960	1965
World War II begins and lasts until 1945	**Kinsey publishes** *Sexual Behavior in the Human Male*	**Kinsey publishes** *Sexual Behavior in the Human Female*	**FDA approves** first birth control pill	(early 1960s) **Second Sexual Revolution**	**U.S. Supreme Court strikes down** Comstock laws

TOLERANCE

review questions

1 Explain how sexuality was viewed during the Enlightenment.

2 How did the Victorian era influence the view of sexuality?

3 Explain how sexuality was repressed during the Victorian era.

SEX IN REAL LIFE

The History of Vibrators

In the late 1800s the vibrator appeared in response to physician demands for more rapid therapies to treat hysteria.

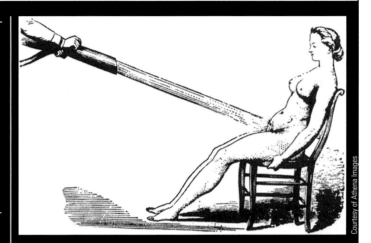

Courtesy of Athena Images

It might surprise you to know that vibrators have a long history dating back to the late 19th century. At that time, many women began voicing complaints to their physicians (who were mostly male) about miscellaneous gynecological problems. Their symptoms typically included fainting, fluid congestion, insomnia, nervousness, abdominal heaviness, loss of appetite for food or sex, and a tendency to cause trouble for others, especially family members (Maines, 1999). Physicians determined that these gynecological complaints were due to "pelvic hyperemia," otherwise known as genital congestion (Maines, 1999). The condition was diagnosed as "hysteria," a common and chronic complaint in women at the time. In fact, it wasn't until 1952 that the American Psychiatric Association dropped hysteria as a diagnosis (Slavney, 1990).

Hysteria was thought best relieved by "intercourse on the marriage bed" or vulvar massage by a physician or midwife (Maines, 1999). Hysteria rates were higher in unmarried, widowed, or chaste women because they did not engage in sexual intercourse. (Notice that there is no mention of lesbian women; physicians felt that hysteria resulted when a woman was not engaging in sexual intercourse with a man.)

To relieve the genital congestion associated with hysteria, physicians used vulvar massage to induce paroxysm (orgasm). This procedure was typically painstaking and time-consuming work, often taking up to one hour per woman. Remember that religious mandates at the time prohibited self-masturbation; therefore, vulvar massage was acceptable only in physicians' offices and was a strictly medical procedure most commonly prescribed for women diagnosed with hysteria (Maines, 1999).

In the late 1800s the vibrator appeared in response to physician demands for more rapid therapies to treat hysteria (Maines, 1999). By the early 1900s, several types of vibrators were available for physicians, from low-priced foot-powered models to more expensive battery and electric models. Advertisements slowly began to appear in women's magazines such as *Needlecraft, Woman's Home Companion,* and *Modern Women* (Maines, 1999). Although the advertisements were primarily directed at women, when they were marketed toward men, they claimed that vibrators made good gifts for women because they could give women a healthy glow with bright eyes and pink cheeks (Maines, 1999).

continued

1966	1969	1973	1973	2004	2008
Masters & Johnson publish *Human Sexual Response*	**Gay Liberation Movement starts** at Stonewall	*Roe v. Wade* **legalizes** abortion	**Homosexuality removed** from DSM	**Massachusetts approves** of same-sex marriage*	Although both **California and Connecticut gave** same-sex couples the right to marry in mid-2008, voters in California eliminated this right in late 2008.

*For more information on the changing legal status of same-sex relationships, see the timeline in Chapter 9.

TOLERANCE

continued

fan, tea kettle, and toaster (Maines, 1999).

In the 1960s, vibrators were openly marketed as sexual aids to improve sexual functioning and satisfaction. This was because of the changing sexual attitudes and increasingly open atmosphere about sexuality. Today vibrators are often marketed as "massagers," with few, if any, references to sexual health. Have you ever seen vibrator packaging that described how the vibrator might improve your sex life? Give you the best orgasm of your life? Help you learn to orgasm? Although sex stores often sell vibrators with sexual images on the packaging, there is typically no discussion of sexual health. Even so, vibrators have come a long way since the beginning of the century!

Social awareness of vibrators also began to build in the 1920s when the devices made their way into pornographic films (Maines, 1999). Soon afterward, vibrators were directly marketed toward women. Vibrators were the 15th household appliance to be electrified, after the sewing machine,

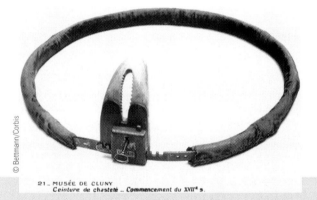

21 - MUSÉE DE CLUNY
Ceinture de chasteté - Commencement du XVIIᵉ s.

Chastity belts first appeared in the 15th century and were used primarily by women so that their husbands were assured the children they fathered were their own.

THE COLONIES: THE PURITAN ETHIC (BEGINNING ABOUT 1600)

The **Puritans** were a religious group that fled England and tried to set up a biblically based society in the New World. They had severe sanctions for sexual transgressions. In New England, for example, the death penalty was applied for sodomy, bestiality, adultery, and rape. In Puritan ideology, the entire community was responsible for upholding morality (D'Emilio & Freedman, 1988). However, the Puritans were not as closed-minded about sex as their reputation suggests, and they believed that sexuality was good and proper within marriage (Escoffier, 2003). In fact, men were obligated to have intercourse with their wives. The Puritans also tolerated most mild sexual transgressions—such as using non-missionary-style sexual positions or engaging in sexual intercourse during menstruation (J. Watkins, 2003).

Puritans
Refers to members of a 16th- and 17th-century Protestant group from England that wanted to purge the church of elaborate ceremonies and simplify worship. It has come to mean any person or group that is excessively strict in regard to sexual matters.

Sex in
American History

American society has been influenced most strongly by Europe, particularly England. Yet it also developed its own unique mix of ideas and attitudes, tempered by the contributions of the many cultures that immigrants brought with them. Let us look at some of these influences, including the colonies, slavery, and the liberalization of sexuality.

REALResearch > In the 1800s, Sylvester Graham (a Presbyterian minister and vegetarian) recommended that to be healthy, a person needed loose clothing, vigorous exercise, a hard mattress, cold night air, chastity, and cold showers. In 1829, he invented the graham cracker, which he believed could reduce sexual desire and increase physical health.

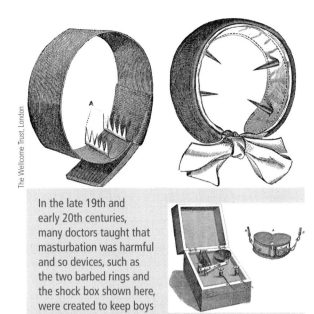

In the late 19th and early 20th centuries, many doctors taught that masturbation was harmful and so devices, such as the two barbed rings and the shock box shown here, were created to keep boys from achieving unwanted erections.

The Wellcome Trust, London

As the New World began to grow, it suffered from a lack of women, and the speculation in Europe was that any woman seeking a man should come to America, which offered women greater independence than Europe. On the island of Nantucket, for example, whaling kept the men at sea for months. The women took over the island's businesses, and prestige was granted to those who managed to make the money grow while their husbands were away (V. L. Bullough, 1973). Still, women were generally expected to tend to their domain of the home and children.

Sexuality was also a bit freer, and courting youth would wander into barns or look for high crops in the field to obscure their necking and groping. There was also a custom called **bundling,** in which young couples were allowed to share a bed as long as they were clothed, wrapped in sheets or bags, or had a wooden "bundling board" between them. The large number of premarital pregnancies suggests that couples found ways to get around their bundling impediments, but in most such cases, the couple would quickly marry (D'Emilio & Freedman, 1988).

THE UNITED STATES: FREEDOM— AND SLAVERY—IN THE NEW WORLD

The pendulum swung back to the liberal side after the Revolutionary War in the late 1700s. This was due mostly to the diminishing power of the church in the United States, leading to more liberal sexual attitudes. This liberalization, along with the continuing slave influx from Africa, had powerful effects on our culture's developing sexuality.

The Liberalization of Sex (About the 1700s)

With the diminished power of the church, came a new period of practical, utilitarian philosophy (as exemplified in Benjamin Franklin's maxims, such as "Early to bed and early to rise. . . ."),

which stressed the individual's right to pursue personal happiness. People began to speak more openly about sexuality and romantic love, and women began to pay more attention to appearance and sexual appeal. Children stopped consulting parents about marriage, and some young women simply became pregnant when they wanted to marry. By the late 18th century, as many as one third of all brides in some parts of New England were pregnant (D'Emilio & Freedman, 1988).

This newfound sexual freedom had many implications. In 1720, prostitution was relatively rare, but by the late 18th century, angry mobs were attacking brothels in cities all over the eastern seaboard (D'Emilio & Freedman, 1988). Contraception, such as early condoms, was readily available (Gamson, 1990), and newspapers and almanacs often advertised contraceptive devices and concoctions to induce abortion. The birth rate dropped, and abortion rates rose through the use of patent medicines, folk remedies, self-induced abortion by inserting objects into the uterus, and medical abortions. Within marriage, sexuality was much celebrated, and in many surviving diaries and letters from that era, couples speak of passion and longing for each other. Extramarital affairs were not uncommon, and some of the diaries quite explicitly record extramarital sexual passion.

Slavery (1600s–1800s)

Before the influx of slaves from Africa, the southern colonies made use of **indentured servants.** Sexual contact with, and even rape of, female indentured servants was fairly common. After 1670, African slaves became common in the South, and many states passed **antimiscegenation** (an-TEE-miss-seg-jen-nay-shun) **laws.** At first the laws were largely ignored. Sexual relations between Whites and Blacks continued, ranging from brutal rape to genuinely affectionate, long-term relationships. By the end of the 18th century, mixed-race children accounted for one fifth of the children born out of wedlock in Virginia (D'Emilio & Freedman, 1988).

The sex lives of slaves were different from those of colonists because of the relative lack of female slaves, the restrictions put on contact with members of the other sex, and the different cultural traditions of Africa. Whites accused African slaves of having loose morals because women tended to have children by different fathers and children slept in the same rooms as their copulating parents. These sexual habits were used as an excuse to rape them, break up their families, and even, at times, kill them. Of course, slave owners did not consider that they were responsible for forcing slaves to live that way. The fear that freed Black men would rape White women (or accusations that they had) was often used as justification to keep Blacks segregated or to lynch them, even though it was far more common for White men to rape Black slaves and servants.

bundling
An American practice of placing a wooden board or hanging sheets in the middle of the bed, or wrapping the body in tight clothes, to allow an unmarried couple to spend the night together without having sex.

indentured servants
People who became servants to pay off a debt and were often treated as little more than slaves.

antimiscegenation laws
Laws forbidding sexuality, marriage, or breeding among members of different races.

The slaves themselves developed a social system to protect their few freedoms. Adults formed and tried to maintain stable unions when possible, although marriage was officially illegal between slaves. Despite harsh conditions, there was a strong sense of morality within the slave community, and slaves tried to regulate sexual behavior as much as possible, forcing men to take care of the women they impregnated and sanctioning girls who were too promiscuous. The myth of slave sexual looseness is disproved by the lack of prostitution and very low venereal disease (STIs) rates among slaves (D'Emilio & Freedman, 1988). It was difficult, however, to maintain sexual unions when the woman's body is legally owned by the White master or when sexual favors might free one from harsh labor in the cotton fields. Despite the fact that plantation owners often condemned the promiscuity of the Blacks (and therefore excused their own sexual exploitation of them), slaves' premarital sexual activity was probably not much different from that of poor Whites (Clinton & Gillespie, 1997).

Settlers throughout early American history used the sexuality of minorities as an excuse to disdain or oppress them. Native Americans had their own cultural system of sexual morality; nonetheless, they were branded as savages for their acceptance of premarital sex and their practice of polygamy, which existed primarily because of the large number of males killed in war. White men freely raped female Native Americans, and Americans used sexual imagery to criticize the Mexicans they encountered in the West and Southwest; one writer claimed that all "darker colored" races were "inferior and syphilitic" (D'Emilio & Freedman, 1988). Mexicans, who were religious Catholics with strict sexual rules, were considered promiscuous by the Protestants because they did not consider it wrong to dance or show affection in public. The settlers often criticized others for sexual behaviors, such as homosexuality and premarital sex, that were not uncommon in their own communities.

THE 19TH CENTURY: POLYGAMY, CELIBACY, AND THE COMSTOCK LAWS (BEGINNING IN THE 1800s)

The pendulum swung back to the liberal side in the 19th century with the rise of a number of controversial social movements focusing on sexuality. The **free love movement,** which began in the 1820s, preached that love, not marriage, should be the prerequisite to sexual relations. Free love advocates criticized the sexual "slavery" of women in marriage, often condemned the sexual exploitation of slaves, and condemned sexuality without love (although their many critics often claimed that they preached promiscuity).

Another controversial group, the Church of Jesus Christ of Latter Day Saints, or Mormons, announced in 1852 that many of its members practiced polygamy, which almost cost Utah its statehood. As with the free love movement, Americans accused the

REALResearch **>** Following in the footsteps of Sylvester Graham, John Kellogg opened a sanitarium (a hospital for the treatment of chronic diseases) in 1906 and preached the "Battle Creek Idea," which was a plan for improving health. He advocated a good diet, exercise, fresh air, adequate sleep, and frequent bowel movements (ZACHARIAS, 2005). He is also credited with the development of Kellogg's Corn Flakes, developed to reduce excitability in the sanitarium's patients.

Mormons of loose morals even though, despite their acceptance of polygamy, they were very sexually conservative (Iverson, 1991). A number of small communities that practiced alternative forms of sexual relations also began during this time. The Oneida community preached group marriage, whereas the Shakers, frustrated with all the arguments over sexuality, practiced strict celibacy (Hillebrand, 2008).

By the close of the 19th century, the medical model of sexuality began to emerge. Americans became obsessed with sexual health, and physicians and reformers began to advocate self-restraint, abstention from masturbation, and eating "nonstimulating" foods (those free from additives and easy to digest). Doctors also argued that women were ruled by their wombs, and many had their ovaries surgically removed to "correct" masturbation or sexual passion. An influential group of physicians even argued that women were biologically designed for procreation and destined only for marriage, for they were too delicate to work or undergo the rigors of higher education. These theories completely ignored the fact that lower-class women often worked difficult labor 12 and 15 hours a day. Male sexuality, however, was viewed as normative.

In the 19th century, homosexuality was underground, although there were some open same-sex relationships that may or may not have been sexual. For example, there are a number of recorded cases in which women dressed and passed as men and even "married" other women (we discuss this more in Chapter 4 on gender). There were also men who wrote of intimate and loving relationships with other men, without an explicit admission of sexual contact. The great poet Walt Whitman, now recognized as a homosexual, at times confirmed his erotic attraction to men but at other times he denied it. In accordance with the developing medical model of sexuality, physicians began to argue that homosexuality was an illness rather than a sin, a view that lasted until the 1970s (D'Emilio, 1998; see Chapter 11).

The movements for more open sexual relationships were countered by strong voices arguing for a return to a more religious and chaste morality, an argument that continues more than a century later. In the 1870s, Anthony Comstock, a dry-goods salesman, single-handedly lobbied the legislature to outlaw obscenity.

free love movement
A movement of the early 19th century that preached love should be the factor that determines whether one should have sex (not to be confused with the free love movement of the 1960s).

Sex in Black America

. . . there have been many myths about the sexuality of African American men and women.

Although there has been significant growth in the scientific study of sexuality within the past 20 years, many specific populations, such as African American men and women, have not been equally studied (Hill, 2005; Parmer & Gordon, 2007). Because of this, there have been many myths about the sexuality of African American men and women. Black men and women are often viewed as "sex-perts" because they are supposed to know a lot about sexuality and engage in a lot of sex (Wyatt, 1998). Many of these myths surfaced during slavery out of the desire to scare White women away from Black men, while allowing White men to sexually exploit black women (Leavy, 1993).

One of the most prominent early sexuality researchers, Alfred Kinsey, did include African Americans in his large-scale study, but his sample size of African Americans was small and select (Kinsey et al., 1953; we discuss more of Kinsey's work in Chapter 2). Studies that followed Kinsey focused on the differences between Black and White sexuality and ignored the diversity and richness of Black sexuality.

Studies on African American sexuality have found that Black men and women are conservative in their sexual behavior (Bowser, 2001; Leavy, 1993; L. Lewis & Kertzner, 2003). Gail Wyatt, a sex therapist, researcher, and professor of psychiatry at the University of California—Los Angeles, has been researching Black sexuality since the early 1980s. In 1998, she published *Stolen Women: Reclaiming Our Sexuality, Taking Back Our Lives.* Although we discuss her book more throughout this textbook, below are some of her interesting findings:

- **83%** of Black women did not masturbate during childhood.

- **74%** of White women and **26%** of Black women (between the ages of 18 and 36) had 13 or more sexual partners.
- **56%** of Black women had only one sexual partner from the time they initiated sexual intercourse until age 17, whereas only **36%** of White women reported a long-term relationship during adolescence.
- Heterosexual Black men are more likely to use condoms for birth control and STI protection (**72%**) than heterosexual White men (**37%**).
- **93%** of White women and **55%** of Black women have had oral sex performed on them, whereas **93%** of heterosexual White women and **65%** of heterosexual Black women have performed oral sex on a man.

In an attempt to educate students about ethnicity and race, some U.S. universities teach courses specifically in African American sexuality. One course, taught at a campus of California State University, explored issues such as the marketing of Black female bodies in the media, representations of Black sexuality in pornography, Black lesbian, gay, and bisexual issues, interracial sexuality, and Black male patriarchy (Andre, 2006).

Rita Melendez, a professor in the Human Sexuality Studies Department at San Francisco State University, believes that subjects and populations studied in sexuality research are determined by race (Andre, 2006). For example, Melendez points out that much of the research on people with HIV is done on people of color by White researchers. To change this focus, Melendez believes universities need to create more courses and programs that encourage research from students of color. In addition, researchers need to be more cognizant of race and ethnicity issues. Throughout this book, we will continue to explore the importance of ethnicity and sexuality.

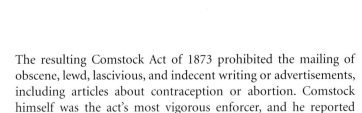

© Rob Levine/Corbis

The resulting Comstock Act of 1873 prohibited the mailing of obscene, lewd, lascivious, and indecent writing or advertisements, including articles about contraception or abortion. Comstock himself was the act's most vigorous enforcer, and he reported hundreds of people to the authorities, even for such things as selling reprints of famous artwork containing nudity or famous books that mentioned prostitution (M. A. Blanchard & Semoncho, 2006). Literally thousands of books, sexual objects, and contraceptive devices were destroyed, denying many people sophisticated contraceptive devices or information for almost 60 years (D'Emilio & Freedman, 1988). It wasn't until 1965 that the U.S. Supreme Court struck down Comstock Laws.

THE 20TH CENTURY:
SEXUAL CRUSADERS AND SEXOLOGISTS (BEGINNING IN THE 1900s)

Even though Comstock laws were in effect at the beginning of the 20th century, one study of 1,000 heterosexual women found that 74% used some form of contraception, most made love at least once a week, and 40% acknowledged masturbating during childhood or adolescence (although others began after marriage; D'Emilio & Freedman, 1988). These statistics reflect the freedom women gradually began to find as they moved to the cities, lived on their own, and began working more outside the home (Irvine, 1990). Yet the overwhelming majority of heterosexual women still considered reproduction the primary goal of sex.

Moral crusaders were also trying to curb newfound sexual freedoms at this time, and those trying to liberalize sexuality further were in an intense struggle, trying to guide the rapid changes taking place in American sexual behaviors. Crusaders pointed to the spread of prostitution and high rates of STIs. Liberalizers argued that modern industrial society could not sustain the coercive sexual standards of past centuries. In one guise or another, these battles are still being fought today.

The Social Hygiene Movement (Beginning in 1905)
In response to high STI rates, a New York physician, Prince Morrow, started a movement in 1905 that was a curious mixture of both liberal and traditional attitudes. The social hygiene movement convinced legislators that scores of virtuous women were catching STIs from husbands who frequented prostitutes, and so laws were passed mandating blood tests before marriage, and a number of highly publicized police actions were brought against prostitutes. Although the movement accepted pleasure as an acceptable motivation for sex, followers were against premarital sex and warned that masturbation harmed one's future sex life. Most important, they were early (if unsuccessful) advocates for sex education in the schools (D'Emilio & Freedman, 1988).

By the close of the 19th century, Americans became obsessed with sexual health . . .

Sexology
Beginning in the early part of the 20th century and increasingly by midcentury, the pioneers of sexual research were beginning to make scientific advances into the understanding of sexuality. Rejecting the religious and moral teachings about how people "should" behave, researchers brought sex out into the open as a subject worthy of medical, scientific, and philosophical debate. We discuss these researchers at length in the following chapter, but here we should note that they had a profound impact on the way people began to talk and think about sexuality.

For example, in the early 1940s Alfred Kinsey's large-scale surveys of American sexual behavior were promising to settle some of the debates and confusion about sexuality by providing scientific answers to questions about how people behaved (we discuss Kinsey's research more in Chapter 2). Kinsey published his research in two volumes in 1948 and 1953, and both were overnight best sellers. Based on thousands of interviews, Kinsey's findings shocked American culture (Kimmel & Plante, 2007). His findings revealed that sex was much more important to peoples' lives than originally thought. Masturbation, homosexuality, and infidelity were not uncommon, and women had more sexual interest and desire than society had been led to believe (Kimmel & Plante, 2007). The popularity of Kinsey's books showed that the American public was hungry for sexual knowledge.

Other researchers, Dr. William Masters and Virginia Johnson, took Kinsey's research a step further and brought sex into a laboratory to study the physiology of sexual response. Their research yielded two important books (Masters & Johnson, 1966, 1970) which were also overnight best sellers (we discuss Masters and Johnson's work more in Chapter 2).

The work of these sexologists helped to demystify sex and make it more respectable to publicly discuss the sexual behaviors and problems of real people. Much of this work was condemned by moral crusaders, who criticized its lack of connection to traditional standards of morality (Irvine, 1990).

The Sexual Revolutions (1920s and 1960s)
The phrase **sexual revolution** was coined in the 1920s by Wilhelm Reich, an Austrian psychoanalyst (Allyn, 2000). Reich was one of the leading figures of the sex reform movement in Europe, and he strongly believed in a sexually liberated society. He founded several clinics throughout Europe to educate people about sexuality and disseminate contraceptive information. Unfortunately, Reich's work was cut short by the political turmoil of the 1930s. Even though his dream for liberation never materialized in full, he did set into motion rapid changes in sexual mores throughout Europe and the United States during the first half of the 20th century (Allyn, 2000).

The values and attitudes about sexuality that were rooted in the Christian tradition slowly began to change as society became more permissive and accepting of sexual freedom. Advertising and other media became more sexualized, and fashion trends changed as the flapper era was ushered in. Flappers were women who typically wore short skirts, had short bob haircuts, and weren't uncomfortable going against societal expectations for women. They wore more makeup than what was generally accepted and had open attitudes about sexuality (Gourley, 2007). The trend toward more liberal ideas and values about sexuality continued in the late 1920s, but it wasn't until the early 1960s when many would say the real sexual revolution took place.

The 1960s were a time when the pendulum swung back to the liberal side; Americans went from "No Sex Until Marriage" to "If It Feels Good, Do It!" Two of the biggest sexuality challenges at this time were the reformulation of male gender roles and an examination of the double-standard of sexuality (Escoffier, 2003).

The modern movement that formed the sexual revolution began in San Francisco, where thousands of young people (who were referred to as "hippies") began to proclaim the power of love and sex. This period of time was an extension of the Enlightenment in the sense that people were searching for knowledge and

sexual revolution
Changes in sexual morality and sexual behavior that occurred throughout the Western world during the 1960s and 1970s.

information (Jong, 2003). There was also an emerging revolt against the moral code of American society, and movements against the status quo were not uncommon (Lipton, 2003). In fact, the Black Civil Rights movement and the growing student protests against the Vietnam War in the mid-1960s proved that people could organize and stand up for what they believed in rather than just going with the crowd.

REALResearch ＞Same-sex sexual expression has been a recognized aspect of Muslim societies for many centuries (ALI, 2002). Medieval Arabic literature had many references to same-sex activities between two men. However, because definitions of sex included penile penetration, sex between two women was not viewed as sex.

There were several events that helped set the stage for the 1960s sexual revolution. One was the discovery of antibiotics in the mid-1930s. This discovery led to decreased fears about sexually transmitted infections, because they were now curable (we discuss sexually transmitted infections in Chapter 15). Another important event was the development of television. In the timeline presented earlier in this chapter, we discuss the invention of the television and the events that helped shift our attitudes about sexuality. By the early 1960s, the majority of U.S. homes had a television set (Abramson, 2003). Television, radio, and other mass media began to broadcast more liberal ideas about sexuality to viewers and listeners. Pornography also became more acceptable, and in 1953 Hugh Hefner began publishing *Playboy* magazine.

Nonfiction sex manuals also began to appear, such as Helen Gurley Brown's *Sex and the Single Girl* (1962; Gurley Brown later went on to publish *Cosmopolitan* magazine), Joan Garrity's *The Sensuous Woman* (1969; although the author only referred to herself as "J" in the book), and David Reuben's *Everything You Always Wanted to Know About Sex (But Were Afraid To Ask)* (1969). There were many others published, and all of them spoke to the changing nature of sexuality. They were all factually written and were best sellers. Mainstream America had been desperate for more information about sexuality. Probably the most important thing these books did was to acknowledge and celebrate one's sexuality.

Another important event that liberated female sexuality at this time was the introduction of the first contraceptive pill in the early 1960s. For the first time, heterosexual women were free to engage in sexual intercourse without the fear of becoming pregnant. No longer was sexual intercourse associated solely with procreation. Fashions changed once again in the mid-1960s, emphasizing women's bodies and showing more skin. Women wore miniskirts, plunging necklines, and see-through blouses, further emphasizing women's sexuality. Some women began to burn their bras and "free their breasts" in an act of defiance.

Soon, poets, writers, and songwriters began to embrace both sensuality and sexual experimentation. Sexuality began to come out of the closet as repressive attitudes began to lessen. All of these influences led to a generation that was much more sexually liberal than those preceding it. At the end of the 1960s, the gay and lesbian civil rights movement officially started with the Stonewall riots (we discuss this more later in the chapter).

Feminism (Beginning in early 1900s)

There have always been women who protested against the patriarchy of their day, argued that women were as capable as men in the realms of work and politics, and defied their culture's stereotypes about women. Yet the 20th century saw the most successful feminist movement in history. The **women's suffrage** movement of the early 20th century first put women's agendas on the national

scene, but it was Margaret Sanger who most profoundly influenced women's sexuality in the first half of the 20th century.

Sanger, a 30-year-old homemaker, attended a lecture on socialism that transformed her into an advocate for the rights of workers and their children. Sanger defied the Comstock laws by arguing that poor workers, who were having child after child, needed birth control. Because she published information about birth control, Sanger was forced to flee to England to avoid arrest for violating the Comstock laws. She finally returned when a groundswell of support in the United States convinced her to come back and face trial. Intellectuals from across Europe wrote to President Woodrow Wilson on her behalf, and the public was so outraged by her arrest that the prosecutors dropped the case. She then opened a birth control clinic in Brooklyn (which eventually evolved into the Planned Parenthood organization) and was repeatedly arrested, evoking much protest from her supporters.

After Sanger, organized feminism entered a quiet phase, not reemerging until the 1960s. In the middle of the 20th century, women increasingly entered institutions of higher education and entered the labor force in great numbers while men were off fighting World War II. At the same time, divorce rates were rising, many women widowed by war were raising children as single parents, and the postwar baby boom relegated middle-class women to their suburban homes. Social conditions had given women more power just as their roles were being restricted again to wife and mother. A backlash was soon to come, and the pendulum would swing back to the conservative side.

The modern feminist movement can best be summarized by the work of three female authors (Ferree & Hess, 1985). In her 1949 book, *The Second Sex,* Simone de Beauvoir showed that women were not granted an identity of their own but were considered the objects of men's wishes and anxieties. Betty Friedan followed in 1963 with *The Feminine Mystique,* a 10-year follow-up of the lives of her graduating class from Smith College in which she found that these educated, bright women felt trapped in the role of housewife and wanted careers to have happier, more fulfilled lives. Finally, at the height of the Vietnam War, Kate Millet's (1969) *Sexual Politics* argued that patriarchy breeds violence and forces men to renounce all that is feminine in them. According to Millet, rape is an act of aggression aimed at keeping women docile and controlling them, and men see homosexuality as a "failure" of patriarchy, so it is violently repressed.

Feminists of the 1960s argued that they were entitled to sexual satisfaction, that the existing relations of the sexes were exploitative, and that women had a right to control their lives and their bodies. Some of the more radical feminists advocated lesbianism

women's suffrage
The movement to get women the right to vote.

The gay liberation movement fights for social acceptance and understanding of gay, lesbian, and bisexual issues.

as the only relationship not based on male power, but most feminists fought for a transformation of the interpersonal relationship of men and women and of the male-dominated political structure. Part of the freedom women wanted was the freedom to choose when to be mothers, and the right to choose abortion became a firm part of the feminist platform.

Feminism has made great cultural and political strides and has changed the nature of American society and sexual behavior. The pursuit of sexual pleasure is now seen as a woman's legitimate right, and heterosexual men are no longer expected to be the sexual experts relied on by docile, virginal mates. Feminists were at the forefront of the abortion debate and hailed the legalization of abortion as a great step in achieving women's rights over their own bodies. More recently, women have begun entering politics in record numbers, and the Senate, Congress, and governorships are increasingly counting women among their members. Even so, women still have many struggles. Men are paid more than women for the same work, poverty is increasingly a problem of single mothers, and rape and spousal abuse are still major social problems in the United States (Lips, 2008). Still, feminism as a movement has had a major impact on the way America views sexuality.

Gay Liberation (Beginning in mid 1900s)

The period after World War II was challenging for homosexuals. Senator Joseph McCarthy, who became famous for trying to purge America of communists, also relentlessly hunted homosexuals. Homosexuals were portrayed as perverts, lurking in schools and on street corners ready to pounce on unsuspecting youth, and many were thrown out of work or imprisoned in jails and mental hospitals. The news media participated in this view, as in a 1949 *Newsweek* article that identified all homosexuals as "sex murderers." Doctors tinkered with a variety of "cures," including lobotomies and castration. Churches were either silent or encouraged the witch hunts, and Hollywood purged itself of positive references to homosexuality. Many laws initiated during this period, such as immigration restrictions for homosexuals and policies banning gays from the military, continued for many years (Adam, 1987).

In 1951, an organization for homosexual rights, the Mattachine Society, was founded in the United States by Henry Hay.

The Daughters of Bilitis, the first postwar lesbian organization, was founded by four lesbian couples in San Francisco in 1955. Although these groups began with radical intentions, the vehement antihomosexuality of American authorities forced the groups to lay low throughout the late 1950s.

Although gay activism increased in America with protests and sit-ins throughout the 1960s, modern gay liberation is usually traced to the night in 1969 when New York police raided a Greenwich Village gay bar called Stonewall. For the first time, the gay community erupted in active resistance, and the police were greeted by a hail of debris thrown by the gay patrons of the bar. There had been previous acts of resistance, but the Stonewall riot became a symbol to the gay community and put the police on notice that homosexuals would no longer passively accept arrest and police brutality.

Following Stonewall, gay activism began a strong campaign against prejudice and discrimination all over the country. Groups and businesses hostile to gays were picketed, legislators were lobbied, committees and self-help groups were founded, legal agencies were formed, and educational groups tried to change the image of homosexuality in America. For example, in 1973, strong gay lobbying caused the American Psychiatric Association to remove homosexuality from the *Diagnostic and Statistical Manual (DSM)*, the official reference of psychiatric disorders. Almost overnight, people who had been considered "sick" were suddenly "normal." The *DSM* change removed the last scientific justification for treating homosexuals any differently from other citizens and demonstrated the new national power of the movement for homosexual rights. Soon the gay movement was a powerful presence in the United States, Canada, Australia, and Western Europe (Adam, 1987).

The 1970s were, in many ways, the golden age of gay life in America. In cities such as San Francisco and New York, gay bathhouses and bars became open centers of gay social life, and gay theater groups, newspapers, and magazines appeared. In 1979, the National March on Washington for Lesbian and Gay Rights was a symbolic step forward for the gay movement (Ghaziani, 2005). The discovery of the AIDS epidemic in the United States and Europe in the beginning of the 1980s doused the excitement of the

As of 2008, same-sex marriage was legal only in Massachusetts and California.

1970s, as thousands of gay men began to die from the disease (see Chapter 15). Historically, when such fearsome epidemics arise, people have been quick to find a minority group to blame for the disease, and homosexuals were quickly blamed by a large segment of the public (Perrow & Guillén, 1990; Shilts, 2000).

In 1990, queer theory developed and grew out of lesbian and gay studies. Although we discuss queer theory more in Chapter 2, the gay rights movement has been at the forefront of trying to change sexual attitudes in the United States not only by pressing for recognition of homosexuality as a legitimate sexual choice, but also by arguing that all sexual minorities have a right to sexual happiness. Although a handful of states allow gay couples to register as "domestic partners" and allow them certain health and death benefits that married couples have, the issue of same-sex marriage is still controversial in American society. As of 2008, same-sex marriage was legal in two states. Still, gays and lesbians are subject to prejudices in the United States, and some states are passing laws making it illegal for homosexuals to be considered a minority group worthy of special protections.

We are the sum total of our history. Our attitudes and beliefs reflect all of our historical influences, from the ancient Hebrews and Greeks to the Christianity of the Middle Ages to the modern feminist and gay liberation movements. Most of us have a hard time recognizing that our own constellation of beliefs, feelings, and moral positions about sex are a product of our particular time and place and are in a constant state of evolution. It is important to keep this in mind as we explore the sexual behaviors of other people and other cultures throughout this book.

review questions

1 Explain how the Puritans viewed sex. Who did they believe was responsible for upholding morality?

2 Explain some of the influences that led to the liberalization of sex in the 1700s.

3 What was the "free love movement" and what did the movement preach?

4 What are the two most important movements to change sexuality in the latter part of the 20th century? What did each contribute?

CHAPTER review

SUMMARY POINTS

1 Human sexuality is grounded in biological functioning, emerges as we develop, and is expressed by cultures through rules about sexual contact, attitudes about moral and immoral sexuality, habits of sexual behavior, patterns of relations between the sexes, and more.

2 The sexual nature of human beings is unique in the animal kingdom. Humans have created ideas, laws, customs, fantasies, and art around the sexual act. Sexuality is a uniquely human trait.

3 American media are the most sexually suggestive in the Western Hemisphere. However, sexuality is one of the most difficult aspects for us to express and explore.

4 The evolution to an upright posture changed forever the way the human species engage in sexual intercourse.

5 Men dominated public life in early history, and we know far more about men's thoughts than women's. The Hebrew Bible contained explicit rules about sexual behavior. The focus on marital sexuality and procreation formed the basis of sexual attitudes in the West for centuries.

6 The Greeks were more sexually permissive than the Hebrews. In Greek culture, pederasty was considered a natural form of sexuality. Rome had few restrictions about sexuality until late in the history of the empire.

7 Chinese civilization's belief in yin and yang taught people how to maximize their sexuality. A woman's essence, or yin, was viewed as inexhaustible, whereas a man's essence, yang, embodied in semen, was limited. Hinduism concentrates on an individual's cycle of birth and rebirth, also known as karma. India's most famous sex manual, the Kama Sutra, appeared sometime during the third or fourth century.

8 Perhaps no single system of thought has had as much impact on the Western world as Christianity. According to early forms of the belief system, sexuality itself was not sinful when performed as part of the marital union, but the ideal situation was celibacy. In fact, with the advent of Christianity, chastity became a virtue for the first time in history.

9 In the early Middle Ages, the influence of the church began to increase. Its teachings began to influence laws, which became much stricter. Perhaps no person from the Middle Ages had a stronger impact on attitudes toward sexuality than the theologian Thomas Aquinas.

10 Muhammad began to preach a religion called Islam in the sixth century. Many Muslim societies have strong rules of modesty for women that involve covering private parts of their bodies. According to the Muslim bible, the Koran, marital sexual intercourse was a good religious deed, and men were encouraged to engage frequently in such behavior. All forms of sexuality were permissible.

11 The Renaissance witnessed a new view of sexuality and of the roles of women in society. Women made great strides in education and became more prominent in political affairs. Pro-female tracts began to circulate, and lively debates about the value of women ensued. However, by the 17th century, witchcraft trails appeared, symbolizing the fear that men held of women's sexuality.

12 In the early 16th century, Martin Luther started Protestantism. Luther saw in the Bible the obligation to reproduce, considered marital love blessed, and considered sexuality a natural function. Sexuality was permissible only in the marital union although it had other justifications besides reproduction.

13 Three important movements that influenced modern sexuality were the Reformation, the Renaissance, and the Enlightenment.

14 The Enlightenment (early 1700s) prized rational thought over traditional authority and suggested that human nature was to be understood through a study of human psychology. Sexual pleasure was considered natural and desirable.

15 During the Victorian era (early 1800s), conservative values were often preached, although not always practiced. The idea of male chivalry returned, and women were considered to be virtuous, refined, delicate, fragile, vulnerable, and remote. Sexuality was repressed in many ways for men and women.

16 The Puritans were a religious group that fled England and tried to set up a biblically based society in the New World. Even though they believed that sexuality was good and proper within marriage, they also believed the entire community was responsible for upholding morality.

17 After the Revolutionary War, the church's power began to diminish in the United States. People began to speak more openly about sexuality, and the liberalization of sexual conduct had many results. Prostitution flourished, and contraception became more readily available.

18 Slavery had a profound effect on post-Revolutionary America. Many slaves developed a social system and formed stable unions, although marriage was officially illegal between slaves. There was a strong sense of morality within the slave community, and sexual behavior was regulated as much as possible.

19 During the 19th century, there was a rise in a number of controversial social movements focusing on sexuality. The free love movement preached that only love should be the prerequisite to sexual relations. However, by the end of the 19th century, the medical model of sexuality began to emerge, and physicians and reformers began to advocate self-restraint, abstention from masturbation, and consumption of "nonstimulating" foods. The Comstock Act of 1873 prohibited the mailing of obscene, lewd, and indecent writings, including articles about contraception or abortion.

20 In 1905, the social hygiene movement convinced legislators to pass laws mandating blood tests before marriage. Premarital sex and masturbation were thought to harm one's future sex life. In the early part of the 20th century, pioneers of sexual research began their work, rejecting the religious and moral teachings about how people "should" behave.

21 The sexual revolution brought changes in values and attitudes about sexuality. Society became more permissive and accepting of sexual freedom. Flappers and hippies helped bring more liberal attitudes about sexuality.

22 Feminism and gay liberation also affected society's attitudes about sexuality. Modern gay liberation is usually traced back to the Stonewall riot of 1969. In 1973, strong gay lobbying caused the American Psychiatric Association to remove homosexuality from the *DSM*.

CRITICAL THINKING questions

1 Explain your goals for this class and how you developed each of these goals. Do you think this class will help you in the future? If so, in what ways?

2 Why do you think "sex sells" when our culture traditionally has had a problem openly talking about sexuality?

3 The Bible has had a profound impact on our attitudes toward sexuality. Do you think that it is still influential? In what ways?

4 How different do China's and India's sexual histories seem to you today? Are they different from our Western views of sexuality?

5 Provide two examples of how cultural images of beauty affect how men and women feel about themselves. Explain how the Chinese practice of foot binding became so widespread and lasted for 1,000 years.

6 Explore the many influences that led to the sexual revolution of the 1960s. Explain how these events shaped the cultural view of sexuality.

7 Compare and contrast both the role of women and the views of sexuality in modern society and in Islam. How does the practice of honor crimes tie into gender issues in society?

WEB resources

Sexuality Now Book Companion Website

Go to www.cengage.com/psychology/carroll for practice quizzes, glossary, flash cards, and more. You can also access the following websites from the companion site.

The Kinsey Institute ■ This official website for the Kinsey Institute is one of only a handful of centers in the world that conducts interdisciplinary research exclusively on sex and has a large library that includes books, films, video, fine art, artifacts, photography, archives, and more.

The Journal of the History of Sexuality ■ This journal has a cross-cultural and cross-disciplinary focus that brings together original articles and critical reviews from historians, social scientists, and humanities scholars worldwide. The website offers a look at recently published articles in the journal.

Salem Witch Trials Documentary Archive ■ This website offers information on the Salem witch trials, including transcripts of court records and maps.

The Sexuality Information and Education Council of the United States (SIECUS) ■ SIECUS is a national organization that promotes comprehensive education about sexuality and advocates the right of individuals to make responsible sexual choices.

CengageNOW

Go to www.cengage.com/login to link to CengageNOW, your online study tool. First take the Pre-Test for this chapter to get your Personalized Study Plan, which will identify topics you need to review and direct you to online resources. Then take the Post-Test to determine which concepts you have mastered and which you still need work on.

Videos in CengageNOW

For additional information on topics discussed in this chapter, check out the videos in CengageNOW on the following topics:

• Politics, Religion, and Sexual Expression—Answers questions about the frequency and nature of sexual practices among churchgoers, non-churchgoers, Republicans, and Democrats in the United States.

CHAPTER 2

Understanding Human Sexuality: Theory and Research

© Bettmann/Corbis

T he untimely death of Dr. Alfred C. Kinsey takes from the American scene an important and valuable, as well as controversial, figure. Whatever may have been the reaction to his findings—and to the unscrupulous use of some of them—the fact remains that he was first, last, and always a scientist. In the long run it is probable that the values of his contribution to contemporary thought will lie much less in what he found out than in the method he used and his way of applying it. Any sort of scientific approach to the problems of sex is difficult because the field is so deeply overlaid with such things as moral precept, taboo, individual and group training, and long established behavior patterns. Some of these may be good in themselves, but they are no help to the scientific and empirical method of getting at the truth. Dr. Kinsey cut through this overlay with detachment and precision. His work was conscientious and comprehensive. Naturally it will receive a serious setback with his death. Let us earnestly hope that the scientific spirit that inspired it will not be similarly impaired.

SOURCE: "Dr. Kinsey Is Dead," *New York Times*, August 26, 1956.

32
Our Mind as a Sex Organ

30
Freud, the Father of Psychoanalysis

49
View in Video

◁ Opposite: © Masterfile

As you learned in the previous chapter, historical attitudes about sexuality depended on many factors, including the media and institutions such as medicine, law, and religion. These factors also affect sexuality research. Alfred Kinsey (1894–1956) was probably the most influential sex researcher of the 20th century. His work changed many of the attitudes that existed about sexuality at the time. Many believe that his early death at age 62 was the result of stress from the constant criticism and struggle he lived under as he tried to legitimize the field of sexuality research. Kinsey was frustrated by the lack of respect many had for his controversial findings in sexuality research, which was then still considered taboo. We discuss more about Kinsey's life and work later in this chapter.

Sex studies seem to appear everywhere today—in magazines, newspapers, and on television. But how do you know whether the research is reliable, that it has been carried out properly? In this chapter, we explore both the major theories and the research methods that underlie the study of sexuality. We also examine some of the most influential sexuality studies that have been done. Theoretical development and ongoing research combine to provide a foundation on which to build further understanding of sexuality.

Before we start, you might wonder why reviewing theory and research in a sexuality textbook is important. Because theories guide our understanding of sexuality and research helps answer our many questions, learning how theories are formulated and research is pursued will give you insight into the information that is provided in the chapters to come. Let's examine the various theories of sexuality and some of the important sex researchers.

Theories about Sexuality

The study of sexuality is multidisciplinary. Psychologists, sexologists, biologists, theologians, physicians, sociologists, anthropologists, and philosophers all perform sexuality research. The questions each discipline asks and how its practitioners transform those questions into research projects can differ greatly. However, the insights of these disciplines complement each other, and no single approach to the study of sexuality is better than another.

A **theory** is a set of assumptions, principles, or methods that help a researcher understand the nature of the phenomenon being

theory
A set of assumptions, principles, or methods that helps a researcher understand the nature of a phenomenon being studied.

studied. A theory provides an intellectual structure to help conceptualize, implement, and interpret a topic, such as human sexuality. The majority of researchers begin with theories about human behavior that guide the kind of questions they ask about sexuality. For example, suppose a researcher subscribes to the theory that sexuality is innate and biologically determined; he or she would probably design studies to examine such things as how the hypothalamus in the brain or the monthly cycle of hormones influences our sexual behavior. It is unlikely he or she would be interested in studying the societal influences on sexuality. A person who believes sexuality is determined by environmental influences, in contrast, would be more likely to study how the media influences sexuality rather than genetic patterns of sexual behavior.

There are several theories—often clashing—that guide much of our thinking about sexuality. These include psychological, biological, sociological, and evolutionary theoretical views of human sexuality. In addition, over the last few years, feminist and queer theories have also become important models for exploring and explaining sexual behavior. We first explore each of these and look at how they influence sexuality research. While we do, however, it is important to remember that many theorists borrow from multiple theoretical perspectives and that these categories often overlap and learn from each other.

PSYCHOLOGICAL THEORIES

Of all the psychological theories of sexuality, the most influential has been Sigmund Freud's psychoanalytic theory. Freud felt that the sex drive was one of the most important forces in life, and he spent a considerable amount of time studying sexuality. His theories affected how society viewed sexual behavior and also helped usher in more liberal attitudes about sexuality.

PSYCHOANALYTIC THEORY

Sigmund Freud (1856–1939) spent most of his life in Vienna, Austria. In the early 1900s, Freud gathered a group of psychologists together to further his ideas, and he became the founder of

Sigmund Freud (1856–1939), the father of psychoanalysis, set the stage for all psychological theories that followed.

the psychoanalytic school. We explore two of Freud's most controversial concepts—personality formation and psychosexual development.

Personality Formation

According to Freud, human behavior is motivated by instincts and drives. The two most powerful drives are **libido** (la-BEED-oh), which is sexual motivation, and **thanatos** (THAN-uh-toes), which is aggressiveness motivation. Of these two, the libido is the more powerful.

Freud believed the personality contained the **id, ego,** and **superego.** At birth, a child has only the id portion of the personality, which functions as the pleasure center. If the id were the only part of the personality that developed, we would always be seeking pleasure and fulfillment with little concern for others; in other words, we would operate in the way most animals do. As humans get older, however, the id balances its desires with other parts of the personality.

By the second year of life, the ego develops as the child begins to interact with his or her environment. The ego keeps the id in check by being realistic about what the child can and cannot have. Because the majority of the id's desires may be socially unacceptable, the ego works to restrain it.

Freud also believed that the last portion of the personality, the superego, develops by the age of 5 years. It contains both societal and parental values and puts more restrictions on what a person can and cannot do. It acts as our conscience, and its most effective weapon is guilt. For example, let's say that a woman was raised in a very religious family, and she wants to wait until she's married to have sex. One night she starts messing around with her boyfriend (an id action). It feels good, and the id is being fulfilled.

libido
According to Freud, the energy generated by the sexual instinct.

thanatos
According to Freud, the self-destructive instinct, often turned outward in the form of aggression.

id
The collection of unconscious urges and desires that continually seek expression.

ego
The part of the personality that mediates between environmental demands (reality), conscience (superego), and instinctual needs (id).

superego
The social and parental standards an individual has internalized; the conscience.

Soon, reality kicks in (the ego), and she realizes that she is about to have sex in the back seat of a car! This causes her to reevaluate the situation, and because she has been taught that premarital sex is wrong, she feels guilty (a superego action). Throughout our lives, the id, ego, and superego are in a constant struggle with each other, but it is the ego, or the realistic portion of our personality, that keeps the other two parts balanced.

If the ego does not keep things in balance the superego could take over, and a person could be paralyzed by guilt. The id could also take over forcing the person to search constantly for pleasure with little concern for others. Freud believed that the only way to bring these conditions into balance was for the person to undergo **psychoanalysis.**

Psychosexual Development

One of Freud's most controversial ideas was his theory of **psychosexual development.** He believed that one's basic personality was formed by events that happened in the first 6 years of life. During each stage of development, Freud identified a different **erogenous** (uh-RAJ-uh-nus) **zone** in which libidinal energy was directed. If the stage was not successfully completed, the libidinal energy was tied up in that zone, and the child could experience a **fixation.** Psychosexual development includes the oral, anal, phallic, and genital stages.

The first stage of psychosexual development, known as the **oral stage,** lasts through the first 18 months of life. According to Freud's theory, problems during this stage could result in an oral fixation, leading to behaviors such as cigarette smoking, overeating, fingernail chewing, or alcohol abuse. The next stage, the **anal stage** begins when a child starts toilet training. Problems during this stage could lead to traits such as stubbornness, orderliness, or cleanliness.

According to Freud, the most important stage is the next one, the **phallic stage,** which occurs between the ages of 3 and 6 years. Freud believed that during the phallic stage, boys go through the **Oedipus** (ED-uh-puss) **complex.** Freud thought girls go through an **Electra complex** and develop penis envy. Freud believed that the Electra stage is never fully resolved, and because of this, women are less psychologically mature than men. At the end of this stage, boys and girls will typically identify with the same-sex parent and adopt masculine or feminine characteristics. The superego begins to develop during this time as well, and most children adopt their parents' values.

*Freud's theories generated **controversy** during the Victorian Era.*

Before puberty, the child passes through the **latency stage,** and sexual interest goes underground. During this stage, little boys often think little girls have "cooties" (and vice versa), and childhood play primarily exists in same-sex groups. Puberty marks the **genital stage,** which is the final stage of psychosexual development. During this stage, sexuality becomes less internally directed and more directed at others as erotic objects.

Freud's ideas were controversial in the Victorian time period in which he lived. His claims that children were sexual from birth and lusted for the other-sex parent caused tremendous shock in the conservative community of Vienna. Remember that at the time when Freud came up with his ideas, there was a strong cultural **repression** of sexuality. Doctors and ministers believed that masturbation would harm your health, and conversations about sex were unheard of. Among modern psychologists, Freud and the psychoanalytic theory have received a considerable amount of criticism. The predominant criticism is that his theory is unscientific and does not lend itself to testing (Myers, 2007). How could a researcher study the existence of the phallic stage? If it is indeed **unconscious,** then it would be impossible to hand out surveys to see when a child was in each stage. Because Freud based his theories on his patients, he has been accused of creating his theories around people who were sick; consequently, they may not apply to healthy people (we discuss this more in the section on research methodology). Finally, Freud has also been heavily criticized because of his unflattering psychological portrait of women (Myers, 2007).

BEHAVIORAL THEORY

Behaviorists believe that it is necessary to observe and measure behavior to understand it. Psychological states, emotions, the unconscious, and feelings are not measurable and therefore are not valid for study. Only overt behavior can be measured, observed, and controlled by scientists. Radical behaviorists (those who believe that we do not actually choose how we behave), such as B. F. Skinner (1953), claim that environmental rewards and punishments determine the types of behaviors in which we engage. This is referred to as **operant conditioning.**

---

psychoanalysis
System of psychotherapy developed by Freud that focuses on uncovering the unconscious material responsible for a patient's disorder.

psychosexual development
The childhood stages of development during which the id's pleasure-seeking energies focus on distinct erogenous zones.

erogenous zones
Areas of the body that are particularly sensitive to touch and are associated with sexual pleasure.

fixation
The tying up of psychic energy at a particular psychosexual stage, resulting in adult behaviors characteristic of the stage.

oral stage
A psychosexual stage in which the mouth, lips, and tongue are the primary erogenous zone.

anal stage
A psychosexual stage in which the anal area is the primary erogenous zone.

phallic stage
A psychosexual stage in which the genital region is the primary erogenous zone and in which the Oedipus or Electra complex develops.

Oedipus complex
A male child's sexual attraction for his mother and the consequent conflicts.

Electra complex
The incestuous desire of a daughter for her father.

latency stage
A psychosexual stage in which libido and sexual interest are repressed.

genital stage
Final psychosexual stage in which a person develops the ability to engage in adult sexual behavior.

repression
A coping strategy by which unwanted thoughts or prohibited desires are forced out of consciousness and into the unconscious mind.

unconscious
All the ideas, thoughts, and feelings to which we have no conscious access.

behaviorists
Theorists who believe that behavior is learned and can be altered.

operant conditioning
Learning resulting from the reinforcing response a person receives following a certain behavior.

We learn certain behaviors, including most sexual behaviors, through reinforcement and punishment. Reinforcements encourage a person to engage in a behavior by associating it with pleasurable stimuli, whereas punishments make it less likely that a behavior will be repeated, because the behavior becomes associated with unpleasant stimuli. For instance, if a man decided to engage in extramarital sex with a colleague at work, it may be because of the positive reinforcements he receives, such as the excitement of going to work. If, in contrast, a man experiences an erection problem the first time he has sexual intercourse outside of his marriage, it may make it less likely he will try the behavior again anytime soon. The negative experience reduces the likelihood that he will engage in the behavior again.

To help change unwanted behavior, behaviorists use **behavior modification.** For example, if a man wants to rid himself of sexual fantasies about young boys, a behavioral therapist might use **aversion therapy.** To do so, the therapist might show the man slides of young boys; when he responds with an erection, an electrical shock is administered to his penis. If this is repeated several times, behaviorists believe the man will no longer respond with an erection. The punishment will have changed the behavior. Contrast this form of therapy to that of a psychoanalytic therapist, who would probably want to study what happened to this man in the first 6 years of his life. A behavior therapist would primarily be concerned with changing the behavior and less concerned with its origins. Much of modern sex therapy uses the techniques developed by behaviorists (MacKenzie, 2008).

Cognitive therapists believe that the biggest sexual organ is between the ears—what turns us on is what we think turns us on.

SOCIAL LEARNING THEORY

Social learning theory actually grew out of behaviorism. Scientists began to question whether behaviorism was too limited in its explanation of human behavior. Many believed that thoughts and feelings had more influence on behaviors than the behaviorists claimed. A noted social learning theorist, Albert Bandura (1969), argued that both external and internal events influence our behavior. By this, he meant that external events, such as rewards and punishments, influence behavior, but so do internal events, such

turn, we are praised and reinforced for these behaviors. Think for a moment about a young boy who identifies with his mother and begins to dress and act like her. He will probably be ridiculed or even punished, which may lead him to turn his attention to a socially acceptable figure, most likely his father. Peer pressure also influences our sexuality. We want to be liked, and therefore we may engage in certain behaviors because our peers encourage it. We also learn what is expected of us from television, our families, even from music.

COGNITIVE THEORY

So far, the theories we have looked at emphasize that either internal conflicts or external events control the development of personality. Unlike these, **cognitive theory** holds that people differ in how they process information, and this creates personality differences. We feel what we think we feel, and our thoughts also affect our behavior. Our behavior does not come from early experiences in childhood or from rewards or punishments; rather, it is a result of how we perceive and conceptualize what is happening around us.

REALResearch **>** Economic and legal changes in the United States (such as increased legal protections, work-related benefits, and social acceptance) have made it more acceptable for American adults, especially women, to select a sex partner of the same sex (BUTLER, 2005).

as feelings, thoughts, and beliefs. Bandura began to bridge the gap between behaviorism and cognitive theory, which we discuss next.

Social learning theorists believe that imitation and identification are also important in the development of sexuality. For example, we identify with our same-sex parent and begin to imitate him or her, which helps us develop our own gender identity. In

behavior modification
Therapy based on operant conditioning and classical conditioning principles, used to change behaviors.

aversion therapy
A technique that reduces the frequency of maladaptive behavior by associating it with aversive stimuli.

cognitive theory
A theory proposing that our thoughts are responsible for our behaviors.

As far as sexuality is concerned, cognitive theorists believe that the biggest sexual organ is between the ears (Walen & Roth, 1987). What sexually arouses us is what we think sexually arouses us. We pay attention to our physical sensations and label these reactions. For example, if a woman does not have an orgasm during partner sex, she could perceive this in one of two ways. She might think that having an orgasm is not really all that important and maybe next time she will have one; or she could think that she is a failure because she did not have an orgasm and feel depressed as a result. What has caused the depression, however, is not the lack of an orgasm but her perception of it.

HUMANISTIC THEORY

Humanistic (or person-centered) psychologists believe that we all strive to develop ourselves to the best of our abilities and to achieve **self-actualization** (Raskin & Rogers, 1989). This is easier to do if we are raised with **unconditional positive regard,** which involves accepting and caring about another person without any stipulations or conditions. In other words, there are no rules a person must follow to be loved. An example of unconditional positive regard would be a child being caught playing sexual games with her friends and her parents explaining that they loved her but disapproved of her behavior.

If, on the other hand, the parents responded by yelling at the child and sending her to her room, she learns that when she does something wrong, her parents will withdraw their love. This is referred to as **conditional love.** The parents make it clear that they will love their child only when she acts properly.

Children who grow up with unconditional positive regard learn to accept their faults and weaknesses, whereas children who have experienced conditional love may try to ignore those traits because they know others would not approve. Accepting our faults and weaknesses leads us toward self-actualization.

Self-actualization occurs as we learn our own potential in life. We want to do things that make us feel good about ourselves. For many of us, casual sex with someone we don't know would not make us feel good; therefore, it does not contribute to our own growth. Sexual intimacy in a loving and committed relationship does feel good and helps contribute to our own self-actualization.

BIOLOGICAL THEORY

The biological theory of human sexuality emphasizes that sexual behavior is primarily a biological process. Sexual functioning, hormonal release, ovulation, ejaculation, conception, pregnancy, and birth are controlled physiologically. All of these events evolved over thousands of years and are deeply embedded in our physiology. Those who advocate this theory also point out that human sexual behavior, including gender roles and sexual orientation, are primarily due to inborn, genetic patterns and are not functions of social or psychological forces. Sexual problems are believed to be due to physiological causes, and intervention often includes medications or surgery.

What sexually arouses us is what we think sexually arouses us.

EVOLUTIONARY THEORY

Unlike biological theory, which contends that our sexuality is biologically based, **evolutionary theory** incorporates both evolution and sociology to understand sexual behavior. To understand sexual behavior in humans, evolutionary theorists study animal sexual patterns and look for evolutionary trends. They believe that sexuality exists for the purpose of reproducing the species, and individual sexuality is designed to maximize the chances of passing on one's genes. According to evolutionary theorists, the winners in the game of life are those who are most successful at transmitting their genes to the next generation.

Think about the qualities you look for in a partner. Students often tell me that they are looking for someone who is physically attractive, monogamous, has a sense of humor, and is intelligent, honest, extroverted, fun, and sensitive. An evolutionary theorist would argue that these qualities have evolved to ensure that a person would be able to provide healthy offspring and care for them well. A physically attractive person is more likely to be fit and healthy. Could this be important to us because of their reproductive capabilities? Evolutionary theorists would say so. They would also argue that qualities such as monogamy, honesty, and sensitivity would help ensure that a partner will be reliable and help raise the offspring.

Some sexual activities have evolved to ensure the survival of the species. For example, evolutionary theorists believe that orgasms have evolved to make sexual intercourse pleasurable; this, in turn, increases the frequency that people engage in it, and the possibility for reproduction is increased. Differences between the sexes in sexual desire and behavior are also thought to have

WHAT DO YOU WANT TO KNOW ?

How can the biological theory explain sexual behavior?
A person who adopts a biological theory would explain differences in sexuality as resulting from brain anatomy, hormones, neurochemicals, or other physical explanations. For example, if a female college student had trouble reaching orgasm, the biological theorist would look to physical reasons for the problem, such as hormonal or neurological causes. If, on the other hand, a biological theorist were trying to explain sexual orientation, he or she might look at hormones, genetics, or brain anatomy for an explanation.

self-actualization
Fulfillment of an individual's potentialities, including aptitudes, talents, and the like.

unconditional positive regard
Acceptance of another without restrictions on their behaviors or thoughts.

conditional love
Conditional acceptance of another, with restrictions on their behaviors or thoughts.

evolutionary theory
A theory that incorporates both evolution and sociology and looks for trends in behaviors.

evolved. The double standard, which states that men are free to have casual sex whereas women are not, exists because men produce millions of sperm per day and women produce only one viable ovum per month. Males try to "spread their seed" to ensure the reproduction of their family line, whereas females need to protect the one ovum they produce each month. When women become pregnant, they have a 9-month biological commitment ahead of them (and some would argue a lifelong commitment as well).

Evolutionary theory has received a considerable amount of criticism, however, particularly because evolutionary theorists tend to ignore the influence of both prior learning and societal influences on sexuality.

SOCIOLOGICAL THEORIES

Sociologists are interested in how the society in which we live influences sexual behavior. Even though the basic capacity to be sexual might be biologically programmed, how it is expressed varies greatly across societies, as we saw in the last chapter. For instance, there are differences in what societies tolerate, men's and women's roles, and how sexuality is viewed. A behavior that may be seen as normal in one society may be considered abnormal in another. For instance, on the island of Mangaia in the South Pacific, women are very sexually assertive and often initiate sexual activity (D. S. Marshall, 1971). From an early age, elders teach them how to have multiple orgasms. However, in Inis Beag in Ireland, sexuality is repressed and is considered appropriate only for procreation (Messenger, 1993). Homosexuality is not tolerated, and heterosexual couples engage in sexual intercourse fully clothed, with only the genitals exposed. Each society has regulated its sexual behaviors.

Sociologists believe that societal influences, such as the family, religion, economy, medicine, law, and the media, affect a society's rules about sexual expression (DeLamater, 1987). Each of these influences dictates certain beliefs about the place of sexuality in one's life and how the culture determines what is sexually "normal."

The family is the first factor that influences our values about what is sexually right and wrong. Our parents and family provide strong messages about what is acceptable and unacceptable. Religion also influences how a society views sexuality. As we discussed in Chapter 1, Christian doctrine stated that sex before marriage was wrong because sex was primarily for procreation. Some religions provide strong opinions on issues such as premarital and extramarital sex, homosexuality, sexual variations, abortion, masturbation, contraception, and sex education. Many people within society look to religious institutions and leaders for answers to their questions about sexuality.

The economy also influences the societal view of sexuality (DeLamater, 1987). The U.S. economy is based on capitalism, which involves an exchange of services for money. This influences the availability of sex-related services such as prostitution, pornography, and sex shops. These services exist because they are profitable.

The medical community also influences how a society views sexuality. For example, many years ago physicians taught that masturbation was a disease that could lead to permanent mental illness. This attitude influenced societal opinions of masturbation. Other behaviors in which physicians urged people not to engage included anal intercourse, extramarital sex, homosexuality, and bisexuality. Society's values about these behaviors were guided by the medical community's attitudes and beliefs.

A fifth influence that regulates sexual behavior in the United States is the law (DeLamater, 1987). The law establishes what sexual behaviors are "officially" right and wrong. For example, laws regulate the availability of certain contraceptive methods, abortion, and certain sexual behaviors. Laws help establish social norms and influence societal attitudes.

As we discussed in Chapter 1, the media influences societal attitudes about sexuality. Television, magazines, music, and even YouTube videos provide valuable information about sexuality. Even though the media have been more inclusive over the past few years, a heterosexual bias still exists (the media tell us that heterosexuality is the most acceptable form of sexual behavior). To be homosexual or even **abstinent** is less acceptable. All of these influence the social views of sexuality and what practices we believe are right and wrong.

FEMINIST THEORY

Feminist theory believes that society has a strong influence on our ideas about sexuality. Many feminists also believe that **sexology** in the United States is dominated by White, middle-class, heterosexist attitudes that permeate sexuality research (Ericksen, 1999; Irvine, 1990). Feminist researchers often claim to have a different view of sexuality that enables them to see things men cannot (Ericksen, 1999; Tiefer, 2004). Several feminist researchers have been leaders in the effort to redefine sexual functioning and remove the medical and biological aspects that permeate sexuality today. Leonore Tiefer, a feminist researcher, has written extensively about the overmedicalization of sexuality. Tiefer argues that there may not be any biological sex drive at all—it may be that our culture is what influences our sexual desire the most (Kaschak & Tiefer, 2001; Tiefer, 2001). We talk more about Tiefer's work in Chapter 14.

Typically there are a number of variations of feminism, with some more liberal or radical than others. Overall, however, feminist scholars believe that the social construction of sexuality is based on power, which has been primarily in the hands of men for centuries (Collins, 1998). They believe there is sexual gender inequality that, for the most part, sees women as submissive and subordinate (Collins, 2000). This power over women is maintained through acts of sexual aggression such as rape, sexual

> **The family** is the **first factor** that influences our values about what is sexually right or wrong.

abstinent
The state of not engaging in sexual activity.

sexology
The scientific study of sexuality.

> Sexual minority youth, particularly boys, report greater levels of school-related problems than their heterosexual peers, which can lead to difficulties in future educational endeavors (PEARSON ET AL., 2007). Although sexual minority girls and boys experience similar levels of emotional distress and problems with social integration, girls tend to internalize distress, whereas boys are more likely to externalize it, leading to more school-related problems.

abuse, sexual harassment, pornography, and prostitution (M. Jackson, 1984; MacKinnon, 1986). In addition, feminists argue that male sexuality consistently views sex as an act that involves only a penis in a vagina. For "sex" to occur, the erect penis must penetrate the vagina and thrust until the male ejaculates. Catharine MacKinnon (1987, p. 75) suggests that male-dominated views of sexuality have resulted in a society that believes that "what is sexual gives a man an erection." All of this led to the repression of female sexuality and, as a result, the lack of attention to the female orgasm.

Feminist researchers also believe that there is much to be gained from collaborative or group research, which uses interviews to gain information, because they can provide rich, qualitative data (di-Mauro, 1995). Controlled laboratory experiments, which have been viewed as more "masculine" in structure (because of the rigid nature of experiments), remove the study from the social context, which affects the outcome of the study (Peplau & Conrad, 1989). We discuss this more later in the chapter.

QUEER THEORY

The feminist and queer theories share a common political interest—a concern for women's and gay, lesbian, bisexual, and transsexual rights. Growing out of lesbian and gay studies, queer theory developed in the 1990s. Queer theory focuses on mismatches between sex, gender, and desire and proposes that

---

SEX IN REAL LIFE

What Questions Would They Ask?

Because theorists from different perspectives are interested in different types of studies, they ask different types of questions.

Because theorists from various perspectives are interested in different types of studies, they ask different types of questions. Following are a few questions that theorists from different schools of thought might ask.

Psychoanalytic: How are sexual problems later in life related to early childhood experiences? How do children resolve the Oedipal and Electra complexes? Does an overactive superego cause college students to feel guilt about sexual behavior?

Behavioral: What reinforces a person's attraction to partners of the same sex? What reinforces a heterosexual college student to use contraception? What are the attractions and hesitancies around the decision to lose one's virginity?

Social Learning: How does peer group pressure influence our sexuality? What effects do the media have on our sexuality? Are children influenced by sexual messages on television?

Cognitive: What is the decision-making process related to contraceptive choice? Do children cognitively understand sexuality? How do men view erectile dysfunction?

Humanist: How do negative parental reactions to first sexual experience affect teenagers? How does self-actualization affect sexuality?

Biological: How does genetics influence sexuality? What are the effects of hormone levels on sexual desire? Does menstruation affect sexual desire in women?

Evolutionary: Why are women the ones who usually control the level of sexual activity? How has monogamy developed?

Sociological: How does religion influence sexuality? How does the threat of HIV/AIDS affect society? Do laws affect sexual behavior?

Feminist: What is the role of rape in repressing female sexuality? How do the media reinforce a male view of sexuality?

Queer: How do homosexual individuals move from a state of identity confusion about their homoerotic feelings to a point at which they accept their lesbian or gay identity? How are same-sex and heterosexual desires interrelated?

As you read through these various questions, which seem of most interest to you? Perhaps these questions can give you insight into which theory makes the most sense to you.

---

domination and its related characteristics, such as heterosexism and homophobia, should be resisted (Isaiah Green, 2007; Schlichter, 2004). Queer theorists believe that studies need to examine how a variety of sexualities are constructed and to abandon various categorizations (homosexual/heterosexual) (Rudy, 2000). Categories are cultural constructions that limit and restrain. Overall, queer theorists and some feminists believe that meaningful societal change can come about only through radical change and cannot be introduced into a society in a piecemeal way (Turner, 2000). (The accompanying Sex in Real Life presents examples of studies that researchers with different theoretical backgrounds might be interested in doing.) Now let's turn our attention to some of the important sexuality studies that have been done.

review questions

1 What is a theory?

2 How does a theory help guide research?

3 Describe the influence of Freud's theories on sexuality.

4 Differentiate between behavioral, social learning, cognitive, humanistic, biological, evolutionary, and sociological theories.

5 Explain how feminist and queer theories have asked a different set of questions about sexuality.

Sexuality Research:
Philosophers, Physicians, and Sexologists

The ancient Greeks, through physicians such as Hippocrates and philosophers such as Aristotle and Plato, may actually be the legitimate forefathers of sex research, because they were the first to develop theories regarding sexual responses and dysfunctions, sex legislation, reproduction and contraception, and sexual ethics. It wasn't until the 18th century, however, that there was increased discussion of sexual ethics and that the first programs of public

and private sex education and classifications of sexual behavior were established.

EARLY SEX
RESEARCH

In the 19th century, researchers (such as Charles Darwin, Heinrich Kaan, Jean-Martin Charcot, and others) from a variety of disciplines laid the foundations of sex research in the modern sense. It was during this time that the study of sex began to concentrate more on the bizarre, dangerous, and unhealthy aspects of sex. In 1843, Kaan, a Russian physician, wrote *Psychopathia Sexualis*, which

timeline Important Developments in the **History of Sex Research**

1843	**1886**	**1892**	**1896**	**1897**	**1897**
Russian physician Heinrich Kaan publishes *Psychopathia Sexualis*, a classification system of sexual diseases.	**Richard von Krafft-Ebing, a German psychiatrist, expands** and refines Kaan's earlier work in *Psychopathia Sexualis*.	**American physician Clelia Mosher begins** a survey among educated middle-class women concerning sexual attitudes and experiences. 	**English private scholar Havelock Ellis begins** *Studies in the Psychology of Sex*. Because they cannot be published in England, they appear in the United States and in Germany.	**Berlin physician Magnus Hirschfeld founds** the Scientific Humanitarian Committee, the world's first "gay rights" organization.	**Berlin physician Albert Moll publishes** *Investigations Into Sexuality*.

Courtesy of Erwin J. Haeberle, Magnus Hirschfeld Archive for Sexology, Humboldt Universitat du Berlin

© Hulton-Deutsch Collection/Corbis

Courtesy of Erwin J. Haeberle, Magnus Hirschfeld Archive for Sexology, Humboldt Universitat du Berlin

presented a classification of what he termed *sexual mental diseases.* This system was greatly expanded and refined more than 40 years later by Richard von Krafft-Ebing in another book with the same title. Sex research during this time almost exclusively focused on people believed to be sick (see nearby Timeline).

During the Victorian period in the 19th century, the majority of sex research was thwarted. Some researchers found that they suddenly lost their professional status, were accused of having the very sexual disorders they studied, or were viewed as motivated solely by lust, greed, or fame. However, as interest in medicine in general grew, researchers began to explore how to improve health and peoples' lives, which included researching various aspects of sexuality.

Physicians were the primary sexuality researchers in the late 19th century (keep in mind that at that time nearly all physicians were male). Because physicians were experts in biology and the body, they were also viewed as the sexuality experts (V. Bullough, 1994). Interestingly, although the majority of physicians had little or no specialized knowledge of sexual topics, most spoke with authority about human sexuality anyway.

The majority of the early sexuality studies were done in Europe, primarily in Germany (V. Bullough, 1994). At the time, sex research was protected because it was considered part of medical research, even though holding a medical degree did not always offer complete protection. Some researchers used pseudonyms to publish their work, some were verbally attacked, and others had their data destroyed.

At the turn of the 20th century, it was the pioneering work of Sigmund Freud, Havelock Ellis, and Iwan Bloch that established the study of sexual problems as a legitimate endeavor in its own right. It is interesting to note that the overwhelming majority of sexology pioneers were Jewish (Haeberle, 1982). The Jewish roots of much of modern sexology have certainly added to its controversial nature in certain countries. As a result of all the negative reactions and problems with sexuality research in Europe, it gradually moved from Germany to the United States, which has led the way in sexuality research ever since.

In 1921, several prominent European doctors attempted to set up an organization called the Committee for Research in Problems of Sex. After much hard work, the organization established itself but experienced problems in low membership rates and a lack of research and publishing support. However, because of strong beliefs and persistence by the founders, the group continued.

*The majority of the **early sexuality studies** were done **in Europe.***

Systematic research into sexuality in the United States began in the early 1920s, motivated by pressures from the social hygiene movement, which was concerned about sexually transmitted infections and their impact on marriage and children. American society was generally conservative and viewed the "sex impulse" as a potential threat to societal stability. Funding for sexuality research was minimal. It wasn't until the beginnings of philanthropy from the fortunes of men such as John D. Rockefeller and Andrew Carnegie that researchers were able to afford to implement large-scale, interdisciplinary projects.

It wasn't until the research of Clelia Mosher, Katharine Bement Davis, Alfred Kinsey, William Masters, and Virginia Johnson in the United States that sexuality research began to be taken seriously. We discuss the impact and research of these scientists later in the chapter.

RECENT STUDIES ON SEXUALITY

Early sex research set the stage for sexuality researchers. We talk about their specific contributions later in this chapter, but as we take a look at the whole picture of sexuality research, it's interesting to note that the majority of research into human sexuality has been *problem driven,* meaning that most of the research that has been done has focused on a specific problem. The research areas of priority include HIV and AIDS, adolescent sexuality, gender, sexual orientation, and sexual coercion (Bancroft, 1996). A review of ongoing research projects at the National Institutes of Health in 2008 revealed several problem-driven types of studies (HIV Prevention Intervention for Couples and Human Papillomavirus (HPV) Infection in Pregnancy; National Institutes of Health, 2008). However, a focus on problems doesn't allow researchers to obtain funds to research topics on healthy sexuality and answer questions such as, "How does normal child sexual development progress?" or "How is sexuality expressed in loving long-term relationships?"

There are many individuals and groups who are opposed to sexuality research today, and some believe that the mystery surrounding sexuality will be taken away by increasing scientific knowledge. Conservative groups believe that research done on topics such as adolescent sexuality would encourage young people to have more sex. Sex researchers are accustomed to pressure from

1899	1903–4	1905	1907	1908	1909
Magnus Hirschfeld begins editing of the *Yearbook for Sexual Intermediate Stages* for the Scientific Humanitarian Committee.	**Magnus Hirschfeld begins** his statistical surveys on homosexuality. They are quickly terminated by legal action.	**Sigmund Freud publishes** *Three Essays on the Theory of Sex,* based on his theory of psychoanalysis. © Hulton-Deutsch Collection/Corbis	**Berlin dermatologist Iwan Bloch coins** the term *Sexualwissenschaft* (sexology) and publishes *The Sexual Life of Our Time.*	**Magnus Hirschfeld publishes** the first issue of *The Journal for Sexology.*	**Albert Moll publishes** *The Sexual Life of the Child,* which challenges Freud's psychoanalytic theory.

conservative groups that oppose their work. In fact, after Alfred Kinsey published his two famous studies about male and female sexuality, which were funded by the Rockefeller Foundation, Congress pushed the foundation to withdraw its financial support from Indiana University, which it did (J. H. Jones, 1997). We discuss politics and sexuality research more later in this chapter.

Sexuality research has become very fragmented over the last few decades, with researchers coming from several different disciplines, such as psychology, sociology, medicine, social work, and public health, to name a few. Oftentimes, researchers are unaware of research being published in other disciplines. Journal articles are often inaccessible to a general audience or to researchers outside the discipline from which the research originated (diMauro, 1995). What tends to happen, therefore, is that the popular media become responsible for disseminating information about sexuality, which is often distorted or sensationalistic.

As you may recall from Chapter 1, **sexologists**—researchers, educators, and clinicians who specialize in sexuality—are scientists who engage in sophisticated research projects and publish their work in scientific journals. Unfortunately, they are sometimes ridiculed, not viewed as "real" scientists, and accused of studying sexuality because of their own sexual hang-ups or because they are voyeurs. Geer and O'Donohue (1987) claim that, unlike other areas of science, sex research is often evaluated as either moral or immoral. Some groups believe that marital sex for procreation is the only acceptable sexual behavior and that many sexual practices (such as masturbation, homosexuality, and premarital and extramarital sex) are immoral. Researchers are often encouraged not to invade the privacy of intimate relationships or to study the sexuality of certain age groups (either young or old). People often resist participating in sexuality research because of their own moral or psychological attitudes toward sex. Methodological problems also have made it difficult for the field of sexuality research. We discuss these issues more later in this chapter.

Academic programs that specialize in human sexuality began appearing in the 1970s (for more information about these programs, see the website listings at the end of this chapter). In addition, several groups exist today to promote sexuality research and education, including the Kinsey Institute for Research in Sex, Gender, and Reproduction; the Society for the Scientific Study of Sexuality (SSSS); American Association for Sexuality Educators, Counselors and Therapists (AASECT); Society for Sex Therapy and Research (SSTAR); and the Sexuality Information and Education Council of the United States (SIECUS). Many medical

Sexuality research has become very fragmented over the last few decades.

schools and universities now teach sexuality courses as a part of the curriculum.

Because the study of sexuality has become so fragmented among disciplines, it is possible that universities will eventually form a separate discipline of "sexual science." Departments of sexual science would include specialists from different disciplines providing students with a comprehensive, multidisciplinary grounding in human sexuality. In addition, they would enable the field to acquire appropriate dedicated research funds (because funding sources are usually unaware of whom and where the researchers of sexuality are). Steady funding for sexuality research is needed to attract new students to the field of sexuality, to continue the work of senior researchers, and to expand research agendas (diMauro, 1995).

Although sexuality research is still in its early stages, it has begun to help remove the stigma and ignorance associated with discussing human sexual behavior. Ignorance and fear can contribute to irresponsible behavior. Sexuality research has helped sex become a topic of discussion rather than a taboo subject. Today, understanding sexuality has become increasingly important to the work of psychologists, physicians, educators, theologians, and scientists.

POLITICS AND SEX RESEARCH

In Chapter 1, we discussed how the changing political climate affects attitudes about sexuality. It won't surprise you to learn that the changing political climate also affects sexuality research. When Kinsey's work was published in the 1950s, several politicians claimed that asking people about their sex lives in a nonjudgmental fashion, like Kinsey did, promoted immorality (Bancroft, 2004). Some conservative politicians believed that heterosexual families were threatened by liberal values inherent in sex research. Negative attitudes such as these affected the public's perception of sex research.

Even so, Kinsey's work helped lead to many societal changes associated with sexuality. The changing roles of women and the development of birth control pills, along with Kinsey's work, led to less acceptance for the double standard of sexuality (Bancroft, 2004). In

sexologist
A professional who studies sexuality.

---

timeline Important Developments in the **History of Sex Research**

1911
Albert Moll publishes *The Handbook of Sexual Sciences.*

Courtesy of Erwin J. Haeberle, Magnus Hirschfeld Archive for Sexology, Humboldt Universitat du Berlin

1912
Iwan Bloch begins publication of the *Handbook of Sexology.*

1913
Magnus Hirschfeld, Iwan Bloch, and others found The *Society of Sexology* in Berlin.

1913
Albert Moll founds *The International Society of Sex Research* in Berlin.

1914
Magnus Hirschfeld publishes *Homosexuality in Men and Women.*

1919
Magnus Hirschfeld opens the first Institute for Sexology in Berlin.

fact, after the publication of Kinsey's second book, the American Law Institute lawyers and judges recommended decriminalizing many forms of sexual behavior (including adultery, cohabitation, and homosexual relationships) (Allyn, 1996). As a result, many states revised their laws about certain sexual practices (Bancroft, 2004).

AIDS research dominated the funded research in the late 1980s and early 1990s. Political resistance to studies on adult and adolescent sexuality grew as conservative views about sexuality once again gained momentum. Several key politicians began to speak out about their opposition to sex research, believing that such research could make deviance less stigmatizing.

The HIV/AIDS crisis that began in the 1980s provided a new opportunity for sex research, leading to one large-scale sexuality study titled the National Health and Social Life Survey (which we discuss later in this chapter) by the National Opinion Research Center at the University of Chicago in the early 1990s (Kimmel & Plante, 2007). This was one of the largest studies of American sexual behavior. However, the original study, which was set to include 20,000 subjects, was cancelled due to mounting political pressure. Funding was acquired from private sources, reducing the number of subjects to 3,500 (Bancroft, 2004).

Although there is a need for an increased understanding of human sexuality today, there are varying levels of political resistance to sex research (Bancroft, 2004). As a result, federal funding for sex research will continue to be problematic, and sex researchers will need to look to private foundations for funding. Many pharmaceutical companies have provided funding for studies on sexual dysfunction, but this has been controversial because the companies have a vested interest in the studies they fund. In fact, pharmaceutical companies have been accused of creating and promoting certain dysfunctions to "medicalize" the conditions and create a need for medication (Tiefer, 2006).

review questions

1 Describe the beginnings of sexuality research, and explain how the focus of sex research has progressed.

2 Explain how sexuality research has been problem driven and give two examples.

3 Explain how politics can influence sexuality research.

Sexuality Researchers

All of the researchers discussed in this section and their publications helped give credibility to the area of sexual research. Some of the researchers adopted Freud's psychoanalytic theory, whereas others developed their research without adopting specific theories of sexuality. Although they had introduced scientific principles into the study of sexual behavior, their influence was mostly limited to the field of medicine.

EARLY PROMOTERS OF SEXOLOGY

Several people were responsible for the early promotion of sexology, including Iwan Bloch, Albert Moll, Magnus Hirschfeld, Richard von Krafft-Ebing, Havelock Ellis, Katharine Bement Davis, Clelia Mosher, Alfred Kinsey, Morton Hunt, William Masters, and Virginia Johnson. All of these researchers made a tremendous contribution to the study of sexology.

Iwan Bloch: *The Journal of Sexology*

Iwan Bloch (1872–1922), a Berlin dermatologist, believed that the medical view of sexual behavior was shortsighted and that both historical and anthropological research could help broaden it. He hoped that sexual science would one day have the same structure and objectivity as other sciences. Along with Magnus Hirschfeld, Bloch and several other physicians formed a medical society for sexology research in Berlin. It was the first sexological society, and it exercised considerable influence (we talk more about this society later). Starting in 1914, Bloch published the *Journal of Sexology,* a scientific journal about sexology. For almost 2 decades, this journal collected and published many important studies. Bloch planned to write a series of sexological studies, but because of World War I and his untimely death at age 50, he never did.

1933
Nazis close the Institute for Sexology and destroy the data.

1938
Alfred Kinsey begins his studies of human sexual behavior.

© Bettmann/Corbis

1947
Alfred Kinsey founds the Institute for Sex Research at Indiana University.

1948
Alfred Kinsey and colleagues publish Sexual Behavior in the Human Male.

1949
Simone de Beauvoir publishes The Second Sex, which helps awaken the feminist movement.

© Michel Philipott/Sygma/Corbis

1951
Clellan S. Ford and Frank A. Beach publish Patterns of Sexual Behavior, in which they compare sexual behavior in 200 human societies.

Albert Moll: *Investigations Concerning the Libido Sexualis*

Albert Moll (1862–1939), a Berlin physician, was another big promoter of sexology. He was a very conservative man who disliked both Freud and Hirschfeld and tried to counter their research at every opportunity. Moll formed the International Society for Sex Research in 1913 to counter Hirschfeld's Medical Society of Sexology. He also organized an International Congress of Sex Research in Berlin in 1926.

Moll wrote several books on sexology, including *Investigations Concerning the Libido Sexualis* in 1897. Unfortunately, it was probably Moll's disagreements with Freud that caused him to be ignored by the majority of English-speaking sexuality researchers, because Freud's ideas were so dominant during the first half of the 20th century (V. Bullough, 1994).

Magnus Hirschfeld (1868–1935) worked hard to establish sexuality as a legitimate field of study.

Magnus Hirschfeld: The Institute for Sexology

Magnus Hirschfeld (1868–1935) was a German physician, whose work with patients inspired him and convinced him that negative attitudes toward homosexuals were inhumane and unfounded. Because Hirschfeld was independently wealthy, all of his work was supported by his own funds (V. Bullough, 1994).

Using a pseudonym, Hirschfeld wrote his first paper on sexology in 1896. In this paper, he argued that sexuality was the result of certain genetic patterns that could result in a person being homosexual, bisexual, or heterosexual. He fought for a repeal of the laws that made homosexuality and bisexuality punishable by prison terms and heavy fines. In 1899, he began the *Yearbook for Sexual Intermediate Stages,* which was published for the purpose of educating the public about homosexuality and other sexual "deviations."

Thousands of people came to him for his help and advice about sexual problems, and in 1900, Hirschfeld began distributing questionnaires on sexuality. By this time, he had also become an expert in the field of homosexuality and sexual variations, and he testified as an expert witness in court cases of sexual offenders. Hirschfeld used only a small amount of his data in the books he published because he hoped to write a comprehensive study of sexuality at a later date. Unfortunately, his data were destroyed by the Nazis before they could be published.

Even though many books had been published by Krafft-Ebing, Ellis, and others, Hirschfeld was the first to develop an Institute for Sexology, which contained his libraries, laboratory, and lecture halls. Over the next few years, the institute continued to grow in size and influence. In 1933, as the political climate heated up, Hirschfeld left Germany and soon learned that his institute in Berlin had been destroyed by the Nazi government, its contents publicly burned, and those who were working there sent to concentration camps. Hirschfeld stayed in France, continuing his work until his death in 1935.

Richard von Krafft-Ebing: *Psychopathia Sexualis*

Richard von Krafft-Ebing (1840–1902) was one of the most significant medical writers on sexology in the late 19th century (V. Bullough, 1994). His primary interest was what he considered "deviant" sexual behavior. Krafft-Ebing believed that deviant sexual behavior was the result of engaging in nonreproductive sexual practices, including masturbation. In 1886, he published an update of a book titled *Psychopathia Sexualis*, which explored approximately 200 case histories of individuals who had experienced **sexual pathology,** including homosexuals and people who had had sex with children (pedophiles).

Although Krafft-Ebing supported sympathetic concern for those who expressed "deviations" and worked to help change existing laws that discriminated against them, he also increased suspicion about differences in sexuality by lumping all forms of sexual variations together as deviant.

sexual pathology
Sexual disorders.

---

timeline Important Developments in the **History of Sex Research**

1953
Alfred Kinsey and his colleagues **publish** *Sexual Behavior in the Human Female.*

1957
American gynecologist Hans Lehfeldt **founds** The Society for the Scientific Study of Sexuality (SSSS).

1964
An American physician, Mary Calderone, founds *The Sexuality Information and Education Council of the United States (SIECUS).*

AP/World Wide Photos

1965
SSSS publishes the first issue of the *Journal of Sex Research.*

1967
The American Association of Sex Educators, Counselors and Therapists (AASECT) is founded.

1970
William Masters and Virginia Johnson publish *Human Sexual Inadequacy.*

© Bettmann/Corbis

Havelock Ellis: *Studies in the Psychology of Sex*

Havelock Ellis (1859–1939), another important sex researcher, was an English citizen who grew up in Victorian society but began to rebel against the secrecy surrounding sexuality. In 1875, when he was 16 years old, he decided to make sexuality his life's work. In fact, it is reported that Ellis sought a medical degree primarily so he could legitimately and safely study sexuality (V. Bullough, 1994). Upon publication of his famous six-volume *Studies in the Psychology of Sex* (1897–1910; H. Ellis, 1910), Ellis established himself as an objective and nonjudgmental researcher. In his collection of case histories from volunteers, he reported that homosexuality and masturbation were not abnormal and should not be labeled as such (Reiss, 1982). In 1901, *The Lancet,* a prestigious English medical journal, reviewed his early volumes and wrote:

> [*Studies in the Psychology of Sex*] *must not be sold to the public, for the reading and discussion of such topics are dangerous. The young and the weak would not be fortified in their purity by the knowledge that they would gain from these studies, while they certainly might be more open to temptation after the perusal of more than one of the chapters. (Grosskurth, 1980, p. 222)*

Unfortunately, Ellis's book was also fairly dry and boring, and as a result, and much to his dismay, Ellis never found the fame and fortune that Freud did.

© Hulton-Deutsch Collection/Corbis

Havelock Ellis (1859–1939) was a key figure in the early study of sexuality.

The rise of behaviorism in the 1920s added a new dimension to sexuality research. The idea of studying specific sexual behaviors became more acceptable. The formulation of more sophisticated scientific research techniques provided researchers with more precise methods for sexual research. Many researchers attempted to compile data on sexual behavior, but the results were inconsistent, and the data were poorly organized. This led Alfred Kinsey, an American researcher, to undertake a large-scale study of human sexuality.

SEXUALITY RESEARCH MOVES TO THE UNITED STATES

Although Alfred Kinsey was mainly responsible for moving large-scale sexuality research to the United States, we also have to give credit to two hardworking female researchers, Clelia Mosher and Katharine Bement Davis, both of whom were working in the United States. Much of their work remained unpublished, although they are also responsible for paving the way for later researchers.

Clelia Mosher: Important Female Questions

By now you have probably realized that men were doing much of the early research into human sexuality. Male sexuality was viewed as normative, and therefore female sexuality was approached through the lens of male sexuality. Clelia Mosher (1863–1940) was ahead of her time, asking questions about sexuality that were quite different from those of her male predecessors. She was actually the first researcher to ask Americans about their sexual behavior (Ericksen, 1999).

In 1892, while Mosher was a student at the University of Wisconsin, she began a research project that lasted 28 years. Her main motivation was to help married women have more satisfying sex lives. She asked upper-middle-class heterosexual women how often they engaged in sexual intercourse, how often they wanted to engage in it, and whether they enjoyed it (MaHood & Wenburg, 1980). One of the questions that Mosher asked the women in her study was, "What do you believe to be the true purpose of intercourse?" (Ericksen, 1999). Although a few women claimed that sexual intercourse was only for procreation, the majority of women said that intercourse was for both sexual pleasure and procreation. However, many of these women reported feeling guilty for wanting or needing sexual pleasure. Ericksen (1999) suggests that this guilt reflected the transition from the repressive Victorian era to the more progressive 20th-century view of sex as an important component of marriage. Much of Mosher's work was never published and never became part of the sex knowledge that circulated during her time (Ericksen, 1999).

Katharine Bement Davis: Defending Homosexuality

Another female researcher, Katharine Davis (1861–1935), began her sexuality research along a slightly different path. In 1920, Davis was appointed superintendent of a prison, and she became interested in prostitution and sexually transmitted infections. Her survey and analysis were the largest and most comprehensive of her time (Ericksen, 1999).

Davis believed that lesbianism was not pathological, and she defended homosexuality as no different from heterosexuality. This idea was considered a threat in the early 1900s because it could mean that women did not need men (Faderman, 1981). Her ideas about lesbianism were largely ignored, but the idea that women might have sexual appetites equal to men's worried many male researchers. Soon the researchers of the day began to turn their attention to married couples and strengthening the family unit (Ericksen, 1999).

Alfred Kinsey: Large-Scale Sexuality Research Begins in the United States

As we discussed in Chapter 1, Alfred Kinsey was probably the most influential sex researcher of the 20th century. His work effectively

> *Kinsey's work changed many of the existing attitudes about sexuality.*

changed many of the existing attitudes about sexuality. By training, Kinsey was a biologist with a PhD from Harvard who was an internationally known gall wasp expert. In 1938, while he was a professor of zoology at Indiana University, he was asked to coordinate a new course on marriage and the family. Before courses like this appeared on college campuses, human sexuality had been discussed only in hygiene courses, in which the focus was primarily on the dangers of STIs and masturbation (V. L. Bullough, 1998).

Soon after the course began, students came to Kinsey with sexuality questions for which he did not have answers, and the existing literature was of little help. This encouraged him to begin collecting data on his students' sex lives. His study grew and before long included students who were not in his classes, faculty members, friends, and non-faculty employees. Soon he was able to obtain grant money that enabled him to hire research assistants. By this time, Kinsey's research had become well established in the scientific community. Kinsey had received a grant in 1941 from the Committee for Research in the Problems in Sex, which was so impressed by his work that it awarded him half of its total research budget in the 1946–1947 academic year (V. L. Bullough, 1998).

In his early work, Kinsey claimed to be **atheoretical.** He felt that because sexuality research was so new, it was impossible to construct theories and hypotheses without first having a large body of information on which to base them. Kinsey's procedure involved collecting information on each participant's sexual life history, with an emphasis on specific sexual behaviors. Kinsey chose to interview participants, rather than have them fill out questionnaires, because he believed that questionnaires would not provide accurate responses. He was also unsure about whether participants would lie during an interview, and so he built into the interview many checks to detect false information. Data collected from husbands and wives were compared for consistency, and the interview was done again 2 and 4 years later to see whether the basic answers remained the same.

Kinsey was also worried about **interviewer bias** (interviewer opinions and attitudes that can influence information collected in the interview). To counter interview bias, only Kinsey and three colleagues conducted the interviews. Of the total 18,000 inter-

Katharine Bement Davis (1861–1935) conducted some of the largest and most comprehensive sexuality studies to date.

atheoretical
Research that is not influenced by a particular theory.

interviewer bias
The bias of a researcher caused by his or her own opinions, thoughts, and attitudes about the research.

timeline Important Developments in the **History of Sex Research**

1986	**1988**	**1989**	**1990**	**1991**
The American Board of Sexology **organizes** in Washington, D.C.	The German *Journal of Sex Research* **is first published.**	The European Federation of Sexology **is founded** in Geneva.	The Asian Federation for Sexology **is founded** in Hong Kong.	Analyse des Comportements Sexuels en France (ACSF) **is begun.**

views, Kinsey himself conducted 8,000 (Pomeroy, 1972). Participants were asked a minimum of 350 questions, and each interviewer memorized each question so that he or she could more easily build rapport with participants and wouldn't continually have to consult a paper questionnaire. Interviewers used appropriate terminology that participants would understand during the interview. Interviews lasted several hours, and participants were assured that the information they provided would remain confidential. A total of 13 areas were covered in the interview, including demographics, physical data, early sexual knowledge, adolescent sexual behaviors, masturbation, orgasms in sleep, heterosexual petting, sexual intercourse, reproductive information, homosexual activity, sexual contact with animals, and sexual responsiveness. See Table 2.1 for information on some of Kinsey's early findings.

The sampling procedures Kinsey used were also strengths of his research. He believed that he would have a high refusal rate if he used **probability sampling.** Because of this, he used what he called "quota sampling accompanied by opportunistic collection" (Gebhard & Johnson, 1979, p. 26). In other words, if he saw that a particular group—such as young married women—was not well represented in his sample, he would find organizations with a high percentage of these participants and add them.

Overall, he obtained participants from colleges and universities; hospitals; prisons; mental hospitals; institutions for young

probability sampling
A research strategy that involves acquiring a random sample for inclusion in a study.

table 2.1

What Did Kinsey Find in His Early Research?

Kinsey's groundbreaking research and the publication of his 1948 and 1953 books revealed many new findings about sexuality. Following are a few of these statistics. Keep in mind that these statistics are based on people's lives in the middle of the 20th century. For more information, visit the Kinsey Institute online at http://www.kinseyinstitute.org:

- Close to **50%** of American men reported engaging in both heterosexual and homosexual activities or having had "reacted to" persons of both sexes in the course of their adult life.

- Whereas about **25%** of males had lost their virginity by the age of 16, only **6%** of females had.

- Married couples reported engaging in sexual intercourse **2.8** times per week in their late teens and only once per week by the age of 50.

- The majority of heterosexual couples reported only having sex in the missionary position.

- By far the majority of men and women reported preferring sex with the lights out (but those who like the lights on were more likely to be men).

- About **50%** of married men reported having sex outside of their marriage, whereas about **25%** of married women did.

- The majority of men and women reported having masturbated.

- The majority of men and women reached their first orgasm during masturbation.

- Close to **70%** of White heterosexual males reported at least one sexual experience with a prostitute.

SOURCE: Kinsey, Pomeroy, & Martin, 1948; Kinsey, Pomeroy, Martin, & Gebhard, 1953.

1993	1994	1994	2002	2007
The Janus Report on Sexual Behavior is published.	**The Robert Koch Institute opens** the Archive for Sexology in Berlin.	**The National Health and Social Life Study is published.**	**Pfizer Pharmaceuticals publishes** the Global Study of Sexual Attitudes and Behaviors.	**Durex publishes** results from its global sex survey.

Alfred Kinsey (1894–1956) implemented the first large-scale survey of adult sexual behavior in the United States.

delinquents; churches and synagogues; groups of people with sexual problems; settlement houses; homosexual groups in Chicago, Los Angeles, New York, Philadelphia, and San Francisco; and members of various groups including the YMCA and the YWCA. Within these groups, every member was strongly encouraged to participate in the project to minimize **volunteer bias.** Kinsey referred to this procedure as **100% sampling.**

INSTITUTE FOR SEX RESEARCH In 1947, Kinsey and his associates established the Institute for Sex Research primarily to maintain the confidential data that had been collected and also to claim royalties from any published work (Gebhard & Johnson, 1979). Not coincidentally, two of Kinsey's most popular and lucrative works were published soon afterward: *Sexual Behavior in the Human Male* appeared in 1948, and *Sexual Behavior in the Human Female* in 1953. These books were overnight best sellers and provided the institute with the financial support to continue its work. Both books helped to break down the myths and confusion surrounding sexuality, while providing scientifically derived information about the sexual lives of men and women.

Many practices that had previously been seen as perverse or unacceptable in society (such as homosexuality, masturbation, and oral sex) were found to be widely practiced; as you might guess, such findings were very controversial and created strong reactions from conservative groups and religious organizations. Eventually, continued controversy about Kinsey's work resulted in the termination of several research grants. The lack of funds was frustrating for Kinsey, who did not like to ask people for money because he felt that to do so would be self-serving (Pomeroy, 1982).

Kinsey's research challenged many of the assumptions about sexuality in the United States, and he stirred up antagonism; in this sense, Kinsey was truly a pioneer in the field of sexuality research (V. L. Bullough, 1998).

Morton Hunt: *Playboy* Updates Dr. Kinsey
In the early 1970s, the Playboy Foundation commissioned a study to update Kinsey's earlier work on sexual behavior. Morton Hunt eventually published these findings in his book *Sexual Behavior* in the 1970s (Hunt, 1974). In addition, he reviewed his findings in a series of articles in *Playboy* magazine.

Hunt gathered his sample through random selection from telephone books in 24 U.S. cities. Although Hunt's sampling technique was thought to be an improvement over Kinsey's techniques, there were also drawbacks. People without listed phone numbers, such as college students or institutionalized persons, were left out of the study. Each person in Hunt's sample was called and asked to participate in a group discussion about sexuality. Approximately 20% agreed to participate.

People participated in small group discussions about sexuality in America and, after doing so, were asked to complete questionnaires about their own sexual behavior and attitudes. A total of 982 males and 1,044 females participated in his study. However, because his sample was such a small percentage of those he contacted, volunteer bias (which we discuss in more detail later in this chapter) prevents his results from being **generalizable** to the population as a whole.

William Masters and Virginia Johnson: Measuring Sex in the Laboratory
Although Alfred Kinsey first envisioned doing physiological studies on sexual arousal and orgasm (and had actually requested funds for a physiologist and a neurologist before his death), it was Masters and Johnson who were actually the first modern scientists to observe and measure the act of sexual intercourse between heterosexual partners in the laboratory. William Masters, a gynecologist, and Virginia Johnson, a psychology researcher, began their sex research in 1954. They were primarily interested in the anatomy and physiology of the sexual response and later also explored sexual dysfunction. Masters and Johnson were a dual sex-therapy team, representing both male and female opinions, which reduced the chance for **gender bias.** Much of the work done by Masters and Johnson was supported by grants, the income from their books, and individual and couple therapy.

Masters and Johnson's first study, published in 1966, was titled *Human Sexual Response.* In an attempt to understand the physiological process that occurs during sexual activity, the researchers actually brought 700 heterosexual people into the laboratory to have their physiological reactions studied during sexual intercourse. The volunteers participated for financial reasons (participants were paid for participation), personal reasons, and even for the release of sexual tension (Masters and Johnson both stated that they felt some volunteers were looking for legitimate and safe sexual outlets). Because Masters and Johnson were studying behaviors they felt were normative (i.e., they happened to most people), they did not feel they needed to recruit a **random sample.**

volunteer bias
A slanting of research data caused by the characteristics of participants who volunteer to participate.

100% sampling
A research strategy in which all members of a particular group are included in the sample.

generalizable
If findings are generalizable, they can be taken from a particular sample and applied to the general population.

gender bias
The bias of a researcher caused by his or her gender.

random sample
A number of people taken from the entire population in such a way to ensure that any one person has as much chance of being selected as any other.

When a volunteer was accepted as a participant in the study, he or she was first encouraged to engage in sexual activity in the lab without the investigators present. It was hoped that this would make him or her feel more comfortable with the new surroundings. Many of the volunteers reported that after a while they did not notice that they were being monitored. During the study they were monitored for physiological changes with an electrocardiograph to measure changes in the heart and an electromyograph to measure muscular changes. Measurements were taken of penile erection and vaginal lubrication with **penile strain gauges** and **photoplethysmographs** (FOH-toh-pleth-iss-mo-grafs).

Through their research, Masters and Johnson discovered several interesting aspects of sexual response, including women's potential for multiple orgasms and the fact that sexuality does not disappear in old age. They also proposed a four-stage model for sexual response, which we discuss in more detail in Chapter 10.

In 1970, Masters and Johnson published another important book, *Human Sexual Inadequacy*, which explored sexual dysfunction. Again they brought couples into the laboratory, but this time only those who were experiencing sexual problems. They evaluated the couples physiologically and psychologically and taught them exercises to improve their sexual functioning. Frequent follow-ups were done to measure the therapeutic results—some participants were even contacted 5 years after the study was completed.

Masters and Johnson found that there is often dual sexual dysfunction in couples (i.e., males who are experiencing erectile problems often have partners who are also experiencing sexual problems). Their studies also refuted Freud's theory that women are capable of both vaginal and clitoral orgasms and that only vaginal orgasms result from intercourse. According to Masters and Johnson, all female orgasms result from direct or indirect clitoral stimulation.

It's important to point out that Masters and Johnson's books were written from a medical, not a psychological, perspective. They also used clinical language, and many professionals speculate this was a tactic to avoid censorship of the books. However, even with this scientific and medical base, their work was not without controversy. Many people viewed Masters and Johnson's work as both unethical and immoral.

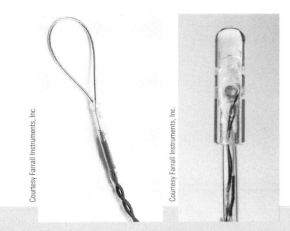

To measure physiological changes during sexual arousal, researchers rely on strain gauges and photoplethysmographs. A penile strain gauge is placed on the base of the penis to measure erectile changes in the penis, while a photoplethysmograph is inserted in the vaginal canal to measure changes in vaginal lubrication.

REALResearch > Studies in evolutionary psychology have found that heterosexual men prefer partners who are younger than themselves to ensure reproductive success. Gay men, on the other hand, have significantly wider age preferences which researchers attributed to the fact that gay men choose partners for reasons other than procreation (GOBROGGE ET AL., 2007).

RESEARCH STUDIES
ON HOMOSEXUALITY

Although many studies have been done on homosexuality, as you will see in Chapter 11, there have been few wide-scale studies. As we stated earlier in this chapter, Katharine Bement Davis researched lesbianism, but her results were largely ignored. Let's now review two classic studies on gay and lesbian sexual behavior.

Evelyn Hooker: Comparing Gay and Straight Men

In the early 1950s, a researcher named Evelyn Hooker (1907–1996) undertook a study on male homosexuality. Hooker compared two groups of men, one gay and the other straight, who were matched for age, education, and IQ levels. She collected information about their life histories, personality profiles, and psychological evaluations and asked professionals to try to distinguish between the two groups on the basis of their profiles and evaluations. They could not, demonstrating that there was little fundamental psychological difference between gay and straight men. Hooker's research helped challenge the widely held view that homosexuality was a mental illness. Today, many studies have shown that there are no psychological differences between heterosexual and homosexual men and women.

Virginia Johnson and William Masters were the first to bring sexuality research into the laboratory.

penile strain gauge
A device used to measure penile engorgement.

photoplethysmograph
A device used to measure vaginal lubrication.

Dr. Evelyn Hooker published the first empirical study to challenge the psychiatric view that homosexuality was a mental illness. Her work ultimately led to the removal of homosexuality from the *Diagnostic and Statistical Manual of Mental Disorders*.

Alan Bell and Martin Weinberg: *Homosexualities*

Alfred Kinsey's death prevented him from publishing a book on homosexuality as he had hoped to do. He had collected a large number of case histories from homosexuals and had learned that many people had participated in same-sex behavior in childhood and adulthood. Homosexuality, to Kinsey, was not an abnormality, as society had thought.

In 1967, a task force was established within the National Institute of Mental Health to examine homosexuality. A total of 5,000 homosexual men and women were interviewed, and 5,000 heterosexual men and women were used for comparison. The interviews contained 528 questions and took 2 to 5 hours to complete. The results of this research were published in 1978 by Alan Bell and Martin Weinberg in a book entitled.

Prior to this research, many people believed that homosexuals were sexually irresponsible and had psychological problems that needed to be cured (Bell & Weinberg, 1978). However, Bell and Weinberg revealed that the majority of homosexuals did not conform to negative stereotypes. They did not push unwanted sexual advances onto people, nor did they seduce children (in fact, heterosexual men were found to be more likely to sexually abuse children than were homosexual men). Intimate relationships in the homosexual community were similar to those in the heterosexual community.

❚ OTHER SEXUALITY STUDIES

A number of other studies have had an impact on how we think about sexuality today. *The Janus Report* and the National Health and Social Life Survey each tried to update Kinsey's large-scale survey of sexual behavior. Let's look at each in turn.

REALResearch > The National Health and Social Life Survey found that **93%** of those who were married in the previous 10 years chose marriage partners of the same race or ethnicity (MAHAY ET AL., 2001).

The Janus Report

In 1993, Drs. Samuel and Cynthia Janus published *The Janus Report on Sexual Behavior* (Janus & Janus, 1993). It was touted as the most comprehensive study of sex in America since Kinsey's work in the 1950s. *The Janus Report* was based on data obtained from nearly 3,000 questionnaires. Overall, the authors claimed that since Kinsey, there had been redistribution of sexual values in American society. They found that people were more willing to engage in a variety of sexual behaviors and that there had been an increase in sexual interest and behavior in elderly Americans. The report also looked at regional differences in sexual behavior.

Although one study cannot fill in all the gaps in knowledge about sexual attitudes and behaviors in the United States, this study did yield valuable information on sexuality, such as the following:

- Americans in their 60s and 70s reported experiencing increased levels of sexual activity.

- Married couples reported the highest level of sexual activity and satisfaction.

- Three out of five married people said their sex lives improved after marriage.

- Areas in which people live influenced overall sexual attitudes and behaviors. Midwesterners were found to have the least sexual activity, whereas those in the South reported the earliest ages of sexual initiation and the highest rates of premarital sex.

- People who are ultraconservative were more likely to be involved in frequent or ongoing extramarital affairs than are those who are ultraliberal.

- Men and women were both initiating sexual activity.

The Janus Report was widely criticized for many reasons. The biggest problems were that the sample was not randomly selected from the general population. Questionnaires were sent out across the United States, and approximately 61% were returned. There has been some question about the representativeness of their sample, because Americans with liberal or more permissive attitudes may have been more likely to respond. Some researchers also claim that many sexual behaviors were overestimated (Greely, 1994).

The National Health and Social Life Survey (NHSLS)

In 1987, facing a devastating AIDS outbreak, the U.S. Department of Health and Human Services called for researchers to study the sexual attitudes and practices of American adults. A group of researchers from the University of Chicago—Edward Laumann, John Gagnon, Robert Michael, and Stuart Michaels—were selected to coordinate this national study of more than 20,000, and funding was provided. Unfortunately, as we discussed earlier in this chapter, financial support was pulled in 1991 by legislation introduced to eliminate federal funding for studies about sexuality.

However, Laumann and his colleagues acquired private funding and continued their research, although with a significantly reduced sample size. A representative sample of 4,369 Americans between the ages of 18 and 59 years was randomly selected and

REALResearch **>** A study comparing college student attitudes about sexual morality from 1940 to 2005 found that students have become more accepting of sex before marriage but less accepting of extramarital affairs (Lance, 2007).

yielded a 79% response rate. A total sample population of 3,432 was used in the final analysis of data. All respondents were interviewed face-to-face, supplemented with brief questionnaires. The National Health and Social Life Survey was the most comprehensive study of sexual attitudes and behaviors since Kinsey, and because the researchers used better sampling procedures, this study is viewed as the most comprehensive, scientifically accurate sexuality study in the United States today.

Preliminary data revealed that Americans were more sexually conservative than previously thought. The majority of people were found to have sex a few times a month or less. The results also indicated the sexual choices that people make are restricted by their social networks (e.g., friends and family). Among the findings are the following:

- The median number of sexual partners since age 18 was 6 for men and 2 for women.

- **75%** of married men and **80%** of married women did not engage in extramarital sexuality.

- **2.8%** of men and **1.4%** of women described themselves as homosexual or bisexual.

- **75%** of men claimed to have consistent orgasms with their partners, whereas **29%** of women did.

- More than 1 in 5 women said they had been forced by a man to do something sexual.

In many of the following chapters, we explore various findings of this important study in more detail.

AGE-SPECIFIC STUDIES:
TEENS AND SENIORS

A few sexuality studies have been done on specific populations, such as adolescents and older adults. We now review some of the more prominent studies.

Teens

Two classic studies on adolescent behavior include work by Robert Sorenson and co-researchers Melvin Zelnick and John Kantner. Sorenson published *Adolescent Sexuality in Contemporary America* in 1973. This study was considered the first comprehensive study of adolescent sexuality and explored teenage masturbation, sexual activity, and homosexual behavior. Specific findings from Sorenson's work are reviewed in Chapter 8.

Another classic study was done by Melvin Zelnik and John Kantner in 1971. They studied the sexual and contraceptive behavior of 15- to 19-year-old females in 1971, 1976, and 1979. The data from this study were used as a comparison for the National Survey of Adolescent Males study, which we discuss later.

The National Longitudinal Study of Adolescent Health (ADD Health, 2002) was initiated in 1994 to study the health and risk behaviors of children in grades 7 through 12. Researchers collected data on adolescents' emotional health, sexuality, experience with violence, and substance use. In 2001 and 2002, ADD health respondents were reinterviewed, and researchers are using the data to explore issues such as first sexual experience, religiosity, self-esteem, and drug and alcohol use.

The National Institute for Child Health and Human Development conducted the National Survey of Adolescent Males (NSAM), a **longitudinal study** on adolescent males, from 1988 to 1995. This study was the first nationally representative survey of the sexual behavior of single adolescent males in the United States since 1979. The NSAM included face-to-face interviews and surveys from a nationally representative group of more than 6,500 adolescent males. Researchers collected information on sexual and contraceptive histories and attitudes about sexuality, contraception, and fatherhood. Respondents over age 18 submitted urine for STI tests. Overall, the findings from this study showed that a significant number of adolescent males engage in sexual activities beyond vaginal intercourse, such as mutual masturbation and oral and anal sex (Gates & Sonenstein, 2000).

Finally, another large-scale study of adolescent behavior, the Youth Risk Behavior Surveillance (YRBS), has been collecting data since 1999. This study includes students in grades 9 through 12, and it is conducted every 2 years. We discuss more about these studies in Chapter 8.

Seniors

Older adults were underrepresented in Kinsey's research. The first study to recognize this, conducted by Bernard Starr and Marcella Weiner in 1981, explored the sexuality of 800 adults who were between the ages of 60 and 91. The questionnaire was composed of 50 open-ended questions about sexual experience, changes in sexuality that have occurred with age, sexual satisfaction, sex and widowhood, sexual interest, masturbation, orgasm, sexual likes and dislikes, and intimacy. The questionnaire was distributed after a lecture about sexuality in the elderly. Each participant was given a questionnaire and a self-addressed, stamped envelope in which to return it.

Sixty-five percent of respondents were female, and 35% were male (Starr & Weiner, 1981). The response rate was 14%, which is very low; therefore, the statistics may not be accurate for all seniors, and it is possible that the sample overrepresented seniors more interested in sex or with more active sex lives.

The study revealed that interest in sexuality continued in the later years, and many older adults felt that sexuality continued to be important for physical and emotional health as they aged. Although Kinsey's research indicated that couples over 60 had sex once every 2 weeks, participants in Starr and Weiner's group reported their frequency was 1.4 times a week. Many reported that they wished this number were higher. In addition, several respon-

longitudinal study
A study done over a certain period of time, wherein participants are studied at various intervals.

REALResearch >Ed Brecher, an expert on elderly sexuality, and Sally Binford, his close personal friend, together made a sexually explicit movie about elderly sexuality in 1974, titled *A Ripple in Time.* Sadly, both Brecher and Binford took their own lives in 1989 and 1993, respectively.

years in a book titled *Love, Sex, and Aging* (Brecher et al., 1984). A total of 4,246 men and women over the age of 50 were included in this study. The survey included questions on attitudes about sex, behaviors, and sexual concerns. Again it was found that older adults were indeed sexually active, even though society still thought of them in nonsexual terms.

dents thought that sexuality was better in the later years, masturbation was acceptable, oral sex was pleasurable, and their sex lives were similar to, or better than, they had been in their younger years. It is also important to point out that many of the studies on sexuality in the elderly failed to explore same-sex behavior. While these studies most probably included gay, lesbian, and bisexual men and women, little was learned about differences in same-sex and heterosexual behavior in the elderly.

In 1983, Edward Brecher and the editors of Consumer Reports Books published another classic study of sexuality in the later

Current research into elderly sexuality supports these earlier studies about sexual interest in aging adults. In a nationally representative survey of men and women over age 60, more than half reported that they were sexually active (defined as engaging in masturbation, oral sex, anal sex, or vaginal intercourse; Dunn & Cutler, 2000). However, the percentages of sexually active elderly men and women decline with each decade (73% among those aged 57–64 years; 53% among those aged 65–74 years; and 26% among those aged 75–85 years; Lindau et al., 2007). We discuss all of these studies more in Chapter 14.

review questions

1 Explain the work done by early promoters of sexology.

2 Differentiate between Alfred Kinsey's work and that of Masters and Johnson's. What did these researchers contribute to our understanding of human sexuality?

3 Discuss the wide-scale research studies that have been done on homosexuality.

4 Compare and contrast *The Janus Report* with the National Health and Social Life Survey.

5 Review the various age-specific and special population studies that have been done, and provide information about populations, type of study, and relevant findings.

Sex Research Methods and Considerations

Now that we have explored some of the findings of studies in sexuality, let us look at the specifics of how these studies are conducted. Each study that we have discussed in this chapter was scientific, yet researchers used different experimental methods depending on the kind of information they were trying to gather. For example, Freud relied on a **case study** methodology, whereas Kinsey used interviews to gather data. There are other ways that researchers collect information, such as questionnaires, laboratory experiments, direct observation, participant observation, and correlations.

Whatever techniques they use, researchers must be certain that their experiment passes standards of validity, reliability, and generalizability. Tests of **validity** determine whether a question or other method actually measures what it is designed to measure. For example, the people who read the question need to interpret it the same way as the researcher who wrote it. **Reliability** refers to the consistency of the measure. If we ask a question today, we would hope to get a similar answer if we ask it again in two

months. Finally, generalizability refers to the ability of samples in a study to have wide applicability to the general population. A study can be generalized only if a random sample is used. All of the methods we review here must fit these three criteria.

CASE STUDIES

When a researcher describes a case study, he or she attempts to explore individual cases to formulate general hypotheses. Freud was famous for his use of this methodology. He would study hysteria in only one patient, because he didn't have several patients with similar complaints. Using this method, however, does not allow researchers to generalize to the wider public because the

case study
A research methodology that involves an in-depth examination of one participant or a small number of participants.

validity
The property of a device measuring what it is intended to measure.

reliability
The dependability of a test as reflected in the consistency of its scores on repeated measurements of the same group.

sample is small. Even so, the case study method may generate hypotheses that can lead to larger, generalizable studies.

QUESTIONNAIRES VERSUS INTERVIEWS

Questionnaire or survey research is generally used to identify the attitudes, knowledge, or behavior of large samples. For instance, Kinsey used this method to obtain information about his many participants, although questions have since been raised about Kinsey's validity and reliability. Kinsey recognized these problems and tried to increase the validity by using interviews to supplement the questionnaires.

Some researchers prefer to use interviews instead of questionnaires; there are advantages and disadvantages to each method. An interview allows the researcher to establish a rapport with each participant and emphasize the importance of honesty in the study. In addition, the researcher can vary the order of questions and skip questions that are irrelevant. However, there are some limitations to interviews. First, they are more time-consuming and expensive than questionnaires. Also, it has been argued that questionnaires provide more honesty because the participant may be embarrassed to admit things to another person that he or she would be more likely to share with the anonymity of a questionnaire. Research has revealed that when people answer sexuality questionnaires, they are likely to leave out the questions that cause the most anxiety, especially questions about masturbation (Catania et al., 1986).

View in Video

"92% of the people who started the survey completed the entire thing."
—*American Sex Lives: 2004 Survey*
To view go to CengageNOW at www.cengage.com/login

DIRECT OBSERVATION

Masters and Johnson used direct observation for their research on sexual response and physiology. This method is the least frequently used because it is difficult to find participants who are willing to come into the laboratory to have sex while researchers monitor their bodily functions. However, if direct observation can be done, it does provide information that cannot be obtained elsewhere. Researchers can actually monitor behavior as it happens, which gives the results more credibility. A man may exaggerate the number of erections per sexual episode in a self-report, but he cannot exaggerate in a laboratory.

Direct observation is expensive and may not be as generalizable, because it would be impossible to gather a random sample. In addition, direct observation focuses on behaviors and, as a result, ignores feelings, attitudes, or personal history.

PARTICIPANT OBSERVATION

Participant observation research involves researchers going into an environment and monitoring what is happening naturally. For instance, a researcher who wants to explore the impact of alcohol on male and female flirting patterns might monitor interactions between and among men and women in bars. This would entail several visits and specific note taking on all that occurs. However, it is difficult to generalize from this type of research because the researcher could subtly, or not so subtly, influence the research findings. Also, this method has limited use in the area of sex research since much of sexual behavior occurs in private.

EXPERIMENTAL METHODS

Experiments are the only research method that allows us to isolate cause and effect. This is because in an experiment, strict control is maintained over all variables so that one variable can be isolated and examined.

For example, let's say you want to teach high school students about AIDS, but you don't know which teaching methodology would be most beneficial. You could design an experiment to examine this more closely. First, you choose a high school and randomly assign all the students to one of three groups. You might start by giving them a questionnaire about AIDS to establish baseline data about what they know or believe. Group 1 then listens to a lecture about AIDS, Group 2 is shown a video, and Group 3 listens to a person with AIDS talk about his or her experience. Strict care is taken to make sure that all of the information that is presented in these classes is identical. The only thing that differs is the teaching method. In scientific terms, the type of teaching method is the **independent variable,** which is manipulated by the researcher. After each class, the students are given a test to determine what knowledge they have gained about AIDS. This measurement is to determine the effect of the independent variable on the **dependent variable,** which in this case is knowledge about AIDS. If one group shows more learning after one particular method was used, we might be able to attribute the learning to the type of methodology that was used.

Experiments can be more costly than any of the other methods discussed, in terms of both finances and time commitment. It is also possible that in an attempt to control the experiments, a researcher may cause the study to become too sterile or artificial (nothing like it would be outside of the laboratory), and the results may be faulty or inapplicable to the real world. Finally, experiments are not always possible in certain areas of research, especially in the field of sexuality. For instance, what if we wanted to examine whether early sexual abuse contributed to adult difficulties with intimate relationships? It would be entirely unethical to abuse children sexually to examine whether they develop these problems later in life.

participant observation
A research methodology that involves actual participation in the event being researched.

independent variable
The variable controlled by the experimenter and applied to the participant to determine its effect on the participant's reaction.

dependent variable
The measured results of an experiment that are believed to be a function of the independent variable.

CORRELATIONS

Correlations are often used when it is not possible to do an experiment. For example, because it is unethical to do a controlled experiment in a sexual abuse study, we would study a given population to see whether there is any correlation between past sexual abuse and later difficulties with intimate relationships. The limitation of a **correlational study** is that it doesn't provide any information about cause. We would not learn whether past sexual abuse causes intimacy difficulties, even though we may learn that these factors are related. The intimacy difficulties could occur for several other reasons, including factors such as low self-esteem or a personality disorder.

> **correlation**
> A statistical measure of the relationship between two variables.
>
> **correlational study**
> A type of research that examines the relationship between two or more variables.

review questions

1 Differentiate between validity and reliability and give one example of each.

2 What makes a study generalizable?

3 Identify the advantages and disadvantages of using interviews and questionnaires.

4 Explain how direct observation and participant observation are used in research studies.

5 Differentiate an experiment from a correlational study.

Problems and Issues in Sex Research

Many problems in sexuality research are more difficult to contend with than they are in other types of research. These include ethical issues, volunteer bias, sampling problems, and reliability.

ETHICAL ISSUES

Ethical issues affect all social science—and sexuality research in particular. Before a person participates in a study of sexuality, researchers must obtain his or her **informed consent.** This is especially important in an area such as sexuality because it is such a personal subject. Informed consent means that the person knows what to expect from the questions and procedures, how the information will be used, that his or her **confidentiality** will be assured, and to whom he or she can address questions. Some things that people reveal in a study, such as their acknowledgment of an affair or a sexual dysfunction, can cause harm or embarrassment if researchers are careless enough to let others find out. Another ethical question that has generated controversy is whether children should be asked questions about sexuality. Overall it is standard procedure in sexuality research to maintain confidentiality and obtain informed consent from all participants, regardless of age.

VOLUNTEER BIAS

Earlier in this chapter we touched on the topic of volunteer bias in our discussion of Morton Hunt's *Sexual Behavior* in the 1970s. Because Hunt's sample was such a small percentage of those he contacted, volunteer bias prevents his results from being generalizable to the population as a whole.

Imagine that we wanted to administer a questionnaire about college students' attitudes toward sexuality, and we recruited volunteers from your biology class. Do you think those who volunteer would be different from those who do not? Research indicates that they may indeed differ.

As early as 1969, Rosenthal and Rosnow (1975) claimed that those who volunteer for psychological studies often have a special interest in the studies in which they participate. Studies that have examined volunteer bias in sexuality research conducted with college students generally support the finding that volunteers differ from nonvolunteers (Catania et al., 1995; Gaither et al., 2003). Volunteers have been found to be more sexually liberal, more sexually experienced, more interested in sexual variety, and more likely to have engaged in sexual behavior, including oral sex, and they report less traditional sexual attitudes than nonvolunteers (Bogaert, 1996; Gaither, 2000; Plaud et al., 1999; Wiederman, 1999).

> **informed consent**
> Informing participants about what will be expected of them before they agree to participate in a research study.
>
> **confidentiality**
> Assurance that all materials collected in a research study will be kept private and confidential.

Research has also found that, overall, men are more likely than women to volunteer for sexuality studies (Gaither et al., 2003).

You might be wondering how a researcher would know whether his or her volunteer sample is different from the nonvolunteer sample. After all, how can the researcher know anything about the nonvolunteers who are not in the study? Researchers have designed ways to overcome this problem. Before asking for volunteers to take part in a sexuality study, researchers ask all participants to fill out a questionnaire that contains personality measures and sexuality questions. Participants are then asked whether they would volunteer for a sexuality study. Because the researchers already have information from both volunteers and nonvolunteers, they simply compare these data.

Because volunteers appear to differ from nonvolunteers, it is impossible to generalize the findings of a study that used a volunteer sample. The Kinsey studies attempted to decrease volunteer bias by obtaining full participation from each member of the groups they studied.

SAMPLING PROBLEMS

Sexuality studies routinely involve the use of college-age populations. Brecher and Brecher (1986) refer to these populations as **samples of convenience,** because the participants used are conve-

samples of convenience
A research methodology that involves using samples that are easy to collect and acquire.

HUMAN SEXUALITY IN A DIVERSE WORLD

Global Sex Research

. . . ratings of sexual satisfaction throughout the world are correlated with overall happiness in both men and women.

There have been a few global studies that have shed some light on cross-cultural sexuality. Global studies are expensive to conduct, and because of this, usually pharmaceutical or contraceptive companies fund them. Here we'll discuss the Global Study of Sexual Attitudes and Behaviors (2002); the Durex Global Sex Survey (2007); and the Global Sex Survey (2007).

The Global Study of Sexual Attitudes and Behaviors studied sexual behavior, attitudes, beliefs, and relationship satisfaction among more than 27,000 men and women age 40 to 80 years (Laumann et al., 2006). Interviews and surveys were conducted in 29 countries representing all world regions.

Results indicated that more than 80% of men and 60% of women thought sex was an important part of their overall lives (see Figure 2.1). Koreans rated sex as most important, and those living in Hong Kong rated it the least important. This survey also found that despite wide cultural variations, there are several predictors of sexual well-being (such as physical and mental health and relationship satisfaction) that are consistent throughout the regions of the world and that ratings of sexual satisfaction throughout the world are correlated with overall happiness in both men and women (Laumann et al., 2006).

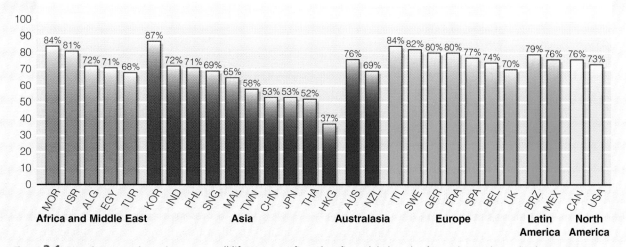

Figure **2.1** How important is sex in your overall life? Source: Pfizer, The Pfizer Global Study of Sexual Attitudes and Behavior, 2002. Used by permission.

continued

continued

Other global studies have also been conducted. One fairly recent one was done in 2007 by the Durex company (see Figure 2.2). This study explored sexual attitudes and behaviors in 41 countries. The study included 26,000 people (categorized as 16+ or 18+ groupings) who responded to a web survey. The Durex study found that the average age for engaging in first penile-vaginal sexual intercourse worldwide is 17.3 (Durex.com, 2007). The age at first intercourse was 15.6 (youngest) in Iceland and 19.8 (oldest) in India. This study also found that heterosexual couples in Greece are the most sexually active, whereas heterosexual couples in Japan are the least.

Whereas both the Global Study and the Durex study investigated sexual attitudes and behaviors in a wide age range, another global study evaluated contraceptive use in adolescents from 24 European and North American countries (Godeau et al., 2008). This study included 34,000 15-year old students who responded by self-report questionnaires. The percentages of students reporting engaging in sexual intercourse ranged from 14% in Croatia to 38% in England. The majority of these students claimed to have used condoms during last sexual intercourse. Condom use in Greece was close to 90%, whereas in Sweden it was closer to 53% (Godeau et al., 2008).

Global studies can help us learn more about societal and cultural factors that influence sexuality. Unfortunately, these studies are expensive, and funding can be difficult to come by.

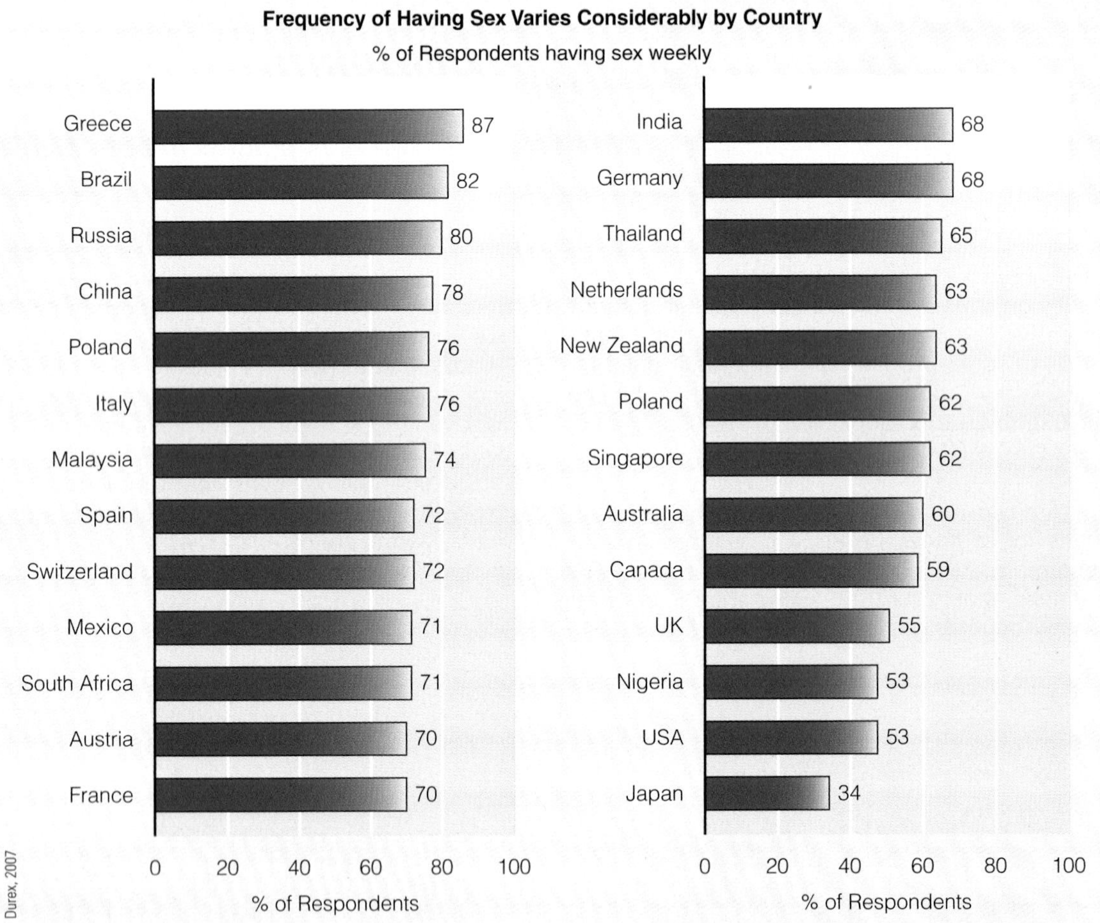

Frequency of Having Sex Varies Considerably by Country

% of Respondents having sex weekly

Country	%		Country	%
Greece	87		India	68
Brazil	82		Germany	68
Russia	80		Thailand	65
China	78		Netherlands	63
Poland	76		New Zealand	63
Italy	76		Poland	62
Malaysia	74		Singapore	62
Spain	72		Australia	60
Switzerland	72		Canada	59
Mexico	71		UK	55
South Africa	71		Nigeria	53
Austria	70		USA	53
France	70		Japan	34

% of Respondents

Durex, 2007

Figure **2.2** Do you engage in sex at least weekly? Source: Retrieved from http://www.durex.com/cm/sexual_wellbeing_graphPrint.asp.

nient for researchers who tend to work at universities. Kinsey used such samples in his initial research at Indiana University. The question is, can these studies be generalized to the rest of the population? Are college students similar to noncollege students of the same age, or people who are older or younger? Probably not. These samples also miss certain groups, such as those who do not go to college, and may also underrepresent minorities and the disabled.

RELIABILITY

How reliable is sex research? Some studies have found that couples who are sexually satisfied tend to overestimate their frequency of sexual behavior, whereas those who are unsatisfied underreport it. In 1967, a study was done to evaluate the reliability of the reporting of sexual activity. Men were required to keep daily logs of when they engaged in sexual activity and also to provide daily urine samples. These samples were microscopically evaluated for semen to substantiate their logs of sexual activity. Reports were found to be consistent with their written logs.

Some critics claim that changes in frequency of sexual behavior over time may be due more to changes in the reporting of behavior than to actual changes in frequency (Kaats & Davis, 1971). For instance, if we had done a study in 1995 about the number of college students that engaged in premarital sex and compared this with data collected in 1963, we would undoubtedly find more people reporting having had premarital sex in 1995. However, it could be that these higher numbers are due in part to the fact that more people felt comfortable talking about premarital sex in 1995 than they did in 1963. To ensure that we know the increase in numbers is actually due to an increase in behavior, it is necessary to take into account the time period of the study when evaluating the results.

Another problem affecting reliability involves the participant's memory. Because many sexuality researchers ask questions about behaviors that might have happened in one's adolescence, people may not always have the capacity to remember information accurately. For instance, if we were to ask a 52-year-old man the age at which he first masturbated, chances are good that he would not remember exactly how old he was. He would probably estimate the age at which he first masturbated. Estimates are not always precise enough for scientific study.

WHAT DO YOU WANT TO KNOW ?

How do researchers know that what people tell them is true?
The fact is that they just don't know, and they hope that people are being honest. Sometimes researchers build into studies little tricks that can catch someone who is lying, such as asking the same questions in different wording again later in a survey. Researchers also anticipate that participants will understand the questions asked and be able to provide the answers. In actuality, researchers may take many things for granted.

review questions

1 Define informed consent and explain the importance of confidentiality.

2 What differences have been found between those who volunteer and don't volunteer for sex research?

3 Define a "sample of convenience" and explain how it is used.

4 How do satisfaction and memory issues potentially affect sex research?

HUMAN SEXUALITY IN A DIVERSE WORLD

Internet-Based Sexuality Research

The accessibility and sense of anonymity of the web have given sexuality researchers access to a wider group of diverse participants.

In 2007, more than 70% of Americans used the Internet and this number continues to grow today (Nielsen NetRatings, 2007). The popularity of the Internet has led to an increase in Internet-based social science research, and sexuality researchers have been relying on the Internet for data collection in many of their studies (Mustanski, 2001). The accessibility and sense of anonymity of the web have given sexuality researchers access to a wider group of diverse participants.

However, there are disadvantages and risks to Internet-based sexuality research. As in other research methods, participants can lie and sabotage research. Because surveys are anonymous, participants could submit multiple responses. To lessen the possibility of this happening, researchers could collect e-mail addresses to check for multiple submissions, but this would negate participants' anonymity. One study that checked for multiple submissions found that participants rarely submitted more than one response (Reips, 2000).

Although more than 70% of people in the United States use the Internet, some caution that Internet users are not representative of all Americans—a variety of minorities are not well represented, nor are those with low socioeconomic status or education (National Telecommunications

continued

continued

and Information Administration & U.S. Department of Commerce, 1999). Wealthier, Caucasian, and better-educated individuals are well represented on the Internet, and this can bias research results. However, even though these differences exist, some researchers claim that the participants pool available online may be more representative of the general population than a group of typical college students (who are the most common research participants; Mustanski, 2001; Reips & Bachtiger, 2000).

One more concern about Internet-based sexuality research is that minors may have access to the studies. However, researchers must ask for informed consent, and participants must agree that they are over the age of 18 before participating.

Even with these cautions, however, Internet-based sexuality research is a dynamic and exciting new frontier for sexuality researchers. It is anticipated that more studies will be done using web-based research methodology in the future.

Source: Mustanski (2001).

While there are advantages and disadvantages to Internet-based sexuality research, many researchers believe that subjects who participate online may be more representative of the general population than the typical college student.

Sexuality Research
Across Cultures

Many studies examine sexuality in cultures outside the United States. Some have been general studies that examine knowledge levels and attitudes in different populations; others have evaluated specific areas such as pregnancy, rape, homosexuality, or sex education. Many times these studies are done by researchers in other countries, but some have also been done by American researchers.

Of all the topics that have been studied cross-culturally, we have probably learned the most about how societies' values and culture influence sexuality. Every culture develops its own rules about which sexual behaviors are encouraged and which will not be tolerated. In 1971, Donald Marshall and Robert Suggs published a classic anthropological study, *Human Sexual Behavior*, which examined how sexuality was expressed in several different cultures. This study remains one of the largest cultural studies ever done on sexuality. Following are some of its interesting findings:

- Masturbation is rare in preliterate cultures (those without a written language).

- Foreplay is usually initiated by males in heterosexual couples.

- Heterosexuals engage in sexual intercourse most commonly at night prior to falling asleep.

- Female orgasmic ability varies greatly from culture to culture.

More recent studies on cross-cultural sexuality have yielded other interesting results. A comprehensive study of sexual behavior titled the *Analyse des Comportements Sexuels en France (ACSF)* was done in 1991 and 1992 (Spira et al., 1993). Funded by a $2.5 million grant from France's health ministry and the national AIDS research agency, it examined the sexual practices of more than 20,000 people between ages 18 and 69 years. Interviews were done primarily by telephone, and the majority of those contacted agreed to participate (an impressive response rate of 76.5% was obtained). Findings revealed that many teenagers do not use condoms during sex because they are too expensive; that rates of extramarital sexual behavior are decreasing; and that the average French heterosexual engages in sex approximately two times per week. This was the largest study done in France in more than 20 years.

In 2001, results gathered from the ACSF were compared with the National Health and Social Life Study done in the United States. Overall, patterns of sexual conduct were similar (Gagnon, 2001). However, there were some areas of difference. The French were found to form monogamous sexual partnerships earlier and to remain in these partnerships for a longer time period than the Americans. The French also had fewer sexual partners over their lifetime and higher frequencies of sexual behavior.

In 2002, Pfizer Pharmaceuticals undertook a comprehensive global study of sexuality. The Global Study of Sexual Attitudes and Behaviors surveyed more than 26,000 men and women in 28 countries. This study was the first global survey to assess behaviors, attitudes, beliefs, and sexual satisfaction. Surveys assessed the importance of sex and intimacy in relationships, attitudes and beliefs about sexual health, and treatment-seeking behaviors for sexual dysfunctions. This survey provided an international baseline regarding sexual attitudes to compare various countries and also monitor cultural changes over time. In 2007, Durex undertook another global study to explore sexual attitudes and behaviors in 41 countries. The study included 26,000 people who responded to a web survey (see the accompanying Human Sexuality in a Diverse World for more information about both of these studies).

Societal influences affect all aspects of sexuality. Throughout this book, we explore more details from cross-cultural studies on sexuality and examine how cultures vary from each other.

WHAT DO YOU WANT TO KNOW ?

How could an entire culture's attitudes about sex differ from those of another culture? I can understand how there might be individual variations, but could there really be significant cultural differences?

Yes, there could. It makes more sense when you think about two very different types of cultures. A collectivist culture (e.g., India, Pakistan, Thailand, or the Philippines) emphasizes the cultural group as a whole and thinks less about the individuals within that society. In contrast, an individualistic culture (e.g., the United States, Australia, or England) stresses the goals of individuals over the cultural group as a whole. This cultural difference can affect the way that sexuality is viewed. For example, a culture such as India may value marriage because it is good for the social standing of members of the society, whereas a marriage in the United States is valued because the two people love each other and want to spend their lives together.

review questions

1 Of all the cross-cultural topics that have been studied, what have we learned the most about?

2 Identify two findings from Marshall and Suggs' large-scale cross-cultural study of sexuality.

3 What differences have been found in the sexuality of the French and Americans?

4 Identify some of the findings from the Pfizer and Durex sex studies.

Sex Research in the Future: Beyond Problem-Driven Research

Many view America as a country "obsessed with sex." As we discussed in Chapter 1, sex is used to sell everything from jeans to iPhones and is oozing from television sitcoms, advertising, music videos, and song lyrics. However, even with this openness and sex all around us, there is a painful lack of solid sexuality research. Our problem-driven approach to sex research has limited what we really know about relationships, love, and human development. Often funding for sexuality research comes from private founda-tions or governmental agencies. Over the past few years, however, there has been a lack of adequate funding.

Overall, it is a trying time for sexuality researchers. Congressional attacks on sexuality research continue, and in 2003 an amendment was proposed that would have cut funding for many grants given to study sexual behaviors. In response, the Coalition to Protect Research was organized to support federal investments in biomedical and behavioral research into human sexual development, sexual health, and sexually transmitted infections (Studwell, 2004).

Religious institutions may also work to impede sexuality research. In fact, in 2003, the Traditional Values Coalition (consisting of more than 43,000 churches) publicly objected to $100 million of government-backed research, much of it focusing on sexual behavior (Carey, 2004). Conservative groups pressure federal agencies to cut funding for sexuality studies, which forces many researchers to turn to pharmaceutical companies for financial support (J. Clark, 2005). Some researchers claim that a reliance on drug company money will reduce sexual functioning to purely physical functions, and the important questions about the psychological and emotional aspects of sexuality will be ignored.

The opinion of many conservatives is that the key to sexual health lies in a lifelong monogamous relationship, and because of this, no research is needed on any sexual behaviors that occur outside of monogamy (Carey, 2004). In fact, according to such beliefs, if researchers do study behaviors outside of this formula, the research will "normalize" deviant behaviors. All of these pressures affect sexuality researchers' ability to do their work. In fact, it has been said that because of these pressures, many sex researchers today operate in a type of "scientific underground," fearing suppression and censure (Carey, 2004).

Our problem-driven approach has resulted in a lack of information in several key areas in human sexuality. We know little about sexual desire and arousal and what makes couples happy long term or about childhood and adolescent sexuality, which has long been a taboo area of research. We also know little about the development of sexual identity, sexual risk taking, and how the increase in sexual material on the Internet affects people's sexual behaviors (Carey, 2004). Infidelity, sexual trauma, and various sexual variations, including sexual predators and people who sexually abuse children, have also been poorly researched.

Funding for sexuality education has been controversial as well. In fact, to get federal funds for sexuality education, a program must discuss abstinence and is often barred from discussing condoms or other contraceptive methods (Kristof, 2005). Since research continues to show that abstinence education does not change teenage sexual behaviors, many states have turned down federal money. By 2008, less than half of U.S. states were accepting federal funding for abstinence education (Freking, 2008). (We discuss this more in Chapter 8.)

The goal of sex research in the future will be to understand the emotional and relational aspects of human sexuality. Instead of focusing primarily on what doesn't work in sexual relationships, such as problems with erections or orgasms, it will help us understand what does work and what keeps couples happy and satisfied. In the future, an increased willingness on the part of the federal government to consider sexuality-related research will help improve our knowledge about sexuality and will aid in bringing sexuality researchers together. An improved collaboration between researchers of various disciplines would help us more fully understand the influences that affect our sexuality and, in turn, would help build the field of sexual science.

In the following chapters of this book, keep in mind the importance of theory and how it guides the questions we have about sexuality. The scientific method helps sexologists find answers to the varied questions we have about human sexual behavior. We will be discussing the results of many more of these scientific studies in upcoming chapters.

REALResearch **>** Sex surveys in magazines, such as *Cosmopolitan,* create new dangers for sex researchers in that they tell readers things that they want to hear. Selected voices that are used in these "analyses" promote sexual joy and passion above all else (ERICKSEN, 1999).

review questions

1 Explain how our "problem-driven" approach to sex research has limited what we know about sexuality.

2 How do religious institutions often impede sexuality research?

3 What direction does sexuality research need to go in the future and why?

CHAPTER **review**

1   A theory is a set of assumptions, principles, or methods that help a researcher understand the nature of a phenomenon being studied. The most influential psychological theory has been the psychoanalytic theory, developed by Sigmund Freud. He discussed personality formation (the development of the id, ego, and superego) and also psychosexual development (oral, anal, phallic, latency, and genital stages).

2   Behavioral theory believes that only overt behavior can be measured, observed, and controlled by scientists. Behaviorists use rewards and punishments to control behavior. A treatment method called behavior modification is used to help change unwanted behaviors.

3   Social learning theory looks at reward and punishment in controlling behavior but also believes that internal events, such as feelings, thoughts, and beliefs, can also influence behavior. Another theory, cognitive theory, holds that people differ in how they process information, and this creates personality differences. Our behavior is a result of how we perceive and conceptualize what is happening around us.

4   Humanistic theory purports that we all strive to develop ourselves to the best of our abilities and to become self-actualized. Biological theory claims that sexual behavior is primarily a biological process, whereas evolutionary theory incorporates both evolution and sociology to understand sexual behavior. Sociological theories are interested in how the society in which we live influences sexual behavior.

5   Feminist theory looks at how the social construction of sexuality is based on power and the view that women are submissive and subordinate to men. Queer theory, another politically charged theory, asserts that domination, such as heterosexism and homophobia, should be resisted.

6   The legitimate forefathers of sexuality research may be Aristotle and Plato, because they were the first to develop theories regarding sexual responses and dysfunctions, sex legislation, reproduction, contraception, and sexual ethics. The majority of the early sex research was done in Europe, primarily in Germany. It wasn't until the 1900s that sexuality research moved to the United States, which has led sexuality research ever since.

7   The majority of sexuality research has been problem driven, and because of this, we know little about what constitutes healthy sexuality. The research has also become fragmented, with researchers coming from several disciplines, many unaware of the work being done by others.

8   The changing political climate affects attitudes about sexuality, as well as sex research. Negative attitudes can affect the public perception of sex research. Politics also can influence what sexuality research gets funded.

9   The most influential early promoters of sexology were Iwan Bloch, Albert Moll, Magnus Hirschfeld, Richard von Krafft-Ebing, and Havelock Ellis. Clelia Mosher did a great deal of sexuality research in the 1800s, but most of her work was never published. Katharine Bement Davis found that homosexuals were no different from heterosexuals, but her work was ignored because it caused fear among male researchers. The focus of sexuality research began to change after her research.

10   Alfred Kinsey was probably the most influential sex researcher of the 20th century. He was the first to take the study of sexuality away from the medical model. Kinsey established the Institute for Sex Research at Indiana University. Morton Hunt updated Kinsey's earlier work on human sexuality.

11   William Masters and Virginia Johnson were the first scientists to observe and measure sexual acts in the laboratory. They discovered several interesting aspects of sexuality, including a model called the sexual response cycle.

12   Research studies have also been done on homosexuality, although there have been very few wide-scale studies. Two classic studies were done by Evelyn Hooker and co-researchers Alan Bell and Martin Weinberg. These studies found that intimate relationships in the homosexual community were similar to those in the heterosexual community.

13   Other sexuality studies include *The Janus Report* (1993) and the National Health and Social Life Survey (1994). Both of these studies were intended to update Kinsey's large-scale survey of sexual behavior.

14   Age-specific studies have been done on teens and seniors. Adolescent health and risk behaviors were the focus of a study by ADD Health. The NSAM studied adolescent males, collecting data between 1988 and 1995. Because seniors were underrepresented in Kinsey's studies, Bernard Starr and Marcella Weiner studied sexuality in 60 to 91 year olds. Edward Brecher et al.'s (1984) study confirmed earlier findings that older adults were indeed sexual.

15   Researchers can use several methods to study sexuality, including case study, questionnaire, interview, participant observation, experimental methods, and correlations.

16   Researchers must be certain that their experiment passes standards of validity, reliability, and generalizability. Several problems can affect sexuality research, such as ethical issues, volunteer bias, sampling and reliability problems. Of all the topics that have been studied cross-culturally, we have learned the most about how societies' values and culture influence sexuality.

17   Pressure from conservative groups has resulted in less support and acceptance of sexuality research. Our problem-driven approach to sexuality research has interfered with what we really know and understand about relationships, love, and human development.

CRITICAL THINKING questions

1 Is sexuality research as valid and reliable as other areas of research? Explain.

2 Do you think that people would be more honest about their sex lives if they were filling out an anonymous questionnaire or if they were being interviewed by a researcher? Which method of research do you think yields the highest degree of honesty? With which method would you feel most comfortable?

3 Why do you think couples might have volunteered to be in Masters and Johnson's study? Would you have volunteered for this study? Why or why not?

4 If you could do a study on sexuality, what area would you choose? What methods of data collection would you use? Why? How would you avoid the problems that many sex researchers face?

WEB resources

Sexuality Now Book Companion Website
Go to www.cengage.com/psychology/carroll for practice quizzes, glossary, flash cards, and more. You can also access the following websites from the companion site.

American Association of Sexuality Educators, Counselors, and Therapists (AASECT) ■ AASECT is devoted to the promotion of sexual health through the development and advancement of the fields of sex therapy, counseling, and education.

Electronic Journal of Human Sexuality ■ Disseminates knowledge to the international community and includes peer-reviewed research articles and dissertations on sexuality.

Sexuality Information and Education Council of the United States (SIECUS) ■ SIECUS is a national, private, nonprofit advocacy organization that promotes comprehensive sexuality education and HIV/AIDS prevention education in the schools.

Society for the Scientific Study of Sexuality (SSSS) ■ SSSS is an interdisciplinary, international organization for sexuality researchers, clinicians, educators, and other professionals in related fields.

CengageNOW
Go to www.cengage.com/login to link to CengageNOW, your online study tool. First take the Pre-Test for this chapter to get your Personalized Study Plan, which will identify topics you need to review and direct you to online resources. Then take the Post-Test to determine what concepts you have mastered and what you still need work on.

Videos in CengageNOW
For additional information on topics discussed in this chapter, check out the videos on the following topics:

- American Sex Lives: 2004 Survey—Listen to how this poll of 1,500 Americans about their sex lives was conducted.

- Studying Sexual Response—Dr. David Barlow and staff psychologists explain how research on sexual dysfunction is conducted.

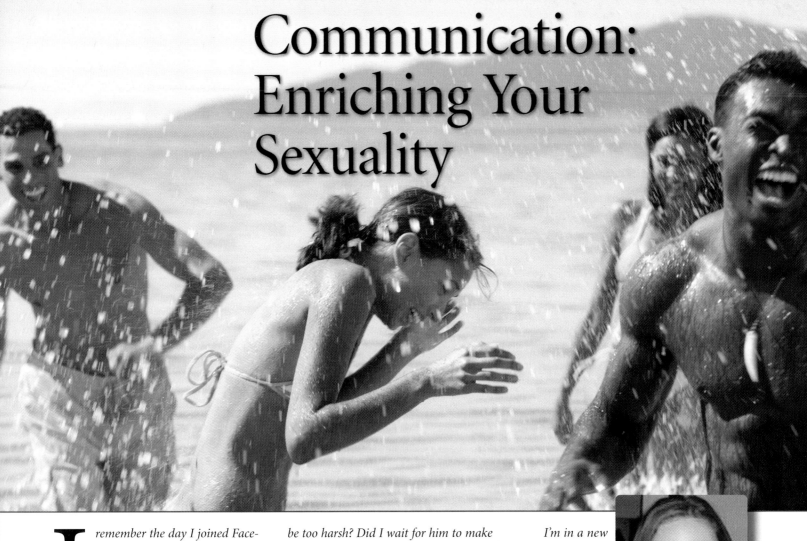

CHAPTER 3

Communication: Enriching Your Sexuality

I remember the day I joined Facebook. Within no time I had 314 friends and 991 photos in my account. I loved being a part of it because I could keep up with my friends, their relationships, recent events, and even see friends' pictures! I could meet new friends and keep in touch with old ones. With a click of a mouse, I instantly know everyone's business. Talk about immediate drama!

When I got into a relationship, I quickly changed my Facebook relationship status to "in a relationship with Dylan." We never really talked about changing our status, we just knew that was what happens when you are in a relationship. After all, a relationship isn't official until it's on Facebook!

Two years later, we broke up. I didn't know what to do. Did I just automatically change my Facebook status, or would that be too harsh? Did I wait for him to make the first move? We were forced to have a conversation about our Facebook status. It was a hard situation for both of us because we were uncomfortable making our breakup public. We knew that as soon as we changed our relationship status, the whole world would know. We could have just broadcasted our breakup on a neon billboard in the middle of New York City! Eventually we did change it, and I was quickly inundated with instant messages—many from people I didn't even consider friends. People kept asking me what happened and how I felt. They hoped I was OK and told me they were sorry. They told me they thought Dylan and I were "perfect" for each other. It was hard for me because after a breakup the last thing you want is a million instant messages. Having to explain the same story over and over again was so painful.

I'm in a new relationship now and I've already told my boyfriend that there is no way we're putting our relationship on Facebook. He had a hard time understanding this at first, but he knows what I went through. At this point, I don't feel that just because I am in relationship it needs to be publicized on Facebook. Although some of my friends think we're not official since we haven't changed our status, my close friends understand. How do a couple of words on a web page make a relationship official anyway? It is truly amazing how communication has changed so dramatically over the past decade and rules our lives today. SOURCE: Author's Files.

© Janell Carroll

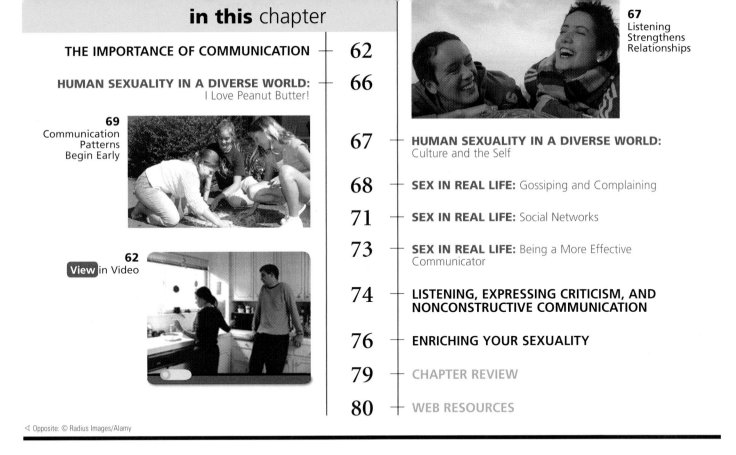
◁ Opposite: © Radius Images/Alamy

Communication has changed drastically over the last few years. In the past if you wanted to talk to people, you went to see them, picked up the phone, or wrote them a letter. Today's college students rely on cell phones, e-mail, instant messaging (IMing), Facebook, and MySpace pages to communicate with friends and family on a daily basis (Diamanduros et al., 2007). Although this technology has allowed more communication between friends, romantic partners, and family members, it has also created many new communication problems. We talk about the advantages and disadvantages of this new technology in this chapter.

Whether you are involved in an intimate relationship now or plan to be at some point in the future, communication is one of the most important elements in a healthy, satisfying relationship. In this chapter, we talk about the importance of communication and improving interpersonal communication, including the ability to communicate about sexual issues. Improving communication has been found to enrich personal sexuality. We discuss other ways to enrich your personal sexuality by learning to feel good about yourself and about your skills in bed and by improving your relationships with others. No one is born a good lover; it takes learning and patience. The information in this chapter may be valuable to you throughout your life, as your relationships change and mature.

Overall, research has shown that couples who know how to communicate with each other are happier, are more satisfied, and have a greater likelihood of making their relationship last (Hahlweg et al., 2000; Rehman & Holtzworth-Munroe, 2007).

© Jupiterimages/Polka Dot/Alamy

Partners who know how to communicate with each other have a better chance of their relationship working out.

However, learning to really communicate with your partner isn't easy. Why is it so hard to talk to your partner? How can you share yourself physically with someone but feel unable to talk about things that are important to you? Why is it difficult to listen to someone when he or she wants to talk about something you don't want to hear?

Let's say you meet someone new tonight. Your eyes find each other across the room, and slowly you make your way over to talk to each other. What would you say? What wouldn't you say? How do you decide? Most likely you make a comment such as, "Pretty loud in here, huh?" or "I can't believe how crowded it is!" The first unwritten rule about communication early in a relationship is that you talk about something relevant but impersonal. You wouldn't walk up to someone you don't know and say, "Do you get along with your parents?" or "Do you ever get acne?" No, these questions are too personal to discuss with a stranger.

When do you start to talk about personal things in relationships? Social psychologists talk about the "onion" theory of communication. We all are onions with many, many layers, and when we first meet someone, we are careful about what we say—our onion layers stay in place. However, as more and more time goes by (and the amount of time differs from person to person), we begin to take off our layers. We take turns sharing personal information.

At first we might talk about the weather ("I can't believe it's still so hot in October") and then progress to certain classes or professors ("I really enjoyed my psychology teacher last semester"). These comments are low risk and really don't involve sharing too much personal information. However, the next layer may include information about politics or family relationships, and the information gets more personal. The key to the onion theory is that as you begin to peel off your layers, so, too, does your partner. If you share something personal about yourself, your partner will probably do the same. If your partner tells you something about a bad experience he or she had, you share a negative experience you've been through.

Some people make the mistake of prematurely peeling back their layers. Have you ever met someone who shared really personal information early, maybe within the first few days of meeting you? Some people talk about personal issues very early in the relationship, which may make you feel uncomfortable (Weisel & King, 2007). Yet there are exceptions to this—have you ever sat next to a stranger on an airplane and shared information that you later realized you've never shared with people you know well? Anxiety may be the culprit here, because you might be a little nervous about flying, and talking might help lessen your anxiety. More important, though, you assume you'll never see this person again, so talk is cheap. There are relatively few risks to sharing so much so soon. When you arrive at your destination, you both go off in different directions and probably won't ever see each other again.

View in Video

"You only seem to care about what you want. . . . I think you're being incredibly selfish."
—*Marriage: "Me" Versus "We"*
To view go to CengageNOW at www. cengage.com/login

The Importance of Communication

Good communication is the principal way in which relationships are created and is the hallmark of a healthy, developing relationship (Duck & Pittman, 1994). These skills can be applied to all aspects of life, such as improving family relationships, being more effective in relationships at school or work, developing a love relationship, or discussing relationship issues and sexuality with a partner. Communication fosters mutual understanding, increases emotional intimacy, and helps deepen feelings of love and intimacy. For love and intimacy to grow, each partner must know how the other feels. In fact, good communication is one of the most important factors in a satisfying relationship (Eaker et al., 2007; Rehman & Holtzworth-Munroe, 2007) Note that having good communication skills and using them are two different things. Partners who have no trouble talking about their feelings in general, for example, may still have trouble telling each other how they want to change certain things in their relationship.

Many relationship problems stem from misunderstandings and poor communication, which lead to anger and frustration. In fact, communication problems are a major source of trouble in relationships. A lack of communication skills contributes to many serious relationship problems, including violence and abuse (Burleson & Denton, 1997). Misunderstandings, anger, and frustration can all lead to a downward spiral in which communication becomes less and less effective.

Relationships between two people inevitably run into difficulties. It's nearly impossible not to experience difficulties when you are sharing your space with another person. This is precisely why many forms of therapy emphasize learning communication skills and why communication self-help books overflow from bookstore shelves. Communication problems usually occur when partners have poor communication skills, feel unable to self-disclose, or have trouble listening. It is also important to point out, however, that not all relationship problems are caused by a lack of communication or poor communication. Sometimes the problems come from an unwillingness to acknowledge a problem or issue that needs to be worked out. In other cases, issues such as poor health or economic stresses can create problems that hinder communication and intimacy.

REALResearch **>** The most common and effective form of communication takes place acoustically when people talk and listen to each other (SALZMANN, 2007). Other forms of communication include tactile (e.g., Braille), optical (e.g., sign language), and even olfactory (e.g., wearing cologne or perfume). Olfactory communication is especially important in social insects, who communicate through odors (SALZMANN, 2007).

IT TAKES SOME LEARNING **TO COMMUNICATE**

Students often tell me they wish they could improve their communication skills. Before we talk about how to do this, let's discuss how we learn to communicate with others. Are we born with the ability to communicate with others, or do we learn it as we grow? If you've ever been around babies, you know that even though they don't have the ability to speak, they know how to communicate with their caregivers. When they are hungry, tired, or just want to be held, they cry. Crying communicates to their caregiver that they need something. As children acquire language, they learn more effective ways of communicating. Yet as we learn to communicate, a host of issues surfaces and interferes with our ability to talk to others. We worry about what others might think, we feel selfish for asking for things we want and need, and we don't know how to talk about ourselves and our needs.

When we communicate with other people, we have three competing goals (Vanfossen, 1996). The first is to "get the job done"—we have a message for someone, and we want to communicate that message. Second, we also have a "relational goal"—we want to maintain the relationship and not hurt or offend someone with our message. Finally, we have an "identity management goal"—that is, we want our communication to project a certain image of ourselves. All of these goals compete with one another (we want to tell someone something, not hurt the relationship, and maintain our image), making the job of communicating our thoughts, needs, or desires even that much tougher. We'll discuss these goals in more detail later in this chapter, but for now, let's explore the effects of gender, sexual orientation, and culture on communication, and perhaps we can uncover guidelines to good communication.

REALResearch > Dating heterosexual couples in which the woman talks less than the man have lower relationship satisfaction than those in which the woman talks the same or more than the man (Sellers et al., 2007). This was found to be due to a violation in traditional gender roles.

HOW WOMEN AND MEN COMMUNICATE

Differences in how men and women communicate has long been a topic of scientific interest (Lakoff, 1975; Litosseliti, 2006; Tannen, 1990). There is a stereotype that women talk more than men. This stereotype was supported by the research of neuropsychiatrist Louann Brizendine, who reported that women used 20,000 words per day, whereas men used only 7,000 (Brizendine, 2006). To determine whether this was true, a group of researchers recently set out to study whether women talk more than men by using electronically activated recorders (Mehl et al., 2007). Electronically activated recorders are digital voice recorders that allow researchers to measure verbal interactions. A total of 396 college students participated in the study. Results indicated that both men and women used about 16,000 words per day, with large individual differences around this mean (Mehl et al., 2007). The researchers suggested that perhaps the fact that all of these subjects were college students may have limited the results of this

REALResearch > A study conducted by Student Monitor looking at the habits and preferences of college students from more than **100** U.S. universities found that beer, Facebook accounts, and text messaging were rated the three most popular things on college campuses (Student Monitor, 2008).

study, but they also pointed out that if the differences are biologically based, they would appear in this sample regardless.

So men and women talk about the same amount. But what about gender differences in conversations? The research supports the fact that conversations between women and men are often more difficult than conversations that occur in same-sex groups (Athenstaedt et al., 2004; Edwards & Hamilton, 2004). Why is this? Do men and women communicate differently? Is part of the communication problem incompatibility between how men and women communicate, so that the content of the communication gets lost in the form it takes?

Linguist Deborah Tannen (1990) has done a great deal of research in the area of communication and gender differences. She has termed the fundamental differences between the way men and women communicate as **genderlects** (JEN-der-lecks). Women have been found to use more rapport-talk, which establishes relationships and connections, whereas men use more report-talk, which imparts knowledge (Eckstein & Goldman, 2001). Tannen (1990)

WHAT DO YOU WANT TO KNOW ?

I am really confused about my relationship with my girlfriend. I thought we communicate really well, but now I don't know what to think. She told me about a problem she is having with another friend. I listened for hours and tried to offer some solutions to help her improve the situation. To my surprise, she became angry with me! What's going on?

If you are a heterosexual man, it could be that there are some gender issues interfering with your ability to communicate here. Research has found that men tend to view conversations as ways to exchange information or fix problems, whereas women tend to try to confirm the other person's feelings and empathize (Gard, 2000). These are tendencies, however, and not all men and women respond the same way. In your case, it sounds as if you listened to your girlfriend and moved on to trying to fix the problem. Perhaps she was looking for your emotional support and some TLC, instead of concrete answers to her dilemma. Unfortunately, women often feel frustrated by men's tendencies to try to fix their problems, whereas men often complain that women refuse to take action to solve their problems. These communication issues can also affect lesbian and gay relationships, and it really depends on the person's individual communication style.

genderlect
Coined by Deborah Tannen, this term refers to the fundamental differences between the way men and women communicate.

A male mode of communication uses more report-talk, which imparts knowledge and helps to establish status.

A female mode of communication uses more rapport-talk, which establishes relationships and maintains intimacy.

REALResearch > Couples who enthusiastically support each other are much happier than those who don't (GABLE ET AL., 2006). Responding to a partner's success energetically ("I knew you could do it!") rather than passively ("Good job") can improve the overall quality of the relationship.

asserts that women use conversations to establish and maintain intimacy, whereas men use conversations to establish status.

Note that often when a gender difference is revealed, it is common to view the male way as normative and the female way as deviating from the norm. When we say "different," it means that there are gender differences in ways of speaking that need to be understood. If they are not, the contrasting conversational styles can lead to frustration, disappointment, and misunderstandings. This is not to imply that one way is better than another—they are simply "different."

Tannen also found that women used less assertiveness in their communication. For example, when stating an opinion, women often end their statement with **tag questions** (e.g., "It's really cold in here, isn't it?" or "That's an interesting idea, isn't it?") to invite discussion and minimize disagreements. They also use **disclaimers** (e.g., "I may be wrong, but. . . ."), **question statements** ("Am I off base here?"; Vanfossen, 1996), and **hedge words** such as "sort of," "kind of," "aren't you," or "would you mind?" All of these tend to decrease the speaker's perceived assertiveness of speech. Although tag questions are frequently used in English, they are not used as much in other languages. In fact, the French and Swedish languages lack an equivalent feature (Cheng & Warren, 2001).

There have been criticisms of Tannen's genderlect theory. One of the biggest criticisms has been in her unidimensional approach of studying gender differences in communication. To Tannen, gender is based on *biological* sex. Therefore, all women communicate one way and all men another way. Another model agrees there are gender differences, but these differences are based on one's *gender role* instead of biological sex (Edwards & Hamilton, 2004). We discuss this research later in this chapter.

Numerous studies on gender and communication have found that differences in many areas of communication are small (Aries, 1996; Dindia & Canary, 2006). Many other factors contribute to our ability to communicate, such as social philosophies, gender roles, dominance, and power. Also keep in mind that many of the studies on gender differences in communication have studied only young, well-educated, middle-class Americans (Mortenson, 2002). Because of this, we do not know whether these findings are generalizable to different groups and cultures within and outside of the United States. We talk more about culture later in this chapter.

THEORIES IN GENDER DIFFERENCES

In the preceding section, we discussed gender differences in communication, but what might contribute to some of these differences? Is it biology? Society? Researchers often disagree about whether gender differences exist, but those who agree that there are

tag question
A way of speaking in which the speaker renounces or denies the validity of what he or she is saying by adding a questioning statement at the end of his or her statement.

disclaimer
A way of speaking in which the speaker renounces or denies the validity of what he or she is saying by including a negative statement.

question statement
A way of speaking in which the speaker renounces or denies the validity of what he or she is saying by adding a question at the end of his or her statements.

hedge word
A way of speaking in which the speaker renounces or denies the validity of what he or she is saying by using certain words to decrease his or her perceived assertiveness.

differences often disagree on the reasons for them. There may be a biological basis—physically innate differences between men and women that cause gender differences in communication. There may be psychological reasons—men and women have experienced different reinforcements for communicating, and these have shaped their patterns of communication. There may also be societal reasons for the differences. Social role theory explains the differences in terms of role expectations about masculinity and femininity in society, whereas societal development theories focus on male dominance in society and its effects on communication patterns.

Although it's true that all of these theories can explain some of the gender differences in communication, gender communication can often be best understood as a form of cross-cultural communication (A. M. Johnson, 2001; Mulvaney, 1994). If you were suddenly in a conversation with a person from another country who had no experience with your culture, you might find this conversation difficult. You wouldn't know the subtleties of that person's communication style, and he or she wouldn't know yours. It's hypothesized that even though men and women grow up in similar environments, they learn different ways of communicating, which resembles a form of cross-cultural communication.

Maltz and Borker (1982) believe that American men and women come from different "sociolinguistic subcultures" and learn different communication rules. They interpret conversations and use language differently. This all begins as children in same-sex play groups, which are often organized very differently. The majority of young girls play in small groups and have "best friends." Reaching higher levels of intimacy is the goal, and their games, such as playing house, less often have winners and losers. Boys, on the other hand, learn to use speech to express dominance and play in hierarchically organized groups that focus on directing and winning (Maltz & Borker, 1982). Boys often jockey for status by telling jokes, showing off, or claiming they are the best at things.

According to Maltz and Borker (1982), during same-sex conversations, girls and boys learn the rules and assumptions about communication, and these rules follow them through life. As adolescents, they begin to communicate in mixed-sex groups with the rules they learned from same-sex communication, which can cause problems. For example, girls learn to nod their head during conversations with other girls. This lets the talker know that she is being listened to. When a woman nods her head during a conversation with a man, he thinks she agrees with him (when she might not agree or disagree—her head nod may simply be showing him that she is listening). When a man doesn't nod his head when a woman is talking to him, she may think he isn't listening to her. All of this can lead to feeling misunderstood and to poor communication. Understanding the differences in communication styles won't automatically prevent disagreements, but it will help keep the disagreements manageable. We will talk more about nonverbal communication techniques in a moment.

THE EFFECTS OF SEXUAL ORIENTATION ON COMMUNICATION

It probably won't surprise you to learn that the majority of research on communication has used heterosexual couples. We actually know very little about communication patterns and strategies in gay and lesbian couples. As we discussed earlier, there are many issues at play when a couple communicates—gender, dominance, gender role, social philosophy, and power. Like heterosexual couples, conversational styles in gay and lesbian relationships have been found to reflect power differences in the relationship more than the biological sex of the communicator (Steen & Schwartz, 1995).

Differences in gay and lesbian communication may also have to do with gender roles. Men who are higher in nurturance engage in more cooperative speech, whereas women who are lower in nurturance engage less in such speech (Edwards & Hamilton, 2004). In addition, stereotypically "feminine" men and women have been found to use more submissive speech patterns, whereas stereotypically "masculine" males have been found to use more dominance language than stereotypically "feminine" or androgenous men and women (Ellis & McCallister, 1980). It may be that gay men and lesbian women are more flexible in their gender roles, and their communication patterns could reflect this comfort.

There has been limited research on speech patterns of gays and lesbians. Research has found that, when compared with heterosexual men's speech, gay men's speech more commonly includes the use of "qualifying adjectives" (such as "adorable" or "marvelous"), a wider-than-usual pitch range, extended vowel length speech (e.g., "maarvelous"), a tendency to avoid reduced forms of speech (e.g., contractions such as "can't" and "won't"), and a greater likelihood of arm and hand gestures (Salzmann, 2007). Lesbian women, on the other hand, have been found to use more hedge words and a narrower pitch range than gay men (Salzmann, 2007). Finally, limited research on self-disclosure in gay men has found that they report more self-disclosure in intimate relationships than heterosexual men (Bliss, 2000). We discuss this more later in the chapter.

In the future, more research is needed to look at the speech and communication patterns of gay men and lesbian women. Research addressing communication strengths and weaknesses in gay and lesbian couples would be helpful to further our understanding of these relationships.

Cultures differ in many ways, and these differences affect communication patterns.

THE EFFECTS OF CULTURE ON COMMUNICATION

Cultures differ in many ways, and these differences affect communication patterns. One important dimension that has been extensively studied is the degree to which a culture encourages individual versus group needs (Cai et al., 2000). Individualistic cultures encourage their members to have individual goals and values and an independent sense of self (Matsumoto, 1996), whereas collectivist cultures emphasize the needs of their members over individual needs. The United States is among the more individualistic countries, along with Canada, Australia, and Great Britain, whereas Asian and Latin cultures tend to be more collectivistic (Adler et al., 2007). This individualistic approach is probably why men and women from the United States disclose more personal information in their communication than members of other cultures (Gudykunst, 1986). Persons from collectivistic cultures, such as the Japanese, disclose little personal information about themselves to others (Seki et al., 2002).

I Love Peanut Butter!

Not all cultures communicate in the same way . . . Wouldn't it be interesting if there were different ways to say I love you?

The story that follows was written by an international student of mine. We had many interesting discussions about the cultural differences in communication. If you have ever traveled to or lived in a different country, you've probably experienced some communication issues. Not all cultures communicate in the same way, and our cultural background affects our communication strategies and patterns. Wouldn't it be interesting if there were different ways to say "I love you"? Can you imagine using the most intimate way only once, or maybe twice, in your lifetime?

I was born in Regensburg, Germany, and I have lived there all of my life. For the past year, I have been living in the United States, and during this time, I have learned a lot about cross-cultural differences in communication. Americans have a very emotional way of using language. They "love" peanut butter—what does this mean? When someone says, "I love you," does this mean that a person loves you as much as peanut butter? Or is it a different kind of love? This was really confusing for me.

I think that special expressions or words lose their real meaning when you use them all the time. This is especially true when it comes to relationships. Americans say, "I love you," but I'm not sure what that really means. A little boy tells his mother he loves her, good friends say it, you hear it being said in advertisements, and everyone loves everyone! But how can you express real deep feelings if you are using the phrase "I love you" all the time? Does it still mean the same thing? How do you know if Americans really love you, if they also love peanut butter? What does "I love you" really mean?

In Germany, we say something that is between "I love you" and "I like you"; maybe it means more, "You are in my heart." You would use the phrase, "Ich hab' dich lieb" to tell your mother and father, your friends, or your new boyfriend how you feel about them. But when someone says, "Ich liebe Dich"—the German "I love you"—then your relationship is really serious. This phrase is reserved only for relationships in which you know your partner really well. Saying "Ich liebe Dich" is very hard for some people, because it can make you more vulnerable. When a man would say "Ich liebe Dich" after three months of dating, it would make me wonder whether he could be taken seriously. Germans only use these words when they really mean it, and this gives the phrase much more respect.

I like how Americans are so open about letting someone know that they care about them, but it's hard to tell when it's really serious. Why is there no phrase in the English language that means something between liking and loving someone? Every culture and every country has its own ways of communicating and expressing ideas. What is most important is learning how to accept and learn from the differences.

SOURCE: Author's files.

REALResearch **>** In a typical conversation, people spend about **80%** of their gaze looking at the eyes, nose, and mouth of the person they're talking to (Wood, 2008). Looking over the person's shoulder or to either side of the person implies disinterest and boredom.

In addition, anthropologists have identified two distinct ways in which individuals from various cultures deliver messages to one another (Adler et al., 2007). A "low-context culture," such as that of the United States, uses language to express thoughts, feelings, and ideas as directly as possible (Hall, 1959). Statements are simple, and the meaning of the statement is in the words that are spoken. A "high-context" culture, which is typical of Asian cultures, relies heavily on subtle and nonverbal cues in its communication (Ambady et al., 1996). Communication is not direct, and a listener's understanding depends on the context of the conversation, nonverbal behavior, relationship history, and social rules. Communicators from high-context cultures may often beat around the bush in their conversations and expect listeners to know what they mean. Remember, however, that culture, sexual orientation, race, ethnicity, and communication styles are all interconnected, and it may be impossible to look at gender without also looking at these other influences.

TYPES OF COMMUNICATION: MORE THAN WORDS

There is much more to communication than words alone. We use nonverbal communication to get our message across, and many of us communicate with others online through e-mail, texting, or IMing. All of these methods of communication raise other important issues.

When our partner listens to us, we feel worthy and cared about, which, in turn, strengthens our relationship.

REALResearch **>** Although same-sex conversations are often easier, women report more difficulties in same-sex conversations than men. Researchers suggest that this is because conversations between women tend to be complex and multilayered, requiring more effort and listening (EDWARDS & HAMILTON, 2004).

The other day a floral delivery truck passed me on the highway with a sign that said, "Increase your vocabulary: Say it with flowers." What does this mean? What does it mean when you send flowers? What does it mean to receive them? Truth is, it can mean several things: "I love you," "I'm sorry," "I'll never do it again," "I'm a jerk," "Sorry I made such a mess." There are many meanings, but what's important to realize is that sending flowers is a **nonverbal communication** technique. In fact, the majority of our communication with others is nonverbal (Guffey, 1999). This is because, even when we say nothing, we are communicating. We communicate through hand gestures, eye contact, silence, and even flowers. We may change our facial expression, tilt our head, or move closer or further away from a person. Nonverbal facial cues are an important and influential part of our communication (Knapp & Hall, 2005).

Culture is also important to consider here, because nonverbal communication differs widely from culture to culture. For example, in Arab cultures, it is common for people to stand very close to one another when conversing, regardless of their gender (Mulvaney, 1994). Although smiling is often a sign of happiness in the United States and many other countries, in many Asian coun-

nonverbal communication
Communication without words (includes eye contact, head nodding, touching, and the like).

HUMAN SEXUALITY IN A DIVERSE WORLD

Culture and the Self

As you read over these cultural differences, consider how these differences might affect communicating with someone from a culture different than your own.

Individualistic Cultures (e.g., United States, Canada, Australia, and Great Britain)

- Individual puts self before others
- Self is unique and separate from others.
- Goal is independence and self-sufficiency
- "ME" orientation
- Reward individual achievement
- Punish and blame individual failure
- High value on issues such as autonomy
- Relatively tolerant of conflict and use a direct approach to handling conflict
- More comfortable talking in public

Collectivistic Cultures (e.g., Asian and Latin cultures)

- Individual puts extended family before self

- People belong to extended families and groups
- "WE" orientation
- Reward for contributions to group goals
- Credit and blame are shared between group members
- Attentive to, and concerned with, opinions of significant others
- Use less direct communication patterns
- Less comfortable talking in public
- High value on issues such as duty, tradition, and hierarchy

   As you read over these cultural differences, consider how they might affect communicating with someone from a culture different from your own. Knowing and understanding these cultural differences can make communication less difficult.

SOURCE: Adapted from Triandis (1990).

Gossiping and Complaining

Next time you stroll through the mall or even your student union, take a look around you. What kinds of communication are the women around you engaging in?

Recently I asked a group of students what it would be like to spend 24 hours with their partner but be able to use only nonverbal communication. Students thought about it, and many didn't know what to make of the question. Would it really be possible for them to be alone with their partner but not (verbally) speak to each other for 24 hours?

Several of the women who were asked this question said that although they'd be willing to try, they didn't think it would work out well. They weren't sure they could be with their partner without verbal communication. The men, on the other hand, enthusiastically responded to my question. "Sure!" many of them said. When pressed for their reasoning, several of the heterosexual men said, "I wouldn't have to hear her complaining!" This made me think—what exactly is "complaining," and do women do this more than men? The answer depends on your definition. Many women say that it's not really "complaining" but rather "discussing" important issues.

Women do more complaining than men and are more likely to commiserate with each other about their complaints (Boxer, 1996; Jaworski & Coupland, 2005). Women report that they enjoy engaging in this type of communication with other women. In fact, these types of communication have been found to be an important bonding tool in women's friendships (Goodwin, 2007; Sotirin, 2000). Many times women complain to each other in an effort to cope with their disappointments, whereas men address troubles by re-sponding with solutions instead of talking at length about the injustice of it all.

Verbal communication is very important in women's lives. Research has found that women's informal talk includes gossip, complaining, "troubles talk," and "bitching" (Sotirin, 2000). Although at first glance these types of talk might seem similar, each appears to have its own structure and function. The focus of gossip is on an absent target and includes contributions from several participants. Gossiping may also have an aggressive component to it, wherein the gossip is meant to hurt or harm a particular relationship (Conway, 2005; Ferguson, 2004). Complaining is usually brief and to the point. "Bitching," in contrast, relates an in-depth account of events, usually about an injustice or something negative that has happened to the speaker, allowing her to express her dissatisfaction (Sotirin, 2000). In "troubles talk," there is one "troubles teller," and the focus of the conversation stays on the teller the entire length of the conversation. Men have been found to engage in gossip too, although they are more likely to gossip to a romantic partner, whereas women were equally likely to share gossip with their romantic partners and their same-sex friends (McAndrew et al., 2007).

Next time you stroll through the mall or even your student union, take a look around you. In what kinds of communication are the women around you engaging? What do you think the purpose of the communication is?

tries, it is a way to cover up emotional pain (Gunawan, 2001). Another common, nonverbal form of communication in the United States is to gesture with a palm up to call another person to come join the group. However, in Korea, the Philippines, and in certain parts of Latin America, this nonverbal behavior is viewed as rude and objectionable (Gunawan, 2001).

Nonverbal communication varies within the United States as well. When a friend tells you, "You're the best" with a smile on her face and a relaxed body posture, you'll probably believe her. However, the same statement coming from a person who has arms crossed, teeth clenched, and eyebrows furrowed has a completely different message. Most likely, in this second situation, you'll think that your friend is angry and being sarcastic. Body language helps fill in the gaps in verbal communication. When a man is uncomfortable, he may have a hard time maintaining eye contact, be unable to sit still, pick his fingernails, or play with his hair (Perry, 2000). When a woman feels positively about you, she will maintain eye contact, smile, or touch you during the conversation. As humans,

Body language helps fill in the gaps in verbal communication.

we are uniquely designed to read these nonverbal cues and respond accordingly.

How well can you read the nonverbal cues people around you share? Are you better at reading your partner's nonverbals than those of, say, a friend? Can you ever know exactly what another person is saying nonverbally? The ability to do so is an important ingredient in successful interpersonal relationships. You might be better at reading your best friend's nonverbal behavior than someone you have known only a short time. Overall, women are better at decoding and translating nonverbal communication (DeLange, 1995). Women's nonverbal communication techniques include more eye contact and head nods, whereas men's has fewer head nods, less eye contact, and minimal "encouragers" (nonverbal cues to let their partner know they are listening; J. C. Pearson et al., 1991). Women have also been found to smile, gaze, lean forward, and touch more often than men in conversation (Wood, 1999).

In one study that looked at first meetings between men and women, women were found to "flirt" using nonverbal cues (such

Communication patterns begin when children play in same-sex groups.

What do the nonverbal cues in this photo tell you?"

as hair flipping and head nodding) to encourage men to reveal more about themselves, which would in turn allow the women to formulate an impression of the men (W. E. Martin, 2001). Men, on the other hand, view flirting as a way to show interest in a potential relationship (Henningsen, 2004).

When it comes to sex, verbal communication about your likes and needs is far better than nonverbal. Yet nonverbal communication can express your sexual desires, and it can be much less threatening than verbal communication. For example, if you would like your partner to touch your breasts more during foreplay, show this by moving your body more when he or she is doing what you like, or moving his or her hands to your breasts. You can moan, or even move more, to communicate your pleasure to your partner. You might also try performing the behavior on your partner that you wish she or he would do to you. However, there are problems with some types of nonverbal communication. As this couple demonstrates, it can often be misunderstood:

REALResearch > Research has found that the menstrual cycle may influence women's ability to pick up on certain nonverbal cues (R. PEARSON & LEWIS, 2005). The accuracy to recognize certain emotions was highest just before ovulation, which may be due to an increase in estrogen.

One woman attempted to communicate her preference for being kissed on the ears by kissing her partner's ears. However, she found that the more she kissed her partner's ears, the less he seemed to kiss hers. Over a period of time her kissing of his ears continued to increase, while his kissing of her ears stopped altogether. Finally she asked him why he never kissed her ears anymore, only to discover that he hated having his ears kissed and was trying to communicate this by not kissing hers. After their discussion, he began to kiss her ears, she stopped kissing his, and both were happier for the exchange (Barbach, 1982, p. 105).

COMPUTER-MEDIATED COMMUNICATION

Computer-mediated communication (CMC) includes communication tools for conveying written text via the Internet. This includes e-mailing, IMing, and communicating through Facebook or MySpace pages. As we discussed earlier in this chapter, today's college students use such CMC methods daily in their communication with their friends and family (Diamanduros et al., 2007). There are questions about these CMC exchanges, however. Is it possible to develop deep and meaningful relationships online? How does it compare to face-to-face communication? Are there differences in how women and men communicate online?

Although we talk about meeting partners online more in Chapter 7, students who like to use the Internet to meet people have told me that they find it easier to meet people online than in a bar or at a party. They like being able to check out a person's website or webpage to get some information about them before the first face-to-face meeting. It seems hard to believe that it would be possible to meet a partner online, given that conversation is reduced to a keyboard or cell phone, yet CMC can be very

computer-mediated communication
Communication produced when people interact with one another by transmitting messages via networked computers.

intimate, and couples can potentially become acquainted faster online than through face-to-face contact. One woman said:

> I found that our relationship progressed very quickly. We became intimate very early on and told each other things about ourselves that "bonded" us. It seemed that there was less risk, since we weren't face-to-face and didn't have to worry about what each other would think. We could also talk all the time—it wasn't unusual for us to find each other online in the wee hours of the morning. (Author's files)

Online communication can also reduce the role that physical characteristics play in the development of attraction and enhance rapport and self-disclosure. Couples who communicate online often have higher rates of self-disclosure and direct questioning that those who meet face-to-face (Antheunis et al., 2007; Gibbs et al., 2006). Some studies claim that online communication, such as texting or IMing, is more intimate than face-to-face communication (Horrigan et al., 2001; Ramirez & Zhang, 2007). Online communication can enhance personal communication by making it easier to stay in touch with people. One study found that more than half of Internet users reported increased communication with their families, and close to 70% reported increased communication with friends (Horrigan et al., 2001).

We do know that when couples overindulge with IMing and texting, the results can often be destructive. One of my students, Whittney, told me that she had dated Bill, a guy she met on MySpace. After a few dates, Bill texted her and asked if she wanted to be his girlfriend. At the time, she was thrilled and texted back a quick "yes!" However, it soon became apparent to her that texting was the only form of communication that Bill used. He texted her hundreds of messages a day. Whittney soon tired of his texting obsession and stopped responding to them. After a few months, her frustration led to a breakup that happened, not surprisingly, via a text message. What's important is that there is a balance in the types of communication strategies you use. Maintaining a relationship through one form of communication such as IMing is not going to be easy.

REALResearch > Researchers have found gender differences in IMing. Overall women are more expressive (Fox et al., 2007), take longer turns, and have longer overall conversations than men (Baron, 2004).

What about gender differences in online communication? Research indicates there are gender differences in online communication styles (Baron, 2004; Sussman & Tyson, 2000). This type of communication has been found to reduce the overly constraining gender roles that are automatically in place in face-to-face conversation. Because of this, women have been found to have an easier time making their voices heard online than in a face-to-face conversation, and use more "smileys" and other **emoticons** (e-MOTE-ick-cons) online than men (B. P. Bailey et al., 2003; Baron, 2004). These often serve to express emotion but may deflect from the seriousness of women's statements. Emoticons can be compared to tag questions during face-to-face conversations. It's

Paul Sakuma/AP Photo

Mark Zuckerberg, a computer programmer and Harvard dropout, founded Facebook in 2004.

also important to point out that researchers who study online communication have no sure way of knowing the gender of the people online. In fact, it has been suggested that people create "virtual identities" online (McAdams, 1996; Vaast, 2007). A man can claim to be a woman or a child could claim to be an adult. Our virtual identities are temporary, but they affect our online personae.

The key to any online relationship is to take it slow and, because you are not meeting the person face-to-face, really get to know your partner as much as you can. Communicate the things that are important to you, and "listen" as your partner talks. Be realistic about the chances the relationship will work out. If you find your partner

---

WHAT DO YOU WANT TO KNOW ?

My boyfriend spends a lot of time on the Internet. The other night, I discovered that he was obsessed with another girl's Facebook page. He had left her several messages and was checking out her photos from a weekend party. I was heartbroken. Do you think this constitutes cheating? It sure feels that way to me.

This is an interesting question. Many people believe that if their partner is having an intimate relationship with someone on the Internet, this is indeed cheating, but this really depends on how you define "intimate." Many online relationships involve sharing personal information about yourself and learning personal information about the person with whom you are communicating. One study that was conducted on "online infidelity" found that usually people who engage in these behaviors are not unhappy with their present relationships (Aviram, 2005). Typically, it has more to do with personality variables, such as a high degree of narcissism. Communication is key here—see whether he can help you understand why he was drawn to engaging in such conversations on Facebook.

emoticons
Facial symbols used when sending electronic messages online; an example would be :-).

SEX IN REAL LIFE

Social Networks

Over the past few years, online social networks have become very popular. A social network is a social structure made up of individuals that are tied together through institutions, friendship, dating, or special interests.

Over the past few years, online social networks have become very popular. Social networks are structures made up of individuals who are tied together through institutions, friendship, dating, or special interests. Social relationships are viewed in terms of "nodes" (individuals) and "ties" (the connections between the individuals) forming a map of individual connections between people (Figure 3.1 contains a social network graphic). Social networks are available for a variety of interests, such as music, cars, sports, clubbing, movies, gaming, business, travel, religion, and books. In addition, there are networks targeted for gay, lesbian, and bisexual members, as well as ethnic and racial groups.

Social network services, such as Facebook, MySpace, Xanga, Yahoo 360, and Friendster are great examples of social networks. These sites allow friends to be connected with others and make new friends. As of 2008, MySpace, the largest social network in North America, had more than 110 million members, and Facebook had more than 60 million members (Owyang, 2008). On college campuses, Facebook is the most popular networking site, and the majority of students check their Facebook accounts daily or several times a day. Since 2006, Facebook has been open to anyone over age 13. It is the most popular website for uploading photos—14 million photos are uploaded on Facebook each day. In 2008, Face-

book added language preferences, allowing users to have their pages translated into Spanish, German, and French (FoxBusiness, 2008).

Research into social networks has found that the shape of a network affects its usefulness to the member. Smaller, tighter networks can be less useful because friends in these types of networks tend to have similar knowledge bases and attitudes. Larger networks often allow more creativity and open discussions about new ideas and concepts. Think about it this way: if you only had friends with similar interests to yours, there would be less chance for learning something new. With a larger, looser network, people are often introduced to new ideas and thoughts.

Early work in the field of social networks found that the average person is able to form only a limited number of connections to other people. "Dunbar's number" proposed that the typical size of a social network is 150 members (Bialik, 2007; Dunbar, 1998). This number originated out of cross-cultural and evolutionary research that found there is a limit to how many friends a person can recognize and about whom he or she can track information. The "small-world phenomenon" claims that through social networks, one random person can connect with another random person anywhere in the world. A study in 1967 by Stanley Milgrim found that there were six degrees of separation between people (Kleinfeld, 2002). Researchers have continued to explore this through Internet-based communication. A study at Columbia University found that there are about five to seven degrees of separation for connecting any two people through e-mail (Watts, 2003).

What are the advantages and disadvantages to using Facebook and other networking sites? Students have told me that although social network sites are great to help them keep in touch and know what's going on, they can also be overwhelming. Once again, balance is the key here—make sure you're not relying on one form of communication, or else you're sure to feel overwhelmed.

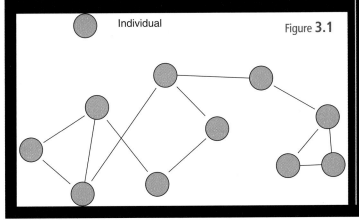

Individual

Figure **3.1**

---

can't communicate offline, it would be a good idea to find a way to talk about these issues before the relationship progresses.

COMMUNICATING MORE EFFECTIVELY

Earlier in this chapter, we discussed the three competing goals of communication. Do you remember what they were? When we communicate with another person, we have a task, a relationship, and an identity management goal. How can we be successful in reaching these various goals?

The first goal is to get the job done. Often men and women are too afraid to share their thoughts with their partner. They do have a message that they would like to share with their partner, but something holds them back. Remember how good communication can make a relationship even better? It is important to put aside your vulnerability and fears and learn to communicate your thoughts to your partner.

The second goal isn't always easy, either. How can we maintain our relationship and not upset the applecart by communicating our thoughts and desires? Think through what you want to say, and realize the impact your message will have on your partner.

How would you feel if your partner shared a similar thought? What might make it easier for you or your partner? Often timing is everything. Make sure that you have the time and energy to talk to your partner before you start. Five minutes before class is probably not the best time to start a conversation.

The third goal, identity management, involves projecting a certain image of ourselves. We might want to tell our partner that we need more space or more time alone, but we don't want to hurt his or her feelings. How can we best share this message with our partner?

Finally, we must also consider the importance of other communication tools. The use of tag questions, which indicate uncertainty in conversation, should be limited (Vanfossen, 1996). Using tag questions can make a partner form an opinion about a person that might not be correct. Nonverbal language is also important. Pay attention to the nonverbal cues that you notice in other people as well as the nonverbal cues that you are sending. What messages are you receiving and sending? Is the other person paying attention? How can you tell? Let's talk about the importance of self-disclosure and asking for what you need.

SELF-DISCLOSURE

Self-disclosure is critical to maintaining healthy and satisfying relationships. Talking with your partner and sharing feelings helps deepen intimacy, feelings of love, and even sexual satisfaction (Dindia, 2002; Macneil, 2004). In addition, opening up and sharing your thoughts and feelings with your partner helps you to grow together as a couple. Self-disclosure lets your partner know what is wrong and how you feel about it, and it enables you to ask for specific change (Fowers, 1998).

Gender has been found to be related to self-disclosure. Overall women tend to disclose more about themselves than men do (Hargie et al., 2001). Not only gender but also sexual orientation play a role. Earlier in this chapter, we discussed self-disclosure in gay relationships. Overall, the research has found that whereas heterosexual and lesbian women differ little in their reported self-disclosing, gay men report more intimate self-disclosures than heterosexual men (Bliss, 2000). In addition, heterosexual women also engage in more self-disclosure than heterosexual men (Dindia, 2000).

Keeping silent about your true feelings and thoughts or criticizing your partner instead of talking is much easier and puts you in a much less vulnerable position. Opening up and talking about yourself makes you vulnerable. Ideally, an intimate partner is one who can hear what you are all about and still love you.

One final note about self-disclosure: it is risky to disclose too much before the relationship is stable and communication skills are in place. This can cause the relationship to deteriorate, as we discussed in regard to the onion theory earlier in the chapter. Problems and issues that are brought up before a couple knows how to communicate and discuss them may only get worse (Butler & Wampler, 1999).

ASKING FOR WHAT YOU NEED

Even though communication is important, it is not always easy. Telling your partner what you really want and need during sexual activity can be difficult. This is because sexuality is an area in which many people feel insecure. People may wonder whether they are good in bed and worry that their partners do not think they are. At the same time, however, they may be hesitant to make suggestions to improve their partner's techniques because they worry that their partner will become insulted and think that his or her sexual skills are being criticized. Anxieties like these do not foster a sense of open and mutual communication. Ultimately, not being open about your likes or dislikes is self-defeating because you may end up feeling resentful of your partner or unhappy in your relationship.

WHAT DO YOU WANT TO KNOW ?

I have been in a relationship with my boyfriend for almost 1 year. We love each other very much, but most of the time I feel that we don't communicate well with each other, mainly because I'm just too afraid to talk about things. I love him very much and want our relationship to last. How can we learn to communicate better?

Communicating our thoughts, needs, hopes, dreams, and desires isn't always easy. Usually intimate or personal information is difficult to share. It's natural to worry about what your boyfriend might think or say. It's best to start slowly. Don't try to tell him everything at one time. You might try sharing a few small details about what you're thinking and feeling. Remember that asking for what you need involves self-disclosure. If you can open up and share your thoughts and listen to what your boyfriend is saying, this can help you grow together as a couple.

self-disclosure
Opening up, talking with your partner, and sharing feelings.

Being a More Effective Communicator

A number of techniques can help us to communicate more effectively. Following we highlight some of the most important ways to become a more effective communicator.

A number of techniques can help us to communicate more effectively. Following we highlight some of the most important ways to become a more effective communicator.

1. Talk about good communication. When you need a good icebreaker to initiate a conversation that will allow you to talk about intimate issues, a safe place to start is to talk about talking. This will let each of you discuss how it is sometimes difficult to talk about things. From there you can move into more personal and sexual areas.

2. Give helpful, supportive feedback. A good listener tries to understand what the speaker is really trying to say and what he or she wants in return. Knowing your partner means knowing when your partner wants advice and when he or she just wants a sympathetic ear.

3. Do not wait until you're angry. According to an ancient Chinese book of wisdom, the truly wise person handles things when they are small, before they grow too big. Let this guide you in your relationships. Discuss problems when you first realize them, while they are still small, and avoid the big, blowout fights.

4. Let go of the need to be right. In relationships, establishing who is "right" and "wrong" is never productive. What is productive is establishing how to improve communication and how to increase intimacy.

5. Ask questions. Remember to ask questions so that you can really understand your partners' needs, desires, and thoughts.

6. Be responsible. Most people cannot read their partner's mind. What is obvious to you may not be obvious to your partner. If you want something, ask for it, and be direct. For example, suppose you want your partner to be more romantic. "You never do anything romantic" is a challenge, whereas "let's plan a romantic evening together" is a more direct and less threatening way to request the same thing.

7. Be supportive. Mix praise with your criticism; say things in positive rather than negative ways. In the previous example, an even better way to put it would be, "I love being alone with you, together, just talking. Let's have a romantic dinner tonight, just the two of us."

8. Learn to say no, gently. People sometimes get into relationship trouble because they do not know how to say "no" to their partners and end up resenting that they are doing things they do not want to do. Every person has a right to say no; in fact, it is a sign of trust and respect for your partner to believe that you can say no and still retain his or her love and affection. But saying no to a request is different from rejecting the person making it. "No" must be said in a way that reassures the partner that it is only the requested action you are refusing.

9. Be forgiving. We all make mistakes in our intimate relationships. We hurt our partners, we do something thoughtless, and we do a thousand little things we wish we could change. We are all human. Bringing up mistakes from the past is never helpful. When communication is done in a spirit of unconditional positive regard (which can be a very difficult state to achieve), all the other qualities of good communication will fall into place.

10. Talk about sex. Although talking about sexual issues can be difficult, it is one of the most important ways to improve your sex life. Location is often key here—don't try talking while lying in the afterglow of a sexual experience. It's often easier to begin a conversation outside the bedroom when you are feeling less vulnerable. An honest conversation about your likes and dislikes can strengthen your relationship.

review questions

1 Explain why good communication is the hallmark of a healthy relationship, and give three examples of how poor communication could lead to a relationship problem.

2 Identify and describe the three competing goals for good communication.

3 What do we know about the impact of gender, sexual orientation, and culture on communication? Describe the theories that have been proposed to explain gender differences in communication styles.

4 Differentiate between individualistic and collectivistic cultures and high- and low-context cultures and describe how these issues can affect communication.

5 What is nonverbal communication? What can you learn from your partner's nonverbal behavior? Provide one example.

6 How can the Internet reduce some of the common communication problems that couples experience in face-to-face conversations?

Listening, Expressing Criticism, and Nonconstructive Communication

The majority of couples spend too much time criticizing each other and not enough time really listening and making affectionate comments (P. Coleman, 2002). One partner often becomes defensive and angry when the other says something that he or she doesn't want to hear. For example, if your partner told you that he felt you weren't giving enough time to your relationship, you could hear this message with an open mind, or you could get angry and think, "What do you know about my time?" Let's now talk about the importance of listening, constructive and nonconstructive communication, and verbal disagreements.

THE IMPORTANCE OF LISTENING

Listening is one of the most important communication skills (Adler et al., 2007). Adults spend nearly 70% of their waking time communicating and 45% of this time listening (Adler et al., 2007; Rankin, 1952). **Active listening** involves using nonverbal communication to let your partner know that you are attentive and present in the conversation. For example, as your partner talks, you can maintain eye contact to let him or her know you are actively listening.

Another important skill is **nondefensive listening,** which involves focusing your attention on what your partner is saying without being defensive (Gottman, 1994). Nondefensive listening relies on self-restraint, which is often absent in distressed couples, who have a difficult time hearing and listening to each other. It can be very difficult to listen fully, but this skill reduces your inclination to interrupt or to defend yourself.

Poor listeners often think that they understand what their partner is trying to say, but they rarely do. Instead they try to find a way to circumvent the discussion and talk about something else. It's very difficult to really listen to someone when you are angry or defensive. Good listening allows you to understand and retain information while building and maintaining your relationships (Adler et al., 2007).

BEING A MORE EFFECTIVE LISTENER

There are many things that interfere with our ability to be an effective listener (Golen, 1990; Hulbert, 1989). These include information overload, preoccupation with personal concerns, rapid thoughts, and noise. It is easy to reach information overload today. We hear so much during the course of our day that it can be difficult to listen carefully to everything we hear. As a result, we must choose what information we will listen and pay attention to.

Figure **3.2** The Chinese characters that make up the verb "to listen" tell us something significant about this skill. From Adler et al., 2007.

A preoccupation with personal concerns may also interfere with our ability to listen. If we are wrapped up in our own thoughts and issues, it's difficult to listen to someone else. Listening is also affected by our brains actively processing information around us. Consider this: we are capable of understanding speech at rates of up to 600 words per minute (Versfeld & Dreschler, 2002), however, the average person speaks between 100 and 140 words per minute. This gives your brain time to think about other things, such as what you'll say to your professor this afternoon, what you'll have for dinner tonight, or when you'll study for the exam tomorrow. So it may be hard to focus on what is being said. Finally, noise also interferes with our ability to listen. Other conversations, music, traffic, and noise significantly interfere with our ability to listen.

Listening and really paying attention can also help you learn important things about your partner. John Gottman, a psychologist known for his research on relationships, gives couples a relationship quiz to see whether they have been paying attention to each other's likes and dislikes (Gottman, 1999). His questions include the following:

- What is the name of your partner's best friend?
- Who has been irritating your partner lately?
- What are some of your partner's life dreams?
- What are three of your partner's favorite movies?
- What are your partner's major current worries?
- What would your partner want to do if he or she suddenly won the lottery?

We don't ever realize how important it is to have others listen to us until someone we really care about doesn't listen to us (P. Coleman, 2002). When others really listen, we are often able to see more clearly what it is that upsets us. Being listened to can make

active listening
Communication and listening technique in which the listener uses nonverbal communication, such as nodding or eye contact, to signal that he or she is attentive to the speaker.

nondefensive listening
Listening strategy in which the listener focuses attention on what his or her partner is saying without being defensive.

us feel worthy, protected, and cared about. As we mentioned earlier, encouraging your partner through active listening, such as eye contact, nodding, or saying "um-hum" (Fowers, 1998) shows your partner that you are "tuned in." It also shows that you believe he or she has something worthwhile to say and encourages him or her to continue talking.

When your partner is finished talking, it is important to summarize what your partner has told you as accurately as possible. This lets your partner know that you heard what he or she was saying and also enables your partner to correct any misunderstandings. Finally, it is also important when listening to validate your partner's statement. Saying "I can understand why you might feel that way" or "I know what you mean" can help you show your partner that you think what he or she is saying is valid. This doesn't necessarily mean that you agree but that you can accept your partner's point of view.

> *In all conversations, **the recipient** of the message **must interpret** the intended meaning of the message . . .*

MESSAGE INTERPRETATION

When walking across campus one day, you trip and fall. Your partner sees you and says, "Be careful!" How do you interpret that? Does it mean you're moving too fast? You need to slow down? Does it mean that your partner is genuinely worried you might hurt yourself? In all conversations, the recipient of the message must interpret the intended meaning of the message (R. Edwards, 1998), which is dependent on several factors, such as the nature of the relationship with the person and your mood at the time.

If you are angry or upset, you may perceive more hostility in ambiguous or benign comments than someone who is not angry or upset (Epps & Kendall, 1995). If you are worried about something or preoccupied with an issue, this can also bias how you interpret a message. In one study, women who were preoccupied with their weight were more likely to interpret ambiguous sentences with negative or "fat" meanings, whereas women who were not preoccupied with their weight did not (Jackman et al., 1995). For example, if a woman who was preoccupied with her weight heard someone say, "You look good today!" she might interpret this to mean that she looked fat yesterday. However, couldn't she also interpret the message in other ways? Perhaps she looked tired yesterday or even stressed out.

NEGATIVE FEELINGS AND CRITICISM

We all get angry sometimes, and we know that not all conversations have happy, peaceful endings. However, the key is in managing the tension. When we disagree with our partner, the opening minutes of a disagreement can indicate whether the conversation will turn angry or simply be a quiet discussion (P. Coleman, 2002). If harsh words are used, chances are the disagreement will build, and the tension will escalate. However, if softer words are used, there is a better chance the disagreement can be resolved.

Negative feelings may also involve sharing or accepting criticism. Accepting criticism isn't an easy thing to do—we are all defensive at times. Although it would be impossible to eliminate all defensiveness, it's important to reduce defensiveness in order to resolve disagreements. If you are defensive while listening to your partner's criticism, chances are good that you will not be able to hear his or her message. Common defensive techniques are to deny the criticism (e.g., "That is just NOT TRUE!"), make excuses without taking any responsibility (e.g., "I was just exhausted!"), deflecting responsibility (e.g., "Me? What about your behavior?"), and righteous indignation (e.g., "How could you possibly say such a hurtful thing?"; P. Coleman, 2002). All of these techniques interfere with our ability to really understand what our partner is trying to tell us. Keeping our defensiveness in check is another important aspect of good communication.

John Gottman, the relationship expert we discussed earlier, found that happy couples experienced 20 positive interactions for every negative one (Nelson, 2005). Couples who were in conflict experienced only five positive interactions for every negative one, and those couples soon to be divorced experienced only 0.8 positive interactions for every negative one. This research suggests that positive and negative interactions can shine light on a couple's relationship happiness.

NONCONSTRUCTIVE COMMUNICATION: DON'T YELL AT ME!

Couples often make many mistakes in their communication patterns that can lead to arguments, misunderstandings, and conflicts. **Overgeneralizations,** or making statements such as "Why do you always . . . ?" or "You never . . . ," generally exaggerate an issue. Telling your partner that he or she "always" (or "never") does something can cause defensiveness and will often lead to complete communication shutdown. Try to be specific about your complaints and help your partner to see what it is that is frustrating you. For example, if you find yourself frustrated by the amount of time your partner spends with friends, find a time when you can discuss your concerns. Try not to be defensive or overgeneralizing and share your thoughts (saying "I feel like I would like to spend more time together" rather than "You always seem to want to be with your friends more than me!").

Try to stay away from **name-calling** or stereotyping words, such as calling your partner a "selfish bastard" or a "nag." These derogatory terms will only help escalate anger and frustration and will not lead to healthy communication. Digging up the past is another nonconstructive communication pattern that accomplishes nothing. It's also important to stay away from old arguments and accusations. The past is just that—the past. So try to leave it there and move forward. Dwelling on past events won't help to resolve them.

overgeneralization
Making statements that tend to exaggerate a particular issue.

name-calling
Using negative or stereotyping words when in disagreement.

Another common mistake that couples make in conversations is to use **overkill.** When you are frustrated with your partner and threaten the worst (e.g., "If you don't do that, I will leave you"), even when you know it is not true, you reduce all communication. Don't make threats if you don't intend to follow through with them. In the same vein, it's important to focus on your frustration in conversation.

Try not to get overwhelmed and throw too many issues in the conversation at once (e.g., the fact that your partner didn't take the trash out last night, forgot to kiss you good-bye, and ignored you when he or she was with friends). This approach makes it really difficult to focus on resolving any one issue because there is just too much happening. Also, avoid yelling or screaming, which can cause your partner to be defensive and angry, and less likely to be rational and understand what you are saying. Even though it's not easy, it's important to stay calm during conversation.

Clinging to any of these communication patterns can interfere with the resolution of problems and concerns. If you recognize any of these patterns in your own relationship, try talking to your partner about it and try to catch yourself before you engage in them.

Disagreements are a common part of relationships.

FIGHTING

Overall, verbal disagreements aren't a bad thing in relationships. In fact, couples who disagree are usually happier than those who say, "We never, ever fight!" Disagreements are a common part of relationships. (It's important to point out, however, that verbal disagreements are different from physical disagreements. We dis-

cuss domestic violence in Chapter 17.) How you handle such disagreements is what is important. Research has shown that happier couples think more positive thoughts about each other during their disagreements, whereas unhappy couples think negatively about each other (P. Coleman, 2002). Even though a happy couple is disagreeing about an issue, the two partners still feel positively about each other.

What happens after an argument? Generally, women are more likely to demand a reestablishment of closeness, whereas men are more likely to withdraw (Noller, 1993). Some couples have developed unique ways to end arguments. One couple told me that when they want to stop arguing, they have agreed that whoever is ready first holds up a pinky finger. This signals to the other that they are ready to end the fight. The other partner must touch his or her pinky to the partner's pinky to acknowledge that the fight is over. This isn't always easy, but it has helped this couple to end arguments amicably.

Other suggestions include taking a time out and coming back to finish a discussion later, learning to compromise, or validating each others' differences in opinions. Also remember that in every relationship, there are some issues that may simply be unresolvable. It's important to know which issues can be worked out and which cannot. The question is, can you live with the irresolvable issues? How can you work on improving these issues?

Let's continue to look at how improved communication can enrich personal sexuality and examine the importance of self-esteem and the qualities we look for in our partners.

overkill
A common mistake that couples make during arguments, in which one person threatens the worst but doesn't mean what he or she says.

review questions

1 Why is listening one of the most important communication skills? What is nondefensive listening?

2 Explain how information overload, personal concerns, rapid thoughts, and noise interfere with our ability to listen.

3 Describe two nonconstructive communication strategies, and explain why they could lead to a communication shutdown.

Enriching Your
Sexuality

So far we've been talking about how difficult it can be to communicate with the people in our lives. What about talking to our partner about sex? Sex can be one of the hardest topics to discuss. Let's talk about why this might be so.

TALKING WITH YOUR PARTNER
ABOUT SEX

How do you let your partner know that you are interested in having sex? The majority of couples show their consent to engage in sex by saying nothing at all (Hickman & Muehlenhard, 1999). Let's face it: it is hard to talk about sex. This is probably because sexuality seems to magnify all the communication problems that exist in any close relationship. We grow up in a society instilled with a sense of shame about our sexuality and are taught at an early age that talking about sex is "dirty." Approaching the subject of sex for the first time in a relationship implies moving on to a new level of intimacy, which can be scary. It also opens the way for rejection, which can be painful.

Too often, we assume that being good in bed also means being a mind reader. Somehow, our partner should just know what arouses us. In reality, nothing could be farther from the truth. Good lovers are not mind readers—they are able and willing to listen and communicate with their partners.

Many people think Johnny Depp and Halle Berry are sexy and attractive.

I LIKE YOU, AND I LIKE MYSELF

Healthy sexuality depends on feeling good about yourself. If you have a poor self-image or do not like certain aspects of your body or personality, how can you demonstrate to a romantic partner why you are attractive? Imagine a man or woman who is overly concerned about his or her body while in bed with a partner. Maybe a woman is worried that her partner will not be attracted to the size or shape of her chest, thighs, or stomach or to her inverted nipples. Perhaps a man is consumed with anxiety over the size of his penis, his weight, or his body hair, worrying that his partner won't find it appealing. All of these fears interfere with our ability to let go, relax, and enjoy the sexual experience. Before anyone else can accept us, we need to accept ourselves.

In American society, learning to like our bodies is often difficult. We talked about the impact of magazines, television, and advertisers all play into our insecurities with their portrayals of the ideal body in Chapter 1. The beauty images that the media present to us are often impossible to live up to and leave many of us feeling unattractive by comparison. We are encouraged to buy products that will make us look more attractive or sexy. To sell products, advertisers must first convince us that we are not OK the way we are—that we need to change our looks, our smells, or our habits. The endless diet products currently on the market also help to increase our dissatisfaction with our bodies. In turn, this has led to a preoccupation with weight and the development of eating disorders such as anorexia and bulimia. Many young women who are convinced that they are overweight consciously starve themselves in an attempt to be thin.

In the United States in particular, we put a high value on physical attractiveness throughout the life cycle, and our body image greatly affects how attractive we feel. The media are primarily responsible for shaping our ideas of the "ideal body." Today the desired body is young, slim, tanned, and pimple-free (Barker & Barker, 2002). Because of this, many American women go on diet after diet, have breast augmentation (or, less often, reduction surgery), or endure liposuction or other types of cosmetic surgery to correct what they see as "flaws" (thighs, eyelids, chests, necks, cheekbones). Men and women use makeup, lie in tanning beds, acquire tattoos and piercings, and undergo surgical procedures to feel more comfortable with their bodies. Many Americans spend hours in gyms lifting weights—some boosting the effects with steroids—to achieve the "perfect" body.

We all have parts of our bodies we wish we could change. In fact, most of us are much more critical of our bodies than our partners would ever be. Not all of us are blessed with the good looks of Halle Berry or Johnny Depp!

Self-esteem is related to our emotional and mental health. Therapists agree that improving mental health includes improving one's self-acceptance, autonomy, and self-efficacy (being able to function in the world), resilience (not to get overburdened by anger, depression, or guilt), interest in one's own career and life, and close relationships with others. All these are important to establish not only good mental health but also good sexual relationships.

Finally, self-esteem has been found to have a powerful effect on how we communicate with others (Adler et al., 2007). A person with positive self-esteem will often think well of others, expect to be accepted by them, and feel comfortable with those whom they feel are superior in some way (Hamachek, 1982). Those with negative self-esteem will often think poorly of others, expect to be rejected by them, and feel threatened by people they view as superior.

WHAT MAKES A GOOD LOVER?

It would be impossible to list all the qualities that make people good lovers. People look for many different things in a partner, and what makes someone a good lover to you might not make that person a good lover to someone else. Overall, good lovers are sensitive to their partner's needs and desires, can communicate their own desires, and are patient, caring, and confident. Being nervous or feeling silly can interfere with sexual abilities. It is hard to concentrate when you are worried about performing.

Men and women sometimes have different views of the same sexual behaviors. In the classic movie *Annie Hall,* the lead characters, Annie and Alvy, each go to see their respective therapists, and are each asked how often they have sex. Annie replies, "Oh, all the time, at least three times a week," whereas Alvy says, "Hardly ever, maybe three times a week." Do you think this reflects a gender difference?

Even sexual techniques can be viewed differently. One man recounts an early sexual experience:

I'll never forget the first time. She was lying on her parents' bed with the lamplight shining on her, naked and suntanned all

Good lovers are sensitive to their partner's needs and desires and can communicate their own desires.

over. . . . I climbed on that bed and I lifted her up onto my thighs—she was so light I could always pick her right up—and I opened up her [vagina] with one hand and I rammed my [penis] up there like it was a Polaris missile. Do you know, she screamed out loud, and she dug her nails in my back, and without being too crude about it I [screwed] her until she didn't know what the hell was happening. . . . She loved it. She screamed out loud every single time. I mean I was an active, aggressive lover. (Masterton, 1987, p. 70)

Yet his partner viewed the sexual activity very differently:

What did I think about it? . . . I don't know. I think the only word you could use would be "flabbergasted." He threw me on the bed as if he were Tarzan, and tugged off all of my clothes, and then he took off his own clothes so fast it was almost like he was trying to beat the world record. . . . He took hold of me and virtually lifted me right up in the air as if I were a child, and then he pushed himself right up me, with hardly any foreplay or any preliminaries or anything. (Masterton, 1987, p. 73)

WHAT DO YOU WANT TO KNOW?

Are there any ways that a person can make himself or herself more attractive to a romantic partner?

Although many people might think the answer to this question lies in a new haircut or outfit, researchers at North Carolina State University have found that rewarding partner interactions through communication will make you more physically attractive to your partner (Albada et al., 2002). Couples who communicated with each other in positive ways (such as giving compliments or expressing affection) rated each other more physically attractive than those who didn't communicate in such ways. The bottom line is that good communication can enhance physical attractiveness.

This is another reason that communication is so important. Here is a man thinking he is doing exactly what his partner wants and a woman wondering why he's doing it. Eventually, this couple's relationship ended, mainly because of a lack of communication, which left both feeling confused and frustrated. As we discussed earlier, communication is one of the most important aspects of a healthy and satisfying relationship.

ENRICHING YOUR SEXUALITY:
IT'S NOT MIND READING

Throughout this chapter, we have discussed the importance of communication and its role in the development of healthy, satisfying relationships. Good communication skills are an integral part of all healthy relationships, and couples who know how to communicate with each other are happier, are more satisfied, and have a better chance of making their relationship last. Many relationship problems stem from poor communication. When it comes to sexual relationships, good communication skills are vital. By talking to your partner, you can share your sexual needs and desires and learn what your partner's sexual needs are. In turn, this can strengthen your overall relationship. It's important to be honest and open and ask for what you need.

It's also important to pay attention to nonverbal cues because we know that much of our communication is interpreted through our nonverbal behavior. Talking about sex isn't easy. We live in a society that believes sex talk is dirty or bad, but talking about sex is one of the best ways to move a relationship to a new level of intimacy and connection.

review questions

1 Why is a healthy self-esteem important in intimate relationships?

2 Identify the ways that good communication can improve your sex life.

3 Why is it often difficult to talk about sex?

CHAPTER review

SUMMARY POINTS

1 Good communication skills are an integral part of all healthy relationships, and couples who know how to communicate with each other are happier, more satisfied, and have a better chance of making their relationship last. Many relationship problems stem from poor communication.

2 Communication fosters mutual understanding, increases emotional intimacy, and helps deepen feelings of love and intimacy. However, a lack of communication skills is a major source of trouble in relationships. Having poor communication skills, an inability to self-disclose, or trouble listening can each lead to communication problems.

3 The three goals of communication include getting the job done, maintaining the relationship, and managing our identity. All of these three goals compete with each other, making communication difficult.

4 Deborah Tannen proposed that there are fundamental differences between the way men and women communicate, and she called these differences "genderlects." She found that women engaged in more rapport-talk, whereas men engaged in more report-talk. Men also tended to use more slang in their communication, whereas women are more supportive and use more words implying feelings.

5 Many theories have been proposed to explain gender differences in communication. However, gender communication is often best understood as a form of cross-cultural communication. Research suggests that men and women may come from different sociolinguistic subcultures and learn different communication rules.

6 Little research has been conducted on communication in gay and lesbian relationships. We do know that power, gender role, and social philosophies all affect communication patterns. Research has found differences between the speech patterns of gay and heterosexual men.

7 Individualistic cultures encourage their members to have individual goals and values and an independent sense of self. Collectivist cultures emphasize the needs of their members over individual needs. Communication patterns have been found to vary depending on cultural orientation.

8 The majority of our communication with others is nonverbal. This form of communication is often done through eye contact, smiling, or touching. Research has found that women are better at decoding and translating nonverbal communication.

9 Women have an easier time making their voices heard during computer-mediated conversation than in face-to-face communication. They have also been found to use more emoticons online. One of the risks of online communication is eroticized pseudo-intimacy, but if things progress slowly, there is a better chance of a relationship working out.

10 There are several ways to communicate more effectively. One of these involves increasing self-disclosure. However, it's important not to disclose too much before the relationship is stable and communication skills are in place. It's also important to ask for what you need, which can be difficult. Partners often worry about hurting feelings or worry that their partner will feel differently about them.

11 Several things can interfere with our ability to listen, including information overload, personal concerns, rapid thoughts, and noise. The majority of couples spend too much time criticizing each other and not enough time really listening and making affectionate comments. Active and nondefensive listening are important.

12 When we express negative feelings, it's important not to use harsh words because tension will escalate. It's also important to learn how to accept criticism without becoming defensive. Mistakes in communication patterns that can get couples into trouble include overgeneralizations, name-calling, and overkill. Overall, verbal disagreements aren't a bad thing in a relationship.

13 One of the hardest topics to discuss in an intimate relationship is sex. The majority of couples show their consent to engage in sexual intercourse by saying nothing. Most of us grow up learning that talking about sex is dirty. Too often we assume that being a good lover means being a mind reader.

14 Healthy sexuality depends on feeling good about yourself. The fact is, before anyone can accept us, we need to accept ourselves; however, one thing that makes this difficult is the media's portrayal of the perfect body.

15 Good lovers are sensitive to their partners' needs and desires and can communicate their own desires. They are also patient, caring, and confident. Overall, we know that communication is one of the most important aspects of a healthy and satisfying relationship.

CRITICAL THINKING questions

1 The research shows that couples who know how to communicate have a greater likelihood of making their relationship last. Apply this to a relationship that didn't work out for you, and explain how poor or absent communication may have affected your relationship.

2 Do you think that men and women have different communication styles and may, in fact, have "cross-cultural" styles of communication? Explain why or why not and give examples.

3 Do you agree with findings claiming that women gossip and complain more than men? Why or why not? Give one example.

4 Why do you think there might be differences in gay and straight communication patterns? What might contribute to some of these differences?

5 Have you ever communicated with someone online and then met later face-to-face? If so, how did your online communication affect your face-to-face communication? What was your online impression of him or her before you met in person?

6 Can you think of any incidence in which a lack of self-esteem on your part negatively affected a relationship? Explain.

7 How have social network services changed communication patterns on today's college campuses? What do you see as the advantages and disadvantages of these services?

WEB resources

Sexuality Now Book Companion Website

Go to www.cengage.com/psychology/carroll for practice quizzes, glossary, flash cards, and more. You can also access the following websites from the companion site.

The American Communication Association ■ The American Communication Association (ACA) has links to the American Communication Journal and the Communication Studies Center, which contains a collection of online resources.

The Positive Way ■ The Positive Way is a resource for helping enhance relationships through communication. This website contains questionnaires and information about communication.

The Journal of Communication ■ *The Journal of Communication* is an interdisciplinary journal with an extensive online offering that focuses communication research, practice, policy, and theory and includes the most up-to-date and important findings in the communication field.

More Self-Esteem ■ This website contains information on how to subscribe to monthly self-esteem newsletters, tips on how to build self-esteem, inspirational words and quotes, information about attitudes and moods and how to cope with them, help with depression, self-confidence tips, articles, and free resources on self-esteem.

CengageNOW

Go to www.cengage.com/login to link to CengageNOW, your online study tool. First take the Pre-Test for this chapter to get your Personalized Study Plan, which will identify topics you need to review and direct you to online resources. Then take the Post-Test to determine what concepts you have mastered and what you still need work on.

Videos in CengageNOW

CengageNOW also contains these videos related to the chapter topics:

- Marriage: "Me" Versus "We"—listen to one couple argue about relocating for the husband's job.

- Communication and Compromise: Planning a Wedding— see how one couple's understanding of each other's point of view helps them compromise on their wedding plans.

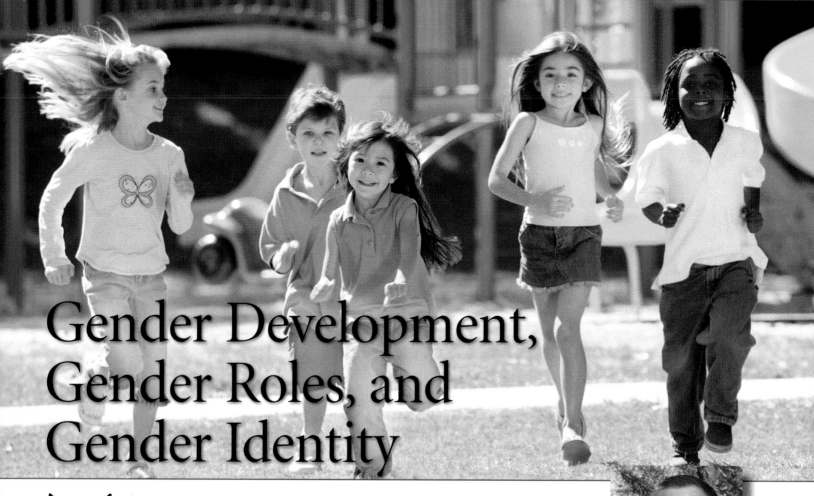

CHAPTER 4

Gender Development, Gender Roles, and Gender Identity

Today I am a grown man. Once upon a time I was a little girl who looked like Shirley Temple. Both those statements are true. I might have been born a girl, but I knew I wasn't meant to be a grown woman.

Knowing that I wasn't a girl did not make the decision to go through gender transition any easier. I had no idea what the end result would be and what my life would look like on the other side. The fact that I chose to take a leap of faith and go forward with transition can give you a sense of how deep the pain was.

Growing up Italian and Roman Catholic, I didn't have sex education. I honestly didn't really understand what the anatomical differences were between boys and girls.

I had no language for my internal sense of myself. I couldn't simply walk up to my parents and say, "Hey this is all well and good, but I'd rather be a boy." I knew I hurt.

I knew I was different. I knew that people would be displeased if I expressed it.

Looking back I can see the things I did to try to "fix" me. Once with the magical thinking that only small children can muster, I asked my grandfather how I could become a jockey. In my mind jockeys were men, and therefore if I grew up to be a jockey, then the boy part would automatically follow.

With adolescence came the beginning of hell. My body started to change in ways for which I was unprepared and couldn't accept. I became acutely suicidal in my early teens and remained so until I made a choice to transition. I abused alcohol into my early 20s as a way of numbing out. Nothing truly gave me peace. I danced around my need for transition for a few years. In my early 30s, I started to meet people who had been born female and medically transitioned to male. Seeing them rocked my world. I now had an idea of what I needed but no idea how to get there.

After 35 years struggling with gender, I finally found the strength to take a leap of faith and start gender transition. It was both the most frightening thing I had ever done and the most loving thing I could do for myself.

Physically changing was only a small part of learning to live my life as a man. I had to learn a new language. I had to learn to relate to men and women within a new social context. At times I felt awkward and uncertain. But never did I regret my decision. Amid all the newness, I sometimes felt raw and exhausted, but at the end of the day I always felt like a kid at Christmas. I had just been given the best gift. I finally got to feel at home in my own skin. I could finally at 37 years old look in the mirror and not hate what I saw.
SOURCE: Author's Files.

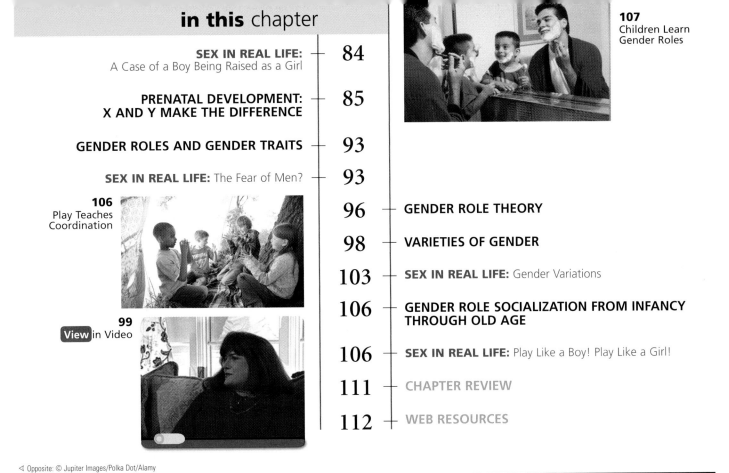

◁ Opposite: © Jupiter Images/Polka Dot/Alamy

I f you're like most college students, you probably don't spend a great deal of time thinking about your gender. You wake up in the morning, and when you catch your reflection in the mirror, you recognize yourself and don't think you're the wrong gender. But what if, when you made that morning trek to the mirror, the face looking back at you wasn't who you thought it should be? How would that feel?

As we begin our discussion about gender, first imagine that as you are reading this, an alien walks into the room. The alien tells you that "zee" (not he or she) is only on Earth for a short time and would like to learn as much as possible about life here during this visit. One of the things "zee" would like to learn about is **gender,** specifically, "What are a man and woman?" How would you answer such a question? You might try to explain how a man and woman look, act, think, or feel. But what is a man, and what is a woman?

When a baby is born, new parents are eager to hear whether "It's a Girl" or "It's a Boy," but what if it was neither? What if a newborn child had ambiguous genitalia, and it was impossible to tell whether it was a boy or a girl? A child with the **gonads** (testes or ovaries) of one gender but with ambiguous external genitalia is often referred to as **intersexed.** Intersexed girls and boys are often reared as members of their chromosomal sex (XX or XY). Throughout history most parents have opted for immediate sur-gery to quickly assign the child's gender to either male or female (Neergaard, 2005). But isn't gender more than anatomy or hormones? What is gender?

Gender raises many issues. For example, if your college or university has on-campus housing, does it allow you to have a roommate who is the other gender? Although many universities assign housing based strictly on a person's birth gender, a growing number of universities are creating gender-neutral housing options. Gender-neutral housing means it doesn't matter what gender you are when it comes to living quarters on campus. These efforts are part of a national movement aimed at helping students who may feel confused or who have questions about their gender. As of late 2007, more than 25 universities offer gender-neutral housing, including Dartmouth, University of Michigan, University of Pennsylvania, Brown University, and University of California-Riverside (GenderBlind, 2008).

gender
The behavioral, psychological, and social characteristics of men and women.

gonads
The male and female sex glands—ovaries and testes.

intersexed
A person who has the gonads (testes or ovaries) of one gender but ambiguous external genitalia; also referred to as a pseudohermaphrodite.

Before we go any further, let's talk about how people tend to use the words **sex** and gender synonymously, even though they have different meanings. When you fill out a questionnaire that asks you "What is your sex?" how do you answer? When you apply for a driver's license and are asked, "What gender are you?" how do you respond? Although your answers here might be the same, researchers usually use the word *sex* to refer to the biological aspects of being male or female and *gender* to refer to the behavioral, psychological, and social characteristics of men and women (Pryzgoda & Chrisler, 2000).

You might wonder why exploring gender is important to our understanding of sexuality. How does gender affect sexuality? Gender stereotypes shape our opinions about how men and women act sexually. For example, if we believe that men are more aggressive than women, we might believe that these gender stereo-types carry over into the bedroom as well. Traditionally, men are viewed as the initiators in sexual activity, and they are the ones who are supposed to make all the "moves." Stereotypes about women, on the other hand, hold that women are more emotional and connected when it comes to sex—more into "making love" than "having sex." Do gender stereotypes really affect how we act and interact sexually? And how do gender stereotypes affect gay and lesbian couples? We explore the relationship between gender and sexuality later in this chapter.

So let's ask again, what is a man? A woman? For many years scientists have debated whether gender is more genetics and biology ("nature") or social environment and upbringing ("nurture"), or is it a combination of the two?

chromosome
A threadlike structure in the nucleus of a cell that carries genetic information.

SEX IN REAL LIFE

A Case of a Boy Being Raised as a Girl

For many years, this Brenda/Bruce case stood as "proof" that children were psychosexually "neutral" at birth and that gender could be assigned, no matter what the genetics or biology indicated.

In 1967, a young Canadian couple brought their two identical twin boys (Bruce and Brian) to the hospital for routine circumcisions; the boys were 8 months old. A surgical mistake during one of the twin's circumcisions resulted in the destruction of his penis. The couple met with Dr. John Money, a well-known medical psychologist, from Johns Hopkins University, who believed that gender was learned and could be changed through child rearing. He did not believe gender was contingent on **chromosomes,** genitals, or even sex hormones (Money, 1975). After meeting with Dr. Money and discussing their options, the couple decided to have their son, Bruce, undergo castration (removal of the testicles) and have surgery to transform his genitals into those of an anatomically correct female. Bruce became Brenda and was put on hormone treatment beginning in adolescence to maintain her feminine appearance. For many years, this Brenda/Bruce case stood as "proof" that children were psychosexually "neutral" at birth and that

gender could be assigned, no matter what the genetics or biology indicated. This case had a profound affect on how children who were born with ambiguous genitalia or who had experienced genital trauma were raised (Colapinto, 2001).

However, even though Money paraded the Brenda/Bruce story as a success and around the globe intersexed children began sex reassignments, no one paid much attention to the fact that Brenda was struggling with her gender identity. In 1997, a study published by Milton Diamond, a reproductive biologist at the University of Hawaii, exposed the case and discussed how Brenda had struggled against her girlhood from the beginning (Diamond & Sigmundson, 1997). Once Brenda reached puberty, despite her hormone treatments, her misery increased. She became depressed and suicidal. She never felt that she was a girl, and she was relentlessly teased by peers. Her parents finally told her the truth, and at 15 years old, she stopped hormonal treatments and changed her name to David.

Soon afterward, David Reimer went public with his medical story in hopes of discouraging similar sex reassignment surgeries. In 2001, John Colapinto wrote the details of this real-life story in a book called *As Nature Made Him: The Boy Who Was Raised as a Girl* (Colapinto, 2001). This book, in conjunction with interviews with David, influenced medical understandings about the biology of gender. Today the Intersex Society of North America opposes the use of sex reassignment surgery for nonconsenting minors.

© Reuters/Corbis

Although David Reimer (left) eventually married and adopted children, his struggles with depression continued. In 2004, at age 38, Reimer took his own life (Burkeman & Younge, 2005).

It is hard to tell infant boys and girls apart, which is why so many parents dress their children in pink or blue.

VLC/Getty Images

The story of Bruce and Brenda discussed in the Sex in Real Life feature in this section illustrates the fact that both nature and nurture are important in the development of gender. In Chapter 2, we discussed evolutionary theory, which argues that many behaviors in men and women have evolved in the survival of the species and that gender differences between men and women may be at least partially a result of heredity.

In this chapter, we explore the nature versus nurture debate as it relates to gender in hopes of finding answers to the questions "What is a man?" and "What is a woman?" We'll start by reviewing prenatal development and sexual differentiation. We will also look at atypical sexual differentiation and chromosomal and hormonal

REALResearch > Video game characters have overwhelmingly been found to be male, even though more female characters have been added to games in the past few years. Gender stereotypes are robust in video games—with men represented as hypermuscular characters and women represented as hypersexualized characters (JANSZ & MARTIS, 2007).

disorders. Although these disorders are not exceedingly common, their existence and how scientists have dealt with them help us learn more about gender. Our biological exploration of gender will help set the foundation on which we can understand how complex gender really is. We will also explore gender roles, theories about gender, and socialization throughout the life cycle.

Prenatal Development:
X and Y Make the Difference

Human beings have a biological urge to reproduce and so are in some sense "designed" to be sexual beings; any species that does not have good reproductive equipment and a strong desire to use

it will not last very long. Simpler organisms, such as amoebas, simply split in two, creating a pair genetically identical to the parent amoeba. More complex organisms, however, reproduce through **sexual reproduction,** in which two parents each donate a **gamete** (GAM-meet), or **germ cell,** the two of which combine to create a new organism.

The tiny germ cells from the male (sperm) and the much larger but also microscopic cell from the female (egg, or ovum) each contain half of the new person's genes and determine his or her sex, hair and eye color, general body shape, the likely age at which he or she will reach puberty, and literally millions of other aspects of the developing fetus's physiology, development, and emotional nature. The genes direct the development of the genitals and the reproductive organs and set the biological clock running to trigger puberty and female **menopause** or male **andropause.** We discuss both of these in the next two chapters.

Most cells in the human body contain 46 chromosomes: 23 inherited from the mother and 23 from the father, arranged in 23 pairs. Twenty-two of the pairs look almost identical and are referred to as **autosomes;** the exception is the 23rd pair, the **sex chromosomes.** The two sex chromosomes, which determine whether a person is male or female, are made up of an X chromosome donated by the mother through the ovum and either an X or a Y chromosome donated by the father's sperm. In normal development, if the male contributes an X chromosome, the child will be female (XX); if he contributes a Y, the child will be male (XY).

All the cells of the body (somatic cells), except gametes, contain all 23 pairs of chromosomes (46 total) and are called diploid (meaning double). However, if a merging sperm and egg also had 23 pairs each, they would create a child with 46 pairs, which is too many (remember that most cells contain only 23 pairs of chromosomes). So gametes are haploid, meaning they

sexual reproduction
The production of offspring from the union of two parents.

gamete
A male or female reproductive cell—the spermatozoon or ovum; also referred to as a germ cell.

germ cell
A male or female reproductive cell—the spermatozoon or ovum; also referred to as a gamete.

menopause
The cessation of menstruation.

andropause
A period of time in a man's life, usually during his 70s or 80s, when testosterone decreases, causing a decrease in spermatogenesis, a thinner ejaculate, a decrease in ejaculatory pressure, decreased muscle strength, increased fatigue, and mood disturbances.

autosome
Any chromosome that is not a sex chromosome.

sex chromosomes
Rod-shaped bodies in the nucleus of a cell at the time of cell division that contain information about whether the fetus will become male or female.

contain half the number of chromosomes (23) of a somatic cell (46). During **fertilization,** a haploid sperm and a haploid egg join to produce a diploid **zygote** (ZIE-goat) containing 46 chromosomes, half from each parent. The zygote can now undergo **mitosis,** reproducing its 46 chromosomes as it grows.

The 46 chromosomes are threadlike bodies made up of somewhere between 20,000 to 25,000 genes, each of which contains **deoxyribonucleic** (dee-OCK-see-rye-bow-new-KLEE-ik) **acid** (**DNA;** Human Genome Project, 2003). DNA acts as a blueprint for how every cell in the organism will develop. At first, the zygote reproduces exact copies of itself. Soon, however, the cells begin a process of differentiation. Differentiation is one of the great mysteries of human biology—suddenly, identical cells begin splitting into liver cells, brain cells, skin cells, and all the thousands of different kinds of cells in the body. The DNA determines the order in which cells differentiate, and a cell's position may determine to some degree which type of cell it will become. Researchers in evolutionary developmental biology explore how and when cells differentiate.

Whether the zygote will develop into a male or female is determined at the moment of conception, and part of the process of differentiation includes the development of our sexual characteristics. If sexual differentiation proceeds without a problem, the zygote will develop into a fetus with typically male or typically female sexual characteristics. However, a variety of things can happen during development that can later influence the person's own sense of being either male or female.

SEXUAL DIFFERENTIATION IN THE WOMB

A human embryo normally undergoes about 9 months of **gestation.** At about 4 to 6 weeks, the first tissues that will become the embryo's gonads develop. Sexual differentiation begins a week or two later and is initiated by the sex chromosomes, which control

View in Video

"Scientists stained the sperm and marked them through a laser, so the X chromosomes may be separated from the Y chromosomes."
—*Choosing Your Child's Gender*
To view go to CengageNOW at www.cengage.com/login

+2.8%

at least four important aspects of sexual development: (1) the internal sexual organs (e.g., whether the fetus develops ovaries or testicles); (2) the external sex organs (such as the penis or clitoris); (3) the hormonal environment of the embryo; and (4) the sexual differentiation of the brain (which includes a cyclic or noncyclic hormonal pattern) (Wilson & Davies, 2007).

Internal Sex Organs

In the first few weeks of development, XX (female) and XY (male) embryos are identical. Around the 5th to 6th week, the primitive gonads form, and at this point they can potentially develop into either **testes** or **ovaries.** Traditional developmental models claim that the "default" development is female; without the specific masculinizing signals sent by the Y chromosome and the SRY (sex-determining region Y) gene, the gonads will develop as female. The SRY is a Y chromosome-specific gene that plays a central role in sexual differentiation and development in males (DiNapoli & Capel, 2008; Krone et al., 2007). However, it may not be only **testosterone** or the SRY gene

REALResearch > The first genetic clue to gender came in 1923 when Theophilus Shickel Painter discovered that all males were XY and all females were XX (DiNapoli & Capel, 2007).

that differentiates males from females—it may also be the presence of ovarian hormones (Blecher & Erickson, 2007).

In most males, the testes begin to differentiate from the primitive gonad by the 7th to 8th week following conception. In most females, the development of the primitive gonad begins to differentiate into ovaries by the 10th or 11th week. The primitive duct system, the **Müllerian** (myul-EAR-ee-an) **duct** (female) or

WHAT DO YOU WANT TO KNOW ?

Does the father's sperm really determine the sex of the child?
Yes, it is the sperm that determines the sex of the child, but the woman's body does have a role to play; there are differences between X and Y sperm (Xs are heavier and slower but live longer; Ys are faster but die more quickly), and a woman's vaginal environment or ovulation cycle may favor one or the other. However, the sex of the child does depend on whether an X chromosome sperm or a Y chromosome sperm, donated by the father, joins with the ovum (which is always an X). The irony is that for many years, in many cultures, men routinely blamed and even divorced women who did not produce a child of a certain sex (usually a boy), when in fact the man's sperm had much more to do with it.

fertilization
The union of two gametes, which occurs when a haploid sperm and a haploid egg join to produce a diploid zygote, containing 46 chromosomes.

zygote
The single cell resulting from the union of sperm and egg cells.

mitosis
The division of the nucleus of a cell into two new cells such that each new daughter cell has the same number and kind of chromosomes as the original parent.

deoxyribonucleic acid (DNA)
A nucleic acid in the shape of a double helix in which all genetic information in the organism is encoded.

gestation
The period of intrauterine fetal development.

testes
Male gonads inside the scrotum that produce testosterone.

ovaries
Female gonads that produce ova and sex hormones.

testosterone
A male sex hormone that is secreted by the Leydig cells of mature testes and produces secondary sex characteristics in men.

Müllerian duct
One of a pair of tubes in the embryo that will develop, in female embryos, into the fallopian tubes, uterus, and part of the vagina.

the **Wolffian** (WOOL-fee-an) **duct** (male), also appears at this time (Krone & Hanley, 2007). Once the gonads have developed, they then hormonally control the development of the ducts into either the female or male reproductive system (we discuss these specifics structures more in Chapters 5 and 6).

In female embryos, the lack of male hormones results in the disappearance of the Wolffian ducts, and the Müllerian duct fuses to form the uterus and inner third of the vagina. The unfused portion of the duct remains and develops into the two oviducts or Fallopian tubes (see Figure 4.1).

In the presence of a Y chromosome, the gonads develop into testes, which soon begin producing **Müllerian inhibiting factor (MIF)** and testosterone. MIF causes the Müllerian ducts to disappear during the 3rd month, and testosterone stimulates the Wolffian duct to develop into the structures surrounding the testicles.

Wolffian duct
One of a pair of structures in the embryo that, when exposed to testosterone, will develop into the male reproductive system.

Müllerian inhibiting factor (MIF)
A hormone secreted in male embryos that prevents the Müllerian duct from developing into female reproductive organs.

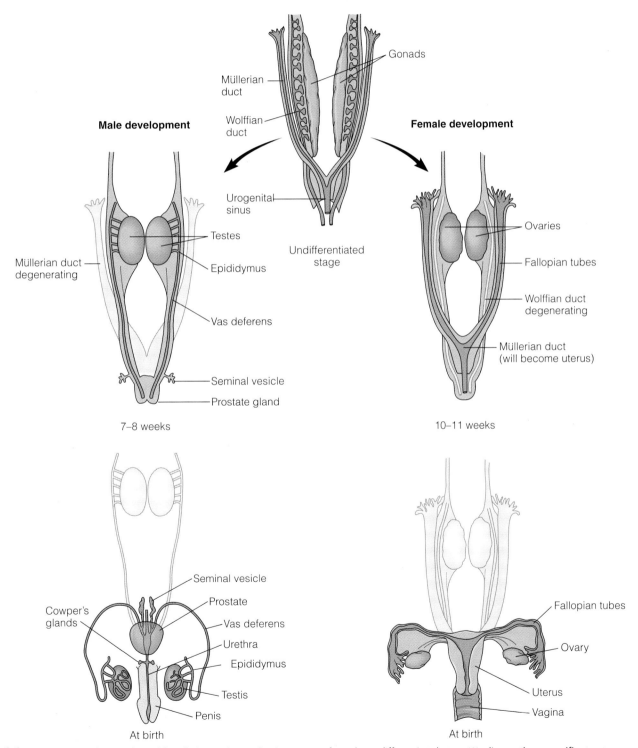

Figure **4.1** Development of the male and female internal reproductive systems from the undifferentiated stage. We discuss these specific structures more in Chapters 5 and 6.

table 4.1

Homologous Tissue

Male and female organs that began from the same prenatal tissue are called homologous. Below are some of the homologous tissues.

Female	Male
clitoral glans	head of the penis (glans)
clitoral hood	foreskin
labia minora	penis
labia majora	scrotum
ovaries	testes

The body converts some testosterone into another **androgen,** called dihydrotestosterone (DHT), to stimulate the development of the male external sex organs.

External Sex Organs

External genitals follow a pattern similar to that of internal organs, except that male and female genitalia all develop from the same tissue. Male and female organs that began from the same prenatal tissue are called **homologous** (HOE-mol-lig-gus; see the nearby Table 4.1 for an overview of homologous tissues). Until the 8th week, the undifferentiated tissue from which the genitalia will develop exists as a mound of skin, or *tubercle,* beneath the umbilical cord. In females, the external genitalia develop under the influence of female hormones produced by the placenta and by the mother and also the lack of influence from the Y chromosome. The genital tubercle develops into the clitoris, the labia minora, the vestibule, and the labia majora (see Figure 4.2)

In males, by the 8th or 9th week the testes begin androgen secretion, which begins to stimulate the development of male genitalia. The genital tubercle elongates to form the penis, in which lies the urethra, culminating in an external opening called the urethral meatus. Part of the tubercle also fuses together to form the scrotum, where the testicles will ultimately rest when they descend.

Hormonal Development and Influences

Hormones play an important role in human development. Table 4.2 lists the various sex hormones and the roles they play. **Endocrine glands,** such as the gonads, secrete hormones directly into the bloodstream to be carried to the target organs. The ovaries, for example, produce the two major female hormones, estrogen and progesterone. **Estrogen** is an important influence in the development of female sexual characteristics throughout fetal development and later life, whereas **progesterone** regulates the menstrual cycle and prepares the uterus for pregnancy. The testicles produce androgens, which are quite important to the male, because even a genetically male embryo will develop female characteristics if androgens are not secreted at the right time or if the fetus is insensitive to androgens.

Brain Differentiation

Most hormonal secretions are regulated by the brain—in particular, by the hypothalamus, which is the body's single most important control center. Yet hormones also affect the development of the brain itself, both in the uterus and after birth. Male and female brains have different tasks and so undergo different development. For example, female brains control menstruation and therefore must signal the release of hormones in a monthly cycle, whereas male brains signal release continuously. With the brain, as with sexual organs, the presence of androgens during the appropriate critical stage of development may be the factor that programs the central nervous system to develop male sexual behaviors (Bocklandt & Vilain, 2007).

> *Most hormonal secretions are regulated by the brain.*

ATYPICAL SEXUAL DIFFERENTIATION: NOT ALWAYS JUST X AND Y

Prenatal development depends on carefully orchestrated developmental stages. At any stage, sex hormone irregularities, genetic abnormalities, or exposure of the fetus to inappropriate maternal hormones can result in atypical sexual differentiation. The result can be a child born with ambiguous genitals or with the external genitals of one sex and the genetic makeup of the other sex. An overview of prenatal sex differentiation syndromes is in the nearby Table 4.3.

Sex Chromosome Disorders

Sometimes a person's sex chromosomes will include an extra X or Y chromosome or will be missing one. Although medical researchers have identified more than 70 such abnormalities of the sex chromosomes, we discuss here the three most common.

Klinefelter's syndrome, which occurs in about 1 in 700 live male births, occurs when an ovum containing an extra X chromosome is fertilized by a Y sperm (designated XXY), giving a child 47 chromosomes altogether. The Y chromosome triggers the development of male genitalia, but the extra X prevents them from developing fully. Although boys and men can be diagnosed at any age with Klinefelter's, older men typically experience with feminized

---

androgen
A hormone that promotes the development of male genitals and secondary sex characteristics. It is produced by the testes in men and by the adrenal glands in both men and women.

homologous
Corresponding in structure, position, or origin but not necessarily in function.

endocrine gland
A gland that secretes hormones into the blood.

estrogen
A hormone that produces female secondary sex characteristics and affects the menstrual cycle.

progesterone
A hormone that is produced by the ovaries and helps to regulate the menstrual cycle.

Klinefelter's syndrome
A genetic disorder in men in which there are three sex chromosomes, XXY, instead of two; characterized by small testes, low sperm production, breast enlargement, and absence of facial and body hair.

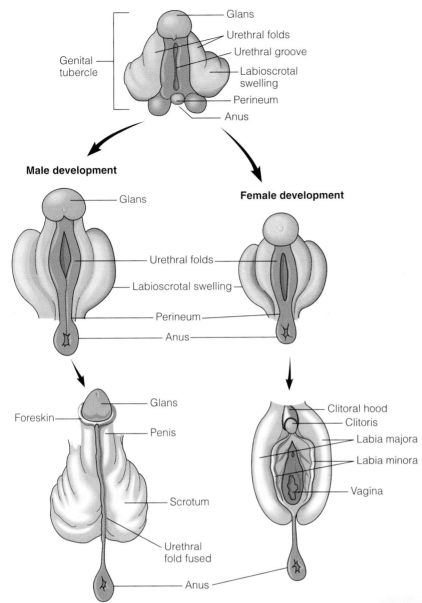

Figure **4.2** Development of the male and female external genitalia from the undifferentiated genital tubercle.

ture breast development, and abnormalities of certain internal organs (Moreno-Garcia et al., 2005). The median age at which a young girl is diagnosed with Turner syndrome is 6.6 years old, although some are not diagnosed until much later (Massa et al., 2005). Because therapeutic administration of estrogen and progesterone, especially during puberty, can help enhance some sexual characteristics and slightly increase height (Sheaffer el al., 2008), early diagnosis of Turner syndrome is important.

XYY syndrome and **triple X syndrome** are very rare disorders. As the names imply, these syndromes occur when a normal ovum is fertilized by a sperm that has two Y chromosomes or two X chromosomes or when an ovum with two X chromosomes is fertilized by a normal X sperm. The XYY individual may grow up as a normal male and the XXX as a normal female, and so often their unusual genetic status is not detected. However, many do suffer from some genital abnormalities, fertility problems, and possible learning difficulties later in life. There is no effective treatment for XYY or XXX syndrome.

Hormonal Irregularities

A **hermaphrodite** (her-MAFF-fro-dite) is born with fully formed ovaries and fully formed testes, which is exceptionally rare. In fact, true hermaphroditism is the rarest form of intersex variations (Krstic et al., 2000). Most people who are called hermaphrodites are actually **pseudohermaphrodites,** those whose external genitals resemble to some degree the genitals of both sexes.

Congenital adrenal hyperplasia (CAH) is a hormonal irregularity that occurs when a genetically normal female (XX) or male (XY) is exposed to large

body contours, small testicles, low levels of testosterone, **gynecomastia,** and infertility (Y. S. Lee et al., 2007). In fact, Klinefelter's syndrome is the most common genetic cause of male infertility (Lanfranco et al., 2004). These men often show low levels of sexual desire, probably due to the lack of testosterone. **Testosterone therapy,** especially if it is begun during adolescence, can enhance the development of **secondary sexual characteristics.**

Turner syndrome is another chromosomal disorder. It is among the most common of the chromosomal disorders, occurring in 1 of every 2,500 live female births. Turner syndrome results from an ovum without any sex chromosome being fertilized by an X sperm (designated XO), which gives the child only 45 chromosomes altogether (if an ovum without a chromosome is fertilized by a Y sperm and so contains no X sex chromosome, it will not survive). Although the external genitalia develop to look like a normal female's, the woman's ovaries do not develop fully, causing **amenorrhea** (aye-men-uh-REE-uh) and infertility. In addition, Turner syndrome is characterized by short stature, imma-

gynecomastia
Abnormal breast development in the male.

testosterone therapy
The use of testosterone to replace missing hormones in males with hormone disorders.

secondary sexual characteristics
The physical characteristics, other than the genitalia, that distinguish male from female.

Turner syndrome
A genetic disorder in females in which there is only one X sex chromosome instead of two, characterized by lack of internal female sex organs, infertility, short stature, and mental retardation.

amenorrhea
The absence of menstruation.

XYY syndrome
A genetic abnormality in which a male has an extra Y sex chromosome; characterized by decreased fertility, some genital abnormality, and slight mental retardation.

triple X syndrome
A genetic abnormality in which a female has an extra X sex chromosome; characterized by decreased fertility, some genital abnormality, and slight mental retardation.

hermaphrodite
Person born with fully formed ovaries and fully formed testes.

pseudohermaphrodite
A person who has the gonads of one sex and the genitalia of the other or is born with ambiguous genitalia; also referred to as intersexed.

congenital adrenal hyperplasia (CAH)
A disorder involving overproduction of androgen in the adrenal glands that can affect males and females. Females born with this condition frequently have masculinized genitals because of excess prenatal androgen exposure, whereas males typically experience early pubertal changes.

table 4.2

The Sex Hormones

Hormone	Purposes
Androgens	A group of hormones that control male sexual development and include testosterone and androsterone. Androgens stimulate the development of male sex organs and secondary sex characteristics such as beard growth and a deepening voice. Testosterone also plays an important part (in both sexes) in stimulating sexual desire. The testes produce androgens in men, although a small amount is also produced by the adrenal glands. Women's ovaries also produce a small amount of androgens, which helps stimulate sexual desire; too much production by the ovaries causes masculinization in women.
Estrogens	A group of hormones that control female sexual development. Estrogen controls development of the female sex organs, the menstrual cycle, parts of pregnancy, and secondary sex characteristics such as breast development. The ovaries produce most of the estrogen in women, although the adrenal glands and the placenta also produce small amounts. Testes also produce a small amount of estrogen in men; if they produce too much, feminization may occur.
Progesterone	A female hormone secreted by the ovaries. Progesterone helps to prepare the lining of the uterus for the implantation of the fertilized ovum, to stimulate milk production in the breasts, and to maintain the placenta. Progesterone works in conjunction with estrogen to prepare the female reproductive system for pregnancy.
Gonadotropin-releasing hormone (GnRH)	A hormone that affects the nervous system. It is produced in the hypothalamus of the brain and transported through the bloodstream to the pituitary gland. Gonadotropin means "gonad stimulating," and GnRH stimulates the pituitary to release hormones, such as follicle-stimulating hormone and luteinizing hormone, which themselves induce the ovaries and testes (as well as other glands) to secrete their hormones.
Follicle-stimulating hormone (FSH)	A hormone released by the pituitary gland when stimulated by GnRH that stimulates the follicular development in females and the formation of sperm in males.
Luteinizing hormone (LH)	A hormone released by the pituitary gland when stimulated by GnRH that stimulates ovulation and the release of other hormones, notably progesterone in the female and testosterone in the male. It also stimulates the cells in the testes to produce testosterone.
Prolactin	A pituitary hormone that stimulates milk production after childbirth and also the production of progesterone.
Oxytocin	A pituitary hormone that stimulates the ejection of milk from the breasts and causes increased contractions of the uterus during labor.
Inhibin	A hormone produced by the cells of the testes that signals the anterior pituitary to decrease FSH production if the sperm count gets too high.

amounts of androgens during crucial stages of prenatal development. It is estimated that 1 in 10,000 to 18,000 children are born with CAH (MedlinePlus, 2004b). CAH is less common in males, and there are often no obvious abnormalities present, but 2 to 3 years before the onset of typical puberty, a CAH boy often experiences increased muscular strength, penile growth, an increase in pubic hair, and a deepening in the voice. The testicles, however, remain small.

CAH may develop in a female when the adrenal glands produce too much androgen. A similar syndrome can also develop if the mother takes male hormones or drugs with effects that mimic male hormones (a number of pregnant women were prescribed such drugs in the 1950s, resulting in a group of CAH babies born during that time).

Depending on the amount of male hormones or drugs, different degrees of masculinization can occur. Although the internal organs remain female and are not affected, the clitoris enlarges, even sometimes developing into a true penis containing a urethra. Underneath the penis, the two labia may fuse to resemble a scrotum, but it contains no testicles.

If the adrenal glands continue to produce excessive androgens, masculinization can continue throughout the CAH female's development. When a child is born with the genital traits of CAH today, a chromosomal analysis is usually performed, so CAH females are typically diagnosed at birth. Corrective surgery can be done to form female genitalia, and drugs can be prescribed to control adrenal output (Warne et al., 2005). Because the internal organs are unaffected, even pregnancy is possible in many CAH females.

Early androgen concentrations may also affect childhood play and adult sexual orientation. Research has shown that CAH girls choose more male-typical toys than girls without CAH (Pasterski

table 4.3

Some Prenatal Sex Differentiation Syndromes

Syndrome	Chromosomal Pattern	External Genitals	Internal Structures	Description	Treatment
CHROMOSOMAL					
Klinefelter's syndrome	47, XXY	Male	Male	Testes are small; breasts may develop; low testosterone levels, erectile dysfunction, and mental retardation are common; people with this disorder have unusual body proportions and are usually infertile.	Testosterone during adolescence may help improve body shape and sex drive.
Turner syndrome	45, XO	Female	Uterus and oviducts	There is no menstruation or breast development; a broad chest with widely spaced nipples, loose skin around the neck, nonfunctioning ovaries, and infertility.	Androgens during puberty can help increase height, and estrogen and progesterone can help promote breast development and menstruation.
XYY syndrome	47, XYY	Male	Male	There is likelihood of slight mental retardation, some genital irregularities, and decreased fertility or infertility.	None.
Triple X syndrome	47, XXX	Female	Female	There is likelihood of slight mental retardation and decreased fertility or infertility.	None.
HORMONAL					
Congenital adrenal hyperplasia (CAH)	46, XX, XY	Some male and some female traits	Internal organs are normal.	While external male genitals are often normal, female infants may have clitoral enlargement and labial fusing.	Surgery can correct external genitals.
Androgen-insensitivity syndrome (AIS)	46, XY	Female	Male gonads in the abdomen	Usually AIS children are raised female. Breasts develop at puberty, but menstruation does not begin. Such a person has a shortened vagina, no internal sexual organs, and is sterile.	Surgery can lengthen vagina to accommodate a penis for intercourse if necessary.

et al., 2005, 2007). CAH girls have been found to have good long-term psychological health and social functioning (J. F. Morgan et al., 2005) and also higher rates of bisexuality and homosexuality than non-CAH girls (Meyer-Bahlburg et al., 2008).

Androgen-insensitivity syndrome (AIS) is, in some ways, the opposite of CAH. It is often first detected when a seemingly normal teenage girl fails to menstruate and chromosomal analysis discovers that she is XY, a genetic male. It is estimated that 1 in 20,000 boys are born each year with AIS (Medline Plus, 2004a). In this syndrome, although the gonads develop into testes and produce testosterone normally, for some reason the AIS individual's cells cannot absorb it; in other words, the testosterone is there but has no effect on the body. Because the Wolffian ducts did not respond to testosterone during the sexual differentiation phase, no male genitalia developed; however, because the gonads, which are male, did produce Müllerian inhibiting factor, the Müllerian ducts did not develop into normal female internal organs either. The AIS individual ends up with no internal reproductive organs except two testes, which remain in the abdomen producing testosterone that the body cannot use.

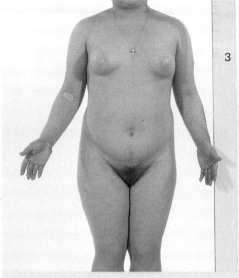

© Wellcome Trust Library/CMSP

Female with Turner syndrome.

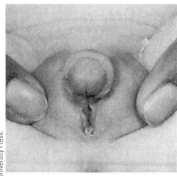

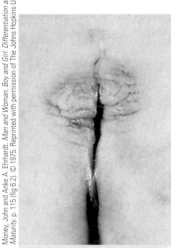

Money, John and Anke A. Ehrhardt. *Man and Woman, Boy and Girl: Differentiation and Dimorphism of Gender Identity from Conception to Maturity.* p. 115 (fig 6.2). © 1975. Reprinted with permission of The Johns Hopkins University Press.

Genitalia of a fetally androgenized female and an androgen-insensitive male with feminized genitals.

The AIS infant has the "default" female genitals, but because the Müllerian ducts also form the last third of the vagina, the infant has only a very shallow vagina. Usually the syndrome is undetected at birth, and the baby is brought up female. Because males do produce a small amount of estrogen, the breasts do develop, so it is only when the teen fails to menstruate that AIS is usually diagnosed. Surgery can then be initiated to lengthen the vagina to accommodate a penis for intercourse, although without any female internal organs, the individual remains infertile. Even though they are genetically male, most AIS individuals seem fully feminized and live as females.

Now that we have discussed the various chromosomal and hormonal conditions that may affect gender, the important question becomes, what can a parent do after a child is born with ambiguous genitals or the genitals of one sex and the genetic makeup of the other? Today's experts recommend that no surgery be performed until the child can consent to it (Neergaard, 2005) because there is too much uncertainty in infancy about intersex conditions (Lorio, 2004; Thyen et al., 2005). This would mean waiting until a child is perhaps 3 to 5 years old or even older to determine whether to proceed with gender reassignment. There has also been a recent movement to use drugs to delay puberty in intersexed and transgendered children (see the nearby Sex in Real Life feature, "Gender Variations," on page 45).

androgen-insensitivity syndrome (AIS)
A condition in which a genetic male's cells are insensitive to androgens, resulting in the development of female external genitalia (but no internal reproductive organs). People with AIS are raised as females.

review questions

1 Differentiate between sex and gender, and explain how the Bruce/Brenda case shed light on the nature versus nurture debate.

2 Describe sexual reproduction, and explain what happens after a sperm fertilizes an ovum.

3 Describe sexual differentiation in a developing fetus.

4 Explain the role that hormones and brain differentiation play in human development.

5 Identify the chromosomal and hormonal factors that may result in an atypical sexual differentiation.

Gender Roles and Gender Traits

Let's go back, for a moment, to that alien you met earlier in the chapter. When you describe what is male and female for the alien, chances are you will talk about stereotyped behavior. You might say, "Men are strong, independent, and assertive, and often have a hard time showing emotion," or "Women are sensitive, nurturing, emotional, and soft." Descriptions like these are based on gender stereotypes. Gender stereotypes are fundamental to our ways of thinking, which makes it difficult to realize how thoroughly our conceptions of the world are shaped by gender issues. For example, when a baby is born, the very first question we ask is, "Is it a boy or a girl?" The parents proudly display a sign in their yard or send a card to friends, proclaiming "It's a girl!" or "It's a boy!" as the sole identifying trait of the child. The card does not state "It's a redhead!" From the moment of birth onward, the child is thought of first as male or female, and all other characteristics—whether the child is tall, bright, an artist, Irish, disabled, gay—are seen in light of the person's gender.

> *Gender stereotypes are fundamental to our ways of thinking . . .*

Overall, we expect men to act like men and women to act like women, and we become confused and uncomfortable when we are denied knowledge of a person's gender. It is very difficult to know how to interact with someone whose gender we do not know because we are so programmed to react to people first according to their gender. If you walked into a party tonight and found yourself face-to-face with someone whom you couldn't tell was male or female, how would you feel? Most likely you'd be confused and search for gender clues. Often our need to categorize people by gender is taken for granted. But why is it so important?

Even our language is constructed around gender. English has no neutral pronoun (neither do many other languages, including French, Spanish, German, and Italian), meaning that every time you refer to a person, you must write either "he" or "she." Therefore, every sentence you write about a person reveals his or her gender, even if it reveals nothing else about that person.

In the gender-variant community, a new language for gender-neutral pronouns has emerged. "Sie" or "ce" (pronounced "see") is proposed for she/he and "hir" (pronounced "here") for hers/his (Feinberg, 1999). So "he is wearing a blue hat" would become "ce is wearing a blue hat," whereas "her book is over there" would become "hir book is over there."

SEX IN REAL LIFE

The Fear of Men?

Many experts today blame this fear of men on the media's image of men as a bad guy, especially when it comes to sexual crimes.

Over the years, many Americans have reacted with panic and fear to countless real and perceived threats to children. These threats include the fear of bullies, drugs, the Internet, and sexual predators (Radford, 2006). The media has helped to stir more fear in parents by pointing out that sexual predators could be lurking anywhere—near schools, churches, malls, or even movie theatres. By 2008, every state imposed notification laws so that communities would be alerted when a convicted sexual offender moved to town. Although we talk more about sexual offender registries in Chapter 16, here let's explore how the rising panic in society about sexual predators has led to a fear of men.

Jeff Zaslow, a columnist with the *Wall Street Journal,* wrote an article in 2007 titled "Are We Teaching Our Children to Be Fearful of Men?" (Zaslow, 2007). In this article, Zaslow points out several ways in which society has contributed to rising fears about men. He discusses how when children get lost in a mall, they are often told to seek out a woman (preferably a "pregnant woman" or a "grandmother"), rather than a man. Or how airlines have changed their policies in seating unaccompanied minor children and now prefer to place them near female passengers. Could this fear of men have led to decreasing rates of male teachers and ad-

ministrators in the elementary schools? Statistics show that the percentage of male elementary school teachers has dropped from 18% to 9% in 2007 (Zaslow, 2007). More fear is instilled by John Walsh, host of *America's Most Wanted*, who advises parents not to hire male babysitters. A soccer club in Michigan requires one female parent on the sidelines at all times to protect children from any unwanted behaviors from men. In Pennsylvania, another soccer coach refrains from hugging his female players after a goal to make sure he's not sending the wrong message (Zaslow, 2007).

Many experts today blame this fear of men on the media's image of men as a bad guy, especially when it comes to sexual crimes. John Walsh defended his position by comparing it to how we choose a dog: "What dog is more likely to bite and hurt you? A Doberman, not a poodle" (Zaslow, 2007).

Do you think that panic and fear about sexual predators have changed men's relationships with children? Do you believe that some men be less likely to coach a female team because they are afraid of their behavior being misinterpreted? These are all valid questions and point to the powerful nature of gender roles and attitudes in society. What do you think needs to be done?

Many of our basic assumptions about gender are open to dispute. Gender research has been growing explosively since the 1980s, and many of the results challenge long-held beliefs about gender differences. Still, research into gender runs into some serious problems. For example, even gender researchers are socialized into accepted gender roles from birth, which may make it difficult for them to avoid projecting their own gender biases onto the research (Allen, 2007). Despite these problems, the data do seem to report certain findings consistently.

Gender roles are culturally defined behaviors that are seen as appropriate for males and females, including the attitudes, personality traits, emotions, and even postures and body language that are considered fundamental to being male or female in a culture. Gender roles also extend into social behaviors, such as the occupations we choose, how we dress and wear our hair, how we talk (as we discussed in Chapter 3), and the ways in which we interact with others.

Note that by saying gender roles are culturally defined, we are suggesting that such differences are not primarily due to biological, physiological, or even psychological differences between men and women but, rather, to the ways in which we are taught to behave. Yet many people believe that various gender differences in behavior are biologically programmed. Who is correct?

Another way to ask the question is this: Which of our gender-specific behaviors are gender roles (that is, culturally determined), and which are **gender traits** (innate or biologically determined)? If gender-specific behaviors are biologically determined, then they should remain constant in different societies; if they are social, then we should see very different gender roles in different societies. The majority of gender-specific behaviors, however, differ widely throughout the world and are determined primarily by culture.

GIRLS ACT LIKE GIRLS, BOYS ACT LIKE BOYS

Typically, we expect that boys and girls will follow stereotypic gender roles and traits. However, the models of femininity and masculinity are quickly changing in our society. Let's now explore our cultural expectations.

Masculinity and Femininity

What is masculine? What is feminine? Not too long ago, the answers would have seemed quite obvious: men naturally have masculine traits, meaning they are strong, stable, aggressive, competitive, self-reliant, and emotionally undemonstrative; women are naturally feminine, meaning they are intuitive, loving, nurturing, emotionally expressive, and gentle. Even today, many would agree that such traits describe the differences between the sexes. These gender stereotypes, however, are becoming less acceptable as our culture changes. **Masculinity** and **femininity** refer to the ideal cluster of traits that society attributes to each gender.

Models of masculinity and femininity are changing rapidly in modern American society. It's not uncommon today to see female police officers on crime scenes or apprehending criminals or women CEOs in the boardroom, nor is it uncommon to find stay-at-home dads at the park with kids or male librarians at the public library shelving books. Yet gender role change can also result in confusion, fear, and even hostility in society. Gender roles exist, in part, because they allow comfortable interaction between the

sexes. If you know exactly how you are supposed to behave and what personality traits you are supposed to assume in relation to the other sex, interactions between the sexes go more smoothly. When things change, determining correct behaviors becomes more difficult.

For example, when construction sites were the exclusive domain of men, a very male-oriented culture arose that included sexual joking, whistling at passing women, and the like. Now that women have become part of the construction team, men complain that they do not know how to behave anymore: are sexual jokes and profanity still OK, or are they considered sexual harassment? Some people yearn for the old days when male and female behaviors were clearly defined, and they advocate a return to traditional gender roles. Other people still see inequality in American society and argue that women need to have more freedom and equality.

Some studies have documented less gender role stereotyping in African American than Caucasian populations. This is probably because African Americans are less sex-role restricted than European American groups and believe that they possess both masculine and feminine traits (Dade & Sloan, 2000; Hill, 2002; Leaper, 2000). In fact, African Americans often view others through a lens of age and competency before gender. We learn about masculinity and femininity from our ethnic group's cultural heritage (M. Crawford, 2006). In one study, Latinas were asked what their parents taught them about how boys and girls *should* behave, and the majority recalled traditional role expectations (Bronstein, 2005).

ARE GENDER ROLES INNATE?

As gender stereotypes evolve, a trait may no longer be seen as the exclusive domain of a single gender. For example, many people have been trying to change our current stereotypes of men as

WHAT DO YOU WANT TO KNOW ?

It seems that the majority of heterosexual women want a guy who is tough, and they don't give the nice guys a chance. Straight guys, on the other hand, tend to look for hot girls instead of thinking about how nice or intelligent the girls are. Why is this?
Men and women always seem to wonder why people of the other sex behave the way they do. Yet society itself supports those kinds of behaviors. Is it really any surprise that men often seem to pursue appearance over substance in women when advertising, television, and women's and men's magazines all emphasize women's appearance? Is it surprising, conversely, that some women pursue the "tough guys" when society teaches them to admire male power?

In the end, it is society that determines the way we view gender relationships, and each of us is responsible to some degree for continuing those attitudes.

gender roles Culturally defined behaviors seen as appropriate for males and females.	**masculinity** The ideal cluster of traits that society attributes to males.
gender traits Innate or biologically determined gender-specific behaviors.	**femininity** The ideal cluster of traits that society attributes to females.

"unemotional" and women as "emotional." The constellation of traits that has been traditionally seen as masculine and feminine may be becoming less rigid. For many centuries, these types of gender traits were seen as innate, immutable, and part of the biological makeup of the sexes. Few scientists suggested that the differences between men and women were primarily social; most believed that women and men were fundamentally different.

REALResearch > Body image in men, like women, is susceptible to social influence. One study found that in competitive tasks against women, men who were less successful at the tasks developed more negative views of their bodies—they viewed themselves as less muscular after "failing" to females (Mills & D'Alfonso, 2007).

Not only did scientists believe that the differences in the sexes were innate, but they also believed that men were superior—having developed past the "emotional" nature of women (Gould, 1981). Unfortunately, these attitudes still exist, both subtly in cultures like our own and overtly in cultures where women are allowed few of the rights granted to men.

How many of our gender behaviors are biological, and how many are socially transmitted? The truth is that the world may not split that cleanly into biological versus social causes of behavior. Behaviors are complex and are almost always interactions between one's innate biological capacities and the environment in which one lives and acts. Behaviors that are considered innately "male" in one culture may be assumed to be innately "female" in another. Even when modern science suggests certain gender traits that seem to be based on innate differences between the sexes, culture can contradict that trait or even deny it.

For example, most researchers accept the principle that males display more aggression than females; adult males certainly demonstrate this tendency, which is probably the result, in part, of higher levels of testosterone. When female bodybuilders, for example, take steroids, they often find themselves acquiring male traits, including losing breast tissue, growing more body hair, and becoming more aggressive. However, the difference is also demonstrated in early childhood, when boys are more aggressive in play, whereas girls tend to be more compliant and docile.

Yet Margaret Mead's (1935/1988/2001) famous discussion of the Tchambuli tribe of New Guinea shows that such traits need not determine gender roles. Among the Tchambulis, the women performed the "aggressive" occupations such as fishing, commerce, and politics, whereas the men were more sedentary and artistic and took more care of domestic life. The women assumed the dress appropriate for their activities—plain clothes and short hair—whereas the men dressed in bright colors. So even if we accept biological gender differences, societies like the Tchambuli show that human culture can transcend biology.

There are some gender differences that are considered purely biological. Physically, males tend to be larger and stronger, with more of their body weight in muscle and less in body fat than females (Angier, 1999). Females, however, are born more neurologically advanced than males, and they mature faster. Females are also biologically heartier than males; more male fetuses miscarry, more

males are stillborn, the male infant mortality rate is higher, males acquire more hereditary diseases and remain more susceptible to disease throughout life, and men die at younger ages than women (although the gender gap in mortality is smaller among the educated and economically advantaged segments of the U.S. population). Males are also more likely to have developmental problems such as learning disabilities. It has long been believed that males are better at mathematics and spatial problems, whereas females are better at verbal tasks; for example, female children learn language skills earlier than males (Weatherall, 2002). Yet many of these differences may be the result of socialization rather than biology.

Another aspect of gender that is said, in some sense, to be innate in females is "mothering" or the "maternal instinct." Do women really have a maternal instinct that men lack? For example, is there a psychological or physical bonding mechanism that happens to women who carry babies in their wombs, one that fathers are unable to experience? Historians have pointed out examples (such as France and England in the 17th and 18th centuries) in which maternal feelings seemed almost nonexistent; children were considered a nuisance, and breast-feeding was seen as a waste of time. Poor children were often abandoned, and the children of the wealthy were sent to the countryside for care by a **wet nurse.**

Boys and girls do show some behavioral differences that appear to be universal. For example, in a study of six cultures, Whiting and her colleagues (Whiting & Edwards, 1988; Whiting & Whiting, 1975) discovered that certain traits seemed to characterize masculine and feminine behavior in 3 to 6 year olds. In almost all countries, boys engaged in more rough-and-tumble play, and boys "dominated egoistically" (tried to control the situation through commands), whereas girls more often sought or offered physical contact, sought help, and "suggested responsibly" (dominated socially by invoking rules or appealing to greater good).

Interestingly, although their strategies were different, both boys and girls often pursued the same ends; for example, rough-and-tumble play among boys and initiation of physical contact among girls are both strategies for touching and being touched. However, Whiting suggests that even these behaviors might be the result of different kinds of pressures put on boys and girls; for example, in their sample, older girls were expected to take care of young children more often than boys, and younger girls were given more responsibility than younger boys. These different expectations from each gender may explain later differences in their behaviors. So even gender behaviors that are spread across cultures may not prove to be innate differences.

There has always been evidence that men's and women's brains were different; autopsies showed that men's brains were more asymmetrical than women's, and women seemed to recover better from damage to the left hemisphere of the brain (as in strokes), where language is situated. Yet it has always been unclear what facts such as these mean. Recently, newer techniques in brain imaging have provided evidence that women's and men's brains

wet nurse
A woman who is able to breast-feed children other than her own.

not only differ in size, but that women and men use their brains differently during certain activities (DeBellis et al., 2001; Hamberg, 2000; F. Schneider et al., 2000). Although it is too early to know what these differences mean, future studies may be able to provide clearer pictures of the different ways men and women think and shed some light on the biological and social influences of these differences.

Aside from the behaviors and physical attributes just discussed, almost no differences between the sexes are universally accepted by researchers. This does not mean that there are not other biological gender differences; we simply do not know for sure. We must be careful not to move too far in the other direction and suggest that there are no innate differences between the sexes. Many of these differences remain controversial, such as relative levels of activity and curiosity and facial recognition skills. These are relatively minor differences, however. Even if it turns out, for example, that female infants recognize faces earlier than males, as has been suggested, or that male children are more active than females, would that really account for the enormous gender role differences that have developed over time? Although biologists and other researchers still study innate differences between the sexes, today more attention is being paid to gender similarities.

This brings up another important concept to keep in mind. Articles on differences between the sexes tend to be easier to publish. For example, which article do you think most people would find more exciting: "Men and Women Have Totally Different Math Abilities" or "Men and Women Have Similar Math Abilities"? Therefore, it may just be that the articles on male/female differences are more likely to be published than those that find no differences.

STUDYING GENDER

During much of the 1970s and 1980s, the focus of gender research was on girls (Warrington & Younger, 2000). Researchers looked at girls' career expectations, how educational curricula reinforced male areas of interest and the effect of this on girls, and how educators responded less frequently to girls in the classroom. Even in the 1990s, this research continued by examining how adolescent girls were losing their sense of self (Pipher, 1994) and how girls have trouble finding peace with their bodies (Brumberg, 1997). Over the past few years, research has expanded to focus on both boys and girls and has examined areas such as alcohol use (C. A. Green, 2004; Veenstra et al., 2007), body image (Mills & D'Alfonso, 2007; Phares et al., 2004), eating disorders (Economos et al., 2008; Wiseman, 2004), athletics (Cunningham, 2008; Hammermeister & Burton, 2004), and video gaming (Ferguson et al., 2008; Dill & Thill, 2007).

review questions

1 Differentiate between gender roles and gender traits, and explain how cross-cultural research helps us identify each.

2 Explain the three ways that the terms *masculinity* and *femininity* are used in society.

3 Which gender behaviors/traits are considered to be biologically based? Are any gender differences universal?

4 What is the focus of both historical and current research on gender?

Gender Role Theory

In Chapter 2, we reviewed general theories of sexuality, and the debates there centered on how much of human sexuality is programmed through our genes and physiology, and how much is influenced by culture and environment. Gender role theory struggles with the same issues, and different theorists take different positions. Social learning theorists believe that we learn gender roles almost entirely from our environment, whereas cognitive development theorists believe that children go through a set series of stages that correspond to certain beliefs and attitudes about gender. Here we will talk about evolutionary, social learning, cognitive development, and gender schema theories.

When a baby is born, he or she possesses no knowledge and few instinctual behaviors. However, by the time the child is about age 3 or 4 years, he or she can usually talk, feed himself or herself, interact with adults, describe objects, and use correct facial expressions and body language. The child also typically exhibits a wide range of behaviors that are appropriate to his or her gender. The process whereby this infant who knows nothing becomes a preschooler who has the basic skills for functioning in society is called **socialization.**

socialization
The process in which an infant is taught the basic skills for functioning in society.

Socialization occurs at various ages and levels of development, and the same is true of gender role socialization. Most boys dress and act like other boys and play with traditionally male toys (guns, trucks), whereas most girls insist on wearing dresses and express a desire to do traditionally "female" things, such as playing with dolls and toy kitchens. Is this behavior innate, or are gender stereotypes still getting through to these children through television and in playing with their peers? The answer depends on which theory of gender role development you accept.

EVOLUTIONARY THEORY:
ADAPTING TO OUR ENVIRONMENT

Recently we have begun to understand more about the biological differences between men and women through the field of evolutionary theory. Evolutionary theory takes into account evolution and our physical nature. Gender differences are seen as ways in which we have developed in our adaptation to our environment.

For example, later in this book we explore how the double standard in sexual behavior developed, in which a man with several partners was viewed as a "player," whereas a woman with several partners was viewed as a "slut." An evolutionary theorist would explain this gender difference in terms of the biological differences between men and women. A man can impregnate several women at any given time, but a woman, once pregnant, cannot become pregnant again until she gives birth. The time investment of these activities varies tremendously. If evolutionary success is determined by how many offspring we have, the men win hands down.

REALResearch > Gender differences in expectations about chastity have been found throughout the world. South Asian, African, Middle Eastern and Latino/a cultures have been found to place a high value on female, but not male, chastity (MAHALINGAM, 2007).

SOCIAL LEARNING THEORY:
LEARNING FROM OUR ENVIRONMENT

Social learning theory suggests that we learn gender roles from our environment, from the same system of rewards and punishments that we learn our other social roles. For example, research shows that many parents commonly reward gender-appropriate behavior and disapprove of (or even punish) gender-inappropriate behavior. Telling a boy sternly not to cry "like a girl," approving a girl's use of makeup, taking a Barbie away from a boy and handing him Spider-Man, making girls help with cooking and cleaning and boys take out the trash—these little, everyday actions build into powerful messages about gender.

Children learn to model their behavior after the same-gender parent to win parental approval. They may learn about gender-appropriate behavior from parents even if they are too young to perform the actions themselves; for example, they see that Mommy does the sewing, whereas Daddy fixes the car. Children also see

models of the "appropriate" ways for their genders to behave in their books, on television, and when interacting with others. Even the structure of our language conveys gender attitudes about things, such as the dominant position of the male; for example, the use of male words to include men and women (using "chairman" or "mankind" to refer to both men and women) or the differentiation between Miss and Mrs. to indicate whether a woman is married. However, people are trying to amend these inequalities today, as evidenced by the growing acceptance of words such as "chairperson" and "humankind," and the title "Ms."

COGNITIVE DEVELOPMENT THEORY:
AGE-STATE LEARNING

Cognitive development theory assumes that all children go through a universal pattern of development, and there really is not much parents can do to alter it. As the child's brain matures and grows, he or she develops new abilities and concerns; at each stage, his or her understanding of gender changes in predictable ways. This theory follows the ideas of Piaget (1951), the child development theorist who suggested that social attitudes in children are mediated through their processes of cognitive development. In other words, children can process only a certain kind and amount of information at each developmental stage.

As children begin to be able to recognize the physical differences between girls and boys and then to categorize themselves as one or the other, they look for information about their genders. Around the ages of 2 to 5, they form strict stereotypes of gender based on their observed differences—men are bigger and stronger and are seen in aggressive roles like policeman and superhero; women tend to be associated with motherhood through their physicality (e.g., the child asks what the mother's breasts are and is told they are used to feed children) and through women's social roles of nurturing and emotional expressiveness. These "physicalistic" thought patterns are universal in young children and are organized around ideas of gender.

As the child matures, he or she becomes more aware that gender roles are, to some degree, social and arbitrary, and cognitive development theory predicts therefore that rigid gender role behavior should decrease after about the age of 7 or 8. So cognitive development theory predicts what set of gender attitudes should appear at different ages; however, the research is still contradictory on whether its predictions are correct (see Albert & Porter, 1988).

Newer theories of gender role development try to combine social learning theory and cognitive development theory, to address weaknesses in both. Cognitive development theory neglects social factors and differences in the ways different groups raise children. On the other hand, social learning theory neglects a child's age-related ability to understand and assimilate gender models and portrays the child as too passive; in social learning theory, the child seems to accept whatever models of behavior are offered without passing them through his or her own thought processes.

GENDER SCHEMA THEORY:
OUR CULTURAL MAPS

Sandra Bem's (1974, 1977, 1981) theory is a good example of a theory that tries to overcome the difficulties posed by the other theories. According to Bem, children (and, for that matter, all of us) think according to **schemas** (SKI-muz), which are cognitive mechanisms that organize our world. These schemas develop over time and are universal, like the stages in cognitive development theory; the difference lies in Bem's assertion that the contents of schemas are determined by the culture. Schemas are like maps in our heads that direct our thought processes.

Bem suggests that one schema we all have is a **gender schema,** which organizes our thinking about gender. From the moment we are born, information about gender is continuously presented to us by our parents, relatives, teachers, peers, television, movies, advertising, and the like. We absorb the more obvious information about sexual anatomy, "male" and "female" types of work and activities, and gender-linked personality traits. However, society also attributes gender to things as abstract as shapes (rounded, soft shapes are often described as "feminine," and sharp, angular shapes as "masculine") and even our drinks (champagne is seen as more feminine, whereas beer is seen as more masculine; Crawford et al., 2004).

Gender schemas are powerful in our culture. When we first meet a man, we immediately use our masculine gender schema and begin our relationship with an already-established series of beliefs about him. For example, we may believe that men are strong or assertive. Our gender schema is more powerful than other schemas and is used more often, Bem argues, because our culture puts so much emphasis on gender and gender differences. This is where she parts company with cognitive development theorists, who argue that gender is important to children because of their naturally physicalistic ways of thinking.

The gender schema becomes so ingrained that we do not even realize its power. For example, some people so stereotype gender concepts that it would never occur to them to say, "My, how strong you are becoming!" to a little girl, whereas they say it easily to a little boy. Bem argues that "strong" as a feminine trait does not exist in the female schema for many people, so they rarely invoke the term "strong" to refer to women.

REALResearch   Playing with "masculine" rather than "feminine" toys and games has been found to be positively related to a woman's future participation in college athletics (GIULIANO ET AL., 2000).

schema
A cognitive mechanism that helps to organize our world.

gender schema
A cognitive mechanism that helps us to understand gender.

sex typing
Cognitive thinking patterns that divide the world into male and female categories and suggest the appropriate behaviors, thoughts, actions, professions, and emotions for each.

review questions

1 Explain how gender role socialization occurs in children.

2 Describe the differences among the evolutionary, social learning, and cognitive development theories.

3 Explain how one's development of a "gender schema" influences his or her view of gender. Give examples to support your answer.

Varieties of Gender

Culture and social structure interact to create **sex typing,** a way of thinking that splits the world into two basic categories—male and female—and suggests that most behaviors, thoughts, actions, professions, emotions, and so on fit one gender more than the other (Liben & Bigler, 2002; Maccoby, 2002). Although there are fewer sex-typed assignments and attitudes today than there were years ago, sex typing still exists.

These stereotypes become so basic to our way of thinking that we do not even realize the powerful hold they have over our conceptions of the world. Many cultures build their entire worldviews around masculinity and femininity. Some cultures have taken these ideas and created models of the universe based on masculine and feminine traits, such as the Chinese concept of yin and yang, which we discussed in Chapter 1.

Because gender is socially constructed, societies decide how gender will be defined and what it will mean. J. E. Williams and Best (1994) collected data about masculinity and femininity in 30 countries and found that throughout the world, people largely agree on gender role stereotypes. In a study of 37 countries, Buss (1994) found that women and men value different qualities in each other. Women place a higher value on the qualities of being "good financial prospects" and "ambitious and industrious" for their mates, whereas men place a higher value on physical attractiveness. We discuss this study more in Chapter 7 (see the Human Sexuality in a Diverse World feature "Good Looks or a Good Prospect? What Do You Want in a Partner?" on page 179).

View in Video

"Inside, I just knew I was a boy."
—Female-to-Male Transsexual: Teo
To view go to CengageNOW at www.cengage.com/login

In American society, conceptions of "masculinity" and "femininity" have been seen as mutually exclusive; that is, a person who is feminine cannot also be masculine and vice versa (Spence, 1984). However, research has shown that masculinity and femininity are independent traits that can exist in people separately (Bem, 1977; Spence, 1984). Bem (1974) suggests that this can lead to four types of personalities: those high in masculinity and low in femininity, those high in femininity and low in masculinity, those low in both ("undifferentiated"), and those high in both ("androgynous"). Such categories may challenge traditional thinking about gender. So may examples of ambiguous gender categories, such as transsexualism or asexuality, which we discuss later in this chapter. In fact, the more one examines the categories of gender that really exist in the social world, the clearer it becomes that gender is more complicated than just splitting the world into male and female.

> *. . . masculinity and femininity are **independent traits** that can exist in people separately.*

MASCULINITY:
THE HUNTER

From the moment of a baby's birth, almost every society has different expectations of its males and females. In many societies, men must go through trials or rights of passage in which they earn their right to be men; few societies have such trials for women.

For example, the !Kung bushmen have a "rite of the first kill" that is performed twice for each boy—once after he kills his first large male animal and once after he kills his first large female animal (Collier & Rosaldo, 1981). During the ceremony, a gash is cut in the boy's chest and filled with a magical substance that is supposed to keep the boy from being lazy. Hunting prowess is ritually connected with marriage, and men acquire wives by demonstrating their ability at the hunt (Lewin, 1988). For example, a boy may not marry until he goes through the rite of first kill, and, at the wedding, he must present a large animal he has killed to his bride's parents. Even the language of killing and marrying is linked; !Kung myths and games equate marriage with hunting and talk of men "chasing," "killing," and "eating" women just as they do animals.

In American society, men are often judged by their "prowess" in business, with successful men receiving society's admiration. Although in many societies men tend to have privileges that women do not, and despite the fact that male traits in many societies are valued more than female traits (which we discuss in further detail soon), it is not easy for men to live up to the strong social demands of being male in a changing society.

Great contradictions are inherent in the contemporary masculine role: the man is supposed to be the provider and yet is not supposed to live entirely for his work; he is often judged by his sexual successes and yet is not supposed to see women as sexual objects to be conquered; he is supposed to be a strong, stable force

View in Video

"I've come to accept this as an important part of my existence."

—*Transgendered: Liz*
To view go to CengageNOW at www. cengage.com/login

yet not cut his emotions off from his loved ones; and he is never supposed to be scared, inadequate, sexually inexperienced, or financially dependent on a woman.

Men in all societies live with these types of gender role contradictions. In some cases, men simplify their lives by exaggerating the "macho" side of society's expectations and becoming hypermasculine males (Farr et al., 2004). To these macho men, violence is manly, danger is exciting, and sexuality must be pursued callously.

Another side of the masculine way of being must also be addressed, however. David Gilmore (1990) notes that men often must go through trials to prove their masculinity, except in those few societies in which people are totally free of predators and enemies and food is plentiful. In those societies, there is no stress on proving "manhood" and little pressure to emphasize differences between men and women. Gilmore concludes that in most societies masculine socialization prepares men to adopt the role of safeguarding the group's survival, to be willing to give their own lives in the hunt or in war to ensure the group's future by protecting the women's ability to reproduce. Gilmore's point is that men are not concerned with being macho as an end in itself but are concerned with the ultimate welfare of society. In fact, Gilmore argues, men are as much nurturers as women, concerned with society's weaker and more helpless members, willing to give their energy and even their lives for the greater social good.

Although masculinity has its privileges, it has its downside, too. Men do not live as long as women, in part because of the demands of the male role. For example, men are more likely to die of stress-related illnesses, including lung cancer (men smoke more than women), motor vehicle accidents (men drive more than women, often because of work), suicide (women attempt suicide more often, but men are more successful at actually killing themselves), other accidents (men do more dangerous work than women), and cirrhosis of the liver (there are more male alcoholics and drug addicts; Courtenay, 2000; D. R. Nicholas, 2000). Men also die more often in wars. School-age boys are twice as likely as girls to be labeled as "learning disabled" (Martin et al., 2008).

In fact, with all the attention on how gender stereotypes harm women, men are equally the victims of society's expectations. Male stereotypes tend to be narrower than female stereotypes, and men who want to conform to society's ideas of gender have less flexibility in their behavior than women (Lips, 2008).

For example, it is still unacceptable for men to cry in public except in the most extreme circumstances. Crying is the body's natural response to being upset. Boys are taught not to cry, but that is difficult when they are emotionally moved; so they stop allowing themselves to be moved emotionally—and then are criticized for not letting their emotions show. Interestingly, when men do cry, their emotions are often seen as more genuine than a woman's (Kallen, 1998). This is probably because a behavior that is inconsistent with a gender stereotype is often seen as more legitimate and "real."

Today men are often judged by how well they do at work, whereas women are often judged by how pretty and thin they are.

FEMININITY:
THE NURTURER

When someone says, "She is a very feminine woman," what image comes to mind? The president of a corporation? A woman in a frilly pink dress? A soldier carrying her gear? In American culture, we associate femininity with qualities such as beauty, softness, empathy, concern, and modesty. In fact, in almost every culture, femininity is defined by being the opposite of masculinity.

On the other hand, ideas of femininity are not static. Sheila Rothman (1978) has argued that modern American society has gone through a number of basic conceptions of what "womanhood" (and, by extension, femininity) should be. For example, the 19th century emphasized the value of "virtuous womanhood," whereby women instilled "morality" in society by starting women's clubs that brought women together and eventually led to the battling of perceived social ills. The Women's Christian Temperance Union, for example, started a movement to ban alcohol that eventually succeeded.

By the early part of the 20th century, the concept of the ideal woman shifted to what Rothman calls "educated motherhood," whereby the woman was supposed to learn all the new, sophisticated theories of child rearing and was to shift her attention to the needs of children and family. Over the next few decades, the woman's role was redefined as a "wife-companion," and she was supposed to redirect her energy away from her children and toward being a sexual companion for her husband. Finally, Rothman argues, the 1960s began the era of "woman as person," in which a woman began to be seen as autonomous and competent and able to decide the nature of her own role in life independent of gender expectations.

View in Video

"I didn't understand that I wasn't a girl."
—Male-to-Female Transsexual: Rachel
To view go to CengageNOW at www.cengage.com/login

Among feminist scholars, ideological battles rage about the meaning of being a woman in today's society. For example, many have faulted feminism for its attitude, at least until recently, that women who choose to stay in the home and raise children are not fulfilling their potential. Yet women with young children who do work often report feelings of guilt about not being with their children (Crittenden, 2001; Lerner, 1998). Many argue that the idea of femininity itself is an attempt to mold women in ways that are determined by men.

For example, the pressure on women to stay thin, to try to appear younger than they are, and to try to appear as beautiful as possible can be seen as reflections of male power (Wolf, 1991). Sexually, as well, women are supposed to conform to feminine stereotypes and be passive, naïve, and inexperienced. The media reinforce the ideals of feminine beauty, and the pressures on women to conform to these ideals lead to eating disorders and the surge in cosmetic surgery (Wolf, 1991). We talk more about the powerful influences of the media in Chapter 18.

The messages a woman receives from modern North American culture are contradictory; she needs a job for fulfillment, but should be home with her children; she is more than her looks, but she had better wear makeup and stay thin; she has every opportunity men have, but only on men's terms. Although femininity has moved away from classic portrayals of women as docile and subservient to men, the pressures are still strong to appeal to those outdated stereotypes.

ANDROGYNY:
FEMININE AND MASCULINE

Up until the 1970s, masculinity and femininity were thought to be on the same continuum. The more masculine you were, the less feminine you were, and vice versa. However, in the 1970s, researchers challenged this notion by suggesting that masculinity and femininity were two separate dimensions and a person could be high or low on both dimensions.

The breakdown of traditional stereotypes about gender has refocused attention on the idea of **androgyny.** Bem (1977), as we mentioned earlier, suggested that people have different combinations of masculine and feminine traits. She considers those who have a high score on both masculinity and femininity to be androgynous. Androgyny, according to Bem, allows greater flexibility in behavior because people have a greater repertoire of possible reactions to a situation. Bem (1974, 1977, 1981) has tried to show that androgynous individuals can display "masculine" traits (such as independence) and "feminine" traits (such as playfulness with a kitten) when situations call for them.

androgyny
Having high levels of both masculine and feminine characteristics.

table 4.4

Transgendered Behaviors

Term	Definition
Female impersonator	A role played by a professional male actor who dresses in women's clothing for a variety of reasons
Drag queens and kings	A drag queen is a role played by a professional actor, typically a gay man, who dresses in flamboyant women's clothing to perform for a variety of reasons; a drag king is a professional female actor who dresses in men's clothing to perform
Gender dysphoric	Having one's gender identity be inconsistent with one's biological sex
Cross-dresser	Living full or part time in the other gender's role and deriving psychosocial comfort in doing so
Transgendered	Engaging in both masculine and feminine behaviors, dress, and/or stereotypic behaviors
Transvestite	Dressing in the clothing of the other gender and deriving sexual pleasure from doing so
Transyouth	A youth who experiences transgenderism or transsexualism
Fetishistic transvestite	Wearing the clothing of the other sex as the preferred or exclusive method of sexual arousal or orgasm
Transsexual	Feeling trapped in the body of the wrong gender; sometimes this will lead to sexual reassignment surgery

REALResearch > To show commitment to gender equality, Norwegian law required **40%** of the country's corporate board seats to be filled by women in 2008 (LAROI & WIGGLESWORTH, 2007). Companies that did not comply risked being shut down by the government. As of 2008, Norway had the highest ratio of female directors worldwide and more women than men in government. Compare this to the United States, where women held about **15%** of board seats in 2007.

Because of Bem's early research on masculinity, femininity, and androgyny, some have suggested that androgyny was a desirable state and androgynous attitudes were a solution to the tension between the sexes. There has been more research on gender roles and androgyny since, and androgyny may not be the answer to the world's gender problems. Suggesting that people should combine aspects of masculinity and femininity may simply reinforce and retain outdated ideas of gender.

Later research questioned whether the masculine and feminine traits that Bem used were still valid nearly 30 years later. One study found that although 18 of 20 feminine traits still qualified as feminine, only 8 of 20 masculine traits qualified as masculine (Auster & Ohm, 2000). Traits originally associated with masculin-

ity, such as analytical, individualistic, competitive, self-sufficient, risk-taking, and defends own beliefs, were no longer viewed as strictly masculine traits. These findings reflect recent societal changes that render some masculine traits desirable for both men and women.

TRANSGENDERISM: LIVING AS THE OTHER SEX

Since 2000, there has been an active increase in attention paid to **transgenderism.** The transgendered community includes those who live full or part time in the other gender's role, **transsexuals,** and **transvestites** (we talk more about transvestites in Chapter 16. See Table 4.4 for more information about transgendered groups). Some professional actors, such as **drag queens** or **female impersonators,** may or may not be transgendered.

A transgendered person is often happy as the biological sex in which he or she was born, yet enjoys dressing up and acting like the other sex (e.g., a man who works during the day as a man and dresses and acts like a man, but who goes home and puts on women's clothing and acts like a woman at night). Although a transvestite often derives sexual pleasure from dressing as a member of the other sex, the majority of transgendered men and women do so for psychosocial pleasure rather than sexual pleasure. Many transgendered people report that they feel more "relaxed" and "at peace" while cross-dressed (Author's files).

Some of the earliest work on transgenderism was done by Magnus Hirschfeld (see Chapter 2). Hirschfeld wrote a book in 1910 called *The Transvestites: An Investigation of the Erotic Desire to Cross Dress.* In this book Hirschfeld explained that there were men and women who thought, felt, or acted like the other sex. John Money, whom we discussed earlier

transgenderism
Living full or part time in the other gender's role and deriving psychosocial comfort in doing so.

transsexual
A person who feels he or she is trapped in the body of the wrong gender.

transvestite
A person who dresses in the clothing of the other gender and derives sexual pleasure from doing so.

drag queen
A professional actor, typically a gay man, who, for a variety of reasons, performs in flamboyant women's clothing.

female impersonator
A professional male actor who dresses in women's clothing for a variety of reasons.

Billy Tipton was a well-known jazz musician who was discovered to be a woman when he died in 1989.

in this chapter, suggested that the majority of people are "gender congruent," which means that their biological sex, gender identity, and gender behaviors are all in sync and there is no transgender behavior (Money, 1955). However, it is estimated that 10% to 15% of the population does not conform to prescribed gender roles (V. L. Bullough, 2001).

At some points in history, transgendered behavior was chosen out of necessity. Billy Tipton (1914–1989), a well-known jazz musician, was discovered to be a female when he died in 1989 (Middlebrook, 1999). He was married to a woman and was the father of three adopted boys who did not learn of his biological gender until after his death. It is believed that Dorothy Tipton changed herself into Billy Tipton sometime around 1934 for professional reasons. Dorothy had been having trouble being taken seriously as a musician and felt that if she were a man, she would have more opportunities to prove herself. Although many people believed that Tipton pretended to be a man out of necessity, some believe that she really had a desire to become a man and was unhappy being a woman.

TRANSSEXUALISM: WHEN GENDER AND BIOLOGY DON'T AGREE

Transsexualism has profound implications for our conceptions of gender categories. In the Western world, we tend to think of gender in terms of biology; if you have XX chromosomes and female genitalia, you are female, and if you have XY chromosomes and male genitalia, you are male. This is not universally true, however. A male transsexual is convinced that he is really a female "trapped" in a man's body. Another way to put it is that a transsexual's gender identity is inconsistent with his or her biological sex. This is called **gender dysphoria** (dis-FOR-ee-uh). Overall, more males than females experience gender dysphoria, although the exact degree of difference in men and women is in dispute (H. Bower, 2001).

Some cases of transsexualism have received great publicity. In 1952, George Jorgensen, a retired Marine, went to Denmark to have his genitals surgically altered to resemble those of a female. George changed his name to Christine, went public, and became the first highly publicized case of a transsexual who underwent **sex reassignment surgery (SRS)**. Jorgensen desired to be a girl

from an early age, avoided rough sports, and was a small, frail child with underdeveloped male genitals (Jorgensen, 1967). Jorgensen's story is typical of other transsexuals, who knew from an early age that they were somehow different.

Another famous case was that of Richard Raskind, an eye doctor and tennis player, who had SRS and then tried to play in a professional women's tennis tournament as Renée Richards. When it was discovered that she was a genetic male, Richards was barred from playing on the women's tennis tour.

More recently, in the early 1990s, the case of Barry Cossey received much publicity. Cossey, who was passing as a female showgirl by age 17, eventually underwent sex reassignment surgery, and became known as "Tula." For a long time, Cossey kept her sex change a secret and went on to become a well-known model, even appearing in bathing suit and brassiere advertisements. After she received a role in the James Bond spy thriller *For Your Eyes Only* (in which she appeared primarily in a skimpy bathing suit), a British tabloid uncovered her past and announced: "James Bond Girl Was a Boy!" Cossey then wrote an autobiography and began appearing on the talk-show circuit as a crusader for the rights of transsexuals. She even appeared fully nude in *Playboy* in 1991.[1]

In the past few years there has been more acceptance for transsexualism in the United States, and this may be due, in part, to an increasingly positive depiction of transsexualism in the media. Television shows such as *Law & Order, Nip/Tuck, Ugly Betty,* and *CSI* have all had transsexual characters in their shows. Outside the

---

[1] It should be noted that Cossey was born with a chromosomal abnormality, XXXY chromosomes, compared with XX for a normal female and XY for a normal male. In most cases of transsexualism, however, no abnormal chromosomes are found.

transsexualism
The condition of feeling trapped in the body of the wrong gender.

gender dysphoria
A condition in which one's gender identity is inconsistent with one's biological sex.

sex reassignment surgery (SRS)
Anatomical surgery to change genitalia on a transsexual; also referred to as gender reassignment.

United States, transsexual men and women experience varying degrees of acceptance. Whereas Iran officially recognized transsexualism in the mid-1980s and began allowing transsexuals to undergo SRS shortly after (Harrison, 2005), Japan has been more reluctant to deal with issues of gender dysphoria. Sex reassignment surgery was not approved in Japan until 1996 (Ako et al., 2001; Matsubara, 2001).

Most transsexuals report a lifelong desire to be a member of the other sex. The desire is often temporarily satisfied by cross-dressing, but, unlike transgenderists, transsexuals do not find cross-dressing satisfying in itself. The personal accounts of transsexuals are usually tales of suffering and confusion over who they are and what gender they belong to, and therapy is useful only in establishing for them that they do, in fact, deeply believe themselves to be emotionally and psychologically of the other sex. Sex reassignment surgery was developed to help bring transsexuals' biology into line with their inner lives.

The process of seeking gender reassignment is long and complicated. The first step is psychological counseling to confirm that the individual is truly gender dysphoric; one cannot simply see a doctor and ask for a sex change. The next step is to live as a member of the other sex, and if a person does so successfully for a designated period, hormones are then administered to masculinize or feminize his or her appearance. Finally, SRS is performed. It may take two or more surgeries to complete the transition.

For male-to-female (MtoF or M2F) transsexuals, the scrotum and testicles are removed. The penis is removed, but the penile skin, with all its sexually sensitive nerve endings, remains attached. A **vaginoplasty** involves using this skin to form the inside of the

vaginoplasty
A transgender operation in which a vagina is artificially constructed.

drag king
A professional actor, who, for a variety of reasons, performs in men's clothing.

SEX IN REAL LIFE

Gender Variations

Perhaps one day gender will be viewed with more fluidity, allowing us to not be quickly categorized into a male or female box.

In the Western world, there are typically only two sexes acknowledged—male and female (Lang & Kuhnle, 2008). This binary gender model is the foundation on which transgender oppression is built (Burdge, 2007). Many men and women deviate from traditional gender norms, but not all identify as transgender (Burdge, 2007). Although many children display gender-variant behavior as children, the majority outgrow these behaviors as they age. In fact, it is estimated that only 15% of these children will continue to have gender identity issues into adulthood (Rosenberg, 2007).

The transgender community typically includes cross-dressers, transvestites, transsexuals, intersex individuals (those born with ambiguous genitals), gender-benders, gender "queers," "butch dyke" lesbians, and **drag kings** and queens. The National Center for Transgender Equality estimates that between 750,000 and 3 million Americans consider themselves to be transgendered (Rosenberg, 2007). The actual number of transgendered people is unknown, because many are not comfortable exposing their true gender identity.

Transgendered youth have often been given the diagnosis of "gender identity disorder," which first appeared in the *Diagnostic and Statistical Manual of Mental Disorders* in 1980 (American Psychiatric Association, 2000). Many researchers today believe that this diagnosis was built on gender stereotypes and implies that these children need to be fixed by aligning their internal sense of gender with their biological sex. Instead of pathologizing these individuals, it might be better to teach them to accept their gender-variant selves (Burdge, 2007).

Transgendered youth often experience depression and low-self-esteem, and some may run away from home to live on the streets (Burgess, 1999). They may also experience social repression, including harassment, physical and sexual abuse, discrimination, and social and family rejection for violating gender categories (Burdge, 2007). Those who are rejected by their family are 4 times more likely to use drugs and attempt suicide (Adriano, 2007).

Today transgendered or questioning youth may be offered hormone blockers to delay puberty and the development of secondary sex characteristics (James, 2008). A growing number of U.S. physicians today are prescribing these hormone blockers to transyouth before the onset of puberty (James, 2008). Delaying puberty can "buy time" for a transyouth to think about his or her gender.

Outside of the United States, these drugs are being used with more frequency. For example, German youths can be given hormone-blocking treatments as young as age 12 years. In the Netherlands, a child must meet certain criteria of wanting to be the other sex at an early age (Brill & Schreirer, 2007). He or she must undergo psychiatric evaluation by multiple experts and is then given a 2-year trial of puberty-delaying drugs.

Throughout this chapter, we explore how traditional gender assignment relies on assumptions about physical anatomy and social behaviors. Perhaps one day gender will be viewed with more fluidity, allowing us not to be quickly categorized into a male or female box.

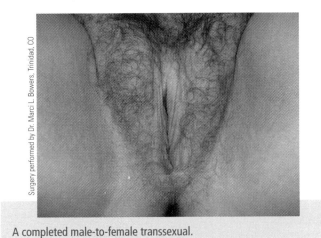

A completed male-to-female transsexual.

A completed female-to-male transsexual.

vagina, which is constructed along with a set of labial lips to simulate female genitalia as closely as possible (Perovic et al., 2005). If desired, silicone implants create breasts. MtoF transsexuals can engage in sexual intercourse as females and achieve orgasm. Many also report that their lovers cannot tell they have had SRS.

Female-to-male (FtoM or F2M) transsexuals have a number of choices to make. A **phalloplasty** can be done, which involves constructing an artificial penis from abdominal skin. Phalloplasty is a difficult procedure and, as a result, is becoming less popular. Penises made from phalloplasty often don't look real, and they cannot achieve a natural erection, so penile implants of some kind are usually used (we discuss these implants more in Chapter 14). A more popular option today is a clitoral release procedure called **metoidioplasty** (Perovic & Djordjevic, 2003). FtoM transsexuals who undergo testosterone therapy typically experience clitoris elongation anywhere from one to three inches in length. A metoidioplasty releases the enlarged clitoris, allowing it to hang like a natural penis.

A **scrotoplasty** can also be done for both of these procedures. This procedure forms a scrotum out of the labia, into which prosthetic testicles can be placed. Overall a metoidioplasty is a simpler procedure than the phalloplasty, which explains its increasing popularity. It also has fewer complications, takes less time, and is less expensive (e.g., a metoidioplasty takes about 1–2 hours and costs about $15,000, whereas a phalloplasty can take 8 hours and

cost approximately $65,000). Overall, the results of female-to-male SRS are rarely as good as that of male-to-female.

In general, SRS has been relatively controversial, with some studies showing healthy postoperative functioning (DeCuypere et al., 2005; Lawrence, 2006), and others showing no alleviation of the psychological suffering that many male and female transsexuals feel (Newfield et al., 2006; Olsson & Möller, 2006). Some clinics have stopped performing transsexual surgery altogether. However, some people seeking sex reassignment have longed for years to bring their bodies into line with their sense of gender identity, and SRS is their ultimate goal. As surgical techniques improve, some SRS problems may be resolved.

THIRD GENDERS: OTHER CULTURES, OTHER OPTIONS

Transsexuals stretch our usual concepts of gender by suggesting that there can be a fundamental and irreconcilable break between our psychological and biological genders. However, some cultures challenge our notions and even have a gender category that is neither male nor female—a third gender.

Many traditional Native American societies had a category of not-men/not-women, known as **berdaches.** The berdache (or "two-spirit") was usually (but not always) a biological male who was effeminate or androgynous in behavior and who took on the social role of female (Blackwood, 1994; W. L. Williams, 1986). The berdache often married a male Native American (and adopted

WHAT DO YOU WANT TO KNOW ?

It seems like there has been very little written over the years about the transgendered experience. Is it true that transgendered men and women were too afraid to write articles or research studies?
Historically, the transgendered community has been relatively quiet in terms of actively publishing research. Before 1990, transgendered men and women made few research contributions to the professional literature. Transsexuals were even quieter—in fact, not one transsexual authored a research study or textbook before 1990 (Denny & Wiederman, 2004). Even so, we have learned much about the transgendered experience through various autobiographies. It is estimated that more than 100 such autobiographies were published from 1952 to 2000 (Denny & Wiederman, 2004). Today the transgendered community is actively engaged in research and continues to contribute rich autobiographies that help us more fully understand the transgendered experience.

phalloplasty
A transgender operation in which a penis is artificially constructed.

metoidioplasty
A clitoral release procedure used in FtoM transsexuals in which the enlarged clitoris is released from its position and moved forward to more closely resemble the position of a penis. In some cases, the urethra is moved to end at the tip of the clitoris.

scrotoplasty
A transgender operation in which a scrotum is made; if desired, silicone implants can be placed in the scrotum.

berdache
A third gender in Native American culture in which an individual takes on the social role of the other gender; also referred to as a "two-spirit."

children), although not all married or engaged in sexual behavior with males. Berdachism was considered a vocation, like being a hunter or warrior, which was communicated to certain boys in their first adult vision. In all social functions, the berdache was treated as a female. The berdache held a respected, sacred position in society and was believed to have special powers.

Biologically female berdaches also lived in Native American tribes. Female berdaches began showing interest in boys' activities and games during childhood (Blackwood, 1984). Adults, recognizing this desire, would teach the girls the same skills the boys were learning. (In one tribe, a family with all girl children might select one daughter to be their "son," tying dried bear ovaries to her belt to prevent conception!)

These females were initiated into puberty as men, and thereafter they were essentially considered men. They hunted and trapped, fought in battle, and performed male ceremonial tasks. Among the Alaskan Ingalik, for example, these biological women would even participate in nude, men-only sweat baths, and the men would ignore the female genitalia and treat the berdache as a man. The female berdache could marry a woman, although the unions remained childless, and the berdache would perform the appropriate rituals when her partner menstruated but would ignore her own menses. Female berdaches became prominent members of some Native American societies, and, in at least one case, a female berdache became chief of the tribe (Whitehead, 1981).

Other cultures have similar roles. The Persian Gulf country of Oman has a class of biological males called the *xani-th* (Wikan, 1977). The *xani-th* are exempt from the strict Islamic rules that restrict men's interaction with women, because they are not considered men. They sit with females at weddings and may see the bride's face; they may not sit with men in public nor do tasks reserved for men. Yet the *xani-th* are not considered females either; for example, they retain men's names.

Another important example are the *hijra* of India. The hijra are men who undergo ritual castration in which all or part of their genitals are removed, and they are believed to have special powers to curse or bless male children. *Hijra* dress as women, although they do not really try to "pass" as women; their mannerisms are exaggerated, and some even sport facial hair. In India, the *hijra* are considered neither men nor women but inhabit a unique third social gender (Nanda, 2001).

In Thailand, there is a group of people called the *kathoey*, who are very similar to Oman's *xani-th*. Two other examples are the *ai-kane* of native Hawaii, who were attached to the court of the chiefs and served sexual, social, and political functions (Morris, 1990), and the *mahu* of Tahiti (Herdt, 1990). The belief in these societies that it is neither obvious nor natural that there are only two genders should make us carefully reconsider our own assumptions about gender.

ASEXUALISM: THE GENETICS BUT NOT THE SEX

A final type of gender category is **asexuality.** On occasion, usually because of a mother's hormone use during pregnancy, a child is born without sexual organs of any kind. This means that the child has no ovaries, uterus, or vagina; has no penis or testicles; and usually has only a bladder and a urethra ending in an aperture for the elimination of urine. Although such a child has a genetic gender (that is, has XX or XY chromosomes), the child has no biological gender. Most are assigned a gender in childhood, are given hormones, and live as male or female.

In 2001, the Asexual Visibility and Education Network (AVEN) was founded to facilitate the growth of the online asexual community and help build acceptance and discussion of these issues (see Chapter Resources for more information). Over the last few years, a growing movement in support of asexuality has been building, helping to develop programs for asexuals and foster research (Prause & Graham, 2007). Today AVEN is the world's largest asexual community.

asexuality
Often refers to the lack of sexual desire but can also refer to a lack of maleness or femaleness.

WHAT DO YOU WANT TO KNOW ?

I don't think there anything wrong with letting boys and girls act like boys and girls! Why try to discourage boys from playing with guns and girls with dolls? Everyone I know grew up that way, and they are OK.

The same people who believe that they "grew up OK" are often the first to complain about the nature of gender relations in the United States. Perhaps we should not forbid boys from ever playing with toy guns (anyway, they would probably just make other toys into guns) or forbid girls to play with dolls, but trying to encourage children to appreciate the activities of the other sex can only help matters. Research has found that parents allow their girls more flexibility in toy choices, whereas they limit the toys that boys play with mainly to masculine toys (Wood et al., 2002).

review questions

1 Describe the stereotypic views of masculinity, and identify the risks associated with these stereotypes.

2 Describe the stereotypic views of masculinity, and identify the risks associated with these stereotypes.

3 Define androgyny, and give one example of androgynous behavior.

4 Differentiate among transgenderism, transsexualism, gender dysphoria, third genders, and asexuality.

Gender Role Socialization
From Infancy Through Old Age

Socialization into gender roles begins at birth and nowadays may begin even before! Parents can now know months before birth whether the fetus is a boy or a girl and can begin to prepare accordingly. Parents even speak to the unborn child—a mother simply by talking and the father by putting his mouth close to the mother's belly—and communicate ideas about their "little boy" or "little girl." In a real sense, then, these parents may begin trying to communicate gender-specific messages before the child is even born (whether the child actually is influenced by these sounds diffusing into the womb is, of course, another question). Parents awaiting the birth of a child are filled with gender expectations, stereotypes, and desires.

SEX IN REAL LIFE

Play Like a Boy! Play Like a Girl!

Toys have been found to be gender stereotyped for all ages, with the exception of infant and toddler toys.

For a child, playing is not a game, it is serious business. Play is what teaches the child physical coordination, hand–eye coordination, the rules of gravity and cause and effect, and other physical and motor skills. As a child matures, playing with peers also teaches lessons of social interaction, sharing, winning and losing, and compromise. Strong gender messages are also typically communicated to children during play, even in infancy.

Toys are gendered, with some toys aimed at boys and some at girls. Walk through a toy store one day. Even though the aisles may not be marked "for boys" and "for girls," it is very clear for which gender an aisle is intended. Boys' toys are often geared toward aggression and destruction, whereas girls' toys are often pink and geared toward domestic life and appearance. Toys have been found to be gender stereotyped for all ages, with the exception of infant and toddler toys (Campenni, 1999).

Studies have found that boys are more rigidly gender typed in their toy play than girls and are often reluctant to interact with feminine toys (V. A. Green et al., 2004). Some of this has been found to be affected by parental influence.

Parents often encourage their children not to choose gender-inappropriate toy choices—more so for their boys than girls. They have also been found to spend more time using masculine toys when playing with boys and have much more flexibility in toys when playing with girls (E. Wood et al., 2002). Boys may be punished for playing with toys intended for girls, whereas girls may be encouraged or even rewarded for cross-gender toy preferences (Pike & Jennings, 2005).

Gender differences in pretend play have also been found. Girls have been found to take on more domestic roles with themes relating to family and home, and boys take on more roles of power, such as superheroes or villains with themes of danger and adventure (Gleason, 2005). Parental differences in acceptance of pretend play have also been found, with mothers holding more positive attitudes toward pretend play overall than fathers (Gleason, 2005).

Gender-stereotyped toy commercials also have been found to influence children. One study found that the gender of the model in a commercial influenced for which gender a child thought the toy was intended (Pike & Jennings, 2005). A girl playing with a doll meant the toy was only for girls, whereas a toy being played with by girls and boys indicated it was for both.

Similar Patterns

Almost every culture has its own gender-appropriate toys. In Russia, the dolls available to the average child are bulky and have simple, bland clothes, but they also have pink or blue hair to indicate whether they are girl or boy dolls. Although Barbie dolls dominate the Russian toy markets, in 2002, the Russian Ministry of Education suggested banning them because they were thought to "awaken sexual impulses in the minds of young girls" (Walsh, 2002). Toys that fostered aggression were also put on the banned list. Even so, many of these toys are still available today.

© Radius Images/Alamy

Children learn much of their gender role behavior from modeling.

CHILDHOOD:
LEARNING BY PLAYING

From the moment parents find out the sex of their baby, a child's life is largely defined by his or her gender. From the baby's name, to how he or she is dressed, to how his or her room is decorated, gender suffuses the newborn's life. Not only do parents construct different environments for boys and girls from birth, they tend to treat them differently as well.

As early as age 2, **modeling behavior** begins to emerge, and children begin to realize that objects and activities are appropriate to specific genders. The rules that a child develops at this point are not flexible but universal; to the child, only women can wear skirts, and only men can shave their face. In fact, cross-gender humor is very funny to young children; a television program that shows a man dressed up in a woman's clothes or a woman who appears on TV sporting a mustache will elicit bursts of laughter. As the child begins to show more complex behaviors, he or she realizes that there are often societal restrictions on acceptable behaviors. Children watch their parents' behavior and learn what are acceptable behaviors for males and females.

Overall, boys are treated more harshly than girls when they adopt cross-gender characteristics (Sandnabba & Ahlberg, 1999). Children who have a strong and persistent identification with the other sex or the gender role of the other sex and are uncomfortable with their own biological sex or gender role may be diagnosed with a **gender-identity disorder.** Overall, the prevalence of gender-identity disorder ranges from .003% to 3% in boys and .001% to 1.5% in girls (Bartlett et al., 2000).

Early in childhood, gender segregation in play, also known as **homosocial play,** begins. Children tend to gravitate to same-sex friends, and as early as 2.5 to 3 years old, children play more actively and more interactively with same-sex playmates (Maccoby & Jacklin, 1987). This tendency is universal. Researchers have tried rewarding children for playing with the other sex, but as soon as the reward is discontinued, play reverts back to same-sex groupings. This segregation may be due to the different playing styles of boys and girls, the attraction of children to others like themselves, or to learned social roles; most probably, it involves a combination of all these factors.

During the school years, gender roles become the measure by which children are judged by their peers. Children who violate sex-typed play are usually rejected (and not kindly) by their peers (Blakemore, 2003). This is especially true of boys, who experience more rejection from their peers when they violate gender stereotypes than girls do. In 2008, a 15-year old boy in California was shot to death in school by a classmate who was not comfortable with the boy's gender identity disorder (Cathcart, 2008).

The classroom itself can also strongly reinforce gender stereotypes. Even though teachers believe they show equal attention to boys and girls, research shows that teachers spend more time with boys, give them more attention, both praise and criticize boys more, use more follow-up questions to boys, and tolerate more bad behavior among boys than girls (Duffy et al., 2001). Girls are also steered away from math and science courses and both boys and girls use biased textbooks that reinforce gender stereotypes (Keller, 2002). Boys who question the teacher are considered curious, whereas girls who question are considered aggressive. Also, teachers stereotype the tasks they ask boys and girls to do; boys may be asked to help move desks, whereas girls are asked to erase the whiteboard.

One of the most comprehensive studies on the well-being of male and female children found that both genders enjoy a higher quality of life than they did in 1985, and that boys and girls have fairly equal quality of life (Meadows et al., 2005). This study reviewed data from various large and ongoing studies, including federal surveys, the census, crime statistics, and other research projects. Between 1985 and 2001, girls and boys were evaluated from childhood through their early 20s. This research comes after several studies claiming that each gender is being shortchanged in society for a variety of reasons. Gender researchers often disagree about whether

modeling behavior
Gender-appropriate behavior that usually emerges in childhood by watching others.

homosocial play
Gender-segregated play.

gender-identity disorder
A disorder in which a child has a strong and persistent identification with the other sex or the gender role of the other sex and is uncomfortable with his or her own biological sex or gender role.

there are advantages or disadvantages to being one gender or the other, and although the findings of this study were widely criticized from both sides of the argument, it is encouraging to see that the quality of life for girls and boys is improving in U.S. society.

ADOLESCENCE: PRACTICE
BEING FEMALE OR MALE

By adolescence, gender roles are firmly established, and they guide adolescents through their exploration of peer relationships and different "love styles" with potential partners. Part of the task of adolescence is to figure out what it means to be a "man" or a "woman" and to try to adopt that role. Boys quickly learn that to be popular, they should be interested in and good at sports, should express interest in sex and women, should not be overly emotional, and should not display interests that are seen as feminine or girlish. Girls, on the other hand, seem to have more latitude in their behavior but are supposed to express interest in boys and men, show concern with their appearance, and exercise a certain amount of sexual restraint. When boys deviate from gender role behavior, the consequences are more severe than when girls deviate. However, when girls deviate from gender stereotypes of sexuality (and have multiple sexual partners, for example), they experience more severe consequences.

*By adolescence, **gender roles** are often firmly established . . .*

Adolescence can be a particularly difficult time for those who are transgendered, homosexual, or bisexual. There tends to be little tolerance for these behaviors in adolescence because they are viewed as the opposite of what the teenagers are "supposed" to do. Teenage boys are supposed to be striving for genuine "masculinity." Although female homosexuality is also seen as deviant and lesbians can be the subject of taunts, females tend to discover their sexual orientation later than males, so fewer "come out" in adolescence.

The life of an emerging gay, lesbian, or bisexual adolescent may be fraught with tension and gender role confusion, which contributes to the high suicide rate among these adolescents. Many gay, bisexual, and transgendered youth survive the adolescent years by concealing their sexual orientation or gender identity (Human Rights Watch, 2001). Many learn that if they don't, they may be subjected to violence or verbal harassment. We discuss the physical and emotional harassment of gay, lesbian, and bisexual students more in Chapter 11.

Teenage gender roles have been changing since the 1970s. For example, heterosexual girls today are much more willing to assert themselves and call boys on the phone or initiate hanging out than they were 25 years ago, when they would have been considered either "desperate" or "sluts."

Yet such changing roles are also confusing; adolescent girls and boys still receive contradictory messages. Traditional male attitudes value sexual achievement, control of the sexual relationship, and suppression of emotions. However, today, as heterosexual teenaged boys are being approached by girls, they are not necessarily more sexually experienced than the girls they date, and they are expected to be sensitive to issues of female equality. Heterosexual teenage girls, on the other hand, have often been taught to be dependent on males but now are expected to assert their

independence. In addition, opportunities for achievement have opened up to the point that many girls who express a wish to become mothers and stay at home may be denigrated for lacking ambition. So even with all the changes that have leveled the playing field between the sexes, it is still not easy for adolescents to negotiate their way into sexual adulthood.

ADULTHOOD:
CAREERS AND FAMILIES

As men and women grow into adulthood, they tend to derive their gender identity primarily in two realms—their careers and their family lives. Although many believe that ideas about gender are firmly established by the time we reach adulthood, recent social changes in sex roles show that adults do have the capacity to revise their thoughts about gender roles.

For many years in Western society, men were encouraged to develop careers, whereas women (insofar as they have been encouraged to work at all) were taught to get a job that would occupy their time until marriage and children remove them from the workforce. The tendency still exists, especially among traditional women who are more feminine, to choose low-prestige occupations or subordinate their careers to those of their husbands.

Men are also socialized into career choices. Society teaches men that career achievement is, in large part, the measure of their worth. Being the breadwinner is a crucial part of male identity, and a man's success is often measured in dollars earned. This is also changing, however, although not as quickly as women's roles in the workplace are changing. In the past few years, men have been entering more female-dominated fields, such as physical therapy and library science, and have also been taking on more childcare responsibilities (U.S. Bureau of the Census, 1999).

Women's roles in the workplace have slowly been changing, and more women are pursuing careers and holding positions of responsibility and leadership. For example, although the percentage of working mothers was about 40% in 1970, it rose to over 63% by 2003 (U.S. Department of Health and Human Services, 2004a). Women have also been moving into more traditionally male-dominated fields, such as law, engineering, and architecture.

More and more women are pursuing professions and looking toward careers for at least part of their personal fulfillment. Yet powerful pressures still exist for heterosexual women to retain primary responsibility for home life, which means that women in high-pressure jobs may have more household responsibilities, unlike men in similar jobs.

Women and Family Life
Throughout most of history, women worked outside the home, and even today, in most countries, women (especially the poor) are a major part of the workforce. Women receive two conflicting messages from American society: the first is the conservative message that a woman must be married and have children to be fulfilled; the second, a feminist message, is that to be fulfilled, women must have a career outside the home. Women who try to do both find themselves with two full-time jobs. Researchers of domestic

life point out that "housework" involves far more than its stereotype of dusting and ironing and includes creating an atmosphere of good family relations, planning the budget, and educating oneself in consumer skills, evaluating educational options, being the liaison between the family and outside services (such as appliance repair) and so on (Epstein, 1988). Single working women with children must assume both roles, but even when a working woman has a working (male) partner, research shows that the woman tends to do a significantly larger percentage of household tasks (Bianchi et al., 2000).

Many women therefore live with a double sense of guilt. If they work, they feel they are not spending the time they should with their children and are leaving the important task of child rearing to a nanny, day-care center, or relatives. If they decide to stay at home and raise their children, they may feel guilty for not being productive members of the workforce. Many women do not even have that choice because economic circumstances require that they work, and most would not be able to stay at home full time without public assistance.

This dispute has been called the "mommy wars," as working mothers and stay-at-home mothers each try to defend their decisions. Nearly half the stay-at-home mothers in one survey said employed mothers did not spend enough time with their children, whereas half of employed mothers said they felt so fulfilled with their jobs that they would keep their jobs even if they could get the same salary without working. The debates over working mothers will not end soon, for women are continuing to enter the workforce in great numbers. As long as society portrays a woman's "real" job as that of mother, women will feel guilty when they choose to be productive outside the family (Warner, 2005).

Men and Family Life

Because of the traditional view that women's primary domain is the family and men's primary domain is the workplace, we have relatively few studies of heterosexual men's roles in the home. For example, enormous amounts of literature have been dedicated to discussing the "unmarried mother," but it is only relatively recently that research has begun to look at the fathers of children born outside of marriage. A growing field of men's studies looks at the role of being a "man" in modern society, including the changing domestic demands on men as more women enter the workforce.

Studies do show that heterosexual men with working wives have begun to share more responsibility for home life. When men become fathers, they begin to carry out many tasks that are stereotypically female, such as feeding and dressing the baby. Even so, fathers have been found to spend less time in direct interaction with infants than do mothers (Laflamme et al., 2003). Women still tend to retain primary responsibility for organizing the daily household and for physical chores such as preparing meals and doing laundry.

Men tend to take on other types of chores, such as heavy-lifting chores and specific projects in the home. Although heterosexual working women still spend more hours on household chores than men do, it is slowly becoming more equitable. Research on same-sex couples has found more equitable divisions of labor than in heterosexual couples (R. J. Green, 2008). This equality of household responsibilities has led to higher levels of relationship satisfaction. We discuss this research more in Chapter 9.

Because of the changing workforce, the number of unemployed heterosexual men whose wives are the primary wage earners is increasing (Fitch, 2003). These stay-at-home dads assume domestic chores and become the primary caretakers for the children. It is interesting, however, that we consider men who choose to keep house "unemployed," whereas women who do the same tasks are usually considered outside the wage-earning workforce. There is still an assumption that a man "should" be working, whereas women have the choice to stay home.

THE SENIOR YEARS

In families with children, the parents can experience either a great sense of loneliness or a newfound freedom as their children grow and leave the home. A few women, especially those with traditional roles as wife and mother, become depressed about losing their primary roles as caretakers and mothers. The phrase "empty nest syndrome" identifies the feelings of sadness and loss that many women experience when their children leave home or no longer need day-to-day care (McBride, 2007). Men and women both may have trouble adjusting to retirement if they derived a

It is becoming more acceptable for fathers to stay at home with their children while their partners go to work.

large sense of their identity from their work. In other words, whether a career or family life is the source of a person's gender identity, significant changes are common in the senior years that may involve difficult adjustments.

As people age, gender roles relax and become less restrictive. For example, older heterosexual men tend to do more housework than younger men. Many are retired and spend more time at home, and some find that their wives are less able to handle the household by themselves. Similarly, heterosexual women who are widowed or whose husbands become disabled must learn to care for their finances or learn other skills that their husbands may have previously handled.

DIFFERENT, BUT NOT LESS THAN:
TOWARD GENDER EQUALITY

Can we create a society that avoids gender stereotypes, a society of total gender equality? Would you want to live in such a society? Does a gender-equal society mean that we must have unisex bathrooms, or is it something subtler, referring to a sense of equal opportunity and respect? Epstein (1986, 1988) believes that gender distinctions begin with basic, human, dichotomous thinking—the splitting of the world into opposites such as good–bad, dark–light, soft–hard, and male–female. This very basic human process tends to exaggerate differences between things, including the sexes, and society invests a lot of energy in maintaining those distinctions.

Many religious and cultural systems clearly define gender roles. Advocates of such systems deny that differentiating gender roles means that one gender is subordinate to the other. For example, Susan Rogers (1978) has argued that we cannot apply Western notions of gender equality to countries with fundamentally different systems. She argues that inequality can exist in society only when women and men are seen in that society as fundamentally similar.

In Oman, for example, women are subject to strict social rules that we in the West would clearly see as subordination. Yet Rogers argues that women in Oman see themselves as quite different from men and are uninterested in the male role and male definitions of power. Is it appropriate for us to impose our categories on their society and suggest that women in Oman are exploited and subordinate even though they themselves do not think so? Such questions go to the heart of the discussion of power in society.

The goal for many is not a society without gender distinctions; a world without differences is boring. Yet a world that restricts people's ability to express difference because of the color of their skin, their religious beliefs, or the type of genitalia they happen to have (or not have!) is unjust. It is the content of gender roles, not their existence, that societies can alter to provide each person an opportunity to live without being judged by stereotypes of gender.

review questions

1 How are children and teenagers socialized about gender roles throughout childhood and adolescence?

2 How are adults socialized about gender roles throughout adulthood, and how does this socialization affect career choice?

3 Describe the conflicting messages that women receive about career and family life.

4 How has the role of the husband/father in the family changed over the past few decades?

5 Explain how gender roles change as people enter later life.

6 Do you think there could ever be a society without gender distinctions? Why, or why not?

CHAPTER review

SUMMARY POINTS

1 Human beings use sexual reproduction to combine 23 chromosomes in the mother's gamete with the 23 in the father's. The zygote then begins to undergo cell differentiation. If the 23rd chromosome pair is XY, the fetus will develop typically female sexual characteristics.

2 Female genitalia develop from the Müllerian duct, whereas male genitalia develop from the Wolffian duct. Both male and female external genitalia develop from the same tubercle so that many male and female genital structures are homologous.

3 Endocrine glands secrete hormones directly into the bloodstream to be carried to the target organs. The ovaries produce estrogen and progesterone, and the testicles produce androgens. The hypothalamus is the body's single most important control center.

4 Atypical sexual differentiation can occur when there are sex hormone irregularities, genetic abnormalities, or exposure of the fetus to inappropriate maternal hormones.

5 Atypical sexual differentiation can be caused by chromosomal or hormonal disorders. Klinefelter's, Turner syndrome, XYY, and triple X are examples of chromosomal disorders, whereas congenital adrenal hyperplasia and androgen-insensitivity syndrome are hormonal disorders.

6 Gender roles are the culturally determined pattern of behaviors that societies prescribe to the sexes. Gender traits are the biologically determined characteristics of gender. Little agreement exists on which gender characteristics are innate and which are learned.

7 The terms "masculinity" and "femininity" are used in three ways in society: first, a masculine or feminine person is said to exemplify characteristics that differentiate the sexes; second, the terms refer to the extent to which adults adhere to socially prescribed gender roles; and third, masculinity and femininity refer to sexual characteristics.

8 Most people agree that males are larger, stronger, and more aggressive, whereas females are neurologically more advanced than males, mature faster, and are biologically heartier. Some also cite evidence that males have better spatial abilities, whereas females have better verbal abilities.

9 Three types of theories about gender role development have been offered: social learning theories, which postulate that almost all gender knowledge is dependent on what children are taught; cognitive development theories, which suggest that children go through a universal set of stages during which they can learn only certain types of information about gender; and newer theories, such as Bem's gender schema theory, which suggests that children do go through developmental stages and that the kinds of things they learn at each stage are largely culturally determined.

10 Gender is socially constructed, and societies decide how it will be defined and what it will mean. In American society, masculinity and femininity are seen as mutually exclusive. Masculine traits include being a good provider, strong, stable, unemotional, fearless, sexually experienced, and financially independent.

11 Feminine traits include being beautiful, soft, empathetic, modest, and emotional. Many traits of femininity are considered to be the opposite of masculinity.

12 Androgyny is high levels of both masculine and feminine characteristics, and some advocate it as a way to transcend gender stereotypes. Transsexuals believe their biological and psychological genders are incompatible, showing us that gender is more complex than simply determining biological gender. Some societies assign gender categories that are neither male or female.

13 The transgendered community includes three groupings: those who live full time or part time in the other gender's role, transsexuals, and transvestites.

14 Infants are socialized into gender roles early through the way they are dressed and treated and through the environment in which they are brought up. They are reinforced for appropriate gender activity through ridiculing of children who violate gender boundaries. Adolescents "try on" adult gender roles and attitudes.

15 In adulthood, careers have been seen as the domain of men, and heterosexual women have gravitated to lower-paying jobs and to subordinate their careers to their husbands. Family life has traditionally been the domain of women, but as women enter the workforce in greater numbers, more men are assuming a larger portion of the child rearing and household duties.

16 As people age, gender roles become more flexible, and the elderly may have to make adjustments to their stereotypes once they retire or their children leave the home. Gender stereotypes are not necessarily bad. In fact, the goal for many societies is not being judged by gender stereotypes.

CRITICAL THINKING questions

1 What questions does the case study example on Brenda/Bruce raise about the nature of gender? Do you feel that gender is innate, socially learned, or a combination of both?

2 How are definitions of masculinity and femininity changing in society? Are many of the old stereotypes still powerful?

3 Why do you think a woman considers the phrase "She's one of the guys" to be a compliment, whereas a man considers the phrase "He's one of the girls" to be a put-down?

4 Which theory of gender development do you favor? Can you relate this theory to your own gender development? What are the theory's strengths and weaknesses?

5 If you met someone at a party tonight who was transgendered, what kind of emotions or thoughts do you think you would have? Would you be interested in pursuing a relationship with him or her? Why, or why not?

WEB resources

Sexuality Now Book Companion Website

Go to www.cengage.com/psychology/carroll for practice quizzes, glossary, flash cards, and more. You can also access the following websites from the companion site.

Asexuality Visibility and Education Network (AVEN) ■ AVEN works to improve public acceptance of asexuality and increase the growth of the asexual community. AVEN hosts the world's largest online asexual community.

FTM International ■ FTM International is one of the largest, longest-running educational organizations serving F2M transgendered people and transsexual men. Information on history, law, and a variety of links about transgenderism are available.

International Foundation for Gender Education (IFGE) ■ Founded in 1987, IFGE is an advocacy and educational organization for promoting expression of individual gender identity. Includes information on F2M and M2F issues spanning health, family, medical, legal, and workplace issues.

Intersex Society of North America ■ The Intersex Society of North America (ISNA) is devoted to ending the shame, secrecy, and unwanted genital surgeries for people born with nonstandard sexual anatomy. Offers information and support for both intersexed people and their friends and family members.

CengageNOW

Go to www.cengage.com/login to link to CengageNOW, your online study tool. First take the Pre-Test for this chapter to get your Personalized Study Plan, which will identify topics you need to review and direct you to online resources. Then take the Post-Test to determine which concepts you have mastered and which you still need work on.

Videos in CengageNOW

For additional information on topics discussed in this chapter, check out the videos in CengageNOW on the following topics:

- **Female-to-Male Transsexual: Teo**—An interview with a female-to-male transsexual about his experiences.

- **Transgendered: Liz**—A transgendered woman discusses her experiences and challenges.

- **Male-to-Female Transsexual: Rachel**—An interview with a male-to-female transsexual about her experiences.

- **Choosing Your Child's Gender**—While it's possible to stain sperm and to separate X and Y chromosomes with 90% accuracy, hear the arguments for and against doing so.

- **Which Is the Real Me? One Woman with Many Hats**—Listen to how one woman has many aspects and roles in her identity.

- **Perceiving Gender Roles: Ages 0–2**—Although research shows that there are early sex differences in behavior, you'll learn how these differences are small but accentuated by environmental influences.

- **Perceiving Gender Roles: Ages 2–5**—Hear how, in the preschool years, children have acquired many gender stereotypes and have different gender role expectations.

- **Perceiving Gender Roles: Ages 5–11**—Learn how, by middle childhood, children have a strong sense of gender identity and gender role expectations.

- **Gender Identity Disorder: Jessica**—Hear how Jessica describes her life both before and after her sex reassignment surgery.

- **As Nature Made Him**—Meet David Reimer, the real Brenda/Bruce that's described in this chapter as he and his biographer discuss his botched sexual reassignment.

- **Transgender Professor**—See how a university professor transitions into living life as a woman while ensuring his marriage continues to thrive.

- **Asexuality**—Listen to people who claim they are asexual and what their feelings are about sexuality.

CHAPTER 5

Female Sexual Anatomy and Physiology

From the time I started puberty I knew something wasn't right. I could have counted on my fingers and toes the number of times I'd had a period between the first one and the age of 22. I knew that I should get it checked out, but because I wasn't sexually active I didn't get my first Pap smear until I was 19. It wasn't until I was 22 that I went to find out what was going on with my periods. It had been 3 years since my last Pap and I told myself I needed to know what was going on with my body. I was diagnosed with polycystic ovarian syndrome (PCOS).

I'm glad I didn't wait any longer. With my diagnosis, things made more sense. I'd always been overweight, and it was mostly in my middle. No one had ever said anything, but I always felt I had more facial hair than a girl "should." After some accompanying blood work, I found out I was also nearly diabetic. I had never thought that not having periods would be related to developing diabetes or high blood pressure. Research is finding that insulin is connected to PCOS, which explains why many women who have the condition will become diabetic. With that, obesity tends to occur. If not managed, PCOS can also lead to hypertension and endometrial cancer.

In a society where body image is everything, I grew up being overweight. Now I have more of an explanation of why, but people don't know that when they see me. Yet PCOS isn't curable. It can be managed, and managed well enough that symptoms virtually disappear, but there is no magic quick fix I had hoped for.

Hearing a diagnosis can be comforting in a "they know what's wrong" sort of way. Yet if you've never heard of the syndrome you're being diagnosed with it, can be an isolating and scary experience. I'm finding there are a lot of women with PCOS, and they've formed communities and groups to talk about how to advocate for themselves and their medical care.

Because my body doesn't work quite right and because it leaves me with some side effects I'm less than thrilled about (and the potential for more as I age!), I'm self-conscious about my body and consequently self-conscious about sex. I'm afraid it'll be hard to find someone willing to learn about how PCOS makes my life different and somewhat challenging. I'm afraid that I won't be able to find someone who is attracted to me because of how I look. I'm afraid I won't be able to find someone who is OK with not having children or having to work for them [using fertility specialists].

Honestly, even though I'm quite hopeful about my prognosis, I can't help but think that PCOS has robbed me of some of my self-esteem. I basically have to take some sort of medication to make my body create a period for the rest of my fertile days, although it doesn't necessarily mean I'm ovulating. I can't always choose what PCOS does to my body, but I can choose to take comfort in the fact that I'm not alone. SOURCE: Author's files.

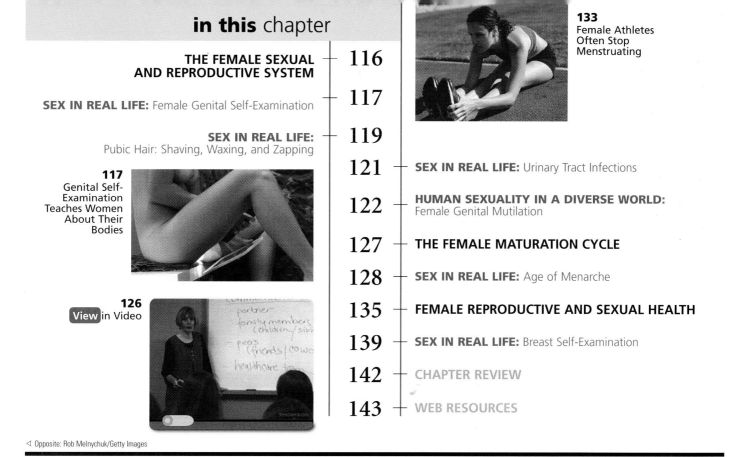

◁ Opposite: Rob Melnychuk/Getty Images

The opening excerpt was written by a 23-year-old woman who was diagnosed with polycystic ovarian syndrome. In this chapter, we talk about this disorder and many others that can affect a woman's reproductive health. It's important to keep in mind that for many years, only physicians were thought to be privileged enough to know about the human body. Today we realize how important it is for all of us to understand how our bodies function. Considering the number of sex manuals and guides that line the shelves of American bookstores, it may seem surprising that the majority of questions that students ask about human sexuality are fundamental, biological questions.[1] Yet it becomes less surprising when we realize that many parents are still uncomfortable discussing sexual biology with their children, and younger people often do not know whom to approach or are embarrassed about the ques-

tions they have (we talk more about this in Chapter 8). Questions about sexual biology are natural, however, for the reproductive system is complex, and there are probably more myths and misinformation about sexual biology than any other single part of human functioning.

Children are naturally curious about their genitals and spend a good deal of time touching and exploring them. However, they are often taught that this exploration is something to be ashamed of. Because girls' genitals are more hidden and recessed, and girls are often discouraged from making a thorough self-examination, they tend to be less familiar with their genitals than boys. This may be reinforced as females mature and are taught that menstruation is "dirty." These attitudes are reflected in ads for "feminine hygiene" products, which suggest that the vagina is unsanitary and has an unpleasant smell.

In this chapter, we explore female anatomy and physiology. Although there are many similarities to male anatomy and physiology, as you will soon learn, female anatomy and physiology are a bit more complicated. Unlike males, females have fluctuating hormone levels, monthly menstruation cycles, and menopause. In Chapter 6, we explore male sexual anatomy and physiology.

---

[1]Consider the questions two students asked during a lecture on human sexual biology: Can a woman pee with a tampon in? (yes) Can a man pee with an erection? (not that well). If you didn't know the answers to these questions, this chapter and the next can help.

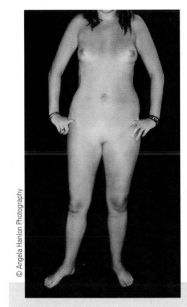
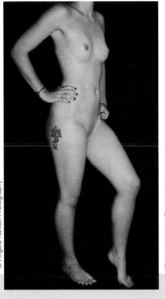
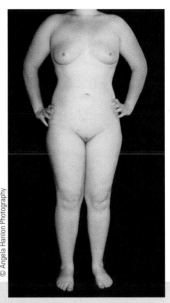

All of the women in the above photos have "normal" bodies. Individual differences in weight and size and shape of hips, breasts, and thighs, and even pubic hair are normal.

The Female Sexual and Reproductive System

It is important for women (and men) to understand the structure of the female reproductive system, which is really a marvel of biological engineering. Women who have not done a thorough genital self-examination should do so not only because it is an important part of the body to learn to appreciate but also because any changes in genital appearance should be brought to the attention of a **gynecologist** or other health care provider. See the accompanying Sex in Real Life for instructions on performing a genital self-exam.

EXTERNAL SEX ORGANS

Although many people refer to the female's external sex organs collectively as the "vagina," this is technically incorrect; the more accurate term for the whole region is **vulva,** or **pudendum** (pue-DEN-dum). The vulva, as we will see, is made up of the mons veneris, the labia majora and labia minora, the vestibule, the perineum, and the clitoris (see Figure 5.1). Although the vagina does open into the vulva, it is mainly an internal sex organ and is discussed in the next section.

Mons Veneris

The fatty cushion resting over the front surface of the pubic bone is called the **mons veneris or mons pubis.** The mons veneris becomes covered with pubic hair after puberty, and although it is considered a stimulating place to caress during lovemaking, it serves largely as a protective cushion for the genitals, especially during sexual intercourse. (See Sex in Real Life, "Pubic Hair: Shaving, Waxing, and Zapping.")

Labia Majora

The **labia majora** (LAY-bee-uh muh-JOR-uh) (outer lips) are two longitudinal folds of fatty tissue that extend from the mons, frame the rest of the female genitalia, and meet at the perineum. The skin of the outer labia majora is pigmented and covered with hair, whereas the inner surface is hairless and contains sebaceous (oil) glands. During sexual excitement, the labia majora fill with blood and engorge, which makes the entire pubic region seem to swell. Because the labia majora are homologous to the male scrotum, the sensation of caressing this area may be similar to that of caressing the scrotum for a male.

Labia Minora

The **labia minora** (LAY-bee-uh muh-NOR-uh) (inner lips) are two smaller pink skin folds situated between the labia majora and the vestibule. They are generally more delicate, shorter, and thinner than the labia majora and join at the clitoris to form the

gynecologist
A physician who specializes in the study and treatment of disorders of the female reproductive system.

vulva
The collective designation for the external genitalia of the female, also referred to as the pudendum.

pudendum
The collective designation for the external female genitalia, also called the vulva.

mons veneris or mons pubis
The mound of fatty tissue over the female pubic bone, also referred to as mons pubis, meaning "pubic mound."

labia majora
Two longitudinal folds of skin extending downward and backward from the mons pubis of the female.

labia minora
Two small folds of mucous membrane lying within the labia majora of the female.

Female Genital Self-Examination

A genital self-examination can teach a woman about her body and make her more comfortable with her genitals.

A genital self-examination can teach a woman about her body and make her more comfortable with her genitals. Many female health problems can be identified when changes are detected in the internal or external sexual organs; therefore, self-examination has an important health function as well.

Begin by examining the outside of your genitals; using a hand mirror can help. Using your fingers to spread open the labia majora, try to identify the other external structures—the labia minora, the prepuce, the introitus (opening) of the vagina, and the urethral opening. Look at the way your genitals look while sitting, lying down, standing up, squatting. Feel the different textures of each part of the vagina,

and look carefully at the coloration and size of the tissues you can see. Both coloration and size can change with sexual arousal, but such changes are temporary, and the genitals should return to normal within a couple of hours after sexual activity. Any changes over time in color, firmness, or shape of the genitals should be brought to the attention of a health professional.

If it is not uncomfortable, you may want to move back the prepuce, or hood, over the clitoris and try to see the clitoral glans. Although the clitoris is easier to see when erect, note how it fits beneath the prepuce. Note also if there is any whitish material beneath the prepuce; fluids can accumulate and solidify there, and so you should gently clean beneath the prepuce regularly.

If you place a finger inside your vagina, you should be able to feel the pubic bone in the front inside part of your vagina. It is slightly behind the pubic bone that the G-spot is supposed to be, but it is hard for most women to stimulate the G-spot with their own fingers. Squat and press down with your stomach muscles as you push your fingers deeply in the vagina, and at the top of the vagina you may be able to feel your cervix, which feels a little like the tip of your nose. Note how it feels to touch the cervix (some women have a slightly uncomfortable feeling when their cervix is touched). Feeling comfortable inserting your fingers into your vagina will also help you if you choose a barrier method of birth control, such as the contraceptive sponge or cervical cap, all of which must be inserted deep within the vagina at the cervix (see Chapter 13).

Genital self-examination can help a woman become more comfortable with her own body.

© Thomas Michael Corcoran/PhotoEdit

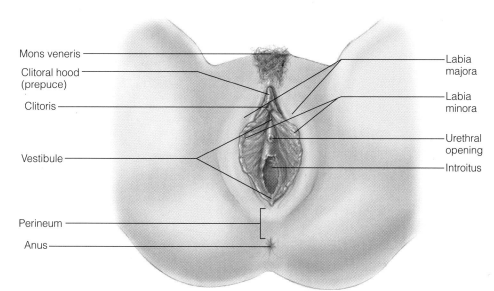

Mons veneris
Clitoral hood (prepuce)
Clitoris
Vestibule
Perineum
Anus
Labia majora
Labia minora
Urethral opening
Introitus

Figure **5.1** The external genital structures of the mature female.

prepuce (PREE-peus), the "hood" over the clitoris. The labia minora contain no hair follicles, although they are rich in sebaceous glands. They also contain some erectile tissue and serve to protect the vagina and urethra. During sexual arousal, the labia minora will darken, although the appearance can differ considerably among women.

The Clitoris

For a long time, people believed that the **clitoris** (KLIT-uh-rus) was only a small pocket of erectile tissue located under the prepuce. The invisibility of the clitoris led many to believe that this was so. However, in 1991, a group of female researchers, using historical and modern anatomical descriptions, created a new definition of the clitoris that encompasses all of the clitoral structures (see Figure 5.2). This group identified 18 structures of the clitoris—some of which are readily visible, and others that are not (Federation of Feminist Women's Health Centers, 1991). In addition to the glans, the clitoris is composed of a body and paired crura (legs). The bulbs of the clitoris lie under the labia. These bulbs, the glans, the body, and crura form an erectile tissue cluster, which altogether is called the clitoris. In 2005, magnetic resonance imaging confirmed this more expansive definition of the clitoris (O'Connell & DeLancey, 2005).

Homologous to the penis, the clitoris is richly supplied with blood vessels as well as nerve endings. The clitoral glans is a particularly sensitive receptor and transmitter of sexual stimuli. In fact, the clitoris, although much smaller than the penis, has twice the number of nerve endings (8,000) as the penis (4,000) and has a higher concentration of nerve fibers than anywhere else on the body, including the tongue or fingertips (Angier, 1999). The body, bulbs, and crura enlarge and engorge with blood in much the same way as the penis does during physical arousal. In addition, the clitoris is the only human organ for which the sole function is to bring sexual pleasure (we talk more about the clitoris and sexual pleasure in Chapter 10).

The clitoral glans is difficult to see in many women unless the prepuce is pulled back, although in some women the glans may swell enough during sexual excitement to emerge from under the prepuce (see Sex in Real Life, "Female Genital Self-Examination"). It is easy to feel the clitoral glans, however, by gently grasping the prepuce and rolling it between the fingers. In fact, most women do not enjoy direct stimulation of the glans and prefer stimulation through the prepuce. It is important to clean under the prepuce, for secretions can accumulate underneath as a material known as smegma. Smegma can harden and cause pain and, if left uncleaned, can produce an unpleasant odor.

In some cultures, the clitoris is removed surgically in a ritual **circumcision,** often referred to as a **clitorectomy.** Other parts of the vulva can also be removed in a procedure known as **infibulation** (in-fib-you-LAY-shun) (see Human Sexuality in a Diverse World on page 122).

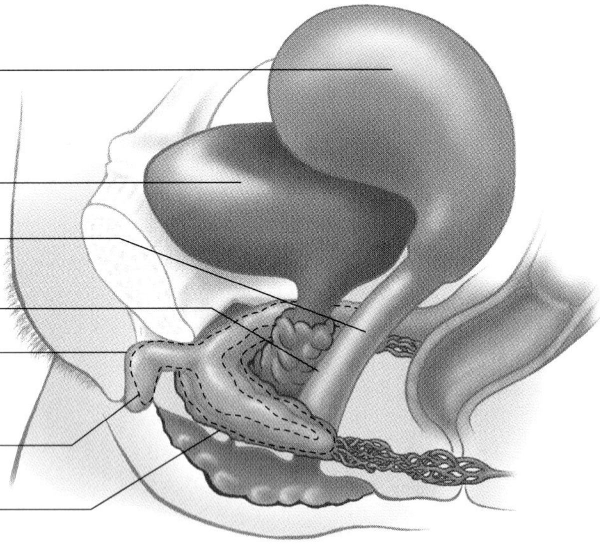

The Vestibule

The **vestibule** is the name for the entire region between the labia minora and can be clearly seen when the labia are held apart. The vestibule contains the opening of the urethra and the vagina and the ducts of Bartholin's glands.

THE URETHRAL MEATUS The opening, or meatus (mee-AYE-tuss), to the urethra (yoo-REE-thruh) lies between the vagina and the clitoris. The urethra, which brings urine from the bladder to be excreted, is much shorter in women than in men, in whom it goes through the penis. A shorter urethra allows more bacteria access into the urinary tract, making women much more susceptible to **urinary tract infections** (see Sex in Real Life, "Urinary Tract Infections").

Uterus

Bladder

Vagina

Area of G-spot

Erect clitoris

Non-erect clitoris (dotted line)

Bulbs of clitoris

Figure **5.2** Side inner view of the erect clitoris. Source: Cass, Vivienne. From *The Elusive Orgasm*. Marlowe & Company, 2007. Copyright © 2007 Marlowe & Company. All rights reserved. Reproduced by permission.

prepuce
A loose fold of skin that covers the clitoris.

clitoris
An erectile organ of the female located under the prepuce; an organ of sexual pleasure.

circumcision
Surgical removal of the clitoris in women; also referred to as clitorectomy.

clitorectomy
Surgical removal of the clitoris; also referred to as circumcision.

infibulation
The ritual removal of the clitoris, prepuce, and labia and the sewing together of the vestibule. Although this is practiced in many African societies, today many are working to eliminate the practice.

vestibule
The entire region between the labia minora, including the urethra and introitus.

urinary tract infection
Infection of the urinary tract, often resulting in a frequent urge to urinate, painful burning in the bladder or urethra during urination, and fatigue.

Pubic Hair: Shaving, Waxing, and Zapping

Products that promote shaving, such as creams, powders, or waxing products, play into the fear that pubic hair is "dirty" or "smelly."

A relatively new development in the sexuality of female college students is pubic hair removal. Products that promote the removal of pubic hair, such as creams, powders, or waxing products, play into the fear that pubic hair is "dirty" or "smelly" and needs to be removed. Changing fashions, such as thong underwear and microscopic bathing suit bottoms, have also contributed to this practice. Outside the United States, perceptions of pubic hair often differ. In fact, women often undergo pubic hair transplants in Korea because pubic hair is seen as a sign of fertility ("Pubic Hair Transplants," 2005).

However, today many students tell me that they have either removed their pubic hair at some point or have decided to remove it forever. Some who have tried it say they like it, but others claim it's uncomfortable because of the new hair growth. There are many ways in which to remove pubic hair. Some women shave, others wax or undergo electrolysis (using electricity to permanently destroy the hair follicle) or laser hair removal. A "Brazilian" wax removes all of a woman's pubic hair, whereas a traditional "bikini" wax removes hair that grows outside the bikini line. Many of these procedures are painful, but the level of discomfort depends on a woman's skin sensitivity. Some gynecological health care providers have noted an increase in pubic hair trimming or removal in their offices (Ursus, 2004).

Following are some opinions on the subject of shaving pubic hair:

"I always thought that pubic hair was like the hair on your head, it grows there, so it was meant to be there. The first time I shaved it, I thought I looked like a 10-year-old little girl, but I thought it looked cool! Now I always shave and think it's a lot "neater" and looks pretty! I have become very good at designing my pubic hair. I can make hearts, and a "J" for my first name. If I'm not seeing anyone, you can bet that it hasn't seen the razor in a while! Sometimes I do that on purpose, because I know that if I'm not trimmed up all nice then there is no way that I will let anyone go near there!"—20-year-old woman

"I have never shaved my pubic hair, nor will I ever. I think it would be too strange and would feel gross. My partners have never complained."—21-year-old woman

"My girlfriend always shaves her pubic hair, and I love it. I can't imagine her being hairy down there, it would be gross. We've experimented with me shaving, but it's really not the same. I think sex feels better for her with no hair to get in the way."—20-year-old man

"I have a Brazilian wax once every couple months and I love it. It feels so clean, and I think it lets my partner know I care about good hygiene."—21-year-old woman

"I have no desire to shave my pubic hair. I think my husband would probably like it, but that's too bad, because it's my body and I don't have the energy to maintain a shaved pussy."—38-year-old woman

SOURCE: Author's Files

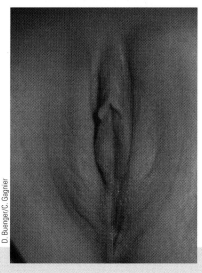
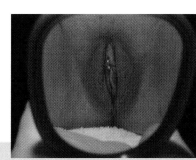
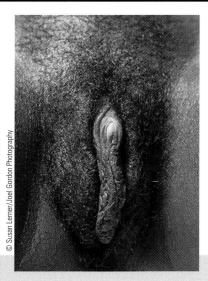

The female vulva comes in various sizes and shapes, and the color and quantity of pubic hair vary as well.

THE INTROITUS AND THE HYMEN The entrance, or **introitus** (in-TROID-us), of the vagina also lies in the vestibule. The introitus is usually covered at birth by a fold of tissue known as the **hymen** (HIGH-men). The hymen varies in thickness and extent and is sometimes absent. The center of the hymen is usually perforated, and it is through this perforation that the menstrual flow leaves the vagina and that a tampon is inserted. If the hymen is intact, it will usually rupture easily and tear at several points during the first sexual intercourse, often accompanied by a small amount of blood. If the woman is sexually aroused and well lubricated, the rupture of the hymen usually does not cause more than a brief moment's discomfort. In rare cases, a woman has an **imperforate hymen,** which is usually detected because her menstrual flow is blocked. A simple surgical procedure can open the imperforate hymen.

An intact hymen has been a symbol of "purity" throughout history, a sign that a woman has not engaged in sexual intercourse. In reality, many activities can tear the hymen, including vigorous exercise, horseback or bike riding, masturbation, or the insertion of tampons or other objects into the vagina. Still, in many cultures during many historical eras, the absence of bloodstained sheets on the wedding night was enough to condemn a woman as "wanton" (promiscuous), and some knowing mothers encouraged their newlywed daughters to have a little vial of blood from a chicken or other animal to pour on the sheet of their bridal bed, just in case. Although virginity "testing" (to check for an intact hymen) is against the law in some countries, illegal virginity tests are routinely performed (Pelin, 1999). Reconstructive surgery to repair a ruptured hymen is practiced in some countries (such as Turkey), but because of fear of repercussions, many physicians are afraid to perform these surgeries (Cindoglu, 1997).

There has been enough demand from women who desire "hymenplasty" that a handful of physicians offer the procedure today. Hymen reconstruction is a procedure in which the mucous membranes in the vagina are sewn together to make a woman appear to be a virgin (Azam, 2000). Women from Middle Eastern cultures and many American and Canadian women have undergone such procedures.

BARTHOLIN'S GLANDS The "greater vestibular glands," or **Bartholin's** (BAR-tha-lenz) **glands,** are bean-shaped glands with ducts that empty into the vestibule in the middle of the labia minora. Historically, Bartholin's glands have been presumed to provide lubrication for penetration of the vagina; however, they do not actually secrete enough lubrication for penetrative sex (H. Blumstein, 2001). It is also thought that they might be responsible for creating a genital scent. The Bartholin's glands can become infected and form a cyst or abscess. When this happens, a woman experiences pain and swelling in the labial and vaginal areas. Bartholin gland cysts are most common in women of reproductive age (Patil et al., 2007).

THE PERINEUM The **perineum** (pear-uh-NEE-um) is the tissue between the vagina and the anus. During childbirth, the baby can stretch the perineum, and in some women, it may tear or a doctor may do an **episiotomy** to allow more room for the baby's head to emerge (we discuss this more in Chapter 12).

WHAT DO YOU WANT TO KNOW?

I've always been worried about the size and shape of my vaginal lips. They just seem too big and floppy. At this point, I'm so embarrassed about them that I can't imagine ever being comfortable showing them to anyone. Is there anything I can do to fix them? It's important to remember that vulvas come in a variety of different shapes and sizes. Some women have long labial lips, whereas others have shorter ones. With the introduction of smaller swimsuits, bikini waxes, and exposure to various pornographic images, many women today are feeling increased pressure to have the "perfect vulva." Concerns like yours are common, and it's important to know that what you describe is perfectly normal.

However, there are some women that are so concerned about their vulva that they opt for "vaginal rejuvenation." Labiaplasty, reduction of the labia minora, is a popular vaginal procedure, even though it can cost up to $8,000 (Wentworth, 2007). Research indicates that labiaplasty procedures are not without risk—reduced sensation or impaired sexual functioning are common side effects (Navarro, 2004). Our fixation with perfection has also led some women to undergo G-spot enhancement (injecting collagen into the area to increase sensitivity) and even anal bleaching (using bleach to restore the anus to a pinkish hue). Because of medical risks and possible complications, the American College of Obstetricians and Gynecologists (2007) recommends against these procedures.

INTERNAL SEX ORGANS

Now that we've covered the female's external sex organs, let's move inside and explore the internal sex organs. The internal female sex organs include the vagina, uterus, Fallopian tubes, and the ovaries (see Figure 5.3).

The Vagina
The **vagina** is a thin-walled tube extending from the cervix of the uterus to the external genitalia and serves as the female organ of intercourse, a passageway for the arriving sperm, and a canal through which menstrual fluid and babies can pass from the uterus. It is tilted toward the back in most women and so forms a 90-degree angle with the uterus, which is commonly tilted for-

introitus Entrance to the vagina.	**perineum** Area between the vagina and the anus.
hymen A thin fold of vascularized mucous membrane at the vaginal opening.	**episiotomy** A surgical incision made in the perineum toward the end of labor to allow the baby to pass through.
imperforate hymen An abnormally closed hymen that usually does not allow the exit of menstrual fluid.	**vagina** A thin-walled muscular tube that leads from the uterus to the vestibule and is used for sexual intercourse and as a passageway for menstrual fluid, sperm, and a newborn baby.
Bartholin's glands A pair of glands on either side of the vaginal opening that open by a duct into the space between the hymen and the labia minora; also referred to as the greater vestibular glands.	

Urinary Tract Infections

Overall, sexually active young women are one of the most at-risk populations for the development of UTIs.

Urinary tract infections (UTIs) are common—in fact, one women in five will develop a UTI in her lifetime, and 20% of these women will experience a recurrence of the UTI after treatment (Hooton, 2003). Overall, sexually active young women are one of the most at-risk populations for the development of UTIs (Ellen-Rinsza & Kirk, 2005; Orenstein & Wong, 1999).

There are several physiological and behavioral reasons why women are more at risk for UTIs than men. Physiologically, women have shorter urethras than men, which allows bacteria to enter into the bladder (Azam, 2000; Kunin, 1997). Bacteria can be present in the rectum or around the vaginal tissues and during sexual intercourse this bacteria is often forced up into the urethra. Other factors that have been found to be related to the development of UTIs include retaining urine for an extended time period (i.e., not going to use the bathroom when a woman first feels the need to urinate), wearing thong underwear, frequent bubble baths, and the use of scented feminine hygiene products.

Normal urine is free from bacteria and viruses. When bacteria do get into the urethra, they can quickly multiply and cause an infection. The majority of UTIs are caused by *Escherichia coli* (*E. coli;* Guneysel et al., 2008). Common symptoms include an increased urge to urinate and pain or burning in the urethra or bladder. Most of the time, there is also pain during urination, and, even though frequency of urinating increases, the volume of urine decreases significantly. The urine may look cloudy and, in severe cases, may even have blood in it.

Any woman who experiences any of these symptoms of UTI should immediately seek medical care. If the pain is severe and a health care provider is unavailable, an over-the-counter medication called Uristat can help lessen the painful symptoms associated with the infection. However, Uristat will not cure a UTI. It is imperative that women who suspect a UTI undergo urine testing for bacteria. If bacteria are present, UTIs are most often treated with antibacterial drugs (such as Bactrim, Amoxil, or Cipro). Additional medications may be prescribed to treat the pain during urination, but if caught early, most UTIs can be cured within a few days. Women who have had three UTIs are likely to continue experiencing them (Foster, 2008). Scientists are currently working on a vaccine to prevent UTIs (Kantele et al., 2008).

To help decrease the likelihood that you or the women you know will acquire a UTI, it is important to:

1. Drink plenty of water.
2. Urinate before and after sexual intercourse.
3. Urinate as soon as you have the urge to go.
4. Wipe the vulva from front to back to avoid bringing bacteria from the anus.
5. Avoid feminine hygiene sprays, douches, and frequent bubble baths.
6. Avoid thong and noncotton underwear.
7. Newer research suggests that because UTIs are caused by an infection with *E. coli* bacteria, it is important to avoid contact with this bacteria by frequent hand washing, keeping pets off the bed, and monitoring chicken intake (Ramchandani et al., 2005). Women who eat more than 4 to 6 servings of chicken per week have been found to be at higher risk for UTIs.
8. Change damp clothing immediately after exercise.
9. Increase intake of unsweetened cranberry juice and/or vitamin C. Both of these can increase the acidity of urine and interfere with the ability of the bacteria to adhere to bladder tissue ("Cranberry and urinary tract infection," 2005).

ward (see Figure 5.3). The vagina is approximately 4 inches in length when relaxed but contains numerous folds that help it expand somewhat like an accordion. The vagina can expand to accommodate a penis during intercourse and can stretch 4 to 5 times its normal size during childbirth.

The vagina does not contain glands but lubricates through small openings on the vaginal walls during engorgement (almost as if the vagina is sweating) and by mucus produced from glands on the cervix. Although the first third of the vaginal tube is well endowed with nerve endings, the inner two thirds are practically without tactile sensation; in fact, minor surgery can be done on the inner part of the vagina without anesthesia.

The Grafenberg Spot and Female Ejaculation

The **Grafenberg spot (G-spot)** and female ejaculation are two controversial issues in the field of human sexuality. The G-spot, first described by Ernest Grafenberg in 1950, is a spot about the size of a dime or quarter in the lower third of the front part of the vagina and is particularly sensitive to stimulation (Whipple, 2000). The G-spot is found about 2 or 3 inches up the anterior

Grafenberg spot (G-spot)
A structure that is said to lie on the anterior (front) wall of the vagina and is reputed to be a seat of sexual pleasure when stimulated.

Female Genital Mutilation

The most common reason given for undergoing such procedures is culture and tradition.

The most common reason given for undergoing such procedures is culture and tradition.

Female genital mutilation involves partial or total removal of the external female genitalia or other injury to the female genital organs for nonmedical reasons (World Health Organization, 2008). The World Health Organization has proposed four classifications of female genital mutilation:

Type I: Partial or total removal of the clitoris and/or prepuce (clitorectomy).
Type II: Partial or total removal of the clitoris and the labia minora with or without excision of the labia majora.
Type III: Narrowing of the vaginal orifice by cutting the labia minora and labia majora with or without excision of clitoris (infibulation).
Type IV: All other harmful procedures to female genitalia for nonmedical purposes including piercing, pricking, scraping, and cauterization.

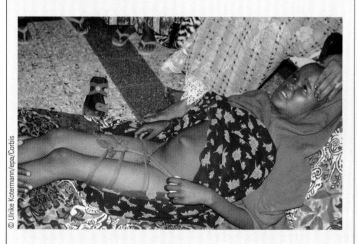

© Ulrike Kotermann/epa/Corbis

Female genital mutilation occurs all over the world, but is most prevalent in the eastern, northeastern, and western regions of Africa, some countries in Asia and the Middle East, and among certain immigrant communities in North America and Europe (see below for statistics from various countries) (World Health Organization, 2008). The following table breaks down the prevalence of female genital mutilation by country in girls and women aged 15 to 49.

Female genital mutilation has been performed throughout history to distinguish "respectable" women and to ensure and preserve a girl's virginity (Gruenbaum, 2006). These procedures are also thought to make the female genitals "clean" and "beautiful" by eliminating masculine parts, such as the clitoris (Johansen, 2007). Worldwide, it is estimated that between 100 and 140 million girls and women have undergone such procedures, and approximately 3 million girls undergo female genital mutilation every year (World Health Organization, 2008). The procedure is usually done on girls between the ages of 4 and 8, although in some cultures, it is performed later (Dare et al., 2004).

Country	Year	Estimated %
Egypt	2005	95.8
Ethiopia	2005	74.3
Gambia	2005	78.3
Guinea	2005	95.6
Kenya	2003	32.2
Sierra Leone	2005	94.0
Somalia	2005	97.9

Female genital mutilation is often done without anesthesia or antiseptic. The majority of these procedures are performed by medically untrained personnel (Dare et al., 2004). The most severe type of circumcision involves the complete removal of the clitoris and labia minora and also the scraping of the labia majora with knives, broken bottles, or razor blades (Carcopino et al., 2004). The remaining tissue is sewn together, leaving a matchstick-sized hole to allow for the passing of urine and menstrual blood. The young girl's legs are then bound together with rope, and she is immobilized for anywhere from 14 to 40 days for the circumcision to heal. The tighter the girl's infibulation, the higher the bride price will be for her.

Female genital mutilation can cause extreme pain, urinary complications or dysfunction, shock, hemorrhage, infection, scarring, recurrent urinary infections, retention of menses at menarche, vulval cysts, and pelvic inflammatory disease (Nour, 2004; World Health Organization, 2008). Of these symptoms, severe pain and bleeding are most common (Dare et al., 2004). A woman who has been infibulated will require surgery during childbirth delivery (Carcopino et al., 2004).

The day that a woman is circumcised is thought to be the most important day in her life, and it is accompanied in

continued

most cultures by rituals. Because menstruation is often difficult through the pinhole opening, marriage usually takes place soon after menstruation begins. Marital penetration of the infibulation can take anywhere from 3 to 4 days to several months, and, in 15% of cases, men are unable to penetrate their wives at all. Often penetration results in severe pain, hemorrhaging, or infection, which may lead to death (Morrone et al., 2002). Anal intercourse is common in some of these cultures, because the vagina may not be penetrable. Approximately one fifth of all women who undergo genital mutilation report wanting their daughters also to undergo the surgery (Dare et al., 2004). Female circumcision is actually illegal in many of the countries where it is practiced, but it is hard to end a deeply ingrained social practice, especially among the rural and tribal peoples who have been performing the ritual for many centuries. The most common reason given for undergoing such procedures is culture and tradition (Carcopino et al., 2004; Dare et al., 2004).

Today female genital mutilation is viewed as a violation of human rights. Many countries have put together policies and legislation to ban it. Although the incidence of FGM has slowly been decreasing over the last few years, the overall decline has been slow (World Health Organization, 2008). Some argue that those outside of Africa have no right to comment on a religious ritual, just as Africans have no right to oppose the circumcision of American males.

Recently, there has been controversy over what Americans and others should do to try to discourage this practice. The United States has been strongly opposed to the practice of female genital mutilation and has worked hard to help reduce the practice. In 2008, the World Health Organization and other United Nations agencies launched a new Interagency Statement on Eliminating Female Genital Mutilation. They hope to see a worldwide end to the practice of female genital mutilation by 2015.

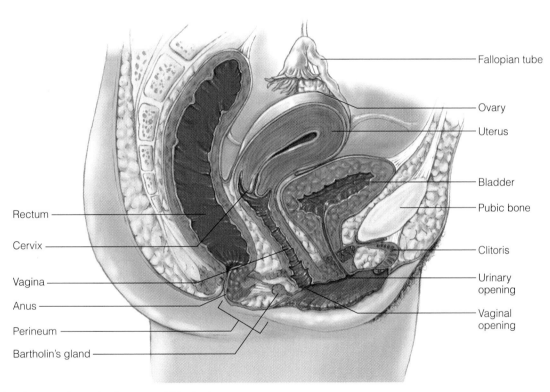

Figure **5.3** The female internal reproductive system (side view).

(front or stomach) side of the vagina, just past the pubic bone (see Figure 5.4). There is some controversy over whether this spot is a separate physiological entity, with some arguing that the entire anterior wall (and even parts of the posterior wall) of the vagina is generally sensitive (Alzate & Hoch, 1986). Others argue that the G-spot is homologous to the male prostate.

Stimulating the G-spot causes pleasant vaginal sensations in some women and may result in powerful orgasms accompanied by the forceful expulsion of fluid (female ejaculation). Women may ejaculate up to 4 ounces of fluid, which may come from the Skenes glands on either side of the urethra (Heath, 1984); however, some researchers argue that female ejaculate is chemically indistinguishable from urine (Alzate, 1985; Whipple, 2000).

The Uterus

The **uterus** is a thick-walled, hollow, muscular organ in the pelvis sandwiched between the bladder in front and the rectum behind. It is approximately the shape of an inverted pear, with a dome-

uterus
The hollow muscular organ in females that is the site of menstruation, implantation of the fertilized ovum, and labor; also referred to as the womb.

shaped top (fundus), a hollow body, and the doughnut-shaped cervix at the bottom. The uterus provides a path for sperm to reach the **ovum,** undergoes a cycle of change every month that leads to menstruation, nourishes and protects the fetus during gestation, and provides the contractions for expulsion of the mature fetus during labor. The uterus is about 3 inches long and flares to about 2 inches wide, but it increases greatly in size and weight during and after a pregnancy and atrophies after menopause.

The uterine wall is about 1 inch thick and made up of three layers (see Figure 5.4). The outer layer, or **perimetrium,** is part of the tissue that covers most abdominal organs. The muscular layer of the uterus, the **myometrium,** contracts to expel menstrual fluid and to push the fetus out of the womb during delivery. The inner layer of the uterus, the **endometrium,** responds to fluctuating hormonal levels, and its outer portion is shed with each menstrual cycle.

THE CERVIX The **cervix** (SERV-ix) is the lower portion of the uterus that contains the opening, or **os,** leading into the body of the uterus. It is through the os that menstrual fluid flows out of the uterus and that sperm gain entrance. Glands of the cervix secrete mucus with varying properties during the monthly cycle;

during **ovulation,** the mucus helps sperm transport through the os, and during infertile periods, it can block the sperm from entering. During childbirth, the cervix softens and the os dilates to allow the baby to pass through. The cervix can be seen with a mirror during a pelvic exam, and women should not hesitate to ask their gynecologist or other medical professional to show it to them. The cervix can also be felt at the top end of the vagina.

The Fallopian Tubes

Fallopian (fuh-LOH-pee-un) **tubes,** also called **oviducts,** are 4-inch-long trumpet-shaped tubes that extend laterally from the sides of the uterus. From the side of the uterus, the tube expands into an ampulla, which curves around to a trumpet-shaped end, the **infundibulum** (in-fun-DIB-bue-lum). At the end of the infundibulum are fingerlike projections that curl around the ovary, poised to accept **ova** when they are released (see Figure 5.4).

Once a month, an ovary releases an ovum that is swept into the Fallopian tube by the waving action of the **fimbriae** (FIM-bree-ee). The fimbriae sense the chemical messages released from the ovary that signal the release of the ovum and begin a series of muscular contractions to help move the ovum down the tube. If the Fallopian tube is long and flexible, it may even be able to catch the released

During childbirth,
the cervix softens *to allow*
the baby to pass through.

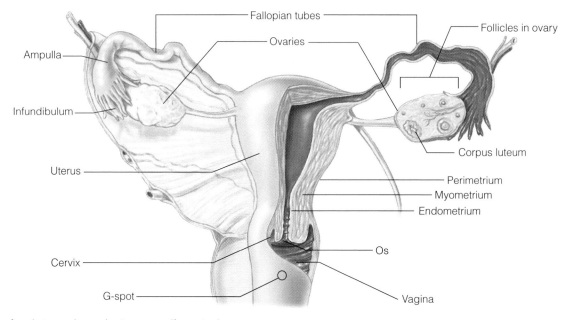

Figure **5.4** The female internal reproductive system (front view).

ovum
The female reproductive cell or gamete; plural is ova.

perimetrium
The outer wall of the uterus.

myometrium
The smooth muscle layer of the uterus.

endometrium
The mucous membrane lining the uterus.

cervix
The doughnut-shaped bottom part of the uterus that protrudes into the top of the vagina.

os
The opening of the cervix that allows passage between the vagina and the uterus.

ovulation
The phase of the menstrual cycle in which an ovum is released.

Fallopian tubes
Two ducts that transport ova from the ovary to the uterus; also referred to as oviducts.

oviducts
Another name for the Fallopian tubes.

infundibulum
The funnel- or trumpet-shaped open end of the Fallopian tubes.

ova
Two or more ovum; singular is ovum.

fimbriae
The branched, fingerlike border at the end of each Fallopian tube.

This photo shows the release of a mature ovum at ovulation. The ovum (red) is surrounded by remnants of cells and liquid from the ruptured ovarian follicle. Mature ova develop in the ovaries from follicles that remained dormant until sexual maturity.

Is there any research on nipple piercing and breast-feeding?

Body piercing has experienced a resurgence over the decade (Armstrong et al., 2004; Caliendo et al., 2005). Men and women today pierce their navels, eyebrows, noses, lips, tongues, nipples, and even genitals! Although the research is sparse, it appears that there are no long-term breast-feeding issues in women with pierced nipples. Each nipple has several milk ducts, so even if there were scarring in one area, other areas could potentially make up for it. In addition, the majority of nipple piercings are done horizontally, which is better for future breast-feeding (J. Martin, 1999). Many piercers recommend not piercing within 1 year of giving birth because piercings need time to heal. Generally this can take anywhere from 3 to 6 months. Jewelry should be removed prior to breast-feeding, although some women choose to breast-feed with jewelry intact. Doing so, however, increases the risk of injury to the child.

ovum from the opposite ovary; some women with a single active ovary on one side and a single functioning Fallopian tube on the other have been known to get pregnant (Nilsson, 1990).

The inner surfaces of the Fallopian tubes are covered by cilia (hairlike projections); the constant beating action of the cilia creates a current along which the ovum is moved toward the uterus. The entire transit time from ovulation until arrival inside the uterus is normally about 3 days. Fertilization of the ovum usually takes place in the ampulla because, after the first 12 to 24 hours, postovulation fertilization is no longer possible. Occasionally, the fertilized ovum implants in the Fallopian tube instead of the uterus, causing a potentially dangerous ectopic pregnancy (see Chapter 12).

The Ovaries

The mature ovary is a light gray structure most commonly described as the size and shape of a large almond shell. With age, the ovaries become smaller and firmer, and after menopause, they may become difficult for gynecologists to feel during an examination. The ovaries have dual responsibilities: to produce ova and to secrete hormones.

The ovary is the repository of **oocytes** (OH-oh-sites), also known as ova, or eggs, in the female. A women is born with approximately 250,000 ova in each ovary, each sitting in its own primary follicle (Rome, 1998). Approximately 300 to 500 of these will develop into mature eggs during a woman's reproductive years (Macklon & Fauser, 2000). The primary follicle contains an

immature ovum surrounded by a thin layer of follicular cells. Follicle stimulating hormone (FSH) and luteinizing hormone (LH) are released in sequence by the pituitary gland during each menstrual cycle, causing about 20 primary follicles at a time to begin maturing. Usually only one follicle finishes maturing each month, which is then termed a secondary follicle, containing a secondary oocyte. At ovulation, the secondary follicle bursts, and the ovum begins its journey down the Fallopian tube. The surface of a mature ovary is thus usually pitted and dimpled at sites of previous ovulations.

Ovulation can occur each month from either the right or left ovary. No one knows why one or the other ovary releases an ovum any given month; sometimes they take turns, and sometimes they do not. It seems to be mostly a matter of chance. If one ovary is removed, however, the other ovary will often ovulate every month (Nilsson, 1990). The ovaries are also the female's most important producer of female sex hormones, such as estrogen, which we discuss later in this chapter.

REALResearch > Men rate women as most attractive during the ovulation portion of their cycle (HASELTON ET AL., 2007). One study found that female dancers at a men's club made approximately **$70** per hour during ovulation, but only **$35** while menstruating (and **$50** per hour during other cycle times) (MILLER ET AL., 2007). However, these pay peaks were only found in women who were not taking birth control pills—women on birth control pills had no midcycle pay peaks or menstrual lows.

oocyte
A cell from which an ovum develops.

nipple
A pigmented, wrinkled protuberance on the surface of the breast that contains ducts for the release of milk.

areola
The pigmented ring around the nipple of the breast.

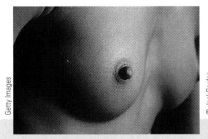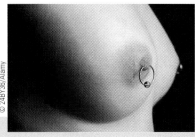

Getty Images

© Joel Gordon

© 24BY36/Alamy

The female breast is mostly fatty tissue and can take various shapes and sizes.

OTHER SEX ORGANS

Reproductive organs are not the only organs involved in a woman's sex life. The secondary sex characteristics of a woman also contribute to sexual pleasure. Although most people consider the breast a sexual part of the body, other erogenous zones may not be as obvious.

The Breasts

Breasts, or mammary glands, are modified sweat glands that produce milk to nourish a newborn child. The breasts contain fatty tissue and milk-producing glands and are capped by a **nipple** surrounded by a round, pigmented area called the **areola** (ah-REE-oh-luh). Each breast contains between 15 and 20 lobes, made up of a number of compartments that contain alveoli, the milk-secreting glands. Alveoli empty into secondary tubules, which in turn pass the milk into the mammary ducts and then into the lactiferous sinuses, where the milk is stored until the lactiferous ducts release it from the nipple (Figure 5.5). When **lactation** begins, infant suckling stimulates the posterior pituitary gland to release **prolactin,** which signals milk synthesis, and **oxytocin,** which allows the milk to be ejected.

Most people see the breasts as an erogenous zone and include stimulation of the breasts in sexual activity. Some women can even experience orgasm from breast and nipple stimulation alone. However, many women in American society are uncomfortable about the size and shape of their breasts. Because breasts are a constant source of attention in our society and are considered an important part of a woman's attractiveness, women may worry that their breasts are unattractive, too small, or too large. Yet the ideal breast differs in other cultures. For example, large breasts are valued in the United States, and so more than 80% of breast surgeries are performed to increase the size of the bust. In France, however, the majority of surgical alterations of the breasts are to decrease their size (Yalom, 1998)!

View in Video

"Women who had low self-esteem, low body image, feelings of low control, low optimism, and a lack of support at home were even more likely to benefit from an education intervention."
—*Breast Cancer: Education and Support Groups*
To view go to CengageNOW at www. cengage.com/login

Other Erogenous Zones

There are many other erogenous zones on the body that can be considered part of a woman's sexual organ system. In fact, the largest sexual organ of all is the skin, and there is no part of it that cannot be aroused if caressed in the right way at the right time during sexual activity. Some of the more common erogenous areas include the lips or the ears, but others, such as the back of the knee, the armpit, or the base of the neck, for example, may be stimulating to certain people. Some people find stimulation of the anus, or anal intercourse, extremely erotic, whereas others do not. Of course, the most important sexual organ is one that you can stimulate only indirectly—the brain.

REALResearch > It is estimated that half of all women experience breast pain during exercise (SCURR, 2007). In one study, a woman's breasts were found to move a vertical distance of approximately eight inches in an overall "figure 8" position during exercise (SCURR, 2007). This bouncing can damage the natural support system, causing significant breast pain. A well-made supportive sports bra can significantly reduce breast movement and reduce breast pain.

lactation
The collective name for milk creation, secretion, and ejection from the nipple.

prolactin
A hormone secreted by the pituitary gland that initiates and maintains milk secretion.

oxytocin
A hormone secreted by the hypothalamus that stimulates contraction of both the uterus for delivery of the newborn and the mammary gland ducts for lactation.

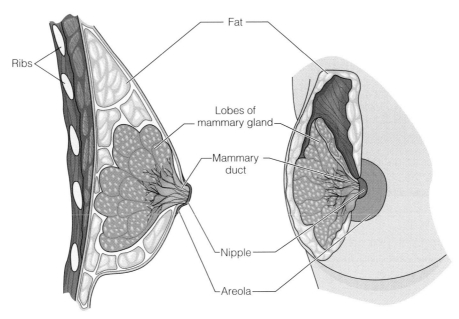

Figure **5.5** The female breast.

review questions

1 Identify and discuss the functions of the external female sexual organs.

2 Identify and discuss the functions of the internal female sexual organs.

3 Explain what breasts are composed of and the various structures contained in them.

4 Discuss female erogenous zones.

The Female
Maturation Cycle

Now that we've discussed the female sexual and reproductive system, let's explore female maturation. The female reproductive system undergoes cyclic hormonal events that lead to pubertal changes, menstruation, and eventually, menopause.

▎ FEMALE
PUBERTY

After birth, the female's sexual development progresses slowly until puberty. The first stirrings of puberty usually begin at about age 8 but can begin as late as 14 or 15. Puberty lasts from 3 to 5 years on average.

No one really knows how the body knows its own age or that it is time for puberty to begin. Newer research suggests that the onset of puberty may be related to weight—girls who are overweight begin menstruating earlier than those who are average or underweight (Kaplowitz, 2008). The onset of puberty can also vary with race. For example, African American girls reach puberty earlier than Caucasian girls (Kaplowitz et al., 2001). African American girls begin puberty between 8 and 9 years of age, a good 1 to 1.5 years earlier than Caucasian girls (Herman-Giddens & Slora, 1997). No one really understands why this is, although some researchers believe it could be due to weight differences (Adair & Gordon-Larsen, 2001).

When puberty begins, a girl's internal clock signals the pituitary gland to begin secreting the hormones FSH and LH, which stimulate the ovaries to produce estrogen while the girl sleeps. Between the ages of 11 and 14, FSH and LH levels begin to increase during the day as well.

As puberty continues, the ovaries, in response to stimulation by the pituitary gland, begin to release more and more estrogen into the circulatory system. Estrogen is responsible for the development and maturation of female primary and secondary sexual characteristics. Under its influence, the Fallopian tubes, the uterus, and the vagina all mature and increase in size. The breasts also begin to develop as fat deposits increase and the elaborate duct system develops. The pelvis broadens and changes from a narrow funnel-like outlet to a broad oval outlet, flaring the hips. The skin remains soft and smooth under estrogen's influence, fat cells in-

affect women's mate preferences (J. CLARK, 2005). During ovulation (high fertility), research has found that women prefer a handsome or creative partner, whereas during low fertility points in the menstrual cycle, she is more likely to prefer earning power over looks and creativity.

crease in number in the buttocks and thighs, and pubic hair develops. Certain bones in the body, which are responsible for height, fuse with the bone shaft, and growth stops. However, in the absence of estrogen, females usually grow several inches taller than average.

The changes that accompany puberty prepare the woman for mature sexuality, pregnancy, and childbirth. At some point during puberty, usually at about the age of 11 or 12, the woman will begin to ovulate. Most women are unable to feel any internal signs during ovulation. In a few women, however, a slight pain or sensation accompanies ovulation, referred to as **mittelschmerz.** The pain may result from a transitory irritation caused by the small amount of blood and fluid released at the site of the ruptured follicle. An increase in female sexual interest around this time may be triggered by a rise in various hormones, most notably testosterone (Halpern et al., 1997).

The beginning of ovulation often closely corresponds to **menarche** (MEN-are-kee) in most girls, although some may begin menstruating a few months before their first ovulation, whereas others may ovulate a few times before their first full menstrual cycle. In the first year after menarche, 80% of menstrual cycles are anovulatory (do not involve ovulation; Oriel & Schrager, 1999).

In some cultures in the past, as soon as a girl reached menarche, she was considered ready to marry and begin bearing children. In our culture, the age of menarche has been steadily decreasing, and most people believe that there is a difference between being physiologically capable of bearing children and being psychologically ready for sexual intercourse and childbearing. In Chapter 8, we discuss the psychological and emotional changes of female puberty.

mittelschmerz
German for "middle pain." A pain in the abdomen or pelvis that some women feel at ovulation.

menarche
The start of menstrual cycling, usually during early puberty.

SEX IN REAL LIFE

Age of Menarche

Moderate to high levels of stress tend to stimulate early maturation in girls.

Menarche is the "hallmark maturation event" in young girls (Towne et al., 2005). The average age of first menarche is 12 to 13 years in most developed countries with minor variations, but the age has been gradually decreasing (Patton & Viner, 2007; Remsberg et al., 2005). One hundred years ago, the average age of first menstruation was about 16 years old. In other, less-developed countries, the age of menarche is later. For example, in rural Chile, the average age of first menarche is close to 14 years old (Dittmar, 2000). Environmental factors, such as high altitudes and poor nutrition, can delay the age at which a girl begins menstruating. In fact, girls with poor nutrition and with substandard living conditions begin menstruating later than girls with either adequate nutrition or adequate living standards (Dittmar, 2000). It is hard to say exactly why this is. There is also a heritability component to the age at which a woman menstruates—many girls reach menarche and menopause at approximately the same age as their biological mothers (Towne et al., 2005). Overall, less than 10% of U.S. girls start menstruating by age 11, and 90% are menstruating by 13.7 years old (Chumlea et al., 2003). As we've discussed in this chapter, severe exercise regimens, such as long distance run-

ning or intense ballet dancing, may delay puberty in young girls. The onset of puberty is triggered by the acquisition of a certain body weight and appropriate fat-to-muscle ratio (Loucks & Nattiv, 2005; Warren et al., 2002). Research has also found that family stress may be associated with an earlier entrance into puberty for girls (K. Kim & Smith, 1999; Ravert & Martin, 1997). Moderate to high levels of stress tend to stimulate early maturation in girls. Even increased television viewing has been blamed for premature puberty and menstruation ("Puberty Inducer?," 2004). One study suggested that the light emitted from televisions lowers the production of melatonin, which may contribute to an earlier puberty. Much more research is needed to explore these possible links.

Girls who have an earlier menarche (before age 11) may be at risk for developing physical problems, including high blood pressure or glucose intolerance (Remsberg et al., 2005). In addition, girls with an earlier menarche tend to have earlier sexual experiences, less academic education in adulthood, and less body satisfaction (Johansson & Ritzen, 2005).

Someone once told me that women who live together often experience menstruation at the same time. Why does this happen?

Menstrual synchronicity, as this phenomenon is called, is common, and women who live in the same apartment or house often notice that they begin to cycle together (however, this will only happen if the women are not using hormonal forms of birth control). Menstrual synchronicity occurs because of pheromones, chemicals that are produced by females (more powerfully in animals) during their fertile periods that signal their reproductive readiness. Women who live together detect each other's pheromones (unconsciously), and slowly their fertile periods begin to converge.

MENSTRUATION

Menstruation (also referred to as a "period") is the name for the monthly bleeding that the majority of healthy women of reproductive age experience. The menstrual cycle lasts from 24 to 35 days, but the average is 28 (meaning there are 28 days from the first day of bleeding to the next first day of bleeding). During the cycle, the lining of the uterus builds up and prepares for a pregnancy. When there is no pregnancy, menstruation occurs, and the lining of the uterus is released in the form of blood and tissue. A cycle of hormones controls the buildup of the uterine lining and the release of fluid. The main reason for a menstrual cycle is to enable a woman to become pregnant.

Earlier we discussed how African American girls often enter puberty earlier than Caucasian girls, so it should come as no surprise that African American girls often begin menstruating earlier than Caucasian girls (Herman-Giddens & Slora, 1997). The ADD

Health (2002) data, which we discussed in Chapter 2, enabled researchers to compare racial and ethnic differences in menarche onset. On average, menarche age is significantly earlier in non-Hispanic Black girls than White or Hispanic girls (Chumlea et al., 2003) and significantly later in Asian girls (Adair & Gordon-Larsen, 2001). Girls with a heavier body mass index (BMI; weight divided by height squared) are more likely to experience an earlier menses (Kaplowitz, 2008) (see Sex in Real Life, "Age of Menarche"). Interestingly, girls whose mothers had their first period by the age of 11 were found to be twice as likely to be obese as those whose mothers did not menstruate until they were 15 or older (Ong et al., 2007) (see Figure 5.6).

The menstrual cycle can be divided into four general phases: the follicular phase, ovulation, the luteal phase, and the menstrual phase (see Figure 5.7). The **follicular phase** begins after the last menstruation has been completed and lasts anywhere from 6 to 13 days. Only a thin layer of endometrial cells remains from the last menstruation. As the follicles in the ovaries begin to ripen with the next cycle's ova, estrogen released by the ovaries stimulates regrowth of the endometrium's outer layer, to about 2 to 5 millimeters thick.

During the **ovulation phase,** an ovum is released, usually about the 14th day of the cycle. The particulars of ovulation were described in the preceding section on the ovaries and Fallopian tubes. The third phase is the **luteal phase.** Immediately following ovulation, a small, pouchlike gland, the **corpus luteum,** forms on

follicular phase
First phase of the menstrual cycle that begins after the last menstruation has been completed.

luteal phase
Third phase of the menstrual cycle, following ovulation, when the corpus luteum forms.

ovulation phase
The second stage of the general menstrual cycle, when the ovum is released.

corpus luteum
A yellowish endocrine gland in the ovary formed when a follicle has discharged its secondary oocyte.

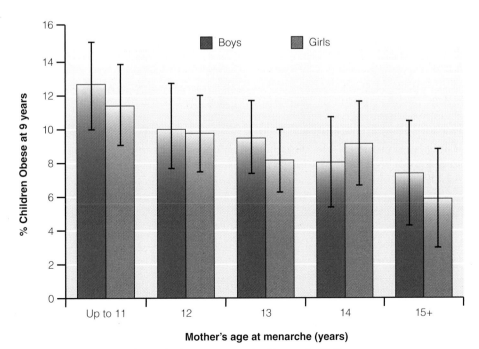

Figure **5.6** Prevalence of obesity in children at age 9, by mother's age at menarche (Ong et al., 2007).

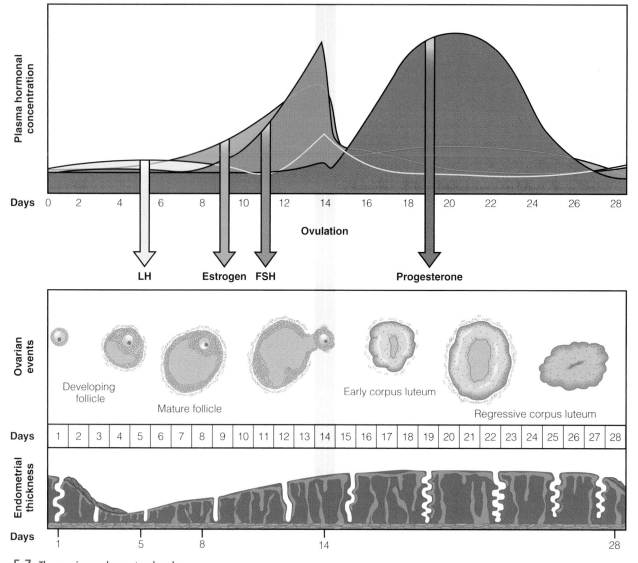

Figure 5.7 The ovarian and menstrual cycles.

the ovary. The corpus luteum secretes additional progesterone and estrogen for 10 to 12 days, which causes further growth of the cells in the endometrium and increases the blood supply to the lining of the uterus. The endometrium reaches a thickness of 4 to 6 millimeters during this stage (about a quarter of an inch) in preparation to receive and nourish a fertilized egg. If fertilization does not occur, however, the high levels of progesterone and estrogen signal the hypothalamus to decrease LH and other hormone production. The corpus luteum begins to degenerate as LH levels decline. Approximately 2 days before the end of the normal cycle, the secretion of estrogen and progesterone decreases sharply as the corpus luteum becomes inactive, and the menstrual phase begins.

In the **menstrual phase,** the endometrial cells shrink and slough off (this flow is referred to as **menses** [MEN-seez]). The uterus begins to contract in an effort to expel the dead tissue along with a small quantity of blood (it is these contractions that cause menstrual cramps, which can be painful in some women). During menstruation, approximately 35 milliliters of blood, 35 milliliters of fluid, some mucus, and the lining of the uterus (about 2 to 4 tablespoons of fluid in all) are expelled from the

uterine cavity through the cervical os and ultimately the vagina. (If a woman is using oral contraceptives, the amount may be significantly smaller; see Chapter 13.) Some women lose too much blood during their menstruation and may develop **anemia.** Menses usually stops about 3 to 7 days after the onset of menstruation.

This monthly cyclical process involves a **negative feedback loop,** in which one set of hormones controls the production of another set, which in turn controls the first (see Figure 5.8). In women, the negative feedback loop works like this: Estrogen and

menstrual phase
Final stage of the general menstrual cycle, when the endometrial cells shrink and slough off.

menses
The blood and tissue discharged from the uterus during menstruation.

anemia
A deficiency in the oxygen-carrying material of the blood, often causing symptoms of fatigue, irritability, dizziness, memory problems, shortness of breath, and headaches.

negative feedback loop
When one set of hormones controls the production of another set, which in turn controls the first, thus regulating the monthly cycle of hormones.

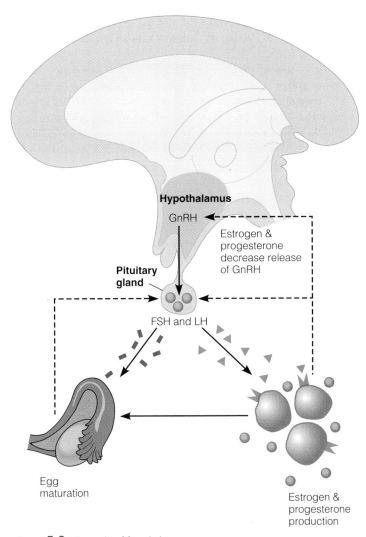

Hypothalamus

GnRH

Estrogen &
progesterone
decrease release
of GnRH

**Pituitary
gland**

FSH and LH

Egg
maturation

Estrogen &
progesterone
production

Figure **5.8** The cycle of female hormones.

Variations in Menstruation

Amenorrhea (Aye-men-oh-REE-uh), the absence of menstruation, can take two forms. In **primary amenorrhea** a woman never even begins menstruation, whereas in **secondary amenorrhea,** previously normal menses stop before the woman has gone through menopause. Primary amenorrhea may result from malformed or underdeveloped female reproductive organs, glandular disorders, general poor health, emotional factors, or excessive exercise. The most common cause of secondary amenorrhea is pregnancy, although it can also occur with excessive exercise, eating disorders, emotional factors, certain diseases, surgical removal of the ovaries or uterus, or hormonal imbalance caused naturally or through the ingestion of steroids. For example, almost all women with anorexia nervosa will experience amenorrhea. When they regain weight, they often will not begin ovulating and menstruating and may need drugs to induce ovulation and start their periods again (Biro et al., 2003). If amenorrhea persists, a physician should be consulted.

Some women suffer from **menorrhagia** (men-or-RAY-gee-uh), or excessive menstrual flow. Often oral contraceptives are prescribed to make menses lighter and more regular. Later in this chapter, we discuss some newer options that women have to avoid menstruation altogether.

Dysfunctional uterine bleeding (DUB), when a woman bleeds for long periods of time or intermittently bleeds throughout her cycle, is another common disorder. DUB is usually caused by conditions such as hormonal imbalance, significant weight loss, eating disorders, stress, chronic illness, and excessive exercise (Oriel & Schrager, 1999). A woman who bleeds throughout her menstrual cycle should see her health care provider. Untreated DUB can lead to medical problems, such as anemia, and can also cause social embarrassment, because some women need to change their sanitary pads and tampons as often as once an hour.

Dysmenorrhea (dis-men-uh-REE-uh), or painful menstruation, may be caused by a variety of inflammations, constipation, or even psychological stress. In the past, there was a tendency to believe that cramps were always the result of a physical problem, and some women even had operations in an attempt to stop the pain, but such strategies usually failed. Today research has found that menstrual cramps are usually caused by prostaglandins, which stimulate the uterus to contract and expel the endometrial lining during menstruation. The uterine muscles are powerful (remember

---

REALResearch > Menstrual cycle–related symptoms, such as cramps, premenstrual syndrome, and other physical and emotional symptoms can have a profound impact on women's quality of life (CLAYTON, 2008). Successful treatments include pain relievers for cramps and discomfort, selective serotonin reuptake inhibitors (SSRIs) for symptoms of depression, and oral contraceptives for ovulation suppression and reduction of menstrual flow and cramping.

---

progesterone are produced by the ovaries at different levels during different parts of the menstrual cycle. As these levels increase, the hypothalamus is stimulated to decrease its production of **gonadotropin-releasing hormone (GnRH),** which sends a message to the pituitary to decrease levels of FSH and LH. The decrease in FSH and LH signals the ovaries to decrease their production of estrogen and progesterone, so the hypothalamus increases its level of GnRH, and it all begins again. This process is similar to a thermostat; when temperatures go down, the thermostat kicks on and raises the temperature, until the rising heat turns off the thermostat and the heat begins slowly to fall.

gonadotropin-releasing hormone (GnRH)
A hormone produced in the hypothalamus which triggers the onset of puberty and sexual development and is responsible for the release of FSH and LH from the pituitary.

amenorrhea
The absence of menstruation.

primary amenorrhea
The lifelong absence of menstruation.

secondary amenorrhea
The absence of menstruation after a period of normal menses.

menorrhagia
Excessive menstrual flow.

dysfunctional uterine bleeding (DUB)
Menstrual bleeding for long periods of time or intermittent bleeding throughout a cycle.

dysmenorrhea
Painful menstruation.

that the muscles help push an infant out at birth), and the menstrual contractions can be strong and sometimes quite painful. However, there are many things that can make the cramps worse. Poor eating habits, an increase in stress, alcohol use, insufficient sleep, and a lack of exercise can aggravate the problem. Reducing salt, sugar, and caffeine intake; moderate exercise; warm baths; and gentle massage of the lower back sometimes help, as do antiprostaglandin pain relievers, such as ibuprofen. Orgasm, either through masturbation or with a partner, also helps many women relieve menstrual cramps. In addition, health care providers recommend relaxation and yoga, which can bring some relief from dysmenorrhea.

Premenstrual Syndrome

The term **premenstrual syndrome (PMS)** refers to physical or emotional symptoms that appear in some women during the latter half of the menstrual cycle that can affect their relationships or ability to function. Estimates of PMS vary widely depending on how it is defined, but only a small number of women find it debilitating. In fact, although close to 75% of reproductive-aged women report premenstrual symptoms, less than 10% have symptoms that would necessitate a diagnosis of PMS (Born & Steiner, 2001; H. Elliott, 2002; Stanford, 2002).

Women who experience PMS often report feeling "out of control," "sad," and "cranky." Their partners often do not understand how to handle their PMS, and many partners report not knowing what to say. Overall a woman who suffers from this syndrome

---

REALResearch > Female athletes experience more injuries during the luteal phase of their menstrual period, presumably because of physiological changes in posture, sway, and knee-joint stability that occur just before the menstrual period (FRIDEN ET AL., 2003).

---

needs a partner to take her symptoms seriously and be loving and supportive. Women who experience PMS may also experience depression, insomnia, excessive sleepiness, restlessness, and feelings of hopelessness (Strine et al., 2005).

The existence of PMS has been controversial (Knaapen & Weisz, 2008). The term became well known in the early 1980s when two separate British courts reduced the sentences of women who had killed their husbands on the grounds that severe PMS reduced their capacity to control their behavior (Rittenhouse, 1991). Although this defense never succeeded in a U.S. trial, publicity over the British trials led to much discussion about this syndrome. Some women objected to the idea of PMS, suggesting that it would reinforce the idea that women were "out of control" once a month and were slaves to their biology, whereas others supported it as an important biological justification of the symptoms they were experiencing each month. The extreme views of PMS have calmed down somewhat, and women who suffer from it can now find sympathetic physicians and a number of suggestions for coping strategies.

In 1994, the American Psychiatric Association introduced the diagnosis of **premenstrual dysphoric disorder (PMDD),** the most debilitating cases of PMS (Rapkin & Winer, 2008). PMDD is now listed in the DSM-IV-TR (American Psychiatric Association, 2000), the latest guide to the accepted disorders of the American Psychiatric Association. To accurately diagnose PMDD, a woman needs to chart her symptoms for at least two menstrual cycles to establish a typical pattern of symptoms (Born & Steiner, 2001; H. Elliott, 2002).

There are four main areas of PMDD symptoms—mood, behavioral, somatic, and cognitive. Mood symptoms include depression, irritability, mood swings, sadness, and hostility. Behavioral symptoms include becoming argumentative, increased eating, and a decreased interest in activities. Somatic symptoms include abdominal bloating, fatigue, headaches, **hot flashes,** insomnia, backache, constipation, breast tenderness, and a craving for carbohydrates. Cognitive symptoms include confusion and poor concentration. PMDD symptoms seem to have both biological and lifestyle components, and so both medication and lifestyle changes can help.

PMDD is often blamed on serotonin dysregulation (Rapkin & Winer, 2008). Serotonin is a neurotransmitter in the brain that is involved in the expression of irritability, anger, depression, and specific food cravings. There is also some evidence that PMDD may have a genetic component—that is, it may run in families (Treloar et al., 2002).

Once documented, the first treatment for PMS or PMDD usually involves lifestyle changes. Dietary and vitamin/nutritional changes such as decreasing caffeine, salt, and alcohol intake; maintaining a low-fat diet; increasing calcium, magnesium, and vitamin E (to decrease negative mood and fluid retention); and taking primrose oil have been found to be helpful. Stress management, increased regular exercise, improved coping strategies, and drug therapy can also help (Stearns, 2001; Yonkers, 1999). It's important to point out that these lifestyle changes would make the majority of us happier, regardless of PMS!

One of the most promising pharmacological treatments has been the SSRIs, such as fluoxetine (Prozac; Clayton, 2008). Fluoxetine has yielded some promising results in the treatment of PMDD, although it can cause side effects, such as headaches and sexual dysfunction (Carr & Ensom, 2002). Overall, the majority of women who suffer from PMS and PMDD do respond well to treatment.

Women who have a history of major depression, **posttraumatic stress disorder,** sexual abuse, or those who smoke cigarettes tend to be more at risk for developing PMS or PMDD (L. Cohen et al., 2002; Koci, 2004; Wittchen et al., 2002). In addition, ethnic variations have also been found. For example, compared with Caucasian women, Hispanic women have been found to have more severe symptoms, whereas Asian women have less (Sternfeld et al., 2002).

Menstrual Manipulation and Suppression

Many years ago, women had fewer periods than they do today. Because of poorer health and nutrition, shorter life spans, more pregnancies, and longer periods spent breast-feeding, women had

---

premenstrual syndrome (PMS)
A group of physiological and psychological symptoms related to the postovulation phase of the menstrual cycle.

premenstrual dysphoric disorder (PMDD)
The most debilitating and severe cases of premenstrual syndrome.

hot flashes
A symptom of menopause in which a woman feels sudden heat, often accompanied by a flush.

posttraumatic stress disorder
A stress disorder that follows a traumatic event, causing flashbacks, heightened anxiety, and sleeplessness.

50 to 150 periods during their lifetime (Ginty, 2005; Thomas & Ellertson, 2000), whereas today they have up to 450. Many women today wish they could schedule their periods around certain events in their lives (e.g., athletic events, dates, or vacations).

Over the last few years, **menstrual manipulation** has become more popular, and in the future it is likely that **menstrual suppression** will make periods optional (Derry, 2007; Ginty, 2005). Birth control pills have been used to reduce menstrual bleeding and to delay the onset of menstruation. Some physicians prescribe continuous birth control pills (in which a woman takes birth control pills with no break), progesterone **intrauterine devices,** and injections to suppress menstrual periods (we will discuss the use of birth control pills in more detail in Chapter 13).

Seasonale, an extended use oral contraceptive, has been available since 2003. It is used for 84 consecutive days instead of the usual 21-day birth control regimen. Another similar extended-use pill, Seasonique, was approved by the FDA. Users of Seasonale and Seasonique experience only 4 periods a year, compared with the usual 13. Many women are excited about the option of reducing the number of menstrual periods; one study found that given a choice of having a period or not, 90% of women would choose not to have periods (Sulak et al., 2002). In 2007, Lybrel, the first continuous-use birth control pills were available to women. Lybrel is taken for 365 days without placebos, allowing a woman to stop menstruating altogether. We discuss these forms of birth control more in Chapter 13.

Methods such as Seasonale, Seasonique, and Lybrel suppress the growth of the uterine lining, leaving little or nothing to be expelled during menstruation. Actually this treatment has been used for years to treat a menstrual condition known as **endometriosis** (en-doe-mee-tree-OH-sus), which can cause severe menstrual cramping and irregular periods. Overall, there is no medical evidence that women need to have a monthly menstrual period, and studies conclude that continuous use of the pill to stop periods is a safe and effective option for preventing pregnancy and reducing menstrual related symptoms (Anderson et al., 2006; Merki-Feld et al., 2008; A. L. Nelson, 2007; Stacey, 2008)

Women with painful periods, intense cramps, heavy menses, migraines, PMS, epilepsy, asthma, rheumatoid arthritis, irritable bowel syndrome, and diabetes all can benefit from menstrual suppression (F. D. Anderson et al., 2006; Merki-Feld et al., 2008; A. L. Nelson, 2007; Stacey, 2008). In addition, menstrual disorders are the number one cause of gynecological disease and affect millions of American women yearly (Clayton, 2008). Some experts suggest that amenorrhea may be healthier than monthly periods because menstrual suppression also avoids the sharp hormonal changes that occur throughout the menstrual cycle.

Originally, birth control pills were designed to mimic the normal menstrual cycle, which is why the cycle includes a period of time for a woman to bleed. This bleeding, called *withdrawal bleed-*ing, is a result of stopping birth control pills for 1 week or taking placebo pills (Stacey, 2008). The bleeding itself bears little biological resemblance to a menstrual period; this is because there is little built-up endometrium to be shed (Thomas & Ellertson, 2000). Even so, most women link having their period with health and fertility. Bleeding has "psychological importance" to many women; it lets a woman know that everything is fine and working the way it should. In fact, abnormal bleeding (spotting or clotting) or an absence of bleeding are important to report to a health care provider promptly.

Sexual Behavior and Menstruation

Many cultures have taboos about engaging in sexual intercourse, or any sexual behaviors, during menstruation. Orthodox Jewish women are required to abstain from sexual intercourse for 1 week after their menstrual period. After this time, they engage in a mikvah bath, following which sexual activity can be resumed.

Although many heterosexual couples report avoiding sexual intercourse during menstruation (Hensel et al., 2004), research has found that this might have to do with personal comfort. Heterosexual couples who are more comfortable with their sexuality report higher levels of sexual intercourse during menstruation (Rempel & Baumgartner, 2003). Menstruation can make things a little messy, so a little preplanning is often needed. Some women use diaphragms or other specially designed products, such as the

© Corbis

Female athletes who significantly reduce their body fat will often stop menstruating. One study found that 65% of long-distance runners on one team stopped menstruating while training (compared with 2%–5% of women in the general population who stop menstruating; Loucks & Nattiv, 2005).

menstrual manipulation
The ability to plan and schedule the arrival of menstruation.

menstrual suppression
The elimination of menstrual periods.

intrauterine devices
Devices that are inserted into the uterus for contraception. Progesterone IUDs often inhibit menstruation.

endometriosis
The growth of endometrial tissue outside the uterus.

The Diva Cup is a silicone menstrual cup that can be used as an alternative to disposable menstrual products such as tampons.

Instead Softcup, to contain menstrual fluid. Others insert a tampon just before sexual activity and then engage in oral or manual sex.

Heterosexual and lesbian couples should talk about this issue and decide what they are comfortable with. As mentioned earlier, however, menstrual suppression might make this question obsolete.

MENOPAUSE

The term **menopause** refers to a woman's final menstrual period but is often (incorrectly) used as a synonym for the **climacteric.** These terms refer to the time in a woman's life in which estrogen production begins to wane, culminating in the cessation of menstruation, usually between the ages of 40 and 58. Women go through **perimenopause** (pear-ee-MEN-oh-pawz) anywhere from 2 to 8 years prior to menopause (Huang, 2007; Twiss, 2007). Typical symptoms of perimenopause include menstrual irregularities, sleep problems, hot flashes, and vaginal dryness (H. D. Nelson, 2008).

As women age, their ovaries become less responsive to hormonal stimulation from the anterior pituitary, resulting in decreased hormone production. Decreased hormone production can lead to irregular cycles or a lack of menstruation. Amenorrhea may occur for 2 or 3 months, followed by a menstrual flow. In most cases, menstruation does not stop suddenly. Hot flashes, headaches, and insomnia can increase, and sexual desire and interest may decrease.

Diminishing estrogen production also results in atrophy of the primary sexual glands. The clitoris and labia become smaller, and degenerative changes occur in the vaginal wall. At the same time, the ovaries and uterus also begin to shrink. Estrogen reduction can also cause changes in the secondary sex characteristics, including pubic hair loss, thinning of head hair, growth of hair on the upper lip and chin, drooping of the breasts and wrinkling of

skin due to loss of elasticity, and **osteoporosis** (ah-stee-oh-po-ROW-sus), resulting in brittle bones.

Decreasing levels of estrogen accelerate bone loss during menopause. It is estimated that 70% of women over age 80 will have osteoporosis (Stanford, 2002). Incidentally, *osteopenia* (a thinning of the bones) also can occur in younger women and is a precursor to osteoporosis. If you smoke, use Depo Provera, or have an eating disorder or a family history of osteoporosis, you might ask your doctor for a bone density test. Today women in their 20s and 30s are advised to get at least 1,000 milligrams of calcium each day and to engage in frequent exercise to maintain bone strength (Lloyd et al., 2004; Manson, 2004).

Certain surgeries, such as removal of the ovaries, can result in a surgically induced menopause because of estrogen deprivation. For this reason, surgeons try to leave at least one ovary in premenopausal women to allow these women to enter menopause naturally.

Many women go through perimenopause and menopause with few problems and find it to be a liberating time, signaling the end of their childbearing years and a newfound freedom from contraception. In fact, the most prevalent sexual problems of older women are not the classic complaints but rather the lack of tenderness and sexual contact with a partner (von Sydow, 2000). In fact, for many menopausal women, life satisfaction is more closely related to relationship with a partner, stress, and lifestyle than menopause status, hormone levels, or hormone replacement therapy (Dennerstein et al., 2000).

Hormone Replacement Therapy

Overall, **hormone replacement therapy (HRT)** has been found to help maintain vaginal elasticity and lubrication, reduce hot flashes, reduce depression, and restore regular sleep patterns. It has also been found to decrease the risk of developing osteoporosis, cardiovascular disease, and colorectal and lung cancers (Brinton & Schairer, 1997; Mahabir et al., 2008; Parry, 2008).

However, in 2002, after the publication of results from the Women's Health Initiative that linked HRT to an increased rate of breast cancer, the use of HRT dropped significantly. Although the use of hormone replacement therapy remains controversial today, some health care providers continue to prescribe it for some pa-

REALResearch **>** Women who have a caffeine-rich diet (consuming more than 300 mg caffeine per day) may experience delayed conception, infertility, and an increased risk of osteoporosis, cardiovascular disease, and cancers later in life (DERBYSHIRE & ABDULA, 2008).

menopause
The cessation of menstrual cycling.

climacteric
The combination of physiological and psychological changes that develop at the end of a woman's reproductive life; usually includes menopause.

perimenopause
Transition period in a woman's life, just before menopause.

osteoporosis
An age-related disorder characterized by decreased bone mass and increased susceptibility to fractures as a result of decreased levels of estrogens.

hormone replacement therapy (HRT)
Medication containing one or more female hormones, often used to treat symptoms of menopause.

tients, others have stopped prescribing it altogether; and some prescribe hormone replacement only for those women with severe menopausal symptoms (Mueck & Seeger, 2008; Zanetti-Dallenbach et al., 2008). Newer therapies containing lower levels of hormones have recently become available, and an increasing number of physicians and health care providers are prescribing these newer options to their menopausal patients (Beck, 2008). Some women use nutritional or vitamin therapy or use herbal remedies containing natural estrogens, such as black cohosh, ginseng, or soy products, to help lessen symptoms instead of hormones (although the use of these products is controversial and may lead to a variety of side effects).

Menopausal women need to weigh the risks and benefits of menopausal treatments and HRT. It is important to discuss these issues with a trusted health care provider. There is no single treatment option that is best for all women.

review questions

1 Identify and explain the physiological changes that signal the onset of puberty.

2 Identify and explain the four phases of the menstrual cycle.

3 Explain what is known about the existence of PMS/PMDD. What treatments are available?

4 Differentiate between menstrual manipulation and menstrual suppression.

5 Explain what causes the physical and emotional changes of perimenopause and menopause.

6 Explain the benefits and risks of hormone replacement therapy.

Female Reproductive and Sexual Health

It is a good idea for every woman to examine and explore her own sexual anatomy. A genital self-exam (see Sex in Real Life, "Female Genital Self-Examination") can help increase a woman's comfort with her genitals. In addition, to maintain reproductive health, all women should undergo routine gynecological examinations with Pap smears beginning within 3 years after first sexual intercourse or at age 21 (E. R. Tuller, personal communication, March 20, 2008).

Routine gynecological exams include a general medical history and a general checkup, a pelvic examination, and a breast examination. During the pelvic examination, the health care provider inspects the genitals, both internally and externally, and manually examines the internal organs.

In a pelvic exam, the health professional will often use a **speculum** to hold open the vagina to examine the cervix (although there is a sense of stretching, this is not generally painful). Many women report discomfort with speculums, and research is currently being done to find alternatives that would allow health care providers access to the cervix. During a pelvic exam, a **Papanicolaou (Pap) smear** is taken from the cervix (see the discussion on cervical cancer that follows). The practitioner will then insert two fingers in the vagina and press down on the lower abdomen to feel the ovaries and uterus for abnormal lumps or pain. A rectovaginal exam may also be performed, in which the practitioner inserts one finger into the rectum and one into the vagina to feel the membranes in between.

It is important to choose a gynecologist or nurse practitioner with care, for this person should be a resource for sexual and birth control information as well. Referrals from friends or family

© Joel Gordon

During a pelvic examination, a device such as a speculum is used to view the cervix.

members, college health services, women's health centers, and Planned Parenthood Centers can direct you to competent professionals. Do not be afraid to change practitioners if you are not completely comfortable.

GYNECOLOGICAL HEALTH CONCERNS

There are several conditions that can interfere with gynecological health. We discuss some of the most prevalent, including endometriosis, toxic shock syndrome, uterine fibroids, vulvodynia, polycystic ovarian syndrome, and vaginal infections.

speculum
An instrument for dilating the vagina to examine the cervix and other internal structures.

Papanicolaou (Pap) smear
A microscopic examination of cells scraped from the cervix. Named after its inventor.

Endometriosis

Endometriosis occurs when endometrial cells begin to migrate to places other than the uterus. They may implant on any of the reproductive organs or other abdominal organs and then engorge and atrophy every month with the menstrual cycle, just like the endometrium does in the uterus. The disease ranges from mild to severe, and women may experience a range of symptoms or none at all.

Endometriosis is most common in women aged between 25 and 40 years who have never had children; it has been called the "career woman's disease" because it is more common in professional women (Simsir et al., 2001). Women who have not had

---

REALResearch >A woman who is scheduled for a yearly pelvic examination with Pap testing should abstain from sexual intercourse, douching, and yeast infection medication for at least 2 days before her pelvic exam. These can all interfere with the reading of a Pap test and make the results difficult to interpret (GLOBERMAN, 2005; L. OBRIZZO, PERSONAL COMMUNICATION, AUGUST 5, 2008).

---

children and those who experience short and heavy menstrual cycles have also been found to be more at risk for endometriosis (Vigano et al., 2004). Among women of childbearing age, the estimated prevalence of endometriosis is as high as 10%; among infertile women, between 20% and 40% (Frackiewicz, 2000; Vigano et al., 2004). If you or someone you know has had symptoms of endometriosis, it is important that complaints are taken seriously.

The cause of endometriosis is still unknown, although some have suggested that it is due to retrograde menstrual flow (a process in which parts of the uterine lining are carried backward during the menstrual period into the Fallopian tubes and abdomen [Frackiewicz, 2000; Leyendecker et al., 2004]). The symptoms of endometriosis depend on where the endometrial tissue has invaded but commonly include painful menstrual periods, pelvic or lower back pain, and pain during penetrative sex; some women also experience pain on defecation (Prentice, 2001). Symptoms often wax and wane with the menstrual cycle, starting a day or two before menstruation, becoming worse during the period, and gradually decreasing for a day or two afterward. The pain is often sharp and can be mistaken for menstrual cramping. Many women discover their endometriosis when they have trouble becoming pregnant. The endometrial cells can affect fertility by infiltrating the ovaries or Fallopian tubes and interfering with ovulation or ovum transport through the Fallopian tube.

Endometriosis is diagnosed through biopsy or the use of a **laparoscope.** Treatment consists of hormone therapy, surgery, or laser therapy to try to remove endometrial patches from the organs. Endometriosis declines during pregnancy and disappears after menopause.

Toxic Shock Syndrome

Toxic shock syndrome (TSS) first hit the news in the early 1980s, when a number of women died or lost limbs to the disease. Many of the infected women used a brand of tampons called Rely, which was designed to be kept in the vagina over long periods of time. Using a single tampon for a long period of time allows bacteria to

build up and can result in infection. The TSS cases of the 1980s were believed to be due to a buildup of toxins produced by an infection of vaginal *Staphylococcus aureus* bacteria (Reingold, 1991).

TSS is an acute, fast-developing disease that can cause multiple organ failure. Symptoms of TSS usually include fever, sore throat, diarrhea, vomiting, muscle ache, and a scarlet-colored rash. It may progress rapidly from dizziness or fainting to respiratory distress, kidney failure, shock, and heart failure and can be fatal if medical attention is not received immediately.

TSS can occur in persons of any age, sex, or race, but most reported cases have occurred in younger menstruating women using tampons. Today TSS is most common in women who forget to remove a tampon, which becomes a breeding ground for bacteria over a few days. TSS can be avoided by using less absorbent tampons, changing tampons regularly, or using sanitary pads instead of tampons.

Polycystic Ovarian Syndrome

This chapter opened with a personal story from a woman who had been diagnosed with **polycystic ovarian syndrome (PCOS).** PCOS is an endocrine disorder that affects approximately 7% of premenopausal women worldwide (Diamanti-Kandarakis, 2007). PCOS causes cyst formation on the ovaries during puberty, which causes estrogen levels to decrease and androgen levels (including testosterone) to increase. A girl with PCOS typically experiences irregular or absent menstruation; a lack of ovulation; excessive body and facial hair or hair loss; obesity; acne, oily skin, or dandruff; infertility; or any combination of these. Many women with PCOS experience fertility issues, and research is ongoing to find ways to help them achieve successful pregnancies (Stadtmauer & Oehninger, 2005). Although the actual cause of PCOS is unknown, researchers continue to explore possible causes.

There are many possible long-term health concerns associated with PCOS, such as an increased risk of diabetes, high blood pressure, and increased cholesterol levels. A variety of treatment options are available, including oral contraception to regulate the period and inhibit testosterone production. Many women find that some of the symptoms associated with PCOS decrease with weight loss (A. M. Clark et al., 1995).

Because many of the symptoms, including increased body and facial hair, acne, and weight gain, affect a woman's sense of self, many women with PCOS experience emotional side effects, including mild depression or self-esteem issues. Getting adequate medical care, education, and support are crucial factors in managing PCOS.

laparoscope
A small instrument through which structures within the abdomen and pelvis can be viewed.

toxic shock syndrome (TSS)
A bacteria-caused illness that can lead to high fever, vomiting, diarrhea, sore throat and shock, loss of limbs, and death if left untreated.

polycystic ovarian syndrome (PCOS)
An endocrine disorder in women that can affect the menstrual cycle, fertility, hormones, a woman's appearance, and long-term health.

Uterine Fibroids

Uterine fibroids, or hard tissue masses in the uterus, affect from 20% to 40% of women aged 35 and older, and as many as 50% of African American women (Laval, 2002). Symptoms include pelvic pain and pressure, heavy cramping, prolonged or heavy bleeding, constipation, abdominal tenderness or bloating, infertility, recurrent pregnancy loss, frequent urination, and painful penetrative sex. Of all of these symptoms, excessive menstrual bleeding is the most common complaint.

Some fibroids can become very large (up to the size of a basketball) and can make a woman look as though she is in her sixth month of pregnancy. Treatment for uterine fibroids is hormone or drug therapy, laser therapy, surgery, or **cryotherapy** (E. A. Stewart, 2001; Viswanathan et al., 2007). It is important to point out that the majority of uterine fibroids are not cancerous and do not cause any problems.

Vulvodynia

At the beginning of the 21st century, many physicians were unaware that a condition known as **vulvodynia** (vull-voe-DY-nia) existed. Vulvodynia refers to chronic vulval pain and soreness. Although a burning sensation in the vagina is the most common symptom, women also report itching, burning, rawness, stinging, or stabbing vaginal/vulval pain (Goldstein & Burrows, 2008). Vulvodynia pain is either intermittent or constant and can range from mildly disturbing to completely disabling. Women who suffer from vulvodynia experience higher levels of psychological distress and depression than those who do not (Jelovsek et al., 2008; Plante & Kamm, 2008).

No one really knows what causes vulvodynia, but there have been several speculations, including injury or irritation of the vulval nerves, hypersensitivity to vaginal yeast, allergic reaction to environmental irritants, or pelvic floor muscle spasms (Arnold et al., 2006; Murina et al., 2008). Treatment options include biofeedback, diet modification, drug therapy, oral and topical medications, nerve blocks, vulvar injections, surgery, and pelvic floor muscle strengthening (Bohm-Starke & Rylander, 2008; Landry et al., 2008; Nair et al., 2008). Newer research indicates that using birth control pills for more than 2 years may increase the risk for vulvar pain during intercourse (Harlow et al., 2008).

Infections

A number of kinds of infections can afflict the female genital system, and those that are sexually transmitted are discussed in Chapter 15. However, some infections of the female reproductive tract are not necessarily sexually transmitted. For example, as we discussed earlier in this chapter, the Bartholin's glands and the urinary tract can become infected, just as any area of the body can become infected when bacteria get inside and multiply. These infections may happen because of poor hygiene practices and are more frequent in those who engage in frequent sexual intercourse. When infected, the glands can swell and cause pressure and discomfort and can interfere with walking, sitting, or sexual intercourse. Usually a physician will need to drain the infected glands with a catheter and will prescribe a course of antibiotics (H. Blumstein, 2001).

REALResearch >Women should change out of their workout clothes—including their underwear—within an hour of exercise (NARDONE, 2004). Sweat glands from the bikini area can lead to dampness, which increases the risk of yeast or bacterial infections. In addition, thong underwear should never be worn during a workout because it can help spread bacteria from the rectum to the vagina.

Douching may put a woman at risk for vaginal infections because it changes the vagina's pH levels and can destroy healthy bacteria necessary to maintain proper balance. Those who reported using douches said they were concerned about vaginal odor and cleanliness. This is typically what drives women to use a variety of feminine hygiene products.

CANCER OF THE FEMALE REPRODUCTIVE ORGANS

Cancer is a disease in which certain cells in the body don't function properly—they divide too fast or produce excessive tissue that forms a tumor (or both). A number of cancers can affect the female reproductive organs. In this section, we look at breast, uterine, cervical, endometrial, and ovarian cancers. We will also review preventive measures for detecting or avoiding common female health problems. In Chapter 14, we discuss how these illnesses affect women's lives and sexuality.

Breast Cancer

Breast cancer is the most prevalent cancer in the world (Parkin et al., 2005). In the United States, an estimated 182,460 new cases of invasive breast cancer were expected to occur in women in 2008 (American Cancer Society, 2008). After continuously increasing for more than 2 decades, the breast cancer rates among women have been decreasing over the past few years. This may be due to a reduction in the use of hormone replacement therapy, which we discussed earlier in this chapter.

Worldwide, breast cancer rates have been found to correlate with variations in diet, especially fat intake. Even with these variations, however, the specific dietary factors that affect breast cancer have not been established. Breast-feeding, on the other hand, has been found to reduce a woman's lifetime risk of developing breast cancer (Eisinger & Burke, 2002).

Unfortunately, there is no known method to prevent breast cancer, so it is extremely important to detect it as early as possible. Every woman should regularly perform breast self-examinations (see the accompanying Sex in Real Life, "Breast Self-Examination"),

uterine fibroids
A (usually noncancerous) tumor of muscle and connective tissue that develops within, or is attached to, the uterine wall.

cryotherapy
The application of extreme cold to destroy diseased tissue, including cancer cells.

vulvodynia
Chronic vulvar pain and soreness.

douching
A method of vaginal rinsing or cleaning that involves squirting water or other solutions into the vagina.

especially after age 35. Women should also have their breasts examined during routine gynecological checkups, which is a good time to ask for instruction on self-examination if you have any questions about the technique.

Another important preventive measure is **mammography,** which can detect tumors too small to be felt during self-examination. There is some controversy about when a woman should begin going for regular mammography examinations, with some claiming that the research shows no significant benefit in women under 50; others suggesting mammograms every 2 years from age 40; still others recommending regular mammograms for women of all ages. The American Cancer Society recommends that a woman begin yearly mammograms every year after age 40. However, you should discuss with your health care provider whether mammography is appropriate for you, and if so, how often.

All women are at risk for breast cancer, even if they have no family history of the disease. Most commonly, breast cancer is discovered by a postmenopausal woman who discovers a breast lump with no other symptoms. However, breast cancer can also cause breast pain, nipple discharge, changes in nipple shape, and skin dimpling. It should be noted here that the discovery of a lump or mass in your breast does not mean you have cancer; most masses are **benign,** and many do not even need treatment. If it is **malignant** and left untreated, however, breast cancer usually spreads throughout the body, which is why it is important that any lump be immediately brought to the attention of your physician or other medical practitioner.

All women are at risk for breast cancer . . .

TREATMENT   In the past, women with breast cancer usually had a **radical mastectomy.** Today few women need such drastic surgery. More often, a partial or modified mastectomy is performed, which leaves many of the underlying muscles and lymph nodes in place (see photo accompanying this section). This procedure, combined with radiation therapy, has similar long-term survival rates as radical mastectomy (American Cancer Society, 2003). If the breast must be removed, many women choose to undergo breast reconstruction, in which a new breast is formed from existing skin and fat or breast implants (see Chapter 14).

If the tumor is contained to its site and has not spread, a **lumpectomy** may be considered. A lumpectomy involves the removal of the tumor, along with some surrounding tissue, but the breast is left intact. Radiation therapy or chemotherapy (or both) are often used in conjunction with a lumpectomy.

RISK FACTORS   Risk factors for breast cancer include age, a family history of breast cancer, a long menstrual history (early menarche and later menopause), never having children, recent use of birth control pills, and having one's first child after age 30 (American Cancer Society, 2008a; Li et al., 2008). An early onset of puberty and menarche may increase the chances of developing breast cancer, probably because of prolonged estrogen exposure (American Cancer Society, 2008). However, newer research claims that obesity, low levels of physical activity, and consuming one or more alcoholic drinks per day may have more to do with the development of breast cancer than do early onsets of puberty or menarche (American Cancer Society, 2008; Verkasalo et al., 2001). A woman's chance of acquiring breast cancer increases significantly as she ages. In fact, 77% of breast cancers appear in women who are 50 years old or older, whereas less than 5% appear in women under age 40 (Jemal et al., 2005).

Family history also may be a risk factor in breast cancer; however, about 90% of women who develop breast cancer do not have any family history of the disease (American Cancer Society, 2008). No study has been large enough to reliably show how the risk of breast cancer is influenced by familial patterns of breast cancer. Although women who have a first-degree relative with breast cancer may have an increased risk of the disease, most of these women will never develop breast cancer (Collaborative Group on Hormonal Factors in Breast Cancer, 2001).

Mutations in a breast cancer gene, either BRCA1 or BRCA2 gene, have been found to lead to high risk for both breast and ovarian cancer. Although these mutations are rare, they are more common in women with relatives who have been diagnosed with

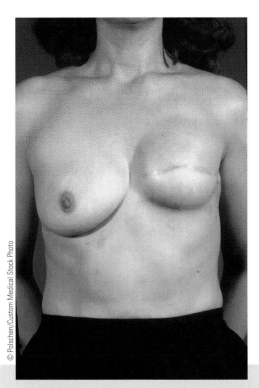

Partial or modified mastectomies are more common today than radical mastectomies.

mammography
A procedure for internal imaging of the breasts to evaluate breast disease or screen for breast cancer.

benign
A nonmalignant, mild case of a disease that is favorable for recovery.

malignant
A cancerous growth that tends to spread into nearby normal tissue and travel to other parts of the body.

radical mastectomy
A surgical procedure that involves removal of the breast, its surrounding tissue, the muscles supporting the breast, and underarm lymph nodes.

lumpectomy
A modern surgical procedure for breast cancer in which only the tumorous lump and a small amount of surrounding tissue are removed.

Breast Self-Examination

Beginning in their 20s, women should become familiar with the shape and feel of their breasts.

A breast self-examination (BSE), along with mammography and a clinical breast exam from a health care provider, can help reduce breast cancer in women. Beginning in their 20s, women should become familiar with the shape and feel of their breasts, so they can report any breast changes to a health care provider. If a woman does detect a thickening or a lump, however, she should not panic; 80% to 90% of all lumps are noncancerous and can be easily treated. After age 40, mammography, clinical breast exams, and even magnetic resonance imaging (MRI) become more useful, although a monthly BSE is still recommended (Saslow et al., 2007). Women with breast implants are also encouraged to perform BSEs (American Cancer Society, 2007).

Because the shape and feel of the breasts change during ovulation and menstruation, it is best to perform a BSE about 1 week after menstruation ceases. BSE should be done at the same time during each cycle (see Figure 5.9 for more information about a breast self exam).

In the Mirror
The first step of a BSE is inspection. Look at your breasts in a mirror to learn their natural contours. With arms relaxed, note any elevation of the level of the nipple, dimpling, bulging, or dimpling. Compare the size and shape of the breasts, remembering that one (usually the left) is normally slightly larger. Next, press the hands down firmly on the hips to tense the pectoral muscles, and then raise the arms over the head looking for a shift in relative position of the

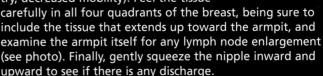

two nipples. These maneuvers also bring out any dimpling or bulging. After doing BSEs over time, any changes will become obvious, which is why it is best to begin BSEs early rather than later in life.

In the Shower
The shower is a good place to do a breast palpation (pressing)—fingers glide well over wet or soapy skin. Press the breast against the chest wall with the flat of the hand, testing the surface for warmth, and moving the hand to test mobility. Pay close attention to increased heat or redness of the overlying skin, tenderness, dilated superficial veins, and retraction (dimpling, asymmetry, decreased mobility). Feel the tissue carefully in all four quadrants of the breast, being sure to include the tissue that extends up toward the armpit, and examine the armpit itself for any lymph node enlargement (see photo). Finally, gently squeeze the nipple inward and upward to see if there is any discharge.

Lying Down
Finally, lie down and put a folded towel or a pillow under your left shoulder. Placing your left hand behind your head, use your right hand to press firmly in small, circular motions all around the left breast, much as you did in the shower. Use three different levels of pressure to feel all the breast tissue. Light pressure allows you to feel the tissues closest to the skin; medium pressure lets you feel a bit deeper; and firm pressure allows you to check the tissue close to your ribs. If you are not sure how firm to press, ask a health care provider to show you. You will feel the normal structures of the breast beneath your fingers, but look for a distinct lump or hardness. Next, do a vertical check by placing your hand on top of the breast and slowly moving it downward from your collarbone to your ribs. Some evidence suggests that this up-and-down movement (vertical pattern) is the most effective part of a breast self exam because it allows a woman to explore the entire breast area (American Cancer Society, 2007). Repeat the entire procedure for your other breast.

Finally, squeeze each nipple again gently, looking for any discharge, whether clear or bloody. Any discharge or any other irregularities or lumps should be reported to your health care provider without delay.

SOURCE: The American Cancer Society, 2007.

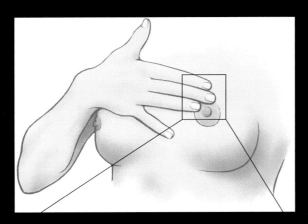

breast or ovarian cancer or who have ethnicity or racial factors. The prevalence of pathogenic genetic mutations was found to be highest in women over age 35 who were of Ashkenazic Jewish ancestry (8.3%) and lowest in Asian Americans (0.5%) (John et al., 2007); other ethnicity findings included Hispanics (3.5%), non-Hispanic Whites (2.2%), and African Americans (1.3%). However, in patients diagnosed before age 35 years, the prevalence rate was particularly high in African American women (17%). Some women who have been found to have a high risk of developing breast cancer choose to undergo prophylactic (preventive) mastectomies before breast cancer can develop (Harmon, 2007; D. A. Levine & Gemignani, 2003; Sakorafas, 2005).

There has also been some controversy over the effect of oral contraceptives on breast cancer rates, with many contradictory studies, some finding an increased risk, and others finding no increased risk (American Cancer Society, 2008; Cabaret et al., 2003; Narod et al., 2002). Although there have been slightly more breast cancers found in women who use oral contraceptives, these cancers have been less advanced and less aggressive (Fraser, 2000). A comprehensive study conducted by the U.S. Food and Drug Administration (FDA) concluded that there is no concrete evidence that the pill causes or influences the development of breast cancer; however, the long-term effects of using oral contraception are not yet certain, and those with a family history of breast cancer might want to consider using other forms of contraception.

Uterine Cancer

Different types of cancer can affect the uterus. Here we discuss cervical, endometrial, and ovarian cancers.

Cervical Cancer

Incidence rates for cervical cancer have decreased steadily over the past several decades. In 2008, it was estimated that there would be roughly 11,000 cases of invasive cervical cancer diagnosed in the United States (American Cancer Society, 2008). A Pap smear, taken during routine pelvic exams, can detect early changes in the cervical cells, which has helped in the early diagnosis of cancer. A few cells are painlessly scraped from the cervix during a Pap smear and are examined under a microscope for abnormalities. Researchers have recently begun evaluating the use of Pap tests in conjunction with a blood test for human papillomavirus (HPV; we discuss this sexually transmitted infection more in Chapter 15). HPV is the primary cause of cervical cancer and using HPV tests identifies 95% of cervical cancers, whereas Pap smears alone identify only 55% (Mayrand et al., 2007; Naucler et al., 2007). Using both tests together has been found to identify cancers nearly 100% of the time.

Cervical cancer has high cure rates because it starts as an easily identifiable lesion, called a **cervical intraepithelial neoplasia (CIN),** which usually progresses slowly into cervical cancer. Better early detection of cervical cancer has led to a sharp decrease in the numbers of serious cervical cancer cases. For some poor or uninsured women in the U.S. and abroad, routine pelvic examinations and Pap smears are not available. It is for this reason that approximately 80% of the 500,000 new cases of cervical cancer are

REALResearch **>**Many women today take herbal supplements, which are unregulated by the FDA. Some of these supplements can interfere with menstrual cycles and the effectiveness of birth control pills (ROAN, 2004). For example, St. John's wort can decrease the pill's effectiveness, and black cohosh has been found to interfere with estrogen levels. It's best to check with your health care provider before taking any herbal supplements.

diagnosed every year in poor countries such as sub-Saharan Africa and Latin America (Nebehay, 2004).

CIN occurs more frequently in women who have had sexual intercourse early in their lives as well as women with multiple sexual partners (American Cancer Society, 2008). Women who begin to have children at an early age, such as teenage mothers, are also at increased risk. Chronic inflammation of the cervix (cervicitis) has also been found to be frequently associated with cervical cancer (American Cancer Society, 2008). As discussed earlier, because of the relationship between the HPV and cervical cancer, it is particularly important for those with a diagnosis of genital warts to have regular Pap smears. Oral contraceptive users have 2 to 4 times the risk for developing cervical cancer, particularly if they have used oral contraceptives for more than 5 to 10 years (American Cancer Society, 2008). The majority of cervical cancers develop slowly, so if a woman has regular Pap tests, nearly all cases can be successfully treated (American Cancer Society, 2008).

There are simple and effective treatments for CIN, such as surgery, radiation, or both, which have resulted in cure rates up to 90% in early-stage disease and a dramatic decline in mortality rate for cervical cancer. If the disease has progressed, treatment commonly includes a **hysterectomy** followed by radiation and chemotherapy.

In 2006, the U.S. FDA approved Gardasil, the first vaccine developed to prevent the most common types of HPV infections that can lead to cervical cancer (American Cancer Society, 2008). We discuss this vaccine more in Chapter 15.

Endometrial Cancer

Cancer of the lining of the uterus is the most frequent gynecological cancer, even though incidence rates for endometrial cancer have also decreased steadily over the past several years. In 2008, it was estimated that there would be approximately 40,000 cases of uterine cancer, most of which involved the endometrial lining (American Cancer Society, 2008). Symptoms include abnormal uterine bleeding or spotting and pain during urination or sexual intercourse. Because a Pap smear is rarely effective in detecting early endometrial cancer, a **D&C (dilation and curettage)** is more reliable. Treatment options for endometrial cancer include surgery, radiation, hormones, and chemotherapy.

Endometrial cancer generally affects women aged over 50 years and is a major reason for hysterectomies in that age group.

cervical intraepithelial neoplasia (CIN)
A change in the cells on the surface of the cervix that may signal early beginnings of cervical cancer; sometimes referred to as cervical dysplasia.

hysterectomy
The surgical removal of the uterus.

dilation and curettage (D&C)
The surgical scraping of the uterine wall with a spoon-shaped instrument.

Estrogen has been found to be a strong risk factor for endometrial cancers, especially when it's used alone, without other hormones, such as progesterone (American Cancer Society, 2008). This would include hormone replacement therapies that only contain estrogens. In addition, the risk is increased for women who experienced an early menarche, late menopause, have not had children, and have a history of polycystic ovarian syndrome. Both pregnancy and the use of birth control pills have been found to offer some protection from endometrial cancers (American Cancer Society, 2008). If detected at an early stage, more than 90% of women will survive at least 5 years.

Ovarian Cancer

Ovarian cancer is the second most common gynecological cancer in women, and it was estimated there were close to 22,000 new cases in the United States in 2008 (American Cancer Society, 2008). Although not as common as uterine or breast cancer, ovarian cancer causes more deaths than any other cancer of the female reproductive system, because the symptoms are usually subtle or nonexistent (American Cancer Society, 2008). Ovarian cancer is more common in northern European and North American countries than in Asia or developing countries.

Most of the time, ovarian cancer invades the body silently, with few warning signs or symptoms until it reaches an advanced stage. However, in 2007, cancer experts began advising women of certain symptoms that may alert them to the presence of ovarian cancer. These symptoms include sudden bloating, increased need to urinate, eating changes, and abdominal or pelvic pain (American Cancer Society, 2008). Since these symptoms are similar to symptoms of irritable bowel syndrome, it's important for a woman to check with her health care provider should she experience a sudden change in these symptoms. A woman in whom an ovarian lump is detected need not panic, however, for most lumps turn out to be relatively harmless **ovarian cysts;** about 70% of all ovarian tumors are benign.

The cause of ovarian cancer is unknown. An increased incidence is found in women who are childless, undergo early menopause, eat a high-fat diet, or who are from a higher socioeconomic status. Women who are lactose-intolerant or who use talc powder (especially on the vulva) have also been found to have higher rates of ovarian cancer. A decreased incidence is associated with having children, using oral contraceptives, or undergoing late menopause (American Cancer Society, 2008). Women who take birth control pills, who were pregnant at an early age, or who had several pregnancies, have particularly low rates of ovarian cancer. One study demonstrated that women who undergo tubal ligation (have their tubes tied to prevent pregnancy) also reduce the risk of ovarian cancer (Narod et al., 2001).

The most important factor in the survival rate from ovarian cancer is early detection and diagnosis. It is estimated that two thirds of cases of ovarian cancer are diagnosed late (Mantica, 2005). Because the ovary floats freely in the pelvic cavity, a tumor can grow undetected without producing many noticeable symptoms (i.e., there is little pressure on other organs; see Figure 5.4).

There are several screening techniques for detecting ovarian cancer. These include blood tests, pelvic examinations, and ultrasound. Unfortunately, pelvic examinations are not effective in the early diagnosis of ovarian cancer, and both blood tests and ultrasound have fairly high **false negatives.** This is why many women with ovarian cancer are diagnosed after the cancer has spread beyond the ovary. Although there are a variety of screening tests available for ovarian cancer, including CA-125 and YKL-40, the United States Preventive Services Task Force recommends against routine screening for ovarian cancer, because the potential benefits of these tests remains low (Mantica, 2005; U.S. Preventive Services Task Force, 2005).

The only treatment for ovarian cancer is removal of the ovaries (with or without accompanying hysterectomy) and radiation and chemotherapy. As we stated earlier, early detection is crucial to maximizing the chance of a cure. Preventive surgery to remove the ovaries in women with a genetic risk has been found to decrease the risk of other gynecologic cancers (American Cancer Society, 2008).

As you have learned throughout this chapter, understanding anatomy and physiology is an important piece in learning about human sexual behavior. It is important to understand all of the physiological and hormonal influences and how they affect the female body before we can move on to the emotional and psychological issues involved in human sexuality. Anatomy and physiology, therefore, are really the foundations of any human sexuality class. We continue laying this foundation in the following chapter when we move on to Chapter 6, "Male Anatomy and Physiology."

> *Ovarian cancer is the second most common gynecological cancer in women.*

ovarian cysts
Small, fluid-filled sacs, which can form on the ovary, that do not pose a health threat under most conditions.

false negatives
Incorrect result of a medical test that wrongly shows the lack of a finding, condition, or disease.

review questions

1 Explain what is done in a yearly pelvic exam and why.

2 Name and explain three gynecological health concerns.

3 Identify and explain the risk factors that have been identified for breast cancer.

4 Explain how a blood test for human papillomavirus along with a Pap smear may help detect cervical cancer.

5 Identify and describe the two most common forms of uterine cancer.

6 Explain why ovarian cancer is the most deadly gynecologic cancer.

CHAPTER **review**

SUMMARY POINTS

1 Endocrine glands produce hormones. Female reproductive hormones include estrogen and progesterone, whereas the primary male reproductive hormone is testosterone.

2 The women's external sex organs, collectively called the vulva, include a number of separate structures, including the mons veneris, labia majora, and labia minora. The clitoris is composed of a glans, body, and paired crura (legs). It is richly supplied with both blood vessels and nerve endings and becomes erect during sexual excitement. The opening of the vagina is also referred to as the introitus.

3 The female's internal sexual organs include the vagina, uterus, Fallopian tubes, and ovaries. The vagina serves as the female organ of intercourse and the passageway to and from the uterus.

4 The uterus is a thick-walled, hollow, muscular organ that provides a path for sperm to reach the ovum and provides a home for the developing fetus. On the sides of the uterus lie two Fallopian tubes, and their job is to bring the ovum from the ovary into the uterus. The mature ovary contains a woman's oocytes and are the major producers of female reproductive hormones.

5 The breasts are modified sweat glands that contain fatty tissue and produce milk to nourish a newborn. Milk creation, secretion, and ejection from the nipple is referred to as breast-feeding, or lactation.

6 Female puberty occurs when the ovaries begin to release estrogen, which stimulates growth of the woman's sexual organs and menstruation. Menstruation can be divided into four general phases: the follicular phase, the ovulation phase, the luteal phase, and the menstrual phase.

7 A number of menstrual problems are possible, including amenorrhea, which involves a lack of menstruation; menorrhagia, which involves excessive menstrual flow; and dysmenorrhea, which is painful menstruation. The physical and emotional symptoms that may occur late in the menstrual cycle are called premenstrual syndrome (PMS). The most debilitating and severe cases of PMS are referred to as premenstrual dysphoric disorder.

8 Menstrual manipulation, the ability to schedule menstrual periods, and menstrual suppression, the ability to completely eliminate menses, are becoming more popular. There are cultural taboos against sexual intercourse during menstruation. However, engaging in sexual intercourse during menstruation is a personal decision; although there is no medical reason to avoid intimacy during this time, couples need to talk about what they are comfortable with doing.

9 As women age, hormone or estrogen production wanes, leading to perimenopause and then menopause, or the cessation of menstruation. Some women use nutritional therapy to help lessen menopausal symptoms, whereas others use hormone replacement therapy, which has its advantages and disadvantages.

10 Regular gynecological examination is recommended for all women to help detect uterine, ovarian, and cervical cancers. Genital self-examination is also an important part of women's health behavior.

11 There are several gynecological health concerns. Endometriosis is a condition in which the uterine cells begin to migrate to places other than the uterus. Toxic shock syndrome is an infection, usually caused by the use of tampons. Symptoms of TSS include high fever, vomiting, diarrhea, and sore throat. If left untreated it can result in death.

12 Uterine fibroids are hard tissue masses in the uterus, and symptoms include pelvic pain, heavy cramping, and prolonged bleeding.

13 The most prevalent cancer in the world is breast cancer. Breast self-examination can help detect breast cancer early. The most common forms of uterine cancer are cervical and endometrial. The most deadly of all gynecologic cancers is ovarian.

CRITICAL THINKING questions

1 What were the early messages that you received (as a man or a woman) about menstruation? Did you receive any information about it when you were growing up? What do you wish would have been done differently?

2 Do you think that PMS really exists? Provide a rationale for your answer.

3 If you are heterosexual or a lesbian, how would you feel about engaging in sex during menstruation? Why do you think you feel this way? Trace how these feelings may have developed.

4 If you are a woman, have you ever practiced a breast self-exam? If so, what made you decide to perform one? If you have never performed one, why not? If you are a man, do you encourage the women in your life to perform breast self-exams? Why or why not?

Sexuality Now Book Companion Website

Go to www.cengage.com/psychology/carroll for practice quizzes, glossary, flash cards, and more. You can also access the following websites from the companion site.

Museum of Menstruation & Women's Health (MUM) ■ An online museum that illustrates the rich history of menstruation and women's health. It contains information on menstruation's history and various aspects of menstruation.

The American College of Obstetricians and Gynecologists (ACOG) ■ ACOG is the nation's leading group of professionals providing health care for women. This site contains information on recent news releases relevant to women's health, educational materials, and links to various other health-related websites.

National Women's Health Information Center (NWHIC) ■ This website, operated by the Department of Health and Human Services, provides a gateway to women's health information services. Information is available on pregnancy, cancers, nutrition, menopause, and hormone replacement therapy, as well as many other health-related areas.

The National Vulvodynia Association (NVA) ■ The National Vulvodynia Association (NVA) is a nonprofit organization created to educate and provide support. NVA coordinates a central source of information and encourages further research.

Cancernet ■ This site contains material for health professionals, including cancer treatments, prevention, and CANCERLIT, a bibliographic database.

Forward USA ■ Forward USA is a nonprofit organization that works to eliminate female genital mutilation (FGM) and provide support services for those young girls and women who are victims of FGM.

CengageNOW

Go to www.cengage.com/login to link to CengageNOW, your online study tool. First take the Pre-Test for this chapter to get your Personalized Study Plan, which will identify topics you need to review and direct you to online resources. Then take the Post-Test to determine what concepts you have mastered and what you still need work on.

Videos in CengageNOW

CengageNOW also contains these videos related to the chapter topics:

- Breast Cancer: Education and Support Groups—Is providing group support or group education more effective in prolonging the lives of women with breast cancer?

- Premature Puberty—Learn about some of the problems associated with the early onset of puberty.

CHAPTER 6

Male Sexual Anatomy and Physiology

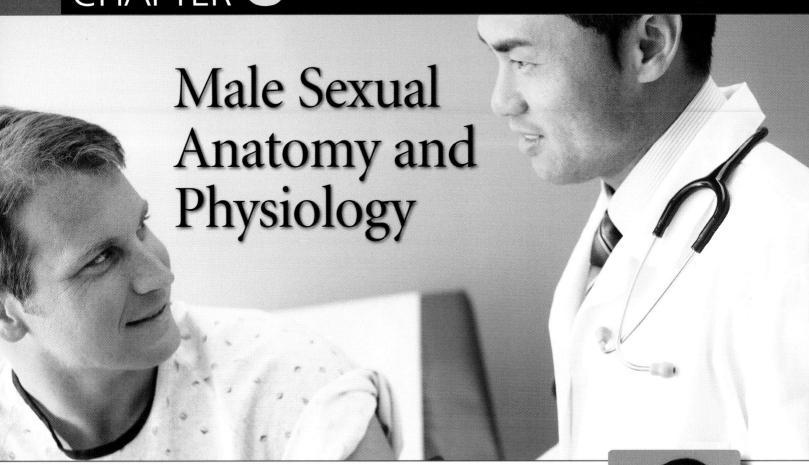

Growing up as a male in society is more difficult than some would think. Starting from the day we are born, boys have separate everything—toys, colors, clothes, haircuts, and even separate ways to deal with emotions. No one really thinks about the pressures guys endure—being forced to conform to society's gender norms for fear of being bullied, abused, or outcasted. We are taught to be emotionally anorexic and never cry. We are taught to play rough sports and be macho.

Growing up I never wanted anything more than to be accepted; but other males aren't accepting of anyone who presents themselves differently. I can remember being in the second grade, I was the only Black boy to have long curly hair, so kids started calling me "Curly Sue." I don't know why, because I didn't think I looked like a girl named Sue. Soon after this, all the boys on the soccer team started to call me this, too. My parents told me it was just stupid humor, but they had no idea how much it bothered me. The next year, I went to a new school and found it was even harsher than the last one. Not only did the nickname follow me, but new, meaner names were made. It went from a harmless nickname to actual outcasting; I was called a "sissy" and "girly boy" because I had long curls, and a "faggot" because of how I looked. I didn't even know what these words meant, and they stayed with me right up until my eighth-grade graduation.

I really didn't understand why everyone hated me. It was so stupid because no one knew me. It got to the point where I would fake being sick just so I wouldn't have to go to school, or throw up in school so they would send me home early. I never talked to my parents about it because I knew I had to just suck it up and take it like a man. I found that going to high school finally shook me of my horrible childhood, and I seriously thought growing up would be a lot easier from there on out. This was true until college—a time when alcohol forces adults to regress back to their preschool ways. Soon I was experiencing physical violence, vandalism, and endless taunting. Strangers who didn't like me, or even know me, would tell me how they felt about me to my face, and try and pick a fight.

Talking to my family about how hard my peers were on me growing up has resulted in a number of conversations that revolve around one cliché: "What doesn't kill you makes you stronger." This may be true, but this way of thinking is used with males way too much. Being told this just forces guys to have a tough exterior. Now that I am getting ready to graduate from college, I can look back and see how I have grown strong because I had to fight so hard to be accepted in my past.
SOURCE: Author's files.

© Janell Carroll

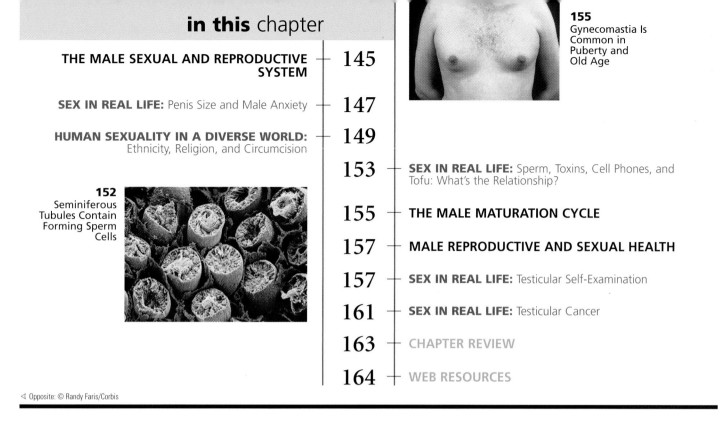

155
Gynecomastia Is Common in Puberty and Old Age

152
Seminiferous Tubules Contain Forming Sperm Cells

◁ Opposite: © Randy Faris/Corbis

Growing up male comes with its own set of challenges, as this student's story tells us. Throughout this book, we explore the challenges of gender and ethnicity. In this chapter, we take a closer look at being male and explore male anatomy and physiology. In the previous chapter, we discussed female anatomy and physiology, and although there are many similarities between the two, there are also many important differences. One obvious difference is the fact that the male gonads (the testes) lie outside of the body, whereas the female gonads (ovaries) are located deep within the abdomen. Because of the location of the male genitalia, boys are often more comfortable than girls with their genitalia. In this chapter, we explore the male reproductive system, maturation, and sexual health issues.

The Male Sexual and Reproductive System

Most men are fairly familiar with their penis and scrotum. Boys learn to hold their penises while urinating, certainly notice them when they become erect, and generally talk more freely about their genitals among themselves than girls do. Yet the male reproductive system is a complex series of glands and ducts, and few men have a full understanding of how the system operates physiologically.

EXTERNAL SEX ORGANS

The external sex organs of the male include the penis (which consists of the glans and root) and the scrotum. Here we discuss these organs and the process of penile erection.

The Penis

The **penis** is the male sexual organ. It contains the urethra, which carries urine and semen to the outside of the body. The penis has the ability to engorge with blood and stiffen, which evolutionary theorists would tell us allows for easier penetration of the vagina to deposit sperm near the cervical os for its journey toward the ovum. Although there is no bone and little muscle in the human

penis
The male copulatory and urinary organ, used both to urinate and move spermatozoa out of the urethra through ejaculation; it is the major organ of male sexual pleasure and is homologous to the female clitoris.

REALResearch > The penis has evolved into a shape that allows it to remove another lover's sperm from the reproductive tract of a woman (SHACKELFORD & GOETZ, 2007). Researchers used two dildos shaped like penises, one with a coronal ridge and one without. The coronal ridge penis removed **56%** more of the (other man's) semen with only one thrust. Sperm competition occurs when the sperm of two or more men is present in the female reproductive tract, and the coronal ridge of the penis helps to push existing sperm out of the way. In addition, researchers found that vaginal intercourse is more vigorous when a partner suspects cheating, allowing the penis to displace more of the existing sperm.

THE GLANS PENIS The corpus spongiosum ends in a conelike expansion called the **glans penis.** The glans penis is made up of the **corona,** the **frenulum** (FREN-yu-lum), and the **meatus** (mee-ATE-us; see Figures 6.1 and 6.2). The glans is very sensitive to stimulation, and some males find direct or continuous stimulation of the glans irritating.

The prepuce of the glans penis is a circular fold of skin usually called the **foreskin.** The foreskin is a continuation of the loose skin that covers the penis as a whole to allow it to grow during erection. The foreskin can cover part or all of the glans and retracts back over the corona when the penis is erect.

penis, the root of the penis is attached to a number of muscles that help eject **semen** and allow men to move the penis slightly when erect. Throughout history, men have experienced anxiety about penis size. In the accompanying Sex in Real Life, "Penis Size and Male Anxiety," we discuss this anxiety.

The penis is composed of three cylinders, each containing erectile tissue—spongelike tissue that fills with blood to cause **erection.** Two lateral **corpora cavernosa** (CORE-purr-uh cav-er-NO-suh) lie on the upper sides of the penis, and the central **corpus spongiosum** (CORE-pus spon-gee-OH-sum) lies on the bottom and contains the urethra. The three are bound together with connective tissue to give the outward appearance of a single cylinder and are permeated by blood vessels and spongy tissues that fill with blood when the penis is erect.

semen
A thick, whitish secretion of the male reproductive organs, containing spermatozoa and secretions from the seminal vesicles, prostate, and bulbourethral glands.

erection
The hardening of the penis caused by blood engorging the erectile tissue.

corpora cavernosa
Plural of corpus cavernosum (cavernous body); areas in the penis (or clitoris) that fill with blood during erection.

corpus spongiosum
Meaning "spongy body," the erectile tissue in the penis that contains the urethra.

glans penis
The flaring, enlarged region at the end of the penis.

corona
The ridge of the glans penis.

frenulum
Fold of skin on the underside of the penis.

meatus
The urethral opening at the opening of the penis.

foreskin
The fold of skin that covers the glans penis; also called the prepuce.

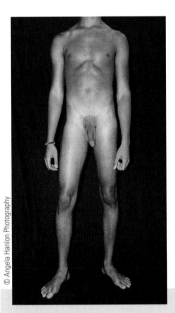 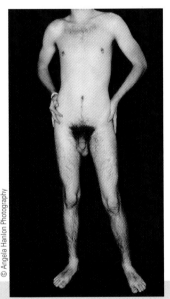 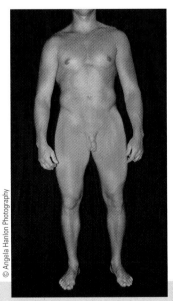 

All of the men in these photos have "normal" bodies. Individual differences in weight, the size and the shape of the torso, and fullness of pubic hair are normal.

Penis Size and Male Anxiety

. . . the vast majority of women and men report that penis size is not a significant factor in the quality of a sex partner.

The penis has been defined as the symbol of male sexuality throughout history. Men have often been plagued by concerns about penis function and size—especially size. Many men assume that there is a correlation between penis size and masculinity, or sexual prowess, and many men assume that their partners prefer a large penis. Others worry about their size and fear that they are not "normal." Although there may be a psychological preference for large penises among some partners (just as some partners desire women with large breasts), penis size has no correlation with the ability to excite a partner sexually during sex.

The average flaccid penis is between 3 and 4 inches long, and the average erect penis is 6 inches. Gary Griffen, the author of *Penis Size and Enlargement,* has found that only 15% of men have an erect penis measuring over 7 inches, and fewer than 5,000 erect penises worldwide measure 12 inches (Griffen, 1995). In the end, penis size has been found to be largely dependent on heredity—the father's penis size correlates well with the sons' (T. Hamilton, 2002).

The exaggerated opinion most men have of average penis size comes from pornographic films (which tend to use the largest men they can find); from men's perspective on their own penis (which, from the top, looks smaller than from the sides); and from overestimates of actual penis size (researchers consistently find that people's estimation of the size of penises they have just seen is exaggerated; Shamloul, 2005).

Still, men continue to be anxious about their penis size. Some succumb to the advertisements for devices promising to enlarge their penises. Men who purchase these devices are bound to be disappointed, for there is no nonsurgical way to enlarge the penis, and many of these techniques (most of which use suction) can do significant damage to the delicate penile tissue (D. Bagley, 2005). Other men with size anxiety refrain from sex altogether, fearing they cannot please a partner or will be laughed at when their partner sees them naked. Yet the vast majority of women and men report that penis size is not a significant factor in the quality of a sex partner.

WHAT DO YOU WANT TO KNOW ?

I've heard that some women can capture a penis in their vagina, using their muscles, so that the man cannot get it out. Is that true?
You are referring to a phenomenon known as "captive penis." Captive penis is found in some animals, in which the penis really is trapped in the vagina once intercourse is initiated. For example, there is a bone in the penis of the male dog that allows the penis to be inserted into the vagina before erection occurs. Once inside, the erection occurs, and the head of the penis enlarges inside the female's vagina. The vagina swells and prevents the male dog from withdrawing until ejaculation occurs and erection of the penis subsides. Although some people and some cultures believe that captive penis can happen in human beings too, there is not one authentic case on record.

In many cultures, the foreskin is removed surgically through a procedure called a **circumcision** (sir-kum-SI-zhun). Circumcision is practiced by many groups, such as Jews and Muslims, as a religious or cultural ritual; however, there are hygienic reasons why other cultures routinely circumcise their infants. If good hygiene is not practiced, **smegma,** secretions from small glands in the foreskin, can accumulate, causing a foul odor and sometimes infections. There is also some medical support for circumcision.

A wide-scale study done in Africa found that male circumcision offered some protection from HIV infection; the risk for HIV infection in circumcised men was 44% lower in circumcised men (M. S. Cohen et al., 2008; Drain, 2006; Morris, 2007; Thomson et al., 2007; Weiss et al., 2000). Another study from Africa found that the odds of HIV infection in circumcised men was 42% lower (Gray et al., 2000). Circumcised men also were found to have lower rates of chlamydia, infant urinary tract infections, penile cancer, and cervical cancer in their female partners (Alanis & Lucidi, 2004; Drain, 2006; Morris, 2007). Keep in mind, however, that these studies were all done with high-risk men, which may affect the studies results.

Even so, as a result of newer research, some medical professionals have begun questioning the health value of circumcision, which was the single most common surgical procedure performed on male patients in the United States in 2002 (Boyle et al., 2002). Since this time, circumcision rates have declined for several reasons, including decreased social pressure and insurance coverage (Mor et al., 2007).

circumcision
The surgical removal of the foreskin from the penis.

smegma
The collected products of sweat and oil glands that can accumulate under the foreskin.

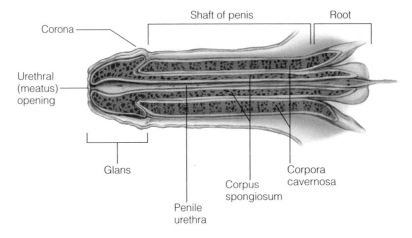

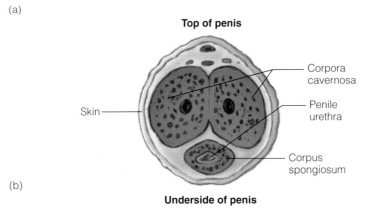

Figure **6.1** The internal structure of the penis.

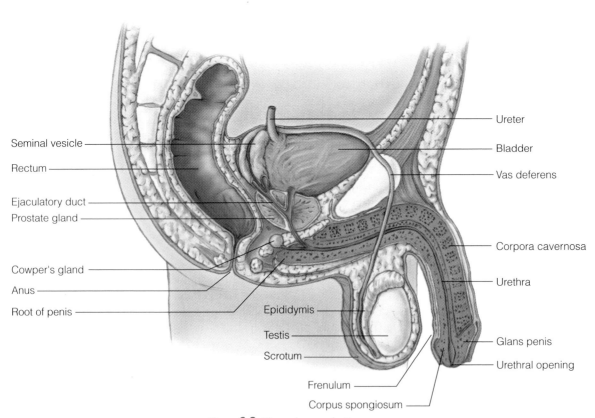

Figure **6.2** The male reproductive organs.

The bottom line is this: Although we do know that there may be some medical benefits to circumcision, they are not strong enough for health care providers to recommend routine circumcision (Kinkade & Meadows, 2005). In 1999, the American Academy of Pediatrics stopped recommending routine male circumcision and suggested that parents make the decision to circumcise based on their own experiences, their family, and religious beliefs (American Academy of Pediatrics, 1999).

THE ROOT The root of the penis enters the body just below the pubic bone and is attached to internal pelvic muscles (see Figure 6.2). The root of the penis goes further into the body than most men realize; it can be felt in the perineum (between the scrotum and anus), particularly when the penis is erect.

ERECTION Erection can occur with any form of stimulation the individual perceives as sexual—visual, tactile, auditory, olfactory, or cognitive. Excitement causes nerve fibers to swell the arteries of the penis, allowing blood to rush into the corpora cavernosa and corpus spongiosum, while veins are compressed to prevent the blood from escaping. The erectile tissues thus will fill with blood, and the penis becomes erect (Japanese folk wisdom claims that men's erection angles change as they age—see Figure 6.3 for more information). The penis returns to its flaccid state when the arteries constrict, the pressure closing off the veins is released, and the sequestered blood is allowed to drain.

Erection is basically a spinal reflex, and men who have spinal injuries can sometimes achieve reflex erections, in which their

penis becomes erect even though they can feel no sensation there. These erections generally occur without cognitive or emotional excitement (see Chapter 14). Also, as we mentioned earlier, most men have regular erections during their sleeping cycle and often wake up with erections, which shows that conscious sexual excitement is not necessary for erection.

HUMAN SEXUALITY IN A DIVERSE WORLD

Ethnicity, Religion, and Circumcision

. . . social considerations have been found to outweigh the medical facts when parents are deciding whether to circumcise their sons.

Circumcision was the single most common surgical procedure performed on male patients in the United States in 2002 (Boyle et al., 2002), and the practice of male circumcision has elicited more controversy than any other surgical procedure in history (Alanis & Lucidi, 2004). Nonreligious circumcision became popular in the 1870s because it was thought to promote hygiene, reduce "unnatural" sexual behaviors, prevent syphilis and gonorrhea, and reduce masturbation (G. Kaplan, 1977; Wallerstein, 1980). An article published in 1947 supporting circumcision reported that cancer was more common in laboratory mice who were not circumcised (Plaut & Kohn-Speyer, 1947). All of these medical reports and social considerations have influenced the incidence of male circumcision.

There have been some differences in circumcision rates across religious groups in the United States (Laumann et al., 2000). For example, Jewish men have the highest rates

of circumcision, whereas Protestant men have the lowest rates. Ethnicity is also related to some differences in circumcision rates. National probability studies done from 1999 to 2004 found that **79%** of men reported being circumcised, including **88%** of non-Hispanic White men, **73%** of non-Hispanic Black men, **42%** of Mexican American men, and **50%** of men of other races and ethnicities (Xu et al., 2007). Various ethnic groups have different preferences concerning circumcising their male children. If circumcision is common in a particular ethnic group, parents may be inclined to circumcise their male children so their sons will look like other boys (Centers for Disease Control and Prevention, 2008). In addition, fathers who are circumcised often have their sons circumcised (Goldman, 1999). These social considerations have been found to outweigh the medical facts when parents are deciding whether to circumcise their sons (M. S. Brown & Brown, 1987).

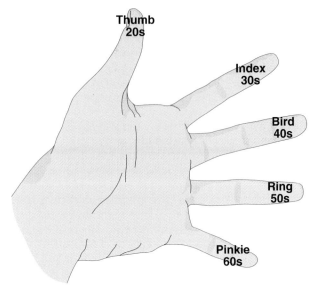

Thumb
20s

Index
30s

Bird
40s

Ring
50s

Pinkie
60s

Figure **6.3** Decades of a man's erection angle. Japanese folk wisdom claims that the fingers of an open hand give clues about erections throughout a man's life. Each finger represents the angle of the erect penis during each decade of a man's life. (*Source:* Hamilton, 2002, *Skin Flutes and Velvet Gloves*, p. 44. St. Martin's Press. © Dr Terri Hamilton. Reprinted by permission of St. Martin's Press LLC.)

The Scrotum

The **scrotum** (SKROH-tum) is a loose, wrinkled pouch beneath the penis, covered with sparse pubic hair. The scrotum contains the testicles, each in a sac, separated by a thin layer of tissue. In the previous chapter, we discussed how a woman's gonads (the ovaries) are located in her abdomen. This is different from the male gonads (the testicles), which sit outside the body. This is because the production and survival of sperm require a temperature that is a few degrees lower than the body's temperature, so the scrotum is actually a kind of cooling tank for the testicles.

When the testicles become too hot, sperm production is halted; in fact, soaking the testicles in hot water has been used as a form of birth control. (Of course, such a technique is highly unreliable, and it takes only a few hardy sperm to undo an hour of uncomfortable soaking. I do not recommend you try it!) Likewise, after a prolonged fever, sperm production may be reduced for as long as 2 months. It has also been suggested that men who are trying to impregnate their partner wear loose-fitting underwear, because tight jockstraps or briefs have been shown to reduce sperm counts somewhat, although the effects are reversible (Shafik, 1991). Semen quality has even been shown to undergo seasonal changes, with decreasing quality of semen and sperm counts during the summer due to the warmer weather (R. J. Levine, 1999).

The scrotum is designed to regulate testicular temperature using two mechanisms. First, the skin overlying the scrotum contains many sweat glands and sweats freely, which cools the testicles when they become too warm. Second, the **cremaster muscle** of the scrotum contracts and expands: When the testicles become too cool, they are drawn closer to the body to increase their tem-

*The **scrotum** is designed to regulate testicular temperature.*

perature; when they become too warm, they are lowered away from the body to reduce their temperature. Men often experience the phenomenon of having the scrotum relax and hang low when taking a warm shower, only to tighten up when cold air hits it after exiting the shower. The scrotum also contracts and elevates the testicles in response to sexual arousal, which may be to protect the testicles from injury during sexual behavior.

INTERNAL SEX ORGANS

The internal sex organs of the male include the testes, epididymis, vas deferens, seminal vesicles, prostate gland, and Cowper's glands. All of these organs play important roles in spermatogenesis, testosterone production, and the process of ejaculation.

The Testicles

The testicles (also referred to as the testes, TEST-eez) are egg-shaped glands that rest in the scrotum, each about 2 inches long and 1 inch in diameter. The left testicle usually hangs lower than the right in most men (T. Hamilton, 2002), although this can be reversed in left-handed men. Having one testicle lower than the other helps one slide over the other instead of crushing together when compressed. The testicles serve two main functions: **spermatogenesis** and testosterone production (see Figures 6.4 and 6.5).

scrotum
External pouch of skin that contains the testicles.

cremaster muscle
The "suspender" muscle that raises and lowers the scrotum to control scrotal temperature.

nocturnal emissions
Involuntary ejaculation during sleep, also referred to as a wet dream.

spermatogenesis
The production of sperm in the testes.

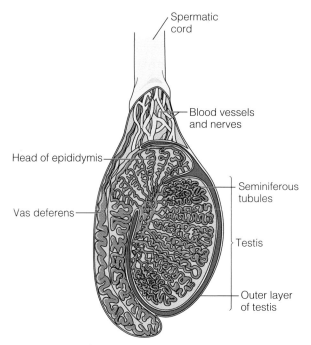

Figure **6.4** Internal structure of the testicle.

SPERMATOGENESIS Sperm are produced and stored in some 300 microscopic tubes located in the testes, known as **seminiferous** (sem-uh-NIF-uh-rus) **tubules.** Uncoiled, this network of tubes would extend over a mile! Figure 6.5 shows the development of the **spermatozoon** in the seminiferous tubules. First, a **spermatogonium** (sper-MAT-oh-go-nee-um) develops in the cells lining the outer wall of the seminiferous tubules and progressively moves toward the center of the tubules. Sertoli cells located in the seminiferous tubules secrete nutritional substances for the developing sperm.

As the spermatogonium grows, it becomes a primary **spermatocyte** (sper-MAT-oh-site) and then divides to form two secondary spermatocytes. As the developing sperm approach the center of the seminiferous tubules, the secondary spermatocytes divide into two **spermatids.** The spermatid then reorganizes its

seminiferous tubules
The tightly coiled ducts located in the testes where spermatozoa are produced.

spermatozoon
A mature sperm cell.

spermatogonium
An immature sperm cell that will develop into a spermatocyte.

spermatocyte
The intermediate stage in the growth of a spermatozoon.

spermatids
The cells that make up the final intermediate stage in the production of sperm.

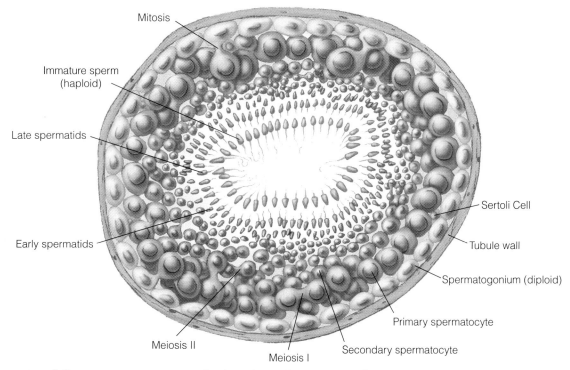

Figure **6.5** Spermatogenesis is continually taking place with various levels of sperm development throughout the testis.

Colored scan of seminiferous tubules, each containing a swirl of forming sperm cells (in blue).

nucleus to form a compact head, topped by an acrosome, which contains enzymes to help the sperm penetrate the ovum. The sperm also develops a midpiece, which generates energy, and a **flagellum** (flah-GEL-lum), which propels the mature spermatozoon. Human sperm formation requires approximately 72 days, yet because sperm is in constant production, the human male produces about 300 million sperm per day (for more information on sperm production, see the nearby Sex in Real Life).

TESTOSTERONE PRODUCTION Testosterone is produced in the testicles in **interstitial** (in-ter-STIH-shul) or **Leydig** (LIE-dig) **cells** and is synthesized from cholesterol. Testosterone is the most important male hormone; we discuss its role when we examine male puberty, later in this chapter.

REALResearch   > The word "testify" originates from the word "testes," the Latin word for testicles. The practice of holding one's testicles while testifying in a court of law was based on the belief that unborn generations would seek revenge if the truth weren't told (T. HAMILTON, 2002). This is why during Greek and Roman times, eunuchs (men whose testicles were removed) were not allowed to testify in court.

THE EPIDIDYMIS Once formed, immature sperm enter the seminiferous tubule and migrate to the **epididymis** (ep-uh-DID-uh-mus; see Figure 6.4), where they mature for about 10 to 14 days and where some faulty or old sperm are reabsorbed. The epididymis is a comma-shaped organ that sits atop the testicle and can be easily felt if the testicle is gently rolled between the fingers. If uncoiled, the epididymis would be about 20 feet in length. After sperm have matured, the epididymis pushes them into the vas deferens, where they can be stored for several months.

The Ejaculatory Pathway

The **vas deferens** (vass DEH-fuh-renz), or ductus deferens, is an 18-inch tube that carries the sperm from the testicles, mixes it with fluids from other glands, and propels the sperm toward the urethra during ejaculation (see Figure 6.2). **Ejaculation** is the physiological process whereby the seminal fluid is forcefully ejected from the penis. During ejaculation, sperm pass successively through the epididymis, the vas deferens, the ejaculatory duct, and the urethra, picking up fluid along the way from three glands—the seminal vesicles, the prostate gland, and the bulbo-urethral gland.

THE SEMINAL VESICLES The vas deferens hooks up over the ureter of the bladder and ends in an **ampulla.** Adjacent to the ampulla are the **seminal vesicles.** The seminal vesicles contribute rich secretions, which provide nutrition for the traveling sperm and make up about 60% to 70% of the volume of the ejaculate. The vas deferens and the duct from the seminal vesicles merge into a common **ejaculatory duct,** a short straight tube that passes into the prostate gland and opens into the urethra.

THE PROSTATE GLAND The **prostate** (PROSS-tayt) **gland,** a walnut-sized gland at the base of the bladder, produces several substances that are thought to aid sperm in their attempt to fertilize an ovum. The vagina maintains an acidic pH to protect against bacteria, yet an acidic environment slows down and eventually kills sperm. Prostatic secretions, which comprise about 25% to 30% of the ejaculate, effectively neutralize vaginal acidity almost immediately following ejaculation.

The prostate is close to the rectum, so a doctor can feel the prostate during a rectal examination. The prostate gland can cause a number of physical problems in men, especially older men, including prostate enlargement and the development of prostate cancer (see the section later in this chapter, "Male Reproductive and Sexual Health"). Annual prostate exams are recommended for men over 35 years of age.

---

flagellum
The tail-like end of a spermatozoon that propels it forward.

interstitial cells
Cells responsible for the production of testosterone; also referred to as Leydig cells.

Leydig cells
The cells in the testes that produce testosterone; also referred to as interstitial cells.

epididymis
A comma-shaped organ that sits atop the testicle and holds sperm during maturation.

vas deferens
One of two long tubes that convey the sperm from the testes and in which other fluids are mixed to create semen.

ejaculation
The reflex ejection or expulsion of semen from the penis.

ampulla
Base of the vas deferens, where the vas hooks up over the ureter of the bladder.

seminal vesicles
The pair of pouchlike structures lying next to the urinary bladder that secrete a component of semen into the ejaculatory ducts.

ejaculatory duct
A tube that transports spermatozoa from the vas deferens to the urethra.

prostate gland
A doughnut-shaped gland that wraps around the urethra as it comes out of the bladder, contributing fluid to the semen.

REALResearch **>** Male social status and female attractiveness have been found to affect sperm quality in red jungle fowl in Asia (a type of bird; CORNWALLIS & BIRKHEAD, 2007). Dominant males produce more sperm than subordinates, and the number and quality of sperm produced is in direct response to female sexual ornamentation—the more elaborate and beautiful the female, the more sperm produced by the male.

COWPER'S GLANDS The **bulbourethral** (bul-bow-you-REE-thral) or **Cowper's glands** are two pea-sized glands that flank the urethra just beneath the prostate gland. The glands have ducts that open right into the urethra and produce a fluid that cleans and lubricates the urethra for the passage of sperm, neutralizing any acidic urine that may remain in the urethra. The drop or more of pre-ejaculatory fluid that many men experience during arousal is the fluid from the Cowper's glands. The fluid may contain some live sperm, especially in a second act of intercourse if the male has not urinated in between.

EJACULATION Earlier in this chapter, we discussed erection as a spinal reflex. Ejaculation, like erection, also begins in the spinal column; however, unlike erection, there is seldom a "partial" ejaculation. Once the stimulation builds to the threshold, ejaculation usually continues until its conclusion.

bulbourethral gland
One of a pair of glands located under the prostate gland on either side of the urethra that secretes a fluid into the urethra; also called a Cowper's gland.

Cowper's gland
One of a pair of glands located under the prostate gland on either side of the urethra that secretes a fluid into the urethra; also called a bulbourethral gland.

SEX IN REAL LIFE

Sperm, Toxins, Cell Phones, and Tofu: What's the Relationship?

Overall, sperm counts have been declining in men throughout the world over the past 20 years.

Spermatogenesis occurs throughout a man's life, although sperm morphology (sperm form and structure) and motility (sperm's ability to swim), along with semen volume, have been found to decline continuously between the ages of 22 and 80 years old (Eskenazi et al., 2003). Researchers have been evaluating changes in total sperm counts, quality, morphology, and motility. Overall, sperm counts have been declining in men throughout the world over the past 20 years (Dindyal, 2004). Decreasing sperm counts and quality may contribute to male infertility—in fact, 25% of infertility cases are due to male factors (Templeton, 1995; we discuss infertility more in Chapter 12). Although declines in sperm counts and quality are a normal function of aging, researchers have begun to look at the impact of environmental and dietary factors, such as environmental toxins, cell phone usage, and certain food products.

Environmental toxins, such as dioxins and phthalates (substances added to plastics to make them more flexible), have also been found to reduce sperm quality (Mocarelli et al., 2008; Taioli et al., 2005). Dioxins are petroleum-derived chemicals that are in herbicides, pesticides, and industrial waste, but they are also commonly found in fish and cow milk products (Taioli et al., 2005). A U.S. study comparing semen quality in various geographic areas found reduced semen quality in areas where pesticides are commonly used (Swan, 2006). Phthalates have also been found to decrease sperm counts and quality (Stahlhut et al., 2007; Voiland, 2008).

Cell phones have also been identified as a possible factor in the decreasing quality of sperm. Cell phones emit radio-frequency electromagnetic waves, which have been found to affect sperm quality. High cell phone usage reduces semen quality in men by decreasing sperm counts, motility, and morphology (Agarwal et al., 2008). A strong association was found between the length of cell phone use and sperm count: Those who talked more than 4 hours a day had lower sperm quality. Other studies claim that cell phone usage may not be harmful to sperm (Deepinder et al., 2007; Erogul et al., 2006; Wdowiak et al., 2007).

Finally, sperm quality is also affected by what one eats and drinks. Men who smoke cigarettes and drink alcohol have significantly lower sperm counts than men who don't use tobacco or alcohol (Kalyani et al., 2007). In addition, men who eat soy products, such as tofu, miso soup, or tempeh, may also have lower sperm counts. A preliminary study found that men who eat a half serving of soy (approximately half a burger) per day have lower sperm counts than men who do not eat soy (Chavarro et al., 2007). Soy products contain high levels of isoflavones, which mimic estrogen in the body, causing hormonal changes in a man's body.

In the next few years, research will continue to monitor these environmental and dietary factors and changes in sperm quality. Some researchers believe that if the sperm decreases were to continue at current rates, widespread male infertility may result (Dindyal, 2004).

When the threshold is reached, the first stage of ejaculation begins: the epididymis, seminal vesicles, and prostate all empty their contents into the urethral bulb, which swells up to accommodate the semen. The bladder is closed off by an internal sphincter so that no urine is expelled with the semen. Once these stages begin, some men report feeling that ejaculation is imminent, that they are going to ejaculate and nothing can stop it; however, others report that this feeling of inevitability can be stopped by immediately ceasing all sensation.

If stimulation continues, strong, rhythmic contractions of the muscles at the base of the penis squeeze the urethral bulb, and the ejaculate is propelled from the body, usually accompanied by the pleasurable sensation of orgasm. Most men have between 5 and 15 contractions during orgasm, and many report enjoying strong pressure at the base of the penis during orgasm. From an evolutionary standpoint, this may be a way of encouraging deep thrusting at the moment of ejaculation to deposit semen as deeply as possible within the woman's vagina.

Once orgasm subsides, the arteries supplying the blood to the penis narrow, the veins taking the blood out enlarge, and the penis usually becomes limp. Depending on the level of excitement, the person's age, the length of time since the previous ejaculation, and his individual physiology, a new erection can be occur anywhere from immediately to an hour or so later. In older men, however, a second erection can take hours or even a day or so (we will discuss aging and sexual function more in chapter 14).

EJACULATE   The male ejaculate, or semen, averages about 2 to 5 milliliters—about 1 or 2 teaspoons. Semen normally contains secretions from the seminal vesicles and the prostate gland and about 50 to 150 million sperm per milliliter. If there are fewer than 20 million sperm per milliliter, the male is likely to be infertile—even though the ejaculate can have up to 500 million sperm altogether! Sperm is required in such large numbers because only a small fraction ever reach the ovum. Also, the sperm work together to achieve fertilization; for example, many die to plug up the os of the cervix for the other sperm, and the combined enzyme production of all sperm are necessary for a single spermatozoon to fertilize the ovum.

During vaginal intercourse, after ejaculation the semen initially coagulates into a thick mucuslike liquid, probably to keep it from leaking back out of the vagina. After 5 to 20 minutes, the prostatic enzymes contained in the semen cause it to thin out and liquefy. If it does not liquefy normally, coagulated semen may be unable to complete its movement through the cervix and into the uterus.

OTHER SEX ORGANS

Like women, men have other **erogenous zones,** or areas of the body that may be responsive to sexual touch. This is often an individual preference, but it can include the breasts and other erogenous zones, including the scrotum, testicles, and anus.

REALResearch   **>** Each ejaculation contains between **300** to **500** million sperm, and it is estimated that **10** to **20** ejaculations contain enough sperm to populate the earth (if, of course, each sperm had one ovum (T. HAMILTON, 2002).

The Breasts

Men's breasts are mostly muscle, and although they do have nipples and areolae, they seem to serve no functional purpose. Transsexual males, who want to change their sex (see Chapter 4), can enlarge their breasts to mimic the female breast by taking estrogen. Some men experience sexual pleasure from having their nipples stimulated, especially during periods of high excitement, whereas others do not.

There are some breast disorders that occur in men, including gynecomastia (guy-neck-oh-MAST-ee-uh), or breast enlargement. Gynecomastia is common both in puberty and old age and usually lasts anywhere from a few months to a few years. It is caused by excessive weight, drug therapy, excessive marijuana use, hormonal imbalances, and certain diseases. Generally gynecomastia disappears in time, and surgical removal is not necessary. However, some men choose to undergo a surgical technique that removes the excessive tissue through suction, which is usually followed by cosmetic surgery.

Breast cancer does affect men, although it is rare and accounts for less than 1% of all cases (American Cancer Society, 2007c). Because it is uncommon, it often progresses to an advanced stage before diagnosis (Frangou et al., 2005). In the previous chapter, we discussed breast cancer in women and the research on the BRCA genes. The presence of these genes can lead to a higher risk for the development of breast cancer. In men, the presence of these genes doubles the normal risk of prostate cancer and increases the risk of breast cancer by 7 times (Tai et al., 2007). Today some men opt for genetic testing to learn whether they have a BRCA mutation and an increased risk of cancer.

WHAT DO YOU WANT TO KNOW ?

Can a male have an orgasm without an ejaculation?

Yes. Before puberty, boys are capable of orgasm without ejaculation. In adulthood, some men report feeling several small orgasms before a larger one that includes ejaculation, whereas other men report that if they have sex a second or third time, there is orgasm without ejaculatory fluid. There are also some Eastern sexual disciplines, such as Tantra, that try to teach men to achieve orgasm without ejaculation because they believe that retaining semen is important for men.

erogenous zone
Any part of the body which, when stimulated, induces a sense of sexual excitement or desire.

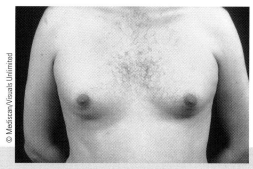

Gynecomastia is common in puberty and old age and can be caused by a variety of factors.

Treatment for breast cancer involves radiation or chemotherapy, and, if the cancer has spread to other parts of the body, surgical removal of the testes may be necessary to eliminate the hormones that could support the growth of the cancer (we talk about this more later in the chapter).

Other Erogenous Zones

Besides the penis, many men experience pleasure from stimulation of the scrotum, testicles (usually through gentle squeezing), and anus. As with women's erogenous zones, there is no part of the male body that is not erogenous if caressed in the right way and at the right time during sex. When the body is sexually stimulated, almost all moderate sensation can enhance excitement—which is why gentle pinching, scratching, and slapping can be exciting for some sexual partners.

review questions

1 Identify the external male sex organs and discuss the functions of each.

2 Explain why the male gonads are located outside of the body.

3 Identify and discuss the functions of the internal male sexual organs.

4 Identify the internal male sex organs and discuss the functions of each.

5 Describe the path taken by a sperm from the moment it is a spermatogonium until it is ejaculated. What other internal male organs contribute to semen along the way?

The Male
Maturation Cycle

Now that we've discussed the male sexual and reproductive system, let's explore male maturation. In the following section, we discuss the physical changes that accompany male puberty. Many of these changes are controlled by hormonal changes that occur and contribute to physical changes in a young boy's body. In Chapter 8, we discuss the psychosexual changes of male puberty.

MALE
PUBERTY

During a boy's early life, the two major functions of the testes—to produce male sex hormones and to produce sperm—remain dormant. No one knows exactly what triggers the onset of puberty or how a boy's internal clock knows that he is reaching the age in which these functions of the testes will be needed. Still, at an average of 10 years of age, the hypothalamus begins releasing gonadotropin-releasing hormone (GnRH), which stimulates the anterior pituitary gland to send out follicle-stimulating hormone (FSH) and luteinizing hormone (LH; see Table 4.2 in Chapter 4).

These flow through the circulatory system to the testes, where LH stimulates the production of the male sex hormone, testoster-

*No one knows exactly what triggers the **onset of puberty** . . .*

one, which, together with LH, stimulates sperm production. A negative feedback system regulates hormone production; when the concentration of testosterone in the blood increases to a certain level, GnRH release from the hypothalamus is inhibited, causing inhibition of LH production and resulting in decreased testosterone production (see Figure 6.6 for more information about the negative feedback loop). Alternately, when testosterone levels decrease below a certain level, this stimulates GnRH production by the hypothalamus, which increases the pituitary's LH production and testosterone production goes up.

As puberty progresses, the testicles grow, and the penis begins to grow about a year later. The epididymis, prostate, seminal vesicles, and bulbourethral glands also grow over the next several years. Increased testosterone stimulates an overall growth spurt in puberty, as bones and muscles rapidly develop. This spurt can be dramatic; teenage boys can grow 3 or 4 inches within a few months. The elevation of testosterone affects a number of male traits: the boy develops longer and heavier bones, larger muscles, thicker and tougher skin, a deepening voice due to growth of the voice box, pubic hair, facial and chest hair, increased sex drive, and increased metabolism.

Spermatogenesis begins at about 12 years of age, but ejaculation of mature sperm usually does not occur for about another 1 to 1.5 years. At puberty, the hormone FSH begins to stimulate sperm production in the seminiferous tubules, and the increased testosterone induces the testes to mature fully. The development of spermatogenesis and the sexual fluid glands allows the boy to begin to experience his first nocturnal emissions, although at the beginning, they tend to contain a very low live sperm count.

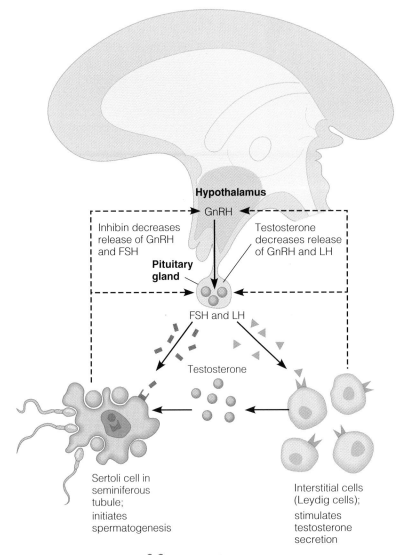

Figure **6.6** The cycle of male hormones.

Image labels:

Hypothalamus
GnRH

Inhibin decreases release of GnRH and FSH

Testosterone decreases release of GnRH and LH

Pituitary gland

FSH and LH

Testosterone

Sertoli cell in seminiferous tubule; initiates spermatogenesis

Interstitial cells (Leydig cells); stimulates testosterone secretion

ANDROPAUSE

As men age, their blood testosterone concentrations decrease. Hormone levels in men have been found to decrease by about 1% each year after age 40 (Daw, 2002). Men do not go through an obvious set of stages, as menopausal women do, but experience a less well-defined set of symptoms in their 70s or 80s called **andropause.** Although men's ability to ejaculate viable sperm is often retained past age 80 or 90, spermatogenesis does decrease, the ejaculate becomes thinner, and ejaculatory pressure decreases. The reduction in testosterone production results in decreased muscle strength, decreased libido, easy fatigue, and mood fluctuations (Seidman, 2007). Men can also experience **osteoporosis** and **anemia** from the decreasing hormone levels (Bain, 2001). Although some men are prescribed testosterone therapy, hormonal treatment for men is still controversial today (Morales, 2004).

andropause
The hormonal changes accompanying old age in men that correspond to menopause in women.

osteoporosis
A disease in which bones become fragile and more likely to break.

anemia
A condition in which there is a deficiency in the oxygen-carrying material of the blood.

review questions

1 Describe the two major functions of the testes, and explain the negative feedback loop in males.

2 Identify the age at which spermatogenesis typically begins. At what age does the ejaculate contain mature sperm?

3 What effect do decreasing levels of testosterone have on men?

Male Reproductive and Sexual Health

It is a good idea for every man to examine and explore his own sexual anatomy. A regular genital self-exam can help increase a man's comfort with his genitals (see Sex in Real Life, "Testicular Self-Examination"). It can also help a man know what his testicles feel like just in case something were to change. We now discuss diseases and other conditions that may affect the male reproductive organs, in addition to cancer of the male reproductive organs.

DISEASES OF THE MALE REPRODUCTIVE ORGANS

There are several conditions that can affect the male reproductive organs, including cryptorchidism, testicular torsion, priapism, and Peyronie's disease. It's important for both men and women to have a good understanding of what these conditions are and what symptoms they might cause.

Cryptorchidism

The testicles of a male fetus begin high in the abdomen near the kidneys, and, during fetal development, descend into the scrotum through the **inguinal canal** (Hutson et al., 1994). In approxi-mately 3% to 5% of full-term male infants, the testes fail to descend into the scrotum, a condition called **cryptorchidism** (krip-TOR-kuh-diz-um; Docimo et al., 2000). (A similar condition can occur in males with an inguinal hernia, in which the intestine enters the scrotum through the inguinal canal and may fill it completely, leaving no room for the testicles.) There is evidence that the incidence of cryptorchidism may be increasing, and research has linked this condition with the use of phthalates (Sharpe & Skakkebaek, 2008; see the nearby Sex in Real Life feature).

The temperature of the abdomen is too high to support sperm production, so if the testes remain in the abdomen much past age 5 years, the male is likely to be infertile (see Figure 6.7 for more information on cryptorchid testes). Cryptorchid testes also carry a 30 to 50 times increased risk of testicular cancer. In most infants, cryptorchidism can be identified and corrected through laparoscopy to find the undescended testis and then surgery to relocate the testis in the scrotum (Hack et al., 2003). It is recommended that this surgery be performed by 6 months (Hutson & Hasthorpe, 2005).

---

inguinal canal
Canal through which the testes descend into the scrotum.

cryptorchidism
A condition in which the testes fail to descend into the scrotum.

SEX IN REAL LIFE

Testicular Self-Examination

Though there are no obvious symptoms of testicular cancer, when detected early, it is treatable.

© Joel Gordon

Although there are no obvious symptoms of testicular cancer, when detected early, it is treatable. The only early detection system for testicular cancer is testicular self-examination (TSE). Yet most men do not do regular TSEs.

Just like breast self-examinations in women, men should examine their testicles at least monthly. This will enable them to have an understanding of what things feel like under normal conditions, which will help them to find any lumps or abnormal growths, should they appear.

To do a testicular exam, compare both testicles simultaneously by grasping one with each hand, using thumb and forefinger. This may be best done while taking a warm shower, which causes the scrotum to relax and the testicles to hang lower. Determine their size, shape, and sensitivity to pressure.

As you get to know the exact shape and feel of the testicles, you will be able to notice any swelling, lumps, or unusual pain. Report any such occurrence to your physician without delay, but do not panic; most lumps are benign and nothing to worry about.

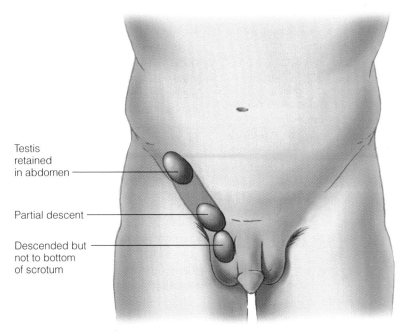

Testis retained in abdomen

Partial descent

Descended but not to bottom of scrotum

Figure **6.7** Although the testicles of a fetus begin high in the abdomen, they must descend into the scrotum during fetal development. If they do not, the male may become infertile.

Testicular Torsion

Testicular torsion refers to a twisting of a testis on its spermatic cord (see Figure 6.8). Usually it occurs when there is abnormal development of the spermatic cord or the membrane that covers the testicle. It is most common in men from puberty to the age of 25, although it can happen at any age. Testicular torsion can occur after exercise, sexual intercourse, or even while sleeping.

Severe pain and swelling are two of the most common symptoms of testicular torsion, although there can also be abdominal pain, nausea, and vomiting (Kapoor, 2008). A physician must diagnose this condition quickly because the twisted cord can cut off the blood supply to the testicle, and surgery to untwist the cord must be performed within 24 hours or else the testicle will atrophy.

REALResearch **>** During vigorous sexual intercourse, it is possible for the penis to slide out of the vagina and slam into the female perineum, resulting in a "vein injury" to the penis (BAR-YOSEF ET AL., 2007). Researchers have found that injuries such as these can lead to pain during erection, curvature of the penis, and potential hardening of the penile arteries. Seeking immediate medical attention may be necessary, especially if the pain increases.

Priapism

Priapism (PRY-uh-pizm) is a painful and persistent erection that is not associated with sexual desire or excitement (Van der Horst et al., 2003). Blood becomes trapped in the erectile tissue of the

penis and is unable to get out. The most common cause of priapism is drug use (erection drugs, cocaine, marijuana, or anticoagulants), but in many cases the cause is unknown.

Treatment for priapism depends on the cause. Draining the blood from the penis is possible with the use of a needle and syringe. If it is related to drug use, the drugs must be discontinued immediately. If there is a neurological or other physiological cause for the priapism, anesthesia or surgery may be necessary. Future sexual functioning may suffer if this condition is not treated effectively.

Peyronie's Disease

Every male has individual curves to his penis when it becomes erect. These curves and angles are quite normal. However, in approximately 1% of men, painful curvature makes penetration

testicular torsion
The twisting of a testis on its spermatic cord, which can cause severe pain and swelling.

priapism
A condition in which erections are long-lasting and often painful.

Normal anatomy   Testicular torsion

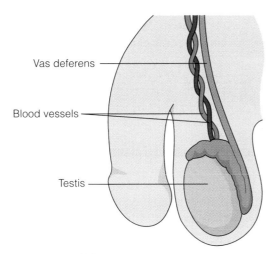
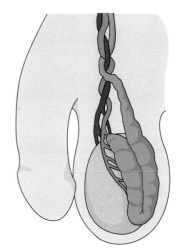

Vas deferens

Blood vessels

Testis

Figure **6.8** Testicular torsion can occur after exercise, sexual intercourse, or even while sleeping.

impossible, leading to a diagnosis of a condition known as **Peyronie's** (pay-row-NEEZ) **disease** (C. J. Smith et al., 2005). Typically this happens between the ages of 45 and 60, although a younger or older man could also experience Peyronie's.

Peyronie's disease occurs in the connective tissue of the penis, and although some cases are asymptomatic, others develop penile nodules, which can cause severe erectile pain (Gelbard, 1988). No one knows what causes Peyronie's disease. It is possible that crystal deposits in the connective tissue, trauma, excessive calcium levels, or calcification may contribute to this disorder (Gelbard, 1988). Usually this disease lasts approximately 2 years and may go away just as suddenly as it appears. It is often treated with medication or surgery (Austoni et al., 2005).

REALResearch > Laptop computers may pose a long-term threat to the fertility of young men. Research has found that keeping a laptop on a man's lap for 1 hour can raise the scrotal temperature enough to have a negative impact on male fertility (SHEYNKIN ET AL., 2005).

OTHER CONDITIONS THAT AFFECT **THE MALE REPRODUCTIVE ORGANS**

Other conditions may also affect the male reproductive organs, including steroid use, hernias, and hydoceles. Over the past few years, steroids have become a controversial topic as more and more male athletes disclose past steroid use. In 2005, congressional hearings began to evaluate steroid use in major league baseball. We discuss this more in the following section.

Anabolic-Androgenic Steroid Use

Before we discuss diseases and cancer of the male reproductive organs, let's talk about the use of steroids (which occur naturally in the body and are known as **androgens**). During puberty in males, the release of androgens increases weight and muscle size, and can also increase endurance and aggressiveness. Some athletes, believing that additional androgens would further increase weight and muscle size and therefore enhance athletic performance, decided to use synthetic steroids.

In the past 3 decades, the use of anabolic-androgenic steroid (AAS), also known as synthetic testosterone, in sport and exercise has increased notably, and it is no longer restricted to elite athletes or adult males. Estimates based on data from the National Survey on Drug Use and Health found that there were more than 1 million current or former AAS users in the United States, with more than half of the lifetime user population 26 years old or older. Studies have found that approximately 12% of adolescent males admit they have used AAS at some point in their lifetime, whereas 1% to 2% of adolescent females admit to using them (Yesalis & Bahrke, 2000). Another study found a significant number of female athletes who were using AAS (Gruber & Pope, 2000). The actual number of people abusing AAS nationwide is unknown (Volkow, 2005).

However, AAS use comes at a high price. It has been associated with many damaging changes in the physiological characteristics of organs and body systems. The best documented effects are to the liver, serum lipids, and the reproductive system, including shrinkage of the testicles (and menstrual cycle changes in women) (Bonetti et al., 2007; Sato et al., 2008). Other areas of concern include cerebrovascular accidents (stroke), prostate gland changes, and impaired immune function (Wysoczanski et al., 2008). In younger athletes, steroids can cause early fusion of the bone-growth plates, resulting in permanently shortened stature. Use of AAS has also been associated with changes in mood and behavior. Schizophrenia, increases in irritability, hostility, anger, aggression, depression, hypomania, psychotic episodes, and guilt have all been reported among AAS users (Venâncio et al., 2008).

Peyronie's disease
Abnormal calcifications in the penis, which may cause painful curvature, often making sexual intercourse impossible.

androgen
The general name for male hormones such as testosterone and androsterone.

Accusations of steroid use in major league baseball circulated in 2005. Photos of before and after supported these claims. Here is Barry Bonds in 1989 (left) and in 2003 (right).

male reproductive organs. Let's now look at testicular, penile, and prostatic cancers. In this section, we also review preventive measures for detecting or avoiding common male health problems. In Chapter 14, we will discuss how these illnesses affect men's lives and sexuality.

Testicular Cancer

Testicular cancer is the most common malignancy in men aged 25 to 34 (Garner et al., 2008). It was estimated that there would be 8,090 new cases of testicular cancer diagnosed in the United States in 2008 (American Cancer Society, 2007a). There are few symptoms until the cancer is advanced, which is why early detection is so important. Most men first develop testicular cancer as a painless testicular mass or a harder consistency of the testes. If there is pain or a sudden increase in testicular size, it is usually due to bleeding into the tumor. Sometimes lower back pain, gynecomastia, shortness of breath, or urethral obstruction may also be found.

Although the incidence of testicular cancer has continuously increased during the last few decades, cure rates have significantly improved. In fact, testicular cancer is one of the most curable forms of the disease (American Cancer Society, 2005). Treatment may involve radiation, chemotherapy, or the removal of the testicle (although radiation and chemotherapy can affect future fer-

The bottom line is this: steroids can cause erectile problems, overly aggressive behavior, mental problems, increased chances of various diseases, shrinkage of the testicles, and even masculinization in women. It is simply not worth the risk.

Inguinal Hernia

An **inguinal hernia** (ING-gwuh-nul HER-nee-uh) is caused when the intestine pushes through the opening in the abdominal wall into the inguinal canal (the inguinal canal was originally used by the testes when they descended into the scrotum shortly before birth). This can happen during heavy lifting or straining. When it does, the intestine pushes down onto the testicles and causes a bulge or lump in the scrotum. The bulge may change shape and size depending on what the man is doing, because it can slide back and forth within the testicle. Other symptoms include pain and possible blockage of the intestine. Depending on the size and the pain associated with the bulge, surgery may be necessary to remove the intestines and restore blood supply to the intestines.

Hydrocele

A **hydrocele** (HI-druh-seal) is a condition in which there is an excessive accumulation of fluid within the tissue surrounding the testicle, which causes a scrotal mass. This accumulation could be due to an overproduction of fluid or poor reabsorption of the fluid. Some men experience pain and swelling within the testicle. Treatment involves removing the built-up fluid.

REALResearch > Women rate muscular men as physically dominating and less likely to be faithful (FREDERICK & HASELTON, 2007). "Toned" men, who were less muscular, were rated the most desirable as mates.

tility, the removal of a testicle does not). If removal of the testicle is necessary, many men opt to get a prosthetic testicle implanted, which gives the appearance of having two normal testicles. Early diagnosis is very important, because the treatment is less severe early on, and one's chance of being cured is greater (review Sex in Real Life, "Testicular Self-Examination").

Penile Cancer

A wide variety of cancers involving the skin and soft tissues of the penis can occur, although cancer of the penis is not common (Mosconi et al., 2005). Any lesion on the penis must be examined by a physician, for benign and malignant conditions can be very similar in appearance, and sexually transmitted infections can appear as lesions. Even though most men handle and observe their penis daily, there is often significant delay between a person's recognition of a lesion and seeking medical attention. Fear and embarrassment may contribute most to this problem, yet almost all of these lesions are treatable if caught early.

CANCER OF THE
MALE REPRODUCTIVE ORGANS

Cancer is a disease in which certain cells in the body don't function properly—they divide too fast or produce excessive tissue that forms a tumor (or both). A number of cancers can affect the

inguinal hernia
A condition in which the intestines bulge through a hole in the abdominal muscles of the groin.

hydrocele
A condition in which there is an excessive accumulation of fluid within the tissue surrounding the testicle, which causes a scrotal mass.

Testicular Cancer

Testicular cancer is the most common type of cancer found in young men between the ages of 25 and 34 . . . Testicular cancer caught early has a 98% success rate.

We have already discussed the importance of testicular self-examination in the early detection of testicular cancer. Testicular cancer is the most common type of cancer found in young men between the ages of 25 and 34. Following are the stories of two men, both of whom were diagnosed with and treated for testicular cancer.

Lance Armstrong, who has won the Tour de France a record number of times, was diagnosed with testicular cancer when he was 25. A scan revealed that the cancer had spread from his testicle to his lungs and brain. Armstrong underwent aggressive surgery, first to remove the malignant testicle and later to remove the cancer that had spread throughout the rest of his body. He was also treated with an aggressive form of chemotherapy. At the time, his doctors gave him a 50/50 chance of survival. One year after his cancer ordeal, he began racing again. Even though Lance had to have a testicle removed and undergo chemotherapy, he was still able to have three children through in-vitro fertilization (see Chapter 12).

When Lance Armstrong was diagnosed with testicular cancer, his physicians advised sperm banking prior to treatment. He was able to father three children through assisted reproduction techniques.

Al Bello/Getty Images

Armstrong is committed to his role as a spokesperson for testicular cancer. Had he known about the importance of early detection, he would have never ignored the swelling and pain in his testicle. Testicular cancer caught early has a 98% success rate. However, many men ignore such pain, thinking that it will go away on its own.

Scott Hamilton, a professional figure skater, was diagnosed with testicular cancer at age 39. His cancer had spread to his abdomen by the time it was discovered. He underwent chemotherapy for 12 weeks and returned to skating shortly after his treatments ended. Hamilton also talks about the importance of early detection and has started a website for people undergoing chemotherapy.

Both Armstrong and Hamilton urge all men to check their testicles regularly for swelling, pain, and any changes in structure or size. Remember, early detection is key!

WHAT DO YOU WANT TO KNOW?

Can a man who has been treated for testicular cancer still have children?

Many men with testicular cancer also have fertility problems. Cancer treatments can cause scarring or ejaculation problems that will interfere with later fertility. During radiation or chemotherapy, sperm production does drop off significantly, and some men have no sperm in their semen. However, for the majority of men, sperm production generally returns to normal within 2 to 3 years. Because many men with testicular cancer are in their reproductive prime, waiting 2 or more years might not be an option. For this reason, many health care providers recommend sperm banking before cancer treatment. Many men who have been treated for testicular cancer do have children after their cancer treatment, as you'll see in Sex in Real Life, "Testicular Cancer."

urethra, BPH may block urination, and surgeons may need to remove the prostate if the condition becomes bad enough. Of far more concern than BPH is prostate cancer, which is the most frequently diagnosed cancer in men, besides skin cancer (American Cancer Society, 2007b). It was estimated that there would be approximately 186,320 new cases of prostate cancer in 2008 (American Cancer Society, 2008). Although rates of prostate cancer increased dramatically between 1988 and 1992 and declined sharply between 1992 and 1995, rates have leveled off since 1995. These changes may be due to the use of prostate cancer screening tests, which we discuss more later.

Although men of all ages can get prostate cancer, it is found most often in men over age 50. In fact, more than 64% of the men with prostate cancer are 65 or older (American Cancer Society, 2007b). For reasons not clearly understood, prostate cancer is about twice as common among African American men as it is among Caucasian Americans (American Cancer Society, 2007b).

Prostate Cancer

As men age, their prostate glands enlarge. In most cases, this natural occurrence, **benign prostatic hypertrophy (BPH),** causes few problems. Because of its anatomical position surrounding the

benign prostatic hypertrophy
The common enlargement of the prostate that occurs in most men after about age 50.

In fact, African American men have the highest prostate cancer rates in the world.

It's important to also realize that there are researchers who believe prostate cancer is not as common as some suggest. For example, one study found that 29% to 44% of men diagnosed with prostate cancer were actually "overdiagnosed" (Etzioni et al., 2002). This is primarily because current testing methods (discussed later) have been yielding high false-positive results.

Although we don't know exactly what causes prostate cancer, we do know that there are several risk factors that have been linked to prostate cancer. These include aging, race, a diet high in fat, and a genetic risk. Signs of possible prostate cancer include lower back, pelvic, or upper thigh pain; inability to urinate; loss of force in the urinary stream; urinary dribbling; pain or burning during urination; and frequent urination, especially at night. Many deaths from prostate cancer are preventable, because a simple 5- or 10-second rectal examination by a physician, to detect hard lumps on the prostate, detects more than 50% of cases at a curable stage. Digital rectal exams are recommended for men each year beginning at the age of 50 (or 45 for men with a history of prostate cancer).

In 1986, the U.S. Food and Drug Administration approved the **prostate-specific antigen** (**PSA**) blood test that measures levels of molecules that are overproduced by prostate cancer cells. This enables physicians to identify prostate cancer and is recommended yearly for men over the age of 50. The PSA test has been one of the most important advances in the area of prostate cancer (American Cancer Society, 2007b). Although not all tumors will show up on a PSA test, a high reading does indicate that something (such as a tumor) is releasing prostatic material into the blood, and a biopsy or further examination is warranted.

There are many treatments for prostate cancer, and almost all are controversial. Some argue that, in older men especially, the best thing is "watchful waiting" in which the cancer is simply left alone, because most men will die of other causes before the prostate cancer spreads. Men who have a history of poor health or who are living in a geographically undesirable location for medical treatment often opt for these more conservative treatments (Harlan et al., 2001).

Others choose **radical prostatectomy** or **radiation** treatment, or **cryosurgery,** which uses a probe to freeze parts of the prostate and has had good success in reducing the occurrence of postsurgical erectile disorder and incontinence (J. K. Cohen et al., 2008). Newer treatments include drugs that attack only cells with cancer, unlike radiation and chemotherapy, which both kill healthy cells in addition to cells with cancer. Research has found that these drugs hold much promise in the treatment of prostate cancer (Bonaccorsi et al., 2004; C. J. Ryan & Small, 2005).

Two of the most common surgical side effects of prostate cancer treatment include erectile dysfunction and the inability to hold one's urine. However, the likelihood of these problems depends on several things, including the extent and severity of the cancer and a man's age at the time of surgery (H. Stewart et al., 2005). Although younger men who experienced satisfactory erections before any prostate cancer treatments have fewer erectile problems after surgery, for most men, erections will improve over time. Difficulty holding urine or urinary leakage may also occur; however, there are treatments available to lessen these symptoms.

As you have learned throughout this chapter and the prior one on female anatomy, understanding anatomy and physiology is an important part of learning about human sexual behavior. We must understand all of the physiological and hormonal influences and how they affect both the female and male body before we can move on to the emotional and psychological issues involved in human sexuality. Anatomy and physiology, therefore, are really the foundations of any human sexuality class. Now we can turn our attention to other important aspects of human sexuality. In Chapter 7, we discuss love and intimacy.

prostate-specific antigen (PSA)
Blood test that measures levels of molecules that are overproduced by prostate cancer cells, enabling physicians to identify prostate cancer early.

radical prostatectomy
The surgical removal of the prostate.

radiation
The use of radioactivity in the treatment of cancer.

cryosurgery
Surgery that uses freezing techniques to destroy part of an organ.

review questions

1 Differentiate between cryptorchidism, testicular torsion, priapism, and Peyronie's disease. Explain what these conditions are and what symptoms they might cause. What are some treatments for these conditions?

2 Explain the side effects of anabolic-androgenic steroid use.

3 Identify the most common cancer in men between the ages of 25 and 34 and describe early symptoms and treatment.

4 Identify which cancer is most frequently diagnosed in men overall and describe early symptoms and treatment.

SUMMARY POINTS

1 Because the male genitalia sit outside the body, unlike female gonads, boys are often more comfortable with their genitalia. The external male sex organs include the penis and the scrotum.

2 The penis has the ability to fill with blood during sexual arousal. It contains the urethra and three cylinders—two corpora cavernosa and one corpus spongiosum. These cylinders are bound together with connective tissue.

3 In many cultures, the foreskin of the penis is removed during circumcision. Although it is the single most common surgical procedure performed on male patients in the United States, medical professionals have questioned the health value of circumcision.

4 An erection is a spinal reflex, and many types of sexual stimulation can lead to this response. When stimulation stops, the penis returns to its unaroused state. Most men have regular erections during their sleeping cycle and often wake up with an erection.

5 The scrotum sits outside the man's body and contains the testicles. Sperm survival requires a temperature that is a few degrees lower than the body's temperature. The cremaster muscle is responsible for the scrotum's positioning. When it's too hot, the muscle allows the scrotum to hang farther away from the body. When it is too cold, the muscle elevates the scrotum so that it is closer to the body.

6 The internal male sex organs include the testes, epididymis, vas deferens, seminal vesicles, prostate gland, and Cowper's glands. All of these organs play important roles in spermatogenesis, testosterone production, and the process of ejaculation.

7 The testicles have two main functions: spermatogenesis and testosterone production. One testicle usually hangs lower (or higher) than the other so that they do not hit each other when compressed. Testosterone is produced in the Leydig cells.

8 Ejaculation is the physiological process whereby the seminal fluid is ejected from the penis. The vas deferens, seminal vesicles, prostate, and Cowper's glands all work together during ejaculation. Most men experience between 5 and 15 contractions during orgasm. After orgasm, the blood that has been trapped in the penis is released, and the penis becomes flaccid.

9 Gynecomastia, or abnormal breast development, is common during male puberty and again in older age. It can be caused by drug therapy, drug abuse, hormonal imbalance, and certain diseases. It will often disappear on its own without surgical intervention. Some men do get breast cancer and, because it is rare, men who are diagnosed are often in advanced stages before their diagnoses.

10 At about the age of 10, a boy enters the first stages of puberty. A negative feedback system regulates hormone production. As puberty progresses, the testicles increase in size, and the penis begins to grow. Increased testosterone stimulates an overall growth spurt in puberty, and the bones and muscles grow rapidly. Spermatogenesis usually begins about the age of 12, but it takes another year or so for an ejaculation to contain mature sperm.

11 Blood testosterone levels decrease as a man ages, and although it is not as defined as menopause, men experience a condition known as andropause. During this time, sperm production slows down, the ejaculate becomes thinner, and ejaculatory pressure decreases.

12 There are several diseases of the male reproductive organs, including cryptorchidism, testicular torsion, priapism, Peyronie's disease, inguinal hernia, and hydrocele. Fortunately, all of these are treatable conditions.

13 Athletes' use of steroids has increased notably over the past 3 decades, even though it had been associated with several damaging changes in the body. This can cause liver and prostate gland changes, testicular shrinkage, and impaired immune function. Research has also found an increased risk of cerebrovascular accidents and, for young people, early fusion of bone growth plates.

14 Testicular cancer is difficult to catch early because there are few symptoms. It is one of the most curable forms of the disease. Penile cancer is relatively uncommon, but it usually appears as a lesion on the penis. Prostate cancer is more common in men over age 50 and is the most common cause of cancer deaths among men over age 60. For unknown reasons, this type of cancer is twice as common in African American men as it is among Caucasians.

CRITICAL THINKING questions

1 We don't seem to need to know how the digestive system works to eat. Why is detailed knowledge of the sexual functioning of men important in human sexuality?

2 If you have a baby boy in the future, would you have him circumcised? Why or why not?

3 Why do you think men are uncomfortable talking about their own body image issues? Why aren't men encouraged to explore these issues?

WEB resources

Sexuality Now Book Companion Website

Go to www.cengage.com/psychology/carroll for practice quizzes, glossary, flash cards, and more. You can also access the following websites from the companion site.

Testicular Cancer Resource Center ■ The Testicular Cancer Resource Center provides accurate information about testicular self-exam and the diagnosis and treatment of testicular cancer. Links are also provided for other cancers and additional websites.

Medical Education Information Center (MEdIC™) ■ The Medical Education Information Center contains information about men's health issues. The site has information on cancer screening, PSA testing, prostate concerns, and other health issues.

MedlinePlus Health Information: Men's Health Topics ■ MedlinePlus contains information on issues such as prostate cancer, circumcision, reproductive health concerns, gay and bisexual health, and male genital disorders.

Lance Armstrong Foundation ■ The Lance Armstrong Foundation (LAF) focuses on cancer information and education. LAF provides services, support, and strives to help cancer patients through diagnosis and treatment, encouraging each

to adopt the same positive attitude that Lance Armstrong adopted in his own battle with cancer.

National Organization of Circumcision Information Resource Centers (NOCIRC) ■ NOCIRC is the first national clearinghouse for information about circumcision. It claims that it owns one of the largest collections of information about circumcision in the world.

CengageNOW

Go to www.cengage.com/login to link to CengageNOW, your online study tool. First take the Pre-Test for this chapter to get your Personalized Study Plan, which will identify topics you need to review and direct you to online resources. Then take the Post-Test to determine what concepts you have mastered and what you still need work on.

Videos in CengageNOW

CengageNOW also contains these videos related to the chapter topics:

• Male Menopause—Learn about a hypothesized "male menopause," or changes in men in midlife.

• Male Ejaculation—See the physical process and stages of male ejaculation.

CHAPTER 7

Love and Intimacy

© Randy Faris/Corbis

Many years ago, a close-knit Italian-American community in Roseto, Pennsylvania, became the subject of an important study (Egolf et al., 1992). Researchers were drawn to this community when they found that Rosetans were healthier than neighboring communities and died of heart attacks at a rate of only half of the rest of Americans (Condor, 1998). The people living in Roseto were the same age as people living in nearby towns. They worked hard at labor-intensive and stressful jobs, smoked cigarettes, drank alcohol, ate fatty foods, and didn't exercise regularly. So why were they healthier?

Researchers found that all of the homes in Roseto contained three generations of families. Roseto was founded in 1882 by Italian immigrants, and the younger generations cared for the older generations. All of the community members watched out for each other as well. Rosetans had a strong sense of community, love, and loyalty, with strong ties to one another. This sense of community and support was found to reduce stress and the diseases that stress can cause. The

"Roseto Effect," as it was known, continued until the 1960s, when social changes in the community led to decreasing bonds and relationships with one another and an increase in health problems.

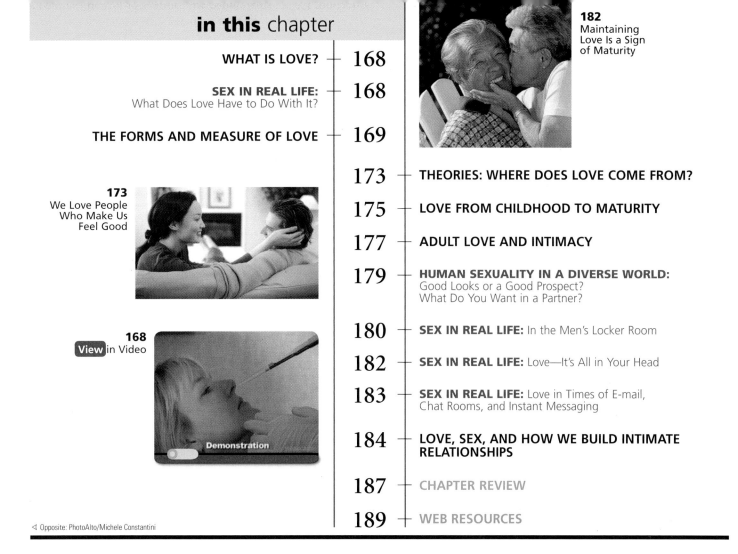

182
Maintaining
Love Is a Sign
of Maturity

173
We Love People
Who Make Us
Feel Good

168
View in Video

Demonstration

◁ Opposite: PhotoAlto/Michele Constantini

You might be wondering why we begin this chapter with such a story. Love and the ability to form loving, caring, and intimate relationships with others are important for both our physical and emotional health. When people love each other, talk to each other, and share their inner selves, their immune systems may actually become stronger than people who isolate themselves or are emotionally withdrawn (Maunder & Hunter, 2008; Ornish, 1999). In this chapter, we talk about the forms and measures of love, where love comes from, love throughout the life cycle, and building intimate relationships. Before we begin, try answering this question: What exactly is *love?*

REALResearch **>** Partners who believe in "love at first sight" become romantically involved more quickly and have partners with less similar personalities than those who don't believe in love at first sight (BARELDS & BARELDS-DIJKSTRA, 2007).

When people love each other they experience less stress in their lives, stronger immune systems, and better overall health.

What Is Love?

One of the great mysteries of humankind is the capacity to love, to make attachments with others that involve deep feeling, selflessness, and commitment. Throughout history, literature and art have portrayed the saving powers of love. How many songs have been written about its passion, and how many films have depicted its power to change people's lives? Yet after centuries of writers discussing love, philosophers musing over its hold on men and women, and religious leaders teaching of the necessity to love one another, how much do we really know about love? Are there different, separate kinds of love—friendship, passion, love of parents—or are they all simply variations on one fundamental emotion? Does love really "grow"? Is love different at age 15 than at 50? What is the relationship between love and sexuality?

View in Video

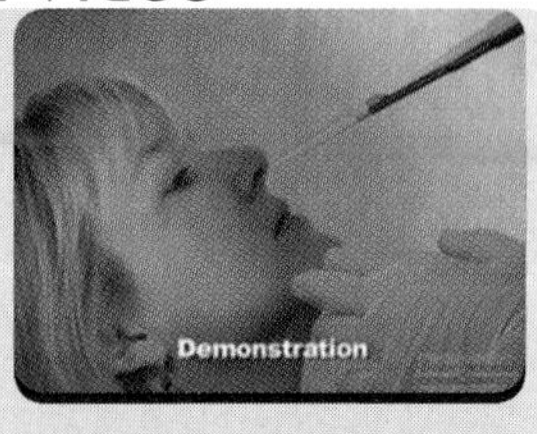

"A cold virus is placed in people's noses, and they are given a sociability scale."
—*Emotions, Stress, and the Immune System*
To view go to CengageNOW at www.cengage.com/login

We go through life trying to come to terms with loving, trying to figure out why we are attracted to certain types or why we fall in love with all the wrong people. The mystery of love is part of its attraction. We are surrounded with images of love in the media and are taught from the time we first listen to fairy tales that love is the answer to most of life's problems. Movies, music, and television inundate us with stories of what love is and these stories have a powerful impact on us (Griffin, 2006). Why should we not try to learn what love really is?

REALResearch > A close father-daughter relationship in childhood has been found to be related to a woman's ability to form strong intimate bonds later in life (Cecchetti, 2007).

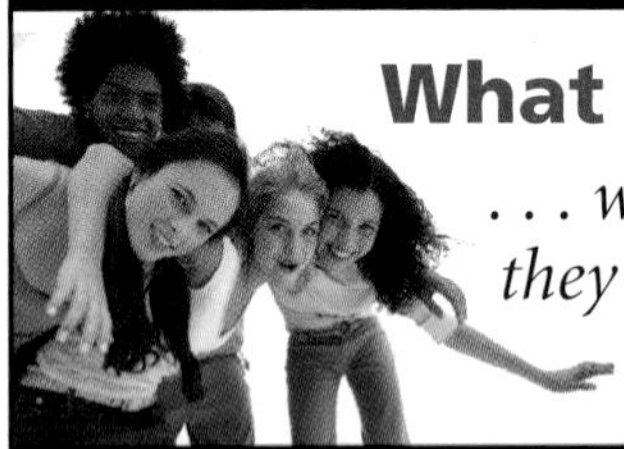

LOVE IN OTHER TIMES AND PLACES

The desire for love is as old as humanity. Each new generation somehow imagines that it is the first, the inventor of "true love," but look at this poem from the late Egyptian empire, written more than 3,000 years ago:

I found my lover on his bed, and my heart was sweet to excess.
I shall never be far away (from) you while my hand is in your hand,
and I shall stroll with you in every favorite place.
How pleasant is this hour, may it extend for me to eternity;

SEX IN REAL LIFE

What Does Love Have to Do With It?

. . . when people open up to each other, talk to each other, and love each other, they become physically healthier.

In his 1999 best-selling book *Love and Survival: Scientific Basis for the Healing Power of Intimacy,* Dean Ornish discusses the importance of love and intimacy. He points to a variety of research studies that claim that when people open up to each other, talk to each other, and love each other, they become physically healthier. Following are just a few of these findings from longitudinal research:

- College students who had distant and nonemotional relationships with their parents had significantly higher rates of high blood pressure and heart disease years later than did students who reported close and emotionally connected relationships.
- Heart patients who felt "loved" had 50% less arterial damage than those who said they did not feel "loved."
- Men and women who reported the least social contact died at the rate of 3 times those who reported the most social contact.
- Women who said they felt "lonely and isolated" were 3.5 times more likely to die of breast, ovarian, or uterine cancer.
- Men who said their wives did not show them "love" suffered 50% more chest pain.
- People with heart disease who have a dog have been found to have 4 times fewer sudden cardiac deaths than those without dogs.

Source: Ornish (1999).

since I have lain with you, you have lifted high my heart.
In mourning or in rejoicing be not far from me.
(Quoted in Bergmann, 1987, p. 5)

The Hebrew Bible speaks of God's love of Israel, and the metaphorical imagery in the Song of Solomon, usually interpreted as depicting God and Israel as lovers, is highly erotic and sexual. The Middle Ages glorified the modern idea of **romantic love,** including loving from afar, or loving those one could not have (**unrequited** [un-ree-KWI-ted] **love**).

Not until the 19th century did people begin to believe that romantic love was the most desirable form of loving relations.

Through most of Western history, marriage was an economic union, arranged by the parents. Once wed, husbands and wives were encouraged to learn love for one another, to develop love. How different that is from the modern romantic ideal of love preceding marriage.

romantic love
Idealized love, based on romance and perfection.

unrequited love
Loving another when the love will never be returned.

review questions

1 What does the chapter opening story about Roseto, Pennsylvania, tell us about the importance of love?

2 Discuss the research on the effects of love and intimacy on physical health.

3 Explain how love today may be different from love that was experienced through most of Western history.

The Forms and Measure of Love

We must admire those researchers who are willing to tackle a difficult subject such as the origins of love or the different forms of love. We all love, and one of the characteristics of love is that we often believe that the intensity of the emotion is unique to us, that no one else has ever loved as we have loved. We also feel many different kinds of love, such as love of a friend, love of a parent, love of a child, love of a celebrity, or love of a pet. Philosophers, historians, social scientists, and other scholars have made attempts to untangle these types of love.

intolerable as those in love; they are just so annoyingly happy all the time! It is not surprising that such a powerful emotion is celebrated in poetry, story, and song. It is also not surprising that such a powerful emotion seems as though it will last forever. After all, isn't that what we learn when the couples in fairy tales "live happily ever after," and when the couples in movies ride off into the sunset?

Unfortunately, perhaps, passion of that intensity fades after a time. If the relationship is to continue, romantic love usually develops into **companionate love,** or **conjugal** (CONN-jew-gull) **love.** Companionate love involves feelings of deep affection, attachment, intimacy, and ease with the partner as well as the development of trust, loyalty, acceptance, and a willingness to sacrifice for the partner (Critelli et al., 1986; Regan, 2006; Shaver & Hazan,

ROMANTIC VERSUS COMPANIONATE LOVE

Romantic love is the all-encompassing, passionate love of romantic songs and poetry, of tearjerker movies and romance novels, and has become the prevailing model of sexual relationships and marriage in the Western world. Romantic love is also sometimes called passionate love, infatuation, obsessive love, and even lovesickness, and with it comes a sense of ecstasy and anxiety, physical attraction, and sexual desire. We tend to idealize the partner, ignoring faults in the newfound joy of the attachment. Passionate love blooms in the initial euphoria of a new attachment to a sexual partner, and it often seems as if we're swept away by it; that is why we say we "fall" in love, or even fall "head over heels" in love.

There are few feelings as joyous or exciting as romantic love. The explosion of emotion is often so intense that people talk about being unable to contain it; it feels as if it spills out of us onto everything we see. Some people joke that there is nothing quite as

© Stockbyte/Picturequest

Companionate love involves deep affection, trust, loyalty, attachment, and intimacy; although passion is often present, companionate love lacks the high and low swings of romantic love.

1987). Although companionate love does not have the passionate high and low swings of romantic love, passion is certainly present for many companionate lovers. Companionate love may even be a deeper, more intimate love than romantic love.

It can be difficult for couples to switch from passionate love to the deeper, more mature companionate love (Peck, 1978). Because the model of love we see on television and in movies is the highly sexual, swept-off-your-feet passion of romantic love, some may see the mellowing of that passion as a loss of love rather than a development of a different kind of love. Yet the mutual commitment to develop a new, more mature kind of love is, in fact, what we should mean by "true love."

THE COLORS OF LOVE:
JOHN ALAN LEE

Psychologist John Alan Lee (1974, 1988, 1998) suggests that in romantic relationships, there are more forms of love than just romantic and companionate love. Lee collected statements about love from hundreds of works of fiction and nonfiction, starting with the Bible and including both ancient and modern authors. He gathered a panel of professionals in literature, philosophy, and the social sciences and had them sort into categories the thousands of statements he found. Lee's research identified six basic ways to love, which he calls "colors" of love, to which he gave Greek and Latin names. Lee's categories are described in Table 7.1.

Lee's colors of love have generated a substantial body of research, much of which shows that his love styles are independent from one another and that each can be measured to some degree (Hendrick & Hendrick, 1989). Lee points out that two lovers with compatible styles are probably going to be happier and more content with each other than two with incompatible styles. Couples who approach loving differently often cannot understand why their partners react the way they do or how they can hurt their partners unintentionally. Imagine how bored an erotic lover would be with a pragmatic lover, or how much a ludic lover would hurt a manic lover. Each would consider the other callous or even cruel, suggests Lee, when people simply tend to love differently. Higher levels of

REALResearch > Birth-order research has found that love styles may be related to where a child is born into a family (McGuirk & Pettijohn, 2008). Middle children have higher rates of ludic love styles, whereas the youngest children are more likely to have pragma, storge, or agape love styles. Finally, only children have higher rates of eros and mania love styles.

manic and ludic love styles are associated with poorer psychological health, whereas higher levels of storge and eros love styles are associated with higher levels of psychological health (Blair, 2000).

LOVE TRIANGLES:
ROBERT STERNBERG

Robert Sternberg (1998, 1999) suggests that different strategies of loving are really different ways of combining the basic building blocks of love. He has proposed that love is made up of three elements—passion, intimacy, and commitment—that can be com-

companionate love
An intimate form of love that involves friendly affection and deep attachment based on a familiarity with the loved one. Also referred to as conjugal love.

conjugal love
An intimate form of love that involves friendly affection and deep attachment based on familiarity with the loved one. Also referred to as companionate love.

table 7.1

Lee's Colors of Love

1. Eros: The Romantic Lover	Eros is like romantic love. Erotic lovers speak of their immediate attraction to their lover, to his or her eyes, skin, fragrance, or body. Most have the picture of an ideal partner in their mind, which a real partner cannot fulfill; that is why purely erotic love does not last. In childhood, erotic lovers often had a secure attachment style with their caregivers.
2. Ludus (LOO-diss): The Game-Playing Lover	Ludic lovers play the "game" of love, enjoying the act of seduction. Commitment, dependency, and intimacy are not valued, and ludic lovers will often juggle several relationships at the same time. In childhood, ludic lovers often had an avoidant attachment style with their caregivers.
3. Storge (STOR-gay): The Quiet, Calm Lover	Storgic love is a quiet, calm love that builds over time, similar to companionate love. Storgic lovers don't suddenly "fall in love" and do not dream of some idealized, romantic lover; marriage, stability, and comfort within love are the goal. Should the relationship break up, the storgic partners would probably remain friends, a status unthinkable to erotic lovers who have split.
4. Mania: The Crazy Lover	Manic lovers are possessive and dependent, consumed by thoughts of the beloved and are often on a roller-coaster of highs and lows. Each encouraging sign from the lover brings joy; each little slight brings heartache, which makes their lives dramatic and painful. Manic lovers fear separation; they may sit by the phone waiting for the beloved to call, or they may call their beloved incessantly. They tend to wonder why all their relationships ultimately fail. In childhood, manic lovers often had an anxious/ambivalent attachment style with their caregivers.
5. Pragma: The Practical Lover	Pragmatic lovers have a "shopping list" of qualities they are looking for in a relationship. They are very practical about their relationship and lovers. Pragmatic lovers want a deep, lasting love but believe the best way to get it is to assess their own qualities and make the best "deal" in the romantic marketplace. They tend to be planners—planning the best time to get married, have children, and even when to divorce ("Well, in two years the house will be paid for and Billy will be in high school, so that would be a good time to get divorced").
6. Agape (AH-ga-pay): The Selfless Lover	Altruistic, selfless, never demanding, patient, and true is agapic love. Never jealous, not needing reciprocity, agapic love tends to happen in brief episodes. Lee found very few long-term agapic lovers. Lee gives the example of a man whose lover was faced with a distressing choice between him and another man, and so he gracefully bowed out.

As you read through these descriptions, where do you think your love style fits in? Are you a pragmatic lover, planning all the details of your love affair? Do you feel stir-crazy in a relationship and end up juggling lovers and playing games? Or do you have a romantic and sensitive love style? It is possible that more than one style will fit you, and also that your love style may change throughout your lifetime. What influences in your life do you think contributed to your love style today?

Source: John Alan Lee, "The Styles of Loving," *Psychology Today,* 8, 43–51. Reprinted with permission from *Psychology Today.* Copyright © 1974 by Sussex Publishers, Inc.

bined in different ways. Sternberg refers to a total absence of all three components as nonlove.

Passion is sparked by physical attraction and sexual desire and drives a person to pursue a romantic relationship. Passion instills a deep desire for union, and, although it is often expressed sexually, self-esteem, nurturing, domination, submission, and self-actualization may also contribute to the experience. Passion is the element that identifies romantic forms of love; it is absent in the love of a parent for a child. Passion fires up quickly in a romantic relationship but is also the first element to fade.

Intimacy involves feelings of closeness, connectedness, and bondedness in a loving relationship. It is the emotional investment one has in the relationship and includes such things as the desire to support and help the other, happiness, mutual understanding, emotional support, and communication. The intimacy component of love is experienced in many loving relationships, such as parent–child, sibling, and friendship relationships.

Commitment, in the short term, is the decision to love someone; in the long term, it is the determination to maintain that love. This element can sustain a relationship that is temporarily (or even permanently) going through a period without passion or intimacy. The marriage ceremony, for example, is a public display of a couple's commitment to each other.

Sternberg combines these elements into seven forms of love, which are described in Table 7.2. A person may experience different forms of love at different times; romantic love may give way to companionate love, or the infatuated lover may find a person to whom he or she is willing to commit and settle down. In the emotionally healthy person, as we shall see, love evolves and changes as we mature (Sternberg, 1998).

table 7.2

Sternberg's Triangular Theory of Love

Robert Sternberg, a professor of psychology at Yale University, believes that love is made up of three elements: passion, intimacy, and commitment, each of which may be present or absent in a relationship. The presence or absence of these components produces eight triangles (seven of these involve at least one component; the eighth represents the absence of any components, referred to as nonlove). Problems can occur in a relationship if one person's triangle differs significantly from the other's. This can happen when one person has more or less of one of the three elements of love. Following are the various types of love proposed by Sternberg.

	Type	Description
	Nonlove	In most of our casual daily relationships, there is no sense of intimacy, passion, or commitment.
	Liking	When there is intimacy without (sexual) passion and without strong personal commitment, we are friends. Friends can separate for long periods of time and resume the relationship as if it had never ended.
	Infatuation	Passion alone leads to infatuation. Infatuation refers to physiological arousal and a sexual desire for another person. Casual hookups and one-night stands would fall into this category. Typically, infatuation quickly fades, often to be replaced with infatuation for someone else!
	Empty love	Empty love involves only commitment, as in a couple who stays together even though their relationship long ago lost its passion and intimacy. However, relationships can begin with commitment alone and develop intimacy and passion.
	Romantic love	Passion and intimacy lead to romantic love, which is often the first phase of a relationship. Romantic love is often an intense, joyful experience.
	Companionate love	Companionate love ranges from long-term, deeply committed friendships to married or long-term couples who have experienced a decrease in the passionate aspect of their love.
	Fatuous (FAT-you-us) love	Love is fatuous (which means silly or foolish) when one does not really know the person to whom one is making a commitment. Hollywood often portrays two people who meet, become infatuated, and make a commitment by the end of the movie. However, a committed relationship continues even after passion fades, so it makes sense to know one's partner before making a commitment.
	Consummate love	Consummate, or complete, love has all three elements in balance. Even after achieving consummate love, we can lose it: passion can fade, intimacy can stagnate, and commitment can be undermined by attraction to another. But it is consummate love we all strive for.

Source: Robert J. Sternberg, "A Triangle Theory of Love," *Psychological Review,* 93, 119–135. Reprinted by permission of the author.

CAN WE MEASURE LOVE?

Based on these types of theories, theorists have tried to come up with scales that measure love. However, you can't just ask people, "How deeply do you love [your partner]?" Each participant will interpret love in his or her own way. One strategy is to create a scale that measures love by measuring something strongly associated with love. Zick Rubin (1970, 1973) was one of the first to try to scientifically measure love. Rubin thought of love as a form of attachment to another person, and created a "love scale" that measured what he believed to be the three components of attachment:

degrees of needing ("If I could never be with _____, I would feel miserable"), caring ("I would do almost anything for _____"), and trusting ("I feel very possessive about _____"). Rubin's scale proved to be an extraordinarily powerful tool to measure love. For example, how a couple scores on the "love scale" is correlated not only with their rating of the probability that they will get married, but their score even predicts how often they will gaze at each other!

Others have since tried to create their own scales. Keith Davis and his colleagues (K. E. Davis & Latty-Mann, 1987; K. E. Davis & Todd, 1982) created the Relationship Rating Scale (RRS), which measures various aspects of relationships, such as intimacy, passion, and conflict. Hatfield and Sprecher (1986) created the Passionate Love Scale (PLS), which tries to measure the degree of intense passion or "longing for union."

Will measures of love eventually tell us what love is made of? Well, as you can imagine, many problems are inherent in trying to measure love. Most love scales really focus on romantic love and are not as good at trying to measure the degree of companionate love (Sternberg, 1987). Also, measuring degrees of love, or types of love, is different from saying what love actually is. Finally, when you ask people questions about love, they can answer only with their conscious attitudes toward love. Many theorists suggest that we don't consciously know why we love, how we love, or even how much we love. Other theorists argue that people do not realize to what degree love is physiological (see the section on physiological arousal theories later in this chapter). So we may be measuring only how people *think* they love.

review questions

1 What is the difference between romantic and companionate, or conjugal, love?

2 Identify and describe John Alan Lee's six colors of love.

3 Identify and describe the three elements of love, according to Robert Sternberg. Explain how these elements combine to make seven different forms of love.

4 Is it possible to measure love? What problems have researchers run into when attempting to do so?

Theories: Where Does Love Come From?

Why do we love in the first place? What purpose does love serve? After all, most animals mate successfully without experiencing "love." Researchers' theories on why we form emotional bonds in the first place can be grouped into five general categories: behavioral reinforcement, cognitive, physiological arousal, evolutionary, and biological.

The behavioral reinforcement theory suggests that we love people we associate with feeling good. Our love for them grows out of doing things together that are mutually reinforcing.

BEHAVIORAL REINFORCEMENT THEORIES

One group of theories suggests that we love because another person reinforces positive feelings in ourselves. Lott and Lott (1961) suggested that a rewarding or positive feeling in the presence of another person makes us like them, even when the reward has nothing to do with the other person. For example, they found that children who were rewarded continually by their teachers came to like their classmates more than children who were not equally rewarded. The opposite is also true. Griffitt and Veitch (1971) found that people tend to dislike people they meet in a hot, crowded room, no matter what those people's personalities are like. Behavioral reinforcement theory suggests that we like people we associate with feeling good and love people if the association is very good. Love develops through a series of mutually reinforcing activities.

COGNITIVE THEORIES

Cognitive theories of liking and loving are based on an interesting paradox: The less people are paid for a task, the more they tend to like it. In other words, a person tends to think, "Here I am washing this car, and I'm not even getting paid for it. Why am I doing this? I must like to wash cars! " The same goes for relationships. If we are with a person often and find ourselves doing things for them, we ask, "Why am I with her so often? Why am I doing her laundry? I must like her—I must even love her!" This theory suggests the action comes first and the interpretation comes later (Tzeng, 1992). Studies have also found that when we think someone likes us, we're more likely to be attracted to them (Ridge & Reber, 2002).

PHYSIOLOGICAL AROUSAL THEORIES

How does love feel? Most people describe physiological sensations: "I felt so excited I couldn't breathe"; "My throat choked up"; "I felt tingling all over." If you look at those descriptions, couldn't they also be descriptions of fear, anger, or excitement? Is there a difference between being in love and being on a roller-coaster?

Perhaps not. In a famous experiment, Schachter and Singer (1962) gave students a shot of epinephrine (adrenaline), which causes general arousal, including sweaty palms, increased heart rate, increased breathing, and so on. They split the students into four groups: one was told exactly what was happening and what to expect, another was told the wrong set of symptoms to expect (itching, numbness, a slight headache), a third group was told nothing, and a fourth group got an injection of saline solution (saltwater) rather than epinephrine.

Each group was put into a waiting room with a student who was actually part of the study. In half the cases, the confederate acted happy, and in half, angry. The interesting result was that the students in the informed group, when they felt aroused, assumed they were feeling the effects of the epinephrine. However, the un-informed groups tended to believe they were experiencing the same emotion as the other person in the room. They thought they were happy, or they thought they were angry. Schachter and Singer concluded that an emotion happens when there is general physiological arousal for whatever reason and a label is attached to it—and that label might be any emotion. In other words, people should be vulnerable to experiencing love (or another emotion) when they are physiologically aroused for whatever reason (Schachter & Singer, 2001). More recent studies confirm the physiological arousal theories (Aron et al., 2005; H. Fisher, 2004). Couples who meet during a crisis (such as during an emergency plane landing) are more likely to feel strongly about one another (Aron et al., 2005; Kluger, 2008). They often incorrectly attribute their high levels of arousal to feelings for the other person.

So, is love just a label we give to a racing heart? The idea may explain why we tend to associate love and sex so closely; sexual excitement is a state of intense physiological arousal. Certainly arousal of some sort is a necessary component of love. Would you want to be in love with someone who wasn't the least bit excited when you entered the room? Love, however, is almost certainly more than arousal alone. Perhaps arousal has a stronger connection to initial attraction than to love. Maybe that is why lust is so often confused with love.

However, this being said, it's also important to point out that the original Schachter and Singer (1962) study has often been challenged and has been difficult to replicate. There is little support for the claim that arousal is a necessary condition for an emotional state, and some would argue that the role of arousal has been overstated (Reisenzein, 1994).

EVOLUTIONARY THEORIES

Evolutionary theorists try to understand the evolutionary advantages of human behaviors. Love, they believe, developed as the human form of three basic instincts: the need to be protected from outside threats, the instinct of the parent to protect the child, and the sexual drive. Love is an evolutionary strategy that helps us form the bonds we need to reproduce and pass our genes on to the next generation (Gonzaga & Haselton, 2008). We love to propagate the species.

To evolutionary theorists, that would explain why we tend to fall in love with people whom we think have positive traits; we want to pass those traits along to our children. In fact, evolutionary theorists argue that their perspective can explain why heterosexual men look for attractive women, and heterosexual women look for successful men, the world over (see the section on cultural influences on attraction later in this chapter). Heterosexual men want a fit, healthy woman to carry their offspring, and heterosexual women want a man with the resources to protect them and help care for the infant in the long period they devote to reproduction. For most of history, this included 9 months of pregnancy and over a year of breast-feeding. Love creates the union that maximizes each partner's chance of passing on their genes to the next generation.

Because the evolutionary theory views love as important for reproduction, you might wonder what this theory has to say about same-sex love, given that gay men and lesbian women are not able to reproduce with each other. Homosexual behavior reinforces bonds between same-sex individuals, which directly and indirectly, contributes to survival and reproduction because it increases the chances of successfully raising offspring (Kirkpatrick, 2000; Muscarella et al., 2001).

BIOLOGICAL THEORIES

Finally, research has shown that biological factors can also influence who we fall in love with (Garver-Apgar et al., 2006; Rodriguez, 2004; Santos et al., 2005; Savic et al., 2005; Thorne & Amrein, 2003). We register the "smells" of people through their **pheromones** (FAIR-oh-moans)—odorless chemicals secreted by both humans and animals (Rodriguez, 2004; Thorne & Amrein, 2003). These pheromones are processed in the hypothalamus, and they influence our choice of sexual partner (Savic et al., 2005). Both men and women respond to pheromones. One study found that women report their male partners are more loving (and jealous) when they were ovulating (Hasleton et al., 2007).

In fact, pheromones have been found to influence attraction, mating, and bonding (Wright, 1994) and have also been found to promote the love bond between a mother and her infant; Kohl & Francoeur, 2002). Research on pheromones and sexual orientation has found that homosexual and heterosexual men respond differently to odors that are involved in sexual attraction, with homosexual men responding in similar ways as heterosexual women (Savic et al., 2005).

Our odor preferences are influenced by our major histocompatibility complex (MHC; Garver-Apgar et al., 2006; Santos et al., 2005). The MHC is a group of genes that helps the body recognize invaders such as bacteria and viruses. Because humans are pro-

pheromones
Chemical substances which are secreted by humans and animals and facilitate communication.

tected by the broadest array of disease resistance, heterosexual men and women may be programmed to mate with a partner whose MHC differs from their own (Garver-Apgar et al., 2006). This way, any offspring have a more complete MHC. We are more likely to be attracted and fall in love with someone whose MHC is different from our own (Garver-Apgar et al., 2006).

Pheromones have been found to influence attraction, mating, and bonding.

Finally, researchers have also been looking at neurotransmitters and various areas of the brain. Magnetic resonance imaging (MRI) has found that certain areas of the brain are stimulated when couples are in love (H. Fisher, 2004). In addition, when these areas of the brain are stimulated, neurotransmitters, such as dopamine, create cravings to be with a particular partner (see the Sex in Real Life feature, "Love—It's All in Your Head," later in the chapter; H. Fisher, 2004). So it appears there may be more to love and attraction than we thought. Certainly more research is needed in these areas.

review questions

1 How does the behavioral reinforcement theory explain love?

2 How do the cognitive theories explain love?

3 How do the physiological arousal theories explain love?

4 How do the evolutionary theories explain love?

5 How do the biological theories explain love?

Love from Childhood to Maturity

Throughout our lives, we love others. First we love our parents or caretakers and then siblings, friends, and romantic partners. At each stage of life, we learn lessons about love that help us mature into the next stage. Love gets more complex as we get older. Let us walk through the different stages of individual development and look at the various ways love manifests itself as we grow.

CHILDHOOD

In infancy, the nature and quality of the bond with the caregiver can have profound effects on the ability of the person to form attachments throughout life (we will discuss this more in the next chapter, "Childhood and Adolescent Sexuality"). Loving, attentive caregivers tend to produce secure, happy children (Rauer & Volling, 2007). Our parents, or the adults who raised us, are our first teachers of love and intimacy. In fact, we tend to relate to others in our love relationships much as we did when we were young. If you grew up in a family in which your parents were unemotional and distant, you learn that love is emotionally risky.

Those who do not experience intimacy growing up may have a harder time establishing intimate relationships as adults (Dorr, 2001). Of course, it is also true that many people who had difficult upbringings are successful at developing deep and intimate relationships.

The type of intimate relationships you form as an adult may be due primarily to the type of attachment you formed as a child (K. Burton, 2005; Mikulincer & Shaver, 2005). Hazan and Shaver (1987) building on the work of Ainsworth and her colleagues (Ainsworth et al., 1978), suggest that infants form one of three types of attachment behaviors that follow them throughout life. *Secure* infants tolerate caregivers being out of their sight because they believe the caregiver will respond if they cry out or need care. Similarly, the secure adult easily gets close to others and is not threatened when a lover goes away. *Anxious/ambivalent* babies cry more than secure babies and panic when the caregiver leaves them. Anxious/ambivalent lovers worry that their partner doesn't really love them or will leave them and that their need for others will scare people away. They tend to desire more closeness than their partners are willing to allow. *Avoidant* babies often have caregivers who are uncomfortable with hugging and holding them and tend to force separation on the child at an early age. In the adult, the avoidant lover is uncomfortable with intimacy and finds trusting others difficult.

© Janell Carroll

A strong and secure bond with a caregiver can have profound effects on the ability of the person to form attachments throughout life.

Hazan and Shaver (1987) found that adults report the same types of behavior as Ainsworth found in infants. People with secure attachment styles also reported more positive childhood experiences and had higher self-esteem than others (Feeney & Noller, 1990). We may develop an attachment style as a child that reemerges as we begin to form romantic attachments in adolescence. Not surprisingly, college students who are securely attached to their parents have an easier time establishing intimate relationships (Neal & Frick-Horbury, 2001).

ADOLESCENCE

There is something attractive about young love, which is why it is celebrated so prominently in novels and movies. The love relationship seems so important, so earnest, and so passionate at the time, and yet so innocent in retrospect. Why are the dips and rises of our loves so important to us in adolescence? Adolescent love teaches us how to react to love, to manage our emotions, and to handle the pain of love. It also lays the groundwork for adult intimacy. Adolescents must learn to establish a strong personal identity separate from their family. Experimentation with different approaches to others is natural, and, during adolescence, we develop the **role repertoire** that follows us into adulthood. Similarly, we experiment with different intimacy styles (J. Johnson & Alford, 1987) and develop an **intimacy repertoire,** a set of behaviors that we use to forge close relationships throughout our lives.

The process of establishing our repertoires can be a difficult task. This helps explain why adolescent relationships can be so

Young love lays the groundwork for adult intimacy.

© Kevin Dodge/Corbis

intense and fraught with jealousy and why adolescents often are unable to see beyond the relationship (J. Johnson & Alford, 1987). Our first relationships often take the form of a "crush" or infatuation and are often directed toward unattainable partners such as teachers or movie stars. Male and female movie stars provide adolescents with safe outlets for developing romantic love before dating and sexual activity begin (Karniol, 2001).

Sometimes the first lessons of love are painful, as we learn that love may not be returned or that feelings of passion fade. Yet managing such feelings helps us develop a mature love style. Many factors have been found to be associated with the ability to find romantic love in adolescence, such as marital status of the parents, the quality of the parental relationship, and comfort with one's body (Cecchetti, 2007; Coordt, 2005; Seiffge-Krenke et al., 2001). In fact, as we discussed earlier, difficulties with attachments in college students' intimate relationships may be caused by poor attachments to one's parents (see the earlier "What Do You Want To Know" feature).

The emotions of adolescent love are so powerful that adolescents may think that they are the only ones to have gone through such joy, pain, and confusion. They may gain some comfort in knowing that almost everyone goes through the same process to some degree. Confusion about love certainly does not end with adolescence.

WHAT DO YOU WANT TO KNOW ?

I have always had a tough time trusting in relationships. Could this have anything to do with the fact that my parents divorced when I was young?

It is possible that the divorce of your parents has made it difficult for you to trust your intimate partners. Research has found that divorce affects a young adult's level of trust in intimate relationships (Coordt, 2005; Ensign et al., 1998). Women whose parents have divorced (compared with women whose parents maintained stable marriages) typically report less trust and satisfaction in intimate relationships (Jacquet & Surra, 2001). Men whose parents have divorced are less likely to experience problems in their intimate relationships unless they have a female romantic partner from a divorced family. Overall, parental divorce may affect trust and intimacy in a close relationship, but it does not put children at an overall disadvantage in the development of love relationships (Coordt, 2005; Sprecher et al., 1998). It may not be the divorce itself that interferes with people's ability to form intimate relationships, but rather the quality of the relationships they have with their mother and father. If they have a good relationship with at least one of their parents, the negative effects in intimate relationships may be reduced (Ensign et al., 1998).

role repertoire
A set of behaviors that we use in our interactions with others. Once we find what works, we develop patterns of interacting with others.

intimacy repertoire
A set of behaviors that we use to forge intimate relationships throughout our lives.

review questions

1 Explain how the nature and quality of our bond with caregivers can affect our ability to form relationships later in life.

2 Identify the various attachment styles. Which of these styles is most like yours?

3 What makes love relationships so difficult and unstable for many adolescents? Why do you think those highs and lows even out as we get older?

Adult Love and Intimacy

Love relationships can last many years. As time goes by, love and relationships grow and change, and trying to maintain a sense of stability and continuity while still allowing for change and growth is probably the single greatest challenge of long-term love relationships.

Attaining intimacy is different from loving. We can love our cat, our favorite musician, or a great leader, but intimacy requires reciprocity—it takes two. Intimacy is a dance of two souls, each of whom must reveal a little, risk a little, and try a lot. In some ways, therefore, true intimacy is more difficult to achieve than true love because the emotion of love may be effortless, whereas the establishment of intimacy always requires effort.

> *. . . intimacy requires reciprocity—it takes two . . .*

Does fate determine whom you will fall in love with, or are there other factors at work? We now talk about physical attraction, proximity, common interests, and other factors that contribute to adult love and intimacy.

ATTRACTION

Imagine that you are in a public place, such as a bar, a museum, or a sports event. Suddenly you see someone and feel an immediate attraction. As you approach him or her with your favorite opening line, you think to yourself, "I wonder why I am so attracted to this person and not to someone else?" We have already discussed the importance of pheromones, and you'll probably agree that smell is an important component of attraction. But what else is going on?

"Haven't I Seen You Here Before?"

One of the most reliable predictors of whom a person will date is proximity: People are most likely to find lovers among the people they know or see around them. Although we might want to believe that we could meet a complete stranger at a bar and fall madly in love, the research tells us this scenario is rare. We are much more likely to meet our romantic partners at a party, religious institution, or friend's house, where the people are likely to come from backgrounds very similar to our own.

"You Know, We Really Have a Lot in Common"

Folklore tells us both that "birds of a feather flock together" and that "opposites attract." Yet only the first saying is supported by the evidence; people tend to be attracted to those who think like they do (Byrne & Murnen, 1988). The majority of people who fall in love share similar educational levels, ethnicity, race, social class, religion and degree of religiousness, desired family size, attitudes toward gender roles, physique and physical attractiveness, family histories, and political opinions (Michael et al., 1994; Z. Rubin, 1973).

"You Have Such Beautiful Eyes"

Physical attractiveness has been found to be one of the most importance influences in forming love relationships for both men and women (Sangrador & Yela, 2000). Physically attractive people are assumed by others to have more socially desirable personalities and to be happier and more successful (Little et al., 2006; Swami & Furnham, 2008). As we discussed in Chapter 4, men have traditionally rated physical attraction as the single most important feature in potential mates (Buss, 1989b).

The "matching hypothesis" claims that people are drawn to others with similar traits and attractiveness to themselves. However, this has been found to be more typical for heterosexual women than men. Heterosexual women have been found to choose men whose overall desirability as a mate matched their own self-perceived physical attractiveness (Todd et al., 2007), whereas heterosexual men are attracted to physically attractive partners even if they are more physically attractive than themselves.

Physical appearance is usually the first thing we perceive about a potential partner, although it tends to fade in importance over the life of the relationship. When considering a romantic partner, both men and women may be willing to compromise on some qualities they are looking for in a partner, but not on physical attractiveness (Sprecher & Regan, 2002). As we discussed in Chapter 4, the media have put such a premium on physical appearance that the majority of people in the United States report they are unhappy with their appearance and would change it if they could.

"You Seem So Warm and Understanding"

On the other hand, it should be some relief to those of us not blessed with runway-model looks that a large percentage of people cite personality as the most important factor in choosing their partners. Although people tend to be attracted to others with personalities like theirs, the general traits cited as most important are openness, sociability, emotional stability, a sense of humor, and receptivity (willing to favorably accept behaviors or emotions).

"By the Way, Have I Shown You My Porsche?"

Financial stability is another quality that many people are attracted to. In fact, for many years, heterosexual women were found to rate men's economic resources as one of the most important requirements in a partner (Buss, 1989b). This was consistent across cultures. However, newer research has shown that heterosexual men want their female partners to have financial resources as well (Buss et al., 2001; Sheldon, 2007). For many of us, having a partner who is financially secure would be a bonus, but it's not the first thing that attracts us to a person.

"So, Can I See You Again?"

What is it, finally, that we really look for in a partner? Men and women report that at the top of their list is mutual attraction and love (Buss et al., 2001). In addition to this, people are in surprising agreement on what other factors they want in an ideal partner. A study of homosexual, heterosexual, and bisexual men and women showed that, no matter what their sexual orientation, gender, or cultural background, all really wanted the same thing. They wanted partners who had similar interests, values, and religious beliefs, who were honest, trustworthy, intelligent, affectionate, warm, kind, funny, financially independent, dependable, and physically attractive (Amador et al., 2005; Toro-Morn & Sprecher, 2003). Now that doesn't seem too much to ask, does it?

ATTRACTION IN DIFFERENT CULTURES

Do men and women in every culture look for the same traits? For example, are more males than females looking for physically attractive mates in Nigeria? Is earning potential more important in males than females in China? David Buss (1989b) did an ambitious study comparing the importance of, among other things, physical attractiveness, earning potential, and age difference to men and women in 37 cultures. His results confirmed the nature of mate attraction (although Buss assumed all his respondents were heterosexual and therefore assumed they were all talking about the other sex). He found that across all 37 cultures, men valued "good looks" in a partner more than women did, and in all 37 cultures, women valued "good financial prospect" in a partner more than men did. Also interesting is that in all 37 cultures, men preferred mates who were younger than they were, whereas women preferred mates who were older. Selected results of Buss's study appear in Human Sexuality in a Diverse World, "Good Looks or a Good Prospect? What Do You Want in a Partner?"

INTIMATE RELATIONSHIPS

What exactly is intimacy? Think about the word; what does it imply to you? The word intimacy is derived from the Latin word *intimus,* meaning "inner" or "innermost" (Hatfield, 1988). Keeping our innermost selves hidden is easy; revealing our deepest desires, longings, and insecurities can be scary. As we discussed in Chapter 3, intimate partners reveal beliefs and ideas to each other, disclose personal facts, share opinions, and admit to their fears and hopes. In fact, self-disclosure is so important to intimacy that early researchers thought that willingness to self-disclose was itself the definition of intimacy (M. S. Clark & Reis, 1988). True self-disclosure, however, involves sharing feelings, fears, and dreams, not just facts and opinions. Individuals who can self-disclose have been found to have higher levels of self-esteem and confidence in their relationship and rate their relationships as more satisfying (Dindia, 2003; Macneil, 2004; Sprecher & Hendrick, 2004).

Intimacy involves a sense of closeness, bondedness, and connectedness (Popovic, 2005; R. J. Sternberg, 1987). People who value intimacy tend to express greater trust in their friends; are more concerned for them; tend to disclose more emotional, personal, and relational content; and have more positive thoughts about others. They also tend to be seen as more likable and noncompetitive by peers; to smile, laugh, and make eye contact more often; and to report better marital enjoyment (M. S. Clark & Reis, 1988).

However, all types of disclosures are risky; the other person may not understand or accept the information offered or may not reciprocate. Thus, risk taking and trust are crucial to the development of intimacy. Because intimacy makes us vulnerable and because we invest so much in the other person, intimacy can also lead to betrayal and disappointment, anger, and jealousy. We explore the dark side of intimacy later in this chapter.

This young girl is from a Longneck tribe in Mae Hong Son, Thailand. In this culture, an elongated neck is viewed as physically attractive.

Good Looks or a Good Prospect? What Do You Want in a Partner?

. . . in the United States, good looks and financial stability are important partner qualities for both men and women.

In a classic study on cultural differences in what men and women look for in a mate, David Buss (1989b) found that, almost universally, men value good looks more in a mate, and women value good financial prospects. More recent research has found that in the United States, good looks and financial stability are important partner qualities for both men and women (Amador et al., 2005; Lacey et al., 2004). As for age, almost universally, men want their mates to be a few years younger than they are, and women want their mates to be a few years older. After taking a look at these graphs, if you were a young, poor, handsome male, what country would you want to live in?

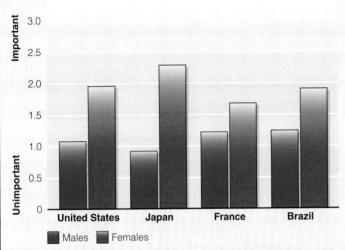

How important is financial stability in a mate?

Males / Females

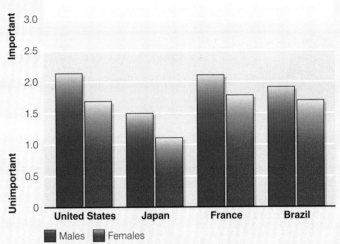

How important are good looks in a mate?

Males / Females

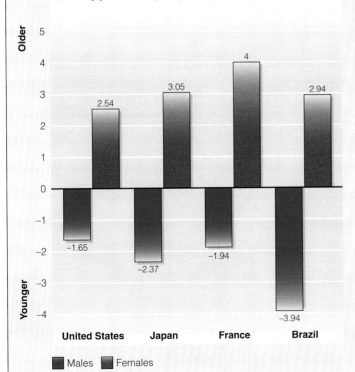

How many years older/younger do you want your partner to be?

Males / Females

In the accompanying graphs, males and females from different countries rate the importance of a mate's looks, financial prospects, and their ideal age difference. In the "Good Looks" and "Good Financial Prospects" graphs, participants rated importance from 0 (unimportant) to 3 (very important). In the "Age Difference" graph, participants rated the importance of age difference in potential mates. A negative number refers to a desire for a mate who is younger by a certain number of years, whereas a higher number refers to a desire for a mate who is older by a certain number of years. Source: Adapted from David Buss, "Sex Differences in Human Mate Preferences: Evolutionary Hypotheses Tested in 37 Cultures." *Behavioral and Brain Sciences, 12,* 149, 1989. Reprinted with permission from Cambridge University Press.

Male and Female Styles of Intimacy

If any area of research in love and intimacy has yielded conflicting findings, it is the question of gender differences. Overall, the research has found that heterosexual women tend to give more importance to the future of intimate relationships than heterosexual men do (Oner, 2001). However, M. S. Clark and Reis (1988) suggest that the subject remains murky because many other variables are at work.

Perhaps the most important factor is culturally transmitted gender roles. Men and women report equally desiring and valuing intimacy, some suggest, but many men grow up with behavioral inhibitions to expressing intimacy. We are taught how to be male and female in society, and, from a very young age, boys are discouraged from displaying vulnerability or doubt about intimacy. As one man's experience reveals in the accompanying Sex in Real Life, "In the Men's Locker Room," it is acceptable for men to talk about sex, but talk of intimacy is often taboo. Although the author's experience may have been extreme, exaggerated by the all-male atmosphere of the athletic team, such attitudes are communicated in subtle ways to most men. Therefore, men may remain unexpressive about intimacy, however strongly they may desire it. It could also be that men simply express intimacy differently—perhaps more through action than words (Gilmore, 1990).

One study compared men and women who scored high on a scale of masculinity or femininity to those who scored high on both (androgyny; Coleman & Ganong, 1985). In Chapter 4, we discussed androgyny. Androgynous people have been found to be more aware of their love feelings, more expressive, and more tolerant of their partner's faults than those who scored high only on the masculinity scale; they were also more cognitively aware, will-

---

SEX IN REAL LIFE

In the Men's Locker Room

Within the locker room subculture, sex and love were seldom allowed to mix.

Following is a story written by a heterosexual man who was reflecting about his experiences growing up as a young boy. As you read through it, consider the impact of gender roles on our expressions of love and intimacy today. Do you think most men are comfortable expressing their emotions today? Why or why not?

I played organized sports for 15 years, and they were as much a part of my growing up as Cheerios, television, and homework. My sexuality unfolded within this all-male social world of sport, where sex was always a major focus. I remember, for example, when we as prepubertal boys used the old "buying baseball cards" routine as a cover to sneak peeks at *Playboy* and *Swank* magazines at the newsstand. We would talk endlessly after practices about "boobs" and what it must feel like to kiss and neck. Later, in junior high, we teased one another in the locker room about "jerking off" or being virgins, and there were endless interrogations about "how far" everybody was getting with their girlfriends.

Eventually, boyish anticipation spilled into real sexual relationships with girls, which, to my delight and confusion, turned out to be a lot more complex than I ever imagined. While sex (kissing, necking, and petting) got more exciting, it also got more difficult to figure out and talk about. Inside, most of the boys, like myself, needed to love and be loved. We were awkwardly reaching out for intimacy. Yet publicly, the message that got imparted was to "catch feels," be cool, and connect with girls but don't allow yourself to depend on them. Once when I was a high school junior, the gang in the weight room accused me of being wrapped around my girlfriend's finger. Nothing could be

further from the truth, I assured them; to prove it, I broke up with her. I felt miserable about this at the time, and I still feel bad about it.

Within the college jock subculture, men's public protests against intimacy sometimes became exaggerated and ugly. I remember two teammates, drunk and rowdy, ripping girls' blouses off at a mixer and crawling on their bellies across the dance floor to look up skirts. Then there were the Sunday morning late breakfasts in the dorm. We jocks would usually all sit at one table and be forced to listen to one braggart or another describe his sexual exploits of the night before. Although a lot of us were turned off by such kiss-and-tell, ego-boosting tactics, we never openly criticized them. Real or fabricated, displays of raunchy sex were also assumed to "win points."

When sexual relationships were "serious," that is, tempered by love and commitment, the unspoken rule was silence. It was rare when we young men shared our feelings about women, misgivings about sexual performance, or disdain for the crudeness and insensitivity of some of our teammates. I now see the tragic irony in this: We could talk about superficial sex and anything that used, trivialized or debased women, but frank discussions about sexuality that unfolded within a loving relationship were taboo. Within the locker room subculture, sex and love were seldom allowed to mix. There was a terrible split between inner needs and outer appearances, between our desire for the love of women and our feigned indifference toward them.

Source: Adapted from Sabo and Runfola, 1980.

ing to express faults, and tolerant than those who scored high only on the femininity scale.

The importance of accepting traditional gender roles is also reflected in comparisons of homosexual and heterosexual men. Although homosexual and heterosexual men agree on the ideal characteristics of love partners and express the same amounts and kinds of love, gay men are more likely to believe that "you should share your most intimate thoughts and feelings with the person you love" (Engel & Saracino, 1986, p. 242). This may be because gay men tend to adopt fewer stereotyped beliefs about gender roles than heterosexual men.

However, some evidence indicates that the differences in attitudes between the genders may be changing. Although in the past women were more comfortable with intimate encounters and men were more comfortable taking independent action, now a new, more androgynous breed of men and women may be emerging who are more comfortable in both roles (Choi, 2004). If so, maybe we can expect greater ease in intimacy between and among the sexes in the upcoming generations of men and women.

Intimacy in Different Cultures

Love seems to be a basic human emotion. Aren't "basic human emotions" the same everywhere? Isn't anger the same in Chicago and Timbuktu, and sadness the same in Paris and Bombay? Although there is evidence that the majority of worldwide cultures experience romantic love (see the nearby "Human Sexuality in a Diverse World"), we do know that one's culture has been found to have a more powerful impact on love beliefs than one's gender (Sprecher & Toro-Morn, 2002). Culture affects how a person defines love, how easily he or she falls in love, who he or she falls in love with, and how the relationship proceeds (Kim & Hatfield, 2004).

As we discussed in Chapter 3, cultural differences in individual versus group needs can affect communication patterns (Cai et al., 2000). It should come as no surprise that these cultural differences can also affect patterns of intimacy. Passionate love is typically emphasized in individualistic cultures, but in collectivist cultures, passionate relationships are often viewed negatively because they may disrupt family traditions (Kim & Hatfield, 2004). For example, although Americans often equate love with happiness, the Chinese have equated love with sadness and jealousy (Shaver et al., 1992). This is because collectivist cultures, such as that of China or Japan, traditionally marry for reasons other than love. Passionate love dies and is not viewed as stable enough to base a marriage on. In a study of France, Japan, and the United States, intimacy style was directly related to whether the culture was individualistic, collectivistic, or mixed (France) and also to how much the culture had adopted stereotypical views of gender roles (how much it tended to see men as assertive and women as nurturing; Ting-Toomey, 1991). The Japanese, with a collectivistic culture and highly stereotypical gender roles, had lower scores in measures of attachment and commitment and were less likely to value self-disclosure than the French or Americans (Kito, 2005). Americans also have stereotypical gender roles, but because of the highly individualistic culture in the United States, Americans tend to have high levels

Love seems to be a basic human emotion.

of confusion and ambivalence about relationships. Interestingly, the French, who have a culture with high individual motivation yet with a strong group orientation, and who also have a more balanced view of masculine and feminine gender roles, had the lowest degree of conflict in intimate relationships.

Culture also affects one's sense of self. For example, in China people's sense of self is entirely translated through their relationships with others. "A male Chinese would consider himself a son, a brother, a husband, a father, but hardly himself. It seems as if. . . . there was very little independent self left for the Chinese" (Chu, 1985, quoted in Dion & Dion, 1988, p. 276). In China, love is thought of in terms of how a mate would be received by family and community, not in terms of one's own sense of romance. Because of this, the Chinese have a more practical approach to love than do Americans (Sprecher & Toro-Morn, 2002).

Finally, a cross-cultural study of college students from Brazil, India, Philippines, Japan, Mexico, Australia, the United States, England, Hong Kong, Thailand, and Pakistan studied the perceived significance of love for the building of a marriage (we talk more about marriage in Chapter 9). Researchers found that love is given highest importance in Westernized nations and the lowest importance in the less developed Asian nations (R. Levine et al., 1995). Thus, culture plays a role in how we experience and express both love and intimacy.

LONG-TERM LOVE AND COMMITMENT

The ability to maintain love over time is the hallmark of maturity. Many people regard love as something that happens to them, almost like catching the flu. This attitude hides an important truth about love: It takes effort and commitment to maintain love—not only commitment to the other person but commitment to continually build on and improve the quality of the relationship. Most long-term relationships that end do so not because the couple "fell out of love" but because, somewhere down the line, they stopped working together on their relationship. In this sense, the old saying is true: The opposite of love is not hate, but indifference.

R. J. Sternberg (1985), you may recall, claimed that passion, intimacy, and commitment are the three elements of love; in consummate love, he says, all three are present. Yet one tends to hear very little talk of commitment in our culture, with its great emphasis on passionate love. Couples going through hard times can persevere and build even stronger and more intimate relationships when their commitment reflects such a deep sense of trust.

If you observe an older couple who have been together for many years, you may have a strong sense of their ease with each other. Couples who continue to communicate with each other, remain committed to each other and the relationship, and remain interested in and intimate with each other build a lasting bond of trust. Those who don't may feel isolated and lonely in relationships that nevertheless endure for many years. Although passionate love may fade over time, love itself does not necessarily diminish. The decline of passion can allow the other components of love to flourish in the relationship.

Love—It's All in Your Head

What does our brain have to do with our feelings of love and romance?

What does our brain have to do with our feelings of love and romance? New research into brain physiology has found that our brain is more involved than you might think. Magnetic resonance imaging (MRI) of brain functioning revealed that certain areas of the brain experience increases in blood flow when a newly in love man or woman looks at a photograph of his or her romantic partner (Aron et al., 2005). More than 2,500 brain images from 17 men and women who rated themselves as "intensely in love" were analyzed using MRI technology (which monitors increases in blood flow indicating neural activity). Strong activity was noted in the motivation areas of the brain, where an overabundance of cells produce or receive the neurotransmitter dopamine (Aron et al., 2005).

Dopamine has been found to be critical for motivation. In fact, neuroscientists have found that men and women who gamble have increased dopamine when they are winning (Carey, 2005b). The researchers concluded that romantic love serves as a motivation for a man or woman to reach a goal. In this case, the goal is to spend time with the love interest.

The area of our brain responsible for sexual arousal was also found to be stimulated in these newly in love participants, but it was the motivation area that received the most stimulation. There is a biological urge that comes from sexual arousal, but also from new love (Carey, 2005b). The researchers hypothesized that when the motivation area is stimulated, a person is motivated to get rewards with his or her love interest above all else. Think about it for a minute.

When we are hungry, thirsty, or tired, the motivation area of our brain is stimulated, motivating us to find food, water, or a place to sleep. When we are romantically in love, this same area motivates us to make the connection and seek out the person we wish to be with.

This may also explain why new love often feels so crazy. Feelings of euphoria, sleeplessness, a preoccupation of thoughts of the partner, and an inability to concentrate are all common when a person is newly in love. Some men and women describe new love as a "drug," one that often leads them to do things they wouldn't normally do. Perhaps it is a result of the increased blood flow to our motivation center—and the increases in dopamine—that motivate us to get more of what we desire.

Although more research is needed on neuroscience, brain activity, and emotions, it has been suggested that this research might help us understand why people with autism often are indifferent to romantic relationships (Carey, 2005b). It could be due to the atypical brain development in the motivation areas of brain that is typical in those with autism. In addition, this research may also help us understand why love changes as the years go by. The strength of activity in the motivation section of the brain has been found to weaken as the length of the relationship increases (Carey, 2005b). In the future, research into brain physiology will continue to teach us more about the physiology of romantic love.

Source: Aron et al., 2005.

LOSS OF LOVE

Popular songs are often about the loss of love; the blues is a whole genre of music built on the experience of losing love, and country-western music is well known for its songs of lost love. People experience loss of love in many ways. The couple may realize that their relationship was based on passion and cannot develop into long-term love. One partner may decide, for his or her own reasons, to end a relationship that is still valued by the other partner. Also, a partner may become ill or die.

The loss of love is a time of mourning, and going through a period of sadness and depression, as well as anger at the partner, is natural. Research has found that most people are critical of their own role in a relationship breakup, although heterosexual women are more likely to blame their partners than are men (Choo et al., 1996). Most people are very vulnerable after the loss of a love relationship—vulnerable to rushing into another relationship to

© David Young-Wolff/Alamy

The ability to maintain love over time is the hallmark of maturity. Couples who have been together a long time often have a sense of ease with each other.

I've always wondered, how can a person stay with only one person his or her whole life and not get bored?

Although it might be hard to believe you could do this, it's also important to remember that love grows and changes when two people commit themselves to work on a relationship. Are you the person you were 10 years ago? What makes you think you'll be the same 10 years from now? When two people allow each other to grow and develop, they find new experiences and new forms of love all the time. People get bored primarily when they lose interest, not because the other person has no mysteries left.

replace the lost partner and vulnerable to self-blame, loss of self-esteem, and distrust of others (Timmreck, 1990).

No easy solutions exist to decreasing the pain of a breakup. Often being good to yourself can help, taking some time to do the things that make you happy. Readjusting your schedule can be difficult, especially if your day revolved around the other person. You may feel the greatest sense of loss at just those times that you used to be together (dinnertime, bedtime). Memories and emotions associated with a breakup often linger on. In fact, researchers have found that painful memories, like a breakup, lead to chemical changes in certain brain receptors, which can strengthen selected memories (Hu et al., 2007). The best thing you can do is be patient and try to find new activities and new patterns in your day. As you go through the grieving process, remember: Almost everyone has experienced what you are feeling at one time or another, and you will pull through.

REALResearch > After a breakup, feelings of sadness, anger, and relief are the most common emotional reactions, and contact with former partners often decreases the feelings of sadness (SBARRA & EMERY, 2005).

SEX IN REAL LIFE

Love in Times of E-mail, Chat Rooms, and Instant Messaging

Today, a person can quickly send an email, text message, or IM without fear of stumbling over his or her words or worrying about reading the body language of rejection.

Technology has changed the dating habits and strategies of establishing love relationships. Years ago, someone who wanted to ask for a date agonized over when and how to phone, what to say, and how to say it. In Chapter 3, we talked about how computer-mediated communication has changed how people communicate with one another. Today a person can quickly send an e-mail, text message, or instant message without fear of stumbling over his or her words or worrying about reading the body language of rejection. The person can meet people, set up dates or "hook-ups," and even break up online today.

But how do these technological changes affect our view of love and relationships? In many ways, this changing technology has made dating and finding love relationships easier. Men and women who are uncomfortable about meeting people or who are new to a school or area often find online dating beneficial. Online dating services can also be beneficial for people who work unusual hours or those who have children or handicaps that might interfere with their ability to meet people. Emotional and intellectual connections are made before any physical interactions. Men and women can get to know specifics about a person, such as hobbies and interests, before they decide whether they want to meet in person.

There are also risks, however. People can present themselves differently online, and what you read may not be what you'll actually get! In Chapter 3, we discussed eroticized pseudo-intimacy and the risks of moving too quickly online. Following is a list of suggestions for dating online:

1. **Guard your anonymity.** Don't give any personal information that would allow someone to find you until you're ready to give this information out.
2. **Watch for red flags.** Pay attention to inconsistencies and stories that just sound too good to be true. If the story sounds too good to be true, it probably is.
3. **Take your time.** There is no reason to rush into anything. The longer you communicate online, the better your opportunity to really get to know each other.
4. **Meet in a public place.** If you do decide to meet, make sure you meet in a public place and tell a friend where you're going and who you are meeting.
5. **Realize that it's easy to be seduced.** The informality of e-mail, instant messaging, and chat rooms can lead to things becoming too serious, too fast.

1 What do we know about why we are attracted to certain people? Explain what factors might be involved.

2 Explain what we know about cross-cultural attraction and identify some of the qualities that men and women may find attractive in other cultures.

3 Explain the importance of self-disclosure on the development of intimacy.

4 Explain what the research has found with respect to gender differences in intimacy styles.

5 Provide three ways in which cultural differences may affect patterns of intimacy.

6 Explain how the ability to maintain love over time is the hallmark of maturity.

Love, Sex, and How We Build Intimate Relationships

One way to express deep love and intimacy is through sexual behavior, but sexual behavior itself is not necessarily an expression of love or intimacy. How do we make the decision to have sex? There are many levels of relationships that can lead to sex. Casual sex and "hooking up" can happen between people who barely know each other, generated by excitement, novelty, and pure physical pleasure.

LOVE AND SEX

Sex can be an expression of affection and intimacy without including passionate love; sex can also be engaged in purely for procreation; or sex can be an expression of love within a loving relationship. Problems can develop when one partner has one view of the developing sexual relationship and the other partner takes a different perspective.

Because the decision to engage in sexual contact involves the feelings and desires of two people, examining your own motivations as well as your partner's is important. When making the decision to initiate a sexual relationship with another person, consider the following:

1. Clarify your values. At some point, each of us needs to make value decisions regarding intimacy, sex, and love. What role does love play in your sexual decisions? How will you reconcile these values with those you have learned from your family, friends, and religion?

2. Be honest with yourself—which is often more difficult than being honest with others. Entering a relationship with another person takes close self-examination. What do you really want out of this encounter? Out of this person? Are you hoping the sexual contact will lead to something deeper, or are you in it simply for the sex? What will you do if you find that you (or your partner) have a sexually transmitted infection? Are you in this because you want to be or because you feel some kind of pressure to be sexual—from yourself or from your partner? Could you say "no" comfortably? Are you ready for a sexual relationship with this person?

3. Be honest with your partner. Another person's feelings and needs are always at issue in any relationship, and part of our responsibility as caring human beings is not to hurt or exploit others. Why is your partner interested in sex with you? Do his or her expectations differ from yours? Will she or he be hurt if your relationship does not develop further? Have you discussed your feelings?

The decision to engage in a sexual relationship may or may not be related to feelings of love. Casual sex has become much more common and accepted than it was 35 or 40 years ago, when young people (especially women) were strongly advised to save their "greatest asset," their virginity, for marriage. Overall the importance of love as an essential condition for sexual relations has diminished. Yet casual sex has become more physically risky with the spread of sexually transmitted infections (we will discuss this more in Chapter 15).

When we begin to feel attracted to someone, we begin to act intimate; we gaze longer at each other, lean on each other, and touch more (Hatfield, 1988). People meeting each other for the first time tend to reveal their levels of attraction by their body language. Perper (1985) observed heterosexual strangers approaching each other in bars. The first stage he called the initial contact and conversation (which, by the way, Perper found to be commonly initiated by the female). If the couple is mutually attracted, they will begin to turn their bodies more and more toward each other, until they are facing one another. The first tentative touches begin, a hand briefly on a hand or a forearm, for example, and increase in duration and intimacy as the evening progresses (again, also often initiated by the female). Finally, the couple shows "full body synchronization"; their facial expressions, posture, and even breathing begin to mirror their partner's. As we discussed in Chapter 3, women smile, gaze, lean forward, and

One way to express deep love and intimacy is through sexual behavior.

How can I tell the difference between being in love and just deeply liking someone?
Unfortunately, no one has come up with a foolproof way of making that distinction. Being "in love" can feel a lot like being "in deep like." One would hope we deeply like those whom we love, and, in fact, we probably love those we deeply like. The element that may be missing from those we deeply like is sexual passion, but sometimes we don't realize that we are not in love with them until after we develop a sexual relationship. The discovery can be painful to both parties, which is why it is advisable to think it through before initiating a sexual relationship with a friend.

touch more often than men in conversation. Women also "flirt" with their nonverbal cues (such as hair-flipping and head-nodding) to encourage their partner to reveal more about themselves, which would in turn allow the women to formulate an impression of the person (W. E. Martin, 2001).

DEVELOPING INTIMACY SKILLS

There are many ways to improve our intimacy skills. As we discussed in Chapter 3, developing intimacy often begins with understanding and liking ourselves—self-love. Other important skills we can develop to enhance our ability to form relationships include receptivity, listening, showing affection, trust, and respect.

Self-Love

Self-love is different from conceit or **narcissism;** it is not a process of promoting ourselves but of being at ease with our positive qualities and forgiving ourselves for our faults. If you are not willing to get to know yourself and to accept your own faults, why would others think you are any more interested in them or that you would judge them any less harshly? Many people look to others for indications of their own self-worth. We must first take responsibility to know ourselves (self-intimacy) and then to accept ourselves as we are. Once we like ourselves, we can reach out to others.

Receptivity

Many of us think we are receptive to others when actually we are sending subtle signals that we do not want to be bothered. Receptivity can be communicated through eye contact and smiling. This allows the other person to feel comfortable and makes us approachable. Taking 5 minutes a day to sit and reconnect with your partner may improve your relationship and help preserve intimacy and passion.

Listening

We discussed in Chapter 3 how true communication begins with listening. Nothing shows you care about another person quite as much as your full attention. It can be very difficult to listen to someone talk only of himself or herself or someone who sees any comment made by another person primarily in terms of how it relates to them. Learning to truly listen enhances intimacy.

Affection

How do we show affection to another person? If you watch a loving parent with his or her child, it is easy to see how affection is displayed. Parents attend to their children, smile at them, touch them in affectionate ways, look in their eyes, and hug and kiss them. Most people want the same things from their intimate friends and lovers. Affection shows that you feel a sense of warmth and security with your partner.

Trust

To trust another is an act of courage because it grants that person the power to hurt or disappoint you. However, intimacy requires trust. Usually trust develops slowly. You trust your partner a little bit at the beginning of your relationship and begin to trust him or her more and more as he or she proves to be dependable and predictable. Having trust in our partner leads to more confidence that the relationship will last. When a couple trusts each other, each expects the partner to care and respond to his or her needs, now and in the future (Zak et al., 1998).

Remember earlier we talked about women from divorced families being less able to trust in intimate relationships? Perhaps it is because these women have seen firsthand what happens in unsuccessful marriages, and they fear intimate relationships just don't work. Men, too, may feel less able to trust when their partner is ambivalent or cautious about trust. The important thing to remember is that often the longer a relationship lasts, the more trust builds between the partners (Jacquet & Surra, 2001).

Respect

We enter into relationships with our own needs and desires, which sometimes cloud the fact that the other person is different from us and has his or her own special needs. Respect is the process of acknowledging and understanding that person's needs, even if you don't share them.

Michael Krasowitz/Getty Images

We are often jealous when we think, fantasize, or imagine that another person has traits we ourselves want.

self-love
Love for oneself; the instinct or desire to promote one's own well-being.

narcissism
Excessive admiration of oneself.

THE DARK SIDE OF LOVE

Love evokes powerful emotions; this is both its strength and its weakness. Many of the emotions that can come from strong feelings about another person can also be destructive to a relationship and may require great maturity or a strong act of will to overcome. Let's now examine three of the dark sides of love: jealousy, compulsiveness, and possessiveness.

Jealousy: The Green-Eyed Monster

Jealousy is a common experience in intimate relationships (Knox et al., 2007). Imagine you are at a party with a person with whom you are in an exclusive, sexual relationship. You notice that person standing close to someone else, talking and laughing, and occasionally putting his or her hand on the other person's arm. At one

---

REALResearch > Research on jealousy has found significant gender differences (KNOX ET AL., 2007). Jealous men are more likely to turn to alcohol and believe that jealousy shows love, whereas jealous women are more likely to turn to food and confide in friends.

---

point, you notice your partner whispering in the other person's ear, and they both laugh.

How does that make you feel? Are you jealous? But wait, I forgot to tell you: The person your partner was talking to and dancing with was of the same sex as your partner (if you are heterosexual) or the other sex (if you are homosexual). Are you still jealous? Oh yes, one more thing. The other person was your partner's younger sibling. Now are you jealous?

Jealousy is an emotional reaction to a relationship that is being threatened (Knox et al., 1999, 2007; Sharpsteen & Kirkpatrick, 1997). A threat is a matter of interpretation; people who deeply trust their partners may not be able to imagine a situation in which the relationship is really threatened. We are most jealous in the situation just described when the person flirting with our partner has traits we ourselves want (or we fantasize that they do). Maybe we imagine our partner will find the other person more desirable than us, sexier, or funnier. A correlation has been found between self-esteem and jealousy; the lower the self-esteem, the more jealous a person feels and in turn the higher his or her insecurity (Knox et al., 1999, 2007). We imagine that the partner sees in the other person all those traits we believe that we lack.

Men and women experience similar levels of jealousy in intimate relationships, yet there is controversy over what triggers jealousy (Fleischmann et al., 2005). Some research supports the fact that heterosexual men are more jealous when they believe that their partner has had a sexual encounter with another man, whereas heterosexual women are often more focused on the emotional or relationship aspects of infidelity (Buss, 2003; Schützwohl, 2008). However, it may have to do with whether the relationship is short or long term (Penke & Asendorpf, 2008). In short-term relationships, both men and women are more threatened by sexual infidelity, whereas emotional infidelity is often more threatening in a long-term relationship (Mathes, 2005).

Other studies have found physiological responses (e.g., increased blood pressure) in both men and women when they imagined scenarios of their partner committing either emotional or sexual infidelity (DeSteno et al., 2002; C. R. Harris, 2003; Turner, 2000). Cheating, either emotional or sexual, can lead to jealousy in both men and women.

Past research on heterosexual couples has found that men report that female–female sexual infidelity was rated the least jealousy-producing—perhaps because a man can fantasize about being with the two women (Sagarin et al., 2003). Unfortunately we know little about infidelity in same-sex relationships and marriages because the majority of the research has been done on heterosexual relationships (Blow & Hartnett, 2005). Overall, we know that people who do not experience jealousy have been found to be more secure, and this security in intimate relationships tends to increase as the couple's relationship grows (Knox et al., 1999, 2007). That is, the longer we are in a relationship with someone, the more our vulnerability to jealousy decreases.

Although many people think that jealousy shows that they really care for a person, in fact it shows a lack of trust in the partner. Jealousy is not a compliment but a demonstration of lack of trust and low self-esteem (Knox et al., 2007; Puente & Cohen, 2003). Jealousy is also a self-fulfilling prophecy; jealous individuals can drive their mates away, which convinces them that they were right to be jealous in the first place. Jealousy can be contained by trying to improve one's own self-image, by turning it around into a compliment (not "she's flirting with other guys" but "look at how lucky I am—other guys also find her attractive"), and by trust of one's partner. Communicating with your partner about your jealous feelings can often help to maintain your relationship (Guerrero & Aff, 1999). Opening up and talking about your uncertainty about the relationship or reassessing the relationship can help restore and strengthen the relationship.

Compulsiveness: Addicted to Love

Being in love can produce a sense of ecstasy, euphoria, and a feeling of well-being, much like a powerful drug (see Sex in Real Life "Love—It's All in Your Head" for more information). In fact, when a person is in love, his or her body releases the drug phenylethylamine, which produces these feelings (Sabelli et al., 1996). (Phenylethylamine is also present in chocolate, which may be why we love it so much, especially during a breakup!) Some people do move from relationship to relationship as if they were love addicted, trying to continually recreate that feeling, or else they obsessively hang on to a love partner long after his or her interest has waned. (See Lee's description of mania in the Colors of Love earlier in the chapter.)

Love addiction is reinforced by the popular media's portrayals (even as far back as Shakespeare's *Romeo and Juliet*) of passionate love as all-consuming. It fosters the belief that only one person is fated to be your "true love," that love is always mutual, and that you'll live "happily ever after." Some people feel the need to be in love because society teaches that only then are they really whole, happy, and fulfilled in their role as a woman or a man. Yet love based solely on need can never be truly fulfilling. In Peele and

REALResearch > Taller men have been found to experience less jealousy than shorter men (BUUNK ET AL., 2008). This may be because male height is associated with attractiveness, dominance, and reproductive success.

Brodsky's (1991) book *Love and Addiction,* they argue that love addiction is more common than most believe and that it is based on a continuation of an adolescent view of love that is never replaced as the person matures. Counseling or psychotherapy may help the person come to terms with his or her addiction to love.

Possessiveness: Every Move You Make, I'll Be Watching You

Because love also entails risk, dependency to some degree, and a strong connection between people, there is always the danger that the strength of the bond can be used by one partner to manipulate the other. Abusive love relationships exist when one partner tries to increase his or her own sense of self-worth or to control the other's behavior by withdrawing or manipulating love.

For intimacy to grow, partners must nurture each other. Controlling behavior may have short-term benefits (you might get the person to do what you want for a while); but, long-term, it smothers the relationship. No one likes the feeling of being manipulated, whether it is subtle, through the use of guilt, or overt, through physical force. Part of love is the joy of seeing the partner free to pursue his or her desires and appreciating the differences between partners. Although every relationship has its boundaries, freedom within those agreed-upon constraints is what encourages the growth and maturation of both partners.

Possessiveness indicates a problem of self-esteem and personal boundaries and can eventually lead to **stalking.** Most states have passed stalking laws, which enable the police to arrest a person who constantly shadows someone (usually, but not always, a woman) or makes threatening gestures or claims (we discuss this more in Chapter 17). Thinking about another person with that level of obsession is a sign of a serious psychological problem, one that should be brought to the attention of a mental health professional.

We started this chapter talking about the importance of love in our lives. The ability to form loving, caring, and intimate relationships with others is important for our emotional health and also our physical health. Love and intimacy are two of the most powerful factors in well-being. Love might not always be easy to understand, but it is a powerful force in our lives, and intimacy is an important component of mature love in our culture.

stalking
Relentlessly pursuing someone, shadowing him or her, or making threatening gestures or claims toward the person when the relationship is unwanted.

review questions

1 What factors might a couple consider when making the decision to initiate a sexual relationship?

2 Why do people feel jealous, and how are jealousy and self-esteem related?

3 Compare and contrast compulsiveness and possessiveness.

CHAPTER review

SUMMARY POINTS

1 We go through life trying to come to terms with loving, trying to figure out why we are attracted to certain types, or why we fall in love with all the wrong people. The mystery of love is part of its attraction.

2 Not until the 19th century did people begin to believe that romantic love was the most desirable form of loving relations. Through most of Western history, marriage was an economic union arranged by the parents. Once wed, husbands and wives were encouraged to learn to love one another, to *develop* love.

3 Romantic love comes with a sense of ecstasy and anxiety, physical attraction, and sexual desire. We tend to idealize the partner, ignoring faults in the newfound joy of the attachment. Passionate love blooms in the initial euphoria of a new attachment to a sexual partner. If a relationship is to continue, romantic love must develop into companionate love.

4 Romantic love is the passionate, highly sexual part of loving. Companionate love involves feelings of affection, intimacy, and attachment to another person. In many cultures, marriages are based on companionate love, assuming that passion will grow as the couple does.

5 John Alan Lee suggests that there are six basic types of love, and Robert Sternberg suggests that love is made up of three elements: passion, intimacy, and decision/commitment, which can combine in different ways in relationships, creating seven basic ways to love and an eighth state, called nonlove, which is an absence of all three elements.

6 The behavioral reinforcement theories suggest that we love because the other person reinforces positive feelings in ourselves. Positive feelings in the presence of another person make us like him or her, even when the reward has nothing to do with the other person.

7 The cognitive theories propose that we love because we think we love. This theory suggests that the action comes first and the interpretation comes later.

8 In the physiological arousal theory, people are vulnerable to experiencing love (or another emotion) when they are physiologically aroused for whatever reason. An emotion happens when there is general physiological arousal for whatever reason and a label is attached to it—and that label might be any emotion.

9 Evolutionary perspectives of love believe that love developed out of our need to be protected from outside threats, to protect children, and from our sexual drive. Love is an evolutionary strategy that helps us form the bonds we need to reproduce and pass our genes on to the next generation.

10 Biological theories believe that pheromones may contribute to feelings of love. Our odor preferences are influenced by our major histocompatibility complex (MHC). Neurotransmitters and the brain also have been found to affect our feelings of love.

11 Love develops over the life cycle. In infancy, we develop attachments to our caregivers; receiving love in return has an influence on our capacity to love later in life. In adolescence, we deal with issues of separation from our parents, and begin to explore adult ways of loving. Adolescents tend to experience romantic love. Attachment styles we learn in infancy, such as secure, avoidant, and ambivalent styles, may last through life and influence how we begin to form adult attachments in adolescence.

12 As we mature and enter adulthood, forming intimate relationships becomes important. Developing intimacy is risky, and men and women have different styles of intimacy, but intimacy is seen as an important component of mature love in our culture. As we grow older, commitment in love becomes more important, and passion may decrease in importance.

13 Relationships take effort, and when a couple stops working on the relationship, both partners can become very lonely, love can fade, and intimacy can evaporate. When love is lost, for whatever reason, it is a time of pain and mourning. The support of family and friends can help us let go of the lost love and try to form new attachments.

14 Men and women may have different intimacy styles. For example, men may learn to suppress communication about intimacy as they grow, or they may learn to express it in different ways.

15 The decision to be sexual is often confused with the decision to love. Values need to be clarified before a sexual relationship is begun.

16 Developing intimacy begins with understanding ourselves and liking ourselves. Receptivity, listening, showing affection, trusting in your partner, and respecting him or her are important in the development of intimacy.

17 Love also has its negative side. Jealousy plagues many people in their love relationships, whereas others seem addicted to love, going in and out of love relationships. Some people also use love as a means to manipulate and control others.

18 Possessiveness indicates a problem of self-esteem and personal boundaries and can eventually lead to stalking. Most states have passed stalking laws, which enable the police to arrest a person who constantly shadows someone or makes threatening gestures or claims.

CRITICAL THINKING questions

1 Using John Alan Lee's colors of love, examine a relationship that you are in (or were in) and analyze the styles of love that you and your partner use(d). Which love style do you think would be hardest for you to deal with in a partner and why?

2 Think of a love relationship that you have been in. Describe how each of the theories proposed in this chapter would explain why you loved your partner. Which theory do you think does the best job, and why?

3 Do you think the research on pheromones fits with your own experiences? Are you attracted (or not attracted) to people by their smell?

4 Explain what gender differences have been found in love, and tie this research to an example from one of your past relationships.

5 How long do you think is appropriate to wait in a relationship before engaging in sex? Why?

6 Have you ever been involved with a partner who was jealous? What was the hardest part of this relationship? How did you handle the jealousy?

Sexuality Now Book Companion Website

Go to www.cengage.com/psychology/carroll for practice quizzes, glossary, flash cards, and more. You can also access the following websites from the companion site.

Love Is Great ■ This website is all about love, dating, romance, and relationships. The website contains information and links to single/dating websites.

Loving You ■ This website contains advice, love poems, and free romantic love notes and quotes. There are also links to dating services, love libraries, and gift shops.

Love Test ■ A nonscientific but fun website that offers a multitude of different "love" tests. Compatibility analysis, astrology reports, fortune tellers, and relationship rating tests are available.

Queendom ■ This site offers the largest online battery of professionally developed and validated psychological assessments. This website is a fun place to find a variety of different quizzes.

CengageNOW

Go to www.cengage.com/login to link to CengageNOW, your online study tool. First take the Pre-Test for this chapter to get your Personalized Study Plan, which will identify topics you need to review and direct you to online resources. Then take the Post-Test to determine what concepts you have mastered and what you still need work on.

Videos in CengageNOW

CengageNOW also contains these videos related to the chapter topics:

• Emotions, Stress, and the Immune System—Learn how social relationships can literally keep you safe from physical ailments.

• How Do I Love Thee? Expressions of Love Styles—Listen to these personal videos and use Lee's love styles to match potential mates.

CHAPTER 8

Childhood and Adolescent Sexuality

Jim Esposito Photography L.L.C./Getty Images

At school I've had some formal sex ed. In health class, at the beginning of the year, we had a discussion about it, and we watched movies—The Miracle of Life and The Miracle of Birth. *People make lots of jokes about those movies because they show a man and a woman having sex, and they have a close-up of the in-and-out. But you don't learn much about the details of sex in school. It's what most of the boys talk about, telling each other how they do it and who they do it with. What I've found is most girls have experienced this stuff before most boys have. There are only a few boys in my school who I've heard talking about kissing someone with the tongue and I've actually believed them. Some of the boys talk about feeling certain parts of the girlfriends' bodies, but I don't believe most of it.*

I'm not sure why, but in conversations I've had with my parents, they've made requests like "not until you're sixteen." I think

it might become a possibility for me at the age of fourteen. I don't think I'll be having sex regularly until I'm fifteen or sixteen. It's not something I'm dying to do, because I question what you're supposed to do. I've seen it on the video, the in-and-outing, but how does that start? I'd say that's the main thing that makes most people my age not quite ready to have sex. Trying to figure out or make up how it works or could work. First there's the question of how girls have sex with you, and then there's the question of how to get girls to have sex with you. The first one is one of the most important things I think about now, how it happens. I've seen enough and heard enough to understand how kissing works, but I don't know how to get from that to having sex. I suppose that's the next bridge to cross, how to turn kissing into sexual intercourse. At school it's perfectly all right to talk about it happening, but there's no way of coming out and asking your friends how it happens. It's one of those things that everyone thinks about, but

no one's able to admit it. You think, maybe everyone else understands this, maybe they're going to think less of me.

On some of the late-night TV shows, I've seen people making out on the couch, and then it cuts off right where the guy unbuttons the girl's top button, and it begins again in the morning, where they're lying in bed. There's no way to figure out how it starts. I don't think girls know either, but I have the feeling that it doesn't matter what the girl does, it's all because of the boy. I can see on TV that the girl doesn't start unbuttoning the boy's shirt, it's always the boy unbuttoning the girl's shirt. They always go home to the boy's apartment. That just gives me the idea the boy is the person who starts it.

SOURCE: Maurer, 1994, p. 34.

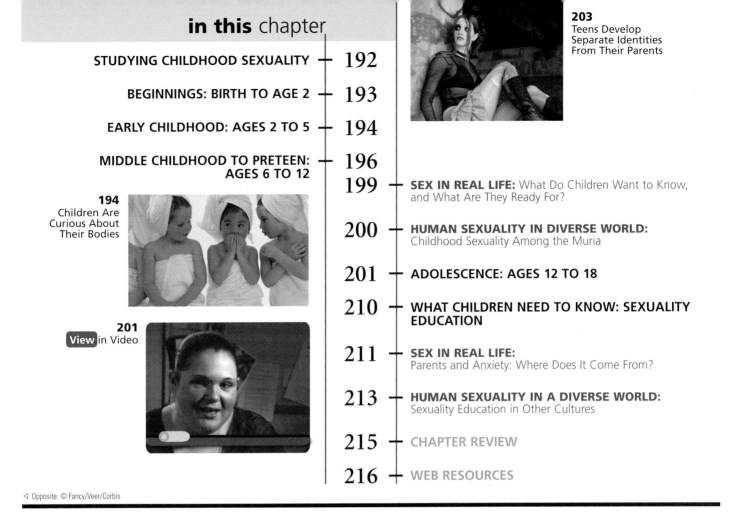

◁ Opposite: © Fancy/Veer/Corbis

This opening story from a 12-year-old boy, published in *Harper's Magazine,* show the struggles of a young boy trying to understand sexuality as he emerges from preadolescence. As you read through his story, try to go back to your own childhood. What were some of the issues you worried about? Thought about? Wanted to know more about?

Children have lots of questions about sexuality—some basic and others more complex. A friend of mine, the mother of two young girls, told me that when one daughter was 3 years old, she asked about a little boy's body. "Why does Brian have a finger sticking out of his bottom?" she asked. Trying her best to keep a straight face and answer the question with as much dignity and respect as she could muster, my friend sat her daughter down and explained that it was a penis, not a finger. She then went on to explain the physiological differences in male and female genitalia.

It's interesting to think about these early questions we all have about sexuality and how we find answers to all of our questions. In this chapter, we look at childhood sexuality from infancy through adolescence. We examine how sexuality develops through-

out childhood and the various influences on adolescent sexuality today. We look at adolescent sexual behavior, contraceptive use, and pregnancy. Finally, we discuss the importance of sexuality education and the controversies surrounding it.

We think of children today as undergoing their own, exclusive stage of development. Children are not just "little adults," and though they can be sexual, children's sexuality is not adult sexuality (Gordon & Schroeder, 1995). Children want love, appreciate sensuality, and engage in behaviors that set the stage for the adult sexuality to come. Nonetheless, we must be careful not to attribute adult motives to childhood behaviors. When a 5-year-old boy and a 5-year-old girl sharing a bath reach out to touch each others' genitals, the meaning that they ascribe to that action cannot be considered "sexual" as adults use the term. As Plummer (1991) notes, a little boy having an erection shows simply that his physiology functions normally; seeing the erection as "sexual" is to overlay an adult social meaning onto the physiology. The child is probably not even aware of the "sexual" nature of his erection and, indeed, may not even be aware that his penis is erect.

Throughout most of history, children were treated as miniature adults, and concepts such as "childhood" and "adolescence" did not exist (Aries, 1962). Most children worked, dressed, and were expected to behave (as much as they were capable) like adults.

table 8.1

Studies of Childhood Sexuality

National Longitudinal Study of Adolescent Health (ADD Health)

- 1994–1995, 1996, 2000–2001, 2008

- School-based sample; 126,000 students in Grades 7–12; 18,000 parents and school administrators

- Interviews and questionnaires

National Survey of Family Growth (NSFG)

- 1973–2002, 2009

- Not limited to teens; females only for 1973–2000; began including males in 2001; 45,000 females, 14–44 years old

- Household-based, in-home interviews and phone interviews

National Longitudinal Study of Adolescent Males (NSAM)

- 1988, 1990–1991, 1995

- Young, never-married males; 6,600 respondents, aged 15–27 years

- In-person interviews and questionnaires; originally designed to correlate with NSFG study

Youth Risk Behavior Surveillance System (YRBS)

- Conducted every 2 years

- Students in Grades 9–12; 14,000 respondents in 2007 survey

- Questionnaires

Every society distinguishes between young and old; every society also creates rules around the sexuality of the young. Sexual growth involves a host of factors—physical maturation of the sexual organs, psychological dynamics, familial relations, and peer relations, all within the social and cultural beliefs about gender roles and sexuality.

Studying
Childhood Sexuality

As we discussed in Chapter 2, it is difficult to carry out research on children's sexuality in American society. Many people oppose questioning children about sexuality, often believing that research on child sexuality will somehow encourage promiscuity. Others seem to believe that if we do not talk about children's sexuality, it will just go away. The truth about American society, however, is that teenagers and even preteens today are often sexually active, with high pregnancy, birth, and abortion rates.

Some researchers have been forging ahead in their study of children's sexual behavior, despite the opposition. The U.S. government has sponsored four large-scale studies to examine adolescent behaviors. These studies include the National Longitudinal Study of Adolescent Health (ADD Health; 1994–1995, 1996, 2001–2002, 2008), the National Survey of Family Growth (NSFG; 1973–2002, 2009), the National Longitudinal Study of Adolescent Males (NSAM; 1988, 1990–1991, 1995), and the Youth Risk Behavior Surveillance System (YRBS, which collects new data every 2 years; see Table 8.1).

ADD Health is the largest, most comprehensive survey of adolescents ever undertaken. It is a nationally representative sample of adolescents in Grades 7 through 12. Interviews and question-naires are used to gather information. The ADD Health study was designed to explore the causes of these behaviors, with an emphasis on the influence of social context. Families, friends, schools, and communities play roles in the lives of adolescents that may encourage healthy choices or lead to unhealthy, self-destructive behavior, and this study explores these influences. Initially the ADD Health study focused only on adolescents, but more recent phases have included data on the transition from adolescence to adulthood.

The NSFG is the only one of these studies that is not limited to teenagers. It provides information on first intercourse, birth control, childbearing, cohabitation, and divorce, among other things, and has examined the behaviors of females between the ages of 14 and 44 (males were included in their analysis beginning in 2001). The NSFG is a household-based survey and uses personal in-home and phone interviews to access information. A third study, the NSAM, which was originally designed to correlate with the NSFG study, was the first nationally representative survey of the sexual and risk-related behavior of young, never-married men in the United States. Males between the ages of 15 and 27 were surveyed through face-to-face interviews in conjunction with questionnaires. In 1995, the NSAM included urine testing for those over 18 years old to test for chlamydia and gonorrhea to collect information about the prevalence of these two sexually transmitted infections (STIs).

The YRBS is another ongoing, longitudinal study that explores the prevalence of certain behaviors that put young people at risk, including sexual behaviors that may result in STIs and unintended pregnancies. This national study is conducted every 2 years and includes students in Grades 9 through 12. In addition to these major studies, the National Health and Social Life Survey also provided limited information on childhood sexuality (see Chapter 2 for more information on the survey).

Together, these studies have helped to shed some light on trends in adolescent sexual behavior. As we discussed in Chapter 2, sexuality research has always been problem driven (i.e., many studies are aimed at decreasing rates of STI or teenage pregnancy), and nowhere is this more apparent than in the research on adolescent sexuality, yet the research has also helped us to understand adolescent sexuality. Although methodologies and populations varied for each of the aforementioned studies, adolescents between the ages of 15 and 17 were a common subpopulation. We discuss many of these findings later in this and upcoming chapters.

In the future, more research is needed on frequency of sexual behaviors other than heterosexual intercourse; differences in gender, ethnicity, race, religion, and social class; same-sex attraction and behavior; cross-cultural research; and the meaning of eroticism and sexuality in young people's lives.

review questions

1 Explain why there has been opposition to childhood sexuality research.

2 Identify the four large-scale studies on adolescent behavior and explain their study populations.

3 Give one example how research into childhood sexuality has been problem driven.

Beginnings:
Birth to Age 2

Let's first take a look at physical and psychosexual changes from birth to age 2. We would not label behavior as "sexual" during this time; however, there are many behaviors that arise out of curiosity.

PHYSICAL DEVELOPMENT:
FULLY EQUIPPED AT BIRTH

Our sexual anatomy becomes functional even before we are born; ultrasound has shown male fetuses with erections in the uterus, and some babies develop erections shortly after birth—even before the umbilical cord is cut (Masters et al., 1982). Female babies are capable of vaginal lubrication from birth (Martinson, 1981). Infant girls produce some estrogen from the adrenal glands before puberty, whereas infant boys have small testes that produce very small amounts of testosterone. Young children are even capable of orgasm!

Kinsey and his colleagues (1948, 1953) established that one half of boys between the ages of 3 and 4 could achieve the urogenital muscle spasms of orgasm (although no fluid is ejaculated), and almost all boys could do it 3 to 5 years before puberty. Kinsey did not collect systematic data on the abilities of young girls to reach orgasm, although he did include some anecdotal stories on

the subject. Still, there is no reason to think that girls should be any less able than boys to orgasm.

PSYCHOSEXUAL DEVELOPMENT:
BONDING AND GENDER IDENTIFICATION

The single most important aspect of infant development is the child's relationship to his or her parents or caregivers. The infant is a helpless creature, incapable of obtaining nourishment or warmth or relieving pain or distress. The bond between the mother and child is more than psychological; a baby's crying actually helps stimulate the secretion of the hormone **oxytocin** in the mother, which releases her milk for breast-feeding (Rossi, 1978; we'll discuss this more in Chapter 12).

Pheromones are also important. Remember that in Chapter 7, we discussed how pheromones promote the bond between a mother and her infant (Kohl & Francoeur, 2002). Equally important as the infant's need for nourishment is the need for holding, cuddling, and close contact with caregivers. An infant's need for warmth and contact was demonstrated in Harlow's (1959) famous experiment, in which rhesus monkeys were separated at birth from their mothers. When offered two surrogate mothers, one a

oxytocin
A hormone secreted by the hypothalamus that may contribute to the physical bond between a mother and her infant.

wire figure of a monkey equipped with milk bottles and one a terrycloth-covered figure, the monkeys clung to the terrycloth figure for warmth and security and ventured over to the wire figure only when desperate for nourishment. The need for a sense of warmth and security in infancy overwhelms even the desire to eat.

As we discussed in Chapter 4, infants between 1 and 2 years of age begin to develop their gender identity (M. Lewis, 1987). After about age 2, it becomes increasingly difficult to change the child's gender identity (which is occasionally done when, for example, a female with an enlarged clitoris is mistakenly identified at birth as a boy). It takes a little longer to achieve **gender constancy,** whereby young children come to understand that they will not become a member of the other sex sometime in the future. Most children develop gender constancy by about age 6, and a strong identification with one gender typically develops that becomes a fundamental part of a child's self-concept (Warin, 2000).

Young girls and boys are curious about their bodies and bodily functions.

SEXUAL BEHAVIOR:
CURIOSITY

In infancy, the child's body is busy making sure all of his or her organs work and learning to control them. The sexual system is no exception. Male babies sometimes have erections during breast-feeding (which can be very disconcerting to the mother), whereas girls have clitoral erections and lubrication (although that is less likely to be noticed). The baby's body (and mind) has not yet differentiated sexual functions from other functions, and the pleasure of breast-feeding, as well as the stimulation from the lips, mouth, and tongue, create a generalized neurological response that stimulates the genital response.

Genital touching is common in infancy, and many infants touch their genitals as soon as their hands are coordinated enough to do so (Casteels et al., 2004). Some babies only occasionally or rarely touch themselves, whereas others do it more regularly. Although babies clearly derive pleasure from this activity; it is not orgasm-based. In fact, it is soothing to the baby and may serve as a means of tension reduction and distraction. In fact, in some cultures, it is a common practice for mothers to calm a baby down by stroking the baby's genitals. Overall, genital touching is normal at this age, and parents should not be concerned about it.

gender constancy
The realization in the young child that one's gender does not normally change over the life span.

review questions

1 Explain how infants have functional sexual anatomy, perhaps even before birth.

2 Identify the single most important aspect of infant development and explain the importance of pheromones, warmth, and contact with caregivers.

3 Differentiate between gender identity and gender constancy.

4 Discuss genital touching in infancy and possible parent concerns about this behavior.

Early Childhood:
Ages 2 to 5

Children continue to develop physically, and in early childhood they begin to understand what it means to be a boy or girl. Curiosity is still the basis for their sexuality during this time. Children also learn that their genitals are private during these years, and they often begin to associate sexuality with secrecy.

PHYSICAL DEVELOPMENT:
MASTERING COORDINATION

Early childhood is a crucial period for physical development. Children of this age must learn to master the basic physical actions, such as eye–hand coordination, walking, talking, and generally learning to control their bodies. Think of all the new things a child must learn: all the rules of speaking and communicating; extremely complex physical skills such as self-feeding, walking, and running; how to interact with other children and adults; control of bodily wastes through toilet training; and handling all the frustrations of not being able to do most of the things they want to do when they want to do them. Although this period of childhood is not a particularly active one in terms of physical sexual development, children may learn more in the first few years of childhood about the nature of their bodies than they learn in the entire remainder of their lives. It is truly a time of profound change and growth.

PSYCHOSEXUAL DEVELOPMENT:
WHAT IT MEANS TO BE A GIRL OR BOY

In early childhood, children begin serious exploration of their bodies. It is usually during this period that children are toilet trained, and they go through a period of intense interest in their genitals and bodily wastes. They begin to ask the first, basic questions about sex, usually about why boys and girls have different genitals and what they are for. They begin to explore what it means to be "boys" or "girls" and turn to their parents, siblings, or television for models of gender behavior. Sometimes children at this age will appear flirtatious or engage in sexual behaviors such as kissing in an attempt to understand gender roles.

SEXUAL BEHAVIOR:
CURIOSITY AND RESPONSIBILITY

Toddlers are not yet aware of the idea of sexuality or genital sexual relations. Like infants, toddlers and young children engage in many behaviors that involve exploring their bodies and doing things that feel good. Both girls and boys at this age continue to engage in genital touching. More than 70% of mothers in one study reported that their children under age 6 touched themselves (Okami et al., 1997).

Genital touching is actually more common in early childhood than later childhood, although it picks up again after puberty (Friedrich et al., 1991). The act may be deliberate and obvious and may even become a preoccupation. Boys at this age are capable of

Laurie A. Watters

Young boys develop strong relationships with same-sex and other-sex friends and relatives, and these relationships set the stage for adult intimate relationships.

erection, and some proudly show it off to visitors. Parental reaction at this stage is important; strong disapproval may teach their children to hide the behavior and to be secretive and even ashamed of their bodies, whereas parents who are tolerant of their children's emerging sexuality can teach them to respect and take pride in their bodies. It is perfectly appropriate to make rules about the times and places that such behavior is acceptable, just as one makes rules about other childhood actions, such as the correct time and place to eat or to urinate.

Child sex play often begins with games exposing the genitals ("I'll show you mine if you show me yours. . . .") and, by the age of 4, may move on to undressing and touching, followed by asking questions about sex around age 5. Sometimes young children will rub their bodies against each other, often with members of the same sex, which seems to provide general tactile pleasure.

SEXUAL KNOWLEDGE AND ATTITUDES:
SEX IS DIFFERENT

During this period of early childhood, children learn that the genitals are different from the rest of the body. They remain covered up, at least in public, and touching or playing with them is either discouraged or to be done only in private. This is the beginning of the sense of secrecy surrounding sexuality.

As we discussed in Chapters 5 and 6, children this age, especially girls, rarely learn the anatomically correct names for their genitals. Why is it that some parents teach their children the correct names for all the body parts except their genitalia? What message do you think it might send children when we use cute play words such as "weiner" or "piddlewiddle" for their genital organs?

In our culture, boys are more likely to be taught a name for their genitals, but girls rarely are taught about the clitoris. This tends to discourage girls from learning more about their sexuality (Ogletree & Ginsburg, 2000). The appearance of the penis seems to fascinate both girls and boys, and although boys tend to be relatively uninterested in girls' genitals, girls are quite interested in boys' penises (Gundersen et al., 1981).

1 Explain how curiosity is still the basis for sexuality in early childhood.

2 What does the research show about genital touching during this age range?

3 Explain how a lack of knowledge about proper anatomical terms for the genitals may affect girls.

4 What is the impact of learning in childhood that the genitals are different from the rest of the body? Explain.

Middle Childhood to Preteen:
Ages 6 to 12

Between ages 6 and 12, the first outward signs of puberty often occur, and both boys and girls become more private about their bodies. Children begin building a larger knowledge base about sexual information—and acquire information from many sources, including their parents/caregivers, peers, and siblings. During the middle childhood to preteen years, children often play in same-sex groups and may begin masturbating, engaging in sexual fantasy, and/or sexual contact.

Puberty is one of the three major stages of physiological sexual development.

PHYSICAL DEVELOPMENT:
PUBERTY

Until a child's body starts the enormous changes involved in puberty, the sexual organs grow in size only to keep up with general body growth and change very little in their physiological activity. Although the body begins internal changes to prepare for puberty as early as age 6 or 7, the first outward signs of puberty begin at 9 or 10. In girls, **breast buds** appear, and pubic hair growth may begin. In boys, pubic hair growth generally starts a couple of years later than in girls, and, on average, girls experience menarche (which we discussed in Chapter 5) before boys experience their first ejaculation (often referred to as **semenarche**; SEM-min-ark). Preadolescent boys experience frequent erections, even to nonerotic stimuli. Common reactions to semenarche include surprise, curiosity, confusion, and pleasure—and typically most boys don't tell anyone about this event (Frankel, 2002; J. H. Stein & Reiser, 1994). Pubertal changes can be frightening for both boys and girls if they are not prepared for them, and, even if prepared, the onset of puberty can be emotionally, psychologically, and physically difficult for some children.

Puberty is one of the three major stages of physiological sexual development, along with prenatal sexual differentiation and menopause. Puberty marks the transition from sexual immaturity to maturity and the start of reproductive ability. In Chapters 5 and 6, we discussed the physiological and hormonal changes that ac-

company puberty, so here we review only those physical changes that have an effect on the nature of adolescent sexuality.

Puberty begins anywhere between the ages of 8 and 13 in most girls and 9 and 14 in most boys. In fact, the age of puberty has been steadily declining, especially among girls, probably because of better nutrition during childhood (Posner, 2006). American girls reach menarche at a mean age of 12 (Posner, 2006; Steiner et al., 2003), and boys experience first semenarche at about age 13 (J. H. Stein & Reiser, 1994; see Figure 8.1 for more information about signs of puberty in boys and girls). In other countries, the age at which children reach puberty may differ. A study in Israel, for example, found the age of semenarche of about 14 (Reiter, 1986). Girls' maturation is, in general, about 1.5 to 2 years ahead of boys (Gemelli, 1996).

The physiological changes of puberty almost seem cruel. At the time when attractiveness to potential sexual partners begins to become important, the body starts growing in disproportionate ways; fat can accumulate before muscles mature, feet can grow before the legs catch up, the nose may be the first part of the face to begin its growth spurt, and one side of the body may grow faster than the other (M. Diamond & Diamond, 1986). Add acne, a voice that squeaks at unexpected moments, and unfamiliarity with limbs that have suddenly grown much longer than one is accustomed to, and it is no wonder that adolescence is often a time of awkwardness and discomfort. Fortunately, the rest of the body soon catches up, so the awkward phase does not last too long.

PSYCHOSEXUAL DEVELOPMENT:
BECOMING MORE PRIVATE

As a child matures, overt sexual behavior lessens. However, such behavior may lessen because it becomes less tolerated by parents and adults as the child grows older. For example, although it may be acceptable for a 3 year old to put his hand down his pants, such behavior would not be as acceptable for a 9 year old.

breast buds
The first swelling of the area around the nipple that indicates the beginning of breast development.

semenarche
The experience of first ejaculation.

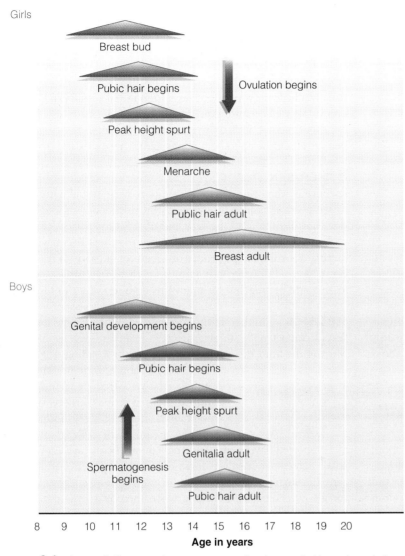

The Age Sequence of Pubertal Maturation in Boys and Girls

Girls

Breast bud

Pubic hair begins

Ovulation begins

Peak height spurt

Menarche

Public hair adult

Breast adult

Boys

Genital development begins

Pubic hair begins

Peak height spurt

Genitalia adult

Spermatogenesis begins

Pubic hair adult

8 9 10 11 12 13 14 15 16 17 18 19 20

Age in years

Figure **8.1** This graph illustrates the average ages when boys and girls go through the major bodily changes of puberty. Source: From *School Age Pregnancy and Parenthood* by Jane Lancaster, p. 20, Aldine de Gruyter, 1986. Reprinted by permission.

Typically, children engage in more sexual exploration behavior up until age 5, and then this behavior decreases. One study found that 2-year-old children of both sexes engaged in more natural sexual exploration than did children in the 10- to 12-year-old range (Friedrich, 1998). Presumably this is due to the fact that children get better at hiding their sexual behaviors.

SEXUAL BEHAVIOR:
LEARNING ABOUT THE BIRDS AND BEES

Children through the middle and late childhood years continue to engage in genital touching and may explore both same- and other-sex contact. Curiosity drives some to display their genitals and seek out the genitals of other children. Prepubescence is the age of sexual discovery; most children learn about adult sexual behaviors such as sexual intercourse at this age and assimilate cultural taboos and prejudices concerning unconventional sexual behavior. For example, it is at this age that children (especially boys) first begin to use sexual insults with each other, questioning their friends' desirability and/or sexual orientation (recall the chapter opener from Chapter 6).

Masturbation

Generally, by the end of this time period, most children are capable of stimulating themselves to orgasm. Although orgasm is possible, not all children in this age range engage in genital touching for the purpose of orgasm.

Boys often learn masturbation from peers, and as they get older, they may masturbate in groups. Girls, on the other hand, typically discover masturbation by accident. When masturbation does begin, both boys and girls may stimulate themselves by rubbing their penis or vulva against soft objects like blankets, pillows, or stuffed animals. Many girls experience pleasure and even orgasm by rhythmically rubbing their legs together.

Sexual Contact

Children from age 6 to puberty engage in a variety of same- and other-sex play. Sex games, such as "spin the bottle" (spinning a bottle in a circle while asking a question such as, "Who is going to kiss Marie?" then the person whom the bottle points to must perform the task), are common and allow children to make sexual contact under the guise of a game. Play, in a sense, is the "work" of childhood, teaching interpersonal and physical skills that will be developed as we mature. Children at this age have some knowledge about sex and are curious about it, but they often have incomplete or erroneous ideas, as expressed by the 12 year old in the chapter opener. Both boys and girls exhibit a range of same-sex sexual behaviors as they move through childhood, from casual rubbing and contact during horseplay to more focused attention on the genitals.

Rates of sexual contact among school-age children are difficult to come by, and most experts still cite Kinsey's data of 1948 and 1953. Kinsey found that 57% of men and 46% of women remembered engaging in some kind of sex play in the preadolescent years. However, the problems with research in this area is that many studies are retrospective (i.e., they asked older adults to remember what they did when they were young), and there are many reasons to think people's recollections of childhood sexuality may not be entirely accurate.

SEXUALITY AND RELATIONSHIPS:
WHAT WE LEARN

All of our intimate relationships influence our sexuality in one way or another. We learn different aspects of sexuality from these varied influences; for example, we may learn behaviors and taboos from our parents, information from our siblings, or techniques from our peers.

In their relationships with each other, boys and girls in middle childhood often imitate adults.

Relationships With Parents and Caretakers

In Chapter 7, we discussed how our parents, or the adults who raised us, are the very first teachers of love and intimacy. As we grow and find relationships of our own, we tend to relate to others in our love relationships much as we did when we were young.

When it comes to childhood sexual behaviors, many parents feel conflicted. Parents want their children to have a positive attitude toward sexuality, but many do not know how to go about fostering this attitude. Children have a natural curiosity about sex, and when parents avoid children's questions, they reinforce children's ideas that sex is secret, mysterious, and bad. As adolescent's bodies continue to change, they may feel anxious about these changes or their relationships with other people. Accurate knowledge about sex may lead to a more positive self-image and self-acceptance. We discuss the importance of sexuality education later in this chapter.

Parents may get upset and confused when they discover that their child engages in sexual play. Sex play in children is perfectly normal, and parents should probably be more concerned if their children show no interest in their own or other children's bodies than if they want to find out what other children have "down there."

*Children have a **natural curiosity** about sex.*

Relationships With Peers

As children age and try to determine how they will fare in the world outside the family, their peer groups increase in importance. Learning acceptable peer-group sexual standards is as important as learning all the other attitudes and behaviors. Children learn acceptable attitudes and behaviors for common games, sports, and even the latest media trends. Friends are very important to adolescents.

SAME-SEX PEERS During middle childhood, adolescents overwhelmingly prefer same-sex to other-sex friends (Hendrick & Hendrick, 2000). Although other-sex friendships do develop, the majority of early play is done in same-sex groupings (Fabes et al., 2003). Early on these friendships tend to be activity-based (friends are made because of shared interests or proximity), but by early adolescence, affective qualities (such as trust, loyalty, honesty) replace the activity-based interests (Bigelow, 1977). With these qualities in place, friendships can tolerate differences in interests or activities and reasonable distance separations (such as not being in the same classroom). As a result, friendships in adolescence become more stable, supportive, and intimate than they were prior to this time (B. B. Brown et al., 1997).

Peers are a major catalyst in the decision to partake in voluntary sexual experimentation with others. Sexual communication and contact are carefully negotiated, because both participants are usually a little nervous about sex. Often initial sexual experimentation takes place among preadolescents of the same sex. Same-sex experimentation is quite common in childhood, even among people who grow up to be predominantly heterosexual.

OTHER-SEX PEERS For most American children, preadolescence is when they begin to recognize their sexual nature and to see peers as potential boyfriends or girlfriends. Although this does not happen until the very end of this time period, children as young as 11 begin to develop interest in others and may begin pairing off within larger groups of friends or at parties. Preadolescence has traditionally been a time of early sexual contact, such as kissing and petting, but for many this does not occur until later.

SIBLINGS Another fairly common childhood experience is sexual contact with siblings or close relatives, such as cousins. Most of the time, this occurs in sex games or fondling, but it can also occur as abuse, with an older sibling or relative coercing a younger one into unwanted sexual activity. Greenwald and Leitenberg (1989) found that among a sample of college students, 17% reported having sibling sexual contact before age 13. Only a small percentage involved force or threat, and penetration was rare. Research on sexual contact between siblings suggests that it can be psychological damaging when there is a large difference between the ages of siblings or coercive force is used (Finkelhor, 1980; Rudd & Herzberger, 1999).

Many cultures have rituals of passage that signify the entry of the child into adulthood. Here a young Jewish boy reads from the Torah at his Bar Mitzvah.

SEX IN REAL LIFE

What Do Children Want to Know, and What Are They Ready For?

... it is important to keep in mind that any particular program must be designed according to the needs of the specific group to which it will be presented.

Because developmental differences influence children's ability to comprehend sexuality education, educators often evaluate what types of questions students ask in order to develop programs that can meet the needs of different age levels (we discuss sex education at greater length later in this chapter). Many proponents of sexuality education programs believe that these programs should be sequential (i.e., there should be a logical order in the curriculum) and comprehensive (i.e., they should include information on bi-

ological, psychological, social, and spiritual components). Following are some typical questions students ask at various ages and suggestions for what to include in sexuality education programs at these levels. Although we've presented these general guidelines for sexuality education programs, it is important to keep in mind that any particular program must be designed according to the needs of the specific group to which it will be presented.

Age Range	Developmental Issues	Questions Children Might Ask	Suggestions for Sexuality Educators
3 to 5 years	Shorter attention spans.	What is that? (referring to specific body parts) What do mommies do? What do daddies do? Where do babies come from?	At this level, sexuality education can focus on the roles of family members, the development of a positive self-image, and an understanding that living things grow, reproduce, and die.
6 to 8 years	Very curious about how the body works.	Where was I before I was born? How does my mommy get a baby? Did I come from an egg?	Sexuality education can include information on plant and animal reproduction, gender similarities and differences, growth and development, and self-esteem.
9 to 12 years	Curiosity about their bodies continues, and heterosexual children are often interested in the other sex and reproduction. Gay, lesbian, and bisexual children may experience same-sex interests at this time.	How does the reproductive system work? Why do some girls have larger breasts than others? Do boys menstruate? Why don't some women have babies?	Sexuality education can include focus on biological topics such as the endocrine system, menstruation, masturbation and wet dreams, sexual intercourse, birth control, abortion, self-esteem, and interpersonal relationships.
12 to 14 years	Preteens may be concerned or confused about the physical changes of puberty, including changes in body shape, body control, reproductive ability, menstruation, breast and penis development, and voice changes.	How can you keep yourself looking attractive? Should your parents know if you're going steady? Why are some people homosexual? Does a girl ever have a wet dream? Does sexual intercourse hurt? Why do people get married?	Sexuality education can focus on increasing knowledge of contraception, intimate sexual behavior (why people do what they do), dating, and variations in sexual behaviors (homosexuality, transvestism, transsexualism).
15 to 17 years	Increased interest in sexual topics and curiosity about relationships with others, families, reproduction, and various sexual activity patterns. Many teenagers begin dating at this time.	What is prostitution? What do girls really want in a good date? How far should you go on a date? Is it good to have sexual intercourse before marriage? Why is sex considered a dirty word?	Sexuality education can include more information on birth control, abortion, dating, premarital sexual behavior, communication, marriage patterns, sexual myths, moral decisions, parenthood, sexuality research, sexual dysfunction, and the history of sexuality.

SOURCE: Based on Breuss & Greenberg, 1981, pp. 223–231.

review questions

1 Explain physical and psychosexual development in middle childhood through the preteen years.

2 Identify and discuss the types of sexual behaviors that are common in middle childhood through the preteen years.

3 Discuss the importance of relationships with parents, peers, and siblings in childhood through preadolescence.

HUMAN SEXUALITY IN A DIVERSE WORLD

Childhood Sexuality Among the Muria

. . . sex—like work, play, food, and sleep—is openly accepted as a normal and natural part of life.

The Muria, a non–Hindu tribal people, live in the state of Basar in the central hill country of India. Their view of childhood sexuality differs from ours in the West.

Beautiful Jalaro, twelve years old, slips out of her parents' thatched-roof hut, heading for the ghotul compound at the edge of the village. . . . Tonight Jalaro hopes to sleep with Lakmu, her favorite of all the ghotul boys. Only last week, she had her first menstrual period, and now all the village boys are eager to sleep with her. She has made love to many of them during her years in the ghotul, but now beautiful Jalaro is a real woman at last. . . .

With a rush of noise and laughter, the girls swarm through the gate, assembling first in front of their own fire and then dispersing to mingle with the boys. One group of boys and girls pairs off and begins singing sexual, taunting songs. Another group settles down by the fire, talking and joking. From a third group, in a different part of the compound, there is the sudden beat of a drum, and half-naked bodies begin to bob and weave in the darkness.

Later on, when the singing and dancing have died down and the smaller children have begun to fall asleep, the Belosa (the girls' headmistress) tells each one whom she will massage and with whom she will sleep. These assignments are made arbitrarily by the headmistress, but Jalaro smiles and lowers her eyes when the Belosa, wise and fair for her seventeen years, orders her to massage Lakmu and then share his sleeping mat.

Before long, Jalaro is kneeling on the ground a short distance from the fire; Lakmu sits on the ground between her thighs. She takes one of the beautiful hand-carved combs from her head and begins to comb out his long, black tangles, talking softly as she works.

When this is done, she massages his back, chest, arms, and legs—slowly at first, but building up to a violent intensity. Then she runs the teeth of her comb all over his body to stimulate his skin. Finally, she finishes by taking each of his arms in turn and cracking every joint from shoulder to fingertip.

This same scene is repeated in a great many other places throughout the compound. Soon the sleeping mats will be unrolled, and the unmarried young of the Muria will be well engrossed in the lovemaking and sexual play. The adults like this arrangement because it gives them privacy in their small, crowded huts at night. And to the [adult] Muria, the enjoyment of sex—in private and without interference from children—is one of the supreme pleasures of married life.

In this technologically simple society, where privacy is all but impossible to find and where sex—like work, play, food, and sleep—is openly accepted as a normal and natural part of life, children of three or four are already familiar with the basic facts of sexual behavior. And by the time a Muria child is twice that age, sexual innocence is a thing of the past. The traditional cultures of the West generally take the attitude that children are not naturally sexual creatures, should not be sexual creatures, and should at all costs be kept away from sexual knowledge and ideas lest they somehow become sexual creatures before their appointed hour arrives. Yet the members of relatively few cultures studied by anthropologists would have anything but derision for such notions. Indeed, the overwhelming majority of preindustrial cultures consider sex to be an inevitable and harmless aspect of childhood.

SOURCE: Richard Currier, "Juvenile Sexuality in Global Perspective," in Constantic and Martin, eds. Children and Sex: New Findings, New Perspectives, 1981, p. 9–19. Used by permission of Lippincott, Williams & Wilkins.

Adolescence:
Ages 12 to 18

Adolescence begins after the onset of puberty and is, in part, our emotional and cognitive reactions to puberty. Adolescence ends when the person achieves "adulthood," signified by a sense of individual identity and an ability to cope independently with internal and external problems (Lovejoy & Estridge, 1987). People reach adulthood at different times; adolescence can end at around age 17 or 18, or it can stretch into a person's 20s. It is recognized the world over as a time of transition, as the entrance into the responsibilities and privileges of adulthood. Most societies throughout history have developed rites of passage around puberty; the Jewish Bar or Bat Mitzvah, Christian confirmation, and the Hispanic Quinceañera come to mind, and other cultures have other rites. The Quinceañera—a 15th birthday celebration for Latina girls—has traditionally been used as an opportunity to discuss female adolescent developmental tasks and challenges, including teenage pregnancy and sexuality (H. Stewart, 2005).

We know the most about this developmental period because, as we discussed earlier in this chapter, there are ongoing research studies on adolescent sexual behavior. Overall, we know there is no other time in the life cycle that so many things happen at once: the body undergoes rapid change; the individual begins a psychological separation from the parents; peer relationships, dating, and sexuality increase in importance; and attention turns to job, career, or college choices.

Many young people have their first experience with partnered sex during this time. It is no wonder that many adults look back on their adolescence as both a time of confusion and difficulty and a time of fond memories.

View in Video

"A lot of teenagers think they're invincible. . . nothing can touch them."
—*Adolescence: Sexual Risk Taking*
To view go to CengageNOW at www.cengage.com/login

WHAT DO YOU WANT TO KNOW ?

I keep reading about how terrible people's adolescence was, and mine was fine—I mean I had the normal problems, but it was no big deal. Am I weird?

Adolescence is a time of great change and development, and how people handle it depends on a host of factors, including their biology (such as fluctuating hormone levels), their family, their personality, and their social relationships. Adolescence, in general, may not be as upsetting or disturbing to most people as theorists tend to portray it (Brooks-Gunn & Furstenburg, 1990). If you had (or are having) a wonderful adolescence, that makes you fortunate, not "weird." Be sympathetic to others who may not have had your resources—whether biological, psychological, or social—as they went through adolescence.

PHYSICAL DEVELOPMENT:
BIG CHANGES

During early adolescence, parents are often shocked at the extreme changes that occur in their children; children can add 5 or 6 inches in height and gain 10 to 20 pounds in less than a year. Boys may develop a lower voice and a more decidedly adult physique, whereas girls develop breasts and a more female physique. Although we tend to concentrate on the development of the sexual organs, biological changes take place in virtually every system of the body and include changes in cardiovascular status, energy levels, sexual desire, mood, and personality characteristics (Hamburg, 1986).

Maturing early or late can also be awkward for boys or girls. Because girls' growth spurts happen earlier than boys', there is a period when girls will be at least equal in height and often taller than boys; this reversal of the cultural expectation of male height often causes both sexes to be embarrassed at dances. Girls who consider themselves to be "on time" in developing feel more attractive and positive about their bodies than those who consider themselves "early" or "late" (Hamburg, 1986).

Being the last boy (or the first) in the locker room to develop pubic hair and have the penis develop can be a humiliating experience that many remember well into adulthood. Similarly, girls who are the first or last to develop breasts often suffer the cruel taunts of classmates, although the messages can be mixed. It may be this combination of beginning of sexual exploration, changing bodies, and peer pressure that results in the average adolescent having a negative **body image** (Brumberg, 1997).

Females

Menarche is the hallmark of female puberty and is often viewed as one of the most important events in a woman's life (we discussed the physiology of menarche in Chapter 5; Ersoy et al., 2005). Menarche can be a scary time for a girl who is uninformed about what to expect and an embarrassing time if she is not taught how to use tampons or pads correctly.

The beginning of menstruation can mean different things to an adolescent girl depending on how her family or her culture explains it to her. It can signify the exciting beginning of adulthood, sexuality, and the ability to have babies—but with all the potential problems that brings as well. Girls who are prepared for menstruation and who are recognized for their intellectual or creative capabilities are more likely to describe pleasurable reactions to the onset of menstruation, whereas girls who are not recognized for other abilities often experience more fear and embarrassment associated with first menstruation (Teitelman, 2004).

Although boys' first sign of sexual maturity—ejaculation—is generally a pleasurable experience that is overtly associated with sexuality, girls' sign of maturity is not associated with sexual plea-

body image
A person's feelings and mental picture of his or her own body's beauty.

sure and may be accompanied by cramps and discomfort, as well as embarrassment if the onset is at an inopportune time (such as in the middle of school). Some girls begin menstruation with little idea of what is happening or with myths about it being bad to bathe, swim, exercise, or engage in sexual activities. Many are unfamiliar with their genital anatomy, making tasks such as inserting tampons difficult and frustrating (Carroll, 2009; M. Diamond & Diamond, 1986).

Males

Adolescent development in males differs in many ways from the development in girls. Boys' voices change more drastically than girls', and their growth spurts tend to be more extreme and dramatic, usually accompanied by an increase in appetite. Because boys' adolescent growth tends to be more uneven and sporadic than girls', the adolescent boy will often appear gangly or awkward. As boys continue to develop, the larynx enlarges, bones grow, and the frame takes on a more adult appearance.

*Adolescence is the **most** **psychologically** and **socially** **difficult** of the life cycle changes.*

For the most part, early development in boys is usually not as embarrassing as it is in girls; beginning to shave may be seen as a sign of maturity and adulthood. However, adolescent boys do experience frequent spontaneous erections, which may have no association with sexuality but are nonetheless quite embarrassing. Their increased sexual desire is often released through **nocturnal emissions** and increased masturbation.

PSYCHOSEXUAL DEVELOPMENT: EMOTIONAL SELF-AWARENESS

Adolescence is, by far, the most psychologically and socially difficult of the life cycle changes. There are a number of tasks that adolescents struggle with: achieving comfort with their bodies, developing an identity separate from their parents', trying to prove their capacity to establish meaningful intimate and sexual relationships, beginning to think abstractly and futuristically, and establishing emotional self-awareness (Gemelli, 1996). We now examine these life cycle changes.

Adolescence (Ages 12 to 18)

In early adolescence, preteens begin to shift their role from child to adolescent, trying to forge an identity separate from their family by establishing stronger relationships with peers. Same-sex friendships are common by the eighth grade and may develop into first same-sex sexual contacts as well (L. M. Diamond, 2000; Lawlis & Lewis, 1987). The importance of a best friend grows as an adolescent matures. In fact, by the end of high school, both girls and boys rated their relationship with their best friend as their most important relationship (B. B. Brown et al., 1997; see Figure 8.2).

Early adolescence, as most of us remember, is often filled with "cliques," as people look to peers for validation and standards of behavior. Dating also often begins at this age, which drives many adolescents to become preoccupied with their bodily appearance and to experiment with different "looks." Young adolescents are often very concerned with body image at this time. Many young girls, in an attempt to achieve the perfect "model" figure, will endlessly diet, sometimes to the point of serious eating disorders. The Youth Risk Behavior Surveillance System (see Chapter 2 for more information about this study) found that many young boys and girls are developing eating disorders and may turn to drugs such as steroids to achieve the perfect body (Pisetsky et al., 2008).

nocturnal emission
Involuntary ejaculation during sleep, also referred to as a "wet dream."

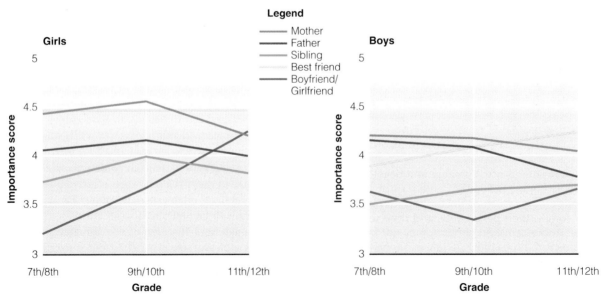

Figure **8.2** This graph shows the age differences in mean ratings of the importance of each type of relationship to one's life during adolescence (1 = not at all important; 5 = extremely important). Source: Brown, Dolcini, & Leventhal, "Transformations in peer relationships at adolescence," p. 169, in Schulenberg et al. (Eds.), *Health Risks and Developmental Transitions During Adolescence*, 1997. Reprinted by permission of Cambridge University Press.

In early and middle adolescence, teens try on different looks, from trendy to rebellious, as they develop an identity separate from their parents.

© Pat Thielen/Alamy

By about age 14, most adolescents experience an increasing interest in intimate relationships. The social environment also helps build this interest through school-sponsored dances and private parties (B. B. Brown et al., 1997). Adolescents who have not yet reached puberty or those who feel they might be gay or lesbian often feel intense pressure to express interest in other-sex relationships at this time (K. M. Cohen & Savin-Williams, 1996). Many adolescents increase the frequency of dating as they try to integrate sexuality into their growing capacity for adult-to-adult intimacy.

For the average middle adolescent, dating consists of going to movies or spending time together after school or on weekends. During this period, couples develop longer-term and more exclusive relationships, and early sexual experimentation (deep kissing, fondling) may also begin. Early dating is often quite informal, and double-dating is popular, as is going out in groups.

Oftentimes, the pattern for gay, lesbian, or bisexual adolescents may be quite different from that of their heterosexual counterparts. They might not fit into the heterosexual dating scene and may try to hide their disinterest in the discussions of the other sex (Faulkner & Cranston, 1998). Rates of depression, loneliness, drug and alcohol abuse, and suicide are significantly higher for gay, lesbian, and bisexual youths (DeAngelis, 2002; Westefeld et al., 2001; we discuss this more in Chapter 11).

Because developing the adolescent sense of self is a delicate process, adolescents may be very sensitive to perceived threats to their emerging ideas of "manhood" or "womanhood." There is an unfortunate tendency among adolescents to portray certain partners as "desirable" and others as undesirable or outcast, which as you can imagine (or remember) can be extremely painful if you are on the wrong side of that judgment. Also, for gay, lesbian, and bisexual youths, family reactions or self-expectations may result in depression or confusion. The development of a gay identity may challenge long-held or socially taught images of the acceptable way to be a man or a woman.

There is no clear line between adolescence and adulthood. Almost all cultures allow marriage and other adult privileges in late adolescence, although there still may be certain restrictions (such as needing parental permission to marry). Late adolescence was, until recently, the stage during which people in Western cultures were expected to begin their search for marital partners through serious dating. As we discuss in Chapter 9, many of today's adults wait longer to establish permanent relationships and perhaps marry (see Figure 8.3 for more information on important sexual and reproductive events for men and women).

SEXUAL BEHAVIOR: EXPERIMENTATION AND ABSTINENCE

Almost every survey shows that sexual activity has increased overall among U.S. teens over the past 50 years, although it may be slowing down somewhat today. Teenagers today are more independent and autonomous than in past generations. As we discussed in Chapter 1, sexual images commonly used in advertising, movies, music, and other media, much of it directed at teens, is constantly bombarding us.

Masturbation

Masturbation is one of the most underreported sexual behaviors in adolescence. This is mainly because adolescent masturbation is a sensitive topic, and adolescents are often somewhat reluctant to admit to doing it (C. J. Halpern et al., 2000). Masturbation during

REALResearch > Adolescent body size has been found to be an important component of friendship. One study found that larger body sizes, especially among adolescent girls, constrained the size of friendship circles because of the stigma attached to body size (CROSNOE ET AL., 2008). As a result, larger female adolescents are often isolated in their school networks.

WHAT DO YOU WANT TO KNOW?

I am 19 years old, and I masturbate at least twice a week, but not as much if I am having good sex with my girlfriend. But she tells me that she never masturbates as much as I do. Why do teenage men masturbate so much more than teenage women?

There are interesting differences in masturbation patterns between the sexes. Although women masturbate more now than they did in years past, girls are less likely than boys to report enjoying masturbation. Also, boys tend to reinforce the social acceptability of masturbation by talking about it more freely among themselves. Historically, girls are socialized not to pay attention to their sexual feelings, and this may also affect masturbation rates. Finally, there may also be biophysical reasons for more frequent male masturbation, such as the obvious nature of the male erection and levels of testosterone.

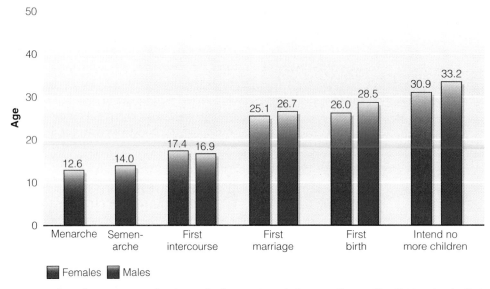

Figure **8.3** Men and women experience important sexual and reproductive events at similar ages. Source: Alan Guttmacher Institute, *In Their Own Right: Addressing the Sexual and Reproductive Health Needs of Men,* 2002, page 8.

adolescence is more likely to be reported during adulthood than during adolescence itself.

As boys and girls enter adolescence, masturbation sharply increases, and the activity is more directed toward achieving orgasm than simply producing pleasurable sensations. Kinsey and his colleagues (1953) found a sharp increase between the ages of 13 and 15 in boys, with 82% of boys having masturbated by age 15. The girls' pattern was more gradual, with 20% having masturbated by age 15 and no sharp increase at any point.

Masturbation is a common sexual behavior for adolescent males (Laumann et al., 1994). In fact, almost all studies find that at every age from adolescence into adulthood, more males masturbate and masturbate more frequently than females. Many boys worry that they masturbate more than other boys, but studies of male adolescents show that the average male teen masturbates between three and five times a week (I. M. Schwartz, 1999). Research on heterosexual adolescent masturbation has found that boys masturbatory activities decrease when they are having regular sexual intercourse, whereas girls' increase; this may be because boys masturbate significantly more than girls in general or because girls are less likely to reach orgasm during sexual intercourse and supplement it with masturbation.

Abstinence

The Sexuality Information and Education Council of the United States (SIECUS) promotes **abstinence** and encourages adolescents to delay sex until they are physically, cognitively, and emotionally ready for mature sexual relationships and their consequences.

Research has found that rates of abstinence in heterosexual high school students increased between 1991 and 2006 (Eaton et al., 2006). In 2006, 54% of high school girls said they never engaged in sexual intercourse (49% in 1991). Among high school boys, 52% said they never engaged in sexual intercourse in 2006 (43% in 1991) (Eaton et al., 2006). Among African American stu-

*As **boys and girls** enter adolescence, **masturbation sharply increases.***

dents, 32% said they never engaged in sexual intercourse in 2006 (compared with 19% in 1991). Some heterosexual teens do, in fact, decide to delay sexual activity, or at least sexual intercourse, until marriage.

Adolescents often think about many factors when deciding to be sexual. Some decide they are not ready because they haven't met the "right" person, whereas others delay sex because of STI or pregnancy fears (Morrison-Beedy et al., 2008). Heterosexual teens who delay sexual intercourse are more likely to live with both biological parents (Upchurch et al., 2001), feel a personal connection to their family (Meschke et al., 2000; Resnick et al., 1997), have discussed sex and abstinence with their parents (Sprecher & Regan, 1996), believe that their mother disapproves of premarital sex, and have higher intelligence levels (C. J. Halpern et al., 2000).

Sexual Contact

Adolescents may engage in a variety of sexual behaviors, including kissing, oral sex, sexual intercourse, and anal sex. Overall, we know considerably more about the adolescent heterosexual behaviors and very little about adolescent same-sex behaviors. It is hopeful that the research in same-sex sexual behavior will continue to grow in the next few years.

KISSING AND PETTING Kissing and touching are the first sexual contact that most adolescents have with potential sexual partners. Coles and Stokes (1985) reported that 73% of 13-year-old girls and 60% of 13-year-old boys had kissed at least once. Because younger girls tend to date older boys, they have higher rates of these kinds of activities at earlier ages than boys do, but the differences diminish over time. For example, 20% of 13-year-

abstinence
Refraining from intercourse and often other forms of sexual contact.

old boys reported touching a girl's breast, whereas 35% of 13-year-old girls reported having their breasts touched, a difference that disappears within a year or two.

ORAL SEX Acceptance of oral sex has increased among young people. Kinsey and his colleagues (1948, 1953) reported that 17% of adolescents reported engaging in **fellatio** (fil-LAY-she-oh) and 11% in **cunnilingus** (kun-nah-LING-gus). More current research from the National Survey of Family Growth (see Chapter 2) found that among teenagers between the ages of 15 and 19, 54% of girls and 55% of boys reported having engaged in oral sex (Flanigan et al., 2005; Lindberg et al., 2008).

For many years, there has been a popular perception in the media that heterosexual teens preferred oral sex over sexual intercourse because it allowed them to preserve their virginity and eliminated pregnancy risk (Stein, 2008; Wind, 2008). However, newer research challenges the myth that heterosexual teens are substituting oral sex for sexual intercourse (Lindberg et al., 2008). An analysis of the sexual practices of 2,271 15 to 19 year olds found that oral sex was more common in adolescent couples who had already initiated sexual intercourse—87% of nonvirgin teens reported engaging in oral sex, whereas only 27% of virgins reported engaging in oral sex (Lindberg et al., 2008). In fact, 6 months after first engaging in sexual intercourse, 82% of heterosexual teens have engaged in oral sex (Lindberg et al., 2008). The majority of heterosexual teens do not substitute oral sex for sexual intercourse and in fact, often engage in oral sex *after* they have already engaged in sexual intercourse.

Other research on adolescent oral sex has found that heterosexual female adolescents are significantly more likely than heterosexual males to indicate they have given oral sex (Lindberg et al., 2008). As for ethnic differences, Caucasian heterosexual females were significantly more likely than their male counterparts to indicate they had given oral sex and significantly more likely than their Hispanic/African American counterparts to have done so (Lindberg et al., 2008). However, these differences were most notable in African American adolescent girls who were twice as likely to report receiving oral sex rather than giving oral sex

*The **average age** for **first** **engaging** in **sexual intercourse** is approximately 17 years.*

(Lindberg et al., 2008). As for socioeconomic differences, heterosexual teens from lower socioeconomic classes and those with more conservative attitudes about sexuality were significantly less likely to report engaging in oral sex, whereas heterosexual adolescents from higher socioeconomic classes and those with more liberal attitudes were more likely to report engaging in oral sex.

ANAL SEX Data from the National Survey of Family Growth (see Chapter 2) found that 11% of heterosexual adolescents have engaged in anal intercourse (Lindberg et al., 2008). Like oral sex, heterosexual adolescent nonvirgins are more likely than virgins to engage in anal intercourse (Lindberg et al., 2008). One in five nonvirgin adolescents have engaged in anal intercourse, whereas only 1% of virgins have done so (Lindberg et al., 2008). Although the overall likelihood of engaging in heterosexual anal intercourse was not found to differ significantly by ethnic or racial group, Hispanic males were more likely than non-Hispanic White males to report ever having engaged in anal intercourse (Lindberg et al., 2008).

Gay adolescents may also engage in anal sex, and for some it is their defining moment of "losing their virginity." One study of college students found that 80% of respondents believed that a man or woman could lose their virginity with a same-sex partner, whereas 10% believed that only a man could do so (Trotter & Alderson, 2007). More research is needed in this area.

HETEROSEXUAL INTERCOURSE The decision to engage in sexual intercourse for the first time is difficult for some teens. They may worry about pregnancy, STIs, their abilities, or how sexual intercourse might change their relationship with their partner.

The average age for first engaging in sexual intercourse is approximately 17 years, although some adolescents engage in intercourse earlier or later (see Figure 8.3 for information on sexual and reproductive events in men and women). However, there are some ethnic differences, with African American males often being younger (15 years old) and Asian American males older (18 years old; Upchurch et al., 1998). Approximately 6% of adolescents engage in sexual intercourse before age 13 (Eaton et al., 2006). Most studies find that females have sex later than males throughout the teen years in all racial groups (Eaton et al., 2006). It is important to realize that all such studies rely on self-report and are made more difficult because definitions of sexuality (even sexual intercourse!) differ among young people (Sanders & Reinisch, 1999).

Today close to half of all high school students have engaged in sexual intercourse nationwide (Eaton et al., 2006; see Figure 8.4), and heterosexual African American males are more likely to have lost their virginity and to have had more lifetime partners than were non–African American heterosexual males (Eaton et al., 2006). The percentage of high school students who have engaged in sexual intercourse is higher among African American males (75%) than females (61%) and among Hispanic males (58%) than females (51%).

WHAT DO YOU WANT TO KNOW ?

Sometimes I feel I should have sex just to get it over with—being a virgin is embarrassing! It's pretty hard to resist when everybody else seems to be doing it.

It used to be that it was shameful (especially for women) to be sexually active; now it often seems equally shameful to admit to being a virgin. The decision to have sex is a serious one. Too often this step is taken without consideration of its consequences—for example, whether we feel psychologically or emotionally ready and whether our partner does. Sex should never be the result of pressure (by our partner, our friends, or ourselves). There may be many reasons that we want to delay sexual experimentation—including moral or religious reasons. Also, teens usually overestimate the numbers of their friends who are sexually active.

---

fellatio
The act of sexually stimulating the male genitals with the mouth.

cunnilingus
The act of sexually stimulating the female genitals with the mouth.

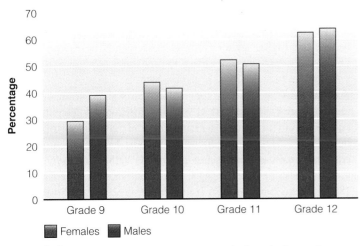

Proportion of High School Students Who Have Had Sex At Least Once, 2005

Figure **8.4** Proportion of high school students who have had sex at least once, 2005 (Grades 9–12). Source: Youth Risk Behavior Surveillance System (YRBS) (2005).

Boys and girls tend to react differently to their first sexual intercourse. The National Health and Social Life Survey found that more than 90% of men said they wanted to have sexual intercourse the first time they did it; more than half were motivated by curiosity, whereas only a quarter said they had sexual intercourse out of affection for their partner (see Chapter 2 for more information on the National Health and Social Life Survey). About 70% of women, too, reported wanting to have sexual intercourse. Nearly half of women said they had sex the first time out of affection for their partner, whereas a quarter cited curiosity as their primary motivation. Twenty-four percent said they just went along with it (fewer than 8% of men said that); 4% reported being forced to have sex the first time, whereas only about 3 men in 1,000 (0.3%) reported being forced. For many, the first sexual intercourse is a monumental occasion. This experience contributes to the redefining of self and the reconfiguration of relationships with friends, family members, and sexual partners (Upchurch et al., 1998).

The first partner with whom a female adolescent engages in heterosexual intercourse is usually slightly older (1–3 years older, 61%) or much older (at least 4 years older, 20%); 15% of partners are the same age (Althaus, 2001). Adolescent males, on the other hand, are likely to have sexual intercourse the first time with a partner who is slightly older (1–3 years older, 36%) or the same age (33%); 24% of partners are 1 to 3 years younger, and 2% of partners are at least 4 years older. Age differences between sex partners are more common in Latinas' relationships than among non-Latinas (Frost & Driscoll, 2006). In fact, these age differences can put younger heterosexual Latinas at an increased risk for early initiation into sexual behavior, unprotected sex, pregnancy, and sexually transmitted infections.

In most of the developed world, the majority of heterosexual men and women engage in sexual intercourse during

their teen years (Alan Guttmacher Institute, 2002b; see Figure 8.5). In fact, the age at which heterosexual teenagers become sexually active is similar across comparable developed countries, such as Canada, France, Sweden, and the United States. Contrast this to Japan, where the majority of heterosexual men and women wait until they are at least 20 years old to begin having sex and use contraception when they do (Althaus, 1997).

SAME-SEX SEXUALITY We know that same-sex contact is common in adolescence, both for those who will go on to have predominantly heterosexual relationships and those who will have predominantly homosexual relationships. Some gay and lesbian adolescents experience sexual intercourse during their teenage years, before they identify themselves as lesbian or gay (Saewyc et al., 1998).

It is difficult to determine actual figures for adolescent same-sex contact. Studies of high school students find that about 10% to 13% report being "unsure" about their sexual orientation, whereas 1% to 6% consider themselves homosexual or bisexual; still, anywhere from 8% to 12% report sexual contact with same-sex partners (Faulkner & Cranston, 1998). Such research, however, relies on self-reports; people may define homosexual differently, or they may deny experiences due to homosexual stigma.

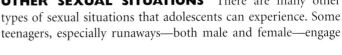

REALResearch > Later initiation of sexual intercourse has been found to be associated with future sexual problems, especially among men (SANDFORT ET AL., 2008).

OTHER SEXUAL SITUATIONS There are many other types of sexual situations that adolescents can experience. Some teenagers, especially runaways—both male and female—engage

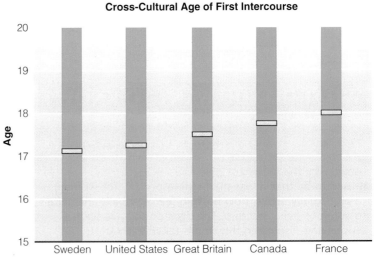

Cross-Cultural Age of First Intercourse

Age by which half of women aged 20–24 had intercourse

Figure **8.5** Half of young women in Canada, France, Great Britain, Sweden, and the United States begin sexual intercourse between the ages of 17 and 18. Source: Reproduced with the permission of The Alan Guttmacher Institute from *Teenage Sexual and Reproductive Behavior in Developed Countries: Can More Progress Be Made?* New York: AGI, 2001, Microsoft® PowerPoint® presentation.

in prostitution. Others make money by becoming involved in child pornography, posing nude for pictures, or performing sexual acts. Although there are few comprehensive studies of the results of engaging in prostitution or pornography as an adolescent (or younger), there is every clinical indication that it results in many sexual and psychological difficulties later on (we discuss coercive sexuality in Chapter 17).

Many of the sexual variations seen in adults, such as transvestism, exhibitionism, and voyeurism, may begin in adolescence, although it is more common for these desires to be expressed in early adulthood. We discuss these sexual variations in depth in Chapter 16.

Ethnic and Racial Differences in Sexual Activity

An adolescent's ethnicity, race, and culture affects his or her sexual attitudes, which sexual behaviors he or she engages in, and the frequency of these behaviors (Quadagno et al., 1998; Zimmer-Gembeck & Helfand, 2008).

Several ethnic and racial differences have been found in participation of certain sexual behaviors, such as oral and anal sex (Lindberg et al., 2008), age of first sexual intercourse (Eaton et al., 2006), and age differences between sexual partners (Frost & Driscoll, 2006). As you will soon see, ethnic and racial differences have also been found in contraceptive use (Mosher et al., 2004), teen pregnancy (Ventura et al., 2007), birth rates (Martin et al., 2007; Martinez et al., 2006; Ventura et al., 2007), abortion (Ventura et al., 2007), and rates of sexually transmitted infections (Buffardi et al., 2008; Forhan, 2008). We explore these issues in more depth in Chapter 10.

INFLUENCES:
PEERS, FAMILY, AND RELIGION

The decision to engage in sexual contact with another person is a personal one, yet it is influenced by many social factors, including peers, family, and religion. There are a number of other social factors that influence sexual behavior as well, and we discuss here a few of the more important ones.

Peer Influences

Peer pressure is often cited as the most important influence on teen sexual behavior, and adolescence is certainly a time when the influence of one's friends and peers is at a peak. Many adolescents base their own self-worth on peer approval (Rudolph et al., 2005). Even among preadolescents, peer influences are strong; among sixth graders who have engaged in sexual intercourse, students were more likely to initiate sexual intercourse if they thought that peers were engaging in it and that it would bring them some kind of social gain. Those who did not initiate sexual intercourse were more likely to believe that their behavior would be stigmatized or disapproved of by their peers (Grunbaum et al., 2002).

Remember, though, that a person's *perceptions* of what his or her peers are doing has a greater influence than peers' actual behavior. Among those subject to and applying peer pressure, many heterosexual adolescent males feel the need to "prove" their mas-

culinity, leading to early sexual activity. Peer pressure is often rated as one of the top reasons that adolescents give for engaging in sexual intercourse.

Relationship With Parents

On the other hand, good parental communication, an atmosphere of honesty and openness in the home, a two-parent home, and reasonable rules about dating and relationships are among the most important factors associated with adolescents delaying their first sexual intercourse (Hahm et al., 2008; Lam et al., 2008; Regnerus & Luckies, 2006). This may be attributed to the fact that close families are more likely to transmit their sexual values and integrate their children into their religious and moral views. Heterosexual children from these homes are also more likely to use contraception when they do engage in sexual intercourse (Halpern-Felsher et al., 2004; Zimmer-Gembeck & Helfand, 2008). This is the case among almost all races and ethnic groups (L. M. Baumeister et al., 1995; Brooks-Gunn & Furstenberg, 1989; Kotchick et al., 1999).

Overall, it is mothers who tend to be the primary communicators about sexuality to children of both sexes; in one study of Latino youths, mothers did the majority of all communication about sexuality to their teenagers (L. M. Baumeister et al., 1995; Raffaelli & Green, 2003). The ADD Health study (2002) has also found that there is a maternal influence on the timing of first sexual intercourse for heterosexual adolescents, especially for females. A mother's satisfaction with her relationship with her daughter, disapproval of her daughter having sex, and frequent communication about sex was found to be related to a delay of first sexual intercourse (Lam et al., 2008; McNeely et al., 2002). Fathers are also important—in fact, girls who have a close relationship with their father are more likely to delay sex (Regnerus & Luchies, 2006).

Religion

The ADD Health study has found that although the relationship between religiosity and sexual activity is complex, in general, more religious heterosexual youths tend to delay first sexual intercourse (S. Hardy & Raffaelli, 2003), have fewer incidents of pre-

REALResearch > Adolescent girls who engage in sexual intercourse before age 16 with an older partner are more likely to acquire a sexually transmitted infection as a young adult than those who delay sexual initiation and have similar-aged sexual partners (RYAN ET AL., 2008).

marital sexual activity, and have fewer sexual partners (Nonnemaker et al., 2003). This correlation may be because young people who attend church frequently and who value religion in their lives are less sexually experienced overall (P. King & Boyatzis, 2004; S. D. White & DeBlassie, 1992). Not only do major Western religions and many other world religions discourage premarital sex, but religious adolescents also tend to develop friendships and relationships within their religious institutions and thus have strong ties to people who are more likely to disapprove of early sexual activity. However, once teens begin engaging in sexual behaviors, religious affiliation and frequency of religious attendance have been found to have little impact on frequency of sexual behaviors (R. Jones et al., 2005).

CONTRACEPTION, PREGNANCY, AND ABORTION: COMPLEX ISSUES

Although we discuss pregnancy, contraception, and abortion more in Chapters 12 and 13, we introduce these concepts here. Overall, heterosexual teens in the United States are less likely to use contraception than teens from other Western developed countries and experience substantially higher levels of adolescent pregnancy and childbearing (Tew & Wind, 2001). Most studies find relatively low rates of parental communication about sex in general and contraception in particular, with adolescents reporting far fewer and less involved discussions about it than their parents report (Jaccard et al., 1998; King & Lorusso, 1997). Adolescents who are able to talk to their mothers about sexuality are more likely to use contraception than adolescents who cannot talk to their mothers (Jaccard & Dittus, 2000; Lam et al., 2008; Meschke et al., 2000). See Figure 8.6 for more information about contraceptive use at first sexual intercourse.

Of all the areas of adolescent sexual behavior, we probably know the most about teenage pregnancy because of its many impacts on the life of the teenager, the teenager's family, and society as a whole. Even though the teenage pregnancy rate in the United States is at its lowest level in 30 years, almost 750,000 teenage (15–19 year olds) women become pregnant each year (Alan Guttmacher Institute, 2006; see Figure 8.7).

The long-term consequences of teenage pregnancy may be difficult for the mother, child, and extended family. Teenage mothers are more likely to drop out of school, have poorer physical and mental health, and be on welfare than their non–childbearing peers, and their children often have lower birth weights, poorer health and cognitive abilities, more behavioral problems, and fewer educational opportunities (Meschke et al., 2000). Teen parenting also has an impact on others, such as the parents of the teens (who may end up having to take care of their children's children), and on society in general, because these parents are more likely to need government assistance.

However, teen pregnancies do not always preclude teen mothers from living healthy, fulfilling lives. In fact, there are examples of teenagers who become pregnant and raise healthy babies while pursuing their own interests. However, the problems a teenage mother faces are many, especially if there is no partner participating in the child's care. A teen who has support from her partner, family, and friends and who is able to stay in school has a better chance of living a fulfilling life.

In studies of teen pregnancy and birth, most of the focus has been on the mothers, who often bear the brunt of the emotional, personal, and financial costs of childbearing (Wei, 2000). Adolescent fathers are more difficult to study. Teenage fathers may run as soon as they learn of their mate's pregnancy or become uninvolved soon after, and thus the problem of single mothers raising children can be traced in part to the lack of responsibility of teen fathers. Society asks little of the teenage male, and there are few social pressures on him to take responsibility for his offspring.

Even so, today many adolescent fathers do accept their role in both pregnancy and parenthood and realistically assess their responsibilities toward the mother and child. Ideally, teenage fathers should be integrated into the lives of their children and should be expected to take equal responsibility for them.

Adolescent parenthood affects every race, every income group, and every part of American society; it is not just a problem of the inner-city poor. Historically, White teenagers have had lower birthrates than African American or Latino adolescents, a trend that continued in the 1990s. Although through much of the 1990s,

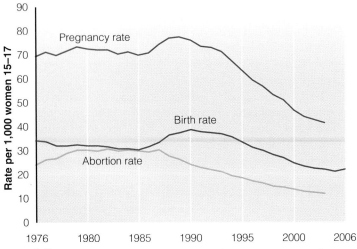

Pregnancy, Birth, and Abortion in U.S. Teens

Figure **8.7** Pregnancy, birth, and abortion rates for U.S. teenagers aged 15–17 years. Source: CDC/NCHS, 2007 Division of Vital Statistics, Published reports.

REALResearch > Black and Hispanic men are approximately twice as likely as White men to father a child before age 20 (MARTINEZ ET AL., 2006).

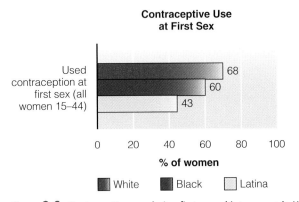

Figure **8.6** Contraceptive use during first sexual intercourse in U.S. women aged 15–44 years old. Reproduced with the permission of The Alan Guttmacher Institute from Teenage Sexual and Reproductive Behavior in Developed Countries: Can More Progress Be Made? New York: AGI, 2001, powerpoint presentation.

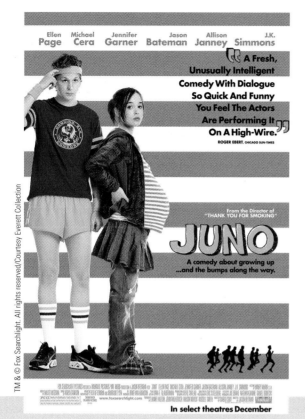

Some teens who experience an unplanned pregnancy decide to put their babies up for adoption. The blockbuster movie *Juno* tells the story of a teenager who unexpectedly finds herself pregnant.

movies and television, yet we hesitate to discuss sex frankly with them. We allow advertising to use blatantly sexual messages and half-dressed models, yet we will not permit advertising for birth control; and there is significant resistance to sex education in the schools.

Today, when teenagers do become pregnant, opportunities may be limited; it is difficult to have a baby and attend high school all day or work at a job. The United States is far behind most other Western countries in providing day-care services that would help single or young parents care for their children. Better counseling, birth control, day-care services, and hope for the future can help ensure that the teenagers who are at risk for unwanted pregnancies and the children of those unwanted pregnancies are cared for by our society.

SEXUALLY TRANSMITTED INFECTIONS: EDUCATION AND PREVENTION

Although we discuss sexually transmitted infections in great detail in Chapter 15, here we briefly talk about adolescent STI rates. Although teenagers represent only 25% of the sexually active population, half of all sexually transmitted infections occur in 15 to 24 year olds each year (Weinstock et al., 2004). In addition, approximately 9 million new STIs occur among teenagers and young adults each year in the United States (Weinstock et al., 2004).

A nationally representative study by the Centers for Disease Control found that one in four teenage girls had a sexually transmitted infection (Forhan, 2008), and African American teenage girls were the most at risk—with 48% infected (Forhan, 2008). Overall, human papillomavirus (HPV) and chlamydia infections were the two most common STIs in teenagers (Forhan, 2008; we discuss these specific STIs in Chapter 15).

Although gay, lesbian, and bisexual youths may not need contraception for birth control purposes, they do need it for protection from sexually transmitted infections. Research has found that gays and lesbians are less likely to use condoms than their straight counterparts (S. M. Blake et al., 2001; Saewyc et al., 1998). Increasing condom use in all teens, regardless of sexual orientation, is imperative in decreasing STIs.

Preventing STIs and teenage pregnancy are both important goals of sex education programs. In the following section, we discuss the importance of sexuality education and what is being taught in schools today.

African American teenagers had the highest rates of pregnancy, birth, and abortion, all three rates dropped by about 20% between 1990 and 1996. Because the birthrate declined more steeply among African American than White teenagers, the gap between these two groups narrowed. Unmarried mothers and their children of all races are more likely to live in poverty than any other segment of the population.

What is it about American society that seems to foster such high rates of teenage pregnancy? A complex series of factors is at work. American society is extremely conflicted about the issue of sexuality in general. Our teens are exposed to sexual scenes in

review questions

1 Explain physical and psychosexual development in adolescence.

2 Explain what we know about the specific sexual behaviors that often occur during adolescence.

3 Identify and explain the influences on adolescent sexuality.

4 Identify and discuss the reasons that adolescents may be erratic users of contraception.

5 Explain how ethnicity, race, and culture are all important influences on adolescent sexual behavior.

What Children Need to Know:
Sexuality Education

Sexuality education inspires powerful emotions and a considerable amount of controversy. In fact, it may be one of the most heated topics in the field of sexuality, as different sides debate whether and how sexuality education programs should be implemented in the schools.

HYGIENE AND SEXUALITY EDUCATION:
THEN AND NOW

People have always been curious about sex. However, it was only in the 20th century that the movement to develop formal and effective sexuality education programs began. Public discussion of sexuality was due, in part, to the moral purity movement of the late 19th century and the medicalization of the sex movement in the early 20th century.

Several developments in the United States set the stage for sexuality education. Concern over skyrocketing rates of venereal diseases (what we now refer to as STIs) in the early 1900s resulted in the formation of two groups, the American Society of Sanitary and Moral Prophylaxis and the American Federation for Sex Hygiene. Although these groups helped to further the cause of sexuality education, they concentrated their attention on STIs. Their approach was to use sexuality education to explain biology and anatomy and to address adolescents' natural sexual curiosity. School sexuality education was very scientific and avoided all discussions of interpersonal sexuality.

Starting in the early 1900s, sexuality education was implemented by various national youth groups, including the YMCA, YWCA, Girl Scouts, Boy Scouts, and 4-H Clubs. These programs were developed mainly to demonstrate to young people the responsibilities required in parenting and to discourage early childbearing. More controversial, however, has been whether to include sexuality education as part of the public school curriculum.

In the United States, for example, the opposition to sexuality education has often been due to two attitudes: first, that sexuality is private, should be discouraged in children, and is best discussed in the context of a person's moral and religious beliefs; and second, that public schools are by their nature public, cannot discuss sex without giving children implicit permission to be sexual, and should not promote the moral or religious beliefs of any particular group. The result of these conflicting attitudes was the belief that sexuality education was best performed by parents in the home.

Attitudes toward sexuality, however, began to change, and sexuality education was seen as more important, due not only to the high teenage pregnancy rate (which shatters the illusion that kids are not actually having sex) but also to STIs and AIDS. Television and other media contributed by being so sex-saturated that sexuality was no longer a private topic. Yet even with all these changes, many still believe that public educational institutions will present a view of sexuality that they object to, and so they still oppose sexuality education in the United States.

Today, the majority of states either recommend or require sexuality education in public schools. Most place requirements on how abstinence or contraception information should be included, and overall, curriculums are heavily weighted toward stressing abstinence (Alan Guttmacher Institute, 2008). As of 2008, 23 states required abstinence be stressed in sexuality education classes, whereas 10 states required it be covered, and no state required that contraception be stressed (Alan Guttmacher Institute, 2008).

EVOLVING GOALS
OF SEXUALITY EDUCATION

Sexuality education can have different goals. Knowledge acquisition, improving personal psychological adjustment, and improving relationships between partners are popular goals. Early sexuality education programs focused primarily on increasing knowledge levels and educating students about the risks of pregnancy (Kirby, 1992), believing that if knowledge levels were increased, then students would understand why it was important for them to avoid unprotected sexual intercourse. Soon sexuality

REALResearch **>** Research on parent-adolescent communication has found that many adolescent boys receive little or no parental communication about sex (M. Epstein & Ward, 2008). Instead, boys learn about sex mostly from their peers and the media.

education programs added values clarification and skills, including communication and decision-making skills. These second-generation sexuality education programs were based on the idea that if knowledge levels were increased and if students became more aware of their own values and had better decision-making skills, they would have an easier time talking to their partners and evaluating their own behavior.

Today, **comprehensive sexuality education programs** try to help students develop a positive view of sexuality. The Guidelines for Comprehensive Sexuality Education (Sexuality Information and Education Council of the United States, 2004a) are a framework designed to help promote the development of comprehensive sexuality education programs nationwide. Originally developed in 1990, the guidelines were revised again in 2004 and include four main goals for sexuality education:

1. To provide accurate information about human sexuality

comprehensive sexuality education programs
Programs that often begin in kindergarten and continue through 12th grade, presenting a wide variety of topics to help students develop their own skills while learning factual information.

2. To provide an opportunity for young people to question, explore, and assess their sexual attitudes

3. To help young people develop interpersonal skills, including communication, decision-making, peer refusal, and assertiveness skills that will allow them to create satisfying relationships

4. To help young people develop the ability to exercise responsibility regarding sexual relationships

The guidelines have also been adapted for use outside the United States and are being used in many countries to help design and implement a variety of sexuality education programs.

WHY SEXUALITY EDUCATION IS IMPORTANT

Although many people claim that knowledge about sexuality may be harmful, studies have found that it is the lack of sexuality education, ignorance about sexual issues, or unresolved curiosity that is harmful (S. Gordon, 1986). Students who participate in comprehensive sexuality education programs are less permissive about premarital sex than students who do not take these courses. Accurate knowledge about sex may also lead to a more positive self-image and self-acceptance. Sexuality affects almost all aspects of human behavior and relationships with other persons. Therefore, if we understand and accept our own sexuality and the sexuality of others, we will have more satisfying relationships. Some experts believe that not talking to children about sex prior to adolescence is a primary cause of sexual problems later in life (Calderone, 1983).

Another reason to support sexuality education is that children receive a lot of information about sex through the media, and much of it is not based on fact. The media and peers are often primary sources of information about sexuality. Sex is present in the songs children listen to, the magazines they read, the shows they watch on television, and on the Internet. Although it is true that there are a growing number of educational sites on the Internet dedicated to sexuality, there are also many poor sources of information on the web.

Proponents of sexuality education believe that sexual learning occurs even when there are no formalized sexuality education programs. When teachers or parents avoid children's questions or appear embarrassed or evasive, they reinforce children's ideas that sex is secret, mysterious, and bad (Milton et al., 2001). As adolescents approach puberty, they may feel anxious about their bodily changes or their relationships with other people. Many teenagers feel uncomfortable asking questions and may be pressured by their peers to engage in sexual activity when they do not feel ready. Giving teenagers information about sex can help them to deal with these changes. The majority of parents, teachers, and students want sexuality education to be taught in secondary schools and high schools and favor comprehensive sex education (Bleakley et al., 2006).

SEXUALITY EDUCATION PROGRAMS

In the United States, each state is responsible for developing its own sexuality education programs. Therefore, the programs vary greatly. Overall, programs are typically either comprehensive or

---

SEX IN REAL LIFE

Parents and Anxiety: Where Does It Come From?

Many parents worry that something bad will happen to their children if they start talking to them about sex.

When parents discuss the concept of sexuality education for their children, many report feeling very anxious and insecure about their own abilities. Anxiety comes from many places, including the following:

• **Fear:** Many parents worry that something bad will happen to their children if they start talking to them about sex. Parents worry that they will wait too long, start too early, say the wrong thing, or give misinformation. They also may worry that talking about sexuality will take away their children's innocence, by making them grow up too fast or become overly interested in sexuality.

• **Lack of comfort:** Because most parents did not talk to their parents about sex, many feel uncomfortable in presenting it themselves. Those who did talk about it usually

talked with their mothers. This causes many fathers to feel especially uncomfortable facing the prospect of educating their sons and daughters.

• **Lack of skills:** Parents often do not know how to say what they want to say. Some resort to a lecture about the "birds and bees," whereas others simply ask their children, "Do you have any questions?"

• **Misinformation:** Many parents do not have the necessary facts about sexuality. Having received little sexuality education themselves, many believe in the myths about sexuality.

SOURCE: Adapted from P. Wilson (1994, pp. 1–2).

abstinence-based. Comprehensive sexuality programs, which we've already been discussing, are those that begin in kindergarten and continue through 12th grade—they include a wide variety of topics and help students to develop their own skills and learn factual information. **Abstinence-only programs** emphasize abstinence from all sexual behaviors, and they typically do not provide information about contraception or disease prevention.

Abstinence-only programs began in the early 1990s when there was a proliferation of sexuality education programs that used fear to discourage students from engaging in sexual behavior. These programs include mottos such as "Do the right thing—wait for the ring," or "Pet your dog—not your date." Important information about topics such as anatomy or STIs is often omitted from these programs, and there is an overreliance on the negative consequences of sexual behavior. These negative consequences are often exaggerated, portraying sexual behavior as dangerous and harmful.

Federal funding for abstinence-based sexuality education has grown significantly since 1996. Federal funds can only be used for sexuality education if they teach abstinence only until marriage, which often excludes information about contraception and sexually transmitted diseases. In fiscal year 2005, the federal government proposed spending approximately $170 million on abstinence-only sexuality education programs, which was more than twice the amount that was spent in fiscal year 2001 (Waxman, 2004a). In 1996, the federal government also passed a law outlining the federal definition of abstinence education. These programs teach:

■ abstinence from sexual activity outside marriage as the expected standard for all school-age children,

■ that sexual activity outside of the context of marriage is likely to have harmful psychological and physical effects, and

■ that bearing children out of wedlock is likely to have harmful consequences for the child, the child's parents, and society.

The majority of Americans believe that sexuality education should emphasize abstinence but also include contraception and STI information (Bleakley et al., 2006). Some of the abstinence-only programs use scare tactics to encourage abstinence, by claiming the consequences of premarital sexual behavior to include

> . . . *loss of reputation; limitations in dating/marriage choices; negative effects on sexual adjustment; negative effects on happiness (premarital sex, especially with more than one person, has been linked to the development of emotional illness [and the] loss of self-esteem); family conflict and possible premature separation from the family; confusion regarding personal value (e.g., "Am I loved because I am me, because of my personality and looks, or because I am a sex object?"); and loss of goals. (Kantor, 1992, p. 4)*

Do abstinence-only programs work? This is the important question, and the responses will differ depending on whom you ask. Supporters of abstinence-only programs often have very strong feelings about comprehensive sexuality education pro-

grams and claim that talking only about abstinence lets children and young adults know that this is the only choice. Those who believe in these programs would say that they are effective. However, a major study done by the National Campaign to Prevent Teen and Unplanned Pregnancy in 2007 found that abstinence-only programs failed to delay sexual behavior and decrease the number of sex partners (Kirby, 2007). Comprehensive sexuality education programs that included abstinence education *along with* contraceptive education were found to delay sexual behavior and to reduce the frequency of sexual behaviors and unprotected sex (Kirby, 2007).

The research has also shown that when students who have had abstinence-based sexuality programs do become sexually active, they often fail to use condoms or any type of contraception (Brückner & Bearman, 2005; Walters, 2005).

> The **majority of Americans** believe that **sexuality education** should emphasize **abstinence.**

STUDYING EFFECTS AND RESULTS

The main way that researchers determine whether a sexuality program is successful is by measuring behavioral changes after a program has been presented. The standard measures include sexual behavior, pregnancy, and contraceptive use (Remez, 2000). If the rates of sexual behavior increase after sexuality education, a program is judged to be ineffective. If these rates decrease, a program is successful. So what are the effects of sex education programs? Do sexuality education courses change people's actual sexual behavior? It is difficult to measure and evaluate these behavioral changes after a sexuality education program, but it appears that there are some limited changes.

Celibacy rings are often worn by those who pledge not to engage in sexual intercourse until marriage.

abstinence-only programs
Sexuality education programs that emphasize abstinence from all sexual behaviors; no information about contraception or disease prevention is provided.

Sexuality Education in Other Cultures

. . . countries that have liberal attitudes toward sexuality. . . have the lowest rates of teenage pregnancy, abortion, and childbearing.

In a study done by the Alan Guttmacher Institute, the United States led nearly all developed countries in the world in the rates of teenage pregnancy, abortion, and teenage childbearing. Overall, countries that have liberal attitudes toward sexuality, easily accessible birth control services for teenagers, and formal and informal sexuality education programs have the lowest rates of teenage pregnancy, abortion, and childbearing. Let's review sexuality education in a variety of places.

The Netherlands

The Netherlands has the world's lowest rates of teenage pregnancy, abortion, and childbearing. This may be because of the liberal attitudes toward sexuality education, high quality of information in sexuality classes, and widely available and confidential contraceptive services. It is estimated that 80% of Dutch secondary schools offer at least 4 to 5 hours of AIDS education (Drenth & Slob, 2004). The Dutch government also supports a variety of sexuality organizations and finances mass-media campaigns aimed at educating the public about sexuality. A Dutch broadcasting company runs a weekly sexuality talk radio show, and it is estimated that there are over 250,000 listeners (Drenth & Slob, 2004).

Sweden

Over the years, Sweden has become known as the world leader in sexuality education. In 1897, the first sex education courses were organized by a female physician (Trost, 2004), and in 1956 sex education became mandatory in all schools. There are national requirements for all sexuality education courses, a national curriculum, and a national handbook to guide teachers' training for these courses. Starting at age 7, students learn about menstruation, intercourse, masturbation, contraception, pregnancy, and childbirth. From ages 10 to 13, students are taught about puberty, sexually transmitted infections, homosexuality, and pedophilia. At the next level of learning, students are taught about sex roles, premarital sex, abortion, pornography, HIV/AIDS, and prostitution. Finally, at the college level, students are taught about sexual desire, sexual orientation, and sexual dysfunction. Sweden also has many youth clinics, offering information, education, and contraceptive services (Trost, 2004). These clinics began forming in an attempt to reduce the teenage abortions rates (a law passed in 1975 allows for free abortions).

England

Sex education in England is a compulsory part of the National Curriculum—Science, and throughout England students participate in a comprehensive sex education program (Hilton, 2003). Studies have found that the programs have effectively prepared students and increased their skills (Douglas et al., 2001).

Brazil

Brazil's annual Carnival is a time of liberation from the sexually repressive ways of Brazilian society. During Carnival, television stations become much less conservative and air naked men and women, many engaging in public sexual activities. Yet even with the open attitudes about sexuality during Carnival, it has been difficult to establish sexuality education in Brazilian schools. The culture is highly patriarchal and has rigid gender roles. There are few sexuality education programs in public schools today, but they first appeared in some of the private schools in the late 1980s (Freitas, 2004).

Japan

In 1974, the Japanese Association for Sexuality Education was founded to help establish comprehensive sexuality education in the schools, although abstinence education was very popular in Japan. As in the United States, popular sources of sex information in Japan include friends and older same-sex peers, magazines, and television.

In 1986, a new sexuality education curriculum was distributed to all middle and high schools in Japan (Kitazawa, 1994). In 1992, the Japanese Ministry of Education revised the sexuality curriculum and approved the discussion of secondary sex characteristics in coeducational fifth-grade classes. In fact, 1992 was called the "First Year of Sexuality Education," and sexuality education was required in schools. Prior to this time, there was no discussion of sexuality in elementary schools (Hatano & Shimazaki, 2004).

Today, however, the number of educators interested in teaching sexuality education is increasing. Teacher workshops and educational programs add to the increasing comfort levels with sexuality. Overall, however, these open attitudes toward sexuality education have not been met without opposition. In fact, sexuality education has been blamed for the changing norms in sexuality that resulted in an increase in divorce and a destruction of the family.

Russia

Although the majority of Russian teenagers and their parents and teachers favor sex education in the schools, Russia has no formal sexuality education program (Kon, 2004). Conservative forces, along with various churches, are adamantly opposed to sex education and have instituted an aggressive campaign against the implementation of sex education programs in the schools. A national opinion poll found that only 13% of parents in Russia have ever talked to their children about sexuality (Kon, 2004).

Comprehensive sexuality programs have been found to be the most successful at helping adolescents delay their involvement in sexual intercourse and help protect adolescents from STIs and unintended pregnancies (Kirby, 2001, 2007; Kohler et al., 2008; Starkman & Rajani, 2002). In addition, sexuality education programs that teach contraception and communication skills have been found to delay the onset of sexual intercourse or reduce the frequency of sexual intercourse, reduce the number of sexual partners, and increase the use of contraception (Kirby, 2007; Kohler et al., 2008). Abstinence-only programs, in contrast, have not yielded successful results in delaying the onset of intercourse (Kirby, 2007; Weed, 2008). In 2007, a federally funded study of abstinence-only programs, conducted by Mathematica Policy Research, found these programs had no effects on sexual abstinence (Trenholm et al., 2007). Overall, there have been no published reports of abstinence-based programs providing significant effects on delaying sexual intercourse. Although many who teach abstinence-only classes claim that these programs are successful, outside experts have found the programs to be ineffective and methodologically unsound (Kirby, 2007; Kohler et al., 2008; Weed, 2008).

Over the past few years, some students have begun taking "virginity pledges" in which they sign pledge cards and promise to remain a virgin until marriage. The ADD Health study, which we discussed earlier in this chapter, found that teenagers who took a virginity pledge were less likely to become sexually active in the months that follow the pledge than students who did not take a pledge (Bearman & Bruckner, 2001). However, these types of programs have also been found to put teenagers at higher risk of pregnancy and sexually transmitted infections (Brückner & Bearman, 2005).

Why do you think this might be? Researchers believe that it is because signing the pledge may make a teenager unable to accept the responsibilities of using contraception when he or she decides to engage in sexual intercourse. One study found that 88% of students who pledged virginity engaged in premarital sex, and when they did they were less likely to use contraception (Brückner & Bearman, 2005; Planned Parenthood Federation of America, 2005).

Measuring attitudes or changes in attitudes and values is difficult at best. Overall, we do know that comprehensive sex education programs can increase knowledge levels, affect the attitudes, and change behaviors (Dailard, 2001b; Kirby, 2007; Kohler et al., 2008). The most successful programs were those in which schools and parents worked together to develop the program. However, many effects of sexuality education programs may not be quantifiable. Programs may help students to feel more confident, be more responsible, improve their mental health, and increase their communication skills. We rarely measure for these changes.

In summary, childhood sexuality is an evolving phenomenon. Sexual knowledge and sexual behavior are common among children in today's society, in which sexuality is so much a part of our culture. However, knowledge does not necessarily mean that children must act on it; there are still very good reasons to encourage children and teenagers to think carefully about sexuality and to advise them to refrain from expressing their sexual feelings physically until the time is right for them.

What we do know is that a close and open parent–adolescent relationship that allows for open communication about sexuality has been found to decrease adolescent sexual behaviors and reduce the influence of peers with regard to sexual issues (Meschke et al., 2000). This is an important finding and is partially responsible for delaying first intercourse, fewer teenage pregnancies, and fewer numbers of sexual partners. Open communication about sexuality, along with a good, solid sexuality education, encourages this kind of responsible sexual behavior.

Childhood sexuality **is an evolving phenomenon.**

review questions

1 Explain both sides of the sexuality education debate.

2 Identify and discuss the various types of sexuality education programs.

3 Discuss research findings on the effects of sexuality education.

CHAPTER **review**

SUMMARY POINTS

1 Throughout most of history, children were treated as miniature adults, and concepts such as childhood did not exist. Children were considered presexual. Four large-scale longitudinal studies have been conducted on adolescent sexuality: the National Survey of Family Growth, the National Longitudinal Study of Adolescent Males, the National Longitudinal Study of Adolescent Health, and the Youth Risk Behavior Surveillance System.

2 Sexual anatomy is functional even before we are born. Male babies are capable of erection, and female babies are capable of vaginal lubrication. The single most important aspect of infant development is the child's relationship with his or her caretakers. Gender identity develops between the ages of 1 and 2 years. It takes a little longer to develop gender constancy, which is the realization that gender will not change during their lifetime. Genital touching is common at this age.

3 In early childhood, physical development continues. In fact, children may learn more in the first few years of childhood about the nature of their bodies than they learn in the entire remainder of their lives. Child sex play is common at this age, and many parents or caregivers need to teach that this behavior is private. Children learn that their genitals are private and must be covered up in public. Boys are often taught about the penis, yet it is rare for girls to be taught about the clitoris.

4 Sometime between the ages of 6 and 12, a child experiences the first outward signs of puberty. In girls the first sign of puberty is the appearance of breast buds, and soon they will experience menarche. Preadolescent boys experience frequent erections, and soon they will experience semenarche. Typically boys do not tell anyone about this event. Prepubescence is the age of sexual discovery.

5 During preadolescence, genital touching continues, and both sexual fantasies and sex games may begin. A sexual script is the sum total of a person's internalized knowledge about sexuality and it can have different themes. All of our intimate relationships influence our sexuality. We learn from our parents and our peers. Sexual contact with siblings is common at this age and has been found to be harmful only when there is coercive force used or a large age difference between siblings.

6 Puberty prepares the body for adult sexuality and reproduction. Adolescence often includes our emotional and cognitive reactions to puberty. There are many physical, emotional, and cognitive changes during this time. The three major stages of physiological sexual development include prenatal sexual differentiation, puberty, and menopause. Some of the first signs of female puberty include the development of breast buds, the appearance of pubic hair, a widening of the hips, a rounding of the physique, and the onset of menstruation.

7 Unlike ovulation, which occurs late in female puberty, spermatogenesis and ejaculation occur early in male puberty. Some of the first signs of male puberty include body changes, increased body hair, a growth spurt, and voice deepening. For the most part, early development in boys is usually not as embarrassing as it is in girls.

8 Adolescents tend to fantasize about sex, and masturbation increases, especially for boys. Mature sexual experimentation begins, often with kissing. Girls' body image tends to improve as they progress through adolescence, whereas boys' tends to worsen. However, girls' general self-image tends to worsen as they grow older, whereas boys' tends to improve.

9 First intercourse is usually unplanned but rarely spontaneous. Adolescents are poor users of contraception, which, coupled with increasing sexual activity, results in high pregnancy rates. The United States has the highest rates of pregnancy, abortion, and childbearing of any Western country.

10 Opposition to sexuality education has often been due to two attitudes: one says that sexuality is private and the second that public schools cannot discuss sex without giving children implicit permission to be sexual and should not promote certain values. Individual states can mandate that schools provide sexuality education.

11 The most common goals for sexuality education include increasing knowledge, understanding one's own attitudes and values, reducing unhealthy sexual behavior, and respecting the attitudes and values of others.

12 Sexuality education programs are often either comprehensive or abstinence-based. Although many Americans believe that contraception should be included in sexuality education, they also believe that information on contraception and STIs should be included.

13 Comprehensive sex education programs can increase knowledge levels, affect attitudes, and change the behaviors of the students who take them.

CRITICAL THINKING questions

1 Should genital touching in young children be encouraged, ignored, or discouraged? What message do you think it sends to a child when parents encourage their child to discover and play with toes, ears, and fingers but pull the child's hands away when he or she discovers his or her genitals?

2 Young children often play sex games, such as "doctor," with each other. What age differences do you think pose the biggest problems? Are sex games acceptable? Why or why not? How should a parent respond?

3 Where should children get their sexual knowledge? Should children learn everything from their parents, school, or the church? Is it better to learn about some things from a particular place? Explain.

4 Why do you think adolescence is a difficult time for many people? What can be done to make the transition through adolescence easier?

5 People today are engaging in sex relatively early in life, often in their middle or early teens. Do you think this is a good time to experiment with sex, or do you think it is too early? What do you think is the "ideal" age to begin experimenting with sex?

WEB resources

Sexuality Now Book Companion Website

Go to www.cengage.com/psychology/carroll for practice quizzes, glossary, flash cards, and more. You can also access the following websites from the companion site.

The Sexuality Information and Education Council of the United States (SIECUS) ■ SIECUS is a national, nonprofit organization that develops, collects, and disseminates information; promotes comprehensive education about sexuality; and advocates the right of individuals to make responsible sexual choices.

Alan Guttmacher Institute (AGI) ■ The mission of the Alan Guttmacher Institute is to provide information and services about issues of sexuality. The institute conducts important research on adolescent and child sexual issues.

All About Sex Discussions ■ This website provides information for preteens, teens, and parents and gives good information on how to talk about and explain such topics as sex, masturbation, sexual orientation, gender, and virginity.

Society for Research on Adolescence ■ The Society for Research on Adolescence's goal is to promote the understanding of adolescence through research and dissemination. Members conduct theoretical studies, basic and applied research, and policy analyses to understand and enhance adolescent development.

The National Longitudinal Study of Adolescent Health ■ This is the official website for the ADD Health study on adolescent sexuality. Information is available on the research design of the study, the research team, publications, data sets, statistics, and research details.

CengageNOW

Go to www.cengage.com/login to link to CengageNOW, your online study tool. First take the Pre-Test for this chapter to get your Personalized Study Plan, which will identify topics you need to review and direct you to online resources. Then take the Post-Test to determine what concepts you have mastered and what you still need work on.

Videos in CengageNOW

For additional information on topics discussed in this chapter, check out the videos in CengageNOW on the following topics:

- Adolescence: Sexual Risk Taking—Listen to teens talk about the reasons adolescents have unprotected sex.

- Teen Slang for Having Sex—Hear the slang terms that teenagers use to describe sexual activity.

- Adolescence: Body Image—Hear interviews with teens about body image, dieting, and eating disorders.

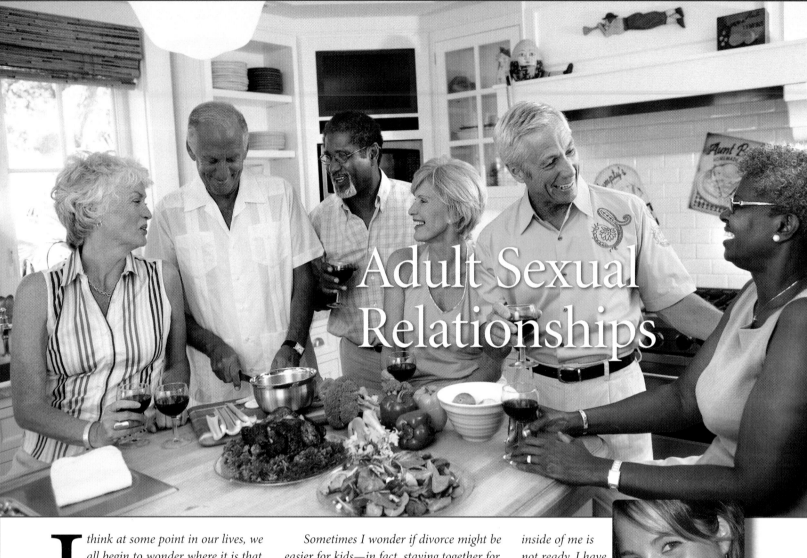

CHAPTER 9

Adult Sexual Relationships

I think at some point in our lives, we all begin to wonder where it is that we get certain qualities and personality characteristics. Many of us reflect upon experiences that may have shaped us into the person we are today. My strong-mindedness, competitiveness, and creativity come from my father, while my work ethic and reliability come from my mother. Together, however, they both have a share in influencing me on one very important domain: marriage.

As a child, I believed I had the ability to put anything back together. So naturally I attempted to put the pieces back together when my mother and father argued. I knew that many parents fought, but I worried about the one monumental fight that would cause my parents to give up and leave the marriage. I worried about my sister and I tried to protect her and reassure her.

Sometimes I wonder if divorce might be easier for kids—in fact, staying together for the kids just doesn't make sense to me. Today my parents are still married, but I often look at their relationship and wonder whether they are still in love. Aside from never witnessing them hold hands or hug and kiss, they have not slept in the same bedroom in over five years. Today, my parents are more like housemates than soulmates. I think about the effect their relationship has had on me and my life.

For over seven years, I have been dating my high school sweetheart, Marcus. He is the most gentle, loving, and sincere man I have ever known. Early on, Marcus and I were inseparable. He became a integral part of my family, and I felt very much a part of his. Now, after over seven amazing years together, it would seem that the next thing to do would be to get married; but something

inside of me is not ready. I have always dreamed of my wedding day just like other girls do; however, knowing that more than 50% of marriages end in divorce and experiencing firsthand my parent's marriage, I wonder if I will ever get the courage to say "I do." It's not just the odds that I am worried about; it is also the idea that marriage might be an unrealistic expectation of society for two people today. After all, who gets married to someone thinking that "until death do us part" really means "until we can't sleep in the same bed anymore"?
SOURCE: Author's Files

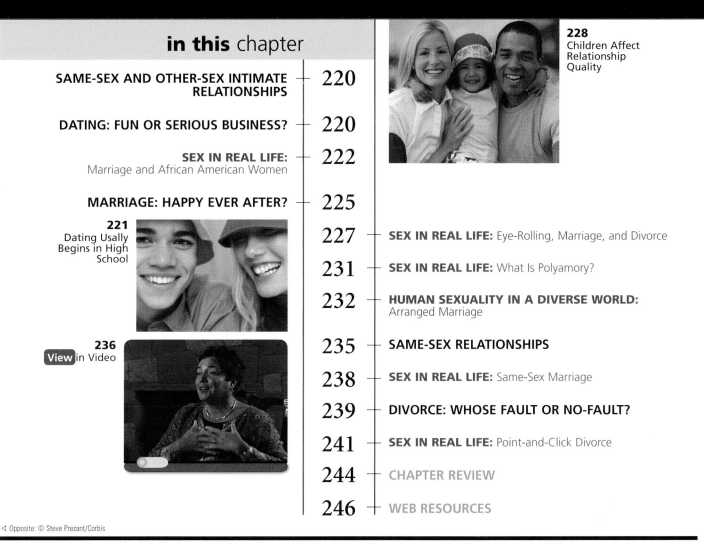
◁ Opposite: © Steve Prezant/Corbis

This story illustrates the importance of our family system. Throughout this book, we've talked about the importance of family and the impact that your family has on your feelings about love, intimacy, and relationships. We also know that other factors, such as society, culture, ethnicity, race, religion, and age also influence our connections with others.

Every society has rules to control the ways that people develop sexual bonds with other people. Until recently, in many parts of the world, parents or other family members arranged for their children to meet members of the other sex, marry them, and begin their sexual lives together. The expectation was that couples would remain sexually faithful and that marital unions would end only in death. In such societies, adult sexual relationships were clearly defined, and deviating from the norm was frowned upon.

In our society today, people openly engage in a variety of adult sexual relationships, including same-sex, other-sex, pre-marital, marital, extramarital, and polyamorous relationships. (Note that a term such as "premarital sex" assumes eventual marriage; for people who never marry, or same-sex couples who are not allowed to marry in most states, their entire lives' sexualities are considered "premarital"!) These relationships can change and evolve over the course of a lifetime, and at different times, a person might live alone and date, cohabit with a partner or partners, marry, divorce, or remarry. In this chapter, we look at adults' sexual relationships with others.

REALResearch ▸ A survey of more than 1,000 undergraduates found that more than **50%** had engaged in a "friends with benefits" relationship (PUENTES ET AL., 2008). Statistically significant results were found between those who reported engaging in such relationships and those who did not. Overall, those who engaged in friends with benefits relationships were more likely to be males, casual daters, juniors or seniors, African American, and nonromantics.

Same-Sex and Other-Sex Intimate Relationships

Intimate relationships are a fundamental part of human development. A person could have an intimate relationship with someone of the same sex or the other sex, and they could date, live together, or marry (although if they are gay or lesbian, they can only legally marry in Massachusetts or California as of 2008). We know that married men and women, gay men, and lesbian women all hold similar positive views about their intimate relationships (Roisman et al., 2008). Even so, there has been considerable debate throughout the years about what type of intimate relationships promote the most healthy psychological adjustment (Roisman et al., 2008).

Although there is not a great deal of research on lesbian and gay intimate relationships, limited studies have been done. One classic study by Blumstein and Schwartz (1983) compared same- and other-sex couples using interviews and questionnaires. Although this study is dated, it remains a classic, because no other studies have undertaken such a large sample population comparing couples in a variety of different relationships. We refer to findings from this study throughout this chapter.

For many years, researchers suggested that same-sex relationships were less stable in adulthood because of negative early life experiences and the challenges of accepting one's sexual orientation (Savin-Williams, 2001). Others claim that societal pressures on same-sex couples, such as the struggle to manage a gay or lesbian identity in a heterosexist culture, lead to weaker intimate relationships (Pachankis & Goldfried, 2004). However, although it may be true that same-sex couples face more relationship challenges than do heterosexual couples, these theories have not been supported by research (Herek, 2006; Roisman et al., 2008). The majority of gay men and lesbian women were found to be secure in both their sexual orientation and childhood experiences and able to connect fully in intimate relationships (Roisman et al., 2008).

It has been suggested that same-sex couples may be more satisfied with their intimate relationships because they are forced to be work harder at them (R. J. Green et al., 1996). Same-sex couples may not have as much family or societal support as heterosexual couples do, which may force them to work harder on their intimate relationships. In addition, relationship satisfaction may be higher in same-sex couples because they share more similar communication styles (Kurdek, 2004; we discuss same-sex relationships more later in this chapter).

review questions

1 Explain how societies try to control the way that people develop sexual bonds with other people.

2 Explain the debate about which relationships promote the most healthy psychological adjustment.

3 Discuss what is known about relationship satisfaction in same-sex couples.

Dating: Fun or Serious Business?

We can understand a lot about a society just by examining the customs and rules it sets up for choosing a partner. For example, just from looking at dating patterns, we can learn about the level of **patriarchy** (PAY-tree-ark-kee) in a society; its ideals about masculinity and femininity; the roles of women and men; the value placed on conformity; the importance of childbearing; the authority of the family; attitudes toward childhood, pleasure, responsibility; and a host of other traits.

In Chapter 7, we discussed the physical benefits of love and intimacy. Dating has been found to provide similar benefits. Relationships provide companionship, emotional support, and even, at times, economic support. Of course, the key may be the kind of people who are in the relationship. For example, people with a strong sense of self have been found to be more satisfied and happy with their dating relationships (Fruth, 2007; Fuller-Fricke, 2007). Not surprisingly, those without a strong sense of self have been found to experience more depression and sadness in their relationships (Fruth, 2007; Fuller-Fricke, 2007).

"Dating" has changed on college campuses today. Today, it is much more common for groups of students to "hang out" rather than go out on a date. Typically, men and women go out with friends and plan on meeting up at a party on campus and going home together, rather than prearranging a date. One study found that 50% of heterosexual female seniors reported being asked out by a man on six or more dates while at college; and one third of respondents said they had been on only two or fewer dates (Glenn & Marquardt, 2001).

Why might there be less "dating" today? Researchers suggest that there are several possible reasons (Glenn & Marquardt, 2001). The sexual revolution has changed society's attitudes about sexuality, making hooking up, casual sex, one-night stands, and "friends with benefits" more acceptable (Puentes et al., 2008). Many students today are also busy and may not want to dedicate the time to pursuing an intimate relationship. We also can't deny the influence of alcohol, which is commonly used on college campuses today and may serve to lower sexual inhibitions.

Overall, commitment in relationships—whether the relationships are between college students in other-sex or same-sex dating

patriarchy
A social system in which the father is the head of the family and men have authority over women and children.

REALResearch > Researchers have found an inverse relationship between smoking marijuana and relationship satisfaction (FERGUSON & BODEN, 2008). The more a person smokes marijuana, the less satisfied he or she tends to be with his or her relationship.

Although the attitudes of college students toward interracial dating are more open, overall there are strong social forces that make it harder for people of different races and cultures to meet.

relationships is dependent on how much individual satisfaction there is in the relationship and the cost-benefit ratio of the relationship (Sprecher, 2001; Zimmer-Gembeck & Petherick, 2006). If the benefits of the relationship outweigh the costs, the couple is generally satisfied.

TYPES OF DATING

The problem with discussing dating behavior is that there are no agreed-on words for different levels of commitment. "Dating," "going out," "hanging out," "seeing each other"—these terms mean different things to different couples.

In traditional heterosexual dating, which occurred before the 1970s, the boy would pick up the girl at her house, the father and mother would meet or chat with the boy, and then the boy and girl would go to a well-defined event (a "mixer"—a chaperoned, school-sponsored dance—or a movie), and she would be brought home by the curfew her parents imposed (Benokraitis, 1993). Today, however, formal dating has given way to more casual dating, in part because of teenagers' almost universal access to cars and parents' more permissive attitudes toward exploring romantic relationships. Teenagers still go to movies and dances, but just as often they will get together at someone's house. Because of the risk of rejection, today's adolescents often use friend networks to find out if someone might be interested in them before asking them out. This way they can assess whether a partner might be interested in them before asking them out. It can be more difficult to meet potential partners as a person gets older. Socializing and

The dating years usually begin in high school in the United States.

going out to bars and clubs may work for some, but others are uncomfortable with this approach. Perhaps the best way to meet others as one gets older is through friends, to get involved in community, religious, and singles groups and to find events and programs where other single people go. As we discussed in Chapter 7, the Internet has provided a new way to meet people, through websites, chat rooms, and online dating services.

Interracial Dating

We live in a multicultural world. As a result, dating someone of a different race, religion, or culture is more common today. This is especially true on college campuses, where close to 25% of students said they were currently in an interracial relationship, and 50% said they'd be open to being romantically involved with someone of a different race (Knox et al., 2000). However, interracial relationships weren't always socially acceptable. In fact, it wasn't until 1967 that the Supreme Court struck down state anti-miscegenation laws, which outlawed interracial relationships (we discussed these laws in Chapter 1).

Those who do date persons from another race or ethnicity have been found to be more politically liberal and less religious than those who would not date such partners (Yancey, 2007). Interestingly, a study using data from the National Survey of Family Growth found that interracial couples who marry have higher rates of divorce compared with same-race couples (Bratter & King, 2008; we discuss divorce more later in this chapter).

WHAT DO YOU WANT TO KNOW ?

Is an e-mail or an instant message an acceptable way to ask someone out?
Today e-mail, text messaging, and IMing are common forms of communication, and research supports that they can help promote intimacy (Hu et al., 2004). Online communication is often easier than face-to-face communication, but it's also easier to misinterpret someone's message online.

Marriage and African American Women

African American women have the lowest marriage rate of any racial group in the United States.

Although marriage rates have been dropping for several years now, there has been a significant decline in marriage among African American women, who have the lowest marriage rate of any racial group in the United States (Kreider, 2005). The 2001 U.S. Census found that whereas 21% of White women were never married, 42% of Black women were never married (Kreider, 2005). These changes have been accompanied by substantial increases in interracial marriage, especially between African American men and non–African American women. Are these events related?

Perhaps so. As more and more African American men marry non–African American women, this reduces the pool of available African American partners for African American women. This is even more true for highly educated African American women, whose marriage prospects (men with similar levels of education) are most likely to choose interracial marriage. However, when African American women are asked which ethnicity they prefer their partner to be, the majority report preferring an African American (Wyatt, 1998).

African American women, in general, often experience a shortage of marriageable men because African American men have higher mortality and incarceration rates (N. E. Bennett et al., 1992). African American men have also been found to have higher rates of unemployment, lower earnings, and lower levels of education than Caucasian men, which further reduces the numbers of desirable African American men for African American women to marry (Tucker & Mitchell-Kernan, 1995).

Some researchers have proposed that rates have dropped because African American women are reluctant to marry. However, the evidence doesn't support this theory. African American men, rather than African American women, have been found to have the strongest reservations about marriage (South, 1993).

African Americans are twice as likely as Caucasians to report being open to the possibility of an interracial relationship (Knox et al., 2000; Rosenblatt et al., 1995), possibly because there are more Whites to choose from and Blacks have a greater exposure to White culture. For heterosexual African American women who want to date African American men, this may lead to less dating and fewer marriages (Crowder & Tolnay, 2000). In the accompanying Sex in Real Life feature, "Marriage and African American Women," we discuss African American women and marriage.

In our multicultural world, race is not the only criterion on which a couple's suitability is judged; there are also issues of different religions, ages, social classes, and disabilities. Couples with these issues may also face some of the same challenges that interracial couples do.

REALResearch > It is estimated that **33%** of college students are involved in a long-distance relationship (STAFFORD & RESKE, 1990). Couples who feel unsure about being long-distance are more distressed, less satisfied with the relationship, and have poorer partner communication than those couples who feel confident and certain their relationship can survive the distance (MAGUIRE, 2007).

WHAT DO YOU WANT TO KNOW?

Why is it that people stare at interracial couples? I just don't understand what the big deal is.

Americans have a history of disapproving of relationships that take place between people of different races. In many other countries, interracial couples are not unusual. In the United States, Latino–White relationships, as well as Asian–White, Native American–White, Latino–Black, and other combinations—although still often looked upon negatively—are more acceptable in the United States than Black–White. Unfortunately, these negative feelings can lead to discrimination against such couples and their children. Social disapproval of interracial couples can also affect the quality of the couple's relationship (Lehmiller & Agnew, 2007).

SEXUALITY IN DATING RELATIONSHIPS

Although we discuss specific sexual behaviors in Chapter 10, here we introduce sexuality in dating relationships. As we have been discussing, sexual practices have been changing on college campuses today. "Hooking up" or having a "friend with benefits" or a "sex buddy" have become more common. Although both men and women report these behaviors are often engaged in purely for the physical pleasures they provide, the research isn't so clear cut (Eshbaugh & Gutt, 2008; Manning et al., 2006).

I once had two heterosexual students in my class who I thought were strangers because they never talked or sat next to each other. However, in reading papers they had handed in, I learned they had been "hooking up" almost every weekend for over 8 months. What was interesting to me, however, was how they each described their relationship. Blye wrote that she was sure Laizon was looking for a commitment because he had sex with her every weekend, whereas Laizon wrote that he was relieved that Blye understood their relationship was purely sexual because he never talked to her during the week. Both Blye and Laizon were evaluating the same behavior differently. Among heterosexuals, it might be easy to assume that it's always the female who is looking for more commitment in these "hookups," but that wouldn't be entirely true. There are many men who hope for more out of a "hookup" but settle for what they can get (see the above What Do You Want to Know? for more information).

> *Sexuality in same-sex dating relationships **is similar** to sexuality in other-sex relationships.*

Sexuality in same-sex dating relationships is similar to sexuality in other-sex relationships. Although some gay men and lesbian women engage in casual sex and hookups, others are more conservative in their sexual behavior. We do know that lesbian women are more likely to self-identify as lesbian before pursuing a sexual relationship with other women, whereas gay men are more likely to pursue sex with men before self-identifying as gay (Savin-Williams & Diamond, 2000).

SEXUALITY IN
OLDER ADULT RELATIONSHIPS

When we picture people engaging in sex, we rarely think of two people over the age of 60. In fact, when I show a film on older adult sexuality, many of my students cover their eyes and feel repulsed. Why is this? Why are we so averse to the idea that older people have healthy and satisfying sex lives? It is probably because we live in a society that equates sexuality with youth. Even so, the majority of older adults maintain an interest in sex and sexual activity, and many engage in sexual activity (Arena & Wallace, 2008; Lindau et al., 2007). There are many similarities in aging among gay, lesbian, and heterosexual populations. In fact, the physical changes of aging affect all men and women, regardless of sexual orientation (Woolf, 2002).

A positive correlation was found between good health and sexual activity, with healthier people reporting higher levels of sexual activity (Lindau et al., 2007). Researchers believe that a healthy sex life in the later years may keep aging adults happy and vibrant (Lindau et al., 2007). We discuss sexuality and the physical and psychological changes of aging in Chapter 10.

COHABITATION:
PROS AND CONS

Like dating, the terminology of cohabiting is also interesting. Is it "living together," "shacking up," "living in sin," "a test drive," or "a trial run"? **Cohabitation** has increased dramatically in the last decade. Some researchers (and partners, for that matter) regard cohabitation as an important part of the pathway to marriage (Manning et al., 2007; Stevenson & Wolfers, 2007), whereas others view it as an end in itself (Mock & Cornelius, 2007).

Until recently, there was little research on nonmarital cohabiting relationships. In fact, researchers documented no rise in cohabitation rates between 1880 and 1970. This was probably because researchers had no labels for such relationships. In the mid-1990s the Census and the Current Population Survey started allowing couples to identify themselves as "unmarried partner" of the homeowner (instead of a roommate), which allowed researchers to get more accurate statistics about cohabitation (Stevenson & Wolfers, 2007). Even so, researchers today believe that statistical data on cohabitation is skewed because of inadequate relationship labels. Some cohabiting heterosexual couples might not think of themselves as "un-

cohabitation
Living together in a sexual relationship when not legally married.

married partners" but rather "boyfriend and girlfriend"; gay and lesbian couples might describe themselves as "roommates." You can see how this terminology can get a little tricky.

The U.S. Census found that cohabiting couples in the United States increased 72% between 1990 and 2000 (U.S. Census Bureau, 2001). Typically the pattern was for young heterosexual couples to live together as a prelude to marriage and not *instead* of marriage (V. King & Scott, 2005; Manning et al., 2007). The National Survey of Family Growth found that 50% of women aged 15 to 44 years had lived with a partner at some point (L. Allen, 2005; Stevenson & Wolfers, 2007). Among those living together, the majority expected to marry their partner. Some couples live together, break up, and live with someone else, referred to as **serial cohabitation.**

U.S. cohabitation rates are highest in the District of Columbia, followed by Vermont and Maine, whereas Utah and Alabama have the lowest cohabitation rates (Jayson, 2005). In 2000, more than 5.2 million U.S. couples were cohabiting (U.S. Census Bureau, 2001). Of these 5.2 million couples, 87% were male–female couples, 6% were male–male couples, and 6% were female–female couples (U.S. Census Bureau, 2000). Although much of the research on cohabitation focuses on younger couples, cohabitation in the United States is more common among the formerly married than the never married (Bumpass & Lu, 2000). There were more than 1 million older adults living together in 2006 in other- and same-sex relationships (S. L. Brown et al., 2006), and 90% of these adults were formerly married. Cohabitation among older adults is likely to continue to increase in the future (S. L. Brown et al., 2006).

Because same-sex marriage isn't available to all same-sex couples, cohabitation is also common among same-sex couples. Unfortunately, there is not a great deal of research on cohabiting same-sex couples but what we do know is taken from census data. This data indicate that same-sex couples who live together have higher and more similar incomes and education levels compared with other-sex couples who live together (Phua & Kaufman, 1999).

There are advantages and disadvantages to cohabitation. Cohabitation allows couples to learn more about each other's habits and idiosyncrasies, share finances, and mature in their relationship. Yet there are also problems. Parents and relatives may not support the union, and society as a whole tends not to recognize people who live together for purposes of health care or taxes. Also, the partners may want different things out of living together: One partner may view it as a stronger commitment to the relationship, whereas the other sees it as a way to have a more accessible sexual partner.

Some people believe that living together can help couples smooth out the rough spots in their relationships and see whether they would be able to take their relationship to the next level. Research indicates, however, that the reverse may be true. Fifty percent of all couples that live together break up within a year or less (Bumpass & Lu, 2000). Heterosexual couples who do marry after living together are at increased risk of divorce, and longer cohabitation has been found to be associated with higher likelihood of divorce (Cohan & Kleinbaum, 2002; Seltzer, 2000; Stevenson & Wolfers, 2007). The research has found that these problems are more common among non-Hispanic White women

but not among Mexican American or African American women (J. Phillips & Sweeney, 2005).

Why might heterosexual couples who live together be less successful as marriage partners? Perhaps these couples develop as separate individuals during that time (because they are not married, they maintain their own "life" outside of the relationship), and this may lead to a higher risk for divorce (Seltzer, 2000). Also, most cohabiting couples do not get joint checkbooks, have mortgages, and so on and may not be prepared for the financial pressures of marriage (disagreements about money are a major reason for divorce).

However, there are several possible shortcomings of the foregoing findings. It may not be that living together itself increases the chance of divorce but that heterosexual couples who choose to live together may have been more likely to divorce even if they didn't live together first (Stevenson & Wolfers, 2007). They may feel that they would not be happy in a marriage; they may be more accepting of divorce; they may be less religious and less traditional in the first place; or they may be less committed in the beginning of the relationship. Because we do not know about the samples in the studies on cohabiting couples, it is difficult to generalize their findings. Some studies have found no correlation between living together and future marital disruption (Teachman, 2003).

> There are **advantages and disadvantages** to cohabitation.

A heterosexual couple's reasons for living together may indicate whether their marriage will be successful. If a couple lives together for economic reasons or because of timing (say they are planning to marry in the near future), this will generally result in a healthy marital relationship. However, complications arise when couples live together because they are nervous about committing to marriage or they want to "test" their relationship. Obviously, if they need to test a relationship to see whether it will work, they are not ready for marriage.

As of 2008, nine states and the District of Columbia recognize **common-law marriage,** which means that if a heterosexual couple lives together for a certain number of years, they are considered married. Typically a couple must present themselves as a married couple (refer to each other as husband and wife; file a joint tax return). There are also cases of individuals who have successfully sued partners they lived with for **alimony** or shared property (called **palimony**), claiming that their partner promised them marriage or lived together with them as though married. If the couple has a child together, of course, both partners are responsible for his or her upbringing, even if they separate. So living together may entangle a couple in legal issues they did not anticipate.

In the United States, same-sex couples who live together are not eligible for common-law marriage, even if they have lived

serial cohabitation
A series of cohabitating relationships with a person living with one partner, breaking up and living with a new partner.

common-law marriage
A marriage existing by mutual agreement between a man and a woman, or by the fact of their cohabitation, without a civil or religious ceremony.

alimony
An allowance for support made under court order to a divorced person by the former spouse, usually the chief provider during the marriage.

palimony
An allowance for support made under court order and given usually by one person to his or her former lover or live-in companion after they have separated.

together for many years. This is different outside the United States, where in some countries cohabitating couples can be given legal status (Bradley, 2001; Godard, 2007; Martin & Théry, 2001). We discuss civil unions and domestic partnerships later in this chapter.

Cohabitation in Other Cultures

Attitudes about cohabitation vary throughout the world. Probably the most acceptance comes from Western European nations where there have been substantial increases in unmarried cohabitation among heterosexual partners (Kiernan, 2001). Instead of viewing these changes as shifts in moral attitudes, however, they are often viewed as simply cultural changes (Björnberg, 2001; Kiernan, 2001; Ostner, 2001).

Probably the most acceptance for heterosexual cohabitation comes from the Scandinavian countries (Noack, 2001). Couples who live together in Norway for a minimum of two years are given similar rights as married couples, including obligations to social security, pensions, and joint taxation. Cohabitation is also common in Sweden where the majority of heterosexual couples live together before marriage (Trost, 2004). In fact, 50% of all Swedish children are born to couples who are living together. In France, cohabitating couples (other and same sex) can apply for legal recognition of their relationship (Martin & Théry, 2001). We discuss the legal recognition of these relationships more later in this chapter.

Cohabitation among heterosexual couples in Spain is lower than most other European countries, mainly because of a trend in delaying residential independence (Tobío, 2001). Many dating Spaniards remain in their family home at least until their 30s (Tobío, 2001). This is also true in Italy, where emerging adults often stay at home with their parents until they marry (Lanz & Tagliabue, 2007). Cohabitation is also rarer in more traditional societies where, even if a couple has sex before or outside of marriage, social customs would never tolerate an unmarried heterosexual couple living together openly. For example, Asian societies still frown on it, although it is sometimes allowed, and it is severely discouraged in Islamic societies.

review questions

1 Explain how dating has changed on college campuses today.

2 Explain how the increased frequency of interracial relationships between African American men and Caucasian women has affected African American women.

3 Identify the differences between cohabiting and married couples, and explain the relationship between cohabitation and eventual divorce rates.

4 What do we know about same-sex dating and cohabitation?

5 Explain what we know about cohabitation outside the United States.

Marriage:
Happy Ever After?

Today, the majority of young people—straight and gay—say they are planning, expecting, or hoping to marry at some point in their lives (D'Augelli et al., 2006/2007; Thornton & Young-DeMarco, 2001). Moreover, 93% of Americans say that a happy marriage is one of their most important life goals (M. Gallagher & Waite, 2000). Although we discuss same-sex marriage later in this chapter, here we focus on heterosexual marriage.

A report from the Centers for Disease Control found that nearly 60% of U.S. adults are married, but marital rates vary by race and ethnicity (Schoenborn, 2004). Approximately 61% of White adults are married, 58% of Hispanic adults, and 38% of Black adults (Schoenborn, 2004).

Couples today are marrying later and are more likely to marry more than once (U.S. Census Bureau, 2007). The age at first marriage has been increasing over the past 30 years, although this number leveled off in the 1990s (Fields & Casper, 2001; see Figure 9.1). In 1970, the median age for first marriage for men and

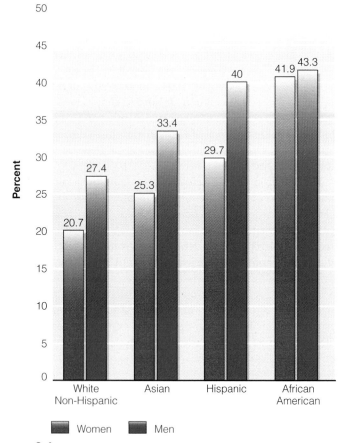

Never Married Rates by Race

Figure **9.1** Percentages of never-married men and women over the age of 15 by race and Hispanic origin. Source: U.S. Census Bureau, 2001.

women was 23 and 21, respectively. In 2005, the age at first marriage went to 27 and 25 for men and women, respectively (U.S. Census Bureau, 2006). However, there are ethnic and racial differences in these ages. For example, Asian and Pacific Islander men and women get married later than other groups (Kreider, 2005).

A survey in 2000 found that marriages in the United States are as happy today as they were 20 years ago (Amato et al., 2003). Marital satisfaction for men has been found to be related to the frequency of pleasurable activities (doing fun things together) in the relationship, whereas for women it was related to the frequency of pleasurable activities that focus on emotional closeness. Other important variables, including being able to talk to each other and self-disclose, physical and emotional intimacy, and personality similarities, are all instrumental in achieving greater relationship quality.

John Gottman, whom we discussed in Chapter 3, found that the quality of the friendship with one's spouse is the most important factor in marital satisfaction for both men and women (Gottman & Silver, 2000). Gottman also found that a couple's ability to resolve conflict added to their marital stability. High rewards, such as emotional support and a satisfying sex life, and low costs (such as arguing, conflicts, and financial burdens) are also important in marital satisfaction (Impett et al., 2001). If a marriage has high costs but low rewards, a person might end the relationship or look outside the marriage for alternative rewards.

People who are married tend to be happier and healthier and have longer lives than either widowed or divorced persons of the same age (Dush & Amato, 2005; Schoenborn, 2004; Zheng & Hart, 2002). In fact, in a study of heterosexual couples, married couples had the highest level of well-being, followed by (in order) cohabitating couples, steady dating relationships, casual dating relationships, and individuals who dated infrequently or not at all (Dush & Amato, 2005). Marriage has also been found to reduce the impact of several potentially traumatic events, including job loss, retirement, and illness.

Overall, marriage provides fewer health benefits to women than men. For instance, although married men have better physical and mental health, more self-reported happiness, and experience fewer psychological problems than either divorced, single, or widowed men (Joung et al., 1995), married women do not receive these same health benefits (Hemstrom, 1996). This may be because women have multiple role responsibilities; for example, married women still tend to do the bulk of the housework and disproportionately take care of the children (see the Real Research feature on page 225). Women, regardless of race, report their marriages are more unfair to them than their husbands do (Forry et al., 2007). The good news is that over the past few years there has been a trend in the mental health benefits of marriage applying equally to men and women (R. W. Simon, 2002; K. Williams & Umberson, 2004). This is probably a result of an increased equality in marriages today (W. B. Wilcox & Nock, 2006).

HAVING CHILDREN OR REMAINING CHILDLESS

Children can be born at any period—while a couple is living apart, living together, or married—and the timing of having children affects the relationship quality. Some couples decide to have children without a formal commitment to each other, some get married to have children, and others get married because the woman is pregnant. Although some couples experience pregnancies as unplanned events, ambivalence and uncertainty is common in couples making decisions about parenthood (Pinquart et

Over time, many married couples experience changes in their sex lives, even though sexuality remains an essential part of the majority of marriages.

al., 2008). In any case, the decision to have or raise children is one that most people face at one time or another.

Parenthood has been increasingly delayed to later ages for many U.S. couples today, and childlessness has become more common (Koropeckyj-Cox et al., 2007). The National Center for Health Statistics (2002) found that in 2000, 29% of women were childless in their 30s, and 19% were childless in their 40s. The number of childless couples is expected to grow in the next few years. In fact, the U.S. Census has projected that the number of married couples with children will decline from 48% to 41% by 2010 (M. Wolf, 2005). Although single parenting has affected these numbers, they are also affected by married couples deciding not to have children. In the past, studies have found that college students have negative attitudes about childless couples, but over the last few years attitudes have become more accepting (Koropeckyj-Cox et al., 2007).

Parents with children often experience decreases in leisure time and time to work on their relationship (Claxton & Perry-Jenkins, 2008; Halfon et al., 2002). Typically, couples with children report lower relationship satisfaction than those without children, and relationship satisfaction levels continue to fall as the number of children increases (Papalia et al., 2002; Twenge et al., 2003). Typically, relationship happiness is higher before the children come, declines steadily until it hits a low when the children are in their teens, and then begins to increase once the children leave the house (Papalia et al., 2002). This may be due to several factors, including reduced time for the relationship or disagreements about child-care responsibilities (Benokraitis, 1993; Halfon et al., 2002).

WHAT DO YOU WANT TO KNOW ?

What is a "prenuptial" agreement?

If a couple divorces, their marriage contract is governed by state law, which determines how assets are divided. However, some couples decide to implement nuptial agreements, or financial plans that couples agree on in marriage, that supersede state laws (Philadelphia, 2000). These agreements can be either prenuptial (drawn up before a marriage) or postnuptial (drawn up after a couple has wed). It is estimated that 20% of couples who plan to marry pursue a prenuptial agreement (A. Dickinson, 2001). These agreements are more common in second marriages, when there is a major change in finances, such as an inheritance (Freedman, 2001).

Proponents of prenuptial agreements believe that because many couples have a hard time talking about financial issues, a prenuptial agreement can help them to sort through these important issues before marriage (Daragahi & Dubin, 2001). However, these types of agreements can also cause problems because they are often initiated by the financially stronger partner and may involve issues of power (Margulies, 2003).

MARITAL SEX CHANGES
OVER TIME

Sexuality is an essential part of most marriages (Sprecher & ToroMorn, 2002). Married men and women both report that sex is integral to a good marriage, although men often report higher sexual needs than women (Elliott & Umberson, 2008). (Figure 9.2 illustrates frequency of sex in marriage compared with other

SEX IN REAL LIFE

Eye-Rolling, Marriage, and Divorce

. . . eye-rolling after a spouse's comments can be a strong predictor for divorce.

John Gottman, a renowned marriage and family therapist, claims that he can predict whether a couple's marriage will succeed or fail from watching and listening to them for just 5 minutes (Gottman, 1999). And 91% of the time, he's right.

Gottman and his colleagues believe that for marriages to succeed, they need to be "emotionally intelligent." They find ways for couples to keep the negative thoughts about each other from overtaking their positive ones. Strong marriages have a 5:1 ratio of positive to negative interactions; when this ratio starts to drop, a couple is headed for di-

vorce. Gottman has also found that certain facial expressions during communication are also important. For example, eye-rolling after a spouse's comments can be a strong predictor for divorce (Parker-Pope, 2002b).

Gottman holds workshops all over the United States for couples who want to improve their relationships. He has recently started offering workshops for gay and lesbian couples as well. He has found that same-sex couples tend to manage relationship conflict in more positive than negative ways.

types of relationships.) However, there is a great deal of variation in who initiates sex, what behaviors a couple engages in, and how often they engage in it (Geer & Broussard, 1990).

Laumann and colleagues (1994) found that 40% of married couples have sexual intercourse two or more times a week, whereas 50% engage in it a few times each month. The frequency of sexual activity and satisfaction with a couple's sex life have been found to be positively correlated (Blumstein & Schwartz, 1983); that is, the more frequent the sexual behavior, the greater the relationship satisfaction. However, it is not known whether increased sexual frequency causes more satisfaction or whether increased relationship satisfaction causes increased sexual behavior.

Typically, marriages (and even long-term relationships) often start out high on passion, but these feelings slowly dissipate over time (Brewis & Meyer, 2005; Starling, 1999). Many couples report

© Jim Craigmyle/Corbis

The introduction of children can affect relationship quality.

engaging in less sex as a marriage progresses. This is consistent with cross-cultural studies that have found that a declining frequency of sexual behavior over time is a common feature of human populations (Brewis & Meyer, 2005).

Some marriages are **asexual relationships,** which means the partners do not engage in sexual behavior (we discussed a slightly different definition of asexuality in Chapter 4, which dealt with the concept of having no assigned gender). This may be because one partner does not have sexual desire anymore, or it may be a mutual decision not to have sex (Donnelly & Burgess, 2008). In either case, most asexual married couples are in stable relationships and feel reluctant to leave (Donnelly & Burgess, 2008). Overall, the majority of married couples report satisfaction with their marital sex (Sprecher, 2002). Typically the reason sex decreases in long-term relationships has less to do with getting bored with one's partner than it has to do with the pressures of children, jobs, commuting, housework, and finances. Later in this chapter, we discuss how having children affects a marital sex life.

MARRIAGES IN LATER LIFE

Marriage has a positive impact on the lives of both aging men and women and this relationship is slightly stronger for men (Schone & Weinick, 1998). Married older adults are happier and have lower rates of disease than their nonmarried counterparts (Dupre & Meadows, 2007). In fact, widowed older adults who have been

asexual relationship
A type of intimate relationship in which the partners do not engage in sexual behavior.

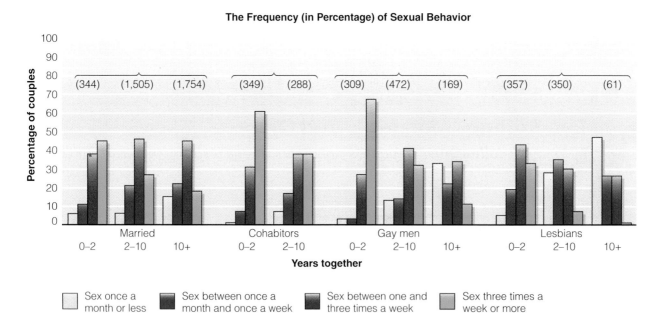

The Frequency (in Percentage) of Sexual Behavior

Note: Very few of the cohabitors had been together more than 10 years.
Numbers in parentheses are the number of couples on which the percentages are based.

Figure **9.2** Frequency of sexual behavior in various types of relationships by years. The numbers above each category represent the total number of respondents. Source: Figure on p. 196: Frequency of Sex in Marriage from American Couples by Philip Blumstein and Pepper Schwartz. Copyright © 1983 by Philip B. Blumstein and Pepper S. Schwartz. Reprinted by permission of HarperCollins Publishers, Inc. and International Creative Management, Inc.

Older couples may experience increased happiness and intimacy when children grow up and leave home.

diagnosed with cancer are more likely to die than married older adults who have been diagnosed with cancer (Ortiz et al., 2007).

Most married older adults report that their marriages improved over time and that the later years are some of the happiest. Older men often report more satisfaction with marriage than do older women, who complain of increased responsibilities in caring for a sick husband or planning activities if he is retired (Schone & Weinick, 1998). This is further complicated by the fact that older adults usually have very few places to turn to for emotional assistance. They have fewer relatives and friends and no coworkers, and their children are often too busy to help. In fact married children are less likely to stay in touch and give emo-

tional, financial, and practical help to their parents, compared with single or divorced children (Sarkisian & Gerstel, 2008).

Many older adults who experience the death of a spouse will remarry. Older men are twice as likely to remarry, however, because women outnumber men in older age and also because older men often marry younger women (M. Coleman et al., 2000). White males remarry more often than other groups; the remarriage rates for African Americans are lower, and they have longer intervals between marriages (South, 1991). Marriages that follow the death of a spouse tend to be more successful if the couple knew each other for a period of time before the marriage, if their children and peers approve of the marriage, and if they are in good health, financially stable, and have adequate living conditions. One 73-year-old man describes his experience:

I can't begin to tell you how happy I am. I am married to a wonderful woman who loves me as much as I love her. My children gave me a hard time of it at first, especially because she is a bit younger than me, but they finally accepted the relationship and came to our wedding. In fact, they gave me away at the ceremony. That's a switch, isn't it? (Janus & Janus, 1993, p. 8)

In 2007, men and women over age 65 were much more likely to be married than at any other time in history (Stevenson & Wolfers, 2007). This is probably because the life expectancy for both men and women has improved. However, there are more older married men than women. This is because women live longer than men and widowhood is more common for them. Seventy-nine percent of men between the ages of 65 to 74 were married in 2004, whereas only 57% of women in the same age group were married (see Figure 9.3 for more information; Federal Interagency Forum on Aging-Related Statistics, 2008).

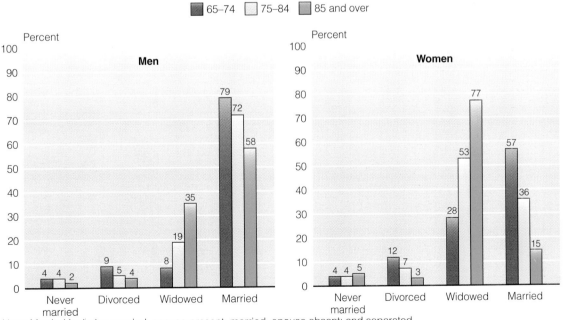

Marital Status of the Population Age 65 and Over, By Age Group and Sex, 2004

65–74   75–84   85 and over

Note: Married includes married, spouse present; married, spouse absent; and separated.
Reference population: These data refer to the civilian noninstitutionalized population.
Source: U.S. Census Bureau, Current Population Survey, Annual Social and Economic Supplement.

Figure **9.3** Marital status of the population age 65 and over, by age group and sex, 2004. Source: Federal Interagency Forum on Aging-Related Statistics. *Older Americans 2008: Key Indicators of Well-Being.* Washington, DC: U.S. Government Printing Office.

Although an estimated 500,000 people over age 65 remarry in the United States every year (M. Coleman et al., 2000), as we discussed earlier in this chapter, more and more older couples decide to live together in place of marriage (S. L. Brown et al., 2006; see Figure 9.4 for more information on living arrangements in men and women aged 65 and over).

EXTRAMARITAL AFFAIRS: "IT JUST HAPPENED"

All societies regulate sexual behavior and use marriage as a means to control the behavior of their members to some degree. Our society is one of the few that have traditionally forbidden sexual contact outside of marriage; research estimates that less than 5% of all societies are as strict about forbidding extramarital intercourse as ours has been (Lance, 2007; Leslie & Korman, 1989).

Almost all couples, whether dating, living together, or married, expect sexual exclusivity from each other. Although extramarital sex refers to sex outside of marriage, we are also referring here to extra-relationship sex, or dating couples who have sex with someone other than their partner. Not surprisingly, adults in the United States are more likely to cheat while living together than while married (Treas & Giesen, 2000). Those who cheat in intimate relationships have been found to have stronger sexual interests, more permissive sexual values, less satisfaction in their intimate relationship, and more opportunities for sex outside the relationship (Treas & Giesen, 2000). Studies on same-sex couples have found that gay men are more likely to cheat than lesbian women (Roisman et al., 2008).

As for extramarital sex, half the states in the United States have laws against sex outside of marriage, although these laws are rarely enforced. If they were enforced, a cheating spouse would be unable to vote, practice law, adopt children, or even raise his or her own children. Engaging in sex outside of a marriage is often rated as a reason for a marriage to breakup (Amato & Previti, 2003).

Laumann and colleagues (1994) found that 20% of women and 15% to 35% of men of all ages reported that they had engaged in extramarital sex while they were married. Even for those couples who never consider sex outside of marriage, the possibility looms, and people wonder about it—what it would be like or whether their partners are indulging in it. Typically, religiosity and church attendance are associated with lower odds of extramarital affairs (Burdette et al., 2007).

How does an extramarital affair typically begin? In the first stage, a person might become emotionally close to someone at school, work, a party, or even on the Internet. As they get to know each other, there is chemistry and a powerful attraction. This moves into the second stage, in which the couple decides to keep the relationship secret. They don't tell their closest friends about their attraction. This secret, in turn, adds fuel to the passion. In the third stage, the couple starts doing things together, even though they would not refer to it as "dating." Each still believes that the relationship is all about friendship. Finally, in the fourth stage, the relationship becomes sexual, leading to an intense emotional and sexual affair (Layton-Tholl, 1998).

Although many people think that sexual desire drives an extramarital affair, research has found that more than 90% of extramarital affairs occur because of unmet emotional needs within the marital relationship (Layton-Tholl, 1998). Laumann and colleagues (1994) found that, overall, couples are faithful to each other as long as the marriage is intact and satisfying. A. P. Thompson (1984) found three types of extramarital affairs: sexual but not emotional, sexual and emotional, and emotional but not

> *Almost all couples* **expect sexual exclusivity** *from each other.*

Figure **9.4** Living arrangements of the population age 65 and over, by sex, race, and Hispanic origin, 2003. Source: Federal Interagency Forum on Aging-Related Statistics, 2004.

sexual. Twenty-one percent of respondents having extramarital sex were involved in predominantly sexual affairs; 19% in both sexual and emotional affairs; and 18% in affairs that were emotional but not sexual (the remaining affairs did not fit clearly into any of these categories). Affairs that are both emotional and sexual appear to affect the marital relationship the most, whereas affairs that are primarily sexual affect it the least.

Gender plays a role in both the type of extramarital affairs in which a person engages and a partner's acceptance of these affairs. Women are more likely than men to have emotional but not sexual affairs, whereas men are more likely to have sexual affairs. When it comes to accepting a partner's extramarital affair, women experience more emotional distress about affairs than men do, but they rate emotional affairs as more harmful than sexual affairs (Guerrero et al., 2004). Men, on the other hand, rate sexual affairs as more harmful than emotional affairs (see Chapter 7 for more information about gender differences in jealousy). Most people who engage in extramarital affairs feel intense guilt about their behavior. Can a marital relationship continue after an extramarital affair? Yes, but it can be difficult. Regaining trust and reestablishing a relationship often takes time after an affair.

OPEN MARRIAGES: SEXUAL ADVENTURING

Some married couples open up their relationships and encourage their partners to have extramarital affairs or to bring other partners into their marital beds, believing that sexual variety and experience enhance their own sexual life. Couples engage in **co-marital sex** (the consenting of married couples to sexually exchange partners), and the partners are often referred to as **swingers** or **polyamorists** (pah-lee-AM-more-rists).

In 1972, George and Nena O'Neill published a book titled *Open Marriage* (O'Neill & O'Neill, 1972). In this book, they explained that "sexual adventuring" was fine, as long as both spouses knew about it. In open marriages, each partner is free to seek out sexual partners outside of the marriage. Many swingers engage in "safe-sex circles" in which they have sex only with people who have tested negative for sexually transmitted infections.

The majority of swingers are White, middle class, middle-aged, and churchgoing (Bergstrand & Williams, 2000). Swinging appears to be increasing in popularity among mainstream married couples in the United States (Bergstrand & Williams, 2000). The North American Swing Club Association claims there are organized swing clubs in almost every U.S. state, as well as in Japan, Canada, England, Germany, and France (Bergstrand & Williams, 2000). In addition, SwingFest, an annual U.S. swinger lifestyle convention, brings in thousands of swingers from around the world (Swingfest.com). Not surprisingly, the Internet is the main source of contact for swingers (R. H. Rubin, 2001).

Most swingers have strict rules meant to protect the marriage; sex in those cases is seen as separate from the loving relations of

comarital sex
The consenting of married couples to exchange partners sexually.

swinger
A man, woman, or couple who openly exchanges sexual partners.

polyamorist
A man, woman, or couple who openly exchanges sexual partners.

SEX IN REAL LIFE

What Is Polyamory?

Polyamorous individuals are not swingers because the emphasis is on a relationship rather than on recreational sex.

If you're in a relationship, do you insist on monogamy from your partner? Most of us would answer this question with a resounding "yes!" We live in a society that expects monogamy from our sexual partners. Serial monogamy, a form of monogamy in which partners have only one sexual partner at any one time, is common on college campuses today. The majority of men and women have more than one sexual partner in their lifetime, but they are monogamous while in these relationships.

A "polyamorous" man or woman has intimate, loving relationships with more than one person at a time, but he or she also has a consensual and agreed-on context to these affairs (Weitzman, 1999). Polyamorous couples are gay and straight, and they are honest with each other about their relationships. These types of relationships are very different from a monogamous couple in which one member cheats while claiming to maintain his or her faithfulness.

Polyamorous individuals are not swingers because the emphasis is on a relationship rather than on recreational sex. Polyamorous relationship could take many forms, including:

1. *Primary-Plus:* One couple in a primary relationship agrees to pursue outside relationships. New lovers are "secondary lovers," and the primary relationship remains the most important.

2. *Triad:* Three people involved in a committed intimate relationship. All three relationships are equal, and there is no primary relationship.

3. *Individual With Multiple Primaries:* This relationship resembles a "V," with one partner at the pivot point with two additional partners who may not relate to each other.

SOURCE: Davidson, 2002.

Arranged Marriage

. . . a significant proportion of all marriages are arranged in large parts of Africa, Asia, and the Middle East.

How would you feel about your mother or father choosing a partner for you to marry? Don't they know you better than anyone else? Although arranged marriages aren't common in the United States today, a significant proportion of all marriages are arranged in large parts of Africa, Asia, and the Middle East (M. Moore, 1994). Marriage partners are chosen by parents, relatives, friends, and matchmakers based on the prospective partner's finances, family values, status, and perceived compatibility (Batabyal, 2001).

Some of the women who are offered as brides come with a dowry (cash or gifts for the groom, or the groom's family at the time of the marriage). Although giving and accepting a dowry is illegal in many countries, it is still widely practiced. In fact, despite the changing roles of women in many countries that have a dowry system, the practice and value of the dowry has increased over the years (Srinivasan & Lee, 2004).

The Manhattan-based *India Abroad Weekly*, which can be accessed online, runs about 125 classified ads every week for families or others searching for Indian brides and grooms. The ads are very specific about what qualities the potential bride or groom has to offer. For example, a recent search yielded the following results:

> [bride] PARENTS seek professional/Doctor match below 27, minimum 59499; for USMD fellow son, 27/69.

> BRIDE needed for well-settled Punjabi boy in US, 42/591199 Ph.D. Healthcare, teetotaler, issueless divorcee; from family-oriented girls.

> [groom] AFFLUENT, Hindu Punjabi parents seek v. tall, v. good-looking, US raised, v. well educated & settled professionals/businessmen match; for v. beautiful, slim, v. fair 29yrs/59899, Dentist daughter.

> [groom] UNMARRIED established young Californians who would like to get married to an established educated Hindu Bengali girl 27/59499, US citizen. Please respond with your accomplishments, family background & photograph.

SOURCE: Retrieved October 21, 2005, from http://www.indiaabroad.com/CLASSIFIED/current-listing/2910.shtml.

---

marriage. The marriage is always viewed as the primary relationship, and sex outside this relationship is thought only to strengthen the marriage (deVisser & McDonald, 2007). In fact, swingers report happier marriages and a higher life satisfaction than nonswingers (Bergstrand & Williams, 2000). Research has found that jealousy increased sexual excitement and arousal in swinging couples, particularly in men (deVisser & McDonald, 2007). However, for some couples, jealousy can be detrimental to the relationship (Bergstrand & Williams, 2000).

MARRIAGES IN OTHER CULTURES

Dating, cohabitation, and marriage are often viewed differently outside the United States. Let's now take a look at courtship, arranged marriages, extramarital sex, and various customs and practices common outside the United States.

Courtship and Arranged Marriages

In most industrialized countries, partner selection through dating is the norm. However, in some countries there are no dating systems. For example, in Sweden, there is no Swedish term for what Americans call "dating"—couples meet at dance clubs, bars, schools, or through friends (Trost, 2004).

There are still a few industrialized cultures in which **arranged marriages** take place. In Iran all marriages are arranged, even those that are based on love (Drew, 2004). A young man will visit the home of the woman he wishes to marry accompanied by three members of his family. The woman is not allowed to speak unless directly questioned. A contract is signed, and although the couple is not formally married, this contract is legally binding. A formal marriage ceremony usually takes place a year later. (For more information about arranged marriage, see the accompanying Human Sexuality in a Diverse World, "Arranged Marriage.")

In some cultures, courtship is a highly ritualized process in which every step is defined by one's kin group or tribe (Hutter, 1981). For example, the marriages of the Yaruros of Venezuela are arranged and highly specified; a man must marry his "crosscousin"—that is, the daughter of either his father's sister or his mother's brother. The marriages are arranged by the shaman or religious leader in consultation with one of the boy's uncles.

The Hottentots of South Africa also marry their cross-cousins, but here the boy can choose which cousin he wants to marry; once he does, he informs his parents, who send someone to seek permission from the girl's parents. Tradition dictates that they must refuse. The youth then approaches the girl, going to her house late at night once everyone is asleep and lying down next to her. She

arranged marriage
Marriage that is arranged by parents or relatives and is often not based on love.

then gets up and moves to the other side of the house. The next night he returns, and if he finds her back on the side where he first lay next to her, he lies down again with her, and the marriage is consummated (Hutter, 1981).

For 2,000 years, marriages in China were arranged by parents and elders, and emotional involvement between prospective marriage partners was frowned upon; if a couple appeared to like having their marriage arranged, the marriage was called off! In China, the primary responsibility of each person was supposed to be to his or her extended family. If there was a marriage bond that was very strong outside of that extended family, it could jeopardize the cohesiveness of the group.

This all began to change with the Communist Revolution of 1949. Through contact with the West, these customs began to erode. Only 8 months after coming to power, the Communist leaders established the Marriage Law of the People's Republic of China, in which, among other things, they tried to end arranged marriages and establish people's right to choose their spouse freely. Today in China, although arranged marriages still take place in the rural areas, people date and meet each other in public places—a condition that was virtually unknown a few generations before.

In many parts of Africa, too, parents used to be involved in mate selection (Kayongo-Male & Onyango, 1984). Marriages were arranged between families, not really individuals, and each family had a set of expectations about the other's role. Courtship was highly ritualized, with the groom's family paying a "bride wealth" to the bride's family. The rituals that preceded marriage were intended to teach the couple what their particular tribe or culture believed married couples needed to know to keep their marriage successful. However, young people did have some say in who they were to marry; in many cases, young people would reject their parents' choices or meet someone they liked and ask their parents to arrange a marriage. One Egyptian boy commented:

> We all know the girls of our village. After all, we played together as kids, and we see them going back and forth on errands as they get older. One favorite place for us to get a glimpse of girls is at the village water source. The girls know that and like to linger there. If we see one we like and think she might be suitable, we ask our parents to try to arrange a marriage, but usually not before we have some sign from the girl that she might be interested. (Rugh, 1984, p. 137)

Today, however, mate selection in most places is a much more individual affair. However much we in the West believe in the right of individuals to choose their own mates, there were some advantages to parental participation in mate selection, and the transition to individual mate selection in traditional societies is often difficult.

Two alarming practices have been on the rise, especially in places such as Afghanistan, Africa, and Bangladesh. Increasing poverty has led some families to either sell their young daughters for a "bride price" or force them into early marriage (Hinshelwood, 2002). Girls between the ages of 8 to 12 years old are sold for between $300 to $800. These young girls can stay with their families

*Today, **mate selection** in most places is a much **more individual affair.***

until their future husband comes to claim them, usually around their first menstrual period. Worldwide, forced marriages of girls below the age of 18 years are common (Nour, 2006). In 2002, 52 million girls aged under 18 years were married (Nour, 2006). In South Asia, close to 50% of all women aged 15 to 24 years are married before age 18, whereas 42% of girls in Africa and 29% of girls in Latin America and the Caribbean are married (Mathur et al., 2003; United Nations Children's Fund, 2005).

Girls who are forced to marry early are less educated, experience more domestic violence, have partners who are significantly older, and have more children (United National Children's Fund, 2005). Another practice, sex trafficking, in which young girls are sold for prostitution, is discussed in Chapter 18. Today many women's groups in the West are working to stop these practices.

Extramarital Sex

Extramarital sex is forbidden in many cultures but often tolerated—even in cultures in which it is technically not allowed. For example, it is considered a grave transgression in Islam and, according to the Koran, is punishable by 100 lashes for both partners (Farah, 1984). However, there are a number of Muslim societies in areas such as Africa and Pakistan where adultery is tacitly accepted as a fact of life (Donnan, 1988; Kayongo-Male & Onyango, 1984).

Those countries that tolerate extramarital sex often find it more acceptable for men than for women. In Zimbabwe, for example, women were asked what they would do if they found out their partners were engaging in extramarital sex: 80% reported they would confront their partners, 15% said they would caution their husbands, and 5% were indifferent. However, when men were asked the same question, 60% replied they would divorce their wives, 20% would severely beat their wives, 18% would severely caution her, and 2% would express disappointment and ask their partner to change (Mhloyi, 1990). In China, elderly neighborhood women keep watch in "neighborhood committees" and report suspicious extramarital activities (Ruan & Lau, 2004).

Customs and Practices

Marriage ceremonies take place in every society, but marriage customs vary widely from culture to culture. In some cultures, girls can be married very young, whereas other cultures mandate marriages between certain relatives, and still others allow multiple spouses.

Most cultures celebrate marriage as a time of rejoicing and have rituals or ceremonies that accompany the wedding process. Among various Berber tribes in Morocco, for example, wedding rituals can include performing a sacrifice, painting the heels of the couple's feet with goat's blood, having a feast, having fish cast at the feet of the bride, or feeding bread to the family dog (Westermarck, 1972). In Iranian culture, a "temporary marriage" allows a Muslim man an opportunity for female companionship outside of legal marriage when he travels or is employed by the military (Drew, 2004). Temporary marriages were formally approved by the Iranian government in 1990.

In many preliterate cultures (and in some literate ones, too), there is a tendency to believe that the main purpose of being female is to get married and have babies. Among the Tiwi, a group of Australian aborigines, this was taken to its logical conclusion; a woman was to get married, and there was no word in their language for a single woman, for there was, in fact, no female—of any age—without at least a nominal husband. The Tiwi believed that pregnancy happens because a spirit entered the body of a female, but one could never be sure exactly when that happened; so the best thing to do was to make sure that the woman was married at all times. Therefore, all Tiwi babies were betrothed before or as soon as they were born, and widows were required to remarry at the gravesides of their husbands, no matter how old they were (Hart & Pilling, 1960).

As we discussed earlier in this chapter, 60% of marriages worldwide are arranged (J. Mackay, 2000), so for many the concept of "loving" one's partner may be irrelevant. In Japan, for example, "love" marriages are often frowned upon because a couple can fall out of love and split up (N. D. Kristof, 1996). Some would argue that Japanese men and women actually love each other less than American couples do. Yet the secret to a strong family, claim the Japanese, is not being in love but rather low expectations, patience, and shame (Kristof, 1996). These factors lead to couples staying together through thick or thin, rather than splitting up when the going gets rough. When one Japanese man, married for 33 years, was asked whether he loved his wife, he replied, "Yeah, so-so, I guess. She's like air or water. You couldn't live without it, but most of the time, you're not conscious of its existence" (Kristof, 1996). This is probably why Japanese couples scored the lowest on what they have in common with each other, compared with couples in 37 other countries (see Figure 9.5).

Some countries allow the practice of **polygamy** (pah-LIGG-uh-mee). Usually, this takes the form of **polygyny** (pah-LIDGE-uh-nee), or having more than one wife, which is a common practice in many areas of Africa and the Middle East, among other places. Although it is rarely practiced in the United States, there are some small Mormon fundamentalist groups that do practice polygyny. Most commonly, a polygynous marriage involves two or three wives, although in Islam a man is allowed up to four.

Some have suggested that polygyny began as a strategy to increase fertility, but the suggestion is controversial. In fact, the majority of studies have found that polygyny is associated with lower fertility among wives (Anderton & Emigh, 1989), although a few studies have found no differences and a few have even found higher rates of fertility (Ahmed, 1986). This is because husbands in polygynous marriages must divide their time between each of their wives, which decreases the chance of impregnation for each individual wife. Therefore, it may be more likely that polygyny developed as a strategy for men to gain prestige and power by having many wives, whereas women could gain the protection of a man in countries where there was a scarcity of men (Barber, 2008).

In Islam, a woman may have sex with only one man, but a man may marry up to four wives. Al-Ghazali, the great Islamic

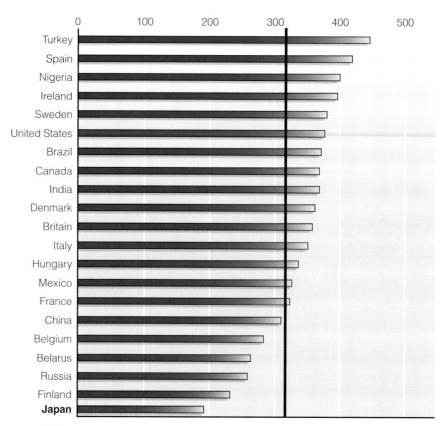

Compatibility of Spouses Index (Average = 316)

Figure **9.5** In a survey by the Dentsu Research Institutes and Leisure Development Center in Japan, spouses answered questions about politics, sex, social issues, religion, and ethics. A score of 500 would indicate perfect compatibility. Source: Who Needs Love! In Japan, Many Couples Don't. *New York Times*, February 11, 1996, p. A1. Copyright © 1996 by *New York Times* Co. Reprinted by permission.

thinker and writer of the 11th century, believed that polygyny was permitted because of the desires of men. What determines whether a Muslim man has multiple wives in most Islamic countries today is his wealth more than anything else, for he usually sets up a different household for each wife. Another reason for polygyny in many Muslim countries is the desire for a male child; if one wife does not deliver a male heir, the man may choose a second and third wife to try for a boy (Donnan, 1988).

One woman commented on the negative aspects of polygamy: "You hear everything, your husband and the other wives. You hear how he behaves with his favorite, usually the new one. The women end up hating the man. Everyone feels bad inside" (M. Simons, 1996, p. A1). However, polygamous husbands have a different view. One polygamous husband says:

My father did it, my grandfather did, so why shouldn't I? When my wife is sick and I don't have another, who will care for me? Besides, one wife on her own is trouble. When there are several, they are forced to be polite and well behaved. If they misbehave, you threaten that you'll take another wife. (M. Simons, 1996, p. A1)

polygamy
The condition or practice of having more than one spouse at one time.

polygyny
The condition or practice of having more than one wife at one time.

Polyandry (PAH-lee-ann-dree), in which a woman has more than one husband, is much less common than polygyny, and it is usually used to consolidate inheritance. For example, in Tibet, a woman may marry several brothers to avoid dividing up the inherited property. The same rationale is used in many **consanguineous** (con-san-GWIN-ee-us) **marriages,** in which a woman marries her own relative to maintain the integrity of family property.

Marriage between certain blood relatives is illegal in all U.S. states and has been since the late 19th century. However, in many Muslim countries in northern Africa; western and southern Asia; north, east, and central India; and the middle Asian republics of the former Soviet Union, marriages take place between relatives between 20% and 55% of the time (Bittles et al., 1991). In Islamic societies marriages between first cousins are most common, whereas in Hindu states of south India uncle–niece and first-cousin marriages are equally common. Incidentally, marriages between certain cousins are legal in many U.S. states.

review questions

1 Explain how marital quality typically changes throughout the life cycle.

2 How does marriage affect a person's health?

3 Explain how sexuality changes throughout marriage and the reasons this might be so.

4 Explain what we know about marital satisfaction in older couples.

5 Explain the gender differences that have been found in reactions to infidelity.

6 Explain what is known about courtship, arranged marriages, extramarital sex, and other customs and practices outside the United States.

Same-Sex Relationships

Although we have been discussing both gay and straight relationships throughout this chapter, in many ways, gay and lesbian relationships have changed more than heterosexual relationships over the last few decades. First, these relationships came "out of the closet" in the 1960s and 1970s, when there was a blossoming and acceptance of a gay subculture. Then, the advent of AIDS resulted in fewer sexual partners and more long-term, monogamous relationships, especially in the gay community.

Intimate relationships between same-sex and other-sex couples are similar in many ways, but there are some areas of difference (Herek, 2006; Pachankis & Goldfried, 2004; Roisman et al., 2008). Compared with heterosexual couples, gay and lesbian couples have higher levels of relationship satisfaction; share more affection, humor, and joy in their relationships; and have less fear and negative feelings about their relationship (Gottman et al., 2003; R. J. Green et al., 1996; Roisman et al., 2008). They report lower levels of conflict and greater relationship quality, compatibility, and intimacy (Balsam et al., 2008), and greater equality and fewer power imbalances than heterosexual relationships (Gottman et al., 2003; R. J. Green, 2008; Kurdek, 1995; Mock & Cornelius, 2007; Soloman et al., 2005).

Lesbian relationships are emotionally closer than gay male couples, who in turn have been found to be emotionally closer than heterosexual married couples (R. J. Green, 2008; Mock & Cornelius, 2007). Women in lesbian relationships have also been found to have higher levels of intimate communication in their relationships compared with other couple types (Mackey et al., 2000).

However, same-sex couples are also more likely to break up than other-sex couples (Cloud, 2008). This may be due to the lack of social and legal recognition of their relationships (Degges-White & Marszalek, 2008; Gottman et al., 2003).

Another interesting area of research has explored "benchmarks," or events that mark important dates, in a couple's relationship (such as first date, engagement, or wedding). For many same-sex couples, the lack of a unified definition for defining the beginning of a gay or lesbian relationship can be difficult. They may celebrate first meeting, first date, first sex, or a commitment ceremony. One lesbian couple said, "we celebrate our anniversary from that day that we acknowledged that we were attracted to each other," whereas a gay couple said, "We use the day we exchanged rings" (Degges-White & Marszalek, 2008). Commitment ceremonies, civil unions, and domestic partnerships have become important celebrations for many same-sex couples because they help establish a couple's relationship (R. J. Green & Mitchell, 2002). Without the availability of formal relationship status, many same-sex couples experience boundary and commitment ambiguity (R. J. Green & Mitchell, 2002). Because there are few same-sex couple role models, many same-sex couples do not know what their relationship should look like and must work together to form relationships that work for them. Although this gives them increased flexibility in defining roles, it also may present additional challenges to

polyandry
The condition or practice of having more than one husband at one time.

consanguineous marriage
A type of marriage between blood relatives, usually to maintain the integrity of family property.

the relationship (Degges-White & Marszalek, 2008). We discuss many more aspects of same-sex relationships in Chapter 11, but here we explore sexuality in these relationships and the advent of civil unions, domestic partnerships, and same-sex marriages.

SEXUALITY IN SAME-SEX RELATIONSHIPS

Earlier in this chapter, we discussed gender differences in initiating sexual activity in heterosexual relationships: Men often do more of the initiating. Does this mean that lesbians may be uncomfortable initiating sex or that gay men never have problems doing so? According to a classic study done by Blumstein and Schwartz (1983), this may be the case. They found that some lesbians do have difficulty initiating or balancing sex in their relationships. Problems with initiating sex in lesbian relationships may be due to the social pressures women have while growing up. In lesbian couples, it is often the more emotionally expressive partner who is responsible for maintaining the couple's sex life.

Similarly, in relationships between gay men the more emotionally expressive partner is usually the one who initiates sexual activity. However, gay men are much less bothered by their role of initiator. Again, this may lead to other problems, with one partner feeling he is always the initiator.

Gay men engage in sexual behavior more often than both lesbian and heterosexual couples (Kurdek, 2006). Lower rates of sexual behavior in lesbian couples have been explained in many ways. It could be that the biological nature of the sex drive is lower in women, that females typically do not initiate sexual activity and may not be comfortable doing so, or that women are less likely than men to express their feelings through sex. Finally, it also

View in Video

"We're not seen as married in the eyes of the state; we're seen as married in the eyes of our family and our church."
—*Same-Sex Marriage*
To view go to CengageNOW at www.cengage.com/login

Rob Melnychuk/Getty Images

The status of same-sex marriage continues to be a contentious issue in the U.S. Although same-sex marriage was legal in three states in mid-2008—including Massachusetts, California, and Connecticut—a constitutional amendment in November of 2008 eliminated the right for same-sex couples to marry in California. It is likely that the political battle over same-sex marriage will continue for some time.

must be pointed out that perhaps lesbian lovemaking lasts longer than heterosexual lovemaking (focusing more on foreplay), and a longer duration of lovemaking could lead to a decrease in the actual number of occurrences.

CIVIL UNIONS AND DOMESTIC PARTNERSHIPS

Many same-sex couples cohabit, whereas others choose **civil unions** and **domestic partnerships** (also referred to as civil partnerships or registered partnerships).These are legally recognized unions that come with varying rights and benefits. The rights and benefits awarded couples varies and depends on the laws of each individual state. Typically, domestic partnerships offer fewer rights than do civil unions.

The terms for same-sex relationships vary around the globe. In Australia, same-sex relationships are referred to as "significant relationships," in the Netherlands they are *geregistreerd partnerschap* ("registered partnerships"), in Germany they are *lebenspartnerschaft* ("life partnerships"), and in Iceland they are *staðfesta samvist* ("confirmed cohabitation"). Not only do the terms for same-sex relationship vary, their legal status does as well. Some countries legalize relationships, whereas others "approve" or "allow" them. See the accompanying timeline of major events in the changing legal status of same-sex relationships.

Legalized relationships are unavailable to the majority of same-sex couples in the United States today (Balsam et al., 2008). In 2000, Vermont was the first state to legalize civil unions, and by 2008, civil unions and domestic partnerships were available in California, Connecticut, Hawaii, Maine, New Hampshire, New Jersey, Oregon, Vermont, Washington, and the District of Columbia (Vestal, 2008). Several other states are considering legislation for legal status of same-sex relationships. See the Timeline "Same-Sex Relationships Around the Globe" for more information.

Typically, civil unions and domestic partnerships that are performed in one state are not recognized in other states, even if they have a civil union or domestic partnership law (Vestal, 2008). The only exception to this is New Hampshire and New Jersey, which both recognize civil unions performed in other states.

Over the past decade, there has been an increase in public support of legal recognition for same-sex couples (Avery et al., 2007). A 2008 CBS News Poll found that the majority of Americans think there should be some legal recognition of gay and lesbian couples (CBS, 2008). Thirty percent of respondents believed that same-sex couples should be allowed to marry, and 28% thought they should be permitted to form civil unions. However, more than one third believe there should be no legal recognition of same-sex relationships (CBS, 2008). Many same-sex couples across the

civil union
A legal union of a same-sex couple, sanctioned by a civil authority.

domestic partner
A person other than a spouse with whom one cohabits. Domestic partners can be either same or other sex.

United States are challenging existing laws that regulate issues such as civil unions, domestic partnerships, same-sex marriage, separation, child custody, and gay adoption. These court cases will continue, some say, until same-sex couples are given the same marital rights as their heterosexual counterparts. The changing legal status of same-sex relationships is especially important to lesbian women, who are more likely than gay men to marry or enter into domestic partnerships and have children (Orlandi, 2008; we discuss these issues more in Chapter 11).

A study of same-sex couples in Vermont found those who had civil unions were more likely to be out about their sexual orientation, have children and joint back accounts with their partner, and have more connections with their families compared with those who did not have civil unions (Balsam et al., 2008). Some researchers suggest that civil unions may increase the stability of same-sex relationships, improve the physical and mental health of the individuals in the relationship, and reduce outside discrimination (M. King & Bartlett, 2005).

SAME-SEX MARRIAGE

In 1996, the U.S. Congress enacted the Defense of Marriage Act, which prohibits federal recognition of civil unions, domestic partnerships, and same-sex marriages. As discussed earlier, even though individual U.S. states may offer these legal options, the federal government will not recognize these unions. In addition, based on the Defense of Marriage Act, each state can recognize or deny any relationship between same-sex couples, recognizing marriage as a "legal union of one man and one woman as husband and wife," by referring to a "spouse" only as a person of the other sex. The Defense of Marriage Act also removes any federal spousal rights of civil unions, domestic partnerships, and same-sex marriage, including social security, federal tax law, and immigration rights for foreign same-sex spouses of American citizens (Mason et al., 2001). As of 2008, 41 states had statutes barring same-sex marriage (Vestal, 2008).

Same-sex marriage was available only in the states of Massachusetts, California, and Connecticut in 2008 (although California voted on an initiative to overturn this ruling in late 2008 by defining a marriage as "between a man and a woman"; McKinley, 2008). By mid-2008, Massachusetts had issued more than 10,000 marriage licenses to same-sex couples (Massachusetts does not allow nonresident same-sex couples to marry; Vestal, 2008). In California, it is estimated that 50 percent of the state's more than 103,000 same-sex couples will get married between 2008 and 2010, and because California will allow nonresidents to marry, during this same time, 67,000 same-sex couples from other states will also marry in California (Sears & Badgett, 2008). Interestingly, economists predicted that same-sex marriage will be good for California's economy by bringing in more than $680 million in wedding and tourism and creating more than 2,000 new jobs (Sears & Badgett, 2008).

In late 2008, the Supreme Court in Iowa was considering same-sex marriage cases. However, same-sex marriages performed in states with legal same-sex marriage are not recognized outside of these states. Think about it this way: A heterosexual couple that gets married in Kansas and moves to Connecticut is still legally married, and their marriage license from Kansas proves it. However, a same-sex couple who gets married in Massachusetts will not be legally recognized when they move to Kansas, even though they have a valid marriage license from the state of Massachusetts. See the accompanying Sex in Real Life, "Same-Sex Marriage," for a moving personal story about the legality of same-sex marriage.

Why should marriage be allowed only for heterosexual couples and not for gay and lesbian couples? Shouldn't same-sex marriages (or an equivalent marriage-like status) be legalized? The answers to these questions go back many years. Aristotle discussed the importance of legislators to establish rules regulating marriage (Dixit & Pindyck, 1994).

Societies have always given preference to heterosexual couples, presumably because of the benefits that heterosexual marriages provide to society (benefits to the couples but also to their offspring). Wardle (2001) discusses eight social interests for marriage, including:

1. Safe sexual relations

2. Responsible procreation

3. Optimal child rearing

4. Healthy human development

5. Protecting those who undertake the most vulnerable parenting roles (i.e., mothers/wives)

6. Securing the stability and integrity of the basic unit of society

7. Fostering civic virtue and social order

8. Facilitating interjurisdictional compatibility

As you can see, heterosexual marriage is strongly linked to procreation, childbirth, and child rearing (Wardle, 2001). The United States has long regulated marriage in an attempt to protect procreative health. This is precisely why marriages between relatives are illegal (birth defects are more prevalent in couples who are related), and marriages between "unfit" or mentally challenged partners are regulated.

Even with all this controversy, many gay and lesbian couples "marry" their partners in ceremonies that are not recognized by the states in which they live. Same-sex marriages, whether legally recognized or not, often suffer from the same jealousies, power

The families of same-sex couples often include children and grandchildren.

Same-Sex Marriage

My employer informed me that a leave of absence would not be granted as care for a dying lover failed to meet guidelines for such consideration.

Below is a letter written by a 39-year-old gay man who lost his long-term partner, Ken. This letter was read to Connecticut lawmakers in support of same-sex marriage.

I define my marital status as widowed, principally as the result of the death of my lover, Ken; his death brought to a close a relationship which had spanned close to seven years. The cause of death was heart failure, the result of a congenital lung condition. Soon after we started dating, he told me of his health condition and of its eventually fatal consequences. He did so not to scare me away, but to prepare me for what lay ahead.

One of my greatest regrets was my inability to place my lover on my health care plan. He was self-employed and found premiums prohibitively expensive. When his health declined to the point that he required around-the-clock care, I lost my job. My employer informed me that a leave of absence would not be granted as care for a dying lover failed to meet guidelines for such con-

sideration. Survival necessitated liquidating, one after another, all of my assets. Upon his death, the estate being insolvent, household items were sold to cover just debts. For those who've experienced the death of a legally defined spouse, if you feel that my relationship with my lover does not equate to the loss that you've sustained, let me tell you this. I remember every restless night, waking up screaming, trembling, and crying; I've lived with the overwhelming loneliness associated with birthdays, anniversaries, and the countless private rituals now remembered only by one; and I can state, unequivocally, that the worst part of widowhood is sleeping alone again—and it has nothing to do with sex—it is literally just sleeping alone again.

The one thing that no one can take away are the last words that Ken spoke, some 20 minutes before he breathed his last, addressed to me, "My beautiful boy, I love you very much."

SOURCE: Author's files.

---

struggles, and "divorces" as heterosexual marriages (P. H. Collins, 1988). In Blumstein and Schwartz's (1983) classic study, gay and lesbian couples complained about their partners' lack of attention, sexual incompatibility, and the same mundane, day-to-day struggles that heterosexual couples deal with. In addition, these couples often have to cope with the disapproval of their families and, sometimes, the stress of hiding their relationship.

SAME-SEX PARENTING

Many gay men and lesbian women express a desire to have and raise children, even though same-sex couples are less likely to have children compared with heterosexual couples (Balsam et al., 2008). One study found that whereas more than 50% of heterosexual men and women had children, under 20% of lesbian and

bisexual women and less than 10% of gay men had children (Balsam et al., 2008).

Studies of lesbian and gay youth have found that two thirds of females and more than 50% of males are interested in raising children at some point in their lives (D'Augelli et al., 2006/2007). Although the majority said they expect to raise their own biological children, others said they would adopt, become foster parents, or help raise a partner's biological children. In Chapter 12, we explore strategies that gay and lesbian couples use to become pregnant.

SAME-SEX RELATIONSHIPS IN OTHER CULTURES

Same-sex relationships outside the United States are supported in some countries and ignored in others. Denmark was the first country to legalize civil unions in 1989, and since then many de-

---

timeline Same-Sex Relationships Around the Globe

1989
Denmark becomes the first country to legally recognize same-sex unions, calling them "registered partnerships."

Doug Menuez/Getty Images

1993
Norway approves civil unions.

1995
Sweden approves registered partnerships.

© Rob Chapple/Thinkstock/Picturequest

1996
Iceland legalizes civil unions.

1996
President Clinton signs the Defense of Marriage Act into law, which upholds states rights to ban same-sex marriage and not recognize marriages performed elsewhere.

veloped countries have established civil unions or similar legal status to provide same-sex couples with benefits and rights similar to marriage (see the nearby Timeline of Same-Sex Relationships for more information).

As of 2008, same-sex marriage was legal in Belgium, Canada, the Netherlands, South Africa, and Spain. Civil unions and domestic or registered partnerships were legal in the Czech Republic, Denmark, Finland, France, Germany, Hungary, Iceland, Norway, Portugal, New Zealand, Switzerland, Sweden, and the United Kingdom (Sterling, 2004; Timberg, 2005). Several other countries are considering legislation for legal status of same-sex relationships.

In Australia, equal rights legislation gives gay and lesbian couples equal rights as heterosexual couples, even though there is no formal terminology for the relationship (Coates, 2004). Strongly religious countries, such as Italy, are not supportive of same-sex relationships. Even so, in the city of Padua, Italy, same-sex couples were allowed to have their relationships legally recognized, which met with strong criticism from the Vatican (Shoffman, 2006). Although homosexuality is outlawed in many countries in Africa, legal marriage rights were nonetheless extended to same-sex couples in 2005.

review questions

1 Explain why same-sex relationships may experience less power imbalances and greater equality and satisfaction than heterosexual relationships.

2 Differentiate between civil unions, domestic partnerships, and same-sex marriage.

3 Explain how and why societies have given preference to heterosexual marriage over same-sex marriage.

4 What do we know about same-sex parenting?

5 Explain what we know about same-sex relationships in other cultures.

REALResearch **>** Divorce is not good for the environment. Research has found that divorce in 12 countries around the world increased the number of households by more than 6 million, increasing the per-person costs for electricity and water by **46%** to **56%** (Yu & Liu, 2007).

Divorce: Whose Fault or No-Fault?

There have been substantial changes in the institution of marriage over the past 30 years. During most of U.S. history, a married couple was viewed as a single, legal entity (M. A. Mason et al., 2001). Today, however, marriage is viewed more as a partnership between a couple. This shift in perception of marriage brought with it a shift in how marriage was dissolved. The liberalization of divorce laws made it easier to obtain a divorce and made it a less expensive process.

By 1985, all states offered couples some type of **no-fault divorce,** which means neither partner needs to be found guilty of a transgression (such as having sex outside marriage) to dissolve the marriage (Krause, 1986). The availability of no-fault divorce contributed to skyrocketing divorce rates (Stevenson & Wolfers, 2007). In an attempt to reduce divorce rates, some states instituted **covenant marriages,** which revolve around restrictive agreed-on

no-fault divorce
A divorce law that allows for the dissolution of a marriage without placing blame on either of the partners.

covenant marriage
A marriage that is preceded by premarital counseling and has strict rules about divorce.

1998	1999	2000	2000	2001
Netherlands legalizes civil unions.	**France approves** civil unions for both same- and other-sex couples with the *Pacte civil de solidarité.*  © Don Mason/Corbis	**Netherlands legalizes** same-sex marriage.	**Vermont governor signs** civil union bill, making it the **first state to** legally recognize same-sex couples. Rob Melnychuk/Getty Images	**Finland approves** registered partnership.

rules and regulations for ending a marriage and also involve premarital counseling and an agreement to pursue additional counseling if marital problems develop. Covenant marriages also extend the wait time for a divorce, in some cases to 2 years or more, unless there is domestic violence involved. We talk more about covenant marriages later in this chapter. Historically divorce rates for married heterosexuals increased sharply between 1970 and 1975 due in part to the liberalization of divorce laws (Kreider, 2005). Rates stabilized after this and began to decrease. By 2005, divorce rates were at the lowest level since 1970 (Stevenson & Wolfers, 2007). Today roughly 1 in 5 adults has ever divorced (Kreider, 2005), and the Census Bureau reports that 50% of U.S. marriages end in divorce (U.S. Census Bureau, 2007).

What causes a couple to end their marriage? The question is complicated because not all unstable or unhappy marriages end in divorce. Couples stay together for many reasons—for the children, because of lack of initiative, because of religious prohibitions against divorce, or financial reasons—even though they have severe problems in their marriages. Similarly, couples with seemingly happy marriages separate and divorce, sometimes to the surprise of one of the partners who did not even know the marriage was in trouble.

Divorce rates vary among age groups. They are highest in women in their teens and decline with increasing age. Generally, divorce occurs early in the marriage; on average, first marriages that end in divorce last about 8 years (U.S. Census Bureau, 2007). Second marriages that end in divorce last about 8.6 years for men and 7.2 years for women (U.S. Census Bureau, 2007).

Divorce rates vary among age groups.

Koreans, Asian Indians, and Chinese couples have the lowest separation rates and divorce rates in the United States, whereas African Americans, Native Americans, and Puerto Ricans show the highest separation and divorce rates in the United States (Kreider, 2005; Skolnick, 1992). Mexican Americans, Cubans, and Whites lie somewhere in between (Skolnick, 1992). Interracial marriages also have higher divorce rates than marriages within racial groups (Bratter & King, 2008). White female–Black male and White female–Asian male couples were more prone to divorce than White–White couples.

A mutually shared decision to divorce is actually uncommon. Usually, one partner wants to terminate a relationship more than the other partner, who is still strongly attached to the marriage and who is more distraught at its termination. In fact, the declaration that a partner wants a divorce often comes as a shock to his or her spouse. When one partner is the initiator, it is usually the female. One study found that women initiated two thirds of all divorces (Brinig & Allen, 2000). The individual who wants his or her marriage to end is likely to view the marriage totally differently from the individual who wants the marriage to continue (H. Wang & Amato, 2000). In addition, the partner who initiated the divorce has often completed the mourning of the relationship by the time the divorce is complete, unlike the partner whose mourning begins once the divorce is finalized.

SAME-SEX DIVORCE

Because same-sex marriage has only recently been legalized in Massachusetts and California there is not a great deal of research on same-sex divorce. We do know that many long-term same-sex couples typically dissolve their relationships privately, married or not. However, without divorce laws, these breakups can be difficult or unfair to one or both partners. A few same-sex married couples began seeking out divorce approximately 7 months after the legalization of same-sex marriage (Gallagher & Baker, 2004).

A Swedish study found a high rate of legal divorce among same-sex couples—both married gay and lesbian couples were more likely to divorce within an 8-year period than heterosexuals (Gallagher & Baker, 2004). Keep in mind, however, that same-sex marriages are less likely to include children than heterosexual marriages, and same-sex couples are generally older than their heterosexual counterparts—both of which may contribute to higher divorce rates (Gallagher & Baker, 2004).

WHY DO PEOPLE GET DIVORCED?

It is difficult to determine why some marriages fail; every couple has its own story. Sometimes the spouses themselves are at a loss to understand why their marriage failed. We now explore some of the social, predisposing, and relationship factors that may contribute to divorce.

timeline Same-Sex Relationships Around the Globe

2001	2001	2001	2002	2002
Germany legalizes civil unions.	**Netherlands gives** same-sex couples the right to adopt children.	**Portugal legalizes** civil partnerships.	**Belgium legalizes** same-sex civil marriage.	**Sweden legalizes** same-sex adoption.
	© Lorne Harris		Ryan Pierse/Getty Images	

Social Factors Affecting Divorce

Divorce rates in the United States are influenced by changes in legal, political, religious, and familial patterns. For example, as we discussed earlier, no-fault divorce laws have made divorce easier for couples to dissolve a marriage. The growth of low-cost legal clinics and the overabundance of lawyers have made divorce cheaper and thus more accessible (see the accompanying Sex in Real Life, "Point-and-Click Divorce"). Additionally, the more equitable distribution of marital assets has made some people less apprehensive about losing everything to their spouses. Changing social issues, such as more women entering the workforce and earning advanced degrees, have also had an impact on divorce rates. Research has found that divorce is more common in couples in which the woman has a professional degree (Wilson, 2008). Another interesting finding in the research is that male college graduates are more likely to have married by age 45 than those without college degrees, whereas female college graduates are less likely to have married than women without college degrees (Stevenson & Wolfers, 2007).

As we discussed earlier in this chapter, a few states have passed laws allowing people to choose a covenant marriage. Because a covenant marriage involves premarital counseling and makes divorce more difficult even if the couple decides later they want one (Wardle, 1999), couples who choose them tend to be more conservative, religious, and have stronger gender-role ideologies than those who choose a traditional marriage (Hawkins et al., 2002).

In recent years, divorce has become generally more acceptable in American society. Whereas 30 or 40 years ago, it was very difficult for a divorced person to attain high political office, Ronald Reagan's divorce was not even an issue in his presidential campaign. Also, many religious groups are less opposed to divorce than they used to be.

2003
Massachusetts Supreme Court rules that state constitution guarantees equal marriage rights for same-sex couples; Massachusetts becomes the **first state to legally recognize same-sex marriage.**

Laurie Swope

2004
New Zealand gives legal recognition to same-sex relationships.

2004
Australia bans same-sex marriage.

Melanie Stetson Freeman/The Christian Science Monitor via Getty Images

2004
New Jersey legalizes domestic partnerships.

2005
Belgium allows same-sex adoption.

Communication avoidance may be one of the first signs that a marriage is in trouble.

Predisposing Factors for Divorce

Certain situations may predispose a couple to divorce. People who have been divorced before or whose parents have divorced have more accepting attitudes toward divorce than those who grew up in happy, intact families (Amato, 1996, 2001; Amato & Hohmann-Marriott, 2007; Wolfinger, 2000). In addition, people who have divorced parents are significantly more likely to report marital problems in their own relationships than people from intact families, and they also tend to be more skeptical about marriage, feeling insecure about the permanence of these relationships (Amato, 2001; Jacquet & Surra, 2001; Weigel, 2007; Wolfinger, 2000).

Other factors that may contribute to divorce are marrying at a young age (S. P. Morgan & Rindfuss, 1985), marrying because of an unplanned pregnancy (G. Becker et al., 1977), alcohol or drug abuse (R. L. Collins et al., 2007), and having children quickly after getting married (S. P. Morgan & Rindfuss, 1985). The interval between marriage and the arrival of children is an important factor; waiting longer promotes marital stability by giving couples time to get accustomed to being a married couple before the arrival of children and may also allow them to become more financially secure (S. P. Morgan & Rindfuss, 1985). Religion is also important: Catholics and Jews are less likely to divorce than Protestants, and divorce rates tend to be higher for marriages of mixed religions. In addition, marriages between people having no religious affiliation have particularly high divorce rates (Skolnick, 1992).

Relationship Factors in Divorce

In general, couples who divorce have known for a long time that there were difficulties in their marriage, although they may not have contemplated divorce. These problems are made worse, in most cases, by communication problems. Some warning signs are communication avoidance (not talking about problems in the relationship); demand and withdrawal patterns of communication, whereby one partner demands that they address the problem and the other partner pulls away; and little mutually constructive communication (Christensen & Shenk, 1991).

Some couples make poor assessments of their partner or believe that the little annoyances or character traits that they dislike in their potential spouses will disappear or change after marriage (Neff & Karney, 2005). Marrying a person with the intention to change his or her personality or bad habits is a recipe for disaster.

ADJUSTING TO DIVORCE

One year after a divorce, 50% of men and 60% of women reported being happier than they were during the marriage (Faludi, 1991). Even 10 years later, 80% of the women and 50% of the men said that their divorce was the right decision. However, for some, divorce can be very painful, both emotionally and physically. Depression is common in those who believe that marriage is permanent (R. W. Simon & Marcussen, 1999).

Women often have an increase in depression after a divorce, whereas men experience poorer physical and mental health (Zheng & Hart, 2002). Illness in men is often attributed to the fact that wives often watch out for their husband's physical health. Depression and sadness also surface when divorced men and women find that they have less in common with married friends as many friends separate into "hers" and "his." Older individuals experience more psychological problems because divorce is less

timeline Same-Sex Relationships Around the Globe

2005
Canada approves same-sex marriage.

AP Photo/CP, Jonathan Hayward

2005
Connecticut authorizes civil unions for same-sex couples.

2006
South Africa legalizes same-sex marriage.

2006
Massachusetts Supreme Court upholds law banning out-of-state couples from marrying in Massachusetts if marriage is illegal in the couple's home state.

Queerstock/Getty Images

2007
Switzerland legalizes civil unions.

common in older populations and because there are fewer options for forming new relationships in older age (H. Wang & Amato, 2000). Older divorced women are more likely to feel anger and loneliness than are younger divorced women. Finally, some racial differences have also been found. Divorced Black men and women adjust more easily and experience less negativity from peers than do Whites (Kitson, 1992).

Another area that is affected after divorce is economics. Financial adjustment is often harder for women because after a divorce a woman's standard of living declines more than a man's (H. Wang & Amato, 2000). Many women who previously lived in a middle-class family find themselves slipping below the poverty line after divorce.

On the other hand, some women's careers improve after a divorce, even more than men's do. Some women who divorce find they have improved performance evaluations and feel more motivated and satisfied with their jobs because they put the time and energy they had invested in their relationship into their work instead. Over time, the majority of people seem to adjust to divorce. Often, social support from friends and family can be very helpful.

Dating after a divorce can be difficult for some. A person may have been involved in committed relationships for many years; consequently, he or she may find that the dating environment has changed drastically since they were younger. It is not uncommon for newly single people to feel frustrated or confused about this unfamiliar environment.

The majority of divorced men and women remarry, and some remarry, divorce, and remarry again (often referred to as **serial divorce**). In fact, the median time between a divorce and a second marriage is about 3.5 years (U.S. Census Bureau, 2007). Overall, 13% to 14% of heterosexuals marry twice, 3% marry three or more times, and less than 1% marry four or more times (Kreider, 2005). Men remarry at higher rates than women, and Hispanics and African Americans remarry at lower rates than whites (M. Coleman et al., 2000). Couples in second marriages report higher relationship satisfaction in their marriages than do couples in first marriages (McCarthy & Ginsberg, 2007).

Divorce and Sex
Few studies have focused on sexual behavior among people who are divorced. Common sense tells us that a person who is depressed or angry about a divorce may have a decrease in both levels of sexual activity and sexual satisfaction. Steven Stack and Jim Gundlach (1992) found that age was inversely related to sex among those who divorced: The older a person was at divorce, the less sexual activity occurred afterward. Another relationship was found between religiosity and sex: The more religious a divorced person was, the less likely he or she was to have another sex partner outside of marriage.

Whether a person has sexual partners after a divorce also depends on his or her sexual attitudes and the presence or absence of children. Divorced persons without children are more likely to have sexual partners than those with children.

*The **majority of divorced** men and women **remarry.***

DIVORCE IN OTHER CULTURES

Divorce is common in almost all societies, but cultural views about it are changing as societies develop. In societies such as the United States, Sweden, Russia, and most European countries, divorce is relatively simple and has little stigma. The exceptions are countries that are largely Roman Catholic; because Catholicism does not allow divorce, it can be difficult to obtain in Catholic countries. Ireland legalized divorce in 1995; before this, it was the only country in the Western world to constitutionally ban divorce (Pogatchnik, 1995). In South America, a heavily Roman Catholic continent, Chile was the last country to legalize divorce in late 2004.

Traditional laws about divorce can still be enforced, especially in more patriarchal cultures. Islamic law, like traditional Jewish law, allows a man to divorce his wife simply by repudiating her publicly three times. A wife, on the other hand, must go to court to dissolve a marriage (Rugh, 1984). In Egypt, it is far easier for men to divorce than for women, and because of this only about 33% of divorces in Egypt are initiated by females. In Israel, women need their husband's permission for a divorce, and councils have been set up to try to convince men to let their wives have a divorce.

serial divorce
The practice of divorce and remarriage, followed by divorce and remarriage.

2007
New Jersey and New Hampshire legalize civil unions.

2007
Oregon legalizes domestic partnerships.

Craig Mitchelldyer/Getty Images

2007
Washington legalizes domestic partnerships.

2008
Norway legalizes same-sex marriage.

2008
Although both California and Connecticut gave same-sex couples the right to marry in mid-2008, voters in California eliminated this right in late 2008.

© Kimberly White/Reuters/Corbis

In 2001, China's government revised its 20-year-old marriage law and included the concept of fault in marriage (Dorgan, 2001; Ruan & Lau, 2004). Before this law was implemented, Chinese couples had an equal division of family property regardless of the reasons for the divorce. Under this new law, however, if a partner is caught engaging in extramarital sex, he can lose everything (research has found that it is mostly men who cheat in China).

The reasons that people get divorced are numerous, although different patterns emerge in different societies. In Egypt, the most common reason given for divorce is infidelity by the husband, whereas among the Hindus of India, the most common reason is cruelty (either physical or mental) from their partner (Pothen, 1989). Arab women's main reasons for divorce include the husband's physical, sexual, or verbal abuse; alcoholism; mental illness; and in-law interference (Savaya & Cohen, 2003). In China, more than 70% of divorces are initiated by women, and the main reason given is an extramarital affair of the husband (Ruan & Lau, 2004). This is also the main reason for divorce in Brazil and many other countries (de Freitas, 2004).

Overall, divorce rates seem to be increasing worldwide as countries modernize and as traditional forms of control over the family lose their power. Only time will tell, however, whether a backlash will stabilize marriage rates, as they seem to be doing in the United States.

Throughout this chapter, we have explored various aspects of adult sexual relationships. Relationships hold a central place in our lives. When people are asked what makes them happy, most say their close relationships and feeling loved and needed (Perlman, 2007). In the next chapter, we turn our attention to adult sexual behaviors.

review questions

1 Explain what makes a no-fault marriage different from a covenant marriage.

2 Identify some of the factors that research has found might predispose a couple to divorce.

3 Explain how men and women adjust to divorce.

4 Identify how dating, cohabitation, marriage, extramarital sex, and divorce are viewed outside the United States.

CHAPTER review

SUMMARY POINTS

1 Intimate relationships are a fundamental part of human development. Overall, married men and women, gay men, and lesbian women all feel positive about their intimate relationships. Although same-sex couples face more relationship challenges than heterosexual couples, the majority of couples are secure and happy in their relationships.

2 By examining the customs and rules a culture sets up for choosing a mate, we can learn about the level of patriarchy in that particular society, ideals about masculinity and femininity,

roles of women and men, the value placed on conformity, the importance of childbearing, the authority of the family, and attitudes toward childhood, pleasure, and responsibility.

3 On college campuses, there have been many recent changes in dating practices. Some researchers argue that college dating doesn't exist. In traditional dating, the boy would pick up the girl at her house, giving her father and mother time to meet with the boy, and then they would go to a well-defined event. The most difficult part of dating is the initial invitation.

4 We are living in a multicultural world. As a result, it is not uncommon to date someone of a different race, religion, or culture. There are still strong social forces that keep the races separate and make it difficult for people to meet. It can be difficult to begin dating again after the end of a marriage or the death of a spouse. Oftentimes this has to do with the fact that the dating environment has changed.

5 Sexual practices have changed on college campuses today. Hooking up, or having a friend with benefits, has become more common. Lesbian women are more likely to self-identify as lesbian before pursuing a sexual relationship with other women, whereas gay men are more likely to pursue sex with men before self-identifying as gay. As people age, their sexual functioning changes, and this can affect their relationships. Sexual inactivity has been found to be a major cause of decreases in sexual functioning.

6 In recent years, cohabitation, or living together outside of marriage, has increased dramatically. In the United States, the typical pattern is to live together before marriage and not in place of marriage. Advantages of cohabitation are that it allows couples to learn more about each other, share finances, and mature in their relationship. Cohabitating couples tend to either marry or separate after just a few years. About 50% of all couples who live together break up within a year or less, and those who marry are at increased risk of divorce. Longer cohabitation has been found to be associated with higher likelihood of divorce.

7 The majority of young people say they are planning and expecting to marry at some point in their lives. The median age for first marriage has been increasing, and in 2000 the age at first marriage went to 27 and 25 for men and women, respectively. Marital satisfaction has been found to be related to the quality of the friendship, frequency of pleasurable activities, being able to talk to each other and offer self-disclosure, physical and emotional intimacy, and personality similarities. High rewards–low costs are also important.

8 Marital quality tends to peak in the first few years of a marriage and then declines until midlife, when it rises again. However, the majority of married couples report that their marriages are happy and satisfying. People who are married tend to be happier, healthier, and have longer lives than either widowed or divorced persons of the same age. Marriage has also been found to reduce the impact of several potentially traumatic events including job loss, retirement, and illness. Overall, marriage provides more health benefits to men than women.

9 Marital happiness is higher before having children, declines steadily until it hits a low when the children are in their teens, and then begins to increase once the children leave the house. Many couples do not realize how time-consuming children are, and they find themselves with little leisure time or time to work on their relationship.

10 The higher the frequency of sexual behavior in marriage, the greater the sexual satisfaction. During the early years, sex is more frequent and generally satisfying. During the next 15 or so years, other aspects of life take precedence over sex, and the couple may experience difficulty in maintaining sexual interest in each other. In the later years, men often report more satisfaction with marriage than do women.

11 Almost all couples, whether dating, living together, or married, expect sexual exclusivity from each other. Those who cheat have stronger sexual interests, more permissive sexual values, less satisfaction in their intimate relationship, and more opportunities for sex outside the relationship. Studies on same-sex couples have found that gay men are more likely to cheat than lesbian women.

12 Women experience more emotional distress about infidelity than men do. A woman is also more likely to be upset about emotional infidelity, whereas a man is more likely to be upset about his partner's sexual infidelity. Some couples engage in comarital sex, but the sex is viewed as separate from the marriage.

13 In many ways, same-sex relationships have changed more than heterosexual relationships over the past few decades. Compared with heterosexual couples, gay and lesbian couples have higher levels of relationship satisfaction; share more affection, humor, and joy; and have less fear and negative feelings about the relationship. These relationships often have more equality as well.

14 Many same-sex couples cohabit, whereas others choose civil unions, domestic partnerships, or same-sex marriage. These are legally recognized unions that come with varying rights and benefits determined by the state in which they live.

15 As of late 2008, same-sex marriage was legal in Massachusetts, California, and Connecticut. The United States has long regulated marriage in an attempt to protect health. Even with all this controversy, many same-sex couples "marry" their partners in ceremonies that are not recognized by the states in which they live.

16 Today, marriage is seen as a partnership between a man and a woman. This shift in perception of marriage has brought with it a shift in divorce. The liberalization of divorce laws has made it easier and less expensive to obtain a divorce. The current U.S. divorce rate remains high compared with earlier times and with other countries. African Americans, Native Americans, and Puerto Ricans show the highest separation and divorce rates in the United States; Korean, Asian Indian, and Chinese Americans have the lowest rates.

17 Certain factors increase the likelihood of divorce. These include marrying at a young age, marrying because of an unplanned pregnancy, having no religious affiliation, being Protestant or a mixed-religion couple, having many communication problems, having divorced before, or having parents who have divorced. Women often have an increase in depression after a divorce, whereas men experience poorer physical and mental health. Men remarry at higher rates than women, and Hispanics and African Americans remarry at lower rates than Whites.

18 In most industrialized countries, dating is the norm. There are still a few industrialized cultures in which arranged marriages take place. Mate selection in most places is a much more individual affair. However, although many in the West believe in the right of individuals to choose their own mates, there were some advantages to parental participation in mate selection, and the transition to individual mate selection in traditional societies is often difficult.

19 Cohabitation is rarer in more traditional societies in which, even if a couple has sex before or instead of marriage, social customs would never tolerate an unmarried heterosexual couple living together openly. In some countries, cohabitation is often a step toward marriage or is seen as a "lower form" of marriage.

20 Marriage ceremonies take place in every society on Earth, but marriage customs vary widely from culture to culture. Some cultures mandate marriages between certain relatives, whereas other cultures allow multiple spouses. Usually, this takes the form of polygyny, or having more than one wife, which is a common practice in many areas of Africa and the Middle East. Attitudes toward marriage vary in different cultures in different times. Same-sex marriages are legal in some countries outside of the United States. The Netherlands was the first country to allow same-sex marriages. Extramarital sex is forbidden in many cultures, but it is often tolerated even in cultures in which it is technically not allowed.

21 Divorce is common in almost all societies, but cultural views about it are changing as societies develop. In societies such as the United States, Japan, Sweden, Russia, and most European countries, divorce is relatively simple and has little stigma. The exceptions are countries that are largely Roman Catholic, because Catholicism does not allow divorce.

CRITICAL THINKING questions

1 What are the qualities you look for in a partner? Why do you think these qualities are important to you? Which could you live without? Which are nonnegotiable?

2 Do you ever want to settle down in a lifelong committed relationship? Why or why not? If so, how long do you think you would want to date someone before settling down for life?

3 How would you feel if your partner cheated on you and engaged in sex outside of your relationship without your knowledge? What would you say to him or her? Have you ever had a conversation about monogamy?

4 Suppose this morning when you woke up, you realized your roommate had another "hookup" last night. How do you feel about his or her frequent hooking up activity? What do you think encourages or discourages hookups on your campus?

5 Pretend you live in a country that practices arranged marriage, and write an informational paragraph about yourself to give to a matchmaker. What would you want the matchmaker to look for in your marriage partner?

6 Jeff and Steve have been dating for 3 years and are ready to commit to each other for life. Do you think their "marriage" should be formally recognized by the law? Why, or why not?

7 There have been many changes in the liberalization of divorce laws. Do you think that divorce has become too easy today? Do couples give up on their marriages too soon because of this?

8 Do you think the expansion of marriage rights to same sex couples erodes or damages heterosexual marriage? Why or why not?

WEB resources

Sexuality Now Book Companion Website
Go to www.cengage.com/psychology/carroll for practice quizzes, glossary, flash cards, and more. You can also access the following websites from the companion site.

The Gottman Institute ■ This website provides information on the work of John Gottman and Julie Schwartz Gottman. They have conducted research on all facets of married life, including parenting issues. The Gottman Institute provides information and training workshops for both gay and straight couples.

Divorce Service Center ■ CompleteCase.com is an online uncontested divorce service center. This site offers assistance with divorce documents without the expenses of a personal lawyer. This is an interesting website that illustrates the changing attitudes about divorce today.

Queendom Tests ■ This Internet magazine includes interactive tests to explore personality, relationships, intelligence, and health. Tests appear in four formats—for lesbians, gay men, heterosexual women, and heterosexual men. Although these tests allow you to explore important issues related to relationships, they are not scholarly or scientific.

Romance 101 ■ Hosted by womensforum.com, this website contains humorous information about relationships, including information about men and women's views on dating, romance, and the "dating bill of rights." This is a fun place to visit for a lighthearted look at romance.

CengageNOW
Go to www.cengage.com/login to link to CengageNOW, your online study tool. First take the Pre-Test for this chapter to get your Personalized Study Plan, which will identify topics you need to review and direct you to online resources. Then take the Post-Test to determine what concepts you have mastered and what you still need work on.

Videos in CengageNOW
For additional information on topics discusses in this chapter, check out the videos in CengageNOW on the following topics:

- Same-Sex Marriage—Hear a lesbian talk about her civil union with her partner and how it is perceived by others.

- Discovering Bisexuality—Hear a woman describe how she gradually realized that she was bisexual.

- Trying Not to Be Gay—Hear a gay man describe his struggle to come to terms with his attraction to men.

- Gay Teens—Gay teens talk about coming out to their families and friends and the difficulties they encountered along the way.

- Sex After 45—Do people become more or less attracted to their partners as they age?

- American Sex Lives: 2004 Poll—Learn the truth about your sex life and everyone else's sex life in this summary of a poll.

- How Frequently Do People Have Sex?—Compare how much sex Americans are having depending on their age, marital status, and whether they have children.

- Who's Cheating?—Hear how differently men and women conceive what cheating is and how people pursue cheating.

- Initiating Sex—Check your intuitions about how and when people initiate sex against the survey data.

- Orgasm: For Real or Not?—Dr. Jennifer Berman and people on the street interviews discuss the whys and hows of orgasms—fake and real.

- Discussing Marriage While Dating—Listen to a young couple discuss whether they are ready for marriage.

- Meeting a Partner's Family—Hear a young man describe his anxiety about meeting his girlfriend's family for the first time.

Sexual Expression: Arousal and Response

Antonio Mo/Getty Images

I am a masochist—I enjoy being tied up and spanked. When a Dominant puts me over his knee and spanks me, first gently, then harder, with escalating force—it's an amazing feeling. At first I feel the warmth of his hand and legs and perhaps I feel his pulse picking up despite his composed expression. Then the pain sets in, and that's all I can think of; that shocking, delicious pain and the knowledge that I could stop it if I really wanted to, but I don't want to. The experience is too wonderful; the spanking itself, the warmth my reddening skin gives off, the intermittent kneading after every ten slaps or so. Now, he changes to a paddle, wood or leather for preference; adding to the shock of pain the surprise of sudden coolness against my hot skin, the flat firmness contrasting the soft contours of his hand. Everything else fades away. Maybe there are others in the dark watching this little tableau, maybe I had a

fight with a friend and it's been haunting me, maybe my foot has fallen asleep—at this moment none of that matters. My world consists solely of the spanker, my body, and the wonderful sensations.

There are a lot of people in the psychological community and the community at large who would say that wanting what I want and doing what I do means that there's something wrong with me, that something happened to me when I was a child to pervert my sexual behavior. But they're wrong; this is who I am. Though I can and do, on occasion, enjoy what is known as "vanilla sex," I just prefer "rocky road."

I became an active member in the "scene," or the sadomasochism community, when I turned 21. Before then, I'd tried a few Internet fetish dating sites, with very limited success. I enjoy myself and life more now then I ever did when I repressed my

"deviant" desires. Like any interest that isn't totally mainstream, it's easier to become more comfortable with yourself once you socialize with your peers. I met some great friends who were interested in similar sexual behaviors, and I learned a terrific amount of stuff about the scene and myself. I soon became more confident and assertive in my everyday life and my sex life. Another terrific factor of being out and about "in the scene" is I can casually ask someone what they're "into." After stumbling through explanations to several boyfriends about wanting to be tied up and spanked, it's a really amazing, really freeing experience to be able to be so open so easily. SOURCE: Author's files.

◁ Opposite: © Solus-Veer/Corbis

The story above was written by a 22-year old student of mine. Her preferences for sadomasochistic sex are clear, and she's finally in a place where she doesn't doubt herself or her sexuality. Human sexuality is a complex part of life, with cultural, psychological, and biological influences shaping how people choose to express their sexuality. Because of the varied influences, it is important to view sexual behaviors in an open, nonjudgmental fashion. In this chapter, we discuss adult sexual behaviors from early adulthood through the senior years. We explore how sexuality is shaped by cultural, ethnic, religious, psychological, and biological influences, and also review the human sexual response cycle and various ways that adults express their sexuality.

REALResearch > Experiencing an orgasm typically produces a physiologically calming effect of sexual satisfaction in men and women, triggered by the release of the hormone prolactin (BRODY & KRÜGER, 2006). The amount of physiological satisfaction depends on the amount of prolactin released. Orgasms have also been found to relieve chronic pain and increase pain thresholds in women (KOMISARUK & WHIPPLE, 1995).

Influences on Sexuality

There are many powerful influences on our sexuality. Here we discuss three of the biggest influences: hormones, ethnicity, and religion.

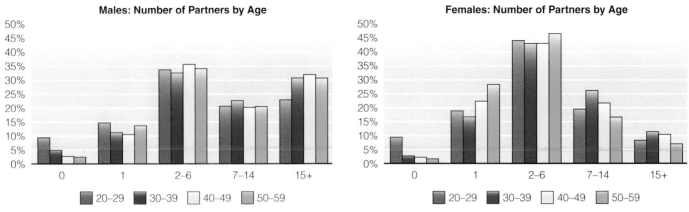

Figure **10.1** Number of sexual partners for men and women by age. Source: Centers for Disease Control (Fryar et al., 2007).

HORMONES AND NEUROTRANSMITTERS

Hormones and **neurotransmitters** both have powerful effects on our bodies. In most animals, the brain controls and regulates sexual behavior chiefly through hormones and neurotransmitters, and these both have an enormous effect on sexual behavior in humans as well (Krüger et al., 2006). We discussed hormones in Chapters 5 and 6 and reviewed the various endocrine glands that secrete hormones into the bloodstream, carrying them throughout the body. Sexologists believe that testosterone is the most influential hormone in the sexual behavior of both men and women. Estrogen also plays a role in regulating the sexual behavior of both sexes. Both men and women produce these hormones, although in differing quantities. For example, in men testosterone is produced in the testes and adrenal glands, and in women testosterone is produced in the adrenal glands and ovaries. Even so, men produce much more testosterone than women: men produce 260 to 1,000 nanograms per deciliter of blood plasma (a nanogram is one-billionth of a gram), whereas women produce around 15 to 70. The amount also varies and decreases with age.

Women's estrogen levels fall during menopause, which can lead to slower growth in the vaginal cells, resulting in thinner vaginal walls, vaginal dryness, and decreased vaginal sensitivity. Despite this decrease in estrogen, testosterone levels often remain constant, which may result in an increase in sexual desire even though the above physical changes can negatively affect sexual functioning.

Hormone replacement therapy (a combination of estrogen and progesterone), although controversial, may help reduce or alleviate some of these physical changes and increase sexual desire (see Chapter 5 for more information about hormone replacement therapy). In men, decreases in testosterone can lead to lessening sexual desire and decreases in the quality and quantity of erections. We discuss aging and sexuality more later in this chapter.

Neurotransmitters, chemical messengers in the body that transmit messages from one nerve cell to another, also have a powerful effect on our bodies. Various neurotransmitters, includ-

ing oxytocin, serotonin, dopamine, and vasopressin, have been found to affect sexual desire, arousal, orgasm, and our desire to couple with certain partners (Ishak et al., 2008; Kosfeld et al., 2005; Lim & Young, 2006; Walch et al., 2001; K. A. Young et al., 2008; L. J. Young & Wang, 2004). Directly following orgasm, levels of serotonin, oxytocin, and vasopressin increase, which can lead to feelings of pleasure, relaxation, and attachment (Fisher, 2004). Researchers have also explored using various neurotransmitters to

REALResearch **>** Compared with other ethnic and racial groups, Mexican Americans have the lowest number of sexual partners in their lifetime, and non-Hispanic Black men and women have the highest number of sex partners (Fryar et al., 2007; see Figures 10.1 and 10.2 for more information about sexual partners).

eliminate sexual urges and desires in sexual offenders (Saleh & Berlin, 2003).

Although hormones and neurotransmitters are important, our social experiences are as well. Unlike animals, humans are strongly influenced by learned experiences and their social, cultural, and ethnic environment.

ETHNICITY

Throughout this book we have explored the impact of ethnicity and race on personal sexual behaviors. We know that ethnicity and sexuality join together to form a barrier, a "sexualized perimeter," that helps us decide who we let in and who we keep out (Nagel, 2003). Ethnicity can also affect which sexual behaviors we engage in, the frequency of these behaviors, our sexual attitudes,

neurotransmitters
Specialized chemical messengers in the body that transmit messages from one nerve cell to another.

Asian American Sexuality

As Asian Americans become more acculturated to the mainstream American culture, their sexual attitudes and behaviors become more consistent with American norms.

In most Asian cultures, sexuality is linked to procreation. However, throughout the years, erotic sexuality has been portrayed in Asian paintings, sculptures, and books (e.g., the Kama Sutra). Japanese and Chinese erotica exists dating back to ancient times. What is noticeably absent is open discussion about sexuality. Sex education in the schools is minimal, and many Asian parents believe that talking about sex is unacceptable (Kulig, 1994). In 2008, I was able to travel to Tokyo to research Japanese sexuality. My research revealed that Japanese culture is very conservative about sexuality. Sex is not talked about openly, and many Japanese men and women are uncomfortable with open discussions about sexuality.

This conservatism is also found in Asian Americans. It is estimated that 4% of the U.S. population is Asian American (Okazaki, 2002), but because this group includes people from many countries, it is difficult to characterize the group as a whole. In 1990, the largest proportions of Asian Americans were (in descending order): Chinese, Filipino, Japanese, Korean, Asian Indian, and Vietnamese (Reeves & Bennett, 2003). Generally speaking, compared with other U.S. ethnic groups, Asian Americans have been found to:

- Be more sexually conservative
- Initiate sexual intercourse later
- Believe the family is of utmost importance
- Believe that sexuality is most appropriate within the context of marriage
- Link sexuality with procreation
- Be more reluctant to obtain sexual and reproductive care

However, beliefs and behaviors are changing. As Asian Americans become more acculturated to the mainstream American culture, their sexual attitudes and behaviors become more consistent with American norms (Okazaki, 2002).

and our ability to communicate about sex (Quadagno et al., 1998).

For example, Black men and women are more likely to have earlier sex and sex with more partners in their lifetimes than other racial and ethnic groups (see Figures 10.2a and 10.2b). Non-Hispanic Black men and women are more likely than Mexican Americans and non-Hispanic Whites to have engaged in sex before age 15 (Fryar et al., 2007). In addition, non-Hispanic Black men and women are more likely than other racial or ethnic groups to have more sexual partners in a lifetime (Eisenberg, 2001; Fryar et al., 2007). However, White and Hispanic women are more likely than African American women to engage in sexual acts besides sexual intercourse, and White women are more likely

to give or receive oral sex than are African American or Hispanic women (Laumann et al., 1994). Ethnicity also affects our sexual attitudes. For example, the sexual attitudes of Mexican American men and women and African American women are more conservative, whereas the attitudes of Whites are less traditional, and those of African American men are the least traditional of all (Mahay et al., 2001).

Finally, ethnicity has also been found to affect our communication patterns about sex. In Chapter 3, we discussed communication and cultural issues. In cultures that are based on male dominance in relationships, women are less likely to bring up the subject of sex or have knowledge about sexual topics. Hispanic women are expected to learn about sex from their husbands, and

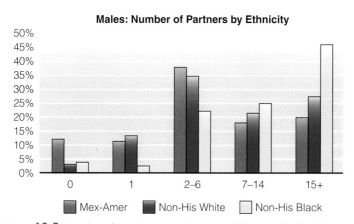

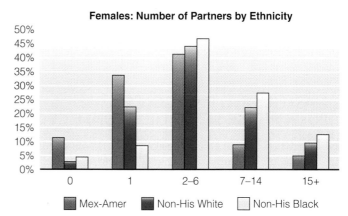

Figure **10.2** Number of sexual partners for men and women by ethnicity. Source: Centers for Disease Control (Fryar et al., 2007).

traditionally, a Hispanic woman who knows about sex is viewed as "sexually permissive" (Forrest et al., 1993). Our culture can also influence how sexually conservative or liberal we are. For example, Asian Americans have been found to be significantly more conservative than non–Asian Americans in their sexual behavior (Okazaki, 2002). We discuss Asian American sexual behavior more in Human Sexuality in a Diverse World, "Asian American Sexuality," and we continue to explore the impact of ethnicity, culture, and sexuality throughout this chapter.

RELIGION

We have already discussed how hormones and ethnicity affect our sexual behavior, but there are many other variables to consider. Our culture, religion, and social, economic, psychological, and biological factors all contribute to the way we behave sexually. As we grow, we learn strong messages about acceptable and unacceptable behaviors from the culture at large, our social classes, and even our language.

Religiosity and strength of religious beliefs also influence sexual behavior (Laumann et al., 1994; Murray et al., 2007; Murray-Swank et al., 2005). Generally, the more religious people are, the more conservative their sexual behavior tends to be. For example, studies on religion and sexuality have found that people with high levels of religiosity engage in less premarital sexual intercourse, are more likely to hold conservative attitudes about sex, are less likely to engage in risky sexual behavior, are less approving of oral sex, and experience more guilt about sexual behavior (Bridges & Moore, 2002; J. Davidson et al., 2004; Janus & Janus, 1993). In addition, religious men and women have fewer partners and are less likely to engage in risky sex (Murray et al., 2007). Finally, in a review of 40 studies, Murray-Swank et al. (2005) found a negative correlation between religiosity and premarital sex—as religiosity increases, premarital sexual activity decreases.

review questions

1 Identify the most influential hormones and neurotransmitters in sexual behavior and explain their roles in sexual behavior.

2 Explain how ethnicity and culture can affect sexual behavior.

3 Explain how religion may influence sexual behavior.

Studying
Sexual Response

There are a series of physiological and psychological changes that occur in the body during sexual behavior, referred to collectively as our **sexual response.** Over the years, several models of these changes have been proposed to explain the exact progression and nature of the human sexual response. These models are beneficial in helping physicians and therapists identify how dysfunction, disease, illness, and disability affect sexual functioning. The most well-known model has been Masters and Johnson's sexual response cycle. Many other sex therapists and sexologists have criticized and suggested changes to this model throughout the years. We review some of these criticisms later in the chapter.

MASTERS AND JOHNSON'S
FOUR-PHASE SEXUAL RESPONSE CYCLE

Based on their laboratory work (see Chapter 2), William Masters and Virginia Johnson proposed a four-phase model of physiological arousal known as the **sexual response cycle** (see Figure 10.3). This cycle occurs during all sexual behaviors in which a person progresses from excitement to orgasm, whether it is through oral or anal sex, masturbation, or vaginal intercourse. These physio-

logical processes are similar for all sexual relationships, whether they are between heterosexual or homosexual partners.

The four phases of the sexual response cycle are **excitement, plateau, orgasm,** and **resolution.** The two primary physical changes that occur during the sexual response cycle are **vasocongestion** (VAZ-oh-conn-jest-shun) and **myotonia** (my-uh-TONE-ee-uh), which we discuss in greater detail shortly.

sexual response
Series of physiological and psychological changes that occur in the body during sexual behavior.

sexual response cycle
Four-stage model of sexual arousal proposed by Masters and Johnson.

excitement
The first stage of the sexual response cycle, in which an erection occurs in males and vaginal lubrication occurs in females.

plateau
The second stage of the sexual response cycle, occurring before orgasm, in which vasocongestion builds up.

orgasm
The third stage of the sexual response cycle, which involves an intense sensation during the peak of sexual arousal and results in a release of sexual tension.

resolution
The fourth stage of the sexual response cycle, in which the body returns to the prearoused state.

vasocongestion
An increase in the blood concentrated in the male and female genitals, as well as in the female breasts, during sexual activity.

myotonia
Involuntary contractions of the muscles.

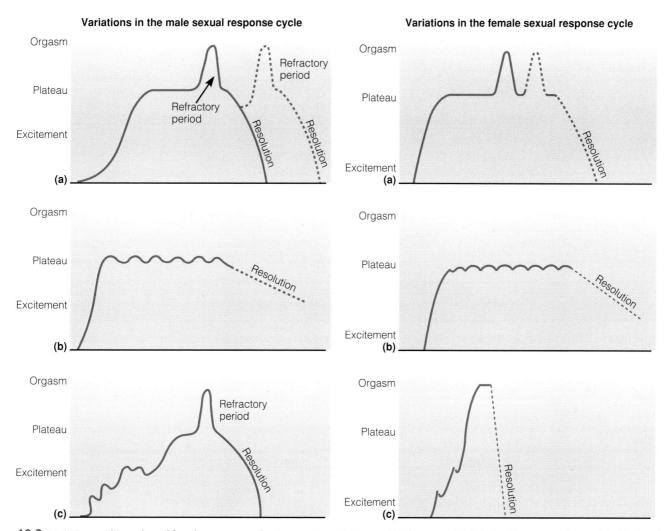

Variations in the male sexual response cycle

(a)

(b)

(c)

Variations in the female sexual response cycle

(a)

(b)

(c)

Figure **10.3** Variations within male and female response cycles. Source: From W. Masters, V. Johnson, and R. Kolodny, *Heterosexuality*, pp. 51–52. Copyright © 1994 by William H. Masters, Virginia E. Johnson, and Robert C. Kolodny. Reprinted by permission of HarperCollins Publishers, Inc.

The Sexual Response Cycle in Women

Sexual response patterns vary among women (and in the same woman depending on her menstrual cycle). These variations can be attributed to the amount of time spent in each phase. For example, more time spent during arousal in foreplay may result in a greater orgasmic response. The intensity of the response may also be affected by factors such as menstrual cycle and previous childbearing. However, even with these differences, the basic physical response is always the same.

EXCITEMENT PHASE The first phase, excitement, begins with vasocongestion, an increase in the blood concentrated in the genitals, breasts, or both. Vasocongestion is the principal physical component of sexual arousal (Frohlich & Meston, 2000). Many circumstances can induce excitement, including hearing your partner's voice, seeing an erotic picture, having a fantasy, or being touched a certain way. Within 30 seconds, vasocongestion causes the vaginal walls to begin lubricating, a process called **transudation** (trans-SUE-day-shun). If a woman is lying down (which is common during foreplay), the process of lubricating the vaginal walls may take a little longer than if she is standing up. This may help explain why it takes most women longer than men to get

ready to have sexual intercourse. During the excitement phase, the walls of the vagina, which usually lie flat together, expand. This has also been called the **tenting effect** (see Figure 10.4).

The breasts also experience changes during this phase. Nipple erections may occur in one or both breasts, and the areolas enlarge (see Figure 10.5). The breasts enlarge, which may cause an increased definition of the veins in the breasts, especially if a woman has large breasts and is fair skinned.

During sexual arousal in women who have not had children, the labia majora (see Chapter 5) thin out and become flattened, and may pull slightly away from the **introitus.** The labia minora often turn bright pink and begin to increase in size. The increase

transudation
The lubrication of the vagina during sexual arousal.

tenting effect
During sexual arousal in females, the cervix and uterus pull up, and the upper third of the vagina balloons open, making a larger opening in the cervix.

introitus
Entrance to the vagina.

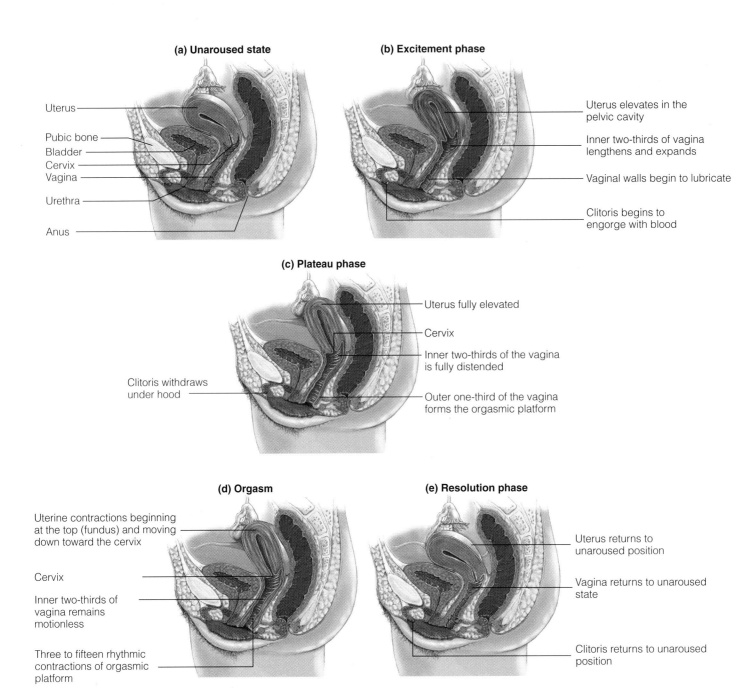

(a) Unaroused state

Uterus
Pubic bone
Bladder
Cervix
Vagina
Urethra
Anus

(b) Excitement phase

Uterus elevates in the pelvic cavity

Inner two-thirds of vagina lengthens and expands

Vaginal walls begin to lubricate

Clitoris begins to engorge with blood

(c) Plateau phase

Clitoris withdraws under hood

Uterus fully elevated

Cervix

Inner two-thirds of the vagina is fully distended

Outer one-third of the vagina forms the orgasmic platform

(d) Orgasm

Uterine contractions beginning at the top (fundus) and moving down toward the cervix

Cervix

Inner two-thirds of vagina remains motionless

Three to fifteen rhythmic contractions of orgasmic platform

(e) Resolution phase

Uterus returns to unaroused position

Vagina returns to unaroused state

Clitoris returns to unaroused position

Figure **10.4** Internal changes in the female sexual response cycle. Source: From W. Masters, V. Johnson, and R. Kolodny, *Heterosexuality,* p. 58. Copyright © 1994 by William H. Masters, Virginia E. Johnson, and Robert C. Kolodny. Reprinted by permission of HarperCollins Publishers, Inc.

in size of the vaginal lips adds an average of .5 to 1 inch of length to the vaginal canal.

Because of the increased vascularity (blood flow) to the genitals during pregnancy and childbirth, women who have had children have a more rapid increase in vasocongestion and enlargement of both the labia majora and minora, which may become two to three times larger by the end of the excitement phase. Vasocongestion may also cause the clitoral glans to become erect, depending on the type and intensity of stimulation. Generally, the more direct the stimulation, the more engorged the entire clitoral organ will become. Sexual arousal may also be facilitated by the neurotransmitter serotonin, which we discussed earlier in this chapter (Frohlich & Meston, 2000).

The excitement phase can last anywhere from a few minutes to hours. Toward the end of the excitement phase, a woman may

experience a **sex flush,** which resembles a rash. This usually begins on the chest and, during the plateau stage, spreads from the breasts to the neck and face, shoulders, arms, abdomen, thighs, buttocks, and back. Women report varied sensations during the excitement phase, which are often felt all over the body, rather than being concentrated in one area.

PLATEAU PHASE Breast size continues to increase during the plateau phase, and the nipples may remain erect. The clitoral glans retracts behind the clitoral hood anywhere from 1 to 3 min-

sex flush
A temporary reddish color change of the skin that sometimes develops during sexual excitement.

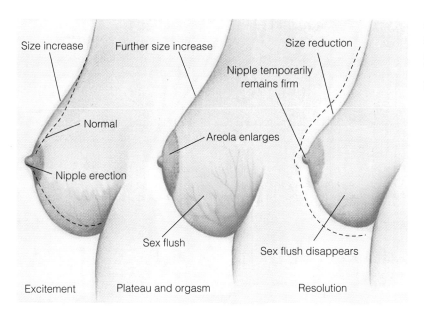

Size increase   Further size increase   Size reduction

Nipple temporarily
remains firm

Normal

Areola enlarges

Nipple erection

Sex flush

Sex flush disappears

Excitement   Plateau and orgasm   Resolution

Figure **10.5** Breast changes in the female sexual response cycle. Source: From W. Masters, V. Johnson, and R. Kolodny, *Heterosexuality*, p. 59. Copyright © 1994 by William H. Masters, Virginia E. Johnson, and Robert C. Kolodny. Reprinted by permission of HarperCollins Publishers, Inc.

utes before orgasm, and, just before orgasm, the clitoris may not be visible at all. Masters and Johnson claim that it is the clitoral hood rubbing and pulling over the clitoris that is responsible for the orgasm during sexual intercourse.

REALResearch > Although orgasms experienced during masturbation are more physiologically intense than orgasms during partner sex, orgasms during masturbation provide less overall sexual satisfaction than orgasms experienced during partner sex (LEVIN, 2007; MAH & BINIK, 2005).

During sexual arousal in women who have not had children, the labia majora are difficult to detect, due to the flattened-out appearance. The labia minora, on the other hand, often turn a brilliant red. In women who have had children, the labia majora become very engorged with blood and turn a darker red, almost burgundy. At this point, if sexual stimulation were to stop, the swelling of the clitoris and labia, which can continue for anywhere from a few minutes to hours, can be very uncomfortable. Orgasm helps to relieve this pressure, whether through masturbation or sexual activity with another person. Overall, the plateau stage may last anywhere from 30 seconds to 3 minutes.

ORGASM PHASE At the end of the plateau phase, vasocongestion in the pelvis creates an **orgasmic platform** in the lower third of the vagina, labia minora (and labia majora in women who have had children), and the uterus (see Figure 10.4). When this pressure reaches a certain point, a reflex in the surrounding muscles is set off, causing vigorous contractions. These contractions expel the blood that is trapped in the surrounding tissues and, in doing so, cause pleasurable orgasmic sensations. Myotonia of the uterine muscles is primarily responsible for these contractions; without these muscles (as in the case of a woman who has had a hysterectomy,

the surgical removal of the uterus), the orgasmic response is significantly reduced.

Muscular contractions occur about every 0.8 seconds during orgasm. In total, there are about 8 to 15 contractions, and the first 5 or 6 are felt most strongly. In women, contractions last longer than in men. A possible explanation for this is that vasocongestion occurs in the entire pelvic region in women (the internal clitoral organ fills the pelvic region), whereas it is very localized in men (mainly in the penis and testicles). Because of this, women need more muscle contractions to remove the built-up blood supply. In Chapter 2, we discussed Freud's two types of orgasms, the clitoral and the vaginal. Today we know that all orgasms in women are thought to be the result of direct or indirect clitoral stimulation, even though orgasms might feel different at different times.

During orgasm, there is a release of vasocongestion and muscle tension. The body may shudder, jerk uncontrollably, or spasm. In addition, orgasms may involve facial grimacing, groans,

---

REALResearch > Male ejaculation has been found to have physiological benefits for both men and women. In men, regular ejaculations help keep sperm morphology (form and structure) and semen volume within normal ranges, and the deposit of sperm in the vaginal canal has been found to regulate ovulatory cycles, enhance mood, and reduce vaginal atrophy (a decrease in tissue firmness) in aging women (LEVIN, 2007).

---

spasms in the hands and feet, contractions of the gluteal and abdominal muscles, and contractions of the orgasmic platform. Peaks in blood pressure and respiration patterns have been found

orgasmic platform
The thickening of the walls of the lower third of the vagina.

during both male and female orgasms. Interestingly, one study that compared couples with high and low orgasmic frequency found that the mortality risk of those who experience more orgasms was 50% lower than the group who experienced fewer orgasms (G. D. Smith et al., 1997). In addition, frequent sexual arousal and orgasm have been found to enhance the functioning of the immune system (Haake, 2004).

RESOLUTION PHASE During the last phase of the sexual response cycle, resolution, the body returns to pre-excitement conditions. The extra blood leaves the genitals, erections disappear, muscles relax, and heart and breathing rates return to normal.

During resolution, women are able to be restimulated to orgasm (and some women can experience multiple orgasms). Kinsey reported that 14% of women regularly experienced **multiple orgasms,** and although Masters and Johnson believed all women were capable of such orgasms, the majority of women they studied did not experience them. If they did, multiple orgasms were more likely to occur from manual stimulation of the clitoral glans, rather than from penile thrusting during sexual intercourse. There has also been some research into the female **G-spot** that indicates that some women may have an area inside the vagina that, when stimulated, causes intense orgasms and possibly female ejaculation of fluid (see Chapter 5).

After orgasm, the skin is often sweaty, and the sex flush slowly disappears. The breasts begin to decrease in size, usually within 5 to 10 minutes. Many women appear to have nipple erections after an orgasm because the breast as a whole quickly decreases in size while the areola are still engorged. The clitoris returns to its original size but remains extremely sensitive for several minutes. Many women do not like the clitoris to be touched during this time because of the increased sensitivity.

Earlier we mentioned that a woman's menstrual cycle may influence her sexual responsiveness. Research has found that sexual excitement occurs more frequently during the last 14 days of a woman's menstrual cycle (Sherfey, 1972). During this time, more lubrication is produced during the excitement phase, which may be due to the increased vasocongestion. As we discussed in Chapter 5, orgasms can be very helpful in reducing cramps during menstruation, presumably because they help to relieve **pelvic congestion** and vasocongestion (Ellison, 2000).

The Sexual Response Cycle in Men

The sexual response cycle in males is similar to that of females, with vasocongestion and myotonia leading to physiological changes in the body (see Figure 10.6). However, in men the four phases are less well defined. During the excitement phase, the penis, like the clitoris in women, begins to fill with blood and become erect. Erection begins quickly during excitement, generally within 3 to 5 seconds (although the speed of this response lengthens with age).

EXCITEMENT PHASE The excitement phase of the sexual response cycle in men is often very short, unless a man uses deliberate attempts to lengthen it. Often this causes a gradual loss of **tumescence** (too-MESS-cents; the swelling of the penis due to vasocongestion), which is referred to as **detumescence** (dee-too-MESS-cents). Distractions during the excitement phase (such as a roommate walking into the room) may also cause detumescence. However, once the plateau stage is reached, an erection is often more stable and less sensitive to outside influences. Women may need more time than men to reach the plateau phase, because they have a larger and more vascular pelvic area, requiring more intense pelvic congestion.

During the excitement phase, the testicles also increase in size, becoming up to 50% larger. This is both a vasocongestive and myotonic response. The cremaster muscle pull the testicles closer to the body to avoid injury during thrusting (see Chapter 6 for more information about this muscle). If sexual stimulation were to stop at this point, the swelling in the testicles may be uncomfortable.

PLATEAU PHASE All of these physical changes continue during the plateau phase. Some men may experience a sex flush, which is identical to the sex flush women experience. In addition, it is not uncommon for men to have nipple erections. Just before orgasm, the glans penis becomes engorged (this is comparable to the engorgement of the clitoral glans in women). At this point, a few drops of pre-ejaculatory fluid may appear on the glans of the penis (see Chapter 6 for more information about pre-ejaculatory fluid).

ORGASM PHASE Orgasm and ejaculation do not always occur together (see Figure 10.6). In fact, there are men who are able to have orgasms without ejaculating and can have several orgasms before ejaculating. Although it is rare, some men are capable of anywhere from 2 to 16 orgasms before ejaculation, although the ability to have them decreases with age (Chia & Abrams, 1997; J. Johnson, 2001).

If orgasm and ejaculation occur at the same time, ejaculation can occur in two stages. During the first stage, which lasts only a

multiple orgasms
More than one orgasm experienced within a short period of time.

G-spot
Grafenberg spot. A controversial structure that is said to lie on the anterior (front) wall of the vagina and is reputed to be a seat of sexual pleasure when stimulated.

pelvic congestion
Pelvic congestion occurs when blood pools in the veins in the uterus, ovaries, and vulva, causing cramping and general discomfort. Typically this pain is lessened after orgasmic release.

tumescence
The swelling of the penis due to vasocongestion, causing an erection.

detumescence
The return of an erect penis to the flaccid state.

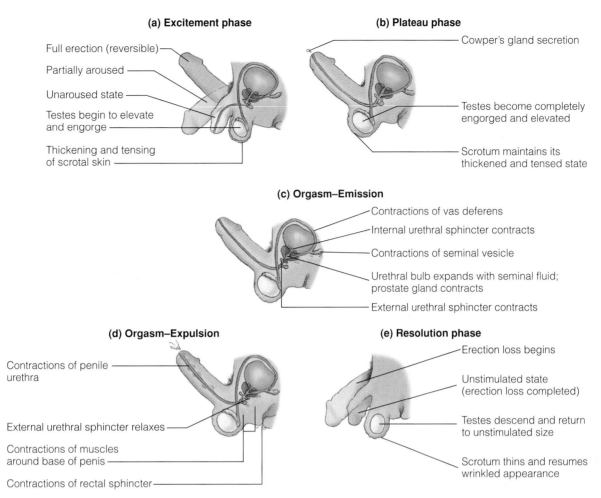

(a) Excitement phase

Full erection (reversible)
Partially aroused
Unaroused state
Testes begin to elevate and engorge
Thickening and tensing of scrotal skin

(b) Plateau phase

Cowper's gland secretion
Testes become completely engorged and elevated
Scrotum maintains its thickened and tensed state

(c) Orgasm–Emission

Contractions of vas deferens
Internal urethral sphincter contracts
Contractions of seminal vesicle
Urethral bulb expands with seminal fluid; prostate gland contracts
External urethral sphincter contracts

(d) Orgasm–Expulsion

Contractions of penile urethra
External urethral sphincter relaxes
Contractions of muscles around base of penis
Contractions of rectal sphincter

(e) Resolution phase

Erection loss begins
Unstimulated state (erection loss completed)
Testes descend and return to unstimulated size
Scrotum thins and resumes wrinkled appearance

Figure **10.6** External and internal changes in the male sexual response cycle. Source: From W. Masters, V. Johnson, and R. Kolodny, *Heterosexuality,* p. 60. Copyright © 1994 by William H. Masters, Virginia E. Johnson, and Robert C. Kolodny. Reprinted by permission of HarperCollins Publishers, Inc.

few seconds, there are contractions in the vas deferens, seminal vesicles, and prostate gland. These contractions lead to **ejaculatory inevitability,** whereby just before orgasm there is a feeling that ejaculation can no longer be controlled. Next, the semen is forced out of the urethra by muscle contractions (the same set of muscles that contract in female orgasm).

The first three or four contractions are the most pleasurable and tend to be the most forceful (various herbal and drug products have recently appeared on the market claiming to increase male orgasmic contractions; see Sex in Real Life, "Sexual Performance Scams"). The force of the ejaculation can propel semen up to 24 inches; this distance is generally longer in younger men (Welch, 1992). After these major contractions, minor ones usually follow, even if stimulation stops. As with women, the muscular contractions during orgasm occur about every 0.8 seconds.

Some men are able to experience multiple orgasms, whereby the orgasm phase leads directly into another orgasm without a refractory period. Research has found that some men are able to teach themselves how to have multiple orgasms (Chia & Abrams, 1997; J. Johnson, 2001). The Chinese were the first to learn how to achieve multiple orgasm by delaying and withholding ejaculation. Some men learn to separate orgasm and ejaculation, thereby allowing themselves to learn to become multiorgasmic. The average number of orgasms a multiorgasmic man can have varies between two and nine orgasms per sexual interaction (Chia & Abrams, 1997; Dunn & Trost, 1989).

RESOLUTION PHASE Directly following ejaculation, the glans of the penis decreases in size, even before general penile detumescence. During the resolution phase of sexual response, when the body is returning to its prearousal state, men go into a **refractory stage,** during which they cannot be restimulated to orgasm for a certain time period. The refractory period gets longer as men get older (we discuss this more later in this chapter).

WHAT DO YOU WANT TO KNOW ?

Does the condition "blue balls" really exist?
The concept of blue balls refers to a pain in the testicles that is experienced by men if sexual arousal is maintained for a significant period but is not followed by an orgasm. It is true that the pressure felt in the genitals, which is caused by vasocongestion, can be uncomfortable (Chalett & Nerenberg, 2000). This discomfort can be relieved through masturbation. Women also experience a similar condition if they are sexually aroused and do not reach orgasm (some of my students refer to such pain as "pink ovaries"). There can be pressure, pain, or a bloating feeling in the pelvic region, which can also be relieved through masturbation.

ejaculatory inevitability
A feeling that ejaculation can no longer be controlled.

refractory stage
The period of time after an ejaculation in which men cannot be stimulated to further orgasm.

SEX IN REAL LIFE

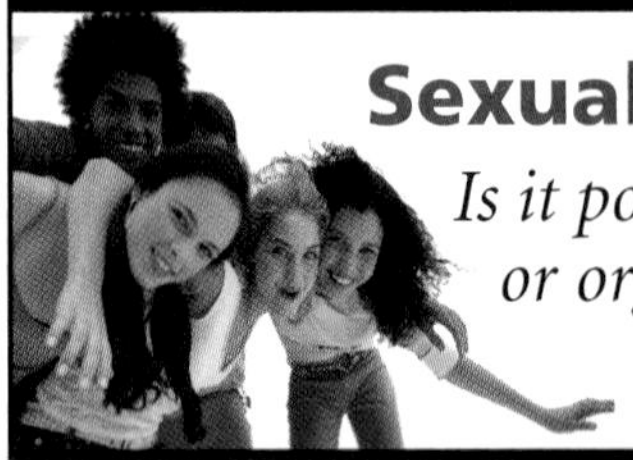

Sexual Performance Scams

Is it possible to take an over-the-counter drug to improve your sex drive, erections, or orgasms?

Is it possible to take an over-the-counter drug to improve your sex drive, erections, or orgasms? Will $59.95 buy you a 1-month supply of awesome orgasms? How much would you pay to find out? Although we discuss the use of aphrodisiacs in Chapter 14, here we consider those advertisements that clog our email accounts and appear in many magazines, promoting better sex.

Over the years, I've had many male students ask me about a drug called Mioplex. This "male orgasm intensifier" has intrigued many college students, a group the company tends to target. Produced in Europe, Mioplex claims that it can increase a man's "ropes," or number of physical ejaculatory contractions during orgasm. It also claims that increasing a man's ejaculatory contractions will help female partners to have better and longer orgasms. Mioplex is a flower seed extract, which has been unavailable in the United States but can be ordered online.

These vitamins or health food supplements are considered "food" items and not drugs—as such, they don't have to be approved by the Food and Drug Administration. There is no guarantee that they work, and they may have side effects. The bottom line on products like this is that many do not work. But an interesting question remains: Why would so many people be so willing to pay for such products?

Younger men, on the other hand, may experience another erection soon after an ejaculation.

Masters and Johnson's model of sexual response is the most comprehensive model sexologists use. It has not been without controversy, however. Many feminist therapists believe that Masters and Johnson's sexual response cycle should not be used universally for classification and diagnosis of sexual dysfunctions (we will discuss this more in a moment). What has happened is that the definition of healthy sexuality has been focused on orgasm and has given less importance to emotions and relationships (Tiefer, 2001). Other researchers would say that the model of sexuality that values performance, penetration, and orgasm is a male model of sexuality (Burch, 1998). Often this belief leads to a view of female sexuality that is passive and even nonexistent.

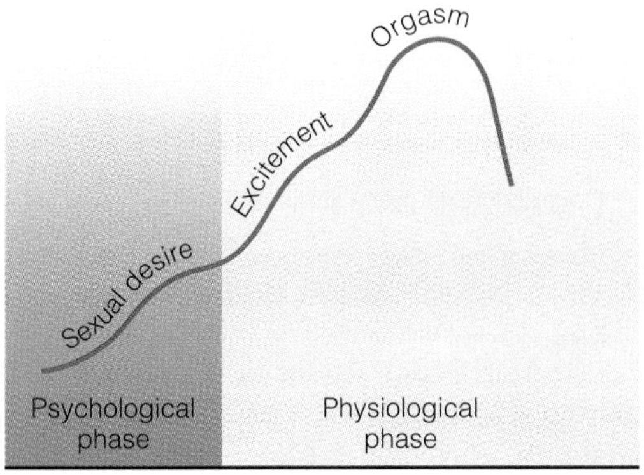

Figure **10.7** Helen Singer Kaplan's three-stage model of sexual response includes the psychological phase of sexual desire and two physiological stages of excitement and orgasm.

OTHER MODELS OF SEXUAL RESPONSE

There have been several other, less comprehensive, models proposed, such as noted sexologist Helen Singer Kaplan's **triphasic model** (Kaplan, 1979), David Reed's Erotic Stimulus Pathway (ESP), and Rosemary Basson's model. Kaplan believed sexual response was not purely physical and also includes sexual desire, excitement, and orgasm (see Figure 10.7). Sexual desire is a psychological component, whereas excitement and orgasm involve physiological processes, including genital vasocongestion and muscular contractions during orgasm. Originally Kaplan's model included only excitement and orgasm, but she later added the desire component in response to the numbers of people who came to therapy with sexual desire problems. Sexual desire was of paramount importance to Kaplan because, without sexual desire, the other two physiological functions would not occur.

Many factors can block sexual desire, such as depression, pain, fear, medications, or past sexual abuse. We discuss the importance of the desire phase and disorders associated with it in Chapter 14. An advantage to Kaplan's model is that the triphasic model is easier to conceptualize than Masters and Johnson's model. For example, most of us can recognize and differentiate desire, excitement, and orgasm but may have a difficult time recognizing when we are in Masters and Johnson's plateau phase.

However, Beverly Whipple, who researched and reported on the G-spot in women (1982), criticized the Kaplan model for being based on the male linear model of sexual function (Sugrue & Whipple, 2001). She contends that women can experience sexual arousal, orgasm, and satisfaction without sexual desire, and they can experience desire, arousal, and satisfaction without orgasm.

David Reed's (1998) ESP model blends features of Masters and Johnson's and Kaplan's models and uses four phases, includ-

triphasic model
A model of sexual response, proposed by Helen Singer Kaplan, which includes three phases.

ing seduction, sensation, surrender, and reflection (see Figure 10.8). Seduction includes all those things that we might do to entice someone to have sex with us—what we wear, perfume or cologne, flowers, and so on. In the next stage of sensation, our senses take over. What we hear, smell, taste, touch, and fantasize about all have the potential to turn us on and enhance our excitement. This, in turn, moves us into the plateau phase. Both the seduction and sensation phase are psychosocial, and they contribute to our physiological response.

In the third phase, surrender—orgasm—occurs. Reed believes that we need to be able to let go and let ourselves reach orgasm. Too much control or not enough may interfere with this response. The final phase of Reed's model is the reflection phase, in which we reflect on the sexual experience. Whether the experience was positive or negative will affect future sexual functioning.

Beverly Whipple expanded Reed's ESP to demonstrate that if the sexual experience was pleasant and produced satisfaction,

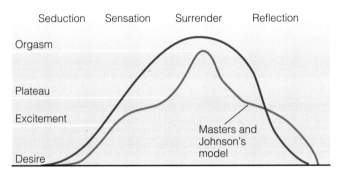

Figure **10.8** David Reeds's Erotic Stimulus Pathway (ESP) model blends features of Masters and Johnson's and Kaplan's models using four phases: seduction, sensation, surrender, and reflection.

then it could lead to the seduction phase of the *next* sexual experience (Whipple & Brash-McGreer, 1997).

Finally, Rosemary Basson (2000) proposed an alternative model of female sexual response. She has developed a sexual response model that attempts to depict a blending of mind and body. In Basson's model, the decision to have sex is driven by the desire for intimacy, not physical lust. Receptiveness to sex leads to sexual activity, which in turn leads to arousal and then desire (Basson, 2000). Basson's model contrasted with Masters and Johnson's focus on predominately physical events in the sexual response cycle.

One of the chief critics of the Masters and Johnson sexual response cycle model is Leonore Tiefer, a noted feminist sexologist who has practiced as a sex therapist for many years in a hospital-based urology department, working with couples in whom the male partner presents with a sexual problem. Tiefer suggests that because both Masters and Johnson's and Kaplan's models are based on the medical model, they leave out important aspects of sexual functioning (Tiefer, 2001). The medical model of sexual functioning focuses exclusively on adequate genital functioning—vasocongestion, myotonia, physical excitement, and orgasm. As Tiefer characterizes the perspective of the medical model, "if it's wet and hard and works, it's normal; if it's not, it's not" (Tiefer, 2001).

Tiefer believes that there are many important aspects of sexual functioning that are left out of these models, including pleasure, emotionality, sensuality, cultural differences, power issues, and communication. Women's sexual experiences do not fit neatly into Masters and Johnson's four stages, according to Tiefer, and as a result women complain of desire and arousal issues and other difficulties in emotionality, sensitivity, or connectedness (Tiefer, 2001). Her work has begun a much-needed dialogue about the importance of gender and sexual functioning.

review questions

1 Identify and describe the four stages of Masters and Johnson's female sexual response cycle and explain what happens in women.

2 Identify and describe the four stages of Masters and Johnson's male sexual response cycle, noting any differences between the male and female cycles.

3 Compare and contrast the various models of sexual response that have been proposed.

Solitary
Sexual Behavior

Adult sexual behavior includes a range of sexual activities. There are some adults who choose not to engage in sexual behavior, whereas others may choose to experiment with sexual partners and behaviors. **Celibacy,** or abstinence, occurs when a person chooses not to engage in sexual intercourse. One 18-year-old man said:

I just don't take my virginity lightly. I want to be sure that the time is right and my partner is right before I decide to have sex. I want to feel completely comfortable and in love with someone before sex enters into the picture. It's that important to me. (Author's files)

celibacy
The state of remaining unmarried; often used today to refer to abstaining from sex.

People may choose abstinence for many reasons (e.g., religious values, fear of physical consequences, past negative experiences, or wanting to "save" themselves for the right person; Rasberry, 2007). For some, the decision to become abstinent comes after a sexual relationship, often referred to as "secondary abstinence." One large-scale college campus study found a 12.5% prevalence rate of secondary abstinence (Raspberry, 2007). Some college students who have had negative experiences in past intimate relationships decide to become abstinent and spend time working on their relationships without sex (L. Elliot & Brantley, 1997; Raspberry, 2007). Some people remain abstinent (or asexual; see Chapter 9) their whole lives and have no sexual partners, whereas others may go through life with just one partner, and still others have multiple partners. Overall, asexual men and women report significantly less desire for sex with a partner and lower sexual arousability (Prause & Graham, 2007).

Sexual fantasies play a role in many people's lives, and may or may not be shared with a partner.

SEXUAL FANTASY:
ENHANCEMENT OR UNFAITHFULNESS?

Sexual fantasy is one of the most common forms of sexual expression in existence (Hicks & Leitenberg, 2001; Frostino, 2007). Whereas Sigmund Freud believed that only sexually unsatisfied people fantasized about sex, today many researchers believe that not only are sexual fantasies normal and healthy, but they may be a driving force behind human sexuality. Liberal attitudes and more sexual experience have been found to be associated with longer and more explicit sexual fantasies (Person et al., 1992; Kahr, 2008). Conversely, those who do not have sexual fantasies have been found to experience a greater likelihood of sexual dissatisfaction and sexual dysfunction (Cado & Leitenberg, 1990). The sexual fantasies of homosexuals and heterosexuals have also been found to be more similar than different, except for the sex of the fantasized partner (Leitenberg & Henning, 1995).

Both men and women may use sexual fantasies both during sexual behavior and at other times, although men tend to have these fantasies more often (Kahr, 2008; Leitenberg & Henning, 1995). Men have also been found to have more **sexual cognitions,** or thoughts about sex, than women (Renaud & Byers, 1999). Studies have found that 54% of men and 19% of women think about sex at least once a day (Laumann et al., 1994).

Overall, research on men's and women's sexual fantasies has shown the fantasies are becoming more similar (Block, 1999;

fantasies can arouse them over and over again, and sexual fantasies are used for a variety of reasons. They can help enhance masturbation, increase sexual arousal, help a person reach orgasm, and allow a person to explore various sexual activities that he or she might find taboo or too threatening to actually engage in.

Women's Sexual Fantasies

Many women report using sexual fantasy on a regular basis, and they use it to increase their arousal, self-esteem, and sexual interest, or to relieve stress (Maltz & Boss, 2001; Shulman & Horne, 2006). Overall, women's sexual fantasies tend to be more romantic and emotional than men's and include more touching, feeling, partner response, and ambiance (Zurbriggen & Yost, 2004). The five most common sexual fantasies for women include sex with current partner, reliving a past sexual experience, engaging in different sexual positions, having sex in rooms other than the bedroom, and sex on a carpeted floor (Maltz & Boss, 2001). Female sexual fantasies tend to be more romantic than male fantasies, as illustrated by this 21-year-old woman's fantasy:

> My ultimate fantasy would be with a tall, strong man. We would spend a whole day together—going to a beach on a motorcycle, riding horses in the sand, and making love on the beach. Then we'd ride the motorcycle back to town, get dressed up and go out to dinner. After dinner we'd come home and make love by the fire. Or we could make love in a big field of tall grass while it is raining softly. (Author's files)

Lesbian and bisexual women also use sexual fantasy. Research has found that relationship quality affects the content of sexual fantasy (J. D. Robinson & Parks, 2003). One 20-year-old lesbian shares her favorite sexual fantasy:

> She has black hair and I stop the car and motion her to get in. She walks quickly, with a slight attitude. She gets in with silence— her hands and eyes speak for her. I take her home, and she pulls me in. I undress her,

REALResearch > Significant gender differences have been found in sexual beliefs. Men are more likely to believe that oral sex is not sex, cybersex is not cheating, and that sex frequency decreases in marriage, whereas women are more likely to believe that oral sex is sex, cybersex is cheating, and that sex frequency in marriage stays high (KNOX ET AL., 2008).

Shulman & Horne, 2006). In fact, women have been reporting more graphic and sexually aggressive fantasies than they have reported in the past (Shulman & Horne, 2006). Overall, however, most men and women have a select few fantasies that are their favorites. These

sexual cognition
Thoughts about sex.

and she is ready for me. Down on the bed she goes, and down on her I go. With legs spread, her clitoris is swollen and erect, hungry for my touch. I give her what she wants. She moans as orgasm courses through her body. (Author's files)

Sexual fantasies are commonly used by older women as well. In fact, using fantasies later in life may help women experience arousal and orgasm (Maltz & Boss, 2001). Studies have shown that age is unrelated to what types of sexual fantasies a person has (Block, 1999). One 50-year-old woman reveals her fantasies at this point in her life:

One big change in my imaginary sex life since I was a young woman: I no longer have those fluffy romantic fantasies where most of the story is about pursuit and the sex at the end is NG, no genitals, in view. Now I picture the genitals, mine and his, and I watch them connect in full juicy color. I see a big penis, always a big penis, and every detail, including the little drops of pre-ejaculate like dew on the head. (Block, 1999, p. 100)

Fantasies about forced sex are common in women (Zurbriggen & Yost, 2004). In one study, more than 50% of participants reported using force fantasies at some point during sex (Strassberg & Lockerd, 1998). Force fantasies are also found in lesbian couples (J. D. Robinson, 2001). Why would a woman incorporate force into her sexual fantasies? Researchers claim it is a way to reduce the guilt women feel for having sexual desires, a way for women to show their "openness" to a variety of sexual experiences, or a result of past sexual abuse (Barner, 2003; Strassberg & Lockerd, 1998).

Women who incorporate force in their sexual fantasies have been found to be less sexually guilty and open to more variety of sexual experiences than those who do not (Shulman & Horne, 2006). There has also been a connection found between force in sexual fantasies and childhood sexual abuse (Shulman & Horne, 2006). It's important to keep in mind that fantasizing about certain sexual behaviors doesn't necessarily mean a person wants to engage in them. In a fantasy, the woman is in control. In her fantasy, she is able to transform something fearful into something pleasurable (Maltz & Boss, 2001).

Men's Sexual Fantasies

Men's sexual fantasies tend to be more active and aggressive than women's (Zurbriggen & Yost, 2004). They are often more frequent and impersonal, dominated by visual images. These fantasies move quickly to explicit sexual acts and often focus on the imagined partner as a sex object. They generally include visualizing body parts, specific sexual acts, group sex, a great deal of partner variety, and less romance.

Compared with women, men's sexual fantasies more often include someone other than their current partner (Hicks & Leitenberg, 2001). The five most common sexual fantasies for men include engaging in different sexual positions; having an aggressive partner; getting oral sex; having sex with a new partner; and having sex on the beach (Maltz & Boss, 2001). Here is a sexual fantasy from a 20-year-old male:

My sexual fantasy is to be stranded on an island with beautiful women from different countries (all of them horny, of course).

I'm the only male. I would make all of them have multiple orgasms, and I would like to have an everlasting erection so I could please them all nonstop. (Author's files)

Sexual fantasy is used by heterosexual, homosexual, and bisexual men. For gay and bisexual men, common sexual fantasies were receiving oral sex from another man, being manually stimulated by another man, engaging in anal intercourse, and kissing another man's lips (Kahr, 2008). When asked about his favorite sexual fantasy, one 21-year-old gay man reports:

My favorite sexual fantasy consists of a purely coincidental meeting between myself and an old friend from high school, Jason. We would eventually end up at my house and talk for hours about what each of us had been up to for the last few years. Eventually, the conversation would become one of his talking about trouble with a girlfriend or something of that nature. Jason tells me that he was always aware that I was gay and that he had been thinking about that a lot lately. He tells me that he has always wondered what it would be like to have sex with another man. I offer to have sex with him. He agrees and we engage in passionate, loving sex. (Author's files)

Are there gender differences in sexual fantasy? On the surface, it appears so. But we have to be careful in interpreting these findings. It could be that men have an easier time discussing their sexual fantasies than women.

MASTURBATION: A VERY INDIVIDUAL CHOICE

For a period in the 19th and early 20th centuries in the United States and Europe, there was a fear that masturbation caused terrible things to happen, such as insanity, death, or even sterility. Parents would go to extremes to protect their children from the sins of masturbation. In fact, aluminum gloves were sold to parents for the purpose of covering children's hands at bedtime so that children wouldn't be able to masturbate (Laqueur, 2003; Stengers & Van Neck, 2001).

Many of these beliefs have persisted, even to the present day. However, today masturbation is beginning to be viewed as one way to promote sexual health and well-being (E. Coleman, 2002; K. Wood, 2005). In fact, one study found that men who ejaculated more than five times per week during their 20s, 30s, and 40s were less likely to develop prostate cancer later in life (Giles et al., 2003). Researchers suggest that this is because frequent ejaculation prevented buildup of semen in the ducts, where it may be carcinogenic (of course, these ejaculations could be a result of frequent sexual activity, masturbation, or both).

Masturbation fulfills a variety of needs for people at different ages, and it can decrease sexual tension and anxiety and provide an outlet for sexual fantasy. It allows people the opportunity to experiment with their bodies to see what feels good and where they like to be touched. It can provide information on what kind of pressure and manipulation give a person the greatest pleasure and orgasmic response. In addition, masturbation can be exciting for couples to use during sexual activity. They may masturbate themselves or each other, either simultaneously or one at a time. **Mutual masturbation** can be very pleasurable, although it may make reaching orgasm difficult because it can be challenging to concentrate both on feeling aroused and pleasuring your partner.

For the majority of American boys, their first ejaculation results from masturbation, and it is often the main sexual outlet during adolescence (see Chapter 8). Janus and Janus (1993) found that 53% of men and 25% of women masturbated for the first time between the ages of 11 to 13. Choosing to masturbate is an entirely personal decision. For some people, masturbation may be unacceptable for personal or religious reasons.

Figure **10.9**

Female masturbation.

mutual masturbation
Simultaneous masturbation of sexual partners by each other.

SEX IN REAL LIFE

Sexual Expression on Spring Break

Research has shown that students on spring break have more permissive attitudes about casual sex than they do when they are in school.

Over the years, there has been a great deal of research on the sexual behavior of college students. As we discussed in Chapter 2, many of the published studies use college students as participants in their research. What we don't know much about, however, is college students' sexual behaviors in specific contexts, such as spring break. Colleges and universities provide students with a 1-week spring-break vacation, usually sometime in March. It is estimated that 1 million U.S. students participate in some form of spring-break vacation (Maticka-Tyndale et al., 1998).

As of 2004, the most popular spring-break locations were Miami Beach, Orlando, Las Vegas, Cancun, San Diego, Daytona, Honolulu, and Phoenix (Rosenberg, 2004). These vacations often consist of several friends traveling together and sharing rooms, with unlimited partying, high alcohol consumption, and many sexually oriented contests (such as wet T-shirt contests). Overall, vacations have been found to be times that people break from typical routines—they might try new things and adopt a more laissez-faire attitude (Eiser & Ford, 1995).

Research has shown that students on spring break have more permissive attitudes about casual sex than they do when they are in school (Maticka-Tyndale et al., 1998). In addition, students who drink alcohol are 7 times more likely to have sexual intercourse than those who don't drink (Center on Addiction and Substance Abuse, 2002) and are more likely to engage in risky sexual behaviors (O'Hare, 2005).

Although more men than women say that they intend to engage in casual sex while on spring break, the number of students that actually do are pretty similar for both sexes. Approximately 15% of men and 13% of women say that they engage in casual sex during spring break (Maticka-Tyndale et al., 1998). Why do you think college students might have more permissive attitudes about casual sex on spring break than the rest of the year?

The National Health and Social Life Survey found that people who are having regular sex with a partner masturbate more than people who are not having regular sex (Laumann et al., 1994). Couples who live together also masturbate—one study found that approximately 85% of men and 45% of women who are living with a partner report masturbating in the last year (Laumann et al., 1994). Other studies have found that for some masturbation complements an active sex life, whereas for others it compensates for a lack of partnered sex or satisfaction with sex (Das, 2007).

Although female masturbation has been found to produce the most physically intense orgasms in women (Masters & Johnson, 1970), women report masturbating less than men overall (Cornog, 2003; Larsson & Svedin, 2002). This may not be entirely true, however, because many women are embarrassed to admit they masturbate. This goes back to the double standard and the stereotype that women are not supposed to enjoy and take pleasure in sexual activities. In Chapter 14, we'll discuss how masturbation is being used in therapy for women who are unable to have orgasms.

Some women and men use vibrators or dildos during masturbation. A vibrator uses batteries and can vibrate at different speeds. Vibrators may be used directly on the genitals, or a woman may insert the vibrator into her vagina. A dildo, which can be made of silicone, rubber, or jelly, and comes in a variety of shapes and sizes, can also be inserted into the vagina or anus but does not use batteries. Vibrators and dildos can also be used during partner sex. We discuss vibrators more in Chapter 14.

Many men and women feel guilty and inadequate about masturbating because of the lasting cultural taboos against this behavior. Outside of the United States, however, attitudes toward masturbation differ. In some cultures, masturbation is acceptable

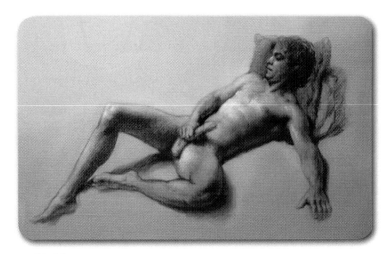

Figure **10.10**
Male masturbation.

and may be practiced openly and casually in public (as in certain areas of Melanesia), whereas in others, it is prohibited. Prohibition often simply relegates masturbation to private locations. In China, Taoist manuals describe masturbation as an essential way to circulate sexual energy in the body (Chia & Abrams, 1997).

In some religious traditions, masturbation is discouraged or forbidden. These cultural views toward masturbation have much to do with whether masturbation is perceived to be "normal" in a particular culture. For example, Asian American women have been found to masturbate significantly less than non-Asian women (Meston et al., 1996). Although masturbation is becoming more acceptable in African American women, research has found that the majority of Black women feel uncomfortable with self-pleasuring (Wyatt, 1998).

review questions

1 Describe the research on sexual fantasy, noting any gender differences.

2 How has masturbation been viewed throughout history? Are there cultural differences in masturbation attitudes?

3 Explain the differences in frequency of male versus female masturbation.

Sexual Behavior with Others

We have already discussed the influence of hormones, neurotransmitters, ethnicity, and religion on sexual behavior. It is also important to understand that cultural factors, such as sex-role stereotypes, may influence sexual behavior. Our culture helps us define what is considered acceptable and unacceptable sexual behavior. Some people experiment with different techniques, whereas others accept a smaller set of sexual behaviors. Overall, research has shown not only that sexual satisfaction is an important component to a happy marriage (Laumann et al., 2006), but it is also linked to satisfaction, love, and commitment in sexually active dating couples as well (Sprecher, 2002).

Keep in mind that each time a couple engages in sexual behavior, there are a variety of needs, feelings, and desires the partners bring together. They may want to stretch out the time and make it last longer, or they may desire a "quickie." They may want a physical release or to feel connected to their partner.

FOREPLAY: THE PRELUDE?

It is interesting to consider how people define "foreplay." Is foreplay all of the sexual behaviors that take place before sexual intercourse? What if sexual intercourse doesn't occur? For the majority of heterosexuals, foreplay is often defined as everything that happens before sexual intercourse (touching, kissing, massage, oral sex, etc.). It has been viewed as something a man has to do to get a woman ready for sexual intercourse.

For many, caressing, fondling, and snuggling are common pieces of foreplay. Hugging can also be an important aspect in caring relationships but also one that is often neglected. In fact, research has shown that married couples have deeper, more relaxed hugs with their young children than they do with each other (Schnarch, 1997).

MANUAL SEX:
A SAFER-SEX BEHAVIOR

Manual sex (also referred to as a "hand job") refers to the physical caressing of the genitals during solo or partner masturbation. Generally, people think of manual sex as something that happens before sexual intercourse, but it has become more popular over the years as a form of safer sex. This is because during manual sex, there is no exchange of body fluids (we discuss safer sex later in this chapter). For partners to learn how best to stimulate each other manually, it can help to watch each other masturbate. After all, most people know best how to stimulate their own bodies. This can be very anxiety-producing for some couples, and in situations in which one partner is hesitant, the other partner can go first, or they can try it again another time.

Manual Sex on Women

Many men (and women, too) may not know exactly what to do with the female genitals. What feels good? Rubbing? Can rubbing hurt? When does a woman like to have her clitoris touched? Where do women like to be touched? Men and women who worry about these questions may become overly cautious or eager in touching a woman's clitoris and vulva.

Because each woman differs in how she likes her clitoris stroked or rubbed, it is important that partners talk openly. The majority of women enjoy a light caressing of the shaft of the cli-

toris, along with an occasional circling of the clitoris, and maybe digital (finger) penetration of the vagina. Other women dislike direct stimulation and prefer to have the clitoris rolled between the lips of the labia. Women report that clitoral stimulation feels best when the fingers are well lubricated. A water-based lubricant, such as K-Y Jelly, or a woman's own lubrication can be used. Some women like to have the entire area of the vulva caressed, whereas others like the caressing to be focused on the clitoris.

Some women like it when their partners begin by lightly caressing their thighs, stomach, and entire mons area. Other women like to have their partners gently part the labia and softly explore the inner vulva. As a woman gets more excited, she may breathe more deeply or moan, and her muscles may become tense. Stopping stimulation when a partner is close to orgasm can be frustrating for her. It is best for partners to communicate openly about what is most enjoyable.

Manual Sex on Men

Many women (and some men) may not know exactly what to do with the penis. Does rubbing feel good? How do men like to have their penis stroked? When do men like to have their penis touched? To reach orgasm, many men like to have the penis stimulated with strong and consistent strokes.

However, at the beginning of sexual stimulation, most men like soft, light stroking of the penis and testicles. The testicles can be very responsive to sexual touch, although out of fear of hurting them oftentimes partners avoid touching them at all. It is true that the testicles can be badly hurt by rough handling, but a light stroking can be pleasurable. A good rule to follow is that most men do not like to have their testicles squeezed any harder than a woman would like to have her breasts squeezed. Remember, also, that the friction of a dry hand can cause irritation, so hand lotion, baby oil, or a lubricant can be used while manually stimulating the penis. However, if manual stimulation leads to vaginal or anal intercourse, any lotion or oil should be washed off, because these products may cause vaginal problems in women and can weaken the strength of latex condoms or diaphragms.

Switching positions, pressures, and techniques often can be frustrating for a man who feels almost at the brink of an orgasm. Another common mistake is to grasp the penis far down near its base. Although this can feel pleasurable, there are fewer nerve endings in the base of the penis than there are in the tip. The most sensitive parts of the male penis are the glans and tip, which are very responsive to touch. In fact, some men can masturbate by rubbing only the glans of the penis. For others, stimulation at the base may help bring on orgasm because it mimics deep thrusting.

All men have their own individual techniques for masturbating. However, the most common techniques involve a quick up-and-down motion that is applied without a great deal of pressure. To emulate this motion, partners should try varying the pressure every once in awhile (harder and then softer). Before orgasm, a

View in Video

"Adventurous sex involves a third person."
—*Styles of Sexually Traditional and Adventurous People*
To view go to CengageNOW at www.cengage.com/login

adventurous sex

manual sex
The physical caressing of the genitals during solo or partner masturbation.

stronger and deeper stroke that focuses on the glans of the penis should be used. At the point of orgasm, it is important to continue firm stroking on the top and sides of the penis but not on the underside. Firm pressure on the underside (the underside is the part of the penis that is "under" when the penis is not erect) of the penis during orgasm can restrict the urethra, which can be uncomfortable during ejaculation.

ORAL SEX:
NOT SO TABOO

Oral sex, also called **cunnilingus** (oral sex on a woman) and **fellatio** (oral sex on a man), has been practiced throughout history. Ancient Greek vases, 10th-century temples in India, and even 19th-century playing cards, all portrayed couples engaging in different types of oral sex. Over the years, however, there have been many taboos associated with oral sex. For some people, oral sex is not an option. It may be against their religion or beliefs, or they may simply find it disgusting. However, for many people, oral sex is an important part of sexual behavior.

REALResearch > Research has found that males are more likely than females to have received oral sex, whereas equal proportions of men and women have given oral sex (Brewster & Tillman, 2008).

The majority of Americans report that they engage in oral sex at least occasionally. Many heterosexual men and women begin engaging in oral sex before their first experience with sexual intercourse (and many teenagers experiment with oral sex, as we discussed in Chapter 8). In one study, 70% of heterosexual males reported performing cunnilingus before their first sexual intercourse, whereas 57% of females reported performing fellatio before their first intercourse (I. M. Schwartz, 1999). Research into racial differences has found that African American women engage in less fellatio, cunnilingus, or both than White women (Wyatt, 1998). African American women who did engage in these behaviors were more likely to be married, whereas White women were more likely to be single if they engage in fellatio. Differences have also been found in educational levels. As educational levels increase, so does experience with oral sex (Laumann et al., 1994).

Some couples use oral sex as a form of foreplay, whereas others engage in oral sex as their main form of sexual behavior. Couples may also engage in **sixty-nine** (see Figure 10.11). This position, however, can be challenging for some couples and may not provide the best stimulation for either of them. **Anilingus** (ain-uh-LING-gus; also called "rimming"), another form of oral sex, involves oral stimulation of the anus. However, hygiene is extremely important to avoid the spread of intestinal infections, hepatitis, and various sexually transmitted infections by an infected partner.

Some heterosexual couples may feel that engaging in oral sex is less intimate than sexual intercourse and may not like it for this reason. Because there is little face-to-face contact during cunnilingus or fellatio, it may make partners feel emotionally distant. Other people report that engaging in oral sex is one of the most intimate behaviors that a couple can engage in because it requires total trust and vulnerability. Not surprisingly, the majority of men and women are more interested in receiving oral sex rather than giving it (Brewster & Tillman, 2008; Laumann et al., 1994). When there is a conflict in a relationship concerning oral sex, partners should talk about it and try to compromise. However, if an agreement cannot be reached, couples should try to find a mutually satisfying alternative.

Before we discuss the types of oral sex, it is important to mention that if the person giving oral sex has a cold sore in his or her mouth or lips, it is possible to transmit this virus to the person on whom they are performing oral sex. In Chapter 15, we discuss how sexually transmitted infections are spread.

Cunnilingus

In the United States, women have historically been inundated with negative messages about their vaginas. Many makers of feminine powders, douches, creams, jellies, and other scented items try to persuade women that their products will make the vagina smell "better." For this reason, many women express concern about the cleanliness of their vaginas during cunnilingus. When their partners try to have oral sex with them, fears and anxieties often prevent women from enjoying the sexual experience. This, coupled with many women's lack of familiarity with their own genitals, contributes to many women's strong discomfort with oral sex.

Many heterosexual men and lesbian women find cunnilingus to be erotic. They report that the taste of the vaginal secretions is arousing to them, and they find the female vulva beautiful and sexy, including its smell and taste. Generally, when we are highly aroused, we are less alert to sensory

Figure **10.11**
The sixty-nine position.

cunnilingus The act of sexually stimulating the female genitals with the mouth.	**sixty-nine** Oral sex that is performed simultaneously between two partners.
fellatio The act of sexually stimulating the penis with the mouth.	**anilingus** Oral stimulation of the anus.

Do women like their partners to kiss them right after they have performed cunnilingus on them?

Some women do; some do not. For some women, sharing a kiss after cunnilingus can be very erotic and sensual. However, other women feel uncomfortable with the taste of their own genitals. It would be best to ask your partner to see what her individual pleasure is.

impressions than when we are not stimulated. This means that when we are aroused, the flavor of the vagina or of semen may be more appealing than it would be if we were not aroused. However, for those who do not find the scent and taste of the vagina arousing, taking a bath or shower together before engaging in oral sex is recommended.

Women report that they like oral sex to begin in a slow and gradual way. They dislike an immediate concentration on the clitoris. Prior to cunnilingus, many women like to be kissed and have their neck and shoulders, breasts, stomach, and finally their vulva, massaged. Kiss the outer lips and caress the mons. A persistent rhythmic caressing of the tongue on the clitoris will cause many women to reach orgasm. During cunnilingus, some women enjoy a finger being inserted into their vagina or anus for extra stimulation. Because pregnant women have an increased vascularity of the vagina and uterus, care should be taken to never blow air into a woman's vagina during cunnilingus. This can force air into her uterine veins, which can cause a fatal condition known as an air embolism, in which an air bubble travels through the bloodstream and can obstruct the vessel (Hill & Jones, 1993; Kaufman et al., 1987; Nicoll & Skupski, 2008; Sánchez et al., 2008).

Cunnilingus is the most popular sexual behavior for lesbian and bisexual women. In fact, the classic study by Blumstein and Schwartz (1983) found that the more oral sex a woman-to-woman couple has, the happier the relationship and the less they fight. Although women in heterosexual relationships often worry that their partners may find the vagina unappealing, this is not so in women-to-women relationships. Perhaps this is because each is more accepting of the other's genitals because they are both

women. As one woman said, "Gay women are very much into each other's genitals. . . . Not only accepting, but truly appreciative of women's genitals and bodies. . . . Lesbians are really into women's bodies, all parts" (Blumstein & Schwartz, 1983, p. 238).

Fellatio

The majority of men enjoy having their genitals orally stimulated, and many are displeased if their partners do not like to perform fellatio (Blumstein & Schwartz, 1983). In gay couples, the more oral sex occurs, the more sexually satisfied the couple is (Blumstein & Schwartz, 1983). Fellatio is the most popular sexual behavior for gay men. However, some men do not desire such stimulation.

Before fellatio, many men enjoy having their partners stroke and kiss various parts of their bodies, gradually getting closer to their penis and testicles. Some men like to have their partner take one testicle gently into the mouth and slowly circle it with the tongue. They may also like to have the head of the penis gently sucked while their partner's hand is slowly moving up and down the shaft. When performing fellatio, partners must be sure to keep their teeth covered with their lips, because exposed teeth can

---

REALResearch > A link has been found between assumptions about Black male sexuality and marketing within the U.S. adult novelty industry. Specifically, phallic representations overstate the size, color, and aggressiveness of the Black penis and, consequently, Black men (ALAVI, 2001).

---

cause pain. Some men like the sensation of being gently scratched with teeth during oral sex, but this must be done very carefully.

Pornographic movies tend to show a sex partner who takes the entire penis into his or her mouth, but this is not necessary. In fact, it may be uncomfortable because of the gagging response. Some men make the mistake, during fellatio, of holding their partners' heads during orgasm. This makes it impossible for the partner to remove the penis and to control the ejaculate.

To avoid a gagging response, it is often helpful to place a hand around the base of the penis while performing fellatio. By placing a hand there, the penis will be kept from entering the back of the mouth, thus reducing the urge to gag. In addition, the hand can be used to provide more stimulation to the penis.

Some partners are concerned about having their partners' ejaculate in their mouths after fellatio. If your partner is free from all sexually transmitted infections, swallowing the ejaculate is fine. Some people enjoy the taste, feel, and idea of tasting and swallowing ejaculate, but others do not. If swallowing is unacceptable, another option may be to spit the ejaculate out after orgasm or not allow your partner to ejaculate in your mouth.

How much semen a man ejaculates during fellatio often depends on how long it has been since his last ejaculation. If a long period of time has gone by, generally the ejaculate will be larger. An average ejaculation is approximately 1 to 2 teaspoons; consists mainly of fructose, enzymes, and different vitamins; and contains approximately 5 calories. The taste of the ejaculate can vary, depending on a man's use of drugs or alcohol, stress level, and diet (Tarkovsky, 2006). Coffee and alcohol can cause the semen to have a bitter taste, whereas fruits (pineapple in particular) can

Do men want their partners to swallow the ejaculate after their orgasms?

Some men do; some don't care. Again, there is more than one way to perform fellatio. Swallowing the ejaculate can be an intimate experience for both partners. Unless a man has a sexually transmitted infection (STI), there is nothing in the ejaculate that could harm a person. However, some people find it uncomfortable to swallow and prefer either to remove the penis before ejaculation or to spit the ejaculate out.

result in sweet-tasting semen. Men who eat lots of red meat often have very acid-tasting semen. The taste of semen also varies from day to day.

Some men and women dislike performing fellatio. There have been some ethnic differences found as well. For example, in Gail Wyatt's study of African American female sexuality, more than 50% of the hundreds of women in her sample had never engaged in fellatio and had no desire to do so (Wyatt, 1998). If you dislike performing fellatio on your partner, try talking about it. Find out if there are things that you can do differently (using your hands more) or that your partner can vary (ejaculating outside of your mouth).

There are many ways that couples engage in sexual intercourse.

Leslie Sponseller/Getty Images

HETEROSEXUAL
SEXUAL INTERCOURSE

People have always wondered how much sex everyone else is having. Overall, Americans fall into three groups: those who have sexual intercourse at least twice a week (one third); those who engage in sexual intercourse a few times a month (one third); and those who engage in sexual intercourse a few times a year or have no sexual partners (one third; Laumann et al., 1994). Age has been found to make a difference—18 to 29 year olds have sex 112 times per year on average, whereas 30 to 39 year olds have sex 86 times per year, and 40 to 49 year olds have sex 69 times per year (Piccinino & Mosher, 1998).

Most heterosexual couples engage in sexual intercourse almost every time they have sex, and when most people think about "sex," they think of sexual intercourse (Sanders & Reinisch, 1999). Sexual intercourse involves inserting the penis into the vagina. However, there are a variety of ways in which couples perform this action. We will discuss the various positions for sexual intercourse shortly.

It is important for couples to delay vaginal penetration until after lubrication has begun. We discussed the sexual response cycle earlier in this chapter, and how, during arousal, the vagina becomes lubricated, making penetration easier and providing more pleasure for both partners. Penetrating a dry vagina, forcefully or not, can be very uncomfortable for both partners. If the woman is aroused but more lubrication is needed, a water-based lubricant should be used.

Pornography helps reinforce the idea that women like thrusting to be fast and rough during sexual intercourse. Video after video shows men engaged in hard and fast thrusting—and women asking for more (we discuss pornography more in Chapter 18). In reality, many women like a slower pace for intercourse. It can be intimate and erotic to make love very slowly, circling the hips, varying pressure and sensations, while maintaining eye contact. Both nonverbal and verbal communication can help ensure that both partners are happy with the timing and pace of intercourse.

Although many men try to delay ejaculation until their partners are satisfied with the length of thrusting, longer thrusting does not always ensure female orgasm. If intercourse lasts for too long, the vagina may become dry, and this can be uncomfortable. Sex therapists report that heterosexual intercourse typically lasts anywhere from 3 to 13 minutes (Corty & Guardiani, 2008). Intercourse that lasts only 1 to 2 minutes was viewed as "too short" while intercourse that lasts more than 13 minutes was "too long." "Adequate" sexual intercourse lasts 3 to 7 minutes, and "desirable" intercourse lasts 7-13 minutes (Corty and Guardiani, 2008).

The majority of couples do not have eye contact during sexual behavior, regardless of their positions (Schnarch, 1997). Schnarch

REALResearch   > Regular sexual intercourse has been found to regulate menstrual cycles in heterosexual women, increasing the likelihood of regular ovulation (Levin, 2007).

proposed that eye contact during sexual behavior intensifies intimacy, and this is difficult for most couples. In addition, over time, we have learned to close our eyes during intimate interactions (such as kissing, sexual intercourse, or oral sex). To increase the intensity of sexual behavior, try keeping your eyes open (it's not as easy as you might think).

Positions for Sexual Intercourse

According to the *Complete Manual of Sexual Positions* (J. Stewart, 1990), there are 116 vaginal entry positions, and, in *The New Joy of Sex* (Comfort & Rubenstein, 1992), 112 positions are illustrated. Of course, we don't have enough room to describe all of these positions, so we will limit this discussion to the four main positions for sexual intercourse: male-on-top, female-on-top, rear entry, and side-by-side. There are advantages and disadvan-

WHAT DO YOU WANT TO KNOW?

I have heard that you can get genital herpes if your partner performs oral sex on you and has a cold sore on his or her lip. Is this true?
It appears that even though oral herpes (a cold sore) is caused by a different strain of the virus than genital herpes, this virus can be passed on during oral sex and lead to genital herpes. Therefore, it is best to avoid performing oral sex when you have a cold sore. We discuss herpes in more depth in Chapter 15.

tages to each of these positions, and couples must choose the sexual positions that are best for them. Keep in mind that although we are discussing positions for heterosexual sexual intercourse here, many gay and lesbian couples use similar positions in their sexual activity.

MALE-ON-TOP The male-on-top (also called the "missionary" or "male superior") position is one of the most common positions for sexual intercourse. In this position, the woman lies on her back and spreads her legs, often bending her knees to make penetration easier. The man positions himself on top of the woman,

---

HUMAN SEXUALITY IN A DIVERSE WORLD

Meet Me in the Love Hotel

A love hotel offers couples privacy and the sexual décor can often help increase sexual interest and desire.

A "love hotel" is a short-stay hotel room that is commonly found in many Asian countries, such as Japan, Hong Kong, or South Korea. Typically rooms are rented for several hours (a "rest") or for the night (a "stay"). Reservations are not accepted; a "rest" typically costs anywhere from 3,000 to 7,000 yen ($30–$70), whereas a "stay" costs approximately 10,000 yen ($100). It is estimated that 1.4 million couples visit a love hotel every day in Japan (Chaplin, 2007). I had the opportunity to explore love hotels on my recent trip to Shibuya, a district of Tokyo, Japan.

Since Japanese homes and apartments are very small and often have paper-thin walls, they offer little privacy to couples wanting to have sex. Many Japanese couples say they have a hard time getting "in the mood" in their traditional homes (Keasler, 2006). A love hotel offers couples privacy and the sexual décor can often help increase sexual interest and desire. Entrances to love hotels are discreet, and there is limited contact with hotel staff. Rooms are selected from an electronic display board posted in the entrance way—if the room is lit up, it is available. Payment is often automated or done through pneumatic tubes, but some hotels offer small windows through which payment can be made discreetly without exposing a customer's face. Identification is not required, and there are no age limits to enter a love hotel. Some love hotels offer specific themes, such as samurai, jungle, pirate, S&M, or even cartoon character themes ("Hello Kitty" is popular).

The rooms in most love hotels are small; in fact, the room I saw was slightly bigger than the double-sized bed. Many rooms come with various amenities, including large televisions with DVD players, slot or karaoke machines, video games, refrigerators, or microwaves. The room I saw even came with a costume rental option offering maid, nurse, stewardess, schoolgirl, or cheerleader costumes (I found it interesting there were no costumes available for men, however). There was also a large electric vibrator attached to the head of the bed, with a sign that said "disinfected." Many rooms also have vending machines that offer a full line of skin care and sex-related products (condoms, lubricants, and sex toys). Couples often talk for a while, play games, have sex, and take a bath (love hotel bathrooms are often fully stocked—the room I saw even offered peppermint bath crystals; Keasler, 2006).

In mid-2008, a crackdown on love hotels in Japan began to explore laws that regulate these hotels. One main issue revolves around collecting personal information from customers. Although Japanese inns and hotels are required to collect personal information from guests, including name and address, love hotels are not (Shimanaka, 2008). As you could guess, many love hotel guests are reluctant to share such information. Lawmakers are also trying to reduce the amount of sexual content both outside and within the love hotels, in an attempt to improve the overall concept of the hotels. Interestingly, many Japanese believe that American motels are like Japanese love hotels—illustrating how commonly we believe our cultural traditions and values are shared (Keasler, 2006).

Figure **10.12**
The male-on-top position.

between her legs (see Figure 10.12). Because his full weight is usually uncomfortable and perhaps even painful for the woman, he should support himself on his arms or elbows and knees.

The male-on-top position allows the male to control the thrusting and permits deep penetration for the man during intercourse. It enables the partners to look at each other, kiss, and hug during sexual intercourse. The woman can move her legs up around her partner or even put them on his shoulders. She can also use a pillow under her hips to increase clitoral stimulation. For some couples, this position is the most comfortable because

the male is more active than the female. This position may also be the most effective for procreation, because the penis can be thrust deep into the vagina, which allows the semen to be deposited as deeply as possible; furthermore, because the woman is lying on her back, the semen does not leak out as easily.

However, there are also some disadvantages to the male-on-top position. If either partner is overweight, or if the female is in the advanced stages of pregnancy, this position can be very uncomfortable. Also, the deep penetration that is possible in this position may be uncomfortable for the woman, especially if her partner has a large penis, which can bump the cervix. This position also makes it difficult to provide clitoral stimulation for the female and may prevent the woman from moving her hips or controlling the strength or frequency of thrusting. Finally, in the male-on-top position, it may be difficult for the man to support his weight, because his arms and knees may get tired.

FEMALE-ON-TOP   In the female-on-top position (also called "female superior") the man lies on his back while his partner positions herself above him (see Figure 10.13). She can either put her knees on either side of him or lie between his legs. By leaning forward, she has greater control over the angle and degree of thrusting and can get more clitoral stimulation. Other variations of this position include the woman sitting astride the man facing his feet or the woman sitting on top of her partner while he sits in a chair.

In the female-on-top position, the female can control clitoral stimulation either by manual stimulation or through friction on her partner's body. She can also control the depth and rhythm of thrusting. Her partner's hands are also free so that he can caress her body during sexual intercourse. Because this position is face-

HUMAN SEXUALITY IN A DIVERSE WORLD

Sex Is Against the Law

In an attempt to fight HIV infection, in 2002 the king resurrected an ancient chastity custom that prohibited single Swazi women from engaging in sexual intercourse or marrying for five years.

Swaziland, a small African nation, has the world's highest HIV infection rate. While the life expectancy was 60 in 1997, it dropped to half of this by 2008 (Bearak, 2008). There are many factors contributing to the high HIV rate, including a high rate of sexually transmitted infections and the practice of having multiple wives (polygamy). The king of Swaziland, a 40-year-old man, currently has 13 wives (it is estimated that his father had somewhere between 70–110 wives; Bearak, 2008). The king believes that the practice of polygamy and having multiple sex partners is unrelated to the skyrocketing AIDS rate. In an attempt to fight HIV infection, the king resurrected an ancient chastity custom in 2001 that prohibited single Swazi women from engaging in sexual intercourse or marrying for five years (Bearak, 2008; Haworth, 2002). All single women in Swaziland were required to wear tasseled headdresses to signify

their compliance with this ban. Virgins under age 19 wore blue and yellow tassels, and women over 19, regardless of virginity status, wore red and black tassels. These headdresses were meant to warn men to stay away from these women.

If this law was not followed, the women faced penalties ranging from surrendering one cow to a cash fine of up to $150. Violators also had to live with the shame of being labeled a "lawbreaker." Women took this law very seriously. One woman said, "I don't think abstaining from sex is a sacrifice if it saves your life." While many men and women took these laws seriously, the king did not. He married a 17-year old girl in 2005 and was promptly fined one cow.

SOURCE: Adapted from Haworth, 2002; Bearak, 2008.

Figure **10.13**
The female-on-top position.

to-face, the partners are able to see each other, kiss, and have eye contact.

Sex therapists often recommend this position for couples who are experiencing difficulties with premature ejaculation or a lack of orgasms, because the female-on-top position can extend the length of erection for men and facilitates female orgasm. It also doesn't require a man to support his weight. For women who are in the advanced stages of pregnancy, the female-on-top position may be a very good position.

There are, however, some drawbacks to the female-on-top position. Some women may feel shy or uncomfortable about taking an active role in sexual intercourse, and this position puts the primary responsibility on the female. Some men may feel uncomfortable letting their partners be on top and may not receive enough penile stimulation in this position to maintain an erection.

SIDE-BY-SIDE   The side-by-side position takes the primary responsibility off both partners and allows them to relax during sexual intercourse. In this position, the partners lie on their sides, and the woman lifts one leg to facilitate penile penetration (see Figure 10.14). This is a good position for couples who want to take it slow and extend sexual intercourse. Both partners have their hands free and can caress each other's bodies. In addition, they can see each other, kiss, and talk during sexual intercourse.

Disadvantages include the fact that sometimes couples in this position have difficulties with penetration. It can also be difficult to get a momentum going, and even more difficult to achieve deep penetration. Women may also have a difficult time maintaining contact with the male's pubic bone during sexual intercourse, which often increases the chances of orgasm.

REAR-ENTRY   There are many variations to the rear-entry position of sexual intercourse. Intercourse can be fast or slow depending on the variation chosen. One variation involves a woman on her hands and knees (often referred to as "doggie style"), while her partner is on his knees behind her. The female can also be ly-

ing on her stomach with a pillow under her hips while the male enters her from behind. Another variation is to use the side-by-side position, in which the male lies behind his partner and introduces his penis from behind (see Figure 10.15).

The rear-entry positions provide an opportunity for clitoral stimulation, either by the male or the female. It may also provide direct stimulation of the G-spot. The rear-entry position also can be good for women who are in the later stages of pregnancy or who are overweight.

Anal Intercourse

During anal intercourse, the man's penis enters his partner's anus (see Figure 10.16). Although many people think of anal sex as a gay male activity (with the anus being used as a substitute for the vagina), anal stimulation is pleasurable for many people and so is practiced by heterosexual, gay, lesbian, and bisexual men and women (Melby, 2007). There are many nerve endings in the anus, and it is frequently involved in sexual response, even if it is not directly stimulated. Some men and women experience orgasm during anal intercourse, especially with simultaneous penile or clitoral stimulation.

The landmark University of Chicago study found that only 1 in 10 heterosexual couples had engaged in anal sex (Laumann et

Figure **10.14**
The side-by-side position.

Figure **10.15**
The side, rear-entry position.

My girlfriend told me that my penis is too large for her vagina and that it causes her pain during intercourse. How far can the vagina expand?

Although it is true that the vagina expands and lengthens during sexual arousal, not every vagina expands to the same degree. If a man's penis is very large, it can bump against the woman's cervix during thrusting, which can cause discomfort. In such cases it is particularly important to make sure the woman is fully aroused before attempting penetration and to try a variety of positions to find which is most comfortable for her. The female superior position or the rear-entry positions may help her control the depth of penetration. Either partner's hand around the base of the penis (depending on the position) may also prevent full penetration, as will some devices such as "cock rings," which are sold through adult catalogues or in adult stores. If the woman's pain continues, she should consult with her gynecologist to rule out a physiological problem and to get more advice and information.

al., 1994), whereas the National Survey of Family Growth (NSFG; see Chapter 2) study found that 1 in 3 heterosexual couples had engaged in anal sex (Melby, 2007). Another analysis of NSFG data found that approximately 22% of 18- to 26-year-old heterosexual couples had engaged in anal sex (Kaestle & Halpern, 2007).

Because the anus is not capable of producing lubrication and the tissue is so fragile, it is important that additional water-based lubricants (such as K-Y Jelly) be used. An oil-based lubricant (such as Vaseline) may cause problems later because the body cannot easily get rid of it, and it can damage latex condoms. Without lubrication, there may be pain, discomfort, and possibly tearing of the tissue in the anus.

During anal intercourse, the **anal sphincter** muscle must be relaxed, which can be facilitated by gentle stroking and digital pen-

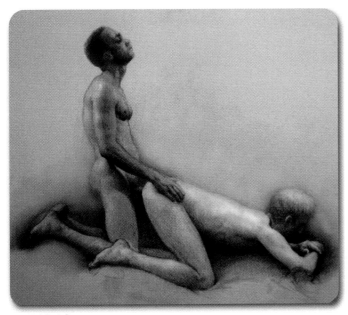

Figure **10.16**
Anal intercourse.

etration of the anus. If it is not, intercourse can be painful. If a couple decides to engage in anal sex, it is important to take it slowly. A condom is a must (unless partners are absolutely sure that both are free from STIs and are HIV-negative). Anal intercourse is one of the riskiest of all sexual behaviors and has been implicated in the transmission of HIV. Research has shown that the risk of contracting HIV through unprotected anal intercourse is greater than the risk of contracting HIV through unprotected vaginal intercourse (Silverman & Gross, 1997; we discuss this more in Chapter 15).

In addition, any couple who decides to engage in anal sex should never transfer the penis from the anus to the vagina or mouth without changing the condom or washing the penis (sex toys should also be washed with antibacterial soap). The bacteria in the anus can cause vaginal infections in women.

Before engaging in anal sex, couples should make sure that they have discussed and agreed on it. Forcing anal sex can be painful and even dangerous. The anal sphincter is delicate tissue that can tear if not treated gently.

SAME-SEX SEXUAL TECHNIQUES

Although the similarities between heterosexual and same-sex sexual behavior are many, there are some differences. The differences have to do with frequency and types of sexual behaviors in which couples engage.

Gay Men

Gay men use a variety of sexual techniques, which refutes the stereotype that most gay men assume only one role (either passive or active) in their relationships. The most frequent techniques used by gay males are fellatio, followed by mutual masturbation, anal intercourse, and body rubbing. Overall, gay and bisexual men engage in oral sex more often than heterosexual or lesbian couples. This is not surprising, given the fact that research has shown that overall, men are more likely than women to have received oral sex (Brewster & Tillman, 2008).

Although many gay men practice anal sex, not all gay men do. Laumann et al. (1994) found that 80% of gay men reported engaging in anal sex, but 20% did not. Some gay men (and other couples, too) engage in **fisting** (also called "hand-balling"), which involves the insertion of the fist and even part of the forearm into the anus or vagina. The use of rubber gloves during fisting has become more common in the last few years (Richters et al., 2003).

Like many other couples, gay men enjoy hugging, kissing, and body caressing; **interfemoral** (in-ter-fem-OR-ull) **intercourse** (thrusting the penis between the thighs of a partner); and **buttockry** (BUT-ock-ree; rubbing of the penis in the cleft of the buttocks).

anal sphincter
A ringlike muscle that surrounds the anus; it usually relaxes during normal physiological functioning.

fisting
Sexual technique that involves inserting the fist and even part of the forearm into the anus or vagina.

interfemoral intercourse
Thrusting the penis between the thighs of a partner.

buttockry
Rubbing of the penis in the cleft of the buttocks.

Figure **10.17**
Gay men use a variety of sexual techniques in their lovemaking.

Gay male sexual behavior changed significantly after AIDS arrived. Undoubtedly because of the massive education efforts initiated in the gay community, in the early 1990s, safe sex practices increased (at least in the major cities) among gay men (Catania et al., 1989). However, researchers believe that STI increases among sexually active gay men in the past few years are due to a decreased fear of acquiring HIV, an increase in high-risk sexual behaviors (e.g., oral sex without a condom), a lack of knowledge about diseases, and increased Internet access to sexual partners (Ciesielski, 2003; Hughes, 2006). We discuss this more in Chapter 15.

Lesbians

Lesbians enjoy a wide range of sexual contact, including body contact, kissing, manual stimulation, oral sex, and penetration using dildos or vibrators. Manual stimulation of the genitals is the most common sexual practice among lesbians, although lesbians tend to use a variety of techniques in their lovemaking. Two-woman couples kiss more than man–woman couples, and two-man couples kiss least of all. After manual stimulation, the next most common practice is cunnilingus, which many lesbians report is their favorite sexual activity. Another common practice is **tribadism** (TRY-bad-iz-um), also called the genital apposition technique, in which the women rub their genitals together. As we noted earlier, some lesbians engage in fisting and also may use dildos or vibrators, often accompanied by manual or oral stimulation.

Although it's rather dated, a nonscientific survey was conducted of more than 100 members of a lesbian social organization in Colorado (Munson, 1987). When asked what sexual techniques they had used in their last 10 lovemaking sessions, 100% reported kissing, sucking on breasts, and manual stimulation of the clitoris; more than 90% reported French kissing, oral sex, and fingers inserted into the vagina; and 80% reported tribadism. Lesbians in their 30s were twice as likely as other age groups to engage in anal stimulation (with a finger or dildo). Approximately a third of women used vibrators, and there were a small number who reported using a variety of other sex toys, such as dildo harnesses,

leather restraints, and handcuffs. Sexual play and orgasm are important aspects of lesbian sexuality (Bolso, 2005).

Lesbian women also report frequently thinking about sex and the use of sexual fantasy. One woman said:

> *I think about sex during the day, staring at my computer screen, while I'm supposed to be writing. Sometimes I call Dana up at work, she picks up the phone, I say, "I'll meet you at home in fifteen minutes, and I'm going to rip off your clothes and throw you down on the couch, and I'm going to eat your pussy. That's what I'm having for lunch." (S. E. Johnson, 1996, p. i)*

There has been some preliminary research done on the existence of **lesbian erotic role identification** (or the roles of "butch" [masculine] and "femme" [feminine] in lesbian relationships). Some scholars believe that such roles are simply social contracts, whereas others believe they are natural expressions of lesbian sexuality (D. Singh et al., 1999). One study examined physiological and behavioral differences of women in these self-identified roles. Butch lesbians were found to have higher saliva testosterone levels, higher waist-to-hip ratios, and recalled more childhood behavior atypical for their gender (D. Singh et al., 1999). It's important to remember that there is no "typical" lesbian couple. Some lesbian couples may engage in role identification, but many others do not.

Overall, lesbians have been found to be more sexually responsive and more satisfied with their sexual relationships and to have lower rates of sexual problems than heterosexual women. Some studies have suggested that the frequency of sexual contact among lesbians declines dramatically in their long-term, committed relationships (Blumstein & Schwartz, 1983; Nichols, 1990). By the beginning of the 1990s, the decreasing sexual interest among lesbian women had become well-established and was referred to as "lesbian bed death" (Nichols, 2004). However, lesbian bed death has not been supported by research, and no overall differences have been found in the sexual frequency of heterosexual and lesbian women (Iasenza, 1991, 2002).

Figure **10.18**
Lesbians have been found to be more sexually responsive and more satisfied in their sexual relationships than heterosexual women.

tribadism
Rubbing genitals together with another person for sexual pleasure.

lesbian erotic role identification
The roles of "butch" and "femme" in lesbian relationships.

1 Explain why manual sex can be a form of safer sex.

2 Describe the differences that have been found in how men and women view oral sex.

3 Identify any gender differences that have been found in the experience of sexual intercourse.

4 Identify various positions for sexual intercourse. Name some advantages and disadvantages of each.

5 Identify the risks of engaging in anal sex.

6 Compare and contrast gay and lesbian sexual behavior.

Sexual Behavior
Later in Life

As men and women age, a variety of physical changes affect sexual functioning and behavior. We now discuss these physical changes and their effect on sexual behavior. (We discuss more of the challenges of aging and health concerns in Chapter 14.)

PHYSICAL CHANGES

As people age, they inevitably experience changes in their physical health, some of which can affect normal sexual functioning (see Table 10.1). Many of these decreases in sexual functioning are exacerbated by sexual inactivity. In fact, research clearly indicates that older adults who have remained sexually active throughout their aging years have a greater potential for a more satisfying sex life later in life (Dimah & Dimah, 2004; Weeks & Hof, 1987). Better knowledge of these changes would help older adults anticipate changes in their sexual activity.

One 50-year-old woman explains how her sex life has improved with age:

When I was in my twenties and early thirties I almost never had an orgasm during intercourse, but I still enjoyed it because of the feeling of the closeness you can't get from anything else. Now, at fifty, I am often orgasmic during intercourse, partly because I have orgasms easier, but mostly because I am more comfortable with stroking my clitoris. (Block, 1999, p. 65)

CHANGES IN SEXUAL BEHAVIOR

Two of the most frequent complaints among older adult women and men are decreases in sexual desire and functioning (Araujo et al., 2004). Because of these changes, masturbation increases, and for heterosexual couples, rates of sexual intercourse decrease (C. B. White, 1982). Research on older gay men has found that

table 10.1
Physical Changes in Older Men and Women

In men:

1. Delayed and less firm erection

2. More direct stimulation needed for erection

3. Extended refractory period (12 to 24 hours before re-arousal can occur)

4. Reduced elevation of the testicles

5. Reduced vasocongestive response to the testicles and scrotum

6. Fewer expulsive contractions during orgasm

7. Less forceful expulsion of seminal fluid and a reduced volume of ejaculate

8. Rapid loss of erection after ejaculation

9. Ability to maintain an erection for a longer period

10. Less ejaculatory urgency

11. Decrease in size and firmness of the testes, changes in testicle elevation, less sex flush, and decreased swelling and erection of the nipples

In women:

1. Reduced or increased sexual interest

2. Possible painful intercourse due to menopausal changes

3. Decreased volume of vaginal lubrication

4. Decreased expansive ability of the vagina

5. Possible pain during orgasm due to less flexibility

6. Thinning of the vaginal walls

7. Shortening of vaginal width and length

8. Decreased sex flush, reduced increase in breast volume, and longer postorgasmic nipple erection

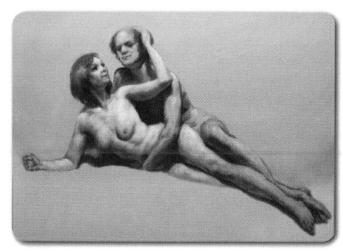

Figure **10.19**
The majority of older adults maintain an interest in sex and sexual activity.

they continue to be sexually active; however, they tend to engage in less anal sex than younger gay men (Van de Ven et al., 1997).

Masturbation may continue among older adults and may fulfill a variety of needs. If an older adult finds that his or her partner is no longer interested in sexual activity, masturbation often becomes an important outlet. This can also be an important activity for older people who have lost their sexual partners because it offers a sexual release that may help decrease depression, hostility, or frustration. Other physical problems, such as arthritis, diabetes, and osteoporosis, can also interfere with sexual functioning. We discuss many other physical problems, such as illness, surgery, and injuries that can affect sexual functioning in Chapter 14.

The stereotype that sex worsens with age is not inevitably true (Dimah & Dimah, 2004). Many older adults are very interested in maintaining an active sex life (Ginsberg et al., 2005). A key to sexual enjoyment later in life is for partners to be patient and understanding with each other. Physical fitness, good nutrition, adequate rest and sleep, a reduction in alcohol intake, and positive self-esteem can all enhance sexuality throughout the life span.

review questions

1 Identify the two most frequent sexual complaints in older men and explain how they affect aging men.

2 Identify and explain some of the physiological changes that occur with aging.

3 Explain how the physical changes of aging might affect the sexual response cycle.

Safer-Sex **Behaviors**

What exactly is **safe sex?** Does it mean wearing a condom? Limiting the number of sex partners? Not engaging in oral, anal, vaginal, or casual sex? Although safe sex does include condom use, it also refers to specific sexual behaviors that are "safe" to engage in because they protect against the risk of acquiring sexually transmitted infections. However, there are no sexual behaviors that protect a person 100% of the time (with the exception of abstinence, solo masturbation, and sexual fantasy). Therefore, maybe the real question is, "Is there really any such thing as safe sex?" In response to that question, it may be more appropriate to refer to **safer-sex** behaviors, because we do know there are some sexual behaviors that are safer than others (see Sex in Real Life, "Safer-Sex Behavior Guidelines"). In Chapter 15, we discuss high-risk sexual behaviors.

All sexually active people should be aware of the risks associated with various sexual behaviors. Not only should people decrease the number of sexual partners, they must learn more about the sexual history of their partners, avoid unprotected vaginal and anal intercourse and other risky activities, and use barrier methods of contraception. In Chapter 13, we discuss what types of lubricants to use with condoms.

Even though most people feel anxious about the possibility of acquiring an STI, casual sexual activity has increased in recent years, and there have been few increases in heterosexual safer-sex behaviors (Moore, 1999). Although there has been a gradual increase in condom use, there have been few changes in the heterosexual behavior of male and female college students; in fact, no significant changes in sexual behavior have been noted. Overall, effective safer-sex negotiation is more an exception than the rule in dating heterosexual couples (Buysse & Ickes, 1999).

Although many people are familiar with condoms, the dental dam, which is a square piece of thin latex, similar to the latex used in condoms, is lesser known and can be used to prevent the transmission of STIs. It is stretched across the vulva or anus to prevent the exchange of bodily fluids. It is available without a prescription in many drugstores and women's health clinics across the United States and now comes in a variety of flavors and colors.

One behavior that has been clearly linked to unsafe sexual behaviors is drinking alcohol, which can impair judgment. In one study, 75% of college students had made decisions that they later regretted while under the influence of alcohol (Poulson et al., 1998). In fact, alcohol use is one of the most important factors that is repeatedly linked to unsafe sexual behavior (Wechsler & Issac, 1992). Young men and women who drink alcohol are 7 times more likely to engage in sexual behaviors (and have more

safe sex
Sexual behaviors that do not pose a risk for the transmission of sexually transmitted infections.

safer sex
Sexual behaviors that reduce the risk of sexually transmitted infections.

Safer-Sex Behavior Guidelines

Remember that engaging in hookups (casual sex) and alcohol use are two activities that can increase your risk of acquiring a sexually transmitted infection.

Following are some sexual activities that are rated for safety. Remember that engaging in "hookups" (casual sex) and alcohol use are two activities that can increase your risk of acquiring a sexually transmitted infection. Typically, unsafe behaviors involve contact with semen, blood, or other body fluids. Those behaviors that are considered safe include activities that involve no exchange of bodily fluids. Contact your local health clinic or AIDS organization for more information.

Safe
massage
hugging
dry kissing
body rubbing, dry humping
sexual fantasy
masturbation (self only)
watching porn or erotica
phone/computer sex
sex toys (provided condoms are used if toys are shared)
taking a bath together

Possibly Safe
French kissing
anal intercourse with condom

vaginal intercourse with condom
fisting with glove
cunnilingus with dental dam
fellatio with condom
anal rimming or anilingus with dental dam
vaginal or anal stimulation with fingers using latex glove

Possibly Unsafe
cunnilingus without a dental dam
vaginal or anal stimulation with fingers without latex glove
fellatio without a condom
sharing sex toys without cleaning or changing condoms in between uses
fisting without a glove
anal rimming or analingus without a dental dam

Unsafe
anal intercourse without condom
vaginal intercourse without condom
blood contact
cunnilingus without a dental dam during menstruation

SOURCE: Adapted from "Safer Sex Basics," 2005.

sexual partners) than those who do not drink (Center on Addiction and Substance Abuse, 2002).

In Chapter 3, we talked about the importance of communication. Communication is key to safer sex relationships. When there is talk about safe sex, women are more likely than men to bring up the topic (M. Allen et al., 2002). However, it's important for all couples to talk about each other's past sexual relationships (such as number of partners and history of STIs) before engaging in sexual intercourse or sexual activity. Such openness will result not only in safer sex, but also a healthier relationship.

Throughout this chapter you have learned that human sexuality is shaped by cultural, ethnic, religious, psychological, and biological influences. All of these factors help us to determine which sexual behaviors we will engage in and which are unacceptable for us. These influences also shape our sexual attitudes and our ability to talk about sexuality.

review questions

1 Define "safe sex" and differentiate it from "safer sex."

2 Give some guidelines for safer sex behaviors.

3 Explain how drinking may be linked to engaging in unsafe sexual behaviors.

SUMMARY POINTS

1 Our hormones have a powerful effect on our bodies. The endocrine glands secrete hormones into the bloodstream. The most influential hormones in sexual behavior are estrogen and testosterone. In most animals, the brain controls and regulates sexual behavior chiefly through hormones, although in humans, learned experiences and social, cultural, and ethnic influences are also important. Hormone levels decrease as we age, and this can cause a variety of problems, such as vaginal dryness and decreased vaginal sensitivity in women and slower and less frequent erections in men.

2 Our ethnic group affects the types of sexual behaviors we engage in, our sexual attitudes, and our ability to communicate about sexuality. Differences have been found between African Americans, Hispanics, Caucasians, and Asian Americans. Religiosity also influences sexual behavior. The more religious people are, the more conservative their sexual behavior tends to be.

3 There are a series of physiological and psychological changes that occur during sexual behavior. Masters and Johnson's sexual response cycle involves four physiological phases, including excitement, plateau, orgasm, and resolution. During these phases, there are changes in both vasocongestion and myotonia. In men, there is a refractory period during resolution, and generally the stages are less well defined. In women, the menstrual cycle may affect the sexual response cycle.

4 Kaplan's model of sexual response has three stages—desire, excitement, and orgasm. It is easier to recognize when a person is going through Kaplan's stages. Reed's ESP model encompasses features of both Kaplan's and Masters and Johnson's models. Phases include seduction, sensation, surrender, and reflection. Tiefer argues that these models are all based on the medical model, and because of this, they leave out important aspects of sexual functioning.

5 The majority of heterosexuals define foreplay as "anything that happens before penetration" or something a man does to get a woman in the mood. Many people use fantasies to help increase their sexual excitement, and people use them both during periods of sexual activity and inactivity. Female sexual fantasies often reflect personal sexual experiences, whereas male fantasies are more dependent on erotica and images.

6 Adult sexual behavior includes a range of sexual activities. Some adults choose to be celibate, or abstinent. Over the past decade, men's and women's sexual fantasies have become more similar. Men masturbate more than women, and women feel more guilt about their masturbatory activity than do men. Masturbation fulfills a variety of needs for different people at different ages. In manual sex, no exchange of bodily fluids occurs. Men and women both have concerns about how best to stimulate their partners manually. Fellatio and cunnilingus are becoming more popular as forms of sexual behavior. Both heterosexual and homosexual couples engage in oral sex.

7 Most heterosexual couples engage in sexual intercourse almost every time they have sex, and when most people think of sex, they think of sexual intercourse. It is important to delay intercourse until after a woman's vaginal lubrication has begun. If a woman needs more lubrication, a water-based lubricant can be used. There are a variety of positions for sexual intercourse.

8 Same-sex couples engage in many of the same sexual activities as heterosexual couples do. Lesbians tend to be more sexually satisfied than heterosexual women and have lower rates of sexual problems. There are more similarities than differences in the sexual behavior of homosexuals and heterosexuals. Both heterosexual and homosexual couples engage in anal sex, and some experience orgasm from this technique. After anal intercourse, the penis should never be transferred from the anus to the vagina because of the risk of infection.

9 The majority of elderly persons maintain an interest in sex and sexual activity, even though society often views them as asexual. A lack of education about the physiological effects of aging on sexual functioning may cause an elderly person to think his or her sex life is over when a sexual dysfunction is experienced.

10 There may be no such thing as safe sex; instead, we refer to "safer" sex. Other than abstinence, solo masturbation, and sexual fantasies, there are no 100% safe sexual behaviors. Few changes in the heterosexual behavior of male and female college students have occurred as a result of the AIDS crisis. Men and women should learn the sexual histories of all their sexual partners and consistently use condoms and dental dams.

CRITICAL THINKING questions

1 Why do you think so many people are hesitant to talk about sexual pleasure? There is no doubt that you talk about sex with friends, but why has it become so taboo and so difficult to talk about what brings you sexual pleasure?

2 Do you think your ethnicity affects your sexuality? In what ways? Why do you think this is?

3 Suppose that your sexual partner shares with you that he or she has been engaging in sexual fantasies during sexual activity with you. How would this make you feel? Would you want to talk to your partner about these fantasies? Why, or why not?

4 Susan has been masturbating regularly since age fifteen, although she feels very guilty about it. She realizes that she is unable to reach orgasm with her partner. After reading this chapter, explain to Susan what you've learned about masturbation, and offer her some advice.

5 Flash forward 30 years and imagine what your life will be like in a committed, long-term relationship. How do you hope your sex life will be? What factors might contribute to any problems you might experience?

6 Suppose you are in a new relationship and have just begun engaging in sexual activity. How can you communicate your desires to keep the sex safe? What problems might come up in this discussion?

WEB resources

Sexuality Now Book Companion Website

Go to www.cengage.com/psychology/carroll for practice quizzes, glossary, flash cards, and more. You can also access the following websites from the companion site.

Electronic Journal of Human Sexuality ■ This online publication of the Institute for Advanced Study of Human Sexuality in San Francisco disseminates information about all aspects of human sexuality. The site offers a database of research articles, book reviews, and posters from various conference presentations.

San Francisco Sex Information Organization ■ San Francisco Sex Information (SFSI) is a free information and referral switchboard providing anonymous, accurate, nonjudgmental information about sex. If you have a question about sex, they will answer it or refer you to someone who can.

Healthy Sex ■ HealthySex.com is an educational site, designed by Wendy Maltz, to promote healthy sexuality based on caring, respect, and safety. The site contains information on sexual health, intimacy, communication, sexual abuse and addiction, sexual fantasies, and midlife sex, and links to a variety of sexuality sites.

Go Ask Alice! ■ Go Ask Alice! is a question-and-answer format website produced by Columbia University's Health Educa-

tion Program. It provides factual, in-depth, straightforward, and nonjudgmental information to improve sexual health. You can visit recently asked questions or search the database.

CengageNOW

Go to www.cengage.com/login to link to CengageNOW, your online study tool. First take the Pre-Test for this chapter to get your Personalized Study Plan, which will identify topics you need to review and direct you to online resources. Then take the Post-Test to determine what concepts you have mastered and what you still need work on.

Videos in CengageNOW

For additional information on topics discussed in this chapter, check out the videos in CengageNOW on the following topics:

- Styles of Sexually Traditional and Adventurous People— Explore the question of sex's importance within a relationship and the styles of sexual expression.

- Sex Toy Parties—The evolution of female sexuality is seen in the rising popularity of sex toy parties involving the display and purchase of sex toys in the host's living room.

CHAPTER 11

Sexual Orientation

The story of my "coming-out" isn't spectacular in any way—I'm an ordinary person with a pretty ordinary life. From the time I was around age 7 or 8, I knew my feelings for other girls were "different." At first I thought the feelings I felt were some strange type of jealousy, but then realized it was attraction.

I developed crushes on female classmates but felt so ashamed and awful that I would cry myself to sleep at night. Girls and boys were pairing off into couples and kissing at middle-school parties, and kids who didn't participate were called "faggot" and "dyke," words that terrified me because I suspected they had something to do with who I was.

My freshman year of high school, I felt like I was on a roller-coaster—I realized I was a lesbian but had no idea where to go from there. During my freshman and sophomore years, I went to parties with friends, but I rarely drank. What if I lost control and told someone who I really was inside? By the middle of my sophomore year, I couldn't take it anymore. I wrote notes to my mother, my father, and my best male friend and hid them where they wouldn't

find the notes for a day or so. I swallowed a bottle of pills, curled up in an out-of-the-way bathroom stall at school while everyone else was at an assembly, and waited to die. A student found me unconscious and got the school nurse.

I recovered, but my life didn't really get better until college. For the first time in my life, I wasn't alone anymore, and it felt incredibly liberating. By my junior year, I knew that I wanted to come out, once and for all, but I was terrified that it would kill my parents—literally. I wanted their love and approval so badly, and all I ever wanted to be was the "perfect" daughter. A few days later, I learned my mom had terminal cancer, and was given 6 months to live. I was crushed—but as strange as this sounds, her diagnosis was a gift to both of us, because I realized I could finally tell her I was a lesbian. Why? Because I knew it wouldn't kill her—she was already dying, and it had nothing to do with my sexual orientation. Shortly after she was diagnosed, I picked up the phone and called her. I said, "Mom, I have something to tell you and it's really difficult. . . . I'm gay." There was a pause, and then she started crying. She completely lost it on the phone and af-

ter an hour or so, she calmed down and told me she loved me and supported me, no matter what. From that day until the day she died, I told my mother everything. I came out to everyone in my life—friends, professors, classmates—and began living my life as the person I had always been inside.

Once I decided to be out in every aspect of my life, everything in my life began to fall in place. I am now in a committed relationship of 4 years, and we have a 2-year-old son through adoption. We live our lives as an openly lesbian couple, and our son knows that he has a Mama and a Mommy that sleep in the same bed. Our families are incredibly supportive, and we have a loving circle of extended family and friends.

As comfortable as I am with myself and my life, I realize that the coming-out journey won't be any easier for the next generation if I don't work to change the way gay and lesbian people are perceived today by living proudly, openly, and without shame. SOURCE: Author's files.

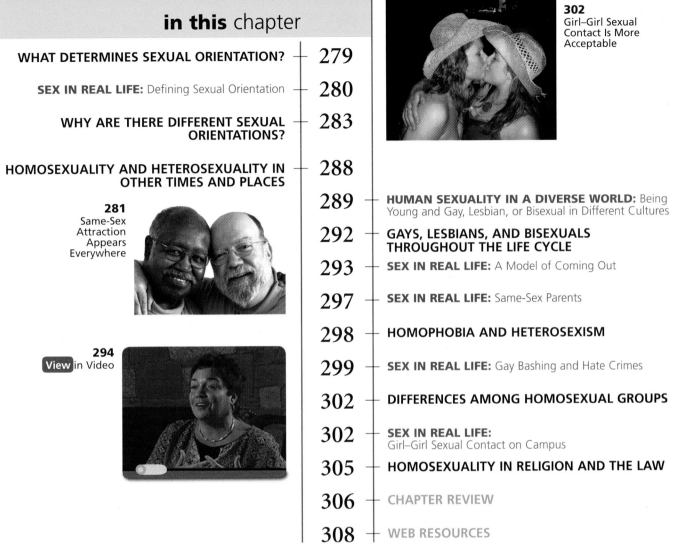

◁ Opposite: Phill Snel/Getty Images

S exual orientation refers to the gender(s) that a person is attracted to emotionally, physically, sexually, and romantically. Heterosexuals are predominantly attracted to members of the other sex; homosexuals to members of the same sex; and bisexuals are attracted to both sexes (the word "gay" is often used to refer to a male homosexual, whereas "lesbian" is often used to refer to a female homosexual).

Although such distinctions may seem simple, as you will soon see, human sexual behavior does not always fit easily into such neat boxes. Today many people use the acronym **GLBTQ** to refer to people whose identity is gay, lesbian, bisexual, transgendered, or questioning (or queer), and we will use the acronym GLB throughout this chapter (we discussed transgender issues in Chapter 4, and here we focus on gay, lesbian, and bisexual issues).

Before the 1980s most of published research on homosexuality focused on the causes or on associated mental disorders (because homosexuality was classified as such until 1973; see Chapter 1), and in the 1990s, HIV and AIDS dominated the research studies (Boehmer, 2002). Today we are learning more about the development of gay, lesbian, and bisexual identities, coming-out issues, aging, and health care, to name a few areas. We discuss this research throughout this chapter.

What Determines Sexual Orientation?

How should we categorize a person's **sexual orientation?** Take a moment to read the Sex in Real Life feature, "Defining Sexual Orientation." Here you will see that the simplest way to categorize a person's

GLBTQ
Acronym for gay, lesbian, bisexual, transgendered, or questioning (or queer) adults or youths.

sexual orientation
The gender(s) that a person is attracted to emotionally, physically, sexually, and romantically.

Defining Sexual Orientation

Who is heterosexual? Who is homosexual? Who is bisexual?

Read through the following descriptions of different sexual lifestyles. How would you categorize these people? Who is heterosexual? Who is homosexual? Who is bisexual?

Susan, 45 years old: I have been in an exclusive, monogamous lesbian relationship with Michele for 21 years. After 8 years with Michele, I decided I wanted a child and had sex a few times with a friend of mine, Jonathan. I now have a 13-year-old son. Seeing how much I enjoyed having a child, my partner decided she wanted one, too, but because she had no desire to have intercourse with a man, she had herself artificially inseminated.

Allie, 25 years old: I had my first sexual experience with a guy when I was 16 years old. I loved sex and enjoyed being with guys. However, I fell madly in love with a woman during my junior year of college. Our sex life was awesome. We drifted apart after college, and now I am sleeping with only men again.

Bill, 21 years old: When I was in my teens, a friend of mine and myself stroked each other to orgasm on three occasions. Although I now date only women, every so often while masturbating, I fantasize about those experiences, which enhances my orgasm. I consider myself heterosexual and feel a bit uneasy about my fantasies.

Anthony, 37 years old: I have been married for 15 years, and I have two children. My wife and I have a healthy sexual life, and I love her very much. I have never had sex with another woman since my marriage. However, about once every 2 or 3 months, I drive to a town about 2 hours away from where I live and pick up a man for quick, anonymous sex. I find these encounters to be the most exciting part of my sex life.

Peter, 26 years old: I have been in prison for 5 years for dealing drugs. While in prison, I've engaged in anal and oral sex with other men, usually fantasizing that they were women. I long for my scheduled release a few months from now, when I plan to resume having sex exclusively with women, as I did before being sent to prison.

Kiko, 45 years old: My partner and I enjoy engaging in group sex with other couples. In these group sex sessions, sexual contact is very free, and often I will give a guy a blow job while my partner engages in sexual contact with women. We are both very comfortable with such contact, feeling that sexual pleasure is sexual pleasure no matter who is administering it.

Are any of these people difficult to categorize?

---

sexual orientation seems to be through sexual behavior: with whom does he or she have sex? However, if that were our sole criterion, we would have to call Peter gay—after all, he has sex exclusively with other men. But because Peter fantasizes only of sex with women, can we really call him gay?

Maybe, then, the secret life of sexual fantasies determines sexual orientation. Bill, however, sometimes fantasizes about sex with men, even though he considers himself **straight** and has sex only with women. Allie is having sex only with men now but has slept with women in the past.

Perhaps we should consider romantic love instead of sex to determine a person's sexual orientation. Whom do you love, or whom could you love? Anthony loves his wife romantically and would never consider an emotional attachment to the men he picks up. Would you consider Anthony 100% **heterosexual** just because he loves only his wife? Maybe we should just let people decide for themselves; if they believe they are heterosexual, they are, no matter how they behave. Yet when people's behavior and beliefs about themselves are in conflict (such as Anthony's), social scientists usually define them by their behavior.

The problem may be that we tend to think of sexual orientation in discrete categories: you are either **homosexual** or heterosexual (or, occasionally, **bisexual**). The full variety and richness of human sexual experience, however, cannot be easily captured in

REALResearch > A CNN/Gallup poll in 2007 found that **42%** of Americans believed homosexuality was caused by upbringing and environment, whereas **39%** believed a person is born gay or lesbian (CABLE NEWS NETWORK, 2007). However, attitudes have been changing—in the 1970s and 1980s, fewer than **20%** of Americans believed a person was born gay.

such restrictive categories. People can show enormous variety in their sexual behavior, sexual fantasies, emotional attachments, and sexual self-concept, and each contributes to a person's sexual orientation.

In this chapter, we explore the nature of sexual orientation and the ways researchers and scholars think about it. Heterosexuality is a sexual orientation, and the question "Why is he or she heterosexual?" is no less valid than "Why is he or she homosexual?" or "bisexual?" Here, however, we focus our attention primarily on the research and writing about homosexuality and bisexuality.

straight
Slang for heterosexual.

heterosexual
Man or woman who is erotically attracted to members of the other sex.

homosexual
Man or woman who is erotically attracted to members of the same sex.

bisexual
Person who is erotically attracted to members of either sex.

If I played sex games with a friend of the same sex when I was 15, am I gay?

Sexual experimentation and sexual orientation are two different things. It is very common, especially in the teenage years and before, to experiment with same-sex contact (and for people who are predominantly gay or lesbian to experiment with the other sex). Yet only a fairly small percentage of people who experiment will become gay, lesbian, or bisexual (Fay et al., 1989).

Sexual orientation refers to the gender that a person is attracted to emotionally, physically, sexually, and romantically. Same-sex attraction has appeared in almost every society throughout history.

MODELS OF SEXUAL ORIENTATION: WHO IS HOMOSEXUAL?

Kinsey and his colleagues (1948) believed that relying on the categories "homosexual" and "heterosexual" to describe sexual orientation was inadequate. They also suggested that using a category such as "homosexual" was not as helpful as talking about homosexual behavior. Trying to decide who is a homosexual is difficult; trying to compare amounts or types of homosexual behavior (including fantasies and emotions) is easier.

So Kinsey introduced a 7-point scale (see Figure 11.1) ranging from *exclusively heterosexual behavior* (0) to *exclusively homosexual behavior* (6). The Kinsey continuum was the first scale to suggest that people engage in complex sexual behaviors that cannot be reduced to simply to "homosexual" and "heterosexual." Many theorists agree that sexual orientation is a continuous variable rather than a categorical variable—that is, there are no natural cutoff points that would easily separate people into categories such as "heterosexual" or "homosexual" (Berkey et al., 1990; L. Ellis et al., 1987).

The Kinsey scale is not without its problems, however. First, Kinsey emphasized people's behavior (although he did consider other factors such as fantasies and emotions), but some researchers suggest that people's emotions and fantasies are the most important determinants of sexual orientation (Bell et al., 1981; F. Klein, 1993; Storms, 1980, 1981). Second, the scale is static in time; how recently must one have had homosexual contact to qualify for "incidents" of homosexual behavior? Or consider Anthony from the Sex in Real Life feature "Defining Sexual Orientation." If Anthony slept with six men over the last year and had sex with his wife once a week, is he in Category 5 (because he had sex with six men and only one woman) or Category 2 (because he had 52 experiences with a woman, but only 6 with men; F. Klein, 1990)?

Other models, such as the Klein sexual orientation grid (KSOG; see Figure 11.2), try to take the Kinsey continuum further by including seven dimensions—attraction, behavior, fantasy, emotional preference, social preference, self-identification, and lifestyle (Horowitz et al., 2001). Each of these dimensions is measured for the past, the present, and the ideal. Take the KSOG to create a profile of your sexual orientation.

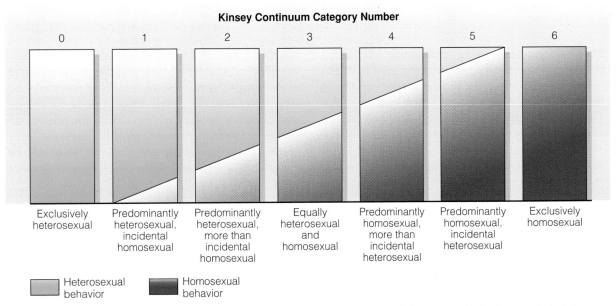

Kinsey Continuum Category Number

| 0 | 1 | 2 | 3 | 4 | 5 | 6 |

| Exclusively heterosexual | Predominantly heterosexual, incidental homosexual | Predominantly heterosexual, more than incidental homosexual | Equally heterosexual and homosexual | Predominantly homosexual, more than incidental heterosexual | Predominantly homosexual, incidental heterosexual | Exclusively homosexual |

☐ Heterosexual behavior ■ Homosexual behavior

Figure **11.1** The Kinsey Continuum. The 7-point scale is based on behaviors ranging from exclusively heterosexual behavior to exclusively homosexual behavior. From H. Kinsey, *Sexual Behavior in the Human Male,* 1948. Reprinted with permission of The Kinsey Institute for Research in Sex, Gender, and Reproduction, Inc.

The Klein Sexual Orientation Grid

	Past	Present	Ideal
A. Sexual attraction			
B. Sexual behavior			
C. Sexual fantasies			
D. Emotional preference			
E. Social preference			
F. Self-identification			
G. Heterosexual/homosexual lifestyle			

0 = other sex only
1 = mostly other sex, incidental same sex
2 = mostly other sex, more than incidental same sex
3 = both sexes equally
4 = mostly same sex, more than incidental other sex
5 = mostly same sex, incidental other sex
6 = same sex only

Figure **11.2** The Klein Sexual Orientation Grid was designed to examine seven dimensions of an individual's sexual orientation to determine whether these dimensions have changed over time and to look at a person's fantasy of his or her "ideal" sexual orientation. The KSOG gives a set of numbers that can be compared to determine rates of different sexual orientations. Use the Kinsey categories in this grid to rate yourself. From Fritz Klein, *Homosexuality/Heterosexuality*, p. 280. Reprinted with permission of The Kinsey Institute for Research in Sex, Gender, and Reproduction, Inc.

range from 2% to 4% to more than 10% in males and 1% to 3% in females, whereas estimates for bisexuality are approximately 3% (M. Diamond, 1993; Hughes, 2006; Seidman & Rieder, 1994; Whitam et al., 1999). Laumann and colleagues (1994) found that although 5.5% of women said they found the thought of having sex with another woman appealing, only about 4% said they had had sex with another woman after the age of 18, and fewer than 2% had had sex with another woman in the past year. Similarly, although 9% of men said they had had sex with another male since puberty, a little more than 5% had had sex with a man since turning 18, and only 2% had had sex with a man in the past year. National studies in France, Britain, Norway, Denmark, and Canada all found same-sex behavior in 1% to 3% of men and a slightly lower percentage of women (Muir, 1993). Overall, surveys indicate that the frequency of same-sex behavior in the United States has remained fairly constant over the years despite changes in the social status of homosexuality (Pillard & Bailey, 1998).

However, there are problems with some of the studies just discussed. For example, many concentrate on same-sex *behavior*, not attraction, fantasies or desires. One national population-based study measured both same-sex attraction and behavior and found 16% to 20% of the adult population of the United States, United Kingdom, and France reported some same-sex attraction or behavior since age 15 (Sell et al., 1995). Researchers claim these statistics were higher because they included same-sex attraction. In addition, these researchers also included men and women who

MEASURING SEXUAL ORIENTATION: **HOW PREVALENT?**

How prevalent are homosexuality, heterosexuality, and bisexuality in society? Kinsey and his colleagues (1948) found that 37% of men and 13% of women reported that they had had at least one adult sexual experience with a member of the same sex that resulted in orgasm and that about 4% of men and 3% of women were lifelong homosexuals. He also reported that 10% of White men had been mostly gay for at least 3 years between the ages of 16 and 55, and this statistic became the one most people cited when estimating the prevalence of homosexuality in the United States. However, because of the problems with Kinsey's sampling (see Chapter 2), these figures may be unreliable.

There continues to be controversy about how many gays, lesbians, or bisexuals there are today. Estimates for homosexuality

REALResearch > Overall, people are fairly good at categorizing others into social groups—such as race, age, gender—especially if the distinction is obvious (Rule, 2008). Being able to recognize whether someone is gay or lesbian is more difficult, and the term *gaydar* has been used to refer to an intuitive sense of another person's sexual orientation (it combines *gay* and *radar*). Research on gaydar has found that U.S. gay men can usually perceive other gay men accurately within a few seconds (Rule, 2008).

were not currently sexually active but reported a history of same-sex behavior in the past (many studies often do not count non-sexually active men and women as being gay or lesbian, even with a history of same-sex behavior; Sell et al., 1995). Although there is much work to be done in determining the prevalence of homosexuality, scholars generally agree that between 3% and 4% of males are predominantly gay, 1.5% to 2% of women are predominantly lesbian, and about 2% to 5% are bisexual (Laumann et al., 1994; Mackay, 2000).

review questions

1 Describe the difficulties involved in our attempts to categorize sexual behavior.

2 Outline the Kinsey model of sexual orientation, and compare and contrast it with the KSOG.

3 Describe the prevalence of gay, lesbian, and bisexual orientations. Explain why this research has been so controversial.

Why Are There Different Sexual Orientations?

In the 1930s and 1940s, a group of scientists tried to explain homosexuality by looking for "masculine" traits in lesbians and "feminine" traits in homosexual men. They claimed that gay men had broad shoulders and narrow hips (indicating "immature skeletal development") and lesbians had abnormal genitalia, including larger-than-average vulvas, longer labia minora, a larger glans on the clitoris, a smaller uterus, and higher eroticism, shown by their tendency to become sexually aroused when being examined (Terry, 1990)! Modern research has failed to find any significant nonneurological physical differences between homosexuals and heterosexuals, although attempts to examine physical differences persist.

Today's theories can be divided into five basic types: biological, developmental, behavioral, sociological, and interactional theories. Biological theories suggest that homosexuals are physically different from heterosexuals. Developmental theories, in contrast, suggest that homosexuality develops in response to a person's upbringing and personal history, and therefore nothing is physically different between the two. Learning theory explores how homosexuality is a learned behavior, whereas sociological theories look at how social forces produce homosexuality in a society. Finally, interactional theories look at the interaction between biology, development, and societal factors.

Scholars in different fields tend to take different approaches to explain why some people are gay, lesbian, or bisexual. Note, however, that almost all the researchers we will discuss assume there are two, exclusive, nonoverlapping categories: homosexual and heterosexual. Most theories on sexual orientation ignore bisexuality or do not offer enough research to explain why bisexuality exists. We discuss bisexuality throughout this chapter.

BIOLOGICAL THEORIES: DIFFERENCES ARE INNATE

Early biological theories implied that homosexuality was an abnormality in development, which contributed to the argument that homosexuality is a sickness. More recently, gay and lesbian scholars, in an attempt to prove that homosexuality is not a "lifestyle choice" as antihomosexual forces have argued, have themselves been arguing that homosexuality is a biologically based sexual variation. Biological theories claim that differing sexual orientations are due to differences in physiology. These differences can be due to genetics, hormones, birth order, or simple physical traits.

Genetics

In 1952, Franz Kallman tried to show that there was a genetic component to homosexuality. Kallman compared identical twins (who come from one zygote and have the same genes (we talk more about twins in Chapter 12), with fraternal twins (who come from two zygotes and have about 50% of the same genes). Although Kallman found a strong genetic component to homosexuality, his study had a number of problems and is unreliable.

Bailey and his colleagues have performed a number of studies of twins to determine the genetic basis of homosexuality. They report that in homosexual males, 52% of identical twins, 22% of fraternal twins, and 11% of adoptive brothers were also gay, show-

---

REALResearch > Research has found differences in homosexual and heterosexual brains—gay men and heterosexual women have similar spatial learning and memory abilities that differ from heterosexual men (RAHMAN & KOERTING, 2008). Another study found that straight men and lesbian women (and gay men and straight women) have similar brain structures (SAVIC & LINDSTRÖM, 2008). Researchers believe that these studies support biological theories of sexual orientation.

WHAT DO YOU WANT TO KNOW ?

Why are men often turned on by watching two females having sex but turned off by watching two males?

Heterosexual men's magazines often feature two women together in sexual positions but almost never two men. In the United States, watching women interact sexually is much more socially acceptable. These pictorials always imply that the women are still attracted to men, waiting for them, just biding their time until a man arrives. An internalized fear of homosexuality in men also makes it difficult for many men to see two men being sexual with each other. It is much less threatening to watch two women. In Chapter 18, we'll discuss gender and the use of pornography.

ing that the more closely genetically related two siblings were, the more likely they were to share a sexual orientation (J. M. Bailey & Pillard, 1993). Among females, 48% of identical twins, 16% of fraternal twins, and 6% of adoptive siblings of lesbians were also lesbians (J. M. Bailey et al., 1993). However, identical twins share much more than genetics. They also share many more experiences than do other kinds of siblings. So the studies cannot tell how much of the concordance is due to genetic factors and how much is due to the identical twins having grown up under similar environmental influences.

Another interesting finding is the one by Hamer and colleagues (1993) of the National Cancer Institute. Hamer found that gay males tended to have more gay relatives on their mother's side, and he traced that to the existence of a gene that he found in 33 of 40 gay brothers. This gene is inherited from the mother's, but not the father's, side (Keller, 2005). In addition, gay men have more gay brothers than lesbian sisters, whereas lesbians have more lesbian sisters than gay brothers (Bogaert, 2005; Pattatucci, 1998). This research has also found evidence of a "gay" gene on the X chromosome but did not find a "lesbian" gene.

If homosexuality were solely a genetic trait, it should have disappeared long ago. Because homosexuals have been less likely than heterosexuals to have children, each successive generation of homosexuals should have become smaller, until genes for homosexuality disappeared from the gene pool. Yet rates of homosexuality have remained constant. Concordance rates for siblings, twins, and adoptees reveal that genes account for at least half of the variance in sexual orientation (Pillard & Bailey, 1998). Even so, Bailey and his colleagues agree that environmental factors are also important.

Hormones

Hormonal theories can concentrate either on hormonal imbalances before birth or on hormone levels in adults. Here we look at both prenatal and adult hormonal levels.

PRENATAL FACTORS When certain hormones are injected into pregnant animals, such as rats or guinea pigs, at critical periods of fetal development, the offspring can be made to exhibit homosexual behavior (Dorner, 1976). Some researchers have found evidence that sexual orientation may be influenced by levels of prenatal hormones in human beings as well (Cohen-Bendahan et al., 2005; Rahman, 2005). (For more information about hormones, see Chapter 4.) In a retrospective study, L. Ellis and colleagues (1988) suggested that stress during pregnancy (which can influence hormonal levels) increased the chances of a homosexual offspring. Early hormone levels have also been found to influence both sexual orientation and related childhood sex-typed behaviors (Berenbaum & Snyder, 1995; Swaab, 2004).

REALResearch > Handedness (being right- or left-handed) has been found to be related to sexual orientation (R. BLANCHARD ET AL., 2006; BOGAERT ET AL., 2007). Right-handed men with older brothers and left-handed men without older brothers have an increased odds of being gay (R. BLANCHARD ET AL., 2006; LALUMIÈRE & BLANCHARD, 2000; LIPPA, 2003).

However, other researchers have concluded that the evidence for the effect of prenatal hormones on both male and female homosexuality is weak (Gooren, 2006; Hall & Schaeff, 2008; Whalen et al., 1990). A study of female rhesus monkeys who were given masculine hormones before birth revealed that their environment after birth was as important to their sexual behavior as the hormones (Money, 1987). In other words, even if prenatal hormones are a factor in sexual orientation, environmental factors may be equally important.

ADULT HORMONE LEVELS Many studies have compared blood androgen levels in adult male homosexuals with those in adult male heterosexuals, and most have found no significant differences (Green, 1988; Mbügua, 2006). Of five studies comparing hormone levels in lesbians and straight women, three found no differences between the two groups in testosterone, estrogen, or

other hormones, and the other two found higher levels of testosterone in lesbians (and one found lower levels of estrogen; Dancey, 1990). Thus, studies so far do not support the idea of adult hormone involvement.

Birth Order

Researchers have also examined effects of birth order. Many gay men have been found to have older brothers, but not older sisters (R. Blanchard, 2004; Bogaert et al., 2007; Camperio-Ciani et al., 2004; Ridley, 2003). Overall it has been estimated that one in seven gay men's sexual orientation was a result of fraternal birth order (the number of older brothers they have; Cantor et al., 2002).

The **maternal immune hypothesis** proposes that in some mothers, there is a progressive immunization to male-specific antigens after the birth of successive sons, which increases the effects of anti-male antibodies on the sexual differentiation of the brain in the developing fetus (R. Blanchard, 2008; Ridley, 2003). This has also been referred to as the fraternal birth order effect. Interestingly, these effects have not been found in left-handed brothers, however (R. Blanchard, 2008).

This research is controversial, but nonetheless research in this direction continues to look for possible interactions. The relationship between sexual orientation and number of older brothers has been found to hold only for males (Blanchard, 2004, 2008).

Physiology

Two articles in the early 1990s reported differences between the brains of homosexual and heterosexual men (S. LeVay, 1991; Swaab & Hofman, 1990). Both studies found that certain areas of the hypothalamus, known to play a strong role in sexual urges, were either larger or smaller in gay men than in straight men. More recent studies have also found brain differences—specifically in the cerebral hemispheres of heterosexual and homosexual men and women (Savic & Lindström, 2008). However, it has not yet been determined whether the differences were there from birth or developed later in life, and the research cannot prove that the differences were due primarily to sexual orientation (Kinnunen et al., 2004; Swaab, 2004).

Physiology studies have also looked at amount of facial hair, size of external genitalia, ear structure, and hearing (Jensen, 1998), body shape and motion (Johnson et al., 2007), eye-blink startle responses (Rahman et al., 2003), spatial ability (Rahman & Koerting, 2008), handedness (R. Blanchard et al., 2006; Martin et al., 2008), and finger-length differences between heterosexual and homosexual men and women (A. Bailey & Hurd, 2005; Hall & Schaeff, 2008; Rahman, 2005). Of all of these, the most research has been done on finger-length differences between heterosexual and homosexual men and women. Researchers found that finger length is affected by prenatal testosterone and estrogen levels, especially in

maternal immune hypothesis
Theory of sexual orientation that proposes that the fraternal birth order effect of gay brothers reflects the progressive immunization of some mothers to male-specific antigens by each succeeding male fetus.

the right hand (McFadden et al., 2005; Rizwan et al., 2007). The typical male-type finger pattern is a longer ring finger than index finger, whereas the typical female-type pattern is similar index and ring finger lengths, or a longer index finger. Lesbian women are more commonly found to have a typical male-type finger length pattern while gay men are more likely to have a typical female-type finger length pattern (Hall & Schaeff, 2008; McFadden et al., 2005). In addition, men with typical female-type finger length patterns have been found to be more emotional than men with a typical male-type finger length (Rizman et al., 2007).

In summary, although there have been some biological differences found among homosexuals, heterosexuals, and bisexuals, findings are inconsistent, and in many cases the evidence is weak. Given the complexity of biological factors, it is impossible to make accurate individual predications because of the randomness of neural connections during development (Pillard, 1998). Because of this, it appears that sexual orientation is the result of an interaction of genetic, biological, and social influences (Schuklenk et al., 1997). We now examine some of the developmental, sociological, and interactional theories of sexual orientation.

DEVELOPMENTAL THEORIES:
DIFFERENCES ARE DUE TO UPBRINGING

Developmental theories focus on a person's upbringing and personal history to find the origins of homosexuality. First we discuss the most influential development theory, psychoanalytic theory, and then we examine gender-role noncomformity and peer-interaction theories of homosexuality.

Freud and the Psychoanalytic School

Sigmund Freud seemed to be of two minds about homosexuality (1953). On the one hand, he believed that the infant was "polymorphous perverse"—that is, the infant sees all kinds of things as potentially sexual. Because both males and females are potentially attractive to the infant, thought Freud, all of us are inherently bisexual. He therefore did not see homosexuals as being sick.

On the other hand, Freud saw male heterosexuality as the result of normal maturation and male homosexuality as the result of an unresolved Oedipal complex (see Chapter 2 for a more complete discussion of this topic). An intense attachment to the mother coupled with a distant father could lead the boy to fear revenge by the father through castration. Female genitalia, lacking a penis, could then represent this castration and evoke fear throughout his life. After puberty, the child shifts from desire for the mother to identification with her, and he begins to look for the love objects she would look for—men.

Like Freud's view of female sexuality in general, his theories on lesbianism were less coherent, but he basically argued that the young girl becomes angry when she discovers she lacks a penis and blames her mother (we discussed the Electra complex in Chapter 2). Unable to have her father, she defensively rejects him and all men and minimizes her anger at her mother by eliminating the competition between them for male affection.

Freud saw homosexuality as partly **autoerotic** and narcissistic; by making love to a body like one's own, one is really making love

Psychoanalytic views of homosexuality dominated for many years.

WHAT DO YOU WANT TO KNOW ?

Is homosexuality found only in humans, or do some animals also exhibit homosexual behavior?

Same-sex activity has been found in 450 species of birds and mammals (Bagemihl, 1999), although some scientists believe this number may be as high as 1,500 (Moskowitz, 2008). In the summer months, killer whales spend one tenth of their time engaging in homosexual activity (Mackay, 2000). Many mammal species, from rats to lions to cows to monkeys, exhibit same-sex mounting behavior. Males mount other males, and females mount other females (although they rarely do it when a male is present). In some penguin species, males have been found to form lifelong same-sex partnerships (Bagemihl, 1999). Bonobo chimpanzees have been found to engage in all types of sexual behaviors, including same- and other-sex behaviors (Waal, 1995). Even so, no one has reliably reported on cases in which individual animals display exclusively homosexual behavior; animal bisexuality is more common (Bagemihl, 1999). However, we should be careful in extending animal analogies to humans.

to a mirror of oneself. Freud's generally tolerant attitude toward homosexuality was repudiated by some later psychoanalysts, especially Sandor Rado (1949). Rado claimed that humans were not innately bisexual and that homosexuality was a mental illness. This view (not Freud's) became standard for the psychiatric profession until at least the 1970s.

Another influential researcher who followed Rado's perspective was Irving Bieber. Bieber and colleagues (1962) studied 106 homosexual men and 100 heterosexual men who were in psychoanalysis. He claimed that all boys had a normal, erotic attraction to women. However, some had overly close and possessive mothers who were also overintimate and sexually seductive. Their fathers, in contrast, were hostile or absent, and this **triangulation** drove the boy to the arms of his mother, who inhibited his normal masculine development. Bieber thus blamed homosexuality on a seductive mother who puts the fear of heterosexuality in her son. However, Bieber's participants were all in psychoanalysis and thus may have had other issues. Also, fewer than two thirds of the homosexual participants fit his model, and almost a third of heterosexual participants came from the same type of family and yet did not engage in homosexual behavior.

The psychoanalytic views of homosexuality dominated for many years. Evelyn Hooker, a clinical psychologist, was a pioneer in gay studies who tried to combat the psychoanalytic view that homosexuality was an illness (see Chapter 2). Hooker (1957) used psychological tests, personal histories, and psychological evaluations to show that homosexuals were as well adjusted as hetero-

autoerotic
The arousal of sexual feeling without an external stimulus.

triangulation
The network of triangles that often occurs among three people (e.g., mother–father–child).

sexuals and that no real evidence existed that homosexuality was a psychological disorder. Although it took many years for her ideas to take hold, many modern psychoanalysts have shifted away from the pathological view of homosexuality. Lewes (1988) demonstrated that psychoanalytic theory itself could easily portray homosexuality as a result of healthy development and that previous psychoanalytic interpretations of homosexuality were based more on prejudice than on science.

Gender-Role Nonconformity

One group of studies that has begun to fuel debate about the role of early childhood in the development of homosexuality is **gender-role nonconformity** research. The studies are based on the observation that boys who exhibit cross-gender traits—that is, who behave in ways more characteristic of girls of that age—are more likely to grow up to be gay, whereas girls who behave in typically male ways are more likely to grow up to be lesbian. As children, gay men on average have been found to be more feminine than straight men, whereas lesbians have been found to be more masculine (J. M. Bailey et al., 1995; Pillard, 1991). Remember, though, that these findings are correlational, meaning that cross-gender traits and later homosexuality appear to be related but do not have a cause-and-effect relationship.

Overall, cross-gender boys are viewed more negatively than cross-gender girls (Sandnabba & Ahlberg, 1999). In addition, cross-gender boys are more often thought to be gay than cross-gender girls are thought to be lesbian. One therapist who works with gay men reports that they saw themselves as:

. . . more sensitive than other boys; they cried more easily, had their feelings more readily hurt, had more aesthetic interests, enjoyed nature, art, and music, and were drawn to other "sensitive" boys, girls and adults. Most of these men also felt they were less aggressive as children than others of their age, and most did not enjoy participating in competitive activities. They report that they experienced themselves as being outsiders since these early childhood years. (Isay, 1989, p. 23)

R. Green (1987) did a prospective study by comparing 66 pervasively feminine boys with 56 conventionally masculine boys as they matured. Green calls the feminine boys "sissy-boys," an unfortunate term. However, he found that these boys cross-dressed, were interested in female fashions, played with dolls, avoided rough play, wished to be girls, and did not desire to be like their fathers from a young age. Three fourths of them grew up to be homosexual or bisexual, whereas only one of the masculine boys became bisexual. The "sissy-boys," however, also tended to be harassed, rejected, and ignored more by their peers; were more sickly than other boys; and had a higher rate of psychological disorders (Zucker, 1990).

One cannot tell from these types of studies whether these boys are physiologically or developmentally different or whether society's reaction to their unconventional play encouraged them to develop a particular sexual orientation. Whether right or wrong, gender-role nonconformity theory cannot be the sole explanation of homosexuality, for many, if not most, gay men were not effeminate as children; not all effeminate boys grow up to be gay; and not all "tomboy" girls grow up to be lesbians.

WHAT DO YOU WANT TO KNOW ?

Is there any therapy that can change a person's sexual orientation?

Some people believe that sexual orientation is determined by social and environmental factors and that a homosexual can change his or her sexual orientation through therapy or religious faith (Newport, 1998). For the past three decades, the ex-gay movement (persons who once identified as gay or lesbian but now identify as straight) has claimed that homosexuals can be changed into heterosexuals through **reparative** (rep-PEAR-at-tiv) **therapy,** or conversion therapy (Cianciotto & Cahill, 2006). These types of therapies are based on the premise that homosexuality is an illness that needs to be cured. "Ex-gay ministries," which use religion to change a gay or lesbian into a heterosexual, have also become more popular in the last few years (Christianson, 2005).

Although the psychoanalyst Irving Bieber (Bieber et al., 1962) reported changing the sexual orientation of 27% of his sample of gay men, more recent psychoanalytic studies have had far less impressive success, and the duration of such "conversions" is questionable. One study found that many teens who participate in such programs report higher levels of depression and thoughts of suicide, along with lower levels of self-esteem and damaged family and peer relationships (Shidlo & Schroeder, 2002). Today reparative therapy is not supported by any reliable research, and the majority of professional organizations are opposed to the use of such therapies (Cianciotto & Cahill, 2006; Cramer et al., 2008; Jenkins & Johnston, 2004).

Peer Group Interaction

Storms (1981) suggests a purely developmental theory of homosexuality. Noting that a person's sex drive begins to develop in adolescence, Storms suggests that those who develop early begin to become sexually aroused before they have significant contact with the other sex. Because dating usually begins around age 15, boys who mature at age 12 still play and interact in predominantly same-sex groupings, and so their emerging erotic feelings are more likely to focus on boys.

Storms's theory is supported by the fact that homosexuals do tend to report earlier sexual contacts than heterosexuals. Also, men's sex drive may emerge at a younger age than women's, if such things as frequency of masturbation are any measure, which may explain why there are fewer lesbians than gay men.

Yet Storms's theory also has its problems. Later in this chapter, we discuss the example of Sambian boys who live communally and have sex with other boys from an early age until they are ready to marry. If Storms is right and a male becomes homosexual because only males are available at the time of sexual awakening, then all male Sambians should be gay. However, almost all go on to lead heterosexual lives.

reparative therapy
Therapy to change sexual orientation; also called conversion therapy.

gender-role nonconformity
Theory that looks at the role of early childhood in the development of homosexuality and explores cross-gendered traits in childhood.

BEHAVIORIST THEORIES: DIFFERENCES ARE LEARNED

Behavioral theories of homosexuality consider it a learned behavior, brought about by the rewarding or pleasant reinforcement of homosexual behaviors or the punishing or negative reinforcement of heterosexual behavior (Masters & Johnson, 1979). For example, a person may have a same-sex encounter that is pleasurable, coupled with an encounter with the other sex that is frightening; in his or her fantasies, that person may focus on the same-sex encounter, reinforcing its pleasure with masturbation. Masters and Johnson (1979) believed that even in adulthood, some men and women move toward same-sex behaviors if they have bad heterosexual encounters and pleasant homosexual ones.

It is interesting to point out, however, that in a society like ours that tends to view heterosexuality as the norm, it would seem that few men and women would be societally reinforced for homosexual behavior. Yet homosexuality exists even without this positive reinforcement from society.

SOCIOLOGICAL THEORIES: SOCIAL FORCES AT WORK

Sociological theories look at how social forces produce homosexuality in a society. They suggest that concepts such as homosexuality, bisexuality, and heterosexuality are products of our social fabric and are dependent on how we as a society decide to define things. In other words, we learn our culture's way of thinking about sexuality, and then we apply it to ourselves.

The idea of "homosexuality" is a product of a particular culture at a particular time; the idea did not even exist before the 19th century (although the behavior did). Some have argued that the use of the term homosexuality as a way to think about same-sex behavior arose only after the Industrial Revolution freed people economically from the family unit and urbanization allowed them to choose new lifestyles in the cities (Adam, 1987). Thus, the idea that people are either "heterosexual" or "homosexual" is not a biological fact but simply a way of thinking that evolves as social conditions change. In other countries, as we note later, these terms are not used, and a person's sexuality is not defined by who his or her partners are.

Sociologists are interested in the models of sexuality that society offers its members and how individuals come to identify with one model or another. For example, maybe effeminate young boys begin to behave as homosexuals because they are labeled homosexual, are called "faggot" by their peers, are ridiculed by their siblings, and even witness the worry and fear on the faces of their parents. They begin to doubt themselves, search for homosexuality in their own behavior, and eventually find it. If American society did not split the sexual world into "homosexual" and "heterosexual" categories, perhaps these boys would move fluidly through same-sex and other-sex contacts without having to choose between the "gay" and "straight" communities.

INTERACTIONAL THEORY: BIOLOGY AND SOCIOLOGY

Finally, the interactional theory proposes that homosexuality results from a complex interaction of biological, psychological, and social factors. Perhaps a child is born after being exposed to prenatal hormones that could predispose him or her toward a particular sexual orientation, but this predisposition, in conjunction with social experiences, either facilitates or inhibits a particular sexual orientation.

Social psychologist Daryl Bem (1996) has proposed an interactional theory that combines both biology and sociological issues. Bem suggests that biological variables, such as genetics, hormones, and brain neuroanatomy, do not cause certain sexual orientations, but rather they contribute to childhood temperaments that influence a child's preferences for sex-typical or sex-atypical activities and peers.

Bem believes that males who engage in "male-typical activities," such as rough-and-tumble play or competitive team sports, prefer to be with other boys who also like these activities. Girls, on the other hand, who prefer "female-typical activities," such as socializing quietly or playing jacks, prefer the company of other girls who like to do the same activities. Gender-conforming children (those who engage in activities typical for their gender) prefer the other gender for romantic interests, whereas nonconforming children prefer the same gender. Bem's "exotic-becomes-erotic" theory suggests that sexual feelings evolve from experiencing heightened arousal in situations in which one gender is viewed as more exotic, or different from oneself (Bem, 1996). Bem asserts that gay and lesbian children had playmates of the other sex while growing up, and this led them to see the same sex as more "exotic" and appealing. However, his research has been contradictory and hasn't been supported by other research (Peplau et al., 1998). Many gay and lesbian children report playmates of both the same sex and the other sex while growing up.

review questions

1 Identify and describe the various areas of research within the biological theory of homosexuality.

2 Identify and describe the various developmental theories of homosexuality.

3 Explain the behavioral theory of homosexuality.

4 Explain the sociological theory of homosexuality.

5 Explain the interactional theory of homosexuality.

6 Differentiate the various theories that have been proposed to explain homosexuality.

Homosexuality and Heterosexuality
in Other Times and Places

When the American Psychiatric Association (APA) decided in 1973 to remove homosexuality from its list of official mental diseases, many psychiatrists were outraged. They demanded a vote of the full APA membership (Bayer, 1981).

For 100 years or so, homosexuality was considered a sickness. Only when scientists dropped that assumption did they make real progress in understanding homosexuality. The enormous complexity of the human brain allows highly flexible human behavior patterns in almost every aspect of life, and human sexuality is not an exception to that rule.

Homosexuality remains controversial in the United States. Some people see homosexuality as a sin. Others argue that homosexuals are a "bad influence" on society and children (and, for example, believe they should not be parents or teachers). Still others defend homosexual rights and attack America's whole view of sexuality.

Many other countries are much more tolerant of homosexuality than the United States—even other Western, predominantly Christian countries (such as Canada or parts of Europe). Western history has included many periods when homosexuality was generally accepted. In fact, Gilbert Herdt (1988), a prominent scholar of homosexuality, states that the modern American attitude is much harsher toward homosexuality than most other countries throughout most of history. The history of social attitudes toward homosexuality can teach us something about our own attitudes today.

*Homosexuality **remains controversial** in the United States.*

Ancient societies left evidence to show that same-sex behavior was not uncommon.

© Mimmo Jodice/Corbis

HOMOSEXUALITY IN HISTORY

Homosexuality has been viewed differently throughout history. Although there have been times when homosexuality has been accepted, there have also been times it has been scorned. The influence of the Church has greatly affected societal tolerance and acceptance of homosexuality.

The Classical Era

Before the 19th century, men who engaged in homosexual acts were accused of **sodomy** (SA-duh-mee), or **buggery,** which were simply seen as crimes and not considered part of a person's fundamental nature. Homosexual activity was common, homosexual prostitution was taxed by the state, and the writers of the time seemed to consider men loving men as natural as men loving women. Even after Rome became Christian, there was no antihomosexual legislation for more than 200 years.

Lesbian love seems to have puzzled ancient writers (who were almost all men). The word "lesbian" itself comes from the island of Lesbos, in Greece, where the poet Sappho lived about 600 B.C. Lesbianism was rarely explicitly against the law in most ancient societies (in fact, two or more unmarried women living together has usually been seen as proper, whereas a woman living alone was viewed with suspicion; Bullough, 1979).

Contrary to popular belief, homosexuality was not treated with concern or much interest by early Christians (Boswell, 1980). Neither ancient Greek nor Hebrew had a word for homosexual; in the entire Bible, same-sex sexual behavior is explicitly mentioned only in the prohibition in Leviticus (and here referring only to men); Saint Paul never explicitly condemned homosexuality, and Jesus made few pronouncements on proper or improper sexuality (except fidelity) and never mentioned homosexuality. Why, then, did Christianity become so antihomosexual?

The Middle Ages

By the ninth century, almost every part of Europe had some sort of local law code based on Church teachings, and although these codes included strong sanctions for sexual transgressions, including rape, adultery, incest, and fornication, homosexual relations were not forbidden in any of them (Boswell, 1980). Church indifference to homosexuality lasted well through the 13th century; in other words, for the first 1,000 years of Christianity, the Church showed little interest in homosexuality and did not generally condemn the behavior (Boswell, 1980; Kuefler, 2006; Siker, 1994). Male brothels appeared, defenses of homosexual relations began

sodomy
Any of various forms of sexual intercourse held to be unnatural or abnormal, especially anal intercourse or bestiality (also called buggery).

buggery
Any of various forms of sexual intercourse held to be unnatural or abnormal, especially anal intercourse or bestiality (also called sodomy).

lesbian
Woman who is sexually attracted to women.

to appear in print, and homosexuality became a fairly accepted part of the general culture until the late Middle Ages.

Homosexuality was completely legal in most countries in Europe in the year 1250 (Boswell, 1980). By 1300, however, there was a new intolerance of differences, and homosexuality was punishable by death almost everywhere (Boswell, 1980; Kuefler, 2006). This view from the late Middle Ages has influenced the Western world's view of homosexuality for the last 700 years.

The Modern Era

From the 16th century on, homosexuals were subject to periods of tolerance and periods of severe repression. In the American colonies, for example, homosexuality was a serious offense. In 1656, the New Haven Colony prescribed death for both males and females who engaged in homosexual acts (Boswell, 1980). The severe attitude toward homosexuality in America reflects its Puritan origins, and America remains, even today, more disapproving of homosexuality than Europe.

Even in times when homosexual acts were condemned, however, homoerotic poems, writings, and art were created. Openly homosexual communities appeared now and then. Other cultures also had periods of relative tolerance of homosexuality. In Japan, for example, the Edo period (1600–1868) saw a flourishing homosexual subculture, with openly gay clubs, geisha houses, and a substantial gay literature (Hirayama & Hirayama, 1986).

During the 19th and early 20th centuries in the United States, it was not uncommon for single, upper-middle-class women to live together in committed, lifelong relationships, although they may not all have engaged in genital sexuality (Nichols, 1990). At the same time, **passing women** disguised themselves as men, entered the workforce, and even married women—who sometimes never knew their husbands were female (remember the discussion of Billy Tipton, the famous jazz musician, from Chapter 4). In most cases, of course, the wife knew, and the couple probably lived as lesbians in a disguised heterosexual marriage. Some of these passing women held offices of great power, and their biological sex was not discovered until their death (Nichols, 1990).

In the 19th and early 20th centuries, physicians and scientists began to suggest that homosexuality was not a sin but an illness, which, if left "untreated," would spread like a contagious disease (Hansen, 1989). The dangers of this perspective were realized in Nazi Germany, where homosexuals were imprisoned and murdered along with Jews, Gypsies, epileptics, and others as part of

passing woman
Woman who disguises herself as a man.

HUMAN SEXUALITY IN A DIVERSE WORLD

Being Young and Gay, Lesbian, or Bisexual in Different Cultures

. . . in different parts of the world GLB adolescents may have very different experiences.

It's important to remember that although we have been exploring the gay, lesbian, and bisexual experiences in the United States, in different parts of the world GLB adolescents may have very different experiences. Here we take a look at adolescents in a variety of places around the globe.

English (male): Between the ages of 13 and 15 I closed myself off from the outside world. I would rarely go out and would never dare to go places where other people of my own age would be. The only thing I knew was that homosexuality was bad. (Plummer, 1989, p. 204)

East Indian (female): My family holds Western culture somehow responsible for offbeat youth. They think my being a lesbian is my being young, and confused, and rebellious. They feel it has something to do with trying to fit into white culture. . . . They're waiting for me to stop rebelling and go heterosexual, go out on dates, and come home early. (Tremble et al., 1989, p. 260)

Mexican (male): I thought myself very bad, and many times I was at the point of suicide. I don't know if I really might have killed myself, but many times I thought about it and believed it was the only alternative. That caused me many problems with my friends. I felt they thought me to be different, homosexual, and really sick. It made me separate from them. I felt myself inferior and thought I was the only one these things happened to. (Carrier, 1989, p. 238)

Chinese (male): I am longing to love others and to be loved. I have met some other homosexuals, but I have doubt about this type of love. With all the pressure I was afraid to reveal myself and ruined everything. As a result, we departed without showing each other homosexual love. As I am growing older my homosexual desire increases. This is too troubling and depressing for anyone. I thought about death many times. When you are young you cannot fall in love and when you are old you will be alone. Thinking of this makes the future absolutely hopeless. (Ruan & Tsai, 1988, p. 194)

Canadian (female): I feel like I am the terrific person I am today because I'm a lesbian. I decided I was gay when I was very young. After making that decision, which was the hardest thing I could ever face, I feel like I can do anything. (Schneider, 1989, p. 123)

Scottish (male): I don't like being gay. I wouldn't choose to be gay, and I don't like the gay scene. It's too superficial. I've got high moral standards. Lust is a sin but love isn't. In the gay scene people use other people and throw them away again. (Burbidge & Walters, 1981, p. 41)

Asian American (gender not identified): I wish I could tell my parents—they are the only ones who do not know about my gay identity, but I am sure they would reject me. There is no frame of reference to understand homosexuality in Asian American culture. (Chan, 1989, p. 19)

the program to purify the "Aryan race" (Adam, 1987). In America, psychiatry continued to view homosexuality as a mental disorder into the 1970s—and some psychiatrists still do today.

Ironically, the medical model's view of homosexuality, which influenced modern ideas of sexual orientation, changed the politics of homosexuality. Because physicians saw homosexuality not as just a behavior but as a built-in trait, it became a primary part of the way people looked at each other (Risman & Schwartz, 1988). Homosexuals began to argue: "If homosexuality is something I am, not just something I do, then I should have a right to be 'who I am' just as Blacks, women, and other groups have a right to be who they are." The new view of homosexuality encouraged homosexuals to band together and press for recognition of their civil rights as a minority group, which led to the modern gay and lesbian liberation movement we discussed in Chapter 1.

> *Same-sex behavior is found in **every culture**.*

HOMOSEXUALITY IN OTHER CULTURES

We all have a natural tendency to believe that others see the world the way we do. Yet what we call "homosexuality" is viewed so differently in other cultures that the word itself might not apply. In many societies, individuals have same-sex sexual relations as a normal part of their lives. This can be minor, as in Cairo, Egypt, where heterosexual men casually kiss and hold hands, or it can be fully sexual, as in the sequential homosexuality of Papua New Guinea, where young males have sexual contact exclusively with other males until getting married at age 18, after which they have sexual contact only with women (see the subsequent discussion on the Sambian tribe).

Same-sex behavior is found in every culture, and its prevalence remains about the same no matter how permissive or repressive that culture's attitude is toward it (Mihalik, 1988). A classic study by Broude and Greene (1976) examined 42 societies for which there were good data on attitudes toward homosexuality. They found that a substantial number of the cultures in the sample have an accepting or only mildly disapproving view of homosexual behavior, and less than half punished homosexuals for their sexual activities.

Remember, too, that the relationship between sexual orientation and gender-related traits is moderated by culture. A culture that has more traditional gender roles tends to have larger homosexual–heterosexual differences in gender-related traits than cultures with less traditional gender roles (Lippa & Tan, 2001). With this in mind, research has found that, in the United States, Hispanic and Asian gays and lesbians show the largest homosexual–heterosexual differences and are more likely to cross gender boundaries (e.g., gay men tend to act more feminine, and lesbian women tend to act more masculine). Cultural factors play an important role in moderating these gender-related differences. We now explore a variety of cultures.

Latin American Countries

In many Central and South American countries, people do not tend to think in terms of homosexuality and heterosexuality, but rather in terms of masculinity and femininity. Male gender roles, for example, are defined by one's **machismo,** which, in terms of sexual behavior, is determined by being the active partner, or penetrator. Therefore, a man is not considered homosexual for taking the active, penetrating role in intercourse, even if he is penetrating other men. As long as he is penetrating, he is masculine.

In Nicaragua, for example, penetrating another man does not make you homosexual; a man who is the active partner in same-sex anal intercourse is called *machista* or *hombre-hombre* ("manly man"), a term used for any masculine male (Murray & Dynes, 1999). In fact, penetrating other men is seen as a sign of manliness and prestige, whereas feminine men allow themselves to be penetrated and are generally scorned.

Note that the implicit message of such cultures is that to mimic female behavior is disgraceful and shameful in a male. This attitude reflects the general nature of these societies, which tend to be patriarchal, with women lacking political and social power. Because women are, in general, considered inferior to men, men who mimic women are to be ridiculed.

In other Latin American countries, homosexuality may be viewed differently. For example, **homophobia** is widespread in Costa Rica, where prior to 1971 the punishment for engaging in sodomy was 1 to 3 years in prison (Arroba, 2004). In Brazil, although male homosexuality is acceptable during Carnival, at other times it is acceptable only for those in the theater, movies, music, or television industry, and it is viewed negatively for those in all other professions (de Freitas, 2004; J. N. Green, 1999).

Arabic Cultures

Although classic works of Arabic poetry use homoerotic imagery, and young boys were often used as the standard of beauty and sexuality in Arabic writing (Boswell, 1980), homosexuality in Arab countries, like sexuality in general, is usually not discussed. It is not uncommon to see men holding hands or walking down the street arm in arm, but for the most part male homosexuality is taboo. Sexual relations in the Middle East are often about power and are based on dominant and subordinate positions. Because of this, similar to some Latin American countries, being the penetrating partner with another man doesn't make a man gay (Sati, 1998).

Gay men in the Arabic world often limit their interactions with other men to sex, instead of emotionally based relationships. Although attitudes about homosexuality are slowly changing in Arabic cultures, many countries still view homosexuality as aberrant (Sherif, 2004). Overall, we know very little about lesbians in Arabic cultures mainly because Arabic women are very reserved and are uncomfortable talking about sex (Sherif, 2004).

Asian Countries

It wasn't until 2001 that the Chinese Psychiatric Association removed homosexuality from its list of mental disorders (Gallagher, 2001). This is a significant change for China, which as recently as 1994 openly opposed homosexuality. Homosexuality was seen as

machismo
Characterized or motivated by stereotypical masculine behavior or actions.

homophobia
Irrational fear of homosexuals and homosexuality.

Ted Ajibe/AFP/Getty Images

The first ever Hong Kong gay rights parade took place in 2005. Many participants wore masks to symbolize the invisibility of gays and lesbians in Hong Kong.

sexuals and lesbians face a maximum of 5 years in jail if they have sex before age 16. Experts claim that the age of consent differences are based on the fact that gay men engage in anal sex, which is more likely to spread sexually transmitted infections (Leonard, 2006). In 2006, a judge ruled that laws prohibiting sex between two men under age 21 were discriminatory (Phillips, 2006).

Sambia

A famous and much discussed example of a very different cultural form of sexual relations, called **sequential homosexuality,** is found in a number of cultures in the Pacific islands. The Sambia tribe of Papua New Guinea has been described in depth by Gilbert Herdt (Herdt, 1981; Stoller & Herdt, 1985). Life in Sambia is difficult because food is scarce and war is common; warriors, hunters, and many children are needed to survive. Sambians believe that mother's milk must be replaced by man's milk (semen) for a boy to reach puberty, and so, at age 7, all Sambian boys move to a central hut where they must fellate the postpubescent Sambian boys and drink their semen. After a boy reaches puberty, he no longer fellates others but is himself sucked by the prepubescent boys until he reaches the age of marriage at about 18. Despite his long period of same-sex activity, he will live as a heterosexual for the rest of his life.

a result of Western influences, and it was considered a "Western social disease" (Ruan & Lau, 2004). In India, although homosexual sex is punishable by up to 10 years in jail, several gay couples have made headlines by publicly declaring themselves married in an attempt to overturn an existing law from 1861 (Predrag, 2005). Not much is known about lesbians in Indian culture, but we do know that lesbians are less accepted than gay men overall (Biswas, 2005). Indian culture has long been patriarchal, and it is not uncommon for some families who fear their daughters might be gay to quickly marry them off (Biswas, 2005). Other Asian societies have different views of homosexuality. Buddhism does not condemn homosexuality, and so Buddhist countries generally accept it. In Thailand, for example, there are no laws against homosexuality, and men may live sexually with boys over 13, who are considered old enough to make their own decisions (W. L. Williams, 1990). In Hong Kong, although the age of consent for heterosexual sex and sex between women is 16, the age of consent for sex between two men is 21 years old (Leonard, 2006). Men who have sex with a man before age 21 risk a life in prison, whereas hetero-

The Lesson of Cross-Cultural Studies of Homosexuality

With all these very different cultural forms of sexuality, trying to pigeonhole people or ways of life into our restrictive, Western "homosexuality–heterosexuality–bisexuality" model seems inadequate. This is a good time to think about your personal theory about homosexuality and to ask yourself: What theory do I believe, and how can it account for the cross-cultural differences in sexual orientation that exist around the world today?

sequential homosexuality
Situation in which heterosexual or bisexual men and women go through a period of homosexuality for a variety of reasons, including cultural and societal.

review questions

1 Explain how our views on homosexuality have changed from ancient times through the Middle Ages.

2 Discuss how the medical model's view of homosexuality during the modern era influenced modern ideas of sexual orientation.

3 Explain how homosexuality has been viewed in other cultures, citing as many examples as possible.

Gays, Lesbians, and Bisexuals
Throughout
the Life Cycle

Gays, lesbians, and bisexuals in America face particular problems that are not faced by most heterosexuals. Many struggle with discrimination, prejudice, laws that do not recognize same-sex unions, lack of spousal benefits for their partners, and families who may reject them. On the other hand, many gay and lesbian couples live together in stable, happy unions, leading lives not really that much different from the heterosexual couple next door. Gay and lesbian lifestyles are as varied and different as those of the rest of society. Here we examine the special challenges and circumstances that gay and lesbian people face.

GROWING UP GAY, LESBIAN, OR BISEXUAL

Imagine what it must be like to be an adolescent and either to believe or know that you are gay, lesbian, or bisexual (a number of you reading this book do not have to imagine it). All your life, from the time you were a toddler, you were presented with a single model of sexual life: you were expected to be attracted to the other sex, to go on dates, and eventually to marry. No other scenario was seriously considered; if you are heterosexual, you probably have never even reflected on how powerfully this "presumption of heterosexuality" (Herdt, 1989) was transmitted by your parents, your friends, television and movies, newspapers and magazines, even the government. Advertisements on TV and in magazines always show heterosexual couples; your friends probably played house, doctor, or spin the bottle, assuming everyone was attracted to the other sex; your grade school, parties, and social activities were organized around this presumption of heterosexuality. There were open questions about many things in your life: what career you would pursue, where you might live, what college you would attend. However, one thing was considered certain: you were going to marry (or at least date) someone of the other sex.

Imagine that while all your friends were talking about the other sex, dating, and sex, you were experiencing a completely different set of emotions. Why, you wondered, can't I join in on these conversations? Why can't I feel the attractions that all my friends feel? Then, at some point in your early teens, you began to realize why you felt differently from your friends. All of a sudden you understood that all the models you had taken for granted your whole life did not apply to you. You began to look for other models that described your life and your feelings—and they simply were not there. In fact, in hundreds of subtle and not-so-subtle ways, society taught you that you were different—and possibly perverted, sinful, illegal, or disgusting. Now what are you supposed to do? Whom do you turn to? How can you possibly tell anyone your deep, painful secret?

The experiences of many lesbians, gays, and bisexuals, at least until recently, followed this scenario, although the timing and intensity varied with individual cases. For example, many gay men

grew up with close male friends, enjoyed sports, and differed only in their secret attraction to other boys, whereas others remember feeling and acting differently from their friends as early as 4 or 5 years old (H. P. Martin, 1991).

Many gay and male bisexual youth report a history of feeling unattached and alienated—most probably because heterosexual dating was often a focal point in peer group bonds (Herdt, 1989). The same is true of young lesbians and female bisexuals, although the pressure and alienation may be felt slightly later in life because same-sex affection and touching is more accepted for girls and because lesbians tend to determine their sexual orientation later than gay men. Overall, gay, lesbian, and bisexual youth have been found to experience higher levels of stigmatization and discrimination than heterosexual youth, which may be responsible for the higher levels of depression in GLB youth (Espelage et al., 2008; Gilman et al., 2001).

WHAT DO YOU WANT TO KNOW ?

Aren't gay men more creative than straight men and more likely to be in the arts? Aren't more female professional athletes lesbian?
If homosexuals are indeed overrepresented in certain professions, it may be because those professions were more accepting of gays and lesbians rather than because they have some "natural talents" in those areas. Jews entered the entertainment industry in the 20th century because the industry was accepting of them during a period when other professions were closed to them; the same may be true for homosexuals, although this has not yet been proved.

PRNewsFoto/Kenneth Cole Productions, Inc.

Positive portrayals of same-sex couples in advertising, such as this ad by Kenneth Cole, can help improve the image of gays and lesbians in society.

COMING OUT
TO SELF AND OTHERS

One of the most important tasks of adolescence is to develop and integrate a positive adult identity. This task is an even greater challenge for gay and lesbian youth because they learn from a very young age the stigma of being different from the heterosexual norm (C. Ryan & Futterman, 2001). Special challenges confront the person who believes he or she is gay, lesbian, or bisexual, including the need to establish a personal self-identity and communicate it to others, known as **coming out** (see the accompanying Sex in Real Life feature, "A Model of Coming Out.") A number of models have been offered to explain how this process proceeds (see for example, Cass, 1979, 1984; E. Coleman, 1982; H. P. Martin, 1991; M. Schneider, 1989; Troiden, 1989).

Coming out refers, first, to acknowledging one's sexual identity to oneself, and many gays, lesbians, and bisexuals have their own negative feelings about homosexuality to overcome. The often difficult and anxiety-ridden process of disclosing the truth to family, friends, and eventually the public at large comes later. Disclosure of identity plays an important role in identity development and psychological adjustment for gay, lesbian, and bisexual men and women.

Although first awareness of sexual orientation typically occurs between the ages of 8 and 9, gays and lesbians come out to others, on average, at around age 18 (Savin-Williams & Diamond, 2000). Some may come out early in their lives, whereas others remain closeted into adulthood (H. E. Taylor, 2000). One study found teens are coming out earlier today than past years and that the average age of coming out for teens was just over 13 years old (Elias, 2007). Coming out does not happen overnight; being homosexual for some may mean a lifetime of disclosing different amounts of information to family, friends, and strangers in different contexts (Hofman, 2005). Deciding whether and how to tell friends and family are difficult decisions. To minimize the risk of rejection, gay and lesbian adolescents choose whom they come out to very carefully (Vincke & van Heeringen, 2002).

coming out
The process of establishing a personal self-identity and communicating it to others.

Overall, gay men and lesbian women have been coming out at earlier ages in the past few years. This is probably in part because of a greater acceptance of homosexuality and an increase of gay role models in the popular media (Elias, 2007). The following story was written by an African American college student who had a positive coming-out story:

I was worried about coming out to my mom since we were so close. I wondered what she would think of me and if she would still love me. One day she picked me up from school early, and asked me if everything was OK. I assured her it was, but she knew something was up. She stopped the car and told me I needed to talk to her. I looked at her concerned face and started to give in. "It is something about me. . . .," I said slowly. "What is it?" she said looking as if she was about to cry. "It's something that you may not like about me. . . .," I said as I started to get teary eyed. "I'm. . . . I'm. . . .," and tears began rolling down my face. "You're. . . . gay. . . .?" I nodded my head and started to cry. My mother unbuckled her seatbelt and hugged me. "Did you think that would change our relationship? You're still my son and I still love you," she said as she wiped the tears away from my eyes. (Author's Files)

View in Video

"I was terrified of going home and telling my parents that I was in a relationship with a woman."
—*Coming Out as a Lesbian*
To view go to CengageNOW at www. cengage.com/login

Not surprisingly, gay and lesbian youth who have a positive coming-out experience have higher self-confidence, lower rates of depression, and better psychological adjustment than those who have negative coming-out experiences (Ryan & Futterman, 2001). Parental rejection during the coming-out process is a major health risk for homosexual and bisexual youth (C. M. Mosher, 2001; Savin-Williams & Dube, 1998). Youth who are rejected by their parents have been found to have increased levels of isolation, loneliness, depression, suicide, homelessness, prostitution, and sexually transmitted infections (Armesto, 2001; D'Augelli, 2005b; Ray, 2007). Some gay, lesbian, and bisexual youth are rejected by friends and family and as a result are forced to run away or live on the streets. Approximately 26% of

REALResearch **>** Same-sex attractions and sexual behaviors are differently related to alcohol and drug use. Although same-sex behavior *without* attraction has been found to be more strongly related to alcohol use, same-sex behavior *with* attraction was more strongly related to drug use (Hegna & Rossow, 2007).

gay youth are forced to leave home because of their sexual orientation (A. T. Edwards, 1997; Remafedi 1987), and more than one in four street youth are gay, lesbian, or bisexual (Kruks, 1991; Lockwood, 2008). Compared with homeless heterosexual youth, GLB homeless youth are more likely to experience depression and loneliness, abuse drugs and alcohol, and to have experienced physical and sexual abuse (Cochran et al., 2002; Gaetz, 2004). In addition, GLB runaway youth are more likely to engage in "survival sex," in which they exchange sex for food or shelter (Gaetz, 2004). Homeless shelters that cater specifically to GLB youth have been set up across the United States, and as of 2007, there were more than 25 such shelters nationwide (Urbina, 2007).

AP Photo/Luis Martinez

In 2004, Rosie O'Donnell and her partner, Kelli Carpenter, along with their four kids, broke new ground by organizing a seven-day gay cruise to the Caribbean. Since then, Rosie has founded "R Family Vacations," a family-friendly vacation service especially for the gay and lesbian community, their family, and friends.

WHAT DO YOU WANT TO KNOW ?

Is homosexuality natural?
The question itself is biased: is heterosexuality "natural"? Also, the question seems to assume that if it is "natural," then it is OK; yet much that is natural, such as killing, is reprehensible. Some people suggest that a human behavior is "natural" if it is found in animals; other animals do display same-sex behavior, and so perhaps it is natural in that sense. Still, many human qualities—humor, language, religion—are not shared by animals and yet are considered "natural." Humans are so immersed in culture and so lacking in instincts that it is impossible to say what is natural. Perhaps the only measure we can use is to ask whether a behavior is found universally—that is, in all or almost all human cultures. By that measure, homosexuality is quite natural.

Many parents of gay, lesbian, or bisexual youth initially react with disappointment, shame, and shock when they learn about a son or daughter's sexual orientation (D'Augelli, 2005b; LaSala, 2000). They may feel responsible and believe they did something to "cause" the nonheterosexual orientation (Fields, 2001a; Strommen, 1989). In one study, more than 50% of gay and lesbian teens experienced a negative reaction from their parents when they came out (Ray, 2007). The family must go through its own "coming out," as parents and siblings slowly try to accept the idea and then tell their own friends. The importance of positive resolution in the family has prompted the formation of a national organization, the Federation of Parents and Friends of Lesbians and Gays (PFLAG), which helps parents learn to accept their children's sexual orientation and gain support from other families experiencing similar events.

View in Video

"I didn't really want to be a faggot."
—*Trying Not to Be Gay*
To view go to CengageNOW at www.cengage.com/login

living in a heterosexual world (Degges-White & Marszalek, 2008). Research on same-sex relationships has found that these relationships are characterized by greater role flexibility, partner equality, and lower levels of sexual jealousy compared to heterosexual relationships (Degges-White & Marszalek, 2008; R. J. Green, 2004; Mock & Cornelius, 2007; Risman & Schwartz, 1988).

Gay and lesbian couples may also work harder at keeping their relationships together. Because they have fewer partners to choose from, they may work harder on their relationships and make the best of them in times of crisis, unlike heterosexual couples who might think there is someone else out there (Kurdek, 2001). After a breakup, same-sex couples also report higher levels of connection to ex-partners than heterosexuals (Harkless & Fowers, 2005).

Gay and Lesbian Sexuality

We discussed gay and lesbian sexuality in Chapter 9, and we know that gay and lesbian men and women, like heterosexuals, engage in sexual behaviors for a variety of reasons and use a variety of positions. Sexuality, for all people, heterosexual, homosexual, or bisexual, can be an expression of deep love, affection, or lust. Because many people tend to identify the homosexual community primarily by its sexuality, sex is always close to the surface. However, gay men and lesbians view their community as much broader, with sexuality as only one component.

As we discussed in Chapter 10, Masters and Johnson (1979) found that arousal and orgasm in homosexuals was physiologically no different from that in heterosexuals. They also found, however, that same-sex partners tend be slower, more relaxed, and less demanding with each other during sex. Gay and lesbian couples spend more time sexually "teasing" and caressing each other, bringing their partners to the brink of orgasm and then withdrawing, before beginning direct genital stimulation. Heterosexuals tend to be more goal-oriented and spend less time at each phase of arousal than same-sex couples. Perhaps, Masters and Johnson suggest, this is because men and women know what pleases them, and so they have an immediate, intuitive understanding of what would please another member of their own sex.

LIFE ISSUES: PARTNERING, SEXUALITY, **PARENTHOOD, AND AGING**

Although growing up and coming out can be difficult for many GLB youth, the next step is establishing intimate relationships. Let's now explore same-sex coupling, sexuality, parenting, and aging.

Looking for Partners

In Chapter 9, we discussed some of the difficulties gay men and lesbian women face in meeting others. Meeting other GLB partners in the heterosexual world can be difficult, so the gay community has developed its own social institutions to help people meet one another and socialize. As we discussed in Chapter 8, many GLB youth have been turning to the Internet in search of partners. Today many schools and universities have clubs, support groups, and meeting areas for gay, lesbian, and bisexual students. Whereas in the mid-1990s, there were only a handful of gay–straight alliance clubs in U.S. high schools, there were 3,200 such clubs in early 2007 (Elias, 2007). Today, adults can meet others at **gay bars** or clubs that cater primarily to GLB couples, through GLB support or discussion groups, and through GLB organizations. Some smaller towns that don't have GLB bars offer gay night at certain bars once a week or so. Gay magazines such as *The Advocate* carry personal ads and ads for dating services, travel clubs, resorts, bed and breakfasts, theaters, businesses, pay phone lines, sexual products, and other services to help gays and lesbians find partners. And of course, gay individuals are introduced through gay and straight friends.

View in Video

"All of a sudden I found myself completely smitten by this woman."
—*Discovering Bisexuality*
To view go to CengageNOW at www.cengage.com/login

Same-Sex Couples

As we discussed in Chapter 9, gay and lesbian couples have happy and fulfilling relationships; their main challenges tend to be issues related to defining their relationship and the societal challenges of

Gay and Lesbian Parents

The 2000 U.S. Census Bureau revealed that there were 601,209 same-sex households, with approximately 301,000 gay male households and 293,000 lesbian households, in the United States (U.S. Census Bureau, 2001). However, actual numbers are most likely significantly higher, because many gays and lesbians may

gay bar
Club or bar that caters primarily to same-sex couples.

Sexuality in gay and lesbian couples can be an expression of deep love, affection, or lust.

© Uwe Krejci/zefa/Corbis

not be comfortable reporting their sexual orientation on the census forms.

Many gay and lesbian couples become parents, and they cite most of the same reasons for wanting to be parents that straight parents do (D'Augelli et al., 2006a). Although fewer lesbian women have children than heterosexual women (18% vs. 50%; Elmslie & Tebaldi, 2008), it is estimated that more than one in three lesbians has given birth and one in six gay men has fathered or adopted a child (Gates et al., 2007).

Gay and lesbian couples who wish to be parents may encounter many problems that heterosexual couples do not face. Because same-sex marriages are not yet legally recognized nationally in the United States, gay couples may have trouble gaining joint custody of a child, and employers may not grant nonbiological parents parental leave or benefits for the child. For the most part, our society assumes a heterosexist view of parenting. Although it is slowly changing, most official forms ask about mothers and fathers today (not mothers and mothers, or fathers and fathers). Yet gay and lesbian couples today are creating new kinds of families, and the social system is going to have to learn how to deal with them.

Lesbian couples may become pregnant through heterosexual intercourse or artificial insemination. It is not uncommon, in fact, for lesbians to ask gay friends to donate sperm for that purpose. However, gay male couples who want children do not have that option. Some gay men try to find surrogate mothers to bear their children, whom they then adopt, but surrogate mothers are expensive and difficult to find. As a result, gay parenting is seldom an individual or couple decision and often involves several negotiations with others (Berkowitz & Marsiglio, 2007). In addition, once they become parents, gay men must often deal with the consequences of breaking social norms by raising children without a woman as a primary caregiver (Mallon, 2003). Organizations,

*. . . **our society** assumes a **heterosexist view** of parenting.*

such as PFLAG and Lambda (a national organization committed to the civil rights of gays, lesbians, and bisexuals) support gay and lesbian parents and are helping to make it easier for homosexuals to adopt.

As for same-sex couple adoption, the Urban Institute, a national research organization, has found there are more than 65,000 adopted children and 14,000 foster children being raised by same-sex couples (Gates et al., 2007). Even so, many same-sex couples find it difficult to adopt children or become foster parents because of the legal and judicial systems where they live. Although it is illegal for same-sex couples to adopt in Florida, Mississippi, and Utah, 11 states and the District of Columbia have policies stating that sexual orientation cannot legally prevent gay and lesbians from adopting (Gandossy, 2007; Gates et al., 2007). In the United States, it is estimated that there are 2 million GLB men and women who are interested in adoption (Gates et al., 2007).

Overall, 57% of Americans believe that same-sex couples should have the legal right to adopt children (Cable News Network, 2007). Outside of the United States, same-sex adoption is legal in Belgium, Iceland, the Netherlands, Norway, Sweden, South Africa, Spain, the United Kingdom, Canada, and some parts of Australia.

Research has found no significant differences between the offspring of lesbian and straight mothers, including their children's sexual orientation (Golombok & Tasker, 1996; Hicks, 2005). In addition, research has found no significant differences in the gender and sexual identities, psychological adjustment, and social relationships between the children of same-sex and heterosexual couples (American Psychological Association, 2005; Greenfeld, 2005). (See the accompanying Sex in Real Life, "Same-Sex Parents.") Yet some courts assume that same-sex couples are emotionally unstable or unable to assume parental roles. All of the scientific evidence suggests that children who grow up with one or two gay and/or lesbian parents do as well emotionally, cognitively, socially, and sexually as do children from heterosexual parents (American Psychological Association, 2005; Greenfeld, 2005; Perrin, 2002). Even so, some gay and lesbian couples find minimal support to parent children and a social stigmatization of children that they do have (Pawelski et al., 2006).

Gay and Lesbian Seniors

In 2006, there were as many as 3 million GLB seniors aged 65 and older in the United States, and this number is expected to grow to 4 million by 2030 (deVries et al., 2006). Many studies have found that having "come out" prior to the senior years often helps a gay or lesbian senior to feel more comfortable with his or her life and sexuality (Quam & Whitford, 1992). Homosexual seniors who have not come out or come to terms with their sexual orientation may feel depressed or alone as they continue to age. In addition, they may experience depression and isolation from the years of internalized homophobia (Altman, 2000; Gross, 2007). For some, hiding their sexual orientation when they are ready for a nursing home is their only choice. One gay man who had been in a relationship with his partner for more than 20 years said, "when I'm at the gate of the nursing home, the closet door is going to slam shut behind me" (Gross, 2007).

Same-Sex Parents

Do you think that gay or lesbian mothers or fathers parent differently from heterosexual mothers or fathers?

Until recently, children raised by same-sex parents were almost always born during their parents' earlier heterosexual marriages. However, today many same-sex couples are creating families through artificial insemination, surrogate mothers, or adoption. As we discuss in the text, more than one in three lesbians have given birth and one in six gay men have fathered or adopted a child (Gates et al., 2007).

Do you think that gay or lesbian mothers or fathers parent differently from heterosexual mothers or fathers? Researchers who have examined this question have found that overall, there are no significant distinctions between children who are raised by same-sex parents and those raised in more traditional homes with a mother and a father.

Some children of same-sex parents experience teasing and taunting during their school years, and some feel isolated because of this. Genevieve Ankeny, a 32-year-old woman, discusses her experiences of being raised by a lesbian mother:

It wasn't until recently that I realized the depth of my grief about the homophobia I endured in high school. Even today, after I've worked through so much of my many feelings about

my mom being lesbian—the old high school feelings still mow me down. I feel like I had been in the closet for my mom for so, so long.

I never spoke to anyone whom I met in high school or outside of my old friends from the city of my mom being a lesbian—not until I was a junior in college. In my high school, I felt no room to be different. I cannot even imagine the isolation, loneliness, fear, and anger I might have felt as a GLB youth. Yet my own feelings about being out of the norm with a gay parent struck me hard. I felt displaced in a suburban high school, being from the city. I had always been so strong and assertive as a young person, but I could not stand up to this—to the undeniable, overt, and covert homophobia in my school.

Looking back, I would change a few things. I would ask my parents and all parents who are gay, lesbian, or bisexual to have consistent conversations with their children about sexuality and sexual orientation, and to acknowledge that the world where we live should all be okay with a family where there is love despite who loves whom. I would also encourage them to talk about homophobia and [the] complexity of being raised in a family that may be very out of the norm. I also would have accepted my mother unconditionally, without question.

SOURCE: Author's files.

There are many issues that confront aging gay and lesbian seniors. Studies have found that nursing home staff often report intolerant or condemning attitudes toward homosexual and bisexual residents (Cahill et al., 2000; Gross, 2007; Röndahl et al., 2004). Because of this, many retirement homes for aging gays, lesbians, bisexual, and transgendered individuals have been established. The first GLB retirement community, The Palms of Manasota, is located in Sarasota, Florida, and Rainbow Vision in Santa Fe, New Mexico, opened in 2006 (deVries et al., 2006). It is anticipated that GLB retirement housing options will increase dramatically in coming years (Gross, 2007).

THE EFFECTS OF STIGMA

GLB youth are more likely than heterosexual youth to think about and to commit suicide (D'Augelli et al., 2005a; Hegna & Rossow, 2007; Russell & Joyner, 2001). Between 48% and 76% of homosexual and bisexual youth have thoughts of committing suicide, and 29% to 42% have attempted it (compared with estimated rates of 7% to 13% among high school students in general; Armesto, 2001; Cochran & Mays, 2000; S. L. Nichols, 1999; Russell & Joyner, 2001). There are also higher rates of substance abuse and alcohol-related problems (Rivers & Noret, 2008; D. F. Roberts et al., 2005), along with more widespread use of marijuana and cocaine than heterosexual youth and adults (Rosario et al., 2004; Ryan & Futterman, 2001) and higher rates of truancy, homelessness, and sexual abuse (D'Augelli et al, 2006b; H. E. Taylor, 2000). Overall, compared with heterosexual and homosexual men and women, bisexuals have been found to be at higher risk for substance abuse (S. T. Russell et al., 2002).

For many years, psychiatrists and other therapists argued that this showed homosexual and bisexual groups had greater psychopathology than heterosexuals. In fact, the problems of GLB life may not be due to psychopathology but to the enormous pressures of living in a society that discriminates against them (Lock & Steiner, 1999). Vulnerable and stigmatized groups in general have higher rates of these types of behaviors, and these problems often result from coping with stigma-related stress. In addition, homosexuals and bisexuals are particularly vulnerable to harassment and other forms of risk, further compounding their stress (Mishna et al., 2008).

Workplace discrimination also adds stress to the lives of gays, lesbians, and bisexuals. Gay men have been found to earn 23% less than married heterosexual men and 9% less than single heterosexual men who are living with a woman (Elmslie & Tebaldi, 2007). However, lesbians were not discriminated against when compared with heterosexual women. Lesbian workers earn more than their heterosexual female peers (Peplau & Fingerhut, 2004), perhaps because employers may believe lesbian women are more career-oriented and less likely to leave the workforce to raise children (Elmslie & Tebaldi, 2008).

As of 2007, 19 states and the District of Columbia have laws that prohibit workplace discrimination based on sexual orientation (Herszenhorn, 2007). However, whereas federal law protects discrimination based on race, religion, ethnicity, age, disability, and pregnancy, it has not included sexual orientation in such legislation. In late 2007, the U.S. House of Representatives approved the Employment Nondiscrimination Act, which prohibits workplace discrimination against GLB men and women (Herszenhorn, 2007).

GAY, LESBIAN, AND BISEXUAL ORGANIZATIONS

Because many organizations misunderstand the needs of homosexuals and bisexuals, gay and lesbian social services, medical, political, entertainment, and even religious organizations have formed. For example, the National Gay and Lesbian Task Force (NGLTF) and its associated Policy Institute advocate for gay civil rights, lobby Congress for such things as a Federal Gay and Lesbian Civil Rights Act, health care reform, AIDS policy reform, and hate-crime laws. In 1987, they helped establish the Hate Crimes Statistics Act, which identifies and records hate crimes. Also well known are the Lambda Legal Defense and Education Fund (for more information see the Web Resources at the end of this chapter) which pursues litigation issues for the gay and lesbian community, and the Human Rights Campaign Fund, which lobbies Capitol Hill on gay and lesbian rights, AIDS, and privacy issues.

Since the advent of the AIDS epidemic, many organizations have formed to help homosexuals and bisexuals obtain medical, social, and legal services. Local GLB organizations—including counseling centers, hotlines, legal aid, and AIDS information— have been established in almost every reasonably sized city in the United States.

The Harvey Milk School in New York City is the first and largest accredited public school in the world devoted to the educational needs of lesbian, gay, bisexual, transgendered, and questioning youth. The school was named after a gay elected official from San Francisco who was murdered in 1978. Fourteen- to eighteen-year-old students from across the country come to the Harvey Milk School to study in an environment in which their sexual orientation is accepted and where they will not be ridiculed, ostracized, or assaulted, as many were in the schools they came from. Universities and colleges have also begun to offer gay and lesbian students separate housing, and as we discussed earlier, many high schools provide gay–straight alliances that help encourage tolerance and provide a place for students to meet.

Gay and lesbian media, including countless magazines and newspapers across the country, have also developed over the past 30 years. The largest and best-known magazine, *The Advocate*, is a national publication that covers news of interest, entertainment reviews, commentaries, gay- and lesbian-oriented products and services, and hundreds of personal ads. Many other specialty magazines are available for GLB men and women, including parenting magazines (such as *Gay Parent* and *Proud Parenting*), travel magazines (such as *Out and About*), and religious magazines (such as *Whosoever*).

Most major cities now have their own gay newspaper, some of which get national exposure; some noteworthy examples are New York's *Next*, Philadelphia's *Gay News*, Chicago's *Free Press*, and the *Seattle Gay News*. These papers are often the best first sources for young gay men and lesbians who are looking for the resources available in their community.

review questions

1 Identify the need for gay, lesbian, and bisexual youth to establish a personal self-identity, and describe the task of coming out.

2 Explain some of the tasks involved in living a GLB life, including looking for partners, sexuality, parenting, aging, and specific problems encountered by GLB individuals.

3 Explain why many GLB groups have set up their own organizations, and give one example of such an organization.

Homophobia and Heterosexism

Gay, lesbian, and bisexual individuals have long been stigmatized. When homosexuality as an illness was removed from the *Diagnostic and Statistical Manual* in 1973 (see Chapter 1), negative attitudes toward homosexuality persisted. It was at this time that researchers began to study these negative attitudes and behaviors.

WHAT IS HOMOPHOBIA?

Many terms have been proposed to describe the negative, often violent, reactions of many people toward homosexuality— antihomosexualism, homoerotophobia, homosexism, homonegativism, and homophobia. The popularity of the term *homophobia* is unfortunate, for phobia is a medical term describing an extreme, anxiety-provoking, uncontrollable fear accompanied by obsessive avoidance. We use this term here to refer to strongly negative attitudes toward homosexuals and homosexuality.

Are people really homophobic? Some might accept homosexuality intellectually and yet still dislike being in the presence of homosexuals, whereas others might object to homosexuality as a practice and yet have personal relationships with individual homosexuals that they accept (Forstein, 1988). When compared with people who hold positive views of gays, lesbians, and bisexuals, people with negative views are less likely to have had contact with homosexuals and bisexuals, and they are more likely to be older and less well educated; be religious and to subscribe to a conservative religious ideology; have more traditional attitudes toward sex roles and less support for equality of the sexes; be less permissive sexually; and be authoritarian (Herek, 1984). Overall, heterosexual men, compared with heterosexual women, have been found to be have significantly more negative attitudes toward gay men (Davies, 2004; Verweij et al., 2008). The accompanying Sex in Real Life, "Gay Bashing and Hate Crimes," discusses violence against homosexuals, which can be the result of extreme homophobia.

It's important to point out that heterosexuals aren't the only people to experience homophobia. Homosexuals who harbor negative feelings about homosexuality experience internalized homophobia. This is especially true in older generations in which there has been less overall acceptance of homosexuality. Overall, older gay men have been found to experience more internalized homophobia (or negative feelings based on sexual orientation directed at oneself) than lesbian women (D'Augelli et al., 2001). Homosexuals with internalized homophobia have been found to have decreased levels of self-esteem and increased levels of shame and psychological distress (D. J. Allen & Oleson, 1999; Szymanski et al., 2001).

An even bigger problem for most gay men and lesbians is **heterosexism.** Heterosexism describes the "presumption of heterosexuality" discussed earlier and the social power used to promote it (Neisen, 1990). Because heterosexual relationships are seen as "normal," a heterosexist person feels justified in suppressing or ignoring those who do not follow that model.

For example, even those with no ill feelings toward homosexuality are often unaware that businesses will not provide health care and other benefits to the partners of homosexuals. In other words, heterosexism can be passive rather than active, involving a lack of awareness rather than active discrimination. One woman said:

> I remember there was a really cute guy in my psychology class. It took me all semester to walk up to him and talk. I was hoping to ask him out for coffee or something. As I walked up behind him to say hello I became aware of a button pinned to the back of his backpack. I was horrified when I read what it said, "How dare you assume I'm heterosexual!!" I nearly tripped and fell over backwards. (Author's files)

heterosexism
The "presumption of heterosexuality" that has sociological implications.

SEX IN REAL LIFE

Gay Bashing and Hate Crimes

Many gay, lesbian, bisexual, and transgendered individuals have suffered from hate crimes and violence.

In this chapter, we are looking closely at sexual orientation and society's views of it, including homophobia, gay bashing, and hate crimes. Many gay, lesbian, bisexual, and transgendered individuals have suffered from hate crimes and violence and, in some cases, been killed because of their assumed sexual orientation and gender identity. Here are a half-dozen examples of victims of various hate crimes:

Teena Brandon—Born female, Teena Brandon chose to live as a man without hormonal or surgical intervention (and changed his name to Brandon Teena). After discovering Brandon's physical sex, John Lotter and Marvin Thomas Nissen kidnapped, assaulted, raped repeatedly, and finally murdered Brandon on December 31, 1993. The movie *Boys Don't Cry* was based on Brandon Teena's life.

Matthew Shepard—This freshman at the University of Wyoming was beaten and left to die on October 12, 1998. Russell Henderson, 21, and Aaron McKinney, 22, beat Shepard and hung him spread-eagled on a fence. Shepard was later found by two bicyclists.

Billy Jack Gaither—This man was bludgeoned to death with an ax handle by Charles Monroe Butler, Jr., 21, and Steven Eric Mullins, 25, on February 19, 1999. They then threw the body of 39-year-old Gaither atop two burning tires.

Private First Class Barry Winchell—This soldier was beaten to death with a baseball bat, while sleeping, by a fellow soldier on July 4, 1999.

Arthur "J.R." Warren—This 26-year-old was murdered on July 4, 2000. Two teens, David Allen Parker and Jared Wilson, admitted that they physically assaulted Warren, including kicks to the head with steel-toed boots, and ran over Warren's body twice with a vehicle.

Danny Lee Overstreet—Overstreet was shot and killed at a bar on September 22, 2000, by 53-year-old Ronald Edward Gay, who eventually confessed to the murder.

The gay rights movement has been successful at changing some of these assumptions, especially in larger cities, but today heterosexism still dictates a large part of the way the average American considers his or her world. Heterosexism can lead to a lack of awareness of issues that can harm GLB individuals today. Let's now turn our attention to hate crimes against GLB people.

HATE CRIMES AGAINST GAY, LESBIAN, AND BISEXUAL PEOPLE

Throughout history, persecution of minorities has been based on philosophies that portrayed those minorities as illegitimate, sub-human, or evil. Likewise, homophobia is not just a set of attitudes; it creates an atmosphere in which people feel they are permitted to harass, assault, and even kill homosexuals. **Hate crimes** are those motivated by hatred of someone's religion, sex, race, sexual orientation, disability, gender identity, or ethnic group. They are known as "message crimes" because they send a message to the victim's affiliated group (American Psychiatric Association, 1998). Typically, hate crimes involve strong feelings of anger (Parrott & Peterson, 2008).

In 2006, there were 7,722 hate crimes reported by the Federal Bureau of Investigation, and 16% of these were motivated by the victims' sexual orientation (U.S. Department of Justice, 2006). The American Psychological Association reports that hate crimes against homosexuals are the most socially acceptable form of hate crimes. One study found that when people are asked whether they have ever used threats or physical violence against a gay, lesbian, or bisexual person, 1 in 10 admit that they have, whereas another 24% acknowledge that they have used name-calling (Franklin, 2000).

Approximately 80% of lesbian, gay, and bisexual youth report verbal victimization, whereas 11% report physical and 9% report sexual victimization (D'Augelli et al., 2006b). Victimization begins on average at age 13, although some verbal attacks began as early as age 6, physical attacks as early as age 8, and sexual attacks as early as age 9 (D'Augelli et al., 2006b). Overall, rates of victimization are higher overall for boys.

After an assault, a homosexual may suffer from what is called "secondary victimization"—losing his or her job, being denied public services, or being harassed by the police in response to being the victim of an antigay attack (Berrill & Herek, 1990). For that reason, a large percentage of hate crimes against homosexuals go unreported (Herek et al., 2002). Whether or not they are reported, hate crimes have a more serious psychological impact on victims than other types of crime (Brienza, 1998).

After a 15-year relationship with the father of her two children, Cynthia Nixon, who played Miranda on the hit TV show *Sex and the City*, revealed she was in a same-sex relationship with Christine Marinoni.

WHY ARE PEOPLE HOMOPHOBIC?

What motivates people to be homophobic? A number of theories have been suggested. Because rigid, authoritarian personalities are more likely to be homophobic, it may be a function of personality type; for such people, anything that deviates from their view of "correct" behavior elicits disdain (K. T. Smith, 1971). Another common suggestion is that heterosexual people fear their own suppressed homosexual desires or are insecure in their own masculinity or femininity (H. E. Adams et al., 1996). Others believe that this explanation is too simplistic (Rosser, 1999). Perhaps people are simply ignorant about homosexuality and would change their attitudes with education. Most likely, all of these are true to some degree in different people.

Another factor that might contribute to homophobia is our confusion of sexual orientation with gender identity. Sexual orientation refers to who your sexual partners are; gender identity has to do with definitions of masculinity and femininity. When a man violates masculine gender roles, people often react negatively (Madon, 1997). Women are often given more flexibility in crossing gender lines, which perhaps explains why there is more acceptance of lesbianism in society today.

HOW CAN WE COMBAT HOMOPHOBIA AND HETEROSEXISM?

Heterosexism is widespread and subtle and therefore difficult to combat. Adrienne Rich (1983), a prominent scholar of lesbian studies, uses the term "heterocentrism" to describe the neglect of homosexual existence, even among feminists. Perhaps we can learn from the history of a similar term: ethnocentrism. Ethnocentrism

WHAT DO YOU WANT TO KNOW ?

Are people really homophobic because they fear that they themselves are homosexuals?
The question is difficult to answer, but many psychologists believe that fear of one's own sexual desires is a factor in homophobia. The best evidence is the level of brutality of gay hate crimes; the degree of violence suggests that there is a deep fear and hatred at work. Why such hatred of somebody you don't even know? The answer must lie within oneself.

hate crime
A criminal offense, usually involving violence, intimidation, or vandalism, in which the victim is targeted because of his or her affiliation with a particular group.

In 2008, Katy Perry's "I Kissed a Girl" was a #1 Billboard hit single, showing how mainstream same-sex sexual behavior in women has become.

Eamonn McCormack/Wire Image

refers to the belief that all standards of correct behavior are determined by one's own cultural background, leading to racism, ethnic bigotry, and even sexism and heterosexism. Although ethnocentrism is still rampant in American society, it is slowly being eroded by the passage of new laws, the media's spotlight on abuses, and improved education. Perhaps a similar strategy can be used to combat heterosexism.

Laws

Hate crimes legislation targets violence that is committed in response to a victim's identity, including sexual orientation. As of 2008, 30 states and the District of Columbia punish perpetrators of hate crimes motivated by sexual orientation and 27 states cover crimes motivated by gender identity (Anti-Defamation League, 2008). However, the punishment varies from state to state.

The Hate Crimes Statistics Act was reauthorized by Congress in 1996. This law requires the compilation of data on hate crimes so that there is a comprehensive picture of these crimes. In 1998, the Hate Crimes Right to Know Act was passed, which requires college campuses to report all hate crimes. However, it's important to point out that "monitoring" or "recording" hate crimes does not necessarily mean putting any resources into improving enforcement or prevention. However, even laws protecting homosexuals from abuse can be thwarted by homophobia.

The Media

The representation of the gay, lesbian, and bisexual community is increasing in the media today (Draganowski, 2004; Freymiller, 2005). Shows like *The L Word, Ugly Betty, Brothers and Sisters,* and *Playing It Straight* have helped pave the way for GLBs on television, resulting in vastly different programming from just a few years ago. Before this, homosexuality was portrayed negatively, with images of GLBs as psychopaths or murderers. Reality television shows, including *Real World* and *The Amazing Race,* have also helped to bring homosexuality out of the closet.

Another important development in the media is the explosion of music, fiction, nonfiction, plays, and movies that portray gay and lesbian life in America more realistically. Whereas once these types of media were shocking and hidden, now they appear on radio stations and in mainstream bookstores and movie theaters.

Education

Another important step to stopping heterosexism is education. Homosexuality remains a taboo subject in many schools, and most proposals to teach sexuality in general—never mind homosexuality in particular—encounter strong opposition by certain parent groups. When sexuality education is taught in schools, there is often very little information included about sexual orientation. Educating today's students about homophobia and heterosexism can help reduce negative attitudes, gay bashing, and hate crimes.

An important step to stopping heterosexism is education.

review questions

1 Define homophobia and explain what factors have been found to be related to its development. Explain how homosexuals can be homophobic.

2 Define heterosexism and heterocentrism and give one example of each.

3 Explain how hate crimes are known as "message crimes" and give one example.

4 Explain how laws, the media, and education have all helped to reduce homophobia and hate crimes.

Differences Among
Homosexual Groups

Because homosexuality exists in almost every ethnic, racial, and religious group, many gays, lesbians, and bisexuals also belong to other minority groups. We now discuss the unique situations of some of these groups.

LESBIANISM:
FACING SEXISM PLUS HOMOPHOBIA

Many women do not fall neatly into homosexual–heterosexual categories. Maybe this is because society is less threatened by lesbian sexuality than by gay sexuality. The research on lesbianism suggests that women's sexual identity is more fluid than men's (see the nearby Sex in Real Life Feature, "Girl–Girl Sexual Contact

on Campus"; Diamond, 2005; Gallo, 2000; Notman, 2002). For some women, an early lesbian relationship is temporarily or permanently replaced by a heterosexual one early in life, or a lifelong heterosexual relationship may be replaced by a lesbian relationship later in life (Notman, 2002). Women have also been found to experience more bisexual attractions and experiences than men (Hoburg et al., 2004).

Lesbian and bisexual women are more likely to be overweight, smoke cigarettes, and have high rates of alcohol consumption; they also report higher levels of depression and antidepressant use than heterosexuals (Case et al., 2004). Some research suggests that much of this hinges on the amount of personal acceptance from their parents. Lesbians who felt that their mothers were accepting of their sexual orientation had higher self-esteem and lower rates of smoking and alcohol consumption than those whose mothers were not accepting (LaSala, 2001). In addition, lesbians who feel supported and accepted have higher levels of self-esteem and well-being overall (Beals & Peplau, 2005). Lesbians have also been found to have lower rates of preventive care (yearly physical examinations) than heterosexual women (Mays et al., 2002), yet

SEX IN REAL LIFE

Girl–Girl Sexual Contact on Campus

. . . sexual behavior between women is more acceptable than sexual behavior between men.

Paula Eureka

Let's imagine you went to a party on campus tonight and while you are there, two heterosexual girls kiss each other deeply. Why do they do it? What would the reaction of the other partygoers be? What if two straight men kissed in the same way? Chances are there would be less support for the two men, but why? Overall, sexual behavior between women is more acceptable than sexual behavior between men (Turner et al., 2005). Girl–girl sexual contact does occur between heterosexual women on college campuses, and it typically occurs in front of friends in public places where the men and women have been drinking alcohol (Hegna & Rossow, 2007). The women might kiss to see what it feels like, to show off to the boys, or to feel more attractive and sexy.

Attitudes about girl–girl sexual behavior have become more liberal in the past few decades. The amount of women responding that sexual behavior between two women is "not wrong at all" rose from 5.6% (for women born before 1920) to 45% (for women born after 1970; men showed a similar increase from 7.5% to 32%; Turner et al., 2005). The actual prevalence of girl–girl sexual contact has also increased sub-

stantially across the 20th century, rising from 1.6% for those U.S. women born before 1920 to 7% for women born in 1970 and afterward (Turner et al., 2005). In surveys from 1996 and 2002, women were significantly more likely to report girl–girl sexual contact, and these differences were more likely in women who were 18 to 29 years old (Turner et al., 2005). The prevalence of girl–girl sexual behavior in the past year for this age group almost tripled (1.5% to 4.2%). Although more males report same-sex sexual behavior, the increases were smaller than they were in women.

Researchers believe that there is more stigmatization of sexual contact between males (Otis & Skinner, 1996), and perhaps this is one reason why young heterosexual women who engage in sexual contact with other women experience fewer negative reactions from others (Hegna & Rossow, 2007). An interesting question is what would the partygoers responses be if the two girls who were kissing in front of the crowd were lesbians and not straight? Would it still garner attention and be socially accepted?

they report high levels of optimism and excitement related to menopause (J. M. Kelly, 2005).

The lesbian community is a vibrant one. Bars, coffeehouses, bookstores, sports teams, political organizations, living cooperatives, media, and lesbian-run and -owned businesses often represent a political statement about the ways in which women can live and work together. A number of lesbian musicians—including k.d. lang, Melissa Etheridge, and Tracy Chapman—sing of issues important to the lesbian community and yet have strong crossover appeal to the heterosexual community. Many lesbian magazines are dedicated to lesbian fiction, erotica, current events, and photography.

Many bisexuals see themselves as having the best of both worlds.

Lesbian and feminist journals provide a forum for the lively and argumentative debates among lesbian scholars. For example, pornography has been the subject of an ongoing dispute among lesbian (and feminist) writers. Some are antiporn, seeing most sexually explicit materials as debasing portrayals of women, whereas the "anti–antiporn" group argues that suppressing expressions of sexuality—even ones we disagree with—is a dangerous practice and limits female and lesbian sexual expression, just as new forms of that expression are beginning to appear (Henderson, 1991).

Bisexuality: Just a Trendy Myth?

Although we have been discussing bisexuality throughout this chapter, bisexuality has really emerged more recently as a separate identity from lesbian, gay, or heterosexual identities, and we are still learning more each year (Bostwick et al., 2007; Ryan & Futterman, 2001). Social and political bisexual groups began forming in the 1970s, but it wasn't until the late 1980s that an organized bisexual movement achieved visibility in the United States (Herek, 2002).

We do know that people who identify as bisexual often first identified as heterosexuals, and their self-labeling generally occurs later in life than either gay or lesbian self-labeling (Weinberg et al., 1994). It is interesting to note that for many years few people noticed the absence of research on bisexuality. This absence stemmed from the fact that researchers believed that sexuality was composed of only two opposing forms of sexuality: heterosexuality and homosexuality (Herek, 2002; Rust, 2000).

Homosexuals have tended to see bisexuals either as on their way to becoming homosexual or as people who want to be able to "play both sides of the fence" by being homosexual in the gay community and heterosexual in straight society. Heterosexuals have tended to lump bisexuals in with homosexuals. Sexuality

scholars have suggested that bisexuality is a myth, or an attempt to deny one's homosexuality; identity confusion; or an attempt to be "chic" or "trendy" (Rust, 2000). Some studies claim that bisexuals are men and women who are ambivalent about their homosexual behavior (Carey, 2005a; Rieger et al., 2005). Bisexuals themselves have begun to speak of **biphobia,** which they suggest exists in both the straight and gay and lesbian communities (Eliason, 1997; Galupo, 2006; Mulick & Wright, 2002; L. Wright et al., 2006). Like gays and lesbians, bisexuals experience hostility, discrimination, and violence in response to their sexual orientation (Herek, 2002). Some researchers suggest that bisexuals experience "double discrimination," because they may experience discrimination from both the heterosexual and homosexual communities (Mulick & Wright, 2002).

Many bisexuals see themselves as having the best of both worlds. As one bisexual put it, "The more I talk and think about it, and listen to people, I realize that there are no fences, no walls, no heterosexuality or homosexuality. There are just people and the electricity between them" (quoted in Spolan, 1991). In our society, fear of intimacy is expressed through either homophobia if you are heterosexual or **heterophobia** if you are gay or lesbian; no matter what your sexual orientation, one gender or another is always taboo—your sexual intimacy is always restricted (F. Klein, 1978). From that perspective, bisexuality is simply lack of prejudice and full acceptance of both sexes.

More people in American society exhibit bisexual behavior than exclusively homosexual behavior (F. Klein, 1990). In **sequential bisexuality,** the person has sex exclusively with one gender, followed by sex exclusively with the other; **contemporaneous bisexuality** refers to having male and female sexual partners during the same time period (J. P. Paul, 1984). Numbers are hard to come by because bisexuality itself is so hard to define. How many encounters with both sexes are needed for a person to be considered bisexual? One? Fifty? And what of fantasies? It is difficult to determine what percentage of people are bisexual because many who engage in bisexual behavior do not self-identify as bisexual (Weinberg et al., 1994).

Some people experience bisexuality through intimate involvement with a close friend of the same sex, even if they have not had same-sex attractions before. Others come to it through group sex or swinging, in which, in the heat of passion, a body is a body and distinctions between men and women easily blur. The new bisexual movement may succeed in breaking through the artificial split of the sexual world into homosexuals and heterosexuals. Perhaps we fear the fluid model of sexuality offered by bisexuals because we fear our own cross-preference encounter fantasies and do not want to admit that most of us, even if hidden deep in our fantasies, are to some degree attracted to both sexes.

WHAT DO YOU WANT TO KNOW ?

Are bisexuals really equally attracted to both sexes?

It depends on the bisexual. Some are more attracted to one sex than the other, whereas others say that they have no preference at all (F. Klein, 1978). Masters and Johnson (1979) found that both heterosexuals and homosexuals have at least some "cross-preference" fantasies; so perhaps if social pressures were not as strong as they are, many more people would be bisexual to some degree.

biphobia
Strongly negative attitudes toward bisexuals and bisexuality.

heterophobia
Strongly negative attitudes toward heterosexuals and heterosexuality.

sequential bisexuality
Having sex exclusively with one gender followed by sex exclusively with the other.

contemporaneous bisexuality
Having sexual partners of both sexes during the same time period.

MINORITY HOMOSEXUALITY: CULTURE SHOCK?

Special problems confront homosexuals who are members of racial or ethnic minorities in the United States. Homosexuality is not accepted by many ethnic groups, and yet the gay community does not easily accommodate expressions of ethnic identity. Minority homosexual youth have been found to experience greater psychological distress than nonminority homosexual youth (Diaz et al., 2001). Many end up feeling torn between the two communities (Nagel, 2003). As one gay Asian American put it, "While the Asian-American community supports my Asian identity, the gay community only supports my being a gay man; as a result I find it difficult to identify with either" (Chan, 1989).

Gay African Americans can find their situation particularly troubling because they often have to deal with the heterosexism of the African American community and the racism of the homosexual and straight communities (Tye, 2006). Some progress is being made, however. Books such as *Brother to Brother: New Writings by Black Gay Men* (Hemphill, 1991) have raised the issue in public. Many feminist and lesbian anthologies and most lesbian and feminist journals include writings explicitly by minority lesbians.

It is also worth pointing out that research has found that although many African American lesbians report positive relationships and pleasant feelings about their sexual relationships, more than half also report feeling guilty about these relationships (Wyatt, 1998). This is consistent with the aforementioned research noting the prevalence of psychological distress in homosexual minorities.

SAME-SEX SEXUAL BEHAVIOR IN PRISON

Homosexual behavior varies greatly in prisons. Sexual contact between inmates, although prohibited, still occurs in prisons today (L. G. Hensley, 2002). Researchers who study prison rape have had difficulties defining it (L. G. Hensley, 2002). If a man is scared for his life and provides sex to a more powerful man for protection, is this rape (see Chapter 17)?

Sexual behaviors in prison are governed by a hierarchy of roles and relationships that define an inmate's position within the prison system (L. G. Hensley, 2002). Although forced sex does oc-

Although there is still hostility toward homosexuality within many major religions, religious scholars have begun to promote a more liberal attitude, including ordination of gay and lesbian clergy and marriage or commitment ceremonies.

cur in prisons, overall it is less common in women's prisons than men's (Girshick, 1999).

Many men and women who engage in same-sex sexual behavior in prison claim that they are not gay or lesbian and that their sexual behavior is an adaptation to their all-male or all-female environments (Girshick, 1999). Many claim they plan to return to heterosexual relationships exclusively once they are released. One female prisoner said:

> I think a lot of [the motivation for gay relationships] is loneliness, despair, and in some cases I know for a fact that it's for financial purposes. I have seen women have relationships with women, leave this dorm hugging and kissing this woman then go out to visitation and hug and kiss their husband. (Girshick, 1999, page 87)

This **situational homosexuality** is also found in other places where men and women must spend long periods of time together, such as on ships at sea.

Same-sex relationships in prison can be strong and jealously guarded (Girshick, 1999; Nacci & Kane, 1983). Inmates speak of loving their inmate partners, and relations can become extremely intimate, even among those who return to a heterosexual life on release.

situational homosexuality
Homosexuality that occurs because of a lack of heterosexual partners.

review questions

1 Explain how women's sexual identity may be more fluid than men's sexual identity and give one example.

2 Some researchers claim that bisexuality is a "trend," but what does the research tell us about bisexuality? Differentiate between sequential and contemporaneous bisexuality.

3 Describe some of the problems that confront GLB minority youth.

4 Explain what is known about same-sex sexual behavior in prisons.

Homosexuality
in Religion and the Law

Religion has generally been considered a bastion of antihomosexual teachings and beliefs, and these beliefs have often helped shape laws that prohibit homosexual behaviors. We now discuss both of these powerful influences.

HOMOSEXUALITY AND RELIGION

There has been a great deal of negativity surrounding homosexuality in religion, and changes in social attitudes toward homosexuality over the past 30 years have provoked conflict over homosexual policies in many religious denominations. Traditionally, both Judaism and Christianity have strongly opposed homosexual behavior.

Some Christian religions are more tolerant, such as the United Church of Christ. This church and its members have welcomed gay, lesbian, and bisexual members; worked for equal rights; and ordained gay, lesbian, and bisexual clergy. They generally view homosexuality as neither a sin nor a choice, and they believe that it is unchangeable. One of the most accepting churches, the Metropolitan Community Churches, promotes itself as the world's largest organization with a primary, affirming ministry to gays, lesbians, bisexuals, and transgendered persons (Metropolitan Community Churches, 2005).

Some Christian religions, such as Presbyterians, Methodists, Lutherans, and Episcopalians, have more conflict over the issue of sexual orientation, resulting in both liberal and conservative views. The Episcopalian church has been sharply divided about the issue of sexual orientation since the consecration of the first openly gay bishop in 2003 (Krueger & Lau, 2008). In fact, by 2008, over 55 conservative parishes have split from the Episcopalian church (Krueger & Lau, 2008). The Presbyterian church has also been working through issues of sexual orientation, and in 2008, it voted to drop the gay clergy ban, which forbids gay ministers, deacons, and elders (Gorski, 2008). However, this vote would require approval from the majority of the 173 regional Presbyterian churches, which will be an ongoing process. In many churches and synagogues, most of the more conservative views, including the idea that homosexuality can be changed through prayer and counseling, come from older members and those living in the southern part of the United States. The conservative Christian faiths, such as Catholics, Southern Baptists, and the Assemblies of God, view homosexuality as a sin and work to restrict gay, lesbian, and bisexual rights.

There is also controversy over sexual orientation in Jewish synagogues throughout the United States. Although Orthodox Jews believe that homosexuality is an abomination forbidden by the Torah, reform congregations are more likely to welcome all sexual orientations. A Reform movement in 1990 allowed the ordaining of gay rabbis (Albert et al., 2001).

There is also no real consensus about gay and lesbian relationships among the various Buddhist sects in the United States. Buddhism differs from Christianity in that it views behaviors as helpful or nonhelpful (whereas Christianity views behaviors as good/evil) and looks at whether there was intent to help or not. As a result of this, Buddhism encourages relationships that are mutually loving and supportive.

Recently, religious scholars, both homosexual and heterosexual, have begun to promote arguments based on religious law and even scripture for a more liberal attitude toward homosexuality. For example, some Jewish scholars have argued that because homosexual orientation is not a free choice but an unalterable feature of the personality, it is immoral to punish someone for it (Kahn, 1989–90).

*Judaism and Christianity have **strongly opposed** homosexual behavior.*

HOMOSEXUALITY AND THE LAW

Throughout history, laws have existed in the Western world that prohibited same-sex sexual behavior, even on pain of death. In the United States, sodomy has been illegal since colonial days, and it was punishable by death until the late 18th century (Boswell, 1980). Fellatio was technically legal until the early 20th century, although it was considered to be "loathsome and revolting" (Murphy, 1990). All 50 states outlawed homosexual acts until 1961.

The Supreme Court overturned the Texas antisodomy law—which made consensual sex between same-sex couples illegal—in 2003. Prior to 2003, under Texas homosexual conduct law, for example, individuals who engaged in "deviate sexual intercourse" with a person of the same sex (even if the partner was consenting) could be charged with a misdemeanor punishable by up to $500 in fines (Lambda, 2001).

Homosexuals are often denied equal housing rights through exclusionary zoning, rent control, and rent stabilization laws. Even in long-term, committed, same-sex couples, partners are routinely denied the worker's compensation and health care benefits normally extended to a spouse or dependents. In addition, without legal marriage, gay and lesbian couples are denied tax breaks, Social Security benefits, and rights of inheritance, all of which are available to married heterosexual couples. Some gay and lesbian couples have even resorted to legally adopting their partners to extend benefits they would otherwise be denied (Harvard Law Review, 1990). Many gay, lesbian, and bisexual employees are also discriminated against on the job, yet they have little legal recourse.

Getty Images

Lesbians, gay men, and bisexual people who also belong to other minority groups must deal with the prejudices of society toward both groups—as well as each group's prejudices toward each other.

Why Do Laws Discriminate Against Homosexuals?
Why are homosexuals in the United States so routinely denied the rights that the rest of the country takes for granted? What is the justification for denying homosexuals protection against housing and job discrimination and denying same-sex marriage?

When it comes to sexual orientation, a liberal–conservative split exists in government as well. The efforts of local, grassroots gay organizations, as well as the national efforts of groups such as the Lambda Legal Defense and Education Fund, may yet break through the wall of legal inaction that prevents homosexuals from fighting the discrimination and victimization they experience in the United States.

Our society is grappling with its acceptance of new forms of sexual relationships. Only time will tell whether that yields increased tolerance or intolerance for people of all sexual orientations.

review questions

1 Explain how changes in social attitudes toward homosexuality have provoked conflict over GLB policies in many religious denominations.

2 Identify some of the more liberal and conservative religions and explain how each religion views homosexuality.

3 Explain how and why laws have discriminated against GLB men and women.

CHAPTER **review**

SUMMARY POINTS

1 Sexual orientation refers to the sex(es) that a person is attracted to emotionally, physically, sexually, and romantically. Heterosexuals are predominantly attracted to members of the other sex; homosexuals to members of the same sex; and bisexuals are attracted to both men and women.

2 Alfred Kinsey introduced a 7-point sexual orientation scale based mostly on people's sexual behaviors, whereas other researchers suggest that people's emotions and fantasies, more than their behaviors, are the most important determinants of sexual orientation. The Klein sexual orientation grid (KSOG) includes the elements of time, fantasy, social and lifestyle behavior, and self-identification.

3 The frequency of gay, lesbian, and bisexual behavior in the United States has remained constant over the years. Scholars generally agree that there are between 3% and 4% of males who are predominantly gay, 1.5% to 2% of women who are predominantly lesbian, and about 2% to 5% who are bisexual. However, many of these studies have methodological flaws and have not taken into account feelings of attraction or fantasies.

4 Several theories have been proposed to explain homosexuality. These include the biological, developmental, behavioral, sociological, and interactional theories.

5 Biological theories claim that differences in sexual orientation are caused by genetics, hormones, birth order, or simple physical traits. Developmental theories focus on a person's upbringing and personal history to find the origins of homosexuality. Developmental theories include psychoanalytic, gender-role nonconformity, and peer-interaction. Behavioral theories view homosexuality as a learned behavior, while the sociological theories explain how social forces produce homosexuality in a society. The interactional theories explore the combined impact of biology and sociology.

6 Same-sex activity was common before the 19th century, and homosexual prostitution was taxed by the state. Homosexuality was not treated with concern or much interest by either early Jews or early Christians. The church's indifference to homosexuality lasted well through the 13th century. By 1300, however, the new intolerance of differences resulted in homosexuality being punishable by death almost everywhere. This view, from the late Middle Ages, has influenced the Western world's view of homosexuality for the past 700 years. In the 19th and early 20th centuries, physicians and scientists began to suggest that homosexuality was not a sin but an illness.

7 Same-sex sexual behavior is found in every culture, and its prevalence remains about the same no matter how permissive or repressive that culture's attitude is toward it. Many homosexuals and bisexuals struggle with discrimination, prejudice, laws that do not recognize their same-sex unions, lack of benefits for their partners, and families who may reject them.

8 Someone who is gay or lesbian must first acknowledge his or her sexual identity to himself or herself, and undergo a process known as coming out. The average age of coming out is about 16 for both men and women, even though there are some youths who remain closeted into late adolescence and even adulthood.

9 Women are more likely to discover their lesbianism through a close relationship with another woman, whereas men are more likely to discover their homosexuality through casual social/sexual contacts. Lesbian couples have a double dose of relationship-enhancing influences, which may contribute to the higher levels of relationship satisfaction among lesbian couples, whereas gay men have a double dose of relationship-destroying influences.

10 Research has found that arousal and orgasm in homosexuals are physiologically no different from that in heterosexual couples. However, gay and lesbian couples tend be slower, more relaxed, and less demanding with each other during sex than heterosexuals.

11 Children who grow up with one or two gay and/or lesbian parents do as well emotionally, cognitively, socially, and sexually as do children from heterosexual parents.

12 Homophobia is an irrational fear of homosexuals and homosexuality, and heterosexism is the presumption of heterosexuality and the social power used to promote it. Hate crimes, also known as "message crimes," are motivated by hatred of someone's religion, sex, race, sexual orientation, disability, or ethnic group. Many states punish perpetrators of hate crimes, but the way they are punished varies from state to state. One of the best ways to stop heterosexism is through education.

13 Society is less threatened by lesbian sexuality, and perhaps this is the reason that women's sexual identity is more fluid than men's. Overall, lesbian and bisexual women have been found to have lower rates of preventative care than heterosexual women.

14 Bisexuals often identify first as heterosexuals, and their self-labeling generally occurs later in life than either gay or lesbian self-labeling. Biphobia is a fear of bisexuals.

15 Minority homosexual youth have been found to experience greater psychological distress than nonminority homosexual youths.

16 Some religions have become more accepting of homosexuals. Laws that prohibited homosexual behavior have existed throughout history in the Western world, even on pain of death. In the United States prior to new legislation, sodomy had been illegal since colonial days.

CRITICAL THINKING questions

1 If you are not gay, lesbian, or bisexual, imagine for a moment that you are. Whom do you think you would approach first to talk about the issues surrounding this discovery? Would you feel comfortable talking with your friends? Parents? Siblings? Teachers? Why, or why not?

2 Suppose that one of your good friends, Tim, comes to you tomorrow and tells you that he thinks he is bisexual. You have seen Tim date only women and had no idea he was interested in men. What kinds of questions do you ask him? After reading this chapter, what can you tell him about the current research on bisexuality?

3 If a person fantasizes only about engaging in same-sex behavior but never has actually done so, would he or she be homosexual? Why, or why not?

4 Where do you fall on Kinsey's continuum? What experiences in your life contribute to your Kinsey ranking, and why?

5 What theory do you think best explains the development of sexual orientation? What features do you feel add to the theory's credibility?

6 Do you think same-sex couples should be allowed to marry each other? Why, or why not? Should they be allowed to have children? Why, or why not?

Sexuality Now Book Companion Website

Go to www.cengage.com/psychology/carroll for practice quizzes, glossary, flash cards, and more. You can also access the following websites from the companion site.

GLBTQ ■ An encyclopedia of gay, lesbian, bisexual, transgender, and queer culture. Contains information about GLBTQ culture, history, and current rulings on same-sex marriage, civic unions, and domestic partnerships.

National Gay and Lesbian Task Force ■ The National Gay and Lesbian Task Force (NGLTF) is a national organization that works for the civil rights of GLBT people. The website contains press releases and information on many GLBT issues, including affirmative action, domestic partnerships, and same-sex marriage.

Gay and Lesbian Association of Retiring Persons ■ The Gay and Lesbian Association of Retiring Persons (GLARP) is an international, nonprofit membership organization that was launched to enhance the aging experience of gays and lesbians. This website provides retirement-related information and services and also works to establish retirement communities for gays and lesbians in the United States and abroad.

Healthy Lesbian, Gay, and Bisexual Students Project ■ This site strives to strengthen the ability of the nation's schools to prevent risk to GLBTQ students. The site contains information about workshops, training, and issues affecting GLBTQ students today.

Lambda Legal Defense and Education Fund ■ The Lambda Legal Defense and Education Fund is a national organization that works for recognition of the civil rights of lesbians, gay men, bisexuals, the transgendered, and people with HIV and AIDS. Their website contains information on a variety of issues related to GLBT issues.

Parents, Families, and Friends of Lesbians and Gays ■ Parents, Families, and Friends of Lesbians and Gays (PFLAG) is a national organization that works to promote the health and well-being of gay, lesbian, bisexual, and transgendered persons, as well as their families and friends. Through education, support, and dialogue, PFLAG provides opportunities to learn more about sexual orientation and helps to create a society that is respectful of human diversity.

CengageNOW

Go to www.cengage.com/login to link to CengageNOW, your online study tool. First take the Pre-Test for this chapter to get your Personalized Study Plan, which will identify topics you need to review and direct you to online resources. Then take the Post-Test to determine what concepts you have mastered and what you still need work on.

Videos in CengageNOW

For additional information on topics discusses in this chapter, check out the videos in CengageNOW on the following topics:

- Coming Out as a Lesbian—Listen to one woman describe coming out as a lesbian at age 38 and how it affected her family and children.

- Trying Not to Be Gay—Hear a gay man describe his struggle to come to terms with his attraction to men.

- Discovering Bisexuality—Hear a woman describe how she gradually realized that she was bisexual.

- Hating People for the People They Love—See how complicated the attitudes toward gay and lesbian people actually are in Dr. Greg Herek's research.

- Coming Out in the Workplace—Interviews with men and women who describe their experiences being "out" in the workplace.

- Don't Ask, Don't Tell—A look at the ongoing debate about gays in the military.

CHAPTER 12

Pregnancy and Birth

Megan Mahoney

My life is not according to plan. I expected that after college, I would get a good job, find a great guy, fall in love, get married, and have three kids while establishing a rewarding career—all before the age of 30. In the real world, I have a successful career that I truly enjoy; I've been in love more than once but never married and never had children. At 43 years old, I was faced with the biggest decision of my life—having a child on my own. This is something I have discussed with friends and family over the years as a possibility but always hoped it wouldn't be necessary. Although I felt nervous, I also was really excited about my decision.

Anonymous sperm donation did not appeal to me. I really wanted to know the father: his personality, sense of humor, looks, intelligence, athleticism, and medical history. I did some research into sperm banks and sperm donation and was actually pleasantly surprised at the amount of information each sperm bank provides (such as height, weight, hair color, eye color, ethnicity, education, occupation, family medical history). In many ways, it felt like an online dating service— but still wasn't the route I wanted to take.

Over the years, I have floated the idea of fathering a child for me to numerous male friends of mine. The man I chose has been a friend for a long time (we dated

briefly many years ago), he is married with children of his own and is a good father. We have agreed to keep his identity secret, and that he will not play a role in the child's life—emotionally or financially. We will remain good long-distance friends, and I will always be thankful for his generosity.

I went through a battery of fertility tests, and the test results were favorable for a woman my age. The entire process took about a year, and the year was full of excitement as well as anguish and disappointment. I estimate that the treatments cost about $30,000 altogether, and my insurance company covered about half these costs, which is pretty good.

After a comprehensive workup, I started fertility drugs in preparation for in vitro fertilization (IVF). I was put on a series of drugs that produced several ova, and when the time was right, I was scheduled for ova retrieval. The doctor used a needle through my vagina to retrieve the four ova that were available. The lab took the ova and immediately attempted to fertilize them. Four embryos resulted, but only three survived to be frozen. I was unable to complete the transfer on that cycle, so we decided to do a new full IVF cycle the following month.

The next month, everything seemed to be going perfectly—the ova retrieval and fertilization resulted in three embryos, and all three were transferred to my uterus (the transfer happened 3 days after the ova re-

trieval). I was sure I was pregnant, and when my period started again I was devastated. Afterward the doctor counseled me that it was highly unlikely my eggs would work and that I should consider egg donation or adoption unless I had unlimited funds and the stamina to keep trying. I said I would look into both options but wanted to transfer my frozen embryos as soon as possible.

The transfer took place that cycle. This time my optimism took a negative turn. In fact I was so certain it failed that I didn't even bother with a home pregnancy test before going to the doctor for testing on the 12th day. To my surprise, while the nurse was drawing my blood, the urine test showed positive. My doctor said I was his oldest patient to get pregnant with her own eggs. As happy and relieved as I was, I tried to keep my joy in check—knowing that miscarriage and genetic abnormalities were not uncommon for someone my age. So I viewed each checkup and test as clearing a hurdle. Even so, the smile didn't leave my face for 9 months.

After a 22-hour labor, I delivered a healthy baby girl. All in all, I feel like I hit the jackpot. Even though life is very different for me today, it is better than I could have ever imagined.

SOURCE: Author's files.

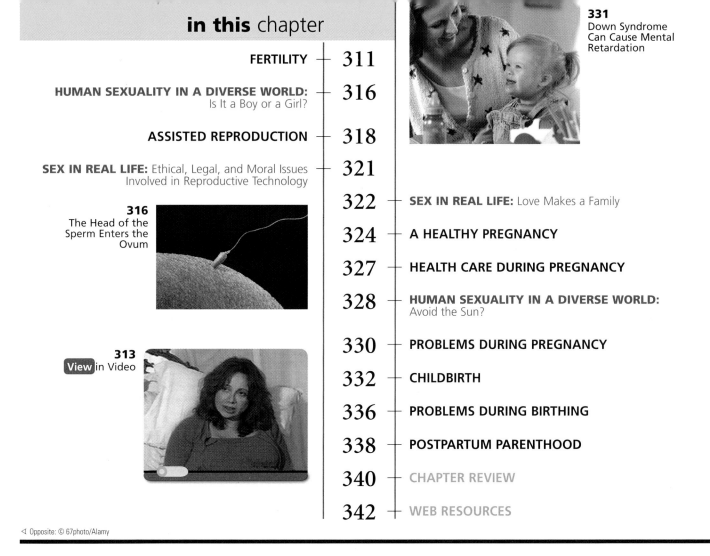

◁ Opposite: © 67photo/Alamy

Traditionally, a family consisted of a father, mother, and their biological children. However, increasing divorce, adoption, teenage pregnancy, and single and same-sex parenting, along with advances in assisted reproductive technologies, have led to a new view of the family. Whereas at one time sexual intercourse was required for pregnancy, this is no longer true today—donor sperm, ova, or embryos can be used. Although the majority of pregnancies and births today occur in heterosexual marriages in the United States (Ethics Committee Report, 2006), there are many variations to this model. In this chapter, we begin to explore issues related to fertility, pregnancy, and childbearing.

Fertility

Most parents, sooner or later, must confront the moment when their child asks, "Where did I come from?" The answer they give depends on the parent, the child, the situation, and the culture.

Every culture has its own traditional explanations for where babies come from. The Australian Aborigines, for instance, believe that babies are created by the mother earth and, therefore, are products of the land. The spirits of children rest in certain areas of the land, and these spirits enter a young woman as she passes by (Dunham et al., 1992). Women who do not want to become pregnant either avoid these areas or dress up like old women to fool the spirits. In Malaysia, the Malay people believe that because man is the more rational of the two sexes, babies come from men. Babies are formulated in the man's brain for 40 days before moving down to his penis for eventual ejaculation into a woman's womb.

In American culture, we take a more scientific view of where babies come from, and so it is important to understand the biological processes involved in conceiving a child, being pregnant, and giving birth. The biological answer to the question, "Where did I come from?" is that we are created from the union of an ovum and a spermatozoon. You may recall from the sexual anatomy and physiology chapters that fertilization and conception are dynamic processes that result in the creation of new life, a process so complex it is often referred to as "the incredible journey."

CONCEPTION:
THE INCREDIBLE JOURNEY

Our bodies are biologically programmed in many ways to help pregnancy occur. For instance, a woman's sexual desire is usually at its peak during her ovulation and just before her menstruation (Bullivant et al., 2004). During ovulation, a **mucus plug** in the cervix disappears, making it easier for sperm to enter the uterus, and the cervical mucus changes in consistency (becoming thinner and stretchy), making it easier for sperm to move through the cervix. The consistency of this mucus also creates wide gaps, which vibrate in rhythm with the tail motion of normal sperm, helping to move the healthy sperm quickly and detain abnormal sperm. The cervical mucus also helps filter out any bacteria in the semen. Finally, the female orgasm may help pull semen into the uterus; once there, continuing muscular contractions of the vagina and uterus help push sperm up toward the Fallopian tubes (pregnancy can certainly still occur, however, without the woman having an orgasm). The consistency of the ejaculated semen also helps. Almost immediately after ejaculation, semen thickens to help it stay in the vagina. Twenty minutes later, when the sperm has had a chance to move up into the uterus, it becomes thin again.

With all the help our bodies are programmed to give, the process of getting pregnant may appear rather easy; however, this is not always the case. The process of becoming pregnant is complex, and things can and do go wrong. For example, the female's immune system itself begins to attack the semen immediately after ejaculation, thinking it is unwanted bacteria. Yet although many sperm are killed by the woman's immune system, this process is usually not a threat to conception. When a fertile woman engages in unprotected sexual intercourse, 30% of the time she becomes pregnant, although a significant number of these pregnancies end in **spontaneous abortion** (Zinaman et al., 1996).

Because the ovum can live for up to 24 hours and the majority of sperm can live up to 72 hours in the female reproductive tract, pregnancy may occur if intercourse takes place either a few days before or after ovulation (A. J. Wilcox et al., 1995). Although most sperm die within 72 hours, a small number, less than 1%, can survive up to 7 days in the female reproductive tract (Ferreira-Poblete, 1997). Throughout their trip into the Fallopian tubes, the sperm haphazardly swim around, bumping into things and each other. When (and if) they reach the jellylike substance that surrounds the ovum, they begin wriggling violently. Although it is not clear how the sperm locate the ovum, preliminary research indicates that the ovum releases chemical signals that indicate its location (Palca, 1991).

Several sperm may reach the ovum, but only one will fertilize it. The sperm secretes a chemical that bores a hole through the outer layer of the ovum and allows the sperm to penetrate for fertilization. The outer layer of the ovum immediately undergoes a physical change, making it impossible for any other sperm to enter. This entire process takes about 24 hours. Fertilization usually occurs in the ampulla (the funnel-shaped open end of the Fallopian tube; see Figure 12.1); after fertilization, the fertilized ovum is referred to as a **zygote.**

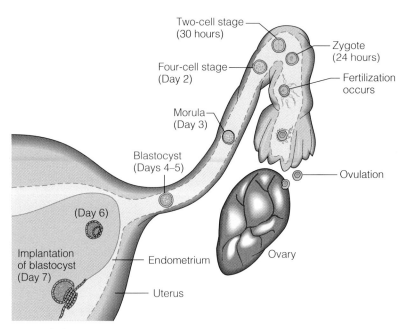

Figure **12.1** After ovulation, the follicle moves through the Fallopian tube until it meets the spermatozoon. Fertilization takes place in the wide outer part of the tube. Approximately 24 hours later, the first cell division begins. For some 3 or 4 days, the fertilized ovum remains in the Fallopian tube, dividing again and again. When the fertilized ovum enters the uterus, it sheds its outer covering in order to be able to implant in the wall of the uterus.

As we discussed in Chapter 4, the sperm carry the genetic material from the male. Each sperm contains 23 chromosomes, including the X or Y sex chromosome, which will determine whether the fetus is male or female. Other information is determined by both the male and female genes, including eye and hair color, skin color, height, and weight.

Approximately 12 hours after the genetic material from the sperm and ovum join together, the first cell division begins. At this point, the collection of cells is referred to as a **blastocyst.** The blastocyst will divide in two every 12 to 15 hours, doubling in size. As this goes on, the cilia in the Fallopian tube gently push the blastocyst toward the uterus. Fallopian tube muscles also help to move the blastocyst by occasionally contracting.

Approximately 3 to 4 days after conception, the blastocyst enters the uterus. For 2 to 3 days, it remains in the uterus and absorbs nutrients secreted by the endometrial glands. On about the sixth day after fertilization, the uterus secretes a chemical that dissolves the hard covering around the blastocyst, allowing it to implant in the uterine wall (R. Jones, 1984). Implantation involves a series of complex interactions between the lining of the uterus and the developing embryo, and this usually occurs 5 to 8 days after fertilization. To facilitate implantation, the endometrium must have been exposed to the appropriate levels of estrogen and

mucus plug
A collection of thick mucus in the cervix that prevents bacteria from entering the uterus.

spontaneous abortion
A natural process through which the body expels a developing embryo.

zygote
The single cell resulting from the union of a male and female gamete; the fertilized ovum.

blastocyst
The hollow ball of embryonic cells that enters the uterus from the Fallopian tube and eventually implants.

progesterone. Most of the time, implantation takes place in the upper portion of the uterus, and after this occurs the woman's body and the developing embryo begin to exchange chemical information. Hormones are released into the woman's bloodstream (these can be detected through pregnancy tests). If implantation does not occur, the blastocyst will degenerate and the potential pregnancy will be terminated.

It is fascinating that a woman's body allows the blastocyst to implant when so many of her body's defenses are designed to eliminate foreign substances. Apparently there is some weakening of the immune system that allows for an acceptance of the fertilized ovum (Nilsson, 1990). Some women do continually reject the fertilized ovum and experience repeat **miscarriages.** We discuss this in greater detail later in this chapter.

After implantation, the blastocyst divides into two layers of cells, the ectoderm and endoderm. A middle layer, the mesoderm, soon follows. These three layers will develop into all the bodily tissues. From the second through the eighth weeks, the developing human is referred to as an **embryo** (EMM-bree-oh). Soon a membrane called the **amnion** begins to grow over the developing embryo, and the amniotic cavity begins to fill with amniotic fluid. This fluid supports the fetus and protects it from shock and also assists in fetal lung development. The **placenta,** which is the portion that is attached to the uterine wall, supplies nutrients to the developing fetus, aids in respiratory and excretory functions, and secretes hormones necessary for the continuation of the pregnancy. The **umbilical cord** connects the fetus to the placenta. By the fourth week of pregnancy, the placenta covers 20% of the wall of the uterus, and at 5 months, the placenta covers half of the uterine wall (R. Jones, 1984). Toward the end of pregnancy, approximately 75 gallons of blood will pass through the placenta daily.

The majority of women deliver a single fetus. However, in 2 out of every 100 couples there is a multiple birth. This can happen in two ways. Sometimes two ova are released by the ovaries, and if both are fertilized by sperm, **fraternal twins** (nonidentical) result. These twins are **dizygotic,** and they can be either of the same or different sex. Two-thirds of all twins are fraternal and are no more closely genetically related than any two siblings. The tendency to have fraternal twins may be inherited from the mother, and older women (over the age of 30) seem to have fraternal twins more often than younger women (due to erratic ovulation and an increased possibility of releasing more than one ovum).

Identical twins occur when a single zygote completely divides into two separate zygotes. This process produces twins who are genetically identical and are referred to as **monozygotic** twins. They often look alike and are always of the same sex. In rare cases, the zygote fails to divide completely, and two babies may be joined together at some point in their bodies; these are known as **conjoined twins,** once referred to as Siamese twins. In some instances, many ova are released and fertilized, and *triplets* (three offspring) or *quadruplets* (four offspring) may result. Recently, the number of multiple births has been increasing as more older women become pregnant and fertility drug use, which can stimulate the

Figure **12.2** Pregnancy and birth rates for unmarried women, by race and Hispanic origin, United States, 2004. Source: *National Vital Statistics Report,* National Center for Health Statistics, 2008; Ventura et al., 2008.

"When you see the babies and hold them, there's no feeling like that."
—*A 57-Year-Old Woman's Successful In Vitro Fertilization*
To view go to CengageNOW at www.cengage.com/login

release of ova, becomes widespread (Wright et al., 2008).

In the United States, minority women had more pregnancies and births than non-minority women (see Figure 12.2). Research from the National Survey of Family Growth found that in 2004, 6.39 million pregnancies resulted in 4.11 million live births in the United States (Ventura et al., 2008). Although the highest pregnancy rates were in women 25 to 29 years old, pregnancy rates increased in older women between 1990 and 2004 (see Figure 12.3).

miscarriage
A pregnancy that terminates on its own; also referred to as a spontaneous abortion.

embryo
The developing organism from the 2nd to the 8th week of gestation.

amnion
A thin, tough, membranous sac that encloses the embryo or fetus.

placenta
The structure through which the exchange of materials between fetal and maternal circulations occurs.

umbilical cord
The long, ropelike structure that connects the fetus to the placenta.

fraternal twins
Two offspring developed from two separate ova fertilized by different spermatozoa.

dizygotic
Pertaining to or derived from two separate zygotes.

identical twins
Two offspring developed from a single zygote that completely divides into two separate, genetically identical zygotes.

monozygotic
Pertaining to or derived from one zygote.

conjoined twins
Twins who are born physically joined together.

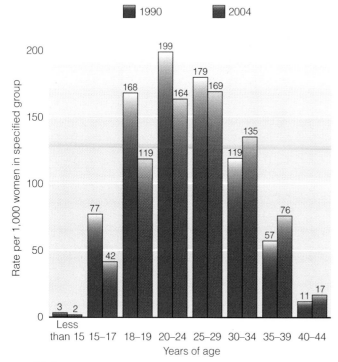

Figure **12.3** Pregnancy rates by age of woman, United States 1990 and 2004. Ventura et al., 2008.

EARLY SIGNS
OF PREGNANCY

If the zygote does implant, most women experience physical signs very early that alert them to their pregnancy. The most common early indicator is missing a period, although some women notice some "spotting" that occurs during the pregnancy (anything more than this is often referred to as irregular bleeding and may indicate a possible miscarriage). Other physical signs include breast tenderness, frequent urination, and **morning sickness** (see Table 12.1).

It is estimated that between 50% and 80% of all pregnant women experience some form of nausea, vomiting, or both, during pregnancy (Atanackovic et al., 2001). This sickness is due to the increase in estrogen and progesterone during pregnancy, which may irritate the stomach lining. It is often worse in the morning because there is no food in the stomach to counter its effects, although it can happen at any point during the day. Researchers believe that morning sickness may protect the fetus from food-borne illness and chemicals in certain foods during the first trimester, which is the most critical time in development (Boyd, 2000). The lowest rates of morning sickness are found in cultures without animal products as a food staple. Some women also develop food aversions, the most common of which are to meat, fish, poultry, and eggs—all foods that can carry harmful bacteria.

In rare cases, **pseudocyesis** (sue-doe-sigh-EE-sis), or false pregnancy, occurs. This is a condition in which a woman believes she is pregnant when she is not. Her belief is so strong that she begins to experience several of the signs of pregnancy (Svoboda, 2006). She may miss her period, experience morning sickness, and gain weight.

morning sickness
The nausea and vomiting that some women have when they become pregnant; typically caused by the increase in hormones. Can occur at any point in the day.

pseudocyesis
A condition in which a woman experiences signs of pregnancy, even though she is not pregnant.

table 12.1

Pregnancy Signs

Physical Sign	Time of Appearance	Other Possible Reasons
Period late/absent	Entire pregnancy	Excessive weight gain or loss, fatigue, hormonal problems, stress, breast-feeding, going off birth control pills
Breast tenderness	1–2 weeks after conception	Use of birth control pills, hormonal imbalance, period onset
Increased fatigue	1–6 weeks after conception	Stress, depression, thyroid disorder, cold or flu
Morning sickness	2–8 weeks after conception	Stress, stomach disorders, food poisoning
Increased urination	6–8 weeks after conception	Urinary tract infection, excessive use of diuretics, diabetes
Fetal heartbeat	10–20 weeks and then throughout entire pregnancy	None
Backaches	Entire pregnancy	Back problems
Frequent headaches	May be entire pregnancy	Caffeine withdrawal, dehydration, eyestrain, birth control pills
Food cravings	Entire pregnancy	Poor diet, stress, depression, period onset
Darkening of nipples	Entire pregnancy	Hormonal imbalance
Fetal movement	16–22 weeks after conception	Bowel contractions, gas

Will guys ever be able to become "pregnant"?
Although *The Oprah Winfrey Show* showcased an oversensationalized case of a pregnant transgendered man in 2008, there have not been any documented pregnancies in a biological man. However, it is possible that newer techniques will enable a biological man to carry a pregnancy to term in the near future. An embryo would have to be implanted into a man's abdomen with the placenta and attached to an internal organ. Hormonal treatment would be necessary to sustain the pregnancy. In addition, the father would have to undergo a cesarean section birth. There may not be many men standing in line to carry a pregnancy, however, because the hormones needed to maintain the pregnancy can cause breast enlargement and penile shrinkage.

Although the majority of cases of pseudocyesis have a psychological basis, there are some that have physical causes. For instance, a tumor on the pituitary gland may cause an oversecretion of prolactin, which in turn can cause symptoms such as breast fullness and morning sickness. Pseudocyesis has been found to be more common in women who believe childbearing is central to their identity, have a history of infertility or depression (or both), or have had a miscarriage (Whelan & Stewart, 1990). Although rare, there are a few cases in which men experienced pseudocyesis, although this is typically due to psychological impairment (Shutty & Leadbetter, 1993). It is more typical for men to experience a related condition called **couvade** (coo-VAHD). Men with this condition experience the symptoms of their pregnant partners, including nausea, vomiting, increased or decreased appetite, diarrhea, or abdominal bloating.

© Universal Pictures/Courtesy Everett Collection

In the film *Junior*, Arnold Schwarzenegger played a scientist who becomes pregnant to further his research. Although men are not yet able to carry a pregnancy to term today, Thomas Beattie, a transgendered man who kept his female reproductive organs, gave birth to a baby girl in 2008 and became pregnant again shortly thereafter.

PREGNANCY TESTING:
CONFIRMING THE SIGNS

If you have had sexual intercourse without using birth control or have experienced any of the signs of pregnancy, it is a good idea to take a pregnancy test. Over-the-counter pregnancy tests can be purchased in drugstores, but sometimes tests are less expensive or even free in university health centers.

Pregnancy tests measure for a hormone in the blood called **human chorionic gonadotropin** (**hCG;** corr-ee-ON-ick go-nad-oh-TRO-pin), which is produced during pregnancy. The hormone hCG is manufactured by the cells in the developing placenta and can be identified in the blood or urine 8 to 9 days after ovulation. The presence of hCG helps build and maintain a thick endometrial layer and so prevents menstruation. Peak levels of hCG are reached in the second and third months of pregnancy and then drop off.

Home pregnancy tests can be inaccurate if taken too soon after conception, and some women who postpone pregnancy tests until after the 12th week may have a **false-negative** pregnancy test because the hCG levels are too low to be detected by the test. If you are using an at-home test, be sure you know how soon after ovulation it can be used. Many tests today can detect hcG levels before a period is late. **False-positive** test results may occur in the presence of a kidney disease or infection, an overactive thyroid gland, or large doses of aspirin, tranquilizers, antidepressants, or anticonvulsant medications (Hatcher et al., 2007).

Of all pregnancy tests, **radioimmunoassay** (**RIA;** ray-dee-oh-im-mue-noh-ASS-say) **blood tests** are the most accurate. RIA tests can detect hCG within a few days after conception and are also useful for monitoring the progress of a pregnancy that may be in jeopardy. The levels of hCG rise early in pregnancy, and if a woman's hormones do not follow this pattern, a spontaneous abortion or an **ectopic pregnancy** may have occurred. We discuss both of these later in this chapter.

After a woman's pregnancy is confirmed, her health care provider helps her to calculate a **due date.** Most physicians date the pregnancy from the first day of the last menstrual period rather than the day of ovulation or fertilization. The standard for due date calculation is called the **Naegele's** (nay-GEL-lays) **rule**—subtract 3 months from the first day of the last period and add

couvade
A condition in which the father (or other relative) experiences the symptoms of pregnancy, childbirth, or both without an actual pregnancy.

human chorionic gonadotropin (hCG)
The hormone that stimulates production of estrogen and progesterone to maintain pregnancy.

false negative
Incorrect result of a medical test or procedure that wrongly shows the lack of a finding.

false positive
Incorrect result of a medical test or procedure that wrongly shows the presence of a finding.

radioimmunoassay (RIA) blood test
Blood pregnancy test.

ectopic pregnancy
The implantation of the fertilized egg outside the uterus, such as in the Fallopian tubes or abdomen.

due date
The projected birth date of a baby.

Naegele's rule
A means of figuring the due date by subtracting 3 months from the first day of the last menstrual period and adding 7 days.

REALResearch ▸ Research on morning sickness has found that it may offer protection from breast cancer. One study found that women who experienced morning sickness during pregnancy had a **30%** lower chance of developing breast cancer later in life, compared with women who did not experience morning sickness (and women who experienced severe morning sickness had even a lower risk; Jaworowicz, 2007). Researchers suggest that changing levels of hCG may be responsible for the nausea and that these levels seem to offer protection from breast cancer later on.

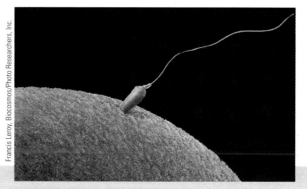

As the head of the spermatozoon enters the ovum, the ovum prevents penetration by another spermatozoon.

7 days for a single birth (Mittendorf et al., 1990; for example, if the last period began on August 1, subtract 3 months and add 7 days, which means that the due date would be May 8). This rule works most effectively with women who have standard 28-day menstrual cycles.

SEX SELECTION:
MYTH AND MODERN METHODS

Throughout time, many couples have searched for ways to choose the sex of their child. A variety of techniques have been proposed by different cultures at different times. Aristotle believed that if a couple had sexual intercourse in the north wind, they would have a male child, and if intercourse took place in the south wind, they would have a female. Hippocrates believed that males formed on the right side of the uterus and females on the left; so, to conceive a daughter, a woman was advised to lie on her left side directly

HUMAN SEXUALITY IN A DIVERSE WORLD

Is It a Boy or a Girl?

Around the world, people use a variety of methods to predict the sex of a baby.

Throughout the world, people have relied on folk wisdom to predict the sex of their baby. Here are some examples:

It's a Girl!
Baby sits on the left side of the womb (Nyinba, Nepal)
Mother puts her left foot first crossing the threshold (Bihar, India)
Baby sits low in the belly (Lepchas, Himalayas, and Bedouin tribes)
Mother is grumpy with women (Dinka, Africa)
Fetus moves slowly and gently (Dustin, North Borneo, and Egypt)
Mother first feels the baby when she is outside (Serbia)
Mother dreams of human skulls (Maori, New Zealand)
Mother dreams of a head kerchief (Egypt)
Mother craves spicy foods (Nyinba, Nepal)
Mother's face has yellow spots (Poland)
Baby "plays in stomach" before sixth month (Nyinba, Nepal)

It's a Boy!
Baby sits on the right side of the womb (Nyinba, Nepal)
Mother puts her right foot first crossing the threshold (Bihar, India)
Baby sits high in the belly (Lepchas, Himalayas, and Bedouin tribes)
Mother is grumpy with men (Dinka, Africa)
Fetus moves fast and roughly (Dustin, North Borneo, and Egypt)
Mother first feels baby move when at home (Serbia)
Mother dreams of huisa feathers (Maori, New Zealand)
Mother dreams of a handkerchief (Egypt)
Mother craves bland foods (Nyinba, Nepal)
Mother looks well (Poland)
Baby first "plays in stomach" after sixth month (Nyinba, Nepal)

SOURCE: Dunham et al., 1992.

I have missed my period now for 2 months in a row. Does this mean that I am pregnant? What should I do?

If you have been engaging in sexual intercourse, there is certainly a chance that you are pregnant. However, there are several reasons for missing your period, including stress, losing weight, active participation in sports, or changes in eating patterns, as well as certain diseases. In any case, it is a good idea to see a gynecologist or your school nurse for an evaluation.

after intercourse. The ancient Greeks thought that if a man cut or tied his left testicle, a couple would not have girls because male sperm were thought to be produced in the right testicle (Dunham et al., 1992). Although some of these suggestions sound absurd today, people in many cultures still hold myths of how to choose and how to know the gender of their child (see Human Sexuality in a Diverse World, "Is It a Boy or a Girl?").

Reasons for wanting to choose a child's sex vary; although some couples simply prefer a male or female child, others desire to choose the sex of their children for medical reasons. For example, certain inherited diseases are more likely to affect one sex (such as hemophilia, which affects more males).

Modern-day methods of gender selection were popularized by Shettles and Rorvik (1970) in their groundbreaking book *Your Baby's Sex: Now You Can Choose.* According to these authors, by taking into account the characteristics of the female (X) and male (Y) sperm, couples can use timing and pH-level adjustments to the vaginal environment (douches) to increase the concentration of X or Y sperm.

Because Y sperm swim faster and thrive in an alkaline environment, Shettles and Rorvik recommended that to have a boy, a couple should have intercourse close to ovulation (to allow the faster-swimming Y sperm to get there first) and douche with a mixture of baking soda and water. Because X sperm tend to live longer and thrive in an acidic environment, for a girl, a couple should time intercourse 2 to 3 days before ovulation and douche with a mixture of vinegar and water.

Medical procedures for sex selection include "microsorting" (also known as "spinning"; separating the X and Y sperm followed by artificial insemination). Other tests that can be used to identify sex include genetic embryo testing and amniocentesis. Microsort-

ing comes at a cost—approximately $3,200 per trial. The reported likelihood of conceiving a male is between 50% and 70% and a female is between 50% to 90% (Pozniak, 2002). Preimplantation genetic diagnosis (PGD) is typically used during assisted reproduction to determine where there are chromosomal or genetic abnormalities in an embryo. Some couples who prefer a child of a certain sex may also use PGD for this preference. As you can imagine, the use of PGD has become controversial because it has also been used for sex selection (Ehrich et al., 2007; Gleicher et al., 2008; Kuliev & Verlinsky, 2008). Finally, an **amniocentesis** (am-nee-oh-sent-TEE-sis) can also determine, among other things, the chromosomal sex of the fetus. These tests raise many moral, sociological, and ethical issues about sex selection. For example, controversy surrounds whether parents should be able to selectively abort a fetus on the basis of sex.

In several places around the world, parents go to extremes to ensure the birth of a male baby. In India, for example, males are valued more than females because of their ability to care for and financially support aging parents. Female offspring, on the other hand, move into a husband's home after marriage and are unavailable to help care for their parents. Early testing has led to an increase in pregnancy termination of female fetuses in India, China, and South Korea (Dubouc & Coleman, 2007; Jha et al., 2006) In fact, India has the lowest ratio of girls to boys in the world (Jha et al., 2006). Some poor families often cannot afford to have girls because parents are expected to provide dowries for their daughters at marriage. In 2008, India's government announced it will pay poor families approximately $3,000 to prevent **female infanticide** ("This Week in Medicine," 2008).

REALResearch >There is evidence that what a woman eats during the time of conception may influence the sex of her child (MATHEWS ET AL., 2008). Women who ate a high-calorie diet along with regular breakfast at the time of conception were more likely to have boys. The researchers believe that trends in low-calorie diets may have influenced the falling proportion of boys in developed countries (MATHEWS ET AL., 2008).

amniocentesis
A procedure in which a small sample of amniotic fluid is analyzed to detect chromosomal abnormalities in the fetus or to determine the sex of the fetus.

female infanticide
The killing of female infants; practiced in some countries that value males more than females.

review questions

1 Explain the process of conception, and describe how the human body is programmed to help pregnancy occur.

2 Identify four signs of pregnancy, and explain why they occur.

3 Explain how pregnancy tests work.

4 Explain the methods for sex selection and define and discuss infanticide.

Assisted Reproduction

Today many couples—married, unmarried, straight, gay, lesbian, young, and old—use assisted reproduction. Some couples use these techniques because they have **infertility** issues, whereas others use them to get pregnant without a partner or with a same-sex partner.

ASSISTED REPRODUCTION IN HETEROSEXUAL COUPLES

Many heterosexual couples use assisted reproduction because of infertility issues. Infertility is defined as the inability to conceive (or impregnate) after 1 year of regular sexual intercourse without the use of any form of birth control (if a woman is over age 35, usually infertility is diagnosed after 6 months of not being able to conceive). In 2007, there were an estimated 6 million infertile couples in the United States (Chavarro et al., 2007).

We know that fertility rates naturally decline in men and women with increasing age, beginning as early as 30 and then decreasing more quickly after age 40—fewer than 10% of women in their early 20s have infertility issues, whereas 30% of women in their 40s do (Chavarro et al., 2007). Sperm quality in men is also affected by aging (Girsh et al., 2008).

Overall, the number of couples seeking assisted reproduction treatment for infertility is increasing each year. In 2005, approximately 12% of U.S. women of childbearing age used assisted reproduction treatments (Centers for Disease Control, 2007). The average age of these women was 36, although the largest group of women was below the age of 35.

Fertility problems can be traced 70% of the time to one of the partners (40% of the time the female, and 30% of the time the male). In 20% of cases, there is a combined problem, and in 10% the reason is unknown (Afek, 1990). Historically, women have been blamed for infertility problems, and up until the last few years, men were not even considered a possible part of the problem.

Infertility has a strong impact on a couple's well-being (Forti & Krausz, 1998). Emotional reactions to infertility can include depression, anxiety, anger, self-blame, guilt, frustration, and fear. Because the majority of people have no experience dealing with infertility, many of those who find out they are infertile isolate themselves and try not to think about it. Overall, women tend to have more emotional reactions to infertility and are more willing to confide in someone about their infertility than are men (Hjelmstedt et al., 1999). Childbearing in the United States is part of what defines being female, and so women who are infertile often feel less valued than fertile women. The term **motherhood mandate** refers to the idea that something is wrong with a woman if she does not play a central role in caregiving and child care (Riggs, 2005).

The most common causes of female infertility include ovulation disorders, blocked Fallopian tubes, endometriosis (see Chapter 5), structural uterine problems, or excessive uterine fibroids. The most common causes for male infertility include problems with sperm production (Lewis et al., 2008). Infertility can also be caused by past infections with gonorrhea, chlamydia, or pelvic inflammatory disease (Chavarro et al., 2007; Hatcher et al., 2004), which is one of the reasons college students are encouraged to have regular medical checkups and women are encouraged to have regular Pap smears. If a sexually transmitted infection is

REALResearch > Unused embryos that result from assisted reproductive techniques, even those of poor quality, can provide stem-cell lines that can be used as a type of repair system in people with defective cells (COHEN ET AL., 2008). One study examined embryo donation and found that whereas **49%** of Spanish couples agreed to donate their embryos, only **3%** of U.S. couples did (CORTES ET AL., 2007).

infertility
The inability to conceive (or impregnate).

motherhood mandate
The belief that something is wrong with a woman if she is not involved in caregiving or child care.

timeline The History of Assisted Reproduction

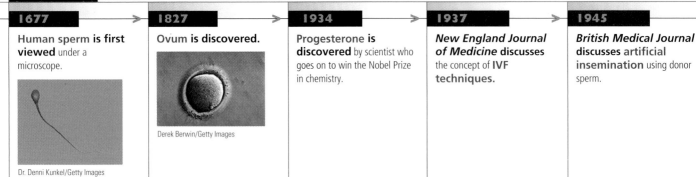

1677	1827	1934	1937	1945
Human sperm is first viewed under a microscope.	**Ovum is discovered.**	**Progesterone is discovered** by scientist who goes on to win the Nobel Prize in chemistry.	*New England Journal of Medicine* discusses the concept of **IVF techniques.**	*British Medical Journal* discusses artificial insemination using donor sperm.

Dr. Denni Kunkel/Getty Images

Derek Berwin/Getty Images

treated early, there is less chance that it will interfere with fertility. Infertility is also affected by age. Women and men who delay pregnancy may experience infertility because of the decreasing quality of their ova and sperm (Coccia & Rizzello, 2008; Girsh et al., 2008). For some men and women who experience reproductive problems, changing lifestyle patterns, reducing stress, avoiding rigorous exercise, and maintaining a recommended weight may restore fertility (Chavarro et al., 2007). For other couples, new medical interventions offer new possibilities.

Finally, whereas in the past single women were denied access to assisted reproductive technologies, this has slowly been changing (Greenfeld, 2005; McManus et al., 2006; L. E. Ross et al., 2006b). In 2006, the Ethics Committee of the American Society for Reproductive Medicine released a statement supporting access to fertility treatment by unmarried, gay, and lesbian persons (Ethics Committee Report, 2006a). As the opening narrative in this chapter illustrated, older, financially stable, and college-educated women are increasingly having children on their own (Hannah-Jones, 2008).

ASSISTED REPRODUCTION
IN SAME-SEX COUPLES

Like unmarried single heterosexuals, many gay, lesbian, and bisexual singles, along with same-sex couples, have also traditionally been denied access to assisted reproductive technologies (Greenfeld, 2005; McManus et al., 2006; L. E. Ross et al., 2006a, 2006b). Whereas gay, lesbian, and bisexual men and women use assisted reproduction for infertility issues, the majority use these techniques to achieve a pregnancy (see the nearby Sex in Real Life feature, "Ethical, Legal, and Moral Issues Involved in Reproductive Technology"). An increasing number of singles and same-sex couples are using assisted reproduction today (see Chapter 9; L. E. Ross et al., 2006a, 2006b). Because U.S. fertility clinics often vary in the willingness and acceptance to treat certain groups (Greenfeld, 2007), GLBs and same-sex couples often seek out clinics that are "gay positive," offering fertility support that is relevant to their lifestyles (L. E. Ross et al., 2006a, 2006b).

REALResearch **>** Diets that restrict types of carbohydrate intake, such as the South Beach Diet, may be bad for fertility. The Nurses' Health Study, a long-term research study that has evaluated the health of more than 100,000 nurses, found that carbohydrate choices can influence fertility (CHAVARRO ET AL., 2007). Women who ate more "fast" carbohydrates, such as white bread, potatoes, and sodas, were **92%** more likely to have had ovulatory infertility than women who ate "slow" carbohydrates (such as whole grains, beans, and vegetables).

Unique issues face gays, lesbians, and bisexuals who want to be pregnant. Lesbian and bisexual women who use infertility services often find that because these centers primarily cater to infertile women, they are required to undergo significant infertility work-ups before any reproductive procedures (Mulligan & Heath, 2007; L. E. Ross et al., 2006a, 2006b). Gay men also face unique issues, because assisted reproduction is often more complicated and expensive than lesbian parenting (C. Friedman, 2007). Although in the past, gay men sought out coparenting arrangements with female friends, today many gay men use adoption and surrogacy (C. Friedman, 2007). Adoption raises several issues, however, because in some states both sexual orientation and state law preclude gay, lesbian, and bisexual couples from being considered as adoptive parents (see Chapter 9). Surrogacy raises additional issues for gay couples because they must choose whose sperm will be used. Some gay men mix their sperm so they don't know which of them is the biological father.

ASSISTED REPRODUCTIVE
OPTIONS

Assisted reproductive technologies that have been developed in the past few years enable some couples to have children even when one of them is infertile or they are of the same sex. However, many of these options are very time-consuming and expensive, and they do not guarantee success. In 2005, 1% of all babies born in the United States were conceived through artificial reproductive technologies (Wright et al., 2008).

1973

IVF is first attempted in the United States. First IVF pregnancy is reported in Australia but does not produce a child.

1978

Louise Brown, the first IVF baby, **is born** in Cambridge, England.

Express/Express/Getty Images

1983

First IVF baby is born in the United States.

Sperm Bank of California is opened to allow donations for unmarried women.

First baby conceived with donor ova is born in Australia.

1984

First baby developed from a frozen embryo is born in Australia.

1987

Embryo transfer procedure is patented.

Although many technologies are available to men and women today, deciding which treatment to use depends on factors such as cost, a woman's age, duration of infertility, and chances of conceiving without treatment.

There are some risks associated with artificial reproductive technologies. **Ovarian hyperstimulation syndrome** and increased multiple births are two of the most common risks (Jakimiuk et al., 2007; Kwan et al., 2008; Van Voorhis, 2006; Wright et al., 2008). In addition, multiple-birth infants born through these techniques have been found to have lower birth rates, increased prematurity, and higher rates of birth defects and infant death (we will discuss birth defects more later in this chapter; see also Allen et al., 2008; Buckett et al., 2007; Centers for Disease Control, 2007; Kelly-Vance et al., 2004; Van Voorhis, 2006). There is also evidence that pregnancies achieved through assisted reproductive techniques are more at risk for miscarriage and delivery problems (Buckett et al., 2007; Van Voorhis, 2006; Wang et al., 2004). In the accompanying Sex in Real Life feature, we discuss some of the legal and ethical issues that have emerged as assisted reproduction has become more common.

Fertility Drugs

Some couples may use fertility drugs to help achieve a pregnancy. As we discussed in Chapters 5 and 6, ovulation and sperm production are a result of a well-balanced endocrine system (pituitary, hypothalamus, and gonads). Some women and men have hormonal irregularities that may interfere with the process of ovulation or sperm production. Although we do not always know why these hormonal problems develop, many problems can be treated with fertility drugs.

Ovarian hyperstimulation syndrome occurs because fertility drugs stimulate the ovaries to produce more ova. This has raised concern about the possible correlation between the use of fertility drugs and the development of breast or ovarian cancer. Whereas some studies have found a possible increased risk in women who have never been pregnant, older women, those with extensive fertility workups, and those with a history of cancer (Brinton, 2007; Pappo et al., 2008), other studies have found no increased risk (Hollander, 2000; Lerner-Geva et al., 2006).

REALResearch > Because many women are delaying first pregnancies, aging ova may contribute to infertility issues (COCCIA & RIZZELLO, 2008). Newer "ovarian reserve" screening tests allow physicians to predict the chances of pregnancy and live birth, allowing them to select treatment options that may have higher success rates.

Surgery

Cervical, vaginal, or endometrial abnormalities that prevent conception may be corrected surgically. Scar tissue, cysts, tumors, or adhesions, as well as blockages inside the Fallopian tubes, may be surgically removed. The use of diagnostic techniques such as **laparoscopy** (la-puh-RAH-ske-pee) and **hysteroscopy** (hiss-stare-oh-OSK-coe-pee) are also common (Coccia et al., 2008). In men, surgery may be required to remove any blockage in the vas deferens or epididymis, or repair a **varicocele** (VA-ruh-coe-seal).

Artificial Insemination

Artificial insemination is the process of introducing sperm into a woman's reproductive tract without sexual intercourse. This is a popular option for both heterosexual and same-sex couples. Ejaculated sperm, collected through masturbation, can come from a partner or from a sperm donor. The sperm is then specially treated and washed, and the healthy sperm are extracted. Several samples may be collected from men with a low sperm count to increase the number of healthy sperm. Once washed, sperm can be deposited in the vagina, cervix, uterus (intrauterine), or Fallopian tubes (intratubal).

ovarian hyperstimulation syndrome
Side effects of excessive hormonal stimulation of the ovaries through fertility drugs. Side effects may include abdominal bloating, nausea, diarrhea, weight gain, abdominal, chest, and leg pain.

laparoscopy
A procedure that allows a direct view of all the pelvic organs, including the uterus, Fallopian tubes, and ovaries; also refers to a number of important surgeries (such as tubal ligation or gall bladder removal) involving a laparoscope.

hysteroscopy
Visual inspection of the uterine cavity with an endoscope.

varicocele
An unnatural swelling of the veins in the scrotum.

artificial insemination
Artificially introducing sperm into a woman's reproductive tract.

timeline The History of Assisted Reproduction

1988
After **a surrogate mother refuses to give up custody** of baby she carried, the New Jersey Supreme Court gives custody of "Baby M" to the genetic father and his wife, and the surrogate is given visitation rights.

AP Photo

1991
A 42-year-old woman **becomes a surrogate** mother for her daughter after becoming pregnant with the daughter's embryo.

1992
Intracytoplasmic sperm injection (ICSI) for male infertility **is introduced.**

© ISM/Phototake

1996
Policy is drawn up by the American Society for Reproductive Medicine on what to do with abandoned embryos.

First baby born that was conceived with intracellular sperm injection (ICSI).

Ethical, Legal, and Moral Issues Involved in Reproductive Technology

Many of the reproductive technologies raise ethical, legal, and moral questions with which many scientists and researchers are grappling.

Many of the reproductive technologies raise ethical, legal, and moral questions with which many scientists and researchers are grappling. Should we be allowed to artificially join the ovum and sperm outside of the uterus? Should older men and women be able to use reproductive technologies to become parents? What about gay, lesbian, bisexual, and transgendered men and women? Should embryos that are not used for artificial reproduction be used in stem-cell research? Should poor women in other countries be encouraged to sell their ova? Will this one day give rise to the manipulation of certain traits or genes in the creation of a "perfect" baby?

In addition, all of these procedures are very expensive. Expensive technologies produce very expensive children. Does expensive mean "better"? Why are people willing to risk their lifesavings on having biologically related children when there are children waiting to be adopted?

In addition to these ethical and moral questions, several legal questions have arisen. What should be done with embryos that are fertilized and frozen for later use if a couple separates? Whose property are they? Should they be equitably distributed to both partners? Should they simply be disposed of? Donated to stem-cell research? Also, because this field is so lucrative, some physicians have been known to perform expensive infertility procedures that may not have a good chance of working.

What do you think about these reproductive techniques? Should a woman be able to "rent" her uterus for the development of someone else's child? Should fertilization be allowed to occur in a petri dish?

Men who decide to undergo sterilization or who may become sterile because of surgery or chemotherapy can collect sperm before the procedure. Sperm can be frozen for up to 10 years in a **sperm bank.** Although the cost of donor sperm varies among sperm banks, typically donor sperm costs between $200 and 600 per insemination. Sperm banks often charge more for "professional" sperm, which has been collected from men with advanced and professional degrees. Some couples buy several vials from the same donor so that offspring can have the same donor father.

A donor may be found through one of the many sperm banks throughout the United States and abroad, usually from an online donor catalog (see Web Resources at the end of this chapter for more information). After a donor is chosen, the sperm bank will typically send sperm to the physician who will be performing the insemination procedure, but in some cases the sperm is sent directly to the buyer. Fertility drugs are often used in conjunction with artificial insemination to increase the chances that there will be healthy ova present when the sperm is introduced.

In Vitro Fertilization

Another reproductive technology is **in vitro fertilization (IVF),** or the creation of a **test-tube baby.** In 1978, Louise Brown, the first test-tube baby, was born in England. Since that time, thou-

sperm bank
A storage facility that holds supplies of sperm for future use.

in vitro fertilization (IVF)
A procedure in which a woman's ova are removed from her body, fertilized with sperm in a laboratory, and then surgically implanted back into her uterus.

test-tube baby
A slang term for any zygote created by mixing sperm and egg outside a woman's body.

1998
First embryonic stem cells **isolated.**

2000
Preimplantation genetic diagnosis (PGD) **is used** to select an embryo to create child who can serve as a bone marrow donor to save a sibling.

2001
Congress **allocates** $900,000 to promote embryo adoption.

2002
Society for Assisted Reproductive Technology **study determines** that there are 400,000 frozen embryos stored at IVF facilities in the United States.

2006
American Society for Reproductive Medicine **publicly supports** access to fertility treatment by unmarried, gay, and lesbian persons.

© Lester Lefkowitz/Corbis

SEX IN REAL LIFE

Love Makes a Family

We believe that our active efforts to interact with other two-mom families has helped our children understand that they are not alone.

Unlike heterosexual couples, same-sex couples cannot become pregnant through sex and must always face the decision of *how* to have children (most heterosexual couples never face this decision unless they find themselves infertile; C. Friedman, 2007). The following is a story written by a woman who, together with her female partner and a sperm donor, has created a family with two moms, an 8-year-old son, and a 4-year-old daughter (see the accompanying family photo).

Besides our love, shared values, common interests and commitment to each other, the fact that we wanted children to be in our lives has always been a part of our relationship. We are at the forefront of the "gayby boom"—gay and lesbian partners deciding to raise children together. The specifics on how to make that happen were long discussed and well planned.

We are fortunate to have a large circle of lesbian couples and friends who were also making similar decisions, and we all shared our experiences with each other. My partner and I spent long hours discussing what was important to us—we believed that certain personality traits and characteristics were inherited. Therefore we wanted a known donor—a friend whom we admired and would be willing to donate his sperm and relinquish all parental decision making and responsibility to us. After having this discussion with several friends, we settled upon one male friend as our donor. Our donor is a carpenter by trade with tremendous visual-spatial skills, athletic ability, and intelligence. He is kind and thoughtful and understood that we would be the parents but that he would get to have the experience of knowing these children and having a relationship with them. He has no other children so this would be his first, and perhaps only opportunity to be a father. He also needed to make a commitment to help us have more than one child.

We had a legal agreement drawn up outlining our conditions so that we were all clear on what to expect. We de-

cided that my partner would go first since she was older than I am but that I would carry the next child. Each couple we know has done things differently for their own personal reasons. We are the only couple amongst our friends who has a known donor; everyone else has used an anonymous sperm donor. The nitty-gritty details of finding a gynecologist that would inseminate with a known donor using live sperm took some research. This whole process requires lesbian and gay couples to be frank advocates for what they want and to seek out resources that meet their needs. Most insurances do not cover inseminations so that cost is out-of-pocket. Also, if additional fertility measures need to be undertaken, as in my case, that is also not a covered expense.

Our children, aged 8 and 4 years old, know their dad and call him by his first name. They see him about once a month, and he is thrilled that they are in his life. We have always been honest about our family configuration. We are also very fortunate to have a network of close friends who are also two-mom families, live in the same town, and whom we participate in shared activities—barbeques, birthday parties, etc.—at least monthly.

While my family has always been supportive of my relationship with my partner and my desire to have children, my partner's parents have slowly accepted this all since the children were born. We can adopt in the state in which we live, so we have each adopted the other's biological child. We interact with lots of relatives, and because our son is now in school, we also interact with heterosexual families. We believe that our active efforts to interact with other two-mom families has helped our children understand that they are not alone and that there are families just like ours within our community.

SOURCE: Author's Files

---

sands of babies have been conceived in this fashion. The name is a bit deceiving, however, because these babies are not *born* in a test tube; rather, they are *conceived* in a petri dish, which is a shallow circular dish with a loose-fitting cover.

Heterosexual and lesbian women with infertility problems may use this method because of blocked or damaged Fallopian tubes or endometriosis (see Chapter 5). Like other artificial reproductive technologies, fertility drugs are typically used before IVF to help stimulate the ovaries. When the ova have matured, 4 to 6 are retrieved with the use of microscopic needles inserted into the abdominal cavity. The ova are put into a petri dish and mixed with washed sperm. Once fertilization has occurred (usually anywhere from 3 to 6 days), the zygotes are either transferred to the woman's uterus or frozen for use at another time (we talk more about this later in the chapter). In 2007, the Centers for Disease Control released a national summary of success rates for assisted reproduction (Centers for Disease Control, 2007). This report showed that of the 134,260 artificial reproductive technology (ART) cycles performed in 2005 in the United States, 38,910 resulted in a live birth (and 52,041 infants).

Earlier we discussed how preimplantation genetic diagnosis can be used on embryos to determine gender. However, this test is more commonly used to screen for chromosomal and genetic abnormalities. A PGD screening costs between $3,000 and $5,000.

Gamete and Zygote Intra-Fallopian Tube Transfer

A small percentage of ART procedures use **gamete intra-Fallopian tube transfer (GIFT)**. GIFT is similar to IVF in that ova and sperm are mixed in an artificial environment. However, after this occurs, both the ova and sperm are placed in the Fallopian tube, via a small incision, prior to fertilization. Fertilization is allowed to occur naturally rather than in an artificial environment. For women who do not desire fertilization to occur outside the body (for religious reasons), GIFT is an attractive option. **Zygote intra-Fallopian tube transfer (ZIFT)** differs slightly from GIFT in that it allows ova and sperm to fertilize outside the body (similar to IVF). However, directly following fertilization, the embryo is placed in the woman's Fallopian tube (and not the uterus, like in IVF), which allows it to travel to the uterus and implant naturally. Although higher success rates were initially reported with these two procedures, they are more invasive than IVF, and today only a small percentage of couples use these procedures (Centers for Disease Control, 2007).

Intracellular Sperm Injections

Couples who experience sperm problems or ova that are resistant to fertilization may use **intracytoplasmic sperm injection (ICSI;** Centers for Disease Control, 2007). ICSI involves injecting a single

© ISM/Phototake

In this enlarged image, a single sperm is injected into the center of an ovum during an intracellular sperm injection procedure.

sperm into the center of an ovum under a microscope. Usually ejaculated sperm are used, but sperm can also be removed from the epididymis or the testes (Devroey & Van Steirteghem, 2004). As of 2005, approximately 60% of ART procedures involved the use of ICSI (Centers for Disease Control, 2007).

Overall, ICSI results have been controversial—with some studies showing no adverse outcomes compared with natural conception (Knoester et al., 2008;

Nauru et al., 2008) and other studies showing increased risks (J. L. Simpson & Lamb, 2001). Research indicates that ICSI may lead to an increased risk of genetic defect, which may be because ICSI eliminates many of the natural barriers to conception, increasing the transmission of abnormal genes (Al-Shawaf et al., 2005; Devroey & Van Steirteghem, 2004; Neri et al., 2008). Scientists do not know how nature chooses one sperm for fertilization, and choosing one randomly may not be appropriate, although physicians usually try to pick one that appears vigorous and healthy.

Oocyte and Embryo Transplants

Women who are not able to produce healthy ova due to ovarian failure or age-related infertility and same-sex couples may use oocyte (egg) and embryo donation. Oocyte donation involves using a donor ova, whereas embryo donation can involve using frozen embryos donated by a couple or the creation of an embryo with a donated ova and sperm. Women over age 40 have a higher chance of achieving pregnancy by using a donated ova than they do using their own aged ova (Lim & Tsakok, 1997).

Surrogate Parenting

Both heterosexual women who cannot carry a pregnancy to term on their own and same-sex couples may use **surrogate parenting.** In this procedure, sperm and ovum are combined, and the zygote is implanted in another woman, called a gestational carrier. In 2005, gestational carriers were used in 1% of assisted reproductive cycles (Centers for Disease Control, 2007).

Women who can neither sustain a pregnancy nor produce their own ova may arrange to have another woman's ova fertilized by either the father's or a donor's sperm. This procedure is also used by gay couples. The woman who carries the fetus is called a **surrogate mother.** At birth, the child is given to the noncarrying woman and her partner.

gamete intra-Fallopian tube transfer (GIFT)
A reproductive technique in which the sperm and ova are collected and injected into the Fallopian tube before fertilization.

zygote intra-Fallopian tube transfer (ZIFT)
A reproductive technique in which the sperm and ova are collected and fertilized outside the body, and the fertilized zygote is then placed into the Fallopian tube.

intracytoplasmic sperm injection (ICSI)
Fertility procedure that involves mechanically injecting a sperm into the center of an ovum.

surrogate parenting
Use of a woman who, through artificial insemination or in vitro fertilization, gestates a fetus for another woman or man.

surrogate mother
A woman who donates her ovum (which is fertilized by the father's sperm) and then carries the zygote to term.

In the United States, individual states are split on the regulation of surrogacy services. Some states, such as New Jersey and New York, refuse to recognize surrogacy contracts, whereas Massachusetts has legalized it (Klimkiewicz, 2008). Outside the United States, surrogacy continues to grow. For example, commercial surrogacy is growing in western India where one clinic matches infertile U.S. couples with local women who are willing to serve as surrogates (Dolnick, 2007). These women are impregnated with the ova and sperm of couples who are unable to conceive on their own. These practices are available in many countries, although they raise many moral, ethical, and legal issues.

Other Options

Other options involve the freezing of embryos and sperm for later fertilization. It is estimated that 30% to 40% of all births from IVF were from frozen embryos (Borini et al., 2008). This can be beneficial for men and women who are diagnosed with illnesses (such as cancer) whose treatment might interfere with their ability to manufacture healthy sperm or ova (recall Lance Armstrong's story in Chapter 6, Sex in Real Life, "Testicular Cancer"). Sperm can be frozen and stored in liquid nitrogen for many years through a process called **sperm cryopreservation.**

The sperm can be collected from the testis, the epididymis, or an ejaculate. The effectiveness of the sperm, once thawed, is variable, and sometimes the sperm do not survive the thawing process. **Embryo cryopreservation** is also possible; but, like sperm, not all embryos can survive the freezing and thawing process (Borini et al., 2008; Leibo, 2008; Youssry et al., 2008).

A growing number of women have been undergoing **ova cryopreservation,** although this is not as common a procedure (Hourvitz et al., 2008; Leibo, 2008; This, 2008). Typically a woman takes drugs to stimulate ovulation, which produces several ova. The ova are surgically extracted, frozen, and stored for in vitro fertiliza-

tion at a later date (Shellenbarger, 2008). However, unlike sperm and embryos, human eggs have a higher water concentration, which makes chromosomal damage more likely during the freezing and thawing processes (Arav & Zvi, 2008; Gook & Edgar, 2007; Gosden, 2005). Even so, by 2008, newer technologies in ova cryopreservation led to the births of approximately 500 newborns (Hourvitz et al., 2008; Shellenbarger, 2008).

Ova cryopreservation can give women the opportunity to preserve their eggs for use later in life. It can also give women undergoing cancer radiation or chemotherapy an option to save ova for a later pregnancy (J. E. Roberts & Oktay, 2005; This, 2008). It is anticipated that ova cryopreservation will become an essential component of assisted reproductive technologies in the future (Hourvitz et al., 2008; Leibo, 2008).

sperm cryopreservation
The freezing of sperm for later use.

ova cryopreservation
The freezing of ova for later use.

embryo cryopreservation
The freezing of embryos for later use.

review questions

1 Define infertility and identify some of the most common causes of both male and female infertility.

2 Explain how same-sex couples, older women, and single women who seek assisted reproduction have been treated unfairly and identify some of the unique issues that confront these groups.

3 Identify and describe the various assisted reproductive options.

4 Differentiate between sperm, ova, and embryo cryopreservation. What are the risks associated with each?

A Healthy Pregnancy

Pregnancy is divided into three periods called **trimesters.** Throughout these trimesters, important fetal development occurs as a pregnant woman's body changes and adjusts to these developments. We now explore these changes.

THE PRENATAL PERIOD: THREE TRIMESTERS

Although you would think a trimester would be a 3-month period, because pregnancies are dated from the woman's last menstrual period, a full-term pregnancy is actually 40 weeks, and

trimester
A term of three months; pregnancies usually consist of three trimesters.

therefore each trimester is approximately 12 to 15 weeks long. Throughout the pregnancy, physicians can use electronic monitoring and **sonography,** or **ultrasound,** to check on the status of the fetus. We now discuss the physical development of the typical, healthy mother and child in each of these trimesters.

First Trimester

The first trimester includes the first 13 weeks of pregnancy (weeks 1–13). It is the trimester in which the most important embryonic development takes place. When a woman becomes pregnant, her entire system adjusts. Her heart pumps more blood, her weight increases, her lungs and digestive system work harder, and her thyroid gland grows. All of these changes occur to encourage the growth of the developing fetus.

PRENATAL DEVELOPMENT   By the end of the first month of pregnancy, the fetal heart is formed and begins to pump blood. In fact, the circulatory system is the first organ system to function in the embryo (Rischer & Easton, 1992). In addition, many of the other major systems develop, including the digestive system, beginnings of the brain, spinal cord, nervous system, muscles, arms, legs, eyes, fingers, and toes. By 14 weeks, the liver, kidneys, intestines, and lungs have begun to develop. In addition, the circulatory and urinary systems are operating, and the reproductive organs have developed. By the end of the first trimester, the fetus weighs .5 ounce and is approximately 3 inches long.

*When a woman becomes pregnant, **her entire system adjusts.***

CHANGES IN THE PREGNANT MOTHER   During the first few weeks of pregnancy, a woman's body adjusts to increased levels of estrogen and progesterone. This can cause fatigue, breast tenderness, constipation, increased urination, and nausea or vomiting (see Table 12.1). Some women experience nausea and vomiting so severe during pregnancy that they must be hospitalized because of weight loss and malnutrition (Sheehan, 2007). This study found that ginger decreased severe nausea associated with pregnancy (Sheehan, 2007). Specific food cravings are normal, as is an increased sensitivity to smells and odors.

Although some women feel physically uncomfortable because of all these changes, many also feel excited and happy about the life growing within them. The final, confirming sign of pregnancy—a fetal heartbeat—can be a joyous moment that offsets all the discomforts of pregnancy. The fetal heartbeat can usually be heard through ultrasound by the end of the first trimester.

Since its introduction in 1950, ultrasound has become a useful tool in obstetrics. It can capture images of the embryo for measurement as early as 5.5 weeks into the pregnancy, and a heartbeat can be seen by 6 weeks. Fetal heartbeat can also be heard through a stethoscope at approximately 9 to 10 weeks, and after a heartbeat is either seen or heard, the probability of miscarriage drops significantly. Ultrasounds help to confirm a pregnancy, rule out abnormalities, indicate gestational age, and confirm multiple pregnancies (we discuss its use as a prenatal screening device more later in this chapter). Newer three-dimensional and even four-dimensional ultrasounds allow parents to view almost lifelike fetal images, including yawns and facial expressions (see the nearby photo). However, the standard two-dimensional images may still offer better diagnostic information than either three- or four-dimensional ultrasounds because it allows physicians to see inside of structures (Handwerk, 2005).

Second Trimester

The second trimester includes the second 15 weeks of pregnancy (weeks 14–28). The fetus looks noticeably more human.

PRENATAL DEVELOPMENT   The fetus grows dramatically during the second trimester and is 13 inches long by the end of the trimester. He or she has developed tooth buds and reflexes, such as sucking and swallowing. Although the sex of the fetus is determined at conception, it is not immediately apparent during development. If the baby is positioned correctly during ultrasound, sex may be determined as early as 16 weeks, although most of the time it is not possible until 20 to 22 weeks.

During the second trimester, soft hair, called **lanugo** (lan-NEW-go), and a waxy substance, known as **vernix,** cover the fe-

An embryo at 7 to 8 weeks. This embryo is approximately 1 inch long.

Although newer ultrasounds can produce both three- and four-dimensional ultrasounds, many physicians believe that standard two-dimensional ultrasounds may provide the best diagnostic information.

sonography
Electronic monitoring; also called ultrasound.

ultrasound
The use of ultrasonic waves to monitor a developing fetus; also called sonography.

lanugo
The downy covering of hair over a fetus.

vernix
Cheese-like substance that coats the fetus in the uterus.

tus's body. These may develop to protect the fetus from the constant exposure to the amniotic fluid. By the end of the second trimester, the fetus will weigh about 1.75 pounds. If birth takes place at the end of the second trimester, the baby may be able to survive with intensive medical care. We discuss premature birth later in this chapter.

CHANGES IN THE PREGNANT MOTHER During the second trimester, nausea begins to subside as the body adjusts to the increased hormonal levels. Breast sensitivity also tends to decrease. However, fatigue may continue, as well as an increase in appetite, heartburn, edema (ankle or leg swelling), and a noticeable vaginal discharge. Skin pigmentation changes can occur on the face. As the uterus grows larger and the blood circulation slows down, constipation and muscle cramps bother some women. Internally, the cervix turns a deep red, almost violet color because of increased blood supply.

As the pregnancy progresses, the increasing size of the uterus and the restriction of the pelvic veins can cause more swelling of the ankles. Increased problems with varicose veins and hemorrhoids may also occur. Fetal movement is often felt in the second trimester, sometimes as early as the 16th week. Usually women can feel movement earlier in their second or subsequent pregnancies because they know what fetal movement feels like.

The second trimester of pregnancy is usually the most positive time for the mother. The early physiological signs of pregnancy such as morning sickness and fatigue lessen, and the mother-to-be finally feels better physically. This improvement in physical health also leads to positive psychological feelings including excitement, happiness, and a sense of well-being. Many women report an increased sex drive during the second trimester, and for many couples, it is a period of high sexual satisfaction.

As the developing fetus begins to move around, many women feel reassured after anxiously wondering whether the fetus was developing at all. In fact, many women report that the kicking and moving about of the developing fetus is very comforting. Finally, the transition to maternity clothes often results in more positive feelings, probably because it is now obvious and public knowledge that the woman is pregnant.

Third Trimester

The third trimester includes the final weeks of pregnancy (weeks 28–40)

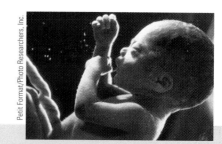

The fetus at 9 months, ready for birth.

and ends with the birth of a child. The fetus gains both fat deposits and muscle mass during this time period.

PRENATAL DEVELOPMENT By the end of the seventh month, the fetus begins to develop fat deposits. She or he can react to pain, light, and sounds. Some fetuses develop occasional hiccups or begin to suck their thumb. If a baby is born at the end of the

---

REALResearch **>** Pregnant women who are exposed to moderate amounts of air pollution have babies with lower birth weights than women who live in areas with low levels of air pollution (BELL ET AL., 2007). Carbon monoxide has been found to have the largest effect on birth weights.

---

seventh month, there is a good chance of survival. In the eighth month, the majority of the organ systems are well developed, although the brain continues to grow. By the end of the eighth month, the fetus is 15 inches long and weighs about 3 pounds. During the third trimester, there is often stronger and more frequent fetal movement, which will slow down toward the ninth month (because the fetus has less room to move around). At birth, an infant on average weighs 7.5 pounds and is 20 inches long.

CHANGES IN THE PREGNANT MOTHER Many of the symptoms from the second trimester continue, with constipation and heartburn increasing in frequency. Backaches, leg cramps, increases in varicose veins, hemorrhoids, sleep problems, shortness of breath, and **Braxton-Hicks contractions** often occur. At first these contractions are scattered and relatively painless (the uterus hardens for a moment and then returns to normal). In the eighth and ninth months, the Braxton-Hicks contractions become stronger. A thin, yellowish liquid called **colostrum** (kuh-LAHS-trum) may be secreted from the nipples as the breasts prepare to produce milk for breast-feeding. Toward the end of the third trimester, many women feel an increase in apprehension about labor and delivery; impatience and restlessness are common.

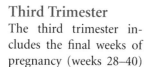

At 5 months, the fetus is becoming more and more lively. It can turn its head, move its face, and make breathing movements. This fetus is approximately 9 inches long.

Braxton-Hicks contractions
Intermittent contractions of the uterus after the third month of pregnancy.

colostrum
A thin, yellowish fluid, high in protein and antibodies, secreted from the nipples at the end of pregnancy and during the first few days after delivery.

In the United States today, partners are allowed and encouraged to participate in the birth. However, this was not always the case. For many years, fathers were told to go to the waiting room and sit until the baby was born. In some other cultures, such as in Bang Chan, Thailand, the father aids in the actual birth of his child (Dunham et al., 1992). The role of the father in pregnancy varies among cultures. Some fathers are required to remain on a strict diet during the course of the pregnancy or to cater to their partner's food cravings at all times.

Pregnancy can be a time of joy and anticipation for the partner of a pregnant woman—but it can also be a time of stress and anxiety. Feelings about parenting in combination with the many changes their partners are undergoing can all add to increased vulnerability.

review questions

1 How many weeks is a typical pregnancy, and how are trimesters determined?

2 Trace prenatal development and changes in the pregnant mother throughout the three trimesters of pregnancy.

3 Explain the changes in a pregnant mother and identify the trimester in which a woman generally feels the most positive and explain why.

Health Care
During Pregnancy

A pregnant woman can do many things to be healthy during her pregnancy, including participating in physical exercise, getting good nutrition, and avoiding teratogens such as drugs and alcohol. Women often maintain sexual interest during pregnancy, although it may begin to wane during the third trimester.

EXERCISE
AND NUTRITION

How much exercise should a woman get during pregnancy? Many physicians strongly advise light exercise during pregnancy; it has been found to result in a greater sense of well-being, enhanced mood, shorter labor, and fewer obstetric problems (Gavard & Artal, 2008; Polman et al., 2007). However, although participation in ongoing exercise throughout pregnancy can enhance birth weight, severe exercise can result in a low-birth-weight baby (Pivarnik, 1998). Most health care providers agree that a woman's exercise routine should not exceed pre-pregnancy levels. Although a woman should always discuss exercise with her health care provider, if she exercised before her pregnancy, keeping up with a moderate amount of exercise during the pregnancy is usually fine.

> . . . a woman's exercise routine **should not exceed** pre-pregnancy levels.

Although it is true that pregnant women are "cardiovascularly challenged" early in pregnancy, it is a myth that too much exercise may cause a miscarriage or harm the developing fetus. Hundreds of pregnant women learned this before the legalization of abortion when they tried to exercise excessively or punch their abdomens in an unsuccessful attempt to dislodge the fertilized ovum. The implanted embryo is difficult to dislodge.

However, there are certain sports that should be avoided during pregnancy, such as waterskiing, scuba diving, vigorous racquet sports, contact sports, and horseback riding, because these may cause injuries in both the mother and her fetus. Aquatic exercise may be the best choice for a pregnant woman because it is non–weight bearing, low impact, and reduces the risk of injury. In addition, aquatic exercise has been found to decrease maternal discomfort and improve body image (S. A. Smith & Michel, 2006). Physical stresses, such as prolonged standing, long work hours, and heavy lifting, can also affect a pregnancy. These stresses can reduce blood flow to the uterus, resulting in lower birth weights and prematurity (Clapp, 1996). It is also important to drink lots of water during pregnancy because water is an essential nutrient and important for all bodily functions.

Nutritional requirements during pregnancy call for extra protein, iron, calcium, folic acid, and vitamin B6 (found in foods such as milk, yogurt, beef, vegetables, beans, and dried fruits). In addition, it is important for a woman to increase her caloric intake during pregnancy. Pregnant women who do not follow nutritional requirements may experience low-birth-weight babies or an increased risk of miscarriage.

Research indicates that poor nutrition during pregnancy may also have long-term consequences for the infant's risk of cardiovascular disease, hypertension, and diabetes (Clapp & Lopez, 2007; Godfrey et al., 1996). Fetuses who are forced to adapt to a limited supply of nutrients may permanently "reprogram" their physiology and metabolism (Barker, 1997).

During the second trimester, an average-weight woman is advised to increase her caloric intake by 300 calories per day, and protein requirements increase. For vegetarians and vegans, it is necessary to increase consumption of vegetables, whole grains, nuts, and seeds and also to include a protein supplement to ensure adequate protein intake. An increase in calcium is also necessary to help with bone calcification of the growing fetus. Because a woman's blood volume increases as much as 50% during pregnancy, iron may be diluted in the blood; thus, many pregnant women are advised to take prenatal vitamins, which include iron supplements.

WHAT DO YOU WANT TO KNOW?

I've heard women say that if the average baby weighs about 7 pounds, then they will gain no more than 10 pounds during pregnancy. Is that safe? How small a weight gain is considered healthy? What about anorexics and bulimics?
It is estimated that a pregnant woman of average size should gain between 15 and 40 pounds throughout a pregnancy, and weight loss or weight maintenance is not recommended (Bish et al., 2008). Pregnancy weight gain accounts for the fetus, amniotic fluid, placenta, breast, muscle, and fat increases. Gaining less than this is not healthy for either the developing baby or the mother—and may actually predispose a baby to obesity later in life (because fetuses learn to restrict calories in the womb, but when nutrition is readily available, overeating is likely; Barker, 1997). In addition, too little weight gain during pregnancy has also been found to be related to a higher blood pressure in offspring once they reach early childhood (P. M. Clark et al., 1998). Although women with eating disorders often experience an improvement in symptoms during a pregnancy (Crow et al., 2008), it's important that anyone with an eating disorder consult with her health care provider before getting pregnant to determine an appropriate weight gain.

DRUGS AND ALCOHOL

There are several substances that physicians recommend avoiding during pregnancy, including caffeine, nicotine, alcohol, marijuana, and other drugs (the accompanying Human Sexuality in a Diverse World, "Avoid the Sun?" describes activities that women in other cultures are told to avoid). All of these substances are teratogens that can cross the placenta, enter into the developing fetus's bloodstream, and cause physical or mental deficiencies. **Fetal alcohol syndrome (FAS),** a condition associated with alcohol intake, occurs when a woman drinks heavily during pregnancy, producing an infant with irreversible physical and mental disabilities. Currently, experts agree that there is no safe level of alcohol use during pregnancy (Sayal et al., 2007).

It is estimated that 10% of U.S. women smoke cigarettes throughout their pregnancy (Weaver et al., 2008). Smoking during pregnancy has been associated with spontaneous abortion, low birth weight, prematurity, and low iron levels (R. P. Martin et al., 2005; Pandey et al., 2005). It has also been found to increase the risk of vascular damage to the developing baby's brain and potentially interfere with a male's future ability to manufacture sperm (Storgaard et al., 2003). Children whose mothers smoked

REALResearch > Research has found that marijuana use can negatively affect sperm development and production, leading to potential fertility problems (BADAWY ET AL., 2008; ROSSATO ET AL., 2008). In addition, marijuana use in both men and women can negatively affect assisted reproduction procedures and contributes to lower infant birth rates (KLONOFF-COHEN ET AL., 2006).

fetal alcohol syndrome (FAS)
A disorder involving physical and mental deficiencies, nervous system damage, and facial abnormalities found in the offspring of mothers who consumed large quantities of alcohol during pregnancy.

during pregnancy have been found to experience an increased aging of the lungs and a higher risk of lung damage later in life (Maritz, 2008). Secondhand smoke has negative effects too, and partners, fathers, friends, relatives, and strangers who smoke around a pregnant woman jeopardize the future health of a developing baby.

PREGNANCY IN WOMEN OVER 30

Until the late 1980s, the majority of women had their first child in their early or mid-20s. Today, it has become common for women to postpone their first pregnancy for a few years (see Figure 12.3; Coccia & Rizzello, 2008). Pregnancies in women over age 35 increased from 1990 to 2004. In 1990, there were 672,000 pregnancies in women of this age group, and this number increased to close to 1 million in 2004, even though the overall pregnancy rate decreased overall during the same period (Ventura et al., 2008).

Earlier in this chapter, we discussed how fertility decreases with age—both ova and sperm quality are affected by age (see Table 12.2; Coccia & Rizzello, 2008; Girsh et al., 2008; Lazarou & Morgentaler, 2008). Remember that a woman is born with a set number of follicles that will develop into ova. As she ages, so do her follicles. On any day of her menstrual cycle, the probability

table 12.2

Risk for Down Syndrome in Live Birth Infant Based on Maternal Age

Age of Mother	Risk of Down Syndrome
20	1 in 1527
25	1 in 1352
30	1 in 895
35	1 in 356
40	1 in 97
45	1 in 23

SOURCE: Hook, E. B. (1981). Rates of chromosome abnormalities at different maternal ages. Obstetrics and Gynecology, 58(3), 282–285.

that a woman who is younger than 27 years old will get pregnant is twice as high as it is for a woman who is over the age of 35 (Dunson et al., 2002).

If an older woman does get pregnant, there are potential risks, including an increase in spontaneous abortion, first-trimester bleeding, low birth weight, increased labor time and rate of **cesarean** (si-ZAIR-ee-un) **section (C-section),** and chromosomal abnormalities (Tough et al., 2002). The likelihood of a chromosomal abnormality increases each year in women over 30 and in men over 55.

SEX DURING PREGNANCY

In some cultures, sex during pregnancy is strongly recommended because it is believed that a father's semen is necessary for proper development of the fetus (Dunham et al., 1992). In an uncomplicated pregnancy, sexual behavior during pregnancy is safe for most mothers and the developing child up until the last several weeks of pregnancy. During a woman's first trimester, sexual interest is often decreased because of physical changes, including nausea and fatigue.

Orgasm during pregnancy is also safe in an uncomplicated pregnancy, but occasionally it may cause painful uterine contractions, especially toward the end of pregnancy. Cunnilingus can also be safely engaged in during pregnancy; however, as we discussed in Chapter 10, air should never be blown into the vagina of a pregnant woman because it could cause an air embolism, which could be fatal to both the mother and baby (Hill & Jones, 1993; Kaufman et al., 1987; Nicoll & Skupski, 2008; Sánchez et al., 2008).

Sexual interest and satisfaction usually begins to subside as the woman and fetus grow during the third trimester (Gokyildiz & Beji, 2005). The increasing size of the abdomen puts pressure on many of the internal organs and also makes certain sexual positions for sexual intercourse difficult. During the first and part of the second trimester, the male-on-top position is used most often during sexual intercourse. However, later in pregnancy, the side-by-side, rear-entry, and female-on-top positions are used more frequently because they take the weight and pressure off the uterus (see Chapter 10 for more information about sexual positions).

cesarean section (C-section)
A surgical procedure in which the woman's abdomen and uterus are surgically opened and a child is removed.

review questions

1 Explain the benefits of exercise in pregnancy, and describe some of the issues that must be considered when exercising during pregnancy.

2 Explain the importance of avoiding drugs and alcohol during pregnancy.

3 Discuss the reasons women are delaying pregnancy more often these days. What are the risks of delayed pregnancy?

4 Discuss the changes in women's sexual interest during pregnancy.

Problems During Pregnancy

The majority of women go through their pregnancy without any problems. However, understanding how complex the process of pregnancy is, it should not come as a surprise that occasionally things go wrong.

ECTOPIC PREGNANCY

Most zygotes travel through the Fallopian tubes and end up in the uterus. In an ectopic pregnancy, the zygote implants outside of the uterus (see Figure 12.4). Ninety-five percent of ectopic pregnancies occur when the fertilized ovum implants in the Fallopian tube (Hankins, 1995). These are called tubal pregnancies. The remaining 3% occur in the abdomen, cervix, or ovaries. Approximately 2% (1 in 50) of all U.S. pregnancies are ectopic, and this number has been steadily increasing primarily because of increases in the incidence of pelvic inflammatory disease caused by chlamydia infections (Tay et al., 2000).

The effects of ectopic pregnancy can be serious. Because the Fallopian tubes, cervix, and abdomen are not designed to support a growing fetus, when one is implanted in these places, they can rupture, causing internal hemorrhaging and possibly death. Symptoms of ectopic pregnancy include abdominal pain (usually on the side of the body that has the tubal pregnancy), cramping, pelvic pain, vaginal bleeding, nausea, dizziness, and fainting (Levine, 2007; Seeber & Barnhart, 2006; Tay et al., 2000). Future reproductive potential is also affected by ectopic pregnancy. A woman who has experienced an ectopic pregnancy is at higher risk for developing another in future pregnancies (Sepilian & Wood, 2004). Today physicians can monitor pregnancies through ultrasound and hCG levels, and many ectopic pregnancies can be treated without surgery (Seeber & Barnhart, 2006).

Before the 19th century, half of all women with an ectopic pregnancy died. Doctors began surgical intervention, and, as a result, only 5% of women with ectopic pregnancy died by the end of the 20th century (Sepilian & Wood, 2004). Today the survival rate is increasing, even though ectopic pregnancy remains the leading cause of maternal mortality in the first trimester, account-ing for 10% to 15% of all maternal deaths (Tenore, 2000). What contributes to the likelihood of an ectopic pregnancy? Although many women without risk factors can develop an ectopic pregnancy (Seeber & Barnhart, 2006), there are some factors that may put a woman more at risk. Women who smoke and those who have had a sexually transmitted infection are at higher risk for an ectopic pregnancy (Ankum et al., 1996). Smoking cigarettes has been found to change the tubal contractions and muscular tone of the Fallopian tubes, which may lead to tubal inactivity, delayed ovum entry into the uterus, and changes in the tubes' ability to transport the ovum (Albers, 2007; Handler et al., 1989; Seeber & Barnhart, 2006;).

REALResearch ▸ Pregnant women who drink too much caffeine have a higher risk of miscarriage (WENG ET AL., 2008). Researchers found that **200** milligrams of caffeine (which is equivalent to one 10-ounce cup of coffee or tea) may double a woman's miscarriage risk. Health care providers today recommend giving up caffeine at least for the first few months of pregnancy.

SPONTANEOUS ABORTION

A spontaneous abortion, or miscarriage, is a natural termination of a pregnancy before the time that the fetus can live on its own. Approximately 15% to 20% of all diagnosed pregnancies end in miscarriage (Friebe & Arck, 2008). Miscarriages can occur anytime during a pregnancy, although the percentage drops dramatically after the first trimester.

In a significant number of miscarriages, there is some chromosomal abnormality (Christiansen, 1996). The body somehow knows that there is a problem in the developing fetus and rejects it. In other cases, in which there are no chromosomal problems, the uterus may be too small, too weak, or abnormally shaped, or the miscarriage may be caused by maternal stress,

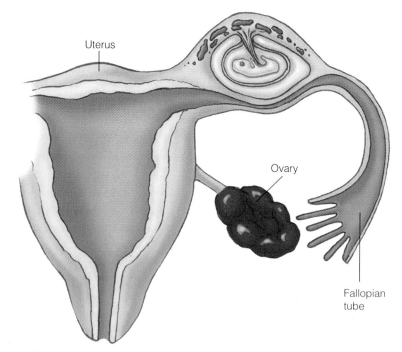

Figure **12.4** In an ectopic pregnancy, the fertilized ovum implants outside the uterus. In most cases, it remains in the Fallopian tube.

Uterus

Ovary

Fallopian tube

nutritional deficiencies, excessive vitamin A, drug exposure, or pelvic infection.

Symptoms of miscarriage include vaginal bleeding, cramps, and lower back pain. Usually a normal menstrual period returns within 3 months after a miscarriage, and future pregnancies may be perfectly normal. However, some women experience repeat miscarriages, often due to anatomic, endocrine, hormonal, genetic, or chromosomal abnormalities (Bick et al., 1998), as well as problems with defective sperm (Carrell et al., 2003). Tests are being developed to try to predict when a miscarriage will occur.

A miscarriage can be emotionally difficult for both a woman and her partner, although research has found that male partners experience less intense emotional symptoms for a shorter period of time (Abboud & Liamputtong, 2003). Lesbian couples have been found to have an especially difficult time with miscarriage, probably because the complexity of planning and achieving a pregnancy are often much more difficult for lesbian couples (Wojnar, 2007).

> *Down syndrome occurs in 1 of every 1,000 live births.*

BIRTH DEFECTS

Although the majority of babies are born healthy, 2% to 3% are born with birth defects (American College of Obstetricians and Gynecologists, 2005). The risk of chromosomal abnormalities increases as a woman ages (see Table 12.2), and chromosomal abnormalities can result in many problems. Sometimes physicians are certain of where the chromosomal problem lies and how it will manifest itself; at other times, they just don't know.

Prenatal diagnostic testing can be used to determine whether there are chromosomal or genetic abnormalities in the fetus. The most common tests include blood work, ultrasound, chorionic villus sampling, maternal-serum alpha-fetoprotein screening, amniocentesis, and cord blood sampling. Most of these tests are used by couples who have an increased risk of birth defects, although some couples may also use them to determine fetal sex. Because older women are more at risk for chromosomal and genetic abnormalities, these tests are often recommended for women over age 35. As we've already discussed, women who have undergone artificial reproductive technologies may choose to use PGD to identify any abnormalities in an embryo before implantation in the uterus (Kuliev & Verlinsky, 2008; Wang, 2007).

Genetic abnormalities include **spina bifida** (SPY-na BIF-id-uh), **anencephaly** (an-en-SEH-fuh-lee), sex chromosome abnormalities (such as Turner and Klinefelter syndromes; see Chapter 4), and many other diseases, such as cystic fibrosis or sickle cell disease. The most common chromosomal ab-

Down syndrome, a chromosomal defect, can cause mental retardation and the characteristics of slanted eyes and a flat face.

©LWA-Dann Tardif/Corbis

normality appears on the 21st chromosome and is known as **Down syndrome.**

Down syndrome occurs in 1 of every 1,000 live births (Irving et al., 2008). In Down syndrome, an extra chromosome has been added to the 21st chromosome; although most of us have 46 chromosomes (23 from each parent), a person with Down syndrome has 47. A child with Down syndrome often exhibits low muscle tone, a flat facial profile, slanted eyes, mental retardation, and an enlarged tongue. Although screening for Down syndrome used to be recommended primarily for women over age 35, in 2007, the American College of Obstetricians and Gynecologists recommended Down syndrome screening for all women, regardless of age (American College of Obstetricians and Gynecologists, 2007). Screening can help determine whether a woman is at risk for having a child with Down syndrome.

If testing is necessary, first-trimester screening typically involves a simple blood test combined with an ultrasound (Malone et al., 2005; Nicolaides et al., 2005; Orlandi et al., 2005). An ultrasound can evaluate the fetal neck thickness, which may indicate an increased risk of Down syndrome. In addition, ultrasound is often used to evaluate structural abnormalities in the fetus and to locate the fetus during other, more invasive tests (Watson et al., 2008). If further testing is warranted, a more invasive test is **chorionic villus sampling (CVS),** which is available between the tenth and twelfth weeks of pregnancy. In this procedure, a sliver of tissue from the chorion (the tissue that develops into the placenta) is removed and checked for abnormalities. Risks of this test include a high false-positive rate, increased risk of miscarriage, and potential limb reduction and deformities (Caughey et al., 2006). CVS can also determine gender.

An amniocentesis may also be used to detect either genetic or chromosomal abnormalities. Although the fetus's gender can be determined, this test is more commonly used to screen for birth defects. It is performed during the second trimester, usually between the fifteenth and twentieth week of pregnancy. In this procedure, **amniotic fluid** is extracted and evaluated for from the womb using a needle and is evaluated for genetic and chromosomal abnormalities.

Another second trimester test, **maternal-serum alpha-fetoprotein screening (MSAFP),** can be performed between the sixteenth and the nineteenth week. MSAFP is a simple blood test that evaluates levels of protein in the blood. High levels may indicate the presence of potential birth defects, including spinal bifida or anencephaly (Reynolds et al., 2008). The MSAFP can provide useful information that can help a woman decide whether she wants to undergo further testing.

spina bifida
A congenital defect of the vertebral column in which the halves of the neural arch of a vertebra fail to fuse in the midline.

anencephaly
Congenital absence of most of the brain and spinal cord.

Down syndrome
A problem occurring on the 21st chromosome of the developing fetus that can cause mental retardation and physical challenges.

chorionic villus sampling (CVS)
The sampling and testing of the chorion for fetal abnormalities.

amniotic fluid
The fluid in the amniotic cavity.

maternal-serum alpha-fetoprotein screening (MSAFP)
A blood test used during early pregnancy to determine neural tube defects such as spina bifida or anencephaly.

Finally, cordocentesis, or cord blood sampling, involves collecting blood from the umbilical cord anytime after the eighteenth week of pregnancy for a chromosome analysis (Berkow et al., 2000). Cordocentesis is an invasive test, although it is a safe and reliable procedure for prenatal diagnosis (Liao et al., 2006).

Researchers are currently working on prenatal testing that is simpler and can be performed earlier in a pregnancy. In the future, pregnant women may be able to have a simple blood test early in their pregnancy to determine whether their fetus has a birth defect (Lo et al., 2007). Keep in mind that if a woman does decide to undergo prenatal testing, she and her partner must decide what to do with the information these tests provide.

RH INCOMPATIBILITY

The Rh factor naturally exists on some people's red blood cells. If your blood type is followed by "+," you are "Rh positive," and if not, you are "Rh negative." This is important when you are having a blood transfusion or when pregnant.

A father or donor who is Rh positive often passes on his blood type to the baby. If the baby's mother is Rh negative, any of the fetal blood that comes into contact with hers (which happens during delivery, not pregnancy) will cause her to begin to manufacture antibodies against the fetal blood. This may be very dangerous for any future pregnancies. Because the mother has made antibodies to Rh-positive blood, she will reject the fetal Rh-positive blood, which can lead to fetal death. After an Rh-negative woman has delivered, she is given **RhoGAM** (row-GAM), which prevents antibodies from forming and ensures that her future pregnancies will be healthy. RhoGAM is also given if an Rh-negative pregnant woman has an amniocentesis, miscarriage, or abortion.

TOXEMIA

In the last 2 to 3 months of pregnancy, 6% to 7% of women experience **toxemia** (tock-SEE-mee-uh), or **preeclampsia** (pre-ee-CLAMP-see-uh). Symptoms include rapid weight gain, fluid retention, an increase in blood pressure, and protein in the urine. If toxemia is allowed to progress, it can result in **eclampsia,** which involves convulsions, coma, and, in approximately 15% of cases, death. Overall, African American women are at higher risk for eclampsia (MacKay et al., 2001).

Women whose mothers experienced preeclampsia are more likely to experience preeclampsia in their own pregnancies, and male offspring from mothers with preeclampsia are twice as likely to father children through a preeclampsia pregnancy as are men who were born from a normal pregnancy (Seppa, 2001). Newer research has found an association between preeclampsia and both partner violence and maternal periodontal disease (Sanchez et al., 2008; Vergnes, 2008).

RhoGAM
Drug given to mothers whose Rh is incompatible with the fetus; prevents the formation of antibodies that can imperil future pregnancies.

toxemia
A form of blood poisoning caused by kidney disturbances.

preeclampsia
A condition of hypertension during pregnancy, typically accompanied by leg swelling and other symptoms.

eclampsia
A progression of toxemia with similar, but worsening, conditions.

review questions

1 Define ectopic pregnancy and spontaneous abortion and discuss what we know about these conditions.

2 Define prenatal diagnostic testing, identify some of the tests, and explain how they can be used to determine whether there are fetal abnormalities.

3 What is Down syndrome and what testing is available to detect it?

4 What is RhoGAM and why would a woman use it?

Childbirth

The average length of a pregnancy is 9 months, but a normal birth can occur 3 weeks before or 2 weeks after the due date. It is estimated that only 4% of American babies are born exactly on the due date predicted (Dunham et al., 1992). Early delivery may occur in cases in which the mother has exercised throughout the pregnancy, the fetus is female, or the mother has shorter menstrual cycles (R. Jones, 1984).

No one knows why, but there is also a seasonal variation in human birth. More babies are conceived in the summer months and in late December (Macdowall et al., 2008). There are also more babies born between the hours of 1 and 7 a.m., and again

this is thought to have evolved because of the increased protection and decreased chances of predator attacks (R. Jones, 1984).

We do not know exactly what starts the birth process. It appears that in fetal sheep, a chemical in the brain signals that it is time for birth (Palca, 1991). Perhaps this may also be true in humans, but the research is still incomplete.

PREPARING FOR BIRTH

As the birth day comes closer, many women (and their partners!) become anxious, nervous, and excited about what is to come. This is probably why the tradition of baby showers started. These gath-

What determines how long a woman will be in labor? Why do they say a woman's first baby is hardest? A friend of mine was in labor for 36 hours!

Usually, first labors are the most difficult. Second and subsequent labors are usually easier and shorter because there is less resistance from the birth canal and the surrounding muscles. Overall, the biggest differences are in the amount of time it takes for the cervix to fully dilate and the amount of pushing necessary to move the baby from the birth canal. Typically, first labors are longer than subsequent labors. We do not know why some women have easier labors than others. It could be the result of diet or exercise during the pregnancy. Ethnic, racial, and maternal age differences have been found in the length of labor. African American women have been found to experience shorter second-stage labors than Caucasian, Asian, and Latina women (Greenberg et al., 2006). In addition, increasing maternal age has been found to be related to prolonged labor (Greenberg et al., 2007).

erings enable women (and more recently, men) to gather and discuss the impending birth. People often share their personal experiences and helpful hints. This ritual may help couples to prepare themselves emotionally and to feel more comfortable.

Increasing knowledge and alleviating anxiety about the birth process are the main concepts behind childbirth classes. In these classes, women and their partners are taught what to expect during labor and delivery and how to control the pain through breathing and massage. Tension and anxiety during labor have been found to increase pain, discomfort, and fatigue. Many couples feel more prepared and focused after taking these courses. However, some same-sex couples report feeling uncomfortable with childbirth classes that cater primarily to heterosexual couples (L. E. Ross et al., 2006a). Having other same-sex couples in the class often makes it a more positive experience.

A few weeks before delivery, the fetus usually moves into a "head-down" position in the uterus (see Figure 12.5). This is referred to as **engagement.** Ninety-seven percent of fetuses are in this position at birth (Nilsson, 1990). If a baby's feet or buttocks are first (**breech position**), the physician may try either to rotate the baby before birth or recommend a cesarean section. We discuss this later in the chapter.

BIRTHPLACE CHOICES

In nonindustrialized countries, nearly all babies are born at home; worldwide, approximately 80% of babies are (Dunham et al., 1992). For low-risk pregnancies, home birth has been found to be as safe as a hospital delivery (K. C. Johnson & Daviss, 2005). Usually, home births are done with the help of a **midwife.** Same-sex couples are more likely to use midwives in their birthing experience, even if they deliver in a hospital setting. This is primarily because many same-sex couples feel that midwives are more accepting of nontraditional families (L. E. Ross et al., 2006b).

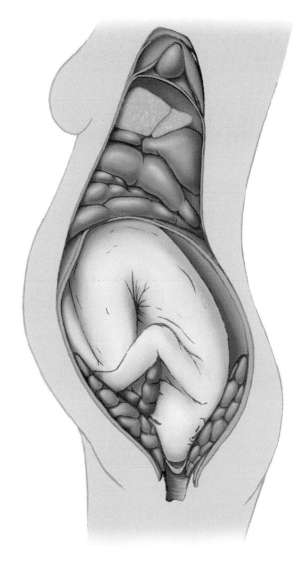

Figure **12.5** The fetus in place in the uterus.

The majority of babies today are born in hospitals in the United States. Most hospitals now offer the use of birthing centers, which include comfortable rooms with a bed for a woman's partner, music, a television, a shower, and perhaps even a Jacuzzi (to help ease labor pains).

INDUCING THE BIRTH

Inducing birth involves using techniques to start the birth process artificially. Usually this is in the form of drugs given in increasing doses to mimic the natural contractions of labor, although in-

engagement
When the fetus moves down toward the birth canal before delivery.

breech position
An abnormal and often dangerous birthing position in which the baby's feet, knees, or buttocks emerge before the head.

midwife
A person who assists women during childbirth.

duced contractions can be more painful and prolonged than natural labor. Birth can occur anywhere from a few hours to several days after induction begins, depending on a woman's prior birth history. Over the past few years, there has been a tremendous increase in childbirth induction. In fact, labor induction is one of the fastest growing medical procedures in the United States (MacDorman et al., 2002). In the United States, labor induction rates reached a high of 21.2% of births in 2003–2004 (Durham et al., 2008).

Labor induction may be done in cases in which labor is slow to progress, pregnancy has lasted beyond 42 weeks, the baby is large, preeclampsia exists, or in cases of fetal death. Unless there is a medical reason, most women are advised to avoid labor induction (Amis, 2007; Durham et al., 2008). Some women elect to have inductions for nonmedical reasons, including anything from wanting to avoid birth on a certain day (such as a holiday) or to accommodate a woman or her partner's work schedule.

BIRTHING POSITIONS

Although women can assume a variety of positions during childbirth, the dominant position in Westernized countries is the semi-reclined position with a woman's feet up in stirrups (DeJonge et al., 2008). Some feminist health professionals claim that this position is easier for the doctor than for the pregnant woman and that it is the most ineffective and dangerous position for labor. Recently, women have been given more freedom in deciding how to position themselves for childbirth in the United States. A woman on her hands and knees or in the squatting position allows her pelvis and cervix to be at its widest. In addition, the force of gravity can be used to help in the birth process. Health care providers today recommend that women use whatever birthing position feels most comfortable for them (DeJonge et al., 2008; Gupta & Nikodem, 2000).

Positions for birth vary in different parts of the world. Rope midwives in rural areas of the Sudan hang a rope from the ceiling and have the mother grasp the rope and bear down in a squatting position. In Bang Chan, Thailand, a husband cradles his pregnant wife between his legs and digs his toes into her thighs. This toe pressure is thought to provide relief from her pain (Dunham et al., 1992).

STAGES OF CHILDBIRTH

Birth itself begins with **cervical effacement** and **dilation,** which leads to expulsion of the fetus and, soon afterward, expulsion of the placenta. The beginning of birth is usually marked by an expulsion of the mucus plug from the cervix. This plug protects the fetus from any harmful bacteria that might enter the vagina during pregnancy. Sometimes women experience false labor, in which contractions are irregular and do not dilate the cervix. In real labor, contractions will be regular and get closer together over time. In a typical birth process, the process is divided into three stages.

Stage One

In the United States, if the birth process is taking too long, physicians may administer the drug pitocin to speed up labor. In Bolivia, however, certain groups of people believe that nipple stimulation helps the birth move quicker. So if a birth is moving too slowly, a woman's nipples may be massaged. Biologically, nipple stimulation leads to a release of oxytocin, which is a natural form of pitocin. This is why many midwives in the United States also practice nipple stimulation during childbirth.

Positions for birth vary in different parts of the world.

In some Guatemalan societies, long and difficult labors are believed to be due to a woman's sins, and so she is asked to confess her sins. If this does not help speed up labor, her husband is asked to confess. If neither of these confessions helps, the father's loincloth is wrapped around the woman's stomach to assure her that he will not leave her once the baby is born (Dunham et al., 1992).

The first stage of labor can last anywhere from 20 minutes to 24 hours and is longer in first births. When true labor begins, the Braxton-Hicks contractions increase. The cervix begins dilation (opening up) and effacement (thinning out) to allow for fetal passage (this phase is called early labor). Throughout the first stage of labor, the entrance to the cervix (the os) increases from 0 to 10 centimeters to allow for the passage of the fetus.

Toward the end of this stage, the amniotic sac usually ruptures (however, this may happen earlier or not at all in some women). Contractions may last for about 30 to 60 seconds at intervals of between 5 and 20 minutes, and the cervix usually dilates to 4 to 5 centimeters. Couples are advised to time the contractions and the interval between contractions and report these to their health care provider.

The contractions will eventually begin to last longer (1 minute or more), become more intense, and increase in frequency (every 1–3 minutes). Dilation of the cervix continues from 4 to 8 centimeters (this phase is called active labor). The contractions that open the os can be very painful, and health care providers will usually monitor the progress of cervical dilation.

The last phase in stage one is called **transition,** which for most women is the most difficult part of the birth process. Contractions are very intense and long and have shorter periods in between, and the cervix dilates from 8 to 10 centimeters. The fetus moves into the base of the pelvis, creating an urge to push; however, the woman is advised not to push until her cervix is fully dilated. Many women feel exhausted by this point.

The woman's body produces pain-reducing hormones called **endorphins,** which may dull the intensity of the contractions.

cervical effacement
The stretching and thinning of the cervix in preparation for birth.

dilation
The expansion of the opening of the cervix in preparation for birth.

transition
The last period in labor, in which contractions are strongest and the periods in between contractions are the shortest.

endorphins
Neurotransmitters, concentrated in the pituitary gland and parts of the brain, that inhibit physical pain.

Should a woman feel the need for more pain relief, she can also be given various pain medications. The most commonly used pain medications include analgesics (pain relievers) and anesthetics (which produce a loss of sensation). Which drug is used depends on the mother's preference, past health history, present condition, and the baby's condition. An epidural block (an anesthetic) is very popular for the relief of severe labor pain. Although there has been an increased use of drugs to reduce the pain of labor in recent years, advances in medical technology today allow physicians to customize pain-relieving drugs for each woman (Leo & Sia, 2008; Moen & Irestedt, 2008).

The fetus is monitored for signs of distress, such as slowed heart rate or lack of oxygen. This is done either through the woman's abdomen with a sensor or by accessing the fetus's scalp through the cervix. Fetal monitoring can determine whether or not the fetus is in any danger that would require a quicker delivery or a C-section.

Stage Two

After the cervix has fully dilated, the second stage of birth, the expulsion of the fetus, begins. Contractions are somewhat less intense, lasting about 60 seconds and spaced at 1- to 3-minute intervals.

Toward the end of this stage of labor, the doctor may perform an **episiotomy** (ee-pee-zee-AH-tuh-mee) to reduce the risk of a tearing of the tissue between the vaginal opening and anus as the fetus emerges. Today episiotomies are very controversial, and the debate centers around several issues. Those who support the practice argue that it can speed up labor, prevent tearing during a delivery, protect against future incontinence, and promote quicker healing. Those who argue against the practice claim that it increases infection, pain, and healing times, and may increase discomfort when intercourse is resumed (Hartmann et al., 2005; Radestad et al., 2008). In 2006, the American College of Obstetricians and Gynecologists recommended against routine use of episiotomy and suggested its use only in limited cases (American College of Obstetricians and Gynecologists, 2006).

WHAT DO YOU WANT TO KNOW ?

Is it safe to use drugs to lessen the pain of labor and birth?

Although some women believe in a "natural" childbirth (one without pain medications), other women want to use medication to lessen the pain. The search for a perfect drug to relieve pain, one that is safe for both the mother and her child, has been a long one. Every year, more and more progress is made. Medication is often recommended when labor is long and complicated, the pain is more than the mother can tolerate or interferes with her ability to push, forceps are required during the delivery, or when a mother is so restless and agitated that it inhibits labor progress. In all cases, the risks of drug use must be weighed against the benefits.

How well a pain medication works depends on the mother, the dosage, and other factors. We do know that the use of some drugs, including epidurals, can increase labor time and may be associated with other risk factors. However, newer lower dosage epidurals have been found to produce fewer side effects and are better tolerated by women (Neruda, 2005).

Seth Resnick/Jupiter Images

There is some controversy over whether lumbar tattoos can interfere with an epidural during labor. Whereas some studies claim they pose no risks (Douglas & Swenerton, 2002), others cite possible risks such as the potential for the epidural to push pigmented tissue into the spinal canal (Kuczkowski, 2006). If the tattoo is large, an anesthesiologist either needs to find a pigment-free area or make a small incision into the tattoo before administering the epidural.

As the woman pushes during contractions, the top of the head of the baby soon appears at the vagina, which is known as **crowning.** Once the face emerges, the mucus and fluid in the mouth and nostrils are removed by suction. The baby emerges and, after the first breath, usually lets out a cry. After the baby's first breath, the umbilical cord, which supplies the fetus with oxygen, is cut; this is painless for the mother and child. Eye drops are put into the baby's eyes to prevent bacterial infection.

Directly following birth, many physicians and midwives place the newborn directly on the mother's chest to begin the bonding process. However, sometimes the woman's partner may be the first to hold the child, or the nurses will perform an **Apgar** test (Finster & Wood, 2005). A newborn with a low Apgar score may require intensive care after delivery.

Stage Three

During the third stage of labor, the placenta (sometimes referred to as the "afterbirth") is expelled from the uterus. Strong contractions continue after the baby is born to push the placenta out of the uterus and through the vagina. Most women are not aware of this process because of the excitement of giving birth. The placenta must be checked to make sure all of it has been expelled. If there was any tearing or an episiotomy was performed, this will

episiotomy
A cut made with surgical scissors to avoid tearing of the perineum at the end of the second stage of labor.

crowning
The emergence of a baby's head at the opening of the vagina at birth.

Apgar
Developed by Virginia Apgar, M.D., this system assesses the general physical condition of a newborn infant for five criteria: (A) activity/muscle tone, (P) pulse rate, (G) grimace and reflex irritability, (A) appearance/skin color, (R) respiration.

need to be sewn up after the placenta is removed. Usually this stage lasts about 30 minutes or so.

In parts of Kenya, the placenta of a female baby is buried under the fireplace, and the placenta of a male baby is buried by the stalls of baby camels. This practice is thought to forever connect the children's future to these locations. Some cultures bury their placentas, whereas others hang the placentas outside the home to show that a baby indeed arrived!

review questions

1 Describe the emotional and physical preparation necessary for the birth of a child, childbirth induction, and the various birthing positions.

2 Identify the three stages of birth and explain what happens at each stage. Generally, how long does each stage last?

3 Which phase of the birthing process is the most difficult for most women and why?

4 What is an episiotomy and why might it be used?

Problems
During Birthing

For most women, the birth of a newborn baby proceeds without problems. However, a number of problems can arise, including premature birth, breech birth, cesarean section delivery, and stillbirth.

PREMATURE BIRTH:
THE HAZARDS OF EARLY DELIVERY

The majority of babies are born late rather than early. Birth that takes place before the 37th week of pregnancy is considered **premature birth.** In 2004, 1 in 8 babies was premature in the United States (Maugh, 2006). Some racial differences have been found in the rates of prematurity—11.5% of births to White women and 17.8% of births to African American women are premature (Maugh, 2006).

Prematurity increases the risk of birth-related defects and infant mortality. In fact, prematurity accounts for 28% of infant deaths worldwide (Menon, 2008). Research into pediatrics has led to tremendous improvements in the survival rates of premature infants. Infants born at 24 weeks' gestation have a greater than 50% chance of survival (Welty, 2005). Unfortunately, more than half of these infants who survive develop complications and long-term effects of prematurity.

Birth may occur prematurely for several reasons, including early labor or early rupture of the amniotic membranes or because of a maternal or fetal problem. It is common for women who have had one premature birth to have subsequent premature births. Approximately 50% of all twin births are premature, and delivery of multiple fetuses occurs about 3 weeks earlier, on average, than single births. In 2004, the world's smallest surviving premature baby was born, weighing in at 8.6 ounces (her twin sister weighed 1 pound, 4 ounces; Huffstutter, 2004). These twins

were delivered via C-section in the 26th week of pregnancy because of medical problems experienced by their mother. Other factors that may lead to premature birth include smoking during pregnancy, alcohol or drug use, inadequate weight gain or nutrition, heavy physical labor during the pregnancy, infections, and teenage pregnancy. In addition, the increase in assisted reproduction and pregnancy in older women may contribute to prematurity rates.

BREECH BIRTH:
FEET FIRST INTO THE WORLD

In 97% of all births, the fetus emerges in the head-down position. However, in 3% to 4% of cases, the fetus is in the breech position, with the feet and buttocks against the cervix (see Figure 12.6). Interestingly, about half of all fetuses are in this position before the seventh month of pregnancy, but most rotate before birth (R. Jones, 1984). Sometimes doctors are aware of the position of the fetus before delivery and can try to change the fetus's position for normal vaginal delivery. However, if this is not possible, or if it is discovered too late into delivery, labor may take an unusually long time. A skilled midwife or physician often can flip the baby or deliver it safely even in the breech position. However, in the United States today, a C-section will often be performed to ensure the health and well-being of both the mother and her child (Ghosh, 2005).

Although no one knows why some fetuses are born in the breech position, there have been some interesting studies done. One study found that there is an intergenerational recurrence of breech births: fathers and mothers who were born breech have more than twice the risk of a breech delivery in their first births (Nordtveit et al., 2008). Another study found that breech births

premature birth
Any infant born before the 37th week of pregnancy.

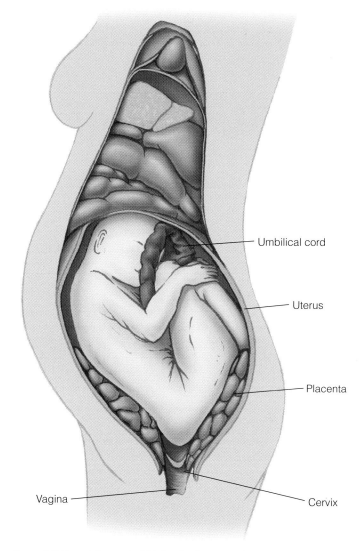

Umbilical cord

Uterus

Placenta

Vagina

Cervix

Figure **12.6** In 3% to 4% of births, the fetus is in the breech position, with feet and buttocks against the cervix.

were twice as high in women who had a past cesarean delivery (Vendittelli et al., 2008).

CESAREAN-SECTION DELIVERY

A cesarean section involves the delivery of the fetus through an incision in the abdominal wall. C-sections have increased in the last few years for several reasons: Women are waiting longer to have children, which increases labor complications; the procedure has become easier and safer to perform than it was several years ago; and doctors perform C-sections to reduce the risks associated with vaginal delivery because of their fear of malpractice suits. In addition, some women decide to undergo a C-section birth to reduce possible pelvic floor trauma that often occurs during vaginal delivery (Dietz, 2006; Herbruck, 2008). Pelvic floor trauma can lead to possible urinary or sexual problems later in life (Herbruck, 2008). The rate of cesarean section was 27% in 2003 (Menacker, 2005) and climbed to 31% by 2006 (Rubin, 2008).

C-sections are necessary when the baby is too large for a woman to deliver vaginally, the woman is unable to push the baby out the birth canal, the placenta blocks the cervix (**placenta previa**), the cervix does not dilate to 10 centimeters, or the baby is in **fetal distress.** If a health care provider decides that a cesarean is necessary, the woman is moved to an operating room and given either a general anesthetic or an epidural. The operation usually lasts between 20 and 90 minutes, and the woman will likely stay in the hospital longer than those who deliver vaginally.

Women who have C-section births may have a higher risk of small fetal size, placental separation from the uterine wall, and uterine rupture in subsequent pregnancies (Daltveit et al., 2008). Even so, some women deliver their next babies vaginally after a C-section (referred to as a VBAC, or vaginal birth after cesarean), whereas others choose another C-section for a variety of reasons, including to avoid the pain or the increased risks of vaginal labor.

Stillbirth: Sad Circumstance

A fetus that dies after 20 weeks of pregnancy is called a **stillbirth** (prior to 20 weeks, it is called a miscarriage). There are many causes for a stillbirth, including umbilical cord accidents, problems with the placenta, birth defects, infections, and maternal diabetes or high blood pressure (Incerpi et al., 1998). Oftentimes the fetal loss is completely unexpected, because half of all stillbirths occur in pregnancies that appeared to be without problems (Pasupathy & Smith, 2005). Approximately 86% of fetal deaths occur before labor even begins, whereas 14% occur during labor and delivery (Fretts et al., 1992). In most cases, a woman goes into labor approximately 2 weeks after the fetus has died; if not, her labor will be induced. Some ethnic differences have been noted: higher rates of stillbirth have been found in African American and interracial couples (Getahun et al., 2005).

The frequency of stillbirths has been decreasing over recent years in the United States, in part because of better treatment of certain maternal medical conditions. Many women are advised to do "kick checks" beginning in the 26th week of pregnancy. If a woman notices that her fetus is kicking fewer than 6 times in an hour or has stopped moving or kicking, fetal monitoring can be performed to check on the status of the fetus. Research has shown that women who have experienced a stillbirth often have a live birth in their next pregnancy, even though they are often viewed as high-risk patients (Black et al., 2008).

In the 1970s, a perinatal bereavement movement began in the United States, which offered parents a way to deal with the death of a newborn (Banerjee, 2007). Since the late 1990s, at least 40 perinatal hospice programs have started in the United States. These groups help families deal with issues related to stillbirth and infant death.

placenta previa
A condition in which the placenta is abnormally positioned in the uterus so that it partially or completely covers the opening of the cervix.

fetal distress
Condition in which a fetus has an abnormal heart rate or rhythm.

stillbirth
An infant who is born dead.

1 Define premature birth and discuss some of the causes and risks associated with premature birth.

2 Define breech birth and identify some of the factors that have been associated with breech birth.

3 Explain some of the reasons for a cesarean-section birth.

4 Differentiate between a miscarriage and a stillbirth.

Postpartum
Parenthood

The majority of women and men are excited about being parents. However, many couples are not prepared for the many physical and emotional changes that occur after the child is born. They may also find changes in their sex lives because of the responsibility and exhaustion that often accompanies parenthood.

MORE PHYSICAL CHANGES
FOR THE MOTHER

Many women report painful contractions for a few days after birth. These contractions are caused by the secretion of oxytocin, which is produced when a woman breast-feeds and is responsible for the shrinking of the uterus. The uterus returns to its original size about 6 weeks postpartum: in breast-feeding women, the uterus returns to its original size quicker than in non-breast-feeding women. A bloody discharge can persist for anywhere from a week to several weeks after delivery. After the bleeding stops, the discharge is often yellow-white and can lasts for a couple of weeks in mothers who breast-feed and up to a month or so in women who do not.

View in Video

"I like children, I love playing with children, but I've never felt the need to have a baby."
—*Deciding Whether to Have Children*
To view go to CengageNOW at www.cengage.com/login

Women may experience an increase in frequency of urination, which can be painful if an episiotomy was performed or natural tearing occurred. Women may be advised to take sitz baths, in which the vagina and perineum are soaked in warm water to reduce the pain and to quicken the healing process. Until the cervix returns to its closed position, full baths are generally not advised.

POSTPARTUM
PSYCHOLOGICAL CHANGES

Many women experience an onset of intense emotions after the birth of a baby. One study found that 52% of new mothers felt excited and elated, 48% reported feeling like they did not need sleep, 37% reported feeling energetic, and 31% reported being more chatty (Heron et al., 2008). At the same time, many women report feeling overwhelmed and exhausted. Minor sadness is a common emotion following the birth of a baby (Howard et al., 2005). However, for some, it is a difficult time with endless crying spells and anxiety. In severe cases, this is referred to as **postpartum depression**. Physical exhaustion, physiological changes, and an increased responsibility of child rearing all contribute to these feelings, coupled with postpartum hormonal changes (including a sudden drop in progesterone). Partner support has been found to decrease postpartum depression in both heterosexual and same-sex couples (Misri et al., 2000; L. E. Ross, 2005a). In the most severe cases, mental disturbances, called **postpartum psychosis,** occur; in rare cases, women have killed or neglected their babies after delivery (Rammouz et al, 2008).

Some ethnic and racial differences have been found in the rates of postpartum depression, with African American and Hispanic mothers reporting more postpartum depression than White mothers (Howell et al., 2005). Studies on postpartum depression in same-sex couples have found that a lack of social support and relationship problems are major sources of stress after the birth of a baby (L. E. Ross et al., 2005a). Relationship problems in same-sex couples often revolved around challenges in negotiating parenting roles. Preliminary research has found that postpartum depression may be more common among lesbian and bisexual women, but more research is needed to support these findings (L. E. Ross et al., 2007).

SEXUALITY
FOR NEW PARENTS

Although most physicians advise their heterosexual patients to wait 6 weeks postpartum before resuming intercourse, in an uncomplicated vaginal delivery (with no tears or episiotomy), intercourse can safely be engaged in 2 weeks after delivery. This period is usually necessary to ensure that no infection occurs and that the cervix has

postpartum depression
A woman's clinical depression that occurs after childbirth.

postpartum psychosis
The rare occurrence of severe, debilitating depression or psychotic symptoms in the mother after childbirth.

F. Villaflor/Jupiter Images

Research has found that body contact during breast-feeding can decrease stress and improve mood for both the mother and her infant.

returned to its original position. If an episiotomy was performed, it may take up to 3 weeks for the stitches to dissolve. Recovery after a C-section birth usually takes approximately 2 weeks, and sexual behavior is safe after this time. To reduce the risk of infection, it is best to avoid cunnilingus until a woman is certain she has no cuts or lacerations as a result of the delivery. In an uncomplicated delivery, 90% of women report resuming sexual activity by 6 months after the baby is born, although those with a complicated labor often wait longer to resume sexual activity (Brubaker et al., 2008). Immediately after delivery, many women report slower and less intense excitement stages of the sexual response cycle and a decrease in vaginal lubrication (Masters & Johnson, 1966). However, at 3 months postpartum, the majority of women return to their original levels of sexual desire and excitement.

BREAST-FEEDING
THE BABY

Within an hour after birth, the newborn baby usually begins a rooting reflex, which signals hunger. The baby's sucking triggers the flow of milk from the breast. This is done through receptors in the nipples, which signal the pituitary to produce prolactin, a chemical necessary for milk production. Another chemical, oxytocin, is also produced, which helps increase contractions in the uterus to shrink it to its original size. In the first few days of breast-feeding, the breasts release a fluid called colostrum, which is very important in strengthening the baby's immune system. This is one of the reasons that breast-feeding is recommended to new mothers.

Breast-feeding rates in the United States increased significantly between 1993 and 2006. Whereas 60% of newborn babies were breast-fed in 1993–1994, 77% were breast-fed in 2005–2006 (McDowell et al., 2008). Although breast-feeding rates were higher in Mexican American and non-Hispanic White infants, rates among non-Hispanic Black infants increased significantly during this time (from 36% in 1993–1994 to 65% in 2005–2006).

Benefits of breast-feeding include strengthening of the infant's immune system and cognitive development and a reduction in infant allergies, asthma, diarrhea, tooth decay, and ear, urinary tract, and respiratory infections (Daniels & Adair, 2005; Khadivzadeh & Parsai, 2005; "50 State Summary," 2008). One study found that breast-fed children attain higher IQ scores than non-breast-fed children (Caspi et al., 2007). Benefits to the mother include an earlier return to pre-pregnancy weight and a lower risk for breast cancer and osteoporosis ("50 state summary," 2008). In addition, the body-to-body contact during breast-feeding has been found to decrease stress and improve mood for both mother and child (Groer, 2005).

For some women, however, breast-feeding is not physically possible. Time constraints and work pressures may also prevent breast-feeding. It is estimated that a baby's primary caregiver loses between 450 and 700 hours of sleep in the first year of the baby's life, and overall, breast-feeding mothers lose the most sleep (Brizendine, 2006; Maas, 1998).

Some women who want to breast-feed but who also wish to return to work use a breast pump. This allows a woman to express milk from her breasts that can be given to her child through a bottle while she is away. Breast milk can be kept in the refrigerator or freezer, but it must be heated before feeding. The majority of U.S. states have laws that allow women to breast-feed in public and to express breast milk while at work in certain areas ("50 State Summary," 2008).

There have been some heated debates about when a child should be **weaned** from breast-feeding. The American Academy of Pediatrics recommends exclusive breast-feeding (no other fluids or food) for 6 months and then continued breast-feeding for a minimum of 1 year, whereas the World Health Organization recommends exclusive breast-feeding for the first 4 to 6 months of life and continued breast-feeding until at least age 2.

Throughout this chapter, we have explored many issues related to fertility, infertility, pregnancy, and childbearing. In the next chapter, we begin to look at limiting fertility through contraception and abortion.

weaned
To accustom a baby to take nourishment other than nursing from the breast.

review questions

1 Describe the physical and emotional changes that women experience after the birth of a child.

2 Differentiate between postpartum depression and postpartum psychosis.

3 How might a woman's sexuality change after the birth of a baby?

4 Identify and explain some of the benefits of breast-feeding.

SUMMARY POINTS

1 Our bodies are biologically programmed to help pregnancy occur: a woman's sexual desire peaks at ovulation, female orgasm helps push semen into the uterus, and semen thickens after ejaculation.

2 Pregnancy can happen when intercourse takes place a few days before or after ovulation, and the entire process of fertilization takes about 24 hours. The fertilized ovum is referred to as a zygote. After the first cell division, it is referred to as a blastocyst. From the second to the eighth week, the developing human is called an embryo.

3 Early signs of pregnancy include missing a period, breast tenderness, frequent urination, and morning sickness. Pregnancy tests measure for a hormone in the blood known as human chorionic gonadatropin (hCG). Pseudocyesis and couvade are rare conditions that can occur in both women and men.

4 Some couples try to choose the sex of their children by using sex-selection methods. During the 16th or 17th week of pregnancy, an amniocentesis can be performed to evaluate the fetus for chromosomal abnormalities, and it can also identify the sex of the fetus.

5 Increased pregnancy terminations have been noted in areas where females are less valued in society and where there are governmental regulations on family size.

6 Many couples, including married, unmarried, straight, gay, lesbian, young, and older men and women, use assisted reproductive technologies. While all couples use assisted reproductive techniques in hopes of achieving a pregnancy, same-sex couples and single women often use these methods in order to create a pregnancy. Infertility is the inability to conceive (or impregnate) after 1 year of regular sexual intercourse without the use of any form of birth control. Although unmarried individuals, gay men, and lesbian women have

historically been denied access to assisted reproductive technologies, this has been changing. An increasing number of singles and same-sex couples are using assisted reproduction today.

7 Couples interested in assisted reproduction have many options today, including fertility drugs; surgery to correct cervical, vaginal, or endometrial abnormalities and blockage in the vas deferens or epididymis; artificial insemination; in vitro fertilization; GIFT; ZIFT; zonal dissection; intracellular sperm injections; oocyte or embryo transplants; surrogate parenting; and cryopreservation.

8 Pregnancy is divided into three 3-month periods called trimesters. In the first trimester, the most important embryonic development takes place. At this time, the fetus grows dramatically and is 3 inches long by the end of this trimester.

9 The mother often feels the fetus moving around inside her uterus during the second trimester. By the end of this period, the fetus is approximately 13 inches long and weighs about 2 pounds. The second trimester of pregnancy is usually the most positive time for the mother.

10 By the end of the eighth month, the fetus is 15 inches long and weighs about 3 pounds. Braxton-Hicks contractions begin, and colostrum may be secreted from the nipples.

11 A woman's exercise routine should not exceed pre-pregnancy levels. Exercise has been found to result in a greater sense of well-being, shorter labor, and fewer obstetric problems. Certain sports should be avoided during pregnancy, such as waterskiing, scuba diving, vigorous racquet sports, contact sports, and horseback riding.

12 Underweight and overweight women are at greater risk of impaired pregnancy outcome, and they are

advised to gain or lose weight before pregnancy.

13 Drugs and alcohol can cross the placenta, enter into the developing fetus's bloodstream, and cause physical or mental deficiencies. FAS occurs when a woman drinks heavily during pregnancy, producing an infant with irreversible physical and mental disabilities.

14 Delaying pregnancy has some risks, including increase in spontaneous abortion, first-trimester bleeding, low birth weight, increased labor time, increased rate of C-sections, and chromosomal abnormalities.

15 Sexual behavior during pregnancy is safe for most mothers and the developing child up until the last several weeks of pregnancy, and maybe up to delivery; orgasm is safe but occasionally may cause painful uterine contractions.

16 In an ectopic pregnancy, the zygote implants outside the uterus, usually in the Fallopian tube. Although many women without risk factors can develop an ectopic pregnancy, some factors may put a woman at increased risk. These include smoking and a history of sexually transmitted infections.

17 The majority of miscarriages occur during the first trimester of pregnancy. The most common reason for miscarriage is a fetal chromosomal abnormality. Prenatal diagnostic testing can be used to determine whether there are chromosomal or genetic abnormalities in the fetus.

18 The risk of chromosomal abnormality increases as maternal age increases. The most common chromosomal abnormality is Down syndrome.

19 An Rh-negative woman must be given RhoGAM immediately after childbirth, abortion, or miscarriage so that she will not produce antibodies and to ensure that her future pregnancies are healthy. Toxemia is a form of blood poisoning that pregnant women can develop; symptoms include weight gain, fluid retention, an increase in blood pressure, and protein in the urine.

20 Increasing knowledge and alleviating anxiety about the birth process are the main concepts behind childbirth classes. Worldwide, the majority of babies are born at home, although most U.S. babies are born in hospitals.

21 Birth itself takes place in three stages: cervical effacement and dilation, expulsion of the fetus, and expulsion of the placenta. The first stage of labor can last anywhere from 20 minutes to 24 hours and is longer in first births. Transition, the last part of stage one, is the most difficult part of the birth process. The second stage of birth involves the expulsion of the fetus. In the third stage of labor, strong contractions continue and push the placenta out of the uterus and through the vagina.

22 The majority of babies are born late, but if birth takes place before the 37th week of pregnancy, it is considered premature. Premature birth may occur early for several reasons, including early labor, early rupture of the amniotic membranes, or a maternal or fetal problem.

23 Problems during birthing include premature birth, breech birth, and stillbirth. A birth that takes place before the 37th week of pregnancy is considered premature and may occur for various reasons. The amniotic membranes may have ruptured, or there may be a maternal or fetal problem. Multiple births also occur earlier than single births. In a breech birth, the fetus has his or her feet and buttocks against the cervix, and either the baby is rotated or a C-section must be performed.

24 A cesarean section involves the delivery of the fetus through an incision in the abdominal wall. C-sections are necessary when the baby is too large for a woman to deliver vaginally, the woman is unable to push the baby out the birth canal, there is placenta previa or placental separation from the baby prior to birth, or if the baby is in fetal distress. Some women also choose to have an elective C-section for a variety of reasons.

25 A fetus that dies after 20 weeks of pregnancy is called a stillbirth. The most common cause of stillbirth is a failure in the baby's oxygen supply, heart, or lungs.

26 Following delivery, the uterus returns to its original size in about 6 weeks. Many women report painful contractions, caused by the hormone oxytocin, for a few days after birth. Breast-feeding women's uteruses return to the original size quicker than those of non-breast-feeding women.

27 The majority of women feel both excitement and exhaustion after the birth of a child. However, for some, it is a very difficult time of depression, crying spells, and anxiety. In severe cases, a woman might experience postpartum depression or postpartum psychosis.

28 Although most physicians advise their heterosexual patients to wait 6 weeks postpartum before resuming sexual intercourse, in an uncomplicated vaginal delivery (with no tears or episiotomy), intercourse can safely be engaged in 2 weeks after delivery. Many women report slower and less intense excitement stages of the sexual response cycle and a decrease in vaginal lubrication immediately after delivery; however, at 3 months' postpartum, most women return to their original levels of desire and excitement.

29 In the first few days of breast-feeding, the breasts release a fluid called colostrum, which is very important in strengthening the baby's immune system. The American Academy of Pediatrics recommends breast-feeding for at least 1 year, whereas the World Health Organization recommends breast-feeding for up to 2 years or longer.

CRITICAL THINKING questions

1 If sex preselection were possible, would you want to determine the sex of your children? Why or why not? If you did choose, what order would you choose? Why?

2 Do you think assisted reproductive techniques should be used in women over 50? Over 60? Do you think older moms can make good mothers? What about older dads?

3 If women can safely deliver at home, should they be encouraged to do so with the help of a midwife, or should they be encouraged to have children in the hospital? If you have children, where do you think you would want them to be born?

4 At what age do you think a child should be weaned? Should a woman breast-feed a child until he or she is 6 months old? Two years old? Four years old? How old?

5 In 2001, a woman ran an ad in a school newspaper at Stanford University offering $15,000 for a sperm donation from the right guy. She required the guy be intelligent, physically attractive, and over six feet tall. The year before an ad ran in the same newspaper from a couple who offered $100,000 for eggs from an athletically gifted female student. Would you have answered either of these ads? Why or why not?

WEB resources

Sexuality Now Book Companion Website

Go to www.cengage.com/psychology/carroll for practice quizzes, glossary, flash cards, and more. You can also access the following websites from the companion site.

American Society for Reproductive Medicine (ASRM) ■ The ASRM is an organization devoted to advancing knowledge and expertise in reproductive medicine, infertility, and assisted reproductive technologies. Links to a variety of helpful websites are available.

BirthStories ■ This interesting website contains true birth stories from a variety of women, including first-time moms, veteran moms, and births after a pregnancy loss. It also has information on birthing, breast-feeding, and newborns.

Childbirth ■ This website contains information about fertility, childbirth complications, pregnancy, labor, epidurals, cesarean sections, newborns, ectopic pregnancies, postpartum care, and a whole lot more.

International Council on Infertility Information Dissemination (INCIID) ■ This website provides detailed information on the diagnosis and treatment of infertility, pregnancy loss, family-building options, and helpful fact sheets on various types of fertility treatments and assisted reproductive techniques. Information on adoption and childfree lifestyles is also included.

RESOLVE ■ RESOLVE: The National Infertility Association was established in 1974. It works to promote reproductive health, ensure equal access to fertility options for men and women experiencing infertility or other reproductive disorders, and provide support services and physician referral and education.

Sperm Bank Directory ■ A national directory of sperm cryo-banks. Provides information on cryopreservation, sperm donation, and donor sperm. There are also links to sperm banks throughout the country, some of which include online donor catalogs.

StorkNet ■ This website provides a week-by-week guide to a woman's pregnancy. For each of the 40 weeks of pregnancy, there is information about fetal development, what types of changes occur within the pregnant body, and suggested readings and links for more information.

CengageNOW

Go to www.cengage.com/login to link to CengageNOW, your online study tool. First take the Pre-Test for this chapter to get your Personalized Study Plan, which will identify topics you need to review and direct you to online resources. Then take the Post-Test to determine what concepts you have mastered and what you still need work on.

Videos in CengageNOW

For additional information on topics discusses in this chapter, check out the videos in CengageNOW on the following topics:

- Deciding Whether to Have Children—Two couples describe how they decided whether to have children.

- A 57-Year-Old Woman's Successful In Vitro Fertilization—Learn the factors considered for whether in vitro fertilization is possible for women, no matter what their age.

CHAPTER 13

Contraception and Abortion

I am a college senior and I have been taking birth control pills for 5 years now. During most of this time, I used pills, with condoms as a backup method. Although I was using only condoms during my first sexual relationship, after a conversation with my mom, we decided it would be best for me to start taking the pill. Birth control pills and condoms are a popular choice among many of my female friends in long-term relationships. A few of my friends also use other methods like the patch and the ring.

When my current relationship began, we used the pill and condoms, but after experiencing one too many broken condoms we gave up on them as a backup method. This was not a decision we took lightly; we had a long conversation about making the commitment to remain faithful to one another and to get tested for STIs [sexually transmitted infections]. We also discussed potential consequences.

Personally, I don't like condoms as a main method of birth control. In my experience, they ruin the mood and have broken several times, which shattered my sense of security and protection when using them. We haven't eliminated condoms all together; we do still use them as backup if I am forgetful in taking my pill, but now we rely on withdrawal as our backup method to the pill.

I think that once you and your partner have been tested, sex should be a truly enjoyable experience for both parties while maintaining spontaneity, excitement, and fun. Sex should not be scheduled or interrupted, and with the birth control pill you can have all the impulsive and uninterrupted sex you want. In addition, withdrawal doesn't get in our way or interrupt the experience. The only downside to withdrawal is the need for some additional cleanup, which to us is worth it in exchange for spontaneous and exciting sex!

While I am very happy with my decision to start taking the pill, there are certainly some downsides. Remembering to take is everyday at the same time is sometimes difficult for me, but I found that setting a cell phone alarm and carrying it with me makes it easier. I also have fears about whether the pill works, and because of this, I've become all too familiar with pregnancy tests and morning after pills for no reason other than my own paranoia. I know that when taken perfectly birth control pills are extremely effective, but I can't help but worry. Using withdrawal as a backup method makes me feel more confident.

Other than allowing for spontaneity, I also like birth control pills because they regulate my period and reduce cramps. I could never take those pills that reduce your periods to only four a year—I would be too worried about pregnancy all the time! The pill gives me a period that I can count on nearly to the day, and I can plan around it a month in advance. For some women, a monthly period may be a nuisance, but to me it's a blessing that is well worth the hassle!

SOURCE: Author's files

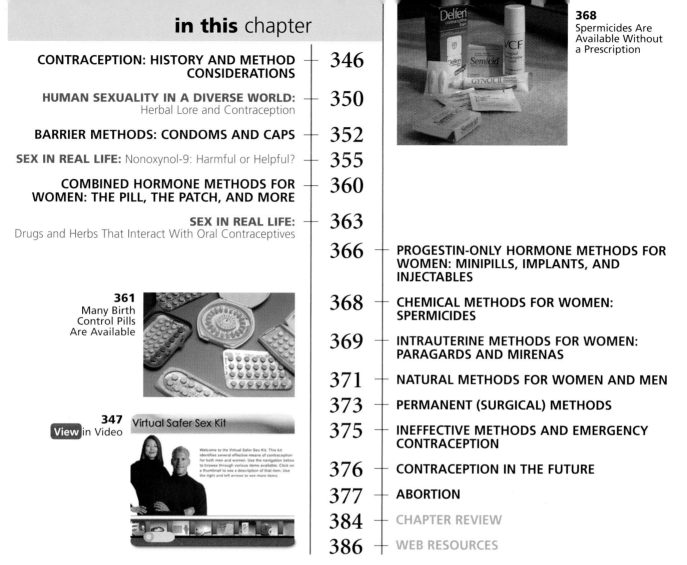

368
Spermicides Are Available Without a Prescription

361
Many Birth Control Pills Are Available

347
View in Video
Virtual Safer Sex Kit

Welcome to the Virtual Safer Sex Kit. This kit identifies several effective means of contraception for both men and women. Use the navigation below to browse through various items available. Click on a thumbnail to see a description of that item. Use the right and left arrows to see more items.

◁ Opposite: © Michelle D. Bridwell/PhotoEdit

The average American woman spends about 30 years trying *not* to get pregnant and only a couple of years trying to become pregnant (see Figure 13.1; Frost et al., 2008). Although some sexually active women are effective contraceptive users during this time, many women use contraception poorly or don't use it at all (Mosher et al., 2004). In fact, many college students take great risks when it comes to **contraception,** even though they are intelligent and educated about birth control. Researchers don't really know why this is, but many factors increase one's motivation to use contraception, including the ability to communicate with a partner, cost of the method, effectiveness rates, frequency of sexual intercourse, motivation to avoid pregnancy, the contraceptive method's side effects, and one's openness about sexuality (Frost et al., 2008; Hatcher et al., 2007). Contraceptive use is further complicated by the fact that an ideal method for one person may not be an ideal method for another, and an ideal method for one person at one time in his or her life may not be an ideal method as he or she enters into different life stages. Having a wide variety of choices available is important to allow couples to choose and change methods as their contraceptive needs change.

As we begin our exploration into contraception and abortion, consider this: Have you thought about whether you ever want to have a child? Maybe you have an exact plan about when you'd like to experience a pregnancy in your life. Or perhaps you have already decided you won't have any children. For many couples, deciding how to plan, and also how to avoid, pregnancies are important issues in their lives. In this chapter, we explore the array of contraceptive methods available today, investigate their advantages and disadvantages, and also discuss emergency contraception and abortion.

contraception
Prevention of pregnancy by abstinence or the use of certain devices or surgical procedures to prevent ovulation, fertilization, or implantation.

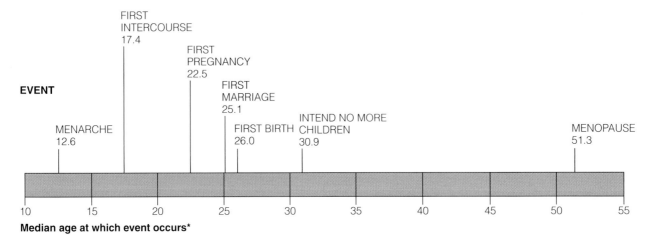

EVENT

MENARCHE
12.6

FIRST
INTERCOURSE
17.4

FIRST
PREGNANCY
22.5

FIRST
MARRIAGE
25.1

FIRST BIRTH
26.0

INTEND NO MORE
CHILDREN
30.9

MENOPAUSE
51.3

Median age at which event occurs*

Note *Age by which half of women have experienced event.

Figure **13.1** The Alan Guttmacher Institute has found that the average woman spends five years pregnant, postpartum, or trying to get pregnant and 30 years avoiding pregnancy. Above is a timeline of reproductive events for the typical American woman. Source: Boonstra et al., *Abortion in Women's Lives,* New York: Guttmacher Institute, 2006, Figure 1.1, p. 7. Reprinted by permission.

Contraception:
History and Method Considerations

Although many people believe that contraception is a modern invention, its origins actually extend back to ancient times. We now explore contraception throughout history, both within and outside of the United States.

CONTRACEPTION IN ANCIENT TIMES

People have always tried to invent ways to control fertility. The ancient Greeks used magic, superstition, herbs, and drugs to try and control their fertility. The Egyptians tried fumigating the female genitalia with certain mixtures, inserting a tampon into the vagina that had been soaked in herbal liquid and honey, and inserting a mixture of crocodile feces, sour milk, and honey (Dunham et al., 1992). Another strategy was to insert objects into

the vagina that could entrap or block the sperm. Such objects include vegetable seed pods (South Africa), a cervical plug of grass (Africa), sponges soaked with alcohol (Persia), and empty pomegranate halves (Greece). These methods may sound far-fetched to us today, but they worked on many of the same principles as modern methods. In the accompanying Human Sexuality in a Diverse World feature, "Herbal Lore and Contraception," we discuss some of these methods.

CONTRACEPTION IN THE UNITED STATES: 1800S AND EARLY 1900S

In the early 1800s, several groups in the United States wanted to control fertility to reduce poverty. However, contraception was considered a private affair, to be discussed only between partners in a relationship. As we learned in Chapter 1, Anthony Comstock worked with Congress in 1873 to pass the Comstock Laws, which prohibited the distribution of all obscene material; this included contraceptive information and devices. Even medical doctors were not allowed to provide information about contraception (although a few still did). Margaret Sanger, the founder of Planned Parenthood, was one of the first people to publicly advocate the importance of contraception in the United States.

REALResearch > Close to **50%** of all pregnancies in the United States are unintended—they occur earlier than planned or after a woman has had her children (FROST ET AL., 2008). It is estimated that half of all women experience one or more unintended pregnancies by the age of 45 (JONES ET AL., 2006; for more information about unintended pregnancy rates see Figure 13.2).

CONTRACEPTION OUTSIDE THE UNITED STATES

Studies of contraceptive use in developing countries have found that close to 71 million married women and 4.2 million never-married women are at risk for unplanned pregnancies and not using contraception (Sedgh et al., 2007a). A woman might not use contraception because she is uneducated about it or doesn't have access to methods; she may also worry about side effects, not understand she is at risk for pregnancy, or believe that she needs to be married to use contraception (Sedgh et al., 2007a). Contraception throughout the world has always been affected by social and economic issues, knowledge levels, religion, and gender roles.

A country's religious views can affect contraceptive use. In fact, many predominantly Catholic regions and countries, such as Ireland, Italy, Poland, and the Philippines, have limited contraceptive devices available. These countries often promote natural methods of contraception, such as withdrawal or natural family planning (Leyson, 2004). Catholic bishops in the Philippines led a massive national protest in 2008 against a bill that would give citizens access to birth control, sex education, and eventually abortion (Burke, 2008; Hoffman, 2008). Many Filipino bishops even refused to give Holy Communion to politicians who approved of the bill (Burke, 2008; Hoffman, 2008).

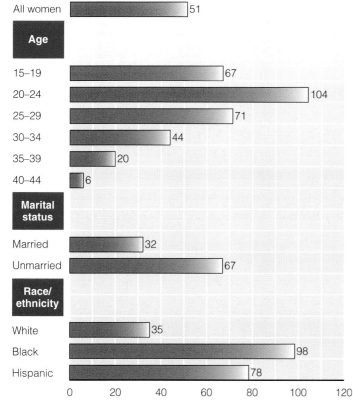

Unintended Pregnancies per 1,000 Women Aged 15–44

Figure **13.2** Some groups of women have higher rates of unintended pregnancies than others. Above are the percentages of women who have experienced an unintended pregnancy in their lifetime by age, marital status, and race/ethnicity. Source: Boonstra et al., *Abortion in Women's Lives,* New York: Guttmacher Institute, 2006, Figure 1.3, p. 9. Reproduced by permission.

> **View** in Video
> Virtual Safer Sex Kit
>
> "This array of safer-sex devices and aids can help you make better decisions."
> —*Virtual Safer-Sex Kit*
> To view go to CengageNOW at www.cengage.com/login

It's also important to point out, however, that not all residents of Catholic countries agree with the Church's contraceptive views (de Freitas, 2004; Tomaso, 2008). One study in Brazil, which contains one of the highest concentrations of Catholics, found that 88% of participants did not follow the Church's contraceptive teachings (in the United States, 75% of Catholics do the same; de Freitas, 2004; Tomaso, 2008). In 2008, 40 years after Pope Paul VI released *Humanae Vitae* (see Table 13.1), more than 50 Catholic groups from around the world joined forces to urge Pope Benedict XVI to lift the Catholic church's ban on birth control (Tomaso, 2008).

Gender roles and power differentials also contribute to a country's contraceptive use. Outside the United States, many women may not be involved in contraception decision making, and contraceptive use is thought to reduce a man's masculinity. For example, in Israel, while Jewish law often opposes family planning, religious law often teaches that men should not "spill their seed." Contraceptive methods that can cause direct damage to sperm, such as vasectomy, withdrawal, condoms, or spermicides, are often not acceptable (Shtarkshall & Zemach, 2004). Contraceptive methods that do not harm sperm, such as oral contraceptives, intrauterine devices (IUDs), and even diaphragms, are more acceptable.

Men are primarily responsible for birth control decisions in Japan, where Japanese women express shock over the liberal views that many American woman hold about birth control pill usage (Hatano & Shimazaki, 2004). In Kenya, married couples report low condom usage because condoms in marriage signify unfaithfulness on the part of the husband (Brockman, 2004).

Scandinavian countries are regarded as some of the most progressive with respect to contraceptive usage. In fact, Finland has been rated as a "model country" in contraceptive use because a variety of contraceptive methods are easily available and students can obtain contraception from school health services (Kontula & Haavio-Mannila, 2004). In the Netherlands and Norway, oral contraceptive use is high and many couples begin taking it prior to becoming sexually active (Drenth & Slob, 2004). In many of these countries, birth control is free and easily accessible (Trost & Bergstrom-Walan, 2004).

REALResearch > Motivations for contraceptive use are often influenced by cultural factors. In some areas of eastern Africa, condom use is extremely low because of the cultural significance of semen (COAST, 2007). Strongly held beliefs about wasting semen have led to low condom use, even when knowledge levels about contraception and STI are high.

 | 3.1

Overview of Contraceptive Methods

Below is an overview of contraceptive methods, including effectiveness rates, prescription requirements, cost, and noncontraceptive benefits. Even though both typical and perfect effectiveness rates are provided here, remember that a method's effectiveness depends on the user's ability to use the method correctly and to continue using it. For many methods, user failures are more common than method failures. Also keep in mind that the cost for each method depends on where it is purchased. Typically, health care clinics are less expensive than pharmacies or private physicians.

Method	Typical Effect	Perfect Effect	MD Visit	Cost	Noncontraceptive Benefits	Male Involved?
Male sterilization	99%	99.9%	Yes	$300–1,000	Possible reduction in risk for prostate cancer	Yes
Female sterilization	99%	99.9%	Yes	$2,000–5,000	Reduces risk of ovarian cancer	No
Implanon	99.5%	99.5%	Yes	$400–800	Can use while breast-feeding; reduced menstrual flow and cramping	No
Mirena IUD	99.2%	99.9%	Yes	$150–300	Decreases menstrual flow and cramping; reduced risk of endometrial cancer; may be beneficial during menopause	No
Paragard IUD	99.2%	99.9%	Yes	$150–300	Reduced risk of endometrial cancer	No
Depo-Provera	97%	99.7%	Yes	$35–70 per month	Reduction in menstrual flow and cramping; decreased risk of PID and ovarian and endometrial cancers; can be used during breast-feeding	No
NuvaRing	92%	99.7%	Yes	$25–35	Decreases menstrual flow and cramping, PMS, acne, ovarian and endometrial cancers, and the development of ovarian cysts	No
Ortho Evra patch	92%	99.7%	Yes	$35–70 for 3 months	Decreases menstrual flow and cramping, PMS, acne, ovarian and endometrial cancers, and the development of ovarian cysts	No
Combined-hormone birth control pills	92%	99.7%	Yes	$15–60 per month	Decreases menstrual flow and cramping, PMS, acne, ovarian and endometrial cancers, and the development of ovarian cysts	No
Progestin-only pills	92%	99.7%	Yes	$15–60 per month	May have similar noncontraceptive benefits as combined pills; reduction of uterine and ovarian cancers	No
Extended-use birth control pills	98%	99.9%	Yes	$90–100 per pack	Four periods per year and fewer menstrual-related problems; may reduce uterine fibroids and endometriosis symptoms	No

timeline History of Contraceptives in the United States

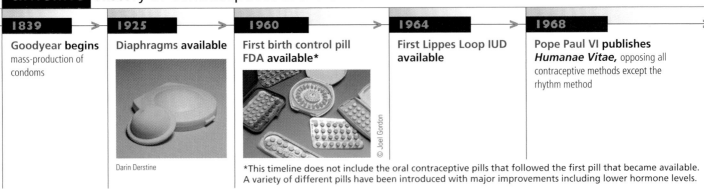

1839
Goodyear begins mass-production of condoms

1925
Diaphrams available

Darin Derstine

1960
First birth control pill FDA available*

© Joel Gordon

1964
First Lippes Loop IUD available

1968
Pope Paul VI publishes *Humanae Vitae,* opposing all contraceptive methods except the rhythm method

*This timeline does not include the oral contraceptive pills that followed the first pill that became available. A variety of different pills have been introduced with major improvements including lower hormone levels.

table 13.1

Overview of Contraceptive Methods—cont'd

Male condom	85%	98%	No	$10–15 per dozen (latex); $20 per dozen (polyurethane)	Protects against STIs; delays premature ejaculation.	Yes
Female condom	79%	95%	No	$2–4 each	Protects against STIs	Possible
Diaphragm	84%	94%	Yes	$30–50	Possible STI protection; may reduce cervical dysplasia	Possible
Today sponge	84%	87%	No	$10–15 for 3	Possible STI protection	Possible
Lea's Shield	80%	n/a	Yes	$65	n/a	Possible
Sympto-thermal method of fertility awareness	97%	91–99%	No	$10–25 for charts and thermometer	Can help a woman learn her cycle and eventually help with pregnancy	Possible
Rhythm method of fertility awareness	88%	91%*	No	n/a	None	Possible
Withdrawal	73%	96%	No	n/a	None	Yes
Spermicides	71%	82%	No	$5-15	n/a	Possible
No Method	15%	15%	No	n/a	n/a	n/a

IUD, intrauterine device; PID, pelvic inflammatory disease; PMS, premenstrual syndrome; STI, sexually transmitted disease.

*Perfect use rates are difficult to determine with the fertility awareness methods because many factors may influence the timing of ovulation.

CHOOSING A METHOD
OF CONTRACEPTION

Several methods of contraception, or **birth control,** are currently available. Prior to the availability of any contraceptive method in the United States, the **Food and Drug Administration (FDA)** must formally approve the method. Let's explore the FDA approval process and individual lifestyle issues that may affect contraceptive method choice.

FDA Approval Process

The FDA is responsible for approving all prescription medications and medical devices in the United States. To get approval for a new drug, a pharmaceutical company must first submit a new drug application (NDA) to the FDA showing that the drug is safe in animal tests and that it is reasonably safe to proceed with human trials of the drug. After this, there are a total of three phases to evaluate the safety of the medication. In Phase 1, the drug is introduced to approximately 20 to 80 healthy volunteers to collect information on the drug's effectiveness. In Phase 2, several hundred people take the drug to evaluate how it works and determine side effects and risks. In Phase 3 trials, the study is expanded, and

birth control
Another term for contraception.

Food and Drug Administration (FDA)
The agency in the U.S. federal government that has the power to approve and disapprove new drugs.

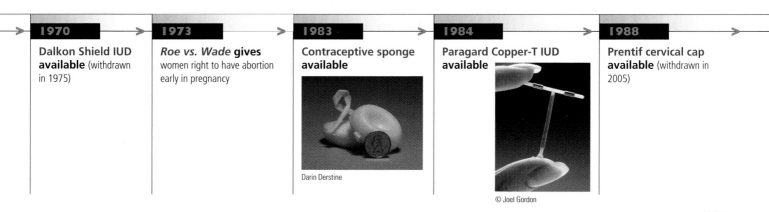

1970
Dalkon Shield IUD available (withdrawn in 1975)

1973
Roe vs. Wade **gives** women right to have abortion early in pregnancy

1983
Contraceptive sponge available

Darin Derstine

1984
Paragard Copper-T IUD available

© Joel Gordon

1988
Prentif cervical cap available (withdrawn in 2005)

Herbal Lore and Contraception

Some of the tested herbs have been found to have high success rates for contraceptive ability.

In many places around the world, herbs are used as contraception. For example, American women in Appalachia drink tea made from Queen Anne's lace directly following sexual intercourse to prevent pregnancy (Rensberger, 1994). They are not alone. Many women from South Africa, Guatemala, Costa Rica, Haiti, China, and India rely on herbal contraceptives (L. Newman & Nyce, 1985). Newer hormonal methods of birth control have reduced fertility around the world, but nonhormonal methods such as natural family planning and herbal methods continue to be used. Some of the tested herbs have been found to have high success rates for contraceptive ability (Chaudhury, 1985).

A common herbal contraceptive in Paraguay is known as *yuyos*. Many types of *yuyos* are taken for fertility regula-tion (Bull & Melian, 1998). The herbs are usually soaked in water and drunk as tea. Older women teach younger women how to use these herbs, but problems sometimes occur when herbal methods are used improperly. Remember that this method works only when using a mix of herbs that have been found to offer contraceptive protection. Drinking herbal tea from the grocery store isn't going to protect you in the same way!

Failure rates from herbal contraceptives are higher than from more modern methods, but many do work better than using nothing at all. What is it that makes the herbal methods effective? We don't know, but perhaps some future contraceptive drugs may come from research into plant pharmaceuticals.

---

hundreds to thousands of people are enrolled in the study. Like drugs, medical devices, such as IUDs and diaphragms, are also subject to strict evaluation and regulation. It is estimated that it takes 10 to 14 years to develop a new contraceptive method (Hatcher et al., 2007; F. H. Stewart & Gabelnick, 2004).

Lifestyle Issues

As we discussed earlier, no single method of birth control is best for everyone—the best one for you is one that you and your partner will use correctly every time you have sexual intercourse. Choosing a contraceptive method is an important decision and one that must be made with your lifestyle in mind. Important issues include your own personal health and health risks, the number of sexual partners you have, frequency of sexual intercourse, your risk of acquiring an STI, how responsible you are, the cost of the method, and the method's advantages and disadvantages.

In Figure 13.3, we review contraceptive choices among U.S. women. Overall, female sterilization, oral contraceptives, and condoms are the most widely used methods among Whites, Afri-can Americans, and Latinos in the United States (Mosher et al., 2004). However, White women are more likely to use birth control pills, whereas Black and Hispanic women are more likely to rely on female sterilization (see Figure 13.7 later in the chapter for more information about race/ethnicity and contraceptive use).

In the following sections, we discuss barrier, hormonal, chemical, intrauterine, natural, permanent, ineffective, and emergency methods of contraception. For each of these methods, we will cover how they work, their **effectiveness rates,** cost, advantages and disadvantages, and cross-cultural patterns of usage. Table 13.1 provides an overview of available contraceptive methods with typical use (which includes user error) and **perfect use** (when a method is used without error).

effectiveness rates
Estimated rates of the number of women who do not become pregnant each year using each method of contraception.

perfect use
Refers to the probability of contraceptive failure for a perfect user of each method.

---

timeline History of Contraceptives in the United States

1990
Norplant **available** (withdrawn in 2002)

1993
Female condom **available**

© Joel Gordon

1994
Polyurethane condoms **available**

1995
Contraceptive sponge **withdrawn** from market

1996
Jadelle 2-rod implant **available** (but not marketed in U.S.)

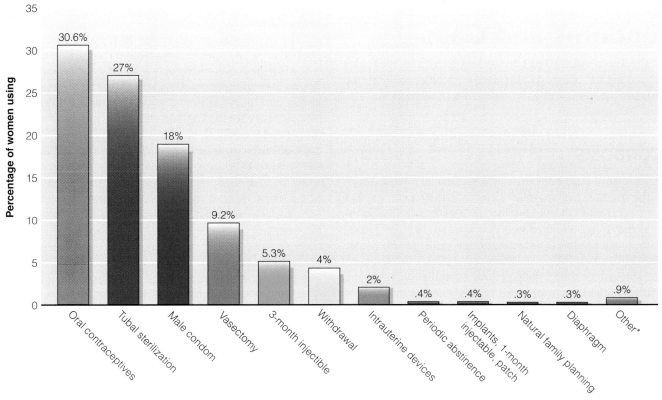

Contraceptive Method Choice Among U.S. Women, 2002

*Includes sponge, cervical cap, female condom and other methods

Figure **13.3** Contraception method of choice among U.S. women, 2002. Source: Adapted from Alan Guttmacher Institute (2005b). Contraceptive use. Retrieved August 13, 2005, from http://www.agi-usa.org/pubs/fb_contr_use.html.

review questions

1 Explain what we know about contraception in ancient times.

2 How was contraception viewed in the United States in the early 1900s?

3 What factors have been found to be related to contraceptive nonuse outside the United States?

4 Identify two important lifestyle issues to consider when choosing a contraceptive method.

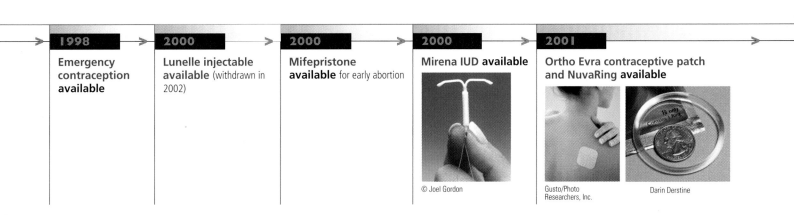

1998

Emergency contraception available

2000

Lunelle injectable available (withdrawn in 2002)

2000

Mifepristone available for early abortion

2000

Mirena IUD available

© Joel Gordon

2001

Ortho Evra contraceptive patch and NuvaRing available

Gusto/Photo Researchers, Inc.

Darin Derstine

Barrier Methods:
Condoms and Caps

Barrier methods of contraception work by preventing the sperm from entering the uterus. These methods include condoms, the diaphragm, the contraceptive sponge, and cervical barriers.

CONDOMS

Penile coverings have been used as a method of contraception since the beginning of recorded history. In 1350 B.C., Egyptian men wore decorative sheaths over their penises. Eventually, sheaths of linen and animal intestines were developed. In 1844, the Goodyear Company improved the strength and resiliency of rubber, and by 1850, rubber (latex) **condoms** were available in the United States (McLaren, 1990). Polyurethane (paul-lee-YUR-ith-ain; nonlatex) condoms were launched in the United States in 1994 and can be used by those with latex allergies. However, if a person does not have a latex allergy, health care providers generally recommend using latex condoms because they have lower rates of slippage and breakage.

When using a condom, space should always be left in the top so that the force of the ejaculate does not break the condom.

Male condoms are one of the most inexpensive and cost-effective contraceptive methods, providing not only high effectiveness rates but also added protection from STIs and HIV (Hatcher et al., 2007). They are the most widely available and commonly used barrier contraceptive method in the United States today. Approximately 97% of male condoms in the United States are made of latex, and the rest are made of lamb intestines ("skins") or polyurethane (Hatcher et al., 2007).

Costs for latex male condoms range from $10 to $15 per dozen; polyurethane and lambskin condoms are more expensive at approximately $20 per dozen; all of these are usually less expensive at family planning clinics.

The first female condom, the Reality Vaginal Pouch (often referred to as "FC"), became available in the United States in 1993. It is made of polyurethane and is about 7 inches long with two flexible polyurethane rings. The inner ring serves as an insertion device, and the outer ring stays on the outside of the vagina. In 2005, a newer female condom (the "FC2") made of a softer and more flexible material, became available in the United States. In 2008, a third female condom made of latex (called the "Reddy") was pending FDA approval. Female condoms cost approximately $3.50 each. In some countries, such as Africa, where the cost is prohibitively high, women have been known to wash and reuse FCs (Potter et al., 2003), although they are not made to be used this way.

How They Work

The male condom ("rubber" or "prophylactic") is placed on an erect penis prior to vaginal penetration. Condoms must be put on before there is any vaginal contact by the penis because sperm may be present in the urethra. After being rolled onto the penis, a half-inch empty space is left at the tip of the condom to allow room for the ejaculatory fluid (see nearby photo). To prevent tearing the condom, the vagina should be well lubricated. Although some condoms come prelubricated, if extra lubrication is needed, water, contraceptive jelly or cream, or a water-based lubricant such as K-Y jelly should be used. Oil-based lubricants such as hand or body lotion, petroleum jelly (e.g., Vaseline), baby oil, massage oil, or vegetable oil should never be used because they may damage the latex and cause the condom to break (polyurethane condoms are not damaged by these products; see Table 13.2).

condom
A latex, animal membrane, or polyurethane sheath that fits over the penis and is used for protection against pregnancy and sexually transmitted infections; female condoms made of either polyurethane or polymer, which protect the vaginal walls, are also available.

timeline History of Contraceptives in the United States

2002
Lea's Shield cervical barrier available (not marketed)

Darin Derstine

2002
Essure permanent sterilization device available

2003
FemCap available (not marketed in U.S.)

2003
Seasonale 3-month birth control available

2004
Depo Provera gets FDA approval for contraceptive use

To avoid the possibility of semen leaking out of the condom, withdrawal must take place immediately after ejaculation, while the penis is still erect, and the condom should be grasped firmly at the base to prevent its slipping off into the vagina during withdrawal. Condom users should always remember to check expiration dates, pull back the foreskin on an uncircumcised penis before putting a condom on, and pinch the reservoir tip to leave a half-inch space in the condom for ejaculation.

There are many types of male condoms on the market, including lubricated, colored, spermicidal, reservoir tip, and ribbed texture condoms. For protection from STIs, the most effective condoms are latex and polyurethane condoms. Spermicidal condoms are lubricated with a small amount of **nonoxynol-9,** but these condoms have not been found to be any more effective than nonspermicidal condoms (Hatcher et al., 2007). Because of the controversy surrounding the use of nonoxynol-9 (see the nearby Sex in Real Life, "Nonoxynol-9: Harmful or Helpful?"), spermicidal condoms are not recommended today (Hatcher et al., 2007).

A female condom is inserted into the vagina prior to penile penetration. The inner ring is squeezed between the thumb and middle finger, making it long and thin, and then inserted into the vagina. Once this is done, an index finger inside the condom can push the inner ring up close to the cervix. The outer ring hangs about 1 inch below the vulva (see Figure 13.4). During intercourse, the penis is placed within the female condom, and care should be taken to make sure it does not slip between the condom and the vaginal wall. It's important that the vagina is well-lubricated so that the female condom stays in place. Female and male condoms should never be used together, because they can adhere to each other and slip or break.

Effectiveness

Effectiveness rates for latex and polyurethane condoms range from 85% (typical use) to 98% (perfect use). Effectiveness rates for female condoms range from 79% (typical use) to 95% (perfect use).

In addition, latex and polyurethane condoms are effective barriers against the transmission of many STIs. However, research has found that the pores in lambskin condoms may be large

nonoxynol-9
A spermicide that has been used to prevent pregnancy and protect against sexually transmitted infections.

table 13.2

What to Use With Condoms

Condoms can be made out of latex, polyurethane, or lambskin. Generally, both latex and polyurethane condoms offer more STI protection than lambskin condoms. All types of lubricants, including oil-based lubricants, can be safely used with polyurethane and lambskin condoms. However, latex condoms should only be used with a water-based lubricant. Following is a listing of products that can be used with all condoms, and products that should never be used with latex condoms.

For Use With All Condoms

- Water-based lubricants (including products such as AquaLube, AstroGlide, or K-Y Jelly)
- Glycerine
- Spermicides
- Saliva
- Water
- Silicone lubricant
- Egg Whites

Do Not Use With Latex Condoms

- Baby oil
- Cold creams
- Edible oils (such as olive, peanut, or canola oil)
- Massage oil
- Petroleum jelly
- Rubbing alcohol
- Suntan oil and lotions
- Vegetable or mineral oil
- Vaginal infection medications in cream or suppository form

SOURCE: Hatcher et al., 2007, p. 307.

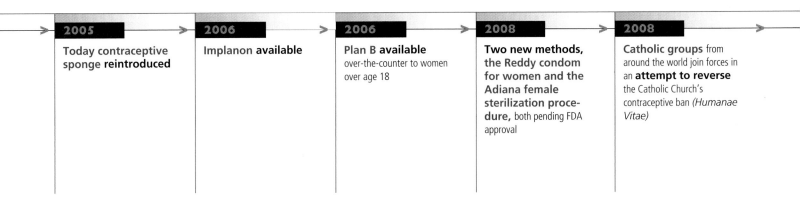

2005	2006	2006	2008	2008
Today contraceptive sponge reintroduced	**Implanon available**	**Plan B available** over-the-counter to women over age 18	**Two new methods, the Reddy condom for women and the Adiana female sterilization procedure,** both pending FDA approval	**Catholic groups** from around the world join forces in an **attempt to reverse** the Catholic Church's contraceptive ban *(Humanae Vitae)*

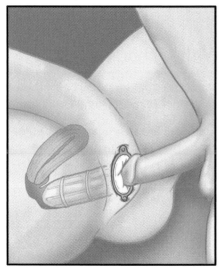
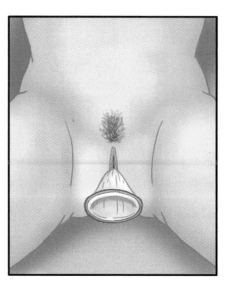

Figure **13.4** Vulva with female condom inserted.

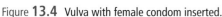

Female condoms, made of polyurethane, have been available since 1993.

© Joel Gordon

enough to permit transmission of some STIs (Hatcher et al., 2007).

Some couples worry that condoms will break. All condoms made in the United States are tested and must meet stringent quality control requirements. Studies have demonstrated that when used correctly (without common errors in use, such as not leaving room at the top of the condom for the ejaculate), the overall risk of condom breakage is very low (Hatcher et al., 2007). Using a condom after the expiration date is the leading cause of breakage.

WHAT DO YOU WANT TO KNOW ?

Do some men have problems maintaining an erection when they use a condom?
Some men do report that they have more difficulties maintaining an erection when they use a latex condom. Some couples complain that wearing a condom is like "taking a shower with a raincoat on," or that it decreases sensitivity during sexual intercourse. Adding two or three drops of a lubricant, such as K-Y jelly, into the condom before rolling it on to the penis can improve penile sensitivity. Many women also report that putting a small amount of a lubricant into their vagina before intercourse helps increase their pleasure and sensitivity while using a condom. Lubricated condoms may help maintain erections by increasing sensitivity, as will polyurethane and lambskin condoms. It's also important to note that men who experience problems with premature ejaculation often find that condoms can help maintain erections.

As we discussed earlier, using certain products with latex condoms may cause them to tear (see the accompanying Sex in Real Life, "What to Use With Condoms"). Creams for vaginal infections (such as Monistat and Vagisil) and exposure to heat can also increase the risk of tearing and breaking. It is not a good idea to carry a condom in your pocket or wallet for an extended period of time.

Advantages

Male condoms offer the most protection from STIs. In addition, they encourage male participation in contraception and may reduce the incidence of premature ejaculation. Other advantages include the fact that they can be purchased over-the-counter, are relatively inexpensive, have minimal side effects, and reduce **postcoital drip** (Hatcher et al., 2007). Polyurethane condoms are more resistant to damage, have a longer shelf life, and, unlike latex condoms, can be used with both oil- and water-based lubricants (Hatcher et al., 2007). Condoms can also be used in conjunction with other contraceptive methods and can be used during oral or anal sex to reduce the risk of STIs (we discuss this more in Chapter 15). Like male condoms, female condoms are over-the-counter, offer STI protection, reduce postcoital drip, and have minimal side effects. The external ring of the female condom may provide extra clitoral stimulation during sexual intercourse, making sex more enjoyable for women. In addition, some women report that they like female condoms because they can use them without partner knowledge. In fact, one international study found that 13% of women used female condoms without their partners knowing (Kerrigan et al., 2000). Finally, female condoms do not require a male erection and can be used during anal sex.

Disadvantages

The male condom decreases spontaneity, may pose sizing and erection problems, and reduces male sensation. In one study, more than 75% of men and nearly 40% of women reported decreased sexual sensation with condom use (Crosby et al., 2008). Condoms may not be comfortable for all men, and some who use polyurethane condoms report slipping or bunching up during use (Hollander, 2001). Finally, some men and women may be embarrassed to suggest using a condom and may feel uncomfortable interrupting foreplay to put one on.

As for female condoms, they can be difficult to insert, uncomfortable, expensive, and may slip during sexual intercourse (Kerrigan et al., 2000; Lie, 2000). One study found that 57% of women and 30% of men reported difficulties with insertion, discomfort during sex, and/or excess lubrication with use (Kerrigan et al., 2000). Some users also report that female condoms can be "noisy" to use (Lie, 2000) and uncomfortable because they hang outside the vulva during use (see Figure 13.4). Newer generation

postcoital drip
A vaginal discharge (dripping) that occurs after sexual intercourse.

female condoms are made of more flexible materials, making them less "noisy," and slippage issues have improved with the addition of a stabilizing sponge in the newer "Reddy" female condoms (J. L. Schwartz & Gabelnick, 2002).

Cross-Cultural Use

Male condoms are popular in many countries throughout the world, including Australia, Canada, Croatia, Czech Republic, Greece, Hong Kong, India, Iran, Italy, Japan, Ireland, Germany, and parts of Africa. In fact, German couples will often avoid intercourse when no condom is available (Lautmann & Starke, 2004), and in Ireland men have been known to make their own condoms out of plastic wrap when they cannot find a condom (something that is not recommended by your author, by the way; Kelly, 2004). Condoms are also popular in Japan, where nearly 80% of couples using contraception choose them (Hatano & Shimazaki, 2004; Hayashi, 2004).

In many other countries, however, male condoms are not widely used. This may be because of embarrassment, lack of availability, or religious prohibition. In Botswana, for example, many couples are embarrassed to purchase condoms (Mookodi et al., 2004), and a similar attitude is found in Brazil, especially among women (de Freitas, 2004). However, these attitudes are slowly changing because of increased condom availability. In Costa Rica, where religious prohibitions discourage condom use, men report not wanting to use condoms and prohibit their partners from using protection as well (Arroba, 2004).

Female condoms have not been popular in developing countries. Several issues may contribute to this, including the fact that

they are expensive, difficult to insert, and require genital touching. Many women in other cultures are not comfortable touching the vagina or inserting anything into it (in fact, tampon use is also much lower in countries outside the United States). However, there are signs that female condom use is increasing in some countries. For example, in Zimbabwe, 15% of couples report that the female condom is their first choice in birth control (Kerrigan et al., 2000).

REALResearch **>** Male condoms help protect future fertility by reducing the risk of STIs and the long-term effects of such infections, which can lead to infertility issues later in life (we discuss this more in Chapter 15; HATCHER ET AL., 2008). In fact, many health care providers today encourage clients to use condoms in addition to a primary contraceptive method.

THE DIAPHRAGM

The **diaphragm** (DIE-uh-fram) is a dome-shaped cup, made of either latex or silicone, with a flexible rim. It is inserted into the vagina before sexual intercourse, and it creates a barrier over the

diaphragm
A birth control device consisting of a latex dome on a flexible spring rim; used with spermicidal cream or jelly.

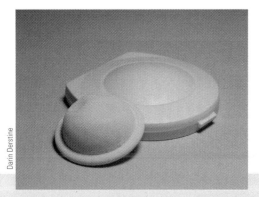

Diaphragms come in a variety of different shapes and sizes and must be fit by a health care practitioner.

cervix so sperm and ova cannot meet. Diaphragms come in several sizes and shapes that must be fitted by a health care provider. Like latex condoms, latex diaphragms should not be used with oil-based lubricants because these can damage the latex (see Table 13.2, "What to Use With Condoms"). In the United States, diaphragms range in cost from $30 to $40 and require spermicidal cream or jelly.

How It Works

The diaphragm is a barrier method of contraception and is used with a spermicidal jelly to ensure that sperm do not live if they should get past the barrier. Prior to insertion, the diaphragm rim is covered with spermicidal jelly, and one tablespoon of the jelly is put into the dome of the diaphragm. Although health care providers typically advise women to insert more spermicidal jelly if in-

tercourse takes place a second time, this may not be necessary because the evidence to support this practice is weak (Hatcher et al., 2007).

The diaphragm is folded in half and inserted into the vagina while a woman is standing with one leg propped up, squatting, or lying on her back (see Figure 13.5). It should be pushed downward toward the back of the vagina, while the front rim is tucked under the pubic bone. Diaphragm insertion may take place immediately before sexual intercourse or up to 6 hours before. Once a diaphragm is in place, a woman should not be able to feel it; if she does, it is improperly inserted. After intercourse, the diaphragm must be left in place for at least 6 to 8 hours, but because of the risk of toxic shock syndrome, it should never be left in place more than 24 hours. To remove the diaphragm, a finger is hooked over the front of the diaphragm rim, and it is then pulled down and out of the vagina. The diaphragm must be washed with soap and water and replaced in its container. If properly cared for, diaphragms can last for several years. However, if a woman loses or gains more than 10 pounds or experiences a pregnancy (regardless of how the pregnancy was resolved—through birth, miscarriage, or **abortion**), she must have her diaphragm refitted by her health care provider.

Effectiveness

Effectiveness rates for the diaphragm range from 84% (typical use) to 94% (perfect use). Correct and consistent use has been found to be an important factor in effectiveness rates. It is estimated that half

abortion
Induced termination of a pregnancy before fetal viability.

(a)
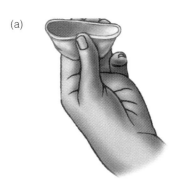

(b)
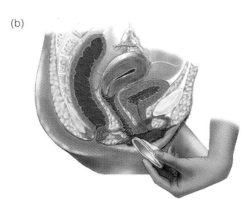

(c)

(d)
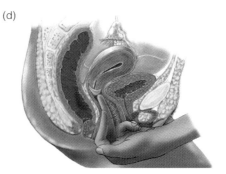

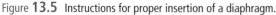

Figure **13.5** Instructions for proper insertion of a diaphragm.

Is it OK to borrow someone else's diaphragm if I can't find mine?

Absolutely not. The diaphragm works by creating a suction on the cervix, which prevents sperm from entering the uterus. To get this suction, a health care provider must measure the cervix and prescribe the right size diaphragm for each individual woman. If you use someone else's diaphragm, it may be the wrong size and thus ineffective. Also, because of the risk of acquiring an STI, it is not a good idea to share diaphragms.

of diaphragm users who become pregnant were using the method incorrectly (Hatcher et al., 2007). In addition, women who have not had children have been found to have higher effectiveness rates than those women who have given birth.

The diaphragm does not affect hormonal levels.

Advantages

The diaphragm does not affect hormonal levels, reduces the risk of cervical dysplasia and cancer, can be inserted before sexual activity, and is relatively inexpensive (Hatcher et al., 2007). In addition, although the diaphragm does not require partner involvement, men can be involved in the insertion of the diaphragm during foreplay (Hatcher et al., 2007).

Disadvantages

A diaphragm requires a visit to a health care provider and increases the risk of toxic shock syndrome and urinary tract infections (Hatcher et al., 2007). It also increases postcoital drip, and users may notice a foul odor if the diaphragm is left in place too long. Diaphragms may also shift during different sexual positions (reducing effectiveness), and an allergic reaction to the spermicide may develop.

Cross-Cultural Use

Because diaphragm use is low in the United States, it shouldn't come as any surprise that it also has low usage rates outside the United States. This is possibly related to the necessity of a health care provider fitting, availability of spermicidal cream or jelly, cost, and the required genital touching. A shortage of health care providers to fit diaphragms may also inhibit their use.

THE CONTRACEPTIVE SPONGE

The Today **contraceptive sponge** was approved by the FDA in 1983; however, it was withdrawn from the market in 1995 because of stringent new government safety rules that had to do with the manufacturing plant. In late 2005, the sponge was reintroduced and is available over-the-counter in the United States. The one-size-fits-all sponge covers the cervix and contains spermicide. A box of three sponges costs approximately $13, depending on where it is purchased.

The Today contraceptive sponge was back on the market in late 2005 in the United States.

Darin Derstine

How It Works

Contraceptive sponges work in three ways: as a barrier, blocking the entrance to the uterus; absorbing sperm; and deactivating sperm. Prior to vaginal insertion, the sponge is moistened with water, which activates the spermicide. It is then folded in half and inserted deep into the vagina (see Figure 13.6). Like the diaphragm, the sponge must be checked to make sure it is covering the cervix. Intercourse can take place immediately after insertion or at any time during the next 24 hours and can occur as many times as desired without adding additional spermicidal jelly or cream. However, the sponge must be left in place for 6 hours after intercourse. For removal, a cloth loop on the outside of the sponge is grasped to gently pull the sponge out of the vagina. Like the diaphragm, the sponge can be inserted and removed by either the woman or her partner and must be removed within 24 hours to reduce the risk of toxic shock syndrome.

Effectiveness

Effectiveness rates for the sponge range from 84% (typical use) to 87% (perfect use). Like the diaphragm, these rates depend on the user, and failure rates are higher in women who have had children (Hatcher et al., 2007).

Advantages

Contraceptive sponges do not affect hormonal levels, can be purchased over-the-counter, can be inserted before sexual intercourse, and allow couples to engage in repeated sexual intercourse during a 24-hour period. In addition, although the sponge does not require partner involvement, men can be involved in the insertion of the sponge during foreplay (Hatcher et al., 2007).

Disadvantages

The contraceptive sponge requires genital touching, may be difficult to insert and remove, and may increase the risk of toxic shock syndrome and urinary tract infections. It also increases postcoital drip, and users may notice a foul odor if the sponge is left in place too long. Some users and their partners may also develop a spermicide-caused allergic reaction.

contraceptive sponge
Polyurethane sponge impregnated with spermicide, inserted into the vagina for contraception.

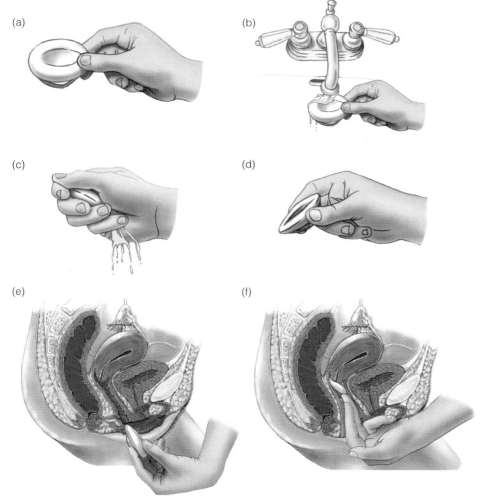

Figure **13.6** Instructions for proper insertion of a contraceptive sponge.

Cross-Cultural Use

The Today contraceptive sponge is available in Canada and many parts of Europe. However, there is little research on cross-cultural use. Women in France have used vaginal sponges dipped in various chemicals to avoid pregnancy for years. These sponges are washed and used over and over. This practice is not recommended, however, because of the risk of infection and toxic shock syndrome. As with diaphragms, sponges tend to have low usage rates outside the United States, which may be because of factors

such as the lack of availability of spermicidal cream or jelly or the required genital touching.

LEA'S SHIELD AND THE FemCap

Both **Lea's Shield** and the **FemCap** are thimble-shaped, silicone devices that are inserted into the vagina and fit over the cervix. Like the diaphragm and sponge, Lea's Shield and the FemCap block sperm from entering the uterus. Both of these devices must be fitted by a health care provider. Lea's Shield comes in one size and has a one-way valve that allows the flow of cervical fluids and air, whereas the FemCap comes in three sizes—small for women who have never been pregnant, medium for women who have been pregnant but have not had a vaginal delivery, and large for

(a) The FemCap is a silicone cup shaped like a sailor's hat that fits securely over the cervix. (b) Lea's Shield is a silicone cup with a one-way valve and a loop for easier removal.

Darin Derstine

Lea's Shield
Reusable silicone barrier vaginal contraceptive that contains a one-way valve.

FemCap
Reusable silicone barrier vaginal contraceptive that comes in three sizes.

women who have had a vaginal delivery of a full-term baby. Both Lea's Shield and the FemCap cost between $35 and $75 and require an health care provider's office visit and spermicidal jelly or cream.

How They Work

Lea's Shield and the FemCap work by blocking the entrance to the uterus and deactivating sperm through the use of spermicidal cream or jelly. After insertion, a woman must check to see that the barrier is covering her cervix. The barriers should be left in place for at least 8 hours after intercourse and can be worn up to 48 hours. Both of these devices have a strap to aid in removal. After use, the devices should be washed with soap and water and allowed to air dry.

Effectiveness

Effectiveness rates for both Lea's Shield and the FemCap are approximately 86% in women who have never had children (Cates & Stewart, 2004). Typical effectiveness rates are lower for women who have had children. At this time, there are no perfect use effectiveness rates for either the Lea's Shield or the FemCap.

Advantages

Like the diaphragm and the sponge, both Lea's Shield and the FemCap do not affect hormonal levels, can be inserted before sexual intercourse, and allow couples to engage in repeated sexual intercourse. In addition, they are made of silicone, and those with latex allergies can safely use them. Lea's Shield has a one-way release valve to reduce the risk of toxic shock syndrome. Finally, although Lea's Shield and the FemCap do not require partner in-

volvement, men can be involved in the insertion of these methods during foreplay (Hatcher et al., 2007).

Disadvantages

The use of these methods requires a medical office visit, and users have an increased risk of toxic shock syndrome and urinary tract infections (Hatcher et al., 2007). They also increase postcoital drip

---

REALResearch > Birth control pills have been found to decrease sexual desire and vaginal lubrication, and these effects may last after a woman has stopped taking the pill (GRAHAM ET AL., 2007; HATCHER ET AL., 2007). However, if a woman is less sensitive to hormonal changes, she may not notice these side effects. If she does, changing birth control pill brands may restore sexual desire.

---

and may shift during sexual intercourse. An allergic reaction to the spermicide may develop, and users may notice a foul odor if the devices are left in place too long.

Cross-Cultural Use

Cervical barriers are widely used in England and in some countries—including Germany, Austria, Switzerland, and Canada—Lea's Shield has been available over-the-counter since 1993 (Long, 2003). However, in less-developed countries, they are used infrequently, probably because of the necessity of a prescription, as well as insertion and removal issues and required genital touching.

cervical barrier
A plastic or rubber cover for the cervix that provides a contraceptive barrier to sperm.

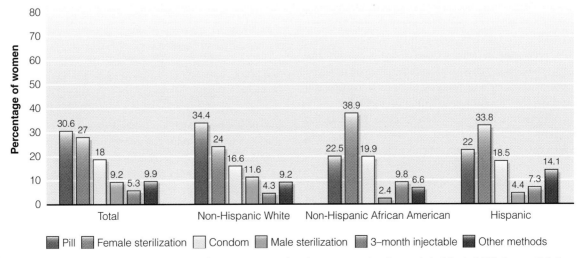

Method of Contraception by Race/Ethnicity

Figure **13.7** Method of contraception among women aged 15 to 44, currently using contraception, by race/ethnicity, in 2002. Source: U.S. Department of Health and Human Services, 2005.

1 Explain how barrier methods of contraception work and identify four barrier contraceptive methods in order of their effectiveness rates.

2 How do male and female condoms work, and what are some of the advantages and disadvantages of these barrier methods?

3 How does the diaphragm work, and what are some of the advantages and disadvantages of this barrier method?

4 How does the contraceptive sponge work, and what are some of the advantages and disadvantages of this barrier method?

5 How do Lea's Shield and the FemCap work, and what are some of the advantages and disadvantages of these barrier methods?

Combined Hormone Methods for Women: The Pill, the Patch, and More

Combined-hormone methods use a blend of hormones (including estrogen and progesterone) to suppress ovulation and thicken the cervical mucus to prevent sperm from joining the ovum. We discuss birth control pills, vaginal rings, and patches. Combined-hormone methods have been found to be effective, safe, reversible, and acceptable to most women. However, for protection against STIs, condoms must also be used.

BIRTH CONTROL PILLS

Margaret Sanger was the first to envision **oral contraceptives** (the birth control pill, or simply "the pill"). Many researchers had been working with chemical methods to inhibit pregnancy in animals, but they were reluctant to try these methods on humans because they feared that increasing hormones could cause cancer. The complexity of a woman's body chemistry and the expense involved in developing the pill inhibited its progress. The birth control pill was federally approved as a contraceptive method in 1960.

At first, the pill was much stronger than it needed to be. In the search for the most effective contraception, more estrogen was seen as more effective. Today's birth control pills have less than half the dose of estrogen the first pills had. After almost 50 years on the market, oral contraceptives still remain the most popular contraceptive method not only in the United States but around the world (Frost et al., 2008; Hatcher et al., 2007). In addition, birth control pills are the most extensively studied type of medication in the history of medicine (Hatcher et al., 2007).

Combination birth control pills, which contain synthetic estrogen and a type of progesterone, are the most commonly used contraceptive method in the United States. They require a pre-

scription and a medical office visit and typically cost between $30 and $60 per month.

In Chapter 5, we discussed menstrual manipulation and menstrual suppression. Typical birth control pills have been designed to mimic an average menstrual cycle, which is why a woman takes them for 21 days and then has 1 week off, when she usually starts her period. Originally, this 3-week-on/1-week-off regimen was developed to convince women that the pill was "natural," which pill makers believed would make the product more acceptable to potential users and reassure them that they were not pregnant every month (Clarke & Miller, 2001; Thomas & Ellertson, 2000). As we discussed in Chapter 5, the bleeding that women experience while on the pill is medically induced and has no physiological benefit (J. L. Schwartz et al., 1999).

Triphasil (try-FAY-sill) **pills** were introduced in the 1990s and continue to grow in popularity today. They contain three sets of pills for each week during the month. Each week, the hormonal dosage is increased, rather than keeping the hormonal level consistent, as with traditional birth control pills. When it was first introduced, many health care providers liked this pill because it seemed to follow a woman's natural cycle. However, many women who use triphasil pills report an increase in breakthrough bleeding because of the fluctuating hormone levels.

Extended-cycle birth control pills became available in 2003 with the FDA approval of Seasonale. Seasonale uses a continuous 84-day active pill with a 7-day placebo pill, which enables women to have only four periods per year. In 2006, Seasonique, a similar extended-cycle pill, was approved by the FDA. The difference between Seasonale and Seasonique is in the placebo pills—although they are inactive in Seasonale, Seasonique placebo pills contain a low dose of estrogen that has been found to cause less spotting during the active pills. Another continuous birth control pill that completely stops menstrual periods, Lybrel, was approved by the FDA in 2007. Lybrel contains lower levels of estrogen than other pills but is taken daily for 365 days a year.

oral contraceptive
The "pill"; a preparation of synthetic female hormones that blocks ovulation.

combination birth control pill
An oral contraceptive containing synthetic estrogen and progesterone.

triphasil pill
A type of multiphasic oral contraceptive with three types of pills, each of which contains a different hormonal dosage.

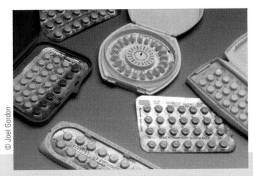

A variety of birth control pills are available, and a health care provider can prescribe the one that's best for you.

Continuous-use birth control pills are not new. In fact, prior to FDA approval of these methods, some health care providers were known to "bicycle" birth control pills (back-to-back use of two packs of active pills with placebo pills at the end of the second pack) or "tricycle" (back-to-back-back use of three packs of active pills with placebo pills at the end of the third pack; Hatcher et al., 2007). In addition, some health care providers have used short-term continuous-use birth control pills for scheduling convenience (i.e., to eliminate the chance of having a period during an athletic event, vacation, or honeymoon; Hatcher et al., 2007).

Birth control pills are also prescribed for noncontraceptive reasons, such as heavy or dysfunctional menstrual bleeding, irregular periods, recurrent ovarian cysts, acne, or polycystic ovary syndrome (see Chapter 5; Hatcher et al., 2007). Today there are more than 70 brands of birth control pills on the market in the United States.

How They Work

The hormones estrogen, progesterone, luteinizing hormone (LH), and follicle stimulating hormone (FSH) fluctuate during a woman's menstrual cycle (see Chapter 5). These fluctuations control the maturation of an ovum, ovulation, the development of the endometrium, and menstruation. The synthetic hormones replace a woman's own natural hormones but in different amounts. The increase in estrogen and progesterone prevent the pituitary gland from sending hormones to cause the ovaries to begin maturation of an ovum. Hormone levels while on the pill are similar to when a woman is pregnant, and this is what interferes with ovulation. Birth control pills also work by thickening the cervical mucus (which inhibits the mobility of sperm) and by reducing the buildup of the endometrium.

Combination birth control pills can either be **monophasic** or **multiphasic.** Monophasic pills contain the same amount of hormones in each pill, whereas multiphasic pills vary the hormonal amount. Traditionally, birth control pills have been used on a monthly cycling plan that involved either a 21-day or 28-day regimen and started on the first or fifth day of menstruation or on the first Sunday after menstruation. **Start days** vary depending on the pill manufacturer. The majority of manufacturers recommend a Sunday start day, which enables a woman to avoid menstruating during a weekend. Each pill must be taken every day at approximately the same time. This is important because they work by maintaining a certain hormonal level in the bloodstream. If this level drops, ovulation may occur (see the accompanying Table 13.3, "What to Do If You Forget," for more information).

monophasic
Describes oral contraceptives containing stable levels of hormones during the entire month; the doses and types of hormones do not vary.

multiphasic
Describes oral contraceptives that contain varying levels of hormones during the month; each week the hormonal dosage is changed.

start day
The actual day that the first pill is taken in a pack of oral contraceptives.

table 13.3

What to Do If You Forget

Many women who take birth control pills forget to take one at some time. As we've discussed throughout this chapter, the pill is most effective if taken everyday at approximately the same time. If you miss a pill, it's a good idea to talk to your health care provider about what would be best to do. In many cases, it depends on several factors including what kind of pill you are on, the dosage of the pill, how many pills you missed, and how soon into the pack you missed them. A backup method or emergency contraception may be necessary.

The following information is for women using a 21- or 28-day combination birth control pill.

Number of Pills Missed	When Pills Were Missed	What to Do	Use a Backup Method?
First 1–2 pills	Beginning of pack	• Take a pill as soon as you remember. • Take the next pill at usual time.	Yes
1–2 pills	Day 3 to 21	• Take the pill as soon as you remember. • Take the next pill at the usual time.	No
3 or more pills	First 2 weeks	• Take the pill as soon as you remember. • Take the next pill at the usual time.	Yes
3 or more pills	Third week	• Do not finish pack. • Start new pack.	Yes

SOURCE: Hatcher et al., 2007; Planned Parenthood, 2008 (http://www.plannedparenthood.org/health-topics/birth-control/if-forget-take-pill-19269.htm).

In most 28-day birth control pill packs, the last seven pills are **placebo pills.** They do not contain hormones, and because of this, a woman usually starts menstruating while taking them. Some health care providers have been advising women to shorten placebo intervals from 7 to 5 days, which has been found to reduce the pill's failure rate (Hatcher et al., 2007). In fact, some low-dose pill brands, such as Mircette, Yaz, and Loestrin, already use only a 2- or 4-day placebo pill regimen (Hatcher et al., 2007).

Women who take birth control pills usually have lighter menstrual periods because the pills decrease the buildup of the endometrium. Menstrual discomfort, such as cramping, is also reduced. Contraceptive pill users may also experience slight breast enlargement due to increases in estrogen. Research has found that 30% of women who take birth control pills experience increased breast size or breast tenderness (Hatcher et al., 2007).

Before starting on birth control pills, a woman must have a full medical examination. Women with a history of circulatory problems, strokes, heart disease, breast or uterine cancer, hypertension, diabetes, and undiagnosed vaginal bleeding are generally advised not to take oral contraceptives (Hatcher et al., 2007). Although migraine headaches have typically been a reason for not using birth control pills, some women may experience fewer migraines while using birth control pills, especially if used continuously without placebo pills (Hatcher et al., 2007). If a woman can use birth control pills, health care providers usually begin by prescribing a low-dose estrogen pill, and they increase the dosage if **breakthrough bleeding** or other symptoms occur.

Because the hormones in birth control pills are similar to those during pregnancy, it is not surprising that many women experience signs of pregnancy. These signs may include nausea, increase in breast size, breast tenderness, water retention, headaches, increased appetite, fatigue, depression, decreased sexual drive, and high blood pressure (Hatcher et al., 2007; see Chapter 12). Symptoms usually disappear within a couple of months, after a woman's body becomes used to the hormonal levels.

If a woman using the pill experiences abdominal pain, chest pain, severe headaches, vision or eye problems, and severe leg or calf pain, she should contact her health care provider immediately. In addition, a woman who takes birth control pills should always inform her health care provider of her oral contraceptive use, especially if she is prescribed other medications or undergoes any type of surgery. Certain drugs may have negative interactions with oral contraceptives (see the accompanying Sex in Real Life, "Drugs and Herbs That Interact With Oral Contraceptives").

Finally, as we discussed in Chapter 5, there has been a very vocal debate in recent years about whether oral contraceptive use increases a woman's risk of developing various cancers. Although the results of many studies are inconsistent, overall, research has found that birth control pills users may be at an increased risk for endometrial and ovarian cancers (Burkman et al., 2004; Emons et al., 2000; Greer et al., 2005; Modan et al., 2001; Schildkraut et al., 2002). However, birth control pill use has also been found to offer possible protection from other cancers, including breast and cervical cancers (Althuis et al., 2003; Deligeoroglou et al., 2003; Franceschi, 2005; Hatcher et al., 2007; Marchbanks et al., 2002; Moreno et al., 2002). These risks may be higher in women with a family history of cancer, who begin taking the pill in their teens,

Women who take birth control pills **have lighter menstrual periods.**

and who continue it for many years, although this research has not been consistent (National Cancer Institute, 2006). Other possible medical complications of the pill include increased risk of cardiovascular disease for certain women (Baillargeon et al., 2005; Hatcher et al., 2007), which is increased in women who smoke cigarettes (Bounhoure et al., 2008; Hatcher et al., 2007).

Effectiveness

Effectiveness rates for combination birth control pills range from 92% (typical use) to 99.7% (perfect use; Hatcher et al., 2007). To be effective, the pill must be taken every day, at the same time of day.

Advantages

If used correctly, oral contraceptives have one of the highest effectiveness rates; do not interfere with spontaneity; reduce the flow of menstruation, menstrual cramps, and premenstrual syndrome; increase menstrual regularity; and reduce the likelihood of ovarian cysts, uterine and breast fibroids, and facial acne (Hatcher et al., 2007). Oral contraceptives also provide important degrees of protection against ovarian and endometrial cancers, **pelvic inflammatory disease,** and benign breast disease (Hatcher et al., 2007). In addition, use of oral contraceptives may increase sexual enjoyment because fear of pregnancy is reduced and they are convenient and easy to use. The pill offers rapid reversibility, and the majority of women who go off the pill return to ovulation within 2 weeks (Hatcher et al., 2007).

Disadvantages

Oral contraceptives must be taken daily, offer no protection from STIs, and put all the responsibility for contraception on the female partner. They can be expensive, and their effectiveness is decreased when certain drugs and herbs are used (see nearby Sex in Real Life feature). In addition, they may contribute to increased risk of STIs because many birth control users tend to be poor users of condoms. Women who are overweight may experience lower effectiveness rates using oral contraceptives (Brunner-Huber & Toth, 2007; Hatcher et al., 2007). This may be because the hormones contained in birth control pills are fat-soluble and may be absorbed by fat and unable to enter the bloodstream (Gardner, 2004).

Another disadvantage of birth control pill use has always been that a medical examination including pelvic examination is necessary to get a prescription in the United States. However, research has found that these tests may not be medically necessary to evaluate whether a woman is an appropriate candidate for birth control pills (Alan Guttmacher Institute, 2004). Some clinics have been exploring prescribing birth control pills via the Internet after a phone consultation with a nurse practitioner (Alan Guttmacher Institute, 2004). In the next few years, a move away from medical evaluations may become more common (Hatcher et al., 2007).

placebo pills
In a pack of 28-day oral contraceptives, the seven pills at the end; these pills are sugar pills and do not contain any hormones; they are used to help a woman remember to take a pill every day.

breakthrough bleeding
Slight blood loss from the uterus that may occur when a woman is taking oral contraceptives.

pelvic inflammatory disease
Widespread infection of the female pelvic organs.

Drugs and Herbs That Interact With Oral Contraceptives

When you take medications, you should always let your health care provider know that you are taking birth control pills.

Many over-the-counter (nonprescription) drugs, prescription medications, and herbal supplements may lower the effectiveness of the pill. Birth control pills may also increase or decrease another drug's effectiveness. When you take medications, you should always let your health care provider know that you are taking birth control pills.

Drugs that interact with oral contraceptives include the following:

Drug	Effect
Acetaminophen (Tylenol)	Decreases effect of pain relief
Alcohol (beer, wine, mixed drinks, etc.)	Increases effect of alcohol
Anticoagulants (Heparin, Coumadin, aspirin)	Decreases anticoagulant effect (Aspirin may be less effective when used with oral contraceptives.)
Antibiotics (Amoxicillin, Tetracycline, Ampicillin)	May decrease effectiveness of oral contraceptives.
Antidepressants (Prozac, Paxil)	Increases blood levels of antidepressant
Antifungal medications (Grisactin)	Can cause breakthrough bleeding and spotting
Barbiturates (Seconal, Nembutal)	Decreases effectiveness of oral contraceptives
Vitamin C	May increase estrogen side effects in daily doses of 1,000 mg or more
St. John's wort (Hypericum)	Decreases effectiveness of oral contraceptives
Caffeine	May reduce caffeine metabolism

SOURCE: Hatcher et al., 2007.

Cross-Cultural Use

The use of birth control pills varies throughout the world (see Figure 13.8). In Great Britain, close to a quarter of reproductive-aged women use birth control pills (T. Taylor et al., 2006), and only 1% of women in Japan use them (Hayashi, 2004). By comparison, approximately 31% of reproductive-aged women in the United States use birth control pills (Alan Guttmacher Institute, 2008a).

Birth control pills are the most popular contraceptive option in many countries—including Australia, Argentina, Austria, Botswana, Brazil, Canada, Costa Rica, Cuba, Denmark, Finland, France, Germany, Hong Kong, Italy, Mexico, the Netherlands, Norway, Puerto Rico, Spain, Sweden, Switzerland, and the United Kingdom (Francoeur & Noonan, 2004). In certain countries, including Costa Rica, Hong Kong, and Mexico, birth control pills are available over-the-counter without a prescription (Arroba, 2004; Ng & Ma, 2004). In 2007, Great Britain announced that it would consider allowing women to get birth control pills through pharmacists or nurses, without a doctor's prescription (Ormsby, 2007).

Fears about safety and reliability issues in countries such as Japan and Russia reduce birth control pill use (Hayashi, 2004; Kon, 2004). Birth control pills were not approved for use in Japan until 1999. However, they have remained unpopular because of

REALResearch > Studies have found that the majority of side effects from birth control pill use, such as headaches, breast tenderness, or bloating, occur during the week when women take their placebo pills and not when they are taking their hormone pills (HATCHER ET AL., 2007; SULAK ET AL., 2000). This is one of the reasons pharmaceutical companies developed continuous-use birth control pills that reduce or eliminate menstrual periods.

WHAT DO YOU WANT TO KNOW?

Last week I lost my pack of birth control pills and did not have time to go to the student health center. My roommate let me take a few of her pills. Is this OK?

This is not a good idea. Because there are many types of pills with different levels of hormones in them, your roommate may not be taking the same kind of pill. Also, with the new triphasil pills, if you took someone else's pills and they were not the same, you could be at risk of getting pregnant. The best idea would be to make time to refill your own prescription and use another method of contraception until you start a new pack of pills.

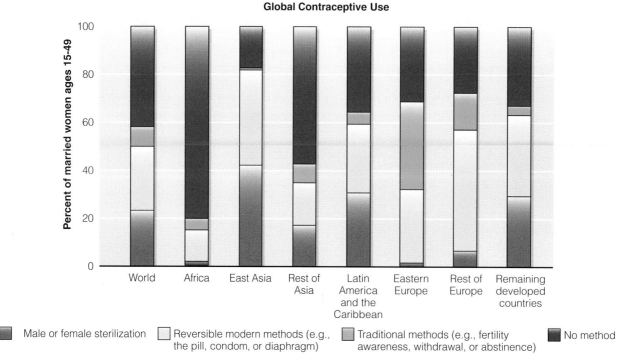

Global Contraceptive Use

Percent of married women ages 15-49

Legend:
- Male or female sterilization
- Reversible modern methods (e.g., the pill, condom, or diaphragm)
- Traditional methods (e.g., fertility awareness, withdrawal, or abstinence)
- No method

Categories: World, Africa, East Asia, Rest of Asia, Latin America and the Caribbean, Eastern Europe, Rest of Europe, Remaining developed countries

Figure **13.8** Women's choice of contraception method worldwide, in 1999. Source: The Alan Guttmacher Institute (AGI), *Sharing Responsibility: Women, Society, and Abortion Worldwide,* Chart 2.4, p. 15. Reproduced with permission.

safety concerns, negative side effects, required daily pill taking, countrywide conservatism, and a lack of advertising (prescription drugs cannot be advertised in Japan; Hayashi, 2004).

HORMONAL
RING

NuvaRing is a hormonal method of birth control that was approved by the FDA in 2001. It is a small plastic ring that is inserted into the vagina once a month and releases a constant dose of estrogen and progesterone. The amount of hormones released into the bloodstream with the NuvaRing is lower than in both oral contraceptives and the patch (we talk more about the patch later in this chapter; Hatcher et al., 2007; van den Heuvel et al., 2005). Each ring costs approximately $25 to $35 and requires a visit to a health care provider.

How It Works
Like birth control pills, NuvaRing works chiefly by inhibiting ovulation, but it is also likely to increase cervical mucus and changes the uterine lining (Hatcher et al., 2007). The ring is inserted deep inside the vagina, where the vaginal muscles hold it in place and moisture and body heat activate the release of hormones. Each ring is left in place for 3 weeks and then taken out for 1 week, during which a woman typically has her period. The used ring is disposed of and a new ring is put back in after the week break.

Although rare, the NuvaRing may fall out of the vagina during a bowel movement, tampon use, or sexual intercourse. If this happens and the ring has been out less than 3 hours, it should be washed and immediately be reinserted. If the ring falls out for more than 3 hours, a backup method of contraception should be used, because contraceptive effectiveness may be reduced.

Researchers continue to evaluate whether the NuvaRing can be used as continuous-use method, although it is not approved for this type of use at present (Hatcher et al., 2007; Mulders & Dieben, 2001). A longer use vaginal ring, that is continuously inserted after being removed for 1 week every month (unlike the shorter-use one that is disposed of after the 1-week break) is currently available outside the United States (Hatcher et al., 2007).

The NuvaRing is inserted deep into the vagina; moisture and heat cause it to time release hormones that inhibit ovulation.

NuvaRing
A small plastic contraceptive ring that is inserted into the vagina once a month and releases a constant dose of estrogen and progestin.

Effectiveness

Effectiveness rates for NuvaRing ranges from 92% (typical use) to 99.7% (perfect use; Hatcher et al., 2007). Effectiveness rates may be lower when other medications are taken, when the unopened package is exposed to high temperatures or direct sunlight, or when the ring is left in the vagina for more than 3 weeks.

Advantages

Like other hormonal methods of birth control, the NuvaRing has a high effectiveness rate; does not interfere with spontaneity; reduces the flow of menstruation, menstrual cramps, and premenstrual syndrome; and increases menstrual regularity (Hatcher et al., 2007). It is easy to use and provides lower levels of hormones than some of the other combined-hormone methods. In addition, NuvaRing may also offer some protection from ovarian and endometrial cancer and ovarian cysts (Hatcher et al., 2007). When a woman stops using NuvaRing, fertility is typically restored within 17 to 19 days after removing the last ring (Mulders et al., 2002).

Disadvantages

The NuvaRing offers no protection against STIs and may cause a variety of side effects, including breakthrough bleeding, weight gain or loss, breast tenderness, nausea, mood changes, headaches, decreased sexual desire, increased vaginal irritation and discharge, and a risk of toxic shock syndrome (Hatcher et al., 2007; Lopez et al., 2008). In addition, NuvaRing use requires an office visit and genital touching. Finally, because this method is new there are no data on extended use.

Cross-Cultural Use

NuvaRing was first approved in the Netherlands in 2001 and has since been approved by many other European countries. Australia approved the NuvaRing in 2007, which brought the total number of countries using NuvaRing to 32 ("NuvaRing now available," 2007). In some countries, usage levels may be low because the NuvaRing requires genital touching. Even so, cross-cultural research has found that the NuvaRing is highly effective, and users report high levels of satisfaction with this method (Brucker et al., 2008; Bruni et al., 2008; Merki-Feld & Hund, 2007; Novák et al., 2003).

HORMONAL PATCH

The **Ortho Evra patch** is a hormonal method of birth control that was approved by the FDA in 2001. It is a thin, peach-colored patch that sticks to the skin and time-releases hormones into the bloodstream. A 1-month supply of the Ortho Evra patch costs about $15 to $50 and must be prescribed by a health care provider.

How It Works

Like birth control pills and the NuvaRing, the Ortho Evra patch uses synthetic estrogen and progestin to inhibit ovulation, increase cervical mucus, and render the uterus inhospitable to implantation. The Ortho Evra patch is placed on the buttock, stom-ach, upper arm or torso (excluding the breast area) once a week for 3 weeks. No patch is used during the fourth week (break week), which usually causes a woman to have her period. A woman can maintain an active lifestyle with the patch in place—she can swim, shower, use saunas, and exercise without the patch falling off (Burkman, 2002; Zacur et al., 2002).

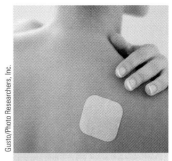

The Orth Evra patch is worn on the buttock, abdomen, or upper torso for 3 weeks each month.

Effectiveness

Effectiveness rates for the Ortho Evra patch are similar to NuvaRing and range from 92% (typical use) to 99.7% (perfect use; Hatcher et al., 2007) The Ortho Evra patch may be less effective in women who weigh more than 198 pounds (Hatcher et al., 2007; Zieman et al., 2002), and as with other hormonal methods, certain medications, such as antibiotic and seizure drugs, can decrease effectiveness.

Advantages

Like other hormonal methods of birth control, the Ortho Evra patch has a high effectiveness rate; does not interfere with spontaneity; reduces menstrual flow, menstrual cramps, and premenstrual syndrome; and increases menstrual regularity (Hatcher et al., 2007). In addition, the patch has a more than 90% perfect dosing level because it is applied to the skin (Burkman, 2002).

REALResearch > A study on the knowledge and beliefs about contraception in Latina women found that less than **50%** of Latinas perceived birth control pills to be safe and had high levels of uncertainty and negative beliefs about the patch, IUD, and hormonal injectables (Venkat et al., 2008). Compared with other ethnic groups, Latina women are more likely to overrate the risks associated with contraceptive use.

Disadvantages

The Ortho Evra patch has been found to expose women to higher levels of estrogen than typical birth control pills (Hitti, 2008; U.S. Food and Drug Administration, 2008), offers no protection from STIs, and may cause a variety of side effects, including breakthrough bleeding, breast tenderness, nausea, mood changes, changes in sexual desire, skin reactions, or headaches (Hatcher et al., 2007). Users of the hormonal patch may also be at risk for the development of blood clots (Hitti, 2008; Food and Drug Admin-

Ortho Evra patch
A thin, peach-colored patch that sticks to the skin and time releases synthetic estrogen and progestin into the bloodstream to inhibit ovulation, increase cervical mucus, and render the uterus inhospitable; also referred to as the "patch."

istration, 2008). Beginning in 2005, lawsuits were filed against the patch's manufacturer, Ortho McNeil, claiming the device caused strokes and blood clots. In 2008, the FDA approved revised labeling to include information about these risks (FDA, 2008). Any woman with a history or risk of blood clots should fully discuss their medical history with health care providers before using the Ortho Evra patch. Finally, because the patch is worn on the skin, it is nearly impossible to conceal, and it can collect fuzz and lint from the user's clothing. Because it is peach-colored, it is also readily apparent on darker skin.

Cross-Cultural Use

We don't know a lot about Ortho Evra's use outside the United States because it is so new. However, early estimates have found that approximately 2 million women worldwide use the contraceptive patch (Bestic, 2005).

review questions

1 Explain how combination hormonal methods of contraception work.

2 Identify three combined-hormonal contraceptive methods in order of their effectiveness rates.

3 What are extended-cycle birth control pills, and how do they work?

4 How have health care providers been using regular birth control pills for extended-cycle use?

5 Identify the advantages and disadvantages of combined-hormonal contraceptive methods.

6 What do we know about the cross-cultural usage of combined-hormone contraceptive methods?

Progestin-Only Hormone Methods for Women: Minipills, Implants, and Injectables

Progestin-only birth control methods are hormonal methods that do not contain estrogen. The methods can be used by women who cannot take estrogen or by women who are breast-feeding because the hormones do not affect the production of breast milk. Progestin-only birth control works by changing a woman's menstrual cycle, which may result in changes in menstrual flow and frequency of periods, as well as an increase in breakthrough bleeding. Over time, many users of progestin-only methods report having no periods at all.

PROGESTIN-ONLY
PILLS

Progestin-only pills (**minipills**) are similar to combination birth control pills, except they contain only a progestin hormone and no estrogen. Unlike combination birth control pills, however, minipills are taken every day with no hormone-free days (Hatcher et al., 2007).

How They Work

Similar to combination birth control pills, minipills work by inhibiting ovulation, thickening cervical mucus, and decreasing Fallopian tube cilia movement and the buildup of the endometrial lining.

Effectiveness

Effectiveness rates for minipills pills range from 92% (typical use) to 99.7% (perfect use; Hatcher et al., 2007). Minipills have always been thought to be less effective than combination birth control pills; however, effectiveness rates are similar to combination pills and failures are often due to user failures rather than method failures.

Advantages

Minipills contain a lower overall hormone level than combination birth control pills and can be safely used by almost all women (Hatcher et al., 2007). They may be safer for women who are older than 35, overweight, smoke, have high blood pressure, a history of blood clots, or women who are breast-feeding. Minipills reduce menstrual symptoms and may eliminate periods altogether. Once discontinued, fertility is quickly restored.

Disadvantages

Because minipills contain lower hormone levels, they require obsessive regularity in pill taking (Hatcher et al., 2007). They offer no protection from STIs and may cause several side effects, including menstrual cycle disturbances (such as breakthrough bleeding or spotting), headaches, nausea, weight gain or loss, breast tenderness, decreased sexual desire, and an increased risk of ovarian cysts (Hatcher et al., 2007). Because progestin affects cilia movement in the Fallopian tubes, women who get pregnant while taking minipills

progestin-only birth control method
Contraceptive hormonal method that does not contain estrogen and works by changing a woman's menstrual cycle.

minipills
A type of birth control pill that contains only synthetic progesterone and no estrogen.

have a higher rate of ectopic pregnancy compared with women taking combination birth control pills (see Chapter 12 for more information about ectopic pregnancy). Finally, minipills may be more difficult to find, because many pharmacies do not stock them.

SUBDERMAL IMPLANTS

Subdermal contraceptive implants are one or more thin tubes or rods that are implanted under the skin and time-release progestin. **Norplant** was the first such method introduced in the United States, in 1990. However, because of multiple lawsuits and court battles, Norplant was withdrawn from the U.S. market in 2002. As of 2008, the only implant available in the United States is a single-rod system called Implanon, which was approved by the FDA in 2006. The cost of Implanon and the insertion ranges from $400 to $800. Another implant, Jadelle, has been approved by the FDA but is not available in the United States at this time (Hatcher et al., 2007). Several other versions are in currently in development both within and outside the United States.

How They Work
The Implanon implant is about the size of a cardboard matchstick and is inserted under the skin of the upper arm during the first 7 days of a woman's menstrual cycle. Like other hormonal methods, it works by suppressing ovulation, thickening cervical mucus, and changing the endometrial lining. The Implanon implant can be left in place for 3 years.

Effectiveness
Subdermal implants are 99.5% effective and have no possibility of user error. However, effectiveness rates may be lower in women who weigh more than 154 pounds.

Advantages
Subdermal implants can be used by women who are unable to use oral contraceptives. They are a highly effective, long-lasting, easily reversible contraceptive method with a rapid onset of protection (Hatcher et al., 2007). Subdermal implants have no estrogen side effects and decrease menstrual flow, cramping, and risk of endometrial cancer. In addition, Implanon implants can be left in place for up to 3 years and can be removed anytime before this. Once removed, ovulation usually returns within 6 weeks (Makarainen et al., 1998).

Subdermal implants have **no possibility of user error.**

Disadvantages
Subdermal implants are relatively new, so we know little about any possible long-term problems with this method. They require a medical office visit to insert the implant, which may be expensive, depending on where it is done. Side effects may include irregular bleeding or other menstrual problems, headaches, dizziness, nausea, weight gain, the development of ovarian cysts, decreases in sexual desire, vaginal dryness, arm pain, and bleeding from the injection site (Hatcher et al., 2007). In the future, scientists hope to develop self-dissolving cylinders so that removal is unnecessary.

Cross-Cultural
Subdermal implants are approved in more than 60 countries and have been used by more than 11 million women worldwide (Hatcher et al., 2007; Meirik et al., 2003). Prior to U.S. FDA approval, Norplant and Implanon had been used throughout Europe, Latin America, Australia, and Asia. In addition, a Chinese version of Norplant has been used by women in China for many years.

HORMONAL INJECTABLES

The most commonly used hormonal injectable is depo-medroxy-progesterone acetate (DMPA, or **Depo-Provera;** DEP-poe PRO-vair-uh) which was approved by the FDA for contraceptive use in 2004 (Hatcher et al., 2007). Depo-Provera is injected once every 3 months, and each injection costs anywhere from $35 to $70.

How It Works
Depo-Provera is injected into the muscle of a woman's arm or buttock and begins working within 24 hours. Like other hormonal methods, it works by suppressing ovulation, thickening cervical mucus, and changing the endometrial lining.

Effectiveness
Effectiveness rates for Depo-Provera range from 97% (typical use) to 99.7% (perfect use; Hatcher et al., 2007).

Advantages
Depo-Provera does not contain estrogen, lasts for 3 months, is only moderately expensive, is reversible, and does not restrict spontaneity (Hatcher et al., 2007). Users of Depo-Provera often notice decreased cramping and pain during menstruation and lighter or absent menstrual periods.

Disadvantages
Women who use Depo-Provera must schedule office visits every 3 months for their injections and experience a range of side effects, including irregular bleeding and spotting, fatigue, dizzy spells, weakness, headaches or migraines, weight gain (it is estimated that a woman will gain an average of 5.4 pounds in the first year of Depo use), and a decrease in bone density (Hatcher et al., 2007). More recent studies have found that bone loss is reversible after a woman stops using Depo-Provera (Kaunitz et al., 2008; Pitts & Emans, 2008). In addition, fertility may not be restored for 9 to 10 months after the last injection (Hatcher et al., 2007; Kaunitz et al., 1998).

subdermal contraceptive implant
Contraceptive implant that time releases a constant dose of progestin to inhibit ovulation.

Norplant
A hormonal method of birth control using doses that are implanted in a woman's arm and that can remain in place for up to 5 years.

Depo-Provera
Depo-medroxyprogesterone, an injectable contraceptive that prevents ovulation and thickens cervical mucus.

Cross-Cultural Use

Depo-Provera has been approved for use in more than 80 countries, including Botswana, Denmark, Finland, Great Britain, France, Sweden, Mexico, Norway, Germany, New Zealand, South Africa, and Belgium (Francoeur & Noonan, 2004; Hatcher et al., 2004). In addition, another combination injectable, Lunelle, is popular cross-culturally but is not available within the United States.

review questions

1 Explain how minipills differ from combined-hormone birth control pills.

2 Explain how minipills, subdermal implants, and hormonal injectables work to prevent pregnancy.

3 Identify the advantages and disadvantages of each of the progestin-only hormone methods.

4 What do we know about the cross-cultural usage of progestin-only hormone methods?

Chemical Methods for Women: Spermicides

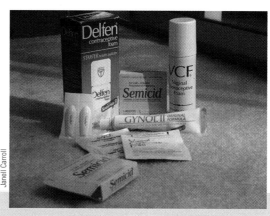

Spermicides are chemical methods of contraception, available without a prescription.

Spermicides come in a variety of forms, including creams, suppositories, gels, foams, foaming tablets, capsules, and films. They are relatively inexpensive and available without a prescription. Nonoxynol-9 is a spermicide that has been used for many years. It is available over-the-counter in many forms (creams, gels, suppositories, film, and condoms with spermicide) and can be used alone or in conjunction with another contraceptive method. However, as you saw from the earlier Sex in Real Life feature, there has been some controversy surrounding the use of nonoxynol-9. Today in the United States, the cost for most spermicides ranges from $5 to $10. They are generally less expensive in clinics.

HOW THEY WORK

Spermicides contain two components: one is an inert base such as jelly, cream, foam, or film that holds the spermicide close to the cervix; the second is the spermicide itself. Foam, jelly, cream, and film are usually inserted into the vagina with either an applicator or a finger. **Vaginal contraceptive film** contains nonoxynol-9 and comes in packages of 12. To use, the film is wrapped around the index finger and inserted into the vagina.

Suppositories are inserted in the vagina 10 to 30 minutes before intercourse to allow time for the outer covering to melt. It is important to read manufacturer's directions for spermicide use carefully. Douching and tampon use should be avoided for 6 to 8 hours following the use of spermicides because they interfere with effectiveness rates.

EFFECTIVENESS

Effectiveness rates for spermicides range from 71% (typical use) to 82% (perfect use). However, effectiveness depends on how correctly and consistently a spermicide is used. Overall, foam is more effective than jelly, cream, film, or suppositories. However, the most successful type of spermicide is one that a couple feels comfortable with and uses consistently.

spermicide
Chemical method of contraception, including creams, gels, foams, suppositories, and films, that works to reduce the survival of sperm in the vagina.

vaginal contraceptive film
Spermicidal contraceptive film that is placed in the vagina.

ADVANTAGES

Spermicides are easy to get and can be purchased over-the-counter. They can easily be carried in one's pocket or purse, do not interfere with a woman's hormones, and can be used by a woman who is breast-feeding. In addition, spermicides can be inserted during foreplay, provide lubrication during intercourse, and have minimal side effects.

DISADVANTAGES

Spermicides must be used each time a couple engages in sexual intercourse, which may be expensive depending on frequency of intercourse. In addition, there is an increase in postcoital drip and some couples may be allergic or have adverse reactions. Spermicides often have an unpleasant taste, and they may cause vaginal skin irritations or an increase in urinary tract infections (Hatcher et al., 2007).

CROSS-CULTURAL USE

Spermicides are widely used in some countries, including Argentina, Australia, Colombia, Costa Rica, Cuba, and many European and Scandinavian countries (Francoeur & Noonan, 2004). However, in many other countries, including Botswana, Brazil, Canada, China, Hong Kong, Japan, Kenya, and Puerto Rico, spermicides are not widely used, probably because of the relatively high cost or required genital touching.

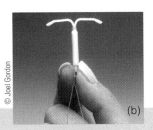

(a) The Copper T is a T-shaped IUD made of flexible plastic; it contains copper and can be left in place for up to 12 years. (b) The Mirena is a T-shaped IUD made of flexible plastic; it continuously releases a small amount of progestin and can be left in place for up to 5 years.

review questions

1 Identify the various forms of spermicidal contraception.

2 What are some of the risks and controversies surrounding the use of nonoxynol-9 spermicide?

3 Explain how spermicides work and discuss effectiveness rates.

4 Identify the advantages and disadvantages of spermidical contraceptive use.

Intrauterine Methods for Women:
Paragards and Mirenas

An **intrauterine device (IUD)** is a small device made of flexible plastic that is placed in the uterus to prevent pregnancy (see Figure 13.9). The Dalkon Shield was a popular type of IUD up until 1975, when the A. H. Robins Company recommended that it be removed from all women who were using them. At that time, users experienced many problems, including severe pain, bleeding, and pelvic inflammatory disease, which even led to sterility in some cases. The problems with the Dalkon Shield were primarily caused by the multifilament string that allowed bacteria to enter into the uterus through the cervix.

As of 2008, there were only two IUDs available in the United States, the ParaGard Copper T and the Mirena. In the United States, the cost for an IUD can range from $150 to $300 and requires an office visit for insertion.

intrauterine device (IUD)
Small, plastic contraceptive device that is inserted into a woman's uterus.

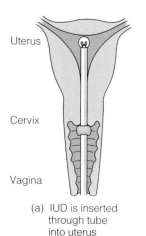 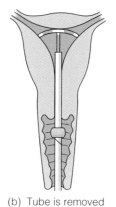 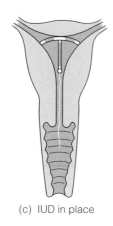

Uterus

Cervix

Vagina

(a) IUD is inserted through tube into uterus

(b) Tube is removed

(c) IUD in place

Figure **13.9** Insertion of an IUD.

ADVANTAGES

IUDs are the least expensive method of contraception over time, and they do not interfere with spontaneity. In addition, they have long-lasting contraceptive effects. In addition, the Mirena IUD reduces or eliminates menstrual flow and cramping. IUDs can also be used as emergency contraception (we discuss emergency contraception later in this chapter). Once the IUD is removed, fertility is quickly restored.

DISADVANTAGES

IUDs require moderately painful insertion and removal procedures, may cause irregular bleeding patterns and spotting (and heavier periods if using the ParaGard IUD), offer no STI protection, and carry a small risk of uterine perforation. The IUD may also be felt by a sexual partner.

CROSS-CULTURAL USE

Worldwide, the IUD is the most commonly used reversible contraceptive method (Hatcher et al., 2007). Whereas an estimated 2% of women in the United States use IUDs, 6% of women in the United Kingdom and 20% of women in France use them (Trussell & Wynn, 2008). In many countries, such as Turkey, China, Nigeria, England, Russia, and Korea, the IUD is the most frequently used form of contraception (Francoeur & Noonan, 2004). The Mirena IUD has been available in Europe for more than 10 years, and it is estimated that at least 3 million women have used it throughout the world. In some countries, including China, Mexico, and Egypt, IUDs are inserted directly after the delivery of a baby (Grimes, 2004). Other countries with high IUD usage include Cuba, Finland, Turkey, Nepal, and the United Kingdom. Low usage has been reported in countries such as Hong Kong, Korea, Ireland, Israel, Japan, and Kenya (Grimes, 2004). Overall, usage rates may vary based on how much the device is marketed in certain countries. For example, a media campaign in Turkey led to a 30% increase in IUD use (Trieman et al., 1995).

GyneFix, an IUD containing a flexible row of copper beads instead of a rigid plastic frame like other IUDs, has been used for many years in countries such as China, Latin America, Asia, and Africa. It is currently awaiting FDA approval in the United States.

HOW THEY WORK

The ParaGard Copper T IUD is placed in the uterus and causes an increase in copper ions and enzymes, which impairs sperm function and prevents fertilization (Hatcher et al., 2007). It can be left in place for up to 12 years. The Mirena IUD time releases progestin, which thickens the cervical mucus, inhibits sperm survival, and suppresses the endometrium (Hatcher et al., 2007). It can be left in place for up to 5 years. The IUD string hangs down from the cervix, and a woman can check the string to make sure the IUD is still properly in place. Both IUDs may also interfere with the implantation of a fertilized ova.

EFFECTIVENESS

IUDs provide some of the highest overall effectiveness rates, ranging from 99.2% to 99.9% (Hatcher et al., 2007). Effectiveness also depends on the age of the woman and her past pregnancy history. A woman who has never been pregnant is more likely to expel the IUD through her cervix.

review questions

1 What is an IUD, and how does it work to prevent pregnancy?

2 How effective is the IUD, and what factors are important in determining effectiveness rates?

3 Identify some of the advantages and disadvantages of IUD use.

4 Are IUDs popular outside the United States? Explain.

Natural Methods
for Women and Men

Natural methods of contraception do not alter any physiological function. They include natural family planning and **fertility awareness,** withdrawal, and abstinence.

▌FERTILITY AWARENESS–BASED METHODS

Fertility awareness–based methods involve identifying a woman's fertile period and either abstaining from sexual intercourse or using another contraceptive method during this time. With the **rhythm method,** a couple simply keeps track of a woman's cycle; other, more intensive methods involve charting and recording physical fertility signs (such as monitoring daily **basal body temperature (BBT)** and checking cervical mucus; Hatcher et al., 2007). Typically these intensive methods are referred to as **natural family planning** (**NFP,** or the **symptothermal method**).

How They Work
With the symptothermal method, a woman takes her BBT every morning before she gets out of bed and records it on a basal body temperature chart. Changes in hormonal levels cause body temperature to rise 0.4° to 0.8°F (0.2°–0.4°C) immediately before ovulation, and it remains elevated until menstruation begins. A woman using this method monitors her cervical mucus, which becomes thin and stretchy during ovulation to help transport sperm. At other times of the month, cervical mucus is thicker. After 6 months of consistent charting, a woman will be able to estimate the approximate time of ovulation, and she can then either abstain from sexual intercourse or use contraception during her high-risk times (usually this period is between 1 and 2 weeks).

Effectiveness
Effectiveness rates for fertility awareness–based methods depend on the accuracy of identifying a fertile period and a couple's ability to avoid intercourse (or use another contraceptive method) during this time. Typical effectiveness rates for these methods range from 97% for symptothermal method to 88% for the rhythm method (Hatcher et al., 2007).

Advantages
Fertility awareness–based methods are an acceptable form of birth control for those who cannot use another method for religious reasons. They can teach couples about the menstrual cycle, are inexpensive, may encourage couples to communicate more about contraception, can involve the male partner, and have no medical side effects. This method can also be helpful when a women is ready to get pregnant because she may be familiar with when she is ovulating. Couples who use these methods often use a variety of sexual expressions when they avoid intercourse during the fertile period.

Disadvantages
Fertility awareness–based methods provide no protection from STIs and restrict spontaneity. In addition, they take time and commitment to learn and require several cycles of records before they can be used reliably. The majority of failures with this method are due to couples engaging in intercourse too close to ovulation. A woman may ovulate earlier or later than usual because of diet, stress, or alcohol use. These methods are often best suited for those needing to space pregnancies, rather than for those who want to avoid pregnancy.

Cross-Cultural Use
What makes fertility awareness–based methods so popular in many areas outside the United States is the fact that it is inexpensive and involves little assistance from health care providers. In addition, these methods may also be the only form of acceptable contraception in Catholic countries such as Ireland, Brazil, and the Philippines. In the Philippines, natural family planning and the rhythm method are thought to improve a couple's relationship because they need to work together to use the method (Leyson, 2004). Societal issues and marketing may also affect the use of this

Darin Derstine

Women using fertility awareness based methods may use CycleBeads to help determine fertile days. To use CycleBeads, a woman moves a ring over a series of color-coded beads that represent her fertile and low-fertility days. The color of the beads lets her know whether she is on a day when she is likely to be fertile.

fertility awareness
Basal body temperature charting used in conjunction with another method of contraception.

fertility awareness–based methods
Contraceptive or family planning method that involves identifying a fertile period in a woman's cycle and either avoiding intercourse or using contraception during this time.

rhythm method
A contraceptive method that involves calculating the period of ovulation and avoiding sexual intercourse around this time.

basal body temperature (BBT)
The body's resting temperature used to calculate ovulation in the symptothermal method of contraception.

natural family planning (NFP)
A contraceptive method that involves calculating ovulation and avoiding sexual intercourse during ovulation and at other unsafe times.

symptothermal method
A contraceptive method that involves monitoring both cervical mucus and basal body temperature to determine ovulation.

method. For example, cultural resistance to condom use has increased the popularity of these methods in Kenya, where it is the most commonly used contraceptive method (Brockman, 2004). Today, many women's groups from the United States travel to developing countries to teach fertility awareness–based methods.

WITHDRAWAL

Withdrawal, or **coitus interruptus,** involves withdrawing the penis from the vagina before ejaculation. Although the National Survey of Family Growth (NSFG; see Chapter 2) estimated that only 2.9% of their sample used withdrawal as their primary contraceptive method, most researchers believe this was underestimated (Kowal, 2004b). When the NSFG study asked sexually active women if they had ever used withdrawal, 56% said yes (Hatcher et al., 2007). Withdrawal can be used in conjunction with another contraceptive method.

How It Works

Withdrawal does not require any advance preparation. A couple engages in sexual intercourse; prior to ejaculation, the male withdraws his penis away from the vaginal opening of the woman. The ejaculate does not enter the vagina.

Effectiveness

The effectiveness of this method depends on a man's ability to withdraw his penis prior to ejaculation (Hatcher et al., 2007). Effectiveness rates range from 73% (typical use) to 96% (perfect use). Originally, scientists believed that high failure rates with this method were due to sperm contained in the pre-ejaculatory fluid. However, although newer research suggests that pre-ejaculatory fluid has no sperm in it, pregnancy can still occur if sperm remains in the urethra from a previous ejaculation (Kowal, 2004b).

Advantages

Withdrawal is another acceptable method of birth control for those who cannot use another method for religious reasons. In addition, it may be a good method for couples who do not mind becoming pregnant, is free, doesn't require any devices or chemicals, and is better than using no method at all (Hatcher et al., 2007).

Disadvantages

Withdrawal provides no protection from STIs, may contribute to ejaculatory problems, and can be difficult and stressful to use. Many men experience a mild to extreme "clouding of consciousness" just before orgasm when physical movements become involuntary (Hatcher et al., 2007). This method also requires trust from the female partner.

Cross-Cultural Use

Withdrawal is a popular contraceptive method throughout the world. It is one of the most frequently used methods in Austria, the Czech Republic, Greece, Ireland, and Italy (Francoeur & Noonan, 2004). In the Czech Republic, more than 40% of women report using withdrawal as their contraceptive method (Zverina, 2004). Overall, it is a popular contraceptive method for couples with limited contraceptive choices or for those who are reluctant to use modern methods of contraception. In other countries, such as Germany, withdrawal remains very unpopular.

ABSTINENCE

Abstinence (or not engaging in sexual intercourse at all) is the only 100% effective contraceptive method (Hatcher et al., 2007). It has probably been the most important factor in controlling fertility throughout history. Abstinence may be primary (never having engaged in sexual intercourse) or secondary (not currently engaging in sexual intercourse). Couples may choose abstinence to prevent pregnancy, to protect against STIs, or for many other reasons (see Chapter 10 for more information about abstinence).

coitus interruptus
A contraceptive method involving withdrawal of the penis from the vagina prior to ejaculation.

review questions

1 Differentiate between the various types of fertility awareness–based methods. What factors influence the effectiveness rates of these methods?

2 Explain how changes in cervical mucus and body temperature provide information about ovulation.

3 Explain the use and effectiveness of withdrawal as a contraceptive method.

4 Identify the advantages and disadvantages of natural contraceptive methods.

5 Explain the cross-cultural use of natural contraceptive methods.

Permanent (Surgical) Methods

Male and female **sterilization** methods are the most commonly used contraceptive methods in the United States (Hatcher et al., 2007). The NSFG (see Chapter 2) reported that 28% of all women aged 15 to 44 years who were using contraception relied on tubal sterilization, whereas 9% relied on a partner's vasectomy (Abma et al., 1997; Hatcher et al., 2007; see Figure 13.3 for more information about sterilization statistics).

The primary difference between sterilization and other methods of contraception is that sterilization is typically considered irreversible. Although some people have been able to have their sterilizations reversed, this can be expensive and time-consuming (Peterson, 2008). The majority of people who request sterilization reversals do so because they have remarried and desire children with their new partners.

FEMALE STERILIZATION

Female sterilization, or **tubal sterilization** (also referred to as "getting one's tubes tied"), is the most widely used method of birth control in the world (Hatcher et al., 2007). In a tubal sterilization, a health care provider may sever or block both Fallopian tubes so that the ovum and sperm can not meet. Blocking the tubes can be done with **cauterization;** a ring, band, or clamp (which pinches the tube together); or **ligation.** In 2002, the U.S. FDA approved the Essure microimplant for tubal sterilization (we discuss this more later in this section), and in 2008 FDA approval was pending for Adiana, a female sterilization procedure that permanently blocks the Fallopian tubes by using radio signals to create Fallopian tube blockage.

In the United States, female sterilization procedures are performed in a hospital under general anesthesia. The sterilization procedure is generally done with the use of a **laparoscope** through a small incision either under the navel or lower in the abdomen. After the procedure, a woman continues to ovulate, but the ovum does not enter the uterus. The costs for female sterilization vary but generally range from $2,000 to $5,000.

In 2002, the FDA approved Essure, the first nonsurgical sterilization method for women. Essure is a tiny, springlike device that is threaded into the Fallopian tubes (see Figure 13.10). This creates tissue growth around the device, which blocks fertilization. Generally this process takes 3 months from the time Essure is placed in the tubes, so it doesn't offer immediate birth control. A woman using this method must undergo testing to make sure that the Fallopian tubes are fully blocked. Although other sterilization procedures may have the possibility of being reversed, placement of Essure is considered an irreversible method of female sterilization (Hatcher et al., 2007; Ledger, 2004).

As with any other surgery, potential risks exist. A woman may feel side effects from the anesthesia or experience bleeding, infection, or possible injury to other organs during the procedure. In a few cases, the surgery is unsuccessful and must be repeated.

Overall, the majority of women who choose permanent sterilization are content with their decision to do so (although the risk for regret is highest in women who undergo these procedures before age 30; Jamieson et al., 2002; Peterson, 2008). In addition, studies on sexual functioning after tubal sterilization have found that women maintain their levels of sexual interest and desire and have more positive than negative sexual effects (Costello et al., 2002). In addition, tubal sterilization has been found to substantially reduce the risk of ovarian cancer, because the blood supply to the ovaries is decreased (Hatcher et al., 2007; Kjaer et al., 2004).

MALE STERILIZATION

Male sterilization, or **vasectomy,** blocks the flow of sperm through the vas deferens (see Chapter 6). Typically, this procedure is simpler, less expensive, and safer than a tubal sterilization (Hatcher et al., 2007; Peterson, 2008). After a vasectomy, the testes continue to produce viable sperm cells, but with nowhere to go, they die and are absorbed by the body. Semen normally contains approximately 98% fluid and 2% sperm, and after a vasectomy, the man still ejaculates semen, but the semen contains no sperm (there is no overall change in volume or texture of the semen after a vasectomy). All other functions, such as the manufacturing of testosterone, erections, and urination, are unaffected by a vasectomy procedure.

The surgery for a vasectomy is performed as **outpatient surgery** with local anesthesia. Two small incisions about a quarter to

REALResearch **>** Although vasectomies were once thought to increase the risk of heart disease, prostate, and testicular cancer, newer research does not support this association (PETERSON, 2008). In addition, vasectomy is less likely than female sterilization procedures to result in serious complications.

sterilization
Surgical contraceptive method that causes permanent infertility.

tubal sterilization
A surgical procedure in which the Fallopian tubes are cut, tied, or cauterized, for permanent contraception.

cauterization
A sterilization procedure that involves burning or searing the Fallopian tubes or vas deferens for permanent sterilization.

ligation
A sterilization procedure that involves the tying or binding of the Fallopian tubes or vas deferens.

laparoscope
A tiny scope that can be inserted through the skin and allows for the viewing of the uterine cavity.

vasectomy
A surgical procedure in which each vas deferens is cut, tied, or cauterized, for permanent contraception.

outpatient surgery
Surgery performed in the hospital or doctor's office, after which a patient is allowed to return home; inpatient surgery requires hospitalization.

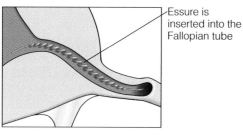
Essure is inserted into the Fallopian tube

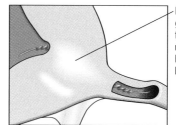
Body tissue grows into the Essure micro-insert, blocking the Fallopian tube

Figure **13.10** Essure is a permanent method of contraception.

a half inch long are made in the scrotum, and the vas deferens is clipped or cauterized, which usually takes approximately 20 minutes (see Figure 13.11). Men are advised to use another form of contraception for 12 weeks following a vasectomy to ensure that there is no sperm left in the ejaculate (Hatcher et al., 2007). Typically, one or two repeat semen analyses are required to evaluate whether there is viable sperm in the sample. However, 35% of men who have vasectomies never return for their first semen analysis, and 70% do not return for their second analysis ("ContraVac," 2008). In 2008, the FDA approved a post-vasectomy home sperm test called SpermCheck, which would enable a man to test his semen sample at home rather than returning to a medical facility ("ContraVac," 2008).

After a vasectomy, a man may experience swelling, bleeding, bruising, or pain but generally these subside within 2 weeks (Hatcher et al., 2007). Although there has been some controversy over whether vasectomies increase a man's risk for prostate cancer, this has not been supported by research (B. Cox et al., 2002; Lynge, 2002). The cost for the procedure varies widely, depending on where it is done. Overall, the cost for a vasectomy ranges from $300 to $1,000.

Effectiveness
Effectiveness for both male and female sterilization procedures ranges from 99% to 99.9% (Hatcher et al., 2007). Tubal sterilizations are effective immediately, whereas vasectomies require semen analysis for 12 weeks after the procedure to ensure no viable sperm remains.

Advantages
Sterilization is a highly effective permanent method of contraception. It offers a quick recovery, few long-term side effects, and, once completed, does not interfere with spontaneity (Peterson, 2008).

Disadvantages
Sterilization requires surgery, can be expensive, provides no protection from STIs, and is considered irreversible.

Cross-Cultural Use
Worldwide, sterilization is used by more people than any other contraceptive method (Peterson, 2008). Although most female sterilizations in the United States are done in a hospital, elsewhere these procedures are often outpatient procedures using local anesthesia (Hatcher et al., 2007).

In Brazil, sterilization is a popular choice in midlife, with more than 42% of women undergoing surgical sterilization (de Freitas, 2004). Sterilization procedures are also common in Australia, Canada, China, Colombia, and Cuba (Francoeur & Noonan, 2004). The Essure method has been used outside the United States in many countries in Europe, Mexico, Brazil, Venezuela, Chile and Uruguay.

In countries where family planning clinics are sparse, many women travel long distances to be sterilized. As we have discussed, access to and promotion of a certain method also contribute to its popularity. In many countries, sterilization is the only method of nonnatural contraception available.

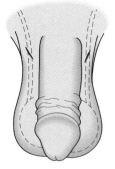
(a) Possible incision sites

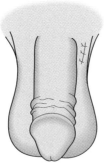
(b) Incision on one side of the testicle and right and left vas are cut

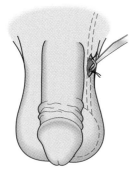
(c) Incision closed

Figure **13.11** In a vasectomy, each vas deferens is clipped, cut, or cauterized.

REALResearch **>** In some countries, unique strategies have been designed to increase vasectomies. For example, in one overpopulated, high-crime area of central India, fast-tracked gun licenses are offered in exchange for a vasectomy (BLAKELY, 2008). This strategy has apparently paid off: A total of **139** men underwent vasectomies in the first month, compared with only **8** in 2007 (BLAKELY, 2008).

1 Identify the two main differences between sterilization and other contraceptive methods.

2 Explain some of the procedures used for female sterilization.

3 Explain some of the procedures used for male sterilization.

4 What are the advantages and disadvantages of sterilization as a contraceptive method?

5 Is sterilization a popular contraceptive method outside the United States? Explain.

Ineffective Methods and Emergency Contraception

Many couples use ineffective methods in an attempt to avoid pregnancy, and some experience unplanned pregnancies. Emergency contraception can be used when a couple fails to use contraception or uses ineffective methods.

UNRELIABLE BIRTH CONTROL

Sometimes couples rely on methods of contraception that are ineffective. They may keep their fingers crossed, hoping that they won't get pregnant. Two of the most common ineffective methods that some couples rely on include douching and breast-feeding.

Douching
Douching involves using a syringe-type instrument to inject a stream of water (which may be mixed with other chemicals) into the vagina (see Chapter 5 for more information about douching). In the mid-1800s, douching was actually recommended by physicians as a contraceptive. However, by the time a woman gets up to douche after intercourse, most of the sperm are already up in her cervix (Cates & Raymond, 2004). Many health care providers recommend that women don't douche at all because it has been found to increase the risk of pelvic infections and STIs.

Breast-Feeding
The **lactational amenorrhea method (LAM)** is a method of avoiding pregnancies based on the postpartum infertility that many women experience when they are breast-feeding (Hatcher et al., 2007). During breast-feeding, the cyclic ovarian hormones are typically suspended which may inhibit ovulation. However, this is not an effective contraceptive method, because ovulation may still occur (Hatcher et al., 2007). Even so, LAM has been practiced throughout the world and has played a role in reducing fertility (see Chapter 12 for more information about breast-feeding; S. Becker et al., 2003).

EMERGENCY CONTRACEPTION

Emergency contraception (EC; also referred to as "morning after" contraception, or ECPs—emergency contraceptive pills) can prevent pregnancy when taken shortly after unprotected vaginal intercourse. It is designed to be used in cases when no contraception was used, contraception was used improperly (such as missed or delayed birth control pills, hormonal injections, replacement vaginal rings or patches), a male condom slipped or broke, a female condom or barrier device was improperly inserted or dislodged during intercourse, an IUD was expelled, or forced sex occurred (Hatcher et al., 2007). The typical user of emergency contraception is single, educated, without children, and between the ages of 15 and 25 (Phipps et al., 2008).

As of 2008, Plan B, a progestin-only method, is the only dedicated emergency contraception available in the United States. The U.S. FDA approved Plan B as an over-the-counter contraception option in women over age 18 in 2006 (FDA, 2006; Kavanaugh & Schwarz, 2008). Concerns about Plan B being available without a prescription have raised fears about increased sexual risk taking in women. However, research has shown this is not the case—having available emergency contraception has not been found to increase sexual risk taking (M. Gold et al., 2004; Hu et al., 2005; Raymond et al., 2006).

Other options for emergency contraception include the use of ordinary combination and progestin-only birth control pills or the insertion of a copper-releasing IUD (Hatcher et al., 2007; Jensen, 2008). ECPs containing estrogen and progestin work by inhibiting or delaying ovulation, making the endometrium less hospitable for implantation of an embryo, thickening the cervical mucus, altering the transportability of the Fallopian tubes, and inhibiting fertilization (Hatcher et al., 2007). ECPs that contain only progestin impair the ovulatory process but may also interfere with sperm functioning in the female reproductive tract (Hatcher

lactational amenorrhea method (LAM)
A method of avoiding pregnancies based on the postpartum infertility that many women experience when they are breast-feeding.

emergency contraception (EC)
Contraception that is designed to prevent pregnancy after unprotected vaginal intercourse.

et al., 2007). ECPs do not interfere with an existing pregnancy; if a woman is already pregnant, taking ECPs will not cause an abortion (we talk more about abortion later in this chapter).

Women who use Plan B typically take two pills, and women who use ECPs may take several at two times. To be effective, emergency contraception should be started within 72 hours of unprotected intercourse, although there is some evidence that it may be effective up until 120 hours (Ellertson et al., 2003; Hatcher et al., 2007; Ngai et al., 2004). A copper-releasing IUD should be inserted within 5 days after unprotected intercourse. The IUD insertion method is used much less frequently than ECPs, mainly because women who need emergency treatment often are not appropriate IUD candidates (F. Stewart et al., 2004). When started within 3 days after unprotected intercourse, Plan B reduces the risk of pregnancy by 89%, whereas ECPs reduce the risk by 75%. A copper-releasing IUD inserted within 5 days reduces the risk of pregnancy by 99%. Emergency hormonal contraception costs vary anywhere from $10 to $45, depending on where it is purchased.

Hormonal emergency contraception methods have several side effects, including nausea, vomiting, cramping, breast tenderness, headaches, abdominal pain, fatigue, and dizziness (Hatcher et al., 2007). The incidence of nausea and vomiting is significantly lower in women who use progestin EC methods, such as Plan B (Hatcher et al., 2007). Women who take ECPs are often advised to take antinausea medicine, such as Dramamine, before taking their ECPs. Side effects for emergency insertion of a copper-releasing IUD include abdominal discomfort and vaginal bleeding or spotting (Hatcher et al., 2007).

Emergency contraception has been available in many countries throughout the world. ECPs are available in Australia, Belgium, Canada, China, Denmark, Finland, France, Greece, Iceland, India, Israel, Jamaica, Libya, New Zealand, the Netherlands, Norway, Portugal, Senegal, South Africa, Sri Lanka, Sweden, Switzerland, Tunisia, the United Kingdom, and many other countries. They can be purchased without a prescription in France (since 1999), Norway (since 2000), Sweden (since 2001), the Netherlands (since 2004), and India (since 2005), and in France they are free of charge.

review questions

1 Explain why douching is an ineffective contraceptive method.

2 Explain why breast-feeding may not offer contraceptive effectiveness.

3 Identify some of the reasons why a woman might use emergency contraception and explain how it works.

4 How soon does a woman need to take emergency contraception to have it be effective?

5 Identify some of the side effects of emergency contraception.

Contraception in the Future

Although many pregnancies occur because couples used no contraception, it is estimated that half of all unintended pregnancies occur because of contraceptive failures (Hatcher et al., 2007). Researchers and scientists today continue to look for effective contraceptive methods that are easy to use and have few or no side effects. A consistent concern has been finding a method that can offer high effectiveness rates along with STI protection (Hatcher et al., 2007).

WHAT'S AHEAD
FOR MEN

Historically, birth control has been considered a female's responsibility, and that may be why the condom and vasectomy are the only birth control methods available to men. Many feminists claim that the lack of research into male methods of birth control has to do with the fact that birth control research is done primarily by men. As a result, women are responsible for using birth control and must suffer through the potential side effects.

Others claim that there are few male methods because it is easier to block the one ovum women produce each month than the millions of sperm in each ejaculation. Other arguments cite the fact that chemical contraception may decrease testosterone production, reduce the male sex drive, and harm future sperm production.

As of 2008, research into male contraception continued to explore chemical and hormonal contraception, reversible vasectomies, vas deferens plugs, and vaccines. **Gossypol,** a nonhormonal agent derived from cottonseed oil, has been used for years in China and reduces sperm production without changing testosterone levels (Hatcher et al., 2007; Song et al., 2006). Anticancer drugs, such as Lonidamine, are also being studied for their ability to reduce sperm production. In Britain, researchers continue to explore the development of a male pill that inhibits male ejaculation, causing an orgasm without ejaculation, or "dry orgasm" (Dawar, 2006).

gossypol
An ingredient in cottonseed oil that, when injected or implanted, may inhibit sperm production.

Contraceptive research is also evaluating the use of hormonal implants and injections for men. Subdermal implants are placed under the skin, and testosterone injections are used to suppress pituitary hormones responsible for spermatogenesis. The first large placebo-controlled study using these methods found successful reductions in sperm production (Mommers et al., 2008). This method was well tolerated by the men in the study, and sperm production was back to normal levels within 15 weeks of discontinuing the method.

Another injectable implant, RISUG (reversible inhibition of sperm under guidance), is also being studied. RISUG has passed both Phase I and II trials in India (Chaudhury et al., 2004). It is injected into the vas deferens where it blocks the passage of sperm. Ongoing research will determine whether this will be a viable contraceptive option for men. Other implants, such as the Intra-Vas Device, are also being studied (Crawford, 2008).

Finally, scientists are evaluating contraceptive vaccines (called **immunocontraceptives**) that would cause infertility until pregnancy is desired (F. Stewart & Gabelnick, 2004). Vaccines could suppress testicular function and eliminate sperm and testosterone production. Unfortunately, vaccines such as these would effectively destroy sexual desire as well. It may be several years before research can correct these problems and vaccines become a valid contraceptive option for men. Although there continues to be ongoing research into new contraception options for men, it is likely that no options will be available until perhaps 2015 at the earliest (Hatcher et al., 2007).

*Women want contraceptives that **are simpler** to use.*

Microbicides will continue to be an important area of research in the next few years. Microbicides could be used by themselves or in conjunction with another method, such as a diaphragm or condom (we will discuss microbicides more in Chapter 15). Other research is evaluating longer acting versions of existing methods, such as the contraceptive patch and hormonal ring. Extended use patches or rings may be options in the next few years.

Immunocontraceptives for women are also being studied. Research is evaluating vaccines to inhibit the function of human chorionic gonadotropin (see Chapter 12) and interrupt a woman's ability to become pregnant (J. L. Schwartz & Gabelnick, 2002). This vaccine is the first contraceptive vaccine to undergo Phase I and II clinical trials in humans. Other vaccines target sex hormones or gamete production (Naz, 2005). Unfortunately, vaccines often negatively affect other functions and do not offer adequate effectiveness yet. New IUDs, implants, injections, and permanent sterilization procedures are also being evaluated. Finally, natural methods of contraception are also being studied. Saliva and urine tests can help natural planning by allowing a woman to determine whether she is ovulating. Fertility computers, which allow a woman to identify fertile periods, are currently undergoing clinical trials for FDA approval. Although we still have a long way to go in making better methods available for controlling whether pregnancy occurs, many improvements are in the works and may be available in the near future.

Financial factors, political pressure, and legal concerns hold back most of the contraceptive research today. Private funding is often difficult because such large amounts are necessary for most research. Unfortunately, the threat of lawsuits (such as the Dalkon Shield situation discussed earlier in the chapter) has effectively scared most big pharmaceutical companies away from contraceptive research (Hatcher et al., 2007; J. L. Schwartz & Gabelnick, 2002).

WHAT'S AHEAD FOR WOMEN

Women report that they want contraceptives that are simpler to use, have fewer side effects, and offer additional non-contraceptive benefits, such as STI protection, clearer skin or less weight gain (Hatcher et al., 2007). Research is ongoing in an attempt to find a contraceptive method that addresses all these concerns.

immunocontraceptives
Vaccines designed to suppress testicular function and eliminate sperm and testosterone production.

microbicide
Chemical that works by inhibiting sperm function; effective against HIV and other STIs, and not harmful to the vaginal or cervical cells.

review questions

1 What do couples look for in new contraceptive methods?

2 Describe why there have been fewer birth control options for men and what the future holds for new male contraception.

3 Describe what the future holds for new female contraceptive methods.

Abortion

Close to half of all pregnancies in the United States are unintended and 40% of these end in abortion (Finer & Henshaw, 2006). Worldwide there were an estimated 42 million abortions performed in 2003—down from 46 million in 1995 (Sedgh et al., 2007b). It is estimated that one in five pregnancies ends in abortion worldwide (Sedgh et al., 2007b).

In the United States, abortion has become the moral issue of the times. In addition, abortion leads many people to question the role that the government should play in their lives. Here we explore the abortion debate.

THE ABORTION
DEBATE

The abortion debate has been very emotional and sometimes even violent. Many on both sides of the issue have strongly held opinions. **Pro-life supporters** believe that human life begins at conception, and thus an embryo, at any stage of development, is a person. Although some pro-life supporters believe that aborting a fetus is murder and that the government should make all abortions illegal, others believe that abortion should only be available for specific cases (such as rape or danger to a mother's life).

REALResearch **>** It is estimated that **50%** of American women will experience an unwanted pregnancy by age **45** (R. Jones et al., 2006), and approximately one-third of them will have an abortion (Alan Guttmacher Institute, 2008b).

On the other side of the issue, **pro-choice supporters** believe that a woman should have control over her fertility. Many people who are pro-choice believe there are a number of situations in which a woman may view abortion as a necessary option. Because not everyone agrees that life begins at conception, pro-choice supporters believe that it is a woman's choice whether to have an abortion, and they strongly believe that the government should not interfere with her decision.

The abortion debate often polarizes people into pro-life and pro-choice camps, with each side claiming moral superiority over the other. College students have generally been viewed as fairly liberal in their attitudes about abortion, but studies have found a normal distribution of abortion attitudes (Carlton et al., 2000). Some students are pro-choice, some are pro-life, and many are somewhere in between.

HISTORICAL
PERSPECTIVES

Abortion has been practiced in many societies throughout history; in fact, there are few large-scale societies in which it has not been practiced (see Chapter 1). Aristotle argued that abortion was necessary as a backup to contraception. He believed that a fetus was not alive until certain organs had been formed; for males, this occurred 40 days after conception, and for females, 90 days. In early Roman society, abortions were also allowed, but husbands had the power to determine whether their wives would undergo abortion.

Throughout most of Western history, religion determined general attitudes toward abortion, and both Judaism and Christianity have generally condemned abortion and punished those who used it. Still, throughout recorded history, abortions were performed. Many women died or were severely injured by illegal surgical abortions performed by semiskilled practitioners. Although it was little discussed publicly, abortion was apparently quite common; the Michigan Board of Health estimated in 1878

that one third of all pregnancies in that state ended in abortion (D'Emilio & Freedman, 1988).

In 1965, all 50 states banned abortion, although there were exceptions that varied by state (for instance, to save the mother's life, in cases of rape or incest, or fetal deformity). Those who could not have a legal abortion either had the baby or had to acquire an illegal abortion. These illegal abortions, known as **back-alley abortions,** were very dangerous because they were often performed under unsanitary conditions and resulted in multiple complications, sometimes ending in death. In 1967, abortion laws in England were liberalized, and many American women traveled to England for an abortion. By 1970, "package deals" appeared in the popular media advertising roundtrip airfare, airport transfers, passport assistance, lodging, meals, and the procedure itself (R. B. Gold, 2003).

In 1973, the Supreme Court ruled in the *Roe v. Wade* decision that women have a constitutionally protected right to have an abortion in the early stages of pregnancy. In the first trimester of pregnancy, a woman can choose abortion without the state interfering. In the second trimester, a state can regulate abortion to protect a woman's health; and, in the third trimester, the potential fetal life enables the state to limit or ban abortion except in cases in which a woman's life or health would be at risk. This decision was enacted to help limit government from controlling a woman's body and ensure the right to privacy.

Since the Supreme Court handed down its decision in *Roe v. Wade* in 1973, individual states have adopted various abortion laws that regulate when and under what circumstances a woman can have an abortion. These regulations include waiting periods, parental involvement for minors, state-mandated counseling, and gestational limits (Alan Guttmacher Institute, 2008c, 2008d). Today pressure continues in the United States from pro-life supporters to reverse the Supreme Court's decision in *Roe v. Wade.*

LEGAL VERSUS
ILLEGAL ABORTIONS

Since the legalization of abortion in the United States in 1973, the number of women's deaths from abortion have declined dramatically—even though the actual number is difficult to determine because so many abortion-related deaths were not noted on death certificates (see Figure 13.12; R. Gold, 1990). Pro-choice supporters believe this is directly due to easier accessibility of abortion. They believe that the legalization of abortion ensured sanitary conditions and immediate treatment for infections.

pro-life supporter
Individual who believes that abortion should be illegal or strictly regulated by the government.

pro-choice supporter
Individual who believes that the abortion decision should be left up to the woman and not regulated by the government.

back-alley abortion
Illegal abortion, which was all that was available prior to the legalization of abortion in the 1970s.

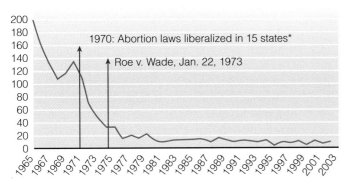

Number of Abortion-Related Deaths

1970: Abortion laws liberalized in 15 states*

Roe v. Wade, Jan. 22, 1973

Figure **13.12** Since abortion was legalized in 1973, the number of deaths from abortion has declined dramatically. Source: Alan Guttmacher Institute, 2008b; Strauss et al., 2004, 2006.

In contrast, pro-life supporters believe that before *Roe v. Wade,* women were more careful about becoming pregnant. Because abortion was not a legal right, many women used birth control consistently, and if they got pregnant, they gave birth. The legalization of abortion, according to the pro-life camp, has caused women and men to become irresponsible about sexuality and contraceptive use. By making abortion illegal, pro-life supporters believe that people will become more responsible about contraception and may delay sexual activity.

WHY DO WOMEN HAVE ABORTIONS?

A woman who experiences an unintended pregnancy has several choices: She can have the baby and keep it or give it up for adoption, or she can terminate the pregnancy through abortion. Making a decision about what to do isn't easy, although situational factors can make it easier for some women. If a woman is in a stable relationship, has adequate finances, or the support of friends and family, sometimes this decision is easier to make. Each year, half of all women who unintentionally become pregnant

WHAT DO YOU WANT TO KNOW ?

In the future, is abortion going to be illegal?
The Supreme Court may eventually overturn the *Roe v. Wade* decision. Should this happen, each state will be responsible for regulating abortion. As of 2008, only seven states had laws that protected the right to choose abortion before fetal viability or when necessary to protect the life or health of the woman if *Roe v. Wade* was overturned (California, Connecticut, Hawaii, Maine, Maryland, Nevada, and Washington; Alan Guttmacher Institute, 2008e). Four states would automatically ban abortion (Louisiana, Mississippi, North Dakota, and South Dakota), 13 states would enforce their existing abortion bans, and 7 states would restrict the right to a legal abortion to the maximum degree possible (Alan Guttmacher Institute, 2008e).

decide to carry their pregnancies to term (approximately 9% of these women place their child up for adoption), whereas others choose to have an abortion (as do a small percentage of women with wanted pregnancies who experience unanticipated issues such as fetal deformity or other medical problems; Boonstra et al., 2006).

Women choosing abortion do so for many different reasons—an inability to care for a child, financial reasons, partner or relationship issues, and work, school, or family issues (Boonstra et al., 2006). There is no simple answer to the question of why a woman decides to have an abortion. We do know that the majority of women—regardless of age, marital status, income, ethnicity, education, or number of children—cite a concern for others as a main factor in their decision to have an abortion (Boonstra et al., 2006).

ABORTION PROCEDURES

Abortion is one of the most common surgical procedures in the United States, and the majority of surgical abortion procedures are performed in specialized abortion clinics (Henshaw & Finer, 2003). However, this has not always been the case. After *Roe v. Wade,* most abortions were performed in hospitals. The move away from hospitals and into clinics has reduced the cost of an abortion. Today a woman can choose between a surgical abortion procedure or medical abortion (the "abortion pill"). The duration of a woman's pregnancy is the most important factor in determining which method a woman should choose. A medical abortion can be used if it is early in the pregnancy (7–9 weeks), whereas surgical abortions are used in both the first and second trimester (see Table 13.4 for more information about early abortion options). Almost 90% of abortions are performed in the first trimester, and 60% of these occur in the first 8 weeks of pregnancy (Hatcher et al., 2007; Henshaw & Kost, 2008; see Figure 13.13).

First-Trimester Surgical Abortion
A **first-trimester surgical abortion** (**vacuum aspiration,** or suction abortion) is performed before 14 weeks of gestation. It is simpler and safer than abortions performed after this time. A first-trimester surgical abortion is often performed on an outpatient basis using local anesthesia.

In a first-trimester surgical abortion procedure, a woman lies on an examining table with her feet in stirrups, and a speculum is placed in her vagina to view the cervix. Local anesthesia is injected into the cervix, which numbs it slightly. **Dilation rods** are used to open the cervix and usually cause mild cramping of the uterus. Following dilation, a **cannula** is inserted into the cervix and is at-

first-trimester surgical abortion
Termination of pregnancy within the first 14 weeks of pregnancy.

vacuum aspiration
The termination of a pregnancy by using suction to empty the contents of the uterus.

dilation rods
A series of graduated metal rods that are used to dilate the cervical opening during an abortion procedure.

cannula
A tube, used in an abortion procedure, through which the uterine contents are emptied.

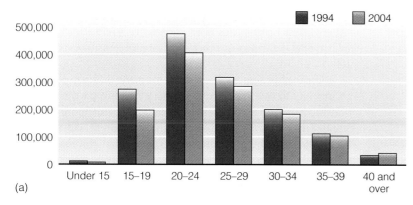

**Abortions by Client Age
1994 and 2004**

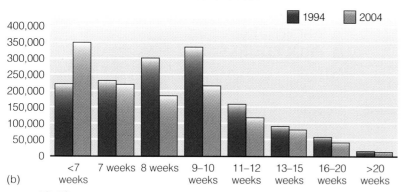

**Abortions by Gestational Age
1994 and 2004**

Figure **13.13** (a) Abortions by Client Age - 1994 and 2004. (b) Abortions by Gestational Age - 1994 and 2004. Source: Reproduced with permission of The Alan Guttmacher Institute from Physicians for Reproductive Choice and Health and The Alan Guttmacher Institute (AGI), *An Overview of Abortion in the U.S.*, New York: AGI, 2008, Microsoft PowerPoint presentation.

tached to a **vacuum aspirator,** which empties the contents of the uterus.

A first-trimester surgical abortion usually takes between 4 and 6 minutes. After it is completed, most clinics require a woman to stay in the clinic, hospital, or doctor's office for a few hours. Once home, she is advised to rest, not to lift heavy objects, to avoid sexual intercourse, not to douche or use tampons for at least 2 weeks, and not to take baths; all of these activities increase the risk of hemorrhaging and infection. She will also experience bleeding and perhaps cramping, as she would during a normal period. Her menstrual period will return within 4 to 6 weeks.

There are several potential risks associated with a first-trimester surgical abortion, including excessive bleeding, possible infection, and uterine perforation. However, because these risks are much lower than for a second-trimester surgical procedure, most health care providers advise women who are considering abortions to have a first-trimester procedure.

Second-Trimester Surgical Abortion

Second-trimester surgical abortions, or late abortions, are those done between 14 and 24 weeks. A woman may undergo a second trimester procedure for several reasons, such as medical complications, fetal deformities that were not revealed earlier, divorce or marital problems, miscalculation of date of last menstrual period, financial or geographic problems (such as not living near a clinic

that offers the procedure), or a denial of the pregnancy until the second trimester.

Between 13 and 16 weeks of pregnancy, a **dilation and evacuation (D&E)** is the most common second-trimester abortion procedure in the United States (Strauss et al., 2004). The procedure is similar to a vacuum aspiration, but it is done in a hospital under general anesthesia. Dilators, such as **laminaria** (lam-in-AIR-ree-uh), may be used to help begin the dilation process and may be inserted into the cervix 12 to 24 hours before the procedure. When a woman returns to the hospital, she may first be given intravenous pain medication and local anesthesia, which is injected into the cervix. The dilators are removed, and the uterus is then emptied with suction and various instruments. Because the fetus is larger in the second trimester, this procedure is more complicated than a first-trimester procedure and involves more risks, including increased pain, blood loss, and cervical trauma.

A procedure known as a "partial-birth abortion" was developed to reduce cervical trauma. This procedure was

vacuum aspirator
A vacuum pump that is used during abortion procedures.

second-trimester surgical abortion
Termination of pregnancy between the 14th and 21st weeks of pregnancy.

dilation and evacuation (D&E)
A second-trimester abortion procedure that involves cervical dilation and vacuum aspiration of the uterus.

laminaria
Seaweed used in second-trimester abortion procedures to dilate the cervix. Used dried, it can swell three to five times its original diameter.

table 13.4

Early Abortion Options

Surgical Abortion	Medical Abortion
Highly effective	Highly effective
Relatively brief procedure	Procedure can take up to several days or more to complete
Involves invasive procedure	No invasive procedure if successful
Allows local or general anesthesia	No anesthesia
Usually requires only one clinic or medical visit	Involves at least two visits
Bleeding is typically lighter after procedure	Bleeding is typically heavier after procedure
Requires medical setting	Can occur in privacy of own home

SOURCE: Hatcher et al., 2007.

The cost for a first-trimester surgical abortion ranges from $350 to $900. These fees usually include an examination, laboratory tests, anesthesia, the procedure, and a follow-up examination. In a private physician's office or hospitals, surgical abortion procedures are more expensive. Medical abortions (those using medications) usually cost anywhere from $350 to $650. A second-trimester surgical abortion can run much higher, depending on whether the procedure is performed in a private clinic or hospital.

typically used between the 18th and the 26th week of pregnancy and involved delivering a live fetus through the vaginal canal but compressing the fetal skull shortly after birth. However, this procedure generated much controversy, and in 2003 the U.S. Supreme Court banned all partial-birth abortion procedures.

Medical Abortion

A medical abortion involves the use of an abortion pill to end a pregnancy. In 2005, medical abortion accounted for 13% of all abortions and 22% of abortions before 9 weeks gestation (R. Jones et al., 2008). Today two drugs have been used for medical abortion, **mifepristone** and **methotrexate.** Mifepristone is usually given as a pill, whereas Methotrexate can be given as a pill or an injection. When one of these drugs is used in conjunction with a **prostaglandin** (misoprostol), the uterus will contract and expel its contents. Early medical abortion is a safe and effective procedure (M. Singh et al., 2008) and research indicates that it may be safer than surgical abortion procedures (Gan et al., 2008).

Mifepristone was first approved for use in pregnancy termination in France in 1988 (during this time it was referred to as RU-486). It was then approved in the United Kingdom in 1991, and in Sweden in 1992. The FDA approved mifepristone for use in the United States in 2000. Methotrexate has not been approved for pregnancy termination in the United States.

A woman taking mifepristone will usually begin bleeding within 4 to 5 hours, and bleeding will continue for up to 13 days, whereas a woman taking methotrexate may continue bleeding for 4 weeks or more. Mifepristone is often more popular because it involves a shorter duration of bleeding; however, a health care provider will decide which method would work best for the patient. Medical abortions may involve two or three office visits, testing, and examinations and can cost anywhere from $350 to $650.

Some women choose medical abortion over surgical abortion because it feels more "natural," offers privacy, can be done earlier, does not use anesthesia, and provides more control (see Table 13.4; F. H. Stewart et al., 2004). However, medical abortions often cause heavier bleeding and cramping than surgical abortions, and some women worry about being away from a medical facility (Lie et al., 2008). Women who undergo a medical abortion must be prepared to have a surgical abortion if they experience an incomplete abortion. Because the drugs for medical abortion are known to cause birth defects, women are not advised to continue a pregnancy after using these drugs.

MIFEPRISTONE Mifepristone (MYFE-priss-tone) has been used in several European countries for more than a decade. Mifepristone is an antiprogestin, which blocks the development of progesterone, causing the lining of the uterus to break down.

Three Mifepristone pills are taken, and 2 days later a woman takes an oral dose of prostaglandin (typically misoprostol). This causes uterine contractions that expel the fertilized ovum. Effectiveness rates range between 95% and 97%. Mifepristone can safely and effectively be used to terminate a pregnancy up until 63 days (9 weeks) from a woman's last menstrual period (F. H. Stewart et al., 2004). There are some potential side effects, however, which include nausea, cramping, vomiting, and uterine bleeding for anywhere from 1 to 3 weeks (M. Singh et al., 2008; F. H. Stewart et al., 2004). The prolonged bleeding and the length of time to expulsion (days compared with minutes) make medical abortion less appealing than a surgical abortion.

METHOTREXATE Methotrexate (METH-oh-trecks-ate) can also be used as an early option for medical abortion. It was approved by the FDA in 1953 as a breast cancer drug and is also used to treat psoriasis and rheumatoid arthritis. When methotrexate is used in combination with misoprostol, it has been found to cause a miscarriage (Bygdeman & Danielsson, 2002). Methotrexate works by stopping the development of the cells of the zygote, and the prostaglandin is used to contract the uterus to expel the pregnancy. As with mifepristone, methotrexate can safely and effectively be used to terminate a pregnancy up to 63 days past a woman's last menstrual period.

REACTIONS TO ABORTION

In the late 1980s, President Ronald Reagan asked Surgeon General Dr. C. Everett Koop to prepare a report on the physical aftereffects of women who have undergone elective abortions. The Surgeon General reported that scientific studies had documented that

Women who undergo an abortion can become pregnant and give birth later on in their life without complications (Boonstra et al., 2006). However, there are rare cases of unexpected complications of abortion that can lead to infertility, such as uterine perforation or severe infection. Women who use medical abortions may have less risk to future fertility because these are nonsurgical abortion options.

mifepristone
Drug used in medical abortion procedures; it blocks development of progesterone, which causes a breakdown in the uterine lining. Mifepristone was also called RU-486 when it was in development.

methotrexate
Drug used in medical abortion procedures; when taken, it stops the development of the zygote.

prostaglandin
Oral or injected drug taken to cause uterine contractions.

physiological health consequences—including infertility, incompetent cervix, miscarriage, premature birth, and low birth weight—are no more frequent among women who experience abortion than they are among the general population of women. The Surgeon General's findings do not support claims by some pro-life advocates who state that there are severe physiological symptoms associated with abortion.

Women's Reactions

The decision to have an abortion is a difficult one. Terminating an unintended pregnancy or an intended pregnancy with a deformed fetus can be very painful. The physiological and psychological effects vary from person to person, and they depend on many factors.

PHYSIOLOGICAL SYMPTOMS Physiological reactions to abortion depend on the type of procedure used. After an early abortion, many women report increased cramping, heavy bleeding with possible clots, and nausea. These symptoms may persist for several days, but if any of these are severe, a health care provider should be seen for an evaluation. Severe complications are much more frequent in late abortion procedures and, as we discussed, include hemorrhaging, **cervical laceration, uterine perforation,** and infection (F. H. Stewart et al., 2004). Of these complications, uterine perforation is the most serious, although the risk of occurrence is small. A woman who has an abortion can get pregnant again and is not at an increased risk for miscarriage or problems in her pregnancy (Hatcher et al., 2007).

A few years back, some pro-life groups began claiming that having an abortion increased a woman's risk of breast cancer. Exhaustive reviews by both the U.S. and British governments concluded there is no association between abortion and breast cancer (or any other type of cancer; Boonstra et al., 2006). Even so, as of 2008, six states required clinics and hospitals that perform abortions to inform patients about the link between breast cancer and abortion (Alan Guttmacher Institute, 2008d).

PSYCHOLOGICAL SYMPTOMS The majority of evidence from scientific studies indicates that most women who undergo surgical abortion have few psychological side effects later on (Adler et al., 1992; Zolese & Blacker, 1992). In fact, relief is the more prominent response for the majority of women. However, although relief may be the immediate feeling, some researchers point out that there are actually three categories of psychological reactions to abortion. Positive emotions include relief and happiness; socially based emotions include shame, guilt, and fear of disapproval; and internally based emotions include regret, anxiety, depression, doubt, and anger, which are based on the woman's feelings about the pregnancy (Thorp et al., 2003). A woman may cycle through each of these reactions—feeling relief one minute, depression or guilt the next.

Some women experience intense, negative psychological consequences that include guilt, anxiety, depression, and regret (Zolese & Blacker, 1992). Other possible negative psychological symptoms include self-reproach, increased sadness, and a sense of loss.

Certain conditions may put a woman more at risk for developing severe psychological symptoms. These include being young, not having family or partner support, being persuaded to have an abortion when a woman does not want one, having a difficult time making the decision to have an abortion, blaming the pregnancy on another person or on oneself, having a strong religious and moral background, having an abortion for medical or genetic reasons, having a history of psychiatric problems before the abortion, and having a late abortion procedure (Dagg, 1991; Mueller & Major, 1989; Zolese & Blacker, 1992).

Thus, although discovering an unplanned pregnancy and deciding to abort are very stressful decisions, in the majority of cases, the emotional aftermath does not appear to be severe (Burnell & Norfleet, 1987; Major et al., 1985; Mueller & Major, 1989). Still, it is very beneficial for a woman (and her partner) who is contemplating an abortion to discuss this with a counselor or health care provider.

It's also important to point out that we know the most about psychological symptoms after surgical abortion and little about reactions to medical abortions. Reactions may be similar, but this will be an area of research that will continue to grow in the next few years.

Men's Reactions

A woman's choice to have an abortion forces a couple to reevaluate their relationship and ask themselves some difficult questions (Naziri, 2007). Do they both feel the same about each other? Is the relationship serious? Where is the relationship going? Keeping the lines of communication open during this time is very important. The male partner's involvement makes the abortion experience less traumatic for the woman; in fact, women whose partners support them and help them through the abortion show more positive responses after abortion (Adler et al., 1990; Moseley et al., 1981). Women who have no support from their partners or who make the decision themselves often experience greater emotional distress. In some cases, women have been found to conceal abortion decisions from their partners, and rates of intimate partner violence have been found to be high in this group (Coker, 2007; Woo et al., 2005).

Some people believe that abortion is a difficult decision only for the woman because she is the one who carries the pregnancy. However, men also have a difficult time with an unplanned pregnancy and the decision to abort, and they often experience sadness, a sense of loss, and fear for their partner's well-being. What makes it even more difficult for most men is that they often do not discuss the pregnancy with anyone other than their partner (Naziri, 2007).

Men also have a difficult time with an unplanned pregnancy.

TEENS AND ABORTION

Each year in the United States, 750,000 teenagers become pregnant, and 85% of these pregnancies are unintended (Alan Guttmacher Institute, 2006; see Figure 13.13). Many states have

cervical laceration
Cuts or tears on the cervix.

uterine perforation
Tearing a hole in the uterus.

passed laws that control teenagers' access to abortion. For instance, some states require **parental notification** or **parental consent.** However, studies have shown that in states without mandatory parental consent or notice requirements, 75% of minors involve one or both parents (Henshaw & Kost, 1992). Those who do not usually have strong reasons for not doing so, and these laws make it difficult for many of them to obtain an abortion. Some states offer a **judicial bypass option,** in which a minor can obtain consent from a judge rather than from her parents.

CROSS-CULTURAL ASPECTS OF ABORTION

Whether a woman will have an abortion often depends on whether her country's laws permit or prohibit the procedure. It is estimated that 25% of women live in countries with significant abortion restrictions. Only a handful of countries, including Canada, Cuba, Puerto Rico, China, Singapore, Vietnam, South Africa, and many of the Scandinavian countries, permit abortion without restriction (Rahman et al., 1998). However, many other countries impose restrictions such as allowing abortion only to save a woman's life (including countries such as Brazil, Mexico, Egypt, Iran, Nepal, Sri Lanka, Ireland, and many areas within sub-Saharan Africa).

Abortion law throughout the world depends on factors such as health care, social factors, religiosity, financial factors, and many other issues. In countries where abortion laws are severely restrictive, some countries allow abortions in cases of rape (such as Brazil and Mexico). A few countries require permission of other family members, such as in Turkey, where a woman cannot have an abortion without the consent of her husband. Still other countries, such as Chile, prohibit abortion altogether, even to save a woman's life, although legal appeals to save a woman's life may be successful in many of these countries (Rahman et al., 1998).

Although the lowest abortion rates are in Europe, especially in Western Europe (Cohen, 2007), the biggest decreases in abortion rates were in Eastern Europe, where the abortion rate fell from 90 to 44 per 1,000 from 1995–2003, mostly because of an increase in contraceptive use (Henshaw et al., 1999; Sedgh et al., 2007a). Although the abortion rate in the United States is 21 per 1,000, rates in Belgium, Germany, and the Netherlands are all below 10 (Cohen, 2007). Abortion is legal and widely available in these countries. However, abortion is less accessible in many countries, such as Africa, Latin America, and the Caribbean, and the abortion rates range from 25 to 39 per 1,000 (see Figure 13.14 for more information about cross-cultural aspects of abortion; Cohen, 2007). Some countries do not have reliable reporting of abortion rates, and unofficial estimates are compiled.

Medical abortion has been widely used outside the United States. In fact, mifepristone has been used in Europe since the late 1990s, and by 2000, it was used in more than 50% of early abortions in some countries (R. K. Jones & Henshaw, 2002). In Germany, women using medical abortion report satisfaction and lower levels of initial anxiety than those using surgical abortion (Hemmerling et al., 2005).

Although many safe and legal abortions occur, approximately 20 million unsafe abortions take place each year (K. Singh & Ratnam, 1998). Unsafe abortion methods include taking drugs, inserting objects into the vagina, flushing the vagina with certain liquids, or having the abdomen vigorously massaged (Tietze & Henshaw, 1986). Deaths from unsafe abortion practices are highest in Africa, where there are 680 deaths per 100,000 abortions (Alan Guttmacher Institute, 1999d).

Abortion remains a controversial procedure in the United States as well as in the rest of the world. Both sides of the issue battle from what they believe are basic principles: one side from a fetus's right to be born, the other from a woman's right to control her own body. The pendulum of this debate continues to swing back and forth. For example, in the early 1970s, the right-to-choose group won an important victory with *Roe v. Wade;* in the early 1990s, the right-to-life group scored a victory with the decision that a state can limit access to abortion.

Current politics may influence whether *Roe v. Wade* is one day overturned. Although new developments like medical abortion may take the fight out of the abortion clinics and into women's homes, the only real certainty about the future of abortion is that it will remain one of the most controversial areas of American public life.

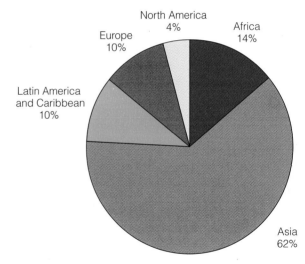

42 million abortions worldwide annually

Figure **13.14** Most abortions occur in Asia, because the world's population is concentrated there. Of the 26 million abortions that occur yearly in Asia, 9 million take place in China. Source: Reprinted from *Lancet,* 370(9595), Sedgh G. et al., Induced abortion: rates and trends worldwide, 1338–1345. Copyright 2007, with permission from Elsevier.

parental notification
Abortion legislation that requires the notification of the parents of a minor prior to an abortion procedure.

parental consent
Abortion legislation that requires the consent of the parents of a minor prior to an abortion procedure.

judicial bypass option
Abortion legislation that allows for a judge to bypass parental consent or notification for a minor to acquire an abortion.

review questions

1 Trace the status of abortion throughout history and differentiate between legal and illegal abortion.

2 Differentiate between first- and second-trimester surgical abortion procedures.

3 Differentiate between surgical and medical abortion and explain how a woman might decide which procedure would be best for her.

4 Identify some physiological and psychological reactions to abortion, and discuss the research on men and abortion.

5 Discuss the laws that have been imposed in an attempt to decrease abortion in adolescent populations.

6 Describe what we know about abortion outside the United States.

CHAPTER review

SUMMARY POINTS

1 Contraception is not a modern invention. The ancient Greeks and Egyptians used a variety of techniques to try to control their fertility. Several groups began to explore controlling fertility in the early 1800s, and Margaret Sanger was one of the first people to advocate the importance of birth control.

2 Contraception throughout the world has always been affected by social and economic issues, knowledge levels, religion, and gender roles. Outside the United States, many women are often not involved in contraceptive decision making, and contraceptive use is thought to reduce a man's masculinity. Scandinavian countries are regarded as some of the most progressive with respect to contraceptive usage. Finland has been rated as a model country in contraceptive use.

3 The FDA has approved several methods of contraception, but no method is best for everyone. These include barrier, hormonal, chemical, intrauterine, natural, permanent, and emergency methods.

4 The FDA is responsible for approving all prescription medicine in the United

States. A pharmaceutical company must submit proof that the drug is safe for human use. It is estimated that it takes 10 to 14 years to develop a new contraceptive method.

5 Issues that must be considered when choosing a contraceptive method include personal health, number of sexual partners, frequency of sexual intercourse, risk of acquiring a STI, responsibility of partners, method cost, and method advantages and disadvantages.

6 Barrier methods of birth control work by preventing the sperm from entering the uterus. Barrier methods include the condom, diaphragm, FemCap, Lea's Shield, and the contraceptive sponge. Male condoms can be made of latex, polyurethane, or lambskin. Female condoms are made of polyurethane.

7 Hormonal methods work by changing hormone levels to interrupt ovulation. Combined-hormone methods include birth control pills, injections, vaginal rings, and patches. Combination birth control pills contain synthetic estrogen and a type of progesterone. The increase in estrogen

and progesterone prevents the pituitary gland from sending hormones to cause the ovaries to begin maturation of an ovum. Other hormonal contraceptive options include a monthly injection of synthetic hormones, including estrogen and progestin; Nuva Ring, a small plastic ring that releases a constant dose of estrogen and progestin and is changed once a month; the Ortho Evra patch, which sticks to the skin and time releases synthetic estrogen and progestin into the bloodstream. All of these work by inhibiting ovulation, increasing cervical mucus, and/or rendering the uterus inhospitable to implantation.

8 Progestin-based methods include subdermal implants, injectables, and minipills. Progestin-only methods include minipills, Norplant, and Depo-Provera. Norplant is a subdermal contraceptive implant, whereas Depo-Provera is a progestin-only injectable contraceptive that works by preventing ovulation and thickening cervical mucus. Norplant was withdrawn from the market in 2005.

9 Chemical methods of contraception include spermicides such as creams, jellies, foams, suppositories, and films. Spermicides work by reducing the survival of sperm in the vagina.

10 IUDs are placed in the uterus and cause an increase in copper ions and enzymes, which impairs sperm function and prevents fertilization. The Mirena IUD also time releases into the lining of the uterus.

11 Natural family planning involves charting menstrual periods by taking a daily basal body temperature and checking cervical mucus in order to determine ovulation. Sexual intercourse is avoided during ovulation. In the rhythm method, there is often no monitoring of the signs of ovulation. Fertility awareness involves charting in conjunction with another form of birth control.

12 Withdrawal is a method of contraception in which the man withdraws his penis from the vagina prior to ejaculation.

13 Couples may choose abstinence to prevent pregnancy, to protect against STIs, or for other reasons such as illness or disease. It is estimated that reported usage rates of this method are low because many couples don't consider it a legitimate method.

14 Tubal sterilization is the most widely used method of birth control in the world. In this procedure, a health care provider may sever or block both Fallopian tubes so that the ovum and sperm cannot meet. A vasectomy blocks the flow of sperm through the vas deferens, and although the testes will continue to produce viable sperm cells, the cells die and are reabsorbed by the body.

15 Unreliable birth control methods include douching and breast-feeding. Some medical providers use a combination of ordinary birth control pills for emergency contraception. Plan B, a progestin-only method, was approved as emergency contraception in 1999, and it must be given within 72 hours of unprotected intercourse. It may be effective for up to 120 hours after unprotected intercourse. An IUD may also be implanted as a form of emergency contraception. Emergency contraception has been available worldwide for more than 2 decades.

16 Contraception has long been thought to be a female's responsibility and that may be why the condom and vasectomy are the only birth control methods available to men. Many feminists claim the lack of male methods is because most of those doing the contraceptive research are men, whereas others claim that most methods are for women because it's easier to interfere with one ovum a month than thousands of sperm a day.

17 There are many new contraceptive methods on the horizon, and many will be easier to use, more long-acting, and have higher effectiveness rates. Immunocontraceptives are also being studied.

18 The abortion debate has been very emotional and even violent. Many on both sides of the issue have strongly held opinions. There are pro-life supporters and pro-choice supporters.

19 Abortion has been practiced in many societies throughout history; in fact, there are few large-scale societies where it has not been practiced. Before abortion was legalized, illegal abortions were common. Throughout most of Western history, religion determined general attitudes toward abortion.

20 In 1973, the court case *Roe v. Wade* gave women a constitutionally protected right to have an abortion in the early stages of pregnancy. In the first trimester of pregnancy, a woman has a right to choose abortion without the state interfering. In the second trimester, a state can regulate abortion to protect a woman's health; in the third trimester, the potential fetal life enables the state to limit or ban abortion except in cases in which a woman's life or health would be at risk.

21 The majority of surgical abortion procedures today are performed in specialized abortion clinics, which is much less expensive than having it done in a hospital. The most serious risks of a surgical abortion include uterine perforation, cervical laceration, severe hemorrhaging, infection, and anesthesia-related complications.

22 Surgical abortions can be either first- or second-trimester procedures. First-trimester abortions are performed before 14 weeks of gestation and are simpler and safer than later procedures. Second-trimester abortions are performed between 14 and 21 weeks.

23 A vacuum aspiration abortion is the most common type of surgical abortion procedure in the United States. There are several potential risks associated with this type of abortion, including excessive bleeding, possible infection, and uterine perforation. A woman may have a second-trimester abortion for several reasons, and a dilation and evacuation is the most commonly used procedure.

24 Medical abortion involves the use of medicine to end a pregnancy. Today mifepristone and methotrexate are used, along with prostaglandin. Mifepristone is used more often because it involves a shorter duration of bleeding. A health care provider determines which drug will work best. Women report that medical abortions feel more natural; however, a woman undergoing a medical abortion must be prepared to undergo a surgical abortion if the procedure is unsuccessful.

25 Women who have abortions do so for many reasons, including the belief that a baby would interfere with other responsibilities, an inability to financially provide for a child, difficulties in the relationship with the father, not wanting people to know they are sexually active, pressure from their partners or families, fetal deformity, risks to mother's health, having several children already, and rape or incest.

26 Physiological reactions to surgical abortion depend on the type of procedure used. Early abortion procedures often result in cramping, heavy bleeding with possible clots, and nausea. Severe complications are much more frequent in late abortion procedures and include hemorrhaging, cervical laceration, uterine perforation, and infections. The majority of women undergoing abortion have very few psychological side effects later on, although there are certain conditions that may put a woman more at risk for developing severe psychological symptoms.

27 The abortion experience is less traumatic when a male partner is involved. Women whose partners support them and help them through the abortion show more positive responses afterward. Women who have no support from their partners often experience greater emotional distress. We know less about a partner's psychological reactions after a medical abortion.

28 Some men have a difficult time with the decision to abort and experience sadness, a sense of loss, and fear for their partner's well-being. Many hold their feelings in and do not discuss the abortion with anyone other than their partner.

29 It is estimated that 4 of every 10 pregnancies throughout the world are unplanned, and 2 in 10 end in an abortion. Whether a woman will have an abortion often depends on whether her country's laws permit or prohibit the procedure. In Russia, the average woman undergoes four or five abortions in her lifetime.

CRITICAL THINKING questions

1 If you found out tomorrow that you (or your partner) were 6 weeks pregnant, what would your options be? Where would you go for help, and whom would you talk to? What would your biggest concerns be?

2 Suppose a good friend of yours, Sylvia, tells you that she is 10 weeks pregnant, and she and her boyfriend have decided that she will have an abortion. She knows that you are taking the sexuality course and asks you about her abortion options. What can you tell her?

3 What method of contraception do you think would work best for you at this time in your life? In 5 years? In 10 years? Why?

4 Do you think women who use herbal contraceptives should be taught about newer, more modern methods of birth control? What if the methods they are using are working for them?

WEB resources

Sexuality Now Book Companion Website
Go to www.cengage.com/psychology/carroll for practice quizzes, glossary, flash cards, and more. You can also access the following websites from the companion site.

Planned Parenthood Federation of America ■ Founded by Margaret Sanger in 1916 as America's first birth control clinic, Planned Parenthood Federation of America is the world's largest voluntary reproductive health care organization. This website offers information on birth control, emergency contraception, STIs, safer sex, pregnancy, abortion, and other health-related concerns.

Alan Guttmacher Institute ■ The Alan Guttmacher Institute (AGI) is a nonprofit organization focused on sexual and reproductive health research, policy analysis, and public education. The Institute's mission is to protect the reproductive choices of all women and men in the United States and throughout the world.

Birthcontrol.Com ■ This Canadian website sells innovative contraceptive products from around the world. Sponges, condoms, spermicides, and barrier methods of contraception can be found, all at relatively inexpensive prices.

National Abortion Federation ■ The National Abortion Federation (NAF) is the professional association of abortion providers in the United States and Canada. NAF members provide the broadest spectrum of abortion expertise in North America.

National Abortion Rights Action League ■ NARAL is a pro-choice league that strives to help find workable answers to ultimately reduce the need for abortions. NARAL believes that ignoring limited access to contraception, reproductive health care, and sex education while taking away a woman's right to choose will only result in more unintended pregnancies and more abortions.

National Right to Life ■ The National Right to Life Committee was founded in response to the U.S. Supreme Court's 1973 decision in *Roe v. Wade*. Since its official beginning, the National Right to Life Committee has grown to more than 3,000 chapters in all 50 states and the District of Columbia. The goal of the National Right to Life Committee is to restore legal protection to human life.

Global Campaign for Microbicides ■ The Global Campaign for Microbicides is an international effort to build support for the development of microbicides. The website contains information about current research and availability of microbicides.

CengageNOW
Go to www.cengage.com/login to link to CengageNOW, your online study tool. First take the Pre-Test for this chapter to get your Personalized Study Plan, which will identify topics you need to review and direct you to online resources. Then take the Post-Test to determine what concepts you have mastered and what you still need work on.

Videos in CengageNOW

For additional information on topics discusses in this chapter, check out the videos in CengageNOW on the following topics:

- Virtual Safer-Sex Kit—Learn the relative benefits and risks of each contraceptive device and safer sex aid depicted.

- Emergency Contraception: The Debate About the Morning-After Pill—The FDA's dilemma about how to make Plan B over-the-counter but still prevent young teens from obtaining it on their own.

CHAPTER 14

Challenges to Sexual Functioning

For years, because of my cerebral palsy and certain other physical difficulties, I doubted my ability to give and receive pleasure in sexual intercourse. For a long time I did not want to ask my doctors about sex because I felt that a negative answer would make me regard myself as nonhuman—such is the value our society places on sexuality. Finally, since I was extremely hazy about what physical movements were involved in sexual intercourse, I decided to go to a movie. After the first two minutes I got the idea down pat and saw that I was perfectly capable of performing. My self-image skyrocketed. I, just like other women, had something sexual to offer a man!

There are various reasons why sexuality of the handicapped was avoided for so long and why it makes many professionals intolerably uncomfortable. First, most physical disabilities alter the looks of the person—deformities, bizarre head and arm motions, drooling, and poor eye contact. Few professionals are able to see their patients as sexu-

ally desirable, and there is even the subtly expressed attitude that there is something a bit wrong with anyone who is sexually attracted to a disabled person. You can imagine what such an attitude does to the self-esteem of the handicapped person—"Anyone who wants me must be nuts!"

The couple too disabled to have sex by themselves must decide whether they want to forgo sex or whether they want to make love in spite of needing help to do so. There are many reasons for making love—recreation, bribery, consolation, procreation, the desire for one-on-one attention, religious experience. Some of the reasons are more amenable than others to third-party participation. But I feel strongly that no couple who wants to have sex should be denied the necessary help to do so, and that, if they live in a health-care facility, it is the duty of the health-care professional to provide such help.

Initial access to potential partners is extremely limited, in large part due to my distorted speech. Opportunities to meet are

few, and when they do exist, men who are not trained to work with handicapped people tend to shy away from me. Somehow I hardly think the father of young children who held me in his arms as he helped me into the YWCA swimming pool was making plans to have me as a future bed partner.

Intellectually, I know that sexually I can perform—the movie proved it. Yet at what might be called the subintellectual level I doubt my body's ability to give another pleasure. Rarely does my body give me pleasure. When I tell it to do something as often as not it does exactly the opposite, or else it flares out in wild, tantrumlike motions. How could my body possibly conform to the wishes of an expectantly excited lover? This is the question I still ask myself.
SOURCE: Sutherland, 1987, pp. 25, 27.

ealthy sexuality depends on good mental and physical functioning. Challenges to sexual functioning include anxiety, sexual dysfunctions, illness, disease, and disability. However, learning to adapt to these challenges is important in maintaining a positive view of sexuality.

It is important to point out that our knowledge about male sexual functioning has advanced far ahead of our knowledge about female sexual functioning. Widespread interest in female sexual dysfunction is fairly recent in the United States and due in part to the success of Viagra. In 2001, the International Society for the Study of Women's Sexual Health (ISSWSH) was established to help foster communication and research into women's sexual health (see the Web Resources at the end of this chapter for more information).

In Chapter 10, we discussed the sexual response cycle—a series of physiological and psychological changes that occur in the body during sexual behavior. Sexual response models help health care providers and therapists identify how dysfunction, disease, illness, and disability affect sexual functioning. Because of continuing concerns over the application of these models to women, many newer models have been designed (Basson, 2005; Tiefer, 2000). In this chapter, we look at these issues and how sexual dysfunctions occur, the treatments used for it, and how illness and disability can interfere with sexual functioning.

Although our sexual response changes as we age, many older couples still enjoy an active, satisfying sex life.

© Roy McMahon/Corbis

Challenges to Sexual Functioning ■ **389**

Sexual Dysfunctions: Definitions, Causes, and Treatment Strategies

Before we discuss sexual dysfunctions, it's important to differentiate between common problems with sexual functioning and true sexual dysfunctions. Common sexual problems include things such as insufficient arousal, lack of enthusiasm for sex, and the inability to relax. These problems often occur infrequently and may or may not interfere with overall sexual functioning. Most of us have experienced a problem that has interfered with our sexual functioning at one point or another, but the problem went away without treatment. Even "normal" couples report periodic problems with sexual functioning (E. Frank et al., 1978). A sexual dysfunction is characterized by a disturbance in the sexual response that typically doesn't go away by itself—in fact, it may get worse over time.

What constitutes a sexual dysfunction? Not being able to get an erection one night? Difficulty having an orgasm during sexual intercourse? Having no sexual desire for your partner? Do sexual dysfunctions have to happen for extended periods of time, or do

---

REALResearch > Research in brain chemistry has found that anti-inflammatory drugs, such as acetaminophen (Tylenol), ibuprofen (Advil), or aspirin, used during a woman's pregnancy may negatively affect an offspring's sexual desire and functioning later in life (AMATEAU & McCARTHY, 2004).

---

they happen only once in a while? There are many types of sexual dysfunctions, and they can happen at any point during sexual activity and throughout the life span.

Sexual dysfunctions are classified by the *Diagnostic and Statistical Manual (DSM)*, the major diagnostic system used in U.S. research and therapy. The *DSM* is occasionally updated, with the last text revision in 2000 (referred to as the *DSM-IV-TR*; American Psychiatric Association, 2000). The *DSM* provides diagnostic criteria for the most common sexual dysfunctions including description, diagnosis, treatment, and research findings. It is anticipated that a revised, fifth edition of the *DSM* (*DSM-V*) will be released in 2012 (American Psychiatric Association, 2008).

One more point needs clarification before moving on—as you will soon realize, the *DSM* classification system for sexual dysfunctions appears rather heterosexist in that often the criteria for diagnosis revolves around an inability to engage in vaginal intercourse. This implies that only heterosexuals experience sexual dysfunction because gay men and lesbian women do not engage in vaginal intercourse. The truth is that we all—gay, straight, and bisexual—can potentially experience a sexual dysfunction. The definition of "penetration" may not always refer to penile–vaginal penetration—it can include anal, oral, or digital penetration. In this chapter, we refer to an inclusive definition of sexual dysfunction.

While some men and women who experience sexual dysfunctions are not distressed by them and do not seek treatment (see the Real Research feature on page 403), some do seek treatment by talking to their health care provider or a sex therapist. A health care provider or sex therapist's first task in evaluating a new client is to ascertain whether a dysfunction exists, and if so, whether the dysfunction is psychological, physiological, or both. This is not always an easy task because psychological and physiological factors can overlap. Let's take a look at some of these factors.

PSYCHOLOGICAL FACTORS IN SEXUAL DYSFUNCTION

Psychological factors that can interfere with sexual functioning include unconscious fears, ongoing stress, anxiety, depression, guilt, anger, fear of infidelity, partner conflict, fear of intimacy, dependency, abandonment, and concern over loss of control, all of which may impair the ability to respond sexually. As we discussed in Chapter 10, the various pressures and time commitments of everyday life may lead to an absence of sexual intimacy. We also know that anxiety plays an important role in developing and maintaining sexual dysfunctions. Both **performance fears** and an excessive need to please a partner interfere with sexual functioning (Bancroft et al., 2005; Kaplan, 1974; Masters & Johnson, 1970). When anxiety levels are high, physiological arousal may be impossible. Therefore, sex therapy usually begins by overcoming performance fears, feelings of sexual inadequacy, and other anxieties. Distractions, shifts in attention, or preoccupation during sexual arousal may interfere with the ability to become aroused, as can **spectatoring.** Therapy may also treat emotional factors such as depression, anger, or guilt. We talk about treatment for psychological factors more later in this chapter.

PHYSICAL FACTORS IN SEXUAL DYSFUNCTION

The prevalence of sexual dysfunction increases with age (Araujo et al., 2004; R. W. Lewis et al., 2004; Yassin & Saad, 2008). This is mainly because of physical factors such as disease, disability, illness, and the use of many commonly used drugs. Prescription drugs may cause erectile or ejaculatory problems in men, orgasm problems in women, and a loss of sexual desire in both. **Psychotropic medications** often lead to sexual dysfunction (Feliciano & Alfonso, 1997). Lowering the drug dosage or changing medications may result in a reversal of these difficulties. Nonprescription

performance fears
The fear of not being able to perform during sexual behavior.

spectatoring
Acting as an observer or judge of one's own sexual performance.

psychotropic medications
Medications prescribed for psychological disorders, such as depression.

Women and Sexual Dysfunction

. . . most sexual problems occur when there is 'discontent or dissatisfaction with any emotional, physical, or relational aspect of sexual experience'.

Masters and Johnson's sexual response cycle (see Chapter 10) and the *DSM* medical classification for sexual dysfunction (see Table 14.1) have long been used as the foundation for treating sexual dysfunction. However, critics challenge how these models apply to female sexuality and contend that they are incomplete by not encompassing psychosocial dimensions of sexual expression (also see Figure 14.2). In 2000, Leonore Tiefer, a leading sex therapist and feminist sexologist, and a group of colleagues proposed the New View of Women's Sexual Problems that included a revision in the classification system for female sexual dysfunction (Kaschak & Tiefer, 2001).

According to Tiefer and colleagues, most sexual problems occur when there is "discontent or dissatisfaction with any emotional, physical, or relational aspect of sexual experience" (Tiefer, 2001). The New View proponents prefer the use of the term "sexual problem" (rather than "sexual dysfunction") for its reduced implication of a medical disease state. The New View of Sexual Problems includes four categories that account for most of the limitations in women's sexual functioning:

I. Sexual Problems Due to Socio-Cultural, Political, Economic Factors
Some contributing factors may include ignorance and anxiety due to lack of sex education, lack of access to reproductive health services, or other social constraints and pressures, perceived inability to meet cultural norms for ideal sexuality, and conflict between the sexual norms of culture of origin and another culture.

II. Sexual Problems Relating to Partner and Relationship Factors may include inhibition, avoidance, or distress arising from betrayal, dislike, or fear of partner; partner's abuse or unequal power; partner's negative patterns of communication; or discrepancies in desire for various sexual activities.

III. Sexual Problems Due to Psychological Factors
These factors include sexual aversion, mistrust, or inhibition of sexual pleasure due to past experiences of physical, sexual, or emotional abuse; depression and anxiety; or general personality problems.

IV. Sexual Problems Due to Medical Factors
Such problems can arise from a wide variety of factors, including numerous local or systemic medical conditions affecting neurological, neurovascular, circulatory, endocrine or other systems of the body; pregnancy, sexually transmitted diseases, or other sex-related conditions; and side effects of many drugs, medications, or medical treatments.

New View proponents believe that an overmedicalization of female sexuality has resulted in an obsessive focus on the physical (genital) aspect of sexuality, leaving psychological and social aspects trivialized or ignored (Tiefer, 1996, 2002). The medical approaches to women's sexual problems has evolved into an increasing emphasis on pills, creams, gels and other pharmaceutical agents, to the dismay of those who believe sexual behavior is multidimensional, complex, and context-dependent (see websites at the end of the chapter for more information on the New View Campaign).

---

drugs such as tobacco, alcohol, marijuana, LSD, and cocaine may also contribute to sexual dysfunction. As we discussed in Chapter 13, research has been evaluating the effects of oral contraceptives on sexual arousal and desire (Graham et al., 2007; Hatcher et al., 2007). We talk about treatment for physical factors more later in this chapter.

CATEGORIZING THE DYSFUNCTIONS

Sexual dysfunctions are categorized as either primary or secondary, and situational or global. A **primary sexual dysfunction** is one that has always existed, whereas a **secondary sexual dysfunction** is one in which a dysfunction developed after a period of adequate functioning. A **situational sexual dysfunction** is a dysfunction that occurs during certain sexual activities or with certain partners (for instance, a man who can get an erection with his

girlfriend but not his wife, or a woman who can have orgasms during masturbation but not during oral sex). A **global sexual dysfunction** is a dysfunction that occurs in every situation, during every type of sexual activity, and with every sexual partner.

It is important to clarify these differences, for they may affect treatment strategies. For instance, primary problems tend to have more biological or physiological causes, whereas secondary problems tend to have more psychological causes. Sex therapists further categorize dysfunctions as those of sexual desire, sexual arousal, orgasm, or pain disorders (many sex therapists use the *DSM-IV-TR* to help in their diagnosing). Each of these may be

primary sexual dysfunction A sexual dysfunction that has always existed.

secondary sexual dysfunction A sexual dysfunction that occurs after a period of normal sexual functioning.

situational sexual dysfunction A sexual dysfunction that occurs only in specific situations.

global sexual dysfunction A sexual dysfunction that occurs in every sexual situation.

| table | 14.1 |

The Sexual Dysfunctions

Sexual Desire Disorders	Symptoms: Sexual Interest
Hypoactive sexual desire disorder	Primary—lifelong diminished or absent feelings of sexual interest or desire; absent sexual thoughts or fantasies Secondary—acquired diminished or absent feelings of sexual interest or desire; diminished or absent sexual thoughts or fantasies
Sexual aversion disorder	Primary—lifelong persistent or recurrent extreme aversion to, and avoidance of, all genital sexual contact with a sexual partner Secondary—acquired persistent or recurrent extreme aversion to, and avoidance of, all genital sexual contact with a sexual partner
Sexual Arousal Disorders	**Symptoms: Physiological Arousal**
Female sexual arousal disorder	Primary—lifelong diminished or absent lubrication response of sexual excitement Secondary—acquired diminished or absent lubrication response of sexual excitement
Male erectile disorder	Primary—lifelong diminished or absent ability to attain or maintain, until completion of the sexual activity, an adequate erection Secondary—acquired diminished or absent ability to attain or maintain, until completion of the sexual activity, an adequate erection
Orgasm disorders	**Symptoms: Orgasm or Ejaculation Problems**
Female orgasmic disorder	Primary—lifelong delay or absence of orgasm following normal sexual excitement Secondary—acquired delay or absence of orgasm following normal sexual excitement
Male orgasmic disorder	Primary—lifelong absence of orgasm in men Secondary—acquired diminished ability to orgasm or markedly decreased orgasmic intensity from any type of stimulation
Premature ejaculation	Primary—lifelong pattern of ejaculating with minimal sexual stimulation before, on, or shortly after penetration and before the person wishes it Secondary—acquired pattern of ejaculating with minimal sexual stimulation before, on, or shortly after penetration and before the person wishes it
Retarded (or inhibited) ejaculation	Primary—lifelong inability to reach orgasm or a prolonged stimulation period to orgasm Secondary—recurrent or persistent inability to reach orgasm or a need for prolonged stimulation period to orgasm
Retrograde ejaculation	Primary—a lifelong pattern of backwards flow of ejaculate into the bladder instead of being released through the urethra Secondary—recurrent or persistent backward flow of ejaculate into the bladder instead of being released through the urethra
Sexual Pain Disorders	**Symptom: Genital Pain**
Dyspareunia	Primary—lifelong recurrent or persistent genital pain associated with sexual intercourse, either in a male or female Secondary—acquired recurrent or persistent genital pain associated with sexual intercourse, either in a male or female
Vaginismus	Primary—lifelong pattern of recurrent or persistent involuntary spasms of the outer third of the vagina that interferes with sexual intercourse Secondary—acquired pattern of recurrent or persistent involuntary spasms of the outer third of the vagina that interferes with sexual intercourse
Sexual Dysfunctions Due to a General Medical Condition	
	Presence of sexual dysfunction that is due to the physiological effects of a general medical condition

primary or secondary, situational or global. See Table 14.1 for an overview of sexual dysfunctions.

TREATING DYSFUNCTIONS

Treatment of most sexual dysfunctions begins with a medical history and workup to identify any physiological causes. In addition to a medical history and examination, it is also important to evaluate any past sexual trauma or abuse that may cause or contribute to the dysfunction. After identifying causes for a sexual dysfunction, the next step is to determine a plan of treatment. Such treatment may be **multimodal,** involving more than one type of therapy. Different types of therapies have different success rates.

Much of the current clinical research today focuses on developing new drugs to treat dysfunctions (even though a number of

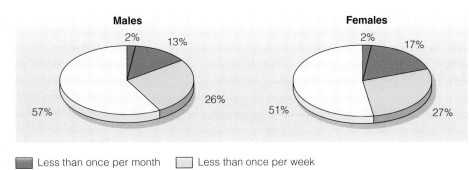

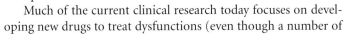

Figure **14.1** How Often Do You Engage in Sex? Sex therapists often rely on norms for sexual behavior to evaluate a client's sexual complaints. Above are the results of a global survey which asked people how often they engaged in sex. However, keep in mind that this type of research may not provide adequate norms, since many people may not be truthful or able to remember their past sexual activity. Data from The Global Study of Sexual Attitudes and Behaviors, funded by Pfizer, Inc. (© 2002 Pfizer, Inc.)

dysfunctions, such as Wellbutrin or Viagra, were originally approved by the FDA to treat other diseases. There is also a brisk business in health supplements to aid in sexual functioning, including aphrodisiacs (see Sex in Real Life, "What Is an Aphrodisiac?" later in the chapter).

We discuss illness and physical causes later in this chapter, but now let us turn to the symptoms and possible causes of various sexual dysfunctions and the current therapies used to treat them.

REALResearch **>** Asian American women have been found to have more sexual complaints than women in other ethnic groups (Woo & Brotto, 2008). However, Asian American men do not have a higher frequency of sexual complaints or problems.

dysfunctions may be caused by or worsened by other medications). As we discussed in Chapter 13, the Food and Drug Administration (FDA) plays a major role in the approval of all new drugs in the United States. Many drug therapies used today for sexual

multimodal
Using a variety of techniques.

review questions

1 Explain how sexual dysfunctions are classified and describe the difference between sexual problems and dysfunctions.

2 Identify some of the psychological factors that have been found to interfere with sexual functioning.

3 Identify some of the physical factors that have been found to interfere with sexual functioning.

4 Differentiate between a primary and secondary sexual dysfunction and explain how these categories may affect treatment strategies.

5 Differentiate between a situational and global sexual dysfunction and explain how these categories may affect treatment strategies.

6 Explain the approach to treatment of sexual dysfunctions.

Sexual Desire Disorders

The *DSM-IV-TR* has two categories of sexual desire disorders, **hypoactive sexual desire (HSD)** and **sexual aversion.** Although there appear to be fewer cases of male HSD than female cases, these lower reports may be attributed to the fact that many men feel less comfortable discussing the problem. Although there are no overall statistics available for prevalence of sexual aversion, researchers believe the condition is relatively rare (Heiman, 2002).

Many therapists consider sexual desire disorders to be the most complicated sexual dysfunction to treat. As we discussed previously, treatment first involves a medical workup to identify any physiological causes. A psychological evaluation will explore any past sexual trauma or abuse that may interfere with sexual desire. Intensive psychotherapy can be undertaken to identify and resolve these causes and can also to explore the motivations for avoiding intimacy. The client may also be assigned homework exercises to help identify these motivations.

HYPOACTIVE SEXUAL DESIRE

When someone has HSD, there are diminished or absent feelings of interest in, or desire for, sexual activity (Heiman, 2002; Gambescia, 2007). However, a person with a HSD can still function sexually even though he or she often does not feel interested in sex. Although studies have found that 33% of women and 16% of men report an ongoing lack of sexual interest (Laumann et al., 1999), decreased desire is one of the most common sexual complaints in women (Frank et al., 2008; Gambescia, 2007). A nationally representative sample of U.S. women found 27% of premenopausal women and 52% of naturally menopausal women experienced HSD (West et al., 2008). Decreases in ovarian hormones may contribute to HSD in menopausal women (Graziottin, 2007; Leiblum et al., 2006).

Many women who experience HSD also experience psychological and emotional distress and lower levels of partner satisfaction (Leiblum et al., 2006). Interestingly, one study found that even though the prevalence of HSD increased with age, the proportion of women distressed about their HSD actually decreased with age (Graziottin, 2007; Hayes et al., 2007).

HSD may manifest in several ways. There may be a lack of sexual fantasies, a reduction of or absence in initiating sexual activity, or a decrease in self-stimulation. Primary HSD, the less common type, is diagnosed when a person has a lifelong pattern of complete disinterest in sex. Secondary HSD, which is more common, refers to a problem in which desire was normal for a certain period of time but then diminished.

Psychological causes for HSD may include a lack of attraction to one's partner, fear of intimacy or pregnancy, marital or relationship conflicts, religious concerns, depression, and other psychological disorders. HSD can also result from negative messages about female sexuality while growing up, treating sex as a chore, a concern over loss of control, or a negative body image (Heiman & LoPiccolo, 1992). Anorexia, sexual coercion, and abuse have all been found to be associated with HSD (Carter et al., 2007; J. F. Morgan et al., 1999). In one study of survivors of sexual assault, more than half had long-lasting problems with sexual desire (Campbell et al., 2006).

HSD in both men and women may also be due to biological factors such as hormonal problems, medication side effects, and illness (Graziottin, 2007; Leiblum et al., 2006). Chronic use of alcohol has also been implicated in HSD (Lutfey et al., 2008).

Treating Hypoactive Sexual Desire

Treatment of HSD disorder depends on many factors, including the individual and his or her relationship. Sex and marital therapy have both been found to be effective, although they may not be as effective in couples experiencing relationship difficulties on top of the sexual dysfunction. Cognitive–behavioral therapy, a form of psychotherapy that emphasizes the importance of how a person thinks and the effect these thoughts have on a person's feelings and behaviors, has offered promising results. These types of therapy are brief (the average number of sessions a client receives is 16), highly instructional, and structured.

Pharmacological (drug) treatment may also be used. Although no drugs are proven to increase sexual desire in men or women, there is evidence that testosterone may be helpful in those who have low testosterone levels (Heiman, 2002; Kingsberg et al., 2007). Because testosterone is largely responsible for male sexual desire, men with low testosterone levels have historically been treated with testosterone injections. However, research has been unable to show a consistent and beneficial role of testosterone in increasing sexual desire in men (Allan et al., 2008; Isidori et al., 2005). Overall, the majority of men who experience low sexual desire have normal levels of testosterone (Wespes & Schulman, 2002).

In women, circulating levels of testosterone decline as they age—in fact, women in their 40s have half the testosterone levels of women in their 20s (Goldstat et al., 2003). Although research has found that low testosterone levels in women contribute to decreased sexual desire, arousal, or orgasm, the use of testosterone therapy in women has also been controversial (Hubayter & Simon, 2008; Talakoub et al., 2002). Some studies have found that testosterone use in women increases sexual desire (S. Davis et al., 2008; Goldstat et al., 2003; Hubayter & Simon, 2008; Kingsberg et al., 2007), whereas other studies have found no improvements in sexual desire levels (S. R. Davis et al., 2005; Panjari & Davis, 2007). However, methodology issues plague many of the studies that support testosterone use, such as small sample sizes and short treatment durations (Panjari & Davis, 2007). Side effects of testosterone use in women include unwanted facial hair, weight gain, acne, and a loss of head hair (Munarriz et al., 2002; Shifren et al., 2000). In addition, there may be an elevated risk of breast cancer

> **The prevalence** of sexual aversion **is relatively rare.**

---

hypoactive sexual desire (HSD)
Diminished or absent sexual interest or desire.

sexual aversion
Persistent or recurrent extreme aversion to and avoidance of all genital sexual contact.

What Is an Aphrodisiac?

. . . it is possible that if a person thinks something will increase his or her sexual desire, it just might do so.

Throughout history, people from primitive—and not so primitive—cultures have searched for the "ultimate" aphrodisiac to enhance sexual interest and performance. Oysters, for example, have been reported to increase sexual desire, although this has never been proven. The idea that oysters are an aphrodisiac may have originated from their resemblance to male testicles—or even to female ovaries. Ancient people believed that food with the shape or qualities of the genitals possessed aphrodisiac qualities; seeds of all kinds were associated with fertility and desire. Scientists have also reported that watermelon can increase sexual desire and interest (Santa Ana, 2008).

In various cultures, carrots, cucumbers, chili peppers, rhino horns, and various seafood, as well as eggs and poppy seeds, were thought to increase sexual desire. The market for so-called aphrodisiacs in some countries has added to the decline of some endangered species, such as the rhinoceros, valued for its horn.

There are no proven aphrodisiacs, but it is possible that if a person thinks something will increase his or her sexual desire, it just might do so. Simply *believing* something will increase desire may cause it to work. Here are some of the most popular substances that have been thought to increase sexual desire. Overall, to increase sexual desire, rely on regular exercise, a healthy diet, candlelight, the use of scents, romantic music, and whatever else enhances your personal sexual arousal.

Alcohol: Although some people believe that alcohol increases their sexual desire, in actuality it merely decreases anxiety and inhibitions, and then only in low doses. In large amounts, alcohol can impair sexual functioning.

In Bangkok, Thailand, a vendor is pushing cobra blood to improve sexual drive. Customers choose their own snake, and then the snake is split open with a razor blade. An incision is made in the major artery of the snake, and all the blood is drained into a wine glass. The blood is then mixed with warm whiskey and a dash of honey. Users believe it helps their sex drive.

AP Photos/Sakchai Lalit

Amyl nitrate: Amyl nitrate (also called "snappers" or "poppers") is thought to increase orgasmic sensations. It is inhaled from capsules that are "popped" open for quick use. Amyl nitrate causes a rapid dilation of arteries that supply the heart and other organs with blood, which may cause warmth in the genitals. Amyl nitrate may dilate arteries in the brain, causing euphoria or giddiness, and relax the sphincter muscle to ease penetration during anal sex. Side effects include severe dizziness, migraine headaches, and fainting. (Amyl nitrate is used by cardiac patients to reduce heart pain.)

Cocaine: Thought to increase frequency of sexual behavior, sexual desire, and orgasmic sensations. In actuality, cocaine may reduce inhibitions, possibly leading to risky sexual behaviors. Long-term use can result in depression, addiction, and increased anxiety.

Ginseng: An herb that has been thought to increase sexual desire. It has not been found to have any specific effects on sexuality.

Marijuana: Reduces inhibitions and may improve mood. No proven effect on sexual desire.

Spanish fly: Consists of ground-up beetle wings (cantharides) from Europe and causes inflammation of the urinary tract and dilation of the blood vessels. Although some people find the burning sensation arousing, Spanish fly may cause death from its toxic side effects.

Yohimbine: From the African Yohimbe tree. Injections have been found to increase sexual arousal and performance in lab animals. It has been prescribed by physicians to increase the frequency of physiological arousal.

(Schover, 2008). The bottom line is that the use of testosterone is not recommended until long-term studies can demonstrate the efficacy and safety of its use (Bitzer et al., 2008a; Schover, 2008).

Sometimes it is not one partner's level of desire that is the problem but the **discrepancy in desire** between the partners. Many couples experience differences in their levels of desire—one partner may desire sex more often than the other. One partner may desire sex only once a month, whereas the other may desire sex once a day. Often, the partner with a lower level of desire will show up at a therapist's office and not the partner with higher

desire (R. C. Rosen & Leiblum, 1987). If the partner with the lower level of desire was paired with someone with an equal level of sexual desire, there would be no problem. People experiencing low levels of sexual desire may turn to **aphrodisiacs** for help (see the accompanying Sex in Real Life, "What Is an Aphrodisiac?").

discrepancy in desire
Differences in levels of sexual desire in a couple.

aphrodisiac
A substance that increases, or is believed to increase, a person's sexual desire.

Treating Sexual Dysfunction in Other Cultures

Sexual goals are different among cultural groups with an egalitarian ideology than among those without.

Sex therapy in the United States has been criticized for its adherence to Western sexual attitudes and values, with an almost total ignorance of cultural differences in sexual dysfunction and therapy. Our view of sex tends to emphasize that activity is pleasurable (or at least natural), both partners are equally involved, couples need and want to be educated about sex, and communication is important to have good sexual relationships (Lavee, 1991; So & Cheung, 2005). It is important to recognize, however, that these ideas might not be shared outside the United States or within different ethnic groups—therefore Masters and Johnson's classic therapy model might be less acceptable to these groups. Sexual goals are different among cultural groups with an egalitarian ideology than among those without (Lau et al., 2005). An egalitarian ideology views mutual sexual pleasure and communication as important, whereas nonegalitarian ideologies view heterosexual intercourse as the goal and men's sexual pleasure as more important than women's (Reiss, 1986). Double standards of sexual pleasure are common, for example, in many Portuguese, Mexican, Puerto Rican, and Latino groups. Some Asian groups also often have strong cultural prohibitions about discussing sexuality. So U.S. values such as open communication, mutual satisfaction, and accommodation to a partner's sexuality may not be appropriate in working with people from these cultures.

In cultures in which low female sexual desire is not viewed as a problem, hypoactive sexual desire wouldn't be viewed as a sexual dysfunction; it would be an acceptable part of female sexuality. In some Muslim groups, for example, the only problems that exist are those that interfere with men's sexual activity (Lavee, 1991).

Approaches to sexual dysfunction also differ outside the United States. Some cultures believe in supernatural causes of sexual dysfunction (such as the man being cursed by a powerful woman or being given the evil eye; So & Cheung, 2005). Malay and Chinese men who experience ED tend to blame their wives for the problem, whereas Indian men attribute their problem to fate (Low et al., 2002). However, Asian culture has also produced the Tantric ceremonial sexual ritual, which might be viewed as therapy for sexual dysfunction.

Tantric sex involves five exercises (Voigt, 1991). First, a couple begins by developing a private ritual to prepare them to share sexual expression: the lighting of candles; using perfume, lotions, music, a special bed or room; certain lighting patterns; massage; reciting poetry together; or meditating. Then they synchronize their breathing by lying together and "getting in touch" with each other. Direct eye contact is sustained throughout the ritual. (Couples often say that they feel uncomfortable using eye contact, but with practice it becomes very powerful.)

Next, "*motionless* intercourse" begins, in which the couple remains *motionless* at the peak of the sensual experience. For many couples, this may be during the time of initial penetration. Initially, this motionlessness may last only a few minutes, building up to increasingly longer periods. The final aspect of the Tantric ritual is to expand the sexual exchange without orgasm, resulting in an intensification of the sexual–spiritual energy (this is similar to Masters and Johnson's technique of delaying orgasm to enjoy the physical sensations of touching and caressing).

SEXUAL AVERSION

Unlike HSD, in which a person might be able to engage in sexual activity even though he or she has little or no desire to do so, a person with a sexual aversion reacts with strong disgust or fear to a sexual interaction. Men and women with sexual aversion seek to avoid any genital contact, and some women may even avoid gynecological examinations (Kingsberg & Janata, 2003). In primary sexual aversion, a man or woman has a negative response to sexual interactions from his or her earliest memory to the present; in a secondary sexual aversion, there was a period of pleasurable and desirable sexual activity before the aversion started.

Overall, sexual aversion affects more women than men, and it is frequently associated with a history of childhood sexual trauma or abuse (Kingsberg & Janata, 2003). This is especially true if the sexual abuse was forced, abusive, guilt producing, or pressured. A history of anorexia has also been found to be associated with sexual aversion (J. F. Morgan et al., 1999).

REALResearch > Sexual dysfunction is common in men and women who experience posttraumatic stress disorder and can affect overall sexual activity, desire, arousal, orgasm, and satisfaction (Chudakov et al., 2008).

Treating Sexual Aversion

Treatment of sexual aversion is difficult, mainly because most men and women would rather not discuss sexuality and are resistant to seeking help. If they do seek help, the most common treatment involves discovering and resolving the underlying conflict. Generally, cognitive–behavioral therapy is most successful at helping to uncover the relationship issues or events from early childhood that contribute to the symptoms of sexual aversion. Treatment often includes goal setting and the completion of homework assignments, both individually and with a partner. It is important that therapy moves at the client's pace and that time is taken to work through his or her issues.

review questions

1 Identify and differentiate the two categories of sexual desire disorders.

2 Explain how hypoactive sexual desire disorder presents and identify some of the possible psychological and physical causes.

3 Identify possible treatment strategies for hypoactive desire disorder.

4 Explain how sexual aversion disorder presents and identify some of the possible psychological and physical causes.

5 Identify possible treatment strategies for sexual aversion disorder.

Sexual Arousal Disorders

The *DSM-IV-TR* has two categories of sexual arousal disorders, female **sexual arousal disorder** and male **erectile disorder.** Sexual arousal disorders occur even when the client reports adequate focus, intensity, and duration of sexual stimulation. The disorder may be primary or, more commonly, secondary in that it only occurs with a certain partner or specific sexual behavior.

FEMALE SEXUAL AROUSAL DISORDER

Female sexual arousal disorder (FSAD) is a persistent or recurrent inability to either obtain or maintain an adequate lubrication response of sexual excitement. In the National Health and Social Life Study, approximately 20% of women reported a lack of sexual lubrication during sexual stimulation (Laumann et al., 1999), whereas 30% of women worldwide report FSAD (Safarinejad, 2008). In addition, FSAD has been found to increase with age (R. W. Lewis et al., 2004). Some women who experience FSAD also experience problems related to desire or orgasmic disorders (Heiman, 2002). Physiological factors in FSAD include decreased blood flow and lubrication in the vulva; psychological factors include fear, guilt, anxiety, and depression. Women who experience female sexual arousal disorder have been found to have a lower sensitivity to touch compared with women without FSAD (Frohlich & Meston, 2005). Further research is needed to determine how this sensitivity might play a role in the development or maintenance of FSAD.

A new category of female sexual arousal has been proposed in which a woman experiences persistent sexual arousal (referred to as **persistent sexual arousal syndrome** or persistent genital arousal disorder; Leiblum, 2007). The opposite of FSAD, a woman's complaint is usually an excessive and unremitting arousal (Goldmeier & Leiblum, 2006). Genital arousal can last for hours or days despite a lack of sexual desire or stimulation (Leiblum, 2007). This persistent arousal can be distressing and worrisome to women and although many may have been reluctant to discuss it with their health care providers in the past, today more women are acknowledging this problem and seeking treatment (Leiblum, 2007). More research is needed to shed more light on this disorder.

Treating Female Sexual Arousal Disorder

In 2000, the EROS clitoral therapy device (CTD) was approved by the FDA for the treatment of FSAD. The device has a small plastic cup that is placed over the clitoris before sex. The cup is attached to a vacuum pump that draws blood into the clitoris, leading to clitoral engorgement. This engorgement increases vaginal lubrication, sexual arousal, and desire. There have not yet been large-scale studies evaluating the benefits of using the EROS-CTD. In addition, there are concerns about the price of this device, which can be over $300 and requires a doctor's prescription. Parallels have been drawn to vibrators and related sex toys, which sell for a fraction of this cost.

sexual arousal disorder Diminished or absent lubrication response of sexual excitation.

erectile disorder Diminished or absent ability to attain or maintain, until completion of the sexual activity, an adequate erection.

persistent sexual arousal syndrome An excessive and unremitting level of sexual arousal. May also be referred to as persistent genital arousal disorder.

There have been many studies evaluating various pharmacological treatments for FSAD. Since the release of Viagra for men in 1998, there has been much interest in using similar drugs to increase sexual arousal in women (Berman et al., 2003; Caruso et al., 2006). However, some studies have shown that although Viagra can increase vasocongestion and lubrication, it provides little overall benefit in the treatment of female sexual arousal disorder (Basson et al., 2002).

In 2006 to 2007, there was growing interest in a nasal spray inhaler dubbed PT-141 (bremelanotide) for treatment of FSAD, which affects the central nervous system, specifically the hypothalamus (Diamond et al., 2006; Pfaus et al., 2007; Safarinejad, 2008; Shadiack et al., 2007). Studies on female rats found increased sexual interest and behaviors (Pfaus et al., 2007). PT-141 claims to work directly on melanocortin receptors in the brain to raise sexual arousal in both men and women. Although preliminary studies suggested PT-141 positively affected desire and arousal in women with FSAD (Diamond et al., 2006; Perelman, 2007; Pfaus et al., 2007; Safarinejad, 2008; Shadiack et al., 2007), the FDA reduced clinical trials of PT-141 in mid-2008 because of safety concerns, including increased blood pressure in participants taking the drug. Limited ongoing trials continue to evaluate this drug and variations of the drug (Clinical Trials, 2008). A few pilot studies have also been conducted on a variety of other **vasoactive agents** to help reduce FSAD, including VasoMax, or phentolamine. Lyriana, a vasoactive cream that is massaged into the

clitoris and labia, gained attention in 2008 for increasing blood flow and reducing FSAD ("About Lyriana," 2008).

A variety of herbal products are available for FSAD, including Zestra, a botanical massage oil formulated to increase female arousal and pleasure, and Avlimil, a nonprescription daily supplement. Both of these claim to be successful at increasing female sexual arousal (D. M. Ferguson et al., 2003). Viacreme, an amino-acid-based cream that contains menthol, has also been used for FSAD. The makers of Viacreme claim that when it is applied to the clitoris, blood flow increases through dilation of clitoral blood vessels. Studies are also testing other agents to increase female sexual arousal, including the aphrodisiac **yohimbine** (yo-HIM-bean; Meston & Worcel, 2002). Yohimbine is a substance produced in the bark of the African yohimbe tree, which has been found to improve sexual functioning. Although these products do not require FDA approval, more research is needed to assess their possible effects and complications (Islam et al., 2001). Despite a great deal of research, few of these hormonal and vasoactive agents have withstood scientific scrutiny (Perelman, 2007). In ad-

vasoactive agent
Medication that causes dilation of the blood vessels.

yohimbine
Produced from the bark of the African yohimbe tree; often used as an aphrodisiac.

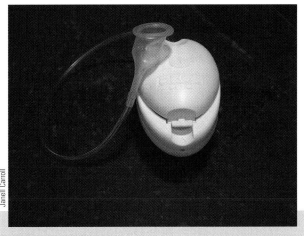

The EROS-CTD is a handheld device that increases blood flow to the clitoris. The plastic cup is placed directly over the clitoris.

Janell Carroll

dition, safety issues have not been addressed for many of these products, adding to concerns of potential harm that these products may produce.

Treating female sexual arousal disorder with pharmaceuticals and herbal products is not always a complete success because the female sexual response cycle is complex (Basson, 2005). Many women are often more focused on the emotional aspects, rather than the genital aspects, of sexual behavior, and thus more effective treatments may be a combination of drugs and psychological therapy (see Figure 14.2; Brotto, 2004; Heiman, 2002; Millner, 2005).

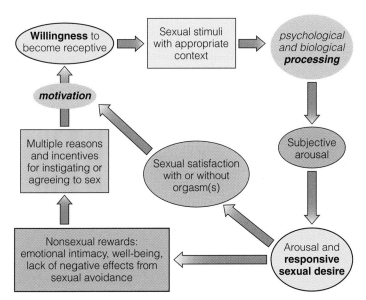

Figure 14.2 Basson sexual response cycle. Rosemary Basson proposes a revised model in the development of sexual desire in women. Although a woman might not begin a sexual interaction feeling sexual desire, her motivations help her develop desire. She may instigate or agree to have sex for a variety of reasons, such as physical pleasure, to express love, or to feel emotionally closer to her partner. This motivation enables her to focus on sexual stimuli, which lead to subjective sexual arousal. Continued stimulation intensifies excitement and pleasure, triggering a desire for sexual behavior. Source: Basson, R. (2001). Using a different model for female sexual response to address women's problematic low sexual desire. *Journal of Sex and Marital Therapy, 27,* 395–403.

WHAT DO YOU WANT TO KNOW ?

Is erectile disorder hereditary?

No, erectile disorder itself is not hereditary. However, certain diseases, such as diabetes, may be inherited and can lead to an erectile disorder or other sexual dysfunctions. It is important to catch these diseases early so that medical intervention can decrease any possible sexual side effects.

MALE ERECTILE DISORDER

Erectile disorder (ED) is defined as the persistent inability to obtain or maintain an erection sufficient for satisfactory sexual behavior (Yassin & Saad, 2008). ED affects millions of men (Costabile et al., 2008; Lue, 2000), and the incidence increases with age—12% of men younger than 59 experience ED, whereas 22% of men aged 60 to 69, and 30% of men over the age of 69 experience ED (Bacon et al., 2003).

We know that normal erectile function involves neurological, endocrine, vascular, and muscular factors. Psychological factors including fear of failure and performance anxiety may also affect erectile functioning. Anxiety has been found to have a cyclical effect on erectile functioning: if a man experiences a problem getting an erection one night, the next time he tries to have intercourse he remembers the failure and becomes anxious. This anxiety, in turn, interferes with his ability to have an erection.

Problems in any of these areas can lead to ED, although newer research has found that 70% of cases have a physical basis, with the major risk factors being diabetes, high cholesterol levels, or chronic medical illnesses (Yassin & Saad, 2008). In many cases, ED is due to a combination of factors (Fink et al., 2002). Unfortunately, when a health care provider identifies a physical problem (such as hypertension) in a patient suffering from ED, he or she might not continue to explore the psychological factors. Or if a psychological problem is found first (such as a recent divorce), the health care provider might not perform a medical evaluation. Overall, EDs in younger men (20–35 years old) are more likely to be psychologically based, whereas EDs in older men (60 and older), they are more likely to be due to physical factors (Lue, 2000).

To diagnose the causes of erectile disorder, health care providers and sex therapists may use tests such as the **nocturnal penile tumescence (NPT) test.** Men normally experience two or three erections a night during stages of rapid eye movement (REM) sleep. If these erections do not occur, it is a good indication that there is a physiological problem; if they do occur, erectile problems are more likely to have psychological causes. The NPT requires a man to spend the night in a sleep laboratory hooked up to several machines, but newer devices allow him to monitor his sleep erections in the privacy of his own home. RigiScan, a portable diagnostic monitor, measures both rigidity and tumescence

nocturnal penile tumescence (NPT) test
A study performed to evaluate erections during sleep that helps clarify the causes of erectile dysfunction.

> Data from a nationally representative sample found that sexual problems among aging men and women are not inevitable consequences of aging, but often develop in response to life stressors, such as relationship and mental health issues (LAUMANN & WAITE, 2008). Overall, women's sexual health has been found to be more sensitive to life stressors than men's.

at the base and tip of the penis. Stamp tests and other at-home devices are also used. A stamp test uses perforated bands resembling postage stamps, which are placed on the base of the penis prior to retiring for the night. In the morning, if the perforations have ripped, this indicates that the man had normal physiological functioning while sleeping.

Treating Male Erectile Disorder

Of all the sexual dysfunctions, there are more treatment options for male erectile disorder than for any other sexual dysfunction. A tremendous amount of research has been dedicated to finding causes and treatment options for ED. Depending on the cause, treatment for ED includes psychological treatment, pharmacological treatment (drugs), hormonal and intracavernous injections, vascular surgery, vacuum constriction devices, and prosthesis implantation. The success rate for treating male erectile disorder (ED) ranges from 50% to 80% (Lue, 2000).

PSYCHOLOGICAL TREATMENT The primary psychological treatments for ED include **systematic desensitization** and sex therapy that includes education, **sensate focus,** and communication training (Heiman, 2002). These treatments can help reduce feelings of anxiety and can evaluate issues that are interfering with erectile response. Relationship therapy can also help explore issues in a relationship that might contribute to erectile dysfunction, such as unresolved anger, bitterness, or guilt.

PHARMACOLOGICAL TREATMENT The first oral medication for ED, Viagra (sildenafil citrate), was approved by the FDA in 1998 and in 2003, Cialis (tadalafil) and Levitra (vardenafil) were approved. These drugs can be used in a variety of ED cases—those that are **psychogenic** (sike-oh-JEN-nick), illness related, or that have physical causes (Heiman, 2002).

All of these drugs produce muscle relaxation in the penis, dilation of the arteries supplying the penis, and an inflow of blood—which can lead to penile erection. They do not increase a man's sexual desire and will not produce an erection without adequate sexual stimulation. Typically, a man must take Viagra about 1 hour before he desires an erection, and Cialis and Levitra often work within 15 to 30 minutes. Erections can last up to 4 hours, although Cialis can aid in erections for up to 36 hours (which is why French media referred to it as "le weekend," because it can be

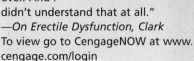

View in Video

"In the process of becoming aroused, all of a sudden it would be over. And I didn't understand that at all."
—*On Erectile Dysfunction, Clark*
To view go to CengageNOW at www.cengage.com/login

taken on a Friday night and last until early Sunday; Japsen, 2003).

There are several side effects with these medications, including headaches, a flushing in the cheeks and neck, nasal congestion, indigestion, and vision changes. Less common side effects include an increased risk of vision problems, including changes in color vision and possible total vision loss, and ringing in the ears, or total hearing loss (Mukherjee & Shivakumar, 2007; Wooltorton, 2006). In fact, the FDA called for revised labeling of all erectile drugs outlining possible vision side effects in 2005 (Kaufman, 2005) and hearing loss in 2007 (Mukherjee & Shivakumar, 2007). Critics of pharmacological treatment for ED point out that drug use focuses solely on an erection and fails to take into account the multidimensional nature of male sexuality (B. W. McCarthy & Fucito, 2005).

Yohimbine, which we discussed earlier in this chapter, has been found to improve erections and is most successful in cases with nonphysical causes (Ernst & Pittler, 1998). It works by stimulating the parasympathetic nervous system, which is linked to erectile functioning. Side effects include dizziness, nervousness, irritability, and an increased heart rate and blood pressure. Nitroglycerin and nitrates have also been used to treat erectile dysfunction in men (Wimalawansa, 2008).

Earlier in this chapter, we discussed the use of PT-141 for female sexual arousal disorder. PT-141 has also been used for erectile dysfunction (Safarinejad & Hosseini, 2008; Shadiack et al.,

---

REAL Research **>** A Finnish study found that regular sexual intercourse in heterosexual men protects against the development of erectile dysfunction among men aged **55** to **75** years (KOSKIMÄKI ET AL., 2008).

2007). In clinical trials, men inhale a nasal spray of PT-141 45 minutes to 2 hours before sexual stimulation. Although preliminary studies suggest PT-141 positively affected erectile functioning (Safarinejad & Hosseini, 2008; Shadiack et al., 2007), as we discussed earlier in this chapter, the FDA reduced clinical trials of PT-141 in mid-2008 because of safety concerns.

systematic desensitization
A treatment method for sexual dysfunction that involves neutralizing the anxiety-producing aspects of sexual situations and behavior by a process of gradual exposure.

sensate focus
A series of touching experiences that are assigned to couples in sex therapy to teach nonverbal communication and reduce anxiety.

psychogenic
Relating to psychological causes.

REALResearch   **>** Research has found that a heterosexual woman's sexual functioning may be affected by a partner's sexual dysfunction. Seventy-eight percent of women whose partners had premature ejaculation had at least one sexual dysfunction themselves, compared with only **43%** of women in a control group (HOBBS ET AL., 2008).

HORMONAL TREATMENTS   Hormonal treatment may help improve erections in men who have hormonal irregularities (such as too much prolactin or too little gonadal hormones; Lue, 2000). Excessive prolactin can interfere with adequate secretion of testosterone and can cause erectile dysfunction. A man with low testosterone levels can be prescribed testosterone therapy through injections, patches, gels, or creams. However, as we discussed earlier, research has been unable to show a consistent and beneficial role of testosterone in increasing sexual functioning in men (Allan et al., 2008; Isidori et al., 2005). Even so, these drugs are commonly used to treat ED.

A testosterone patch is applied directly to the scrotum, whereas gels and creams can be applied to other parts of the body such as the arms or stomach. AndroGel, a clear, colorless, odorless gel, was approved by the FDA in 2000 for the treatment of low testosterone (Morley & Perry, 2000). It is applied daily and is absorbed into the skin. Some men prefer this type of application over a painful injection or patch. Side effects are rare but include headaches, acne, depression, gynecomastia, and hypertension. None of these testosterone preparations should be used by men with prostate cancer because they can exacerbate this condition.

INTRACAVERNOUS INJECTIONS   Also used to treat ED are **intracavernous** (in-truh-CAV-er-nuss) **injections** (Alexandre et al., 2007; Lue, 2000). Men and their partners are taught to self-inject these preparations directly into the corpora cavernosa (see Chapter 6) while the penis is gently stretched out. The injections cause the blood vessels to relax, which increases blood flow to the penis. The majority of patients report very minor pain from these injections. However, each time a man desires an erection, he must use this injection. The higher the dosage of medication, the longer the erection will last.

Priapism, a possible side effect of treatment, occurs in some men using intracavernous injections. Other side effects are more related to the injection than to the drug itself and may include pain, bleeding, or bruising (Alexandre et al., 2007; Israilov et al., 2002). Prostaglandin pellets have also been used to increase blood flow to the penis. The pellets are inserted directly into the urethra where they are absorbed. Erections with these methods will typically occur within 20 minutes and can last for an hour and a half.

VACUUM CONSTRICTION DEVICES   In the past several years, **vacuum constriction devices,** which use suction to induce erections, have become more popular, in part because they are less invasive and safer than injections. One such device, the ErecAid System, involves putting the flaccid penis into a vacuum cylinder and pumping it to draw blood into the corpora cavernosa (similar to the one Austin Powers was caught with in *International Man of Mystery*). To keep the blood in the penis, a constriction ring is rolled onto the base of the penis after it is removed from the vacuum device. This ring is left on the penis until the erection is no longer desired. When it is removed, the man will lose his erection. Side effects include possible bruising and, in rare cases, testicular entrapment in the vacuum chamber (Lue, 2000). Overall, these devices can be expensive, bulky and noisy, and they reduce spontaneity, which some couples find unappealing.

SURGICAL TREATMENTS   Surgical intervention has increased as a treatment for erectile dysfunction. In some cases, physicians perform **revascularization** to improve erectile functioning; in other cases, **prosthesis** (pross-THEE-sis) **implantation** may be recommended. Acrylic implants for erectile dysfunction were first used in 1952, but they were replaced by silicone rubber in the 1960s and then by a variety of synthetic materials in the 1970s. Today there are two main types of implants: **semirigid rods,** which provide a permanent state of erection but can be bent up and down; and inflatable devices that become firm when the man pumps them up (Simmons & Montague, 2008). Penetrative sexual behaviors may safely be engaged in 4 to 8 weeks after surgery. After prosthesis implantation, a man is still able to orgasm, ejaculate, and impregnate (Simmons & Montague, 2008).

Sexual satisfaction after a prosthesis implantation has been found to be related to several factors, such as a man's relationship with his partner and feelings about his own masculinity (Kempeneers et al., 2004). Between 10% and 20% of patients remain dissatisfied, dysfunctional, or sexually inactive even after prosthetic surgery (Minervini et al., 2006). In some cases, if a man has psychological factors that contribute to his erectile difficulties, these issues are likely to resurface after a prosthesis is implanted.

intracavernous injection
A treatment method for erectile dysfunction in which vasodilating drugs are injected into the penis for the purpose of creating an erection.

priapism
A condition in which erections are long lasting and often painful.

vacuum constriction device
Treatment device for erectile dysfunction used to pull blood into the penis.

revascularization
A procedure used in the treatment of vascular erectile dysfunction in which the vascular system is rerouted to ensure better blood flow to the penis.

prosthesis implantation
A treatment method for erectile dysfunction in which a prosthesis is surgically implanted into the penis.

semirigid rod
A flexible rod that is implanted into the penis during prosthetic surgery.

WHAT DO YOU WANT TO KNOW ?

A couple of guys I know have some Viagra, and they have been trying to get me to take it. Is it safe to use this drug if you don't have ED?

There is evidence that some men use Viagra or other erectile drugs in conjunction with other recreational drugs, such as marijuana (Eloi-Stiven et al., 2007). Although recreational use of Viagra and other erectile drugs is not uncommon, it does not always live up to expectations (Albert, 2005; Crosby & Diclemente, 2004; Eloi-Stiven et al., 2007; Fisher et al., 2006; Musacchio et al., 2006). Men who use these drugs are often disappointed since it doesn't always lead to longer and firmer erections and can often contribute to physical side effects, such as harmful changes in blood pressure (Crosby & Diclemente, 2004; D. Fisher et al., 2006). In addition, men who use these drugs recreationally are more likely to engage in unsafe sex compared with those not using these drugs, which puts them more at risk for sexually transmitted infections (Swearingen & Klausner, 2005).

REALResearch > Sexual dysfunction is common in aging adults, with hypoactive sexual desire disorder and pain disorders most common in women and erectile dysfunction most common in men (Bitzer et al., 2008b).

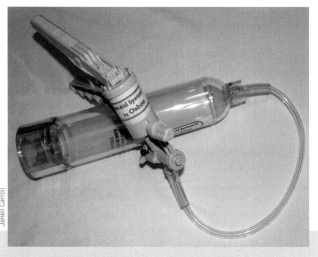

Vacuum constriction devices, such as the ErecAid, are often used in the treatment of erectile dysfunction. A man places his penis in the cylinder, and vacuum suction increases blood flow to the penis causing an erection.

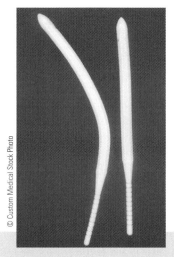

These semirigid prostheses are surgically implanted in the penis and can enable a man with erectile dysfunction to have an erection suitable for penetrative sexual behavior.

review questions

1 Identify and explain the two categories of sexual arousal disorders.

2 Explain how female sexual arousal disorder presents and identify some of the possible psychological and physical causes.

3 Identify possible treatment strategies for female sexual arousal disorder.

4 Explain how male sexual arousal disorder presents and identify some of the possible psychological and physical causes.

5 Identify some of the tests used to diagnose male erectile disorder and explain some of the pharmacological and hormonal treatments for erectile dysfunction.

6 Identify how intracavernous injections, vacuum constriction devices, and surgery are used in the treatment of erectile dysfunction.

Orgasm
Disorders

Every individual reaches orgasm differently and has different wants and needs to build sexual excitement. Some people need very little stimulation, others need a great deal of stimulation, and some never reach orgasm. The *DSM-IV-TR* has three categories of **orgasmic disorders:** female orgasmic disorder, male orgasmic disorder, and **premature ejaculation.**

FEMALE ORGASMIC DISORDER

Historically, this female sexual dysfunction was referred to as "frigidity," which had negative implications about the woman. *DSM-IV-TR* defines female orgasmic disorder as a delay or absence of orgasm following a normal phase of sexual excitement. This is a common complaint among women, and studies have found that approximately one quarter of women report orgasmic disorder (Laumann et al., 1994; Meston et al., 2004). Remember though, that the DSM definition does not indicate that orgasm must occur during sexual intercourse. In fact, the majority of heterosexual women are unable to orgasm during sexual intercourse. If a woman is unable to orgasm during all sexual activities after a normal phase of sexual excitement, she may be experiencing orgasmic disorder. Some women who take certain psychotropic drugs, including many types of antidepressants, experience delayed or absent orgasms (Labbate, 2008).

Primary orgasmic disorder describes a condition in which a woman has never had an orgasm. Secondary orgasmic dis-order refers to a condition in which a woman was able to have orgasms previously but later has trouble reaching orgasm. Situational orgasmic disorder refers to a condition in which a woman can have orgasms only with one type of stimulation.

Women with orgasmic disorders, compared with orgasmic women, often report less relationship satisfaction and lower levels of emotional closeness (González et al., 2006). They also have more difficulties in asking their partners for direct clitoral stimulation, discussing how slow or fast they want to go, or how hard or soft stimulation should be. Some women worry about what their partners might think if they made sexual suggestions or feel uncomfortable receiving stimulation (such as cunnilingus or manual stimulation) without stimulating their partners at the same time. Distracting thoughts, such as "his hand must be falling asleep" or "he can't be enjoying this" can increase existing anxiety and interfere with orgasm (Birnbaum et al., 2001; M. P. Kelly et al., 1990).

Physical factors can also cause female orgasmic disorder. Severe chronic illness and disorders such as diabetes, neurological problems, hormonal deficiencies, and alcoholism can all interfere with orgasmic response. Certain prescription drugs can also impair this response.

Treating Female Orgasmic Disorder

Today the majority of treatment programs for orgasmic disorder involve a combination of different treatment approaches, such as homework assignments, sex education, communication skills training, cognitive restructuring, desensitization, and other techniques (Meston et al., 2004). The most effective treatment for female orgasmic disorder was developed by LoPiccolo and Lobitz (1972) and involves teaching a woman to masturbate to orgasm.

On a psychological level, masturbation also helps increase the pleasurable anticipation of sex. Education, self-exploration, communication training, and body awareness are also included in masturbation training for orgasmic problems. Masturbation exercises begin with a woman examining her body and vulva with mirrors. Then she is instructed to find which areas of her body feel the most pleasurable when touched and to stroke them. If this does not result in orgasm, a vibrator is used. As a woman progresses through these stages, she may involve her sexual partner so that the partner is able to learn which areas are more sensitive than others.

Although masturbation training is the most effective treatment for female orgasmic disorder, some therapists do not incorporate it into their treatment for a variety of reasons (including patient or therapist discomfort). Interestingly, improving orgasmic responsivity does not always increase sexual satisfaction. Many heterosexual women enjoy engaging in sexual intercourse over masturbation because it provides more intimacy and close-

REALResearch > A nationally representative study of U.S. women found that while **40%** of women reported experiencing low sexual desire, decreased sexual arousal, and/or problems reaching orgasm, only **12%** indicated these issues were a source of personal distress (SHIFREN ET AL., 2008).

ness (Jayne, 1981), even though masturbation may be a better means of reaching orgasm (Dodson, 1993).

Two additional treatments involve systematic desensitization and **bibliotherapy.** Both of these have been found to be helpful in cases in which there is a great deal of sexual anxiety. In systematic desensitization, events that cause anxiety are recalled into imagination, and then a relaxation technique is used to dissipate the anxiety. With enough repetition and practice, eventually the anxiety-producing events lose the ability to create anxiety. Both masturbation training and systematic desensitization have been found to be effective; however, masturbation training has higher effectiveness rates (Heiman & Meston, 1997).

orgasmic disorder
A delay or absence of orgasm following a normal phase of sexual excitement.

premature ejaculation
Pattern of ejaculating with minimal sexual stimulation before, on, or shortly after penetration and before the person wishes it.

bibliotherapy
Using books and educational material for the treatment of sexual dysfunction or other problems.

I seem to have problems achieving orgasm with my partner, yet I am able to with the help of a vibrator. Are there different levels of orgasms? Sometimes it is so deep and complete and emotional; other times it is very satisfying but not to the tips of my toes! Is this normal? I would love to be able to achieve the same satisfaction with my partner as I can by myself or with a vibrator.

There are different levels of sexual satisfaction that result from orgasms. Orgasms differ based on stress, emotions, thoughts, physical health, menstrual cycles, sexual position, and method of stimulation. However, Masters and Johnson did find that masturbation usually evoked more powerful orgasms than intercourse. To experience these orgasms with your partner, you might try masturbating together or using a vibrator with your partner.

Bibliotherapy has also been found to be helpful for not only orgasmic dysfunctions but other dysfunctions as well. It can help a person regain some control and understand the problems she is experiencing. Although the results may be short-lived, bibliotherapy has been found to improve sexual functioning (van Lankveld et al., 2001).

MALE ORGASMIC DISORDER

Male orgasmic disorder is relatively rare, with only 8% of men reporting problems reaching orgasm (Laumann et al., 1994). It is defined as a delay or absence of orgasm following a normal phase of sexual excitement. As we discussed previously, many men who take psychotropic medications experience problems with orgasm.

Treating Male Orgasmic Disorder

Male orgasmic disorder is uncommon and is rarely treated by sex therapists (Heiman, 2002). Treatment options include psychotherapy and, if necessary, changing medications.

PREMATURE EJACULATION

Ejaculatory dysfunction is a common sexual problem but may often be overlooked (Bettocchi et al., 2008). Premature ejaculation (PE) is the most common ejaculatory dysfunction, although it is often difficult to define (Renshaw, 2005). Does it depend on how many penile thrusts take place before orgasm, how many minutes elapse between actual penetration and orgasm, or whether a man reaches orgasm prior to his partner? All of these definitions are problematic because they involve individual differences in sexual functioning and also make the assumption that a man is heterosexual and engaging in sexual intercourse.

Although the time it takes to ejaculate may vary based on a man's age, sexual experience, health, and stress level, PE usually refers to a man reaching orgasm just before, or directly following,

penetration (Grenier & Byers, 2001). Occasional or substance-induced early ejaculation often does not qualify for a diagnosis of PE. However, usually if a couple believes there is a problem, then it is often treated like one.

Premature ejaculation is the most common sexual dysfunction in men under age 40 (Jannini & Lenzi, 2005; Vardi et al., 2008). In the United States, estimates are that close to 30% of men report experiencing PE in the previous year (Laumann et al., 1994). Although we don't know exactly what causes premature ejaculation, some evolutionary theorists claim that PE may actually provide a biological advantage in that a male will be able to mate quickly, decreasing his chances of being killed or pushed away. Masters and Johnson (1970) originally proposed that PE develops when a man's early sexual experiences are rushed because of the fear of being caught or discovered. These fears, they believed, could condition a man to ejaculate rapidly. Others have pointed out that PE occurs in men who are unable to accurately judge their own levels of sexual arousal, which would enable them to use self-control and avoid rapid ejaculation (H. S. Kaplan, 1989). Like other erectile problems, PE has been found to be associated with depression, anxiety, drug and alcohol abuse, and personality disorders.

Treating Premature Ejaculation

Premature ejaculation is often treated in a variety of ways. Treatment methods today include behavioral cognitive therapy and pharmaceutical treatments (Shindel et al., 2008; Wylie & Ralph, 2005). Two behavioral techniques are also popular, including the **squeeze technique** and the **stop–start technique** (Shindel et al., 2008). Both involve stimulating the penis to the point just before ejaculation. Usually a man practices these techniques alone during masturbation and then with a partner (Heiman, 2002).

With the squeeze technique, sexual intercourse or masturbation is engaged in just short of orgasm and then stimulation is stopped. The man or his partner puts a thumb on the frenulum and the first and second fingers on the dorsal side of the penis (see Figure 14.3). Pressure is applied for 3 to 4 seconds, until the urge to ejaculate subsides. With the stop–start technique, stimulation is simply stopped until the ejaculatory urge subsides. Stimulation is then repeated up until that point, and this process is repeated over and over. Using these methods, a man can usually gain some control over his erection within 2 to 10 weeks and can have excellent control within several months.

It is believed that these techniques may help a man get in touch with his arousal levels and sensations. Suggested effectiveness rates have been as high as 98%, although it is unclear how this effectiveness is being measured (Masters & Johnson, 1970). In addition, many studies fail to mention whether the treatment permanently solves the problem or if periodic repetition of the techniques is necessary. Directly following treatment for premature ejaculation, men showed significant gains in length of sex play, satisfaction with sexual relationships, and increased mate acceptance (DeAmicis et al., 1985). However, these improvements

squeeze technique
A technique in which the ejaculatory reflex is reconditioned using a firm grasp on the penis.

stop–start technique
A technique in which the ejaculatory reflex is reconditioned using intermittent pressure on the glans of the penis.

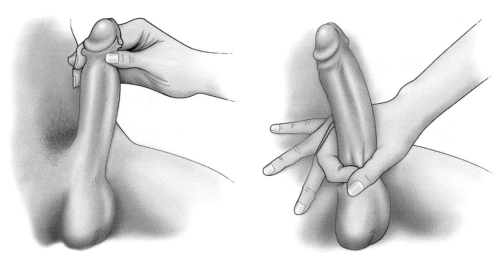

Figure **14.3** The squeeze technique is often recommended in the treatment of premature ejaculation. Pressure is applied either at the top or to the base of the penis for several seconds until the urge to ejaculate subsides.

were not maintained 3 years later, and the frequency and desire for sexual contact in all couples, duration of sexual intercourse in heterosexual couples, and marital satisfaction in married couples all decreased.

As discussed, health care providers have been exploring pharmaceutical treatments for PE (Renshaw, 2005; Shindel et al., 2008; Wylie & Ralph, 2005). Selective serotonin reuptake inhibitors (SSRIs) are the most commonly used pharmaceutical treatment for premature ejaculation (Shindel et al., 2008). However, long-term use of SSRIs is associated multiple side effects, including dry mouth, nausea, drowsiness, reduced libido, and the development of other sexual dysfunctions (Hellstrom, 2006). Erectile drugs, such as Viagra, have also been used to treat premature ejaculation. Another drug, called DPS, has undergone Phase III trials and may be approved by the FDA for the treatment of premature ejaculation (Hellstrom, 2006).

Finally, topical agent trials are also underway. Many of these agents contain either anesthetic properties or other ingredients that prolong erections. However, long-term safety issues have not yet been addressed with these topical agents (Hellstrom, 2006).

Other Ejaculatory Dysfunctions

There is a wide spectrum of ejaculatory dysfunction, ranging from premature ejaculation that we just discussed to a delay or absence of ejaculation. A man with **retarded** (or inhibited) **ejaculation** is either unable to reach orgasm or requires a prolonged stimulation period (30–45 minutes; Rowland et al., 2004). **Retrograde ejaculation** involves the backward flow of ejaculate into the bladder instead of its being released through the urethra. Typically men with retrograde ejaculation still experience orgasm but have very little ejaculate (or a "dry" orgasm). Not surprisingly, men with retrograde ejaculation often experience fertility problems (Ohl et al., 2008). Some men may experience painful ejaculation, which is often caused by infections or medical issues (Lee et al., 2008; Schultheiss, 2008).

*Retarded and retrograde ejaculation **are relatively rare.***

Both retarded and retrograde ejaculation are relatively rare. In fact, less than 3% of men experience retarded ejaculation (Perelman & Rowland, 2006). However, those who do experience these ejaculatory dysfunctions often experience considerable anxiety and distress and may also experience relationship problems related to the dysfunction.

Causes for these ejaculatory dysfunctions include psychological issues, medications, drug use, diseases, injuries, and various urological surgeries (Bettocchi et al., 2008; Lee et al., 2008; Mufti et al., 2008; Perelman & Rowland, 2006; Schultheiss, 2008). Psychological factors include a strict religious upbringing, unique or atypical masturbation patterns, fear of pregnancy, or ambivalence over sexual orientation.

Treating Ejaculatory Dysfunctions

Although psychological factors have been primarily implicated in retarded ejaculation, we still do not really understand what causes this problem, which makes treatment difficult. In many cases, psychotherapy is used to help work through some of these issues as a part of treatment. Unfortunately, retarded ejaculation is often difficult to treat, and there are no evidence-based treatments proved to eliminate this dysfunction (Nelson et al., 2007; Richardson et al., 2006). A novel treatment for retarded ejaculation includes penile vibratory stimulation, which involves using a small vibrator to increase penile sensations during sexual activity (Nelson et al., 2007). It has been found to be an effective treatment, although more research is needed. Animal studies are currently being done to evaluate experimental drugs that have been found to accelerate ejaculation (Waldinger & Schweitzer, 2005). In addition, various pharmacological studies are being conducted to

retarded ejaculation
Condition in which ejaculation is impossible or occurs only after strenuous efforts.

retrograde ejaculation
The backward flow of ejaculate into the bladder instead of being released through the urethra.

evaluate possible medications to treat retarded ejaculation (Chan et al., 2008; Waldinger, 2005). For some men, changing their daily medications can often improve ejaculatory function.

Psychological issues can also be challenging to treat. One 43-year-old man shared with me his lifelong problem in reaching orgasm with his partner. He had been sexually abused as a child for many years by an uncle who was a few years older than he. During this abuse, the uncle tried to make him reach orgasm. However, the boy learned to withhold the orgasmic response, much to the dismay of the uncle. Later on in life, this pattern continued even though he was not consciously trying to do so.

One psychological treatment involves instructing a man to use situations in which he is able to achieve ejaculation to help him during those in which he is not. For example, if a man can ejacu-late during masturbation while fantasizing about being watched during sexual activity, he is told to use this fantasy while he is with his partner. Gradually, the man is asked to incorporate his partner into the sexual fantasy and to masturbate while with the partner.

Retrograde ejaculation is not harmful, and because of this, some heterosexual men do not seek treatment unless they are trying to get a partner pregnant. However, we do know that many medical conditions, such as diabetes, spinal cord injuries, surgeries, and medications can contribute to retrograde ejaculation. Therefore, changing medications or controlling medical conditions can be helpful. The use of certain antidepressants and antihistamines have also been found to be helpful in the treatment of retrograde ejaculation, because these medications help restrict muscles of the bladder during ejaculation.

review questions

1 Define female orgasmic disorder and explain possible psychological and physical factors that might contribute to it.

2 Identify the various treatments for female orgasmic disorder.

3 Define male orgasmic disorder and explain treatments for this dysfunction.

4 Define premature ejaculation and explain possible psychological and physical factors that might contribute.

5 Identify the various treatments for premature ejaculation.

6 Discuss other ejaculatory dysfunctions.

Pain
Disorders

Genital pain disorders can occur at any stage of the sexual response cycle. Although pain disorders are more frequent in women, they also occur in men. *DSM-IV-TR* has two categories of pain disorders, **vaginismus** (vadg-ih-NISS-muss), which occurs in women, and **dyspareunia** (diss-par-ROON-ee-uh), which can affect both men and women.

VAGINISMUS

The **pubococcygeus** (pub-oh-cock-SIGH-gee-us) **muscle** surrounds the entrance to the vagina and controls the vaginal opening. Vaginismus involves involuntary contractions of this muscle, which can make penetration during sexual intercourse virtually impossible (Ozdemir et al., 2008). Forced penetration can be difficult and may cause a woman severe pain. Vaginismus may be situation-specific, meaning that a woman may be able to allow penetration under certain circumstances but not in others (say, during a pelvic exam but not during sexual intercourse; LoPiccolo & Stock, 1986).

The muscle contractions that occur during vaginismus are in reaction to anticipated vaginal penetration. One woman had been in a relationship with her partner for more than 3 years, but they had never been able to engage in penile–vaginal intercourse because she felt as if her vagina "was closed up" (author's files). Penetration of her vagina with her partner's fingers was possible and enjoyable, but once penile penetration was attempted, her vagina was impenetrable. She also shared that she had been forced to engage in sex with her stepfather for several years of her early life.

Vaginismus is common in women who have been sexually abused or raped, and it is often present along with other sexual difficulties such as sexual aversion and difficulties becoming aroused. Women who experience vaginismus often experience dyspareunia, or painful intercourse, as well (Heiman, 2002).

Treating Vaginismus
People who experience any of the pain disorders often believe that they have to live with the problem. As a result, they do not seek help. However, medical evaluations and counseling can help isolate possible causes and solutions. Women who are experiencing vaginismus should consult with a health care provider and bring

vaginismus
Involuntary spasms of the muscles around the vagina in response to attempts at penetration.

dyspareunia
Genital pain associated with intercourse.

pubococcygeus muscle
A muscle that surrounds and supports the vagina.

their partner. A physical examination will check for any medical problems that may be contributing to the pain.

After the diagnosis is confirmed, one of the most effective treatments is the use of **dilators.** After a health care provider instructs a woman to use these dilators, they can be used at home and inserted by the woman or her partner. The size of the dilators is slowly increased, and they can even be left in place overnight if necessary. These dilators help to open and relax the vaginal muscles. If these procedures are successful, penile or digital penetration can be attempted. In some cases, however, it may be necessary to use a dilator on a regular basis just before penetration. It is estimated that between 75% and 100% of women who use this technique are able to experience penetrative sex by the end of treatment (Heiman, 2002). Women without a sexual partner can also be treated and are taught to insert dilators on their own. Although sex surrogates are not commonly used in the U.S. today, one study from Israel found that incorporating surrogate sex partners into the treatment of single women with vaginismus yielded successful treatment rates (Ben-Zion et al., 2007).

It is also helpful for women and their partners to become educated about vaginismus and sexuality to reduce their anxiety or tension. If a history of sexual abuse or rape exists, it is important to work through the trauma before beginning work with the dilators, or treatment for vaginismus may be unsuccessful.

DYSPAREUNIA
AND VULVODYNIA

Dyspareunia may occur before, during, or after sexual behavior and may involve only slight pain, which does not interfere much with sexual activity. However, when it is extreme, it may make sexual behavior difficult, if not impossible. It is estimated that close to 15% of heterosexual women experience pain during sexual intercourse (Laumann et al., 1999). Contrary to popular belief, men can also experience dyspareunia, which may cause pain in the testes or penis, either during or after sexual behavior.

A number of things may cause such pain, from physical problems to allergies or infections. Psychological problems can also cause dyspareunia, and so a full diagnosis from a health professional is imperative. In Chapter 5, we discussed vulvodynia, which can be another cause of dyspareunia. **Vulvar vestibulitis** (vess-tib-u-LITE-is) **syndrome,** a type of vulvodynia, is considered one of the most common causes of dyspareunia today (Perrigouard et al., 2008).

Dyspareunia in men is caused by the same physiological and psychological factors as in females. It can also be due to Peyronie's disease (which we discussed in Chapter 6). Severe cases can cause significant curvature in the penis, which can make penetrative sex impossible.

Treating Dyspareunia and Vulvodynia

Like vaginismus, dyspareunia should be evaluated medically prior to treatment. Several physical and psychological issues can contribute to painful intercourse. If there is a physical problem, such as an infection, medical treatment will usually result in a lessening or total elimination of the pain. As we discussed earlier in this chapter, women suffering from dyspareunia should also be evalu-

ated for vulvodynia prior to any treatment for their sexual dysfunction. Treatment for vulvar vestibulitis, including psychotherapy, biofeedback, and surgery, have resulted in significant reduction in dyspareunia after treatment and in follow-up studies (Gunter, 2007). Psychological causes of dyspareunia, such as performance anxieties or a fear of intimacy, must be treated through counseling or psychotherapy.

dilators
A graduated series of metal rods used in the treatment of vaginismus.

vulvar vestibulitis syndrome
Syndrome that causes pain and burning in the vaginal vestibule and often occurs during sexual intercourse, tampon insertion, gynecological exams, bicycle riding, and wearing tight pants.

review questions

1 Explain how genital pain occurs during the sexual response cycle.

2 Identify the two main categories of pain disorders.

3 Define vaginismus and identify potential causes.

4 Identify treatments for vaginismus.

5 Define dyspareunia and identify potential causes.

6 Identify treatments for dyspareunia.

Illness, Disability, and Sexual Functioning

We all need love, and we all need touching and contact with others. Yet somehow we have grown to think that sexuality is the privilege of the healthy. As the chapter opening story illustrated, we tend to exclude ill or disabled people from our visions of the sexual, and so we deny them a basic human right. If you were suddenly disabled or developed a chronic illness, would you lose your desire to be regarded by another as sexy and desirable?

Health care providers often rely on the International Classification of Diseases (ICD), an official system of identifying various illnesses. Several of these illnesses and their treatments can interfere with a person's sexual desire, physiological functioning, or both. Sexual functioning involves a complex physiological process, which can be impaired by pain, immobility, changes in bodily functions, or medications (LeVay et al., 1981). More often, though, the problems are psychological. Sudden illness causes shock, anger, resentment, anxiety, and depression, all of which can adversely affect sexual desire and functioning. Many illnesses cause disfiguration and force a person to deal with radical changes in body image; after removal of a limb, breast, testicle, or the need to wear an external bag to collect bodily waste, many people wonder: How could anyone possibly find me sexually attractive?

Serious illness often puts strains on loving relationships. A partner may be forced to become nurse, cook, maid, and caretaker as well as lover. The caretaker of an ill person may worry that the sick partner is too weak or fragile for sex or be too concerned with his or her illness to want sexual contact. Still, many couples do enjoy loving, full relationships.

Another common assumption is that all patients are heterosexual, and so, for example, disabled lesbians may be given contraceptive advice without being asked if they need it (O'Toole & Bregante, 1992). Heterosexual women looking for information about sexuality and their particular disability may find little, and lesbians may find none at all.

The real questions that sick people and their partners have about their sexuality are too often ignored by medical professionals. They may be questions of mechanics, such as "What positions can I get into now that I have lost a leg?"; questions of function: "Will my genitals still work now that I have a spinal cord injury?"; questions of attractiveness: "Will my husband still want me now that I have lost a breast?"; even questions of appropriateness: "Should I allow my mentally ill teenage daughter to pursue a sex life when she may not understand the consequences?" We now review a sample of physical and mental challenges that confront people and also some of the sexual questions and problems that can arise.

CARDIOVASCULAR PROBLEMS: HEART DISEASE AND STROKE

Heart disease, including **hypertension, angina,** and **myocardial infarction (MI),** is the number one cause of death in the United States. A person with heart disease—even a person who has had a heart transplant—can return to a normal sex life shortly after recovery. Most cardiologists allow sexual behavior as soon as the patient feels up to it, although they usually recommend that heart transplant patients wait from 4 to 8 weeks to give the incision time to heal. However, researchers have found that the frequency of sexual behavior after MIs does decrease. In fact, only 1 in 4 couples returns to their previous levels of sexual behavior (Ben-Zion & Shiber, 2006). Why does this occur?

One reason is fear. Many patients (or their partners) fear that their damaged (or new) heart is not up to the strain of sexual behavior or orgasm (Evada & Atwa, 2007; Kazemi-Saleh et al., 2007). This fear can be triggered by the fact that, when men and

hypertension
Abnormally high blood pressure.

angina
Chest pains that accompany heart disease.

myocardial infarction (MI)
A cutoff of blood to the heart muscle, causing damage to the heart; also referred to as a heart attack.

women become sexually excited, their heartbeat and respiration increases, and they may break out into a sweat (these are also signs of a heart attack). Some people with heart disease actually do experience some angina during sexual activity. Although not usually serious, these incidents may be frightening. Research has found that although sexual activity can trigger a MI, this risk is extremely low (Baylin et al., 2007; Muller et al., 1996). In fact, except for patients with very serious heart conditions, sex puts no more strain on the heart than walking up a flight or two of stairs.

Some problems also involve physical factors. Because penile erection is a vascular process, involving the flow of blood into the penis, it is not surprising that erectile dysfunction is a common problem in male patients with cardiovascular problems (Hebert et al., 2008). Some heart medications also can dampen desire or cause erectile problems, or, less often, women may experience a decrease in lubrication. Sometimes, adjusting medications can help couples who are experiencing such problems.

Erectile dysfunction is a **common problem** *in male patients with cardiovascular problems.*

After a heart attack or other heart problems, it is not uncommon to have feelings of depression, inadequacy (especially among men), or loss of attractiveness (especially among women; Evada & Atwa, 2007; Schover & Jensen, 1988). In addition, in older patients, a partner often assumes the responsibility of enforcing the doctor's orders: "Watch what you eat!" "Don't drink alcohol!" "Don't put so much salt on that!" "Get some exercise!" This is hardly a role that leads to sexual desire. Any combination of these factors may lead one or both partners to avoid sex.

Strokes, also called cerebral vascular accidents (CVAs), happen when blood is cut off from part of the brain, usually because a small blood vessel bursts. Although every stroke is different depending on what areas of the brain are damaged, some common results are **hemiplegia** (he-mi-PLEE-jee-uh), **aphasia** (uh-FAY-zhee-uh), and other cognitive, perceptual, and memory problems. As with other types of brain injury (such as those caused by automobile accidents), damage to the brain can affect sexuality in a number of ways.

In most cases of stroke, sexual functioning itself is not damaged, and many stroke victims do go on to resume sexual activity. After a stroke, the problems that confront a couple with normal functioning are similar to those with cardiovascular disease: fear of causing another stroke, worries about sexual attractiveness, and the stresses and anxieties of having to cope with a major illness. However, a stroke can also cause physiological changes that affect sexuality. Some men find that after a stroke, their erections are crooked because the nerves controlling the erectile tissue on one side of the penis are affected. Hemiplegia can result in spasticity (jerking motions) and reduced sensation on one side of the body. Paralysis can also contribute to a feeling of awkwardness or unattractiveness. In addition, aphasia can affect a person's ability to communicate or understand sexual cues.

Some stroke victims also go through periods of **disinhibition,** in which they exhibit behavior that, before the stroke, they would have been able to suppress. Often this includes **hypersexuality,** in which the patient may make lewd comments, masturbate in public, disrobe publicly, or make inappropriate sexual advances (Larkin, 1992). Others may experience **hyposexuality,** in which they show decreased sexual desire, or they may experience ED. Sexual intervention programs have been designed for use in reha-

bilitation hospitals, and they can be of great help in teaching couples how to deal with the difficulties of adjusting to life after a stroke.

CANCER

Cancer can involve almost any organ of the body and has a reputation of being invariably fatal. In fact, cure rates have increased dramatically, and some cancers are now more than 90% curable. Still, cancer can kill, and a diagnosis of cancer is usually accompanied by shock, numbness, and gripping fear. Also, as in other illness, partners may need to become caretakers, and roles can change. Cancer treatments are likely to disrupt a patients' sexual functioning (Burns et al., 2007; Ofman, 2004). These disruptions may be temporary or long lasting.

For example, surgery is required for a number of cancers of the digestive system, and it can lead to **ostomies** (OST-stome-mees). People with cancer of the colon often need to have part or all of the large intestine removed; the rectum may be removed as well. A surgical opening, called a **stoma** (STOW-mah), is made in the abdomen to allow waste products to exit the body. This is collected in a bag, which, for many patients, must be worn at all times (others can take it off periodically). Ostomy bags are visually unpleasant and may emit an odor, and the adjustment to their presence can be difficult for some couples. Having a new opening on the body to eliminate bodily wastes is itself a hard thing to accept for many people, but most eventually adjust to it and, barring other problems related to their disease, go on to live healthy and sexually active lives.

Cancer can affect sexual functioning in other ways as well. Physical scars, the loss of limbs or body parts, changes in skin texture when radiation therapy is used, the loss of hair, nausea, bloatedness, weight gain or loss, and acne are just some of the ways that cancer and its treatment can affect the body and one's body image. In addition, the psychological trauma and the fear of death can lead to depression, which can inhibit sexual relations. Perhaps the most drastic situations, however, occur when cancer affects the sexual organs themselves.

stroke
Occurs when blood is cut off from part of the brain, usually because a small blood vessel bursts.

hemiplegia
Paralysis of one side of the body.

aphasia
Defects in the ability to express and/or understand speech, signs, or written communication, due to damage to the speech centers of the brain.

disinhibition
The loss of normal control over behaviors such as expressing sexuality or taking one's clothes off in public.

hypersexuality
Abnormally expressive or aggressive sexual behavior, often in public; the term usually refers to behavior due to some disturbance of the brain.

hyposexuality
Abnormal suppression of sexual desire and behavior; the term usually refers to behavior due to some disturbance of the brain.

ostomies
Operations to remove part of the small or large intestine or the bladder, resulting in the need to create an artificial opening in the body for the elimination of bodily wastes.

stoma
Surgical opening made in the abdomen to allow waste products to exit the body.

Breast Cancer

In American society, breasts are a focal part of female sexual attractiveness, and women often invest much of their feminine self-image in their breasts. For many years, a diagnosis of breast cancer usually meant that a woman lost that breast; **mastectomy** was the preferred treatment. **Simple mastectomies** meant that the breast tissue alone was removed, whereas radical mastectomies involved the removal of the breast along with other tissues and lymph nodes. As we discussed in Chapter 5, the numbers of mastectomies have decreased today, and many women are opting for lumpectomies. These are often coupled with chemotherapy, radiation therapy, or both. Still, some women must undergo radical mastectomies and must contend not only with having cancer, but also with an altered image of their sexual identity.

There might be very little time to prepare oneself psychologically for the loss of a breast. A woman who loses a breast may worry that her partner will no longer find her attractive or desirable. Some go so far as to wear their bras during sexual activity or to avoid looking in mirrors when nude.

To wear the clothes they are used to wearing, many women missing a breast (or both breasts) will wear a prosthesis or a specially designed bra. Other women choose to undergo breast reconstruction, in which tissue and fat from other parts of the body are molded into the shape of a breast and implanted under a fold of skin, or fluid-filled implants are added. Years ago, reconstructed breasts were not very satisfactory, but recent advances in reconstructive techniques can create a much more natural-looking breast. Surgery can

*A mastectomy can have **a negative impact** on a woman's sexuality.*

An advertising campaign by the Breast Cancer Fund parodied the fact that society routinely represents women's breasts as only sexual in nature, whereas breast cancer is treated with secrecy.

Courtesy of www.breastcancerfund.org/Heward Jue

also create a realistic looking nipple, although some women are satisfied with just the form of a breast (Sandowski, 1989).

A mastectomy can have a negative impact on a woman's sexuality and body image (Brandberg et al., 2008). Even so, however, the most important factor in resuming a normal sexual life is the encouragement and acceptance from the woman's sexual partner.

Pelvic Cancer and Hysterectomies

Cancer can also strike a woman's vagina, uterus, cervix, or ovaries. Although women with vaginal and cervical cancers often experience more sexual problems than women without these cancers, rates of sexual activity and partnering are similar (Lindau et al., 2007). Negative changes in sexual functioning have been found in some studies (Donovan et al., 2007; Gamel et al., 2000), but not in others (Greenwald & McCorkle, 2008). Common sexual issues include insufficient vaginal lubrication, shortened vaginas, reduced vaginal elasticity, and dyspareunia (Bergmark et al., 1999). Although the majority of cervical cancer survivors have a positive attitude toward sexuality (Greenwald & McCorkle, 2008), those who do not commonly have issues with negative views of themselves as sexual beings (Donovan et al., 2007). Overall, a woman's feelings about her cancer treatment and her social support network are both important in sexual recovery from these treatments. In addition, women who had conversations about the sexual effects of cancer with their health care providers had significantly fewer sexual problems (Lindau et al., 2007).

Cancer of the reproductive organs may result in a hysterectomy. In a total hysterectomy, the uterus and cervix (which is part of the uterus) are removed; in a radical hysterectomy, the ovaries are also removed (**oophorectomy;** oh-uh-for-RECT-toe-mee), along with the Fallopian tubes and surrounding tissue. Hysterectomies are also performed for conditions other than cancer. In fact, they are done so often that hysterectomy is the second most frequently performed surgical procedure performed on women in the United States (Keshavarz et al., 2002; Kuppermann et al., 2004).

A hysterectomy may or may not affect sexual functioning (Jongpipan & Charoenkwan, 2007), but oftentimes health care providers neglect to discuss the sexual implications of hysterectomy. A hysterectomy can affect sexual functioning and pleasure in a number of ways. The ovaries produce most of a woman's estrogen and progesterone; so, when they are removed, hormonal imbalances follow. Even with hormone replacement therapy, reduced vaginal lubrication, mood swings, and other bodily changes can occur. Also, many women find the uterine contractions of orgasm very pleasurable, and when the uterus is removed, they lose that aspect of orgasm. In Chapter 10, we discussed myotonia and the importance of the uterine muscles during sexual response. Although research supports the fact that removing the uterus and these muscles can decrease physical sexual response (Maas et al., 2004), there is also research that claims it does not

mastectomy
Surgical removal of a breast.

simple mastectomy
Surgical removal of the breast tissue.

oophorectomy
Surgical removal of the ovaries.

affect sexual functioning (Jongpipan & Charoenkwan, 2007; Srivastava et al., 2008). Women with a history of depression or sexual problems are often at increased risk for a worsening of these symptoms after a hysterectomy (Shifren & Avis, 2007).

Prostate Cancer

As we discussed in Chapter 6, almost all men will experience a normal enlargement of the prostate gland if they live long enough. Prostate cancer is one of the most common cancers in men over age 50. When prostate cancer is diagnosed or if the normal enlargement of the prostate progresses to the point at which it affects urination, a **prostatectomy** (pross-tuh-TECK-toe-mee) must be performed, sometimes along with a **cystectomy.** In the past, a prostatectomy involved cutting the nerves necessary for erection, resulting in erectile dysfunction. Newer techniques, however, allow more careful surgery, and fewer men suffer ED as a result.

One result of prostatectomy may be **incontinence,** sometimes necessitating an **indwelling catheter.** Many couples fear that this means the end of their sex life because removing and reinserting the catheter can lead to infection. However, the catheter can be folded alongside the penis during sexual behavior or held in place with a condom (Sandowski, 1989). For men who experience erectile dysfunction from the surgery, penile prostheses or intracavenous injections are possible. As in all surgeries of this kind, the man must also cope with the fear of disease, concern about his masculinity and body image, concern about the reactions of his sexual partner, and the new sensations or sexual functioning that can accompany prostate surgery.

Testicular Cancer

Cancer of the penis or scrotum is rare, and cancer of the testes is only slightly more common. Still, the sexual problems that result from these diseases are similar to those from prostate cancer. Testicular cancer is most common in men who are in their most productive years. Research has found that although sexual issues, including ejaculatory problems, are common after treatment for testicular cancer (Dahl et al., 2007), research has shown there is considerable improvement 1 year after diagnosis (van Basten et al., 1999).

In Chapter 6, we discussed testicular cancer, and, although the surgical removal of a testicle (orchiectomy) because of cancer usually does not affect the ability to reproduce (sperm can be banked, and the remaining testicle may produce enough sperm and adequate testosterone), some men do experience psychological difficulties. This is mainly because of feelings that they have lost part of their manhood or fears about the appearance of their scrotum. The appearance of the scrotum can be helped by inserting a testicular prosthesis that takes the place of the missing testicle. In some rare cases, cancer of the penis may necessitate a partial or total **penectomy** (pee-NECK-toe-mee). In a total penectomy, the man's urethra is redirected downward to a new opening that is created between the scrotum and anus. Even with a penectomy, some men can have orgasms by stimulating whatever tissue is left where the penis was, and the ejaculate leaves the body through the urethra (Schover & Jensen, 1988).

It is well documented that sexual dysfunctions can occur as a result of any type of cancer or cancer treatment (Ofman, 2004; Sheppard & Wylie, 2001). Sexual problems and dysfunctions may

be a temporary result of the stress associated with the situation, but they may also be long lasting (Ofman, 2004).

CHRONIC ILLNESS AND CHRONIC PAIN

Many people born with chronic diseases, or those who develop them later in life, suffer for many years with their condition. They must learn to make adjustments in many parts of their lives, including their sexual behaviors. Chronic pain from illnesses such as arthritis, migraine headaches, and lower back pain can make intercourse difficult or impossible at times.

RESPIRATORY ILLNESSES

Other conditions that affect sexual functioning are the respiratory illnesses, including **chronic obstructive pulmonary disease (COPD),** asthma, and tuberculosis. These diseases affect sexual functioning not only because they may make physical exertion difficult, but also because perceptual and motor skills can be impaired. Millions of people who have COPD learn to take medicine before sexual activity and slow down their pace of sexual activity; their partners learn to use positions that allow the person with COPD to breathe comfortably.

Many other chronic illnesses call for special types of sexual counseling and understanding. To understand the challenges that chronic illness poses to sexual functioning, we now review a sample of such conditions and examine the types of sexual challenges they present.

DIABETES

Diabetes is caused by the inability of the pancreas to produce insulin, which is used to process blood sugar into energy, or by the inability of the body to use the insulin produced. Diabetes may affect children (Type I diabetes), who must then depend on insulin injections for the rest of their lives, or it may appear later (Type II diabetes) and may then be controlled through diet or oral medication. Diabetes is a serious condition that can ultimately lead to blindness, renal failure, and other problems.

Diabetes is often used to demonstrate the effects of disease on sexuality because diabetics tend to exhibit multiple and complex

---

prostatectomy
The surgical removal of the prostate gland.

cystectomy
The surgical removal of the bladder.

incontinence
Lack of normal voluntary control of urinary functions.

indwelling catheter
A permanent catheter, inserted in the bladder, to allow the removal of urine in those who are unable to urinate or are incontinent.

penectomy
Surgical removal of the penis.

chronic obstructive pulmonary disease (COPD)
A disease of the lung that affects breathing.

sexual difficulties. In fact, sexual problems (especially difficulty in getting an erection for men and vaginitis or yeast infections in women) may be one of the first signs of diabetes. A large number of men in the later stages of diabetes have penile prostheses implanted. Women with Type I diabetes, aside from some problems with vaginal lubrication, do not seem to have significantly more problems than unaffected women. However, women with Type II diabetes show loss of desire, difficulties in lubrication, less satisfaction in sex, and difficulty reaching orgasm (Schover & Jensen, 1988).

One third of American families have at least one problem drinker in the family.

Differentiating between how much of a person's sexual difficulty is due to underlying physiological problems and how much is due to psychological issues is often difficult. Depression, fear of erectile disorder, lack of sexual response, anxiety about the future, and the life changes that diabetes can bring can all dampen sexual desire. Sexual counseling is an important part of diabetes treatment.

MULTIPLE SCLEROSIS

Multiple sclerosis (MS) involves a breakdown of the myelin sheath that protects all nerve fibers, and it can be manifested in a variety of symptoms, such as dizziness, weakness, blurred or double vision, muscle spasms, spasticity, and loss of control of limbs and muscles. Symptoms can come and go without warning, but MS is progressive and may worsen over time. MS often strikes people between the ages of 20 and 50, at a time when they are establishing sexual relationships and families (M. P. McCabe, 2002).

Multiple sclerosis can affect sexual functioning in many ways. Most commonly, men with MS experience erectile dysfunction (M. P. McCabe, 2002), whereas women with MS experience difficulties reaching orgasm (Tepavcevic et al., 2008; Tzortzis et al., 2008). Both men and women may become hypersensitive to touch, experiencing even light caresses as painful or unpleasant. Fatigue, muscle spasms, and loss of bladder and bowel function can also inhibit sexual contact. Sexual counseling, penile prostheses in men, and artificial lubrication in women can help overcome some of these difficulties.

ALCOHOLISM

Alcohol is the most common type of chemical dependency in the United States and Western Europe; about one third of American families have at least one problem drinker in the family, and alcohol is the third leading cause of death in the United States. Ethyl alcohol is a general nervous system depressant that has both long- and short-term effects on sexual functioning. It can impair spinal reflexes and decrease serum testosterone levels, which can lead to erectile dysfunction. Paradoxically, even as serum testosterone levels drop during alcohol abuse, luteinizing hormone (LH) levels can increase, leading to increased libido (George & Stoner, 2000).

Long-term alcohol abuse can have drastic consequences. **Hyperestrogenemia** (high-per-ess-troh-jen-EE-mee-uh) can result from the liver damage due to alcoholism, which, combined with lower testosterone levels, may cause gynecomastia (which we dis-

cussed in Chapter 6), testicular atrophy, sterility, ED, and the decreased libido seen in long-term alcoholic men. In women, liver disease can lead to decreased or absent menstrual flow, ovarian atrophy, loss of vaginal membranes, infertility, and miscarriages. Alcohol can affect almost every bodily system; after a while, the damage it causes, including the damage to sexual functioning, can be irreversible, even if the person stops drinking alcohol.

Alcoholism also has a dramatic impact on families. It often coexists with anger, resentment, depression, and other familial and relationship problems. Some people become abusive when drunk, whereas others may withdraw and become noncommunicative. For both sexes, problem drinking may lead them into a spiral of guilt, lowered self-esteem, and even to thoughts of suicide. Recovery is a long, often difficult process, and one's body and sexuality need time to recover from periods of abuse.

SPINAL CORD INJURIES

The spinal cord brings impulses from the brain to the various parts of the body; damage to the cord can cut off those impulses in any areas served by nerves below the damaged section. Therefore, to assess the dysfunctions that result from a spinal cord injury (SCI; or a spinal tumor), a physician must know exactly where on the spine the injury occurred and how extensively the cord has been damaged (Benevento & Sipski, 2002). Although some return of sensation and movement can be achieved in many injuries, most people are left with permanent disabilities. In more extreme cases, SCI can result in total or partial **paraplegia** (pah-ruh-PLEE-jee-uh) or total or partial **quadriplegia** (kwa-druh-PLEE-jee-uh). In these cases, the person is rendered extremely dependent on his or her partner or caretaker.

Men are four times more likely than women to experience SCI. If the injury is above a certain vertebra and the cord is not completely severed, a man may still be able to have an erection through the body's reflex mechanism, although it may be difficult to maintain because he will not be able to feel skin sensations in the penis. Injuries to the lower part of the spine are more likely to result in erectile difficulties in men, but they are also more likely to preserve some sensation in the genitals. Men without disabilities maintain erections in part through psychic arousal, such as sexual thoughts, feelings, and fantasies; however, with SCI, psychic arousal cannot provide continuing stimulation. Most men with SCI who are capable of having erections are not able to climax or ejaculate, which involves a more complex mechanism than an erection (Benevento & Sipski, 2002).

Women with SCI remain fertile and can bear children, and heterosexual women need to continue to use contraception. However, women with SCI can also lose sensation in the genitals and

hyperestrogenemia
Having an excessive amount of estrogens in the blood.

paraplegia
Paralysis of the legs and lower part of the body, affecting both sensation and motor response.

quadriplegia
Paralysis of all four limbs.

with it the ability to lubricate during sexual activity. However, many men and women with spinal cord injuries maintain orgasmic ability (M. Alexander & Rosen, 2008). A number of men report experiencing orgasm without ejaculation (Sipski et al., 2006). "Phantom orgasm," a psychic sensation of having an orgasm without the corresponding physical reactions, is also common. Skin sensation in the areas unaffected by the injury can become greater, and new erogenous zones can appear (D. J. Brown et al., 2005; Ferreiro-Velasco et al., 2005).

Sexual problems develop over time as the full impact of their situation takes effect. Although men with SCI can resume sexual activity within a year of their injury, their frequency of sexual activity decreases after the injury (C. J. Alexander et al., 1993). Many men and women enjoy a variety of sexual activities after SCI, including kissing, hugging, and touching. A healthy sex life after spinal cord injury is possible if a man or woman can learn to overcome the physical and psychological obstacles of their injuries (Kreuter et al., 2008).

Rehabilitation from SCI is a long, difficult process. Still, with a caring partner, meaningful sexual contact can be achieved. Men incapable of having an erection can still use their mouths and sometimes their hands. If vaginal intercourse is desired, couples can use the technique of "stuffing," in which the flaccid penis is pushed into the vagina. Newer treatment methods include prosthesis implantation, vacuum erection devices, and the injection of vasoactive drugs. Prosthesis implantation in men with spinal cord injuries have shown good patient satisfaction and low complication rates (Kim et al., 2008) Research has found that Viagra can significantly improve erections in men with spinal cord injury (Fink et al., 2002).

Sexual issues among the mentally ill ***are often neglected.***

AIDS AND HIV

In other chapters, we discuss the influence that AIDS has had on the sexual behaviors and attitudes of people in the United States. Because HIV can be passed to others through sexual activity, millions of Americans have changed their sexual lifestyles to include safer sex practices. But what of those who discover that they are HIV-positive or have developed AIDS? Although we discuss HIV and AIDS in depth in Chapter 15, here we review how the knowledge about HIV and the virus itself affect sexual functioning.

Caught up in the tragedy of their situation, their fear of infecting others, and often their shame, some people cease all sexual activity. Others limit their sexual contact to hugging, kissing, and caressing. Although people with HIV often experience sexual dysfunction (Catalan & Meadows, 2000), the existence of HIV in the bloodstream need not mean the end of one's sexual life. HIV-positive people need to be careful and considerate with their partners, avoiding exchange of body fluids and accidental infection. However, there is ample opportunity for loving, sexual relations while maintaining safety.

Wearing condoms and dental dams reduces (although it does not eliminate) the risk of sexually transmitting the virus during oral, vaginal, or anal sex (Schover & Jensen, 1988). Mutual massage, mu-

tual masturbation, the use of vibrators or other sex toys, and kissing without the exchange of saliva are all safe practices if care is taken (for example, the ejaculate of an infected partner should not come into contact with skin if the skin has cuts or abrasions; Sandowski, 1989). Sexuality can be important to those infected with HIV, for in the midst of the world's fear and rejection, sexuality reaffirms that they are loved, cared for, and accepted by their partners.

MENTAL ILLNESS AND RETARDATION: SPECIAL ISSUES

People with psychological disorders have sexual fantasies, needs, and feelings, and they have the same right to a fulfilling sexual expression as others do. However, historically they have either been treated as asexual, or their sexuality has been viewed as illegitimate, warped, or needing external control (Apfel & Handel, 1993). Yet a sudden or drastic change in sexual habits may be a sign of mental illness or a sign that a mentally ill person is getting worse (or better, depending on the change).

People with **schizophrenia,** for example, can be among the most impaired and difficult psychiatric patients. **Neuroleptics,** antipsychotic drugs such as Thorazine and Haldol, can cause increased or decreased desire for sex; painful enlargement of the breasts, reproductive organs, or testicles; difficulty in achieving or maintaining an erection; delayed or retrograde ejaculation; and changes, including pain, in orgasm.

Outside of the effects of neuroleptics, however people with schizophrenia have been found to grapple with the same sexual questions and dysfunctions as other people. The same is true of people with **major depression** and other **affective disorders.** They may experience hyposexuality when depressed or hypersexuality in periods of mania. Both can also occur as a result of antidepressant medications. Otherwise, their sexual problems do not differ significantly from those of people without major psychiatric problems (Schover & Jensen, 1988).

Sexual issues among the mentally ill are often neglected in psychiatric training, and health care providers who treat the mentally ill have often spent more time trying to control and limit patients' sexual behavior than they have been in treating sexual dysfunction. For years, the mentally retarded population has been kept from learning about sexuality and having sexual relationships. It is as if an otherwise healthy adult is supposed to display no sexual interest or activity at all. Educators have designed special sexuality education programs for the mentally retarded and developmentally disabled to make sure that they

schizophrenia
Any of a group of mental disorders that affect the individual's ability to think, behave, or perceive things normally.

neuroleptics
A class of antipsychotic drugs.

major depression
A persistent, chronic state in which the person feels he or she has no worth, cannot function normally, and entertains thoughts of or attempts suicide.

affective disorders
A class of mental disorders that affect mood.

express their sexuality in a socially approved manner (Monat-Haller, 1992). However, to deny people with psychiatric problems or retardation the pleasure of a sexual life is cruel and unnecessary.

Many people with mental disabilities (and physical disabilities) must spend long periods of their lives—sometimes their entire lives—in institutions, which makes developing a sex life difficult. Institutions differ greatly in the amount of sexual contact they allow; some allow none whatsoever, whereas others allow mutually consenting sexual contact, with the staff carefully overseeing the patients' contraceptive and hygienic needs (Trudel & Desjardins, 1992).

Another aspect of institutional life involves the sexual exploitation of patients with mental illness or mental retardation. This is well known but seldom discussed by those who work in such institutions. About half of all women in psychiatric hospitals report having been abused as children or adolescents, and many are then abused in a hospital or other institutional setting. Children who grow up with developmental disabilities are between 4 and 10 times more likely to be abused than children without those difficulties (Baladerian, 1991). Therefore, it is difficult to separate the sexual problems of mental illness, developmental disability, and psychiatric illness from histories of sexual abuse (Apfel & Handel, 1993; Monat-Haller, 1992).

review questions

1 Explain how physical illness and its treatment can interfere with sexual desire, physiological functioning, or both.

2 Explain how stroke and heart disease can psychologically and physiologically affect sexual functioning.

3 Explain how the various cancers in women and men can psychologically and physiologically interfere with sexual functioning.

4 Explain how chronic illnesses can psychologically and physiologically interfere with sexual functioning.

Getting Help for Sexual Problems and Dysfunctions

People who are ill or disabled have the same sexual needs and desires as everyone else. In the past, these needs have too often been neglected not because the disabled themselves were not interested in sexuality but because health care providers and other health care professionals were uncomfortable learning about their sexual needs and discussing them with their patients. Fortunately, this has been changing, and now sexuality counseling is a normal part of the recuperation from many diseases and injuries in many hospitals. It is important for all of us to learn that those with disabilities are just like everybody else and simply desire to be treated as such.

If you are experiencing problems or dysfunctions with sexual functioning, it is important to seek help as soon as possible. Often, when the problems are ignored, they lead to bigger problems down the road. If you are in college and have a student counseling center available to you, this may be a good place to start looking for help. Request a counselor who has received training in sexuality or ask to be referred to one who has.

Today, many therapists receive specific training in sexuality. One of the best training organizations in the United States is the American Association of Sexuality Educators, Counselors, and Therapists (AASECT). This organization offers certification programs in human sexuality for counselors, educators, and therapists and can also provide information on those who are certified as therapists or counselors.

review questions

1 Explain how the sexual needs of people who are ill or disabled have been neglected over the years.

2 Explain why sexuality counseling is an important part of the recovery process.

3 Why might it be beneficial to seek help and not ignore a sexual problem?

CHAPTER **review**

1 Healthy sexuality depends on good mental and physical functioning. Sexual problems and dysfunctions are common, and anxiety plays an important role in developing and maintaining sexual dysfunctions.

2 Therapists often use the sexual response cycle to help identify how sexual dysfunction, disease, illness, and disability affect sexual functioning. However, there have been concerns about how this model applies to women and female sexual functioning. Therapists also use the *DSM-IV-TR* to diagnose sexual dysfunction.

3 A health care provider or sex therapist first must determine whether a problem is psychological or physiological, and often these two can overlap. Psychological causes include unconscious fears, ongoing stress, anxiety, depression, guilt, anger, fear of infidelity, partner conflict, fear of intimacy, dependency, abandonment, or loss of control. Physical causes for sexual dysfunction include disease, disability, illness, and many commonly used drugs. Nonprescription drugs such as tobacco, alcohol, marijuana, LSD, and cocaine can also cause sexual dysfunctions.

4 Sexual dysfunctions can be primary or secondary and situational or global. Research has found that primary problems have more biological or physiological causes, whereas secondary problems tend to have more psychological causes. Situational problems occur during certain sexual activities or with certain partners, whereas global problems occur in every situation, during every type of sexual activity, and with every sexual partner. Sex therapists further categorize dysfunctions as those of sexual desire, sexual arousal, orgasm disorders, and pain disorders.

5 Sexual desire disorders include hypoactive sexual desire and sexual aversion. In hypoactive sexual desire (HSD), there is a low or absent desire for sexual activity. Secondary HSD is more common than primary HSD. Many women who experience HSD have lower levels of partner satisfaction.

6 Psychological causes for HSD include a lack of attraction to one's partner, fear of intimacy or pregnancy, marital or relationship conflicts, religious concerns, depression, and other psychological disorders. HSD can also result from negative messages about female sexuality while growing up, treating sex as a chore, a concern over a loss of control, or a negative body image. There are fewer cases of male hypoactive sexual desire than female. Cognitive–behavioral therapy and medications to increase testosterone have been found to be beneficial in the treatment of HSD.

7 Sexual aversion disorder involves an actual fear or disgust associated with sexual activity, and it affects more women than men. This condition is often caused by past sexual abuse. The most common treatment for sexual aversion involves discovering and resolving the underlying conflict that is contributing to the sexual aversion.

8 Sexual arousal disorders include female sexual arousal disorder (FSAD) and male erectile disorder. FSAD is an inability to either obtain or maintain an adequate lubrication response of sexual excitement; it can have both physiological and psychological causes. Several medications are being evaluated in the treatment of FSAD. The EROS-CTD is available to women who are diagnosed with FSAD.

9 Erectile disorder is defined as the persistent inability to obtain or maintain an erection sufficient for satisfactory sexual performance. It can be caused by neurological, endocrine, vascular, or psychogenic factors, and often there is a combination of these factors at play. Of all the sexual dysfunctions, there are more treatment options for male erectile disorder than for any other sexual dysfunction. Treatment options include psychological treatment (including systematic desensitization and

sex therapy); psychopharmacological, hormonal, and intracavernous injections; transurethral therapy; vascular surgery; vacuum constriction devices; and prosthesis implantation. The treatment of ED has changed considerably since erectile drugs became available.

10 Orgasmic disorders include female orgasmic disorder, male orgasmic disorder, and premature ejaculation. Female orgasmic disorder is a delay or absence of orgasm following a normal phase of sexual excitement. There are both physiological factors (such as chronic illness, diabetes, neurological problems, hormonal deficiencies, or alcoholism) and psychological factors (such as a lack of sex education, fear or anxiety, or psychological disorders) that may interfere with a woman's ability to reach orgasm. The majority of treatment programs for orgasmic disorder involve a combination of different treatment approaches, such as homework assignments, sex education, communication skills training, cognitive restructuring, desensitization, and other techniques.

11 Male orgasmic disorder is relatively rare and involves a delay or absence of orgasm following a normal phase of sexual excitement. Psychotropic medications have been found to interfere with orgasmic ability. Treatment options include psychotherapy and, if necessary, changing medications.

12 Premature ejaculation (PE) refers to a condition in which a man reaches orgasm just before, or immediately following, penetration. It is the most common sexual dysfunction in men under age 40. Treatment methods for PE include behavioral cognitive therapy and pharmaceutical treatments. Two popular behavioral techniques include the stop–start and the squeeze techniques.

13 Other ejaculatory dysfunctions range from PE to a delay or absence of ejaculation. Retarded ejaculation refers to a situation in which a man may be entirely unable to reach orgasm during certain sexual activities or may be able to ejaculate only after prolonged intercourse. Retrograde ejaculation involves the backward flow of ejaculate into the bladder instead of being released by the urethra. Some men also experience painful ejaculation. Causes for all of these ejaculatory dysfunctions include psychological issues, medications, drug use, disease, injuries, and various urological surgeries. Retarded ejaculation can be challenging to treat.

14 The genital pain disorders include vaginismus and dyspareunia. Vaginismus involves involuntary contractions of the vaginal muscles, which can make vaginal penetration virtually impossible. One of the most effective treatments for vaginismus includes the use of dilators.

15 Dyspareunia is pain before, during, or after sexual intercourse; it can occur in men and women. Vulvar vestibulitis syndrome is considered one of the most common causes of dyspareunia today. Dyspareunia should be evaluated medically to determine whether there are any medical problems contributing to the pain.

16 Other problems can interfere with sexual functioning. Faking orgasms often occurs as a result of a dysfunction, and generally the dysfunction should be discussed with sexual partners. Sleep sex is a condition in which a person commits sexual acts in his or her sleep. Peyronie's disease is not a sexual dysfunction in and of itself, but it can cause sexual dysfunction.

17 Bibliotherapy, hypnosis, relaxation training, and medications also show some promise in the treatment of sexual dysfunction. Much of the current clinical research today focuses on developing new drugs to treat dysfunctions.

18 Physical illness and its treatment can interfere with a person's sexual desire, physiological functioning, or both. Cardiovascular problems, including hypertension, myocardial infarctions, strokes, and cancer can all affect sexual functioning. There can be physical problems that interfere with physiological functioning, or there can be psychological problems or fear of sexual activity that can interfere with sexual functioning.

19 Chronic illnesses, such as diabetes, multiple sclerosis, muscular dystrophy, and alcoholism can also negatively affect sexual functioning. Spinal cord injuries, mental illness and retardation, and infection with HIV and AIDS all present specific challenges to sexual functioning. People who are ill or disabled have the same sexual needs and desires that healthy people do.

20 People who are experiencing sexual dysfunction, illness, disease, or disability should seek treatment as soon as possible to avoid the development of further problems.

CRITICAL THINKING questions

1 Suppose that one night you discover that you are having trouble reaching orgasm with your partner. What do you do about it? When it happens several times, what do you do? Who would you feel comfortable talking to about this problem?

2 If you were suddenly disabled or developed a chronic illness, would you lose your desire to love and be loved, to touch and be touched, to be regarded by another as sexy and desirable?

3 Do you think insurance plans should cover erectile drugs? Do you think college students without erectile disorder should recreationally take erectile drugs? Why, or why not?

4 Do you think that drug companies could convince us that a dysfunction exists when there is none? Should researchers be doing more work to uncover the causes of female sexual dysfunction, even if the pharmaceutical companies are paying for this research? Why, or why not?

5 Although women may be diagnosed with persistent sexual arousal syndrome, there is no companion diagnosis for men. Why do you think this is? Do you think there should be such a diagnosis for men? Why, or why not?

WEB resources

we discussed in this chapter, challenges the myths promoted by the pharmaceutical industry and calls for research on the many causes of women's sexual problems. A variety of links to sexual health organizations are available.

Masters and Johnson's Therapy Program ■ Masters and Johnson's website provides information on relational and sex therapy, trauma-based disorders, eating disorders, sexual compulsivity, and dissociative disorders. A question-and-answer section of the site answers the most frequently asked questions about sex therapy and the treatment of various disorders.

Dr. Carne's Resources for Sex Addiction & Recovery ■ Dr. Patrick Carne is a pioneer in the field of sexual addiction. This website offers information, research, and assistance for sex addiction and recovery. Several online tests are available for sexual addiction (gay and straight), Internet sexual addiction, and betrayal bonds.

The Sexual Health Network ■ The Sexual Health Network is dedicated to providing easy access to sexuality information, education, mutual support, counseling, therapy, health care, products, and other resources for people with disabilities, illness, or natural changes throughout the life cycle and those who love them or care for them.

CengageNOW

Go to www.cengage.com/login to link to CengageNOW, your online study tool. First take the Pre-Test for this chapter to get your Personalized Study Plan, which will identify topics you need to review and direct you to online resources. Then take the Post-Test to determine what concepts you have mastered and what you still need work on.

Videos in CengageNOW

For additional information on topics discussed in this chapter, check out the videos in CengageNOW on the following topics:

- Erectile Dysfunction: Clark—Hear how various factors affect Clark's erectile dysfunction, including physical symptoms, depression, and cultural expectations.

- Sex Patch for Women—Acting on the brain, this sex patch slowly releases testosterone in the skin, allowing women to experience sexual desire and improve the quality of their sex lives.

- Sex Devices for Women—Hear how the 43% of women between ages 18 and 59 who have sexual dysfunction may experience sexual desire and arousal again with these aids.

- Herbal Sexual Enhancements: Do They Work?—Learn how the effectiveness of sexual enhancements is unproven and their safety is unknown.

CHAPTER 15

Sexually Transmitted Infections and HIV/AIDS

My story starts when I started hooking up with one of my friends, Jason. He was hot, athletic, and had the most unique combination of qualities I've found in one person. The first night Jason and I kissed, I asked, "To get this out of the way, do you have any STDs?" I thought the answer would be a simple no, but he said, "Well, I had chlamydia back in the day."

A few weeks later, Jason's ex-girlfriend called me at five in the morning—she was another mutual friend. In one breath she said, "Jason has herpes. He gave it to me too, and that's just the way it is." I was shocked, scared, and sad that I wouldn't get to see where this relationship could go. Having an STD and lying about it was an obvious deal-breaker, right? Yet I felt sort of powerful with my new information. A line in the sand had to be drawn eventually, but its terms and conditions were up to me. But I didn't want herpes, but I didn't want this awesome person out of my life or sex life, either. So I wrote Jason letters; I practiced calling it off in my mirror. But I couldn't go through with it. The parts that held me back said, "Smart and sexually responsible people have STDs, too." I didn't want fear to be the reason why I didn't give him a chance. The real, core reason I didn't do anything is shameful to admit. I needed his attention, his touch, his compliments,

and his confidence. So I ignored the problem.

Four months went by before I noticed the bumps. It burned when I peed and afterward. I thought I had another bad urinary tract infection; I'd been getting a lot of those lately. I decided to take a look, and that's when I saw them. White, cauliflowery bumps at the corners of my vagina. This is it, I thought. I've waited too long to make up my mind, and now it's too late. I'll have herpes for the rest of my life because I wasn't strong enough to say no and walk away.

I went to the doctor, a terrifying visit I'd imagined over and over in my mind. Dreaded. But it wasn't herpes. It was HPV [human papillomavirus]. The doctor told me I also had a lesion on my cervix, which meant I had at least two different types of HPV. Apparently the types of HPV that cause genital warts don't cause abnormal cells on the cervix. It took eight months and two surgeries before I had a normal Pap smear. Before getting it, I knew nothing. I had no idea that "genital warts" was the same thing as HPV. HPV silently progresses. I also had no idea a vaccine was recently developed. Was it my fault I didn't know? Was I the only woman who didn't know? Jason said he didn't know. He never had an outbreak, at least not one he could distinguish from herpes. We found out that his ex gave it to him, the one who had called me. The night she called, she also told me how she and Jason had "made a

pact" against ever telling anyone about herpes but she decided to warn me. However, the HPV she kept to herself. When kept secret, every STD is dangerous.

It dawned on me that when I met Jason, I didn't trust myself at all. Things seemed to happen to me by accident; I didn't lead a deliberate life. Since I wasn't in charge of my life, how could I be in charge of, responsible for, my body? How was I qualified to determine whether I trusted anyone else? I put my confidence in what made me feel better. I didn't have many things besides Jason to give me confidence. Jason and I didn't use condoms every time. Sometimes it would only be right at the end, when it really mattered. I valued ensuring he still wanted me more than I valued my sexual health. Even though I still don't have herpes, it's only because I'm lucky.

I've realized that my body is my personal responsibility. Telling people in the future that I have HPV is my responsibility.

The experience with HPV and herpes has taught me that STDs are real. The information is there. That is the value of education. But education doesn't mean anything if you don't care enough about yourself to use it diligently.
SOURCE: Author's files

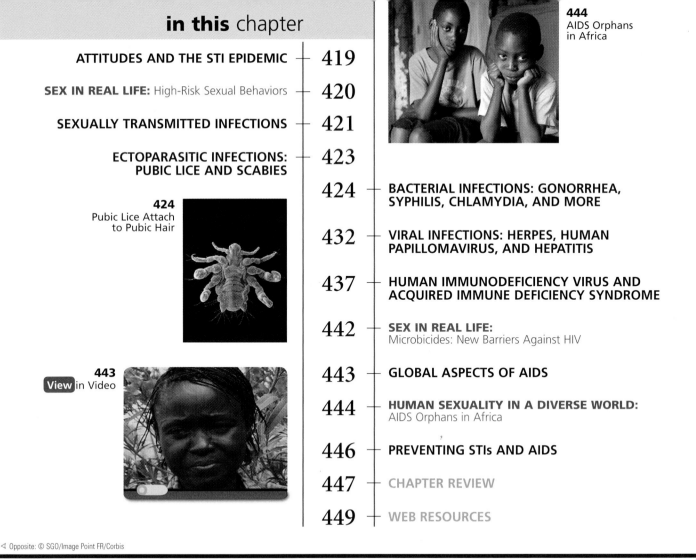

444
AIDS Orphans
in Africa

424
Pubic Lice Attach
to Pubic Hair

443
View in Video

◁ Opposite: © SGO/Image Point FR/Corbis

There are more than 65 million men and women living with a sexually transmitted infection (STI) in the United States, and it is estimated that 19 million new infections will occur each year (Centers for Disease Control and Prevention [CDC], 2007a; Montgomery et al., 2008; Weinstock et al., 2004). Although there are more than 25 infections spread primarily through sexual activity, in this chapter we limit our discussion to pubic lice, scabies, gonorrhea, syphilis, chlamydia, vaginal infections, herpes, human papilloma-virus, viral hepatitis, and the human immunodeficiency virus. We explore attitudes, incidence, diagnosis, symptoms, treatment, and the prevention of STIs.

Attitudes and the STI Epidemic

The sudden appearance of a new disease has always elicited fear about the nature of its **contagion.** Cultural fears about disease and sexuality in the early 20th century gave way to many theories about casual trans-

REALResearch > When it comes to choosing a sex partner, college students may not care as much about possible STIs as they do about other factors. One study of 400 men and women found that students rated potential partners infected with STIs as more appealing than partners who were overweight (CHEN & BROWN, 2005).

contagion
Disease transmission by direct or indirect contact.

High-Risk Sexual Behaviors

Drinking alcohol and engaging in sexual activity under the influence of alcohol often increases the risk of acquiring an STI...

High-risk sexual behaviors are those practices that increase the risk of acquiring a sexually transmitted infection. Engaging in sexual activity under the influence of alcohol often increases the risk of acquiring an STI because alcohol can increase the likelihood that a person will participate in high-risk sexual activity.

Engaging in safer-sex behaviors can decrease the risk of acquiring an STI. Safer sex behaviors include knowing your partner's STI history, being in a monogamous sexual relationship, using condoms and barriers for all sexual activity, and avoiding alcohol use (see Chapter 10, Sex in Real Life, "Safer-Sex Behavior Guidelines").

Following are some of these high-risk behaviors:

- Unprotected sexual intercourse without the use of a male or female condom unless this occurs in a long-term, single-partner, monogamous relationship in which both partners have been tested for STIs

- Engaging in oral sex with a male or female partner without using a condom or dental dam unless this occurs in a long-term, single-partner, monogamous relationship in which both partners have been tested for STIs

- Engaging in sexual intercourse before age 18

- Having multiple sex partners

- Engaging in sexual intercourse with a partner who has multiple sex partners

- Engaging in anal sex without a condom

- Engaging in sexual activity with a partner who has anal sex with multiple sex partners

- Engaging in oral sex with a partner who has multiple sex partners

- Engaging in sexual activity with a partner who has ever injected drugs

- Engaging in sex work or sexual activity with a partner who has ever engaged in sex work

- Engaging in sexual activity with a partner who has a history of STIs

- Engaging in sexual activity with a partner with an unknown STI history

mission (Brandt, 1985). At the turn of the 20th century, physicians believed that STIs could be transmitted on pens, pencils, toothbrushes, towels, and bedding. In fact, during World War I, the U.S. Navy removed doorknobs from its battleships, claiming that they were responsible for spreading sexual infections (Brandt, 1985).

Sexually transmitted infections have historically been viewed as symbols of corrupt sexuality (P. A. Allen, 2000). When compared with other illnesses, such as cancer or diabetes, attitudes about STIs have been considerably more negative, and many people believe that people so afflicted "got what they deserved." This has been referred to as the **punishment concept** of disease. To acquire an STI, it was generally believed, one must break the silent moral code of sexual responsibility. Those who become ill therefore have done something bad, for which they are being punished.

Kopelman (1988) suggested that this conceptualization has endured because it serves as a defense mechanism. By believing that a person's behavior is responsible for acquiring an STI, we believe ourselves to be safe by not engaging in whatever that behavior is. For example, if we believe that herpes happens only to people who have more than 10 sexual partners, we may limit our partners to 2 or 3 to feel safe. Whether we are safe, of course, depends on whether our beliefs about the causes of transmission are true. Negative beliefs and stigma about STIs persist. One study found that many people who are diagnosed with STIs experience "self-stigmatization," which is an acceptance of the negative aspects of stigma (feeling inadequate and ashamed; Fortenberry et al., 2002). These negative feelings can also interfere with the act of getting tested at all.

College students are often apprehensive about getting tested for STIs, especially when they think they might be positive. One study found that social stigma and negative consequences of testing often cause college students to delay or avoid getting tested for STIs (Barth et al., 2002). Students report that they would feel "embarrassed" and worried that other people would perceive them as "dirty." This is probably why in one study, many students said they would "rather not know" if they had an STI (Barth et al., 2002).

College students often act as though they are invincible; they may believe that although others may get STIs, it will not happen to

punishment concept
The idea that people who had become infected with certain diseases, especially STIs, did something wrong and are being punished.

them. In fact, the majority of young people believe that they are not at risk for contracting an STI (Ku et al., 2002). Yet we know that college students are a part of the population that is most at risk for contracting an STI (Revzina & DiClemente, 2005). This is because, as the opening story illustrates, college students often have difficulties talking about these issues. In addition, many students engage in high-risk sexual behaviors, such as having multiple partners and inconsistent condom use (see the accompanying Sex in Real Life, "High-Risk Sexual Behaviors," for more information).

The truth is that young adults are disproportionately affected by STIs, and the incidence of these infections continues to grow in this population (Casey et al., 2008; T. Hall et al., 2008). Studies have found that close to half of the nearly 19 million STIs that occur in the United States each year occur in people 15 to 24 years old (Crosby & Danner, 2008; Revzina & DiClemente, 2005; Weinstock et al., 2004).

Overall, adolescent and young females are more biologically at risk for developing an STI than older women (Santelli et al., 1999). This is because the cervix of a young girl is more vulnerable to certain STIs (Arrington-Sanders et al., 2007). Even so, many female adolescents often do not believe they are at risk for contracting a sexually transmitted infection (Ethier et al., 2003).

REALResearch > The Centers for Disease Control reported that one in four U.S. teenage girls was infected with an STI; the ratio for African American teenage girls was one in two (CDC, 2007A).

review questions

1 Define the punishment concept of disease.

2 Explain how the punishment concept might make a person neglect protecting themselves from STIs.

3 Explain why college students might be apprehensive about STI testing.

Sexually Transmitted Infections

In the United States, cases of syphilis, gonorrhea, chancroid, chlamydia, the human immunodeficiency virus (HIV), and acquired immune deficiency syndrome (AIDS) must be reported to the CDC. Reporting these infections helps to identify disease trends and communities that may be at high risk. The required reporting for other STIs varies by state.

Women experience more long-term consequences of STIs (CDC, 2007a). They are more susceptible to gonorrhea, chlamydia, and HIV, although the spread of syphilis and genital warts is usually shared equally between the sexes. Although the prevalence of HIV was higher in men in the late 1980s, heterosexual women are still more susceptible than men if they have sexual intercourse with an infected male partner. Studies have found that women are at greater risk for long-term complications from STIs because the tissue of the vagina is much more fragile than the skin covering the penis, and infected semen can stay in the female reproductive tract (Bolton et al., 2008; CDC, 2007a). In addition, many more women are **asymptomatic;** therefore, they do not know that they are infected. Some infections, such as herpes and HIV, also have properties of **latency.** A person can have the virus

that causes the disease but not have symptoms, and tests may even show up negative. As a result, the person may be unaware that he or she is infecting others. This is why it is important to tell all sexual partners about an STI if you find yourself infected. In fact, the CDC formally recommended testing for men and women whose partners have been infected with HIV, syphilis, Chlamydia, or gonorrhea in 2008 (Dooley, 2008).

STIs can adversely affect pregnancy as well. In fact, certain untreated STIs, such as syphilis, gonorrhea, chlamydia, herpes, hepatitis B, and HIV, can cause problems such as miscarriage, stillbirth, early onset of labor, premature rupture of the amniotic sac, mental retardation, and fetal or uterine infection (CDC, 2007a). Some STIs, such as syphilis, can cross the placenta and infect a developing fetus, whereas other STIs, such as gonorrhea, chlamydia, and herpes, can infect a newborn as he or she moves through the vagina during delivery. HIV can cross the placenta, infect a newborn at birth, or, unlike other STIs, be transmitted during breast-feeding (Arias et al., 2003).

asymptomatic
Without recognizable symptoms.

latency
A period in which a person is infected with an STI but does not test positive for it.

Bacterial STIs can be treated during pregnancy with antibiotics, and if treatment is begun immediately, there is less chance the newborn will become infected. Viral infections cannot be treated, but antiviral medications can be given to pregnant women to lessen the symptoms of these infections (Bardeguez et al., 2008; Kriebs, 2008). If there are active vaginal lesions or sores from an STI at the time of delivery, a health care provider may recommend a cesarean section. Women who do not know their partner's STI history should always use latex condoms during pregnancy.

Although STIs occur in all racial and ethnic groups, there are some racial and ethnic differences in prevalence rates. African Americans have higher rates of most STIs than Whites and Hispanics. Gonorrhea and syphilis are as much as 44 times higher in African Americans than Whites. These differences may partially be because African Americans are more likely to be treated in public clinics, which are more likely to report STIs (Arrington-Sanders et al., 2007). Even so, this can't explain all of these ethnic and racial differences in STI rates. Other factors, such as access to health care, the ability to seek help, poverty, and sexual practices are also responsible for some of the rate disparities (Laumann & Youm, 2001).

Over the past several decades, the rates of STIs in men who have sex with men (MSM) have been increasing. Researchers believe that STI increases in MSM are due to several factors, including a lack of knowledge about STIs, increased Internet access to sexual partners, a decreased fear of acquiring HIV, the increased use of alcohol and other drugs because of discrimination and social pressures about orientation, and an increase in high-risk sexual behaviors, including oral sex (Brooks et al., 2008; Ciesielski, 2003; Daneback et al., 2007; Mackesy-Amiti et al., 2008; Ogilvie et al., 2008). Compared with heterosexual men and women, MSM report significantly more sexual risk taking (i.e., inconsistent condom use and multiple sexual partners; Brooks et al., 2008).

Although few studies have examined the incidence of STIs in women who have sex with women, transmission risk varies by STI and certain sexual practices (e.g., oral sex, penetrative sex, or shared sex toy use; Fethers et al., 2000; Marrazzo et al., 2001, 2002, 2005). Overall, the research has found that several STIs can be transmitted during vulva-to-vulva sex, including trichomoniasis, bacterial vaginosis (BV), herpes, human papillomavirus, hepatitis C, and HIV (Fethers et al., 2000; A. Johnson et al., 1992; Kellock & O'Mahony, 1996; Marrazzo et al., 2005; O'Hanlan & Crum, 1996; Troncoso et al., 1995). Lesbian women are more likely to have fewer sexual partners than heterosexual women (VanderLaan & Vasey, 2008), and they also engage in less penetrative sex, which reduces their overall risk of STI infection. However, many lesbian women do not believe regular Pap smears are necessary and are less likely than heterosexual women to obtain yearly pelvic exams (Bauer & Welles, 2001; Marrazzo, 2004; Tjepkema, 2008). This may put them more at risk for adverse complications of STIs. Overall the incidence of STIs is significantly higher in bisexual women than among lesbians (Koh et al., 2005; Morrow & Allsworth, 2000; Tao, 2008).

For men and women who need contraception, birth control methods offer varying levels of protection from sexually transmitted infections. In 1993, the Food and Drug Administration (FDA) approved labeling contraceptives for STI protection. Barrier methods, such as condoms, diaphragms, or contraceptive sponges, can decrease the risk of acquiring an STI, although the FDA recommended revised labeling on condom packaging in 2005 to indicate that condoms must be used "consistently and correctly" to decrease STI risk (Alonso-Zaldivar & Neuman, 2005).

Although nonoxynol-9 (N-9) spermicide was once thought the most effective at reducing the risk of acquiring an STI, there is good evidence that it does not protect against STIs and may, in fact, increase the rate of genital ulceration, causing a higher risk of STI infection (Boonstra, 2005; FDA, 2007; Jain et al., 2005; B. A. Richardson, 2002; Wilkinson et al., 2002; see Chapter 13 for more information about N-9).

Condoms are the most effective contraceptive method for reducing STI risk. The degree of protection, however, depends on several factors, including the types of sexual behaviors engaged in and correct and consistent use (Mindel & Sawleshwarkar, 2008). The role of oral contraceptives in preventing STIs is complicated. The increased hormones change the cervical mucus and the lining of the uterus, which can help prevent any infectious substance from moving up into the genital tract. In addition, the reduced buildup of the endometrium decreases the possibility of an infec-

---

REALResearch **>** Female African American adolescents whose male partner was intoxicated during sex were significantly more likely to test positive for an STI than were adolescents whose partners were not intoxicated (CROSBY ET AL., 2008).

---

tious substance growing (because there is less nutritive material for bacteria to survive). However, oral contraceptives may also cause the cervix to be more susceptible to infections because of changes in the vaginal discharge.

STIs can be caused by several agents, some of which are bacterial, others viral. The causal agents are important in treating STIs. The most effective way to avoid STI transmission is to abstain from oral, vaginal, and anal sex or to be in a long-term, mutually monogamous relationship with someone who is free from STIs.

WHAT DO YOU WANT TO KNOW?

Can STIs be transmitted through oral sex?
If there are open sores on the penis or vulva, it is possible that an STI may be transmitted to the mouth through oral sex. If there are active cold sores in the mouth or on the lips and a person performs oral sex, it is possible to transmit the virus to the genitals. Oral sex with a partner infected with gonorrhea or chlamydia may cause an infection in the throat. As for HIV, some researchers have found that oral sex is an unlikely method of transmission for the virus (Kohn et al., 2002), whereas others have found that HIV transmission through oral sex is possible (CDC, 2003a).

1 Explain why women are more susceptible to STIS and more at risk for long-term complications.

2 Define the "asymptomatic" and "latent" aspects of STI and explain how these may affect a man or woman.

3 Explain what we know about STIs in men who have sex with men and women who have sex with women.

4 How might birth control methods help or hurt a person's STI risk?

Ectoparasitic Infections: Pubic Lice and Scabies

Ectoparasitic infections are those that are caused by parasites that live on the skin's surface. The two ectoparasitic infections that are sexually transmitted are pubic lice and scabies.

PUBIC LICE

Pubic lice (or "crabs") are a parasitic STI; the lice are very small, wingless insects that can attach themselves to pubic hair with their claws. They feed off the tiny blood vessels just beneath the skin and are often difficult to detect on light-skinned people. Under closer observation, it is possible to see the movement of their legs. They may also attach themselves to other hairy parts of the body, although they tend to prefer pubic hair. When not attached to the human body, pubic lice cannot survive more than 24 hours. However, they reproduce rapidly, and the female cements her eggs to the sides of pubic hair. The eggs hatch in 7 to 9 days, and the newly hatched nits (baby pubic lice) reproduce within 17 days.

Incidence
Pubic lice are common and regularly seen by health clinics and various health care providers. Although there are no mandated reporting laws, pubic lice affect millions of people worldwide.

Symptoms
The most common symptom is a mild to unbearable itching, which often increases during the evening hours. This itching is thought to be a result of an allergic reaction to the saliva that the lice secrete during their feeding. People who are not allergic to this saliva may not experience any itching.

Diagnosis
The itching usually forces a person to seek treatment, although some people detect the lice visually first. Diagnosis is usually made fairly quickly because the pubic lice and eggs can be seen with the naked eye.

Treatment
To treat pubic lice, it is necessary to kill both the insects and their eggs. In addition, the eggs must be destroyed on sheets and clothing. Health care providers can prescribe Kwell ointment, which comes in a shampoo or cream. The cream must be applied directly to the pubic hair and left on for approximately 12 hours, whereas the shampoo can be applied and directly rinsed off. There are also some fairly effective over-the-counter products that can be purchased in drugstores; however, these products are usually not as effective as Kwell. Sheets and all articles of clothing should be either dry cleaned, boiled, or machine washed in very hot water. As with the other STIs, it is important to tell all sexual partners to be checked for lice because they are highly contagious.

SCABIES

Scabies is an ectoparasitic infection of the skin with the mite *Sarcoptes scabiei*. It is spread during skin-to-skin contact, both during sexual and nonsexual contact. The mites can live for up to 48 hours on bed sheets and clothing and are impossible to see with the naked eye.

WHAT DO YOU WANT TO KNOW?

Can crabs be spread through casual contact, such as sleeping on the same sheets or sharing clothes? What if someone with crabs sat on my couch and I sat down right after them?

If you slept in the bed of a person who was infected with pubic lice or wore the same clothes without washing them, there is a chance that you could become infected.

Although crabs are usually spread through sexual contact, it is possible to acquire them if you share a bed or towels, linens, articles of clothing, combs and brushes, or toilet seats with a person who is infected.

pubic lice
A parasitic STI that infests the pubic hair and can be transmitted through sexual contact; also called crabs.

scabies
A parasitic STI that affects the skin and is spread during skin-to-skin contact, both during sexual and nonsexual contact.

The Wellcome Medical Photo Library, London

Pubic lice attach to pubic hair and feed off the tiny blood vessels beneath the skin.

Incidence

Infection with scabies occurs worldwide and among all races, ethnic groups, and social classes. Like pubic lice, there are no mandated reporting laws, but scabies affects millions of people worldwide.

Symptoms

Usually the first symptoms include a rash and intense itching. The first time a person is infected, the symptoms may take between 4 and 6 weeks to develop. If a person has been infected with scabies before, the symptoms usually develop more quickly.

REALResearch **>** The global cost of treating chlamydia is **$10 billion** annually (CHIARADONNA, 2008).

Diagnosis

A diagnosis can usually be made on examination of the skin rash. A skin scraping can be done to confirm the diagnosis. A delay in diagnosis can lead to a rapid spread of scabies, so immediate diagnosis and treatment are necessary (Tjioe & Vissers, 2008).

Treatment

Topical creams are available to treat scabies. All bed sheets, clothing, and towels must be washed in hot water, and all sexual partners should be treated. Usually itching continues for 2 to 3 weeks after infection, even after treatment.

review questions

1 Identify the two ectoparasitic STIs and describe how common they are.

2 Identify the most common symptoms associated with ectoparasitic STIs and explain what a person should do if they experience any of these symptoms.

3 Identify the treatment for ectoparasitic STIs.

Bacterial Infections:
Gonorrhea, Syphilis, Chlamydia, and More

Some sexually transmitted infections are caused by bacteria, including gonorrhea, syphilis, chlamydia, chancroid, and a variety of vaginal infections. Here we explore the incidence, symptoms, diagnosis, and treatment for these bacterial infections.

GONORRHEA

Gonorrhea (the "clap" or "drip") is caused by the bacterium *Neisseria gonorrhoeae,* which can survive only in the mucous membranes of the body. These areas, such as the cervix, urethra, mouth, throat, rectum, and even the eyes, provide moisture and warmth that help the bacterium survive. *N. gonorrhoeae* is actually fragile and can be destroyed by exposure to light, air, soap, water, or a change in temperature, and so it is nearly impossible to transmit gonorrhea nonsexually. The only exception to this is the transmission of gonorrhea from a mother to her baby as the baby passes through the vagina during delivery. Transmission of gonorrhea occurs when mucous membranes come into contact with each other; this can occur during sexual intercourse, oral sex, vulva-to-vulva sex, and anal sex.

Incidence

Although gonorrhea rates hit a record low a few years ago, rates are increasing again and today, gonorrhea is the second most commonly reported infectious disease in the United States (chlamydia, which we will discuss shortly, is the first). In 2006, there were 358,000 reported cases of gonorrhea in the United States (CDC, 2007a). However, because gonorrhea is underdiagnosed and underreported, experts believe that the actual prevalence is more than 700,000 per year (Weinstock et al., 2000).

Several factors, including sex, race and ethnicity, and geographical area, have been found to affect gonorrhea rates. Women are more at risk for gonorrhea and in 2006 were more likely to be diagnosed with gonorrhea than men (see Figure 15.1; CDC, 2007a). Geographic differences have also been found, with higher gonorrhea rates in parts of the South and Midwest (see Figure 15.2). Finally, the incidence of gonorrhea also varies by race and ethnicity. The incidence of gonorrhea in African Americans was 18 times higher than in Whites in 2006 (which was down from 2002 when gonorrhea was 23 times more prevalent in African Americans; CDC, 2007a; see Figure 15.3).

gonorrhea
A bacterial STI that causes a puslike discharge and frequent urination in men; many women are asymptomatic.

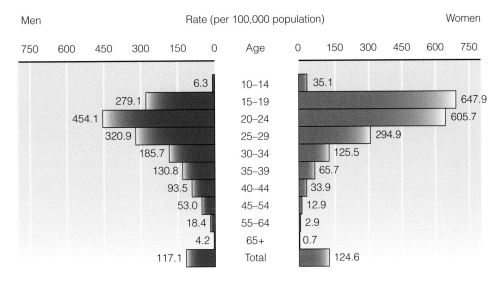

Figure **15.1** Gonorrhea—Age- and sex-specific rates: United States, 2006. Source: Centers for Disease Control and Prevention, 2007a.

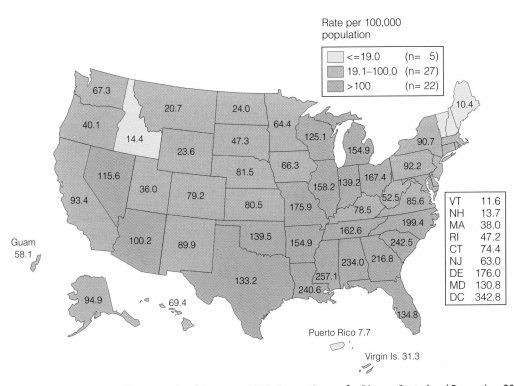

Figure **15.2** Gonorrhea—Rates by state: United States and outlying areas, 2006. Source: Centers for Disease Control and Prevention, 2007a.

Symptoms

The majority of women who are infected with gonorrhea are asymptomatic and do not know that they are carrying the disease; however, they are still able to infect their partners. In women, the cervix is the most common site of infection, and a pus-filled cervical discharge may develop. If there are any symptoms, they develop within 3 to 5 days and include an increase in urinary frequency, abnormal uterine bleeding, and bleeding after sexual intercourse, which results from an irritation of the cervix. The cervical discharge can irritate the vaginal lining, causing pain and discomfort. Urination can be difficult and painful. (This is different from the pain caused by a urinary tract infection; see Chapter 5.) If left untreated, gonorrhea can move up into the uterus and Fallopian tubes and may lead to pelvic inflammatory disease

(PID). In fact, gonorrhea is a major cause of PID in women (we discuss PID later in this chapter).

Approximately 25% of infected men are asymptomatic, although they are still able to transmit the disease to their partners (Cates, 2004). When a man experiences symptoms, these would include **epididymitis** (epp-pih-did-ee-MITE-us), urethral discharge, painful urination, and an increase in the frequency and urgency of urination. Symptoms usually appear between 2 and 6 days after infection.

epididymitis
An inflammation of the epididymis in men, usually resulting from STIs.

Sexually Transmitted Infections and HIV/AIDS ■ **425**

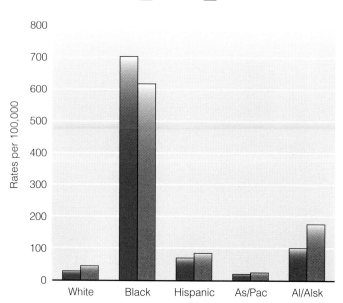

Figure **15.3** Gonorrhea—Rates by race, ethnicity, and gender: United States, 2006. Source: Centers for Disease Control and Prevention, 2007a.

Rectal gonorrhea, which can be transmitted to men and women during anal intercourse, may cause bloody stools and a puslike discharge. If left untreated, gonorrhea can move throughout the body and settle in various areas, including the joints, causing swelling, pain, and pus-filled infections.

Diagnosis

Testing for gonorrhea involves collecting a sample of the discharge from the cervix, urethra, or another infected area with a cotton swab. The discharge is incubated to allow the bacteria to multiply. It is then put on a slide and examined under a microscope for the presence of the **gonococcus bacterium.** DNA testing using a person's urine has become common for gonorrhea testing (Hawthorne et al., 2005).

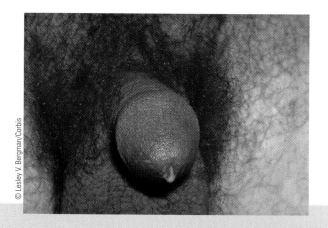

The majority of men infected with gonorrhea experience symptoms and will seek out treatment. However, this may not happen until they have already infected others.

What STIs do gynecologists check for during a regular exam?
During a woman's yearly visit, health care providers perform a Pap testing, which is designed to evaluate the cervical cells. Although it is possible that some STIs, such as cervical warts and herpes, may show up during Pap testing, many will not. If you think that you may have been exposed to any STIs, it is important for you to ask your health care provider to perform specific tests to screen for these. Specific tests can be run for syphilis, gonorrhea, chlamydia, herpes, genital warts, or HIV. All sexually active young people (under age 25) should have a chlamydia test performed annually (Couldwell, 2005).

Treatment

Gonorrhea can be treated effectively with antibiotics, either orally or via injection. Although several types of antibiotics have been successfully used in the past, drug-resistant strains forced the CDC to revise its gonorrhea treatment guidelines and recommend the use of only a single class of antibiotics in 2007 ("Update to CDC's STDs Treatment Guidelines," 2007). Sexual partners must also be treated, or else reinfection and further infection of others will occur (Golden et al., 2005).

SYPHILIS

Syphilis is caused by an infection with the bacterium *Treponema pallidum.* Like *N. gonorrhoeae,* these bacteria can live only in the mucous membranes of the body. The bacteria enter the body through small tears in the skin and are able to replicate themselves. Syphilis is transmitted during sexual contact, and it usually first infects the cervix, penis, anus, lips, or nipples. **Congenital syphilis** may also be transmitted through the placenta during the first or second trimester of pregnancy.

Incidence

Syphilis rates decreased in 1990 and in 2000 were the lowest since reporting began in 1941. In the last decade, the overall national syphilis rates have increased, primarily among gay men. The rate of both primary (the first stage of infection) and secondary (the later stages of infection) syphilis among men increased 54% since 2001 (we discuss primary and secondary syphilis later in this section; Heffelfinger et al., 2007). Although the rates of syphilis in men and women were similar a decade ago, today syphilis rates in men are close to 6 times higher than in women (CDC, 2007a).

gonococcus bacterium
The bacterium that causes gonorrhea (*Neisseria gonorrhoeae*).

syphilis
A bacterial STI that is divided into primary, secondary, and tertiary stages.

congenital syphilis
A syphilis infection acquired by an infant from the mother during pregnancy.

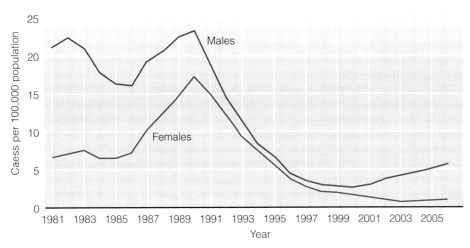

Primary and Secondary Syphilis Rates By Gender, 1981–2006

Figure **15.4** Primary and secondary syphilis rates by gender, 1981–2006. Source: Centers for Disease Control, 2007d.

Experts believe that men having sex with men may primarily be responsible for these increases.

In 2006, there were close to 10,000 reported cases of primary and secondary syphilis (CDC, 2007a; see Figure 15.4). By far, the majority of these cases were reported in men (CDC, 2007a). In fact, 64% of all cases of primary and secondary syphilis were in men who have sex with men (CDC, 2007a). Rates in women have either declined or remained stable.

Although racial and ethnic differences in syphilis rates exist, these differences have been declining overall. The rate of syphilis in African Americans was 29 times greater than Whites in 1999, whereas rates were only 6 times greater in African Americans in 2006 (CDC, 2007a). This represents both a decrease in the rates of syphilis in the African American community and an increase in syphilis rates in White males. African Americans continue to be disproportionately affected by syphilis at a rate that is 3 times that of Hispanics, who have the second highest infection rate (CDC, 2007a). The rate of primary and secondary syphilis in African American women is 16 times higher than in White women.

Like gonorrhea, syphilis rates differ geographically, with lower rates in the Midwest and higher rates in the South. There are also racial and ethnic variations, with higher rates in African Americans (see Figure 15.5 for more information on syphilis and racial and ethnic groups).

Symptoms

Infection with syphilis is divided into three stages. The first stage, primary or early syphilis, occurs anywhere from 10 to 90 days after infection (typically this happens within 2 to 6 weeks after infection). During this stage, there may be one or more small, red-brown sores, called chancres, that appear on the vulva, penis, vagina, cervix, anus, mouth, or lips. The **chancre** (SHANK-ker), which is a round sore with a hard, raised edge and a sunken center, is usually painless and does not itch. If left untreated, the chancre will heal in 3 to 8 weeks. However, during this time the person can still transmit the disease to other sexual partners.

After the chancre disappears, the infected person enters the second stage, secondary syphilis, which begins anywhere from 3 to 6 weeks after the chancre has healed. During this stage, the syphi-

lis invades the central nervous system. The infected person develops reddish patches on the skin that look like a rash or hives. There may also be wartlike growths in the area of infection (D. L. Brown & Frank, 2003). If the rash develops on the scalp, hair loss can also occur. The lymph glands in the groin, armpit, neck, or other areas enlarge and become tender. Additional symptoms at this stage include headaches, fevers, anorexia, flulike symptoms, and fatigue.

In the third and final stage of the disease, tertiary or late syphilis, the disease goes into remission. The rash, fever, and other symptoms go away, and the person usually feels fine. He or she is still able to transmit the disease for about 1 year, but after this time the person is no longer infectious. Left untreated, however, tertiary or late syphilis can cause neurological, sensory, muscular, and psychological difficulties and is eventually fatal.

Diagnosis

Anyone who develops a chancre should immediately go to a health care provider to be tested for the presence of the syphilis-causing bacteria. This diagnosis can be made in several ways. A culture can be taken from one of the lesions and microscopically examined. Today the most common tests used for the detection of syphilis are blood tests. These tests check for the presence of antibodies, which develop after a person is infected with the bacteria.

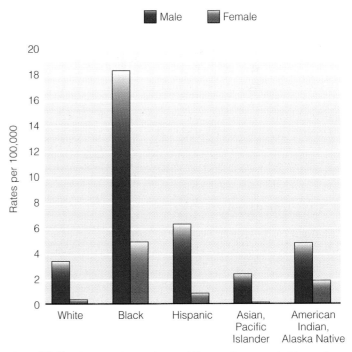

Figure **15.5** Primary and secondary syphilis rates by race, ethnicity, and gender, 2006.

chancre
A small, red-brown sore that results from syphilis infection; the sore is actually the site at which the bacteria entered the body.

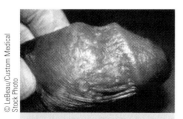

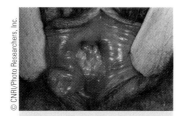

The chancre, which appears on the underside of the penis in this photo, is the classic painless ulcer of syphilis.

Typical syphilis chancre on a woman's labia.

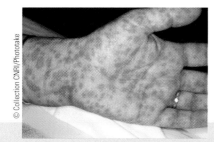

A secondary syphilis infection produces rashes on the palms or soles, as well as a generalized body rash.

During late syphilis, blood tests may be negative or weakly positive even if the infection exists (Singh et al., 2008). If a person thinks that he or she may have been exposed to syphilis but tests negative, he or she should engage only in safer-sex activity and consult with his or her health care provider immediately.

Treatment

In its early stages, syphilis is relatively easy to treat. If a person has been infected for less than a year, treatment typically involves a single injection of an antibiotic. Additional doses may be required if a person has been infected longer than a year (CDC, 2007a). However, if syphilis is allowed to progress to the later stages, it is no longer treatable and is often fatal.

though experts believe that the majority of cases went unreported because many infected men and women do not experience symptoms and do not get tested (CDC, 2007a). It is estimated there are closer to 2.8 million new cases of chlamydia each year (Weinstock et al., 2004). Chlamydia affects all socioeconomic and ethnic groups, and like some other STIs, is highest among African Americans (see Figure 15.7). Chlamydia rates are 8 times higher in African American women than White women (CDC, 2007a). Chlamydia rates are also higher in younger women than in younger men (see Figure 15.8). The highest chlamydia rates are in females aged 15 to 19, followed by females aged 20 to 24 (CDC, 2007a).

However, higher rates in women may be a result of screening programs aimed at women. Chlamydia infection in men is substantially underdiagnosed, and experts claim that if men were routinely screened, the rates for men and women would be more similar (Dunne et al., 2008; Joffe et al., 2008; Ku et al., 2002). Lesbians also are at risk for chlamydia, although it is most common in heterosexual populations (K. M. Freund, 1992).

Symptoms

Chlamydia has been called a "silent disease" because approximately 75% of women and 50% of men are asymptomatic (CDC, 2007a). Those who do have symptoms usually develop them within 1 to 3 weeks after becoming infected. Even without symptoms, chlamydia is contagious, which explains why rates are increasing.

Female symptoms can include burning during urination, pain during sexual intercourse, and pain in the lower abdomen. In most women, the cervix is the site of infection with chlamydia, and so cervical bleeding or spotting may occur. Some women do experience a vaginal discharge; however, this is rare and is more likely an indication of another STI (K. M. Freund, 1992). Male symptoms may include a discharge from the penis, burning sensation during urination, burning and itching around the opening of the penis, and a pain or swelling in the testicles. The bacterium

REALResearch **>** A study of 411 sexually active 14 to 19 year olds from various U.S. public health clinics found that **53%** were infected with chlamydia (Niccolai et al., 2007).

CHLAMYDIA

Chlamydia is the common name for infections caused by a bacterium called *Chlamydia trachomatis*. Risk factors for chlamydia are similar to those for other STIs and include multiple sexual partners, a partner who has had multiple sexual partners, being under age 25, inconsistent use of barrier contraceptives (such as condoms), and a history of STIs. Chlamydia can be transmitted during vaginal intercourse, oral sex, or anal sex. In addition, an infected woman can pass the infection to her newborn during childbirth.

Incidence

Chlamydia is the most commonly reported infectious disease in the United States (CDC, 2007a; see Figure 15.6). In 2006, there were more than 1 million new cases of chlamydia reported, al-

that causes chlamydia can also cause epididymitis and **nongonococcal urethritis (NGU)** in men.

In women, the bacteria can move up from the uterus to the Fallopian tubes and ovaries, leading to pelvic inflammatory disease. In fact, infection with chlamydia is thought to be one of the agents most responsible for the development of PID (CDC, 2007b; Terán et al., 2001). Forty percent of women with untreated chlamydia will develop PID, and approximately 20% of them will become infertile (Hillis & Wasserheit, 1996). Women who are in-

chlamydia
A bacterial STI; although often asymptomatic, it is thought to be one of the most damaging of all the STIs.

nongonococcal urethritis (NGU)
Urethral infection in men that is usually caused by an infection with chlamydia.

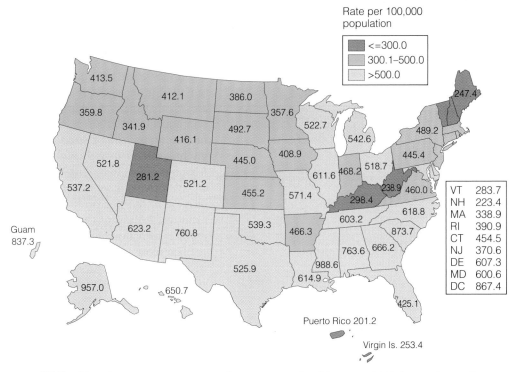

Figure **15.6** Chlamydia—Rates among women by U.S. state and outlying areas, 2006. Source: Centers for Disease Control, 2007a.

VT	283.7
NH	223.4
MA	338.9
RI	390.9
CT	454.5
NJ	370.6
DE	607.3
MD	600.6
DC	867.4

fected with cervical chlamydia and who undergo an elective (or possibly spontaneous) abortion or vaginal birth are also at increased risk of developing pelvic inflammatory disease (Boeke et al., 2005).

Diagnosis

Because of the increasing rates of chlamydia in the United States today, the CDC has recommended yearly screening for all sexually active women under age 26, as well as women over age 26 who have risk factors, such as multiple partners (CDC, 2007b). There are several tests available to detect chlamydia. The most common involves taking a sample of the cells from the infected area to evaluate microscopically for the presence of the bacteria. Recently, urine-based tests have become available, which are easier and less invasive (Joffe et al., 2008; Trigg et al., 2008). Research to find a home-based screening test for chlamydia is ongoing.

Treatment

Antibiotics are used to treat chlamydia, but, like gonorrhea, chlamydia has become highly resistant. Antibiotics are usually taken for a certain period of time (usually at least 7–10 days). The CDC recommends that women be retested for chlamydia 3 months after treatment to make sure they are no longer infected (CDC, 2007b). In addition, sexual partners from the last 3 months should also be tested for chlamydia, whether or not they are experiencing symptoms. This is necessary to avoid reinfection, further complications, and the spread of chlamydia to others (Gilson & Mindel, 2001).

CHANCROID

Although a **chancroid** (SHANK-kroyd) may look similar to a syphilis chancre, the difference lies in its soft edges compared with the hard edges of a syphilis sore. Chancroids are sexually transmitted through the *Hemophilus ducreyi* bacterium.

Incidence

This STI is relatively rare in the United States but worldwide 7 million cases occur each year (Steen, 2001). The reported cases of chancroid in the United States were approximately 5,000 in 1987, but only 33 in 2006 (CDC, 2007a). However, this bacterial infection is underreported, and many clinics do not have screening kits.

The majority of cases diagnosed in the United States involve a person who has traveled to a country where the disease is more common. Chancroid is one of the most prevalent STIs in many poor countries, such as those in Africa, Asia, and the Caribbean (Trees & Morse, 1995). Chancroid has also been found to be associated with HIV transmission and is common in areas with high rates of HIV.

Symptoms

Both women and men infected with chancroid develop a small lesion or several lesions at the point of entry. Four to seven days after infection, a small lump appears and ruptures within two or

chancroid
A bacterial STI characterized by small bumps that eventually rupture and form painful ulcers.

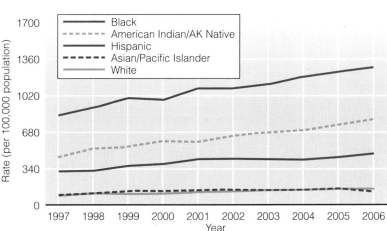

Figure **15.7** Chlamydia—Rates by race and ethnicity, 1997–2006. Source: Centers for Disease Control, 2007a.

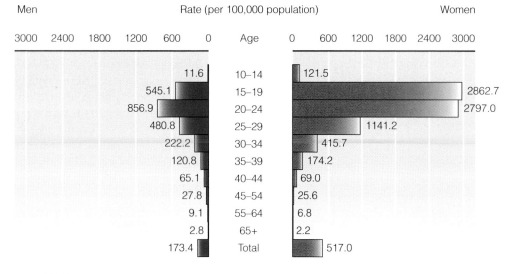

Men	Rate (per 100,000 population)					Age					Women	
3000	2400	1800	1200	600	0		0	600	1200	1800	2400	3000
					11.6	10–14	121.5					
		545.1				15–19						2862.7
	856.9					20–24						2797.0
		480.8				25–29		1141.2				
			222.2			30–34	415.7					
			120.8			35–39	174.2					
				65.1		40–44	69.0					
				27.8		45–54	25.6					
				9.1		55–64	6.8					
				2.8		65+	2.2					
				173.4		Total		517.0				

Figure **15.8** Chlamydia—Age and sex-specific rates: United States, 2006.

three days, forming a shallow ulcer. These ulcers are painful, with ragged edges, and may persist for weeks and even months (D. A. Lewis, 2000). The infection may spread to the lymph nodes of the groin, which can cause swelling and pain.

Diagnosis

Diagnosis is often difficult, mainly because of difficulties culturing *H. ducreyi*, the responsible bacteria (Schulte et al., 1992). As a result, chancroid may be significantly underdiagnosed. A fluid sample from the ulcers is collected to examine for the presence of *H. ducreyi*.

Treatment

Chancroids are treated with antibiotics. Counseling about HIV and testing are often recommended because chancroids can increase the risk of HIV infection. Regular follow-ups are advisable until the ulcer is completely healed. All recent sexual contacts should be told to seek testing and treatment.

VAGINAL INFECTIONS

There are several common vaginal infections that may also be associated with sexual intercourse, including trichomoniasis, hemophilus, bacterial vaginosis, and candidiasis. All of these may cause a vaginal discharge, vulvar itching and irritation, and vaginal odor.

Trichomoniasis (trick-oh-mun-NYE-iss-sis; also called trich, or TV) is a form of vaginitis that is caused by *Trichomonas vaginalis*. Women can contract trichomoniasis from an infected man or woman, whereas a man usually contracts it only from an infected woman. Even though the actual number of women seeking health care visits for trichomoniasis is fairly low, experts estimate that there are 7.4 million new cases of trichomoniasis every year (CDC, 2007c). The organism is acquired through heterosexual or lesbian sexual activity and is rarely transmitted through gay male sexual activity; symptoms usually appear anywhere from 3 to 28 days after infection.

The most common symptom for women is an increase in vaginal discharge, which may be yellowish or green-yellow, frothy, and foul smelling; it may cause a burning or itching sensation in the vagina. Some women are asymptomatic or have minimal symptoms (CDC, 2007c). In men, the most common site of infection is the urethra, although trichomoniasis infection is often asymptomatic. If there are symptoms, there may be a slight increase in burning on the tip of the penis, mild discharge, or slight burning after urination or ejaculation.

The most common treatment for trichomoniasis is metronidazole (Flagyl), which can cause side effects such as nausea, headaches, loss of appetite, diarrhea, cramping, and a metallic taste in the mouth. Anyone taking this medication should not drink alcohol until 24 hours after treatment. It is recommended that all partners should be treated, and sex should be avoided until after treatment.

Bacterial vaginosis (BV) is the most common vaginal infection in women of childbearing age (Allsworth & Peipert, 2007; Schwebke, 2000). Rates of BV are higher in African and Mexican American women and also in all women who have douched in the past 6 months (Allsworth & Peipert, 2007). Symptoms may include an increase in vaginal discharge and a fishy odor to the discharge. However, approximately half of infected women are asymptomatic. BV occurs when there is an overabundance of certain types of bacteria that are present normally in the vagina (Holzman et al., 2001). Overall, multiple sex partners, douching, and low concentrations of beneficial vaginal bacteria have been found to increase a woman's susceptibility to BV. In addition, research has found that occurrences of BV are more common in the first week of the menstrual cycle (Keane et al., 1997). Women who have sex with women are also at risk for BV, and studies have found they may be at increased risk because there is more exposure to vaginal secretions (Evans et al., 2007; Marrazzo et al., 2008).

Women with BV have been found to have an increased risk of endometriosis and PID. Treatment is generally metronidazole or clindamycin, either orally or vaginally (Brandt et al., 2008). Alcohol should be avoided during the course of treatment. Treatment of male sex partners has not been found to be beneficial in the treatment of BV. New research is evaluating the use of probiotics in the treatment of BV (Bolton et al., 2008; Marrazzo et al., 2007). Probiotics are dietary supplements, such as the bacterium *Lactobacillus*, that help regulate bacteria and yeast in the body.

trichomoniasis
A vaginal infection that may result in discomfort, discharge, and inflammation.

bacterial vaginosis (BV)
Bacterial infection that can cause vaginal discharge and odor but is often asymptomatic.

Lactobacillus
Bacterium in the vagina that helps maintain appropriate pH levels.

Vulvovaginal candiasis (can-DIE-ass-sis; yeast infections, also called moniliasis or candidiasis) can be very troubling to women who are prone to them. **Yeast infections** can be difficult to get rid of, and recurrences are common. The infections are caused by a variety of different fungi, but one of the most common is *Candida albicans*. This fungus is normally present in the vagina, but it multiplies when the pH balance of the vagina is disturbed because of antibiotics, regular douching, pregnancy, oral contraceptive use, diabetes, or careless wiping after defecation (yeast is present in fecal material, and so it is important to make sure it does not come into contact with the vulva). Although yeast infections are usually not sexually transmitted during heterosexual sex, if a woman experiences multiple infections, her partner should be evaluated and treated with topical antifungal creams (C. Wilson, 2005). While male partners are less likely to transmit yeast since the penis does not provide the right environment for the growth of the yeast, female partners can transmit yeast infections during sexual activity (R. Bailey et al., 2008).

A yeast infection often causes burning, itching, and an increase in vaginal discharge. The discharge may be white, thin, and watery and may include thick white chunks. It is estimated that 75% of women will experience a yeast infection at least once in their life, and 40% to 45% will have two or more yeast infections (C. Wilson, 2005).

Treatment includes either an antifungal prescription or over-the-counter drugs (such as Monistat, Gyne-Lotrimin, or Mycelex), which are applied topically on the vulva and are inserted into the vagina. However, research has shown that a widespread use of these over-the-counter antifungal medications has caused a large increase in recurrent infections (MacNeill & Carey, 2001). Misuse of over-the-counter drugs can contribute to medication-resistant strains of yeast (Hoffstetter et al., 2008).

Like BV, probiotics have also been used in the treatment of yeast infections (Falagas et al., 2006; Watson & Calabretto, 2007). Earlier we discussed the use of *Lactobacillus* in the treatment of BV. It is a type of "good" bacteria found in the vagina of healthy women and also in yogurt. Eating one cup of yogurt daily may help reduce yeast infection recurrences (Falagas et al., 2006; Watson & Calabretto, 2007).

PELVIC
INFLAMMATORY DISEASE

In Chapter 12, we discussed PID, an infection of the female genital tract, including the endometrium, Fallopian tubes, and the lining of the pelvic area. Here we look at the role of STIs in the development of pelvic inflammatory disease. Pelvic inflammatory disease can be caused by many agents, but the two that have been most often implicated are chlamydia and gonorrhea (J. Ross, 2001).

WHAT DO YOU WANT TO KNOW?

I have a vaginal discharge that is yellowish white, but there is no odor. I think it's a yeast infection because it's kind of itchy. Should I use an over-the-counter cream?

Remember that having a discharge doesn't always mean that you have a vaginal infection. Normal vaginal discharge can range from white to slightly yellow, and it varies throughout the menstrual cycle. Symptoms of a yeast infection can include vaginal itching and burning, pain during sex and urination, and a thick, white discharge. Keep in mind, however, that research has found only one in four women who seek treatment for a yeast infection actually has one (Hoffstetter et al., 2008). Other causes of vaginal itching include inflammation, dry skin, and other STIs, including bacterial vaginosis. Like a yeast infection, bacterial vaginosis can sometimes be triggered by the use of antibiotics or the use of feminine hygiene products. Over-the-counter medications for yeast infections, which fight fungus, are ineffective against bacterial vaginosis.

Although the exact rates of PID are unknown, it has been estimated that there are 1 million U.S. cases of PID each year. However, two thirds of PID cases remain unrecognized by women and their health care providers (CDC, 2008). Long-term complications of PID include ectopic and tubal pregnancies, chronic pelvic pain, and infertility. Approximately 100,000 women become infertile each year due to PID (CDC, 2008).

Sexually active young women are most at risk for PID because their cervix is not mature and may be more susceptible to PID (CDC, 2008). A woman's risk for PID increases if she has multiple sex partners.

Symptoms of PID vary from none to severe. The most common symptom is lower abdominal pain. Severe symptoms may include acute pelvic pain, fever, painful urination, and an abnormal vaginal bleeding or discharge. Treatment for PID includes antibiotics for 14 days, which effectively eliminates the symptoms of PID (J. Ross, 2001). If the symptoms continue or worsen, hospitalization may be necessary. Sexual partners should be also be treated, even if they have no symptoms.

Sexually active young women are most at risk for PID.

vulvovaginal candidiasis
A vaginal infection that causes a heavy discharge; also referred to as a yeast infection.

yeast infection
Vaginal infection that causes an increase in vaginal discharge, burning, and itching and may be sexually transmitted; also referred to as vulvovaginal candidiasis.

1 Identify the bacterial STIs and describe those that are most common today.

2 Explain how age, gender, race, ethnicity, geographic area, and sexual orientation have been found to affect incidence rates.

3 Explain the asymptomatic nature of the bacterial STIs and identify possible symptoms. How many people who are infected with a bacterial STI are typically asymptomatic?

4 Identify the common treatments for bacterial STIs.

5 Differentiate among the common vaginal infections, including trichomoniasis, hemophilus, bacterial vaginosis, and vulvovaginal candiasis. Explain symptoms and treatments for each.

6 Explain what pelvic inflammatory disease is, and identify causes, symptoms, and long-term risks.

Viral Infections:
Herpes, Human Papillomavirus, and Hepatitis

Sexually transmitted infections can also be caused by viruses. Once a virus invades a body cell, it is able to reproduce itself, so a person will have the virus for the rest of his or her life. Viruses can live in the body, and although a person may not experience symptoms, he or she is still infected with the virus. We now discuss herpes, human papillomavirus, and viral hepatitis, and later in this chapter, we explore the human immunodeficiency virus and AIDS.

▌HERPES

Herpes (herpes simplex, herpes genitalis) is caused by an infection with the **herpes simplex virus (HSV)**. Typically the virus prefers to infect the mouth and face (**herpes simplex I, or HSV-1**) or the genitals (**herpes simplex II, or HSV-2**), where it causes sores to appear. HSV is contained in the sores that the virus causes, but the virus may also be released between outbreaks from the infected skin (often referred to as **viral shedding**). Because of this, it is possible to transmit the virus even when the infected partner doesn't have any active symptoms (Mertz, 2008; Wald et al., 2000).

Although HSV-2 is almost always sexually transmitted, HSV-1 is usually transmitted during childhood through nonsexual contact (Xu et al., 2006). In fact, by age 5, it is estimated that more than 35% of African American children and 18% of Caucasian children are infected with HSV-1 (Whitley & Roizman, 2001). This is probably a result of kissing HSV-1 infected relatives and friends.

Although HSV-1 prefers the mouth and lips and HSV-2 prefers the genitals, both can affect nonpreferred sites as well (e.g., people can become infected with HSV-1 on their genitals if they receive oral sex from a person with HSV-1 on his or her lip; Corey & Handsfield, 2000). If the virus infects a less preferred site the symptoms are usually less severe.

HSV is highly contagious. Pregnant mothers can pass HSV-2 on to their infants while the baby is in the uterus, during delivery from exposure to active sores in the birth canal, or directly following birth (Corey & Handsfield, 2000). A person can also **autoinoculate** themselves. If infected persons touch an HSV sore and then rub another part of their body, they may infect themselves in that location as well. A person could also transmit HSV to their partner's genitals in this manner.

Incidence

There are no mandatory reporting regulations for herpes simplex virus in the United States, but we do know that HSV is common. Close to 60% of people between the ages of 14 and 49 years old are infected with HSV-1 (Xu et al., 2006). HSV-2 is also common and in the United States, as many as 1 million people, age 12 and older, are infected each year (CDC, 2007a; Fleming, 1997). HSV-2 is one of the most prevalent STIs in the world (J. Smith & Robinson, 2002). Keep in mind, however, actual infection rates are higher than reported because many people infected with HSV-2 have not been diagnosed or reported.

herpes
A highly contagious viral infection that causes eruptions of the skin or mucous membranes.

herpes simplex virus (HSV)
The virus that causes herpes.

herpes simplex I (HSV-I)
A viral infection that causes cold sores on the face or lips.

herpes simplex II (HSV-2)
A viral infection that is sexually transmitted and causes genital ulcerations.

viral shedding
The release of viral infections between outbreaks from infected skin.

autoinoculate
To cause a secondary infection in the body from an already existing infection.

HSV rates are often higher in women, mainly because male-to-female routes of transmission are more efficient than female-to-male routes. It is estimated that one in four women and one in five men have genital herpes (CDC, 2007a). However, there is evidence that HSV prevalence has been increasing in males aged 20 to 39, primarily through men having sex with men (Xu et al., 2006).

Symptoms

The first symptoms of herpes usually appear within 4 days after infection, but they can appear anywhere from 2 to 12 days later. However, many of those infected with HSV-1 and HSV-2 may not experience any noticeable symptoms (Whitley & Roizman, 2001). If a person does develop HSV sores, the first occurrence is generally the most painful. Overall, women tend to have more severe symptoms with HSV-2 than men.

At the onset, there is usually a tingling or burning feeling in the affected area, which can grow into an itching and a red, swollen appearance of the genitals (this period is often referred to as the **prodromal phase**). The sores usually last anywhere from 8 to 10 days, and the amount of pain they cause can range from mild to severe. Pain is usually most severe at the onset of the infection and improves thereafter. Depending on the amount of pain, urination may be difficult. Small blisters may appear externally on the vagina or penis. The blisters, which are usually red and sometimes have a grayish center, will eventually burst and ooze a yellowish discharge. As they begin to heal, a scab will form over them. Other symptoms of HSV include a fever, headaches, pain, itching, vaginal or urethral discharge, and general fatigue. These symptoms peak within 4 days of the appearance of the blisters. A few patients with severe symptoms require hospitalization.

The frequency and severity of recurrent episodes of herpes depend on several things, including the amount of infectious agent (how much of the virus was contained in the original infecting fluids), the severity of the infection, the type of herpes, and the timing of treatment (Mark et al., 2008). Over time the frequency of recurrent outbreaks diminishes. There are certain triggers that may increase the likelihood of an HSV outbreak and these include exposure to sunlight (natural or tanning beds), lip trauma or chapping, sickness, menstruation, fatigue, and persistent anxiety and stress (F. Cohen et al., 1999).

Psychological reactions to herpes outbreaks can include anxiety, guilt, anger, frustration, helplessness, a decrease in self-esteem, and depression (Dibble & Swanson, 2000). Persons with supportive partners and social relationships tend to do better psychologically. In addition, those who receive psychological support services experience a greater reduction in recurrent episodes of herpes and an improvement in their emotional health (Swanson et al., 1999).

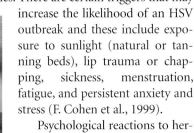

This is a typical patch of HSV-1 blisters, which often appear on the lips or mouth.

HSV rates are often higher in women.

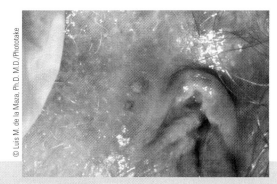

HSV-2 infection in women can cause blisters on the vulva, vagina, or any place the virus entered the body.

Diagnosis

The presence of blisters caused by the herpes virus is often enough to diagnose the disease. Oftentimes, however, health care providers will take a scraping of the blisters to evaluate for the presence of HSV (Whitley & Roizman, 2001). No tests for the detection of HSV-1 or HSV-2 are 100% accurate because tests depend on the amount of infectious agent and the stage of the disease. Success rates for detecting HSV-2 antibodies vary from 80% to 98%, and there are high false-negative results, mainly because the tests are performed too early.

Treatment

There is no cure for infection with the herpes virus. Once infected, a person will always carry the virus in his or her body. The standard therapy for HSV infection today is oral antiviral drugs, such as aciclovir (Zovirax or an available generic), valacyclovir (Valtrex), and famciclovir (Famvir). All of these drugs shorten the duration of outbreaks, prevent complications (such as itching or scarring), and reduce viral shedding (Corey et al., 2004; Sacks et al., 2005). In addition, antiviral therapy can significantly reduce sexual transmission of the virus (Patel, 2004). These drugs can be used as needed when an outbreak occurs or can be taken daily to suppress outbreaks (Bren, 2004; Wald, 1999; Whitley & Roizman, 2001).

Natural remedies for herpes outbreaks include applying an ice pack to the affected area during the prodromal phase and applying cooling or drying agents such as witch hazel. Increasing intake of foods rich in certain amino acids, such as L-lysine, which includes fish or yogurt, and decreasing the intake of sugar and nuts (which are high in arginine) may also help reduce recurrences (Griffith et al., 1987; Vukovic, 1992). Lysine can also be purchased from the vitamin section of any drugstore. Although research has been ongoing to find a vaccine to prevent HSV, it will likely be several more years before an effective vaccine for HSV is available (Brittle et al., 2008; Cattamanchi et al., 2008).

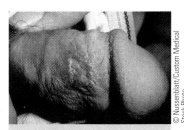

Here HSV-2 blisters appear on the penis.

prodromal phase
The tingling or burning feeling that precedes the development of herpes blisters.

Because herpes is not curable, when people are in their "downtime" between flare-ups, can they still transmit it?

Although many people believe that the herpes virus cannot be transmitted if there are no active lesions, there is now evidence that it can be transmitted even in the absence of active lesions (Boselli et al., 2005; Mertz, 2008; Whitley & Roizman, 2001). Herpes simplex viruses are often asymptomatic, and therefore men and women who are infected with genital herpes should always use condoms so that they do not infect their partners.

HUMAN PAPILLOMAVIRUS

There are more than 30 types of the **human papillomavirus (HPV)** that can infect the genital tract. "Low-risk" HPV (Types 6 and 11), can cause genital warts (condyloma acuminata, venereal warts), which are similar to warts that appear on other parts of the body. "High-risk" HPV (types 16 and 18) can cause abnormal Pap

---

REALResearch > It has been estimated that by age 50, **80%** of women will be infected with HPV (CDC, 2005D).

---

tests and increase cancer risks, especially cervical cancer (Grce & Davies, 2008; Tovar et al., 2008). The human papillomavirus can be transmitted through sexual intercourse, oral sex, vulva-to-vulva sex, or anal sex.

Although there is ample evidence that almost all cervical cancers can be attributed to HPV infection (Peyton et al., 2001; Walboomers et al., 1999), we also know that HPV can infect the throat, mouth, and anus, contributing to oral and anal cancers. Oral HPV can be sexually transmitted during oral-genital contact. Because of this, those who have given oral sex to six or more partners have been found to be at higher risk for throat cancer than persons who have not given oral sex (D'Souza et al., 2007). Anal HPV has been increasing in both men and women in the past few years (D'Hauwers & Tjalma, 2008). Studies have found that anal HPV-associated anal cancer in men who have sex with men may be as common as HPV-associated cervical cancer risk in heterosexually active women (Goodman et al., 2008; Palefsky, 2008). Another study found that HPV-associated anal cancer is more common in men who have sex with men than cervical cancer is among women (Chin-Hong et al., 2008). Several factors have been found to be related to HPV infection, including early age of first intercourse (before age 16), having more than two sexual partners within the previous year, or having a sexual partner who has had multiple sex partners (Goodman et al., 2008; J. A. Kahn et al., 2002; Peyton et al., 2001).

Incidence

Human papillomavirus is the most common sexually transmitted infection in the United States (Dunne et al., 2007). The CDC (2008a) estimates that approximately 6.2 million Americans are infected with HPV each year. It is estimated that 45% of women between the ages of 20 and 24 years are infected with HPV (the overall prevalence rate in girls and women between the ages of 14 to 59 years old is 27%; Gostin & DeAngelis, 2007; see Figure 15.9). Rates of HPV are particularly high in college-age women and men as well (Revzina & DiClemente, 2005).

Although there have been limited studies on HPV in lesbians and men, studies have found that HPV infection is prevalent in both of these groups (Dunne et al., 2006; Marrazzo et al., 2001). Whereas one study found a 53% prevalence rate in U.S. men (Giuliano et al., 2008a), another study evaluating HPV prevalence in men in the United States, Mexico, and Brazil found an overall prevalence rate of 65%, which was higher in Brazil (72%) than in the United States (61%) and Mexico (62%; Giuliano et al., 2008b). In gay men, HPV infections have been found to co-occur with HIV infection (Pierangeli et al., 2008).

Symptoms

Although some men and women who are infected with HPV are asymptomatic, those who do develop symptoms do so as late as 6 weeks to 9 months after infection. It is estimated that 10% of HPV infections lead to **genital warts** (Koutsky, 1997; see Figure 15.10). Genital warts are usually flesh colored and may have a bumpy surface. Warts develop in women on the vagina, vulva, or cervix, and in men on the penile shaft, head, scrotum, and rarely, the urethra (Krilov, 1991). Warts can also appear on the anus in both men and women. In some areas, warts may grow together and have a cauliflower like appearance. These lesions are generally asymptomatic, and unless the warts are large, many people do not notice them and unknowingly infect other sexual partners. Because of the contagious na-

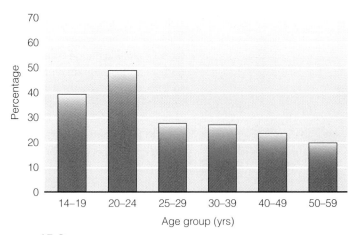

Figure **15.9** Human papillomavirus in U.S. women by age group, 2007. Source: National Health and Nutrition Examination Survey, 2003–2004. Available at http://www.cdc.gov/nchs/about/major/nhanes/nhanes2003-2004/nhanes03_04.htm; Dunne, et al., 2007.

human papillomavirus (HPV)	genital wart
A sexually transmitted viral infection that can cause genital warts, cervical cancer, or both.	Wartlike growth on the genitals; also called venereal wart, condylomata, or papilloma.

Warts that appear on the penis are usually flesh-colored and may have a bumpy appearance.

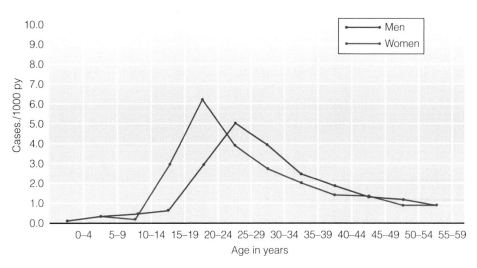

Figure **15.10** Rate of genital wart diagnosis in the United States by age group and sex, 2000. Source: Dunne E.F., Unger E.R., Sternberg M., et al. Prevalence of HPV infection among females in the United States. *JAMA* 2007, 297: 813–819. Copyright © 2007 AMA. All rights reserved. Reproduced by permission.

ture of genital warts, approximately 65% of sexual partners of people with cervical warts develop warts within 3 to 4 months of contact (Krilov, 1991).

HPV can also cause a foul-smelling discharge, which may cause some itching and pain. Children who are infected with HPV at birth during exposure in the birth canal are at risk of developing viral growths in the respiratory tract, which can cause respiratory distress and hoarseness (Fletcher, 1991).

Diagnosis

Although HPV may show up on Pap testing, 80% to 90% of the time, it does not (Kassler & Cates, 1992). The FDA approved an HPV DNA test in 2003 that can identify 13 of the high-risk types of HPV associated with cervical cancer (L. Johnson et al., 2008). Cells are collected during a woman's Pap testing and sent to a lab for analysis. Health care providers recommend that women who have more than one sexual partner should ask their medical provider for an HPV DNA test. A health care provider may be able to detect warts on visual inspection. If not, a high-risk detection kit can also be performed to aid in diagnosis. A health care provider may also soak the infected area with acetic acid (white vinegar), which turns the skin of the warts white and makes them easier to

see under magnification. An examination of the cervix under magnification (called colposcopy) can also be used. Biopsies are also performed to check for HPV.

Treatment

As we've discussed, HPV infection can cause genital warts (low-risk types) or abnormal changes in the cervical cells (high-risk type). It is important to seek treatment immediately if a person notices the development of genital warts because they can quickly grow and multiply. Genital warts can be treated in several ways, and no treatment method is superior to another or best for all patients with HPV. Important factors for a health care provider to consider when deciding treatment options include the number and size of the warts, patient preference, treatment costs, convenience, and side effects.

Treatment alternatives include chemical topical solutions (to destroy external warts), cryotherapy (freezing the warts with liquid nitrogen), electrosurgical interventions (removal of warts using a mild electrical current, often referred to as a LEEP or "loop electrosurgical excision procedure"), or laser surgery (high-intensity lasers to destroy the warts). It may be necessary to try several treatment methods, and repeat applications are common (CDC, 2008a).

Although the majority of sexual partners of those infected with HPV are already infected, if they are not, an infected person should use condoms during sexual behavior for at least 6 months following treatment (Lilley & Schaffer, 1990). Some couples decide to use condoms long term because of the possibility of transmitting the virus when no warts are present. It is possible that a low-risk type infection may be cleared up by the immune system over time (CDC, 2008a; Dunne, 2007). In fact, one study found that the low-risk type HPV infection was cleared in 90% of women within 2 years (Ho et al., 1998).

Women who have been diagnosed with a high-risk type of HPV are encouraged to have pelvic exams and Pap tests at least once a year. This will allow health care providers to monitor pre-

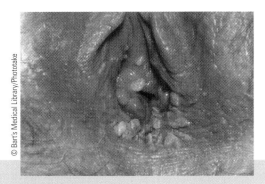

Here genital warts appear on the outside of the vulva.

cancerous changes in the cervical cells (often referred to as **cervical dysplasia**).

In 2006, the FDA approved Gardasil, the first vaccine developed to prevent certain types of HPV that have been found to cause cervical cancer and genital warts. This vaccine is effective against HPV Types 6 and 11 (which cause 90% of genital warts) and HPV Types 16 and 18 (which have been found to cause 70% of cervical cancers). In the United States, the Advisory Committee on Immunization Practices recommends HPV vaccines for females 11 to 12 years old (Bayas et al., 2008; T. Wright et al., 2008). In addition, vaccines are also recommended for females between ages 13 and 26 years. Gardasil is given in three doses over a 6-month period and is 95% to 100% effective in protecting women from these types of HPV (Gostin & DeAngelis, 2007; Govan, 2008). As of late 2008, the CDC reported that 1 in 4 teenage girls (13–17-years old) in the U.S. have had the HPV vaccine.

1 in 4 teenage girls in the U.S. have had the HPV vaccine.

Ideally a girl should have the HPV vaccine before becoming sexually active, although there is evidence that sexually active women may also benefit from the vaccine (T. Wright et al., 2008). The vaccine is currently effective for a period of 5 years, and maybe longer (Harper & Paavonen, 2008). Because it is new, the actual duration of the vaccine protection is unknown, and it is possible that a vaccine booster will be necessary at some point. Women who have the HPV vaccine still need to have regular Pap tests because the vaccine does not protect against all types of HPV that can cause cancer (Tovar et al., 2008).

Gardasil is a safe and effective vaccine, and it is continuously monitored and evaluated by both the CDC and the FDA. Side effects include arm soreness, possible joint and muscle pain, fatigue, and general weakness. There have also been some cases of fainting and lightheadedness after the injection (CDC, 2008b). Because of this, many health care providers recommend women wait 15 minutes before they leave their health care provider's office after getting this vaccine.

WHAT DO YOU WANT TO KNOW ?

Could I get HPV from the HPV vaccine? Can I get the vaccine if I've already had sex?

Unlike most vaccines, Gardasil does not contain a live or dead virus. It contains only virus-like particles and is noninfectious. The particles in the vaccine stimulate a woman's body to produce antibodies against HPV (Schlegel, 2007; FDA, 2006). Currently recommendations are for women to have the vaccine before age 26, and ideally before becoming sexually active (CDC, 2008c; FDA, 2006). However, if you are already sexually active but have not been exposed to HPV types 6, 11, 16, and 18, the vaccine will protect you from these types (Schlegel, 2007). If you have already been exposed to some of these types, the vaccine will protect you from the types you have not been exposed to. It is important to discuss these issues with your medical provider, but keep in mind that physicians' opinions and attitudes about the vaccine influence whether they offer or promote the vaccine (Ishibashi et al., 2008). Overall, college students report high intent to receive the HPV vaccine, with women reporting a significantly higher intent than men (Jones & Cook, 2008).

Another promising vaccine, Cervarix, is still in development and has not yet been approved by the FDA. This new vaccine is similar to Gardasil but may last longer (Cadman, 2008; Tovar et al., 2008). As of 2008, Cervarix had been approved for use in 67 countries and was seeking approval in 35 more countries (Tovar et al., 2008).

There are several issues that have made HPV vaccine controversial. One involves the issue of mandatory vaccination in public schools. Some groups have tried to institute mandatory vaccinations for young girls before attending public schools (Casper & Carpenter, 2008; Gostin & DeAngelis, 2007; Javitt et al., 2008). This has also brought up the issue of whether boys and men should be required to have the vaccines (as of 2008 they were not; Ferris et al., 2008; R. Fisher et al., 2008; M. A. Goldstein, 2008; Laurence, 2008). Another controversial issue involves mandatory vaccination for immigrants. In late 2008 the U.S. government made Gardasil vaccinations mandatory for young women who sought to immigrate to the U.S. (Jordan, 2008). All of these issues have led to a continued debate about the use of HPV vaccines.

VIRAL HEPATITIS

Viral hepatitis is an infection that causes impaired liver function. The three main types of viral hepatitis include hepatitis A (HAV), hepatitis B (HBV), and hepatitis C (HCV). Hepatitis A is transmitted through fecal–oral contact and is often spread by food handlers but can also be spread through anal–oral contact. Hepatitis B is predominantly spread during high-risk sexual behaviors (see Sex in Real Life, "High-Risk Sexual Behaviors," earlier in the chapter; Kellerman et al., 2003). Although hepatitis C can be spread through sexual behavior, it is mostly caused by illegal intravenous drug use or unscreened blood transfusions.

Incidence

In 2006, there were approximately 3,500 symptomatic cases of HAV in the United States, which was the lowest rate ever recorded (CDC, 2008d). This is probably a result of the HAV vaccine, which became available in 1995. After asymptomatic cases and probable underreporting have both been calculated in, the total HAV cases is probably closer to 32,000 cases (CDC, 2008d).

Rates of HBV have also been declining. Close to 5,000 cases of acute HBV were reported in the United States in 2006, which was the lowest ever recorded (CDC, 2008e). However, after adjusting for asymptomatic cases and underreporting, this number may be closer to 46,000 (CDC, 2008e). Globally, HBV affects close to 350 million people (CDC, 2008e).

Finally, in 2006 there were only 802 confirmed cases of HCV reported, although when asymptomatic cases and probable underreporting were both calculated in, there were approximately

cervical dysplasia	viral hepatitis
Disordered growth of cells in the cervix, typically diagnosed with Pap testing.	A viral infection; three main types of viral hepatitis include hepatitis A (HAV), hepatitis B (HBV), and hepatitis C (HCV).

19,000 new HCV infections (CDC, 2008f). It is estimated there are approximately 3.2 million men and women in the United States with chronic HVC infection (CDC, 2008f).

Symptoms

Symptoms of HAV usually occur within 4 weeks after a person is infected and include fatigue, abdominal pain, loss of appetite, and diarrhea. HAV has no chronic long-term infection. Symptoms of HBV usually occur anywhere from 6 weeks to 6 months after infection, although infection with HBV is usually asymptomatic. Possible symptoms may include nausea, vomiting, jaundice, headaches, fever, a darkening of the urine, moderate liver enlargement, and fatigue. It is estimated that 15% to 25% of those infected with HBV will die from chronic liver disease (CDC, 2008e). Finally, most people infected with HCV are asymptomatic or have a mild illness and develop this illness within 8 to 9 weeks. The CDC estimates that between 75% and 85% of those infected with HCV will develop a chronic liver infection (CDC, 2008f).

Diagnosis

Blood tests are used to identify viral hepatitis infections.

Treatment

Antiviral therapies are available for the treatment and management of hepatitis. These therapies have been designed to reduce viral load by interfering with the life cycle of the virus and also causing the body to generate an immune response against the virus (Guha et al., 2003). Health care providers generally recommend bed rest and adequate fluid intake so that a person doesn't develop dehydration. Usually after a few weeks, an infected person feels better, although this can take longer in persons with severe and chronic infections.

Vaccines are available for the prevention of both hepatitis A and B, and persons at high risk of contracting either of these should have the vaccine. Young children are often routinely vaccinated against both hepatitis A and B (Lee et al., 2008). High-risk individuals include health care workers who may be exposed to blood products, intravenous drug users and their sex partners, people with multiple sexual partners, people with chronic liver disease, and housemates of anyone with hepatitis (CDC, 2008g). Men who have sex with men should also be vaccinated against HAV and HBV (C. Diamond et al., 2003). Research continues to explore a vaccine for hepatitis C (Kang & Nicolay, 2008; Lang & Weiner, 2008).

review questions

1 Identify the viral STIs and describe those that are most common today.

2 Explain how age, gender, race, ethnicity, geographic area, and sexual orientation have been found to affect the incidence of viral STIs.

3 Differentiate between "high-risk" and "low-risk" HPV and explain long-term consequences of these risk types.

4 Explain how the Gardasil vaccine works. What are current recommendations for its use?

5 Differentiate between HAV, HBV, and HCV. What hepatitis vaccines are available and what are current recommendations for its use?

Human Immunodeficiency Virus and Acquired Immune Deficiency Syndrome

Although the **human immunodeficiency virus (HIV)** is a viral infection, there are several factors that set it apart from other STIs and also shed some light on why the **acquired immune deficiency syndrome (AIDS)** debate became so politically charged. HIV/AIDS appeared in the early 1980s, a time when modern medicine was believed to be well on its way to reducing epidemic disease (D. Altman, 1986). In addition, AIDS was first identified among gay and bisexual men and intravenous drug users. Because of this early identification, the disease was linked with "socially marginal" groups in the population (D. Altman, 1986; Kain, 1987). The media gave particular attention to the lifestyle of "victims"

and implied that social deviance has a price. One study found that one in five people believed that people who got AIDS through sex or drugs got what they deserved (Valdiserri, 2002). Although the stigma of HIV/AIDS decreased in the 1990s, in 1999, nearly one in five American adults said they "fear" a person with AIDS (Herek et al., 2002). We talk more about public attitudes about AIDS later in this chapter.

AIDS is caused by a viral infection with HIV, a virus primarily transmitted through body fluids, including semen, vaginal fluid, breast milk, and blood. During vaginal or anal intercourse, this virus can enter the body through the vagina, penis, or rectum. Oral sex may also transmit the virus, although it is difficult to measure the risk associated with oral sex because few people en-

human immunodeficiency virus (HIV)
The retrovirus responsible for the development of AIDS; can be transmitted during vaginal or anal intercourse.

acquired immune deficiency syndrome (AIDS)
A condition of increased susceptibility to opportunistic diseases; results from an infection with HIV, which destroys the body's immune system.

gage exclusively in oral sex. Even so, the research has consistently shown that the risk of HIV transmission from unprotected oral sex is lower than that of unprotected vaginal or anal sex (Kohn et al., 2002; E. D. Robinson & Evans, 1999). Kissing has been found to be low risk for transmitting HIV, especially when there are no cuts in the mouth or on the lips. It is also possible to transmit the virus during intravenous drug use by sharing needles.

Like the herpes virus, HIV never goes away; it remains in the body for the rest of a person's life. However, unlike the herpes virus, an untreated HIV infection is often fatal. After a person is infected, the virus may remain dormant and cause no symptoms. This is why some people who are infected may not realize that they are. However, a blood test can be taken to reveal whether a person is HIV-positive. Even a person who does not know that he or she has been infected can transmit the virus to other people immediately after infection.

HIV attacks the **T-lymphocytes** (tee-LIM-foe-sites; **T-helper cells**) in the blood, leaving fewer of them to fight off infection. When there is a foreign invader in our bloodstream, antibodies develop that are able to recognize the invader and destroy it. However, if the antibodies cannot do this or if there are too many viruses, a person will become ill. These antibodies can be detected in the bloodstream anywhere from 2 weeks to 6 months after infection, which is how the screening test for HIV works. The immune system also releases many white blood cells to help destroy invaders.

REALResearch **>** Studies have found that the virus responsible for HIV infection has low infectivity in the lab, but a factor in human semen can potentially enhance the infectivity of the virus by more than **100,000** times (Roan & Greene, 2007).

HIV attaches itself to the T-helper cells and injects its infectious RNA into the fluid of the helper cell. The RNA contains an enzyme known as **reverse transcriptase** (trans-SCRIPT-ace), which is capable of changing the RNA into DNA. The new DNA takes over the T-helper cell and begins to manufacture more HIV.

The attack on the T-helper cells causes the immune system to be less effective in its ability to fight disease, and so many **opportunistic diseases** infect people with AIDS that a healthy person could easily fight off (we discuss these diseases later in this chapter). No one knows exactly why some people acquire the virus from one sexual encounter, whereas others may not be infected even after repeated exposure. Research has shown that a person who has an STI is at greater risk of acquiring HIV (Gilson & Mindel, 2001; Hader et al., 2001; Pialoux et al., 2008).

It is unknown exactly where HIV came from, although scientists have many different theories. None of these theories has been proved, however. In the early 1980s, a number of gay men, mostly in Los Angeles and New York City, began coming down with rare forms of pneumonia and skin cancer. Physicians began calling the disease GRID, for "gay-related immunodeficiency syndrome." It was hypothesized that there was a new infectious agent causing the disease, that the immune system was being suppressed by a drug that the infected persons were using, or that perhaps a sexual

lubricant was involved. Many physicians felt that this infectious agent would quickly be isolated and wiped out. Today it is anticipated that the AIDS virus will continue to infect people for the next several decades without a cure.

INCIDENCE

As mentioned earlier in this chapter, all 50 U.S. states require that HIV and AIDS cases be reported to local or state health departments. These statistics help to track the spread of the virus. Some experts were worried that mandatory HIV reporting would deter men and women from being tested. To help encourage testing, some states use confidential codes to keep HIV-positive people anonymous.

At the end of 2003, there were close to 1 million people living with HIV in the United States (Glynn & Rhodes, 2005), and approximately 25% of them were unaware they were infected with HIV (CDC, 2008i). By the end of 2005, there were approximately 1.2 million people living with AIDS in the United States (UNAIDS, 2008). In 2008, the CDC reported there were 56,000 new HIV infections in the United States.

The CDC implemented a new plan in 2008 for determining HIV incidence. The Serological Testing Algorithm for Recent HIV Seroconversion (STARHS) can distinguish recent from long-standing infections (CDC, 2008h). Because a person can be infected with HIV for years before a diagnosis is made, this new formula helped determine when an individual was actually infected with HIV. Although the CDC had estimated approximately 40,000 new HIV infections since the 1990s, this new testing revealed there were 56,300 men and women newly infected with HIV in 2006 alone (CDC, 2008h; H. I. Hall et al., 2008). This new testing revealed the HIV/AIDS epidemic was worse than the CDC previously had estimated.

Although there were few women affected by HIV and AIDS early in the epidemic, the prevalence of HIV/AIDS in women increased significantly during the 1990s but has been steadily decreasing since 2001. Even so, today women account for more than one quarter of new HIV/AIDS cases in the United States, and women of color are especially affected (CDC, 2008j). In fact, HIV was the leading cause of death for women of color aged 25 to 34 in 2004 (CDC, 2008j).

An infected mother can also transmit HIV to her fetus. It is estimated that approximately 750,000 children have become infected with HIV worldwide, and most of these are through mother-to-child transmission (Newell, 2005). Although infection

T-lymphocyte (T-helper cell)
Type of white blood cell that helps to destroy harmful bacteria in the body.

reverse transcriptase
A chemical that is contained in the RNA of HIV; it helps to change the virus's DNA.

opportunistic disease
Disease that occurs when the immune system is depressed; often fatal.

may be possible through breast-feeding, it is more likely that transmission takes place during pregnancy through the placenta or through the birth-canal during delivery (Newell, 2005). Fortunately, because of improvements in obstetric care, rates of maternal–infant transmission have decreased. Today HIV tests are routinely offered to pregnant women, and if a test is positive, medications can be used to reduce **viral load,** and a planned cesarean section can be done to reduce the risk of transmission to the infant during delivery.

Overall, the majority of people infected with HIV in 2008 were men who had sex with men (45%), followed by heterosexuals who engaged in high-risk sexual behaviors (27%), and intravenous drug users (22%; see Figure 15.11; CDC, 2008i). Overall, gay and bisexual men, African Americans, and Hispanics/Latinos are disproportionately affected by HIV (H. I. Hall et al., 2008). Although African Americans make up only 12% of the total U.S. population, in 2006, 46% of new HIV infections were in African Americans (see Figure 15.12; CDC, 2008h). Like other STIs, the incidence of HIV in the African American and Hispanic/Latino communities may result from several factors, including poverty, limited access to health care, and higher rates of other STIs or drug use (CDC, 2008h). HIV also disproportionately affects younger people: More than half of those infected with HIV in the United States are between age 25 and 44 years (Centers for Disease Control and Prevention, 2008i).

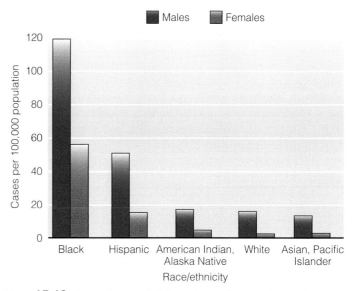

Figure **15.12** Human immunodeficiency virus—diagnoses by race/ethnicity and gender in the United States, 2006. Source: McQuillan & Kruszon-Moran, 2008.

KNOWLEDGE AND ATTITUDES ABOUT AIDS

College students are at risk for HIV because of high rates of sexual activity, multiple sexual partners, inconsistent condom use, and the use of alcohol during sexual activity (LaBrie et al., 2002). Knowledge levels about HIV/AIDS among U.S. college students are generally high, although higher knowledge levels have not been found to be consistently correlated with behavior changes or the practice of safer sex (Caron et al., 1992).

Although fewer people hold negative attitudes about people with AIDS today, AIDS remains a stigmatized condition in the United States (Herek et al., 2002). We've discussed that many Americans hold negative opinions of those infected with STIs; today we find that many people are also afraid and uncomfortable around someone with AIDS and have many mistaken beliefs about how it is transmitted.

REALResearch >In sub-Saharan Africa, male circumcision has been found to reduce the risk of acquiring HIV by **60%** (J. Bailey et al., 2008). Although two thirds of African men are circumcised, many are circumcised by unqualified practitioners, and safety is a growing concern.

SYMPTOMS

HIV infection results in a gradual deterioration of the immune system through the destruction of T-helper lymphocytes (Friedman-Kien & Farthing, 1990). For those who are not being treated, this decline in T-helper lymphocytes takes an average of 3 years in those who are emotionally depressed and more than 5 years in those who are nondepressed (B. Bower, 1992).

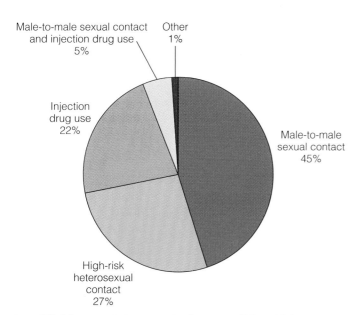

Figure **15.11** Transmission categories for persons living with human immunodeficiency virus in the United States, 2003. Source: Centers for Disease Control, 2008i.

viral load
The amount of viral particles in a sample of blood. A person with high viral load usually develops AIDS faster than a person with a low viral load.

The average person who is HIV-positive and is not on any type of treatment will develop AIDS within 8 to 10 years. Flulike symptoms such as fever, sore throat, chronic swollen lymph nodes in the neck or armpits, headaches, and fatigue may appear. After this period, an infected person will seem to recover, and all symptoms will disappear. Later symptoms may include significant weight loss, severe diarrhea that persists for more than 1 month, night sweats, **oral candidiasis,** gingivitis, oral ulcers, and persistent fever (Friedman-Kien & Farthing, 1990). In addition, a person might experience persistent dizziness, confusion, and blurring of vision or hearing.

In an untreated person, the deterioration of the immune system makes it easier for opportunistic diseases to develop. In general, the incidence of opportunistic illnesses (those that can make someone

---

REALResearch **>** A genetic variation found in people of African descent increases the odds of becoming infected with HIV by **40%** (WEIJING ET AL., 2008). However, once infected, this genetic variation can slow the progression of the disease and increase life expectancy. This may help explain some of the racial and ethnic differences in the incidence and fatality rates of HIV.

---

sick when their immune system is compromised) are similar in men and women with a few exceptions (Hader et al., 2001). In women, cervical cancer may develop as an AIDS-defining condition (Hader et al., 2001). *Pneumocystis carinii* **pneumonia (PCP)** is one type of opportunistic illness that may develop in untreated men and women who are infected with HIV. PCP is a type of pneumonia that was uncommon before 1980. Other opportunistic diseases include **toxoplasmosis, cryptococcosis, cytomegalovirus,** and **Kaposi's sarcoma (KS).** KS is a rare type of blood vessel cancer that occurs in gay men but is rarely seen in other populations. Lesions from KS frequently occur around the ankle or foot, or they may be on the tip of nose, face, mouth, penis, eyelids, ears, chest, or back. Without treatment, two thirds of male patients with AIDS develop KS lesions on the head and neck (Alkhuja et al., 2001). Other STIs may appear or progress quickly, such as genital warts or syphilis, which may be resistant to treatment.

DIAGNOSIS

Tests for HIV can either identify the virus in the blood or, more commonly, detect whether the person's body has developed antibodies to fight HIV. The most widely used test for antibodies is the **ELISA (enzyme-linked immunoabsorbent assay).** To check for accuracy, if an ELISA test result is positive, a second test, known as the **Western Blot,** is used. These tests can determine the presence or absence of HIV antibodies. If there are none, the test results are negative, indicating that the person is probably not infected with HIV. It takes some time for the body to develop antibodies, and so there is a period in which a person is infected with HIV but the test will not reveal it. If the test is positive, antibodies are present in the body, and the person has HIV. It should be noted that **false-negative** and **false-positive** test results are also possible, although tests done within 6 months of infection have a higher accuracy than those performed later.

Probably the biggest development in diagnosis in the past few years has been the development of rapid HIV testing (Greenwald et al., 2006). Both the ELISA and Western Blot HIV tests require as much as 2 weeks before a result is possible. The OraQuick Rapid HIV Antibody test was the first FDA-approved, noninvasive HIV antibody test. This test detects the presence of antibodies to HIV and requires only a drop of blood. Test results are available within 20 minutes. An oral version of this test, called the OraQuick Advance Antibody Device, has also been approved by the FDA. The oral test collects antibodies from the blood vessels in mucous membranes in the mouth (it does not collect saliva). All of these tests must be used by trained professionals and cannot be used at home. Those who test positive are encouraged to follow up with an AIDS blood test.

TREATMENT

Since 1995, there has been a tremendous decrease in HIV- and AIDS-related deaths, primarily because of the development of **highly active antiretroviral therapy** (**HAART;** Crum et al., 2006;

---

oral candidiasis
An infection in the mouth caused by the excess growth of a fungus that naturally occurs in the body.

Pneumocystis carinii **pneumonia (PCP)**
A rare type of pneumonia; an opportunistic disease that often occurs in people with AIDS.

toxoplasmosis
A parasite that can cause headache, sore throat, seizures, altered mental status, or coma.

cryptococcosis
An acute or chronic infection that can lead to pulmonary or central nervous system infection.

cytomegalovirus
A virus that can lead to diarrhea, weight loss, headache, fever, confusion, or blurred vision.

Kaposi's sarcoma (KS)
A rare form of cancer that often occurs in untreated men with AIDS.

ELISA (enzyme-linked immunoabsorbent assay)
The screening test used to detect HIV antibodies in blood samples.

Western Blot
A test used to confirm a positive ELISA test; more accurate than the ELISA test, but too expensive to be used as the primary screening device for infection.

false negative
A negative test result that occurs in a person who is positive for the virus.

false positive
A positive test result that occurs in a person who is negative for the virus.

highly active antiretroviral therapy (HAART)
The combination of three or more HIV drugs.

M. H. Katz et al., 2002; Venkatesh et al., 2008). HAART is the combination of three or more HIV drugs, often referred to as "drug cocktails." This development, in conjunction with the development of **HIV RNA testing** (which allows health care providers to monitor the amount of virus in the bloodstream), has allowed for better control of HIV and has slowed the disease progression. Between 1990 and 2003, these treatments reduced the AIDS annual death rate by 80% (Crum et al., 2006).

HAART therapy has also significantly increased the life expectancy of children infected with HIV at birth ("Trends in HIV/AIDS Diagnoses," 2005). Without treatment, 1 in 3 HIV-positive African newborns die before the age of one, half die before their second birthday, and the majority die by the age of 5-years old (Newell et al., 2004). Today children infected with HIV are surviving longer than earlier in the epidemic, mainly due to HAART therapy (Davies et al., 2008).

Before starting treatment for HIV infection, a person should be given both a viral load test and **CD4+ T cell count.** These tests can determine how much HIV is in a person's system and also estimate the T-helper white blood cell count (which can show how well a person's immune system is controlling the virus). A baseline CD4+ cell count will also give a health care provider a starting measure to compare with later viral load estimates after a person has started drug therapy. This will enable the health care provider to see whether the drug combinations are effective.

In the mid-1990s HAART therapy involved taking 20 to 30 or more pills with food restrictions (some drugs must be taken on an empty stomach, and others must be taken just after eating). This therapy often include side effects such as fatigue, nausea, fever, nightmares, headaches, diarrhea, changes in a person's fat distribution, elevated cholesterol levels, the development of diabetes, decreased bone density, liver problems, and skin rashes. Over the past few years, newer drug regimens have used fewer pills, and in 2006 the FDA approved the first HIV triple-drug treatment comprised of only 1 pill (Laurence, 2006; Sternberg, 2006). Atripla is a one-pill, once-a-day medicine that combines three antiretroviral drugs.

However, in many places these newer drug regimens are not yet available, and it is estimated that close to 60% of those infected with HIV are on a 3-pill-a-day treatment (Sternberg, 2006). Once a person starts this type of drug therapy, it is very important that the dosages are taken every day at the same time (unlike other medications that require an 80% adherence, HIV drugs require a near-perfect adherence to dosing schedules; Mannheimer et al., 2002). Missed dosages can cause a drug resistance, which will destroy the drug's effectiveness. A missed dose could also cause the virus to survive and mutate into a resistant strain that will not respond to drug therapy. A person who begins drug therapy will most probably continue it for his or her entire life.

There are side effects to HAART therapy. Two to eight weeks after starting HAART therapy, a person should have his or her viral load test redone. This will enable a health care provider to see how effective the drugs are. After this initial test, a person should have a viral load test every 3 to 4 months and a CD4+ T cell count every 3 to 6 months to make sure the drugs are still effective. If the viral load is still detectable 4 to 6 months after starting treatment, the drug therapy should be changed. How fast the viral load de-

creases depends on several factors, including baseline CD4+ T cell count, whether the person has any AIDS-related illnesses, and how closely the person has followed the drug-therapy protocol.

Many health care providers believe that after a patient has been diagnosed with HIV, it is important that he or she receive psychological counseling to provide information on the virus, promote a healthier lifestyle, reduce the risk of transmission to others and help him or her learn coping strategies and abstain from high-risk behaviors. Without this intervention, it is possible that people who are diagnosed with HIV will become depressed and may even attempt suicide (Benton, 2008; Pyne, 2008; Rabkin, 2008).

Finally, it is also important to point out that the advent of HAART therapy in the late 1990s brought with it a substantial increase in high-risk behavior among HIV-positive gay men (Elford et al., 2000; Elford & Hart, 2005; M. H. Katz et al., 2002; Stephenson et al., 2003; Wolitski et al., 2001). These behavioral changes were thought to be due to increased feelings of optimism and reduced levels of HIV. However, this trend has once again reversed over the past few years and risky sexual behaviors in HIV-positive gay men have decreased (Elford, 2006). Some experts are fearful that newer once-a-day pill treatments may again lead to an increase in risky sexual behaviors (Elford, 2006).

> *To prevent the further spread of HIV, **people's behavior must change.***

PREVENTION

To prevent the further spread of HIV, people's behavior must change. Many programs have been started to achieve this goal, including educational programs, advertising, and mailings. Public service announcements about AIDS have increased on radio stations, and many television programs have agreed to address HIV/AIDS in upcoming episodes. A variety of television shows have also included the topic of HIV/AIDS in their programming.

Schools are also working to help prevent HIV and AIDS through education. Many schools today include HIV education in their classes. These programs provide students with information about HIV, risky sexual behaviors, and prevention strategies. Different educational programs emphasize different messages.

After a diagnosis of HIV has been made, it is important to inform all past sexual contacts to prevent the spread of the disease. Because the virus can remain in the body for several years before the onset of symptoms, some people may not know that they have the virus and are capable of infecting others.

It seems reasonable that before we can determine what will reduce high-risk behaviors that contribute to increases in HIV and AIDS, we need to know the behaviors in which people are engaging. Yet data on sexual practices are lacking in the United States. As you remember from Chapter 2, many of our assumptions about current sexual behaviors are based on the Kinsey

HIV RNA testing
Test that allows health care providers to monitor the amount of virus in the bloodstream.

CD4+ T cell count
Test that can determine the T-helper white blood cell count, which will show how well a person's immune system is controlling HIV.

studies from the 1940s and 1950s. We know little about current rates of high-risk behaviors, such as anal intercourse, extramarital or teenage sexuality, and homosexuality. The National Health and Social Life Survey helped shed some light on these behaviors, and two ongoing surveys, the Behavioral Risk Factor Surveillance Survey (BRFSS) and the Youth Risk Behavior Surveillance Survey (YRBS), continue to collect and monitor information about risk behaviors at the state level (see Chapters 2 and 8 for more information about these studies).

In 2006, more than a dozen AIDS vaccine trials were moving through the evaluation process (see Chapter 13 for more information about the FDA approval process). One of the most promising vaccines, MRKAd5, has been halted at this time because of a failure of the vaccine to reduce HIV levels or prevent transmission of the virus (McEnery, 2008). Today research continues to search for an AIDS vaccine. In the United States, the majority of AIDS vaccine research is funded through the National Institutes of Health (NIH). In 2006, the NIH spent close to $500 million for AIDS vaccine research and development (Kresge, 2008). Ongoing national and international trials are taking place for the development of an HIV vaccine. Unfortunately, such a vaccine could take years. The polio vaccine took 47 years to produce, and it is anticipated that the HIV vaccine may take just as long (Markel, 2005).

*There is a **great stigma** attached to HIV.*

FAMILIES AND HIV

Families and friends of people with HIV often do not receive the same social support as do families and friends of people with other devastating illnesses, such as cancer or Alzheimer's disease. There is a great social stigma attached to HIV, and many caregivers find that they have to deal with this pain on their own. Children whose parents become infected with the HIV/AIDS often have difficulties sorting through their own personal feelings about this.

As we have discussed, with the help of HAART therapies many parents with HIV are living longer today. This has brought up many new issues, such as disclosure (when and how to tell family members) and adjusting to having a parent with HIV. The majority of parents living with AIDS have discussed their illness with their family members. Mothers are more likely to disclose their HIV status earlier than fathers, and they disclose more often to their daughters than their sons (Lee & Rotheram-Borus, 2002). Many people with HIV-positive family members find it helpful to become involved in support groups. The names of several organizations are provided at the end of this chapter.

SEX IN REAL LIFE

Microbicides: New Barriers Against HIV

Microbicides are chemical substances that can significantly reduce STI transmission when applied vaginally or rectally.

Microbicides are one of the most promising new developments in the fight against STIs (Olsen et al., 2007; Trager, 2003). Microbicides are chemical substances that can significantly reduce STI transmission when applied vaginally or rectally. They come in many forms, such as creams, gels, suppositories, lubricants, and dissolving film (Gottemoeller, 2001). Microbicides work by killing microbes, or pathogens that are present in semen or vaginal fluids. These products can be used by couples trying to avoid a pregnancy and an STI, and also by couples who are infected with STIs but are trying to become pregnant.

Some traditional spermicides have antimicrobial properties, including nonoxynol-9 (N-9). As we discussed in Chapter 13, frequent use of N-9 spermicide has been found to cause irritation of the cervix and vagina, which may actually help in the transmission of HIV (Gayle, 2000; Van Damme et al., 2002).

Condoms have always been the number one defense against STIs; however, their use must be negotiated with a partner, and because of this, they aren't used as often as they should be (remember that in Chapter 13, we learned that many young heterosexual women don't feel they can refuse intercourse without a condoms; Rickert et al., 2002). Microbicides can be used by one partner without negotiation, and studies have shown that microbicides are more accepted than condoms. In fact, 90% of men in one study said they would not object to their partners using these products (Callahan, 2002). Microbicides could help to reduce the number of HIV infections by 2.5 million over 3 years (DePineres, 2002).

As of 2008, microbicides were not yet available to the public. However, several Phase II and III level trials were ongoing (we discussed how FDA approval works in Chapter 13). Experts are hopeful that a microbicide will be available for public use by 2013.

review questions

1 Explain how HIV is transmitted and how the virus affects the body.

2 Identify the various routes of transmission for HIV, and identify the groups with the highest rates of infection today.

3 Explain what we know about the public's knowledge levels and attitudes about HIV and AIDS.

4 Identify the various symptoms and opportunistic diseases that develop as a result of HIV and AIDS.

5 Explain how HAART therapy and the new one pill once-a-day treatment work. What other factors are important in the treatment of HIV and AIDS?

6 Identify and explain some of the important issues that face the family of a person with HIV.

Global Aspects of AIDS

The United Nations Program on HIV/AIDS estimates that unless improvements are made in treatment and prevention, from 2000 to 2020, 68 million people in the 45 most heavily affected countries will die of AIDS. The global total of young people living with HIV/AIDS could experience a 70% increase by 2010 (Summers et al., 2002). What makes the global numbers even more threatening is that 95% of those infected with HIV have no access to treatment, mostly because of financial and cultural reasons (Kreinin, 2001). Other problems may also interfere with access to treatment, including transportation issues and possible drug confiscation to sell for profit in other markets.

Children are grossly affected by the AIDS epidemic worldwide. In fact, it is estimated that every minute a child becomes infected with HIV and another child dies of an AIDS-related illness (UNAIDS, 2008). By 2005, an estimated 15 million children had lost at least one parent to AIDS worldwide; but by 2010 it is estimated that there will be 18 million children who have lost a parent to AIDS in sub-Saharan Africa alone (see the nearby Human Sexuality in a Diverse World feature; UNAIDS, 2005b). The number of children who have been orphaned throughout the world because of AIDS is equivalent to the total number of children under age 5 living in the United States. Here we explore HIV/AIDS in Asia, Eastern Europe and Central Asia, North America, Western and Central Europe, sub-Saharan Africa, Latin America, the Caribbean, the Middle East and Latin America.

View in Video

"Now they don't want me anymore."
—AIDS in Africa

To view go to CengageNOW at www. cengage.com/login

ASIA

Over 5 million people were living with HIV in Asia in 2007 (UNAIDS, 2008). The main mode of HIV transmission in Asian countries is unprotected sex, both with intimate partners and paid sex workers. A large proportion of HIV infections occur in married women whose husbands frequent sex workers. Recently there has been a push to increase condom use in sex workers, and this has been fairly successful in Cambodia and Thailand (UNAIDS, 2008). Other modes of infection include injecting drug use and men having sex with men.

EASTERN EUROPE AND CENTRAL ASIA

As of 2007, there were approximately 1.5 million adults and children living with HIV in this area (UNAIDS, 2008). The Russian Federation has the largest AIDS epidemic in all of Europe, which is mainly fueled by intravenous drug use and prostitution. An increase in media coverage in the Russian Federation has helped bring some attention to the increasing numbers of HIV infection. The main modes of HIV transmission in Eastern Europe and Central Asia are injecting drug use, sex workers and their partners, heterosexual intercourse, and men having sex with men (UNAIDS, 2008).

NORTH AMERICA AND WESTERN AND CENTRAL EUROPE

The United States comprises 1.2 of the 2 million people living with HIV in North America and Western and Central Europe (UNAIDS, 2008). Fewer people are dying from HIV infection in these countries because of antiretroviral therapy. Overall, the main mode of HIV transmission is men having sex with men, heterosexual intercourse, and injecting drug use.

SUB-SAHARAN AFRICA

The majority of the world's HIV-positive people live in sub-Saharan Africa, where close to 67% of the global number of people with HIV are living (UNAIDS, 2008; see Figure 15.13). The

AIDS Orphans in Africa

It is estimated that by 2010 there will be more than 25 million AIDS orphans globally.

The effects of the AIDS epidemic have been particularly hard on children, many who have been orphaned. Although we typically think of an orphan as a child without parents, the word is used a bit differently by those involved in the AIDS epidemic. A *maternal orphan* is a child who has lost a mother to AIDS, a *paternal orphan* has lost a father to AIDS, and a *double orphan* has lost both parents to AIDS (Fredriksson et al., 2008). It is estimated that by 2010 there will be more than 25 million AIDS orphans globally (Sherr et al., 2008), and at least 18.4 million of these orphans will be from sub-Saharan Africa alone (Andrews et al., 2006; Cluver & Gardner, 2007). While only 10% of the world's population lives in sub-Saharan Africa, close to 80% of AIDS orphans come from this area (Roby & Shaw, 2006). AIDS orphans are often young—15% are newborn to 4 years old, 35% are 5–9 years old, and 50% are 10–14 years old (Monasch & Boerma, 2004).

At the beginning of the AIDS epidemic in the 1980s, orphanages were set up in many African communities to help care for the many children whose parents had died. However, the number of orphans quickly surpassed the amount of space available in the orphanages. Today 90% of orphans in sub-Saharan Africa are cared for by extended family members (Heymann et al., 2007). In fact, over one third of working adults in sub-Saharan Africa care for orphans in their households, but the majority of these families live in poverty and are unable to meet the essential caregiving needs of the orphans in their care (Heymann et al., 2007; Kidman et al., 2007; Roby & Shaw, 2006). Ongoing poverty in sub-Saharan Africa has forced some orphans either into the labor market or to the streets where they may beg, steal, or prostitute themselves for money (Amanpour, 2006).

African orphans are at increased risk for many physical, socioeconomic, and psychological problems (Sherr et al.,

© Friedrich Stark/Alamy

2008). Many experience anxiety, depression, fear, anger, and guilt, which can contribute to long-term mental health issues (Foster, 2006). One study found that 12% of orphans wished they were dead, compared to 3% of non-orphans (Atwine et al., 2005). Orphans are also at increased risk of social isolation, abuse, neglect, malnutrition, and homelessness, and many lose their opportunities for health care, future employment, and adequate education (Andrews et al., 2006; Cluver & Gardner, 2007; Foster, 2006; Li et al., 2008; Rivers et al., 2008). In fact, since many extended families are unable to afford school and uniform fees, orphans are less likely to attend school than non-orphans (Kürzinger et al., 2008).

Orphans are also at higher risk for negative sexual health outcomes compared to non-orphans. They are more likely to initiate sex early and have multiple sex partners, are less likely to use condoms, and more likely to experience teenage pregnancy (Birdthistle et al., 2008; Gregson et al., 2005). They are also more at risk for forced sex and have a higher prevalence of HIV and herpes infections (Birdthistle et al., 2008).

As the HIV/AIDS rates continue to climb in many countries around the globe, it is imperative to find ways to both reduce HIV/AIDS infections and to increase access to antiretroviral treatment. In addition to this, however, finding care and assistance for orphans also remains a priority. Local and global communities continue to reach out to help AIDS orphans around the globe, ensuring adequate access to services and providing support services for caregivers and families (Roby & Shaw, 2006; UNAIDS, 2008). Some groups provide psychological support, food, and/or clothing and offer resources to keep orphans in school (Foster, 2002). Many believe that finding ways to keep orphans in school may be the key to this crisis, since an adequate education can increase self-esteem and help ensure financial independence in the future (Fredriksson et al., 2008).

main mode of HIV transmission is heterosexual intercourse, but injecting drug use, sex work, and men having sex with men also contribute to transmission.

Children are also hard hit in sub-Saharan Africa, where it is estimated 90% of children younger than 15 years who are HIV-positive live (UNAIDS, 2008). One study found that a 15-year-old in Botswana has an 80% chance of dying from AIDS

(Piot, 2000). Because sub-Saharan Africa has the world's largest population of HIV-positive children, South Africa's *Sesame Street* unveiled an HIV-positive Muppet character, Kami. Kami is a 5-year-old orphan whose parents died of AIDS. Kami's character was designed to help children in South Africa understand AIDS and teach them that it's OK to play with HIV-positive children.

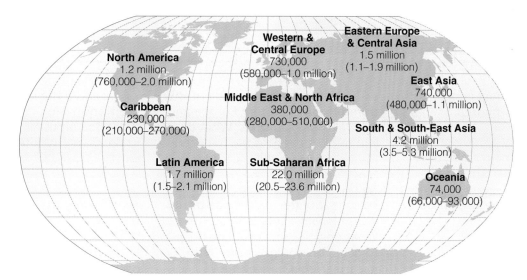

Figure **15.13** Human immunodeficiency virus (HIV)—Adults and children estimated to be living with HIV worldwide, 2007. Source: Joint United Nations Programme on HIV/AIDS (2008). Report on the global AIDS epidemic. UNAIDS. Retrieved on September 18, 2008 from http://www.unaids.org/en/KnowledgeCentre/HIVData/GlobalReport/2008/2008_Global_report.asp. Reprinted with permission.

AP/Wide World Photos

In South Africa, an HIV-positive Muppet was added to the cast of *Sesame Street*. Her name is Kami, which is derived from the Tswana word for "acceptance."

One of the biggest problems in many parts of Africa is that because of cost, only a small percent of the many people with HIV are receiving HAART therapy. In addition, millions of infected men and women are not being treated for opportunistic diseases. Dangerous cultural myths exist in some parts of South Africa. Groups of HIV-positive men believe that sex with a young virgin will cure them of AIDS (Sidley, 2002; Zulu, 2007). As a result, dozens of babies in South Africa have been raped by HIV-positive men, and the crime is increasing. In 2002, a 9-month-old baby was raped by a group of HIV-positive men and reconstructive surgery was necessary to repair her vagina (Sidley, 2002).

LATIN AMERICA

There were 1.7 million people living with HIV in Latin America in 2007 (UNAIDS, 2008). The main mode of HIV transmission is men having sex with men, injecting drug use, and sex work. Hidden epidemics of men having sex with men exist in several Central American countries, including El Salvador, Mexico, Costa Rica, and Nicaragua (Bastos et al., 2008).

THE CARIBBEAN

There were 230,000 people living with HIV in the Caribbean in 2007 (UNAIDS, 2008). The majority of HIV-positive men and women live in the Dominican Republic and Haiti. The main mode of HIV transmission in this area is heterosexual intercourse with both intimate partners and paid sex workers, along with men having sex with men.

THE MIDDLE EAST

Although there is limited information about HIV in these areas, we know there were approximately 380,000 men and women living with HIV in 2007 (UNAIDS, 2008). The main mode of HIV transmission was unprotected paid sex, men having sex with men, and injecting drug use. In Iran, drug-related epidemics have contributed to rising HIV rates. Although Sudan has increased efforts at educating the public about HIV and AIDS, one study found that only 5% of women knew that condom use could protect them from HIV infection, and more than two thirds of the women had never heard of a condom (UNAIDS, 2005b).

In summary, recent research suggests that counseling is being increasingly recognized as an important part of care for people with HIV and their families in developing countries. Provision of education and information is also increasing. In some countries, home-based health care is being established to remove some of the burden from the hospitals, increase quality health care, and reduce costs.

1 Explain the global impact of the AIDS epidemic on children.

2 Identify the main mode of HIV transmission in Asian countries. What do you think could be done to decrease HIV infections in this particular area?

3 Identify the main mode of HIV transmission in Eastern Europe and Central Asian countries. What do you think could be done to decrease HIV infections in this particular area?

4 Identify the main mode of HIV transmission in sub-Saharan Africa. What do you think could be done to decrease HIV infections in this particular area?

5 Identify the main mode of HIV transmission in Latin America. What do you think could be done to decrease HIV infections in this particular area?

6 Identify the main mode of HIV transmission in the Middle East. What do you think could be done to decrease HIV infections in this particular area?

Preventing STIs and AIDS

You might be feeling pretty overwhelmed with all this new information about STIs. It's important not to lose sight of the fact that there is much that you can do to help prevent a sexually transmitted infection. If you are sexually active, one of the most important things you can do is to get yourself tested. When you get into a sexual relationship, make sure your partner is also tested. Today's experts recommend full testing for STIs for sexually active men and women, including HIV testing (L. A. Johnson, 2005).

You can also make sure that you carefully choose your sexual partners and use barrier methods such as condoms to reduce your chances of acquiring an STI. Unless you are in a monogamous relationship, it's important to avoid high-risk sexual behaviors (see Sex in Real Life, "High-Risk Sexual Behaviors," earlier in the chapter). In addition, it's also important to be sure you are knowledgeable about STIs. Knowledge and education are powerful tools in decreasing the frequency of STIs.

EARLY DETECTION

If you already have an STI, early detection and management of the infection are important and can help lessen the possibility of infecting others. Be sure to notify your sexual partners as soon as a positive diagnosis is made to help reduce the chances that someone else will become infected. As we discussed earlier in this chapter, many college students are apprehensive about getting tested for STIs, especially when they think they might be positive. It's important to be proactive in these matters and seek testing and treatment if you think you may have become infected. Many of the bacterial STIs can be treated with antibiotics. However, delaying treatment may result in more long-term consequences to your health, such as PID or infertility (for you or your partner).

TALKING ABOUT STIs

Talking about STIs isn't always easy to do, and although people might not always respond positively to such a discussion, it is important. Honesty, trust, and communication are key elements to any successful relationship. To begin a conversation about STIs, choose a time when you can be alone and uninterrupted. Sometimes it's a little easier to start by bringing up the importance of honesty in relationships. You could talk about what you've learned in this class and how it's made you think about your current and future health. Talk about any infections, diseases, and past behaviors that may have put you or your partner at risk. Suggest STI testing and the importance of monogamy in your relationship.

Overall, as we discussed at the beginning of this chapter, it's important that we continue to try to break the silence about sexually transmitted infections and work to reduce the negative beliefs and stigma associated with them. Only then can we help encourage responsibility and safe behaviors.

review questions

1 Identify some strategies that a person can use to decrease the possibility of acquiring an STI.

2 If you have already been infected with an STI, what can you do to help manage the infection?

3 Explain how communication can be an important tool in decreasing STIs.

CHAPTER **review**

SUMMARY POINTS

1 STIs have historically been viewed as symbols of corrupt sexuality, which is why there has been a "punishment concept" of disease. College students are at an increased risk of acquiring STIs because they engage in many behaviors that put them at higher risk, such as having multiple partners and engaging in unprotected sexual behaviors.

2 The majority of STIs occur in those under 25 years old; adolescents have a higher biological risk for developing an STI.

3 All states require that syphilis, gonorrhea, chlamydia, HIV, AIDS, and chancroid be reported to public health centers. In addition, many states require reporting cases of HSV and HPV.

4 Women are at greater risk for long-term complications from STIs because of the fragility of the female reproductive tract. More women are asymptomatic and are more susceptible to gonorrhea, chlamydia, and HIV, although the spread of syphilis and genital warts is usually equal between the sexes. African Americans have higher rates of most STIs than Caucasians, even though STIs occur in all racial and ethnic groups.

5 HIV infection has declined in men who have sex with men, although there have been increases in the rates of gonorrhea, syphilis, and chlamydia in HIV-infected members of this population. Women who have sex with women can become infected with hepatitis C, herpes, trichomoniasis, and HPV.

6 Nonoxynol-9 has been found to increase the rate of genital ulceration, causing a higher risk of STI infection. Condoms are the most effective contraceptive method for reducing the risk of acquiring an STI.

7 Ectoparasitic infections are those that are caused by parasites that live on the skin's surface and include pubic lice and scabies. Treatment is with topical creams to kill the parasites and their larvae.

8 The majority of women who are infected with gonorrhea are asymptomatic, whereas men are symptomatic. Testing for gonorrhea involves collecting a sample of the discharge from the cervix, urethra, or another infected area with a cotton swab. Gonorrhea can be treated effectively with antibiotics. Antibiotics are usually administered orally, but in severe cases, intramuscular injections may be necessary.

9 Syphilis usually infects the cervix, penis, anus, or lips first. It can also infect a baby during birth. Syphilis has decreased over the past few years in the United States and may soon be eliminated. Infection with syphilis is divided into three stages: primary or early syphilis, secondary syphilis, and tertiary or late syphilis. Antibiotics are the treatment of choice today.

10 Chlamydia is the most frequently reported infectious disease in the United States and the most commonly diagnosed bacterial STI in the developed world. The majority of men and women with a chlamydia infection are asymptomatic. Antibiotics are the treatment of choice today for chlamydia.

11 Chancroid is relatively rare in the United States but is one of the most prevalent STIs in many developing countries. Once infected, women and men often develop small lesions where the infection entered the body. The infection may spread to the lymph nodes of the groin, which can cause swelling and pain. Chancroids are treated with antibiotics.

12 Vaginal infections include trichomoniasis, hemophilus, bacterial vaginosis, and candidiasis. The majority of women have symptoms, whereas the majority of men are asymptomatic. Hemophilus is caused by bacteria; although the majority of women are asymptomatic, some may experience a vaginal discharge, soreness, itching, and burning. Treatment includes oral antibiotics or vaginal suppositories.

13 Bacterial vaginosis (BV) is the most common cause of vaginal discharge and odor. Women with BV have been found to have an increased risk of endometriosis and pelvic inflammatory disease. Vaginal candidiasis is caused by a fungus that is normally present in the vagina, but it multiplies when the pH balance of the vagina is disturbed. Treatment includes either an antifungal prescription or over-the-counter drugs.

14 Viral infections include HSV, HPV, viral hepatitis, and HIV. Herpes is caused by either HSV-1 or HSV-2; however, once a person is infected, the symptoms can overlap. HSV-2 is one of the most common STIs in the United States. The virus can be transmitted even when a person does not have symptoms. Once infected, a person will always carry the virus in his or her body. The standard therapy for HSV infection today are antiviral drugs.

15 There are more than 100 types of HPV, and 30 of these are sexually transmitted. Almost all cervical disease can be attributed to HPV infection. Many people who are infected with HPV are asymptomatic, whereas others develop symptoms as late as 6 weeks to 9 months after infection. The majority of sexual partners of people with cervical warts develop warts within 3 to 4 months of contact. Genital warts can be treated in several ways. An HPV vaccine is now available and recommended for young girls and women.

16 Viral hepatitis is an infection that causes impaired liver function. There are three types of viral hepatitis: hepatitis A (HAV), hepatitis B (HBV), and hepatitis C (HCV). HAV infection is usually symptomatic, whereas infection with HBV and HCV is asymptomatic. Blood tests are used to identify viral hepatitis infections. Vaccines are available for the prevention of both HAV and HBV, and research on a vaccine for hepatitis C is in progress.

17 Pelvic inflammatory disease (PID) is an infection of the female genital tract.

Today chlamydia is the leading cause of PID; 1 in 7 women of reproductive age are found to have at least one episode of PID by age 35. Treatment for PID includes antibiotics.

18 AIDS is caused by an infection with the human immunodeficiency virus and is primarily transmitted through body fluids, including semen, vaginal fluid, and blood. HIV attacks the T-helper cells in the blood, and antibodies can be detected in the bloodstream anywhere from 2 weeks to 6 months after infection. The attack on the T-helper cells causes the immune system to be less effective in its ability to fight disease, and so many infected people develop opportunistic diseases.

19 Women are the fastest growing U.S. group with AIDS, and heterosexual transmission is the most common way a woman is infected with HIV. AIDS is most dramatically affecting African Americans and continues to affect minority communities disproportionately throughout the world. College students are at risk for HIV because of high rates of sexual activity, multiple sexual partners, lack of protection during sexual activity, and sexual activity that takes place after a couple has been drinking.

20 Later symptoms of untreated AIDS may include significant weight loss, severe diarrhea, night sweats, oral candidiasis, gingivitis, oral ulcers, and persistent fever. The deterioration of the immune system makes it easier for opportunistic diseases to develop.

21 Tests for HIV can look for either the virus itself or for antibodies that the body has developed to fight HIV. One of the biggest developments in diagnosis has been the development of rapid HIV testing. These tests detect the presence of antibodies to HIV and require either a drop of blood or oral fluids. Research continues to work toward developing a home AIDS tests.

22 The development of highly active antiretroviral therapy has significantly reduced the number of deaths from HIV/AIDS. However, HAART therapy is much more common in North America and Europe. Newer treatments involve a one-a-day pill. An HIV-infected man or woman must undergo drug therapy for life.

23 Prevention and educational programs have begun to help reduce the spread of AIDS. Educational programs, advertising, mailings, public service announcements, and television shows all have helped to increase knowledge

levels about HIV/AIDS. Many schools are beginning to include AIDS education in their classes.

24 Families and friends of people with AIDS often do not receive the same social support as do families and friends of people with other devastating diseases. Today, with the help of HAART therapies, many parents with HIV are living longer, and this has brought up issues of disclosure and adjusting to having a parent with HIV.

25 The worldwide number of people living with HIV is more than 38 million, and by far the majority of people infected with HIV have no access to treatment, mostly because of financial and cultural reasons. Children have also been affected by the AIDS epidemic; 90% of these orphans live in sub-Saharan Africa.

26 There are ways to protect yourself from becoming infected with an STI. If you do become infected, early treatment can reduce long-term consequences. Although it's not always easy to talk to a sexual partner about STIs, it's important to do so. We need to continue to break the silence about STIs and work to reduce the negative beliefs and stigma associated with these infections.

CRITICAL THINKING questions

1   How will reading this chapter affect your own sexual practices? What material has had the biggest impact on you, and why?

2   Suppose that your best friend has never heard of chlamydia. What can you tell him or her about the symptoms, long-term risks, diagnosis, and treatment of chlamydia? Should he or she be worried?

3   Suppose that one late night when you are talking to a group of friends, the topic of sexually transmitted infections comes up. In your argument to encourage your friends to use condoms, what can you say about

the asymptomatic nature of STIs? The properties of latency? How women are more at risk? How do you think your friends will respond?

4   Do you think the United States should provide medication to AIDS-infected men and women in sub-Saharan Africa who cannot afford it? Or should the United States provide sexuality education on AIDS prevention to those who do not have the virus? How would the money be best spent, and why?

5   Have you ever dated someone with an STI? If so, when did you find out about it? How did you feel? Did it affect your sex life? How so?

6   The vaccine Gardasil, which protects women from strains of HPV that can cause cervical cancer, has been available for a few years now. If you had female children, would you get them vaccinated? Health care providers are recommending vaccinating girls as young as 9 years old. If you would give your daughter the vaccine, at what age do you think you'd want her to have it and why? If it were available for boys and men, would you want your son to have it? At what age?

WEB resources

Sexuality Now Book Companion Website

Go to www.cengage.com/psychology/carroll for practice quizzes, glossary, flash cards, and more. You can also access the following websites from the companion site.

American Social Health Association ■ The American Social Health Association provides information on sexually transmitted infections. The website contains support, referrals, resources, and in-depth information about sexually transmitted infections.

Centers for Disease Control and Prevention ■ The Centers for Disease Control and Prevention's division of STI prevention provides information about sexually transmitted infections, including surveillance reports and disease facts. The CDC's division of HIV/AIDS prevention provides information about HIV and AIDS, including surveillance reports and facts about the infection.

Herpes.org ■ Herpes.org is an online resource for people with herpes and the human papillomavirus. The website provides information about the infections, what nonprescription and prescription treatments work and where to find medical help and medication.

Joint United Nations Program on HIV and AIDS (UNAIDS) ■ The Joint United Nations Program on HIV and AIDS provides monitoring and evaluation of AIDS research

and also provides access to various links and information about AIDS. Information on AIDS scenarios for the future, antiretroviral therapy, and HIV/AIDS in children and orphans is available.

LesbianSTDs ■ This website provides information and resources regarding sexual health and sexually transmitted infections in women who have sex with women.

CengageNOW

Go to www.cengage.com/login to link to CengageNOW, your online study tool. First take the Pre-Test for this chapter to get your Personalized Study Plan, which will identify topics you need to review and direct you to online resources. Then take the Post-Test to determine what concepts you have mastered and what you still need work on.

Videos in CengageNOW

For additional information on topics discussed in this chapter, check out the videos in CengageNOW on the following topics:

- AIDS in Africa—Describes HIV/AIDS as related to gender, poverty, stigma, education, and justice.

- HIV/AIDS: Orel—Listen to Orel describe how strong social support and pursuing personal interests helps to mitigate the effects of HIV/AIDS.

CHAPTER 16

Varieties of Sexual Expression

I am a rubber fetishist and professional therapist, in that order. This combination has given me a special view of unusual sexual practices both through my own personal experience and as a result of the large number of other individuals whom I have encountered professionally and personally.

I have four clear vignettes of memory associated with my early delight with rubber, which I present either because they stimulate me in the telling or because they may be important to a therapist or client. One is of a woman with long dark hair playing with my penis by stroking it with soft rubber panties and moving her long hair gently and playfully over it. The whole image is intense and all involving. It is loving, fun, sexually exciting (I have no image of the state of my penis), secure, and safe. For me, rubber most often provides all of these experiences in one simultaneous concert of sensations. A second image is that of a moment of pleasant security when I pull back the bed covers far enough to place my hand gently on the rubber sheet. . . . to exchange the upset of a forgotten and unpleasant encounter with an adult for the quiet tranquility of the soft rubber and its loving associations. A third image is sliding under the cotton sheet to enjoy the rubber after I have been "tucked in" at night and then engaging in what my mother called "bounding up and down," still my favorite

form of stimulation with my face and whole body gently moving over the rubber, skillfully massaging my penis between the rubber and my stomach. The fourth image is of a birthday. The rubber was in the form of solid rubber animals, smooth and rubber smelling but rather hard and of little sexual use. By the time I was three I was a full-blown rubber fetishist. No raincoat, bathing cap, or pair of baby panties was (or is) safe from me. My pediatrician was warm and kind about it, and I appreciate the impact of his support on my life. I had no inkling of being weird, no guilt, in contrast with many of my fellow fetishists at the hands of their professionals. I hoped that I wouldn't outgrow it, and I didn't. . . . Simply stated, my life involved rubber as a central element from my earliest years and still does as I enter my sixties. Neither my mother nor professionals stimulated any guilt.

In my own presentations of my rubber fetish I do not fail to enjoy some good laughs at myself. This is because I take myself seriously, seriously enough to laugh at things that are absurd. For example, I have received disapproving looks from women wearing rubber raincoats who thought I was looking at them, and from men who mistook my absorbed gaze as sexual attraction to them. . . . Or the small department store that always had a supply of various kinds of rubber coats (if I don't have a particular size or color, I must [get one]). The

salesman took me to a private loft upstairs where there were hundreds of rubber coats. I do not know if someone there shared my fetish, but it was my idea of heaven. I took lots of time, so the salesman asked if it was all right if he left me alone. All right? I went around my heaven with a delightful erection and sampled the softness of the rubber against my penis. Every coat in the collection. Then I took a few and laid them on a flat surface and made love to them. It was incredible. It's all silly, and fun.

Laughter, particularly at the self, dislodges the judgments and fears that are associated with most sexual behaviors because it provides a new perspective. The fetishes offer the therapist the opportunity to dislodge the seriousness which entrenches a distressed perspective, and discover the effectiveness of these approaches even to serious sexual difficulty and offenses. It is also effective. At best, a six-foot man looks ridiculous in ten-inch heels and knows it. If the therapist can't laugh, the message is clear to the client that it is as weird as he thought. SOURCE: From Thomas Sargent, "Fetishism," Journal of Social Work and Human Sexuality, 1988, pp. 27–42. Reprinted by permission of The Haworth Press, Inc.

467
Media Images May Sexualize Kids

456
Children Sometimes Dress As the Other Sex

452
View in Video

◁ Opposite: © Roger Cracknell 19/Shambhala/Alamy

Human sexuality can be expressed in many ways. We tend to celebrate individual and cultural differences in most aspects of human life—in what people eat, how they dress, or how they dance, for example. Yet we have been less tolerant of sexual diversity, and we have historically considered such behavior "deviant" or "perverted" (Laws & O'Donohue, 1997). More modern views of sexuality, however, do not categorize people as "deviant" versus "normal." For example, the sexual world is not really split into those who become sexually excited from looking at others naked or having sex and those who do not; most people get aroused to some degree from visual sexual stimuli. Some people get more aroused than others, and at the upper limits are those who can get aroused only when watching sexual scenes; such people have taken a normal behavior to an extreme. In this chapter, we explore variations of sexual behavior, including differences in sexual desire and the **paraphilias.**

What Is "Typical" Sexual Expression?

Some medical and sexuality texts still categorize certain kinds of behavior as sexual deviance. Many undergraduate texts discuss these behaviors in chapters that includes words such as "abnormal," "unusual," or "atypical" sexual behavior in their titles. Yet how exactly do we decide whether a behavior is "normal"? What is "typical" sexual activity? Where do we draw the line? Do we call

paraphilia
Clinical term used to describe types of sexual expressions that are seen as unusual and potentially problematic. A person who engages in paraphilias is often referred to as a paraphiliac.

it "atypical" if 5% of sexually active people do it? Ten percent? Twenty-five percent?

Sexual behaviors increase and decrease in popularity; oral sex, for example, was once considered a perversion, but now it is a commonly reported sexual behavior in adolescent populations (Prinstein et al., 2003). Perhaps, then, we should consider as "deviant" only behaviors that may be harmful in some way. Masturbation was once believed to lead to mental illness, acne, and stunted growth; now it is considered a normal, healthy part of sexual expression. If many of these desires exist to some degree in all of us, then the desire itself is not atypical, just the degree of the desire.

View in Video

"In bondage, her life can literally be in my hands with rope, fire play, or more extreme kinds of S&M."
—*Bondage and S&M*
To view go to CengageNOW at www.cengage.com/login

WHAT DO YOU WANT TO KNOW ?

If I fantasize about watching other people having sex or if I get turned on by being spanked, does that mean I have a paraphilia?
A strong and varied fantasy life is the sign of healthy sexuality, and acting out fantasies in a safe sexual situation can add excitement to one's sex life. Problems may arise when the fantasy or desire becomes so prominent or preoccupying that you are unable to function sexually in its absence; sexual play is taken to the point of physical or psychological injury; you feel extreme levels of guilt about the desire; or your compulsion to perform a certain type of sexual behavior interferes with everyday life, disrupts your personal relationships, or risks getting you in trouble with the law. Under any of these circumstances, it is advisable to see a qualified sex therapist or counselor.

Social value judgments, not science, primarily determine which sexual behaviors are considered "normal" by a society. For example, in 1906, Krafft-Ebing defined sexual deviance as "every expression of (the sexual instinct) that does not correspond with the purpose of nature—i.e., propagation" (J. C. Brown, 1983, p. 227). Certainly, most people would not go so far today. Freud himself stated that the criterion of normalcy was love and that defenses against "perversion" were the bedrock of civilization because perversion trivializes or degrades love (A. M. Cooper, 1991). Note that Freud's objections to perversion are not medical, as they were to most other mental disturbances, but moral.

Even "modern" definitions can contain hidden value judgments: "The sexually variant individual typically exhibits sexual arousal or responses to inappropriate people (e.g., minors), objects (e.g., leather, rubber, garments), or activities (e.g., exposure in public, coercion, violence)" (Gudjonsson, 1986, p. 192). "Appropriate" or "inappropriate" people, objects, or activities of sexual attention differ in different times, in different cultures, and for different people.

Despite these objections, certain groups of behaviors are considered the most common deviations from conventional heterosexual or homosexual behavior. The people who engage in these activities may see them as unproblematic, exciting aspects of their sexuality, or they may be very troubled by their behavior. Society may see the behavior as either solely the business of the individual in the privacy of his or her bedroom (e.g., sexual excitement from shoes or boots), as a sign that the person is mentally ill (e.g., having sex with animals), or as dangerous and illegal (e.g., sex with underage children). Today many states have passed laws that require sex offenders to register with the towns in which they live (see the nearby Sex in Real Life feature). In this chapter, we explore sexual behaviors that are fairly rare, theories of why people are attracted to unusual sexual objects, and how therapists have tried to help those who are troubled by their sexual desires.

review questions

1 Explain how medical and sexuality texts categorize sexual behaviors and how this might affect popular opinions.

2 Explain how sexual behaviors increase and decrease in frequency and how this affects society's view of perversions.

3 How do social value judgments determine which sexual behaviors are viewed as normal?

Megan's Law

Many convicted sex offenders have protested the law, claiming that it violates their constitutional rights.

In 1994, 7-year-old Megan Kanka was lured into her neighbor's home in Hamilton Township, New Jersey, by the promise of a puppy. There she was raped, strangled, and suffocated by a two-time convicted sexual offender. Shortly thereafter, the governor of New Jersey, Christine Todd Whitman, signed the toughest sex offender registration act in the country, known as "Megan's Law." In 1996, Megan's Law became federal law and mandated that every community have access to information about the presence of convicted sex offenders in their neighborhoods. Two years earlier, in 1994, a federal statute known as the Jacob Wetterling Crimes against Children and Sexually Violent Offender Registration Program was passed, which also requires all states to create registration programs for convicted sex offenders (Trivits & Reppucci, 2002).

Today, all 50 states require that convicted sex offenders register on their release from prison into the community and require the listing (with the offenders' names, addresses, photographs, crimes, and sometimes physical descriptions) to be made available to the public. Although all require sex offenders to register, the statutes vary in what information is made available and for how long (Trivits & Reppucci, 2002). In some states, sexual offenders must register for the rest of their lives.

Many convicted sex offenders have protested the law, claiming that it violates their constitutional rights; however, the government has decided that the safety of children is a higher priority than the privacy of convicted sex offenders. Critics also argue that these listings encourage violent behavior directed at the offenders, although studies have found that the actual incidence of such events is low (Klaas, 2003; J. Miller, 1998). In addition, some argue that having such lists creates instant mailing lists for those who wish to connect with other offenders (Sommerfeld, 1999).

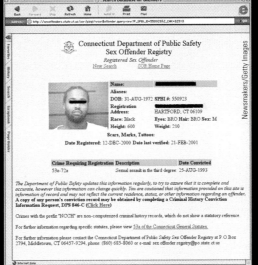

All 50 states require convicted sex offenders to register upon their release to the community. Sexual offender registry profiles often contain personal information including name, address, date of birth, offense, and physical description.

Some states continue to add regulations to their sex offender registry laws. For example, in 2005, certain towns in New York, Florida, and New Jersey banned convicted child molesters from being within 2,500 feet of any school, day-care center, playground, or park (Koch, 2005). Other states use electronic monitoring in addition to their online registries. For example, Florida, Alabama, New Jersey, Missouri, Ohio, and Oklahoma all passed laws requiring electronic monitoring (ankle bands that monitor the offender's whereabouts).

Unfortunately, the registries may have given many parents and caregivers a false sense of security. Of the 551,000 sex offenders who were registered in 2005, 100,000 were missing or had failed to supply a current address (Koch, 2005). In addition, sex offender registries contain only those offenders who have been convicted of sexual offenses and not all who commit such crimes. Nonetheless, many of these new laws and tracking devices may help to discourage sexual offenders from engaging in these behaviors.

Paraphilias: Moving from
Exotic to Disordered

The word paraphilia (pear-uh-FILL-ee-uh) is derived from the Greek "para" (besides) and "philia" (love or attraction). In other words, paraphilias are sexual behaviors that involve a craving for an erotic object that is unusual or different. According to the *Diagnostic and Statistical Manual of Mental Disorders* (4th ed., text revision; *DSM-IV-TR*), the essential features involved in a paraphilia are recurrency and intensity of the sexual behavior that involves a nonhuman object or the suffering or humiliation of oneself or one's partner, a child, or a nonconsenting person (American Psychiatric Association, 2000). This behavior causes significant distress and interferes with a person's ability to work, interact with friends, and other important areas of one's life. To be diagnosed with a paraphilia, a person must be experiencing symptoms for 6 months or more. For some people with paraphilias, the fantasy or presence of the object of their desire is necessary for arousal and orgasm; in others, the desire occurs periodically or exists separately from their other sexual relationships.

Research has shown that there are no "classic" profiles of people with paraphilias (Scheela, 1995). Individuals who engage in paraphiliac behavior are a heterogeneous group with no true factors that set them apart from nonparaphiliacs, with the exception of gender—the majority of those with paraphilias are men. Other than this, people with paraphilias come from every socioeconomic bracket, every ethnic and racial group, and from every sexual orientation (Seligman & Hardenburg, 2000). It is estimated that half of those who engage in paraphiliac behavior are married, and the majority report sexual problems and dysfunctions in their marital sexual relationships (S. B. Levine et al., 1990).

There are no "classic" profiles of people with paraphilias.

Although there are no classic profiles that fit all paraphilias, there are some factors that have been found to be related to the development of a paraphilia. Research has found that many people with paraphilias have grown up in a dysfunctional family and experienced significant family problems during childhood that contribute to the poor social skills and distorted views of sexual intimacy often seen in those with paraphilias (Seligman & Hardenburg, 2000). This is not to say that everyone who grows up in such a household will develop a paraphilia; rather, it may be a related factor. The severity of paraphilias varies; someone with a mild case might use disturbing sexual fantasies during masturbation, whereas someone with a severe case may engage in unwanted sexual behavior with a child or may even commit murder.

Paraphilias are similar to many impulse-control disorders, such as substance abuse, gambling, and eating disorders (A. Goodman, 1993). Many people with paraphilias feel conflicted over their behavior, and they develop tension and a preoccupation with certain behaviors. They repeatedly try to suppress their sexual behaviors but are unable to do so (Seligman & Hardenburg, 2000).

Many people find lingerie exciting, enjoy watching sexual scenes, or enjoy being lightly bitten or scratched during sex. For people with paraphilias, however, the lingerie itself becomes the object of sexual attention, not a means of enhancing the sexuality of the partner. For this reason, some have suggested that the defining characteristic of paraphilia is that it replaces a whole with a part, that it allows the person to distance himself or herself from complex human sexual contact and replace it with the undemanding sexuality of an inanimate object, a scene, or a single action (L. J. Kaplan, 1991).

Motivations for paraphiliac behaviors vary. Some people with paraphilias claim that their behaviors provide meaning to their lives and give them a sense of self (A. Goodman, 1993), whereas others say the behaviors relieve their depression and loneliness or help them express rage (S. B. Levine et al., 1990). Many violent or criminal people with paraphilias have little ability to feel empathy for their victims and may convince themselves that their victims enjoy the experiences, even though the victims do not consent to them (Seligman & Hardenburg, 2000).

Research on paraphilias has been drawn mostly from clinical and incarcerated samples, which are almost certainly not representative of the population as a whole. The number of people who live comfortably with uncommon sexual habits is hard to determine because people tend to be reluctant to admit to their sexual inclinations, even in confidential questionnaires, especially if they seem unusual. What is known is that people who do have para-

philias usually have more than one (American Psychiatric Association, 2000).

People with paraphilias are often portrayed as sick, perverted, or potential sex offenders. There is thus an attempt to draw a clear line between those with paraphilias and "normal" people; yet the line is rarely that clear. Certainly, there are paraphiliac behaviors that can be dangerous or can threaten others. Men who expose themselves to young girls, people who violate corpses, strangers who rub against women on buses, or adults who seduce underage children must not be allowed to continue their behavior. There can even be legal problems with the paraphilias that are not in themselves dangerous; some **fetishists** resort to stealing the object of interest to them, and occasionally a voyeur will break into people's homes. Also, paraphiliacs are often compulsive masturbators, even up to 10 times a day or more, which can make it difficult to hold a job, for example. A number of therapies have been developed to help these people; but, as you will see, it is difficult to change a person's arousal patterns.

Other people live comfortably with their paraphilias. It's important for us to differentiate between paraphilias that are consensual (those that involve a partner's consent) and nonconsensual (those that do not involve a partner's consent). A man who has a fetish for lingerie, for example, may find a partner who very much enjoys wearing it for him. As you saw in the chapter opener, rubber brings comfort, excitement, and a sense of well-being to this man, and he has no desire to see his fetish go away. Why should he want to put it to an end just because some other people find it distasteful, perverted, or abnormal? In what sense is such a person sick?

For this reason, paraphilias have become controversial. Some theorists suggest that the term describes a society's value judgments about sexuality and not a psychiatric or clinical category (Silverstein, 1984). Some theorists deny that terms such as paraphilia really describe anything at all. Robert J. Stoller, a well-known psychoanalytic theorist, objected to the idea of trying to create psychological explanations that group people by their sexual habits (Stoller, 1996).

WHAT DO YOU WANT TO KNOW?

Don't women also engage in these behaviors? Why are paraphilias more common in men?

No one really knows, although theories abound. Some researchers suggest that perhaps paraphilias are developed visually, and the male tends, for some biological reason, to be more sexually aroused by visual stimuli than the female. Maybe cultural variables give men more sexual latitude in expressing what excites them. It could also have something to do with the way we look at it; women may express their paraphilias in different, less obvious ways than men. There could also be power differentials that contribute to higher rates in men.

fetishist
One who focuses intensely on an inanimate object or body part (the fetish) for the arousal of sexual desire.

Paraphilias Throughout the World

The majority of information available concerns pedophilia, transvestism, and transsexualism.

Although there has not been much research documenting the incidence, expression, and treatment of paraphilias outside the United States, there have been limited studies. The majority of information available concerns pedophilia, transvestism, and transsexualism. A limited amount of research exists on other paraphilias, such as sadomasochism. Here, we explore what we do know about paraphilias in a variety of countries.

Brazil

In Chapter 9, we discussed the conservative and religious background of many Brazilians, so it shouldn't come as any surprise that there is not a great deal of acceptance for paraphiliac behaviors. Although there are no legal restrictions against transvestism, researchers estimate that there are few who engage in this practice (de Freitas, 2004). Transsexualism is viewed negatively, and it is against the law to undergo sexual reassignment surgery (SRS). In fact, both the patient and surgeon would be charged with a felony if SRS were to take place (de Freitas, 2004). Because of this, some transsexuals travel to Europe to undergo SRS. We do know that throughout history, zoophilia has been found to occur in Brazil, and it has been found to be more common in both men and those living in rural areas (de Freitas, 2004).

China

China has very strict policies against behaviors it deems inappropriate, and paraphilias certainly fall into this category. Sex offenders in China are often charged with "hooliganism," which is a term that includes a wide range of uncivil and sexually unrestrained behavior (Ruan & Lau, 2004). China has very severe penalties for those who engage in such behaviors, and harsh punishments are common. For example, one review reported that the Chinese government enforced the death penalty for certain sexual crimes, including forced sex and pedophilia (Ruan & Lau, 2004).

Germany

Although transvestites are considered deviant in Germany, they don't get much attention (Lautmann & Starke, 2004). Transsexuals, however, are often treated with disdain. Even so, new laws established in 2002 have provided two possibilities of sex change for transsexuals. In the first, often referred to as the "small solution," a transsexual changes his or her name without changing gender. To do so, he or she would need expert opinions from two people, confirming that he or she has been transsexual for at least 3 years. A "major solution" involves sexual reassignment surgery, which is widely available in Germany. This would lead to legal recognition of gender reassignment on official documents, including passports and birth certificates.

Denmark

Denmark, and many of the Scandinavian countries, have much more liberal attitudes about sexuality, so they are less likely to sweep behaviors under the carpet if they don't agree with them. Paraphilias are viewed as criminal behaviors, and those found engaging in such behaviors are appropriately charged. Denmark also has high reporting and treatment rates for paraphilias (Graugaard et al., 2004). In reaction to increased rates of child sexual abuse, Denmark opened a center for the treatment of sexually abused children at the University Hospital in Copenhagen in 2000, and today many groups actively educate professionals and the lay public about incest and child sexual abuse (Graugaard et al., 2004).

Czech Republic

Paraphiliacs in the Czech Republic have many more opportunities for communication and contact with other paraphiliacs than they did in when they were under communist control (Zverina, 2004). This would include clubs, magazines, newspapers, and the Internet. Sadomasochism and fetishes are the most common paraphilias in the Czech Republic (Zverina, 2004). Sexual offenders who are charged with crimes are referred for counseling and treatments, which are covered under national health insurance plans.

Japan

Sadism and masochism are well-known in Japanese art and literature (Hatano & Shimazaki, 2004). Thousands of S&M magazines are sold each month, and many nightclubs cater to the S&M subculture. Like China, Japan has strict laws and punishments for people who engage in child sexual abuse. In 1999, Japan enacted a Child Prostitution and Child Pornography Prohibition Law that prohibits sexual activity with minors and enforces strict punishments for those charged with these behaviors (Hatano & Shimazaki, 2004).

Hong Kong

Although transvestism is not illegal in Hong Kong, a transvestite will be arrested if his or her appearance or behaviors disrupts the peace (Ng & Ma, 2004). Transvestites and transsexuals are often eyed with suspicion and treated differently than nonparaphiliacs. Transsexuals are allowed to undergo sexual reassignment surgery, but they are not legally recognized and must continue to use their chromosomal sex (Ng & Ma, 2004). This often leads to a reduction in social rights, such as tax deductions and child adoptions.

SOURCE: Francoeur & Noonan, 2004.

It is common for young children to play around with clothing and sometimes dress as the other sex. The majority of them, however, will not become cross-dressers.

THEORIES ABOUT
WHERE PARAPHILIAS BEGIN

Many researchers have theorized as to why and how paraphilias develop, but very little consensus has been reached. Paraphilias are undoubtedly complex behavior patterns, which may have biological, psychological, or social origins—or aspects of all three.

Biological Theories

Biological researchers have found that a number of conditions can initiate paraphiliac behavior. Men without previous paraphilias began to display paraphiliac behavior when they developed temporal lobe epilepsy, brain tumors, and disturbances of certain areas of the brain (Kreuter et al., 1998; Rahman & Symeonides, 2008; Sartorius et al., 2008; G. Simpson et al., 2001). This does not mean that everyone with a paraphilia has one of these diseases. Researchers have found that some paraphiliacs have differences in brain structure and brain chemistry and possible lesions in certain parts of the brain (Kennet, 2000). Researchers have also been studying whether higher levels of certain hormones, such as testosterone, may contribute to the development of a paraphilia (Giotakos et al., 2005). However, at most these are factors that may lead some people to be more likely to develop a paraphilia, and they do not explain the majority of paraphiliac behaviors.

Psychoanalytic Theory

Psychoanalytic thought suggests that paraphilias can be traced back to the difficult time the infant has in negotiating his way through the Oedipal crisis and castration anxiety. This can explain why paraphilias are more common among men because both boys and girls identify strongly with their mothers, but girls can continue that identification, whereas boys must, painfully, separate from their mothers to establish a male identity.

Louise Kaplan, a psychoanalyst, suggests that every paraphilia involves issues of masculinity or femininity; as she writes, "every male perversion entails a masquerade or impersonation of masculinity and every female perversion entails a masquerade or impersonation of femininity" (1991, p. 249). For example, a man who exposes himself in public may be coping with castration anxiety by evoking a reaction to his penis from women. The exhibitionist in this view is "masquerading" as a man to cover up feelings of nonmasculinity; he is saying, in effect, "Let me prove that I am a man by showing that I possess the instrument of masculinity." He even needs to demonstrate that his penis can inspire fear, which may be why exhibitionists disproportionately choose young girls, who are more likely to display a fear reaction (Kline, 1987). This confirms to the exhibitionist the power of his masculinity.

In contrast, voyeurs, who are excited by looking at others nude or having sex, may be fixated on the experience that aroused their castration anxieties as children—the sight of genitals and sexuality (Kline, 1987). Looking allows the person to gain power over the fearful and hidden world of sexuality while safe from the possibility of contact. The visual component of castration anxiety occurs when the boy sees the power and size of the father's genitals and the lack of a penis on his mother or sisters. The act of looking initiates castration anxiety, and in the voyeur, the looking has never ceased. Yet looking itself cannot really relieve the anxiety permanently, and so the voyeur is compelled to peep again and again.

Developmental Theories

Freud suggested that children are polymorphously perverse; that is, at birth we have a general erotic potential that can be attached to almost anything. We learn from an early age which sexual objects society deems appropriate for us to desire, but society's messages can get off track. For example, advertising tries to "sexualize" its products—we have all seen shoe commercials, for example, that emphasize the long, sexy legs of the model while focusing on the shoes she wears. Some boys may end up focusing on those shoes as objects of sexual fantasy, which can develop into a fetish.

A theory that builds on similar ideas is John Money's (1984, 1986, 1990) **lovemaps.** Money suggests that the auditory, tactile, and (especially) visual stimuli we experience during childhood sex play form a template in our brain that defines our ideal lover

lovemap
Term coined by John Money to refer to the template of an ideal lover and sexual situation we develop as we grow up.

and ideal sexual situation. If our childhood sex play remains undisturbed, development goes on toward heterosexual desires. If, however, the child is punished for normal sexual curiosity or if there are traumas during this stage, such as sexual abuse, the development of the lovemap can be disrupted in one of three ways.

In **hypophilia** (high-po-FILL-ee-uh), negative stimuli prevent the development of certain aspects of sexuality, and the genitals may be impaired from full functioning. Overall, females are more likely to experience hypophilia than men, resulting in an inability to orgasm, vaginal pain, or lubrication problems later in life. A lovemap can also be disrupted to cause a condition called **hyperphilia** (high-per-FILL-ee-uh), in which a person defies the negative sexual stimulus and becomes overly sexually active, even becoming compulsively sexual (we discuss hypersexuality later in this chapter). Finally, a lovemap can be disrupted when there is a substitution of new elements into the lovemap, and a paraphilia can develop. Because normal sexual curiosity has been discouraged or made painful, the child redirects erotic energy toward other objects that are not forbidden, such as shoes, rubber, or just looking; in other cases, the child turns his or her erotic energy inward and becomes excited by pain or humiliation.

Females are more likely to experience hypophilia than men.

Once this lovemap is set, it becomes very stable, which explains why changing it is so difficult. For example, Money (1984) suggests that sexual arousal to objects may arise when a parent makes a child feel shame about interest in an object. For example, a boy may be caught with his mother's panties in the normal course of curiosity about the woman's body, but when he is severely chastised, the panties become forbidden, dirty, promising of sexual secrets, and he may begin to seek them out.

Another theory about how these fixations occur is the idea of **courtship disorders** (K. Freund & Blanchard, 1986; K. Freund et al., 1983, 1984). Organizing paraphilias into "courtship" stages suggests that the paraphiliac's behavior becomes fixed at a preliminary stage of mating that would normally lead to sexual intercourse. Thus, a person becomes fixated on a particular person, object, or activity and does not progress to typical mating behaviors.

Behavioral Theories

Behaviorists suggest that paraphilias develop because some behavior becomes associated with sexual pleasure through conditioning (G. D. Wilson, 1987). For example, imagine that a boy gets a spanking. While receiving it, the boy has an erection, either by coincidence or because he finds the stimulus of the spanking plea-surable (it becomes a reinforcement). Later, remembering the spanking, he becomes excited and masturbates. As he repeats his masturbatory fantasy, a process called **conditioning** occurs, whereby sexual excitement becomes so associated with the idea of the spanking that he has trouble becoming excited in its absence.

You can imagine how similar situations could lead to other types of fetishes: A boy lies naked on a fur coat, or takes a "pony" ride on his aunt's leg while she's wearing her black leather boots, or puts on his sister's panties, or spies on a female houseguest through the bathroom keyhole. All of these behaviors become positively reinforced and thus are more likely to be repeated.

Sociological Theories

Another way of looking at the causes of paraphilias is to examine the ways society encourages certain behaviors. Feminists, for example, argue that in societies that treat women as sexual objects, it can be a natural development to replace the woman with another, inanimate sexual object. When men and their sexual organs are glorified, some men may need to reinforce their masculinity by exposing themselves and evoking fear.

American society is ruled by images, saturated with television, movies, commercials, advertisements, and magazines; most of these images have highly charged sexual imagery (R. Collins, 2005). The result, some argue, is a world where the image takes the place of the reality, where it becomes common to substitute fantasies for reality. Surrounded by media, the society experiences things vicariously, through reading about it or seeing it rather than actually doing it. In such a climate, representations of eroticism may be easily substituted for sex itself, and so paraphilias become common.

hypophilia
Lack of full functioning of the sexual organs due to missing stages of childhood development.

hyperphilia
Compulsive sexuality due to overcompensating for negative reactions to childhood sexuality.

courtship disorder
A theory of paraphilias that a person's paraphilia stems from being stuck in a preliminary stage of normal courtship progression.

conditioning
In behaviorism, the process whereby a person associates a particular behavior with a positive response; for example, if food repeatedly is served to a dog right after the sound of a bell, the dog will salivate at the sound of the bell even when no food is served.

review questions

1 Define a paraphilia and explain the essential features of a paraphilia as determined by the *DSM*.

2 Identify and explain some of the motivations for paraphiliac behaviors.

3 Differentiate between consensual and nonconsensual paraphilias.

4 Compare and contrast how the biological and psychoanalytic theories explain paraphilias and provide an example.

5 Compare and contrast how the developmental and sociological theories explain paraphilias and provide an example.

Types of Paraphilias

Paraphilias have been grouped into a number of major categories by researchers and clinicians. We review here some of the more common types of paraphilias, including fetishism, sadism and masochism, exhibitionism and voyeurism, transvestic fetishism, and pedophilia.

FETISHISM

A fetish is an inanimate object or a body part not usually associated with the sex act that becomes an individual's primary or exclusive focus of sexual arousal and orgasm. The fetishist (FEH-tish-ist) can develop a sexual response to an object, such as shoes, boots, panties, or bras; to a fabric, such as leather, silk, fur, or rubber; or to a body part, such as feet, buttocks, or hair (Wasserman, 2001). As with most paraphilias, the majority of fetishists are male (Darcangelo, 2008; Laws & O'Donohue, 1997). The strength of the preference for the object varies from thinking about or holding the object to a need to use it during all sexual acts. In the absence of the object, a male with a fetish may experience erectile dysfunction (American Psychiatric Association, 2000).

Many people enjoy using lingerie or even rubber or other fabrics as part of their lovemaking without becoming dependent on them for arousal. The fetishist, in contrast, needs the presence or the fantasy of the object to achieve arousal and sometimes cannot achieve orgasm in its absence. Some fetishists integrate the object of their desire into their sexual life with a partner; for others it remains a secret fetish, with hidden collections of shoes, or panties, or photographs of a body part, over which they masturbate in secret, ever fearful of discovery.

Many fetishists see their sexual habits as a major part of their life, a source of their sense of identity; yet because fetishism is often regarded by society as shameful, they may be embarrassed to admit to their sexual desires. It is therefore rare to find a person who is open about their fetish and even has a sense of humor about it, as the man in the chapter-opening story does in his description of his rubber fetish.

Different cultures hold up different body parts, objects, colors, or smells as symbols of attraction and sexuality for mating (see Chapter 7 for more information about attraction in different cultures). Fetishism involves a person becoming sexually attracted to a symbol itself instead of what it represents. Put another way, for the fetishist, the object—unlike the living, breathing person—is itself erotic, rather than the person, which also eliminates having to deal with another person's feelings, wants, and needs. It can be a refuge from the complexity of interpersonal sexual relations. In that sense, all the paraphilias we discuss can be seen as a type of fetishism; pain and humiliation, or women's clothes, or looking at people having sex can each be a substitute for interpersonal sexuality.

Transvestic Fetishism

In Chapter 4, we discussed the concept of transgenderism. Typically, a transvestite obtains sexual pleasure from dressing in the clothing of the other sex (see Table 4.4). As the nearby Sex in Real Life illustrates, a transgendered person typically feels a sense of comfort, whereas a transvestite typically feels sexual arousal (Seligman & Hardenburg, 2000). Both may be comfortable being the sex they are and not in search of sex reassignment surgery.

True transvestism is often referred to as **transvestic fetishism** (trans-VESS-tick FEH-tish-iz-um) to emphasize the fact that the cross-dresser has an erotic attraction to the clothing he or she wears. Clothes are, in all cultures, symbols of sexual identity and gender roles. Many transvestites are not comfortable with the gender roles that society forces on them because of their biological gender, and many men feel that cross-dressing liberates them from the expectations society puts on them (Wheeler et al., 2008).

---

transvestic fetishism
A paraphilia in which the preferred or exclusive method of sexual arousal or orgasm is through wearing the clothing of the other sex.

Most drag kings are female performance artists who dress in masculine drag and personify the male gender as part of their performance. Their cross-dressing behavior is mostly for their work and the majority of drag kings are content with their birth gender.

WHAT DO YOU WANT TO KNOW?

Aren't transvestites, deep down, really homosexual?

No. Some male homosexuals enjoy dressing as females, and some may derive a certain sexual satisfaction from it. Most heterosexual transvestites are not at all interested in sex with men. They seem all absorbed by women; they want to look, act, and behave like women and get a strong sexual attraction from women's clothes. Some like it when men approach them when they are cross-dressed but only because it affirms their abilities to pass as women.

Transgenderism

Being transgendered has given me the chance to see life from both sides, male and female.

Below, Barbara, a 50-year-old transgendered woman discusses her upbringing, her crossdressing, and her feelings about growing up male with a desire to crossdress as a woman.

Before I was born, my gender was up for grabs. I know that my mother had had two miscarriages before me, and she was given doses of estrogen during her first trimester of pregnancy with me. My guess is that while my body formed on the "XY" track, my brain did the backstroke in a pool of hormonal femininity. Still when I was born the doctor took one look between my legs and announced "It's a BOY!", but he had NO idea how wrong he was.

As early as I can remember (around age 5), I knew I was "different". I quickly learned that my family did not accept my gender variant perspective. That didn't stop my wanting to explore my feminine side, it just meant I had to always do it in secret. With those secrets came enormous guilt and shame. To everyone around me I grew up a normal heterosexual male—but all the while I recognized my ever-present perception of a second self. It remained my secret. It wasn't until age 25, when I met the person I wanted to spend my life with that I felt compelled to share my secret with another person. Very shortly after meeting her, I sat down to explain a lifetime of doubt, but I was immediately paralyzed. I found myself with no vocabulary to describe a lifetime of emotions. All those years of shame and guilt won out, and my mind was blank when I tried to impart the wholeness I felt dressed

Nigel Dickson

as a woman (even if only for a few minutes). I was frustrated at my own inability to articulate the core of my being—to tell my story so someone else could understand. Ultimately, she listened and heard more than I could say. The conversation ended in her generously offering me unconditional acceptance and love—the single greatest gift possible.

Being transgendered has given me the chance to see life from both sides, male and female. It is not something I chose. I feel like I was drawn to it much like a moth to a flame. However, today I no longer let my genitalia define my gender, I live two lives and celebrate each of them. As a woman, I am active in the community and in a church. By being happy and proud of who I am, I have experienced acceptance and success in almost everything I attempt. In turn it has brought peace to my male personae, too. Slowly my "secret" has been discovered by many people around me. Although I wouldn't go so far to say that it has been fully embraced and accepted, most of my friends and co-workers have respected my life choices and supported me.

Unlike most of my generation who lived their lives in hiding plagued with shame and guilt, today I meet many young transmen and transwomen who put an emphasis on their personal happiness and fulfillment. For the last several years I have been active on a speaker's bureau. I travel to various schools and universities and discuss my personal experiences and various trans-issues. I do this in hopes of making the path to acceptance for tomorrow's transyouth more manageable than it was for me growing up.

SOURCE: Author's files

A true transvestite is almost always a heterosexual male (Docter, 1988; Wheeler et al., 2008), although perhaps this is because cross-dressing for women is much more acceptable in our society. For example, in the United States, women often wear traditionally male clothing such as pants, suits, or ties, and they are free to wear pink, blue, or whatever colors they choose.

Transvestites differ from transsexuals in that they do not desire to change their biological gender. Their differences also seem to begin early in life; one study found that transsexuals, but not transvestites, lacked interest in playing with other boys while young, and transvestites, but not transsexuals, cross-dressed very early in life (Bullough et al., 1983). A small number of transvestites will go to great lengths to feminize their appearance, employing electrolysis (hair removal), taking hormones, or even getting

surgical implants to simulate female breasts. However, even most of these transvestites would stop at sex reassignment surgery because they enjoy heterosexual intercourse and being men.

Many theorists believe that transvestism evolves from an early childhood experience, such as a male masturbating with or in some item of female clothing (Stayton, 1996; Wheeler et al., 2008). Some transvestites report childhood experiences of being punished or humiliated by women and being forced to dress as a woman (Maxmen & Ward, 1995). This behavior soon develops into a sexual experience with the male getting physically aroused while holding, touching, or wearing the item of clothing.

Some transvestites then move beyond the sexual arousal and begin to feel less anxious and stressed when around the particular item of clothing (Wheeler et al., 2008). Cross-dressing may allow these men to relax, freed from the societal pressures of being male. Most transvestites began cross-dressing at a very young age and began masturbating while wearing women's clothing during adolescence and these behaviors continue to grow into a paraphilia in adulthood (Dzelme & Jones, 2001; Wheeler et al., 2008). Many transvestites are secretive about their habits, fearing that others will censure or ridicule them. Many have private collections of female clothes, and married transvestites may even hide their habit from their wives, although the majority do tell (Newring et al., 2008).

It's not uncommon for transvestites to marry and raise families, and the majority of partners of transvestites know about the cross-dressing behavior and are accepting of it (A. L. Reynolds & Caron, 2005). Most had learned of their partner's habit early in the relationship and tolerated or even supported it to some degree, although some expressed resentment and fear of public exposure (Newring et al., 2008). However, the majority characterized their marriage as happy and described their husbands as loving and good fathers. Some women married to transvestites fully support their husband's feminine identity, seeing "her" as a separate partner and friend from "him." In some families, the male's transvestism is completely open, and the children know about it (M. P. Allen, 1989).

Transvestism is usually harmless, and most transvestites are not anxious to seek out therapy to stop their behavior (Newring et al., 2008). Many times treatment is sought only when a transvestite's partner is upset or the cross-dressing causes stress in the relationship (Dzelme & Jones, 2001). Many female partners of male transvestites do not understand his need to dress in women's

---

---

clothing (Dzelme & Jones, 2001; Newring et al., 2008), even though they are accepting of the behavior. In any case, transvestism is usually so firmly fixed in a man's personality that eradication is neither possible nor desirable. The goal of therapy is to cope with the anxieties and guilt of the transvestite and the way he relates interpersonally and sexually with his partner and family (Newring et al., 2008). Transvestite support groups have been organized in cities all over the country and may offer a good support system for these men (Newring et al., 2008).

SADISM
AND MASOCHISM

Sadism refers to the intentional infliction of physical or psychological pain on another person to achieve sexual excitement. The *DSM-IV-TR* describes sadism as a condition in which a person has sexual fantasies, urges, or behaviors that involve an infliction of pain, suffering, or humiliation to enhance or achieve sexual

excitement (Yates et al., 2008). Sadistic fantasies or acts may include restraint, blindfolding, strangulation, spanking, whipping, pinching, beating, burning, and electrical shocks (Kleinplatz & Moser, 2006).

The term sadism is derived from a man named Donatien Alphonse François de Sade (1740–1814), known as the Marquis de Sade. De Sade was sent to prison for kidnapping and terrorizing a beggar girl and then later for tricking some prostitutes into eating "Spanish fly," supposedly an aphrodisiac, but which caused such burning and blistering that one threw herself out a window (see Chapter 14 for more information about Spanish fly and other aphrodisiacs). While in prison, de Sade wrote novels describing such tortures as being bound hand and foot, suspended between trees, set upon by dogs, almost being eviscerated (cut open), and so on. De Sade believed that the highest form of sexual activity for women was pain, not pleasure, because pleasure could be too easily faked. Marquis De Sade spent much of his life in prison and died in a lunatic asylum (Bullough, 1976).

Masochism (MASS-oh-kiz-um), the achievement of sexual pleasure through one's own physical pain or psychological humiliation, was named after another novelist, Leopold Baron Von Sacher-Masoch (1836–1895). Sacher-Masoch believed that women were created to subdue men's "animal passions," and he describes the whippings he himself experienced at the hands of his mistresses (Bullough, 1976). Masochism involves the act of being humiliated, beaten, bound, or made to suffer (American Psychiatric Association, 2000).

Sadism and masochism both associate sexuality and pain, and most people who practice one are also involved with the other. Therefore, the phenomenon as a whole is often referred to as **sadomasochism** (say-doe-MASS-oh-kiz-um), or S&M. The acronym BDSM—bondage, discipline, sadism, and masochism—is commonly used today because it illustrates the diverse range of possible experiences (Kleinplatz & Moser, 2006; Wiseman, 2000). Some individuals may only participate in one aspect of BDSM, whereas others may engage in a variety of BDSM practices (Kleinplatz & Moser, 2006; Wiseman, 2000).

Because BDSM encompasses a wide variety of behaviors, the number of people who engage in it depends on how one defines it. Kinsey and his colleagues (1953) found that 3% to 12% of women and 10% to 20% of men reported getting sexually aroused to S&M narratives. However, because many couples may not feel comfortable sharing information about these behaviors, researchers today believe that BDSM is much more prevalent than studies indicate (Chancer, 2006; Kleinplatz & Moser, 2006; Yates et al., 2008).

sadism
Focus on administering pain and humiliation as the preferred or exclusive method of sexual arousal and orgasm.

masochism
Focus on receiving pain and humiliation as the preferred or exclusive method of sexual arousal and orgasm.

sadomasochism
The sexual activities of partners in which one takes a dominant, "master," position, and the other takes a submissive, "slave," position.

Freud and his followers made sadomasochism central to their theories about adult sexuality. Freud believed that to some degree we all feel ambivalent about the ones we love and even, at times, feel the desire to hurt them. However, we also feel guilty about it, especially in early childhood, and the guilt we feel is satisfied by turning that hurt on ourselves. Later psychoanalytic theorists believed that the goal of masochism was not pain or punishment itself but rather relinquishing the self to someone else to avoid responsibility or anxiety for sexual desires.

Sexual responses to pain exist, to some degree, in many sexual relationships. Kinsey and his colleagues (1953), for example, found that about half the men and women in his sample experienced erotic response to sexual biting, and 24% of men and 12% of women had some erotic response to sadomasochistic stories. Another study found that 25% of men and women reported occasionally engaging in sadomasochistic behavior (L. Rubin, 1990). For example, some couples use bondage as a variation on their lovemaking without any other strong sadomasochistic elements (Comfort, 1987).

Bondage and restraint are the most common expressions of BDSM.

The paraphiliac sadomasochist takes these natural tendencies to an extreme. S&M involves the use of physical pain, psychological humiliation, or both as part of sexuality. In most S&M encounters, one partner plays the **dominant** role ("master") and the other the **submissive** ("slave"). Female dominants are often referred to as *Mistress,* and male dominants are referred to as *Master* or *Lord.* Oftentimes, a submissive will wear a collar, made of leather or chain, to signify submission to a dominant (Cross & Matheson, 2006; Wiseman, 2000).

Overall, bondage and restraint are the most common expressions of BDSM, although spanking and exposure to urine and feces may also be involved (Seligman & Hardenburg, 2000). However, it is power, rather than pain, that is the most important aspect of BDSM behaviors (Cross & Matheson, 2006).

A variety of techniques are commonly used to physically dominate the submissive partner. Tying the submissive partner up or using restraints to render him or her helpless is often referred to as B&D (for bondage and discipline). B&D is often accompanied by **flagellation, caning, birching,** or other painful or shocking stimuli on the skin such as the use of hot wax, ice, or biting (Wiseman, 2000). Psychological techniques can include sensory deprivation (through the use of face masks, blindfolds, earplugs), humiliation (being subject to verbal abuse or being made to engage in embarrassing behaviors such as boot-licking, **scatophagic** [scat-oh-FAJ-ick] behavior, **urolagnia** [yur-oh-LOG-nee-uh], or acting like a dog), forced cross-dressing, or **infantilism** (American Psychiatric Association, 2000; Moser, 1988). This is accompanied by verbal descriptions of what is to come and why the person deserves it, increasing in intensity over time to eventual sexual climax. Note that the pain is used as part of a technique to enhance sexuality—the pain itself is not exciting. If the submissive partner slammed his hand in the car door on his way home from a sexual encounter, he would not find the resultant pain in any way sexually arousing.

People can participate in BDSM to different degrees. For some couples, BDSM is an occasional diversion in their lovemaking. Others pursue it outside of a committed relationship; for example, most big cities have newspapers with advertisements for sadomasochistic services, in which a **dominatrix** will offer her services to submissive men. For these men, the opportunity to absolve themselves of decision making and put their sexual lives completely in the hands of a dominant woman is exciting.

A sadomasochistic subculture exists for those who have adopted BDSM as a lifestyle (see the chapter opener in Chapter 10). Partners meet in BDSM clubs, read BDSM newsletters and magazines, and join organizations (such as the Eulenspiegel Society, the Society of Janus, or the lesbian S&M group SAMOIS). Specialty shops cater to BDSM advocates, selling restraints, whips, leather clothing, and other items. The sadomasochistic encounter, which is really a kind of drama or performance, is enhanced by both sides knowing their roles and dressing the part.

Much of BDSM is about playing roles, usually with appropriate attitude, costuming, and scripted talk (Hoff, 2003). The BDSM encounter is carefully planned, and the dominant partner is usually very careful not to actually hurt the submissive partner while "torturing" him or her. A "safe word" is usually agreed on so that the submissive partner can signal if he or she is in real distress (Wiseman, 2000). The *Master's and Mistress' Handbook,* a guide to S&M encounters, offers a set of rules on how to torture one's partner without really causing harm:

Remember that a slave may suddenly start to cough or feel faint. If masked and gagged, choking or lack of oxygen may result in se-

© Peter Marlow/Magnum Photos

Sadomasochists often use props, like leather clothes, studs, chains, and nipple clamps.

dominant
Describes the active role in sadomasochistic sexuality.

submissive
Describes the passive role in sadomasochistic activity.

flagellation
Striking a partner, usually by whipping.

caning
Beating someone with a rigid cane.

birching
Whipping someone using the stripped branch of a tree.

scatophagia
The ingestion of feces, often as a sign of submission.

urolagnia
The ingestion of urine, often as a sign of submission.

infantilism
Treating the submissive partner as a baby, including dressing the person in diapers in which he or she is forced to relieve himself or herself.

dominatrix
A professional dominant woman who charges money to engage in bondage and discipline fantasy play with submissive clients.

A dominatrix is paid by submissive clients to engage in bondage and discipline fantasy play.

rious consequences within seconds.... Never leave a bound and gagged slave alone in a room.... It is essential that gags, nostril tubes, enema pipes, rods and other insertions should be scrupulously clean and dipped into mild antiseptic before use.... Never use cheap or coarse rope. This has no "give" and can quickly cause skin-sores. (Quoted in Gosselin, 1987, pp. 238–239)

Sadomasochistic subcultures exist among gays, lesbians, and heterosexuals (Sandnabba et al., 2002; Nordling et al., 2006). In heterosexual BDSM, power relations between the sexes may be overturned, with the female being the dominant partner and the male submissive. The sadomasochistic drama is used to explore the nature of social relations by using sex as a means to explore power (Truscott, 1991). Gay men who engage in BDSM have been found to prefer the use of leather, dildos, and wrestling, whereas heterosexual men tend to prefer humiliation, masks, gags, and straight jackets (Nordling et al., 2006). Both heterosexual and homosexual BDSM practitioners derive sexual excitement from playing with power relations, from either being able to dominate another completely or to give in completely to another's will.

The BDSM subculture takes symbols of authority and dominance from the general culture, such as whips, uniforms, and handcuffs, and uses them in a safe erotic drama in which scripted roles take the place of "real self." It even mocks these symbols of authority by using them for erotic pleasure. Well-known social psychologist R. F. Baumeister (1988) suggests that sadomasochism is a reaction to modern society itself. Noting that sexual masochism proliferated when Western culture became highly individualistic, Baumeister suggests that it relieves the submissive partner of a sense of responsibility for the self by placing one's behavior completely under someone else's control (which may be why many businessmen pay a dominatrix to humiliate them).

Overall, men and women who engage in BDSM behaviors have been found to be well adjusted and well educated (Allison et al., 2001; Kleinplatz & Moser, 2006; Santilla et al., 2000). However, some studies have found that many females who engage in BDSM have a history of sexual abuse (Nordling et al., 2000).

EXHIBITIONISM AND VOYEURISM

Visual stimuli are basic aspects of sexuality; most sexually active people enjoy looking at the nude bodies of their partners, and such things as lingerie and the act of undressing one's partner can enhance the sexual nature of the human form. The enormous industry of adult magazines and books, the almost obligatory nude scene in modern movies, the embarrassment most people feel when seen naked inappropriately, and even the common nighttime dream of being caught naked in public all show the fundamental psychological power of visual sexual stimuli.

For some people, looking at nudity or sexual acts, or being seen naked or engaging in sex, become the paramount activities of sexuality. The person who becomes sexually aroused primarily from displaying his (or, more rarely, her) genitals, nudity, or sexuality to strangers is an **exhibitionist;** the person whose primary mode of sexual stimulation is to watch others naked or engaging in sex is called a **voyeur.** Langevin and Lang (1987) reviewed a number of studies that show that there is a close connection between exhibitionism and voyeurism; most exhibitionists engaged in voyeuristic habits before beginning to expose themselves.

Exhibitionism

Exhibitionism involves exposing the genitals to a stranger (American Psychiatric Association, 2000). As such, this behavior is nonconsensual. The exhibitionist (or "flasher"), who is usually male, achieves sexual gratification from exposing his genitals in public or to unsuspecting people, who are usually female (Murphy & Page, 2008). What excites the exhibitionist is not usually the nu-

REALResearch > One study found that sadists and masochists have been found to have unique personality styles that contribute to their behaviors. Sadists are more likely to have aggressive personality styles, whereas masochists are more likely to experience self-image problems (RASMUSSEN, 2005).

dity itself but the lack of consent of the victim as expressed in her shocked or fearful reaction. True exhibitionists would not get the same sexual charge being naked on a nude beach, for example, where everyone is naked.

exhibitionist
A person who exposes his or her genitals to strangers as a preferred or exclusive means of sexual arousal and orgasm.

voyeur
One who observes people undressing or engaging in sex acts without their consent as a preferred or exclusive means of sexual arousal and orgasm.

Exhibitionists usually have erections while exposing themselves, and they masturbate either then and there or later, while thinking about the reactions of their victims. Usually exhibitionism begins in the teen years and decreases as a man ages; however, it may worsen in times of stress or disappointment (American Psychiatric Association, 2000; Murphy & Page, 2008; Seligman & Hardenburg, 2000).

Exhibitionism is legally classified as "indecent exposure" and accounts for up to one third of all sex convictions in the United States, Canada, and Europe (Bogaerts et al., 2006; Langevin & Lang, 1987; Murphy & Page, 2008). However, it's important to keep in mind that exhibitionists have a witness to their crimes, unlike some of the other paraphilias (such as voyeurism). As such, there is a higher likelihood of being caught. Research has failed to confirm any personality characteristics that might be common to exhibitionists except that the behavior is compulsive and very difficult to stop (Rabinowitz et al., 2002). Many exhibitionists have normal dating and sexual histories, are married or in committed partnerships and have normal sexual relations with their spouses or partners (Langevin & Lang, 1987). The majority of exhibitionists are shy and withdrawn, and many have been found to have borderline or avoidant personality disorders (or both; Bogaerts et al., 2008; Murphy & Page, 2008). Although we don't know exactly how many exhibitionists there are, we do know that many women are "flashed"—in fact, 40% to 60% of female college students report having been exposed to (Murphy & Page, 2008).

Exhibitionism in women is rare, although cases of it are reported in the literature (Grob, 1985; Rhoads & Boekelheide, 1985). Rhoads and Boekelheide (1985) suggest that the female exhibitionist may desire to feel feminine and appreciated, and seeing men admire her naked body reinforces her sense of sexual value and femininity. Perhaps, then, exhibitionism in women just takes a different form than in men. Another factor may be that women have much more opportunity to expose their bodies in social settings without being arrested. Exposing breast (and even buttock) cleavage is often acceptable by today's fashion standards.

*Exhibitionism **in women** is rare.*

Although female exhibitionism is rare, it is interesting how much more acceptable it is for a woman to expose her body in U.S. society. Few people would complain about this woman exposing her breasts in public.

Women, therefore, have more legitimate ways to expose their bodies than men do. This type of exposure may be enough for female exhibitionists.

Obscene Telephone Callers

The exhibitionist must have the courage to confront his victims in person; the telephone allows a more anonymous kind of contact for the timid paraphiliac. **Scatolophilia** (scat-oh-low-FILL-ee-uh), the technical name for obscene telephone calling, is a form of exhibitionism in which a person, almost always male, calls women and becomes excited as the victims react to his obscene suggestions. Most scatolophiliacs masturbate either during the call or afterward. Like exhibitionism, scatophilia is nonconsensual, and the scatolophiliac becomes excited by the victim's reactions of fear, disgust, or outrage.

Most scatolophiliacs have problems in their relationships and suffer from feelings of isolation and inadequacy. For many, scatolophilia is the only way they can express themselves sexually (Holmes, 1991). Scatolophiliacs often have coexisting paraphilias, such as exhibitionism or voyeurism (M. Price et al., 2002).

The obscene telephone caller may boast of sexual acts he will perform on the victim, may describe his masturbation in detail, may threaten the victim, or may try to entice the victim to reveal aspects of her sexual life or even perform sexual acts such as masturbating while he listens on the phone. Some callers are very persuasive; many have great success in talking women into performing sexual acts while posing as product representatives recalling certain products, as the police, or even as people conducting a sexual survey (please note: no reputable sexuality researchers conduct surveys over the phone. If you receive such a call, do not answer any sexually explicit questions.). Others threaten harm to the victim or her family if she does not do what he asks (obscene callers often know the victim's address, if only from the phone book). Some will get a woman's phone number while observing her writing a check at a place like the supermarket and then will frighten her more because he knows her address, appearance, and even some of her food preferences (Matek, 1988; see the accompanying Sex in Real Life, "Reactions to an Obscene Telephone Caller").

WHAT DO YOU WANT TO KNOW?

What should I do if I receive an obscene telephone call?
You should react calmly and not exhibit the reactions of shock, fright, or disgust that the caller finds exciting. Do not slam the phone down; simply replace it gently in the cradle. An immediate ring again is probably a callback; ignore it, or pick up the phone and hang up quickly without listening. Sometimes a gentle suggestion that the person needs psychological help disrupts the caller's fantasy. Persistent callers can be discouraged by suggesting that you have contacted the police. If you do get more than one call, notify the telephone company. Caller ID has been helpful in reducing the rates of obscene phone calls.

scatolophilia
Sexual arousal from making obscene telephone calls.

Reactions to an Obscene Telephone Caller

I was very scared, because I didn't know who this person was, whether he was hiding in the bushes...

Obscene telephone callers become sexually aroused as their victims respond to their obscene suggestions. Below is a personal account from a 28-year-old woman who tells about her experiences with an obscene telephone caller when she was sharing a home with two roommates.

One day I noticed several very explicit and perverted messages on my phone machine. The guy who left them knew my name and said he was watching me, following all my moves, and had seen me taking a shower before. The whole time he kept breathing heavily. I was very scared, because I didn't know who this person was, whether he was hiding in the bushes, or how he could know who I was.

His calls became more frequent and persisted for months. Each time he called he was very disgusting—saying things about pussy, vagina, breasts, nipples, wanting to fuck me. He described what he thought it would be like to have sex with me—in fact, he also threatened to rape me. It was really disgusting. I was so scared and would cry all the time. I felt as if he were everywhere, because I didn't know who he was. The police told me to be careful about where I went and whom I talked to.

He called at all different times of the day. He'd tell me what I had worn on particular days and knew what I looked like. I felt his closeness. . . . I felt as though I was a threat to the safety of my roommates, who were frightened as well. My Dad brought over a shotgun and slept in the house one night. Actually that

was the night that this guy told me he was going to come over and rape me.

The phone company eventually traced the incoming calls to a specific phone number. It turned out the calls were coming from a home number and one of the kids living at the home was making the calls. He was about 19 and the grocery clerk at the store that I shopped at. Every time I went there and checked out, he saw what I was wearing and also took all of the information off my checks.

The arrest was made. He admitted to harassing about six other women over the phone. The charges that were filed against him were called harassment by communication. We began the trial, and although it was hard to go over everything that happened again, I felt that everyone I interacted with respected and believed in me, which made me feel stronger.

In the end, the guy was found guilty, sentenced to community service, had to go to therapy two to three times a week, and pay a fine of $500. One month later, he started calling again. I couldn't believe it! I called the police, and he was picked up and thrown in jail again.

In thinking about this now, I just wish that I hadn't waited so long to call the police the first time. I endured a whole month of his calls before I called the police. This guy's phone calls totally took away the trust and compassion I had for other people.

SOURCE: Author's files.

Voyeurism

Voyeurs, or those who engage in **scopophilia,** are people whose main means of sexual gratification is watching unsuspecting persons undressing, naked, or engaging in sexual activity. Some would argue that we are a voyeuristic society; our major media—newspapers, television, movies, advertisements—are full of sexual images that are intended to interest and arouse us. Magazines and movies featuring nude women or couples are popular. Even television shows display far more nudity and sexuality than would have been allowed just a few years ago. In modern society, it seems, we have all become casual voyeurs to some degree.

Clinical voyeurs, however, are those for whom watching others naked or viewing erotica is a compulsion. Voyeurs are often called "Peeping Toms," a revealing term because implicit in it are two important aspects of voyeurism. First, a "peeper" is one who looks without the knowledge or consent of the person being viewed, and true voyeurs are excited by the illicit aspect of their peeping. Second, the voyeur is usually male. Although it is becoming more acceptable for women in society to read magazines such as *Playgirl,* which show nude men, or to spend an evening watching male strippers such as the Chippendales, clinically speaking there are very few "Peeping Janes" (Lavin, 2008).

The typical voyeur is a heterosexual male who begins his voyeuristic behaviors before age 15 (Lavin, 2008; Seligman & Hardenburg, 2000). **Primary voyeurism** is apparently rare. More often, voyeurism is mixed in with a host of other paraphiliac behaviors (Langevin & Lang, 1987; Lavin, 2008). Still, voyeurs are generally harmless and are satisfied just with peeping, although they certainly can scare an unsuspecting person who sees a strange man peering in the window. In a few cases, however, voyeurism can lead to more and more intrusive sexual activity, including rape (Holmes, 1991). Voyeurs, when caught, are usually not charged with a sex crime but with trespassing or sometimes breaking and entering (Lavin, 2008). Therefore, how many actually get in trouble with the law is difficult to determine.

Many voyeurs satisfy some of their urges by renting pornographic videos or going to live sex shows. For most voyeurs, however, these are ultimately unsatisfying, for part of the excitement is the knowledge that the victim does not know or approve of the

scopophilia
The psychoanalytic term for voyeurism, literally "the love of looking."

primary voyeurism
Voyeurism as the main and exclusive paraphilia.

fact that the voyeur sees them. Like exhibitionists, voyeurs tend to be immature, sexually frustrated, poor at developing relationships, and chronic masturbators (Lavin, 2008). Some voyeurs have turned to voyeuristic webcam sites that capture unsuspecting sexual activity and broadcast it live over the Internet (M. D. Griffiths, 2000).

Although it technically refers to a single couple copulating in front of others, **troilism** (TROY-ill-iz-um) has come to mean any sex sessions involving multiple partners. Troilism is not new; in 1631, Mervyn Touchet, the Second Earl of Castlehaven, was executed in England for ordering his servants to have sex with his wife while he watched. The fact that they were servants and thus

troilism
Any sex sessions involving multiple partners, typically witnessed by others.

SEX IN REAL LIFE

Pedophilia: An Autobiography

I believe that I was born a pedophile because I have had feelings of sexual attraction toward children and love for them as long as I can remember.

Many people don't understand what would motivate a pedophile to want to have intimate relationships with young children. Below is a personal account from Dr. Silva (not his real name), a physician incarcerated for having sex with a minor.

I believe that I was born a pedophile because I have had feelings of sexual attraction toward children and love for them as long as I can remember. I was not traumatized into this age orientation nor, certainly, did I ever make a conscious decision to be attracted in this way. Just as homosexuals and heterosexuals discover their sexual orientation, I discovered my age orientation as I grew, and I have been aware of it from a young age.

My developing experience with sex was occurring when I was 14 and 15 years old, and it was during this time that we in my peer group were befriended by a neighborhood man, about 25, who was known to "like boys." He drove us around and treated us to snacks and movies. At times, we went to his apartment, in pairs or as a group, where he took us individually into his bedroom to fellate us. I once spent the night with him. His mother and sister, with whom he lived, barely reacted to my presence there in the morning, as if it were not unusual for him to appear in the morning with a boy. While I enjoyed the oral sex he performed on me, the overall experience was unfulfilling. I was disappointed that he did not feel the emotional bond for me that I expected after such an intimate encounter. I felt satisfied physically but used. Subsequent experiences with him became acceptable once I adjusted my expectations and sought only sexual gratification.

In my second semester in medical school, I befriended Peter, a fellow medical student whose family lived in a nearby town. He invited me to meet his family and see the town. I will never forget the first time I met his brother Allen, who was 11 or 12 at the time. I loved the whole family, but what I felt for Allen was stronger than anything I had ever known before. During one of the earliest [visits to Peter's family], I had the opportunity to share a single bed with Allen. In future encounters he was wide awake and actively participated in our sexual relationship, which went on during the next two years and even later when I returned to visit. My relationship with him was the first true pedophilic/pedosexual relationship. After our sexual activity ceased, we maintained a close friendship that endures to this day.

In my fourth semester at medical school, I moved into a boarding house. Other students lived there with the host family, which consisted of a mother and three sons, ages 11, 12, and 13; the boys certainly were a factor in my choice. Thirteen-year-old John

showed much interest in me. We became excited, and it was not long before we had our clothes off and began fondling each other. By now it was clear to me that I loved children, especially boys, and was happiest when I was in their company. What I took pleasure in most was seeing them happy and developing healthy in mind and body. So, I encouraged their interests if I felt these interests were healthy, or I exposed them to experiences that I thought would contribute to their educational or cultural edification.

It was in this period that I became friends with Eric, just about to turn 9, whose family recently had moved onto our street. I had been dating Cathy [at the time], a foreign-born peer female who lived in my city and worked near our house. I enjoyed a good relationship, sexual and otherwise, with Cathy for about six months. Before we broke up, my relationship with Eric had become sexual and more pleasing than that with Cathy, and also she and I had been growing apart emotionally. I began to feel that I was maintaining our relationship for the sake of appearances and that young males were my true love—especially Eric.

Eric and I had become increasingly close. What made our relationship so beautiful and precious was the way in which it developed so gradually and so naturally. Most of the time, he just came over to my house and lay down with me for a few moments. One special time was a morning that he was on his way to school. He climbed into my room through my window, as he frequently did, removed his book bag, and lay down next to me. We embraced for a few moments until we were satisfied, and it was time for him to get to school. Not a word was spoken; all of our communication was physical on that occasion. Clearly, it was not sex that attracted me to him but, rather, our great emotional bond, which made sex so gratifying. Sex was a small but incredibly beautiful part of our relationship. The vast majority of the time we engaged in many other recreational and constructive activities.

The demise of our relationship began when his mother suspected some friends of mine were using marijuana in his presence. Eric was told we could no longer be friends. The next time I came over, she told me he did not want to see me anymore. Not long afterward, he moved out of the country with his family. It still hurts me to think about him, and I do not think I will ever fully recover.

SOURCE: From *Pedophilia: Biosocial Dimensions* by Donald C. Silva, 1990. With kind permission of Springer Science+Business Media.

beneath his station was as damaging to him as the actual act (Bullough, 1976).

Troilism may involve aspects of voyeurism, exhibitionism, and, sometimes, latent homosexual desires; an observer who gets excited, for example, by watching his wife fellate another man may be subconsciously putting himself in his wife's place. Some

---

REALResearch   > In 2000, police arrested more than **100** people in more than 21 countries for possession of over **750,000** images of child pornography, including children as young as **18** months old (O'GRADY, 2001).

---

troilists install ceiling mirrors, video cameras, and other means to capture the sexual act for viewing later on. Others engage in sharing a sexual partner with a third party while they look on, or they engage in swinging (see Chapter 9). Many couples experiment with group sex, but to the troilist, engaging in or fantasizing about such sexual activity is the primary means of sexual arousal.

PEDOPHILIA

Pedophilia (pee-doh-FILL-ee-uh; meaning "love of children") has been called many things throughout history: child-love, cross-generational sex, man/child (or adult/child) interaction, boy-love, pederasty, and Greek love (Bullough, 1990). The variety of terms shows how differently adult–child sexual interactions have been viewed in different periods of history. In Chapter 17, we discuss child sexual abuse and incest, whereas here we concentrate our attention on pedophilia.

Pedophilia is one of the most common paraphilias and is most likely to be seen in treatment due to its harmful and illegal nature (O'Grady, 2001). Pedophiles are often 16 years old or older and at least 5 years older than their victims (American Psychiatric Association, 2000). However, even though many people consider sexual contact between adults and children to be one of the most objectionable of crimes today, in many periods of history and in different cultures today, various types of child–adult sexual contact have been seen as acceptable (see Chapter 1 for more information about Greek pederasty, or Chapter 11 for more information on the Sambian culture). Even so, pedophilia is illegal in every country in the world (O'Grady, 2001).

What exactly constitutes such contact in a society may be unclear. For example, as recently as the 1980s, a girl in the state of New Mexico could get married at age 13. If a 30-year-old man marries a 13-year-old girl and has legal, consensual marital intercourse with her, is it pedophilia? What if they have consensual sex but are not married? Why should a piece of paper—a marriage certificate—make a difference in our definition?

Throughout most of history, a girl was considered ready for marriage and an adult sexual relationship as soon as she "came of age," that is, at menarche. It was common for much older men to be betrothed to very young women, and such marriages were seen as proper. For example, Saint Augustine decided to get married to try to curb his sexual promiscuity, and so he was betrothed to a

prepubertal girl. Although intercourse was not permitted until she reached puberty, such early marriages were apparently common (Bullough, 1990). In England in the 18th to 19th centuries, 12 years was considered the age of consent. In the 18th century as well, adult–child sex (especially same-sex pairings) were accepted in China, Japan, parts of Africa, Turkey, Arabia, Egypt, and the Islamic areas of India (Ames & Houston, 1990).

To some degree or another, then, what legally constitutes pedophilia is a matter of the laws in different societies. Yet, clinically speaking, pedophilia refers to sexual activity with a prepubescent child (under age 13). Many times these behaviors are also referred to as child sexual abuse. Attraction to postpubertal boys and girls is called **ephebephilia** (ef-fee-be-FILL-ee-uh), but it is not usually considered pathological. In fact, it has been shown that heterosexual males in almost all cultures are attracted to younger females, and homosexual males are attracted to younger or younger appearing males (O'Grady, 2001).

Pedophiles often report an attraction to children of a particular age range, most often 8 to 10 year olds in those attracted to girls, and slightly older in those attracted to boys (attraction to prepubescent girls is more common; Murray, 2000). Some pedophiles are unable to function sexually with an adult, whereas others also maintain adult sexual relationships (Seligman & Hardenburg, 2000). Many pedophiles believe that pedophilia will become more socially acceptable over time, much like homosexuality did (O'Grady, 2001).

Pedophiliac behavior is often obsessive (O'Grady, 2001). Pedophiles are usually obsessed with their fantasies, and these fantasies tend to dominate their lives. They are also predators—they know which child they like, and they work hard to get the trust and support from the parents or caretakers first. Pedophiles are good at winning the trust of parents. In fact, parents often trust the pedophile so much that they often take the pedophile's word over their own child's (O'Grady, 2001).

Many pedophiles threaten their victims and tell them they must keep their sexual activity secret. One therapist tells of a patient who had been repeatedly threatened by her assailant:

> as a young teen, she and a friend were raped repeatedly by a friend of their parents. It went on for years. He would rape the girls in front of each other and threatened the lives of both of them if they told. They didn't. They were both afraid of him and convinced they wouldn't be believed anyway, given his high standing in the community and his friendship with their parents. There is a song she still hates, she tells me, because he used to sing it as he undressed them. (Salter, 2003, p. 13)

In the United States, an adult who has sexual contact with a boy or girl under the age of consent (see Table 17.1 for more in-

pedophilia
Sex with children as a preferred or exclusive mode of sexual interaction in an adult; child molestation. People who engage in this behavior are called pedophiles, or sexual offenders.

ephebephilia
Attraction to children who have just passed puberty; also called hebephilia.

formation about the age of consent) to whom he or she is not married is guilty of child sexual abuse. A child sexual abuser may or may not be a pedophile; a person may sexually abuse a child because an adult is not available, because children are easier to seduce than adults, out of anger, or because of other sexual, psychological, or familial problems.

Girls are twice as likely as boys to be victims of pedophiliac behavior (Murray, 2000). In one study, 44% of pedophiles chose only girls, 33% chose only boys, and 23% abused both boys and girls (Murray, 2000). Boys are less likely to reject sexual advances and to report their sexual advances to authorities than girls (Brongersma, 1990). This may be the reason that violence is less common in sexual contact between men and boys than between men and girls.

Some pedophiles only look at children and never touch, whereas others engage in a variety of sexual acts with their victims, with the most common behavior being fondling and exhibitionism, rather than penetration (Murray, 2000). As we discussed earlier, pedophiles often have a lack of empathy and believe that their behavior does not cause any negative psychological or physical consequences for their victims (Miranda & Fiorello, 2002).

Unfortunately, some pedophiles, realizing the chance of the child reporting the act, kill their victims. After one such murder of a young New Jersey girl named Megan Kanka in July 1994, her parents spearheaded "Megan's Law," which was signed into state law in October 1994. This law made it mandatory for authorities in New Jersey to tell parents when a convicted child molester moved into the neighborhood and increased penalties for child molesters. In 1996, Megan's Law became federal law. See the Sex in Real Life feature on page 453 for more information.

Female pedophiles also exist, although they often abuse children in concert with another person, usually their male partner. They may act to please their adult sexual partners rather than to satisfy their own pedophilic desires. Although less common, female pedophiles have been found to have a higher incidence of psychiatric disorders than male pedophiles (Chow & Choy, 2002).

A number of small organizations in Western countries, usually made up of pedophiles and ephebephiles, argue that man–boy love should be legalized, usually under the pretense of guarding "the sexual rights of children and adolescents" (Okami, 1990). In America, the North American Man–Boy Love Association (NAMBLA) supports the abolition of age-of-consent laws. NAMBLA believes that there is a difference between those who simply want to use children for sexual release and those who develop long-lasting, often exclusive, and even loving relationships with a single boy. Suppe (1984) agrees that pederasty among postpubescent boys need not necessarily be harmful (which is not to deny that it often may be). On the other hand, those who work with sexually abused children vehemently deny the claim, pointing to children whose lives were ruined by sex with adults.

Several factors may go into pedophilic behavior (Murray, 2000). Pedophiles have been described as having had arrested psychological development, which makes them childlike with childish emotional needs. They may also have low self-esteem and poor social relations with adults, may be trying to overcome their own humiliations and pains from their childhood, or may exaggerate the social male role of dominance and power over a weaker sexual partner. Conditions such as alcoholism may lessen the barriers to having sex with children. In one study, pedophiles were asked why they engaged in sex with children. The most common response was that the children didn't fight it, followed by a lack of sexual outlets with adults, intoxication, and victim-initiation of sexual behavior (Pollack & Hashmall, 1991).

Over the years, research has found that being a victim of sexual abuse in childhood is one of the most frequently reported risk factors for becoming a pedophile (Glasser et al., 2001; Langstrom et al., 2000; Seto, 2004). It is estimated that 35% of pedophiles were sexually abused as children (Keegan, 2001). Studies have also found that the choice of gender and age of victims often reflects the pattern of past sexual abuse in the pedophile's life (Pollock & Hashmall, 1991). Although past sexual abuse is a risk factor, it's important to point out that the majority of male victims of child sexual abuse do not become pedophiles (Salter et al., 2003). Pedophiles have high **recidivism** (re-SID-iv-iz-um) rates, and for some unknown reason, these rates are higher in homosexual men

---

REALResearch > Undercover investigations on the Internet, in which police officers pose as underage youth, account for **25%** of all arrests for Internet sex crimes against minors (MITCHELL ET AL., 2005).

(Murray, 2000). The recidivism rate is the main impetus for legislation such as Megan's Law (M. A. Alexander, 1999).

The Internet has been a two-edged sword when it comes to pedophilia. On one hand, it has helped pedophiles find each other

Many media images sexualize children and associate sexuality with youth. These media images may encourage pedophiliac fantasies.

recidivism
A tendency to repeat crimes, such as sexual offenses.

and talk about their behaviors. This can validate their behaviors because they are no longer feeling isolated, as though they are the only person who engages in child sex behaviors. Pedophiles are also able to gather information and can actually share images with each other (O'Grady, 2001). On the other hand, the Internet has also become a powerful tool to combat pedophilia, both in the online reporting of sex offenders and the ability of law officials to go undercover and seek out pedophiles online (Trivits & Reppucci, 2002; see the nearby Real Research).

Women-only passenger cars are subway and railway cars which do not allow male passengers. Problems with groping and frotteurism on public transportation has led to the establishment of women-only passenger cars in places such as Tokyo, Japan and Seoul, South Korea.

OTHER PARAPHILIAS

People can be sexually attracted to almost anything. An article in the *Journal of Forensic Sciences* tells of a man who was erotically attracted to his tractor; he wrote poetry to it, he had a pet name for it, and his body was found after he was asphyxiated by suspending himself by the ankles from the tractor's shovel to masturbate (O'Halloran & Dietz, 1993). However, there are a number of other paraphilias that are relatively more common, although all are rare, and we now review a sample of them.

Frotteurism

Frotteurism (frah-TOUR-iz-um) involves a man rubbing his genitals against a woman's thighs or buttocks in a crowded place (such as a subway) where he can claim it was an accident and get away quickly. In some cases, he may fondle a woman's breasts with his hand while he is rubbing up against her. This is similar to **toucheurism,** which is the compulsive desire to touch strangers with one's hands for sexual arousal. This desire, usually in men, finds expression on buses, trains, in shopping malls, while waiting in line, at crowded concerts, anywhere where bodies are pressed together. There have also been cases of frotteurism or toucheurism among doctors or dentists who rub against or touch their patients. Frotteurism, however, does not usually appear in isolation but as one of a number of paraphilias in an individual (Langevin & Lang, 1987).

Necrophilia

Tales of **necrophilia** (neck-row-FILL-ee-uh), or having sex with corpses, have been found even in ancient civilizations. The Egyptians prohibited embalmers from taking immediate delivery of corpses of the wives of important men for fear that the embalmers would violate them (Rosman & Resnick, 1989). More recently, the legends of the vampires imply necrophilia in the highly sexual approaches of the "undead." The stories of Sleeping Beauty, Snow White, and Romeo and Juliet all convey a sense of the restorative powers of loving the dead and thereby bringing the corpse back to life.

Rosman and Resnick (1989) suggest that necrophiliacs desire a partner who is unresisting and unrejecting; to find one, many seek out professions that put them in contact with corpses. They identify three types of genuine necrophilia: necrophiliac fantasy, in which a person has persistent fantasies about sex with dead bodies without actually engaging in such behavior; "regular" necrophilia, which involves the use of already-dead bodies for sexual pleasure; and necrophiliac homicide, in which the person commits murder to obtain a corpse for sexual pleasure. However, necrophilia is extremely rare and accounts for only a tiny fraction of murders (Milner et al., 2008).

An infamous case of necrophiliac homicide was that of serial killer Jeffrey Dahmer. Dahmer, who admitted to killing

---

REALResearch > Frotteurism is most common in people between the ages of **15** and **25** years and decreases as a person ages (SELIGMAN & HARDENBURG, 2000).

Zoophilia

Zoophilia (zoo-uh-FILL-ee-uh; also referred to as **bestiality**), or sexual contact with animals, is rare, although Kinsey and his colleagues (1948, 1953) found that one man in every 13 engages in this behavior. Contact between people and animals has been both practiced and condemned since earliest times.

Studies of people who engage in sex with animals have found that a male dog is the most popular animal sex partner for both men and women (Miletski, 2002). Sexual behaviors included masturbating the animal, submitting to anal sex performed by the animal, or active or passive oral sex with the animal (Miletski, 2002).

---

frotteurism
An intense and recurrent fantasy or behavior that involves touching and rubbing the genitals against a nonconsenting person in a crowded place.

toucheurism
The act of compulsively touching strangers with the hands to achieve sexual arousal.

zoophilia
The sexual attraction to animals in fantasy or through sexual contact as a preferred or exclusive means of sexual arousal and orgasm (also referred to as bestiality).

bestiality
A paraphilia that involves engaging in sexual relations with an animal (also referred to as zoophilia).

necrophilia
The sexual attraction to dead bodies in fantasy or through sexual contact as a preferred or exclusive means of sexual arousal and orgasm.

17 men and having sex with their corpses; he also mutilated their bodies, tried to create a "shrine" out of their organs that he thought would give him "special powers," and ate their flesh. In keeping with Rosman and Resnick's claim that necrophiliacs desire a partner who is unresisting and unrejecting, Dahmer bored holes into his victims' skulls while they were alive and poured in acid or boiling water, trying to create "zombies" who would fulfill his every desire.

On the other hand, Dahmer also had sex with his victims while they were alive; perhaps he was an **erotophonophiliac,**

which is someone who gets sexual excitement from the act of murder itself. Dahmer admitted his deeds but claimed he was insane. A jury found him sane and guilty, and he was sentenced to life in prison with no chance of parole; he was killed by another inmate in 1994.

erotophonophiliac
A person who derives sexual excitement from murdering others.

review questions

1 Define a fetish and identify the key features of this paraphilia. What are the most common fetish items? Define transvestic festishism.

2 Define sadism and masochism and identify the key features of these paraphilias.

3 Define exhibitionism and voyeurism and identify the key features of these paraphilia.

4 Define pedophilia and identify the key features of this paraphilia.

5 Identify some of the other less common paraphilias and identify the key features of these disorders.

Assessing and Treating Paraphilias

Although the majority of those with paraphilias do not seek treatment and are content with balancing the pleasure and guilt of their paraphilia, others find their paraphilia to be an unwanted disruption to their lives. Their sexual desires may get in the way of forming relationships, may get them into legal trouble, or may become such a preoccupation that they dominate their lives. For these people, a number of therapeutic solutions have been tried, with varying success.

ASSESSMENT

It is very difficult to assess and measure sexual variations (Laws & O'Donahue, 2008). Part of the problem is that many people tend to feel uncomfortable reporting their sexual practices, especially if they are socially stigmatized. In addition, sexual behaviors often occur in private and may involve the use of sexual fantasy, which is nearly impossible to measure (Laws & O'Donahue, 2008). There are also ethical issues that make assessment difficult.

Although some people with paraphilias are referred to clinicians by law enforcement, for others, assessment is often done through self-report, behavioral observation, or by physiological tests or personality inventories (Laws & O'Donahue, 2008;

Seligman & Hardenburg, 2000). Self-reports may not be reliable, however; individuals under court order to receive treatment for pedophilia may be highly motivated to report that the behavior has ceased. Also, people are not necessarily the best judge of their own desires and behavior; some may truly believe they have overcome their sexual desires when in fact they have not. The second technique, behavioral observation, is limited by the fact that it cannot assess fantasies and desires; also, most people can suppress these behaviors for periods of time.

Physiological tests may be a bit more reliable. The most reliable technique for men is probably **penile plethysmography,** which is often used with male sex offenders. For example, a pedophile can be shown films of nude children and the plethysmograph can record his penile blood volume. If he becomes excited at the pictures, then he is probably still having pedophilic desires and fantasies. A similar test is also available to test the sexual response of female offenders. However, both of these physiological tests have been found to be of limited use in this population because there are no outward signs of arousal (Laws & O'Donahue, 2008; Seligman & Hardenburg, 2000).

Personality inventories, such as the **Minnesota Multiphasic Personality Inventory (MMPI),** can help establish personality

penile plethysmography
A test performed by measuring the amount of blood that enters the penis in response to a stimulus, which can indicate how arousing the stimulus is for the male.

Minnesota Multiphasic Personality Inventory (MMPI)
Psychological test used to assess general personality characteristics.

patterns and determine whether there are additional psychological disorders (Seligman & Hardenburg, 2000). Other psychological inventories for depression and anxiety are often also used. In the future, the development of methodologies to assess these behaviors will be a priority in this field (Laws & O'Donahue, 2008).

TREATMENT
OPTIONS

For the most part, treatment for paraphilias today is multifaceted and may include group, individual, and family therapy; medication; education; and self-help groups (Laws & O'Donahue, 2008; Seligman & Hardenburg, 2000; see Table 16.1). Overall, treatment is aimed at the reduction or elimination of the paraphiliac symptoms, relapse prevention, and increasing victim empathy (d'Amora & Hobson, 2003).

Whatever the technique, the most important goal of therapy must be to change a person's behavior. If behavior can be changed, even if fantasies and inner emotional life are not altered, then at least the person will not be harming others or himself or herself. That is why behavioral techniques have been the most commonly used and most successful of the paraphilia treatments.

Therapy to resolve earlier childhood trauma or experiences that help maintain the paraphiliac behaviors is also helpful (H. Kaplan et al., 1994). This therapy can help increase self-esteem and social skills, which are often lacking in people with paraphilias. Positive behaviors can be encouraged by teaching them how to improve their social skills, allowing them to meet more men or women as potential sexual partners. To change emotions and thoughts, counseling, modeling (taking after a positive role model), or feedback can be used to change a person's attitudes toward the sexual object. In empathy training, which is useful when there is a victim, the person is taught to increase his or her compassion by putting himself or herself in the same situation as the victim. Incarcerated sex offenders may be exposed to relapse prevention therapies, which focus on controlling the cycle of troubling emotions, distorted thinking, and fantasies that accompany their activities (Goleman, 1992). These techniques can be used in either group psychotherapy or individual counseling sessions. Group therapy has been found to be an important tool in reducing isolation, improving social skills, and reducing shame and secrecy (Seligman & Hardenburg, 2000).

Yet most find their desires difficult to suppress, and for them aversion therapy is one of the most common treatment strategies (Laws & O'Donahue, 2008; Seligman & Hardenburg, 2000). In aversion therapy, the undesirable behavior is linked with an unpleasant stimulus. For example, the person might be shown pictures of nude boys or asked to fantasize about exposing himself to a girl, while an unpleasant odor, a drug that causes nausea, or an electric shock is administered. This technique has had some success, although its effectiveness decreases over time (Laws & O'Donahue, 2008). In **shame aversion,** the unpleasant stimulus is shame; for example, an exhibitionist may be asked to expose himself in front of an audience.

*The most important goal of therapy must be **to change a person's behavior.***

Although removing the behavior itself may protect any victims, the person who still fantasizes about the behavior or has the same underlying attitude that led to it (such as fear of women) may not really be that much better off. The psychological underpinnings of the paraphilia also must be changed. In **systematic desensitization** (Wolpe, 1958), the person is taught to relax and is then taken through more and more anxiety-provoking or arousing situations until eventually the person learns to relax during even the most extreme situations (Hawton, 1983).

A number of therapies incorporate masturbation to try to reprogram a person's fantasies. In **orgasmic reconditioning,** the paraphiliac masturbates; just as he feels orgasm is inevitable, he switches his fantasy to a more socially desirable one, hoping thereby to increasingly associate orgasm and, later, erection with the desirable stimulus. Similarly, in **satiation therapy,** the person masturbates to a conventional fantasy and then right away masturbates again to the undesirable fantasy (Marshall, 1979). The decreased sex drive and low responsiveness of the second attempt makes the experience less exciting than usual, and eventually the behavior may lose its desirability.

In addition to these behavioral therapies, pharmacotherapy (drug therapy) has become more popular in the past several years (Chopin-Marcé, 2001). Several drugs have been found to reduce the urges to act out on paraphiliac behaviors and can maintain a reduction in undesirable behavior even when drug therapy is stopped (Terao & Nakamura, 2000). Testosterone-suppressing drugs (antiandrogen) have been used to treat paraphilias in men. These drugs can produce castration levels of testosterone for up to 5 years (Reilly et al., 2000). The research shows that certain drugs can lead to a significant decrease in deviant sexual fantasies, urges, and behaviors (Keegan, 2001).

Antidepressants have also been found to be helpful. In fact, many therapists believe that the compulsive nature of many paraphilias is related to a psychological condition known as **obsessive–compulsive disorder (OCD).** Because of these similarities, treatment options for sexual paraphilias have begun to evaluate the use of serotonin reuptake inhibitors (SSRIs; these antidepressant drugs have been successful in the treatment of OCD; Abouesh & Clayton, 1999). SSRIs have been found to reduce deviant sexual fantasies, urges, and behaviors (Keegan, 2001).

Surgery has also been used in the treatment of paraphilias. Castration may not be the answer to the violent or pedophilic of-

shame aversion
A type of aversion therapy in which the behavior that one wishes to extinguish is linked with strong feelings of shame.

systematic desensitization
A technique by which a person learns to relax while experiencing arousal or anxiety-provoking stimuli.

orgasmic reconditioning
A sex therapy technique in which a person switches fantasies just at the moment of masturbatory orgasm to try to condition himself or herself to become excited by more conventional fantasies.

satiation therapy
A therapy to lessen excitement to an undesired stimulus by masturbating to a desired stimulus and then immediately masturbating again, when desire is lessened, to an undesired stimulus.

obsessive–compulsive disorder (OCD)
A psychological disorder in which a person experiences recurrent and persistent thoughts, impulses, or images that are intrusive and inappropriate and that cause marked anxiety and repetitive behaviors.

table 16.1

Paraphilia Treatment Options

Treatment for paraphilias may often involve several approaches. Overall, the goal of treatment is to reduce or eliminate the paraphiliac behaviors, reduce or eliminate the chances of relapse, and increase personal feelings of self-esteem as well as victim empathy. Although many sexual offenders are mandated by courts to go to therapy, those who seek out therapy on their own have been found to be more motivated and successful in their treatment. Although many convicted sex offenders will reduce their paraphiliac behavior after treatment, some may not. Those who are engaging in high levels of paraphiliac behavior and/or those with multiple psychological disorders are often less successful in therapy. Following are the various treatment options for paraphilias.

Type of Therapy	Therapeutic Methods
Individual	One-on-one therapy with a psychologist or counselor; work on improving self-esteem and social skills. Often uses modeling, empathy, and social skills training, controlling the cycle of troubling emotions, distorted thinking, and fantasies that accompany their activities.
Group	A form of psychotherapy in which a therapist works with multiple paraphiliacs with similar conditions. The interactions between the members of the group are analyzed and considered to be therapeutic.
Family	Treatment of more than one member of a family in the same session. Family relationships and processes are explored and evaluated for their potential role in the paraphiliac's behavior.
Cognitive behavioral	Combination of cognitive and behavior therapy. Works to help weaken the connections between certain situations and emotional/physical reactions to them (including depression, self-defeating, or self-damaging behaviors), while also examining how certain thinking patterns help contribute to behavior. Emphasizes relaxation and improving emotional health.
Systematic desensitization	A technique used in behavior therapy to treat behavioral problems involving anxiety. Clients are exposed to threatening situations under relaxed conditions until the anxiety reaction is extinguished.
Aversion	A behavior-modification technique that uses unpleasant stimuli in a controlled fashion to change behavior in a therapeutic way. An example would be a pedophile who is given an electric shock or a nausea drug while looking at naked pictures of children.
Shame aversion	A behavior-modification technique that uses shame as the unpleasant stimuli to change behavior in a therapeutic way. An example would be an exhibitionist that is asked to expose himself in front of an audience.
Orgasmic reconditioning	A behavioral technique that involves reprogramming a person's fantasies. An example would be to have a paraphiliac masturbate, and when orgasm is inevitable, he would switch his fantasy to a more socially desirable one, hoping thereby to increasingly associate orgasm and, later, erection with the desirable stimulus.
Satiation	A behavioral technique in which a person masturbates to a conventional fantasy and then immediately masturbates again to an undesirable fantasy. The decreased sex drive and low responsiveness of the second attempt makes the experience less exciting than usual, and eventually the behavior may lose its desirability.
Pharmacotherapy	Medications may be used to improve symptoms, delay the progression, or reduce the urge to act on paraphiliac behaviors. A variety of medications have been used, including antidepressants and testosterone-suppressing drugs.
Surgical	Procedures such as castration are used to stop the paraphiliac behavior.
Chemotherapy	Using medication to either decrease sexual drive or to treat psychological pathologies that are believed to underlie the paraphiliac behavior.

fender; some use foreign objects on their victims, and so the inability to achieve erection is not necessarily an impediment to their activity. Others cite the fact that although castration may cause a decrease in testosterone, it does not always result in a decrease in sex drive (Santen, 1995). To the degree that such crimes are crimes of aggression, rather than of sex, castration may not address the underlying cause.

Ultimately, there is no certain way to change a person's sexual desires. For many people with paraphilias whose desires are socially or legally unacceptable, life is a struggle to keep their sexuality tightly controlled. As we mentioned earlier, recidivism rates for those with paraphilias are generally high, so long-term treatment is often necessary (McGrath, 1991; Rabinowitz et al., 2002). Those who do best are motivated and committed to treatment (as opposed to being mandated by the court to appear in therapy), seek treatment early, and have normal adult sexual outlets (Seligman & Hardenburg, 2000). Those with less treatment success often have multiple psychological disorders, low empathy levels, and a high frequency of paraphiliac behavior (H. Kaplan et al., 1994).

Overall, this is an area of research that is also in need of further study. Unfortunately, there have been few studies showing promising treatment results for paraphilias. In fact, current research does not support the fact that treatments lead to long-term behavioral changes (Laws & O'Donahue, 2008). Treatment modalities for paraphilias will be another priority research area in the future.

review questions

1 Explain some of the reasons a paraphiliac may, or may not, seek out therapy.

2 How are paraphilias assessed? Are self-reports reliable? Why or why not?

3 Identify the various treatment options for the paraphilias.

4 Explain how aversion therapy has been used for the treatment of the paraphilias.

5 What is often the main goal of therapy for a paraphiliac?

Hyposexuality and **Hypersexuality: Understanding the Ranges of Sexual Frequency**

Another variation of human sexuality is sexual frequency. Although there is a great range in frequency of sexual contact in the general population (see Chapter 10), some argue that certain people cross over the line from a vigorous sex life to an obsessed sex life. On the other side are those who, for various reasons, seem to have little or no sex drive at all.

HYPERSEXUALITY:
DOES OBSESSION IMPLY ADDICTION?

Sexuality, like drugs, alcohol, gambling, and all other behaviors that bring a sense of excitement and pleasure, should involve some degree of moderation. Yet for some people, the need for repeated sexual encounters, which often end up being fleeting and unfulfilling, becomes almost a compulsion (Bancroft & Vukadinovic, 2004; G. H. Golden, 2001). An addiction involves an uncontrollable craving and compulsive need for a specific object. A typical sexual addict is a married man whose obsession with masturbation increases to an obsession with pornography, cybersex, prostitute visits, or multiple sexual affairs (Keane, 2004).

In the past, derogatory terms, mostly for women, were used to describe these people; an example is **nymphomaniac.** Terms for men were more flattering and included **Don Juanism, satyriasis,** or, in other cases, "studs." Perhaps nowhere else is the double standard between the sexes so blatant—women who enjoy frequent sexual encounters are considered "whores" or "sluts," whereas

men who enjoy similar levels of sexual activity have been admired. However, on some college campuses across the United States, men who engage in sex with many partners are often referred to as "man whores" or male "sluts" (Author's files).

The *DSM-IV-TR* does not recognize sexual addiction. Even so, an increasing number of clinicians and researchers recognize the syndrome (Birchard, 2006; Kwee et al., 2007), which was first written about by Patrick Carnes (2001) in his book, *Out of the Shadows: Understanding Sexual Addiction.* Carnes wrote about the parallels between sexual addiction and compulsive gambling, both of which involve an obsessive and compulsive addiction.

In 2008, actor David Duchovny sought help for sexual addiction. Ironically, Duchovny had just won a Golden Globe for his portrayal of a sexually compulsive womanizer on the hit television show *Californication.*

nymphomaniac
A term used to describe women who engage in frequent or promiscuous sex; usually used pejoratively.

Don Juanism, or satyriasis
Terms used to describe men who engage in frequent or promiscuous sex.

SEX IN REAL LIFE

Internet Sexual Addiction

It's not hard to understand how an addiction might develop when we learn that about 200 new sex-related sites are added to the Internet every day...

The convenience of the Internet has helped shape compulsive patterns of online use, especially in the area of sexuality (Boies et al., 2004; Young et al., 2000). Today men and women can search online for information about sex, engage in online chats, and buy sexual products and materials. Some of these Internet activities may be potentially addictive, especially those that involve sexually related Internet crimes, such as cyberstalking (Griffiths, 2001). It's not hard to understand how an addiction might develop when we learn that about 200 new sex-related sites are added to the Internet every day, and sex on the Internet generates $1 billion each year (Carnes, 2003).

A person who has an Internet sexual addiction routinely spends significant amounts of time in chat rooms and instant messaging with the intent of getting sex; feels preoccupied with using the Internet to find online sexual partners; discusses personal sexual fantasies not typically expressed offline; masturbates while engaging in online chats; obsesses about the next opportunity to engage

in online sex; moves from cybersex to phone sex or face-to-face meetings; hides online chat sessions from others; obsessively seeks out Internet pornography sites; feels guilty; and has decreasing interest in real-life sexual partners (Griffiths, 2001). Men and women with low self-esteem, a distorted body image, an untreated sexual dysfunction, or a prior diagnosed sexual addiction are more at risk for developing an Internet sexual addiction (Young et al., 2000), and those who seek out Internet pornography have been found to have higher levels of loneliness, compared with those who do not (Yoder et al., 2005).

Many people with paraphilias turn to the Internet as a "safe" outlet for their sexual fantasies and urges. Psychotherapy and support groups often offer the most help for those with Internet sexual addictions. More research is needed into this new and growing problem. Research has shown that there is a small minority of men and women who experience significant disturbances caused by their online sexual activity (Griffiths, 2001).

According to Carnes, a sexual addict goes through four cycles repeatedly: a preoccupation with thoughts of sex; ritualization of preparation for sex (such as primping oneself and going to bars); compulsive sexual behavior over which the addict feels he or she has no control; and despair afterward as the realization hits that he or she has again repeated the destructive sequence of events.

Today sexual addiction is often referred to as compulsive sexual behavior (CSB; Miner et al., 2007). It is characterized by recurrent and intense sexual urges, fantasies, and behaviors that typically interfere with a person's daily functioning (Coleman et al., 2003; Miner et al., 2007). For some people, CSB may involve compulsive masturbation or an obsession with pornography, whereas for others it may progress to multiple sex partners or exhibitionistic behaviors. CSB can cause emotional suffering and can lead to problems in one's occupational functioning (Miner et al., 2007), and marital and family relationships are often negatively affected or jeopardized by these behaviors (Bird, 2006).

Although there are no definite numbers, the Society for the Advancement of Sexual Health estimates that 3% to 5% of Americans have CSB, with men outnumbering women five to one (Beck, 2008; Society for the Advancement of Sexual Health, 2008). However, these numbers are based only on those who seek treat-

ment so actual numbers are probably much higher. The availability of sex on the Internet has increased the number of cases of sexual addiction (Landau, 2008).

Typically treatment for CSB involves individual or group therapy as part of a 12-step recovery process (similar to the Alcoholics Anonymous program), originated by Carnes (2001). Medications may also be used, especially if a person also has bipolar disorder or depression, which are commonly associated with CSB. The main goal of treatment is to get a person to have sex in a relationship, which can be challenging (Landau, 2008). It is yet to be seen whether compulsive sexual behavior will be put back in the next edition of the *DSM*, due out in 2012.

Many have criticized the idea of sexual addiction, however. They argue that terms such as "sexual addiction" are really disguised social judgments. Sexual addiction may be nothing more than an attempt to "repathologize" sexual behaviors (Keane, 2004). Before the sexual freedom of the 1960s, those who engaged in promiscuous sex were often considered physically, mentally, or morally sick. Some scholars suggest that there has been an attempt to return to a pathological model of sexuality using the concept of addiction (Irvine, 1995). Although this is a growing area of research, there is limited research available on sexual addicts. Clinicians have found that sexual addicts tend to have a low opinion of themselves, distorted beliefs, a desire to escape from unpleasant emotions, difficulty coping with stress, a memory of an intense "high" that they experienced at least once before in their life (and that they are looking for again), and an uncanny ability to deny that they have a problem, even when it severely disrupts their lives

(Earle & Crow, 1990). In response, a number of self-help groups have been organized, including Sexaholics Anonymous, Sex Addicts Anonymous, Sex and Love Addicts Anonymous, and Co-Dependents of Sexual Addicts.

WHAT DO YOU WANT TO KNOW ?

I think about sex a lot—it seems like it is almost all the time. I also like to have sex as often as I can. Do I have sex addiction?
Probably not. Thinking about sex is a universal human pastime, especially when a person is younger and just beginning to mature as a sexual being. Sexual addiction becomes a problem when people find their sexual behavior becoming dangerous or uncomfortable. People who find that they cannot stop themselves from engaging in behaviors that put them at physical risk, that they find immoral, that make them feel extremely guilty, or that intrude on their ability to do other things in their life should probably seek counseling—but that is true whether or not the behavior is sexual.

HYPOSEXUALITY: LACKING DESIRE AND AVOIDING SEX

On the other side of the spectrum are those who have lost their sexual desire or never had it in the first place. People with hyposexuality have low sexual fantasies or desire for sexual activity. In Chapter 14, we discussed sexual aversion disorder, in which a person cannot engage in sex, feeling disgust, aversion, or fear when confronted by a sexual partner (American Psychiatric Association, 2000). People with such conditions are different from those who choose celibacy as a sexual lifestyle, which we also discussed in Chapter 10; in contrast to those who choose to be celibate, people with hyposexuality often have low sexual desire or lack sexual desire altogether. Their problems may be due to substance abuse, hormonal disturbances, or psychological causes, and various therapies may be recommended, depending on the cause.

review questions

1 Explain how sexuality can be viewed as a behavior that brings excitement and pleasure, similar to gambling, drugs, and alcohol.

2 What is hypersexuality, and how is it manifested in a man or woman? Explain any gender differences in the perceptions of hypersexuality.

3 Explain Carne's treatment methods and the four cycles of repair.

4 Explain the issues contributing to the debate about whether sexual addiction exists.

5 What is hyposexuality?

Variations, Deviations, and **Who Gets to Decide?**

What criteria should we use to decide whether a sexual behavior is "normal"? The number of people who engage in it? What a particular religion says about it? Popular opinion? Should we leave it up to the courts or psychiatrists? Stoller (1991) suggests that we are all perverse to some degree. Why should some people be singled out as being too perverse, especially if they do no harm to anyone else?

Perhaps the need we feel to brand some sexual behaviors as perverse is summed up by S. B. Levine and colleagues (1990, p. 92): "Paraphiliac images often involve arousal without the pre-

tense of caring or human attachment." We tend to be uncomfortable with sex for its own sake, separate from ideas of love, intimacy, or human attachment (Laws & O'Donohue, 2008), which is one reason that masturbation was seen as evil or sick for so many years.

Paraphilias are still labeled "perversions" by law and often carry legal penalties. Because even consensual adult sexual behavior, such as anal intercourse, is illegal in some states, it is not surprising that paraphilias are as well. Yet these laws also contain contradictions; for example, why is it illegal for men to expose themselves, yet women are not arrested for wearing a see-through blouse? We must be careful deciding that some sexual behaviors are natural and others are unnatural, or some normal and others abnormal. Those that we call paraphilias may simply be part of human sexual diversity, unproblematic unless they cause distress, injury, or involve an unconsenting or underage partner.

review questions

1 Identify some of the ways that people may determine whether a sexual behavior is "normal."

2 Explain how there are contradictions in laws regulating sexual behaviors.

3 How might paraphilias be viewed as a normal variation of human sexual behavior?

CHAPTER review

SUMMARY POINTS

1 People celebrate individual differences for most aspects of human life, with the exception of sexual diversity. Sexual behavior can be viewed as a continuum, but social value judgments, rather than science, determine which sexual behaviors are considered acceptable in society. Attitudes about which behaviors are acceptable vary over time, and there are cultural variations.

2 Paraphilias are recurrent, intense sexually arousing fantasies, sexual urges, or behaviors that involve a craving for an erotic object for 6 months or more that involves a nonhuman object, the suffering or humiliation of oneself or one's partner, or children or other nonconsenting persons. This behavior causes significant distress and interferes with a person's ability to work, interact with friends, and other important areas.

3 People with paraphilias come from every socioeconomic bracket, every ethnic and racial group, and every sexual orientation. The factors that have been found to be related to the development of a paraphilia include a person's sex, growing up in a dysfunctional family or experiencing family problems during childhood, and past sexual abuse.

4 Several theories attempt to explain the development of paraphilias. The biological theories claim physical factors are responsible for the development of paraphiliac behavior. Psychoanalytic theorists suggest that the causes can be traced back to problems during the Oedipal crisis and with castration anxiety. Developmental theories claim that a person forms a template in his or her brain that defines his or her ideal lover and sexual situation, and this can be disrupted in several ways. Paraphilias may also be due to courtship disorders in which the behavior becomes fixed at a preliminary stage of mating that would normally lead to sexual intercourse. Behaviorists suggest that paraphilias develop because a behavior becomes associated with sexual pleasure through conditioning. Sociologists look at the ways in which society shapes and encourages certain behaviors.

5 Some of the most common paraphilias include fetishism, sadism, masochism, exhibitionism, voyeurism, transvestism, and pedophilia. A fetish is an inanimate object or a body part (not usually associated with the sex act) that becomes the primary or exclusive focus of sexual arousal and orgasm in an individual. Sadism refers to the intentional infliction of physical or psychological pain on another person in order to achieve sexual excitement. A masochist derives sexual pleasure through his or her own physical pain or psychological humiliation. Exhibitionism is the most common of all reported sexual offenses, and it involves a person becoming sexually aroused primarily from displaying his (or, more rarely, her) genitals. Voyeurs' main means of sexual gratification are in watching unsuspecting persons undressing, naked, or engaging in sexual activity.

6 Transvestism (also called transvestic fetishism) is another type of paraphilia in which a person obtains sexual pleasure from dressing in the clothing of the other sex. The biggest difference between a cross-dresser and a transvestite is the fact that the transvestite feels sexual pleasure during cross-dressing, whereas a cross-dresser usually does not. Most of the time, neither desires sexual reassignment surgery.

7 Pedophilia refers to a persistent and intense need to engage in sexually arousing fantasies, sexual urges, or behaviors involving sexual activity with a prepubescent child. Pedophiles most often report an attraction to children of a particular age range. Many choose children because they are available and vulnerable; some pedophiles are unable to function sexually with an adult. The Internet has been both helpful and detrimental in the elimination of pedophilia: Pedophiles use it to find each other and talk about their behaviors, but it has also helped to identify pedophiles.

8 Treatment for paraphilias first involves an assessment. This can be done through self-report, behavioral observation, physiological tests, or personality inventories. Overall, the most important goal of therapy must be to change a person's behavior. Treatments for paraphilias may include group, individual, and family therapy, medication, education, and self-help groups. Behavioral methods are most common; techniques include aversion therapy, shame aversion, systematic desensitization, orgasmic reconditioning, and satiation therapy. Pharmacological and surgical interventions, such as testosterone-suppressing drugs, antidepressants, and chemotherapy are also used.

9 Hypersexuality and hyposexuality are two variations in sexual behavior. Some have called hypersexuality a sexual addiction because it involves compulsive sexual behavior. Patrick Carnes (1981) argues that people who engage in many of the paraphilias are really sexual addicts whose need for constant sexual encounters is similar to any addictive behavior.

10 It is difficult to determine how to decide whether a sexual behavior is normal or abnormal. Much of society feels uncomfortable with the idea of sex for its own sake, separate from love, intimacy, and human attachment.

CRITICAL THINKING questions

1 How do you decide whether a sexual behavior is "normal"? What is your definition of "typical" sexual activity, and where do you draw the line for yourself?

2 Do you think people should be allowed to engage in any sexual behaviors they choose, as long as they don't hurt anyone? Explain.

3 If the majority of people feel that the behavior of Dr. Sargent (the rubber fetishist who told his story at the beginning of the chapter) is distasteful, perverted, or abnormal, should we as a society make him stop doing it? Do you think he is sick? Do you think he needs help to stop this behavior? Why, or why not?

4 Which theory do you think best explains why a paraphilia might develop? What aspects of this theory make the most sense to you, and why?

5 Suppose that tonight when you are walking by yourself, you are approached by a middle-aged man who flashes you and begins stroking his erect penis. What do you think you would be thinking as he stands in front of you stroking his penis? What do you do? Whom do you tell?

6 Do you think a pedophile's address and photograph should be made public so that neighbors can be aware of his or her crimes against young children? How long should this information be listed? For 1 year? 5 years? 10 years? The rest of his or her life? Explain.

WEB resources

Sexuality Now Book Companion Website
Go to www.cengage.com/psychology/carroll for practice quizzes, glossary, flash cards, and more. You can also access the following websites from the companion site.

Center for Sex Offender Management ■ The Center for Sex Offender Management's (CSOM) goal is to enhance public safety by preventing further victimization through improving the management of adult and juvenile sex offenders in the community.

Sex Addicts Anonymous ■ Sex Addicts Anonymous (SAA) is a fellowship of men and women who share their experience, strength, and hope with each other so they may overcome their sexual addiction and help others recover from sexual addiction or dependency.

Silent Lambs ■ Silent Lambs is a website dedicated to reducing the ability of churches to adopt a "code of silence" when it comes to child sexual abuse that occurs within the church. This website has a variety of links and helpful information; a variety of videos and transcripts are available from recent clergy sexual abuse cases.

Vegan Erotica ■ VeganErotica.com manufactures handcrafted vegan bondage gear, whips, belts, harnesses, and other vegan leather (a.k.a. "pleather") items. Vegan condoms and other sex products are also available. All products are 100% vegetarian and do not contain animal products, nor were they tested on animals.

National Sex Offender Public Registry ■ The National Sex Offender Public Registry, coordinated by the Department of Justice, is a cooperative effort between the state agencies hosting public sexual offender registries and the federal government. This website's search tool has a number of search options that allow a user to submit a single national query to obtain information about sex offenders.

CengageNOW
Go to www.cengage.com/login to link to CengageNOW, your online study tool. First take the Pre-Test for this chapter to get your Personalized Study Plan, which will identify topics you need to review and direct you to online resources. Then take the Post-Test to determine what concepts you have mastered and what you still need work on.

Videos in CengageNOW

For additional information on topics discussed in this chapter, check out the videos in CengageNOW on the following topics:

- Bondage and S&M—Check your ideas about bondage, domination, and sadomasochism against a couple who engages in these practices.

- A Professional Dominatrix—Listen to a professional dominatrix describe her job.

CHAPTER 17

Power and Sexual Coercion

O ne of the most difficult emotional decisions to understand is why, at the first sign of aggression or mistreatment, a woman does not or cannot leave a man who abuses her. It sounds straightforward and easy, but is it?

Let me begin by saying that abusive relationships do not start with violence. Women do not enter into a relationship saying, "It's okay to hurt me." Even abusive relationships usually start romantically, sharing love and trust, building dreams together, and often having children—just as in a normal relationship.

Often, the spouse's controlling behavior is not seen immediately but develops slowly over time. When a woman realizes how damaging her relationship is, she often has really made an emotional commitment and developed a sense of loyalty to her partner. The bonds between the couple have been built over time and do not suddenly cease to exist. Once abuse enters the relationship, her emotional ties are a great source of turmoil. I know when I took my marriage

vows, I meant "for better or for worse." But when "until death do us part" suddenly became a frightening reality, I was faced with some terrifying decisions.

There are myriad and complex reasons for staying in an abusive relationship. Many women have no other source of financial support or housing. We ask them to leave their homes behind, cloaked only by the temporary safety of darkness, to hide in community shelters (when there is room) or to live in the streets. How many people would choose to take their children from their home, with no guarantee of food or shelter? How realistic are the options that we insist are the "obvious solutions" to this problem?

The fear of retaliation and further victimization by the abuser is another serious concern. Once, when I tried to leave, my ex-husband took my dachshund puppy and beat him against the wall. He told me to remember those cries because if I ever left him or tried to get help, those cries would haunt me because they would be cries of my young niece. At that moment, I knew he was capa-

ble of every horrible threat he had ever made and my life was in grave danger.

Abuse by an intimate partner, either emotional or physical, is a commonly unrecognized cause of illnesses and injury among women. Recent estimates reveal that from 2 million to 4 million women are battered by their "significant other" each year. How long can we continue to ignore this horrifying crime? We must realize that our actions, or lack of action, can have a huge impact on a woman's life. Be aware that by not asking a woman about it, you could be closing your eyes to the fact that this woman will most likely return home, only to be beaten again and again.

SOURCE: From G. Bundow, 1992, "Resident Forum: Why Women Stay," Journal of the American Medical Association, 267, p. 23. Reprinted with permission.

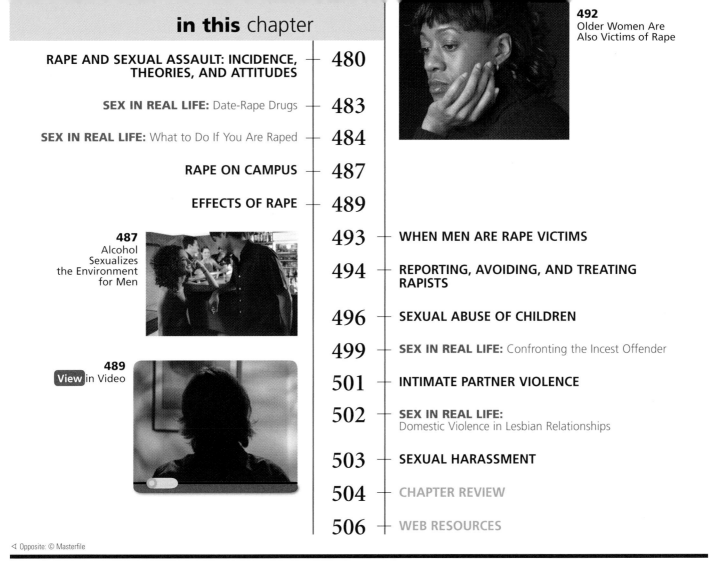

in this chapter

◁ Opposite: © Masterfile

P ower is an aspect of all sexual relationships. Sexual relationships are healthy when power is shared and when the relationship empowers the partners. In sexuality, however, as everywhere in human life, power can also be used to degrade and oppress. For example, the act of seduction is usually an interaction between each partner's power, which is partly what makes dating and sexual anticipation so exciting. However, coercive sexuality involves the clash of personal power, with one partner overpowering the other.

Physically or psychologically forcing sexual relations on another person is usually referred to as rape. Sexual contact with a minor by an adult is called child sexual abuse and, in some societies, is also considered rape. There are also instances in which a person with more power entices, pressures, or encourages another person with less power into sexual activities, ranging from an

WHAT DO YOU WANT TO KNOW ?

Why do people rape?
There are several theories as to why rape exists in our society. Feminists argue that the nature of the relationships between the sexes fosters rape. Others argue that it exists because of the rapist's psychopathology. Still others claim it is because of how women dress, act, or behave. Today most theorists agree that rape is a crime of power in which sex is used as a weapon.

unwanted glance or word to actual sexual contact. This is sexual harassment. This chapter begins with rape and sexual assault and goes on to explore other ways that power can be misused in relationships.

Rape and Sexual Assault: Incidence, Theories, and Attitudes

For most mammals, penile penetration of a female by a male is done only when the female is in estrus, or "heat," as it is commonly called. However, forced penetration is common in a wide variety of animal species (Lalumière et al., 2005b); for instance, male orangutans often engage in forced mating and vicious biting of the female. Humans can have sexual intercourse at any point in the menstrual cycle, which means other motivations determine when intercourse might take place. However, in humans, male and female desire for sexual contact may not coincide.

DEFINING RAPE AND SEXUAL ASSAULT

The line that separates **rape** from other categories of sexual activity can be blurry because of the fine distinctions between forced and consensual sex, as well as societal patterns of female passivity and male aggression (LaFree, 1982). For instance, societal and cultural rules often dictate that men, not women, should initiate sexual activity. These beliefs about how sex is supposed to be can make defining rape a difficult task. Defining rape is also complicated by the fact that not all unwanted sex is nonconsensual. In one study, a significant percentage of college students (25% of men and 50% of women) reported consensually engaging in unwanted sexual activity in a dating relationship (O'Sullivan & Allgeier, 1998).

The U.S. Department of Justice defines rape as forced sexual intercourse that can include psychological and physiological coercion. This would include forced vaginal, anal, or oral penetration. Psychological coercion would include pressuring someone who has not consented to sexual activity or taking advantage of someone because of their intellectual abilities, intoxication, or age (see Table 17.1). **Sexual assault** is defined as any type of sexual contact or behavior that occurs without the consent of the recipient of the unwanted sexual activity. Behaviors that are included in the definition of sexual assault are unwanted penetration, forced oral sex, masturbation, touching, fondling, or kissing. It would also include forcing someone to view sexually explicit materials, such as pornography. These definitions apply to both male and female victims and include heterosexual and homosexual rape and sexual assault.

However, these definitions are proposed as guidelines by the U.S. Department of Justice and exact definitions of rape and sexual assault are determined by individual states. Typically, state definitions include lack of consent, force or threat of force, and vaginal penetration in the definition of rape and sexual assault. Regardless of state definitions, some women do not consider an assault to be rape if there was no penis involved (Bart & O'Brien, 1985). This is because many women view rape as something that

WHAT DO YOU WANT TO KNOW ?

My ex-boyfriend forced me to have sex with him. Since I dated him in the past, does that mean this is not rape?
It does not matter if you have had a sexual relationship with someone in the past—if it is nonconsensual, it is rape. Rape can, and does, occur between an offender and victim who have a preexisting relationship (often referred to as "date rape" or "acquaintance rape"), and even between spouses, which we talk about later in this chapter.

is done by a penis (intercourse, fellatio, anal sex) rather than something done to a vagina (digital penetration, cunnilingus, touching).

There has been a debate about the appropriate term for a person who has experienced a rape or sexual assault. Although the word "victim" emphasizes the person's lack of responsibility for the incident, it may also imply that the person was a passive recipient of the attack. The term "victim" can also become a permanent label. Some prefer the term "survivor," which implies that the person had within herself or himself the strength to overcome and to survive the rape. It also confirms that the person made important decisions—for example, not to fight and possibly be killed—during the assault and thus was not completely passive. However, for clarity, in this chapter we use the term "victim" to refer to a person who has survived a rape.

RAPE STATISTICS

In 2006, the U.S. Department of Justice reported more than 270,000 cases of rape or sexual assault (Rand & Catalano, 2007). This translated into someone being sexually assaulted every 2 minutes in the United States (Rape, Abuse, & Incest National Network, 2008). It is difficult, however, to assess the actual number of rapes because rape has been one of the most underreported crimes in the United States (U.S. Department of Justice—Office

REALResearch > The United States has the highest rape rate of all industrialized nations—it is **4** times higher than in Germany, **12** times higher than in England, and **20** times higher than in Japan (ROZEE, 2005).

of Justice Programs, 2002). Even so, rape victims today are significantly more likely to report a rape than they were in the past. Whereas 35% of rapes were reported from 1993 to 1997, this per-

rape
Forced sexual behavior without a person's consent.

sexual assault
Coercion of a nonconsenting victim to have sexual contact.

table 17.1

Age of Consent

Many countries, and states within the United States, have legal ages of consent. The age of consent is how old a person must be to be considered capable of legally giving informed consent to engage in sexual acts with another person. It is considered a crime for a person to engage in sexual behavior with someone below the age of consent. Many countries and states provide ages of consent for male–male and female–female sex. In some countries, there is no information on specific ages for certain behaviors.

Country	Male–Female Sex	Male–Male Sex	Female–Female Sex
Queensland, Australia	16	18	16
Austria	14	18	14
Bahamas	16	18	18
Botswana	16 for females 14 for males	Illegal for all ages	No information
Denmark	15	15	15
Hong Kong	16	21	No information
Croatia	14	14	14
India	16	Illegal for all ages	Illegal for all ages
Italy	14	14	14
Kenya	16	Illegal for all ages	Illegal for all ages
Madagascar	21	21	21
Puerto Rico	14	Illegal for all ages	Illegal for all ages
Saudia Arabia	No age minimum but must be married	Illegal for all ages	Illegal for all ages
South Africa	16	19	19
Swaziland	18	Illegal for all ages	Illegal for all ages
U.S.A.—California	18	18	18
U.S.A.—Connecticut	16	16	16
U.S.A.—Illinois	17	17	17
U.S.A.—New Hampshire	16	18	18
U.S.A.—Pennsylvania	16	16	16

SOURCE: "Legal age of consent." (1998–2000). Retrieved November 30, 2005, from http://www.ageofconsent.com/ageofconsent.htm

centage was up to 42% from 2002 to 2007 (Rand & Catalano, 2007).

Why are close to half of victims unlikely to report rape? Some do not report it because they feel shameful, guilty, embarrassed, or humiliated and don't want people to know (Sable et al., 2006; Shechory & Idisis, 2006). Many also worry that their reports won't be taken seriously, their confidentiality won't be maintained, or the attacker will retaliate (Sable et al., 2006). Finally, because victims knows their attacker in more than 73% of rapes, they might not feel comfortable reporting (see Figure 17.1; Catalano, 2006).

CHARACTERISTICS OF RAPISTS

Who is it that rapes? What is your image of a "rapist"? A drunk at a fraternity party? A stranger who jumps out of a bush? What drives someone commit rape? Anger? Frustration? Even today, the question of why someone would rape is still largely unanswered.

Research has shown that the majority of rapists are primarily male, young, single, and between the ages of 15 and 30 (Amir, 1971; D. E. H. Russell, 1984). Antisocial personality patterns and high levels of impulsivity and aggression are common (Giotakos

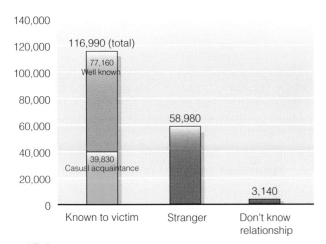

Figure **17.1** Number of rapes/sexual assaults by relationship to offender, 2003. Source: U.S. Department of Justice—Office of Justice Programs, 2003.

et al., 2005; Lalumière et al., 2005d), and many rapists have experienced overwhelmingly negative early interpersonal experiences, most of which were with their fathers (McCormack et al., 2002). Sexist views about women are common, and rape myth acceptance, low self-esteem, and political conservatism have also been found (Beech et al., 2006; Masser et al., 2006). There are also correlations found between rapists and past sexual abuse (Stevenson & Gajarsky, 1992) and between the use of violent and degrading pornography and a negative view of women (Millburn et al., 2000). Research on birth order and parental age of sex offenders has found that rapists tend to be later born to older mothers and fathers (Langevin et al., 2007). Even so, despite the assumption that rapists are psychologically disturbed individuals, research does not support the assumption that they are very different from nonoffenders (Cornett & Shuntich, 1991; Oliver et al., 2007).

Studies have found that there are a variety of types of rapists—power, anger, and sadistic (J. Douglas & Olshaker, 1998; Hazelwood & Burgess, 1987; McCabe & Wauchope, 2005; Pardue & Arrigo, 2008). Power rapists are motivated by domination and control; anger rapists use anger in overt ways, such as through a macho image, force, or a weapon; and sadistic rapists are motivated by sexual and aggressive fantasies.

Convicted rapists are not the only ones who are attracted to the idea of forcing or coercing a woman to engage in sex. In a classic study about the potential to rape, 356 college-age heterosexual men were asked, "If you could be assured that no one would know and that you could in no way be punished for forcing a woman to do something she really didn't want to do (rape), how likely, if at all, would you be to commit such acts?" Sixty percent indicated that under the right circumstances, there was some likelihood that they would use force, or rape, or both (Ceniti & Malamuth, 1984). This study is dated, however, so it is difficult to know whether the results would be significantly different today. Other, more recent studies have found similar results. In a study of male university students, 30% admitted they might force sex under certain circumstances (Lev-Wiesel, 2004), whereas another study found that 58% of heterosexual male college students acknowledged forcing sex on a woman who was unable to consent or who had made her lack of consent clear (Parkhill & Abbey, 2008).

THEORIES ABOUT RAPE

What drives someone to rape another person? We discuss the most prominent theories of why rape occurs, including rapist psychopathology, victim precipitation, feminist, sociological, and evolutionary theories.

Rapist Psychopathology: A Disease Model

Modern ideas about why rape occurs evolved first from psychiatric theories, which suggested that men rape because of mental illness, uncontrollable sexual urges, or alcohol intoxication. This theory of **rapist psychopathology** suggests that it is either disease or intoxication that forces men to rape and that if they did not have these problems, they would not rape.

REALResearch > Women who speak out about their rape experiences to friends, family, and support providers and experience negative reactions are often silenced and stop talking about their experiences to anyone (AHRENS, 2006). Negative reactions lead to increased self-blame and uncertainty about whether their experience qualified as rape, which increase the likelihood of the development of posttraumatic stress disorder (ULLMAN ET AL., 2007).

According to this theory, the rape rate can be reduced by finding these sick individuals and rehabilitating them. The theory makes people feel safer because it suggests that only sick individuals rape, not "normal" people. However, research consistently fails to identify any significant distinguishing characteristics of rapists (Fernandez & Marshall, 2003). Having psychological or alcohol problems does not predispose a person to be a rapist. In fact, men who rape are often found to be nearly "normal" in every other way. Perhaps it is easier to see rapists as somehow sick than realize that the potential to rape exists in many of us.

Theories of rapist psychopathology were very common until the 1950s, when feminist researchers began to refocus attention on rape's effect on the victim rather than on the offender. However, there are still those who accept psychopathological theories today. In fact, college students often report that this theory helps to explain stranger rape but doesn't help us to understand date or acquaintance rape (Cowan, 2000).

rapist psychopathology
A theory of rape that identifies psychological issues in a rapist that contribute to rape behavior.

Date-Rape Drugs

With higher doses, convulsions, vomiting, loss of consciousness, and coma and/or death can occur.

The term "date-rape drug" is slang for any drug that may be used during a sexual assault. This would include Rohypnol (also called roofies, Forget Pill, or Mind Eraser), gamma hydroxybutyric acid (GHB; also called Liquid Ecstasy, Georgia Home Boy, or Easy Lay), and Ketamine (also called Special K, Kit Kat, or Cat Valium). Today experts refer to rapes using these drugs as "drug-facilitated sexual assault." The effects of these drugs are similar to those of Valium, but they are much more powerful. The drugs go to work quickly, and the time they last varies. If a person has been drinking alcohol when the drugs were ingested, the drug effects will last longer. Side effects of these drugs may include drowsiness, memory problems, lower blood pressure, sleepiness, problems talking, dizziness, and impaired motor functions. With higher doses, convulsions, vomiting, loss of consciousness, and coma or death can occur. In late 2005, reports circulated about fatal levels of GHB given to women at Colorado fraternity parties ("Date Rape Drug Served," 2005).

Rohypnol is illegal in the United States, but is legal in several countries and has been smuggled into the United States. Rohypnol comes in tablet form and is typically placed in a drink,

These and similar coasters include test patches that can show the presence of date-rape drugs in a drink.

where it quickly dissolves. Once dissolved, the tablets are undetectable—there is no taste or color change to the liquid. Ketamine is a white powder that easily dissolves in a drink, whereas GHB can come in tablet, liquid, or powder form. Ketamine and GHB are both legal and used for different medical purposes. The effects of these drugs usually begin within 30 minutes, peak within 2 hours, and can last a total of 8 hours. An individual may feel nauseous, hot or cold, and dizzy within 10 minutes after ingesting these drugs.

You can protect yourself from drug-facilitated sexual assault by never accepting drinks from other people, opening your drinks yourself, and by never leaving your drink unattended. If you think you have been drugged, it's important to go to a police station or hospital as soon as possible. A urine test can check for the presence of the drugs. These drugs can leave your body within 12 to 72 hours, so it's important to get a urine test as soon as possible. For more information about date-rape drugs, check the website listings at the end of this chapter.

Victim Precipitation Theory: Blaming the Victim

Victim precipitation theory explores the ways victims make themselves vulnerable to rape, such as how they dress, act, or where they walk (Wakelin, 2003). By focusing on the victim and ignoring the motivations of the attacker, many have labeled this a "blame the victim" theory.

The victim precipitation theory of rape shifts the responsibility from the person who knowingly attacked to the innocent victim (Sawyer et al., 2002): "She was walking home too late at night," "She was drunk," "She was wearing too much makeup," or "She was flirting." One study found that women who wore suggestive clothing and were drinking alcohol were perceived as having greater sexual intent, and more blame, than women who wore neutral attire and were not drinking (Maurer & Robinson, 2008). College students often rate women who are dressed suggestively and drinking alcohol as more responsible for a sexual assault (Maurer & Robinson, 2008).

The victim precipitation theory also serves to distance people from the reality of rape and lulls them into the false assumption that it could not happen to them or someone close to them because they would not act like "those other women." If we believe bad things happen to people who take risks, then we are safe if we

do not take those risks. In the majority of rapes, however, women are not engaging in risky behavior.

In Susan Brownmiller's (1975) classic work on gender and rape, she argues that rape forces a woman to stay in at night, to monitor her behavior, and to look to men for protection. This attitude also contributes to a rape victim's guilt because she then wonders: "If I hadn't worn what I did, walked where I walked, or acted as I did, maybe I wouldn't have been raped." Overall, men are more likely than women to believe in the victim precipitation theory and to view sexual coercion as acceptable (Auster & Leone, 2001; Proto-Campise et al., 1998).

Feminist Theory: Keeping Women in Their Place

Feminist theorists contend that rape and the threat of rape are tools used in our society to keep women in their place. This fear keeps women in traditional sex roles, which are subordinate to

victim precipitation theory
A theory of rape that identifies victim characteristics or behaviors that contribute to rape.

feminist theory
A theory of rape contending that rape is a tool used in society to keep a woman in her place.

What to Do If You Are Raped

When a woman is raped, she often spends a long time trying to figure out exactly what she did to put herself at risk for a rape.

1. Know that it was not your fault. When a woman is raped, she often spends a long time trying to figure out exactly what she did to put herself at risk for a rape. This is probably because women have always been told to "be careful," "watch how you dress," or "don't drink too much." In reality, a rape might happen anywhere and at any time. No one asks to be raped.

2. Talk to a rape crisis counselor. Some women like to talk to a rape crisis counselor before going to the hospital or police. This is very helpful because counselors can often give you advice. Besides this, they are knowledgeable about rape and the aftermath of symptoms. Many hospitals have on-site counselors, usually volunteers from Women Organized Against Rape. Talking to a counselor also helps give the victim back her sense of control (see the Web Resources at the end of this chapter).

3. Go to a hospital for a medical examination. An immediate medical evaluation is imperative. If there is a nurse or health care provider on campus, you can see either of them, but it is better to go to a local emergency room to have a thorough physical examination. New federal requirements beginning in 2009 have made states pay for "Jane Doe Rape Kits," which allow for an anonymous collection of evidence during the medical evaluation (United States Department of Justice, 2008; Wyatt, 2008). This allows women to have a medical examination, but the evidence will only be released if she decides to press charges. Medical evaluations are important for two reasons: to check for STIs that may have been transmitted during the rape and to check for the presence of date-rape drugs. Because some of the STIs

take time to show up positive on a culture, it is important to be retested in the following weeks. Recently, some women have requested AIDS tests postrape, although infection with HIV also takes time to show up. If a woman was not using birth control or has reason to suspect that she may have become pregnant, the hospital can administer the morning-after pill (see Chapter 12 for more information about the morning-after pill). Also, if you think you might have been drugged, you can also have a urine test to check for the drug's presence. Try not to urinate before having this test.

4. Do not throw away any evidence of the rape. Do not shower before you go to the hospital. If you decide to change your clothes, do not wash or destroy what you were wearing. If anything was damaged in the assault, such as glasses, jewelry, or book bags, keep these, too. Put everything in a plastic bag, and store it in a safe place. It is necessary to preserve the evidence of the rape, which will be very important if you decide to press charges against the rapist.

5. Decide whether you want to file a police report. You have a choice of filing either a formal or informal report. This is something that you will need to sort through and decide. A rape crisis counselor can be very helpful in this decision process.

6. Decide whether you want to press charges. Although you do not need to decide this right away, you will need to think about it as soon as possible. It is important to review this decision with a lawyer experienced in rape cases.

men's. Feminist theorists believe that the social, economic, and political separation of the genders has encouraged rape, which is viewed as an act of domination of men over women (Hines, 2007; Murnen et al., 2002). Sex-role stereotyping—which reinforces the idea that men are supposed to be strong, aggressive, and assertive, whereas women are expected to be slim, weak, and passive— encourages rape in our culture (Murnen et al., 2002).

Sociological Theory: Balance of Power

Sociological theory and feminist theory have much in common; in fact, many feminist theorists are sociologists. Sociologists believe that rape is an expression of power differentials in society (T. A. Martin, 2003). When men feel disempowered by society, by changing sex roles or by their jobs, overpowering women with the symbol of their masculinity (a penis) reinforces, for a moment, men's control over the world.

Sociologists explore the ways people guard their interests in society. For example, the wealthy class in a society may fear the

poorer classes, who are larger in number and envy the possessions of the upper class. Because women have been viewed as "possessions" of men throughout most of Western history, fear of the lower classes often manifested itself in a belief that lower-class males were "after our wives and daughters." During the slavery period in the United States, for example, it was widely believed that, if given the chance, Black males would rape White women, whereas White males did not find Black women attractive. Yet the truth was just the opposite; rape of White women by black males was relatively rare, whereas many White slave masters routinely raped their Black slaves. Once again, this supports the idea that rape is a reflection of power issues rather than just sexual issues.

sociological theory
A theory of rape that identifies power differentials in society as causing rape.

Evolutionary Theory: Product of Evolution

Finally, a controversial theory on the origins of rape comes out of evolutionary theory. Randy Thornhill and Craig Palmer, authors of *Natural History of Rape: Biological Bases of Sexual Coercion*, propose that rape is rooted in human evolution (Thornhill & Palmer, 2000). According to evolutionary theory, men and women have developed differing reproductive strategies, wherein men desire frequent mating to spread their seed, and women are designed to protect their eggs and be more selective in choosing mates (see Chapter 2 for more information about evolutionary theory). Rape has developed as a consequence of these differences in reproductive strategies. The majority of rapists are male, Thornhill and Palmer assert, because men are designed to impregnate and spread their seed.

As you might guess, this theory is controversial, and many feminists and sociologists alike are upset about ideas proposed in this theory (Brownmiller, 2000; Roughgarden, 2004). However, controversial or not, it's an interesting argument for us to consider when discussing theories on the development of rape.

GENDER DIFFERENCES IN ATTITUDES ABOUT RAPE

Researchers have used many techniques to measure attitudes about rape and rape victims, such as questionnaires, written vignettes, mock trials, videotaped scenarios, still photography, and newspaper reports. Gender research has found that overall, men are less empathetic and sensitive than women toward rape, and they attribute more responsibility to the victim (Nagel et al., 2005; Whatley, 2005; B. H. White & Kurpius, 2002). Men believe more rape myths (stereotypical beliefs that blame the victim; Burgess et al., 2007; Burt, 1980; Franiuk et al., 2008), and they also believe that a woman is signaling sexual availability when the woman thinks her behavior is simply friendly or even neutral (B. E. Johnson et al., 1997; Saal et al., 1989). Women rate a rape as more justified and see the victim as more responsible for the rape when the woman was seen as "leading a man on" (Muehlenhard & MacNaughton, 1988; Muehlenhard & Schrag, 1991). One study found that some women may not support female rape victims because of traditional attitudes about men and a belief in the idea that a woman needs a man to feel fulfilled (which would lead to more support for the man; Chapleau et al., 2007).

However, there is some hope in changing these attitudes about rape. One longitudinal study found that all men experienced a decline in negative rape attitudes over the 4 years they were in college (Pamm, 2001). This may be due in part to rape education workshops, which have been found to increase awareness and decrease rape myths (Foubert & Cremedy, 2007; Katz, 2006; Klaw et al., 2005).

ETHNIC DIFFERENCES IN ATTITUDES ABOUT RAPE

Although the majority of the research has examined gender differences in attitudes about rape, there is also research on ethnicity differences in rape attitudes. Overall, ethnic minorities have been found to have more traditional attitudes toward women, which has been found to affect rape attitudes (Fischer, 1987). For example, among college students, non-Hispanic Whites are more sympathetic than African Americans to women who have been raped (Nagel et al., 2005). However, African Americans are more sympathetic than either Hispanic (Fischer, 1987; Littleton et al., 2007) or Japanese American college students (Yamawaki & Tschanz, 2005). Asian American students have the least sympathy for women who have been raped and are more likely to hold a rape victim responsible for the rape and excuse the rapist (Devdas & Rubin, 2007; J. Lee et al., 2005; Yamawaki & Tschanz, 2005).

Researchers suggest that these differences are due to variations in cultural gender roles and conservative attitudes about sexuality. It's important to keep in mind that within these ethnic groups,

REALResearch > "Persecutory" rape occurs in the context of a political conflict (DUNKLEY, 2005). This would include rape that occurs during times of war, when men are indifferent to the fate of women they view as enemies (HYNES, 2004; LALUMIÈRE ET AL., 2005C). Although men are also raped during wartime, women are more frequently targeted (BORCHELT, 2005).

there are also gender differences in attitudes about rape, with women more supportive of rape victims than men.

RAPE IN DIFFERENT CULTURES

Rape is defined differently around the world, so the incidence of rape varies depending on a culture's definition. One culture might accept sexual behavior that is considered rape in another culture. For example, rape has been accepted as a punishment in some cultures throughout history. Among the Cheyenne Indians, a husband who suspected his wife of infidelity could put her "out to field," where other men were encouraged to rape her (Hoebel, 1954). In the Marshall Islands of the Pacific Ocean, women were seen as the property of the males, and any male could force sexual intercourse upon them (Sanday, 1981). In Kenya, the Gusii people view intercourse as an act in which males overpower their female partners and

REALResearch > Racist and sexist stereotypes influence rape blame attribution. The "jezebel stereotype," which originated during slavery, views Black women as promiscuous and therefore more at fault for sexual assault (DONOVAN, 2007).

cause them considerable pain. In fact, if she has difficulty walking the next morning, the man is seen as a "real man" and will boast of his ability to make his partner cry (Bart & O'Brien, 1985). In 2002, an 11-year-old Pakistani boy was found guilty of walking unchaperoned with a girl from a different tribe. His punishment involved the gang raping of his 18-year-old sister, which was done to shame his family. The gang rape took place in a mud hut while hundreds of people stood by and laughed and cheered (Tanveer, 2002).

Rape has also been used for initiation purposes. In East Africa, the Kikuyu used to have an initiation ritual in which a young boy was expected to rape to prove his manhood (Broude & Greene, 1976). Until he did this, he could not engage in sexual intercourse or marry a woman. In Australia, among the Arunta, rape serves as an initiation rite for girls. After the ceremonial rape, she is given to her husband, and no one else has access to her (Broude & Greene, 1976).

Child rape is also common in some places around the globe. In Chapter 15, we discussed the South African myth about curing AIDS through sex with a virgin child (Posel, 2005). It is estimated that sexual violence against children, including infant rape, has increased 400% over the past decade in South Africa (Dempster, 2002). Some studies have found that 1 million women and children are raped in South Africa each year (Meier, 2002).

Many cultural beliefs and societal issues are responsible for the high rape rates in South Africa, including the fact that South African women have a difficult time saying no to sex; many men believe they are entitled to sex and believe that women enjoy being raped (Meier, 2002). South Africa has the highest reported rape rates in the world (and probably a higher unreported rape rate), and experts have been looking for ways to help deter men from committing rape (Dixon, 2005). Because of this, in 2005, an anti-rape female condom was unveiled in South Africa (Dixon, 2005; see nearby photo). This device is con-

troversial: Some believe that it puts the responsibility for the problem on the shoulders of South African women, whereas others believe that the device may help lessen the climbing rape rates in South Africa.

In Asian cultures there are often more conservative attitudes about sex; because of this, there is often more tolerance for rape myths (M. A. Kennedy & Gorzalka, 2002; Uji et al., 2007; Yamawaki, 2007). Research by Sanday (1981) indicates that the primary cultural factors that affect the incidence of rape in a society include relations between the sexes, the status of women, and male attitudes in the society. Societies that promote male violence have higher incidences of rape because men are socialized to be aggressive, dominating, and to use force to get what they want.

Rapex, an antirape condom worn by women, was unveiled in South Africa in 2005. The South African inventor, shown here, advises women to insert the device as part of their daily security routine. During rape, metal barbs in the condom will hook into the skin of the penis and immediately disable the man, allowing the woman to get away. The barbs must be surgically removed, so a rapist will need to seek medical attention, enabling the police to identify him.

review questions

1 Explain why there is no single definition of rape.

2 Describe the problems that have been encountered in attempting to identify the actual number of rapes.

3 Identify what researchers have found about the characteristics of rapists.

4 Identify and differentiate between the five theories of rape.

5 Discuss gender and ethnicity differences in rape attitudes and how these attitudes might be changed.

6 Explain how the rates of rape vary depending on how each culture defines rape.

Rape on Campus

Rape is prevalent on U.S. college campuses. It is estimated that approximately 3% of women experience a completed or attempted rape during a typical college year (B. S. Fisher et al., 2000). Studies on college campuses have found high rates of both verbal and forced sexual behavior in dating relationships (DeGue & DiLillo, 2005; Forbes & Adams-Curtis, 2000; Hines, 2007). Sanday (1990) refers to verbal sexual coercion as "working a yes out." Some men have been found to use nonphysical methods of coercion to obtain sexual contact with an unwilling partner, such as continual arguments, verbal pressure, or deceit (DeGue & DiLillo, 2005). Men who use verbal sexual coercion have been found to believe in more rape myths, report more hostility toward women, and have more sexual partners than men who do not use such coercion (DeGue & DiLillo, 2005).

A study done in 2000 looked at sexual coercion on college campuses across the United States and found that 2% of women reported they had been raped, whereas 1% reported they were victims of an attempted rape—meaning that 35 women are raped or experience an attempted rape for every 1,000 college students each year (B. S. Fisher et al., 2000). As we discussed earlier, the majority of these women knew the person who sexually victimized them; the majority were ex-boyfriends, classmates, friends, or coworkers (B. S. Fisher et al., 2000).

In Chapter 7, we discussed stalking in intimate relationships. Some women report being stalked on campus, either physically, or through notes and e-mails. Overall, a total of 8% to 16% of women and 2% to 7% of men report being stalked at some point in their lives (Dennison & Thomson, 2005). What's interesting is that college-age men and women often have differing definitions for stalking, and typically, men are not as quick to define unwanted attention and interest as stalking (Hills & Taplin, 1998). Stalking is a serious problem, especially given that 81% of women who have been stalked by a lover were also physically assaulted by that lover, whereas 31% were sexually assaulted by him (Tjaden & Thoennes, 1998). See Figure 17.2 for more information about stalking on college campuses.

Alcohol can sexualize the environment for men. A man who has been drinking may believe that a woman is signaling she is available when she is acting friendly.

WHAT DO YOU WANT TO KNOW ?

What if you are drunk and she is too, and when you wake up in the morning, she says you raped her?
Claims of rape must be taken seriously. This is why men and women should be very careful in using alcohol and engaging in sexual activity. The best approach would be to delay engaging in sexual activity if you have been drinking. This way, you will not find yourself in this situation.

Because the majority of women know their assailants on college campuses, it won't come as any surprise that few feel comfortable reporting or pressing charges. Studies have found that although two thirds of the women talked to someone else about the incident, the majority told only a friend (B. S. Fisher et al., 2000).

ALCOHOL AND RAPE

Alcohol use is one of the strongest predictors of acquaintance rape on college campuses, where at least half of all rape cases involve the use of alcohol by the rapist, victim, or both (Benson et al., 2007; Klein et al., 2007; Parkhill & Abbey, 2008). One study found that 79% of college students who reported being sexually assaulted were using alcohol use at the time of the assault (Benson et al., 2007).

For men, alcohol seems to "sexualize" the environment around them. Cues that might be taken as neutral if the men were not drunk (such as a certain woman talking to them or dancing with them) may be seen as an indication of sexual interest (Abbey et al., 2005; Montemurro & McClure, 2005; Peralta, 2008). In addition, alcohol increases the chances of engaging in risky sexual behaviors (Klein et al., 2007; O'Hare, 2005).

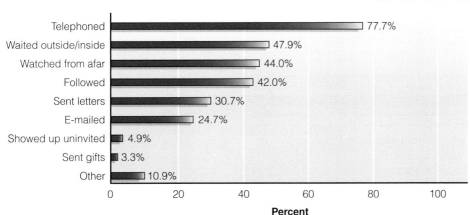

Figure **17.2** Percentages of stalking behaviors on college campuses. Source: B. S. Fisher et al., 2000; Stalking Resource Center, 2000.

For women, alcohol may lead to increased teasing and flirting, which sends ambiguous messages. Like alcohol use in men, women under the influence of alcohol engage in risky sexual behaviors (Klein et al., 2007; Maisto et al., 2004; O'Hare, 2005; see Chapter 15 for a discussion of high-risk sexual behaviors). For a woman, being drunk is one of the strongest risk factors for being sexually victimized (B. S. Fisher et al., 2000). Women who get drunk are more likely to be viewed as "loose" or sexually "easy" (Parks & Scheidt, 2000). These views help put blame on women who have been raped. Unfortunately, when a woman experiences a rape while drunk she is more likely to blame herself and often will not label the attack as a rape even when it clearly was (L. G. Hensley, 2002).

Alcohol use on college campuses, as it relates to rape, is viewed very differently for men and women. A man who is drunk and is accused of rape is seen as less responsible because he was drinking ("Lighten up; he didn't even know what he was doing"); a woman who has been drinking is seen as more responsible for her behavior ("Can you believe her? She's had so much to drink that she's flirting with everyone—what a slut!"; Peralta, 2008; D. Richardson & Campbell, 1982; Scully & Marolla, 1983).

In 2006, several members of Duke University's lacrosse team were accused of raping a female stripper. As a result, three team members were charged with rape. In 2007, after an emotional year, the North Carolina Attorney General dropped all charges and declared the three players innocent of rape.

FRATERNITIES AND RAPE

Initially, Greek organizations were established to help students join together to participate in social issues that they felt were largely ignored by their respective universities (Bryan, 1987). Today, however, many fraternities and sororities operate primarily for socializing. It is estimated that 10% of college rapes happen in fraternities (B. S. Fisher et al., 2000).

Although rape does occur in residence halls and off-campus apartments, there are several ways in which fraternities create a riper environment for rape. Many fraternities revolve around an ethic of masculinity. Values that the members see as important

---

REALResearch > Research has found there is more blame aimed at rape victims if their sexual orientation suggests a possible attraction to the rapist (WAKELIN & LONG, 2003). In a male perpetrated rape, gay men and heterosexual women receive the most blame, whereas lesbians and heterosexual men receive the least blame.

---

include competition, dominance, willingness to drink alcohol, and sexual prowess. There is considerable pressure to be sexually successful, and the members gain respect from other members through sex (P. Y. Martin & Hummer, 1989; Murnen & Kohlman, 2007). The emphasis on masculinity, secrecy, and the protection of the group often provides a fertile environment for coercive sexuality (Adams-Curtis & Forbes, 2004; Murnen & Kohlman, 2007). In addition, fraternity men have been found to be more accepting of rape myths (Bleecker & Murnen, 2005).

Some fraternities have begun to institute educational programs for their members. Others invite guest speakers from **rape crisis centers** to discuss the problem of date rape. Until members of

fraternities learn to use peer pressure against those who violate the rights of women, rape will certainly continue to be a problem.

ATHLETES AND RAPE

Participation in college athletics has been found to be associated with rape-supportive attitudes and, to a lesser degree, sexually aggressive behavior (Murnen & Kohlman, 2007). Male athletes have been found to be disproportionately overrepresented as assailants of rape by women surveyed (Locke & Mahalik, 2005; Sawyer et al., 2002). In addition, athletes who participate on teams that produce revenue have higher rates of sexually abusive behavior than athletes on teams that don't produce revenue (Koss & Gaines, 1993; McMahon, 2004). Researchers suggest that perhaps it is the sense of privilege that contributes to a view of the world in which rape is legitimized. Playing sports may also help connect aggression and sexuality.

Some researchers suggest that all male groups may foster "hypermasculinity," which promotes the idea that violence and aggression are "manly" (Muehlenhard & Cook, 1988). The need to be aggressive and tough while playing sports may also help create problems off the field (Boeringer, 1999; T. J. Brown et al., 2002). One male athlete explains:

rape crisis centers
Organizations that offer support services to victims of sexual assault, their families, and friends. Many offer information, referrals, support groups, counseling, educational programs, and workshops.

You can be the nicest guy, but when you step on that mat, you've gotta flip a switch. You've gotta go nuts, and you've gotta become an animal. Within the rules, but you've gotta go out there and you've gotta be so intense. You have to just break that guy. (McMahon, 2004, p. 10)

Many male athletes may also have a distorted view of women, which often revolves around views expressed in the locker room. Locker-room talk often includes derogatory language about women (including the use of words such as "sluts" or "bitches" to describe them), whereas those athletes who are not playing well are referred to as "girls" (McMahon, 2004; Murnen & Kohlman, 2007).

Studies have also been done on female athletes, who often believe they are less at risk than female nonathletes (McMahon,

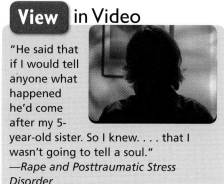

View in Video

"He said that if I would tell anyone what happened he'd come after my 5-year-old sister. So I knew. . . . that I wasn't going to tell a soul."
—*Rape and Posttraumatic Stress Disorder*
To view go to CengageNOW at www.cengage.com/login

2004). When asked about the potential for a female athlete to be raped, one woman said:

I think it would be a shock to a female athlete—because, we feel that we're so tough. . . . I always am kidding around that like, I could sit on a guy and knock the wind out of him and the idea of a guy taking advantage of me seems. . . . well, that could never happen. . . . I work out all the time, I'm so strong. . . . I'm not some little girl. I'm tough. (McMahon, 2004, p. 16)

Compared with female nonathletes, female athletes are more likely to blame the victim for a rape and believe that some women who are raped have put themselves in a bad situation (McMahon, 2004). Overall, female athletes have more negative attitudes about date rape than male athletes (Holcomb et al., 2002).

review questions

1 Explain what we know about rape on campus.

2 Explain the role that alcohol plays in rape on college campuses.

3 Explain the research on fraternity membership and rape on college campuses.

4 Explain the research on athletes, athletics, and rape on college campuses.

Effects of Rape

Rape is an emotionally, physically, and psychologically shattering experience for the victim. Immediately after a rape, many victims report feeling numb and disorganized. Some deny that the rape occurred at all, to avoid the pain of dealing with it. Others express self-blame, disbelief, anger, vulnerability, and increased feelings of dependency. As time goes by, the healing process begins, and feelings may shift to self-pity, sadness, and guilt. Anxiety attacks, nightmares, and fear slowly begin to decrease, although the incident is never forgotten. Women with a history of sexual abuse, including rape, have a lower health-related quality of life and more psychological symptoms than those who have no history of sexual abuse (L. M. Dickinson et al., 1999). Some women never return to prior functioning levels and must create an entirely new view of themselves.

RAPE TRAUMA SYNDROME

Researchers Burgess and Holmstrom (1974) coined the term **rape trauma syndrome (RTS),** which describes the effects of rape. RTS is a two-stage stress response pattern characterized by physical, psychological, behavioral, sexual problems, or a combination of these, and it occurs after forced, nonconsenting sexual activity. Although the *Diagnostic and Statistical Manual of Mental Disorders* (*DSM;* American Psychiatric Association, 2000) does not recognize RTS, it is similar to **posttraumatic stress disorder (PTSD),** which

rape trauma syndrome (RTS)
A two-stage stress response pattern that occurs after a rape.

posttraumatic stress disorder (PTSD)
Anxiety disorder recognized by the *DSM-IV-TR* that can develop after a life threatening or anxiety-producing event and can cause ongoing emotional and psychological symptoms, such as insomnia, depression, flashbacks, and nightmares.

During the first stage of rape trauma syndrome, victims may feel depressed, confused, angry, guilty, or humiliated. Talking to a counselor can be very helpful in working through these feelings.

occurs after a traumatic event. Research has found that a significant number of rape survivors develop posttraumatic stress syndrome within 2 weeks after the rape (Resnick et al., 1999).

Although not all victims respond to rape in the same manner, what follows is a description of what typically occurs. During the first stage of RTS, the **acute phase,** most victims fear being alone, strangers, or even their bedroom or their car if that is where the rape took place. Other emotional reactions to rape include anger (at the assailant, the rape, health care workers, family, one's self, court), anxiety, depression, confusion, shock, disbelief, incoherence, guilt, humiliation, shame, and self-blame (Frazier, 2000). A victim may also experience wide mood fluctuations. Difficulties with sleeping, including recurrent nightmares, are common. This phase begins immediately following the assault, may last from days to weeks and involves several stress-related symptoms.

The majority of victims eventually talk to someone about the rape (B. S. Fisher et al., 2003). However, in one study, half of the women who were raped waited years before telling anyone (Monroe et al., 2005). Most of the time a victim will talk to friends or family members rather than to the police. Younger victims are more likely to tell someone than are older victims, perhaps because older victims blame themselves more for the rape and may fear that others, too, will blame them. Some victims initially tell someone right after the rape and then, because of negative reactions from support persons, halt their disclosure and never mention it again (Ahrens, 2002).

Depression often follows a rape, and some victims report still feeling depressed 8 to 12 months postrape. Women who have been raped are more likely to experience depression than women who never experience sexual abuse (Cheasty et al., 2002). Several factors have been found to be related to the development of a significant depression after a rape, including having a history of prior psychological problems or prior victimization and a tendency to self-blame (Frazier, 2000).

Sometimes depressive feelings are so severe that victims' thoughts turn to suicide. In fact, research has found an association between rape and attempted suicide (Bridgeland et al., 2001). Poverty, prior depression, and prior sexual assaults also increase feelings of depression, anxiety, and overall problems associated with the rape (Cheasty et al., 2002).

Emotional reactions also vary depending on whether the victim knew his or her assailant. Women who report being raped by strangers experience more anxiety, fear, and startle responses, whereas those raped by acquaintances usually report more depression and guilt and a decrease in self-confidence (Sorenson & Brown, 1990). A woman who knew her assailant may have initially trusted him and agreed to be with him, and so after the rape she may wonder how she could have had such bad judgment, why she did not see it coming, and she may feel a sense of betrayal. There are also many physical symptoms experienced by men and women who have been raped. Some of these include general body soreness, bruises, difficulties with swallowing and throat soreness if there was forced oral sex (in women), genital itching or burning, rectal bleeding or pain, sexually transmitted infection symptoms, and eating disorders. In women, the emotional stress of the rape may also cause menstrual irregularities. However, some of these symptoms (nausea and menstrual irregularities) are also signs of pregnancy, which is why a pregnancy test is of utmost importance after a victim has been raped.

Recent research reveals that there is a higher incidence of pregnancy in women who have been raped than in women who engage in consensual unprotected sexual intercourse (Gottschall & Gottschall, 2003). We do know that women who are in prime fertile ages are overrepresented in rape victim statistics. This, in conjunction with the fact that women who are ovulating may be more physically attractive to rapists, may contribute to the higher pregnancy rates (Gottschall & Gottschall, 2003; the hormones involved in ovulation, which we discussed in Chapter 5, often make a woman appear more attractive). A young, healthy woman will have a higher chance of pregnancy than an older woman.

Long-term reorganization, stage two of RTS, involves restoring order in the victim's lifestyle and reestablishing control. Many victims report that changing some aspect of their lives, such as changing their address or phone number, helped them to gain control. Symptoms from both stages can persist for 1 to 2 years after the rape (Nadelson et al., 1982), although Burgess and Holmstrom (1979) found that 74% of rape victims recovered within 5 years. Recovery is affected by the amount and quality of care that the victim received after the rape. Positive crisis intervention and the support of others decrease the symptoms of the trauma.

Depression often follows a rape.

acute phase
First stage of the rape trauma syndrome, in which a victim often feels shock, fear, anger, or other related feelings.

long-term reorganization
The second stage of the rape trauma syndrome, which involves a restoration of order in the victim's lifestyle and reestablishment of control.

Do women who are raped eventually have a normal sex life?
Although it may take anywhere from a few days to months, most rape victims report that their sex lives get back to what is normal for them (van Berlo & Ensink, 2000). However, research indicates that lesbian women may have more difficulties with sexual problems postrape (Long et al., 2007). Counseling, a supportive partner, and emotional support are extremely helpful.

In the past, many researchers have argued that rape is a violent crime, not a sexual one. "Desexualizing" rape, or taking the sexual aspect out of it, has deemphasized postrape sexual concerns (Wakelin, 2003). Rape is indeed both a violent and a sexual crime, and the majority of victims report experiencing sexual problems postrape, even though these problems may not be lifelong (J. V. Becker et al., 1986; Holmstrom & Burgess, 1978; Van Berlo & Ensink, 2000).

Changes in sexual behaviors and sexual difficulties can persist for a considerable period after the rape (Campbell et al., 2004). It can take weeks, months, or even years to work through sexual difficulties such as fear of sex, desire and arousal disorders and specific problems with sexual behaviors such as sexual intercourse, genital fondling, and oral sex. Counseling can be helpful for women suffering from postrape sexual difficulties. It is not uncommon for a woman to seek help for a sexual problem, such as anorgasmia (lack of orgasm) and, during the course of therapy, reveal an experience with rape that she had never discussed. Some women may become more sexual after a rape. In fact, one study found an increase in alcohol consumption postrape, which increased the likelihood of engaging in risky sexual behaviors with multiple partners (Deliramich & Gray, 2008).

Some victims never discuss their rape.

SILENT RAPE REACTION

Some victims never discuss their rape with anyone and carry the burden of the assault alone. Burgess and Holmstrom (1974) call this the **silent rape reaction,** and in many ways, it is similar to RTS. Feelings of fear, anger, and depression and physiological symptoms still exist; however, they remain locked inside. In fact, those who take longer to confide in someone usually suffer a longer recovery period (L. Cohen & Roth, 1987).

The silent rape reaction occurs because some victims deny and repress the incident until a time when they feel stronger emotionally. This may be months or even years later. A student of mine, who had been raped 3 years earlier, was taking a course in psychology and noticed with frustration that as she read each chapter of the textbook, she would become extremely anxious when she saw the word therapist. When she explored why this produced anxiety, she realized that she could read the word only as the rapist, and it frightened her. Perhaps her subconscious was letting her know that she was finally ready to work through the repressed experience. Slowly the memories of the rape came back, as did all of the pain

and sorrow from the attack. After 2 months in counseling, she had worked through the memories sufficiently to feel that she was on her way to resolving her feelings about the rape.

RAPE OF PARTNERS AND OTHER SPECIAL POPULATIONS

Although we have learned from the research that there are certain groups more at risk for rape and sexual assault, we also know that there are special populations who are also at risk, including spouses, lesbians, older women, women with disabilities, and prostitutes.

Marital Rape

As of 1993, marital rape is considered a crime in all 50 states, even though it may be treated differently in various states. It has been estimated that 10% to 14% of all married women are raped by their husbands, although this number is much higher in battered women (D. E. H. Russell & Howell, 1983; Yllo & Finkelhor, 1985).

Overall, college-aged men and women are less likely to view marital rape as a serious crime (Auster & Leone, 2001; Ferro et al., 2008; Kirkwood & Cecil, 2001; Whatley, 2005). College students rate married women more responsible for rape when they dressed seductively (Whatley, 2005) or had been unfaithful in the marriage (Munge et al., 2007).

Although their symptoms are similar to those who are victims of nonmarital rape, many of these women report feeling extremely betrayed and may lose the ability to trust others, especially men. In addition, there is often little social support for wives who are raped, and those who stay with their husbands often endure repeated attacks (Bergen & Bukovec, 2006). Unfortunately, marital rape may be one of the least discussed types of rape.

Lesbians and Bisexuals

Similar to heterosexual women, rape is a common experience in both lesbian and bisexual women. In fact, adult sexual assault is slightly higher in lesbian and bisexual women compared with heterosexual women (Balsam et al., 2005). Lesbian and bisexual women also report a higher rate of completed rape than heterosexual women (Balsam et al., 2005). It is estimated that 35% of lesbian and bisexual women who have been raped seek help after a rape, mostly from friends (Bradford et al., 1994).

Like heterosexual women, lesbian and bisexual women also experience rape trauma syndrome following a rape. The emotional repercussions after a rape can be more intense in lesbian and bisexual women compared with heterosexual women, with bisexual women experiencing the most intense reactions (Long et al., 2007). Lesbians may also experience difficulties in assimilating the experience of rape into their own self-image (Long et al., 2007; Orzek, 1988). They may be "feminist-identified" in most areas of their lives, and the rape may force them to reexamine the patriarchal society and their feelings about men. Some lesbians may have never experienced sexual intercourse with a man and may be un-

silent rape reaction
A type of rape trauma syndrome in which a victim does not talk to anyone after the rape.

Older women are also victims of rape and may experience increased trauma due to declining physical health and more conservative attitudes about sexuality.

accustomed to dealing with the fear of pregnancy, let alone the extreme feelings of being violated and abused.

Older Women

Many people believe that rape only happens to younger women. It is difficult to think about our mothers or grandmothers being raped. The stereotype that only young, attractive women are raped prevents our thinking about the risk of rape for older women. Although it is true that younger women are more at risk for rape, older women are also raped (Ball, 2005; Burgess & Morgenbesser, 2005; Jeary, 2005). Older women are likely to be even more traumatized by rape than younger women because many have very conservative attitudes about sexuality, have undergone physical changes in the genitals (lack of lubrication and/ or thinning of the walls of the vagina) that can increase the severity of physical injury, and have less social support after a rape, which reinforces and intensifies their sense of vulnerability (Burgess & Morgenbesser, 2005).

Women With Disabilities

Women with disabilities, regardless of their age, race, ethnicity, sexual orientation, or socioeconomic class, are assaulted, raped, and abused at a rate 2 times greater than women without disabilities (Cusitar, 1994; Sobsey, 1994; Wacker et al., 2008). They may be more vulnerable because of their diminished ability to fight back. In addition, mentally handicapped persons may have a more difficult time reading the preliminary cues that would alert them to danger. The impact of a rape may be intense for these people because of a lack of knowledge about sexuality, loss of a

sense of trust in others, and the lack of knowledgeable staff who can effectively work with them. In many cases, women with severe mental disabilities who have been sexually assaulted may not realize that their rights have been violated and therefore may not report the crime. Because of these factors, the intensity and length of time of RTS is usually prolonged.

Prostitutes

Studies have found that between 68% and 70% of female prostitutes have been victims of rape (Farley & Barkan, 1998; Silbert, 1998). Because a prostitute's job is to provide sex in exchange for payment, the question of consent is often difficult to judge. Also, because of the general disapproval of prostitution, a prostitute who reports rape is often treated with disdain. People tend not to believe that she was raped or may think that she is angry because she was not paid. Many prostitutes who are raped begin to question their involvement in prostitution. Believing and trusting her experience and performing a comprehensive medical checkup are imperative.

HOW PARTNERS REACT TO RAPE

When a man or woman's sexual partner is raped, the partner often feels anger, frustration, and intense feelings of revenge (M. E. Smith, 2005). Many partners express a strong desire to "kill him" (the rapist), "make him pay," and the like. In addition, some partners experience a sense of loss, guilt, self-blame, and jealousy. Emotional reactions to the rape may affect a man's or woman's feelings about his or her partner and view of men in the world (M. E. Smith, 2005). In cases of acquaintance rape, a man or woman may lose trust in his or her partner, feeling that because the partner knew the assailant, she may have expressed sexual interest in him. Overall, after a date rape experience, negative judgments and reactions by a rape victim's partner are common (A. Brown & Testa, 2008). These reactions further isolate the victim and reinforce her feelings of guilt.

All in all, rape places a great deal of stress on a relationship. Couples often avoid dealing with rape entirely, believing that talking about it would be too stressful. Many men feel uncomfortable sharing their feelings about a rape because they worry about burdening their partners. However, open communication is extremely beneficial and should be encouraged. Even though dealing with a rape in a relationship can be traumatic, it has been found that women who have a stable and supportive partner recover from a rape more quickly than those who do not.

review questions

1 Define and describe the rape trauma syndrome.

2 Identify the stages of the rape trauma syndrome and explain what typically happens during these stages.

3 Define and describe the silent rape reaction and discuss the long-term effects of the silent rape reaction.

4 Describe the effects of rape in special populations, including married partners, lesbians, older women, women with disabilities, and prostitutes.

5 Describe the typical reactions of men and women whose partners have been raped.

When Men Are Rape Victims

Can a man be raped? Each year in the United States, more than 14,000 men report being victims of rape or attempted rape (Rennison, 2001; this means that 5% of all reported rapes are reported by men). However, male rape is even more underreported than female rape (Wiwanitkit, 2005). Typically, men who are raped are viewed more negatively than women who have been raped (I. Anderson, 2004). Like women, long-term effects of rape are common in men and can include depression, anger, anxiety, self-blame, and increased vulnerability (J. Walker et al., 2005).

RAPE OF MEN
BY WOMEN

Students often laugh at the idea that a man could be raped by a woman because they believe the myth that men are always willing to have sex, and so a woman would never need to rape a man. However, the myth actually serves to make male rape more humiliating and painful for many men. One study found that 1 in 33 men report having experienced an attempted or completed rape in their lifetime (L. G. Hensley, 2002).

Female rapists have been found to engage in a wide range of sexually aggressive behaviors, including forced sex and the use of verbal coercion (P. B. Anderson & Savage, 2005). In a study of male college students, 34% reported coercive sexual contact: 24% from women, 4% from men, and 6% from both sexes (Struckman-Johnson & Struckman-Johnson, 1994). The majority of male rapes by women use psychological or pressured contact, such as verbal persuasion or emotional manipulation, rather than physical force. Although the majority of college men had no or very mild negative reactions to the unwanted female contact, 20% of the men experienced strong negative reactions. Because men who are raped by women are often unwilling to define themselves as victims, many do not report these rapes even though physical and psychological symptoms are common (P. B. Anderson & Savage, 2005).

*The rape of men is **infrequently reported.***

WHAT DO YOU WANT TO KNOW?

Technically, can a man really be raped?
Some people think that it is impossible for a woman to rape a man because he just would not get an erection. Even though men are anxious, embarrassed, or terrorized during a rape, they are able to have erections. Having an erection while being raped may be confusing and humiliating, just as an orgasm is for females. In fact, for some it may be the most distressing aspect of the assault (Sarrel & Masters, 1982). Women who rape men can also use dildos, hands, or other objects to penetrate the anus. In addition, men can be orally or anally raped by men and forced to perform various sexual behaviors.

RAPE OF MEN
BY MEN

It is estimated that between 5% and 10% of all reported rapes in the United States involve male victims (Scarce, 1997). However, this is probably an underrepresentation of the true incidence because the rape of men by men is infrequently reported to the police (Hodge & Canter, 1998; Tewksbury, 2007). Men who are raped are often less likely than women to report the rape or seek out medical care. For many men who have been raped by a man, the fear that others will think they are gay is a barrier to reporting (Sable et al., 2006).

Male victims of rape are likely to be young (late teens to late 20s) and African American (Scarce, 1997). However, the higher frequency of rape in African Americans may be because much of the research on male rape has been done in African American communities. Although attackers are often known by the victim, multiple attackers are more common in the rape of men than the rape of women.

Gay men have been found to be raped at a higher rate than heterosexual men (Scarce, 1997). Hickson and colleagues (1994) found that in a sample of 930 gay men, close to 30% claimed they had been sexually assaulted at some point in their lives. Close to one third of the victims had been sexual with the perpetrator prior to the sexual assault. The victims reported forced anal and oral sex and masturbation to ejaculation. The most common type of activity in the sexual assault of men by men is anal penetration followed by oral penetration (N. Groth & Burgess, 1980; Scarce, 1997).

As in the case of female rape, male rape is an expression of power, a show of strength and masculinity that uses sex as a weapon. The most common emotional reactions to the rape of men by men include shame, embarrassment, self-blame, hostility, and depression (Scarce, 1997; Tewksbury, 2007). Like women, men who have been raped may go through the rape trauma syndrome (Tewksbury, 2007). Many victims question their sexual orientation and feel that the rape makes them less of a "real man." The risk of suicide and alcoholism in men who have been raped has been found to be higher than in women (Holmes & Slap, 1998; Scarce, 1997). Also, unlike women, some male rape victims may increase their subsequent sexual activity to reaffirm their manhood.

PRISON
RAPE

The Prison Rape Elimination Act, a federal law that reduces tolerance for prison sexual assault, became effective in 2003. It mandated the collection of national data on the incidence of prison rape, and provides funding for research and program development. This law has helped reduce prison rape and support those who have been raped in prison. Studies have found that approximately 18% of prison inmates report sexual threats from other prisoners, whereas 8.5% report sexual assaults in prison (C. Hensley et al., 2005).

Although prison rape occurs most frequently in the male population, it also occurs between female inmates using a variety of different objects to penetrate the vagina or anus. Women who are in U.S. prisons are often victims of sexual harassment, molestation, coercive sexual behaviors, and forced sexual intercourse, with the majority of this abuse being perpetuated by prison staff (Struckman-Johnson & Struckman-Johnson, 2002). Female inmates also experience sexual pressure in their interactions with other female inmates (Alarid, 2000). Some researchers have pointed out that incarcerated women are viewed as "bad girls" and because of this they are viewed as sexually easy (Struckman-Johnson & Struckman-Johnson, 2002). The majority of women who are raped in prison never report the crime for fear of retaliation.

Men in prison learn avoidance techniques that women use in society—physical modesty, no eye contact, no accepting of gifts, and tempering of friendliness (Bart & O'Brien, 1985). Prison rape has been found to be an act of asserting one's own masculinity in an environment that rewards dominance and power (Peeples & Scacco, 1982). Sex, violence, and conquest are the only avenues open to men in the restrictive confines of prison. To rape another man is seen as the "ultimate humiliation" because it forces the victim to assume the role of a woman. The victim becomes the "property" of his assailant, who will, in turn, provide protection in return for anal or oral sex. However, the rapist often will "sell" sexual favors from his man to other inmates in exchange for cigarettes or money.

Like rape in other populations, prison rape has been found to have a significant role in the development of posttraumatic stress disorder (Kupers, 2001). Inmates who have been raped also experience rape trauma syndrome. As mentioned previously, the acute phase is characterized by feelings of fear, anxiety, anger, and guilt, as well as numerous physical problems. Because these men and women must continue to interact with their assailants, long-term reorganization may take longer to work through. In addition, oftentimes there are no rape crisis services for those who have been raped in prison and little sympathy from prison employees.

Prison rape has also contributed to the increased prevalence of HIV and other sexually transmitted infections in U.S. prisons (Pinkerton et al., 2007). Rectal and vaginal trauma is common during prison rape, which increases the risk of sexually transmitted infections and HIV (Dumond & Dumond, 2002).

review questions

1 How has the myth that a man could never be raped by a woman made male rape more humiliating for the victims?

2 Explain how female rapists use verbal persuasion or emotional manipulation more often than physical force.

3 Explain how the male rape of men has been viewed as an expression of power.

4 What does the research tell us about rape in prison?

5 Explain how prison rape has been associated with posttraumatic stress disorder.

Reporting, Avoiding, and Treating Rapists

As we learned earlier in the chapter, the majority of rape victims do not report the rape to the police. We now explore reporting statistics and reasons for nonreporting and the process of telling the police, pressing charges, and going to court. We also look at rape avoidance strategies and rapist treatment.

REPORTING A RAPE

It is estimated that about one in seven rapes is reported (Resnick et al., 2005); the likelihood of reporting is increased if the assailant was a stranger, if there was violence, or if a weapon was involved (U.S. Department of Justice—Office of Justice Programs, 2002). This probably has to do with the fact that victims are clearer about intent under these conditions.

Gender differences in reporting are also common. Women are less likely to report a rape if it does not fit the stereotypical rape scenario, whereas men are less likely to report if it jeopardizes their masculine self-identity (Pino & Meier, 1999).Women who report their rapes to the police have been subsequently found to have a better adjustment and fewer emotional symptoms than those who do not report (Sable et al., 2006).

It is also important for a victim to write out exactly what happened in as much detail as possible. When did the rape occur? Where was the victim? What time was it? Who was with the victim? What did the rapist look like? What was he or she wearing? Exactly what happened? Was alcohol involved? Was anyone else present? The victim should keep this for his or her own records, for if he or she decides to press charges it will come in handy. Over time memories fade, and the victim can lose the important small details.

Telling the Police

On college campuses, campus police are often notified before the local police. Campus police may be able to take disciplinary action, such as fines or dismissal if the assailant is a student, but they are not able to press formal charges. Pressing charges with the local police may be important for two reasons. First, it alerts the police to a crime and thus may prevent other women from being victimized. Second, if the victim decides to take legal action, he or she will need to have a formal report from the local police (not the campus police).

Although police officers have become more sensitive to the plight of rape victims in the past few years, some victims still report negative experiences (Monroe et al., 2005). Society's victim-precipitated view of rape also affects the attitudes of the police. To make sure that a crime did indeed occur, police must interrogate each case completely, which can be very difficult for a victim who has just been through a traumatic experience. Still, many report that taking such legal action makes them feel back in control, that they are doing something about their situation.

Re-living a rape during a legal trial is emotionally draining. Many victims feel isolated and alone with increased feelings of guilt and self-blame.

Pressing Charges

The decision to press official charges is a difficult one that takes much consideration. It has often been said that a rape victim goes through a second rape because he or she seems to be put on trial more than the accused rapist. Court proceedings take up a great deal of time and energy, and they create considerable anxiety.

Victims of rape report that they pressed charges because they were angry, to protect others, or they wanted justice to be served. Reasons for refusing to press charges include being afraid of revenge, wanting to just forget, feeling sorry for the rapist, or feeling as though it would not matter anyway because nothing would be done. Victims of rape can also file a civil lawsuit and sue the assailant for monetary damages. Civil lawsuits are generally easier to prove than criminal lawsuits (Wagner, 1991).

*Rape trials **can be extremely difficult** for all involved.*

Going to Court

If a victim is undecided about whether to press charges, it may be helpful to sit in on a rape trial. Rape trials can be extremely difficult for all involved. However, the purpose of sitting in is not to scare a person but to prepare oneself. It is not easy to proceed with legal action, so it can be really helpful to gather support from friends and family.

Avoidance Strategies

Rape is the only violent crime in which we expect a person to fight back. If a woman does not struggle, we question whether she wanted to have sex. Only with visible proof of a struggle (bruises and cuts) does society seem to have sympathy. Some victims of rape have said that at the time of the rape, they felt frozen with fear, that it was impossible to move because they just could not believe what was happening to them. One victim explains:

Did you ever see a rabbit stuck in the glare of your headlights when you were going down a road at night? Transfixed— like it knew it was going to get it—that's what happened. (Brownmiller, 1975, p. 358)

How does a person know when to fight back? What should his or her strategies be? If you are confronted with a potential or attempted rape, the first and best strategy is to try to escape. However, this may not be possible if you are in a deserted area, if there are multiple attackers, or if your attacker has a weapon. If you cannot escape, effective strategies include verbal strategies such as screaming, dissuasive techniques ("I have my period" or "I have herpes"), empathy (listening or trying to understand), negotiation ("Let's discuss this"), and stalling for time. However, if the rapist does not believe the victim, these techniques may cause more harm than good.

Prentky and Knight (1986) assert that the safest strategy is to attempt to talk to the attacker and try to make yourself a real person to him ("I'm a stranger; why do you want to hurt me?"). Self-defense classes can help a person to feel more confident in his or her ability to fight back. One study found that women who had taken a self-defense class felt more prepared and less scared during the rape than women who had never taken such a class (Brecklin & Ullman, 2005).

Treating the Rapist

Can a person who rapes be treated so that he or she loses the desire to rape? Because the majority of rapists are male, we concentrate on treating male rapists in this section.

Many therapies have been tried, including shock treatment, psychotherapy, behavioral treatment, support groups, and the use of Depo-Provera, a drug that can diminish a man's sex drive. The idea behind Depo-Provera is that if the sex drive is reduced, so, too, is the likelihood of rape. So far these treatments have yielded inconclusive results. Many feminists argue that because violence, not sexual desire, causes rape, taking away sexual desire will not decrease the incidence of rape. For many men in treatment, the most important first step is to accept responsibility for their actions.

Many programs have been developed to decrease myths about rape and increase knowledge levels. All-male programs have been found to reduce significantly the belief in rape myths (Foubert & Cremedy, 2007; Foubert & Marriott, 1997). In another study evaluating posteducation outcomes, among the 20% of men who indicated a possible likelihood of raping before participating in an educational program, 75% reported less likelihood of raping after the program (Foubert & McEwen, 1998). However, although attitudes about rape myths appear to change after these programs, research has yet to show that these attitude changes result in changes in sexually coercive behavior (Foubert, 2000; Foubert & Cremedy, 2007). Treatments for high-risk rapists (those who are repeat offenders) have not been found to be overwhelmingly successful (Lalumière et al., 2005a).

1 What gender differences have been found in the reporting of rape?

2 Explain how a victim-precipitated view of rape might affect police attitudes.

3 Identify some of the reasons a victim might press (and not press) charges after a rape.

4 Explain the process of telling the police, pressing charges, and going to court. What are some of the problems a rape victim might experience along the way?

5 Explain some of the strategies given for avoiding a rape. When might these strategies cause more harm than good?

6 Identify some of the therapies that have been used in the treatment of rapists.

Sexual Abuse of Children

So far we have been talking about forced sexual relations between adults. But what happens when the coercive behavior involves children? **Child sexual abuse** is defined as sexual behavior that occurs between an adult and a minor. One important characteristic of child sexual abuse is the dominant, powerful position of the adult or older teen that allows him or her to force a child into sexual activity. The sexual activity can include inappropriate touch, removing a child's clothing, genital fondling, masturbation, digital penetration with fingers or sex toys, oral sex, vaginal intercourse, or anal intercourse (Valente, 2005). These behaviors are all illegal because the child is not old enough or mature enough to consent to this behavior.

As straightforward as this seems, the definition of child sexual abuse can become fuzzy. For instance, do you consider sexual play between a 13-year-old brother and his 7-year-old sister sexual abuse? How about an adult male who persuades a 14-year-old girl to fondle his genitals? Or a mother who caresses her 2-year-old son? How about a 14-year-old-boy who willingly has sex with a 25-year-old woman? How would you define the sexual abuse of children? Personal definitions of sexual abuse affect how we perceive those who participate in this behavior (Finkelhor, 1984).

Many researchers differentiate between child sexual abuse, which usually involves nonrelatives; pedophilia, which involves a compulsive desire to engage in sex with a particular age of child; and **incest,** which is sexual contact between a child or adolescent who is related to the abuser. There are several types of incest, including father–daughter, father–son, brother–sister, grandfather–grandchild, mother–daughter, and mother–son. Incest can also occur between stepparents and stepchildren or aunts and uncles and their nieces and nephews. Sexual activity between a child and someone who is responsible for the child's care (such as a babysitter) may also be considered incest, although definitions for incest vary from state to state.

Because most children look to their parents for nurturing and protection, incest involving a parent, guardian, or someone else the child trusts can be extremely traumatic. The incestuous parent exploits this trust to fulfill sexual or power needs of his or her own. The particularly vulnerable position of children in relation to their parents has been recognized in every culture. The **incest taboo**—the absolute prohibition of sex between family members—is universal (J. L. Herman, 1981).

Sociologists suggest that social restrictions against incest may have originally formed to reduce role conflicts (Henslin, 2005). A parent who has a sexual relationship with his or her child will have one role (i.e., parent) that conflicts with another (i.e., lover), which can interfere with responsibilities. We must also understand, however, that definitions of incest vary cross-culturally. A tribal group in tropical Africa called the Burundi believe that a mother causes her son's erectile dysfunction by allowing the umbilical cord to touch his penis during birth (Henslin, 2005). To rectify this situation, the mother must engage in sexual intercourse with the son. Although this practice may sound crazy to us, the culture of the Burundi supports this practice. The incest taboo still exists in this culture, but this practice is not viewed as incestuous behavior.

In the United States, we typically believe that father–daughter incest is the most common type, but research has shown that today the most common offenders are uncles and male first cousins (Henslin, 2005). Sibling incest also occurs and is more likely to occur in families in which there is a dominating father, a passive mother, and a dysfunctional home life (Carlson et al., 2006; Phillips-Green, 2002). Many siblings play sex games with each other while growing up, and there is some disagreement over whether this sex play between siblings is traumatic. Some believe that it is not traumatic unless there is force or exploitation, whereas others believe that it may lead to long-term difficulties in both interpersonal and sexual relationships (Cyr et al., 2002; Daie et al., 1989).

child sexual abuse
Sexual contact with a minor by an adult.

incest
Sexual contact between persons who are related or have a caregiving relationship.

incest taboo
The absolute prohibition of sex between family members.

Although the majority of offenders are male, some women do engage in incest. Mother–son incest is more likely to be subtle, including behaviors that may be difficult to distinguish from normal mothering behaviors (including genital touching; R. J. Kelly et al., 2002). Men who have been sexually abused by their mothers often experience more trauma symptoms than do other sexually abused men.

Finally, it's also important to mention that the increased time that children spend unsupervised on the Internet has given rise to a new type of child sexual abuse (Seymour et al., 2000). Online sexual predators lurk in chat rooms and post sexually explicit material on the Internet in hopes of making contact with children. Aggressive predators will dedicate much time to the development of relationships with vulnerable children and will try to alienate these children from their families. Some predators have even bought plane tickets for children to set up meetings (Seymour et al., 2000).

INCIDENCE OF
CHILD SEXUAL ABUSE

Accurate statistics on the prevalence of child sexual abuse are difficult to come by for many reasons: Some victims are uncertain about the precise definition of sexual abuse, might be unwilling to report, or are uncomfortable about sex and sexuality in general (Ephross, 2005; Finkelhor, 1984). The overall reported incidence has been increasing over the past 30 years. In the Kinsey and colleagues (1953) study of 441 females, 9% reported sexual contact with an adult before the age of 14. By the late 1970s and early 1980s, reports of child sexual abuse were increasing dramatically; 1,975 cases were reported in 1976, 22,918 in 1982 (Finkelhor, 1984), and 130,000 by 1986 (Jetter, 1991). It is estimated that 1 of every 4 girls and 1 of every 10 boys experiences sexual abuse as a child (Fieldman & Crespi, 2002; Valente, 2005).

Perhaps the increase in the incidence of child sexual abuse is a reflection of the changing sexual climate (in which there is less tolerance for such behavior), rather than an actual increase in the number of sexual assaults on children. The women's movement and the child protection movement both have focused attention on child sexual abuse issues (Finkelhor, 1984). Women's groups often teach that child sexual abuse is due to the patriarchal social structure and must be treated through victim protection. The child protection movement views the problem as one that develops out of a dysfunctional family and is treated through family therapy.

The reported incidence of child sexual abuse in other countries is much lower than in the United States (Finkelhor, 1984). However, note that the rate in the United States increased as the sexual climate changed. The incidence in other countries may be similar to the United States, but the United States may be more receptive to reports of abuse or may define child sexual abuse differently.

Recently there has been some doubt about the credibility of child sex abuse reporting. Would a child ever "make up" a story of sexual abuse? Research has shown that false reports occur in fewer than 10% of reported cases (Besharov, 1988). This is important because a child's report of sexual abuse remains the single most important factor in diagnosing abuse (Heger et al., 2002).

VICTIMS OF
CHILD SEXUAL ABUSE

Although research is limited because of sampling and responding rates, we do know that the median age for sexual abuse of both girls and boys is around 8 or 9 years old (Feinauer, 1988; Finkelhor et al., 1990). Boys are more likely to be sexually abused by strangers (40% of boys, 21% of girls), whereas girls are more likely to have family members as assailants (29% of girls, 11% of boys; Finkelhor et al., 1990).

Finkelhor proposes three reasons why the reported rates of male sexual abuse may be lower than those for females: (a) Boys grow up believing that they must be self-reliant and may feel that they should be able to handle the abuse; (b) male sexual abuse gets entwined with the stigma of homosexuality, because the majority of offenders are male; and (c) because boys often have more freedom than girls in our society, they may have a great deal to lose by reporting a sexual assault (1984, pp. 156–157).

Reactions to abuse vary. Many victims are scared to reveal the abuse, because of shame, fear of retaliation, belief that they themselves are to blame, or fear that they will not be believed. Some incest victims try to get help only if they fear that a younger sibling is threatened. When they do get help, younger victims are more likely to go to a relative for help, whereas older victims may run away or enter into early marriages to escape the abuse (J. L. Herman, 1981). Victims of incest with a biological father delay reporting the longest, whereas those who have been victims of stepfather or live-in partners have been found to be more likely to tell someone more readily (Faller, 1989).

*The overall reported incidence of child sexual abuse **has been increasing.***

HOW CHILDREN
ARE AFFECTED

There have been conflicting findings regarding the traumatic effects of sexual abuse. Some studies indicate that children are not severely traumatized by sexual abuse (Fritz et al., 1981), whereas more recent studies indicate that it may have long-lasting effects that may lead to other psychological problems, including antisocial behavior, drug abuse, and prostitution (Hardt et al., 2008; Lu et al., 2008). A. N. Groth (1978) suggests that sexual abuse is the most traumatic when it exists over a long period of time, the offender is a person who is trusted, penetration occurs, and there is aggression.

Keep in mind that what follows is a discussion of what is typically experienced by a victim of childhood sexual abuse or incest. As we have discussed before, it is impossible to predict what a child's experience will be; the reaction of each child is different. There are a few factors that make the abuse more traumatic, including the intensity of the sexual contact and how the sexual abuse is handled in the family. If a family handles the sexual abuse in a caring and sensitive manner, the effects on the child are often reduced.

PSYCHOLOGICAL AND EMOTIONAL REACTIONS

Sexual abuse can be devastating for a child and often causes feelings of betrayal, powerlessness, fear, anger, self-blame, low self-esteem, and problems with intimacy and relationships later in life (Valente, 2005). Children who hide their sexual abuse often experience shame and guilt and fear the loss of affection from family and friends (Seymour et al., 2000). They also feel frustrated about not being able to stop the abuse.

Whether they tell someone about their sexual abuse, many victims experience psychological symptoms such as depression, increased anxiety, nervousness, emotional problems, and personality and intimacy disorders. Similar to reactions of rape victims, depression is the most prevalent emotional symptom, which may be higher in victims who are abused repeatedly (Cheasty et al., 2002). Guilt is usually severe, and many children blame themselves for the sexual abuse (Valente, 2005). Victims of sexual abuse are also more likely than nonabused children to commit suicide (Valente, 2005).

Victims may also try to cut themselves off from a painful or unbearable memory, which can lead to what psychiatrists refer to as a **dissociative disorder.** In its extreme form, dissociative disorder may result in **dissociative personality disorder (DPD),** in which a person maintains two or more distinct personalities. Although it has long been a controversial issue in psychology (McNally, 2003), there is research to support the claim that some abuse victims are unable to remember past abuse. In one study of incest victims, 64% were found to partially repress their abuse, whereas 28% severely repressed it (J. Herman & Schatzow, 1987). Some experts claim that although the memories are classified as bad, disgusting, and confusing, many times they are not "traumatic." Because of this, the memories are simply forgotten and not repressed (McNally et al., 2004, 2005). This issue continues to be controversial even though many victims of sexual abuse often report an inability to remember details or the entirety of the abuse.

Women who were sexually abused as children have higher rates of personality disorders and posttraumatic stress disorder than those who experienced sexual abuse later in life (McLean & Gallop, 2003). Earlier in this chapter we discussed the increased risk of engaging in risky sexual behaviors postrape. Both antisocial and promiscuous sexual behavior are also related to a history of childhood sexual behavior (Deliramich & Gray, 2008; Valente, 2005). The most devastating emotional effects occur when the sexual abuse is done by someone the victim trusts. In a study of the effects of sexual abuse by relatives, friends, or strangers, it was found that the stronger the emotional bond and trust between the victim and the assailant, the more distress the victim experienced (Feinauer, 1989).

Long-Term Effects

It is not uncommon for children who are sexually abused to display what Finkelhor and Browne (1985) refer to as **traumatic sexualization.** Children may begin to exhibit compulsive sex play or masturbation and show an inappropriate amount of sexual knowledge. When they enter adolescence they may begin to show promiscuous and compulsive sexual behavior, which may lead to sexually abusing others in adulthood (Valente, 2005). These children have learned that it is through their sexuality that they get attention from adults. Children who have been sexually abused are also more vulnerable to revictimization later in life (Valente, 2005).

Children who are sexually abused have been found to experience sexual problems in adulthood. The developmentally inappropriate sexual behaviors that they learned as children can contribute to a variety of sexual dysfunctions later in life (Najman et al., 2005). Research has found that a large proportion of patients who seek sex therapy have histories of incest, rape, and other forms of sexual abuse (Maltz, 2002).

Eating disorders are also common. Research reveals a connection between eating disorders and sexual abuse (Wonderlich et al., 2001). In one study sexually abused children were found to eat less when they were emotionally upset and were more likely than nonabused children to desire a thinner body type (Wonderlich, 2000). The obsessions about food become all-consuming and may temporarily replace the original trauma of the sexual abuse. When these patients discussed their past sexual abuse, they were often able to make significant changes in their eating patterns.

Children who are sexually abused also commonly develop problems such as drug and alcohol addiction or prostitution. In fact, victims of sexual abuse have been found to have higher rates of alcohol and drug use, even as early as age 10 (Valente, 2005). Finkelhor and Browne (1985) hypothesize that because of the stigma that surrounds the early sexual abuse, the children believe they are "bad," and the thought of "badness" is incorporated into their self-concept. As a result, they often gravitate toward behaviors that society sees as deviant.

It is not unusual for adults who had been abused as children to confront their offenders later in life, especially among those who have undergone some form of counseling or psychotherapy to work through their own feelings about the experience. They may feel a strong need to deal with the experience and often get help to work through it. The accompanying Sex in Real Life, "Confronting the Incest Offender," is a letter written by an 18-year-old incest victim to her father. She had been sexually assaulted by him throughout her childhood, and this was the first time that she had confronted him.

Many children blame themselves for the sexual abuse.

dissociative disorder
Psychological disorder involving a disturbance of memory, identity, and consciousness, usually resulting from a traumatic experience.

dissociative personality disorder (DPD)
A dissociative disorder in which a person develops two or more distinct personalities.

traumatic sexualization
A common result of sexual abuse in which a child displays compulsive sex play or masturbation and shows an inappropriate amount of sexual knowledge.

Confronting the Incest Offender

You took my childhood away from me by making me lock my childhood away in the dark corners of my mind.

The following letter was written by an 18-year-old college student to her father. She had just begun to recall past sexual abuse by her father and was in counseling working on her memories. She decided to confront her father with this letter.

Dad: I can't hide it any longer! I remember everything about when I was a little girl. For years I acted as if nothing ever happened; it was always there deep inside but I was somehow able to lock it away for many years. But Daddy, something has pried that lock open, and it will never be able to be locked away again. I remember being scared or sick and crawling into bed with my parents only to have my father's hands touch my chest and rear. I remember going on a Sunday afternoon to my father's office, innocently wanting to spend time with him, only to play with some machine that vibrated.

I remember sitting on my father's lap while he was on the phone. I had a halter top on at the time. I remember wondering what he was doing when he untied it then turned me around to face him so he could touch my stomach and chest. I remember many hugs, even as a teenager, in which my father's hand was on my rear. I remember those words, "I like what is underneath better," when I asked my father if he liked my new outfit. But Daddy, more than anything, I remember one night when mom wasn't home. I was scared so I crawled into bed with my father who I thought was there to protect me. I remember his hands caressing my still undeveloped breast. I remember his hand first rubbing the top of my underwear then the same hand working

its way down my underwear. I remember thinking that it tickled, but yet it scared me.

Others had never tickled me like this. I felt frozen until I felt something inside me. It hurt, and I was scared. I said stop and started shaking. I remember jumping out of bed and running to my room where I cried myself to sleep. I also remember those words I heard a few days later, "I was just trying to love you. I didn't mean to hurt you. No one needs to know about this. People would misunderstand what happened."

You don't have to deal with the memories of what this has done to my life, my relationships with men, my many sleepless nights, my days of depression, my feelings of filth being relieved through making myself throw up and the times of using—abusing—alcohol in order to escape. You haven't even had to see the pain and confusion in my life because of this. I have two feelings, pain and numbness. You took my childhood away from me by making me lock my childhood away in the dark corners of my mind. Now that child is trying to escape, and I don't know how to deal with her.

I felt it was only fair that you know that it is no longer a secret. I have protected you long enough. Now it is time to protect myself from all of the memories. Daddy, I must tell you, even after all that has happened, for some reason I'm not sure of, I still feel love for you—that is, if I even know what love is.

Source: Author's files.

CHARACTERISTICS
OF CHILD SEXUAL ABUSERS

Many of us would like to believe that sexual abusers are identifiable by how they look. They are not. Sexual abusers look like nice people. Yet there are things that distinguish abusers from those who do not abuse children. Research comparing child molesters to nonmolesters has shown us that molesters tend to have poorer social skills, lower IQs, unhappy family histories, lower self-esteem, and less happiness in their lives (Finkelhor et al., 1990; Hunter et al., 2003; Langevin et al., 1988; Milner & Robertson, 1990). The majority of abusers are heterosexual males (Valente, 2005). As surprising as it may seem, many abusers have strict religious codes yet still violate sexual norms. In one study, for example, an incest offender who had been having sexual interactions with his daughter for 7 years was asked why he had not had vaginal intercourse with her. He replied: "I only had anal sex with her because I wanted her to be a virgin" (Dwyer & Amberson, 1989, p. 112).

Denying responsibility for the offense and claiming they were in a trancelike state is also common. The majority of offenders are also good at manipulation, which they develop to prevent discovery by others. One man told his 13-year-old victim, "I'm sorry this

had to happen to you, but you're just too beautiful," demonstrating the typical abuser's trait of blaming the victim for the abuse (Vanderbilt, 1992, p. 3). Ironically, those who abuse children also often report disdain for other sex offenders (Dwyer & Amberson, 1989).

The Development of a Sexual Abuser

Three prominent theories—learning, gender, and biological—propose factors that make abuse more likely. Proponents of learning theories believe that what children learn from their environment or those around them contributes to their behavior later in life. Many child sex abusers were themselves sexually abused as children (Seto, 2008). Many reported an early initiation into sexual behavior that taught them about sex at a young age. Many learned that such behavior was how adults show love and affection to children.

Proponents of gender theories identify gender as an important aspect in the development of an abuser—sexual abusers are overwhelmingly male (Finkelhor et al., 1990; Seto, 2008). Males often are not taught how to express affection without sexuality, which leads to needing sex to confirm their masculinity, being more focused on the sexual aspect of relationships, and being socialized to

REALResearch > Victims of childhood sexual, physical, and emotional abuse lose at least 2 years of quality of life (CORSO ET AL., 2008). This typically occurs because of the increased risk of obesity, depression, and heart disease, in addition to the development of unhealthy behaviors such as substance abuse or sexual promiscuity.

be attracted to mates that are smaller (Finkelhor, 1984; Seto, 2008). Keep in mind that the incidence of female offenders may be lower because of lower reporting rates for boys or because society accepts intimate female interaction with children as normal (A. N. Groth, 1978). Although we used to think that about 4% of offenders were female (D. E. H. Russell, 1984), newer studies have found that these numbers may be significantly higher. In one study, a review of 120,000 cases of child sexual abuse, 25% of cases were found to involve a female offender (Boroughs, 2004).

Proponents of biological theories suggest that physiology contributes to the development of sexual abusers (see Chapter 16). One study found that male offenders had normal levels of the male sex hormone testosterone but elevated levels of other hormones (Lang et al., 1990). There have also been reports of neurological differences between incest offenders and non–sex-criminal offenders that are thought to contribute to violence (Langevin et al., 1988).

TREATING
CHILD SEXUAL ABUSE

We know that sexual abuse can have many short- and long-term consequences—for victims as well as abusers. As a result, it is important to help victims of child sexual abuse to heal and help abusers learn ways to eliminate their abusive behaviors.

Helping the Victims Heal

Currently, the most effective treatments for victims of child sexual abuse include a combination of cognitive and behavioral psychotherapies, which teach victims how to understand and handle the trauma of their assaults more effectively. Many victims of sexual abuse also have difficulties developing and maintaining intimate relationships. Being involved in a relationship that is high in emotional intimacy and low in expectations for sex is beneficial (W. Maltz, 1990). Learning that they have the ability to say no to sex is very important and usually develops when they establish relationships based first on friendship, rather than sex. Many

times the partners of victims of sexual abuse are confused; they do not fully understand the effects of abuse in the lives of their mates, and so they may also benefit from counseling (L. Cohen, 1988).

Treating Abusers

In Chapter 16, we discussed treatment for pedophilia. The treatment of child sexual abusers is similar in that the primary goal is to decrease the level of sexual arousal to inappropriate sexual objects—in this case, children. This is done through behavioral treatment, psychotherapy, or drugs. Other goals of therapy include teaching sexual abusers to interact and relate better with adults; assertiveness skills training; empathy and respect for others; increasing sexual education; and evaluating and reducing any sexual difficulties that they might be experiencing with their sexual partners (Abel et al., 1980). Because recidivism is high in these abusers, it is also important to find ways to reduce the incidence of engaging in these behaviors (Firestone et al., 2005).

PREVENTING
CHILD SEXUAL ABUSE

How can we prevent child sexual abuse? One program that has been explored is the "just say no" campaign, which teaches young children how to say no to inappropriate sexual advances by adults. This program has received much attention. How effective is such a strategy? Even if we can teach children to say no to strangers, can we also teach them to say no to their fathers or sexually abusive relatives? Could there be any negative effects of educating children about sexual abuse? These are a few questions that future research will need to address.

Increasing the availability of sex education has also been cited as a way to decrease the incidence of child sexual abuse. Children from traditional, authoritarian families that have no sex education are at higher risk for sexual abuse. Education about sexual abuse—teaching that it does not happen to all children—may help children to understand that it is wrong. Telling children where to go and whom to talk to is also important.

Another important factor in prevention is adequate funding and staffing of child welfare agencies. Social workers may be among the first to become aware of potentially dangerous situations. Physicians and educators must also be adequately trained to identify the signs of abuse.

review questions

1 Define child sexual abuse and discuss its incidence.

2 Discuss victims' psychological and emotional reactions to child sexual abuse.

3 Explain what the research tells us about sexual abusers and the development of such behavior.

4 Describe the most effective treatments for victims and perpetrators of childhood sexual abuse.

5 Identify some ways in which society can help prevent childhood sexual abuse.

REALResearch **>** One study on violence in college dating relationships found that men and women who had shoved, punched, or physically abused a sibling were more likely to engage in intimate partner violence later in life (NOLAND ET AL., 2004). As siblings compete with one another for family resources, they use violence as a form of manipulation and control and then carry these behaviors into future intimate relationships.

Intimate Partner Violence

Intimate partner violence (**IPV,** which may also be referred to as domestic violence) is found among all racial, ethnic, and socio-economic classes, and it is estimated that more than 2 million people—1.5 million women and 834,732 men—are victims of IPV each year (Gazmararian et al., 2000; Sormanti & Shibusawa, 2008; Tilley & Brackley, 2005; Tjaden & Thoennes, 2000; Tonelli, 2004). The American Public Health Association reported that women experience close to 5 million intimate partner related physical assaults each year (Armour et al., 2008). However, the numbers of unreported IPV incidents are much higher. In fact, national studies have found that 29% of both women and men have experienced intimate partner violence in their lifetime (Coker et al., 2002; Reid et al., 2008). Studies have found that women with disabilities are significantly more likely to report experiencing IPV in their lifetime, compared to women without disabilities (Armour et al., 2008). Although IPV is common in adolescent and college-age populations, it can happen to men and women at any age (Bonomi et al., 2007; Forke et al., 2008). Many women and men are killed by their violent partners—76% of IPV homicide victims were women, whereas 24% were men (Fox & Zawitz, 2004).

Victims of IPV experience both physical and psychological symptoms, and the symptoms depend on both the frequency and severity of the violence (J. C. Campbell et al., 2002). Common psychological symptoms, similar to those experienced by victims of other coercive sexual behaviors, include depression, antisocial behavior, increased anxiety, low self-esteem, and a fear of intimacy (Tjaden & Thoennes, 2000). Physical symptoms may include headaches, back pain, broken bones, gynecological disorders, and stomach problems.

DEFINING INTIMATE PARTNER VIOLENCE AND COERCION

Intimate partner violence is coercive behavior that uses threats, harassment, or intimidation. It can involve physical (shoving, hitting, hair pulling), emotional (extreme jealousy, intimidation, humiliation), or sexual (forced sex, physically painful sexual behaviors) abuse. Some offenders even are violent toward pets, especially pets that are close to the victim. Generally there is a pattern of abuse, rather than a single isolated incident.

As the chapter opening story indicated, many women in abusive relationships claim their relationship started off well. They believe the first incidence of violence is a one-time occurrence that won't happen again. They often excuse their partner's behavior and accept their partner's apologies. In time, the abuser convinces his partner that it is really her fault that he became violent and that if she changes, it won't happen again.

Most women in this situation begin to believe that the problems are indeed their fault, so they stay in the abusive relationship. Many actually believe that it's safer in the relationship than outside of it. Things that may make it more difficult for a woman to leave include issues such as finances, low self-esteem, fear, or isolation.

This type of violence and abuse also occurs among college students. One 21-year-old college student talks about her relationship:

> *No one could understand why I wanted my relationship with Billy to work. After all, no relationship is perfect. He didn't mean to slam me that hard. Why would he want to leave bruises on me? Look at him. He's a big guy. Anyone can tell he might have trouble seeing his own strength. He means well. He gives the best hugs, like a big sweet bear. He always says he's sorry. He loves me and tells me this in letters all the time. He thinks I'm sweet, pretty, and kind. Maybe my friends are just jealous. After all, he is a really good-looking guy. I know a lot of girls who want him. He tells me girls throw themselves at him every day. Why would he lie? (Author's files)*

Intimate partner violence in same-sex relationships looks similar to IPV in heterosexual relationships (Eaton et al., 2008; A. Robinson, 2002). However, in same-sex relationships there are additional issues that may arise, including being "outed" if a partner tries to get help or leave the relationship (C. Brown, 2008). Outing when a person is not ready could result in employment or social issues (National Coalition of Anti-Violence

Although less is known about the prevalence and experience of intimate partner violence in lesbian relationships, we do know that IPV in lesbian relationships looks similar to IPV in heterosexual relationships.

© Joel Gordon

intimate partner violence (IPV)
A pattern of coercive behavior designed to exert power and control over a person in an intimate relationship through the use of intimidation, threats, or harmful or harassing behavior.

Domestic Violence in Lesbian Relationships

. . . domestic violence occurs at about the same rate in lesbian relationships as it does in heterosexual relationships.

Although we don't often hear much about it, domestic violence occurs at about the same rate in lesbian relationships as it does in heterosexual relationships (Eaton et al., 2008; Hewlett, 2008). Many women in same-sex relationships do not feel comfortable discussing the violence with others and worry about being outed by their partner (C. Brown, 2008). Following is one woman's story about the violence in her relationship.

I met my girlfriend at a party that a friend hosted. She was intelligent, beautiful, and had a wonderful sense of humor. Our relationship developed rapidly and the closeness we shared was something I had never experienced before. It is difficult to remember exactly when the abuse began because it was subtle. She criticized me because she didn't like my cooking, and she occasionally called me names when we argued. I didn't think much about it because she had recently lost custody of her daughter to her ex-husband because of her sexual orientation and was angry, irritable, and depressed. She often threatened suicide and attempted it during an argument that we had and then blamed me for calling 911 for help. Despite the stress she was experiencing, she was very supportive of me when my family "disowned" me after I came out to them. When I bought my first car, she insisted I put it in her name. Although we had periods of profound happiness, our arguments increased in frequency as did her

drinking and drug use. I kept telling myself that things would get better but they never did. She continually accused me of being unfaithful (I wasn't) and even once raped me after claiming I had flirted with a supermarket cashier. The first time she hit me I grabbed her wrist and twisted her arm to keep from being hit again. My response frightened me so much I suggested we see a couple's counselor, and she agreed.

Couple counseling was not helpful, and although things felt worse, our therapist said that was normal so we persevered. I began scrutinizing my own behavior believing that if I could only do things better or differently, our life together would improve. It wasn't until she pulled a knife on me that I realized that it wasn't going to change for the better. . . . it was only going to get worse. I called a crisis line and the counselor suggested that what I was experiencing was domestic violence. That had actually never occurred to be because we were both women. Leaving her was the hardest thing I have ever done.

It's still difficult to think of my situation as domestic violence but with the help of my counselor and support group, I am learning that women can be violent to other women, that anger, stress, depression, alcohol and drugs do not cause violence, that violence is a choice the abuser makes, and finally, that I am not to blame.

SOURCE: National Coalition of Anti-Violence Programs, 1998

Programs, 1998). Although we know less about intimate partner violence in gay relationships, studies have found that one in three men in same-sex relationships have been abused (Houston & McKirnan, 2008). Unfortunately, many gay and bisexual men are reluctant to seek help for violence in intimate relationships, because there is often little social support to do so (Cruz, 2003).

REALResearch > A nationally representative study of adults and children in India found a relationship between domestic violence and the development of asthma (SUBRAMANIAN ET AL., 2007). Exposure to psychological stressors, such as violence, can affect the immune system, which can influence the development of asthma.

❚ PREVENTING INTIMATE PARTNER VIOLENCE

Several factors have been found to be related to IPV, including a history of IPV in the offender's family and excessive alcohol use (Leonard, 2005; Lipsky et al., 2005). Educational programs can

help educate the public about intimate partner violence. Safe housing for victims of IPV can also reduce the likelihood of future abuse. Today there are thousands of battered women's shelters across the United States. These shelters provide women with several important things, including information and a safe haven. Often these centers have 24-hour hotlines that can help women who are struggling with issues related to domestic violence (see the Web Resources at the end of this chapter for other hotline options). Increasing the availability of safe houses and counseling and education is imperative. In addition, increasing the availability of services for gay, lesbian, bisexual, transgendered, elderly, and disabled women and men will help ensure that help is available for all who may need it.

REALResearch > Researchers have found that there are approximately **5.3** million incidents of intimate partner violence each year among U.S. women; **3.2** million occur among U.S. men (NATIONAL CENTER FOR INJURY PREVENTION AND CONTROL, 2005). Common behaviors include pushing, grabbing, slapping, and hitting.

review questions

1 Define intimate partner violence and give one example.

2 Identify some common psychological and physiological symptoms of IPV.

3 How is IPV in same-sex relationships similar to, and different from, heterosexual relationships?

4 Explain how intimate partner violence relates to sexual and physical abuse.

Sexual Harassment

Sexual harassment is a very broad term that includes anything from jokes, unwanted sexual advances, a "friendly" pat, an "accidental" brush on a person's body, or an arm around a person (Cammaert, 1985). It can also include unwanted sexual attention online (Barak, 2005). Because of the wide variety of actions that fall under this definition, many people are confused about what exactly constitutes sexual harassment.

In the United States, the courts recognize two types of sexual harassment, including **quid pro quo harassment** and **hostile environment harassment.** Quid pro quo (meaning "this for that") harassment occurs when a person is required to engage in some type of sexual conduct in exchange for a certain grade, employment, or other benefit. For example, a teacher or employer might offer you a better grade for engaging in sexual behavior. Another type of sexual harassment involves being subjected to unwelcome repeated sexual comments or visually offensive material that creates a hostile work environment and interferes with work or school. For example, a student or employee might repeatedly tell sexual jokes or send them via the Internet.

It may seem that sexual harassment is not as shocking as other forms of sexual coercion, but the effects of harassment on the victim can be traumatic and often cause long-term difficulties. Fitzgerald and Ormerod claim that "there are many similarities between sexual harassment and other forms of sexual victimization, not only in the secrecy that surrounds them but also in the [myth] that supports them" (1991, p. 2). Severe or chronic sexual harassment can cause psychological side effects similar to rape and sexual assault, and in extreme cases, it has been known to contribute to suicide.

INCIDENCE AND REPORTING OF HARASSMENT

It is estimated that 25% to 30% of college students report experiences of sexual harassment (Mènard et al., 2003). Sexual harassment on campus usually involves sexist comments, jokes, or touching, and the majority of students do not report it (Mènard et al., 2003). Federal law prohibits the sexual harassment of college students, and victims of sexual harassment can sue their schools for damages for sexual harassment (Hogan, 2005).

In the United States, sexual harassment has increased in recent years, probably in relation to the increase in women in the workforce. Because of sexual harassment, women are 9 times more likely than men to quit a job, 5 times more likely to transfer, and 3 times more likely to lose their jobs (Parker & Griffin, 2002). Although the majority of people who are sexually harassed are female, it can also happen to men. Same-sex harassment also occurs (Foote & Goodman-Delahunty, 2005).

As we have discussed, many victims of sexual harassment never say anything to authorities, although they may tell a friend. This may be in part because women are socialized to keep harmony in relationships. Others verbally confront the offender or leave their jobs to get away from it. Assertiveness is the most effective strategy, either by telling someone about it or confronting the offender. Many fear, however, that confronting a boss or teacher who is harassing them could jeopardize their jobs or their grades. Also, although these strategies increase the chances that the behavior will stop, they do not guarantee it. If you are being sexually

REALResearch **>** Cross-cultural studies on attitudes about sexual harassment have found that students from individualist countries (such as the United States, Canada, Germany, and the Netherlands) are less accepting of sexual harassment, whereas students from collectivist countries (such as Ecuador, Pakistan, the Philippines, Taiwan, and Turkey) are more accepting (SIGAL ET AL., 2005).

sexual harassment
Unwanted sexual attention from someone in school or the workplace; also includes unwelcome sexual jokes, glances, or comments, or the use of status or power to coerce or attempt to coerce a person into having sex.

quid pro quo harassment
A type of sexual harassment that involves submission to a particular type of conduct, either explicitly or implicitly, to get education or employment.

hostile environment harassment
A type of sexual harassment that occurs when an individual is subjected to unwelcome repeated sexual comments, innuendoes, or visually offensive material or touching that interferes with school or work.

harassed by someone in a university setting, the best advice is to talk to a counselor or your advisor about it. Remember that you are protected by federal law. Colleges and universities today will not tolerate the sexual harassment of any student, regardless of gender, ethnicity, religion, or sexual orientation.

Women and men think differently about sexual harassment. In one study, females were more likely than males to experience sexual harassment and to perceive it as harmful (Hand & Sanchez, 2000). Researchers have found that a behavior might be interpreted as sexual harassment by a woman, whereas it's interpreted as flattering to a man (Lastella, 2005).

PREVENTING SEXUAL HARASSMENT

The first step in reducing the incidence of sexual harassment is to acknowledge the problem. Too many people deny its existence. Because sexual harassers usually have more power, it is difficult for victims to come forward to disclose their victimization. University officials and administrators need to work together to provide educational opportunities and assistance for all students, staff, and employees. Establishing policies for dealing with these problems is necessary. Workplaces also need to design and implement strong policies against sexual harassment.

Education, especially about the role of women, is imperative. Studies have shown that sexual harassment education and training can reduce these behaviors (Lonsway et al., 2008). As our society continues to change and as more and more women enter the workforce, we need to prepare men for this adjustment. Throughout history, when women have broken out of their traditional roles, there have always been difficulties. Today we need research to explore the impact of women on the workforce.

Throughout this chapter we have explored how power can be used in sexual relationships to degrade and oppress. Rape, the sexual abuse of children, incest, intimate partner violence, and sexual harassment are problems in our society today. The first step in reducing these crimes is to acknowledge the problems and not hide them. Education, especially about the role of women, is necessary; without it, these crimes will undoubtedly continue to escalate.

review questions

1 Define sexual harassment and differentiate between the various types of sexual harassment.

2 Explain how sexual harassment can affect a woman's employment.

3 Identify gender differences in thoughts about sexual harassment.

4 Identify some strategies for dealing with, and preventing, sexual harassment.

CHAPTER review

SUMMARY POINTS

1 Physically or psychologically forcing sexual relations on another person is usually referred to as rape. Sexual assault refers to sexual penetration (vaginal, oral, anal) as well as unwanted sexual touching.

2 On the average, a rape occurs every 2 minutes in the United States. Actual incidence rates for rape are difficult to determine because forcible rape is one of the most underreported crimes in the United States. Women do not report rape for several reasons, including

that they do not think that they were really raped, they blame themselves, they fear no one will believe them, they worry that no legal action will be taken, or they feel shame or humiliation. However, today more and more women are reporting their rapes.

3 Four theories that explain why rape occurs are the rapist psychopathology, victim precipitation, feminist, and sociological theories. The rapist psychopathology theory suggests that either disease or intoxication forces

men to rape. Victim precipitation theory shifts the responsibility from the person who knowingly attacked to the innocent victim.

4 Feminists believe that rape and the threat of rape are tools used in our society to keep women in their place. The social, economic, and political separation of the sexes has also encouraged rape, which is viewed as an act of domination of men over women. Finally, sociologists believe that rape is an expression of power differentials in society. When men feel disempowered by society, by changing sex roles, or by their jobs, overpowering women with the symbol of their masculinity (a penis) reinforces, for a moment, men's control over the world.

5 There are also strong gender differences in attitudes toward rape. Men have been found to be less empathetic and sensitive toward rape than women and to attribute more responsibility to the victim than women do, especially those men who often view pornography. During a man's college years, he will experience a decline in negative rape attitudes. Rape awareness workshops can also help decrease the acceptability of rape myths.

6 The United States has the highest rate of reported rapes in the world. In some cultures, rape is accepted as a punishment for women or is used for initiation purposes. Rape has also been used during times of war as a weapon. This is referred to as persecutory rape. The rape of children is also common in some places around the globe.

7 Almost a quarter of college women report that they were forced to have sexual intercourse at some point in their lives. The majority of these women knew the person who sexually victimized them. Some women also report being stalked on campus, either physically or through notes and e-mails. Because many of these women know their attackers, few feel comfortable reporting or pressing charges.

8 Alcohol use is one of the strongest predictors of acquaintance rape on college campuses. At least half of all rape cases involve alcohol consumption by the rapist, victim, or both. Alcohol use on college campuses, as it relates to rape, is viewed very differently for men and women.

9 Fraternities tend to tolerate and may actually encourage the sexual coercion of women, because they tend to host large parties with lots of alcohol and little university supervision. The ethic of masculinity also helps foster an environment that may increase the risk of rape.

10 Male athletes have been found to be disproportionately overrepresented as assailants of rape by women surveyed.

Many athletes have been found to view the world in a way that helps to legitimize rape, and many feel a sense of privilege. Female athletes have been found to be more likely than nonathletes to believe in the blame-the-victim theory of rape and believe that some women put themselves in a bad situation.

11 Rape is an emotionally, physically, and psychologically shattering experience for the victim. Rape trauma syndrome is a two-stage stress response pattern characterized by physical, psychological, behavioral, or sexual problems (or a combination of these). Two stages, the acute and long-term reorganization, detail the symptoms that many women feel after a rape. Rape may cause sexual difficulties that can persist for a considerable period after the rape. Some victims have a silent rape reaction because they never report or talk about their rape.

12 The effects of rape are similar in special populations, including rape between marital partners and rape of lesbians, older women, women with disabilities, and prostitutes. Partners of women who have been raped also experience emotional symptoms. All in all, rape places a great deal of stress on a relationship.

13 Men can be raped by women and also by other men. The majority of male rapes by women use psychological or pressured contact, such as verbal persuasion or emotional manipulation, rather than physical force. The true incidence is unknown because the rape of men by men is infrequently reported to the police. Male rape is an expression of power, a show of strength and masculinity, that uses sex as a weapon. Rape also occurs in prison.

14 Rapists are primarily from younger age groups and tend to reduce their rape behavior as they get older. They have also been found to have experienced overwhelmingly negative early interpersonal experiences, most of which were with their fathers; have sexist views about women; accept myths about rape; have low self-esteem; and be politically conservative.

15 Different therapies for rapists include shock treatment, psychotherapy, behavioral treatment, support groups,

and the use of medications. Many programs have been developed to decrease myths about rape and increase knowledge levels. All-male programs have been found to reduce significantly the belief in rape myths.

16 The likelihood that a rape will be reported increases if the assailant was a stranger, if there was violence, or if a weapon was involved. Women who report their rapes to the police have been found to have a better adjustment and fewer emotional symptoms than those who do not report. Some victims refuse to press charges because they are afraid of revenge, want to forget the event, feel sorry for the rapist, or feel as though it would not matter anyway because nothing will be done.

17 Incest refers to sexual contact between a child or adolescent and a parent, stepparent, uncle, cousin, or caretaker. Child sexual abuse can include undressing, inappropriate touch, oral and genital stimulation, and vaginal or anal penetration. The most common incest offenders are uncles and male first cousins.

18 The overall reported incidence of child sexual abuse has been increasing over the past 30 years. This may be because of the changing sexual climate rather than an actual increase in the number of sexual assaults on children.

19 The median age for sexual abuse of both girls and boys is around 8 or 9 years old, and many victims are scared to reveal the abuse. Victims of incest with a biological father delay reporting the longest, whereas those who have been victims of stepfathers or live-in partners tell more readily.

20 Children who hide their sexual abuse often experience shame and guilt and fear the loss of affection from family and friends. They also have low self-esteem and feel frustrated about not being able to stop the abuse.

21 Whether or not they tell someone about their sexual abuse, many victims experience psychological symptoms such as depression, increased anxiety, nervousness, emotional problems, low self-esteem, and personality and intimacy disorders. Guilt is usually severe, and many females develop a tendency to blame themselves for the sexual abuse. Men and women who have been sexually abused may not be able to recall the abuse. The most devastating emotional effects occur when the sexual abuse is done by someone the victim trusts.

22 Research comparing child molesters to nonmolesters has shown that molesters tend to have poorer social skills, lower IQs, unhappy family histories, lower self-esteem, and less happiness in their lives. As surprising as it may seem, many abusers have strict religious codes yet still violate sexual norms. Three prominent theories that propose factors that make abuse more likely are learning, gender, and biological theories.

23 Currently, the most effective treatments for victims of sexual abuse include a combination of cognitive and behavioral psychotherapies. Many victims of sexual abuse also have

difficulties developing and maintaining intimate relationships. Goals for therapy of child sex abusers include decreasing sexual arousal to inappropriate sexual objects, teaching them to interact and relate better with adults; assertiveness skills training; empathy and respect for others; increasing sexual education; and evaluating and reducing any sexual difficulties that they might be experiencing with their sexual partners.

24 Increasing the availability of sex education can also help decrease child sexual abuse. Adequate funding and staffing of child welfare agencies may also be helpful.

25 Women are 6 times more likely to experience violence from a partner or ex-partner than from a stranger. Intimate partner violence is coercive behavior that is done through the use of threats, harassing, or intimidation. It can be physical, emotional, or sexual.

When intimate partner violence occurs in gay or lesbian relationships, one fear is being outed if a partner tries to get help or leave the relationship.

26 Sexual harassment includes anything from jokes, unwanted sexual advances, a friendly pat, an "accidental" brush on a person's body, or an arm around a person. Severe or chronic sexual harassment can cause psychological side effects similar to rape and sexual assault, and in extreme cases it has been known to contribute to suicide. It is estimated that 25% to 30% of college students report experiences with sexual harassment.

27 The first step in reducing the incidence of sexual harassment is to acknowledge the problem. Too many people deny its existence. Because sexual harassers usually have more power, it is difficult for victims to come forward to disclose their victimization.

CRITICAL THINKING questions

1 If a woman is raped who was alone and drunk at a bar dancing very seductively with several men, do you think she is more to blame than a woman who was raped in the street by an unknown assailant? Explain.

2 In 2003, a woman accused Kobe Bryant of the Los Angeles Lakers of rape. Do you think professional athletes make poor decisions with women who flock to them? Do you think a woman would cry rape without just cause? Why, or why not?

3 Do you consider a 17-year-old male who has sexual intercourse with his 14-year-old girlfriend sexual abuse? How would you define the sexual abuse of children?

4 In 2003, Max Factor heir Andrew Luster, who had jumped bond for rape and sexual assault, was captured and sentenced to over 120 years in prison for rape. His personal worth at the time was around $30 million. Why do you think such a person would rape? Using the theories presented in this chapter,

explain what factors might have led to these behaviors.

5 In a handful of divorce cases, one spouse accuses the other of child sexual abuse. Do you think that these accusations originate from a vengeful ex-spouse wanting custody, or do you think it might be easier to discuss the sexual abuse once the "bonds of secrecy" have been broken, as they typically are during divorce?

WEB resources

Sexuality Now Book Companion Website

Go to www.cengage.com/psychology/carroll for practice quizzes, glossary, flash cards, and more. You can also access the following websites from the companion site.

Adult Survivors of Child Abuse (ASCA) ■ Designed specifically for adult survivors of physical, sexual, and emotional child abuse or neglect, ASCA offers an effective support program. This website's mission is to reach out to as many survivors of child abuse as possible, and it offers information on individual and group support groups.

American Women's Self-Defense Association (AWSDA) ■ The AWSDA began with the realization that women's self-defense needs were not being met. Founded in 1990, AWSDA is an educational organization dedicated to furthering women's awareness of self-defense and rape prevention.

National Violence Against Women Prevention Research Center ■ The National Violence Against Women Prevention Research Center provides information on current topics related to violence against women and its prevention. The website contains statistics and information on many topics, including evaluations of college sexual assault programs across the nation.

Rape, Abuse & Incest National Network (RAINN) ■
RAINN is the nation's largest anti–sexual assault organization. It operates the National Sexual Assault Hotline at 1-800-656-HOPE and carries out programs to prevent sexual assault, help victims, and ensure that rapists are brought to justice. Their website includes statistics, counseling resources, prevention tips, news, and more.

Men Can Stop Rape (MCSR) ■ MCSR is a nonprofit organization that works to increase men's involvement and efforts to reduce male violence. MCSR empowers male youth and the institutions that serve them to work as allies with women in preventing rape and other forms of men's violence. MCSR uses education and community groups to build men's capacity to be strong without being violent.

Security on Campus ■ Security on Campus is a nonprofit organization that works to make campuses safe for college and university students. It was cofounded in 1987 by Connie and Howard Clery, following the murder of their daughter at Lehigh University. Jeanne Clery was a freshman when she was beaten, raped, and murdered by another student in her dormitory room. Security on Campus educates students and parents about crime on campus and assists victims in understanding laws pertaining to these crimes.

Male Survivor ■ Male Survivor works to help people better understand and treat adult male survivors of childhood sexual abuse. Information about male sexual abuse and a variety of helpful links are available.

Northwest Network of Bi, Trans, Lesbian and Gay Survivors of Abuse ■ The Northwest Network provides support and advocacy for bisexual, transsexual, lesbian, and gay survivors of abuse. Information about sexual abuse and a variety of helpful links are available.

CengageNOW

Go to www.cengage.com/login to link to CengageNOW, your online study tool. First take the Pre-Test for this chapter to get your Personalized Study Plan, which will identify topics you need to review and direct you to online resources. Then take the Post-Test to determine what concepts you have mastered and what you still need work on.

Videos in CengageNOW

For additional information on topics discussed in this chapter, check out the videos in CengageNOW on the following topics:

- Rape and Posttraumatic Stress Disorder—Learn how the effects of rape affect this woman's life in the 10 years since it happened.

- Gang-Rape in Pakistan—Hear how a Pakistani woman challenged the existing power structures after being gang raped.

- Does He Treat You Right?—Listen to a woman voice concern about the way her friend's boyfriend treats her.

CHAPTER 18

Sexual Images and Selling Sex

I t's not like I've always wanted to be a porn star. Of course I've wondered what the lifestyle would be like, and how I would perform if I were one. One night I find out that a famous porn star, Ginger Lynn, is dancing at a local strip club. We go to see her, and after her dance she offers to sign autographs. She also mentions that she is sponsoring a competition to earn a chance to star in an adult porno film with her. I was intrigued and decided to approach her to ask her about it. After speaking with her for a while about the opportunity she took some information from me and told me that she would call me.

After a battery of tests to check for STIs, I flew out west to make my porn debut a few months later. I was given $700 to pay for travel expenses and my "services." My head was spinning on the plane because I was consumed by anticipation, excitement, nervousness, and fear. I was mostly worried about my relationship with my girlfriend. I knew that she was having a hard time understanding why I wanted to do this. To be honest, I wasn't even sure why I wanted to do it. I guess I looked at it as the opportunity of a lifetime. But I still questioned it. Was I trying to prove something?

It is hard to explain the feelings I had when I first arrived to the set where the filming would take place. There were many peo-ple walking around freely observing the sex scenes while they were being filmed. The people there were all very courteous and professional. Each of us was taken aside and asked about what types of scenes and sex acts we were willing to participate in. The producers stressed that we should not participate in anything we were uncomfortable with.

The days on the set were long. There were about a dozen each males and females participating, and each of us had to do a minimum of three scenes, each scene lasting about an hour. The male performers were encouraged to take a Viagra pill for insurance after consulting the onsite doctor.

On this first day I participated in two scenes. The first involved an oral sex competition with seven girls and seven guys. The guys serviced the girls first while the girls were blindfolded. We had to kneel and perform cunnilingus on each girl for three minutes. By a show of fingers in the air the girls were asked to "score" the guys on a scale of 1 to 10. There was a cash prize for the guy with the highest score.

The second scene was much like the first only it involved the guys seated on the couches and the girls on their knees. I was blindfolded and each of the seven girls came around and gave me oral sex for three minutes each. When each of the girls had given action to each of us, we removed our blind-folds to watch the grand finale— our ejaculations. During all the scenes the cam-eramen moved around freely filming video and taking still photos.

My third scene was filmed on the final day of shooting. I was to be dominated by two women. We participated in a kinky threesome the likes of which I have never known. The women performed oral sex on each other and on me. We switched positions repeatedly, and there was much grop-ing and licking. The scene lasted for about an hour, but the time seemed to go by very quickly. At one point I was lying down and one girl was sitting on my face while the other was sucking my cock.

The experience was very interesting. Although I was glad to have the experience I did not find that it was an appealing career for me to pursue, and I have been troubled by the potential aftermath of my participation. I realize that I might lose my relationship with my girlfriend. I wonder if she'll decide to let me go because she is so unhappy that I'd want to star in a porn film. SOURCE: Author's files.

in this chapter

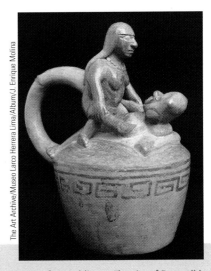

533
Legal Prostitution
in Amsterdam

514
Sex and Drugs
on TV

523
View in Video

◁ Opposite: © Atlantide Phototravel/Corbis

O ur lives today are full of visual media: magazines, newspapers, book covers, CD and DVD packaging, cereal boxes and food products—even medicines are adorned with pictures of people, scenes, or products. Advertisements peer at us from magazines, billboards, buses, matchbook covers, and anywhere else that advertisers can buy space. Television, movies, computers, and other moving visual images surround us almost everywhere we go, and we will only depend on them more as information technology continues to develop. We live in a visual culture with images we simply cannot escape.

We begin this chapter with a brief history of erotic representations. Next we take a look at how erotic representations are presented to us every day in books, television, advertising, and other media. Only then do we turn to the graphic sexual images of pornography. We also explore how sex itself is sold today, from lap dances in strip clubs to prostitution. Along the way ask yourself the following: What influence do sexual representations and selling sex have on us? What are they trying to show us about ourselves? How do they subtly affect the way we think about men, women, and sexuality?

The Art Archive/Museo Larco Herrera Lima/Album/J. Enrique Molina

Early erotic art was often public art. The city of Pompeii included large, erect phalluses on street corners, and erotic frescoes adorned many people's homes.

Erotic Representations in History

Human beings have been making representations of themselves and the world around them since ancient times. Many of the earliest cave drawings and animal bone sculptures have been representations of the human form, usually scantily dressed or naked. Often the poses or implications of the art seem explicitly erotic. Yet it is hard to know to what degree these images were considered erotic by preliterate people, for early erotic art was also sacred art in which the purpose was to represent those things most important to early people—the search for food and the need to reproduce (Lucie-Smith, 1991). However, by the dawn of the great ancient civilizations such as Egypt, people were drawing erotic images on walls or pieces of papyrus just for the sake of eroticism (Manniche, 1987). Since that time, human beings have been fascinated with representations of the human form naked or engaged in sexually explicit behavior; in turn, many governments have been equally intent on limiting or eradicating those images.

Erotic representations have appeared in most societies throughout history, and they have been greeted with different degrees of tolerance. Ancient cultures often created public erotic tributes to the gods, including temples dedicated to phallic worship. India's sacred writings are full of sexual accounts, and some of the most explicit public sculptures in the world adorn its temples. Greece is famous for the erotic art that adorned objects like bowls and urns. When archaeologists in the 18th and 19th centuries uncovered the Roman city of Pompeii, buried in a volcanic blast in 79 A.D., they were startled and troubled to find that this jewel of the Roman Empire, which they had so admired, was full of brothels, had carved phalluses protruding at every street corner, and had private homes full of erotic **frescoes** (FRESS-cohs; Kendrick, 1987). Authorities hid these findings for years by keeping the erotic objects in locked museum rooms and publishing pictures of the city in which the phalluses were made to taper off like candles.

Not all sexual representations are explicit, and many of our greatest artists and writers included sexual components in their creations. The plays of Shakespeare, although hardly shocking by today's standards, do contain references to sexuality and sexual intercourse. The art of Michelangelo and Leonardo da Vinci also included graphic nudity without being titillating. Still, in their day, these pictures caused controversy: in the 16th century, for example, priests painted loincloths over nude pictures of Jesus and the angels. What people in one society or one period in history see as obscene, another group—or the same group later—can view as great art.

THE DEVELOPMENT OF PORNOGRAPHY

Most sexual representations created throughout history had a specific purpose, whether it was to worship the gods, to adorn pottery, or, later, to criticize the government or religion. Very little erotic art seems to have been created simply for the purpose of arousing the viewer, as much of modern erotic art is. So most of history's erotic art cannot be considered "pornographic" in the modern sense (L. Hunt, 1993).

Pornography, which tends to portray sexuality for its own sake, did not emerge as a distinct, separate category until the middle of the 18th century in the United States. For most of history, sexuality itself was so imbedded in religious, moral, and legal contexts that it was not thought of as a separate sphere of life (Kendrick, 1987). Explicit words and pictures (along with other forms of writing, such as political writings) were controlled in the name of religion or in the name of politics, not in the name of public **decency** (L. Hunt, 1993). For example, **obscenity** was illegal among the Puritans (punishable originally by death and later by boring through the tongue with a hot iron) because it was an offense against God. That is why before the 19th century, **hardcore** sexual representations were extremely rare.

Another strong influence on the development of pornography in the United States was the development of the printing press and the mass availability of the printed word (sexually explicit books were printed within 50 years of the invention of movable type in the Western world). For most of history, written or printed work was available only to a small elite because only they could afford it and, more important, only they could read.

The most famous pornographic work of the 18th century was John Cleland's *Memoirs of a Woman of Pleasure* (better known as *Fanny Hill*), first published in 1748. Cleland's work was solely aimed at sexually arousing the reader. Before Cleland, most sexually explicit books were about prostitutes because these women did "unspeakable" things (that could be described in graphic detail) and because they could end up arrested, diseased, and alone, thereby reinforcing society's condemnation of their actions. In fact, the word "pornography" literally means "writing about harlots."

Cases such as *Fanny Hill* teach us that to really understand the meaning of "pornography," we must understand the desire of the U.S. government and other groups to control it and suppress it. In other words, the story of pornography is not just about publishing erotic material but also about the struggle between those who try to create it and those who try to stop them. Both sides must be included in any discussion of pornography; without those who try to suppress it, pornography just becomes erotic art. In fact, the term **erotica,** often used to refer to sexual representations that are

> **Erotic representations have appeared** in most societies throughout history.

fresco
A type of painting done on wet plaster so that the plaster dries with the colors incorporated into it.

pornography
Any sexually oriented material that is created simply for the purpose of arousing the viewer.

decency
Conformity to recognized standards of propriety, good taste, and modesty—as defined by a particular group (standards of decency differ among groups).

obscenity
A legal term for materials that are considered offensive to standards of sexual decency in a society.

hard core
Describes explicit, genitally oriented sexual depictions; more explicit than soft core, which displays sexual activity often without portrayals of genital penetration.

erotica
Sexually oriented media that are considered by a viewer or society as within the acceptable bounds of decency.

not pornographic, really just means pornography that a particular person finds acceptable. One person's pornography can be another person's erotica. As we shall see in this chapter, the modern arguments about pornography are some of the most divisive in the country, pitting feminists against feminists, allying some of the most radical feminist scholars with fundamentalist preachers of the religious right, and pitting liberals against liberals and conservatives against conservatives in arguments over the limits of free speech.

But sexually explicit representations are not the only sexual images in U.S. society. Sexuality is present in almost all of our **media,** from the model sensuously sipping a bottle of beer to the offhand sexual innuendos that are a constant part of television sitcoms. In fact, the U.S. entertainment media seems to be almost obsessed by sexual imagery; Michel Foucault (1987), French philosopher and historian of sexuality, has called it a modern compulsion to speak incessantly about sex. Before we discuss the sexually explicit representations of "pornography" with the heated arguments they often inspire, let us turn to the erotic images that present themselves to us in the popular media every day.

media
All forms of public communication.

review questions

1 Explain how erotic representations have appeared throughout history.

2 Differentiate among pornography, obscenity, and erotica.

3 Describe the development of pornography.

Sexuality in the Media and the Arts

Since the early 1990s, representations in the U.S. **mass media** have become more explicitly erotic. Many of the images we see today are explicitly or subtly sexual. Barely clothed females and shirtless, athletic males are so common in our ads that we scarcely notice them anymore. Some even feature full nudity (in fact, some clothing companies, such as Abercrombie, are notorious for using naked models or models with very little clothing—which appears rather odd when you remember they want to sell clothes!). The majority of movies, even those directed at children, have sexual scenes that would not have been permitted in movie theaters even 20 years ago. The humor in television sitcoms has become more and more sexual, and nudity has begun to appear on prime-time network television shows. In addition, graphic depictions of sexuality, which until recently could only be found in adult bookstores and theaters, are now available at neighborhood video stores.

We like to believe that we are so used to the media that we are immune to its influences. Does sex (or violence) on television, for example, really influence how promiscuous (or violent) our society becomes? Do the constant sexual stereotypes paraded before us in commercials and advertisements really help shape our attitudes toward gender relations? Does constant exposure to sexual images erode family life, encourage promiscuity, and lead to violence against women, as some conservative and feminist groups claim? Also, if we find out that sex and violence in the media do have an effect on how we behave, what should we do about it?

Vince Bucci/AFP/Getty Images

Although now in reruns, the HBO hit *Sex and the City* broke new ground by openly discussing the sex lives of four single women living in New York City. In 2008, the official *Sex and the City* movie was released and was also a big hit.

EROTIC LITERATURE: **THE POWER OF THE PRESS**

Although the portrayal of sexuality is as old as art itself, pornography and censorship are more modern concepts, products of the mass production of erotic art in society. Throughout Western history, reactionary forces (usually the clergy) often censored nudity in public art, especially when it featured religious figures. For example, on the walls of Michelangelo's Sistine Chapel, clerics painted over the genitals of nudes with loincloths and wisps of fabric. Still, because there was no way to mass produce these kinds of art, the Church's reactions varied on a case-by-case basis.

Pornography in the modern sense began to appear when printing became sophisticated enough to allow fairly large runs of popular books, beginning in the 16th century. Intellectuals and clergy were often against this mass production of books. They worried

mass media
Media intended for a large, public audience.

that if everybody had books and could learn about things for themselves, why would anyone need teachers, scholars, or theologians? Religious and secular intellectuals quickly issued dire warnings about the corrupting effects of allowing people direct access to knowledge and established censorship mechanisms. By the 17th century, the Church was pressuring civic governments to allow them to inspect bookstores, and soon forbidden books, including erotica, were being removed; such books then became rarer and more valuable, and a clandestine business arose in selling them. It was this struggle between the illicit market in sexual art and literature and the forces of censorship that started what might be called a pornographic subculture, one that still thrives today.

TV and movie producers in the U.S. believe that "sex sells."

Today, erotic literature of almost any kind is readily available in the United States. The sexual scenes described in the average romance novel today would have branded it as pornographic only a few decades ago. One would think that such books would be the main targets of people trying to censor sexually explicit materials. Yet most censorship battles over sexually explicit material involve images rather than written word.

Although the early court cases that established the American legal attitudes toward pornography in the United States were often about books (especially about sending them through the mail), modern debates about pornography tend to focus more on explicit pictures and movies. Still, it was the erotic novel that first established pornographic production as a business in the Western world and provoked a response from religious and governmental authorities.

TELEVISION AND FILM: STEREOTYPES, SEX, AND THE DECENCY ISSUE

The advent of television in the United States only increased our dependence on visual media, and it is probably no exaggeration to say that television is the single strongest influence on the modern American outlook toward life. American teenagers watch an average of 3 hours of television each day, and one in four teens says that television influences his or her behavior (Henry J. Kaiser Family Foundation, 2003; D. F. Roberts et al., 2005).

Television allows us to have the world delivered to us in the comfort of our home. But the world we see on TV is only a small slice of the real world; television, like the movies, edits and sanitizes the world it displays. For example, although literally hundreds of acts of sexual intercourse are portrayed or suggested on television shows and in the movies every day, we rarely see a couple discuss or use contraception, discuss the morality of their actions, contract a sexually transmitted infection (STI), worry about AIDS, experience erectile dysfunction, or regret the act afterward. Most couples fall into bed shortly after initial physical attraction and take no time to build an emotional relationship before becoming sexually active. Values and morals about sexuality seem nonexistent.

In an attempt to capture American viewers back from cable and satellite stations, the major television networks have been increasing the sexual content of their programming (Kunkel et al., 2005). Television talk shows have also become decidedly more graphic in their content. As the number of talk show hosts has increased, so has competition for provocative guests, and a good sexual confession—men who cross-dress, mothers who sleep with their teenage sons' best friends, women who leave their spouses for other women, teenage prostitutes—are guaranteed at least to catch some attention. The HBO hit *Sex and the City* broke new ground by having four women openly discussing their sexuality. Popular nightly dramas such as *Grey's Anatomy* and *Desperate Housewives* both use sex to entice viewers.

Television magazine shows that imitate news reports but concentrate on two or three stories (for example, *Dateline* or *20/20*) often search for stories with lurid content, and if there is a sexual scandal or a rape accusation in the news, they are sure to feature it. Even the "hard" news shows, such as the networks' evening news reports, have turned a corner in their willingness to use graphic descriptions of sexual events. News shows, after all, also need ratings to survive, and one way to interest audiences is to report legitimate news stories that have a sexual content in a graphic and provocative way. These news reports deliver the sexually explicit information with the implicit message that they disapprove of it; but they still deliver it.

Television and movie producers in the United States believe that "sex sells," and so they fill their programming with it. In 2005, *Sex on TV4*, a biennial study of sexual content on American television, analyzed more than 1,000 hours of programming including all genres of television shows. Overall, 70% of the shows studied included some sexual content; and shows averaged five sexual episodes per hour (Kunkel et al., 2005). These numbers were up from 1998, when 56% of shows included sexual content, and 3.2 sexual episodes occurred every hour. During prime-time programming, 77% of shows included sexual content and averaged close to 6 sexual episodes per hour (Kunkel et al., 2005; see Figures 18.1, 18.2, and 18.3). This study also found that only 11% of

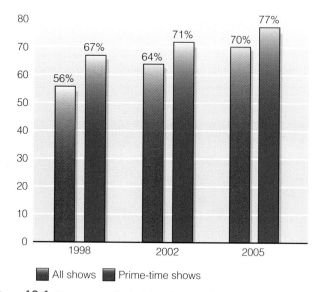

Percentage of Television Shows with Sexual Content

Figure **18.1** Percentage of television shows with sexual content over time, 1998–2005. Source: From "Sex on TV4, A Kaiser Family Foundation Report" (#7398), Chart 1, Nov. 2005, The Henry J. Kaiser Family Foundation. This information was reprinted with permission from the Henry J. Kaiser Family Foundation. The Kaiser Family Foundation is a non-profit private operating foundation, based in Menlo Park, California, dedicated to producing and communicating the best possible information, research and analysis on health issues.

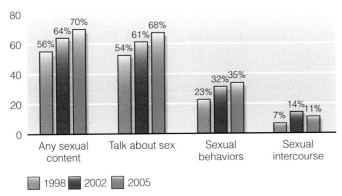

Percentage of Shows with Sexual Content Over Time

Figure **18.2** Percentage of television shows with sexual content over time, 1998–2005, by type of content. Source: From "Sex on TV4, A Kaiser Family Foundation Report" (#7398), **Chart 3**, Nov. 2005, The Henry J. Kaiser Family Foundation. This information was reprinted with permission from the Henry J. Kaiser Family Foundation. The Kaiser Family Foundation is a non-profit private operating foundation, based in Menlo Park, California, dedicated to producing and communicating the best possible information, research and analysis on health issues.

prime-time network shows made references to sexual risks or responsibilities, and this percentage has remained virtually the same since 1998 (Kunkel et al., 2005). Interestingly, approximately 53% of sexual scenes that included intercourse were between couples with an established relationship; 20% were between couples who have met but who have no relationship; 15% were between couples who have just met; and in 12% of cases it was unclear what the couple's relationship is (Kunkel et al., 2005).

The AIDS epidemic was a key factor in opening up the way news organizations speak about sexuality (for example, the word "condom" would never have appeared on a major news network before AIDS). Another landmark came in 1998 when news broke of a sex scandal between then-President Bill Clinton and Monica Lewinsky. The Clinton–Lewinsky story was one of the biggest of the decade and was covered by most evening news shows in explicit detail. This story broke precedent and allowed the networks to use language and sexual references that would have been unthinkable just a few years earlier.

The new frankness on television can, of course, be used to transmit important sexual information and help demystify sexuality through educational programming. In the past, shows such as *Talk Sex With Sue Johanson* on Oxygen and other educational shows have helped teach the public about sex. However, the vast majority of sexual references are made to titillate, not to inform, and much of the sex portrayed on television is provided in an artificial and unrealistic light (Kunkel et al., 2005).

Television, Film, and Minority Sexuality

As sexually explicit as the U.S. visual media have become, they have generally had a very poor track record in their portrayals of cer-

tain sexual behaviors, such as same-sex behavior and sexuality among certain minorities, such as the elderly, the disabled, and racial and ethnic minorities. Today popular shows such as *House*, *Nip/Tuck, Brothers and Sisters,* and the *L Word* help bisexual, lesbian, and gay men become more mainstream on television.

Unfortunately, the sexual lives of ethnic and racial minorities have historically been neglected by the major American media. African Americans complained for many years that television and movies tend to portray them as criminals, drug pushers, or pimps; only recently have black actors begun appearing in stable television roles and sitcoms. African American filmmakers continue to release movies showing African American sexual life from the African American perspective, and the popularity of Black film stars such as Will Smith, Halle Berry, Denzel Washington, Queen Latifah, and Samuel L. Jackson have broken the barriers and encouraged movies with African American romantic leads.

Although the roles for African Americans have improved, today other minorities, such as Asian Americans, Latinos, and Native Americans, are less common, and they are rarely portrayed as romantic leads. Even in films that feature minority populations, such as *Dances with Wolves* and *The Last Samurai*, a white actor plays the romantic leads. Can you even think of a movie (outside of Kung Fu movies) in which an Asian man is the romantic lead?

Television, Film, and Gender

American television offers its viewers sexual information both explicitly (through such things as news, documentaries, and public service announcements) and implicitly (through the ways it portrays sexuality or gender relations in its programming; Gunter & McAleer, 1990; Peter & Valkenburg, 2007). One implicit message of American television programming, almost since its inception, has been that men are in positions of leadership (whether they are chief legal counsel or the head of the family), whereas women, even if they are high-ranking, are sexual temptations for men. Even today, the stereotyping of women is often extreme in

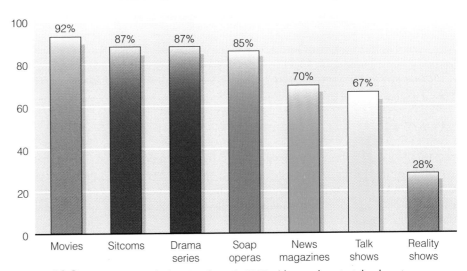

Percentage of Shows with Sexual Content by Genre

Figure **18.3** FL.Percentage of television shows in 2005 with sexual content, by show type. Source: From "Sex on TV4, A Kaiser Family Foundation Report" (#7398), **Chart 4**, Nov. 2005, The Henry J. Kaiser Family Foundation. This information was reprinted with permission from the Henry J. Kaiser Family Foundation. The Kaiser Family Foundation is a non-profit private operating foundation, based in Menlo Park, California, dedicated to producing and communicating the best possible information, research and analysis on health issues.

Spuiten en Slikken—Sex and Drugs on Television

Typical sex storylines for the show involve oral and anal sex, partner swapping, pornography, and semen tasting.

Each culture has rules about how much sex is tolerated on television. In more conservative cultures, such as Japan, there is less tolerance, while in more liberal cultures, such as the Netherlands, there is more tolerance. I recently had the opportunity to attend the taping of a popular Dutch television show *Spuiten en Slikken*. The title of the show is a play on words which can mean either "Shoot Up and Swallow" or "Ejaculate and Swallow," referencing sex and drugs. *Spuiten en Slikken* explores sex and drugs in a very open and matter-of-fact fashion and is aimed at 13 to 19 year olds. The show airs once a week at 11 p.m. and it has between 500,000 and 750,000 viewers each week (P. Castelijn, personal communication, September 26, 2008).

On each show, *Spuiten en Slikken* has professional actors experiment with sex and drugs, while young audience members watch to learn what can happen. Typical sex storylines for the show involve oral and anal sex, partner swapping, pornography, and semen tasting, while typical drug storylines include exploring the effects of psychedelic mushrooms, hash, or marijuana. On one show, the host smoked pot to show audience members the effect of marijuana use on memory (she forgot most of her lines).

A group of researchers at *Spuiten en Slikken* pay attention to sexual and drug trends in the young adult population for content ideas. One show they were

working on was about the popularity of young adults taping themselves having sex (A. Gnocchi, personal communication, September 26, 2008). In this show, they explored what could go wrong if you tape yourself having sex (i.e., it could get into the wrong hands) as well as how to do it right (i.e., get the right lighting) if you're going to do it.

I asked Pim Castelijn, the director of programming for the station that broadcasts the show in the Netherlands, if he thought the show "glorified" sex and drugs. Did it make kids want to try the things they talked about on the show? He told me that both sex and drugs *are* glorious, and he wondered why people were afraid to tell adolescents about the bad *and* the good. Pim felt that Americans spend too much time talking about the negatives when it comes to sex, and not enough time talking about the positives (P. Castelijn, personal communication, September 26, 2008). *Spuiten en Slikken* attempts to highlight both the good and the bad associated with various sexual behaviors (and drug use) and doesn't automatically claim that all sex and drugs are bad. It presents a balanced approach in hope that kids who watch will be able to make up their own minds.

Probably the most interesting thing I learned about the show that day was that the station it airs on, BNN, is a publicly funded station, funded with taxpayer money. Do you think a show like this would air in the United States? Why or why not?

---

television commercials, which we consider in the section on advertising. Although the types of portrayals of women's roles are changing and improving on television today, men still outnumber women in major roles, and the traditional role of woman as sex object still predominates on television.

Many gender stereotypes persist on American television. The only place they often don't show up is on soap operas. Because soap operas are aimed at women, they tend to portray women as more competent than other programming does (Geraghty et al., 1992; Stern et al., 2006). Yet even soap operas send subtle messages about keeping women in their place; women who are more sexually active and independent of men tend to be portrayed as evil or unsympathetic.

Fortunately, some gender stereotypes on other television shows are changing. Men are now being shown as single or stay-at-home dads, and there is a tendency to mock the old "macho man" stereotypes on shows such as *The Family Guy*. Shows like *Bones*, *CSI*, and *Law & Order* regularly feature women in leading roles and have helped establish the new television woman: forceful, working outside the home, and dealing with the real-life problems of balancing social life, personal issues, and work. These women are smart, motivated, and self-confident. Gender stereotypes have also been changing with the increasing popularity of reality television shows, such as *Survivor* and *The Amazing Race*. Shows like these portray the majority of women as strong, independent, and self-confident people who are willing to take risks.

Television and Children

Earlier we mentioned the number of hours that American teenagers watch television. Although most watch 3 hours per day, during a typical school day, teenagers spend 4 hours and 41 minutes in front of some form of media (TV Turnoff Network, 2005). By the time today's youths are 70 years old, they will have spent about 7 years of their lives watching television! Television viewing begins early in the United States: 2 to 5 year olds spend almost 28 hours a

---

REALResearch > Even with Internet blocks and filters, **70%** of teenagers (aged 10–17-years old) claim to have viewed pornography on the Internet (DELMONICO & GRIFFIN, 2008).

---

week watching television and teenagers about 22 hours. In 1961, the average age to begin watching television was 3 years old, but by 2007 it was 9 months old (Zimmerman et al., 2007).

Researchers have begun to ask serious questions about the impact of all this television watching, especially because television is so inundated with sexuality and sexual stereotypes. For example, children are concerned with gender roles, and they often see the world in terms of "boy's" behavior and "girl's" behavior. As we discussed in Chapter 4, children are taught early to behave in gender-appropriate ways, and they quickly begin to tease other children who do not follow these stereotypes (such as effeminate boys). Still, research shows that when children are exposed to books or films that portray nonstereotyped gender behaviors, their gender stereotypes are reduced (Comstock & Paik, 1991).

Historically, many children's shows lacked positive female role models and offered stereotyped portrayals of men and women. For example, although *Sesame Street* has had a human cast of mixed ethnicities and genders and even a number of female Muppets, its most notable Muppet figures (from Kermit to Bert and Ernie to Big Bird to the Count) have all been male. It was only with the introduction of Zoe in 1993 that a female Muppet managed to gain a high profile.

Television executives argue that boys will not watch cartoons with a female lead, but girls will watch cartoons with a male lead, and so it makes more economic sense to produce cartoons featuring males. The result is that it is hard for young girls to find good gender role models in cartoons. It is understandable that researchers have found that more television viewing is correlated with greater sexual stereotyping in certain groups of children (Gunter & McAleer, 1990). However, the situation is slowly improving, with *Blue's Clues* (Blue is a girl), *Dora the Explorer,* and *Bob the Builder* (Wendy, Bob's sidekick, is more handy than Bob).

One might also wonder what effect television has on the developing sexuality of children and adolescents. We know that sex is a common theme on many television programs today. How does this affect the sexual behavior of teens? Research has shown that increasing sexual content on television is related to early sexual initiation in adolescents (Collins et al., 2004). Teens who watch a lot of television are likely to believe their peers are sexually active. One study found that the more hours of television

teens watched, the more likely they were to perceive their peers as being sexually active (Eggermont, 2005).

The Movement Against the Sexualization of the Visual Media

The irony is that American networks have turned to sex to increase their ratings, yet the constant presence of sexual themes on television is beginning to turn viewers away. The majority of Americans want stronger regulation of sexual content and profanity (Kunkel et al., 2005).

Portrayal of sexuality in movies has also long been a source of controversy. There was no control over motion picture content until the 1930s, when the industry began policing itself with the Motion Picture Code. However, the rating system has not stopped the filmmakers from trying to be as sexually explicit as they can within their rating categories. Hollywood seems to try to push the limits of the R rating as far as possible, and a number of directors have had to cut sexually explicit scenes out of their movies. In fact, some movies are made in two or three versions; the least sexually explicit version is for release in the United States, a more explicit copy is released in Europe (where standards are looser), and a third, even more explicit version, is released on DVD.

A backlash does seem to be developing, and Hollywood has been reducing the sexual explicitness of its general release movies. Michael Medved (1992), a noted movie critic, argued in his book *Hollywood vs. America* that the movie and television industries are out of touch; too dedicated to violence, profanity, and sex; and do not really understand what consumers want to see on television and in the movies. He claimed that G- and PG-rated movies actually make more money than R-rated movies.

However, some of the shows boycotted by groups such as the American Family Association get high ratings for the very reasons

---

REALResearch > Studies have shown that people are less likely to remember the brand name of a product in an ad with sex and violence than in an ad without (BUSHMAN & BONACCI, 2002).

WHAT DO YOU WANT TO KNOW ?

Most kids today know all about sex at an early age. So why are people so uptight about showing nudity on television? What do they think it will do to their kids?

Even in a society like ours, which has begun to discuss sex more openly, it is still a difficult subject for children to understand. Many parents believe that it is their job to introduce the topic to their children, to explain it to them, and to teach their children whatever values the parents believe are appropriate. This may be undermined when children see fairly uncensored sexuality on television, which is usually shown without any discussion of values and without any way to address the children's questions about what they are seeing. In the accompanying Sex in Real Life, "Generation M," we talk about research on the media consumption habits of children and teenagers.

The face of media is quickly changing all around us. Today we can hear music from devices smaller than our finger and access the Internet through our cell phones. Newer cars have optional built-in television monitors on seat backs, and today's cell phones download e-mails and take digital pictures. Today's adolescents spend an average of 6.5 hours per day using media, including television, movies, Internet, video, cell phones, iPods, MP3 players, GameCubes, and PlayStations (Rideout et al., 2005). What is the effect of all this media on the lives of young people today?

In 2005, the Henry J. Kaiser Family Foundation released *Generation M: Media in the Lives of 8–18-Year-Olds,* the results of a study that included responses to anonymous questionnaires from more than 2,000 8 to 18 year olds. In addition, 700 adolescents were asked to keep private journals detailing their use of various media. Thirty-nine percent of adolescents were found to have their own cell phone, and 55% owned their own video game player. Following are other interesting findings from this important study. On average, adolescents between the ages of 8 to 18 were found to:

© Janell Carroll

- Watch 4 hours of television each day

- Listen to 1.75 hours of music each day

- Use the computer for recreational use 1 hour each day

- Play video games for 50 minutes per day

- Read recreational material for 43 minutes a day

In the average home in America, 80% have cable or satellite, and 55% of these also get premium cable channels, such as HBO. What is interesting, however, is the number of adolescents who have access to this material in their bedrooms. Fifty-three percent of 8 to 18 year olds report there are no rules about television watching (Rideout et al.,

2005). The study also found that in the average adolescent bedroom:

- 68% have a television

- 54% have a DVD/VCR

- 49% have a video game console

- 31% have a computer

- 65% have an MP3, iPod, CD player, or tape player

Gender differences were found: boys were twice as likely as girls to play video games, but girls spent more time listening to music than boys. As for the overall types of music listened to by both girls and boys, rap and hip-hop were the clear favorites (60% of Caucasians, 70% of Hispanics, and 81% of African Americans reported this genre of music as their favorite; Rideout et al., 2005). Ethnic differences revealed that African American youths spent more time watching television than Hispanic or Caucasian Americans.

Adolescents' increased access to computers, and the Internet gives them much greater access to information. Many adolescents report that their parents are unaware of what they see online (Cameron et al., 2005). In addition, instant messaging has become one of the most popular computer activities in this age group (Rideout et al, 2005). Because research has shown that the exposure to sexuality in the media has been found to be related to adolescent sexual behavior (Pardun et al., 2005), the content of these media is worth exploring. This generation of adolescents is certainly a media generation, but now the question for researchers is this: What long-term impact will this have on adolescents?

SOURCE: Rideout et al., 2005.

---

that they are boycotted: because they are willing to deal with complex issues such as abortion and homosexuality in a frank and honest (if sometimes sensationalistic) manner. It will be interesting to see whether advertisers are scared away by these groups or continue to sponsor provocative and controversial programs.

ADVERTISING:
SEX SELLS AND SELLS

Advertising is a modern medium, and its influence pervades modern life. There is practically no area free from its effects, from mass media to consumer products and even to nature itself—

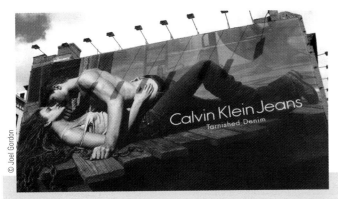

Calvin Klein was one of the first to use nudity and sex in its advertising.

billboards obscure our views from highways, and planes drag advertising banners at our beaches. People proudly wear advertisements for soft drinks or fashion designers on their shirts, sneakers, or hats, not realizing that they often spend more for such clothing, paying money to help the company advertise!

According to estimates, children see up to 40,000 advertisements on television every year (TV Turnoff Network, 2005). Studies have shown that advertising has a profound effect on the way children think about the world (forming a mind-set of "products I want to have," for example), and it influences the way they begin to form their ideas of sexuality and gender roles (Durkin, 1985; Gunter & McAleer, 1990).

Advertising and Gender Role Portrayals

In his groundbreaking book *Gender Advertisements,* Erving Goffman (1976) used hundreds of pictures from print advertising to show how men and women are positioned or displayed to evoke sexual tension, power relations, or seduction. Advertisements, Goffman suggested, do not show actual portrayals of men and women but present clear-cut snapshots of the way we *think* they behave. Advertisements try to capture ideals of each sex: Men are shown as more confident and authoritative, whereas women are more childlike and deferential (Belknap & Leonard, 1991). Since Goffman's book was published, advertisements have become more blatantly sexual, and analyzing the gender role and sexual content of advertisements has become a favorite pastime of those who study the media.

Although studies indicate that advertising is becoming less sexist today, gender differences still exist (Wolin, 2003). Studies of television commercials, for example, still show differences between the way men and women are portrayed. Men are pictured in 3 times the number of occupational categories as women, and women are more likely than men to be in commercials that feature the home. Male spokespersons are also commonly used for female products; however, female spokespersons are rarely used to advertise male products (Peirce, 2001).

As you flip through popular magazines today, it's obvious that advertising companies are trying to put more women into ads in positions of authority and dominance. Men are also being shown in traditionally female roles, such as cuddling babies or cooking. However, the naked body is still a primary means of selling products, and even if gender roles are becoming more egalitarian, portrayals of sexuality are still blatant.

***Advertisements try to capture** ideals of each sex.*

Advertising and Portrayals of Sexuality

The purpose of advertising is threefold—to get your attention, to get you physiologically excited, and to associate that excitement with the product being advertised. The excitement can be intellectual, emotional, physical (sports, for example), or visual (fast-moving action, wild colors); but when you think of "getting excited," what immediately comes to mind? Well, that is what comes to the mind of advertising executives also, and so ads often use sexual images or suggestions to provoke, to entice—in short, to *seduce.*

Sexuality (especially female sexuality) has been used to sell products for decades. In an analysis comparing magazine advertisements in 1964 with advertisements in 1984, Soley and Kurzbard (1986) found that although the percentage of advertisements portraying sexuality did not change, sexual illustrations had become more overt and visually explicit by 1984. By the late 1990s, a variety of advertisers, including Calvin Klein and Abercrombie, were challenging the limits with advertising campaigns that featured graphic nudity or strong sexual implications. Although Abercrombie was forced to withdraw many of its catalogs because of public outcry, today clothing manufacturers and perfume companies constantly try to out-eroticize each other. Today ads with nudity and sexual innuendo are commonplace.

Not all portrayals of sexuality are this blatant, however. Some are suggestive, such as sprays of soda foam near the face of an ecstatic looking woman, models posing with food or appliances placed in obviously phallic positions, models posed in sexual positions even if clothed, or ads that show women and, less often, men whose faces are contorted in sexual excitement. Some authors even claim that advertisements have tried to use **subliminal** sexuality—pictures of phalluses or breasts or the word *sex* worked into advertisements so they cannot be seen without extreme scrutiny (J. Levine, 1991).

Whether these strategies work is a matter of much debate, but Calvin Klein's ads were so provocative that news reports about them appeared in newspapers and on television news shows—and

A recent advertising campaign for the Pirelli fashion collection featured Naomi Campbell and Tyson Beckford naked, wearing only sneakers.

subliminal
Existing or functioning below the threshold of consciousness, such as images or words, often sexual, that are not immediately apparent to the viewer of an advertisement, intended to excite the subconscious mind and improve the viewer's reaction to the ad.

that is just what advertisers want most for their ads and the products they represent, for people to talk and think about them.

OTHER MEDIA: MUSIC VIDEOS, VIRTUAL REALITY, AND MORE

There are other forms of media that we have not discussed. Because sexuality pervades our lives, it also pervades our art and our media. Today sex-advice columns run in many newspapers and magazines across the country. There are also thousands of "900 number" telephone lines offering sexual services of various kinds across the country. People call the number and pay a certain amount per minute (or use their credit cards for a flat fee) and can talk either to other people who have called in on a party line or to professionals who will discuss sex or play the part of the caller's sexual fantasy. These phone lines cater to men and women (although more commonly to men) and to heterosexuals and homosexuals. Even cell phones are now capable of receiving pornographic images and video clips (see the accompanying Sex in Real Life, "Portable Pornography").

We have discussed the power of the Internet throughout this text, but we mention it here once again because the Internet allows for completely unregulated interaction between millions of people. The Internet has generated whole new forms of communications, and, as new forms of media are developed, sexual and gender issues are arising there, too. Literally thousands of sexually explicit conversations, artworks, and computer games go zipping through the Internet between the users of computer networks every day. Today anyone with access to a computer, from 10 year olds to college professors, can have virtually unlimited access to explicit sexual materials on the web.

Computer technology has been taken even one step further: virtual reality (VR). In VR, pictures generated by computer are projected into goggles put over the eyes, and as the head and eyes move, the picture moves accordingly. The user is given the illusion of actually being in the scene before him or her. Recently, enterprising VR producers have been making sexually explicit VR movies that are coordinated with "stimulators" (vibrators) attached to sensors at the groin; one can actually feel as though one is acting in the pornographic scene while the computer responds to the user's own physical states of excitement and stimulates the user to orgasm. Certainly, new forms of media will present challenges to those who want to regulate or control the public's access to sexually explicit materials.

SEX IN REAL LIFE

Portable Pornography

What makes porn manufacturers optimistic about cell phone porn is that many U.S. consumers are willing to spend extra money for cell phone content.

You've probably heard people complain that "porn is everywhere today." Although it's a bit of an exaggeration, pornography *has* been creeping into a variety of new places, including cell phones and video iPods. Analysts believe that in the next few years, these will become popular devices for accessing pornography because they are small and easy to conceal (P. Hall, 2005; K. Regan, 2005), and many of today's cell phones have high-resolution screens and increased memory capabilities that enable them to play videos.

In Europe, cell phone pornography brings in over $100 million a year (Regan, 2005). What makes porn manufacturers optimistic about cell phone porn is that many U.S. consumers are willing to spend extra money for cell phone content. In fact, ringtone sales topped $450 million in the United States in 2005 (Regan, 2005). Consumers are willing to spend money on a variety of other content, including interactive games, downloadable music, sports and weather, instant messaging, and other services.

The major wireless telecommunication carriers are devising a ratings system to prepare for the onslaught of cell phone pornography (this rating system will be similar to the movie rating system). Companies such as Hotphones, Pornforyourphone, Voooyeur, Xobile, and Vivid Entertainment have all been working on pornographic content for cell phones. Xobile now offers 2-minute pornographic video clips for 44 cents each (Regan, 2005). Another company, Dirty-Text, Inc., offers pornographic text messaging to cell phones for a fee (Korzeniowski, 2005).

At the same time, other companies are scrambling to develop cell phone blocks for underage cell phone users. Over the next few years, it will be interesting to keep an eye on these developments. Experts predict that by 2009, sales of portable pornography will reach $200 million in the United States (P. Hall, 2005; K. Regan, 2005) and will probably top $2.5 billion worldwide (Korzeniowski, 2005).

1 Identify the early reactionary forces that began a censorship of erotic literature.

2 Explain how television uses sex to attract viewers and increase their ratings.

3 In what ways do television and movies influence our perceptions of gender?

4 Identify and explain how television has been found to socialize children from a young age.

5 Explain how gender roles have been portrayed in various types of advertising.

6 Explain how advances in technology have provided people with greater access to sexual content.

WHAT DO YOU WANT TO KNOW ?

I've heard that men and women who are looking for child pornography often use the Internet. What kind of images do they look for? How often do they get caught?

Although the distribution of child pornography is illegal and banned by federal law in all 50 states, the crimes still occur. Research has found that from 2000 to 2001 an estimated 1,713 nationwide arrests were made for Internet-related crimes involving the possession of child pornography (Wolak et al., 2005). Those who were arrested all had access to minor children, either by living with them, through a job, or in organized youth activities. The majority were Caucasian (91%), older than 25 (86%), and unmarried (Wolak et al., 2005). When law officials reviewed the child pornography that offenders had in their possession, they found 83% had images of 6 to 12 year olds; 39% had images of 3 to 5 year olds; and 19% had images of children under age 3. These images contained children involved in a range of sexual behaviors including oral sex, genital touching, and penetration (Wolak et al., 2005).

Graphic Images: Pornography **and the Public's Response**

Pornography has always aroused passions, but the debate over pornography is particularly active today because pornography is so widely available. Pornography can be purchased in stores, and viewed and downloaded online. Worldwide, over $3,000 is spent on pornography each second, and in the United States a new pornographic video is created every 39 minutes (Ropelato, 2008). In addition, throw in arguments from free-speech advocates, antiporn (and anti-antiporn) feminists, religious groups, presidential commissions, the American Civil Liberties Union, and a powerful pornography industry, and you can begin to see the extent of the fights that have developed over this issue.

DEFINING OBSCENITY: **"BANNED IN BOSTON"**

We begin this section by reviewing the disputes over the legal and governmental definitions of pornography as they have been argued in presidential commissions and in the highest courts in the country. Then we look at how those same debates are discussed among the scholars and activists who try to influence the country's policies toward pornography. We also examine the basic claim of modern opponents of pornography: that pornography is harmful in its effects on individuals and society as a whole. Finally, we examine the public's attitudes toward pornography.

Court Decisions

The First Amendment to the Constitution of the United States, enacted in 1791, includes the words: "Congress shall make no law. . . . abridging the freedom of speech, or of the press." Ever since, the court system has struggled with the meaning of those words, for it is obvious that they cannot be taken literally; we do not have the right to make false claims about other people, lie in court under oath, or, in the most famous example, "yell 'fire' (falsely) in a crowded theater," even though that limits our freedom of speech.

Court cases in the United States have established the following three-part definition of obscenity that has determined how courts define pornography. For something to be obscene it must (a) appeal to the **prurient** (PRURE-ee-ent) interest; (b) offend contemporary community standards; and (c) lack serious literary, artistic, political, or scientific value.

However, these criteria are not without critics. Important questions remain about topics such as the definitions of commu-

---

REALResearch > Gender differences have been found in pornography exposure and usage. Men are exposed to pornography at earlier ages than women and are more likely watch pornography on their own while masturbating (HALD, 2006).

---

prurient
Characterized by lascivious thoughts; used as criterion for deciding what is pornographic.

nity standards and prurient interest, and who gets to decide. Some argue that the criteria of prurience, offensiveness, and community standards turn moral fears into legal "harms," which are more imaginary than real, and so we end up with arbitrary discussions of what is "prurient" and which speech has "value" (I. Hunter et al., 1993). In contrast, antiporn feminists argue that pornography laws were made to reflect a male preoccupation with "purity" of thought and insult to moral sensibilities and to ignore the true harms of pornography: the exploitation of women (which we'll explore shortly; R. J. Berger et al., 1991).

Presidential Commissions

Although presidential commissions date back to George Washington, they became more popular in the 20th century (Rosenbaum, 2005). As of 2005, a total of 46 presidential commissions had been established, examining issues such as bioethics, chemical warfare, and terrorist attacks. These commissions issued detailed reports and recommended changes in public policy. Even though presidential commissions often do not lead to an adoption of new policies, they do help educate Americans about important issues. Now we'll explore two of the commissions on pornography.

1970 COMMISSION ON OBSCENITY AND PORNOGRAPHY

In 1967, President Lyndon Johnson set up a commission to study the impact of pornography on American society. The commission was headed by a behavioral scientist who brought on other social scientists, and although the commission also included experts in law, religion, broadcasting, and publishing, its findings were based on empirical research, and much of its $2 million budget was used to fund more scientific studies (Einsiedel, 1989). The commission (which used the terms "erotica" or "explicit sexual material" rather than "pornography"), studied four areas: pornography's effects, traffic and distribution of pornography, legal issues, and positive approaches to cope with pornography (R. J. Berger et al., 1991).

The 1970 Commission operated without the benefit of the enormous research on pornography that has appeared in the last 30 years, and so it has been criticized for such things as not distinguishing between different kinds of erotica (for example, violent vs. nonviolent); for including homosexuals, exhibitionists, and rapists all under the same category of "sex offenders"; and for relying on poor empirical studies. Still, although calling for more research and better designed and funded studies in the future, the commission did perform the most comprehensive study of the evidence up until that time and concluded that no reliable evidence was found to support the idea that exposure to explicit sexual materials is related to the development of delinquent or criminal sexual behavior among youths or adults, so adults should be able to decide for themselves what they will or will not read (Einsiedel, 1989).

In other words, the commission recommended that the state stop worrying so much about pornography, which it saw as a relatively insignificant threat to society. The U.S. Senate was not happy with the commission's conclusions and condemned them.

THE 1986 ATTORNEY GENERAL'S COMMISSION ON PORNOGRAPHY (THE "MEESE COMMISSION")

In 1985, President Ronald Reagan appointed Attorney General Edwin Meese to head a new commission that he expected to overturn the 1970 Commission's findings. In fact, the official charter of the Meese Commission was to find "more effective ways in which the spread of pornography could be contained" (R. J. Berger et al., 1991, p. 25) and so already assumed that pornography was dangerous or undesirable and needed containment. Whereas the 1970 Commission focused on social science, the Meese Commission listened to experts and laypeople through public hearings around the country, most of whom supported restricting or eliminating sexually graphic materials. Virtually every claim made by antipornography activists was cited in the report as fact with little or no supporting evidence, and those who did not support the commission's positions were treated rudely or with hostility (R. J. Berger et al., 1991).

The Meese Commission divided pornography into four categories: violent pornography, "degrading" pornography (e.g., anal sex, group sex, homosexual depictions), nonviolent/nondegrading pornography, and nudity. The commission used a selection of scientific studies to claim that the first two categories are damaging and may be considered a type of social violence, and that they hurt women most of all. Overall, the Meese Commission came to the opposite conclusions of the 1970 Commission and made a number of recommendations:

- Antipornography laws were sufficient as they were written, but law enforcement efforts should be increased at all levels.
- Convicted pornographers should forfeit their profits and be liable to have property used in production or distribution of pornography confiscated, and repeat offenses against the obscenity laws should be considered felonies.
- Religious and civic groups should picket and protest institutions that peddle offensive materials.
- Congress should ban obscene cable television, telephone sex lines, and child pornography in any form.

Reaction to the Meese Commission was immediate and strong. Many of the leading sexuality researchers cited by the commission in support of its conclusions condemned the report and accused the commission of intentional misinterpretation of their scientific evidence. The Moral Majority, the religious right, and conservative supporters hailed the findings as long overdue. Women's groups were split on how to react to the report. On the one hand, the report used feminist language and adopted the position that pornography damages women. Antiporn feminists saw in Meese a possible ally to get pornography banned or at least restricted and so supported the Meese Commission's conclusions, if not its spirit. Other women's groups, however, were very wary of the commission's antigay postures and conservative bent, and they worried that the report would be used to justify wholesale censorship.

REALResearch > One study found that **87%** of male students and **31%** of female students reported using pornography in their lifetimes (Carroll et al., 2008). However, while **20%** of male students reported using pornography daily or almost daily, only **3%** of women did so.

In 2005, Jenna Jameson, one of the most successful female porn stars in the world, recorded "moan tones" to sell as downloadable ringtones for cell phones.

THE PORNOGRAPHY DEBATES:
FREE SPEECH AND CENSORSHIP

The religious conservative opposition to pornography is based on a belief that people have an inherent human desire to sin and that pornography reinforces that tendency and so undermines the family, traditional authority, and the moral fabric of society (R. J. Berger et al., 1991). Unless strong social standards are kept, people will indulge themselves in individual fulfillment and pleasure, promoting material rather than spiritual or moral values (Downs, 1989). Users of pornography become desensitized to shocking sexual behaviors, and pornography teaches them to see sex as simple physical pleasure rather than a part of a loving, committed relationship. This leads to increased teen pregnancy rates, degradation of females, and rape; in this, at least, the religious conservative antipornography school agrees with the antiporn feminists.

WHAT DO YOU WANT TO KNOW?

I've watched pornography, and I'm just curious about condom use. Are there any rules about using condoms on the sets of pornographic movies?

Male and female adult film actors are not legally required to wear condoms during filming. Some production companies may require condoms, but producers argue that viewers don't want to watch safe sex in porn and scenes with condoms take too long to shoot (Liu, 2004; Madigan, 2004). Actors are required to undergo monthly testing for STIs, but as you learned from Chapter 15, many infections may not show up in testing until many weeks after a person becomes infected. Some states have begun exploring legislation to require condom use during filming. In fact, in 2004 the California Assembly warned the pornographic-film industry that condoms must be worn or they will write a law to require it (Liu, 2004; Madigan, 2004).

Nowhere has the issue of pornography been as divisive as among feminist scholars, splitting them into two general schools. The antipornography feminists see pornography as an assault on women that silences them, renders them powerless, reinforces male dominance, and indirectly encourages sexual and physical abuse against women. The other side, which includes groups such as the Feminist Anticensorship Taskforce (FACT), argues that censorship of sexual materials will eventually (if not immediately) be used to censor such things as feminist writing and gay erotica and would therefore endanger women's rights and freedoms of expression (Cowan, 1992). Some who argue against the antipornography feminists call themselves the "anti-antiporn" contingent, but for simplicity's sake we refer to them simply as the "anticensorship" group.

Antipornography Arguments

One of the scholars who has written most forcefully and articulately against pornography is Catherine MacKinnon (1985, 1987, 1993). MacKinnon argues that pornography cannot be understood separately from the long history of male domination of women and that it is in fact an integral part and a reinforcing element of women's second-class status. According to MacKinnon, pornography is less about sex than power. She argues that pornography is a discriminatory social practice that institutionalizes the inferiority and subordination of one group by another, the way segregation institutionalized the subordination of Blacks by Whites.

MacKinnon suggests that defending pornography on First Amendment terms as protected free speech is to misunderstand the influence of pornography on the everyday life of women in society. She suggests thinking of pornography itself as a violation of a woman's right not to be discriminated against, guaranteed by the Fourteenth Amendment. Imagine, she suggests, if the thousands of movies and books produced each year by the pornographic industry were not showing women, but rather Jews, African Americans, the handicapped, or some other minority splayed naked, often chained or tied up, urinated and defecated on, with foreign objects inserted into their orifices, while at the same time physical assaults and sexual assaults against that group were epidemic in society (as they are against women). Would people still appeal to the First Amendment to prevent some kind of action?

Other feminists take this argument a step further and claim that male sexuality is by its nature subordinating; Andrea Dworkin (1981, 1987), for example, is uncompromising about men and their sexuality. Dworkin, like MacKinnon, sees pornography as a central aspect of male power, which she sees as a long-term strategy to elevate men to a superior position in society by forcing even strong women to feign weakness and dependency. Even sexuality reflects male power: Dworkin sees every act of intercourse as an assault, because men are the penetrators and women are penetrated.

Because pornography is harmful in and of itself, such authors claim, it should be controlled or banned. Although they have not had much success passing such laws in the United States, their strong arguments have set the agenda for the public debate over pornography.

Anticensorship Arguments

A number of critics have responded to the arguments put forth by people like MacKinnon and Dworkin (Kaminer, 1992; Posner, 1993; Wolf, 1991). First, many argue that a restriction against pornography cannot be separated from a restriction against writing or pictures that show other oppressed minorities in subordinate positions. Once we start restricting all portrayals of minorities being subordinated, we are becoming a society ruled by censorship. Many Hollywood movies, television shows, and even women's romance novels portray women as subordinate or secondary to men; are all of those to be censored, too? MacKinnon seems to make little distinction between *Playboy* and movies showing violent rape; are all sexual portrayals of the female body or of intercourse harmful to women?

Also, what about lesbian pornography, in which the models and the intended audience are female, and men almost wholly excluded? Many of these portrayals are explicitly geared toward resisting society's established sexual hierarchies; should they also be censored (Henderson, 1991)? Once sexually explicit portrayals are suppressed, anticensorship advocates argue, so are the portrayals that try to challenge sexual stereotypes.

A more complicated issue is the antiporn group's claim that pornography harms women. One response is to suggest that such an argument once again casts men in a more powerful position than women and, by denying women's power, supports the very hierarchy it seeks to dismantle. But the question of whether it can be demonstrated that pornography actually harms women is a difficult one.

STUDIES ON
PORNOGRAPHY AND HARM

Both sides of the pornography debate produce reams of studies that support their side; the Meese Report and antiporn feminists such as MacKinnon and Dworkin produce papers showing that

---

REALResearch **>** The average age for a child's first exposure to online pornography is 11-years old (MITCHELL ET AL., 2003).

---

pornography is tied to rape, assault, and negative attitudes toward women, and others produce studies showing that pornography has no effects or is secondary to more powerful forces (W. A. Fisher & Barak, 1991). More recent experts argue that pornography is linked to failed relationships and negative attitudes about women (P. Paul, 2005). Who is right?

Society-Wide Studies
In 1969, J. Edgar Hoover, director of the FBI, submitted evidence to the Presidential Commission on Obscenity and Pornography claiming that police observation had led him to believe the following:

A disproportionate number of sex offenders were found to have large quantities of pornographic materials in their residences. . . . more, in the opinion of witnesses, than one would expect to find in the residences of a random sample of non-offenders of the same sex, age, and socioeconomic status, or in the residences of a random sample of offenders whose offenses were not sex offenses. (Quoted in I. Hunter et al., 1993, p. 226)

Correlations like these have been used since the early 19th century to justify attitudes toward pornography (I. Hunter et al., 1993). Such claims are easily criticized on scientific grounds because a "witness's opinion" cannot be relied on (and there has never been a study that has reliably determined the amount of pornography in the "average" nonoffender or non–sex offender's home). Better evidence is suggested in the state-by-state studies (L. Baron & Straus, 1987; J. E. Scott & Schwalm, 1988). Both groups of researchers found a direct nationwide correlation between rape and sexually explicit magazines: Rape rates are highest in those places with the highest circulation of sex magazines.

However, Denmark, which decriminalized pornography in the 1960s, and Japan, where pornography is sold freely and tends to be dominated by rape and bondage scenes, have low rates of reported rape, relative to the United States (Davies, 1997; Posner, 1993). In a study of four countries over 20 years, Kutchinsky (1991) could find no increase in rape relative to other crimes in any of the countries, even as the availability of pornography increased dramatically. L. Baron (1990), the same researcher who found that rape rates correlated with explicit magazines, did a further study, which showed that gender equality was higher in states with higher circulation rates of sexually explicit magazines. This may be because those states are generally more liberal. Women in societies that forbid or repress pornography (such as Islamic societies) tend to be more oppressed than those in societies in which it is freely available. All in all, the effects of pornography on a society's violence toward women are far from clear.

Individual Studies
Several laboratory studies have sought to determine the reactions of men exposed to different types of pornography. In most cases, men are shown pornography, and then a test is done to determine whether their attitudes toward women, sex crimes, and the like are

altered. Although little evidence indicates that nonviolent, sexually explicit films provoke antifemale reactions in men (Davies, 1997; Padgett et al., 1989), many studies have shown that violent or degrading pornography does influence attitudes. Viewing sexual violence and degradation increases fantasies of rape, the belief that some women secretly desire to be raped, acceptance of violence against women, insensitivity to rape victims, desire for sex without emotional involvement, the treatment of women as sex objects, and desire to see more violent pornography (R. J. Berger et al., 1991; W. A. Fisher & Barak, 1991; Linz, 1989).

However, these studies take place under artificial conditions (would these men have chosen to see such movies if not in a study?), and feelings of sexual aggression in a laboratory may not mirror a person's activities in the real world. It is also unclear how long such feelings last and whether they really influence behavior (Kutchinsky, 1991). Other studies show that men's aggression tends to increase after seeing any violent movie, even if it is not sexual, and so the explicit sexuality of the movies may not be the important factor (Linz & Donnerstein, 1992). A recent study on the self-perceived effects of pornography use in Danish men and women 18–30 years old found few negative effects (Hald & Malamuth, 2008). In fact, participants reported that the use of pornography had an overall positive effect on various aspects of their lives.

Are We Missing the Point?

Lahey (1991) argues that the attempt to determine the effects of viewing pornography misses the point because, once again, the focus is on men and their reactions; is it not enough that women feel belittled, humiliated, and degraded? The voice of women is silent in pornography studies. The questions focus on whether pornography induces sexual violence in men. Pornography, Lahey (after MacKinnon and Dworkin) argues, harms women by teaching falsehoods about them (that they enjoy painful sex, are not as worthy as men, secretly desire sex even when they refuse it, and do not know what they really like); it harms women's self-esteem; and it harms women by reproducing itself in men's behavior toward women.

Certainly, there is an argument to be made that certain kinds of sexually explicit materials contribute little to society and cause much pain directly and indirectly to women. Many who defend sexually explicit materials that show consensual sex abhor the violent and degrading pornography that is the particular target of feminist ire. Whether the way to respond to such materials is through new laws (which may do little to stop its production; for example, child pornography, which is illegal, flourishes in the United States; Wolak et al., 2005) or through listening to the voices of women, who are its victims, is an open question.

ONLINE PORNOGRAPHY

The online pornography industry is quickly growing and was worth approximately $2 billion in 2003 (Swartz, 2004). The number of online porn sites increased 18-fold since 1998, from approximately 70,000 to 1.3 million (Swartz, 2004). Many of the online buying features available through websites today (such as real-time credit card processing) were developed by the pornography industry (Griffiths, 2003). The accessibility, anonymity, and ease of use have all contributed to the growing popularity of the Internet. Some view pornographic images online, visit sexually oriented chat rooms, or may engage in sexual activities with an anonymous person online (J. P. Schneider, 2000a).

Online sex users can be either *recreational users* (those who enter sites out of curiosity or for entertainment), *at-risk users* (those who are increasingly drawn to usage of online sexually oriented materials), or *compulsive users* (those who spend over 11 hours per week engaging in online sexual activities; Cooper et al., 1999). Research has found that approximately 83% of online sex users are recreational users; 11% are at-risk users, and 6% are compulsive users (A. Cooper et al., 1999). Individuals who engage in compulsive online sex often experience changes in their intimate relationships. In fact, one study found 68% of users lost interest in sex with their partner (J. P. Schneider, 2000b). Partners and children of users also experience psychological side effects as well, including depression and loneliness (P. Paul, 2005; see Chapter 16 for more information about Internet sexual addictions). Users of online pornography also report a desensitization to pornography over time (J. P. Schneider, 2000b).

Over the next few years it will be interesting to see what happens to online pornography. Two of the pornography industry's biggest challenges—distribution and privacy—have been solved with the Internet (Chmielewski & Hoffman, 2006). Online pornography reduces embarrassment and allows individuals to watch and buy pornography in the privacy of their own home.

REALResearch > Heterosexual men who watch pornographic videos containing images of naked men with a woman have been found to have higher quality sperm than heterosexual men who watch similar videos containing only women (KILGALLON & SIMMONS, 2005). Researchers suggest this is due to a perceived sperm competition, wherein a heterosexual male produces higher quality sperm when there is a threat of a female choosing another male.

WHAT THE PUBLIC THINKS
ABOUT PORNOGRAPHY

It is not only scholars and activists who disagree about pornography; the general public seems profoundly ambivalent about it as well. The majority want to ban violent pornography and feel that such pornography can lead to a loss of respect for women, acts of violence, and rape. Female erotica and soft-core pornography are generally not viewed as negatively. One of the biggest producers of female erotica is Candida Royalle, who had previously been an adult film actress. Royalle is the founder of Femme Productions, which has produced more than 16 soft-core pornography videos for women and couples.

Unlike many other businesses today, America's pornography industry continues to do well. One study found that the porn industry generated $97 billion in 2006 alone (Ropelato, 2008). Video and computer technology continues to open doors to millions and millions of customers throughout the world. Even so, pornography is a difficult, controversial problem in American society. By arguing that sex is the only part of human life that should not be portrayed in our art and media, the core conflict over sexuality is revealed: people seem to believe that although sexuality is a central part of human life, it should still be treated differently than other human actions, as a category unto itself.

review questions

1 Explain how courts define pornography and obscenity.

2 Discuss and differentiate between the two commissions on pornography, and explain the findings of each.

3 Identify the two schools of thought regarding the pornography debate.

4 Differentiate the antipornography and anticensorship argument.

5 Describe the studies that have been done examining pornography and harm.

6 Discuss public attitudes about pornography.

Selling Sex: Prostitution, **Pimps, and the Government**

Thus far we have explored how sexual images have been used to sell everything from blue jeans to perfume and how sex has been used in television and films to increase viewership and ratings. We also looked at pornography's history, its growing presence on the Internet, and the public's response to it. Now we turn our attention to the selling of sex through prostitution.

DEFINING
PROSTITUTION

Researchers have found the study of prostitution a challenge, because the exact size of the population is unknown, making a representative sample difficult to come by (Shaver, 2005). Also, because prostitution is illegal in the United States, except for certain counties in Nevada, many prostitutes are hidden, so their behaviors cannot be measured.

Defining prostitution is not easy. The U.S. legal code is ambiguous about what constitutes prostitution; for instance, some state penal codes define prostitution as the act of hiring out one's body for sexual intercourse, whereas other states define prostitution as sexual intercourse in exchange for money or as any sexual

behavior that is sold for profit. Some consider erotic dancers and models to be a form of prostitution (Dalla, 2002).

Dictionaries also have different definitions for prostitution. For example, the *Oxford English Dictionary* defines prostitution as "offering of the body to indicate lewdness for hire," whereas the *American Heritage Dictionary* defines a prostitute as "a person who solicits and accepts payment for sexual intercourse." For our purposes in this chapter, we define prostitution as the act of a male or female engaging in sexual activity in exchange for money or other material goods. Although the use of prostitutes is significantly underreported, studies have found that 2% to 3% of adult male residents of large metropolitan areas in the United States have patronized local prostitutes (Brewer et al., 2008).

Over the course of time, prostitutes have been called many slang terms, such as "whores," "hookers," "sluts," or "hustlers." Some other terms often used when discussing prostitution include a **pimp,** who may act as a protector and business manager for many prostitutes; and a **madam,** who is in charge of managing a home, **brothel,** or group of prostitutes. A **john** is a person who hires a prostitute, and a **trick** is the service that the prostitute

pimp
A slang term that refers to the male in charge of organizing clients for a female prostitute.

madam
A slang term that refers to the woman who is responsible for overseeing a brothel or a group of prostitutes.

brothel
A house of prostitution.

john
A slang term that refers to a prostitute's client.

trick
A slang term that refers to the sexual services of a prostitute; also may refer to a john.

performs (although recently "trick" has come to mean the same as "john"). Historically, most prostitutes worked in brothels, although with the exception of certain areas of Nevada, few brothels remain in the United States. However, brothels are still widespread in the Asian world.

SOCIOLOGICAL ASPECTS OF PROSTITUTION

Society has created social institutions such as marriage and the family in part to regulate sexual behavior. However, it is also true that throughout history, people have had sexual relations outside these institutions. Prostitution has existed, in one form or another, as long as marriage has, which has led some to argue that it provides a needed sexual release. Whether a society should recognize this by allowing legal, regulated prostitution, however, raises a number of controversial social, political, economic, and religious questions.

Some sociologists suggest that prostitution developed out of the **patriarchal** nature of most societies. In a society in which men are valued over women and men hold the reins of economic and political power, some women exploit the only asset that cannot be taken away from them—their sexuality. Other sociologists used to claim that women actually benefited from prostitution because, from a purely economic point of view, they get paid for giving something away that is free to them. Kingsley Davis, one of the most famous sociologists of the 20th century, wrote:

The woman may suffer no loss at all, yet receive a generous reward, resembling the artist who, paid for his work, loves it so well that he would paint anyway. Purely from the angle of economic return, the hard question is not why so many women become prostitutes, but why so few of them do. (As quoted in Benjamin, 1961, p. 876)

WHO BECOMES A PROSTITUTE?

It is estimated that there are as many as 2 million prostitutes working in the United States today, some full time and some part time. Although there are more female prostitutes with male clients than all other forms combined, there are also gay, lesbian, and straight male prostitutes (Goode, 1994; Perkins & Bennett, 1985).

What motivates a man or woman to sell sex for money? Is it the money? Is it fear? Is it necessity? The majority of prostitutes say that their primary and maybe even sole motivation for prostituting is for the money (Rio, 1991). Prostitutes can make more money, on average, than their peers who work conventional jobs.

Many prostitutes say that the major drawback to their job is having to engage in sex with their clients. It is a myth that women become prostitutes because they love sex or because they are "sex addicts." Those involved in the prostitution subculture say that if a prostitute enjoys sexual intercourse with clients, it "gets in her way" (Goode, 1994) because she may lose sight of the importance of client pleasure, or she might want to spend more time with a particular client, which could reduce her income. One prostitute said:

I would say that nothing could prompt me to have an orgasm or even become excited with a john. . . . I doubt that I would be able to manage it. . . . I will always pretend to be excited, and to come at the moment he comes, but if I really got excited I would be all involved with myself, and the timing would be thrown off, and actually he wouldn't have a good time as if I were faking it. It's funny to think of, but he gets more for his money if it's a fake than if he were to get the real thing. (Wells, 1970, p. 139)

The majority of prostitutes do not enjoy their work. In fact, one study found that 89% of female prostitutes reported wanting to escape from prostitution (Farley et al., 2003). Most prostitutes work full time, with 49% of their clients repeat customers, including some long-term customers (M. Freund et al., 1989). A regular customer visits the prostitute at least once a week, and some have sexual encounters two or three times each week with the prostitute or spend several hours at a hotel (or one of their homes) together.

FEMALE PROSTITUTES

In the United States, most female prostitutes are young. The average age of entry into female prostitution is 14 years old (Dittmann, 2005). One study found that 75% of prostitutes were younger than 25 (Potterat et al., 1990). The majority of female prostitutes are single (Medrano et al., 2003).

Typically, female prostitutes live in an apartment or home with several other prostitutes and one pimp. This is known as a **pseudofamily** (Romenesko & Miller, 1989). The pseudofamily

WHAT DO YOU WANT TO KNOW?

Do prostitutes enjoy having sex?
Having sex with whom? Eighty percent of prostitutes have sexual lives outside of their professional lives (Savitz & Rosen, 1988). As for sex with clients, some prostitutes report that they enjoy both sexual intercourse and oral sex, although the majority do not. Some do experience orgasms in their interactions with clients, but again, the majority do not. In fact, in Masters and Johnson's early research on sexual functioning, they included prostitutes (see Chapter 2) but found that the pelvic congestion in prostitutes, which resulted from having sex without orgasms, made them poor subjects for their studies.

patriarchal
Of or pertaining to a society or system that is dominated by male power.

pseudofamily
A type of family that develops when prostitutes and pimps live together; rules, household responsibilities, and work activities are agreed on by all members of the family.

Female Prostitution in Australia

My occupation is not all that different from any nine-to-five worker except the hours are better, I'm my own boss, and the pay's better.

Lee is a 37-year-old prostitute in Sydney, Australia. She also raises a family at home. Here she talks about her life of prostitution.

I began prostituting when I was nineteen and met some working ladies. I was intrigued by what they were doing and saw the money they had and what they could do with it. . . .

I've made $2,000 in one week, which is very good money. I charge $20 minimum, short time, just for straight sex. That's ten minutes, which will not sound very long to most people, but when you consider that the average male only needs two or three minutes in sex—I had some guys finishing even before they get on the bed. I make all my clients wear a condom and I've put the condom on them and by the time I've turned around to get on the bed they've already blown it. In most of these cases it's the guys who are most apologetic and feel they have fallen down on the job.

I always check my clients both for any disease or body lice. If I am at all wary of a client I always get another girl to double-check. I go to the doctor once a week and get a report within ten minutes. There are some girls who will take anybody and don't use any protection, and they don't know how to check a client properly anyway. Girls on drugs are less careful than they should be, and in the parlors condoms are generally not insisted on.

Clients ask for a range of different sexual activities. It can range from good old-fashioned straight-out sex to swinging from the chandeliers. Apart from bondage and discipline there are some weird requests such as golden showers, spankings and whippings, and the guy who wants a girl to shit on a glass-top table with him underneath the table. There's money to be made in these things but I won't do them because it's my own individual choice.

As for a typical day for me, I get up between seven and seven-thirty and have the usual argument with getting kids off to school. I do my housework like any other housewife. I have pets, and I have a normal home. I eat, sleep and breathe like any normal human being. I enjoy cooking a lot. I keep my business quite separate from my home life, and the kids don't know what I do, my husband doesn't want to know about it and I don't want to discuss it with him. Work is work. I go to work to work and when I go home and close the doors on the house that's it. My occupation is not all that different from any nine-to-five worker except the hours are better, I'm my own boss, and the pay's better.

SOURCE: Perkins & Bennett, 1985, pp. 71–85.

---

operates much like a family does; there are rules and responsibilities for all family members. The pimp is responsible for protecting the prostitutes, whereas the prostitutes are responsible for bringing home the money. Other household responsibilities are also agreed on. When the female ages or the pimp tires of her, she may be traded like a slave or simply disowned.

Psychological problems are more common in prostitutes than nonprostitutes and more common in older prostitutes (de-Schampheleire, 1990). There are dangers associated with a life of prostitution—stressful family situations and mistreatment by clients or pimps. To deal with these pressures, many prostitutes turn to drugs or alcohol, although many enter prostitution to enable them to make enough money to support their preexisting addictions. One study found that 95% of prostitutes used drugs, including crack, heroin, alcohol, and marijuana (Dalla, 2002). One prostitute said: "It would take a real strong person to prostitute without drugs." Many women who become prostitutes have drug addictions and use the prostitution as a way to help pay for their drugs (Potterat et al., 1998).

REALResearch **>** As a prostitute's drug addictions increase, her willingness to accept less money or drugs in return for services also increases (DALLA, 2002).

Entry into prostitution is often a gradual process (Goode, 1994). At first, the activity may bother them, but, as time goes by, they become accustomed to the life and begin to see themselves and the profession differently. In the accompanying Human Sexuality in a Diverse World, "Female Prostitution in Australia," one woman shares her feelings about her work.

Predisposing Factors

Some common threads run through the lives of many prostitutes. The most common factor, according to researchers, is an economically deprived upbringing (Goode, 1994). However, because high-class prostitutes, who often come from wealthy backgrounds, are less likely to be caught and arrested, research studies may concentrate too much on poorer women.

Early sexual contact with many partners in superficial relationships has also been found to be related to prostitution. Prostitutes are also more often victims of sexual abuse, initiate sexual activity at a younger age, and experience a higher frequency of rape. Intrafamilial violence and past physical and sexual abuse are also common (Earls & David, 1990; R. L. Simons & Whitbeck, 1991). Overall, Black women who have a history of emotional or physical abuse have been found to be more likely to engage in prostitution than White or Hispanic women with similar abuse (Medrano et al., 2003).

Sexually abused children who run away from home have been found to be more likely to become prostitutes than those who do not run away (Seng, 1989). Perhaps these experiences also affect a woman's decreasing sense of self-esteem. Parents of prostitutes often report experiencing stress because of a history of failed intimate relationships, economic problems, and unstable relationships. In addition, many prostitutes grow up in poor neighborhoods, which provide easy access to prostitution careers because active prostitution circles are common.

> Streetwalkers are **the most common type** of prostitute.

Keep in mind that though these factors contribute to a predisposition to prostitution, they do not *cause* a woman to become a prostitute. For example, we know that many prostitutes have had no early sex education either in school or from their family; however, this does not mean that the lack of sex education *caused* them to become prostitutes. Many different roads lead to a life of prostitution.

Types of Female Prostitution

Female prostitutes can solicit their services in the street, bars, hotels, brothels, massage parlors; as **call girls** or **courtesans;** or out of an **escort agency** (Perkins & Bennett, 1985). These types of prostitutes differ with respect to the work setting, prices charged, and safety from violence and arrest. Streetwalkers make up about 20% of all prostitutes; bar girls, 15%; massage-parlor prostitutes, 25%; hotel prostitutes, 10%; brothel prostitutes, 15%; and call girls, 15% (C. P. Simon & Witt, 1982).

STREETWALKERS Also called street prostitutes, streetwalkers are the most common type of prostitute. To attract customers, they dress in tight clothes and high heels and may work on street corners or transportation stops (Riccio, 1992). This type of prostitution is considered the most dangerous type because streetwalkers are often victims of violence, rape, and robbery (Dalla, 2002; Romero-Daza et al., 2003). For this reason, they usually have a pimp for protection (we discuss pimps in greater detail shortly).

Streetwalkers generally approach customers and ask them questions such as, "Looking for some action?" or "Do you need a date?" If the client is interested, the prostitute will suggest a price, and they will go to a place where the service can be provided (an alley, car, or cheap hotel room). Typically, streetwalkers are looking to make as much money as possible, and they will try to "hustle" to make more (by suggesting more expensive types of sexual activity).

BAR PROSTITUTES Also called bar girls, bar prostitutes work in bars and hustle patrons for drinks and sexual activity. Because they usually work for the bar owner, they try to build up a client's bar bill. Unlike streetwalkers, bar girls have more protection from violence and police arrests. Bar prostitutes typically hand over 40% to 50% of their nightly earnings to the bar manager.

HOTEL PROSTITUTES These prostitutes may be referred to hotel patrons by a bellboy or hotel manager. They keep 40% to 50% of the money they charge clients, and the hotel manager keeps the rest.

BROTHEL PROSTITUTES Brothel prostitutes work out of a home or apartment that is shared by a group of prostitutes. A madam or pimp generally runs the house. Brothels offer more protection for prostitutes than the street.

In the United States, Nevada is the only state with counties in which brothels are legal. Prostitutes carry identification cards and are routinely examined for STIs. When a customer walks into a brothel in Nevada, he may be given a "menu" of choices. From this menu he picks an appetizer (such as a hot bath or a pornographic video) and a main course (such as the specific sexual position). Then he can choose a woman from a **lineup,** and the couple go into a private room.

The typical rate is $2 per minute, with more exotic services being more expensive. Usually conventional sexual intercourse costs $30 to $40, and oral sex may cost $50 or more. Prostitutes inspect the client's genitals for signs of STIs and collect payment. The brothel prostitute keeps between 50% and 60% of her earnings, and the rest goes to the brothel owner.

MASSAGE PARLOR PROSTITUTES Some prostitutes are masseuses who also provide sexual services. The owners of the massage parlor act as though they are unaware of this sexual activity. The most common service offered in massage parlors is fellatio or fellatio accompanied by sexual intercourse (Perkins & Bennett, 1985). Prices in massage parlors are typically higher than those charged by streetwalkers, and security guards provide additional protection. However, the trade-off is that a parlor keeps more of the profit earned for working in their establishment.

ESCORTS Escort services, agencies that provide prostitutes who serve as escorts, operate in ways similar to massage parlors, except that escort services do not have to take the responsibility for sexual activity because it does not occur on their premises. Prices for an escort vary widely and are dependent on location and hours worked.

CALL GIRLS AND COURTESANS Higher-class prostitution involves both call girls and courtesans (Dalla, 2002). In 2008, New York governor Eliot Spitzer was found to have had multiple liaisons with a variety of prostitutes working with the Emperor's Club V.I.P. The Emperor's Club operated out of New York, Washington, Miami, Paris, and London that offered prostitutes for anywhere from $1,000 to $5,500 per hour.

OTHER TYPES OF PROSTITUTES Other, less common types of prostitutes include **bondage and discipline (B&D) prostitutes** who engage in bondage and discipline services, using such

call girl
A higher-class female prostitute who is often contacted by telephone and may either work by the hour or the evening or for longer periods.

courtesan
A prostitute who often interacts with men of rank or wealth.

escort agency
An agency set up to arrange escorts for unaccompanied males; sexual services are often involved.

lineup
The lining up of prostitutes in a brothel so that when clients enter a brothel, they can choose the prostitute they want.

bondage and discipline (B&D) prostitute
A prostitute who is paid to engage in bondage and discipline fantasy play with clients.

things as leather, whips, and chains. Women who specialize in B&D will advertise with pseudonyms such as Madam Pain or Mistress Domination (Perkins & Bennett, 1985). B&D prostitutes may have dungeons, complete with whips, racks, and leg irons and wear black leather, studded belts, and masks. Many B&D prostitutes charge money to engage in bondage and discipline fantasy play with their clients.

*The majority of male prostitutes **begin with street hustling.***

Lesbian prostitutes also exist, but we know little about them. Lesbian prostitutes tend to be older, and many take a younger woman on as a paid sexual partner (Perkins & Bennett, 1985). Lesbian prostitutes often have only one client at any given time.

MALE PROSTITUTES

Male prostitutes who service women are referred to as **gigolos** (JIG-uh-lows). Traditionally, gigolos are young men who are hired by older women to have an ongoing sexual relationship. Male prostitutes who service other men are referred to as hustlers or "boys." Some male prostitutes service both men and women.

Male prostitutes who have sex with men may be otherwise heterosexual. Ironically, many of these heterosexual, masculine bodybuilders are homophobic, which causes many conflicts between their attitudes and behaviors. Approximately 50% of male prostitutes are homosexual, and 25% each are bisexual or heterosexual (Pleak & Meyer-Bahlburg, 1990). Like women, men tend to enter into the life of prostitution early, usually by the age of 16 (with a range from 12 to 19; J. A. Cates & Markley, 1992). The majority of male prostitutes are between the ages of 16 and 29 and White (D. J. West, 1993). Like the pimp for female prostitutes, many male prostitutes also have mentors, or "sugar daddies."

When male prostitutes are asked what types of sexual behavior they engage in with their clients, 99% say that they perform fellatio, either alone or in combination with other activities; 80% say that they engage in anal sex, and 63% participate in **rimming** (Morse et al., 1992). In addition, many reported other activities including **water sports** and sadomasochistic behavior.

Predisposing Factors

Like females, males become prostitutes mainly for the money (Kaye, 2007). However, many factors predispose a man to become a prostitute. Early childhood sexual experience (such as coerced sexual behavior), combined with a homosexual orientation, increases the chances of choosing prostitution (Earls & David, 1989). Male prostitutes often experience their first sexual experience at a young age (approximately 12 years old) and have older partners. Male prostitutes also have fewer career aspirations than do nonprostitutes and are more likely to view themselves as addicted to either drugs or alcohol (Cates & Markley, 1992). More than 50% of male prostitutes report using alcohol and a variety of drugs with their clients and commonly accept drugs or alcohol as a trade for sex (Morse et al., 1992).

Like female prostitutes, male street prostitutes have more psychopathology than nonprostitute peers (P. M. Simon et al., 1992), which may have to do with their dangerous and chaotic environments. They are more suspicious, mistrustful, hopeless, lonely,

and often lack meaningful interpersonal relationships (Leichtentritt & Arad, 2005). These feelings may develop out of the distrust that many have for their clients; clients may refuse to pay for services, hurt them, or force them to do things that they do not want to do. In fact, more than half of male prostitutes report that they are afraid of violence while they are hustling (J. R. Scott et al., 2005). The majority live alone, with no partner. This may be because of the type of lifestyle they lead or the sense of hopelessness they carry with them. Although many would like to stop prostituting, they feel that they would not be able to find other employment (P. M. Simon et al., 1992).

Types of Male Prostitution

Male prostitutes, like females, may engage in street hustling, bar hustling, and escort prostitution. The differences between these types of prostitution are in income potential and personal safety.

STREET AND BAR HUSTLERS Male street and bar hustlers solicit clients on the street or in parks that are known for the availability of the sexual trade. The majority of male prostitutes begin with street hustling, especially if they are too young to get into bars. Male prostitutes, like female prostitutes, ask their clients if they are "looking for some action."

Because of increasing fear and danger on the streets, many street hustlers eventually move into bars. One male prostitute explains:

> You got a lot of different kinds of assholes out there. When someone pulls up and says "get in," you get in. And you can look at their eyes, and they can be throwing fire out of their eyes, and have a knife under the seat. You're just in a bad situation. I avoid it by not hustling in the street. I hustle in the bars now. (Luckenbill, 1984, p. 288)

Male prostitutes also report that bar hustling enables them to make more money than street hustling because they get to set their own prices. The average price for a bar trick ranges from $50 to $75.

ESCORTS A natural progression after bar hustling is escort prostitution, which involves finding someone who arranges clients but also takes a share of the profits. Each date that is arranged for an escort can bring from $150 to $200, and the prostitute usually keeps 60% for himself. However, escort services are not always well-run or honest operations, and problems with escort operators may force a male prostitute to return to bar hustling. Compared with other types of male prostitutes, however, escort prostitutes are least likely to be arrested.

gigolo
A man who is hired to have a sexual relationship with a woman and receives financial support from her.

rimming
Oral stimulation of the anus.

water sports
Sexual services that involve urinating on or inside one's sexual partner.

Adolescent Prostitution

. . . they always made some remark about my age because I'm so young. Being thirteen has been a strong selling point for me.

More than 85% of teenagers who run away eventually become involved in prostitution. Below is an account from Lynn, a 13-year-old adolescent prostitute.

It was freezing cold that Friday afternoon as I stood on the street corner looking for buyers. The harsh wind made the temperature feel as though it were below zero, and I had been outdoors for almost two and a half hours already. I was wearing a short fake fur jacket, a brown suede miniskirt and spike heels. Only a pair of very sheer hose covered my legs, and I shook as I smiled and tried to flag down passing cars with male drivers. The cold bit at my skin, but if I had come out dressed in jeans and leg warmers, I'd have never gotten anywhere. After all, I was selling myself, and the merchandise had to be displayed.

Finally, a middle-aged man in an expensive red sports car pulled up to the curb. He lowered the car window and beckoned me over to him with his finger. I braced myself to start my act. Trying as hard as I could to grin and liven up my walk, I went over to his car, rested my chest on the open window ledge and said, "Hi ya, Handsome."

He answered, "Hello, Little Miss Moffet. How'd you like Handsome to warm you up on a cold day like this?" I wished that I could have told him that I wouldn't like it at all. That even the thought of it made me sick to my stomach. He had called me Little Miss Moffet—they always made some remark about my age because I'm so young. Being thirteen has been a strong selling point for me. In any case, I hid my feelings and tried to look enthusiastic. They all want a happy girl who they think wants them. So with the broadest smile I could manage, I answered,

"There's nothing I'd like better than to be with you, Sir." I started to get into his car, but he stopped me, saying, "Not so fast, Honey, how much is this going to cost me?" I hesitated for a moment. I really wanted twenty dollars, but it had been a slow day and I had a strong feeling that this guy wasn't going to spring for it, so I replied, "Fifteen dollars, and the price of the hotel room."

We had sex in the same run-down dirty hotel that I always take my tricks to. It doesn't cost much, and usually that's all that really matters to them. Being with that guy was horrible, just like it always turns out to be. That old overweight man sweated all over me and made me call him Daddy the whole time. He really smelled bad too, once he got started. He may have thought that he was kissing me, but actually he just slobbered on my body. He kept calling me Marcy, and later he explained that Marcy was his youngest daughter.

Once he finished with me, the guy seemed in a big hurry to leave. He dressed quickly, and just as he was about to rush out the door, I yelled out, "But what about my money?" He pulled a ten-dollar bill out of his back pocket and laid it on the dresser, saying only, "Sorry, kid, this is all I've got on me right now."

At that moment I wished that I could have killed him, but I knew that there was nothing I could do. The middle-class man in the expensive red sports car had cheated his 13-year-old hooker. That meant that I had to go back out on the street and brave the cold again in order to find another taker.

SOURCE: Landau, 1987, pp. 25–26.

CALL BOYS Like call girls, **call boys** keep a small group of clients with whom they have sex occasionally to earn money. Many of these prostitutes have had experience working both on the street and in bars, but they leave to go into business for themselves.

TRANSSEXUAL AND TRANSVESTITE PROSTITUTES

Transsexual and transvestite prostitution is more common among male-to-female transsexuals than female-to-male (Perkins & Bennett, 1985). Some male transvestite prostitutes adopt an exaggerated female appearance and work beside female prostitutes (Elifson et al., 1993a), luring unsuspecting clients who do not always realize he is male. Most are homosexual males, but some are **she-males.** After being on hormonal therapy before sex reassignment surgery, they develop breasts but also still have a penis.

▌ADOLESCENT PROSTITUTES

What we know about adolescent prostitution is disheartening. For adolescents who run away from home, prostitution offers a way to earn money and to establish their autonomy. Many of these adolescents have been sexually abused and have psychological problems (Gibson-Ainyette et al., 1988; S. J. Thompson, 2005). Adolescent prostitution can have long-term psychological and sociological effects on the adolescents and their families (Landau, 1987).

It is estimated that between 750,000 and 1,000,000 minors run away from home each year in the United States and that more than 85% eventually become involved in prostitution (Landau, 1987). Others prostitute while living at home. See the accompanying Sex in Real Life, "Adolescent Prostitution," for one adolescent's account.

Pimps look for scared adolescent runaways at train and bus stations and lure them with promises of friendship and potential love relationships. A pimp will approach a runaway in a very caring and friendly way, offering to buy her a meal or give her a place to stay. At first, he makes no sexual demands whatsoever. He buys her

call boy
A higher-class male prostitute who is often contacted by telephone and may work by either the hour or the evening or for longer periods.

she-male
A slang term that refers to a male who has been on hormones for sex reassignment but has not undergone surgery; she-males often have both a penis and breasts.

clothes and meals and does whatever it takes to make her feel in-debted to him. To him, all of his purchases are a debt she will one day repay. As soon as the relationship becomes sexual and the girl has professed her love for the pimp, he begins asking her to "prove" her love by selling her body. The girl may agree to do so only once, not realizing the de-structive cycle she is beginning. This cycle is based on breaking down her self-esteem and increasing her feelings of helplessness. Male adolescents may enter into the life of prostitution in similar ways. Some may choose a life of prostitution to meet their survival needs or to support a drug habit.

Outside the United States, adolescent prostitution is prevalent in many countries, such as Brazil and Thailand. Female adoles-cents in Brazil are drawn to prostitution primarily for financial and economic reasons (Penna-Firme et al., 1991). (See Sex in Real Life: "Sexual Trafficking" later in the chapter.) In Thailand, some parents sell their daughter's virginity for money or act as their managers and arrange jobs for them. One Thai prostitute said:

> I started to work when I was fourteen years old. I worked at a "steakhouse," an entertainment place which was half a night-club and half a restaurant. During this time, I went out with customers only when I wanted to. I had worked there for about one year before I met one man who took me to a brothel. This man was a friend of a friend. He said he would like to show me the beach. He took us four girls. He did not take us to the beach but to a brothel and he sold us to the owner. Every day I had to receive fifteen men. If I did not obey the owner or did not get many men, I got beaten. I could finally escape from that brothel because one man helped me. (Pheterson, 1989, p. 64)

OTHER PLAYERS IN THE BUSINESS

Prostitutes are not the only people involved in the business. Other players include pimps, clients, and the government.

The Pimp

Pimps play an important role in prostitution, although not all prostitutes have pimps. In exchange for money, a pimp offers the prostitute protection from both clients and the police. Many pimps take all of a prostitute's earnings and manage the money, providing her with clothes, jewels, food, and sometimes a place to live. A pimp recruits prostitutes and will often manage a group of prostitutes, known as his "stable." His women are known by each other as "wives-in-law" (Ward et al., 1994).

Many pimps feel powerful within their peer group and enjoy the fact that their job is not particularly stressful for them. Pimps often require that their prostitutes make a certain amount of money (Dalla, 2002). In addition, a pimp often has several women working for him, many of whom he is involved with sexually.

The Client

As we discussed earlier, clients of prostitutes are often referred to as "johns" or "tricks"; another term is "kerb crawlers" (Brooks-Gordon & Geisthorpe, 2003). As noted earlier, the term "trick" has

The majority of clients of prostitutes are male.

also been used to describe the behavior requested by the client. This term originated from the idea that the client was being "tricked" out of something, mainly his money (Goode, 1994).

What motivates people to go to pros-titutes? An abnormally high sex drive? Variety in their sexual lives? Sigmund Freud believed that some men preferred sex with prostitutes because they were incapable of sexual arousal without feeling that their partner was inferior or a "bad" woman. Carl Jung went a step further and claimed that prostitution was tied to various unconscious **arche-types,** such as the "Great Mother." This archetype includes feelings of hatred and sexuality, which are connected to mother figures. This in turn leads men to have impersonal sex with partners whom they do not love or to whom they have no attraction.

There is much confusion about clients and the reasons they visit prostitutes (Brooks-Gordon & Geisthorpe, 2003). What we do know is that the majority of clients of prostitutes are male (Monto, 2001), and they visit prostitutes for a variety of reasons: for guaranteed sex, to eliminate the risk of rejection, for greater control in sexual encounters, for companionship, to have the un-divided attention of the prostitute, because they have no other sexual outlets, because of physical or mental handicaps, and for adventure, curiosity, or to relieve loneliness (Jordan, 1997; McKeganey & Bernard, 1996; Monto, 2000). They may also be turned on by engaging in the illicit or risky sex with prostitutes (Monto, 2001). Married men sometimes seek out prostitutes when their wives will not perform certain behaviors, when they feel guilty about asking their wives to engage in an activity, or when they feel the behaviors are too deviant to discuss with their wives (Jordan, 1997). A nonscientific study done in 2008 interviewed men who had paid for sex and found that the majority of men felt highly conflicted about their behavior (Heinzmann, 2008). Eighty-three percent of men said they kept returning to prostitution because it was an "addiction," and 40% said they were drunk when they went to the prostitutes. One client felt it was all about business: "Prosti-tutes are a product, like cereal. You go to the grocery, pick the brand you want and pay for it. It's business" (Heinzmann, 2008).

When men who were arrested for prostitution were asked which sexual behaviors they engaged in with a prostitute, 81% had received fellatio, 55% had engaged in sexual intercourse, whereas others engaged in a little of both, or manual masturba-tion (i.e., hand jobs; Monto, 2001). Clients from this study also reported that they believed that oral sex had a lower risk of STI or AIDS transmission than other sexual behaviors.

Sadomasochistic behavior, with the woman as dominant and the man submissive, is the most common form of "kinky" sexual behavior requested from prostitutes (Goode, 1994). Other com-monly requested behaviors from prostitutes include clients dress-ing as women, masturbating in front of nude clients, and rubber fetishes. One prostitute recalled a job in which she was paid $300 to dress up in a long gown and urinate in a cup while her client masturbated, and another was asked to have sex with a client in his daughter's bed (Dalla, 2002).

Clients may also seek out prostitutes because they are afraid of emotional commitments and want to keep things uninvolved; to

archetypes
Ancient images that Carl Jung believed we are born with and influenced by.

build up their egos (many prostitutes fake orgasm and act very sexually satisfied); because they are starved for affection and intimacy; or because they travel a great deal or work in heavily male-populated areas (such as in the armed services) and desire sexual activity.

Kinsey found that clients of prostitutes are predominantly White, middle-class, unmarried men who are between the ages of 30 and 60 (Kinsey et al., 1948). More recent research supports Kinsey's findings—the majority of men who visit prostitutes are middle-aged and unmarried (or unhappily married; Monto & McRee, 2005). They also tend to be regular or repeat clients: almost 100% go monthly or more frequently, and half of these go weekly or more frequently (M. Freund et al., 1991). "Regulars" often pay more than new customers and are a consistent source of income (Dalla, 2002).

Male clients are most often solicited in their car on street corners in areas where female prostitution is common, but solicitation can also happen in hotels or transportation stops (Riccio, 1992). Of the clients who seek male prostitutes, almost 75% also go to female prostitutes for sex (Morse et al., 1992). Anal sex and oral sex are the two most popular sexual behaviors requested from male prostitutes (M. Freund et al., 1991).

The majority of clients are not concerned with the police because law enforcement is usually directed at prostitutes rather than clients. However, today more and more police are turning to the clients to stop prostitution. Some authorities have gone so far as videotaping license plates and enrolling clients in "john school" to stop their behaviors (B. Fisher et al., 2002).

REALResearch > The National Health and Social Life Survey found a substantial discrepancy between men's and women's interest in fellatio. Although **45%** of men reported receiving fellatio very appealing, only **17%** of women found giving it appealing (Monto, 2001). Not surprisingly, fellatio is the most requested sexual behavior from prostitutes (Monto, 2001).

The Government: Prostitution and the Law

Prostitution is illegal in every state in the United States, except, as noted earlier, for certain counties in Nevada. However, even though it is illegal, it still exists in almost every large U.S. city. In general, the government could address the issue of prostitution in two ways. Prostitution could remain a criminal offense, or it could be legalized and regulated. If prostitution were legalized, it would be subject to government regulation over such things as licensing, location, health standards, and advertising.

The biggest roadblock to legalized prostitution in the United States is that prostitution is viewed as an immoral behavior by the majority of people (Rio, 1991). Laws that favor legal prostitution would, in effect, be condoning this immoral behavior. Overall, however, the strongest objections to legalized prostitution are reactions to streetwalking. Today the majority of Americans believe that the potential benefits of legalized prostitution should be evaluated.

Those who feel that prostitution should be legalized believe that this would result in lower levels of sexually transmitted infec-

tions (because prostitutes could be routinely checked for STIs) and less disorderly conduct. Another argument in favor of legalization is that if prostitution were legal, the government would be able to collect taxes on the money earned by both prostitutes and their pimps. Assuming a 25% tax rate, this gross income would produce $20 billion each year in previously uncollected taxes.

When college students were asked how they felt about the legalization of prostitution, those who scored high on scales of feminist orientation were more likely to view prostitution as an exploitation and subordination of women; they were also less likely to believe that women engage in prostitution for economic needs, and they believed that prostitution should not be legalized (Basow & Campanile, 1990). Overall, women are more likely than men to believe that prostitution should not be legalized and to see prostitution as exploitation and subordination of women.

In parts of Nevada where prostitution is legal, the overwhelming majority of people report that they favor legalized prostitution. Ordinances for prostitution in Nevada vary by county, with each county responsible for deciding whether prostitution is legal throughout the county, only in certain districts, or not at all.

For instance, there are no legal brothels in Reno or Las Vegas, perhaps because these cities enjoy large conventions and because many men attend these conventions without their partners. City officials felt that if a convention was held in a town with legalized prostitution, many partners might not want the men to attend; thus, there would be a decrease in the number of convention participants. Even so, there are several brothels near Reno and Las Vegas and also several that are close to state borders. Usually, these are the largest of all the Nevada brothels. Brothels are locally owned small businesses that cater to both local and tourist customers. Although prostitution in Nevada is not a criminal offense, there are laws against enticing people into prostitution, such as pimping or advertising for prostitutes (H. Reynolds, 1986).

Crackdowns on prostitution in other areas of the United States (where prostitution is not legal) often result in driving it further underground. This is exactly what happened in New York City in the 1980s. After law officials cracked down on prostitution in Manhattan, many brothels moved to Queens. Some of the prostitutes began operating out of "massage parlors" or private homes, which were supported through drug money.

Many groups in the United States and abroad are working for the legalization of prostitution. In San Francisco in 1973, an organization called COYOTE ("Call Off Your Old Tired Ethics") was formed by an ex-prostitute named Margo St. James to change the public's views of prostitution. Today, COYOTE is regarded as the best-known prostitutes' rights group in the United States. COYOTE's mission is to repeal all laws against prostitution, to reshape prostitution into a credible occupation, and to protect the rights of prostitutes. Members argue that contrary to popular belief, not all prostitution is forced—some women voluntarily choose to prostitute, and so prostitution should be respected as a career choice.

Delores French, a prostitute, author, president of the Florida COYOTE group, and president of HIRE ("Hooking Is Real Employment") argues that:

A woman has the right to sell sexual services just as much as she has the right to sell her brains to a law firm when she works as a lawyer, or to sell her creative work to a museum when she works as an artist, or to sell her image to a photographer when she works as a model, or to sell her body when she works as a ballerina. Since most people can have sex without going to jail, there is no reason except old fashioned prudery to make sex for money illegal. (Quoted in Jenness, 1990, p. 405)

review questions

1 Define prostitution and some of the terms associated with it.

2 Identify the factors that sociologists believe helped foster the development of prostitution.

3 Describe what the research has found about female male, and adolescent prostitutes, and differentiate among the various types of prostitutes.

4 Describe the responsibilities of a pimp.

5 Identify the factors that research has found motivate people to use prostitutes.

6 Identify the pros and cons of legalized prostitution.

Prostitution: Effects and Cultural Differences

No discussion of prostitution can be complete without examining STIs and life after prostitution. In addition, because prostitution occurs throughout the world, it's important to explore cultural differences in the practice of prostitution.

PROSTITUTION AND SEXUALLY TRANSMITTED INFECTIONS

Most U.S. prostitutes are knowledgeable about STIs and AIDS. They try to minimize their risks by using condoms, rejecting clients with obvious STIs, and routinely taking antibiotics. However, although female prostitutes often do feel they are at risk of infection with STIs or AIDS with clients, they usually do not feel this way with their husbands or boyfriends (Dorfman et al., 1992). Condoms are used less frequently with their own sexual partners than with clients. Among homosexual male prostitutes, receptive anal intercourse without a condom is the most common mode of HIV transmission (Elifson et al., 1993a), whereas among female prostitutes, intravenous drug use is the most common mode of HIV transmission.

Many opponents of legalized prostitution claim that legalization would lead to increases in the transmission of various STIs. However, STI transmission and prostitution have been found to have less of a relationship than you might think. Rates of STIs in Europe were found to *decrease* when prostitution was legalized and to *increase* when it was illegal (Rio, 1991). This is probably because when prostitution is legal, restrictions can be placed on the actual practice, and medical evaluations are often required. Many prostitutes take antibiotics sporadically to reduce the risk of STIs; however, this practice has led some strains of STIs to become resistant to many antibiotics. Long-term use of antibiotics diminishes their effectiveness in an individual. Also, viral STIs, such as AIDS and herpes, are not cured by antibiotics.

Male prostitutes have sex with multiple partners, are exposed to blood and semen, frequently practice high-risk sexual behaviors, and may continue prostituting even after they find out they are HIV-positive. In addition, many have been infected with other STIs, which may make HIV transmission easier (Morse et al., 1991).

Outside the United States, increasing prostitutes' condom use and knowledge about AIDS has been an important task. There has been a lot of attention to AIDS transmission among prostitutes in Africa, for example. In Nigeria, AIDS prevention programs, which include health education, condom promotion and distribution, and a STI treatment clinic, resulted in two thirds of prostitutes using condoms (E. Williams et al., 1992). In Somalia, the prevalence of HIV in nonprostitute populations is 16 per 1,000; in prostitutes, it is 30 per 1,000 (Corwin et al., 1991). Men and nonprostitute women knew more about AIDS and preventive information than female prostitutes. In Zaire, 99% of prostitutes reported hearing of AIDS, but only 77% knew that sex was the predominant mode of transmission (Nzila et al., 1991). Seventy-five percent of prostitutes had at least one STI, and 35% were HIV-positive.

REALResearch > More than **1** in **12** U.S. men report exchanging drugs, money, or a place to stay for sex with a female in the last year (DECKER ET AL., 2008). Swapping sex is a common risk factor for HIV/STIs.

LIFE AFTER PROSTITUTION

Potterat and colleagues (1990) found that female prostitutes stay in the life for a relatively short time, usually 4 or 5 years. Some feel ready to leave, whereas others are forced out because of a deteriorating physical appearance or because of addiction to drugs or alcohol. Life after prostitution is often grim because most prostitutes have little money and few skills (which is why they turned to prostitution in the first place; Farley et al., 2003). In addition, there is usually little to show for the years they spent prostituting. Some seek psychotherapy as a way to handle leaving prostitution, and others spend a great deal of time in and out of prison for shoplifting or robbery.

Research has found that many prostitutes are raped and physically assaulted as a result of their work. One study found that between 60% and 75% of female prostitutes were raped, whereas 70% to 95% were physically assaulted (U.S. Department of State, 2005). Overall, 68% qualified for a diagnosis of posttraumatic stress disorder. As a result, some resort to suicide as a way out.

Even so, there is a lot of disagreement about whether mandatory treatment programs should exist for prostitutes. If a person voluntarily chooses to engage in prostitution and he or she does not feel it is a problem, should the government require that he or she undergo treatment? Even if it were possible to make prostitutes stop prostituting, few resources are available for them to establish a similarly salaried occupation (Rio, 1991). We need to evaluate how to best help a prostitute if he or she decides to stop prostituting. Also, because we have learned that the backgrounds of many prostitutes include a history of sexual abuse, familial violence, and alcohol abuse, perhaps we can offer intervention early on to help these people find alternative ways to make a living.

PROSTITUTION IN OTHER CULTURES

Prostitution exists all over the globe. We now explore how different countries handle prostitution and the different problems they encounter.

Window prostitutes in Amsterdam, Holland, solicit customers in the red-light district, where prostitution is legal.

At a beach resort in Thailand, young prostitutes wait for a buyer.

During World War II, it is estimated that 200,000 women from Japan, Korea, China, the Philippines, Indonesia, Taiwan, and the Netherlands were taken by the Imperial Japanese Army from their hometowns and put in brothels for Japanese soldiers (Kakuchi, 2005). In 1993, Japan finally admitted to having forced women to prostitute themselves as **comfort girls,** and now these women are demanding to be compensated for the suffering they were forced to endure. In 2005, the Women's Active Museum on War and Peace in Tokyo was opened to honor the women who worked as sex slaves during World War II.

A group named GABRIELA (General Assembly Binding Women for Reforms, Integrity, Equality, Leadership, and Action) has formed in the Philippines in an attempt to fight prostitution, sexual harassment, rape, and battering of women. More than 100 women's organizations belong to GABRIELA, which supports the economic, health, and working conditions of women. GABRIELA operates free clinics for prostitutes and also provides seminars and activities to educate the community about prostitution (L. West, 1989).

Prostitution has long been a part of the cultural practices in Thailand. Many countries, including the United States, Japan, Taiwan, South Korea, Australia, and Europe, organize "sex tours" to Thailand. Prostitution is endorsed by both men and women in Thailand mainly because of the prevailing belief that men have greater sex drives than women (Taywaditep et al., 2004). In fact, college students in Thailand often report that prostitution protects "good women" from being raped (Taywaditep et al., 2004). It is estimated that there are between 500,000 and 700,000 female sex workers and between 5,000 and 8,000 male sex workers in

comfort girl
A woman in Japan or the Philippines during World War II who was forced into prostitution by the government to provide sex for soldiers; also called a hospitality girl.

SEX IN REAL LIFE

Sexual Trafficking

Worldwide, thousands of women and children are sold into sexual trafficking or sexual slavery every year.

Worldwide, between 600,000 and 800,000 people are trafficked across international borders every year—80% of whom are female and 50% children (Hodge, 2008). Victims tend to come from countries such as Asia, the former Soviet Union, Africa, and Eastern Europe and are most commonly trafficked to Italy, the U.S., Germany, and the Netherlands (Hodge, 2008). Some individuals are recruited via false-front agencies (such as modeling or employment agencies that pose as legitimate organizations) or they are approached because they are already working in prostitution in their native country and are promised more money in wealthier nations (Hodge, 2008). Since many cannot afford the trip, they agree to work off their debts once they arrive in their new location (referred to as *debt bondage;* Hodge, 2008). For many others, there is no choice involved in the process—they are sold by poor family members or kidnapped.

The physical and psychological costs to victims of sexual trafficking are high. Many are beaten and raped and experience broken bones, bruises, cuts, and vaginal bleeding (Raymond & Hughes, 2001). In addition, emotional symptoms of depression, anxiety, and PTSD are common (Hodge, 2008).

In the U.S., the Victims of Trafficking and Violence Protection Act of 2000 has helped protect victims of sexual trafficking by increasing awareness and enforcing laws against sexual trafficking (Hodge, 2008). This statute has also helped to create a "T-visa" which allows victims to stay in the U.S. to assist federal authorities in the prosecution of traffickers. Victims may be moved into the witness protection program and granted permanent residency after 3 years (Hodge, 2008).

Following is one young woman's testimony before the U.S. Senate Foreign Relations Committee in 2000:

When I was 14, a man came to my parents' house in Veracruz, Mexico, and asked me if I was interested in making money in the United States. He said I could make many times as much money doing the same things that I was doing in Mexico. At the time, I was working in a hotel cleaning rooms and I also helped around my house by watching my brothers and sisters. He said I would be in good hands, and would meet many other Mexican girls who had taken advantage of this great opportunity. My parents didn't want me to go, but I persuaded them.

A week later, I was smuggled into the United States through Texas to Orlando, Florida. It was then the men told me that my employment would consist of having sex with men for money. I had never had sex before, and I had never imagined selling my body.

And so my nightmare began. Because I was a virgin, the men decided to initiate me by raping me again and again, to teach me how to have sex. Over the next three months, I was taken to a different trailer every 15 days. Every night I had to sleep in the same bed in which I had been forced to service customers all day.

I couldn't do anything to stop it. I wasn't allowed to go outside without a guard. Many of the bosses had guns. I was constantly afraid. One of the bosses carried me off to a hotel one night, where he raped me. I could do nothing to stop him.

Because I was so young, I was always in demand with the customers. It was awful. Although the men were supposed to wear condoms, some didn't, so eventually I became pregnant and was forced to have an abortion. They sent me back to the brothel almost immediately.

I cannot forget what has happened. I can't put it behind me. I find it nearly impossible to trust people. I still feel shame. I was a decent girl in Mexico. I used to go to church with my family. I only wish none of this had ever happened. (Polaris Project, 2005)

Thailand—working "direct" (in brothels or massage parlors) or "indirect" (available for dates and also offering sex for their customers). Direct sex workers make between $2 and $20 for a service, whereas indirect sex workers make between $20 and several hundred dollars (Taywaditep, 2004). Sex workers in Thailand are required to participate in the governmental STI monitoring system, which has helped decrease STI prevalence.

Thailand has instituted a "100% condom use" program targeted at the prostitution industry (Sharma, 2001). Although HIV infections have been decreasing in Thailand, the World Health Organization (2001) estimates that prostitution will be the key factor in future HIV transmission. Adding to the problem is the fact that Thai men generally do not wear condoms. Some maintain that they are immune to AIDS, and prostitutes are too afraid to ask their clients to wear condoms. Prostitution is so prevalent

in Thailand that Thai men view a trip to a prostitute almost in the same regard as going to the store for milk (Sexwork.com, 2008). It has also been suggested that because many Thais are Buddhists, they believe in reincarnation and hope that they will not be a prostitute in their next life. This belief in reincarnation often reduces the fear of death (Kirsch, 1985; Limanonda et al., 1993).

In Amsterdam, Holland, De Wallen is the largest and best known red-light district. This area is crowded with sex shops, adult movie and live theater shows, and street and window prostitutes. These prostitutes are called "window" prostitutes because they sit behind a window and sell their bodies. There are approximately 200 such windows in the red-light district, which is one of the biggest tourist attractions in Amsterdam. Travel services run tours through the red-light district, although these tourists do not generally use the prostitutes' services. Prostitution in Amsterdam is loosely regulated by authorities. Prostitutes pay taxes, get regular checkups, and participate in government-sponsored health and insurance plans (McDowell, 1986).

In Cuba, male and female prostitutes who solicit tourists are known as *jineteros* (Espín et al., 2004). *Jineteros* exchange sex for clothing or other luxuries brought over from other countries. In Havana, teenagers offer sex to older tourists in exchange for a six-pack of cola or a dance club's cover charges. Female prostitutes in Cuba also ply the tourist trade.

In New Zealand, prostitution is not illegal, but several laws exist to restrict solicitation to certain places. This is a description of one prostitute from Dunedin, New Zealand:

Lynne, a 24-year-old, strolled into the sex industry from a normal childhood in a rural town in Southland. She has worked as an escort and in massage parlours for the last five years and would like nothing more than to "retire" and buy her own home in her old town. The trouble is the money is very, very good and it is hard for her to turn her back on such a highly paid job. Besides, once you have worked in the business it is not easy to find a job elsewhere. How do you tell a prospective employer where you have worked for the last five years when you have no reference? How do you explain your range of skills in relating to people? ("Working Girls," 1992, p. 21)

Although prostitution exists all over the world, it is dealt with differently in each culture. We have much to learn from the way that other cultures deal with prostitution. There are many places throughout the world where young girls are forced into sexual slavery against their will (see the accompanying Sex in Real Life, "Sexual Trafficking"). In 2003, the Bush administration established a task force to help fight these practices in 165 countries throughout the world.

Throughout this chapter, we have explored erotic representations in books, television, advertising, other media, and how sex is used to sell products. We have also examined the sale of sex itself through prostitution and strip bars. There are many effects to living in a society so saturated with sexual representations, and these effects certainly help shape our opinions and thoughts about men, women, and sexuality today.

review questions

1 Explain what has been found about STI knowledge and condom usage in prostitutes.

2 Identify and explain the issues that arise after a prostitute stops prostituting.

3 Describe what is known about prostitution outside the United States.

CHAPTER review

SUMMARY POINTS

1 Erotic representations have existed in almost all societies at almost all times; they have also been the subject of censorship by religious or governmental powers.

2 Pornography emerged as a separate category of erotic art during the 18th century. The printing press made it more readily available. The erotic novel first established pornography production as a business in the Western world, and it provoked a response of censorship from church and governmental authorities.

3 Television and, to a lesser extent, movies have become the primary media in the United States, and they contain enormous amounts of sexually suggestive material. Certain groups have begun to organize to change the content of television programming.

4 Advertising has commercialized sexuality and uses an enormous amount of sexual imagery to sell products. Advertisements are becoming more sexually explicit in the general media in the United States.

5 Pornography is one of the most difficult issues in public life in America. Feminists, conservatives, and the religious right argue that pornography is destructive, violates the rights of women, corrupts children, and should be banned or severely restricted. Liberals and critics of banning pornography argue that creating a definition of pornography that protects art and literature is impossible, that people have the right to read whatever materials they want in their own homes, and that censorship is a slippery slope that leads to further censorship. The public is split between these positions.

6 The online pornography industry is quickly growing. The accessibility, anonymity, and ease of use have all contributed to the growing popularity of the Internet. Some view online pornography, visit sexually oriented chat rooms, or may engage in sexual activities with an anonymous person online. Online sex users can be either *anonymous users* (those who enter sites out of curiosity or for entertainment), *at-risk users* (those who are increasingly drawn to usage of online sexually oriented materials), or *compulsive users* (those who spend over 11 hours per week engaging in online sexual activities). Users of online pornography also report a desensitization to pornography over time.

7 It is often difficult to define prostitution, and many slang terms have been developed. According to sociologists, society has created social institutions to regulate sexual behavior. Prostitution may have developed out of a patriarchal society.

8 Many prostitutes claim their sole motivation for prostituting is the money. Many also claim the major drawback of their job is engaging in sex with their clients.

9 There are several types of female prostitutes, including streetwalkers; bar, hotel, and brothel prostitutes; call girls; and escorts and courtesans. Streetwalkers are considered to have the most dangerous job because they are often victims of violence, rape, and robbery. Bondage-and-discipline and lesbian prostitutes also exist.

10 Male prostitutes are often referred to as hustlers, gigolos, or "boys." There are different types of male prostitutes. They may engage in street or bar hustling or escort prostitution or may

work as call boys. Straight, gay, bisexual, transvestite, and transsexual prostitutes exist. The majority of males begin in street prostitution and may eventually move into bar and escort prostitution.

11 Of the estimated 750,000 to 1,000,000 minors who run away from home each year, more than 85% eventually become involved in prostitution to make money. Many of them have been sexually abused and have psychological problems. Outside of the United States, adolescent prostitution is prevalent.

12 Pimps play an important role in prostitution. They offer protection, recruit other prostitutes, may manage a group of prostitutes, and try to keep prostitutes hustling to make money. Successful pimps can make a great deal of money and often feel powerful in their role as a pimp.

13 Clients go to prostitutes for a variety of reasons, including guaranteed sex, to eliminate the risk of rejection, for companionship, to have the undivided attention of the prostitute, because they have no other sexual outlets, for adventure or curiosity, or to relieve loneliness.

14 Many people believe that prostitution should be legalized so that it can be subjected to government regulation and taxation. However, others think that it would be immoral to legalize prostitution.

15 Different groups, such as COYOTE, have organized to change the public's views of prostitution and to change the laws against it. These groups are also common outside the United States.

16 Prostitutes are at high risk for acquiring STIs and AIDS. Overall, they

are knowledgeable about these risks and use condoms some of the time. STIs have been found to decrease when prostitution is legal and to increase when it is illegal.

17 Female prostitutes stay in the life for a relatively short time; some feel ready to leave, whereas others are forced out because of a deteriorating physical appearance or because of addiction to drugs or alcohol. Prostitutes have few skills after a life of prostitution, and there is usually little to show for the years they spent prostituting. Some seek psychotherapy, and others spend a great deal of time in and out of prison for shoplifting or robbery.

18 Prostitution exists all over the world. "Comfort girls" were forced into prostitution in Japan during World War II. "Hospitality girls" were used for the same purposes in the Philippines.

19 Prostitution has long been a part of the cultural practices in Thailand. Prostitution is legal and supported by both men and women in Thailand mainly because of the prevailing belief that men have greater sex drives than women. College students in Thailand often report that prostitution protects "good women" from being raped. Sex workers in Thailand are required to be under a governmental STI monitoring system, which has helped decrease STI prevalence.

20 Worldwide, 600,000 to 800,000 people, mostly women and children, are sold into sexual trafficking each year. Some are kidnapped or sold by poor family members, while others are recruited from false-front agencies or are already working as prostitutes. Since they cannot afford to travel, many become involved in debt bondage.

CRITICAL THINKING questions

1 When you read through one of your favorite magazines and see the various advertisements that use sex to sell their products, what effect do these ads have on you? Do you think there are any effects of living in a society so saturated with sexual images? Why or why not?

2 Do you think that sex or violence on television influences how promiscuous

or violent our society becomes? Do the sexual stereotypes paraded before us in commercials and advertisements shape our attitudes toward gender relations? What do you think can be done about this?

3 What television shows did you watch as a child? What messages about gender, sexuality, and relationships did you learn

from these shows? Would you let your own child watch these shows today? Why or why not?

4 Would you ever want to go to a strip club? If so, what would be your reasons for going? For not going? If you have been, what types of reactions did you have?

Sexuality Now Book Companion Website

Go to www.cengage.com/psychology/carroll for practice quizzes, glossary, flash cards, and more. You can also access the following websites from the companion site.

STORM: Sex Trade Opportunities for Risk Minimization ■ STORM is a harm reduction advocacy, education, direct services, and activist organization for individuals and issues involving the sex trade. Its website contains harm reduction information and strategies offered by current or former sex workers.

Coalition Against Trafficking in Women (CATW) ■ Founded in 1988, CATW was the first international, nongovernmental organization to focus on human sex trafficking, especially in women and children. CATW promotes women's human rights by working internationally to combat sexual exploitation in all its forms.

GABRIELA Network, USA (GABNet) ■ The GABRIELA (General Assembly Binding Women for Reform, Integrity, Equality, Leadership, and Action) Network is a United States–based multiracial, multiethnic women's solidarity organization that works on issues that affect women and children of the Philippines but have their roots in decisions made in the United States. The Purple Rose Campaign, spearheaded by GABRIELA, addresses the issue of sex trafficking of Filipino women and children.

Henry J. Kaiser Family Foundation ■ The Kaiser Foundation conducts original survey research on a wide range of topics related to health policy and public health, as well as major social issues, including sexuality. In 2005, the Kaiser Foundation published *Sex on TV4,* the fourth study on sex on television. The goal of Kaiser's surveys is to better understand the public's knowledge, attitudes, and behaviors.

Prostitution Research and Education ■ Prostitution Research and Education, sponsored by the San Francisco Women's Centers, develops research and educational programs to document the experiences of people in prostitution through research, public education, and arts projects. Links are provided to fact sheets about prostitution, arguments for and against legalization, outreach programs for those who want to leave the business, information on female slavery outside the United States, and many other important topics.

Victims of Pornography ■ Victims of Pornography is a website aimed to educate and create awareness that there are real victims of pornography. The site includes news, letters from men, women, and children who have been involved with pornography, and links to advocacy and outreach groups.

CengageNOW

Go to www.cengage.com/login to link to CengageNOW, your online study tool. First take the Pre-Test for this chapter to get your Personalized Study Plan, which will identify topics you need to review and direct you to online resources. Then take the Post-Test to determine what concepts you have mastered and what you still need work on.

Videos in CengageNOW

For additional information on topics discussed in this chapter, check out the videos in CengageNOW on the following topics:

- My Best Friend Is an Exotic Dancer—Listen to how two friends resolve their differing opinions about one's part-time job.

- Sex Worker (Loretta)—A woman talks about how she got into the business, the dangers, and why she stays.

- Sex Workers—Listen to how addiction and poverty contribute to the prevalence of sex work in the United States and China.

- Bondage and S&M—Evaluate your ideas about bondage, domination, and sadomasochism against these couples who engage in these practices.

REFERENCES

Abbey, A., Zawacki, T., & Buck, P. O. (2005). The effects of past sexual assault perpetration and alcohol consumption on men's reactions to women's mixed signals. *Journal of Social & Clinical Psychology, 24*(2), 129–155.

Abboud, L. N., & Liamputtong, P. (2003). Pregnancy loss: What it means to women who miscarry and their partners. *Social Work in Health Care, 36*(3), 37–62.

Abel, G., Becker, J., & Skinner, L. (1980). Aggressive behavior and sex. *Psychiatric Clinics of North America, 3*, 133–135.

Abma, J. C., Chandra, A., Mosher, C. W., & Peterson, L. (1997). Fertility, family planning, and women's health: New data from the 1995 National Survey of Family Growth. *Vital and Health Statistics*, Series 23, No. 19, 1–114.

Abouesh, A., & Clayton, A. (1999). Compulsive voyeurism and exhibitionism: A clinical response to paroxetine. *Archives of Sexual Behavior, 28*(1), 23–30.

About Lyriana. (2008). Retrieved August 29, 2008, from http://www.lyriana.com/about-lyriana/.

Abramson, A. (2003). *The history of television: 1942–2000.* Jefferson, NC: McFarland Publishers.

Adair, L. S., & Gordon-Larsen, P. (2001). Maturational timing and overweight prevalence in U.S. adolescent girls. *American Journal of Public Health, 91*(4), 642–645.

Adam, B. D. (1987). *The rise of a gay and lesbian movement.* Boston: Twayne.

Adams, H. E., Wright, L. W., Jr., & Lohr, B. A. (1996). Is homophobia associated with homosexual arousal? *Journal of Abnormal Psychology, 105*, 440–445.

Adams-Curtis, L. E., & Forbes, G. B. (2004). College women's experiences of sexual coercion: A review of cultural, perpetrator, victim, and situational variables. *Trauma, Violence & Abuse, 5*(2), 91–122.

Add Health. (2002). Add Health and Add Health 2000: A national longitudinal study of adolescent health. Retrieved June 14, 2002, from http://www.cpc.unc.edu/addhealth.

Adler, N. E., David, H. P., Major, B. N., et al. (1992). Psychological factors in abortion. *American Psychologist, 47*, 1194–1204.

Adler, N. E., David, H. P., Major, B. N., Roth, S. H., Russo, N. F., & Wyatt, G. E. (1990). Psychological responses after abortion. *Science, 248*, 41–44.

Adler, R. B., Rosenfeld, L. B., & Proctor, R. F. (2007). *Interplay: The process of interpersonal communication* (10th ed.). New York: Oxford University Press.

Adriano, J. (2007, April 27). Transgender children face unique challenges. ABC News. Retrieved February 24, 2008, from http://abcnews.go.com/2020/story?id=3091754.

Afek, D. (1990). Sarah and the women's movement: The experience of infertility. *Women and Therapy, 10*, 195–203.

Agarwal, A., Deepinder, F., Sharma, R. K., Ranga, G., & Li, J. (2008). Effect of cell phone usage on semen analysis in men attending infertility clinic: An observational study. *Fertility and Sterility, 89*, 124–128.

Ahmed, J. (1986). Polygyny and fertility differentials among the Yoruba of western Nigeria. *Journal of Biosocial Sciences, 18*, 63–73.

Ahrens, C. E. (2002). Silent and silenced: The disclosure and non-disclosure of sexual assault. *Dissertation Abstracts,* University of Illinois at Chicago, #0-493-62204-7.

Ahrens, C. E. (2006). Being silenced: The impact of negative social reactions on the disclosure of rape. *American Journal of Community Psychology, 38*, 263–274.

Ainsworth, M. D. S., Blehar, M. C., Waters, E., & Wall, S. (1978). *Patterns of attachment: A psychological study of the strange situation.* Hillsdale, NJ: Erlbaum.

Ako, T., Takao, H., Yoshiharo, M., Osamu, I., & Yutaka, U. (2001). Beginnings of sexual reassignment surgery in Japan. *International Journal of Transgenderism.* Retrieved June 1, 2003, from http://www.symposion.com/ijt/ijtvo05no01_02.htm.

Alan Guttmacher Institute. (1999a). Facts in brief: Teen sex and pregnancy. Retrieved September 9, 2003, from http://www.agi-usa.org/pubs/fb_teen_sex.pdf.

Alan Guttmacher Institute. (1999b). Sexually transmitted disease surveillance. Unpublished tabulations of the 1988–1994 National Health and Nutrition Examination Surveys. Atlanta, GA: Centers for Disease Control and Prevention.

Alan Guttmacher Institute. (2002). Facts in brief: Contraceptive use. Retrieved January 14, 2003, from http://www.agi-usa.org/pubs/fb_contr_use.html.

Alan Guttmacher Institute. (2004). *The unfinished revolution in contraception: Convenience, consumer access, and choice.* Washington, DC: Alan Guttmacher Institute. Retrieved October 28, 2008, from http:// www.guttmacher.org/pubs/2004/09/20/UnfinRevInContra.pdf.

Alan Guttmacher Institute. (2006). U.S. Teenage pregnancy statistics: National and state trends and trends by race and ethnicity. Retrieved May 29, 2008, from http://www.guttmacher.org/pubs/2006/09/12/USTPstats.pdf.

Alan Guttmacher Institute. (2006, September). U.S. teenage pregnancy statistics: National and state trends and trends by race and ethnicity. Retrieved October 28, 2008, from http://www.guttmacher.org/pubs/2006/09/12/USTPstats.pdf.

Alan Guttmacher Institute. (2008a, January). Facts in brief: Facts on contraceptive use. Retrieved July 20, 2008, from http://www.guttmacher.org/pubs/fb_contr_use.html.

Alan Guttmacher Institute. (2008b, July 1). State Policies in Brief: Abortion policy in the absence of Roe. Retrieved July 28, 2008, from http://www.guttmacher.org/statecenter/spibs/spib_APAR.pdf.

Alan Guttmacher Institute. (2008c). State Policies in Brief: An overview of abortion laws. Retrieved October 28, 2008, from http://www.guttmacher.org/statecenter/spibs/spib_OAL.pdf.

Alan Guttmacher Institute. (2008d). State Policies in Brief: Counseling and waiting periods for abortion. Retrieved October 28, 2008 from http://www.guttmacher.org/statecenter/spibs/spib_MWPA.pdf.

Alan Guttmacher Institute. (2008e, May 1). State Policies in Brief: Sex and STI/HIV education. Retrieved May 29, 2008, from http://www.guttmacher.org/statecenter/spibs/spib_SE.pdf.

Alan Guttmacher Institute. (2008f). Trends in abortion in the United States, 1975–2005. Retrieved August 3, 2008, from http://www.guttmacher.org/presentations/trends.html.

Alanis, M. C., & Lucidi, R.S. (2004, May). Neonatal circumcision: A review of the world's oldest and most controversial operation. *Obstetrical & Gynecological Survey, 59*(5), 379–395.

Alavi, A. K. (2001). Little white lies: Racialized images of the phallus in the U.S. *Dissertation Abstracts,* Georgia State University, #0-493-36368-4.

Albada, K. F., Knapp, M. L., & Theune, K. E. (2002). Interaction appearance theory: Changing perceptions of physical attractiveness through social interaction. *Communication Theory, 12*, 8–40.

Albers, K. (2007). Comprehensive care in the prevention of ectopic pregnancy and associated negative outcomes. *Midwifery Today with International Midwife. (84)*, 26–27, 67.

Albert, A., & Porter, J. R. (1988). Children's gender-role stereotypes: A sociological investigation of psychological models. *Sociological Forum, 3,* 184–210.

Albert, R. T., Elwell, S. L., & Idelson, S. (2001). *Lesbian rabbis: The first generation.* Piscataway, NJ: Rutgers University Press.

Albright, J. (2008). Sex in American online: An exploration of sex, marital status, and sexual identity in Internet sex seeking and its impacts. *Journal of Sex Research, 45,* 175–186.

Alexander, C. J., Sipski, M. L., & Findley, T. W. (1993). Sexual activities, desire, and satisfaction in males pre- and post-SCI. *Archives of Sexual Behavior, 22,* 217–228.

Alexander, M., & Rosen, R. (2008). Spinal cord injuries and orgasm: A review. *Journal of Sex and Marital Therapy, 24,* 308–324.

Alexander, M. A. (1999). Sexual offender treatment efficacy revisited. *Sexual Abuse: A Journal of Research and Treatment, 11,* 101–116.

Alexandre, B., Lemaire, A., Desvaux, P., & Amar, E. (2007). Intracavernous injections of prostaglandin E1 for erectile dysfunction: Patient satisfaction and quality of sex life on long-term treatment. *Journal of Sexual Medicine, 4,* 426–431.

Ali, K. (2002). Muslim sexual ethics: Same-sex sexual activity and lesbian and bisexual women. The Feminist Sexual Ethics Project. Retrieved January 2, 2008, from http://www.brandeis.edu/projects/fse/muslim/mus-essays/mus-ess-homosex.html.

Alkhuja, S., Mnekel, R., Patel, B., & Ibrahimbacha, A. (2001). Stidor and difficult airway in an AIDS patient. *AIDS Patient Care and Sexually Transmitted Diseases, 15*(6), 293–295.

Allan, C., Forbes, E., Strauss, B., & McLachlan, R. (2008). Testosterone therapy increases sexual desire in ageing men with low-normal testosterone levels and symptoms of androgen deficiency. *International Journal of Impotence Research, 20,* 396–401.

Allen, C. (2007). It's a boy! Gender expectations intrude on the study of sex determination. *DNA and Cell Biology, 26,* 699–705.

Allen, C., Bowdin, S., Harrison, R., Sutcliffe, A., Brueton, L., Kirby, G., et al. (2008, June 3). Pregnancy and perinatal outcomes after assisted reproduction: A comparative study. *Irish Journal of Medical Science,* 177(3), 233–241.

Allen, D. J., & Oleson, T. (1999). Shame and internalized homophobia in gay men. *Journal of Homosexuality, 37*(3), 33–34.

Allen, L. (2005). Increased frequency in cohabitating couples raises new legal concerns. Retrieved September 17, 2005, from http://www.lawyers.com/lawyers/A~1026044~LDS/COHABITATING+lEGAL+CONCERNS.html.

Allen, M. P. (1989). *Transformations.* New York: Dutton.

Allen, M., Emmers-Sommer, T. M., & Crowill, T. L. (2002). Couples negotiating safer sex behaviors: A meta-analysis of the impact of conversation and gender. In M. Allen & R. Preiss (Eds.), *Interpersonal communication research.* Mahwah, NJ: Erlbaum.

Allen, P. L. (2000). *The wages of sin: Sex and disease, past and present.* Chicago: University of Chicago Press.

Allison, L., Santilla, P., Sandnabba, N., & Nordling, N. (2001). Sadomasochistically oriented behavior: Diversity in practice and meaning. *Archives of Sexual Behavior, 30,* 1–12.

Allsworth, J. E., & Peipert, J. F. (2007). Prevalence of bacterial vaginosis: 2001–2004 national health and nutrition examination survey data. *Obstetrics and Gynecology, 109,* 114–120.

Allyn, D. (1996). Private acts—public policy: Alfred Kinsey, the American Law Institute and the privatization of American sexual morality. *Journal of American Studies, 30,* 405–428.

Allyn, D. (2000). *Make love not war: The sexual revolution: An unfettered history.* Boston: Little, Brown.

Aloni, M., & Bernieri, F. J. (2004). Is love blind? The effects of experience and infatuation on the perception of love. *Journal of Nonverbal Behavior, 28*(4), 287–295.

Alonso-Zaldivar, R., & Neuman, J. (2005, November 11). FDA suggests warning for condoms. *Los Angeles Times,* p. A-15.

Al-Shawaf, T., Zosmer, A., Dirnfeld, M., & Grudzinskas, G. (2005). Safety of drugs used in assisted reproduction techniques. *Drug Safety, 28*(6), 513–528.

Althaus, F. (1997). Most Japanese students do not have intercourse until after adolescence. *Family Planning Perspectives, 29*(3), 145–147.

Althaus, F. (2001). Levels of sexual experience among U.S. teenagers have declined for the first time in three decades. *Family Planning Perspectives, 33*(4), 180–182.

Althuis, M. D., Brogan, D. D., Coates, R. J., Daling J.R., Gammon M.D., Malone K.E., et al. (2003). Breast cancers among very young premenopausal women (United States). *Cancer Causes and Control, 14,* 151–160.

Altman, C. (2000). Gay and lesbian seniors: Unique challenges of coming out in later life. *SIECUS Report, 4,* 14.

Altman, D. (1986). *AIDS in the mind of America.* New York: Anchor Press, Doubleday.

Alzate, H., & Hoch, Z. (1986). The "G spot" and "female ejaculation": A current appraisal. *Journal of Sex and Marital Therapy, 12,* 211–220.

Amador, J., Charles, T., Tait, J., & Helm, H. (2005). Sex and generational differences in desired characteristics in mate selection. *Psychological Reports, 96*(1), 19–25.

Amanpour, C. (2006). World fails to save Africa's AIDS orphans: Africa's HIV-infected children also ignored. *CNN Online.* Retrieved November 3, 2008 from http://www.cnn.com/2006/WORLD/africa/07/17/amanpour.africa.btsc/index.html.

Amateau, S. K., & McCarthy, M. M. (2004). Induction of PGE$_2$ by estradiol mediates developmental masculinization of sex behavior. *Nature Neuroscience, 7*(6), 1–8.

Amato, P. (1996). Explaining the intergenerational transmission of divorce. *Journal of Marriage and the Family, 58,* 628–640.

Amato, P. R. (2001, January). What children learn from divorce. *Population Today.* Washington, DC: Population Reference Bureau.

Amato, P. R., & Hohmann-Marriott, B. (2007). A comparison of high- and low-distress marriages that end in divorce. *Journal of Marriage and Family, 69,* 621–639.

Amato, P. R., & Previti, D. (2003). People's reasons for divorcing: Gender, social class, the life course, and adjustment. *Journal of Family Issues, 24,* 602–626.

Ambady, N., Koo, J., Lee, F., & Rosenthal, R. (1996). More than words: Linguistic and nonlinguistic politeness in two cultures. *Journal of Personality and Social Psychology, 70,* 996–1011.

American Academy of Pediatrics. (1999). Task Force on Circumcision. Circumcision Policy Statement (RE 9850), *Pediatrics, 103,* 686–693.

American Cancer Society. (2003). How to perform a breast self-exam. Retrieved October 7, 2005, from http://www.cancer.org/

docroot/CRI/content/CRI_2_6x_How_to_perform_a_breast_self_exam_5.asp?sitearea=.

American Cancer Society. (2005). Testicular cancer has high cure rate—in America. Retrieved April 6, 2008, from http://www.cancer.org/docroot/NWS/content/update/NWS_1_1xU_Testicular_Cancer_Has_High_Cure_Rate_%E2%80%94_In_America.asp.

American Cancer Society. (2007a). How to perform a breast self exam. Retrieved March 22, 2008, from http://www.cancer.org/docroot/CRI/content/CRI_2_6x_How_to_perform_a_breast_self_exam_5.asp.

American Cancer Society. (2007b). Overview: Prostate Cancer. Retrieved October 15, 2008, from http://www.cancer.org/docroot/CRI/CRI_2_1x.asp?dt=36.

American Cancer Society. (2007c). Overview: Testicular cancer. Retrieved April 6, 2008, from http://www.cancer.org/docroot/CRI/content/CRI_2_2_1x_How_Many_People_Get_Testicular_Cancer_41.asp?sitearea=.

American Cancer Society. (2007d). What are the Key Statistics about Breast Cancer in Men? Retrieved August 11, 2008, from http://www.cancer.org/docroot/CRI/content/CRI_2_4_IX_What_are_the_key_statistics_for_male_breast_cancer_28.asp.

American Cancer Society. (2008). Cancer: Facts and figures. Retrieved March 18, 2008, from http://www.cancer.org/downloads/STT/2008CAFFfinalsecured.pdf.

American College of Obstetricians and Gynecologists. (2005). Diagnosing birth defects. ACOG educational publications. Retrieved from http://www.acog.org/publications/patient_education/bp164.cfm.

American College of Obstetricians and Gynecologists. (2007). Screening for fetal chromosomal abnormalities. Washington, DC: American College of Obstetricians and Gynecologists (ACOG); 2007 Jan. 11 p. (ACOG Practice Bulletin; No. 77).

American College of Obstetrics and Gynecology. (2007). Vaginal "rejuvenation" and cosmetic vaginal procedures (ACOG committee opinion No. 378). Obstetrics and Gynecology, 110, 737–738.

American Psychiatric Association. (1994). Diagnostic and statistical manual of mental disorders (4th ed.). Washington, DC: Author.

American Psychiatric Association. (1998). Media information: Position statement on hate crimes. Retrieved October 4, 2008, from http://www.apa.org/releases/hate.html.

American Psychiatric Association. (2000). Diagnostic and statistical manual of mental disorders (4th ed., Text. Rev.). Washington, DC: Author.

American Psychiatric Association. (2008). DSM-V: The future manual. Retrieved August 25, 2008, from http://www.psych.org/dsmv.asp.

American Psychological Association. (2005). Lesbian and gay parenting. Committee on Lesbian, Gay, and Bisexual Concerns. Retrieved September 1, 2008, from http://www.apa.org/pi/lgbc/publications/lgparenting.pdf.

Ames, M. A., & Houston, D. A. (1990). Legal, social, and biological definitions of pedophilia. Archives of Sexual Behavior, 19, 333–342.

Amir, M. (1971). Patterns in forcible rape. Chicago: University of Chicago Press.

Amis, D. (2007). Care practice #1: Labor begins on its own. Journal of Perinatal Education, 16, 16–20.

Anderson, F. D., Gibbons, W., & Portman, D. (2006). Long-term safety of an extended-cycle oral contraceptive (Seasonale): A 2-year multimember open-label extension trial. American Journal of Obstetrics and Gynecology, 195, 92–96.

Anderson, I. (2004). Explaining negative rape victim perception: Homophobia and the male rape victim. Current Research in Social Psychology, 10(4), 43–57.

Anderson, P. B., & Savage, J. S. (2005). Social, legal, and institutional context of heterosexual aggression by college women. Trauma, Violence, & Abuse, 6(2), 130–140.

Anderton, D., & Emigh, R. (1989). Polygynous fertility: Sexual competition vs. progeny. American Journal of Sociology, 94(4), 832–855.

Andre, A. (2006). The study of sex. Retrieved January 2, 2008, from http://www.alternet.org/story/33347/.

Andrews, G., Skinner, D., Zuma, K. (2006). Epidemiology of health and vulnerability among children orphaned and made vulnerable by HIV/AIDS in sub-Saharan Africa. AIDS Care, 18(3), 269–276.

Angier, N. (1999). Woman: An intimate geography. New York: Anchor Books.

Ankum, W. M., Hajenius, P. J., Schrevel, L. S., & Van der Veen, F. (1996). Management of suspected ectopic pregnancy. Impact of new diagnostic tools in 686 consecutive cases. Journal of Reproductive Medicine, 41(10), 724–728.

Antheunis, M., Valkenburg, P. M., & Peter, J. (2007). Computer-mediated communication and interpersonal attraction: An experimental test of two explanatory hypotheses. CyberPsychology & Behavior, 10, 831–836.

Anti-Defamation League. (2008). State hate crime statutory provisions. Retrieved October 2, 2008, from http://www.adl.org/learn/hate_crimes_laws/map_frameset.html.

Apfel, R. J., & Handel, M. H. (1993). Madness and loss of motherhood. Washington, DC: American Psychiatric Press.

Araujo, A. B., Mohr, B. A., & McKinlay, J. B. (2004). Changes in sexual function in middle-aged and older men: Longitudinal data from the Massachusetts male aging study. Journal of the American Geriatrics Society, 52(9), 1502–1509.

Arav, A., & Zvi, R. (2008). Do chilling injury and heat stress share the same mechanism of injury in oocytes? Molecular Cell Endocrinology, 282, 150–152.

Arena, J. M., & Wallace, M. (2008). Issues regarding sexuality. In E. Capezuti, D. Zwicker, M. Mezey, T. Fuller, D. Gray-Miceli, & M. Kluger (Eds.). Evidence-based geriatric nursing protocols for best practice (3rd ed., pp. 629–647). New York: Springer Publishing Company.

Arias, R. A., Munoz, L. D., & Munoz-Fernandez, M. A. (2003). Transmission of HIV-1 infection between trophoblast placental cells and T-cells take place via an LFA-1-mediated cell to cell contact. Virology, 307(2), 266–277.

Aries, E. (1996). Men and women in interaction: Reconsidering the differences. New York: Oxford University Press.

Aries, P. (1962). Centuries of childhood: A social history of family life. New York: Vintage Books.

Armesto, J. C. (2001). Attributions and emotional reactions to the identity disclosure of a homosexual child. Family Process, 40(2), 145–162.

Armour, B.S., Wolf, L., Mitra, M., Brieding, M. (2008). Differences in intimate partner violence among women with and without a disability. American Public Health Association's 136th Annual Meeting, San Diego, CA. October 27. Retrieved November 14, 2008, from http://apha.confex.com/apha/136am/webprogram/Paper182004.html.

Armstrong, M. L., Roberts, A. E., Owen, D. C., & Koch, J. R. (2004). Toward building a composite of college student influences with body art. Issues in Comprehensive Pediatric Nursing, 27, 277–295.

Arnold, L.D., Bachmann, G., Rosen, R., Kelly, S., Rhoads, G. (2006). Vulvodynia: Characteristics and associations with comorbidities and quality of life. *Obstetrics and Gynecology, 107*(3), 617–624.

Aron, A., Fisher, H., Mashek, D, Strong, G., Li, H., & Brown, L. (2005). Reward, motivation and emotion systems associated with early-stage intense romantic love. *Journal of Neurophysiology, 94*(1), 327–337.

Arondekar, A. (2007). The voyage out: Transacting sex under globalization. *Feminist Studies, 33*, 337–424.

Arrington-Sanders, R., Dyson, J., & Ellen, J. (2007). STDs in adolescents. In J. Klausner & E. Hook (Eds.), *Current diagnosis and treatment of STDs* (pp. 160–166). New York: McGraw-Hill.

Arroba, A. (2004). Costa Rica. In R. T. Francoeur & R. J. Noonan (Eds.), *The Continuum international encyclopedia of sexuality* (pp. 227–240). New York/London: Continuum International.

Atanackovic, G., Wolpin, J., & Koren, G. (2001). Determinants of the need for hospital care among women with nausea and vomiting of pregnancy. *Clinical and Investigative Medicine, 24*(2), 90–94.

Athenstaedt, U., Haas, E., & Schwab, S. (2004). Gender role self-concept and gender-typed communication behavior in mixed-sex and same-sex dyads. *Sex Roles, 50*(1–2), 37–52.

Atwine, B., Cantor-Graae, E., Banjunirwe, F. (2005). Psychological distress among AIDS orphans in rural Uganda. *Social Science and Medicine, 61*, 555–564.

Auster, C. J., & Leone, J. M. (2001). Late adolescents' perspectives on marital rape. *Adolescence, 36*, 141–152.

Auster, C. J., & Ohm, S. C. (2000). Masculinity and femininity in contemporary American Society. *Sex Roles, 43*(7–8), 499–528.

Austoni, E., Colombo, F., Romano, A. L., Guarneri, A., Goumas, I. K., & Cazzaniga, A. (2005). Soft prosthesis implant and relaxing albugineal incision with saphenous grafting for surgical therapy of Peyronie's disease. *European Urology, 47*(2), 223–230.

Avery, A., Chase, J., Johansson, L., & Litvak, S. (2007). America's changing attitudes toward homosexuality, civil unions, and same-gender marriage: 1977–2004. *Social Work, 52*, 71–80.

Aviram, I. (2005). Online infidelity: Aspects of dyadic satisfaction, self-disclosure, and narcissism. Retrieved May 9, 2005, from http://jcmc.indiana.edu/vol10/issue3/aviram.html.

Azam, S. (2000). What's behind retro virginity? The Toronto Star Life Story. Retrieved December 29, 2002, from http://www.psurg.com/star2000.html.

Bacon, C. G., Mittleman, M. A., Kawachi, I., et al. (2003). Sexual function in men older than 50 years of age: Results from the health professionals follow-up study. *Annals of Internal Medicine, 139*, 161–168.

Badawy Z. S., Chohan K. R., Whyte D. A., Penefsky H. S., Brown O. M., Souid A. K. (2008). Cannabinoids inhibit the respiration of human sperm. Fertility and Sterility, Retrieved October 13, 2008, from http://www.fertstert.org/article/S0015-0282(08)00750-4/abstract.

Bagemihl, B. (1999). *Biological exuberance: Animal homosexuality and natural diversity.* New York: St. Martin's Press.

Bagley, D. (2005). Personal communication.

Bailey, A., & Hurd, P. (2005). Finger length ratio correlates with physical aggression in men but not in women. *Biological Psychology, 68*(3), 215–222.

Bailey, B. P., Gurak, L. J., & Konstan, J. A. (2003). Trust in cyberspace. In J. Ratner (Ed.), *Human factors and Web development* (2nd ed., pp. 311–321). Mahwah, NJ: Erlbaum.

Bailey, J., Benato, R., Owen, C., & Kavanagh, J. (2008). Vulvovaginal candidiasis in women who have sex with women. *Sexually Transmitted Diseases, 35*, 533–536.

Bailey, J., Farquhar, C., Owen, C., & Mangtani, P., (2004). Sexually transmitted infections in women who have sex with women. *Sexually Transmitted Infections, 80*(3), 244–246.

Bailey, J. M., & Pillard, R. C. (1993). A genetic study of male sexual orientation. *Archives of General Psychiatry 50*(3), 240–241.

Bailey, R., Egesah, O., & Rosenberg, S. (2008). Male circumcision for HIV prevention: A prospective study of complications in clinical and traditional settings in Bungoma, Kenya. *Bulletin of the World Health Organization, 86*, 669–677.

Baillargeon, J., McClish, D., Essah, P., & Nestler, J. (2005). Association between the current use of low-dose oral contraceptives and cardiovascular arterial disease: A meta-analysis. *Journal of Clinical Endocrinology & Metabolism, 90*, 3863–3870.

Bain, J. (2001). Testosterone replacement therapy for aging men. *Canadian Family Physician, 47*, 91–97.

Baladerian, N.J. (1991). Sexual abuse of people with developmental disabilities. *Sexuality and Disability, 9*, 323–335.

Ball, H. (2005). Sexual offending on elderly women: A review. *Journal of Forensic Psychiatry & Psychology, 16*(1), 127–138.

Balsam, K., Rothblum, E., & Beauchaine, T. (2005). Victimization over the life span: A comparison of lesbian, gay, bisexual and heterosexual siblings. *Journal of Counseling and Clinical Psychology, 73*, 477–487.

Balsam, K. F., Beauchaine, T., Rothblum, E., & Solomon, S. (2008). Three-year follow-up of same-sex couples who had civil unions in Vermont, same-sex couples not in civil unions, and heterosexual married couples. *Developmental Psychology, 44*, 101–116.

Bancroft, J. (1996). Sex research in the U.S. *Journal of Sex Research, 33*(4), 327–328.

Bancroft, J. (2004). Alfred C. Kinsey and the politics of sex research. *Annual Review of Sex Research, 15*, 1–39.

Bancroft, J., Herbenick, D., Barnes, T., Hallam-Jones, R., Wylie, K., & Janssen, E. (2005). The relevance of the dual control model to male sexual dysfunction: The Kinsey Institute/BASRT collaborative project. *Sexual & Relationship Therapy, 20*(1), 13–30.

Bancroft, J., & Vukadinovic, Z. (2004). Sexual addiction, sexual compulsivity, or what? Toward a theoretical model. *Journal of Sex Research, 41*(3), 225–234.

Bandura, A. (1969). *Principles of behavior modification.* Austin, TX: Holt, Rinehart & Winston.

Banerjee, N. (2007, March 13). A place to turn when a newborn is fated to die. *New York Times.* Retrieved from http://www.nytimes.com/2007/03/13/health/13hospice.html.

Barak, A. (2005). Sexual harassment on the Internet. *Social Science Computer Review, 23*(1), 77–92.

Barbach, L. (1982). *For each other: Sharing sexual intimacy.* New York: Penguin Group.

Barber, N. (2008). Explaining cross-national differences in polygyny intensity. *Cross-Cultural Research, 42*, 103.

Bardeguez, A., Lindsey, J., Shannon, M., Tuomala, R., Cohn, S., Smith, E., et al. (2008). Adherence to antiretrovirals among US women during and after pregnancy. *Journal of Acquired Immune Deficiency Syndrome, 48*, 408–417.

Barelds, D., & Barelds-Dijkstra, P. (2007). Relations between different types of jealousy and self and partner perceptions of relationship quality. *Clinical Psychology and Psychotherapy, 14*, 176–188.

Barker, D. J. (1997). Maternal nutrition, fetal nutrition, and disease in later life. *Nutrition, 13*(9), 807–813.

Barker, D. J., & Barker, M. J. (2002). The body as art. *Journal of Cosmetic Dermatology, 1*(2), 88.

Barner, J. M. (2003). Sexual fantasies, attitudes, and beliefs: The role of self-report sexual aggression for males and females. *Dissertation Abstracts International, 64*(4-B), 1887 (#0419–4217).

Baron, L. (1990). Pornography and gender equality: An empirical analysis. *The Journal of Sex Research, 27,* 363–380.

Baron, L., & Straus, M. A. (1987). Four theories of rape: A macrosociological analysis. *Social Problems, 34,* 467–489.

Baron, N. S. (2004). See you online: Gender issues in college student use of instant messaging. *Journal of Language & Social Psychology, 23*(4), 397–423.

Bart, P. B., & O'Brien, P. H. (1985). *Stopping rape: Successful survival strategies.* New York: Pergamon Press.

Barth, K. R., Cook, R. L., Downs, J. S., Switzer, G. E., & Fischoff, B. (2002). Social stigma and negative consequences: Factors that influence college students' decision to seek testing for STIs. *Journal of American College Health, 50*(4), 153–160.

Bartlett, N.H., Vasey, P.L., Bukowski, W. (2000). Is gender identity disorder in children a mental disorder. *Sex Roles, 43*(11–12), 753–785.

Bar-Yosef, Y., Greenstein, A., Beri, A., Lidawi, G., Matzkin, H., & Chen, J. (2007). Doral vein injuries observed during penile exploration for suspected penile fracture. *Journal of Sexual Medicine, 4,* 1142–1146.

Basow, S. A., & Campanile, F. (1990). Attitudes toward prostitution as a function of attitudes toward feminism in college students: An exploratory study. *Psychology of Women Quarterly, 14,* 135–141.

Basson, R. (2000). The female sexual response: A different model. *Journal of Sex and Marital Therapy, 26,* 51–65.

Basson, R. (2001). Using a different model for female sexual response to address women's problematic low sexual desire. *Journal of Sex and Marital Therapy, 27,* 395–403.

Basson, R., Berman, J., Burnett, A., Derogaris, L., & Ferguson, D. (2000). Report of the international consensus development conference on female sexual dysfunction: Definitions and classifications. *Journal of Urology, 163,* 888–893.

Basson, R., McInnes, R., Smith, M., Hodgson, G., & Koppiker, N. (2002). Efficacy and safety of sildenafil citrate in women with sexual dysfunction associated with female sexual arousal disorder. *Journal of Women's Health and Gender-Based Medicine, 11*(4), 367–377.

Bassoon, R. (2005). Women's sexual dysfunction: Revised and expanded definitions. *Canadian Medical Association Journal, 172,* 1327–1333.

Bastos, F., Caceres, C., Galvao, J., Veras, M., & Castilho, E. (2008). AIDS in Latin America: Assessing the current status of the epidemic and the ongoing response. *International Journal of Epidemiology, 37,* 729–737.

Batabyal, A. A. (2001). On the likelihood of finding the right partner in an arranged marriage. *Journal of Socio-Economics, 30*(3), 273–281.

Bauer, G. R., & Welles, S. L. (2001). Beyond assumptions of negligible risk: STDs and women who have sex with women. *American Journal of Public Health, 91*(8), 1282–1287.

Baumeister, L. M., Flores, E., & Marin, B. V. (1995). Sex information given to Latina adolescents by parents. *Health Education Research, 10*(2), 233–239.

Baumeister, R. F. (1988). Masochism as escape from self. *Journal of Sex Research, 25,* 28–59.

Bayas, J., Costas, L., & Munoz, A. (2008). Cervical cancer vaccination indications, efficacy, and side effects. *Gynecological Oncology, 110*(Suppl. 2), S11–S14.

Bayer, R. (1981). *Homosexuality and American psychiatry: The politics of diagnosis.* New York: Basic Books.

Baylin, A., Hernandez-Diaz, S., Siles, X., Kabagambe, E., & Campos, H. (2007). Triggers of nonfatal myocardial infarction in Costa Rica: Heavy physical exertion, sexual activity, and infection. *Annals of Epidemiology, 17,* 112–118.

BBC News. (2006). Turkish boys commit "honour" crimes. *BBC News.* Retrieved December 31, 2007, from http://news.bbc.co.uk/2/hi/europe/5285726.stm?ls.

Beals, K. P., & Peplau, L. A. (2005). Identity support, identity devaluation, and well-being among lesbians. *Psychology of Women Quarterly, 29*(2), 140–148.

Bearak, B. (2008, September 5). In destitute Swaziland, leader lives royally. *New York Times.* Retrieved October 3, 2008, from http://www.nytimes.com/2008/09/06/world/africa/06king.html?pagewanted=1&_r=1&sq=mswati&st=cse&scp=3.

Bearman, P., Bruckner, H. (2001). Promising the future: Virginity pledges and first in-tercourse. *American Journal of Sociology, 106*(4), 859–912.

Beck, M. (2008, March 11). Sorting through the choices for menopause hormones. *Wall Street Journal,* p. D1.

Beck, M. (2008, September 30). Is sex addiction a sickness, or excuse to behave badly? *Wall Street Journal,* (Eastern edition). New York, p. B.9.

Becker, G., Landes, E., & Michael, R. (1977). An economic analysis of marital stability. *Journal of Political Economy, 85,* 1141–1187.

Becker, J. V., et al. (1986). Level of postassault sexual functioning in rape and incest victims. *Archives of Sexual Behavior, 15,* 37–50.

Becker, S., Rutstein, S., & Labbok, M. (2003). Estimation of births averted due to breast-feeding and increases in levels of contraception needed to substitute for breast-feeding. *Journal of Bios Science, 35,* 559–574.

Beech, A., Ward, T., & Fisher, D. (2006). The identification of sexual and violent motivations in men who assault women: Implication for treatment. *Journal of Interpersonal Violence, 21,* 1635.

Belknap, P., & Leonard II, W. M. (1991). A conceptual replication and extension of Erving Goffman's study of gender advertisements. *Sex Roles, 25,* 103–118.

Bell, A. P., & Weinberg, M. S. (1978). *Homosexualities: A study of diversity among men and women.* New York: Simon & Schuster.

Bell, A. P., Weinberg, M. S., & Hammersmith, S. K. (1981). *Sexual preference: Its development in men and women.* Bloomington: Indiana University Press.

Bell, M. L., Ebisu, K., & Belanger, K. (2007). Ambient air pollution and low birth weight in Connecticut and Massachusetts. *Environmental Health Perspectives, 115,* 1118–1124.

Bem, S. L. (1974). The measurement of psychological androgyny. *Journal of Consulting and Clinical Psychology, 42,* 155–162.

Bem, S. L. (1977). On the utility of alternative procedures for assessing psychological androgyny. *Journal of Consulting and Clinical Psychology, 45,* 196–205.

Bem, S. L. (1981). Gender schema theory: A cognitive account of sex-typing. *Psychological Review, 88,* 354–364.

Bem, S. L. (1989). Genital knowledge and gender constancy in preschool children. *Child Development, 60,* 649–662.

Benevento, B. T., & Sipski, M. L. (2002). Neurogenic bladder, neurogenic bowel, and sexual dysfunction in people with spinal cord injury. *Physical Therapy, 82*(6), 601–612.

Benjamin, H. (1961). *Encyclopedia of sexual behavior.* New York: Hawthorn Books.

Bennett, N. E., Bloom, D. A., & Craig, E. H. (1992). American marriage patterns in transition. In S. J. South & S. E. Tolnay (Eds.), *The changing American family: Sociological and demographic perspectives* (pp. 89–108). Boulder, CO: Westview.

Benokraitis, N. V. (1993). *Marriages and families.* Englewood Cliffs, NJ: Prentice Hall.

Benson, B., Gohm, C., & Gross, A. (2007). College women and sexual assault: The role of sex-related alcohol expectancies. *Journal of Family Violence, 22,* 341–351.

Benton, T. (2008). Depression and HIV/AIDS. *Current Psychiatry Reports, 10,* 280–285.

Ben-Zion, I., Rothchild, S., Chudakov, B., & Aloni, R. (2007). Surrogate versus couple therapy in vaginismus. *Journal of Sexual Medicine, 4,* 728–733.

Ben-Zion, I., & Shiber, A. (2006). Heart to heart: Rehabilitation of sexuality in cardiac patients. *Harefuah, 145,* 350–351.

Berenbaum, S. A., & Snyder, E. (1995). Early hormonal influences on childhood sex-typed activity and playmate preferences. *Developmental Psychology, 31*(1), 31–43.

Bergen, R., & Bukovec, P. (2006). Men and intimate partner rape: Characteristics of men who sexually abuse their partner. *Journal of Interpersonal Violence, 21,* 1375.

Berger, R. J., Searles, P., & Cottle, C. E. (1991). *Feminism and pornography.* New York: Praeger.

Bergmann, M. S. (1987). *The anatomy of living.* New York: Fawcett Columbine.

Bergmark, K., Avall-Lundqvist, E., Dickman, P., Henningsohn, L., & Steineck, G. (1999). Vaginal changes and sexuality in women with a history of cervical cancer. *New England Journal of Medicine, 340,* 1383–1389.

Bergstrand, C., Williams, B. (2000, October 10). Today's alternative marriage styles: The case of swingers. *Electronic Journal of Human Sexuality, 3.* Retrieved September 14, 2008, from http://www.ejhs.org/volume3/swing/body.htm.

Berkey, B. R., Perelman-Hall, T., & Kurdek, L. A. (1990). The multidimensional scale of sexuality. *Journal of Homosexuality, 19,* 67–87.

Berkow, R., Beers, M. H., Fletcher, A. J., & Bogin, R. M. (Eds). (2000). *Merck manual of medical information* (Home ed.). Whitehouse Station, NJ: Merck & Co.

Berkowitz, D., & Marsiglio, W. (2007). Gay men: Negotiating procreative, father, and family identities. *Journal of Marriage and Family, 69,* 366–382.

Berman, J., Berman, L., Toler, S., Gill, J., Haughie, S., & the Sildenafil Study Group. (2003). Safety and efficacy of sildenafil citrate for the treatment of female sexual arousal disorder: A double-blind, placebo controlled study. *Journal of Urology, 170*(6 Pt 1), 2333–2338.

Berrill, K. T., & Herek, G. M. (1990). Primary and secondary victimization in anti-gay hate crimes. *Journal of Interpersonal Violence, 5,* 401–413.

Besharov, D. (1988). *Protecting children from abuse and neglect: Policy and practices.* Springfield, IL: Charles C. Thomas.

Bestic, L. (2005). When a patch works. Retrieved August 30, 2005, from http://www.timesonline.co.uk/article/0,,8124-1716899,00.html

Bettocchi, C., Verze, P., Palumbo, R., Arcaniolo, D., & Mirone, V. (2008). Ejaculatory disorders: Pathophysiology and management. *Nature Clinical Practice: Urology, 5,* 93–103.

Bialik, C. (2007). Sorry you have gone over your limit of network friends. *Wall Street Journal.* Retrieved February 10, 2008, from http://online.wsj.com/article/SB119518271549595364.html?mod=googlenews_wsj.

Bianchi, S. M., Milkie, M. A., Sayer, L. C., & Robinson, J. P. (2000). Is anyone doing the housework? Trends in the gender division of household labor. *Social Forces, 29*(1), 191–229.

Bick, R. L., Maden, J., Heller, K. B., & Toofanian, A. (1998). Recurrent miscarriage: Causes, evaluation, and treatment. *Medscape Women's Health, 3*(3), 2.

Bieber, I., et al. (1962). *Homosexuality: A psychoanalytic study.* New York: Basic Books.

Bigelow, B. J. (1977). Children's friendship expectations: A cognitive developmental study. *Child Development, 48,* 246–253.

Birchard, T. (2006). Addictions without substance series part II: Sexual addiction. *Drugs and Alcohol Today, 6,* 32–35.

Bird, M. H. (2006). Sexual addiction and marriage and family therapy: Facilitating individual and relationship healing through couple therapy. *Journal of Marital and Family Therapy, 32*(3), 297–310.

Birdthistle, I., Floyd, S., Machingura, A., Mudziwapasi, N., Gregson, S., Glynn, J.R. (2008). From affected to infected? Orphanhood and HIV risk among female adolescents in urban Zimbabwe. *Epidemiology and Social AIDS, 22*(6), 759–766.

Birnbaum, G., Glaubman, H., & Mikulincer, M. (2001). Women's experience of heterosexual intercourse. *Journal of Sex Research, 38*(3), 191–194.

Biro, R. M., Lucky, A. W., Simbartl, L. A., Barton, B. A., Daniels, S. R., Striegel-Moore, R., et al. (2003). Pubertal maturation in girls and the relationship to anthropometric changes: Pathways through puberty. *Journal of Pediatrics, 142*(6), 643–646.

Bish, C. L., Chu, S. Y., Shapiro-Mendoza, C., Sharma, A., & Blanck, H. (May 1, 2008). Trying to lose or maintain weight during pregnancy—United States, 2003. *Maternal and Child Health Journal.* Retrieved October 14, 2008, from http://www.springerlink.com/content/n76tk678r07j87v1/?p=13a04154744143e6be60537c74733c0d&pi=1.

Biswas, S. (2005, May 17). Fear and loathing in gay India. *BBC News.* Retrieved September 15, 2008, from http://news.bbc.co.uk/2/hi/south_asia/4304081.stm.

Bittles, A. H., Mason, W. M., & Greene, J. (1991). Reproductive behavior and health in consanguineous marriages. *Science, 252*(5007), 789–794.

Bitzer, J., Kenemans, P., Mueck, A., & the FSD Education Group (2008a). Breast cancer risk in postmenopausal women using testosterone in combination with hormone replacement therapy. *Maturitas, 59,* 209–218.

Bitzer, J., Platano, G., Tschudin, S., & Alder, J. (2008b). Sexual counseling in elderly couples. *Journal of Sexual Medicine, 5*(9), 2027–2043.

Björnberg, U. (2001). Cohabitation and marriage in Sweden—does family form matter. *International Journal of Law, Policy and the Family, 15,* 350–362.

Black, M., Shetty, A., & Bhattacharya, S. (2008). Obstetric outcomes subsequent to intrauterine death in the first pregnancy. *British Journal of Gynecology, 115,* 269–274.

Blackwood, E. (1994). Sexuality and gender in Native American tribes: The case of cross-gender females.In A.C. Herrmann & A.J. Stewart (Eds.), *Theorizing feminism: Parallel trends in the humanities and social sciences.* (pp. 301–315). Boulder, CO: Westview Press.

Blair, A. (2000) Individuation, love styles and health-related quality of life among college students. *Dissertation Abstracts International,* University of Florida, #0-599-91381-9.

Blake, S. M., Ledsky, R., Lehman, T., Goodenow, C., Sawyer, R., & Hack, T. (2001). Preventing sexual risk behaviors among gay, lesbian, and bisexual adolescents: The benefits of gay-sensitive HIV instruction in schools. *American Journal of Public Health, 91,* 940–946.

Blakely, R. (2008). India offers firearms permits for vasectomies. *Times Online.* Retrieved October 27, 2008, from http://www.timesonline.co.uk/tol/news/world/asia/article3593874.ece.

Blakemore, J. E. (2003). Children's beliefs about violating gender norms: Boys shouldn't look like girls, and girls shouldn't act like boys. *Sex Roles, 48*(9–10), 411–419.

Blanchard, M. A., & Semoncho, J. E. (2006). Anthony Comstock and his adversaries: The mixed legacy of the battle for free speech. *Communication and Public Policy, 11,* 317–366.

Blanchard, R. (2004). Quantitative and theoretical analyses of the relation between older brothers and homosexuality in men. *Journal of Theoretical Biology, 230*(2), 173–187.

Blanchard, R. (2008). Review and theory off-handedness, birth order, and homosexuality in men. *Laterality, 13,* 51–70.

Blanchard, R., Cantor, J. M., Bogaert, A., Breedlove, S., & Ellis, L. (2006). Interaction of fraternal birth order and handedness in the development of male homosexuality. *Hormones & Behavior, 49,* 405–414.

Bleakley, A., Hennessey, M., & Fishbein, M. (2006). Public opinion on sex education in U.S. schools. *Archives of Pediatrics and Adolescent Medicine, 160,* 1151–1156.

Blecher, S. R., & Erickson, R. P. (2007). Genetics of sexual development: A new paradigm. *American Journal of Medical Genetics, 143,* 3054–3068.

Bleecker, E., & Murnen, S. (2005). Fraternity membership, the display of degrading sexual images of women, and rape myth acceptance. *Sex Roles, 53,* 487–493.

Bliss, G. K. (2000). Self-disclosure and friendship patterns: Gender and sexual orientation differences in same-sex and opposite-sex friendships. *Dissertation Abstracts International, 1 (5-A),* 1749.

Block, J. D. (1999). *Sex over 50.* Paramus, NJ: Reward Books.

Blow, A. J., & Hartnett, K. (2005). Infidelity in committed relationships: A methodological review. *Journal of Marital and Family Therapy, 31*(2), 183–216.

Blumstein, H. (2001). Bartholin gland disease. Retrieved September 9, 2002, from http://www.emedicine.com/emeg/topic54.htm.

Blumstein, P., & Schwartz, P. (1983). *American couples.* New York: William Morrow.

Bocklandt, S., & Vilain, E. (2007). Sex differences in brain and behavior: Hormones versus genes. *Advances in Genetics, 59,* 245–266.

Boehmer, U. (2002). Twenty years of public health research: Inclusion of lesbian, gay, bisexual and transgender populations. *American Journal of Public Health, 92*(7), 1125–1131.

Boeke, A. J., van Bergen, J. E., Morre, S. A., & van Everdingen, J. J. (2005). The risk of pelvic inflammatory disease associated with urogenital infection with chlamydia trachomatis: Literature review. *Ned Tijdschr Geneeskd, 149*(16), 878–884.

Boeringer, S. (1999). Associations of rape-supportive attitudes with fraternal and athletic participation. *Violence Against Women, 5*(1), 81–90.

Bogaert, A. (1996). Volunteer bias in human sexuality research: Evidence for both sexuality and personality differences in males. *Archives of Sexual Behavior, 25*(2), 125–140.

Bogaert, A. F. (2005). Gender role/identity and sibling sex ratio in homosexual men. *Journal of Sex and Marital Therapy, 31,* 217–227.

Bogaert, A. F., Blanchard, R., & Crosthwait, L. (2007). Interaction of birth order, handedness, and sexual orientation in the Kinsey interview data. *Behavioral Neuroscience, 121,* 845–853.

Bogaerts, S., Vanheule, S., Leeuw, F., & Desmet, M. (2006). Recalled parental bonding and personality disorders in a sample of exhibitionists: A comparative study. *Journal of Forensic Psychiatry and Psychology, 17,* 636–646.

Bohm-Starke, N., & Cylinder, E. (2008). Surgery for localized, provoked vestibulodynia: A long-term follow-up study. *Journal of Reproductive Medicine, 53,* 83–89.

Boies, S. C., Knudson, G., & Young, J. (2004). The Internet, sex, and youths: Implications for sexual development. *Sexual Addiction & Compulsivity, 11,* 343–363.

Bolso, A. (2005). Orgasm and lesbian sexuality. *Sex Education, 5*(1), 29–48.

Bolton, F. G., & MacEachron, A. E. (1988). Adolescent male sexuality: A developmental perspective. *Journal of Adolescent Research, 3,* 259–273.

Bolton, M., van der Straten, A., Cohen, C. (2008). Probiotics: Potential to prevent HIV and sexually transmitted infections in women. *Sexually Transmitted Diseases, 35*(3), 214–225.

Bonaccorsi, L., Marchiani, S., Muratori, M., Forti, G., & Baldi, E. (2004*). Journal of Cancer Research and Clinical Oncology, 130*(1), 604–614.

Bonetti, A., Tirelli, F., Catapano, A., Dazzi, D., Dei Cas, A., Solito, F., et al. (2007). Side effects of anabolic androgenic steroids abuse. *International Journal of Sports Medicine, 29*(8), 679–687.

Bonomi, A., Anderson, M., Reid, R., Carrell, D., Fishman, P., Rivara, F., & Thompson, R. (2007). Intimate partner violence in older women. *The Gerontologist, 47,* 34–41.

Boonstra, H. (2005, May). Condoms, contraceptives and nonoxynol-9: Complex issues obscured by ideology. *The Guttmacher Report on Public Policy,* 8(2), pp. 4–7.

Boonstra, H. D., Gold, R. B., Richards, C. L., & Finer, L. B. (2006). *Abortion in women's lives.* New York: Alan Guttmacher Institute.

Borchelt, G. (2005). Sexual violence against women in war and armed conflict. In A. Barnes (Ed.), *Handbook of women, psychology, and the law* (pp. 293–327). New York: Wiley.

Borini, A., Cattoli, M., Bulletti, C., & Coticchio, G. (2008). Clinical efficiency of oocyte and embryo cryopreservation. *Annals of the New York Academy of Sciences, 1127,* 49–58.

Born, L., & Steiner, M. (2001). Current management of premenstrual syndrome and premenstrual dysphoric disorder. *Current Psychiatry Reports, 3*(6), 463–469.

Bornstein, D. (Ed.). (1979). *The feminist controversy of the Renaissance.* Delmar, NY: Scholars' Facsimiles & Reprints.

Boroughs, D. S. (2004). Female sexual abusers of children. *Children & Youth Services Review, 26*(5), 481–487.

Boselli, F., Choissi, G., Bortolamasi, M., & Callinelli, A. (2005). Prevalence and determinants of genital shedding of herpes simplex virus among women attending Italian colposcopy clinics. *European Journal of Obstetrics and Reproductive Biology, 118*(1), 86–90.

Bostwick, W., Esteban, S., Horn, S., Hughes, T., Johnson, T., & Valles, J. R. (2007). Drinking patterns, problems, and motivations among collegiate bisexual women. *Journal of American College Health, 56,* 285–292.

Boswell, J. (1980). *Christianity, social tolerance, and homosexuality: Gay people in western Europe from the beginning of the Christian* era to the fourteenth century. Chicago: The University of Chicago Press.

Bounhoure, J., Galinier, M., Roncalli, J., Assoun, B., & Puel, J. (2008). Myocardial infarction and oral contraceptives. *Bulletin of the Academy of National Medicine, 192,* 569–579.

Bower, B. (1992). Depression, early death noted in HIV cases. *Science News, 142,* 53.

Bower, H. (2001). The gender identity disorder in the DSM-IV classification: A critical evaluation. *Australian and New Zealand Journal of Psychiatry, 35*(1), 1–8.

Bowser, B. (2001). Social class in black sexuality. In R. Satow (Ed.), *Gender and social life* (pp. 120–124). Needham Heights, MA: Allyn & Bacon.

Boxer, D. (1996). Ethnographic interviewing as a research tool in speech act analysis: The case of complaints. In S.M. Gass and J. Neu (Eds.), *Speech Acts Across Cultures* (pp. 217–239). New York: de Gruyter.

Boyd, L. (2000). Morning sickness shields fetus from bugs and chemicals. *RN, 63*(8), 18–20.

Boyle, G. J., Goldman, R., Svoboda, J. S., & Fernandez, E. (2002). The acceptability of male circumcision to reduce HIV infections in Nyanza Province, Kenya. *AIDS Care, 14*(1), 27–40.

Bradford, J., Ryan, C., & Rothblum, E. (1994). National Lesbian Health Care Survey: Implications for mental health care. *Journal of Consulting and Clinical Psychology, 62,* 228–242.

Bradley, D. (2001). Regulation of unmarried cohabitation in west-European jurisdictions—Determinants of legal policy. *International Journal of Law, Policy and the Family, 15,* 22–50.

Brandberg, Y., Sandelin, K., Erikson, S., Jurell, G., Liljegren, A., Lindblom, A., et al. (2008). Psychological reactions, quality of life, and body image after bilateral prophylactic mastectomy in women at high risk for breast cancer: A prospective 1-year follow-up study. *Journal of Clinical Oncology, 26,* 3943–3949.

Brandt, A. M. (1985). *No magic bullet: A social history of venereal disease in the United States.* New York: Oxford University Press.

Brandt, M., Abels, C., May, T., Lohmann, K., Schmidts-Winkler, I., & Hoyme, U. (2008). Intravaginally applied metronidazole is as effective as orally applied in the treatment of bacterial vaginosis, but exhibits significantly less side effects. *European Journal of Obstetrics, Gynecology, and Reproductive Biology.* Epub ahead of print.

Retrieved November 6, 2008, from http://www.ncbi.nlm.nih.gov/pubmed/18775597.

Bratter, J. L., & King, R. B. (2008). "But will it last?": Marital instability among interracial and same-race couples. *Family Relations, 57,* 160–172.

Brecher, E., & the Editors of Consumer Reports Books. (1984). *Love, sex and aging.* Boston: Little, Brown.

Brecher, E. M., & Brecher, J. (1986). Extracting valuable sexological findings from severely flawed and biased population samples. *Journal of Sex Research, 22,* 6–20.

Brecklin, L. R., & Ullman, S. E. (2005). Self-defense or assertiveness training and women's responses to sexual attacks. *Journal of Interpersonal Violence, 20*(6), 738–762.

Bren, L. (2004). Genital herpes: A hidden epidemic. U.S. Food and Drug Association. *FDA Consumer Magazine.* Retrieved September 17, 2008, from http://www.fda.gov/Fdac/features/2002/202_herp.html.

Breuss, C. E., & Greenberg, S. (1981). *Sex education: Theory and practice.* Belmont, CA: Wadsworth.

Brewer, D., Roberts, J., Muth, S., & Potterat, J. (2008). Prevalence of male clients of street prostitute women in the United States. *Human Organization, 67,* 346–357.

Brewis, A., & Meyer, M. (2005). Marital coitus across the life course. *Journal of Biosocial Sciences, 37,* 499–518.

Brewster, K. L., & Tillman, K. H. (2008). Who's doing it? Patterns and predictors of youths' oral sexual experiences. *Journal of Adolescent Health, 42,* 73–80.

Bridgeland, W. M., Duane, E. A., & Stewart, C. S. (2001). Victimization and attempted suicide among college students. *College Student Journal, 35*(1), 63–76.

Bridges, L. J., & Moore, K. A. (2002). *Religious involvement and children's well-being: What research tells us (and what it doesn't).* Washington, DC: ChildTrends Research Brief.

Brienza, J. (1998). Hate crimes against gays hurt body and soul. *Trial, 34*(10), 95–98.

Brigham and Women's Hospital. (2008, April 11). High risk pregnancy over age 30. Retrieved from http://brighamandwomens.staywellsolutionsonline.com/RelatedItems/91,P07007.

Brill, S., & Schreier, H. (2007, November 18). Gender identity and the chemical delay of puberty. *San Francisco Chronicle.* Retrieved December 18, 2008, February 24, 2008, from http://www.sfgate.com/cgi-bin/article.cgi?file=/c/a/2007/11/18/IN-VMT7C9C.DTL.

Brinig, M. F., & Allen, D. A. (2000). "These boots are made for walking": Why most divorce filers are women. *American Law and Economics Review, 2,* 126–169.

Brinton, L. (2007). Long-term effects of ovulation-stimulating drugs on cancer risk. *Reproductive Biomedicine Online, 15,* 38–44.

Brinton, L. A., & Schairer, C. (1997). Postmenopausal hormone-replacement therapy: Time for a reappraisal? *New England Journal of Medicine, 336*(25), 1821–1822.

Brittle, E., Wang, F., Lubinski, J., Bunte, R., & Friedman, H. (2008). A replication-competent, neuronal spread-defective, live attenuated herpes simplex virus type 1 vaccine. *Journal of Virology, 82,* 8431–8441.

Brizendine, L. (2006). *The Female Brain.* New York, NY: Broadway Publishing.

Brockman, N. (2004). Kenya. In R. T. Francoeur & R. J. Noonan (Eds.), *The Continuum international encyclopedia of sexuality* (pp. 679–691). New York/London: Continuum International.

Brody, S., & Krüger, T. (2006). The post orgasmic prolactin increase following intercourse is greater than following masturbation and suggests greater satiety. *Biological Psychology, 71,* 312–315.

Brongersma, E. (1990). Boy-lovers and their influence on boys: Distorted research and anecdotal observations. *Journal of Homosexuality, 20,* 145–173.

Bronstein, P. (2005). The family environment: Where gender role socialization begins. In J. Worell & C. Goodheart (Eds.), *Handbook of girls' and women's psychological health* (pp. 262–271). New York: Oxford University Press.

Brooks, R., Lee, S., Newman, P., & Leibowitz, A. (2008). Sexual risk behavior has decreased among men who have sex with men in Los Angeles but remains greater than that among heterosexual men and women. *AIDS Education and Prevention, 20,* 312–324.

Brooks-Gordon, B., & Geisthorpe, L. (2003). What men say when apprehended for kerb crawling: A model of prostitutes' clients' talk. *Psychology, Crime and Law, 9*(2), 145–171.

Brooks-Gunn, J., & Furstenberg, F. F. (1989). Adolescent sexual behavior. *American Psychologist, 44,* 249–257.

Brooks-Gunn, J., & Furstenberg, F. F. (1990). Coming of age in the era of AIDS: Puberty, sexuality, and contraception. *Milbank Quarterly, 68,* 59–84.

Brotto, L. A. (2004). Genital and subjective sexual arousal in women: Effects of menopause, sympathetic nervous system activation, and arousal disorder. *Dissertation Abstracts International, 64*(11-B), #0419–4217.

Broude, G. J., & Greene, S. J. (1976). Cross-cultural codes on twenty sexual attitudes and practices. *Ethnology, 15,* 409–428.

Brown, A., & Testa, M. (2008). Social influences on judgments of rape victims: The role of the negative and positive social reactions of others. *Sex Roles, 58,* 490–501.

Brown, B. B., Dolcini, M. M., & Leventhal, A. (1997). Transformations in peer relationships at adolescence: Implications for healthrelated behavior. In J. Schulenberg, J. L. Maggs, & K. Hurrelmann (Eds.), *Health risks and developmental transitions during adolescence* (pp. 161–189). Cambridge, U.K.: Cambridge University Press.

Brown, C. (2008). Gender-role implications on same-sex intimate partner abuse. *Journal of Family Violence, 23,* 457–463.

Brown, D. J., Hill, S. T., & Baker, H. W. (2005). Male fertility and sexual function after spinal cord injury. *Progress in Brain Research, 152,* 427–439.

Brown, D. L., & Frank, J. E. (2003). Diagnosis and management of syphilis. *American Family Physician, 68*(2), 283–290.

Brown, H. G. (1962). *Sex and the single girl.* New York: Giant Cardinal.

Brown, J. C. (1983). Paraphilias: Sadomasochism, fetishism, transvestism and transsexuality. *British Journal of Psychiatry, 143,* 227–231.

Brown, M. S., & Brown, C. A. (1987). Circumcision decision: Prominence of social concerns. *Pediatrics, 80,* 215–219.

Brown, S. L., Lee, G. R., & Bulanda, J. R. (2006). Cohabitation among older adults: A national portrait. *Journals of Gerontology Series B: Psychological Sciences and Social Science, 61,* S71–S79.

Brown, T. J., Sumner, K. E., & Nocera, R. (2002). Understanding sexual aggression against women: An examination of the role of men's athletic participation and related variables. *Journal of Interpersonal Violence, 17*(9), 937–952.

Brownmiller, S. (1975). *Against our will: Men, women, and rape.* New York: Simon & Schuster.

Brownmiller, S. (2000). Rape on the brain: A review of Randy Thornhill and Craig Palmer. Retrieved December 5, 2005, from http://www.susanbrownmiller.com/html/review-thornhill.html.

Brubaker, L., Handa, V., Bradley, C., Connolly, A., Moalli, P., Brown, M., & Weber, A.

(2008). Sexual function 6 months after first delivery. *Obstetrics and Gynecology, 111,* 1040–1044.

Brucker, C., Karck, U., & Merkle, E. (2008). Cycle control, tolerability, efficacy and acceptability of the vaginal contraceptive ring, NuvaRing: Results of clinical experience in Germany. *European Journal of Contraceptive Reproductive Health Care, 13,* 31–38.

Brückner, H., & Bearman, P. (2005). After the promise: The STD consequences of adolescent virginity pledges. *Journal of Adolescent Health, 36*(4), 271–278.

Brumberg, J. J. (1997). *The body project: An intimate history of American girls.* New York: Vintage Books.

Bruni, V., Pontello, V., Luisi, S., & Petraglia, F. (2008). An open-label multicentre trial to evaluate the vaginal bleeding pattern of the combined contraceptive vaginal ring NuvaRing. *European Journal of Obstetrics and Gynecological Reproductive Biology, 139,* 65–71.

Brunner-Huber, L., & Toth, J. (2007). Obesity and oral contraceptive failure: Findings from the 2002 National Survey of Family Growth. *American Journal of Epidemiology, 166,* 1306–1311.

Bryan, W. A. (1987). Contemporary fraternity and sorority issues. *New Directions for Student Services, 40,* 37–56.

Buckett, W., Chian, R., Holzer, H., Dean, N., Usher, R., & Tan, S. (2007). Obstetric outcomes and congenital abnormalities after in vitro maturation, IVF, and ICSI. *Obstetrics and Gynecology, 110,* 885–891.

Buffardi, A. L., Thomas, K. K., Holmes, K. K., & Manhart, L. E. (2008). Moving upstream: Ecosocial and psychosocial correlates of sexually transmitted infections among young adults in the United States. *American Journal of Public Health, 98,* 1128–1137.

Buhrich, N., & McConaghy, N. (1985). Preadult feminine behaviors of male transvestites. *Archives of Sexual Behavior, 14,* 413–419.

Bull, S. S., & Melian, L. M. (1998). Contraception and culture: The use of Yuyos in Paraguay. *Health Care for Women International, 19*(1), 49–66.

Bullivant, S., Sellergren, S., Stern, K., Spencer, N., Jacob, S., Mennella, J., McClintock, M. (2004). Women's sexual experience during the menstrual cycle: Identification of the sexual phase by noninvasive measurement of luteinizing hormone. *Journal of Sex Research, 41*(1), 82–93.

Bullough, V. (1994). *Science in the bedroom: The history of sex research.* New York: Basic Books.

Bullough, V. L. (1973). *The subordinate sex: A history of attitudes toward women.* Urbana: University of Illinois Press.

Bullough, V. L. (1976). *Sexual variance in society and history.* New York: Wiley.

Bullough, V. L. (1979). *Homosexuality: A history.* New York: New American Library.

Bullough, V. L. (1990). History in adult human sexual behavior with children and adolescents in Western societies. In J. Feierman (Ed.), *Pedophilia biosocial dimensions* (pp. 69–90). New York: Springer-Verlag.

Bullough, V. L. (1998). Alfred Kinsey and the Kinsey Report: Historical overview and lasting contributions. *Journal of Sex Research, 35*(2), 127–131.

Bullough, V. L. (2001). Transgenderism and the concept of gender. Retrieved May 24, 2003, from http://www.symposium.com/ijt/gilbert/bullough.htm.

Bullough, V. L., Bullough, B., & Smith, R. (1983). A comparative study of male transvestites, male to female transsexuals, and male homosexuals. *Journal of Sex Research, 19,* 238–257.

Bumpass, L., & Lu, H.-H. (2000). Trends in cohabitation and implications for children's family contexts in the U.S. *Population Studies, 54,* 29–41.

Bundow, G. L. (1992). Why women stay. *Journal of the American Medical Association, 267*(23), 3229.

Burbidge, M., & Walters, J. (1981). *Breaking the silence: Gay teenagers speak for themselves.* London, U.K.: Joint Council for Gay Teenagers.

Burch, B. (1998). Lesbian sexuality. *Psychoanalytic Review, 85*(3), 349–372.

Burdette, A. M., Ellison, C. G., Sherkat, D. E., & Gore, K. A. (2007). Are there religious variations in marital infidelity? *Journal of Family Issues, 28,* 1553.

Burdge, B. J. (2007). Bending gender, ending gender: Theoretical foundations for social work practice with the transgender community. *Social Work, 52,* 243–250.

Bureau of Justice. (2004). *Criminal victimization, 2003.* Washington, DC: Author.

Burgess, A. W., & Holmstrom, L. L. (1979). *Rape: Crisis and recovery.* Bowie, MD: Robert J. Brady.

Burgess, A. W., & Morgenbesser, L. I. (2005). Sexual violence and seniors. *Brief Treatment & Crisis Intervention, 5*(2), 193–202.

Burgess, C. (1999). Internal and external stress factors associated with the identity development of transgendered youth. *Journal of Gay and Lesbian Social Services, 10*(3–4), 35–47.

Burgess, G. (2007). Assessment of rape-supportive attitudes and beliefs in college men. *Journal of Interpersonal Violence, 22,* 973.

Burke, D. (2008, July 26). Birth control ban marks 40 years. *The Ledger.* Retrieved October 28, 2008, from http://www.theledger.com/article/20080726/NEWS/807260367/1326&title=Birth_Control_Ban_Marks_40_Years.

Burkeman, O., & Younge, G. (2005). Being Brenda. Retrieved February 24, 2005, from http://www.godspy.com/life/Being-Brenda.cfm.

Burkman, R., Schlesselman, J. J., & Zieman, M. (2004). Safety concerns and health benefits associated with oral contraception. *American Journal of Obstetrics and Gynecology, 190*(Suppl. 4), S5–22.

Burkman, R. T. (2002). The transdermal contraceptive patch: A new approach to hormonal contraception. *International Journal of Fertility and Women's Medicine, 47*(2), 69–76.

Burleson, B.R., Denton, W.H. (1997). The relationship between communication skill and marital satisfaction some moderating effects. *Journal of Marriage and Family, 59*(4), 884–894.

Burnell, G. M., & Norfleet, M. A. (1987). Women's self-reported response to abortion. *Journal of Psychology, 121,* 71–76.

Burns, M., Costello, J., Ryan-Woolley, B., & Davidson, S. (2007). Assessing the impact of late treatment effects in cervical cancer: An exploratory study of women's sexuality. *European Journal of Cancer Care, 16,* 364–372.

Burt, M. (1980). Cultural myths and support for rape. *Journal of Personality and Social Psychology, 38,* 217–230.

Burton, K. (2005). Attachment style and perceived quality of romantic partner's opposite-sex best friendship: The impact on romantic relationship satisfaction. *Dissertation Abstracts International, 65*(8-B), 4329, # 0419-4217.

Bushman, B., & Bonacci, A. M. (2002). Violence and sex impair memory for television ads. *Journal of Applied Psychology, 87*(3), 557–564.

Buss, D. (1989). Sex differences in human mate preferences: Evolutionary hypotheses tested in 37 cultures. *Behavioral and Brain Sciences, 12,* 1–49.

Buss, D. M. (1994). *The evolution of desire: Strategies of human mating.* New York: Basic Books.

Buss, D. M. (2003). The dangerous passion: Why jealousy is as necessary as love and sex. *Archives of Sexual Behavior, 32*(1), 79–80.

Buss, D. M., Shackelford, T. K., Kirkpatrick, L., & Larsen, R. J. (2001). A half century of mate preferences: The cultural evolution of values. *Journal of Marriage & the Family, 63*(2), 491–503.

Butler, A. C. (2005). Gender differences in the prevalence of same-sex sexual partnering: 1988–2002. *Social Forces, 84,* 421–449.

Butler, M. H., & Wampler, K. S. (1999). A metaanalytic update of research on the couple communication program. *American Journal of Family Therapy, 27*(3), 223.

Buunk, A. P., Park, J. H., Zurriaga, R., Klavina, L., & Massar, K. (2008). Height predicts jealousy differently for men and women. *Evolution and Human Behavior, 29,* 133–139.

Buunk, B. P., Angleitner, A., & Oubaid, V. (1996). Sex differences in jealousy in evolutionary and cultural perspective: Tests from the Netherlands, Germany, and the United States. *Psychological Science, 7*(6), 359–363.

Buysse, A., DeClerq, A., & Verhofstadt, L. (2000). Dealing with relational conflict: A picture in milliseconds. *Journal of Social and Personal Relationships, 17*(4–5), 574–597.

Buysse, A., & Ickes, W. (1999). Communication patterns in laboratory discussions of safer sex. *Journal of Sex Research, 36*(2), 121.

Bygdeman, M., & Danielsson, K. G. (2002). Options for early therapeutic abortion. *Drugs, 62*(17), 2459–2470.

Byrne, D., & Murnen, S. K. (1988). Maintaining loving relationships. In R. Sternberg & M. L. Barnes (Eds.), *Psychology of love* (pp. 293–310). New Haven, CT: Yale University Press.

Cabaret, A. S., Leveque, J., Dugast, C., Blanchot, J., & Grall, J. Y. (2003). Problems raised by the gynaecologic management of women with BRCA 1 and 2 mutations. *Gynecology, Obstetrics and Fertility, 31*(4), 370–377.

Cable News Network. (2007, June 27). Poll majority: Gays' orientation can't change. *CNN.com.* Retrieved September 15, 2008, from http://www.cnn.com/2007/US/06/27/poll.gay/index.html.

Cadman, L. (2008). The future of cervical cancer prevention: Human papillomavirus vaccines. *Journal of Family Health Care, 18,* 131–132.

Cado, S., & Leitenberg, H. (1990). Guilt reactions to sexual fantasies during intercourse. *Archives of Sexual Behavior 19*(1), 49–63.

Cahill, S., South, K., & Spade, J. (2000). *Outing age: Public policy issues affecting gay, lesbian, bisexual and transgender elders.* Washington, DC: National Gay and Lesbian Task Force.

Cai, D., Wilson, S. R., & Drake, L. E. (2000). Culture in the context of intercultural negotiation: Individualism-collectivism and paths to integrative agreements. *Human Communication Research, 26*(4), 591–617.

Calderone, M. (1983). On the possible prevention of sexual problems in adolescence. *Hospital and Community Psychiatry, 34,* 528–530.

Caliendo, C., Armstrong, J. L., & Roberts, A. E. (2005). Self-reported characteristics of women and men with intimate body piercings. *Journal of Advanced Nursing, 49*(5), 474–484.

Callahan, M. M. (2002). Safety and tolerance studies of potential microbicides following multiple penile applications. Annual Conference on Microbicides, May 12–15, 2002, Antwerp, Belgium.

Cameron, K. A., Salazar, L. F., Bernhardt, J. M., Burgess-Whitman, N., Wingood, G. M., & DiClemente, R. J. (2005). Adolescents' experience with sex on the web: Results from online focus groups. *Journal of Adolescence, 28*(4), 535–540.

Cammaert, L. (1985). How widespread is sexual harassment on campus? Special issue, Women in groups and aggression against women. *International Journal of Women's Studies, 8,* 388–397.

Campbell, J. C., Webster, D., Koziol-McLain, J., Block, C., Campbell, D., Curry, M. A., et al. (2002). Intimate partner violence and physical health consequences. *Archives of Internal Medicine, 162*(10), 1157–1163.

Campbell, K., & Ponzetti, J. J. (2007). The moderating effects of rituals on commitment in premarital involvements. *Sexual and Relationship Therapy, 22,* 415–418.

Campbell, R., Lichty, L., Sturza, M., & Raja, S. (2006). Gynecological health impact of sexual assault. *Research in Nursing and Health, 29,* 399–413.

Campbell, R., Sefl, T., & Ahrens, C. E. (2004). The impact of rape on women's sexual health risk behaviors. *Health Psychology, 23*(1), 67–74.

Campenni, C. E. (1999). Gender stereotyping of children's toys: A comparison of parents and nonparents. *Sex Roles, 40*(1–2), 121–138.

Camperio-Ciani, A., Corna, F., & Capiluppi, C. (2004). Evidence for maternally inherited factors favouring male homosexuality and promoting female fecundity. *Proceedings: Biological Sciences, 271*(1554), 2217–2221.

Cantor, J. M., Blanchard, R., Paterson, A. D., & Bogaert, A. (2002). How many gay men owe their sexual orientation to fraternal birth order? *Archives of Sexual Behavior, 31*(1), 63–71.

Carcopino, X., Shojai, R., & Boubli, L. (2004). Female genital mutilation: Generalities, complications and management during obstetrical period. *Journal of Gynecology, Obstetrics, & Biological Reproduction, 33*(5), 378–383.

Carey, B. (2004, November 9). Long after Kinsey, only the brave study sex. Retrieved April 2, 2005, from http://query.nytimes.com/gst/abstract.html?res=FA0D11F638580C7A8CDDA80994DC404482.

Carey, B. (2005). Straight, gay or lying? Bisexuality revisited. Retrieved July 5, 2005, from http://www.thetaskforce.org/downloads/07052005NYTBisexuality.pdf.

Carlson, B., Maciol, K., & Schneider, J. (2006). Sibling incest: Reports from forty-one survivors. *Journal of Child Sexual Abuse, 15,* 19.

Carlton, C. L., Nelson, E. S., & Coleman, P. K. (2000). College students' attitudes toward abortion and commitment to the issue. *Social Science Journal, 37*(4), 619–625.

Carnes, P. (2001). *Out of the shadows: Understanding sexual addiction.* Center City, MN: Hazelden Information Education.

Carnes, P. (2003). Understanding sexual addiction. *SIECUS Report, 31*(5), 5–7.

Caron, S. L., Davis, C. M., Wynn, R. L., & Roberts, L. W. (1992). America responds to AIDS, but did college students? Differences between March, 1987, and September 1988. *AIDS Education and Prevention, 4,* 18–28.

Carr, R. R., & Ensom, M. H. (2002). Fluoxetine in the treatment of premenstrual dysphoric disorder. *Annuals of Pharmacotherapy, 36*(4), 713–717.

Carrell, D. T., Wilcox, A. L., Lowry, L., Peterson, C. M., Jones, K. P., Erickson, L., et al. (2003). Elevated sperm chromosome aneuploidy and apoptosis in patients with unexplained recurrent pregnancy loss. *Obstetrics and Gynecology, 101*(6), 1229–1235.

Carrier, J. M. (1989). Gay liberation and coming out in Mexico. *Journal of Homosexuality, 17,* 225–252.

Carroll, J. (2009). *The day Aunt Flo comes to visit.* Avon, CT: Best Day Media.

Carroll, J., Padilla-Walker, L., Nelson, L., Olsen, C., Barry, C., Madsen, S. (2008). Generation XXX. *Journal of Adolescent Research, 23*(1), 6–30.

Carter, F., Carter, J., Luty, S., Jordan, J., McIntosh, V., Bartram, A., et al. (2007). What is worse for your sex life: Starving, being depressed, or a new baby? *International Journal of Eating Disorders, 40,* 664–667.

Caruso, S., Rugolo, S., Agnello, C., Intelisano, G., DiMari, L., & Cianci, A. (2006). Sildenafil improves sexual functioning in premenopausal women with type 1 diabetes who are affected by sexual arousal disorder: A double-blind, crossover, placebo-controlled pilot study. *Fertility and Sterility, 85,* 1496–1501.

Case, P., Austin, S. B., Hunter, D., Manson, J., Malpeis, S., Willett, W., & Spiegelman, D. (2004). Sexual orientation, health risk factors, and physical functioning in the nurses' health study II. *Journal of Women's Health, 13*(9), 1033–1047.

Casey, B., Getz, S., & Galvan, A. (2008). The adolescent brain. *Developmental Review, 28,* 62–77.

Casper, M., & Carpenter, L. (2008). Sex, drugs, and politics: The HPV vaccine for cervical cancer. *Sociology of Health and Illness, 30,* 886–899.

Caspi, A., Williams, B., Kim-Cohen, J., Craig, I., Milne, B., Poulton, R., et al. (2007). Moderation of breastfeeding effects on the IQ by genetic variation in fatty acid metabolism. *Proceedings of the National Academy of Sciences of the United States of America, 104,* 18860–18865.

Cass, V. C. (1979). Homosexual identity formation: A theoretical model. *Journal of Homosexuality, 4,* 219–235.

Cass, V. C. (1984). Homosexual identity formation: Testing a theoretical model. *The Journal of Sex Research, 20,* 143–167.

Casteels, K., Wouters, C., VanGeet, C., & Devlieger, H. (2004). Video reveals self-stimulation in infancy. *Acta Paediatrics, 93*(6), 844–846.

Catalan, J., & Meadows, J. (2000). Sexual dysfunction in gay and bisexual men with HIV infection: Evaluation and treatment. *AIDS Care, 12*(3), 279–286.

Catalano, S. (2006). *National Crime Victimization Survey: Criminal victimization, 2005.* Bureau of Justice Statistics, September. Retrieved October 4, 2008, from http://www.ojp.usdoj.gov/bjs/pub/pdf/cv05.pdf.

Catania, J. A., Binson, D., Van Der Straten, A., & Stone, V. (1995). Methodological research on sexual behavior in the AIDS era. *Annual Review of Sex Research, 6,* 77–125.

Catania, J. A., Coates, T. J., Kegeles, S. M., et al. (1989). Implications of the AIDS risk-reduction model for the gay community: The importance of perceived sexual enjoyment and help-seeking behaviors. In V. M. Mays, G. W. Albee, & S. F. Schneider (Eds.), *Primary prevention of AIDS: Psychological approaches* (pp. 242–261). Newbury Park, CA: Sage.

Catania, J. A., McDermott, L. J., & Pollack, L. M. (1986). Questionnaire response bias and face-to-face interview sample bias in sexuality research. *Journal of Sex Research, 22,* 52–72.

Cates, J. A., & Markley, J. (1992). Demographic, clinical, and personality variables associated with male prostitution by choice. *Adolescence, 27,* 695–706.

Cates, W. (2004). Reproductive tract infections. In R. A. Hatcher et al. (Eds.), *Contraceptive technology* (18th Rev. ed., pp. 191–220). New York: Ardent Media.

Cates, W., & Raymond, E. G. (2004). Vaginal spermicides. In R. A. Hatcher et al. (Eds.), *Contraceptive technology* (18th Rev. ed., pp. 355–363). New York: Ardent Media.

Cates, W., & Stewart, F. (2004). Vaginal barriers. In R. A. Hatcher et al. (Eds.), *Contraceptive technology* (18th Rev. ed., pp. 365–389). New York: Ardent Media.

Cathcart, R. (2008, February 23). Boy's killing, labeled a hate crime, stuns a town. *New York Times.* Retrieved February 23, 2008, from http://www.nytimes.com/2008/02/23/us/23oxnard.html?ref=us.

Cattamanchi, A., Posavad, C., Wald, A., Baine, Y., Moses, J., Higgens, T., et al. (2008, September 10). A Phase I study of DNA vaccine for herpes simplex virus type 2 (HSV-2) in healthy HSV-2 seronegative adults using a needle-free injection system. *Clinical Vaccine Immunology.* Epub ahead of print. Retrieved November 5, 2008, from http://www.ncbi.nlm.nih.gov/pubmed/18784341?ordinalpos=2&itool=EntrezSystem2.PEntrez.Pubmed.Pubmed_ResultsPanel.Pubmed_DefaultReportPanel.Pubmed_RVDocSum.

Caughey, A., Hopkins, L., & Norton, M. (2006). Chorionic villus sampling compared with amniocentesis and the difference in the rate of pregnancy loss. *Obstetrics and Gynecology, 108,* 612–616.

CBS. (2008, June 15). Changing views on gay marriage. *CBS News Poll.* Retrieved September 14, 2008, from http://www.cbsnews.com/htdocs/pdf/MAYB-GAYMARRIAGE.pdf.

Cecchetti, J. A. (2007). Women's attachment representations of their fathers and the experience of passionate love in adulthood. *Dissertation Abstracts International: Section B: The Sciences and Engineering, 68,* 3389.

Ceniti, J., & Malamuth, N. (1984). Effects of repeated exposure to sexually violent or nonviolent stimuli on sexual arousal to rape or nonrape depictions. *Behavior Research and Therapy, 22,* 535–548.

Center on Addiction and Substance Abuse. (2002, February). Substance use and risky sexual behavior: Attitudes and practices among adolescents and young adults. Retrieved September 30, 2002, from http://www.casa.columbia.org.

Centers for Disease Control and Prevention. (2003). Can I get HIV from oral sex? Retrieved November 22, 2005, from http://www.cdc.gov/hiv/pubs/faq/faq19.htm.

Centers for Disease Control and Prevention. (2005a). Recommended childhood and adolescent immunization schedule—United States. *Morbidity and Mortality Weekly Report, 53*(51, 52), Q1–Q3.

Centers for Disease Control and Prevention. (2005b). Sexually transmitted disease surveillance, 2004. Retrieved November 25, 2005, from http://www.cdc.gov/std/stats/04pdf/2004SurveillanceAll.pdf.

Centers for Disease Control and Prevention. (2007). *2005 assisted reproductive technology success rates: National summary and fertility clinic reports.* Atlanta, GA: Author.

Centers for Disease Control and Prevention. (2007a). *Chlamydia—CDC fact sheet.* Retrieved September 18, 2008, from http://www.cdc.gov/std/Chlamydia/STDFact-Chlamydia.htm.

Centers for Disease Control and Prevention, Division of STD Prevention. (2007a). *Sexually transmitted disease surveillance, 2006.* Retrieved September 17, 2008, from http://www.cdc.gov/STD/stats/toc2006.htm.

Centers for Disease Control and Prevention. (2007b). *Trends in reportable sexually transmitted diseases in the U.S., 2006.* Retrieved September 18, 2008, from http://www.cdc.gov/STD/STATS/pdf/trends2006.pdf.

Centers for Disease Control and Prevention. (2007c). Trichomoniasis—CDC fact sheet. Retrieved September 18, 2008, from http://www.cdc.gov/std/trichomonas/STDFact-Trichomoniasis.htm.

Centers for Disease Control and Prevention. (2008). *Pelvic inflammatory disease—CDC fact sheet.* Retrieved September 18, 2008, from http://www.cdc.gov/std/PID/STDFact-PID.htm.

Centers for Disease Control and Prevention. (2008, February). Male circumcision and risk for HIV transmission and other health conditions: Implications for the United States. Department of Health and Human Services. Retrieved December 18, 2008, from http://www.cdc.gov/hiv/resources/factsheets/circumcision.htm.

Centers for Disease Control and Prevention. (2008a). *Genital HPV infection—CDC fact sheet.* Retrieved September 18, 2008, from http://www.cdc.gov/std/HPV/STDFact-HPV.htm.

Centers for Disease Control and Prevention. (2008b). Syncope after vaccination—United States, January 2005–July 2007. *Morbidity and Mortality Weekly Report, 57,* 457–460.

Centers for Disease Control and Prevention. (2008c). *HPV vaccine—questions and Answers.* Retrieved September 18, 2008, from http://www.cdc.gov/vaccines/vpd-vac/hpv/vac-faqs.htm.

Centers for Disease Control and Prevention. (2008d). *Hepatitis A.* National Center for HIV/AIDS, Viral Hepatitis, STD, and TB Prevention, Division of Viral Hepatitis. Retrieved September 16, 2008, from http://www.cdc.gov/hepatitis/HAV/HAV-faq.htm#general.

Centers for Disease Control and Prevention. (2008e). *Hepatitis B.* National Center for HIV/AIDS, Viral Hepatitis, STD, and TB Prevention, Division of Viral Hepatitis. Retrieved September 16, 2008, from http://www.cdc.gov/hepatitis/HBV/HBV-faq.htm#overview.

Centers for Disease Control and Prevention. (2008f). *Hepatitis C.* National Center for HIV/AIDS, Viral Hepatitis, STD, and TB Prevention, Division of Viral Hepatitis. Retrieved September 16, 2008, from http://www.cdc.gov/hepatitis/HCV.htm.

Centers for Disease Control and Prevention. (2008g). *Viral hepatitis.* National Center for HIV/AIDS, Viral Hepatitis, STD, and TB Prevention, Division of Viral Hepatitis. Retrieved September 16, 2008, from http://www.cdc.gov/hepatitis/index.htm.

Centers for Disease Control and Prevention. (2008h). MMWR analysis provides new details on HIV incidence in U.S. populations. *CDC HIV/AIDS Facts.* Retrieved September 16, 2008, from http://www.cdc.gov/hiv/topics/surveillance/resources/factsheets/pdf/mmwr-incidence.pdf.

Centers for Disease Control and Prevention. (2008i). *HIV and AIDS in the U.S.: A picture of today's epidemic.* Retrieved on September 18, 2008, from http://www.cdc.gov/hiv/topics/surveillance/united_states.htm.

Centers for Disease Control and Prevention. (2008j). HIV/AIDS among women. *CDC HIV/AIDS Fact Sheet.* Retrieved September 16, 2008, from http://www.cdc.gov/hiv/topics/women/resources/factsheets/pdf/women.pdf.

Chalett, J. M., & Nerenberg, L. T. (2000). "Blue balls": A diagnostic consideration in testiculoscrotal pain in young adults: A case report and discussion. *Pediatrics, 106,* 843.

Chan, C. S. (1989). Issues of identity development among Asian-American lesbians and gay men. *Journal of Counseling and Development, 68,* 16–20.

Chan, J., Olivier, B., deJong, R., Snoeren, E., Kooijman, E., vanHasselt, F., et al. (2008). Translational research into sexual disorders: Pharmacology and genomics. *European Journal of Pharmacology, 585,* 426–435.

Chancer, L. S. (2006). *Sadomasochism in everyday life: The dynamics of power and powerlessness.* New Brunswick, NJ: Rutgers University Press.

Chapleau, K., Oswald, D., & Russell, B. (2007). How ambivalent sexism toward women and men support rape myth acceptance. *Sex Roles, 57,* 131–136.

Chaplin, S. (2007). *Japanese love hotels: A cultural history.* London: Routledge.

Chaudhury, K., Bhattacharyya, A., & Guha, S. (2004). Studies on the membrane integrity of human sperm treated with a new injectable male contraceptive. *Human Reproduction, 19,* 1826–1830.

Chaudhury, R. R. (1985). Plant contraceptives translating folklore into scientific application. In D. B. Jelliffe & E. F. Jelliffe (Eds.), *Advances in international maternal and child health* (pp. 107–114). Oxford, U.K.: Claredon Press.

Chavarro, J., Sadio, S. M., Toth, T. L., & Hauser, R. (2007, October). Soy food and soy isoflavone intake in relation to semen quality parameters. Presentation at the Annual

Meeting of the American Society for Reproductive Medicine, Washington, D.C.

Chavarro, J. E., Willett, W. C., & Skerrett, P. J. (2007). *The fertility diet.* New York: McGraw Hill.

Cheasty, M., Clare, A. W., & Collins, C. (2002). Child sexual abuse: A predictor of persistent depression in adult rape and sexual assault victims. *Journal of Mental Health, 11*(1), 79–84.

Chen, E. Y., & Brown, M. (2005). Obesity stigma in sexual relationships. *Obesity Research, 13,* 1393–1397.

Cheng, W., & Warren, M. (2001). She knows more about Hong Kong than you do isn't it: Tags in Hong Kong conversational English. *Journal of Pragmatics, 33,* 1419–1439.

Cherulli, K. C. (2004). *A rough guide on history and human sexuality.* Retrieved January 2, 2008, from http://www.historyofsexuality.com/PrintArticle20.phtml.

Chia, M., & Abrams, D. (1997). *The multiorgasmic man: Sexual secrets every man should know.* San Francisco: HarperCollins.

Chiaradonna, C. (2008). The Chlamydia cascade: Enhanced STD prevention strategies for adolescents. *Journal of Pediatric Adolescent Gynecology, 21*(5), 233–241.

Chin-Hong, P., Berry, J., Cheng, S., Catania, J., DaCosta, M., Darragh, T., et al. (2008). Comparison of patient- and clinician-collected anal cytology samples to screen for human papillomavirus-associated anal intraepithelial neoplasia in men who have sex with men. *Annals of Internal Medicine, 149,* 300–306.

Chmielewski, D. C., Hoffman, C. (2006). Porn industry again at the tech forefront. *Los Angeles Times,* p. A1. Retrieved November 15, 2008, from http://articles.latimes.com/2006/apr/19/business/fi-porn19.

Choi, N. (2004). Sex role group differences in specific, academic, and general self-efficacy. *Journal of Psychology: Interdisciplinary & Applied, 138*(2), 149–159.

Choo, P., Levine, T., & Hatfield, E. (1996). Gender. Love schemas, and reactions to romantic break-ups. *Journal of Social Behavior and Personality, 11,* 143–160.

Chopin-Marcé, M. J. (2001). Exhibitionism and psychotherapy: A case study. *International Journal of Offender Therapy & Comparative Criminology, 45*(5), 626–633.

Chow, E. W., & Choy, A. L. (2002). Clinical characteristics and treatment response to SSRI in a female pedophile. *Archives of Sexual Behavior, 31*(2), 211–215.

Christianson, A. (2005). A re-emergence of reparative therapy. *Contemporary Sexuality, 39*(10), 8–17.

Christensen, A., & Shenk, J. L. (1991). Communication, conflict, and psychological distance in nondistressed, clinic, and divorcing couples. *Journal of Consulting and Clinical Psychology, 59*(3), 458–463.

Christiansen, O. B. (1996). A fresh look at the causes and treatments of recurrent miscarriage, especially its immunological aspects. *Human Reproduction Update, 2*(4), 271–293.

Chudakov, B., Cohen, H., Matar, M., & Kaplan, Z. (2008). A naturalistic prospective open study of the effects of adjunctive therapy of sexual dysfunction in chronic PTSD patients. *Israel Journal of Psychiatry Related Sciences, 45,* 26–32.

Chumlea, W. C., Schubert, C. M., Roche, A. F., Kulin, H. E., Lee, P. A., Himes, J. H., & Sun, S. S. (2003). Age at menarche and racial comparisons in U.S. girls. *Pediatrics, 111,* 110–113.

Cianciotto, J., & Cahill, S. (2006). *Youth in the crosshairs: The third wave of the ex-gay movement.* National Gay and Lesbian Task Force Policy Institute. Retrieved October 2, 2008, from http://www.thetaskforce.org/downloads/reports/reports/YouthInTheCrosshairs.pdf.

Ciesielski, C. A. (2003). STDs in men who have sex with men: An epidemiologic review. *Current Infectious Diseases Report, 5*(2), 145–152.

Cindoglu, D. (1997). Virginity tests and artificial virginity in modern Turkish medicine. *Women's Studies International Forum, 20*(2), 253–261.

Clapp, I., & Lopez, B. (2007). Size at birth, obesity and blood pressure at age five. *Metabolic Syndrome and Related Disorders, 5,* 116–126.

Clapp, J. F. (1996). Morphometric and neurodevelopmental outcome at age five years of the offspring of women who continued to exercise regularly throughout pregnancy. *Journal of Pediatrics, 129*(6), 856–863.

Clark, A. M., Ledger, W., Galletly, C., Tomlinson, L., Blaney, F., Wang, X., & Norman R.J. (1995). Weight loss results in significant improvement in pregnancy and ovulation rates in anovulatory obese women. *Human Reproduction, 10,* 2705–2712.

Clark, J. (2005). The big turnoff. *Psychology Today, 38*(1), 17–19.

Clark, M. S., & Reis, H. T. (1988). Interpersonal processes in close relationships. *Annual Review of Psychology, 39,* 609–672.

Clark, P. M., Atton, C., Law, C. M., Shiell, A., Godfrey, K., & Barker, D. J. (1998). Weight gain in pregnancy, triceps skinfold thickness, and blood pressure in offspring. *Obstetrics and Gynecology, 91*(1), 103–107.

Clarke, A. K., & Miller, S. J. (2001). The debate regarding continuous use of oral contraceptives. *Annals of Pharmacotherapy, 35,* 1480–1484.

Claxton, A., & Perry-Jenkins, M. (2008). No fun anymore: Leisure and marital quality across the transition to parenthood. *Journal of Marriage and Family, 70,* 28–44.

Clayton, A. H. (2008). Symptoms related to the menstrual cycle: Diagnosis, prevalence, and treatment. *Journal of Psychiatric Practices, 14,* 13–21.

Clinical Trials. (2008, August 28). *Evaluate the safety and efficacy of bremelanotide in women with female sexual arousal disorder (FSAD).* National Institutes of Health. Retrieved August 29, 2008, from http://clinicaltrials.gov/ct2/show/NCT00425256?term=female+sexual+arousal+disorder&rank=6.

Clinton, C., & Gillespie, M. (1997). *Sex and race in the early South.* Oxford, England: Oxford University Press.

Cloud, J. (2008, January 28). Are gay relationships different? *Time Magazine, 171,* 78.

Cluver, L., Gardner, F. (2007). Risk and protective factors for psychological well-being of children orphaned by AIDS in Cape Town: A qualitative study of children and caregivers' perspectives. 19(3), 318–325.

Coast, E. (2007). Wasting semen: Context and condom use among the Maasai. *Culture, Health and Sexuality, 9,* 387–401.

Coates, R. (2004). Australia. In R. T. Francoeur & R. J. Noonan (Eds.), *The Continuum international encyclopedia of sexuality* (pp. 27–41). New York/London: Continuum International.

Coccia, M., & Rizzello, F. (2008). Ovarian reserve. Assessment of human reproductive function. *Annals of the New York Academy of Science, 1127,* 27–30.

Coccia, M., Rizzello, F., Cammilli, F., Bracco, G., & Scarselli, G. (2008). Endometriosis and infertility surgery and ART: An integrated approach for successful management. *European Journal of Obstetrics, Gynecology, and Reproductive Biology, 138,* 54–59.

Cochran, B. M., Ginzler, J., & Cauce, A. (2002). Challenges faced by homeless sexual minorities: Comparison of gay, lesbian, bisexual, and transgendered homeless sexual minorities with their heterosexual counterparts. *Journal of Public Health, 92,* 773–777.

Cochran, S. D., & Mays, V. M. (2000). Lifetime prevalence of suicide symptoms and affective disorders among men reporting samesex sexual partners: Results from NHANES III. *American Journal of Public Health, 90*(4), 573–578.

Cohan, C., & Kleinbaum, S. (2002). Toward a greater understanding of the cohabitation effect. *Journal of Marriage and Family, 64*(1), 180–193.

Cohen, C., Brandhorst, B., Nagy, A., Leader, A., Dickens, B., Isasi, R., Evans, D., & Knoppers, B. (2008). The use of fresh embryos in stem cell research: Ethical and policy issues. *Cell Stem Cell, 2,* 416–421.

Cohen, F., Kemeny, M., Kearney, K., Zegans, L., Neuhaus, J., & Conant, M. (1999). Persistent stress as a predictor of genital herpes recurrence. *Archives of Internal Medicine, 159,* 2430–2436.

Cohen, J. K., Miller, R. J., Ahmed, S., Lotz, M. J., & Baust, J. (2008). Ten-year biochemical disease control for patients with prostate cancer treated with cryosurgery as primary therapy. *Urology, 71,* 515–518.

Cohen, K. M., & Savin-Williams, R. C. (1996). Developmental perspectives on coming out to self and others. In R. C. Savin-Williams & K. M. Cohen (Eds.), *The lives of lesbians, gays, and bisexuals: Children to adults* (pp. 113–151). Fort Worth, TX: Harcourt Brace.

Cohen, L. (1988). Providing treatment and support for partners of sexual-assault survivors. *Psychotherapy, 25,* 94–98.

Cohen, L., & Roth, S. (1987). The psychological aftermath of rape: Long-term effects and individual differences in recovery. *Journal of Social and Clinical Psychology, 5,* 525–534.

Cohen, L. S., Soares, C., Otto, M., Sweeney, B., Liberman, R., Harlow, B. (2002). Prevalence and predictors of premenstrual dysphoric disorder (PMDD) in older premenopausal women. The Harvard Study of Moods and Cycles. *Journal of Affective Disorders, 70*(2), 125–132.

Cohen, M. S., Hellmann, N., Levy, J. A., Decock, K., & Lange, J. (2008). The spread, treatment, and prevention of HIV-1: Evolution of a global pandemic. *Journal of Clinical Investigation, 118,* 1244–1254.

Cohen, S. A. (2007). New data on abortion incidence, safety illuminate key aspects of worldwide abortion debate. *Guttmacher Policy Review,* 10. Retrieved October 28, 2008, from http://www.guttmacher.org/pubs/gpr/10/4/gpr100402.html.

Cohen-Bendahan, C., van de Beek, C., & Berenbaum, S. (2005). Prenatal sex hormone effects on child and adult sex-typed behavior: Methods and findings. *Neuroscience & Biobehavioral Reviews, 29*(2), 353–384.

Coker, A. L. (2007). Does physical intimate partner violence affect sexual health? A systematic review. *Trauma Violence Abuse, 8,* 149–177.

Coker, A. L., Davis, K. E., Arias, I., Desai, S., Sanderson, M., Brandt, H. M., et al. (2002). Physical and mental health effects of intimate partner violence for men and women. *American Journal of Preventive Medicine, 23*(4), 260–268.

Colapinto, J. (2001). *As nature made him: The boy who was raised as a girl.* New York: HarperCollins.

Coleman, E. (1982). Developmental stages of the coming-out process. *American Behavioral Scientist, 25,* 469–482.

Coleman, E. (2002). Masturbation as a means of achieving sexual health. *Journal of Psychology and Human Sexuality, 14*(2–3), 5–16.

Coleman, E., Gratzer, T., Nesvacil, L., Raymond, N. (2000). Nafazodone and the treatment of nonparaphilic compulsive sexual behavior: A retrospective study. *The Journal of Clinical Psychiatry, 61*(4), 282–285.

Coleman, E., Raymond, N., & McBean, A. (2003). Assessment and treatment of compulsive sexual behavior. *Minnesota Medicine, 86,* 42–47.

Coleman, M., & Ganong, L. H. (1985). Love and sex role stereotypes: Do macho men and feminine women make better lovers? *Journal of Personality & Social Psychology, 49*(1), 170–176.

Coleman, M., Ganong, L., & Fine, M. (2000). Reinvestigating remarriage: Another decade of progress. *Journal of Marriage and Family, 62*(4), 1288–1308.

Coleman, P. (2002). *How to say it for couples.* New York: Prentice Hall Press.

Coles, R., & Stokes, G. (1985). *Sex and the American teenager.* New York: Harper & Row.

Collaborative Group on Hormonal Factors in Breast Cancer. (2001). Familial breast cancer. *The Lancet, 358*(9291), 1389–1399.

Collier, J. F., & Rosaldo, M. Z. (1981). Politics and gender in simple societies. In S. Ortner & H. Whitehead (Eds.), *Sexual meanings* (pp. 275–329). Cambridge, U.K.: Cambridge University Press.

Collins, P. H. (1998). The tie that binds: Race, gender and U.S. violence. *Ethnic and Racial Studies, 21*(5), 917–939.

Collins, P. H. (2000). It's all in the family. *Women and Language, 23*(2), 65–69.

Collins, R. (1988). *Sociology of marriage and the family.* Chicago: Nelson-Hall.

Collins, R. (2005). Sex on television and its impact on American youth: Background and results from the RAND television and adolescent sexuality study. *Child & Adolescent Psychiatric Clinics of North America, 14*(3), 371–385.

Collins, R. L., Ellickson, P. L., & Klein, D. J. (2007). Research report: The role of substance use in young adult divorce. *Addiction, 102,* 786.

Collins, R. L., Elliott, M. N., Berry, S. H., Kanouse, D. E., Kunkel, D., Hunter, S. B., & Miu, A. (2004). Watching sex on television predicts adolescent initiation of sexual behavior. *Pediatrics, 114*(3), 280–289.

Comfort, A. (1987). Deviation and variation. In G. D. Wilson (Ed.), *Variant sexuality: Research and theory* (pp. 1–20). Baltimore: Johns Hopkins University Press.

Comfort, A., & Rubenstein, J. (1992). The new joy of sex: A gourmet guide to lovemaking in the nineties. New York: Simon & Schuster.

Comstock, G., & Paik, H. (1991). *Television and the American child.* San Diego, CA: Academic Press.

Condor, B. (1998, April 2). Romantic Rx Studies link love and intimacy to improved cardiovascular health. *Chicago Tribune* page 3.

ContraVac receives FDA approval for post-vasectomy home sperm test. (2008, March 3). *Reuters.* Received October 28, 2008, from http://www.reuters.com/article/pressRelease/idUS255680+03-Mar-2008+BW20080303.

Conway, A.M. (2005). Girls, aggression, and emotional regulation. *American Journal of Orthopsychiatry, 75*(2), 334–339.

Cooper, A., Delmonico, D., & Burg, R. (2000). Cybersex users, abusers, and compulsives: New findings and implications. *Sexual Addiction and Compulsivity, 7,* 5–29.

Cooper, A., Putnam, D. E., Planchon, L., & Boies, S. C. (1999). Online sexual compulsivity: Getting tangled in the net. *Sexual Addiction & Compulsivity, 6*(2), 79–104.

Cooper, A. M. (1991). The unconscious core of perversion. In G. I. Fogel & W. A. Myers

(Eds.), *Perversions and near-perversions in clinical practice: New psychoanalytic perspectives* (pp. 17–35). New Haven: Yale University Press.

Coordt, A. K. (2005). Young adults of childhood divorce: Intimate relationships prior to marriage. *Dissertation Abstracts International, Section A: Humanities and Social Sciences, 66,* 500.

Corey, L., & Handsfield, H. (2000). Genital herpes and public health. *Journal of the American Medical Association, 283,* 791–794.

Corey, L., Wald, A., Patel, R. Sacks, S., Tyring, S., Warren, T., Douglas, J., Paavonen, J., Morrow, R., Beutner, K., Stratchounsky, L., Mertz, G., Keene, O., Watson, H., Tait, D., & Vargas-Cortes, M. (2004). Once-daily Valacyclovir to reduce the risk of transmission of genital herpes. *The New England Journal of Medicine, 350*(1), 11–20.

Cornett, M., & Shuntich, R. (1991). Sexual aggression: Perceptions of its likelihood of occurring and some correlates of selfadmitted perpetration. *Perceptual & Motor Skills, 73,* 499–507.

Cornog, M. (2003). *The big book of masturbation: From angst to zeal.* San Francisco, CA: Down There Press.

Cornwallis, C. K., Birkhead, T. R. (2008). Plasticity in reproductive phenotypes reveals status-specific correlations between behavioral, morphological, and physiological sexual traits. *Evolution, 62*(5), 1149–1161.

Corso, P., Edwards, V., Fang, X., & Mercy, J. (2008). Health-related quality of life among adults who experience maltreatment during childhood. *American Journal of Public Health, 98,* 1094–1100.

Cortes, J., Antinolo, G., Martinez, L., Cobo, F., Barnie, A., Zapata, A., & Menendez, P. (2007). Spanish stem cell bank interviews examine the interest of couples in donating surplus human IVF embryos for stem cell research. *Cell Stem Cell, 1,* 17–20.

Corty, E. W., & Guardiani, J. M. (2008). Canadian and American sex therapists' perceptions of normal and abnormal ejaculatory latencies: How long should intercourse last? *Journal of Sexual Medicine, 5,* 1251–1256.

Corwin, A. L., Olson, J. G., Omar, M. A., Razaki, A., et al. (1991). HIV-1 in Somalia: Prevalence and knowledge among prostitutes. *AIDS, 5,* 902–904.

Costabile, R., Mammen, T., & Hwang, K. (2008). An overview and expert opinion on the use of alprostadil in the treatment of sexual dysfunction. *Expert Opinions in Pharmacotherapy, 9,* 1421–1429.

Costello, C., Hillis, S. D., Marchbanks, P. A., Jamieson, D. J., & Peterson, H. B. (2002). The effect of interval tubal sterilization on sexual interest and pleasure. *Obstetrics and Gynecology, 100*(3), 511–518.

Couldwell, D. L. (2005). Management of unprotected sexual encounters. *The Medical Journal of Australia, 183*(10), 525–528.

Coulson, N. J. (1979). Regulation of sexual behavior under traditional Islamic law. In Al- Sayyid-Marsot & A. Lutfi (Eds.), *Society and the sexes in medieval Islam* (pp. 63–68). Malibu, CA: Undena Publications.

Courtenay, W. H. (2000). Behavioral factors associated with disease, injury, and death among men: Evidence and implications for prevention. *The Journal of Men's Studies, 9*(1), 81–142.

Covey, H. C. (1989). Perceptions and attitudes toward sexuality of the elderly during the Middle Ages. *The Gerontologist, 29,* 93–100.

Cowan, G. (1992). Feminist attitudes toward pornography control. *Psychology of Women Quarterly,* 165–177.

Cowan, G. (2000). Beliefs about the causes of four types of rape. *Sex Roles, 42*(9–10), 807–823.

Cox, B., Sneyd, M., Paul, C., Delahunt, B., & Skegg, D. (2002). Vasectomy and risk of prostate cancer. *Journal of the American Medical Association, 287,* 3110–3115.

Cramer, R., Golom, F., LoPresto, C., & Kirkley, S. (2008). Weighing the evidence: Empirical assessment and ethical implications of conversion therapy. *Ethics & Behavior, 18,* 93–114.

Cranberry and urinary tract infection. (2005). *Drug Therapy Bulletin, 43*(3), 17–19.

Crawford, A. (2008, July 13). Male fertility options growing. *Chicago Tribune.* Retrieved July 29, 2008, from http://www.chicagotribune.com/features/lifestyle/chi-0713-guy-birth-control-for-mjul13,0,1337399.story.

Crawford, J. T., Leynes, P. A., Mayhorn, C. B., & Bink, M .L. (2004). Champagne, beer, or coffee? A corpus of gender-related and neutral words. *Behavior Research Methods, Instruments & Computers, 36*(3), 444–459.

Crawford, M. (2006). *Transformations: Women, Gender & Psychology.* New York: McGraw-Hill.

Critelli, J. W., Myers, E. J., & Loos, V. E. (1986). The components of love: Romantic attraction and sex role orientation. *Journal of Personality, 54*(2), 354–370.

Crittenden, A. (2001). *The price of motherhood.* New York: Metropolitan Books.

Crosby, R., & Danner, F. (2008). Adolescents' STD protective attitudes predict sexually transmitted disease acquisition in early adulthood. *Journal of School Health, 78,* 310–313.

Crosby, R., Diclemente, R. (2004). Use of recreational Viagra among men having sex with men. *Sexually Transmitted Infections, 80,* 466–468.

Crosby, R., Diclemente, R., Wingood, G., Salazar, L., Lang, D., Rose, E., et al. (2008). Co-occurrence of intoxication during sex and sexually transmitted infections among young African American women: Does partner intoxication matter? *Sexual Health, 5,* 285–289.

Crosby, R., Milhausen, R., Yarber, W., Sanders, S., & Graham, C. (2008). Condom "turn offs" among adults: An exploratory study. *International Journal of STDs and AIDS, 19,* 590–594.

Crosnoe, R., Frank, K., & Mueller, A. S. (2008). Gender, body size and social relations in American high schools. *Social Forces, 86,* 1189–1217.

Cross, P., & Matheson, K. (2006). Understanding sadomasochism: An empirical examination of four perspectives. *Journal of Homosexuality, 50,* 133–166.

Crow, S., Agras, W., Crosby, R., Halmi, K., Mitchell, J. (2008). Eating disorder symptoms in pregnancy: A prospective study. *International Journal of Eating Disorders, 41,* 277–279.

Crowder, K. D., & Tolnay, S. E. (2000). A new marriage squeeze for black women: The role of racial intermarriage by black men. *Journal of Marriage and Family, 62*(3), 792–817.

Crum, N., Riffenburgh, R., Wegner, S., Agan, B., Tasker, S., Spooner, K., et al., and the Triservice AIDS Clinical Consortium. (2006). Comparisons of causes of death and mortality rates among HIV-infected patients. Analysis of the pre-, early, and late HAART (highly active antiretroviral therapy) eras. *Journal of Acquired Immune Deficiency Syndromes, 41,* 194–200.

Cruz, J. M. (2003). "Why doesn't he just leave?": Gay male domestic violence and the reasons victims stay. *Journal of Men's Studies, 11,* 309.

Cullinan, K. (2003). Swaziland grapples with AIDS. Retrieved August 29, 2003, from http://www.csa.za.org/article/articleview/194/1/1/.

Cunningham, G. B. (2008). Creating and sustaining gender diversity in sport organizations. *Sex Roles, 58,* 136–145.

Cusitar, L. (1994). *Strengthening the link: Stopping the violence.* Toronto: Disabled Women's Network.

Cyr, M., Wright, J., McDuff, P., & Perron, A. (2002). Intrafamilial sexual abuse. *Child Abuse and Neglect, 26*(9), 957–973.

d'Amora, D., & Hobson, B. (2003). Sexual offender treatment. Retrieved March 31, 2003, from http://www.smith-lawfirm.com/Connsacs_ offender_treatment.htm.

D'Augelli, A., Grossman, A., & Starks, M. (2005). Parents' awareness of lesbian, gay, and bisexual youths' sexual orientation. *Journal of Marriage & Family, 67*(2), 474–482.

D'Augelli, A. R. (2005). Stress and adaptation among families of lesbian, gay, and bisexual youth: Research challenges. *Journal of GLBT Family Studies, 1,* 115–135.

D'Augelli, A. R., Grossman, A. H., Hershberger, S., & O'Connell, T. (2001). Aspects of mental health among older lesbian, gay, and bisexual adults. *Aging and Mental Health, 5,* 149–158.

D'Augelli, A. R., Grossman, A., Salter, N., Vasey, J., Starks, M., & Sinclair, K. (2005). Predicting the suicide attempts of lesbian, gay, and bisexual youth. *Suicide and Life-Threatening Behavior, 35,* 646–660.

D'Augelli, A. R., Grossman, A. H., & Starks, M. (2006). Childhood gender atypicality, victimization, and PTSD among lesbian, gay, and bisexual youth. *Journal of Interpersonal Violence, 21,* 1462–1482.

D'Augelli, A. R., Rendian, J., Sinclair, K., & Grossman, A. (2007). Lesbian and gay youth's aspirations for marriage and raising children. *Journal of LGBT Issues in Counseling, 1*(4), 77–98.

D'Emilio, J. (1998). *Sexual politics, sexual communities.* Chicago: University of Chicago Press.

D'Emilio, J., & Freedman, E. (1988). *Intimate matters: A history of sexuality in America.* New York: Harper & Row.

D'Hauwers, K., & Tjalma, W. (2008). HPV in men. *European Journal of Gynecological Oncology, 29,* 338–340.

D'Souza, G., Kreimer, A., Viscidi, R., Pawlita, M., Fakhry, C., Koch, W., et al. (2007). Case-control study of human papillomavirus and oropharyngeal cancer. *New England Journal of Medicine, 356,* 1944–1956.

Dade, L. R., & Sloan, L. R. (2000). An investigation of sex-role stereotypes in African Americans. *Journal of Black Studies, 30*(5), 676.

Dagg, P. K. B. (1991). The psychological sequelae of therapeutic abortion—denied and completed. *American Journal of Psychiatry, 148,* 578–585.

Dahl, A., Bremnes, R., Dahl, O., Klepp, O., Wist, E., & Fossa, S. (2007). Is the sexual function compromised in long-term testicular cancer survivors? *European Urology, 52,* 1438–1447.

Daie, N., Wilztum, E., & Eleff, M. (1989). Longterm effects of sibling incest. *Journal of Clinical Psychiatry, 50,* 428–431.

Dalla, R. L. (2002). Night moves: A qualitative investigation of street-level sex work. *Psychology of Women Quarterly, 26*(1), 63–74.

Daltveit, A., Tollances, M., Pihlstrom, H., & Irgens, L. (2008). Cesarean delivery and subsequent pregnancies. *Obstetrics and Gynecology, 111,* 1327–1334.

Dancey, C. P. (1990). Sexual orientation in women: An investigation of hormonal and personality variables. *Biological Psychology, 30,* 251–264.

Daneback, K., Mansson, S., & Ross, M. (2007). Using the Internet to find offline sex partners. *Cyberpsychological Behavior, 10,* 100–107.

Daniels M. C., Adair, L. S. (2005). Breast-feeding influences cognitive development in Filipino children. *Journal of Nutrition, 135*(11), 2589–2595.

Daragahi, B., & Dubin, A. (2001). Can prenups be romantic? *Money, 30*(2), 30–38.

Darcangelo, S. (2008). Fetishism: Psychopathology and theory. In D. Laws & W. O'Donohue (Eds.), *Sexual deviance: Theory, assessment and treatment* (2nd ed., pp. 108–118). New York: Guilford Press.

Dare, R. O., Oboro, V. O., Fadiora, S. O., Orji, E. O., Sule-Edu, A. O., & Olabode, T. O. (2004). Female genital mutilation: An analysis of 522 cases in South-Western Nigeria. *Journal of Obstetrics & Gynaecology, 24*(3), 281–283.

Das, A. (2007). Masturbation in the United States. *Journal of Sex and Marital Therapy, 33,* 301–317.

Date rape drug served at Colorado fraternity parties: One dose potentially fatal, investigation finds. (2005). Retrieved December 3, 2005, from http://www.thedenverchannel.com/news/5068195/detail.html.

Davidsen, L., Vistulien, B., & Kastrup, A. (2007). Impact of the menstrual cycle on determinants of energy balance: A putative role in weight loss attempts. *International Journal of Obesity, 31,* 1777–1785.

Davidson, J. (2002). Working with polyamorous clients in the clinical setting. *Electronic Journal of Human Sexuality, 5.* Retrieved September 13, 2008, from http://www.ejhs.org/volume5/polyoutline.html.

Davidson, J., Moore, N., & Ullstrup, K. (2004). Religiosity and sexual responsibility: Relationships of choice. *American Journal of Health Behavior, 28*(4), 335–346.

Davies, K. A. (1997). Voluntary exposure to pornography and men's attitudes toward feminism and rape. *Journal of Sex Research, 34*(2), 131–138.

Davies, M., Boulle, A., Fakir, T., Nuttall, J., Eley B. (2008). Adherence to antiretroviral therapy in young children in Cape Town, South Africa, measured by medication return and caregiver self-report: a prospective cohort study. *BMC Pediatrics, 4*(8), 34.

Davis, K. E., & Latty-Mann, H. (1987). Love styles and relationship quality: A contribution to validation. *Journal of Social & Personal Relationships, 4*(4), 409–428.

Davis, K. E., & Todd, M. J. (1982). Friendship and love relationships. *Advances in Descriptive Psychology, 2,* 79–122.

Davis, S., Papalia, M., Norman, R., O'Neill, S., Redelman, M., Williamson, M., et al. (2008). Safety and efficacy of a testosterone metered-dose transdermal spray for treating decreased sexual satisfaction in premenopausal women: A randomized trial. *Annals of Internal Medicine, 15,* 569–577.

Davis, S. M., & Greenstein, T. N. (2007). Effects of union type on division of household labor. *Journal of Family Issues, 28,* 1246–1272.

Davis, S. R., Davison, S. L., Donath, S., & Bell, R. J. (2005). Circulating androgen levels and self-reported sexual function in women. *Journal of the American Medical Association, 294*(1), 91–96.

Daw, J. (2002). Hormone therapy for men? *Monitor on Psychology, 33*(9), 53.

Dawar, A. (2006, November 28). British scientists invent male pill. *Telegraph.* Retrieved October 28, 2008, from http://www.telegraph.co.uk/news/migrationtemp/1535304/British-scientists-invent-male-pill.html.

DeAmicis, L. A., Goldberg, D. C., LoPiccolo, J., Friedman, J., & Davies, L. (1985). Clinical follow-up of couples treated for sexual dysfunction. *Archives of Sexual Behavior, 14,* 467–489.

DeAngelis, T. (2002). New data on lesbian, gay, bisexual mental health. *Monitor on Psy-*

chology, 33. Retrieved May 26, 2008, from http://www.apa.org/monitor/feb02/new-data.html.

de Beauvoir, S. (1952). *The second sex.* New York: Vintage Books.

DeBellis, M. D., Keshavan, M. S., Beers, S. R., Hall, J., Frustaci, K., Masalehdan, A., et al. (2001) Sex differences in brain maturation during childhood and adolescence. *Cerebral Cortex, 11*(6), 552-557.

Decker, M., Raj, A., Gupta, J., & Silverman, J. (2008). Sex purchasing and associations with HIV/STI among a clinic-based sample of U.S. men. *Journal of Acquired Immune Deficiency Syndrome, 48*(3), 355–359.

DeCuypere, G., T'Sjoen, G., Beerten, R., Selvaggi, G., Sutter, P., Hoebeke, P., et al. (2005). Sexual and physical health after sex reassignment surgery. *Archives of Sexual Behavior, 34,* 679–690.

Deepinder, R., Makker, K., Agarwal, A. (2007). Cell Phones and Male Infertility: Dissecting the Relationship. *Reproductive BioMedicine Online, 15*(3), 266–270.

de Freitas, S. (2004). Brazil. In R. T. Francoeur & R. J. Noonan (Eds.), *The Continuum complete international encyclopedia of sexuality* (pp. 98–113). New York/London: Continuum International.

Degges-White, S., & Marszalek, J. (2008). An exploration of long-term, same-sex relationships: Benchmarks, perceptions, and challenges. *Journal of Lesbian, Gay, Bisexual, and Transgendered Issues in Counseling, 1,* 99–119.

DeGue, S., & DiLillo, D. (2005). "You would if you loved me": Toward an improved conceptual and etiological understanding of nonphysical male sexual coercion. *Aggression & Violent Behavior, 10*(4), 513–532.

DeJonge, A., Teunissen, D., van Diem, M., Scheepers, P., & Lagro-Janssen, A. (2008). Woman's positions during the second stage of labour: Views of primary care midwives. *Journal of Advanced Nursing, 63,* 347–356.

DeLamater, J. (1987). A sociological approach. In J. H. Geer & W. T. O'Donohue (Eds.), *Theories of human sexuality* (pp. 237–253). New York: Plenum Press.

DeLamater, J. D. (1989). The social control of human sexuality. In K. McKinney & S. Sprecher (Eds.), *Human sexuality* (p. 30–62). Norwood, NJ: Ablex.

DeLange, J. (1995). Gender and communication in social work education: A cross-cultural perspective. *Journal of Social Work Education, 31*(1), 75–82.

Deligeoroglou, E., Michailidis, E., & Creatsas, G. (2003). Oral contraceptives and reproductive system cancer. *Annals of New York Academy of Science, 997,* 199–208.

Deliramich, A., Gray, M. (2008). Changes in women's sexual behavior following sexual assault. *Behavior Modification, 32*(5), 611–621.

Delmonico, D. L., Griffin, E. J. (2008). Cybersex and the e-teen: What marriage and family therapists should know. *Journal of Marital and Family Therapy, 34*(4), 431–444.

Dempster, C. (2002). Silent war on South African women. Retrieved April 10, 2003, from www.new.bbc.co.uk/hi/english/world/africa/newsid_190900011909220.stm.

Dennerstein, L., Dudley, E., Guthrie, J., & Barrett-Connor, E. (2000). Life satisfaction, symptoms, and the menopausal transition. *Medscape Women's Health, 5*(4), E4.

Dennison, S. M., & Tomson, D. M. (2005). Criticisms of plaudits for stalking laws? What psycholegal research tells us about proscribing stalking. *Psychology, Public Policy, & Law, 11*(3), 384–406.

Denny, D., & Wiederman, M. W. (2004). A chorus of transgender voices. *Journal of Sex Research, 41*(4), 410–412.

DePineres, T. (2002). Reproductive health 2002: Update on contraception and medical abortion from the ARHD Annual Meeting. *Medscape Ob/Gyn and Women's Health, 7*(2). Retrieved May 20, 2003, from http://www. medscape.com/viewarticle/442100.

Derbyshire, E., & Abdul, S. (2008). Habitual caffeine intake in women of childbearing age. *Journal of Human Nutrition and Dietetics, 21,* 159–164.

Derry, P. S. (2007). Is menstruation obsolete? *British Medical Journal, 334*(7600), 955.

de-Schampheleire, D. (1990). MMPI characteristics of professional prostitutes: A cross-cultural replication. *Journal of Personality Assessment, 54,* 343–350.

DeSteno, D., Barlett, M. T., Braverman, J., & Salovey, P. (2002). Sex differences in jealousy: Evolutionary mechanism or artifact of measurement? *Journal of Personality and Social Psychology, 83*(5), 1103–116.

Devdas, N., & Rubin, L. (2007). Rape myth acceptance among first-and second-generation south Asian American women. *Sex Roles, 56,* 701–705.

deVisser, R., & McDonald, D. (2007). Swings and roundabouts: Management of jealousy in heterosexual "swinging" couples. *British Journal of Social Psychology, 46,* 459–476.

deVries, B., Croghan, C., & Worman, T. (2006). Always independent, never alone: Serving the needs of gay and lesbian elders. *Journal on Active Aging, 5,* 44–47.

Devroey, P., & Van Steirteghem, A. (2004). A review of ten years experience of ICSI. *Human Reproduction Update, 10,* 19–28.

Diamanduros, T., Jenkins, S. J., & Downs, E. (2007). Analysis of technology ownership and selective use among undergraduates. *College Student Journal, 41,* 970–976.

Diamanti-Kandarakis, E. (2007). Role of obesity and adiposity in polycystic ovary syndrome. *International Journal of Obesity, 31,* s8–s13.

Diamond, C., Thiede, H., Perdue, T., Secura, G. M., Valleroy, L., Mackellar, D., Corey, L., & Seattle Young Men's Survey Team. (2003). Viral hepatitis among young men who have sex with men: Prevalence of infection, risk behaviors, and vaccination. *Sexually Transmitted Diseases, 30*(5), 424–432.

Diamond, L., Earle, D., Heiman, J., Rosen, R., Perelman, M., & Harning, R. (2006). An effect on the subjective sexual response in premenopausal women with sexual arousal disorder by bremelanotide (PT-141), a melanocortin receptor agonist. *Journal of Sexual Medicine, 3,* 628–638.

Diamond, L. M. (2000). Sexual identity, attractions, and behavior among young sexual minority women over a 2-year period. *Developmental Psychology, 36*(2), 241–250.

Diamond, L. M. (2005). A new view of lesbian subtypes: Stable versus fluid identity trajectories over an 8-year period. *Psychology of Women Quarterly, 29*(2), 119–128.

Diamond, M. (1993). Homosexuality and bisexuality in different populations. *Archives of Sexual Behavior, 22,* 291–310.

Diamond, M., & Diamond, G. H. (1986). Adolescent sexuality: Biosocial aspects and intervention. In P. Allen-Meares & D. A. Shore (Eds.), *Adolescent sexualities: Overviews and principles of intervention* (pp. 3–13). New York: Haworth Press.

Diamond, M., & Sigmundson, H. K. (1997). Sex reassignment at birth: Long-term review and clinical implications. *Archives of Pediatric Medicine, 151,* 290–297.

Diaz, R. M., Ayala, G., Bein, E., Henne, J., & Marin, B. V. (2001). The impact on homophobia, poverty, and racism on the mental health of gay and bisexual Latino men. *American Journal of Public Health, 41*(6), 927–933.

Dibble, S. L., & Swanson, J. M. (2000). Gender differences for the predictors of depression in young adults with genital herpes. *Public Health Nursing, 17*(3), 187–194.

Dickinson, A. (2001, July 23). Take a pass on the postnup: The latest trend in marriage is to negotiate your divorce in advance. *Time, 148*(3), 73.

Dickinson, L. M., DeGruy, F. U. III, Dickinson, W. P., & Candib, L. M. (1999). Health related quality of life and symptom profiles of female survivors of sexual abuse. *Archives of Family Medicine, 8*(1), 35–43.

Dietz, H. P. (2006). Pelvic floor trauma following vaginal delivery. *Current Opinions in Obstetrics and Gynecology, 18,* 528–537.

Dill, K. E., & Thill, K. P. (2007). Video game characters and the socialization of gender roles. *Sex Roles, 57,* 851–865.

Dimah, K., & Dimah, A. (2004). Intimate relationships and sexual attitudes of older African American men and women. *The Geronotologist, 44,* 612–613.

diMauro, D. (1995). *Sexuality research in the United States: An assessment of the social and behavioral sciences.* New York: Social Science Research Council.

DiNapoli, L., & Capel, B. (2008). SRY and the standoff in sex determination. *Molecular Endocrinology, 22,* 1–9.

Dindia, K. (2002). Self-disclosure research: Knowledge through meta-analysis. In M. Allen & R. W. Preiss (Eds.), *Interpersonal communication research: Advances through meta-analysis* (pp. 169–185). Mahwah, NJ: Erlbaum.

Dindia, K., & Allen, M. (2006). Sex differences in self-disclosure: A meta-analysis. *Psychological Bulletin, 112,* 106–124.

Dindia, K. & Canary, D.J. (2006). (Eds.), *Sex differences and similarities in communication* (2nd. ed.). Mahwah, NJ: Erlbaum.

Dindyal, S. (2004). The sperm count has been decreasing steadily for many years in Western industrialised countries: Is there an endocrine basis for this decrease? *The Internet Journal of Urology 2*(1). Retrieved December 18, 2008, from http://www.is-pub.com/ostia/index.php?xmlFilePath=journals/iju/vol2n1/sperm.xml.

Dion, K. L., & Dion, K. K. (1988). Romantic love: Individual and cultural perspectives. In R. J. Sternberg & R.J. Barnes (Eds.), *Psychology of love* (pp. 264–289). New Haven, CT: Yale University Press.

Dittmann, M. (2005). Getting prostitutes off the streets. *Monitor on Psychology, 35*(9), 71.

Dittmar, M. (2000). Age at menarche in a rural Aymara-speaking community located at high altitude in northern Chile. *Mankind Quarterly, 40*(4), 38–52.

Dixit, A. K., & Pindyck, R. S. (1994). *Investment under uncertainty.* Princeton, NJ: Princeton University Press.

Dixon, R. (2005). Controversy in South Africa over device to snare rapists. Retrieved October 19, 2005, from http://www.smh.com.au/news/world/controversy-in-south-africa-over-device-to-snare-rapists/2005/09/01/1125302683893.html.

Docimo, S. G., Silver, R. S., & Cromie, W. (2000, November 1). The undescended testicle: Diagnosis and management. Retrieved April 10, 2005, from http://www.aafp.org/afp/ 20001101/2037.html.

Docter, R. F. (1988). *Transvestites and transsexuals: Mixed views.* Los Angeles, CA: Delacorte.

Dodson, B. (1993). *Sex for one: The joy of selfloving.* New York: Crown.

Dolnick, S. (2007, December 31). India leads way in making commercial surrogacy a viable industry. *Hartford Courant,* p. A3.

Donnan, H. (1988). *Marriage among Muslims: Preference and choice in Northern Pakistan.* New York: E. J. Brill.

Donnelly, D. A., & Burgess, E. O. (2008). The decision to remain in an involuntarily celibate relationship. *Journal of Marriage and Family, 70,* 519–536.

Donovan, K., Taliaferro, L., Alvarez, E., Jacobsen, P., Roetzheim, R., & Wenham, R. (2007). Sexual health in women treated for cervical cancer: Characteristics and correlates. *Gynecological Oncology, 104,* 428–434.

Donovan, R. (2007). To blame or not to blame: Influences of target race and observer sex on rape blame attribution. *Journal of Interpersonal Violence, 22,* 772.

Dooley, S.W. (2008). Recommendations for partner services programs for HIV infection, syphilis, gonorrhea, and chlamydial infection. *Morbidity and Mortality Weekly, 57*(RR09), 1–63.

Dorfman, L. E., Derish, P. A., & Cohen, J. B. (1992). Hey girlfriend: An evaluation of AIDS prevention among women in the sex industry. *Health Education Quarterly, 19,* 25–40.

Dorgan, M. (2001, June 13). New divorce laws in China give rise to spying. *Hartford Courant,* A13.

Dorner, G. (1978). Hormones and sexual differentiation of the brain. Ciba Foundation Symposium, Mar 14–16, (62), 81–112.

Dorr, C. (2001). Listening to men's stories: Overcoming obstacles to intimacy from childhood. *Families in Society, 82,* 509–515.

Douglas, J., & Olshaker, M. (1998). *Obsession.* Sydney: Pocket Books.

Douglas, M., & Swenerton, J. (2002). Epidural anesthesia in three parturients with lumbar tattoos: A review of possible implications. *Canadian Journal of Anesthesia, 49,* 1057–1060.

Douglas, N., Kemp, S., Aggleton, P., & Warwick, I. (2001). The role of external professionals in education about sexual orientation—towards good practice. *Sex Education, 1*(2), 149–162.

Downs, D. A. (1989). *The new politics of pornography.* Chicago: The University of Chicago Press.

Doyle, D. (2005). Ritual male circumcision: A brief history. *Journal of the Royal College of Physicians, 35,* 279–285. Retrieved April 8, 2008, from http://www.rcpe.ac.uk/publications/articles/journal_35_3/doyle_circumcision.pdf.

Doyle, R. (2005). Gay and lesbian census. *Scientific American, 292*(3), 28.

Dr. Kinsey Is Dead; Sex Researcher, 62: Dr. Alfred C. Kinsey Dies at 62; Did Research on Sex Behavior. (1956, August 26). *New York Times.* Retrieved January 26, 2008, from ProQuest Historical Newspapers, *The New York Times* (1851–2004) database. (Document ID: 91647143).

Draganowski, L. (2004). Unlocking the closet door: The coming out process of gay male adolescents. *Dissertation Abstracts International, 64*(11-B). (#0419-4217)

Drain, P. K., Halperin, D. T., Hughes, J. P., Klausner, J. D., & Bailey, R. C. (2006). Male circumcision, religion, and infections diseases: An ecologic analysis of 118 developing countries. *BMC Infectious Diseases, 6,* 172.

Drenth, J. J., & Slob, A. K. (2004). Netherlands and the autonomous Dutch Antilles. In R. T. Francoeur & R. J. Noonan (Eds.), *The Continuum international encyclopedia of sexuality* (pp. 725–751). New York/London: Continuum International.

Drew, P. E. (2004). Iran. In The International Encyclopedia of Sexuality. In R. T. Francoeur & R. J. Noonan (Eds.), *The Continuum international encyclopedia of sexuality* (pp. 554–568). New York/London: Continuum International.

Dubuc, S., & Coleman, D. (2007). An increase in the sex ratio of births to India-born mothers in England and Wales: Evidence for sex-selective abortion. *Population and Development Review, 33,* 383–400.

Duck, S., & Pittman, G. (1994). Social and personal relationships. In M. L. Knapp & G. R. Miller (Eds.), *Handbook of interpersonal communication* (2nd ed., 655–686.). Newbury Park, CA: Sage.

Duffy, J., Warren, K., & Walsh, M. (2001). Classroom interactions: Gender of teacher, gender of student and classroom subject. *Sex Roles, 45*(9–10), 579–593.

Dumond, R., & Dumond, D. (2002). The treatment of sexual assault victims. In C. Hensley (Ed.), *Prison sex: Practice and policy* (pp. 67–87). Boulder, CO: Lynne Reinner.

Dunbar, R. (1998). *Grooming, gossip, and the evolution of language.* Boston: Harvard University Press.

Dunham, C., Myers, F., McDougall, A., & Barnden, N. (1992). *Mamatoto: A celebration of birth.* New York: Penguin Group.

Dunkley, C. (2005). Rape as a method of torture. *British Journal of Guidance & Counselling, 33*(1), 142–143.

Dunn, M. E., Cutler, N. (2000). Sexual issues in older adults. *AIDS Patient Care and STDs, 14*(2), 67–69.

Dunn, M. E., & Trost, J. E. (1989). Male multiple orgasms: A descriptive study. *Archives of Sexual Behavior, 18,* 377–387.

Dunne, E. (2007). *Genital warts.* U.S. Centers for Disease Control, Division of STD Prevention. Retrieved September 17, 2008, from http://www.cdc.gov/vaccines/recs/acip/downloads/mtg-slides-oct07/23HPV.pdf.

Dunne, E., Chapin, J., Rietmeijer, C., Kent, C., Ellen, J., Gaydos, C., et al. (2008). Rate and predictors of repeat *Chlamydia trachomatis* infection among men. *Sexually Transmitted Diseases 35(11* Suppl), 540–4.

Dunne, E., Nielson, C., Stone, K., Markowitz, L., Giuliano, A. (2006). Prevalence of HPV infection among men: A systematic review of the literature. *Journal of Infectious Diseases, 194,* 1044–1054.

Dunne, E. F., Unger, E. R., Sternberg, M., McQuillan, G., Swan, D. C., Patel, S. S., Markowitz, L. E. (2007). Prevalence of HPV infection among females in the United States. *Journal of the American Medical Association, 297,* 813–819.

Dunson, D. B., Colombo, B., & Baird, D. D. (2002). Changes with age in the level of duration of fertility in the menstrual cycle. *Human Reproduction, 17*(5), 1399–1403.

Dupre, M. E., & Meadows, S. O. (2007). Disaggregating the effects of marital trajectories on health. *Journal of Family Issues, 28,* 623–652.

Durex.com. (2007). *Sexual wellbeing global study 2007–2008.* Retrieved on January 20, 2008, from http://durex.com/cm/sexual_wellbeing_globeflash.asp.

Durham, L., Veltman, L., Davis, P., Ferguson, L., Hacker, M., Hooker, D., et al. (2008). Standardizing criteria for scheduling elective labor inductions. *American Journal of Maternal Child Nursing, 33,* 159–165.

Durkin, K. (1985). *Television, sex roles, and children.* Milton Keynes, UK: Open University Press.

Dush, C., & Amato, P. R. (2005). Consequences of relationship status and quality for subjective well-being. *Journal of Social and Personal Relationships, 22,* 607.

Dworkin, A. (1981). *Pornography: Men possessing women.* New York: Putnam.

Dworkin, A. (1987). *Intercourse.* New York: The Free Press.

Dwyer, S. M., & Amberson, J. I. (1989). Behavioral patterns and personality characteristics of 56 sex offenders: A preliminary study. *Journal of Psychology and Human Sexuality, 2,* 105–118.

Dzelme, K., & Jones, R. A. (2001). Male crossdressers in therapy: A solution-focused perspective for marriage and family therapists. *American Journal of Family Therapy, 29,* 293–305.

Eaker, E. D., Sullivan, L. M., Kelly-Hayes, M., D'Agostino, R. B., Sr., & Benjamin, E. J. (2007). Marital status, marital strain and the risk of coronary heart disease or total mortality: The Framingham Offspring Study. *Psychosomatic Medicine, 69,* 509–513.

Earle, R. H., & Crow, G. M. (1990). Sexual addiction: Understanding and treating the phenomenon. *Contemporary Family Therapy, 12,* 89–104.

Earls, C. M., & David, H. (1989). A psychosocial study of male prostitution. *Archives of Sexual Behavior, 18,* 401–419.

Eaton, D. K., Kann, L., Kinchen, S., Ross, J., Hawkins, J., Harris, W., et al. (2006, June 9). Youth risk behavior surveillance—United States, 2005. Surveillance Summaries. *Morbidity and Mortality Weekly Report,* 55(no. SS-5). Hyattsville, MD: U.S. Department of Health and Human Services, Centers for Disease Control. Retrieved September 2, 2008, from http://www.cdc.gov/mmwr/PDF/SS/SS5505.pdf.

Eaton, L., Kaufman, M., Fuhrel, A., Cain, D., Cherry, C., Pope, H., & Kalichman, S. (2008). Examining factors co-existing with interpersonal violence in lesbian relationships. *Journal of Family Violence, 23,* 697–706.

Eckstein, D., & Goldman, A. (2001). The couples' gender-based communication questionnaire. *Family Journal of Counseling and Therapy for Couples and Families, 9*(1), 62–74.

Economos, C. D., Hildebrandt, M., & Hyatt, R. (2008). College freshman stress and weight change: Differences by age. *American Journal of Health Behavior, 32,* 16–26.

Edwards, A. T. (1997). Let's stop ignoring our gay and lesbian youth. *Educational Leadership, 54*(7), 68–71.

Edwards, R. (1998). The effects of gender, gender role, and values. *Journal of Language and Social Psychology, 17*(1),52–72.

Edwards, R., & Hamilton, M. A. (2004). You need to understand my gender role: An empirical test of Tannen's model of gender and communication. *Sex Roles, 50*(7–8), 491–504.

Egolf, B., Lasker, J., Wolf, S., & Potvin, L. (1992). The Roseto effect: A 50-year comparison of mortality rates. *American Journal of Public Health, 82*(8), 1089–1092.

Ehrich, K., Williams, C., Farsides, B., Sandall, J., & Scott, R. (2007). Choosing embryos: Ethical complexity and relational autonomy in staff accounts of PGD. *Sociology of Health and Illness, 29,* 1091–1106.

Einsiedel, E. (1989). Social science and public policy: Looking at the 1986 commission on pornography. In S. Gubar & J. Hoff (Eds.), *For adult users only* (pp. 87–107). Bloomington: Indiana University Press.

Eisenberg, M. (2001). Differences in sexual risk behaviors between college students with same-sex and opposite-sex experience. *Archives of Sexual Behavior, 30*(6), 575–589.

Eiser, J. R., & Ford, N. (1995). Sexual relationships or holiday: A case of situational disinhibition? *Journal of Social and Personal Relationships, 12,* 323–339.

Eisinger, F., & Burke, W. (2002). Breast cancer and breastfeeding. *Lancet, 360*(9328), 187–195.

Elford, J. (2006). Changing patterns of sexual behaviour in the era of highly active anti-retroviral therapy. *Current Opinions in Infectious Disease, 19*(1), 26–32.

Elford, J., Bolding, G., Maguire, M., & Sherr, L. (2000). *Combination therapies for HIV and sexual risk behavior among gay men.* Journal of Acquired Immune Deficiency Syndrome, 23, 266–271.

Elford, J., & Hart, G. (2005). HAART, viral load and sexual risk behavior. *AIDS, 19,* 205–207.

Elias, M. (2007, February 11). Gay teens coming out earlier to peers and family. *USA Today.* Retrieved October 2, 2008, from http://www.usatoday.com/news/nation/2007-02-07-gay-teens-cover_x.htm.

Eliason, M. J. (1997). The prevalence and nature of biphobia in heterosexual undergraduate students. *Archives of Sexual Behavior, 26,*(3), 317–326.

Elifson, K. W., Boles, J., Posey, E., Sweat, M., et al. (1993). Male transvestite prostitutes and HIV risk. *American Journal of Public Health, 83,* 260–261.

Ellen-Rinsza, M., & Kirk, G. M. (2005). Common medical problems of the college student. *Pediatric Clinics of North America, 52*(1), 9–24.

Ellertson, C., Evans, M., Ferden, S., Leadbetter, C., Spears, A., Johnstone, K., & Trussell, J. (2003). Extending the time limit for starting the Yuzpe regimen of emergency contraception to 120 hours. *Obstetrics & Gynecology, 101,* 1168–1171.

Elliott, H. (2002). Premenstrual dysphoric disorder: A guide for the treating physician. *North Carolina Medicine Journal, 63*(2), 72–75.

Elliott, L., & Brantley, C. (1997). *Sex on campus.* New York: Random House.

Elliott, S., & Umberson, D. (2008). The performance of desire: Gender and sexual negotiation in long-term marriages. *Journal of Marriage and Family, 70,* 392–407.

Ellis, D. G., & McCallister, L. (1980). Relational control sequences in sex-typed and androgynous groups. *Western Journal of Speech Communication, 44,* 35–49.

Ellis, H. (1910). *Studies in the psychology of sex* (Vols. I–VI). Philadelphia: F. A. Davis.

Ellis, L., Ames, M., Ashley, P. W., & Burke, D. (1988). Sexual orientation of human offspring may be altered by severe maternal stress during pregnancy. *The Journal of Sex Research, 25,* 152–157.

Ellis, L., Burke, D., & Ames, M. (1987). Sexual orientation as a continuous variable: A comparison between the sexes. *Archives of Sexual Behavior, 16,* 523–529.

Ellison, C. R. (2000). *Women's sexualities.* Oakland, CA: New Harbinger.

Elmslie, B., & Tebaldi, E. (2007). Sexual orientation and labor market discrimination. *Journal of Labor Research, 28*(3), 436–453.

Eloi-Stiven, M., Channaveeraiah, N., Christos, P., Finkel, M., & Reddy, R. (2007). Does marijuana use play a role in the recreational use of sildenafil? *Journal of Family Practitioner, 56,* E1–E4.

Emons, G., Fleckenstein, G., Hinney, B., Huschmand, A., & Heyl, W. (2000). Hormonal interactions in endometrial cancer. *Endocrine-Related Cancer, 7,* 227–242.

Engel, J. W., & Saracino, M. (1986). Love preferences and ideals: A comparison of homosexual, bisexual, and heterosexual groups. *Contemporary Family Therapy: An International Journal, 8*(3), 241–250.

Ensign, J., Scherman, A., & Clark, J. (1998). The relationship of family structure and conflict to levels of intimacy and parental attachment in college students. *Adolescence, 33*(131), 575–582.

Ephross, P. H. (2005). Group work with sexual offenders. In G. L. Greif (Ed.), *Group work with populations at risk* (pp. 253–266). New York: Oxford University Press.

Epps, J., & Kendall, P. C. (1995). Hostile attributional bias in adults. *Cognitive Therapy and Research, 19,* 159–178.

Epstein, C. F. (1986). Symbolic segregation: Similarities and differences in the language and non-verbal communication of women and men. *Sociological Forum, 1,* 27–49.

Epstein, C. F. (1988). *Deceptive distinctions: Sex, gender, and the social order.* New Haven, CT: Yale University Press.

Epstein, M., & Ward, L. M. (2008). "Always use protection": Communication boys receive about sex from parents, peers, and the media. *Journal of Youth and Adolescence, 37,* 113–127.

Ericksen, J. A. (1999). *Kiss and tell: Surveying sex in the twentieth century.* Cambridge, MA: Harvard University Press.

Erogul, O., Oztas, E., Yildirim, I., Kir, T., Aydur, E., Komesli, G., et al. (2006). Effects of electromagnetic radiation from a cellular phone on human sperm motility: An in vitro study. *Archives of Medical Research, 37,* 840–843.

Ersoy, B., Balkan, C., Gunay, T., & Egemen, A. (2005). The factors affecting the relation between the menarcheal age of mother and daughter. *Child: Care, Health & Development, 31*(3), 303–308.

Escoffier, J. (2003). *Sexual revolution.* New York: Thunder's Mouth Press.

Eshbaugh, E. M., & Gute, G. (2008). Hookups and sexual regret among college women. *Journal of Social Psychology, 148,* 77–89.

Eskenazi, B., Wyrobek, A. J., Sloter, E., Kidd, S. A., Moore, L., Young, S., & Moore, D. (2003). The association of age and semen quality in healthy men. *Human Reproduction, 18,* 447–454.

Espelage, D. L., Aragon, S. R., Birkett, M., & Koenig, B. W. (2008a). Homophobic teasing, psychological outcomes, and sexual orientation among high school students: What influence do parents and schools have? *School Psychology Review, 37,* 202–216.

Espín, M. C., Llorca, M. D. C., Simons, B. C., Borrego, N. G., Cueto, G. M., Guerra, E. A., Rodríguez, B. T., et al. (2004). Cuba. In R. T. Francoeur & R. J. Noonan (Eds.), *The Continuum complete international encyclopedia of sexuality* (pp. 259–327844). New York/London: Continuum International.

Ethics Committee Report. (2006). *Access to fertility treatment by gays, lesbians, and unmarried persons.* Ethics Committee of the American Society for Reproductive Medicine. Retrieved from http://www.asrm.org/Media/Ethics/fertility_gayslesunmarried.pdf.

Ethier, K. A., Kershaw, T., Niccolai, L., Lewis, J. B., & Ickovics, J. R. (2003). Adolescent women underestimate their susceptibility to sexually transmitted infections. *Sexually Transmitted Infections, 79,* 408–411.

Etzioni, R., Penson, D. F., Legler, J. M., Tommaso, D., Boer, R., Gann, P. H., et al. (2002). Overdiagnosis due to prostate-specific antigen screening. *Journal National Cancer Institute, 94,* 981–990.

Evada, M., & Atwa, M. (2007). Sexual function in female patients with unstable angina or non-ST-elevation myocardial infarction. *Journal of Sexual Medicine, 4,* 1373–1380.

Evans, A., Scally, A., Wellard, S., & Wilson, J. (2007). Prevalence of bacterial vaginosis in lesbians and heterosexual women in a community setting. *Sexually Transmitted Infections, 83,* 424–425.

Fabes, R., Martin, C., & Hanish, L. (2003). Young children's play qualities in same-, other-, and mixed-sex peer groups. *Child Development, 74*(3), 921–932.

Faderman, L. (1981). *Surpassing the love of men: Romantic friendship and love between women from the Renaissance to the present.* New York: William Morrow.

Falagas, M., Betsi, G., Athanasiou, S. (2006). Probiotics for prevention of recurrent vulvovaginal candidiasis: A review. *Journal of Antimicrobial Chemotherapy, 58*(2), 266–272.

Faller, K. C. (1989). The role relationship between victim and perpetrator as a predictor of characteristics of intrafamilial sexual abuse. *Child and Adolescent Social Work Journal, 6,* 217–229.

Faludi, S. (1991). *Backlash: The undeclared war against American women.* New York: Crown.

Farah, M. (1984). *Marriage and sexuality in Islam.* Salt Lake City: University of Utah Press.

Farley M., Cotton A., Lynne, J., et al. (2003). Prostitution and trafficking in nine countries: An update on violence and posttraumatic stress disorder. In M. Farley (Ed.), *Prostitution, trafficking and traumatic stress* (pp. 33–74). Binghamton, NY: Haworth Press.

Farr, C., Brown, J., & Beckett, R. (2004). Ability to empathise and masculinity levels: Comparing male adolescent sex offenders with a normative sample of non-offending adolescents. *Psychology, Crime & Law, 10*(2), 155–168.

Faulkner, A. H., & Cranston, K. (1998). Correlates of same-sex sexual behavior in a random sample of Massachusetts high school students. *American Journal of Public Health, 88*(2), 262–266.

Fay, R. E., Turner, C. F., Klassen, A. D., & Gagnon, J. H. (1989). Prevalence and patterns of same-gender sexual contact among men. *Science, 243,* 338–348.

Federation of Feminist Women's Health Centers. (1991). *A new view of a woman's body: An illustrated guide.* Los Angeles: The Feminist Press.

Feeney, J. A., & Noller, P. (1990). Attachment style as a predictor of adult romantic relationships. *Journal of Personality & Social Psychology, 58*(2), 281–291.

Feierman, J. (1990). *Pedophilia: Biosocial dimensions.* New York: Springer-Verlag.

Feinauer, L. (1988). Relationship of long term effects of childhood sexual abuse to identity of the offender: Family, friend, or stranger. *Women and Therapy, 7,* 89–107.

Feinauer, L. (1989). Comparison of long-term effects of child abuse by type of abuse and by relationship of the offender to the victim. *American Journal of Family Therapy, 17,* 46–48.

Feinberg, L. (1999). *Trans liberation: Beyond blue and pink.* Boston: Beacon Press.

Feliciano, R., & Alfonso, C. A. (1997). Sexual side effects of psychotropic medication: Diagnosis, neurobiology, and treatment strategies. *International Journal of Mental Health, 26*(1), 79–89.

Ferguson, C. J., Cruz, A. M., & Rueda, S. M. (2008). Gender, video game playing habits and visual memory tasks. *Sex Roles, 58,* 279–287.

Ferguson, D., & Boden, J. (2008). Cannabis use and later life outcomes. *Addiction, 103,* 969–975.

Ferguson, D. M., Steidle, C. P., Singh, G. S., Alexander, J. S., Weihmiller, M. K., & Crosby, M. G. (2003). Randomized placebo-controlled, double blind, crossover design trial of the efficacy and safety of Zestra for women with and without female sexual arousal disorder. *Journal of Sex and Marital Therapy, 29*(Suppl. 1), 33–44.

Ferguson, R. B. (2004). The associations among members' perceptions of intragroup relationship conflict, leader-member exchange quality, and leader gossiping behavior. *Dissertation Abstracts International, 64*(10-A), (#0419-4209).

Fernandez, Y. M., & Marshall, W. L. (2003). Victim empathy, social self-esteem, and psychopathology in rapists. *Sexual Abuse: Journal of Research and Treatment, 15*(1), 11–26.

Ferree, M. M., & Hess, B. B. (1985). *Controversy and coalition: The new feminist movement.* Boston: Twayne.

Ferreira-Poblete, A. (1997). The probability of conception on different days of the cycle with respect to ovulation: An overview. *Advances in Contraception, 13*(2–3), 83–95.

Ferreiro-Velasco, M. E., Barca-Buyo, A., de la Barrera, S. S., Montoto-Marques, A., Vazquez, X. M., & Rodriguez-Sotillo, A. (2005). Sexual issues in a sample of women with spinal cord injury. *Spinal Cord, 43*(1), 51–55.

Ferris, D., Waller, J., Miller, J., Patel, P., Jackson, L., Price, G., & Wilson, C. (2008). Men's attitudes toward receiving the human papillomavirus vaccine. *Journal of Lower Genital Tract Diseases, 12,* 276–281.

Ferro, C., Cermele, J., & Saltzman, A. (2008). Current perceptions of marital rape. *Journal of Interpersonal Violence, 23,* 764.

Fethers, K., Marks, C., Mindel, A., & Estcourt, C. (2000). Sexually transmitted infections and risk behaviours in women who have sex with women. *Sexually Transmitted Infections, 77,* 390.

Fethers, K., Marks, C., Mindel, A., & Estocourt, C. S. (2000). STI and risk behaviors in women who have sex with women. *Sexually Transmitted Infections, 76*(5), 345–349.

Fieldman, J. P., & Crespi, T. D. (2002). Child sexual abuse: Offenders, disclosure and school-based initiatives. *Adolescence, 37*(145), 151–160.

Fields, J. (2001). Normal queers: Straight parents respond to their children's "coming-out." *Symbolic Interaction, 24*(2), 165–188.

Fields, J., & Casper, L. M. (2001). America's families and living arrangements. *Current Population Reports.* Washington, DC: U.S. Census Bureau.

Finer, L. B., & Henshaw, S. K. (2006). Disparities in rates of unintended pregnancy in the United States, 1994 and 2001. *Perspectives on Sexual and Reproductive Health, 38,* 90–96.

Fink, H. A., MacDonald, R., Rutks, I. R., & Nelson, D. B. (2002). Sildenafil for male erectile dysfunction: A systematic review and meta-analysis. *Archives of Internal Medicine, 162*(12), 1349–1360.

Finkelhor, D. (1980). Sex among siblings: A survey on prevalence, variety, and effects. *Archives of Sexual Behavior, 9,* 171–194.

Finkelhor, D. (1984). *Child sexual abuse: New theory and research.* New York: The Free Press.

Finkelhor, D., & Browne, A. (1985). The traumatic impact of child sexual abuse. *American Journal of Ortho-Psychiatry, 55,* 530–541.

Finkelhor, D., Hotaling, G., Lewis, I. A., & Smith, C. (1990). Sexual abuse in a national survey of adult men and women: Prevalence, characteristics, and risk factors. *Child Abuse and Neglect, 14,* 19–28.

Finster, M., & Wood, M. (2005). The Apgar score has survived the test of time. *Anesthesiology, 102*(4), 855–857.

Firestone, P., Nunes, K. L., Moulden, H., Broom, I., & Bradford, J. M. (2005). Hostility and recidivism in sexual offenders. *Archives of Sexual Behavior, 34*(3), 277–283.

Fischer, G. J. (1987). Hispanic and majority student attitudes toward forcible date rape as a function of differences in attitudes toward women. *Sex Roles, 17*(1–2), 93–101.

Fisher, B., Wortley, S., Webster, C., & Kirst, M. (2002). The socio-legal dynamics and implications of "diversion": The case study of the Toronto "John School" diversion programme for prostitution offenders. *Criminal Justice: International Journal of Policy and Practice, 2*(34), 385–410.

Fisher, B. S., Cullen, F. T., & Daigle, L. E. (2005). The discovery of acquaintance rape: The salience of methodological innovation and rigor. *Journal of Interpersonal Violence, 20*(4), 493–500.

Fisher, B. S., Cullen, F. T., & Turner, M. G. (2000). *Sexual victimization of college women.* Washington, DC: U.S. Department of Justice, National Institute of Justice.

Fisher, B. S., Daigle, L. E., Cullen, F. T., & Turner, M. G. (2003). Reporting sexual victimization to the police and others: Results from a national-level study of college women. *Criminal Justice & Behavior, 30*(1), 6–38.

Fisher, D., Malow, R., Rosenberg, R., Reynolds, G., Farrell, N., & Jaffe, A. (2006). Recreational Viagra use and sexual risk among drug abusing men. *American Journal of Infectious Disease, 2,* 107–114.

Fisher, H. (2004). *Why we love: The nature and chemistry of romantic love.* New York: Henry Holt.

Fisher, R., Darrow, D., Tranter, M., & Williams, J. (2008). Human papillomavirus vaccine: Recommendations, issues, and controversies. *Current Opinions in Pediatrics, 20,* 441–445.

Fisher, W. A., & Barak, A. (1991). Pornography, erotica, and behavior: More questions than answers. *International Journal of Law and Psychiatry, 14,* 65–83.

Fitch, M.T. (2003). Levels of family involvement and gender role conflict among stay-at-home dads. *Dissertation Abstracts International Section A: Humanities & Social Sciences, 64*(2-A), #AA13080872.

Fitch, R. H., & Denenberg, V. H. (1998). A role for ovarian hormones in sexual differentiation of the brain. *Behavioral Brain Science, 21*(3), 311–327.

Fitzgerald, L. F., & Ormerod, A. J. (1991). Perceptions of sexual harassment: The influence of gender and academic context. *Psychology of Women Quarterly, 15,* 281–294.

Flanigan, C., Suellentrop, K., Albert, B., Smith, J., & Whitehead, M. (2005, September 15). Science says #17: Teens and oral sex. Retrieved September 17, 2005, from http://www.teenpregnancy.org/works/pdf/ScienceSays_17_OralSex.pdf.

Fleck, F. (2004). Microbicides preventing HIV infection could be available by 2010. *Bulletin of the World Health Organization, 82*(5), 393–394.

Fleischmann, A. A., Spitzberg, B. H., Andersen, P. A., Roesch, S. C., & Metts, S. (2005). Tickling the monster: Jealousy induction in relationships. *Journal of Social and Personal Relationships, 22*(1), 49–73.

Fleming, D., McQuillian, G., Johnson, R., Nahmias, A. J., Aral, S. O., Lee, F. K., St. Louis, M.E. (1997). Herpes simplex virus type 2 in the U.S., 1976 to 1994. *New England Journal of Medicine, 337,* 1105–1111.

Fletcher, J. L. (1991). Perinatal transmission of human papillomavirus. *American Family Physician, 43,* 143.

Food and Drug Administration, Office of Women's Health. (2006, June). *Human papillomavirus.* Retrieved September 16, 2008, from http://www.fda.gov/WOMENS/getthefacts/hpv.html.

Food and Drug Administration. (2006, August 24). *FDA approves over-the-counter access for Plan B for women 18 and older: Prescription remains required for those 17 and under.* Retrieved October 28, 2008, from http://www.fda.gov/bbs/topics/news/2006/new01436.html.

Food and Drug Administration. (2007a, December 18). *FDA mandates new warning for nonoxynol 9 OTC contraceptive products.* Retrieved October 28, 2008, from http://www.fda.gov/bbs/topics/NEWS/2007/NEW01758.html.

Food and Drug Administration. (2007b). Over-the-counter vaginal contraceptive and spermicide drug products containing nonoxynol 9; required labeling. Final rule. *Federal Register, 72,* 71769–71785.

Food and Drug Administration. (2008, January 18). *FDA approves update to label on birth control patch.* Retrieved October 28, 2008, from http://www.fda.gov/bbs/topics/NEWS/2008/NEW01781.html.

Foote, W. E., & Goodman-Delahunty, J. (2005). Harassers, harassment contexts, same-sex harassment, workplace romance, and harassment theories. In W. E. Foote & J. Goodman-Delahunty (Eds.), *Evaluating sexual harassment: Psychological, social, and legal considerations in forensic examinations* (pp. 27–45). Washington, DC: American Psychological Association.

Forbes, G. B., & Adams-Curtis, L. E. (2001). Experiences with sexual coercion in college males and females: Role of family conflict, sexist attitudes, acceptance of rape myths, self-esteem, and the Big-Five personality factors. *Journal of Interpersonal Violence, 16,* 865–889.

Forhan, S. (2008, March). *Prevalence of STIs and bacterial vaginosis among female adolescents in the U.S.: Data from the National Health and Nutritional Examination Survey 2003–2004.* Presented at the 2008 National STD Prevention Conference, Chicago, IL. Retrieved May 29, 2008, from http://www.cdc.gov/STDConference/2008/media/summaries-11march2008.htm#tues1.

Forke, C., Myers, R., Catallozzi, M., & Schwarz, D. (2008). Relationship violence among female and male college undergraduate students. *Archives of Pediatric Adolescent Medicine, 162,* 634–641.

Forrest, K., Austin, D., Valdes, M., Guentes, E., & Wilson, S. (1993). Exploring norms and beliefs related to AIDS prevention among California Hispanic men. *Family Planning Perspectives, 25,* 111–117.

Forry, N. D., Leslie, L. A., & Letiecq, B. L. (2007). Marital quality in interracial relationships. *Journal of Family Issues, 28,* 1538.

Forstein, M. (1988). Homophobia: An overview. *Psychiatric Annals, 18,* 33–36.

Fortenberry, J. D. (2002). Unveiling the hidden epidemic of STDs. *Journal of the American Medical Association, 287*(6), 768–769.

Forti, G., & Krausz, C. (1998). Clinical review 100: Evaluation and treatment of the infertile couple. *Journal of Clinical Endocrinology Medicine, 83*(12), 4177–4188.

Foster, G. (2002). Supporting community efforts to assist orphans in Africa. *New England Journal of Medicine, 346,* 1907–1911.

Foster, G. (2006). Children who live in communities affected by AIDS. *The Lancet, 367*(9511), 700–1.

Foster, R. T. (2008). Noncomplicated urinary tract infections in women. *Obstetrics and Gynecology Clinics of North America, 35,* 235–248.

Foubert, J., & Cremedy, B. (2007). Reactions of men of color to a commonly used rape prevention program. *Sex Roles, 57,* 137–144.

Foubert, J. D. (2000). The longitudinal effects of a rape: Prevention program on fraternity men's attitudes. *Journal of American College Health, 48*(4), 158–163.

Foubert, J. D., & Marriott, K. A. (1997). Effects of sexual assault peer education program on men's belief in rape myths. *Sex Roles, 36,* 257–266.

Foubert, J. D., & McEwen, M. K. (1998). An all-male rape prevention peer education program: Decreasing fraternity men's behavioral intent to rape. *Journal of College Student Development, 39,* 548–556.

Fowers, B. J. (1998). Psychology and the good marriage. *American Behavioral Scientist, 41*(4), 516.

Fox, A.B., Bukatko, D., Hallahan, M., Crawford, M. (2007). The medium makes a difference: Gender similarities and differences in instant messaging. *Journal of Language and Social Psychology, 26*(4), 389.

Fox, J. A., & Zawitz, M. W. (2004). Homicide trends in the United States. Retrieved October 23, 2005, from www.ojp.usdoj.gov/bjs/homicide/homtrnd.htm.

FoxBusiness.com. (2008). Facebook releases site in Spanish; German and French to follow. Retrieved February 10, 2008, from http://www.foxbusiness.com/article/facebook-releases-site-spanish-german-french-follow_471333_1.html.

Frackiewicz, E. J. (2000). Endometriosis: An overview of the disease and its treatment. *Journal of the American Pharmaceutical Association, 40*(5), 645–657.

Franceschi, S. (2005). The IARC commitment to cancer prevention: The example of papillomavirus and cervical cancer. *Recent Results in Cancer Research, 166,* 277–297.

Francoeur, R. T., & Noonan, R. J. (Eds.). (2004). *The Continuum international encyclopedia of sexuality.* New York/London: Continuum International.

Frangou, E. M., Lawson, J., & Kanthan, R. (2005). Angiogenesis in male breast cancer. *World Journal of Surgical Oncology, 3*(1), 16.

Franiuk, R., Seefelt, J., & Vandello, J. (2008). Prevalence of rape myths in headlines and their effects on attitudes toward rape. *Sex Roles, 58,* 790–802.

Frank, E., Anderson, C., & Rubinstein, D. N. (1978). Frequency of sexual dysfunction in normal couples. *New England Journal of Medicine, 299,* 111–115.

Frank, J. E., Mistretta, P., & Will, J. (2008). Diagnosis and treatment of female sexual dysfunction. *American Family Physician, 77,* 635–642.

Frankel, L. (2002). "I've never thought about it": Contradictions and taboos surrounding American males' experiences of first ejaculation (semenarche). *Journal of Men's Studies, 11*(1), 37–54.

Franklin, K. (2000). Antigay behaviors among young adults. *Journal of Interpersonal Violence, 15*(4), 339–363.

Fraser, I. S. (2000). Forty years of combined oral contraception: Evolution of a revolution. *Medical Journal of Australia, 173*(10), 541–544.

Frazier, P. A. (2000). The role of attributions and perceived control in recovery from rape. *Journal of Personal and Interpersonal Loss, 5*(2/3), 203–225.

Frederick, D., & Haselton, M. (2007). Why is muscularity sexy? Tests of the fitness indicator hypothesis. *Personality and Social Psychology Bulletin, 33,* 1167–1183.

Fredriksson, J., Kanabus, A., Pennington, J., Pembrey, G. (2008). AIDS orphans. Avert International AIDS Charity. Retrieved November 3, 2008, from http://www.avert.org/aidsorphans.htm.

Freedman, M. (2001). For love and money. *Forbes, 167*(14), 202.

Freitas, S. L. G. (2004). Brazil. In R. T. Francoeur & R. J. Noonan (Eds.), *The Continuum complete international encyclopedia of sexuality* (pp. 98–113). New York/London: Continuum International.

Freking, K. (2008, June 24). States turn down U.S. abstinence education grants. Associated Press, Yahoo News. Retrieved December 18, 2008, from http://www.oegis.com/news/ads/2008/AD081302.html.

Fretts, R.C., Boyd, M. E., Usher, R. H., & Usher, H. A. (1992). The changing pattern of fetal death, 1961–1988. *Obstetrics and Gynecology, 79*(1), 35–39.

Freud, S. (1953). Three essays on the theory of sexuality. In J. Strachey (Ed. & Trans.), *The standard edition of the complete psychological works of Sigmund Freud* (Vol. 7, pp. 130–243). London: Hogarth Press. (Original work published 1905)

Freund, K., & Blanchard, R. (1986). The concept of courtship disorder. *Journal of Sex and Marital Therapy, 12,* 79–92.

Freund, K., Scher, H., & Hucker, S. (1983). The courtship disorders. *Archives of Sexual Behavior, 12,* 369–379.

Freund, K., Scher, H., & Hucker, S. (1984). The courtship disorders: A further investigation. *Archives of Sexual Behavior, 13,* 133–139.

Freund, K. M. (1992). Chlamydial disease in women. *Hospital Practice,* 175–186.

Freund, M., Lee, N., & Leonard, T. (1991). Sexual behavior of clients with street prostitutes in Camden, New Jersey. *Journal of Sex Research, 28,* 579–591.

Freund, M., Leonard, T. L., & Lee, N. (1989). Sexual behavior of resident street prostitutes with their clients in Camden, New Jersey. *Journal of Sex Research, 26,* 460–478.

Freymiller, L. (2005, May). Separate or equal?: Gay viewers respond to same-sex and gay/straight relationships on TV. Presented at the 2005 Annual Meeting of the International Communication Association, New York, NY.

Friden, C., Hirschberg, A. L., Saartok, T., Backstrom, T., Leanderson, J., & Renstrom, P. (2003). The influence of premenstrual symptoms on postural balance and kinesthesia during the menstrual cycle. *Gynecological Endocrinology, 17*(6), 433–440.

Friebe, A., Arck, P. (2008). Causes for spontaneous abortion: What the bugs 'gut' to do with it? *International Journal of Biochemistry and Cell Biology, 40*(11), 2348–2352.

Friedin, J., V. (2007). Psychologists' beliefs and advocacy regarding the formation of romantic relationships through internet communication. *Dissertation Abstracts International, 67*(10-B), #0419-4217.

Friedman, C. (2007). First comes love, then comes marriage, then comes baby carriage: Perspectives on gay parenting and reproductive technology. *Journal of Infant, Child, and Adolescent Psychotherapy, 6,* 111–123.

Friedman-Kien, A. E., & Farthing, C. (1990). Human immunodeficiency virus infection: A survey with special emphasis on mucocutaneous manifestations. *Seminars in Dermatology, 9,* 167–177.

Friedrich, W. N. (1998). Behavioral manifestations of child sexual abuse. *Child Abuse and Neglect, 22*(6), 523–531.

Friedrich, W. N., Grambsch, P., Broughton, D., Kuiper, J., & Beilke, R. L. (1991). Normative sexual behavior in children. *Pediatrics, 88,* 456–464.

Fritz, G. S., Stoll, K., & Wagner, N. N. (1981). A comparison of males and females who were sexually molested as children. *Journal of Sex & Marital Therapy, 7*(1), 54–59.

Frohlich, P. F., & Meston, C. M. (2000). Evidence that serotonin affects female sexual functioning via peripheral mechanisms. *Physiology and Behavior, 71*(3–4), 383–393.

Frohlich, P. F., & Meston, C. M. (2005). Tactile sensitivity in women with sexual arousal disorder. *Archives of Sexual Behavior, 34*(2), 207–217.

Frost, J. J., Darroch, J. E., & Remez, L. (2008). Improving contraception use in the United States. *In Brief, 1.* New York: Alan Guttmacher Institute.

Frost, J. J., & Driscoll, A. K. (2006). *Sexual and reproductive health of U.S. Latinas: A literature review.* New York: Alan Guttmacher Institute. Retrieved May 27, 2008, from http://www.guttmacher.org/pubs/2006/02/07/or19.pdf.

Frostino, A. (2007). Guilt and jealousy associated with sexual fantasies among heterosexual married individuals. Widener University. *Dissertation Abstracts International: Section B: The Sciences and Engineering, 68*(3-B), 1924.

Fruth, A. (2007). Dating and adolescents' psychological well-being. *Dissertation Abstracts International Section A: Humanities and Social Sciences, 68*(1-A), 360.

Fryar, C. D., Hirsch, R., Porter, K. S., Kottiri, B., Brody, D., & Louis, T. (2007, June 28). Drug use and sexual behaviors reported by adults: United States, 1999–2002. Advance Data from Vital and Health Statistics, Centers for Disease Control, 384. Retrieved October 3, 2008, from http://www.cdc.gov/nchs/data/ad/ad384.pdf.

Fuller-Fricke., R.L. (2007). Interaction of relationship satisfaction, depressive symptoms, and self-esteem in college-aged women. *Fuller Theological Seminary, Dissertation Abstracts,* UMI #3267404.

Gable, S.L., Gonzaga, G.C., Strachman, A. (2006). Will you be there for me when things go right? Supportive responses to positive event disclosures. *Journal of Personality and Social Psychology, 91*(5), 904–917.

Gaetz, S. (2004). Safe streets for whom? Homeless youth, social exclusion, and criminal victimization. *Canadian Journal of Criminology and Criminal Justice, 46,* 423–456.

Gagnon, J. H. (2001). A comparative study of the couple in the social organization of sexuality in France and the United States—statistical data included. *Journal of Sex Research, 38*(1), 24–34.

Gaither, G. A. (2000). The reliability and validity of three new measures of male sexual preferences (Doctoral dissertation, University of North Dakota). *Dissertation Abstracts International, 61,* 4981.

Gaither, G. A., Sellbom, M., & Meier, B. P. (2003). The effect of stimulus content on volunteering for sexual interest research among college students. *Journal of Sex Research, 40*(3), 240–249.

Gallagher, M., & Baker, J. K. (2004, May 4). Same-sex unions and divorce risk: Data from Sweden. *iMAPP Policy Brief.* Retrieved September 14, 2008, from http://www.marriagedebate.com/pdf/SSdivorcerisk.pdf.

Gallagher, M., & Waite, L. (2000). *The case for marriage.* New York: Doubleday.

Gallo, R. V. (2000). Is there a homosexual brain? *Gay and Lesbian Review, 7*(1), 12–16.

Galupo, M. P. (2006). Sexism, heterosexism, and biphobia: The framing of bisexual women's friendships. *Journal of Bisexuality, 6,* 35–45.

Gambescia, N. (2007). Sexual dysfunction. In N. Kazantzis, L. L'Abate (Eds.). *Handbook of Homework Assignments in Psychotherapy* (pp. 351–368). Spring Ceince and Business Media, New York, NY.

Gamel, C., Hengeveld, M., Davis, B. (2000). Informational needs about the effects of gynaecological cancer on sexuality: A review of the literature. *Journal of Clinical Nursing, 9*(5), 678–688.

Gamson, J. (1990). Rubber wars: Struggles over the condom in the United States. *Journal of the History of Sexuality, 1,* 262–282.

Gan, C., Zou, Y., Wu, S., Li, Y., & Liu, Q. (2008). The influence of medical abortion compared with surgical abortion on subsequent pregnancy outcome. *International Journal of Gynecology and Obstetrics, 101,* 231–238.

Gandossy, T. (2007, June 27). Gay adoption: A new take on the American family. CNN. Retrieved October 2, 2008, from http://www.cnn.com/2007/US/06/25/gay.adoption/index.html.

Gard, C. (2000). What is he/she saying? *Current Health, 26*(8), 18–20.

Gardner, A. (2004). *Excess weight can compromise birth control pills.* Sexual Health Network. Retrieved October 1, 2008, from http://sexualhealth.e-healthsource.com/?p=news1&id=523135.

Garner, M., Turner, M. C., Ghadirian, P., Krewski, D., & Wade, M. (2008). Testicular cancer and hormonally active agents. *Journal of Toxicology and Environmental Health, 11,* 260–275.

Garrity, J. (1969). *The sensuous woman.* New York: Dell Publishers.

Garver-Apgar, C. E., Gangestad, S. W., Thornhill, R., Miller, R. D., & Olp, J. J. (2006). Major histocompatibility complex alleles, sexual responsivity, and unfaithfulness in romantic couples. *Psychological Science, 17,* 830–835.

Gates, G., Badgett, L., Macomber, J. E., & Chambers, K. (2007, March 27). Adoption and foster care by lesbian and gay parents in the United States. Urban Institute. Retrieved October 2, 2008, from http://www.urban.org/url.cfm?ID=411437.

Gates, G. J., & Sonenstein, F. L. (2000). Heterosexual genital sexual activity among adolescent males: 1998–1995. *Family Planning Perspectives, 32*(6), 295–304.

Gavard, J., & Artal, R. (2008). Effect of exercise on pregnancy outcome. *Clinical Obstetrics and Gynecology, 51,* 467–480.

Gayle, H. (2000). Letter to colleagues from Helene Gayle, M.D. Retrieved March 4, 2000, from http://www.cdc.gov/washington/testimony/ha030200.htm.

Gazmararian, J. A., Petersen, R., Spitz, A. M., Goodwin, M. M., Saltzman, L. E., & Marks, J. S. (2000). Violence and reproductive health: Current knowledge and future research directions. *Maternal and Child Health Journal, 4*(2), 79–84.

Gebhard, P., & Johnson, A. (1979). *The Kinsey data: Marginal tabulations of the 1938–1963 interviews conducted by the Institute for Sex Research.* Philadelphia: W. B. Saunders.

Geer, J. H., & Broussard, D. B. (1990). Scaling heterosexual behavior and arousal: Consistency and sex differences. *Journal of Personality and Social Psychology, 58,* 664–671.

Geer, J. H., & O'Donohue, W. T. (1987). A sociological approach. In J. H. Geer & W. T. O'Donohue (Eds.), *Theories of human sexuality* (pp. 237–253). New York: Plenum Press.

Gelbard, M. (1988). Dystrophic penile classification in Peyronie's disease. *Journal of Urology, 139,* 738–740.

Gemelli, R. J. (1996). *Normal child and adolescent development.* Arlington, VA: American Psychiatric Press.

GenderAIDS. (2003). Swaziland king's polygamy remarks condemned. Retrieved August 29, 2003, from http://archives.healthdev.net/gender-aids/msg00495.html.

GenderBlind. (2008). National Student GenderBlind Campaign. Research Data Update Summer 2007. Retrieved February 17, 2008, from http://www.genderblind.org/research.pdf.

Geraghty, C., et al. (1992). A woman's space: Women and soap opera. In F. Bonner, L. Goodman, & R. Allen (Eds.), *Imagining women* (pp. 221–236). United Kingdom: Polity Press.

Getahun, D. Ananth, C. V., Selvam, N., & Demissie, K. (2005). Adverse perinatal outcomes among interracial couples in the United States. *Obstetrics and Gynecology, 106*(1), 81–88.

Ghaziani, A. (2005). Breakthrough: The 1979 national march. *Gay & Lesbian Review Worldwide, 12*(2), 31–33.

Ghosh, M. K. (2005). Breech presentation: Evolution of management. *Journal of Reproductive Medicine, 50*(2), 108–116.

Gibbs, J. L., Ellison, N. B., & Heino, R. D. (2006). Self-presentation in online personals: The role of anticipated future interaction, self-disclosure, and perceived success in Internet dating. *Communication Research, 33,* 152–177.

Gibson-Ainyette, I., Templer, D. I., Brown, R., & Veaco, L. (1988). Adolescent female prostitutes. *Archives of Sexual Behavior, 17,* 431–438.

Giles, G., English, D., McCredie, M., Borland, R., Boyle, P., & Hopper, J. (2003). Sexual factors and prostate cancer. *British Journal of Urology, 92*(3), 211–216.

Gilman, S. E., Cochran, S. D., Mays, V., Hughes, M., Ostrow, D., & Kessler, R. C. (2001). Risk of psychiatric disorders among individuals reporting same-sex sexual partners in the national comorbidity survey. *American Journal of Public Health, 91*(6), 933–940.

Gilmore, D. D. (1990). *Manhood in the making: Cultural concepts of masculinity.* New Haven, CT: Yale University Press.

Gilson, R. J., & Mindel, A. (2001). Sexually transmitted infections. *British Medical Journal, 322*(729S), 1135–1137.

Ginsberg, T. B., Pomerantz, S. C., & Kramer-Feeley, V. (2005). Sexuality in older adults: Behaviours and preferences. *Age and Ageing, 34,* 475–480.

Ginty, M. M. (2005). New pills launch debate over menstruation. Retrieved March 19, 2005, from http://www.womensenews.org/article.cfm/dyn/aid/1879/context/archive.

Giotakos, O., Markianos, M., & Vaidakis, N. (2005). Aggression, impulsivity, and plasma sex hormone levels in a group of rapists, in relation to their history of childhood attention-deficit/hyperactivity disorder symptoms. *Journal of Forensic Psychiatry & Psychology, 16*(2), 423–433.

Girsh, E., Katz, N., Genkin, L., Girtler, O., Bocker, J., Bezdin, S., & Barr, I. (2008). Male age influences oocyte-donor program results. *Journal of Assisted Reproductive Genetics, 25*(4), 137–143.

Girshick, L. B. (1999). *No safe haven: Stories of women in prison.* Lebanon, NH: University Press of New England.

Giuliano, A., Lazcano-Ponce, E., Villa, L., Flores, R., Salmeron, J., Lee, J., et al. (2008a). The human papillomavirus infection in men study: Human papillomavirus prevalence and type distribution among men residing in Brazil, Mexico, and the United States. *Cancer Epidemiology Biomarkers Prevention, 17,* 2036–2043.

Giuliano, A., Lu, B., Nielson, C., Flores, R., Papenfuss, M., Lee, J., et al. (2008b). Age-specific prevalence, incidence, and duration of human papillomavirus infections in a cohort of 290 U.S. men. *Journal of Infectious Disease, 198,* 827–835.

Giuliano, T. A., Popp, K. E., Knight, J. L. (2000). Footballs versus barbies: Childhood play activities as predictors of sport participation by women. *Sex Roles, 42*(3–4), 159–181.

Glasser, M., Kolvin, I., Campbell, D., Glasser, A., Leitch, I., & Farrelly, S. (2001). Cycle of child sexual abuse: Links between being a victim and becoming a perpetrator. *British Journal of Psychiatry, 179,* 482–494.

Gleason, T. R. (2005). Mothers' and fathers' attitudes regarding pretend play in the context of imaginary companions and of child gender. *Merrill-Palmer Quarterly, 51,* 412–437.

Gleicher, N., Weghofer, A., & Barad, D. (2008). Preimplantation genetic screening: "Established" and ready for prime time? *Fertility and Sterility, 89,* 780–788.

Glenn, N., & Marquardt, E. (2001). Hooking up, hanging out and hoping for Mr. Right: College women on mating and dating today. Retrieved October 19, 2005, from http://www. americanvalues.org/Hooking_Up.pdf.

Globerman, S. (2005, March). Right test, wrong results: When little things can mean a lot. *O, The Oprah Magazine,* p. 116.

Glynn, M., & Rhodes, P. (2005). *Estimated HIV prevalence in the United States at the end of 2003.* Programs and abstracts of the 2005 National HIV Prevention Conference (Atlanta). Abstract 545. Atlanta, GA: Centers for Disease Control and Prevention.

Gobrogge, K. L., Perkins, P. S., Baker, J. H., Balcer, K. D., et al. (2007). Homosexual mating preferences from an evolutionary perspective: Sexual selection theory revisited. *Archives of Sexual Behavior, 36,* 717–724.

Godard, J. (2007). Pacs seven years on: Is it moving toward marriage? *International Journal of Law, Policy and the Family, 21,* 310–321.

Godeau, E., Gabhainn, S. N., Vignes, C., Ross, J., Boyce, W., & Todd, J. (2008). Contraceptive use by 15-year-old students at their last sexual intercourse. *Archives of Pediatric Medicine, 162,* 66–73.

Godfrey, K., Robinson, S., Barker, D. J., Osmond, C., & Cox, V. (1996). Maternal nutrition in early and late pregnancy in relation to placental and fetal growth. *British Medical Journal, 312*(7028), 410–414.

Goffman, E. (1976). *Gender advertisements.* New York: Harper Colophon Books.

Gokyildiz, S., & Beji, N. K. (2005). The effects of pregnancy on sexual life. *Journal of Sex and Marital Therapy, 31*(3), 201–215.

Gold, J. C. (2004). Kiss of the yogini: "Tantric sex" in its South Asian contexts. *Journal of Religion, 84*(2), 334–336.

Gold, M., Wolford, J., Smith, K., Parker, A. (2004). The effects of advance provision of emergency contraception on adolescent women's sexual and contraceptive behaviors. *Journal of Pediatric and Adolescent Gynecology, 17,* 87–96.

Gold, R. (1990). *Abortion and women's health, a turning point for Americans.* New York: Alan Guttmacher Institute.

Gold, R. B. (2003, March). Lessons from before Roe: Will past be prologue? Retrieved September 3, 2005, from http://www.agi-usa.org/pubs/ib_5-03.html.

Golden, G. H. (2001). Dyadic-dystonic compelling eroticism: Can these relationships be saved? *Journal of Sex Education & Therapy, 26*(1), 50.

Golden, M. R., Whittington, W. L., Handsfield, H. H., Hughes, J. P., Stamm, W. E., Hogben, M., Clark, A., Malinski, C., Helmers, J., Thomas, K., & Holmes, K. (2005). Effect of expedited treatment of sex partners on recurrent or persistent gonorrhea or chlamydial infection. *The New England Journal of Medicine, 352*(7), 676–685.

Goldman, R. (1999). The psychological impact of circumcision. *British Journal of Urology International, 83,* 93–102.

Goldmeier, D., & Leiblum, S. (2006). Persistent genital arousal in women: A new syndrome entity. *International Journal of STDs and AIDS, 17,* 215–216.

Goldstat, R., Briganti, E., Tran, J., Wolfe, R., & Davis, S. (2003). Transdermal testosterone therapy improves well-being, mood, and sexual function in premenopausal women. *Menopause, 10,* 390–398.

Goldstein, A. T., & Burrows, L. (2008). Vulvodynia. *Journal of Sexual Medicine, 5,* 5–15.

Goldstein, M. A. (2008). Human papillomavirus vaccine in males. *New England Journal of Medicine, 359,* 863–864.

Goleman, D. (1992, April 14). Therapies offer hope for sexual offenders. *The New York Times,* pp. C1, C11.

Golen, S. (1990). A factor analysis of barriers to effective listening. *Journal of Business Communication, 27,* 25–36.

Golombok, S., & Tasker, F. (1996). Do parents influence the sexual orientation of their children? *Developmental Psychology, 32*(1), 3–12.

Gonzaga, G., Haselton, M., Smurda, J., Davies, M., & Poore, J. (2008). Love, desire, and the suppression of thoughts of romantic alternatives. *Evolution and Human Behavior, 29,* 119–126.

González, M., Viáfara, G., Caba, F., Molina, T., & Ortiz, C. (2006). Libido and orgasm in middle-aged women. *Maturitas, 53,* 1–10.

Goode, E. (1994). *Deviant behavior.* Englewood Cliffs, NJ: Prentice Hall.

Goodman, A. (1993). Diagnosis and treatment of sexual addiction. *Journal of Sex and Marital Therapy, 19*(3), 225–251.

Goodman, M., Shvetsov, Y., McDuffie, K., Wilkens, L., Zhu, X., Ning, L., et al. (2008). Acquisition of anal human papillomavirus infection in women: The Hawaii HPV cohort study. *Journal of Infectious Diseases, 197,* 957–966.

Goodwin, J. (2007, June). Kill yourself or your family will kill you. *Marie Claire,* 155–157.

Goodwin, M. H. (2007). Participation and embodied action in preadolescent girls' assessment activity. *Research on Language & Social Interaction, 40,* 353–375.

Gook, D. A., & Edgar, D. H. (2007). Human oocyte cryopreservation. *Human Reproductive Update, 13,* 591–605.

Gooren, L. (2006). The biology of human psychosexual differentiation. *Hormones & Behavior, 50,* 589–601.

Gooren, L. J., & Bunck, M. C. (2004). Transsexuals and competitive sports. *European Journal of Endocrinology, 151*(4), 425–429.

Gordon, B. N., & Schroeder, C. S. (1995). *Sexuality: A developmental approach to problems.* Chapel Hill, NC: Clinical Child Psychology Library.

Gordon, H. (2008). The treatment of paraphilias: A historical perspective. *Criminal Behaviour and Mental Health, 18,* 79–87.

Gordon, S. (1986). What kids need to know. *Psychology Today, 20,* 22–26.

Gorski, E. (2008, June 28). Presbyterian assembly votes to drop gay clergy ban. *USA Today.* Retrieved October 2, 2008, from http://www.usatoday.com/news/religion/2008-06-30-presbyterians-gay_N.htm.

Gosden, R. G. (2005). Prospects for oocyte banking and in-vitro maturation. *Journal of the National Cancer Institute Monograph, 34,* 60–63.

Gosselin, C. C. (1987). The sadomasochistic contract. In G. D. Wilson (Ed.), *Variant sexuality: Research and theory* (pp. 229–257). Baltimore: Johns Hopkins University Press.

Gostin, L. O., & DeAngelis, C. D. (2007). Mandatory HPV vaccination. *Journal of the American Medical Association, 297,* 1921–1923.

Gottemoeller, M. G. (2001). Microbicides: Expanding the options for STD prevention. *SIECUS Report, 30*(1), 10–13.

Gottman, J., Levenson, R., Swanson, C., Swanson, K., Tyson, R., & Yoshimoto, D.

(2003). Observing gay, lesbian and heterosexual couples' relationships: Mathematical modeling of conflict interaction. *Journal of Homosexuality, 45,* 65–91.

Gottman, J., & Silver, N. (2000). *The seven principles for making marriage work.* New York: Crown.

Gottman, J. M. (1994). *Why marriages succeed or fail.* New York: Simon & Schuster.

Gottman, J. M. (1999). *The seven principles for making marriage work.* New York: Random House.

Gottschall, J. A., & Gottschall, T. A. (2003). Are per-incident rape-pregnancy rates higher than per-incident consensual pregnancy rates? *Human Nature, 14*(1), 1–20.

Gould, S. J. (1981). *The mismeasure of man.* New York: Norton.

Gourley, C. (2007). *Flappers and the new American woman: Perceptions of women from 1918 through the 1920s.* Breckenridge, CO: Twenty-First Century Books.

Govan, V. A. (2008). A novel vaccine for cervical cancer: Quadrivalent human papillomavirus recombinant vaccine. *Therapeutics and Clinical Risk Management, 4,* 65–70.

Graham, C., Bancroft, J., Doll, H., Greco, T., & Tanner, A. (2007). Does oral contraceptive-induced reduction in free testosterone adversely affect the sexuality or mood of women? *Psychneuroendocrinology, 32,* 246–255.

Graugaard, C., Eplov, L. F., Giraldi, A., Mohl, B., Owens, A., Risor, H., & Winter, G. (2004). Denmark. In R. T. Francoeur & R. J. Noonan (Eds.), *The Continuum complete international encyclopedia of sexuality* (pp. 329–344). New York/London: Continuum International.

Gray, R. H., Kiwanuka, N., Quinn, T. C., Kiwanuka, N., Quinn, T. C., Sewankambo, N. K., et al. (2000). Male circumcision and HIV acquisition and transmission: Cohort studies in Rakai, Uganda. *AIDS, 14,* 2371–2381.

Graziottin, A. (2007). Prevalence and evaluation of sexual health problems—HSDD in Europe. *Journal of Sexual Medicine, 4*(Suppl 3), 211–219.

Grce, M., & Davies, P. (2008). Human papillomavirus testing for primary cervical cancer screening. *Expert Review of Molecular Diagnostics, 8,* 599–605.

Greely, A. (1994). Review of the Janus report on sexual behavior. *Contemporary Sociology, 23,* 221–223.

Green, C. A. (2004). Gender differences in the relationships between multiple measures

of alcohol consumption and physical and mental health. *Alcoholism: Clinical & Experimental Research, 28*(5), 754–765.

Green, J. N. (1999). *Beyond carnival: Male homosexuality in twentieth-century Brazil.* Chicago: University of Chicago Press.

Green, R. (1987). *The "sissy boy syndrome" and the development of homosexuality.* New Haven, CT: Yale University Press.

Green, R. (1988). The immutability of (homo)sexual orientation: Behavioral science implications for a constitutional (legal) analysis. *The Journal of Psychiatry and the Law, 16,* 537–575.

Green, R. (2004). Risk and resilience in lesbian and gay couples: Comment on Solomon, Rothblum, and Balsam (2004). *Journal of Family Psychology, 18,* 290–292.

Green, R. J. (2008). Gay and lesbian couples: Developing resilience in response to social injustice. In M. McGoldrick & K. Hardy (Eds.), *Revisioning family therapy: Race, culture, and gender in clinical practice* (2nd ed.). New York: Guilford Press.

Green, R. J. (2008, January 11). *What straights can learn from gays about relationships and parenting.* San Francisco: Rockway Institute. Retrieved December 19, 2008, from http://www.newswise.com/articles/view/536799/.

Green, R. J., Bettinger, M., & Zacks, E. (1996). Are lesbian couples fused and gay male couples disengaged? Questioning gender straightjackets. In J. Laird & R. J. Green (Eds.), *Lesbians and gays in couples and families: A handbook for therapists* (pp. 185–230). New York: Jossey-Bass.

Green, R. J., & Mitchell, V. (2002). Gay and lesbian couples in therapy: Homophobia, relational ambiguity, and social support. In A. S. Gurman & N. S. Jacobson (Eds.), *Clinical handbook of couple therapy* (3rd ed., pp. 546–568). New York: Guilford Press.

Green, V. A., Bigler, R., & Caterwood, D. (2004). The variability and flexibility of gender-typed toy play: A close look at children's behavioral response to counter-stereotypic models. *Sex Roles, 51,* 371–386.

Greenberg, M., Cheng, Y., Hopkins, L., Stotland, N., Bryant, A., & Caughey, A. (2006). Are there ethnic differences in the length of labor? *American Journal of Obstetrics and Gynecology, 195,* 743–748.

Greenberg, M., Cheng, Y., Sullivan, M., Norton, L., & Caughey, A. (2007). Does length of labor vary by maternal age? *American*

Journal of Obstetrics and Gynecology, 197, 428.

Greenfeld, D. A. (2005). Reproduction in same sex couples: Quality of parenting and child development. *Current Opinions in Obstetrics and Gynecology, 17,* 309–312.

Greenfeld, D. A. (2007). Gay male couples and assisted reproduction: Should we assist? *Fertility and Sterility, 88,* 18–20.

Greenwald, E., & Leitenberg, H. (1989). Long-term effects of sexual experiences with siblings and nonsiblings during childhood. *Archives of Sexual Behavior, 18,* 289–400.

Greenwald, H., & McCorkle, R. (2008). Sexuality and sexual function in long-term survivors of cervical cancer. *Journal of Women's Health, 17,* 955–963.

Greenwald, J. L., Burstein, G., Pincus, J., & Branson, G. (2006). A rapid review of rapid HIV antibody tests. *Current Infectious Disease Reports, 8,* 125–131.

Greer, J. B., Modugno, F., Allen, G. O., & Ness, R. B. (2005). Androgenic progestins in oral contraceptives and the risk of epithelial ovarian cancer. *Obstetrics and Gynecology, 105,* 731–740.

Gregson, S., Nyamukapa, C., Garnett, G., Wambe, M., Lewis, J., Mason, P., Chandiwana, S., Anderson, R. (2005). HIV infection and reproductive health in teenage women orphaned and made vulnerable by AIDS in Zimbabwe. *AIDS Care, 17*(7), 785–794.

Grenier, G., & Byers, E. (2001). Operationalizing premature or rapid ejaculation. *Journal of Sex Research, 38*(4), 369–378.

Griffin, S. A. (2006). A qualitative inquiry into how romantic love has been portrayed by contemporary media and researchers. *Dissertation Abstracts International Section A: Humanities and Social Sciences, 67,* 2272.

Griffith, R. S., Walsh, D. E., Myrmel, K. H., Thompson, R. W., & Behforooz, A. (1987). Success of L-lysine therapy in frequently recurrent herpes simplex infection. Treatment and prophylaxis. *Dermatologica, 175*(4), 183–190.

Griffiths, M. (2001). Sex on the Internet: Observations and implications for Internet sex addiction. *Journal of Sex Research, 38*(4), 333–343.

Griffiths, M. (2003). Internet abuse in the workplace and concern for employers and employment counselors. *Journal of Employment Counseling, 40*(2), 87–97.

Griffiths, M. D. (2000). Excessive Internet use: Implications for sexual behavior. *Cyberpsychology and Behavior, 3,* 537–552.

Griffitt, W., & Veitch, R. (1971). Hot and crowded: Influences of population density and temperature on interpersonal affective behavior. *Journal of Personality and Social Psychology, 17,* 92–98.

Grimes, D. A. (2004). Intrauterine devices (IUDs). In R. A. Hatcher et al. (Eds.), *Contraceptive technology* (18th Rev. ed., pp. 495–530). New York: Ardent Media.

Grob, C. S. (1985). Single case study: Female exhibitionism. *Journal of Nervous and Mental Disease, 173,* 253–256.

Groer, M. W. (2005). Differences between exclusive breastfeeders, formula-feeders, and controls: A study of stress, mood, and endocrine variables. *Biological Research for Nursing, 7*(2), 106–117.

Gross, J. (2007, October 9). Aging and gay, and facing prejudice in twilight. *New York Times.* Retrieved September 3, 2008, from http://www.nytimes.com/2007/10/09/us/09aged.html.

Grosskurth, P. (1980). *Havelock Ellis: A biography.* New York: Alfred A. Knopf.

Groth, A. N. (1978). Patterns of sexual assault against children and adolescents. In A. W. Burgess, A. N. Groth, L. L. Holmstrom, & S. M. Sgroi (Eds.), *Sexual assault of children and adolescents.* Toronto: Lexington Books.

Groth, N., & Burgess, A. (1980). Male rape: Offenders and victims. *American Journal of Psychiatry, 137,* 806–810.

Gruber, A. J., & Pope, H. G. (2000). Psychiatric and medical effects of anabolic-androgenic steroid use in women. *Psychotherapy and Psychosomatics, 69*(1), 19–26.

Gruenbaum, E. (2006). Sexuality issues in the movement to abolish female genital cutting in Sudan. *Medical Anthropology Quarterly, 20,* 121.

Grunbaum, J. A., Kann, L., Kinchen, S. A., Williams, B., Ross, J. G., Lowry, R., & Kolbe, L. (2002). Youth risk behavior surveillance: United States, 2001. *Morbidity and Mortality Weekly Report, 51*(no. SS-4).

Gudjonsson, G. H. (1986). Sexual variations: Assessment and treatment in clinical practice. *Sexual and Marital Therapy, 1,* 191–214.

Gudykunst, W. B. (1986). The influence of cultural variability on perceptions of communication behavior associated with relationship terms. *Human Communication Research, 13,* 147–166.

Guerrero, L. K., & Afifi, W. (1999). Toward a goal-oriented approach for understanding communicative responses to jealousy.

Western Journal of Communication, 63(2), 216–248.

Guerrero, L. K., Spitzberg, B. H., & Yoshimura, S. M. (2004). Sexual and emotional jealousy. In J. H. Harvey, A. Wenzel, & S. Sprecher (Eds.), *The handbook of sexuality in close relationships* (pp. 311–345). Mahwah, NJ: Erlbaum.

Guffey, M. E. (1999). *Business communication: Process & product* (3rd ed.). Belmont, CA: Wadsworth.

Guha, C., Shah, S. J., Ghosh, S. S., Lee, S. W., Roy-Chowdhury, N., & Roy-Chowdhury, J. (2003). Molecular therapies for viral hepatitis. *BioDrugs, 17*(2), 81–91.

Guilleminault, C., Moscovitch, A., & Poyares, D. (2002). Atypical sexual behavior during sleep. *Psychosomatic Medicine, 64,* 328–336.

Gunawan, M. H. (2001). Nonverbal communication: The "silent" cross-cultural contact with Indonesians. Retrieved September 29, 2005, from http://www.ialf.edu/kipbipa/papers/MuhamadHandiGunawan.doc.

Gundersen, B. H., Melas, P. S., & Skar, J. E. (1981). Sexual behavior of preschool children: Teachers' observations. In L. L. Constantine & F. M. Martinson (Eds.), *Children and sex: New findings, new perspectives* (pp. 45–61). Boston: Little, Brown.

Guneysel, O., Onur, O., Erdede, M., & Denizbasi, A. (2008). Trimethoprim/sulfamethoxazole resistance in urinary tract infections. *Journal of Emergency Medicine* [Epub]. Retrieved March 22, 2008, from http://www.ncbi.nlm.nih.gov/pubmed/18325714?ordinalpos=3&itool=EntrezSystem2.PEntrez.Pubmed.Pubmed_ResultsPanel.Pubmed_RVDocSum.

Gunter, B., & McAleer, J. L. (1990). *Children and television: The one-eyed monster?* London: Routledge, Chapman, Hall.

Gunter, J. (2007). Vulvodynia: New thoughts on a devastating condition. *Obstetrics and Gynecological Survey, 62,* 812–819.

Gupta, J. K., & Nikodem, V. C. (2000). Woman's position during second stage of labour. *Cochrane Database of Systematic Reviews, 2,* CD002006.

Haake, P., Tillmann, H. C., Krueger, M., Goebel, K., Heberling, U., Schedlowski, M. (2004). Effects of sexual arousal on lymphocyte subset circulation an cytokine production in men. *Neuroimmunomodulation, 11,* 293–298.

Hack, W. W., Meijer, R. W., Bos, S. D., & Haasnoot, K. (2003). A new clinical classification for undescended testis. *Scandinavian Journal of Nephrology, 37*(1), 43–47.

Hader, S. L., Smith , D. K., Moore, J. S., & Holmberg, S. D. (2001). HIV infection in women in the U.S.: Status at the millennium. *Journal of the American Medical Association, 285*(9), 1186–1192.

Haeberle, E. J. (1982). The Jewish contribution to the development of sexology. *Journal of Sex Research, 18,* 305–323.

Hahlweg, K., Kaiser, A., Christensen, A., Fehm-Wolfsdorf, G., & Grother, T. (2000). Self-report and observational assessment of couples' conflict. *Journal of Marriage and Family, 62*(1), 61.

Hahm, H., Lee, J., Zerden, L., & Ozonoff, A. (2008). Longitudinal effects of perceived maternal approval on sexual behaviors of Asian and Pacific Islander (API) young adults. *Journal of Youth and Adolescence, 37,* 74–85.

Hald, G. M. (2006). Gender differences in pornography consumption among young heterosexual Danish adults. *Archives of Sexual Behavior, 35*(5), 577–585.

Hald, G. M., Malamuth, N. M. (2008). Self-perceived effects of pornography consumption. *Archives of Sexual Behavior, 37*(4), 614–626.

Halfon, N., McLearn, K. T., & Schuster, M. A. (2002). *Child rearing in America: Challenges facing parents with young children.* New York: Cambridge University Press.

Hall, E. T. (1959). *Beyond culture.* New York: Doubleday.

Hall, H. I., Song, R., Rhodes, P., Prejean, J., An, Q., Lee, L., et al. (2008b). Estimation of HIV incidence in the United States. *Journal of the American Medical Association, 300,* 520–529.

Hall, P. (2005, December 14). Porta-porn: Smut finding it's way onto video iPods in a big way. *Hartford Courant,* p. D1.

Hall, P., & Schaeff, C. (2008). Sexual orientation and fluctuating asymmetry in men and women. *Archives of Sexual Behavior, 37,* 158–165.

Hall, T., Hogben, M., Carlton, A., Liddon, N., & Koumans, E. (2008a). Attitudes toward using condoms and condom use: Difference between sexually abused and non-abused African American female adolescents. *Behavioral Medicine, 34,* 45–54.

Halpern, C. J., Udry, J. R., Suchindran, C., & Campbell, B. (2000). Adolescent males' willingness to report masturbation. *Journal of Sex Research, 37*(4), 327–333.

Halpern, C. T., Udry, J. R., & Suchindran, C. (1997). Testosterone predicts initiation of coitus in adolescent females. *Psychosomatic Medicine, 59*(2), 161–171.

Halpern-Felsher, B., Kropp, R., Boyer, C., Tschann, J., Ellen, J. (2004). Adolescents' self-efficacy to communicate about sex: Its role in condom attitudes, commitment, and use. *Adolescence, 39*(155), 443–457.

Halsall, P. (1996). *Thomas Aquinas: Summa theologiae.* Retrieved April 10, 2008, from http://www.fordham.edu/halsall/source/aquinas1.html.

Hamachek, D. E. (1982). *Encounters with others: Interpersonal relationships and you.* New York: Holt, Rinehart & Winston.

Hamberg, K. (2000). Gender in the brain: A critical scrutiny of the biological gender differences. *Lakartidningen, 97,* 5130–5132.

Hamburg, B. A. (1986). Subsets of adolescent mothers: Developmental, biomedical, and psychosocial issues. In J. B. Lancaster & B. A. Hamburg (Eds.), *School-age pregnancy and parenthood: Biosocial dimensions* (pp. 115–145). New York: Aldine DeGruyter.

Hamer, D. H., et al. (1993). A linkage between DNA markers on the X chromosome and male sexual orientation. *Science, 261,* 321–327.

Hamilton, T. (2002). *Skin flutes and velvet gloves.* New York: St. Martin's Press.

Hammermeister, J., & Burton, D. (2004). Gender differences in coping with endurance sport stress: Are men from Mars and women from Venus? *Journal of Sport Behavior, 27*(2), 148–165.

Hand, J. Z., & Sanchez, L. (2005). Badgering or bantering? Gender differences in experience of, and reactions to, sexual harassment among U.S. high school students. *Gender & Society, 14*(6), 718–746.

Handler, A., Davis, F., Ferre, C., & Yeko, T. (1989). The relationship of smoking and ectopic pregnancy. *American Journal of Public Health, 79,* 1239–1242.

Handwerk, B. (2005, February 25). 4-D ultrasound gives video view of fetuses in the womb. *National Geographic News.* Retrieved October 14, 2008, from http://news.nationalgeographic.com/news/pf/80752382.html.

Hankins, G. (1995). *Operative Obstetrics.* Appleton and Lange, Stamford, CT.

Hannah-Jones, N. (2008, January 1). Bringing up baby all by momself. *The Oregonian.* Retrieved from http://www.oregonlive.com/oregonian/stories/index.ssf?/base/news/1199161513105830.xml&coll=7.

Hansen, B. (1989). American Physicians' earliest writings about homosexuals, 1880–1900. *Milbank Quarterly, 67*(Suppl 1), 92–108.

Hardt, J., Sidor, A., Nickel, R., Kappis, B., Petrak, P., & Egle, U. T. (2008). Childhood adversities and suicide attempts: A retrospective study. *Journal of Family Violence, 23,* 713–719.

Hardy, S., & Raffaelli, M. (2003). Adolescent religiosity and sexuality: An investigation of reciprocal influences. *Journal of Adolescence, 26*(6), 731–739.

Hargie, O. D., Tourish, D., & Curtis, L. (2001). Gender, religion, and adolescent patterns of self-disclosure in the divided society of Northern Ireland. *Adolescence, 36,* 665–679.

Harkless, L. E., & Fowers, B. J. (2005). Similarities and differences in relational boundaries among heterosexuals, gay men, and lesbians. *Psychology of Women Quarterly, 29*(2), 167–176.

Harlan, L. C., Potosky, A., Cilliland, F. D., Hoffman, R., Albertsen, P. C., Hamilton, A. S., Eley, J. W., Stanford, J. L., & Stephenson, R. A. (2001). Factors associated with initial therapy for clinically localized prostate cancer: Prostate cancer outcomes study. *Journal of the National Cancer Institute, 93*(24), 1864–1871.

Harlow, B. L., Vitonis, A. F., & Stewart, E. G. (2008). Influence of oral contraceptive use on the risk of adult-onset vulvodynia. *Journal of Reproductive Medicine, 53,* 102–110.

Harlow, H. F. (1959). Love in infant monkeys. *Scientific American, 200,* 68–70.

Harmon, A. (2007, September 16). Cancer free at 33, but weighing a mastectomy. *New York Times.* Retrieved March 20, 2008, from http://www.nytimes.com/2007/09/16/health/16gene.html.

Harper, D., & Paavonen, J. (2008). Age for HPV vaccination. *Vaccine, 26*(Suppl. 1), A7–11.

Harris, C. R. (2003). A review of sex differences in sexual jealousy, including self-report data, psychophysiological responses, interpersonal violence, and morbid jealousy. *Personality and Social Psychology Review, 7*(2), 102–128.

Harrison, F. (2005). Iran's sex-change operations. *BBC News.* Retrieved May 25, 2008, from http://news.bbc.co.uk/2/hi/programmes/newsnight/4115535.stm.

Hart, C. W. M., & Pilling, A. R. (1960). *The Tiwi of North Australia.* New York: Holt, Rinehart & Winston.

Harvard Law Review. (1990). *Sexual orientation and the law.* Cambridge, MA: Harvard University Press.

Haselton, M. G., Mortezaie, M., Pillsworth, E. G., Bleske-Recheck, A. E., & Frederick, D. A. (2007). Ovulation and human female ornamentation: Near ovulation, women dress to impress. *Hormones and Behavior, 51*, 40–45.

Hatano, Y., & Shimazaki, T. (2004). Japan. In R. T. Francoeur & R. J. Noonan (Eds.), *The Continuum international encyclopedia of sexuality* (pp. 636–678). New York/London: Continuum International.

Hatcher, R. (2004). Depo-Provera injections, implants, and progestin-only pills (minipills). In R. A. Hatcher et al. (Eds.), *Contraceptive technology* (18th Rev. ed., pp. 461–494). New York: Ardent Media.

Hatcher, R., & Nelson, A. (2004). Combined hormonal contraceptive methods. In R. A. Hatcher et al. (Eds.), *Contraceptive technology* (18th Rev. ed., pp. 361–460).

Hatcher, R. A., Trussell, J., Nelson, A., Cates, W., Steward, F., & Kowal, D. (2007). *Contraceptive technology* (19th ed.). New York: Ardent Media.

Hatcher, R. A., Trussell, J., Stewart, F. H., Nelson, A. L., Cates, W., Guest, F., & Kowal, D. (2004). *Contraceptive technology* (18th Rev. ed.). New York: Ardent Media.

Hatfield, E. (1988). Passionate and companionate love. In R. J. Sternberg & R. J. Barnes (Eds.), *Psychology of love* (pp. 191–217). New Haven, CT: Yale University Press.

Hatfield, E., & Sprecher, S. (1986). Measuring passionate love in intimate relationships. *Journal of Adolescence, 9*(4), 383–410.

Hawkins, A. J., Nock, S. L., Wilson, J. C., Sanchez, L., & Wright, J. D. (2002). Attitudes about covenant marriage and divorce: Policy implications from a three-state comparison. *Family Relations, 51*(2), 166–176.

Haworth, A. (2002, September). Where sex is against the law. *Marie Claire*, pp. 108–116.

Hawthorne, C. M., Farber, P. J., & Bibbo, M. (2005). Chlamydia/gonorrhea combo and HR HPV DNA testing in liquid-based pap. *Diagnostic Cytopathology, 33*(3), 177–180.

Hawton, K. (1983). Behavioural approaches to the management of sexual deviations. *British Journal of Psychiatry, 143*, 248–255.

Hayashi, A. (2004, August 20). Japanese women shun the use of the pill. *CBS News*. Retrieved October 28, 2008, from http://www.cbsnews.com/stories/2004/08/20/health/main637523.shtml.

Hayes, R., Dennerstein, L., Bennett, C., Koochaki, P., Leiblum, S., & Graziottin, A. (2007). Relationship between hypoactive sexual desire disorder and aging. *Fertility and Sterility, 87*, 107–112.

Hazan, C., & Shaver, P. (1987). Romantic love conceptualized as an attachment process. *Journal of Personality & Social Psychology, 52*(3), 511–524.

Hazelwood, R., & Burgess, A. (1987). *Practical aspects of rape investigation: A multidisciplinary approach.* New York: Elsevier.

Heath, D. (1984). An investigation into the origins of a copious vaginal discharge. *Journal of Sex Research, 20*, 194–210.

Hebert, K., Lopez, B., Castellanos, J., Palacio, A., Tamariz, L., & Arcement, L. (2008). The prevalence of erectile dysfunction in heart failure patients by race and ethnicity. *International Journal of Impotence Research, 20*(5), 507–511.

Heffelfinger, J., Swint, E., Berman, S., & Weinstock, H. (2007). Trends in primary and secondary syphilis among men who have sex with men in the U.S. *American Journal of Public Health, 97*, 1076–1083.

Heger, A., Ticson, L., Velasquez, O., & Bernier, R. (2002). Children referred for possible sexual abuse: Medical findings in 2384 children. *Child Abuse & Neglect, 26*(6–7), 645–659.

Hegna, K., & Rossow, I. (2007). What's love got to do with it? Substance use and social integration for young people categorized by same-sex experience and attractions. *Journal of Drug Issues, 37*, 229–256.

Heiman, J. (2002). Sexual dysfunction: Overview of prevalence, etiological factors, and treatments. *Journal of Sex Research, 39*(1), 73–79.

Heiman, J., & LoPiccolo, J. (1992). *Becoming orgasmic: A sexual and personal growth program for women.* New York: Simon & Schuster.

Heiman, J., & Meston, M. (1997). Empirically validated treatment for sexual dysfunction. *Annual Review of Sex Research, 8*, 148–194.

Heinzmann, D. (2008, May 6). Some men say using prostitutes is an addiction: 200 take part in a study about motivation. *Chicago Tribune.* Retrieved October 7, 2008, from http://libill.hartford.edu:2083/pqdweb?index=7&did=1473639221&SrchMode=1&sid=4&Fmt=3&VInst=PROD&VType=PQD&RQT=309&VName=PQD&TS=1223437846&clientId=3309.

Hellerstein, E., Olafson, L., Parker, H., & Offen, K. M. (1981). *Victorian women: A documentary account of women's lives in nineteenth-century England, France, and the United States.* Stanford, CA: Stanford University Press.

Hellstrom, W. J. (2006). Current and future pharmacotherapies of premature ejaculation. *Journal of Sexual Medicine, 3*(Suppl 4), 332–341.

Hemmerling, A., Siedentopf, F., & Kentenich, H. (2005). Emotional impact and acceptability of medical abortion with mifepristone: A German experience. *Journal of Psychosomatic Obstetrics & Gynecology, 26*(1), 23–31.

Hemphill, E. (1991). *Brother to brother: New writings by black gay men.* Boston: Alyson.

Hemstrom, O. (1996). Is marriage dissolution linked to differences in mortality risks for men and women? *Journal of Marriage and the Family, 58*, 366–378.

Henderson, L. (1991). Lesbian pornography: Cultural transgression and sexual demystification. *Women and Language, 14*, 3–12.

Hendrick, C., & Hendrick, S. S. (1989). Research on love: Does it measure up? *Journal of Personality & Social Psychology, 56*(5), 784–794.

Hendrick, C., & Hendrick, S.S. (2000). *Close relationships: A sourcebook.* Thousand Oaks, CA: Sage.

Henningsen, D. D. (2004). Flirting with meaning: An examination of miscommunication in flirting intentions. *Sex Roles, 50*(7–8), 481–489.

Henry J. Kaiser Family Foundation. (2003). Sex on TV 3: Content and context. Executive summary. Retrieved May 23, 2003, from http://www.kff.org/content/2003/20030204a/FINAL_EX.PDF.

Hensel, D. J., Fortenberry, J. D., Harezlak, J., Anderson, J. G., & Orr, D. P. (2004). A daily diary analysis of vaginal bleeding and coitus among adolescent women. *Journal of Adolescent Health, 34*(5), 392–394.

Henshaw, S. K., & Finer, L. B. (2003). The accessibility of abortion services in the United States, 2001. *Perspectives on Sexual and Reproductive Health, 35*(1), 16–24.

Henshaw, S. K., & Kost, K. (1992). Parental involvement in minors' abortion decisions. *Family Planning Perspectives, 24*, 200.

Henshaw, S.K., Kost, K. (2008). Trends in the characteristics of women obtaining abortions, 1974 to 2004. Alan Guttmacher Institute. Retrieved October 28, 2008, from http://www.guttmacher.org/pubs/2008/09/23/TrendsWomenAbortions-wTables.pdf.

Henshaw, S. K., Singh, S., & Haas, T. (1999). The incidence of abortion worldwide. *In-*

ternational Family Planning Perspectives, 25(Suppl.), S30–S38.

Hensley, C. (2002). Prison rape: Practice and policy. Boulder, CO: Lynne Rienner.

Hensley, C., Koscheski, M., & Tewksbury, R. (2005). Examining the characteristics of male sexual assault targets in a Southern maximum-security prison. Journal of Interpersonal Violence, 20(6), 667–679.

Hensley, L. G. (2002). Treatment of survivors of rape: Issues and interventions. Journal of Mental Health Counseling, 24(4), 331–348.

Henslin, J. M. (2005). The sociology of human sexuality. In J. M. Henslin, Sociology: A down-to-earth approach. Online chapter retrieved November 30, 2005, from http://www.ablongman.com/html/henslintour/henslinchapter/ahead3.html.

Herbruck, L. F. (2008). The impact of childbirth on the pelvic floor. Urlogical Nursing, 28, 173–184.

Herdt, G. (1981). Guardians of the flutes: Idioms of masculinity. New York: McGraw-Hill.

Herdt, G. (1988). Cross-cultural forms of homosexuality and the concept "gay." Psychiatric Annals, 18, 37–39.

Herdt, G. (1989). Introduction: Gay and lesbian youth, emergent identities, and cultural scenes at home and abroad. In G. Herdt (Ed.), Gay and lesbian youth (pp. 1–42). New York: Harrington Park Press.

Herek, G. (2002). Heterosexuals' attitudes toward bisexual men and women in the United States. Journal of Sex Research, 39(4), 264–274.

Herek, G. (2006). Legal recognition of same-sex relationship in the United States: A social science perspective. American Psychologist, 61, 606–621.

Herek, G., Cogan, J. C., & Gillis, J. (2002). Victim experiences in hate crimes based on sexual orientation. Journal of Social Issues, 58(2), 319–339.

Herek, G. M. (1984). Beyond "homophobia": A social psychological perspective on attitudes toward lesbians and gay men. In J. P. DeCecco (Ed.), Homophobia: An overview (pp. 1–21). New York: The Haworth Press.

Herek, G. M., Capitanio, J. P., & Widaman, K. F. (2002). HIV-related stigma and knowledge in the U.S., 1991–1999. American Journal of Public Health, 92, 371–377.

Herman, J., & Schatzow, E. (1987). Recovery and verification of memories of childhood sexual trauma. Psychoanalytic Psychology, 4, 1–14.

Herman, J. L. (1981). Father–daughter incest. Cambridge, MA: Harvard University Press.

Herman-Giddens, M. E., & Slora, E. J. (1997). Secondary sexual characteristics and menses in young girls seen in office practice. Pediatrics, 99(4), 505–513.

Heron, J., McGuinness, M., Blackmore, E., Craddock, N., & Jones, I. (2008). Early postpartum symptoms in puerperal psychosis. British Journal of Obstetrics and Gynecology, 115, 348–353.

Herszenhorn, D. M. (2007, November 8). House approves bill outlawing workplace discrimination against gays. International Herald Tribune. Retrieved October 2, 2008, from http://www.iht.com/articles/2007/11/08/america/congress.php.

Hewlett, M. (2008, September 17). Getting help is hard for gay domestic violence victims. McClatchy—Tribune Business News. Retrieved October 5, 2008, from http://libill.hartford.edu:2083/pqdweb?index=2&did=1556431461&SrchMode=1&sid=1&Fmt=3&VInst=PROD&VType=PQD&RQT=309&VName=PQD&TS=1223252228&clientId=3309.

Heymann, J., Earle, A., Rajaraman, D., Miller, C., Bogen, K. (2007). Extended family caring for children orphaned by AIDS: Balancing essential work and caregiving in a high HIV prevalence nation. AIDS Care, 19(3), 337–345.

Hickman, S. E., & Muehlenhard, C. L. (1999). By the semi-mystical appearance of a condom: How young women and men communicate sexual consent in heterosexual situations. Journal of Sex Research, 36(3), 258–272.

Hicks, S. (2005). Is gay parenting bad for kids? Responding to the "very idea of difference" in research on lesbian and gay parents. Sexualities, 8(2), 153–168.

Hicks, T., & Leitenberg, H. (2001). Sexual fantasies about one's partner versus someone else: Gender differences in incidence and frequency. Journal of Sex Research, 38, 43–50.

Hickson, F. C. I., Davies, P. M., & Hunt, A. J. (1994). Gay men as victims of nonconsensual sex. Archives of Sexual Behavior, 23(3), 281–294.

Hill, B. F., & Jones, J. S. (1993). Venous air embolism following orogenital sex during pregnancy. American Journal of Emergency Medicine, 11, 155–157.

Hill, S. (2005). Black intimacies: A gender perspective on families and relationships. Walnut Creek, MD: AltaMira Press.

Hill, S. A. (2002). Teaching and doing gender in African American Families. Sex Roles, 47, 493–506.

Hillebrand, R. (2008). The Oneida community. Retrieved April 10, 2008, from http://www.nyhistory.com/central/oneida.htm.

Hillis, S., & Wasserheit, J. (1996). Screening for chlamydia—a key to the prevention of pelvic inflammatory disease. New England Journal of Medicine, 334, 1399–1401.

Hills, A. M., & Taplin, J. L. (1998). Anticipated responses to stalking: Effect of threat and target-stalker relationship. Psychiatry, Psychology & Law, 5(1), 139–146.

Hilton, G. (2003). Listening to the boys: English boys' views on the desirable characteristics of teachers of sex education. Sex Education, 3(1), 33–45.

Hines, D. (2007). Predictors of sexual coercion against women and men: A multilevel, multinational study of university students. Archives of Sexual Behavior, 36, 403–422.

Hinshelwood, M. (2002). Early and forced marriage: The most widespread form of sexual exploitation of girls? Retrieved August 27, 2003, from http://www.kit.nl/ils/exchange_content/html/forced_marriage_-_sexual_healt.asp.

Hirayama, H., & Hirayama, K. (1986). The sexuality of Japanese Americans. Special issue: Human sexuality, ethnoculture, and social work. Journal of Social Work and Human Sexuality, 4(3), 81–98.

Hirschfeld, M. (1910). The transvestites: An investigation of the erotic desire to cross dress. Amherst, NY: Prometheus Books.

Hitti, M. (2008, January 18). FDA strengthens warning on blood clot risk for users of Ortho Evra birth control skin patch. WebMD. Retrieved October 28, 2008, from http://www.webmd.com/sex/birth-control/news/20080118/birth-control-patch-stronger-warning.

Hjelmstedt, A., Andersson, L., Skoog-Syanberg, A., Bergh, T., Boivin, J., & Collins, A. (1999). Gender differences in psychological reactions to infertility among couples seeking IVF and ICSI treatment. Acta Obstetricia et Gynecologica Scandinavica, 78(1), 42–48.

Ho, G. Y., Bierman, R., Beardsley, L., Chang, C. J., Burk, R. D., et al. (1998). Natural history of cervicovaginal papillomavirus infection in young women. New England Journal of Medicine, 338(7), 423–428.

Hobbs, K., Symonds, T., Abraham, L., May, K., & Morris, M. (2008). Sexual dysfunction in partners of men with premature ejaculation. International Journal of Impotence Research, 20(5):512–517.

Hoburg, R., Konik, J., Williams, M., & Crawford, M. (2004). Bisexuality among self-identified heterosexual college students. *Journal of Bisexuality, 4,* 25–36.

Hodge, D. R. (2008). Sexual trafficking in the U.S.: A domestic problem with transnational dimensions. *Social Work, 53*(2), 143–152.

Hodge, S., & Canter, D. (1998). Victims and perpetrators of male sexual assault. *Journal of International Violence, 13,* 222–239.

Hoebel, E. A. (1954). *The law of primitive man.* Cambridge, MA: Harvard University Press.

Hoff, G. (2003). Power and love: Sadomasochistic practices in long-term committed relationships. *Dissertation Abstracts: Section B, 64*(1-B), #0419–4217.

Hoffman, M. C. (2008, July 23). Philippines in struggle against abortionist population control initiative. *LifeSite News.com.* Retrieved October 28, 2008, from http://www.lifesitenews.com/ldn/2008/jul/08072201.html.

Hoffstetter, S., Barr, S., LeFevre, C., Leong, F., & Leet, T. (2008). Self-reported yeast symptoms compared with clinical wet mount analysis and vaginal yeast culture in a specialty clinic setting. *Journal of Reproductive Medicine, 53,* 402–406.

Hofman, B. (2005). "What is next?": Gay male students' significant experiences after coming-out while in college. *Dissertation Abstracts International Section A: Humanities & Social Sciences, 65*(8-A), #0419–4209.

Hogan, H. (2005). Title IX requires colleges & universities to eliminate the hostile environment caused by campus sexual assault. Retrieved October 25, 2005, from http://www.securityoncampus.org/victims/title-ixsummary.html.

Holcomb, D. R., Savage, M. P., Seehafer, R., & Waalkes, D. M. (2002). A mixed-gender date rape prevention intervention targeting freshmen college athletes. *College Student Journal, 36*(2), 165–179.

Hollander, D. (2000, March/April). Fertility drugs do not raise breast, ovarian or uterine cancer risk. *Family Planning Perspectives, 32*(2), 100–103.

Hollander, D. (2001). Users give new synthetic and latex condoms similar ratings on most features. *Family Planning Perspectives, 33*(1), 45–48.

Holmes, R. (1991). *Sex crimes.* Newbury Park, CA: Sage.

Holmes, W., & Slap, G. (1998). Sexual abuse of boys: Definition, prevalence, correlates, sequelae, and management. *Journal of the American Medical Association, 280,* 1855–1862.

Holzman, C., Leventhal, J. M., Qiu, H., Jones, N., & Wang, J. (2001). Factors linked to bacterial vaginosis in nonpregnant women. *American Journal of Public Health, 91*(10), 1664–1671.

Hooker, E. (1957). The adjustment of the male overt homosexual. *Journal of Projective Techniques, 21,* 18–31.

Hooton, T. M. (2003). The current management strategies for community-acquired urinary tract infection. *Infectious Disease Clinics of North America, 17*(2), 303–332.

Horowitz, S. M., Weis, D. L., & Laflin, M. T. (2001). Differences between sexual orientation behavior groups and social background, quality of life, and health behaviors. *Journal of Sex Research, 38*(3), 205–219.

Horrigan, J. B., Rainie, L., & Fox, S. (2001). Online communities: Networks that nurture long-distance relationships and local ties. Pew Internet and American Life Project. Retrieved April 26, 2008, from http://www.pewinternet.org/pdfs/pip_communities_report.pdf.

Hourvitz, A., Maman, E., Meiri-Farber, B., & Dor, J. (2008). Oocyte cryopreservation. *Harefuah, 147,* 149–154.

Houston, E., & McKirnan, D. (2008). Intimate partner abuse among gay and bisexual men: Risk correlates and health outcomes. *Journal of Urban Health, 84,* 681–690.

Howard, L. M., Hoffbrand, S., Henshaw, C., Boath, L., & Bradley, E. (2005). Antidepressant prevention of postnatal depression. *The Cochrane Database of Systematic Reviews, 2,* art. no. CD004363.

Howell, E. A., Mora, P. A., Horowitz, C. R., & Leventhal, H. (2005). Racial and ethnic differences in factors associated with early postpartum depressive symptoms. *Obstetrics & Gynecology, 105*(6), 1442–1450.

Hu, H., Real, E., Takamiyak, J., Kang, M., Ledoux, J., Huganir, R., & Malinow, R. (2007). Emotion enhances learning via norepinephrine regulation of AMPA-receptor trafficking, *Cell, 131,* 160–173.

Hu, X., Cheng, L., Hua, X., & Glasier, A. (2005). Advanced provision of emergency contraception to postnatal women in China makes no difference in abortion rates: A randomized controlled trial. *Contraception, 72,* 111–116.

Hu, Y., Wood, J., Smith, V., & Westbrook, N. (2004). Friendships through IM: Examining the relationship between instant mes-saging and intimacy. *Journal of Computer-Mediated Communication, 10*(1), art. 6.

Huang, J. (2007). Hormones and female sexuality. In M. Tepper & A. F. Owens (Eds.), *Sexual Health, Vol 2: Physical Foundations* (pp. 43–78). Westport, CT: Praeger.

Hubayter, Z., & Simon, J. (2008). Testosterone therapy for sexual dysfunction in postmenopausal women. *Climacteric, 11,* 181–191.

Huffstutter, P. J. (2004). Smallest surviving preemie will go home soon. Retrieved December 23, 2004, from http://www.latimes.come/news/nationworld/nation/la-na-baby22dec,0,3320847,print.story.

Hughes, J. R. (2006). A general review of recent reports on homosexuality and lesbianism. *Sexuality and Disability, 24,* 195–205.

Hughes, L. M., Griffith, R., Aitken, R. (2007). The search for a topical dual action spermicide/microbicide. *Current Medicinal Chemistry, 14,* 775–786.

Hulbert, F. (1989). Barriers to effective listening. *Bulletin for the Association for Business Communication, 52,* 3–5.

Human Genome Project. (2003). How many genes are in the human genome? Retrieved October 1, 2005, from http://www.ornl.gov/sci/techresources/Human_Genome/faq/genenumber.shtml.

Human Rights Watch. (2001). Hatred in the hallways. Retrieved May 14, 2003, from http://www.hrw.org/reports/2001.

Hunt, L. (1993). Introduction: Obscenity and the origins of modernity, 1500–1800. In L. Hunt (Ed.), *The invention of pornography* (pp. 9–45). New York: Zone Books.

Hunt, M. (1974). *Sexual behavior in the 1970's.* New York: Dell.

Hunter, I., Saunders, D., & Williamson, D. (1993). *On pornography: Literature, sexuality and obscenity law.* New York: St. Martin's Press.

Hunter, J. A., Figueredo, A. J., Malamuth, N. M., & Becker, J. V. (2003). Juvenile sex offenders: Toward the development of a typology. *Sexual Abuse: Journal of Research & Treatment, 15*(1), 27–48.

Hutson, J. M., Baker, M., Terada, M., Zhou, B., & Paxton, G. (1994). Hormonal control of testicular descent and the cause of cryptorchidism. *Reproduction, Fertility and Development, 6*(2), 151–156.

Hutson J. M., & Hasthorpe S. J. (2005). Testicular descent and cryptorchidism: The state of the art in 2004. *Pediatric Surgery, 40*(2), 297–302.

Hutter, M. (1981). *The changing family: Comparative perspective.* New York: Wiley.

Hynes, H. P. (2004). On the battlefield of women's bodies: An overview of the harm of war to women. *Women's Studies International Forum, 27*(5–6), 431–445.

Iasenza, S. (1991). The relations among selected aspects of sexual orientation and sexual functioning in females. New York University. *Dissertation Abstracts International,* #9134752.

Iasenza, S. (2002). Beyond "lesbian bed death": The passion and play in lesbian relationships. *Journal of Lesbian Studies, 6,* 111–120.

Impett, E. A., Beals, K. P., & Peplau, L. A. (2001). Testing the investment model of relationship commitment and stability in a longitudinal study of married couples. *Current Psychology, 20*(4), 312–327.

Incerpi, M. H., Miller, D. A., Samadi, R., Settlage, R. H., Goodwin, T. M. (1999). Stillbirth evaluation: What tests are needed? *American Journal of Obstetrics and Gynecology, 180*(6 Pt 1), 1595–1596.

Irvine, J. (1990). *Disorders of desire, sex, and gender in modern American sexology.* Philadelphia: Temple University Press.

Irvine, J. (1995). Reinventing perversion: Sex addiction and cultural anxieties. *Journal of the History of Sexuality, 5*(3), 429–449.

Irving, C., Basu, A., Richmond, S., Burn, J., & Wren, C. (2008, July 2). Twenty-year trends in prevalence of survival of Down syndrome. *European Journal of Human Genetics.* Retrieved October 14, 2008, from http://www.nature.com/ejhg/journal/vaop/ncurrent/abs/ejhg2008122a.html.

Isaiah Green, A. (2007). Queer theory and sociology: Locating the subject and the self in sexuality studies. *Sociological Theory, 25,* 26–45.

Isay, R. A. (1989). *Being homosexual.* New York: Farrar, Straus, & Giroux.

Ishak, W. W., Berman, D. S., & Peters, A. (2008). Male anorgasmia treated with oxytocin. *Journal of Sexual Medicine, 5,* 1022–1024.

Ishibashi, K. L., Koopmans, J., Curlin, F. A., Alexander, K., & Ross, L. (2008). Paediatricians' attitudes and practices towards HPV vaccination. *Acta Paediatrician, 97*(11), 1550–1556.

Isidori, A., Giannetta, E., Gianfrilli, D., Greco, E., Bonifacio, V., Aversa, A., et al. (2005). Effects of testosterone on sexual function in men: Results of a meta-analysis. *Clinical Endocrinology, 63,* 381–394.

Islam, A., Mitchel, J., Rosen, R., Phillips, N., Ayers, C., Ferguson, D., et al. (2001). Topical alprostadil in the treatment of female sexual arousal disorder. *Journal of Sex and Marital Therapy, 27*(5), 531–540.

Israilov, S., Niv, E., Livne, P. M., Shmeuli, J., Engelstein, D., Segenreich, E., & Baniel, J. (2002). Intracavernous injections for erectile dysfunction in patients with cardiovascular diseases and failure or contraindications for sildenafil citrate. *International Journal of Impotence Research, 14*(1), 38–43.

Iverson, J. S. (1991). A debate on the American home: The antipolygamy controversy, 1880–1890. *Journal of the History of Sexuality, 1,* 585–602.

Jaccard, J., Dittus, P. J., & Gordon, V. V. (1998). Parent–adolescent congruency in reports of adolescent sexual behavior and in communications about sexual behavior. *Child Development, 69*(1), 247–261.

Jaccard, J., Dittus, P. J., & Gordon, V. V. (2000). Parent–teen communication about premarital sex: Factors associated with the extent of communication. *Journal of Adolescent Research, 15*(2), 187–209.

Jackman, L. P., Williamson, D. A., Netemeyer, R. G., & Anderson, D. A. (1995). Do weight-preoccupied women misinterpret ambiguous stimuli related to body size? *Cognitive Therapy and Research, 19,* 341–355.

Jackson, B. (1998). *Splendid slippers: A thousand years of an erotic tradition.* Berkeley, CA: Ten Speed Press.

Jackson, M. (1984). Sex research and the construction of sexuality: A tool of male supremacy? *Women's Studies International Forum, 7,* 43–51.

Jacquet, S. E., & Surra, C. A. (2001). Parental divorce and premarital couples: Commitment and other relationship characteristics. *Journal of Marriage and Family, 63*(3), 627–639.

Jain, J. K., Minoo, P., Nucatola, D. L., & Felix, J. C. (2005). The effect of nonoxynol-9 on human endometrium. *Contraception, 71*(2), 137–142.

Jakimiuk, A., Fritz, A., Grzybowski, W., Walecka, I., & Lewandowski, P. (2007). Diagnosing and management of iatrogenic moderate and severe ovarian hyperstymulation syndrome in clinical material. *Polish Academy of Sciences, 45*(Suppl. 1), S105–108.

Jamanadas, K. (2008). Sati was started for preserving caste. Retrieved April 8, 2008 from http://www.ambedkar.org/research/Sati_Was_Started_For_Preserving_Caste.htm.

James, A. (2008, February 26). Life without puberty: Hormone blockers for minors, the trans movement's new frontier. *Advocate.* Retrieved February 26, 2008, from http://www.advocate.com/issue_story_ektid51685.asp.

Jamieson, D., Kaufman, S., Costello, C., Hillis, S., Marchbanks, P., & Peterson, H. (2002). A comparison of women's regret after vasectomy versus tubal sterilization. *Obstetrics and Gynecology, 99,* 1073–1079.

Janeway, E. (1971). *Man's world, woman's place: A study in social mythology.* New York: W. Morrow.

Jannini, E. A., & Lenzi, A. (2005). Epidemiology of premature ejaculation. *Current Opinions in Urology, 15*(6), 399–403.

Jansz, J., & Martis, R. G. (2007). The Lara phenomenon: Powerful female characters and video games. *Sex Roles, 56,* 141–148.

Janus, S. S., & Janus, C. L. (1993). *The Janus report on sexual behavior.* New York: Wiley.

Japsen, B. (2003). Viagra faces 1st rivals by year's end. Retrieved July 18, 2003, from http://www.webprowire.com/summaries/5357111.html.

Javitt, G., Berkowitz, D., & Gostin, L. (2008). Assessing mandatory HPV vaccination: Who should call the shots? *Journal of Law, Medicine and Ethics, 36,* 384–395.

Jaworowicz, D. (2007). Novel risk factors for breast cancer. Presented at the 40th Annual Meeting of the Society for Epidemiologic Research, Boston, MA.

Jaworski, A., & Coupland, J. (2005). Othering in gossip: "You go out you have a laugh and you can pull yeah okay but like…." *Language and Society, 34,* 667–695.

Jayne, C. (1981). A two-dimensional model of female sexual response. *Journal of Sex and Marital Therapy, 7,* 3–30.

Jayson, S. (2005, July 17). Cohabitation is replacing dating. *USA Today.* Retrieved September 13, 2008, from http://www.usatoday.com/life/lifestyle/2005-07-17-cohabitation_x.htm.

Jeary, K. (2005). Sexual abuse and sexual offending against elderly people: A focus on perpetrators and victims. *Journal of Forensic Psychiatry & Psychology, 16*(2), 328–343.

Jelovsek, J. E., Walters, M. D., & Barber, M. D. (2008). Psychosocial impact of chronic vulvovaginal conditions. *Journal of Reproductive Medicine, 53,* 75–82.

Jemal, A., Murray, T. Ward, E., Samuels, A., Tiwari, R. C., Ghafoor, A., Feuer, E. J., & Thun, M. J. (2005). Cancer statistics, 2005. *CA: A Cancer Journal for Clinicians, 55,* 10–30.

Jenkins, D., & Johnston, L. (2004). Unethical treatment of gay and lesbian people with conversion therapy. *Families in Society, 85*(4), 557–561.

Jenness, V. (1990). From sex as sin to sex as work: COYOTE and the reorganization of prostitution as a social problem. *Social Problems, 37,* 403–420.

Jensen, J. T. (2008). A continuous regimen of levonorgestrel/ethinyl estradiol for contraception and elimination of menstruation. *Drugs Today, 44,* 183–195.

Jensen, M. N. (1998). Heterosexual women have noisy ears. *Science News, 153*(10), 151–152.

Jepsen, L. K., & Jepsen, C. A. (2002). An empirical analysis of the matching patterns of same-sex and opposite-sex couples. *Demography, 39,* 435–454.

Jetter, A. (1991). Faye's crusade. *Vogue,* 147–151, 202–204.

Jha, P., Kumar, R., Vasa, P., Dhingra, N., Thiruchelvam, D., & Moineddin, R. (2006). Low male-to-female sex ratio of children born in India: National survey of 1.1 million households. *The Lancet, 367,* 211–218.

Joffe, A., Rietmeiger, C., Chung, S., Willard, N., Chapin, J., Lloyd, L., et al. (2008). Screening asymptomatic adolescent men for Chlamydia trachomatis in school-based health centers using urine-based nucleic acid amplification tests. *Sexually Transmitted Diseases, 35*(11 Suppl):S19–23.

Johansen, R. E. B. (2007). Experiencing sex in exile—can genitals change their gender? In Y. Hernlund & B. Shell-Duncan (Eds.), *Transcultural bodies: Female cutting in global context* (pp. 248–277). New Brunswick, NJ: Rutgers University Press.

Johansson, T., & Ritzen, E. M. (2005). Very long-term follow-up of girls with early and late menarche. *Endocrine Development, 8,* 126–136.

John, E. M., Miron, A., Gong, G., Phipps, A. I., Felberg, A., Li, R. P., et al. (2007). Prevalence of pathogenic BRCA1 mutation carriers in 5 U.S. racial/ethnic groups. *Journal of the American Medical Association, 298,* 2910–2911.

Johnson, A., Wadsworth, J., Wellings, K., Bradshaw, S., & Field, J. (1992). Sexual lifestyles and HIV risk. *Nature, 360,* 410–412.

Johnson, A. M. (2001). Popular belief in gender-based communication differences and relationship success. *Dissertation Abstracts,* University of Massachusetts, Amherst, #0-599-95739-5.

Johnson, B. E., Kuck, D. L., & Schander, P. R. (1997). Rape myth acceptance and sociodemographic characteristics: A multidimensional analysis. *Sex Roles, 36*(11–12), 693–707.

Johnson, J. (2001). *Male multiple orgasm: Step by step* (4th ed). Jack Johnson Seminars.

Johnson, J., & Alford, R. (1987). The adolescent quest for intimacy: Implications for the therapeutic alliance. *Journal of Social Work and Human Sexuality* (Special issue: Intimate Relationships), 5, 55–66.

Johnson, K., Gill, S., Reichman, V., Tassinary, L. (2007). Swagger, sway, and sexuality: Judging sexual orientation from body motion and morphology. *Journal of Personality and Social Psychology, 93*(3), 321–334.

Johnson, K. C., & Daviss, B. A. (2005). Outcomes of planned home births with certified professional midwives: Large prospective study in North America. *British Medical Journal, 330*(7505), 1416–1420.

Johnson, L., Starkey, C., Palmer, J., Taylor, J., Stout, S., Holt, S., et al. (2008). A comparison of two methods to determine the presence of high-risk HPV cervical infections. *American Journal of Clinical Pathology, 130,* 401–408.

Johnson, L. A. (2005). Experts urge routine HIV tests for all. Retrieved February 11, 2005, from http://abcnews.go.com/Health/wireStory?id=485527.

Johnson, S. E. (1996). *Lesbian sex: An oral history.* Tallahassee, FL: Naiad Press.

Jones, J. H. (1997). *Alfred C. Kinsey: A public/private life.* New York: W. W. Norton.

Jones, M., & Cook, R.(2008). Intent to receive an HPV vaccine among university men and women and implications for vaccine administration. *Journal of American College Health, 57,* 23–32.

Jones, R. (1984). *Human reproduction and sexual behavior.* Englewood Cliffs, NJ: Prentice Hall.

Jones, R., Darroch, J., & Singh, S. (2005). Religious differentials in the sexual and reproductive behaviors of young women in the United States. *Journal of Adolescent Health, 36*(4), 279–288.

Jones, R., Singh, S., Finer, L., Frohwirth, L. (2006). Repeat abortion in the U.S. Occasional Report. Guttmacher Institute, 29, New York, NY.

Jones, R., Zolna, M., Henshaw, S., & Finer, L. B. (2008). Abortion in the United States: Incidence and access to services, 2005. *Perspectives on Sexual and Reproductive Health, 40,* 6–16.

Jones, R. K., & Henshaw, S. K. (2002). Mifepristone for early medical abortion: Experiences in France, Great Britain and Sweden. *Perspectives on Sexual and Reproductive Health, 34*(3). Retrieved September 9, 2003, from http://www.agi-usa.org/pubs/journals/3415402.html.

Jong, E. (2003). Pure possibility. In J. Escoffier (Ed.), *Sexual revolution* (p. xxxvii). New York: Thunder's Mouth Press.

Jongpipan, J., & Charoenkwan, K. (2007). Sexual function after radical hysterectomy for early-stage cervical cancer. *Journal of Sexual Medicine, 4,* 1659–1665.

Jordan, J. (1997). User buys: Why men buy sex. *Australian and New Zealand Journal of Criminology, 30,* 55–71.

Jordan, M. (2008, October 1). Gardasil requirement for immigrants stirs backlash. *Wall Street Journal Online.* Retrieved November 5, 2008, from http://online.wsj.com/article/SB122282354408892791.html.

Jorgensen, C. (1967). *Christine Jorgenson: Personal biography.* New York: Erickson.

Joung, I. M., Stronks, K., & van de Mheen, H. (1995). Health behaviours explain part of the differences in self-reported health associated with partner/marital status in the Netherlands. *Journal of Epidemiology and Community Health, 49*(5), 482–488.

Julien, D., Chartrand, E., Simard, M., Bouthillier, D., & Begin, J. (2003). Conflict, social support, and relationship quality: An observational study of heterosexual, gay male, and lesbian couples' communication. *Journal of Family Psychology, 17,* 419–428.

Kaats, G. R., & Davis, K. E. (1971). Effects of volunteer biases in studies of sexual behavior and attitudes. *Journal of Sex Research, 7,* 26–34.

Kafka, M. (2001). The paraphilia-related disorders: A proposal for a united classification of nonparaphilic hypersexuality disorders. *Sexual Addiction and Compulsivity, 8,* 227–239.

Kahlor, L., & Morrison, D. (2007). Television viewing and rape myth acceptance among college women. *Sex Roles, 56,* 729–739.

Kahn, J. A., Rosenthal, S. L., Succop, P. A., Ho, G., & Burk, R. D. (2002). Mediators of the association between age of first sexual intercourse and subsequent HPV infection. *Pediatrics, 109*(1), 132–134.

Kahn, Y. (1989–90). Judaism and homosexuality: The traditionalist/progressive debate. *Journal of Homosexuality, 18,* 47–82.

Kahr, B. (2008). *Who's been sleeping in your head: The secret world of sexual fantasies.* New York: Basic Books.

Kain, E. L. (1987). A note on the integration of AIDS into the Sociology of Human Sexuality. *Teaching Sociology, 15,* 320–323.

Kakuchi, S. (2005). New museum documents lives of Japan's "comfort women." Retrieved November 6, 2005, from http://www.womensenews.org/article.cfm?aid=2509.

Kallen, L. (1998). Men don't cry, women don't fume. *Psychology Today, 31*(5), 20.

Kalyani, R., Basavaraj, P. B., & Kumar, M. L. (2007). Factors influencing quality of semen: A two year prospective study. *Indian Journal of Pathology and Microbiology, 50,* 890–895.

Kaminer, W. (1992, November). Feminists against the first amendment. *Atlantic Monthly,* pp. 111–117.

Kang, M., & Nicolay, U. (2008). Evaluation of operational chronic infection endpoints for HCV vaccine trials. *Contemporary Clinical Trials, 29,* 671–678.

Kantele, A., Palkola, N., Arvilommi, H., Honkinen, O., Jahnukainen, T., Mertsola, J., & Kantele, J. (2008). Local immune response to upper urinary tract infections in children. *Clinical and Vaccine Immunology, 15,* 412–417.

Kantor, L. (1992). Scared chaste? Fear based educational curricula. *SIECUS Reports, 21,* 1–15.

Kaplan, G. (1977). Circumcision: An overview. *Current Problems in Pediatrics, 1,* 1–33.

Kaplan, H., Sadock, B., & Grebb, J. (1994). *Synopsis of psychiatry* (7th ed.). Baltimore, MD: Williams and Wilkins.

Kaplan, H. S. (1974). *The new sex therapy.* New York: Bruner/Mazel.

Kaplan, H. S. (1979). *Sexual desire disorders: Dysfunctional regulation of sexual motivation.* New York: Brunner-Mazel.

Kaplan, L. J. (1991). Women masquerading as women. In G. I. Fogel & W. A. Meyers (Eds.), *Perversions and near-perversions in clinical practice: New psychoanalytic perspectives* (pp. 127–152). New Haven, CT: Yale University Press.

Kaplowitz, P. B. (2008). Link between body fat and the timing of puberty. *Pediatrics, 121*(Suppl 3), S208–217.

Kaplowitz, P. B., Slora, E. J., Wasserman, R. C., Pedlow, S. E., & Herman-Giddens, M. E. (2001). Earlier onset of puberty in girls: Relation to increased body mass index and race. *Pediatrics, 2108*(2), 347–354.

Kapoor, S. (2008). Testicular torsion: A race against time. *International Journal of Clinical Practices, 62,* 821–827.

Karniol, R. (2001). Adolescent females' idolization of male media stars as a transition into sexuality. *Sex Roles, 44*(1–2), 61–77.

Kaschak, E., & Tiefer, L. (2001). *A new view of women's sexual problems.* Binghamton, NY: Haworth Press.

Kasestle, C. E., & Halpern, C. T. (2007). What's love got to do with it? Sexual behaviors of opposite-sex couples through emerging adulthood. *Perspectives on Sexual and Reproductive Health, 29,* 134–140.

Kassler, W. J., & Cates, W. (1992). The epidemiology and prevention of sexually transmitted diseases. *Urologic Clinics of North America, 19,* 1–12.

Katz, J. (2006). *The macho paradox: Why some men hurt women and how all men can help.* New York: Sourcebook.

Katz, M. H., Schwarcz, S. K., Kellogg, T. A., Klausner, J. D., Dilley, J. W., Gibson, S., et al. (2002). Impact of highly active antiretroviral treatment on HIV seroincidence among men who have sex with men. *American Journal of Public Health, 92*(3), 388–395.

Kaufman, B. S., Kaminsky, S. J., Rackow, E. C., & Weil, M. H. (1987). Adult respiratory distress syndrome following orogenital sex during pregnancy. *Critical Care Medicine, 15,* 703–704.

Kaufman, M. (2005). FDA investigates blindness in Viagra users. Retrieved November 15, 2005, from http://www.washingtonpost.com/wp-dyn/content/article/2005/05/27/AR2005052701246_pf.html.

Kaunitz, A. M., Arias, R., & McClung, M. (2008). Bone density recovery after depot medroxyprogesterone acetate injectable contraception use. *Contraception, 77,* 67–76.

Kavanaugh, M. L., & Schwarz, E. B. (2008). Counseling about and use of emergency contraception in the United States. *Perspectives on Sexual Reproductive Health, 40,* 81–86.

Kaye, K. (2007). Sex and the unspoken in male street prostitution. *Journal of Homosexuality, 53,* 37–73.

Kayongo-Male, D., & Onyango, P. (1984). *The sociology of the African family.* London: Longman.

Kazemi-Saleh, D., Pishgou, B., Assari, S., & Tavallaii, S. (2007). Fear of sexual intercourse in patients with coronary artery disease: A pilot study of associated morbidity. *Journal of Sexual Medicine, 4,* 1619–1625.

Keane, F., Thomas, B., Whitaker, L., Renton, A., Taylor-Robinson, D. (1997). An association between non-gonococcal urethritis and bacterial vaginosis and the implications for patients and their sexual partners. *Genitourinary Medicine, 73*(5), 373–377.

Keane, H. (2004). Disorders of desire: Addiction and problems of intimacy. *Journal of Medical Humanities, 25*(3), 189–197.

Keasler, M. (2006). *Love hotels.* San Francisco: Chronicle Books.

Keegan, J. (2001). The neurobiology, neuropharmacology and pharmacological treatment of the paraphilias and compulsive sexual behavior. *Canadian Journal of Psychiatry, 46*(1), 26–33.

Keller, J. (2002). Blatant stereotype threat and women's math performance. *Sex Roles, 47*(3–4), 193–198.

Keller, J. C. (2005). Straight talk about the gay gene. *Science & Spirit, 16,* 21.

Kellerman, S. E., Hanson, D. L., McNaghten, A. D., & Fleming, P. L. (2003). Prevalence of chronic hepatitis B and incidence of acute hepatitis B infection in human immunodeficiency virus-infected subjects. *Journal of Infectious Disease, 188*(4), 571–577.

Kellock, D., & O'Mahony, C. P. (1996). Sexually acquired metronidazole-resistant trichomoniasis in a lesbian couple. *Genitourinary Medicine, 72,* 60–61.

Kelly, J. M. (2005). *Zest for life: Lesbians' experiences of menopause.* North Melbourne, Australia: Spinifex Press.

Kelly, M. P., Strassberg, D. S., & Kircher, J. R. (1990). Attitudinal and experiential correlates of anorgasmia. *Archives of Sexual Behavior, 19,* 165–177.

Kelly, R. J., Wood, J., Gonzalez, L., MacDonald, V., & Waterman, J. (2002). Effects of mother–son incest and positive perceptions of sexual abuse experiences on the psychosocial adjustment of clinic-referred men. *Child Abuse and Neglect, 26*(4), 425–441.

Kelly, T. P. (2004). Ireland. In R. T. Francoeur & R. J. Noonan (Eds.), *The Continuum international encyclopedia of sexuality* (pp. 569–580). New York/London: Continuum International.

Kelly-Vance, L., Anthis, K. S., & Needelman, H. (2004). Assisted reproduction versus spontaneous conception: A comparison of the developmental outcomes in twins. *Journal of Genetic Psychology, 165*(2), 157–168.

Kempeneers, P., Andrianne, R., & Mormont, C. (2004). Penile prosthesis, sexual satisfaction and representation of male erotic value. *Sexual & Relationship Therapy, 19*(4), 379–392.

Kendrick, W. M. (1987). *The secret museum: Pornography in modern culture.* New York: Viking.

Kennedy, M. A., & Gorzalka, B. B. (2002). Asian and non-Asian attitudes toward rape, sexual harassment and sexuality. *Sex Roles, 46*(7–8), 227–238.

Kennet, G. A. (2000). *Serotonin receptors and their function.* Bristol, U.K.: Tocris.

Kerrigan, D., Mobley, S., Rutenberg, N., Fisher, A., & Weiss, E. (2000). The female condom: Dynamics of use in urban Zimbabwe. New York: The Population Council. Retrieved July 24, 2008, from http://www.popcouncil.org/pdfs/horizons/fcz.pdf.

Keshavarz, H., Hillis, S., Kieke, B., & Marchbanks, P. (2002). Hysterectomy surveillance—United States, 1994–1999. *MMWR Surveillance Summaries, 51*(SS05), 1–8.

Khadivzadeh, T., & Parsai, S. (2005). Effect of exclusive breastfeeding and complementary feeding on infant growth and morbidity. *Eastern Mediterranean Health Journal, 10*(3), 289–294.

Kidman, R., Petrow, S., Heymann, S. (2007). Africa's orphan crisis: Two community-based models of care. *AIDS Care, 19*(3), 326–329.

Kiernan, K. (2001). The rise of cohabitation and childbearing outside marriage in Western Europe. *International Journal of Law, Policy and the Family, 15*, 1–21.

Kilgallon, S., & Simmons, L. (2005). Image content influences men's semen quality. *Biology Letters, 1*(3), 253–255.

Kim, J., & Hatfield, E. (2004). Love types and subjective well-being: A cross-cultural study. *Social Behavior and Personality, 32*, 173–182.

Kim, K., & Smith, P. K. (1999). Family relations in early childhood and reproductive development. *Journal of Reproductive and Infant Psychology, 17*(2), 133–149.

Kim, Y., Yang, S., Lee, J., Jung, T., & Shim, H. (2008). Usefulness of a malleable penile prosthesis in patients with a spinal cord injury. *International Journal of Urology, 15*(10), 919–923.

Kimmel, M. S., & Plante, R. F. (2007). Sexualities. *Contexts, 6,* 63–65.

King, B. M., & Lorusso, J. (1997). Discussions in the home about sex: Different recollections by parents and children. *Journal of Sex and Marital Therapy, 23*(1), 52–60.

King, M., & Bartlett, A. (2005). What same sex civil partnerships may mean for health.

Journal of Epidemiology & Community Health, 60, 188–191.

King, P., & Boyatzis, C. (2004). Exploring adolescent spiritual and religious development: Current and future theoretical and empirical perspectives. *Applied Developmental Science, 8,* 2–6.

King, V., & Scott, M. (2005). A comparison of cohabiting relationships among older and younger adults. *Journal of Marriage & Family, 67*(2), 271–285.

Kingsberg, S., Shifren, J., Wekselman, K., Rodenberg, C., Koochaki, P., & Derogatis, L. (2007). Evaluation of the clinical relevance of benefits associated with transdermal testosterone treatment in postmenopausal women with hypoactive sexual desire disorder. *Journal of Sexual Medicine, 4,* 1001–1008.

Kingsberg S. A., & Janata, J. W. (2003). Sexual aversion disorder. In S. Levine (Ed.), *Handbook of clinical sexuality for mental health professionals* (pp. 153–166). New York: Brunner-Routledge.

Kinkade, S., & Meadows, S. (2005). Does neonatal circumcision decrease morbidity? *The Journal of Family Practice, 54*(1), 81–82.

Kinnunen, L. H., Moltz, H., Metz, J., & Cooper, M. (2004). Differential brain activation in exclusively homosexual and heterosexual men produced by the selective serotonin reuptake inhibitor, fluoxetine. *Brain Research, 1024*(1–2), 251–254.

Kinsey, A., Pomeroy, W. B., & Martin, C. E. (1948). *Sexual behavior in the human male.* Philadelphia: Saunders.

Kinsey, A. C., Pomeroy, W., Martin, C. E., & Gebhard, P. (1953). *Sexual behavior in the human female.* Philadelphia: Saunders.

Kirby, D. (1992). Sexuality education: It can reduce unprotected intercourse. *SIECUS Report, 21,* 19–25.

Kirby, D. (2001, May). Emerging answers: Research findings on programs to reduce teen pregnancy. National Campaign to Prevent Teen Pregnancy.

Kirby, D. (2007). Emerging Answers: 2007. *Research Findings on Programs to Reduce Teen Pregnancy and Sexually Transmitted Diseases.* Washington, DC: National Campaign to Prevent Teen and Unplanned Pregnancy. Retrieved May 29, 2008, from http://www.thenationalcampaign.org/EA2007/EA2007_full.pdf.

Kirkpatrick, R. C. (2000). The evolution of human homosexual behavior. *Current Anthropology, 41,* 385–414.

Kirkwood, M., & Cecil, D. (2001). Marital rape: A student assessment of rape laws and marital exemption. *Violence Against Women, 7,* 1234–1253.

Kirsch, A. T. (1985). Text and context: Buddhist sex roles/culture of gender revisited. *American Ethnologist, 12*(2), 302–320.

Kitazawa, K. (1994). Sexuality issues in Japan. *SIECUS Report,* 7–11.

Kito, M. (2005). Self-disclosure in romantic relationships and friendships among American and Japanese college students. *Journal of Social Psychology, 145,* 127–140.

Kitson, G. C. (1992). *Portrait of divorce: Adjustment to marital breakdown.* New York: Guilford Press.

Kjaer, S., Mellemkjaer, L., Brinton, L., Johansen, C., Gridley, G., & Olsen, J. (2004). Tubal sterilization and risk of ovarian, endometrial and cervical cancer. A Danish population-based follow-up study of more than 65,000 sterilized women. *International Journal of Epidemiology, 33,* 596–602.

Klaas, M. (2003). *Klaas Action Review Newsletter, 9*(1). Retrieved May 23, 2003, from http://www.pollyklaas.org/newsletter.htm.

Klaw, E. L., Lonsway, K. A., Berg, D. R., Waldo, C. R., Kothari, C., Mazurek, C. J., & Hegeman, K. E. (2005). Challenging rape culture: Awareness, emotion and action through campus acquaintance rape education. *Women & Therapy, 28*(2), 47–63.

Klein, F. (1978). *The bisexual option: A concept of one-hundred percent intimacy.* New York: Arbor House.

Klein, F. (1990). The need to view sexual orientation as a multivariable dynamic process: A theoretical perspective. In D. P. McWhirter, S. A. Sanders, & J. M. Reinisch (Eds.), *Homosexuality/ heterosexuality: Concepts of sexual orientation* (pp. 277–282). New York: Oxford University Press.

Klein, F. (1993). *The bisexual option* (2nd ed.). Philadelphia: Haworth Press.

Klein, W., Geaghan, T., & MacDonald, T. (2007). Unplanned sexual activity as a consequence of alcohol use: A prospective study of risk perceptions and alcohol use among college freshman. *Journal of American College Health, 56,* 317–323.

Kleinfeld, J. (2002). Six degrees: Urban myth? *Psychology Today.* Retrieved February 10, 2008, from http://psychologytoday.com/articles/pto-20020301-000038.html.

Kleinplatz, P., Moser, C. (2006). *Sadomasochism: Powerful pleasures,* Routledge, NY: Haworth Press.

Klimkiewicz, J. (2008, April 24). Outsourcing labor. *Hartford Courant,* p. D1–D4.

Kline, P. (1987). Sexual deviation: Psychoanalytic research and theory. In G. D. Wilson (Ed.), *Variant sexuality: Research and theory* (pp. 150–175). Baltimore: Johns Hopkins University Press.

Klonoff-Cohen, H., Natarajan, L., Chen, R. (2006). A prospective study of the effects of female and male marijuana use on in vitro fertilization (IVF) and gamete intrafallopian transfer (GIFT) outcomes. *American Journal of Obstetrics and Gynecology, 194*(2), 369–376.

Kluger, J. (2008, January 17). The science of romance: Why we love. *Time Magazine.* Retrieved August 17, 2008, from http://www.time.com/time/magazine/article/0,9171,1704672-2,00.html.

Knaapen, L., & Weisz, G. (2008). The biomedical standardization of premenstrual syndrome. *Studies in History and the Philosophy of Biology and Biomedical Science, 39,* 120–134.

Knapp, M. L., & Hall, J. A. (2005). *Nonverbal communication in human interaction* (6th ed.). Belmont, CA: Wadsworth.

Knoester, M., Helmerhorst, F., Vandenbroucke, J., van der Westerlaken, L., Walther, F., Veen, S., et al. (2008). Perinatal outcome, health growth, and medical care utilization of 5- to 8- year old intracytoplasmic sperm injection singletons. *Fertility and Sterility, 89,* 1133–1146.

Knox, D., Breed, R., & Zusman, M. (2007). College men and jealousy. *College Student Journal, 41,* 435–444.

Knox, D., Zusman, M., & McNeely, A. (2008). University student beliefs about sex: Men vs. women. *College Student Journal, 42,* 181–186.

Knox, D., Zusman, M. E., Buffington, C., & Hemphill, G. (2000). Interracial dating attitudes among college students. *College Student Journal, 434*(1), 69–72.

Knox, D., Zusman, M. E., & Mabon, L. (1999). Jealousy in college student relationships. *College Student Journal, 33*(3), 328–329.

Ko, D. (2001). *In every step a lotus: Shoes for bound feet.* Berkeley: University of California Press.

Ko, D. (2007). *Cinderella's sisters: A revisionist history of footbinding.* Berkeley: University of California Press.

Koch, W. (2005). Despite high-profile cases, sex-offense crimes decline. Retrieved October 9, 2005, from http://www.usatoday.com/news/nation/2005-08-24-sex-crimes-cover_x.htm?POE=NEWISVA.

Koci, A. F. (2004). Marginality, abuse and adverse health outcomes in women. *Dissertations Abstracts International,* 0419–4217.

Koh, A. S., Gomez, C. A., Shade, S., & Rowley, E. (2005). Sexual risk factors among self-identified lesbians, bisexual women, and heterosexual women accessing primary care settings. *Sexually Transmitted Diseases, 32*(9), 563–569.

Kohl, J. V., & Francoeur, R. (2002). *The scent of eros: Mysteries of odor in human sexuality.* Lincoln, NE: iUniverse, Author's Choice Press.

Kohler, P. K., Manhart, L. E., & Lafferty, W. E. (2008). Abstinence-only and comprehensive sex education and the initiation of sexual activity and teen pregnancy. *Journal of Adolescent Health, 42,* 344–351.

Kohn, C., Hasty, S., & Henderson, C. W. (2002, September 3). Study confirms infection from receptive oral sex occurs rarely. *AIDS Weekly,* 20–22.

Komisaruk, B. R., & Whipple, B. (1995). The suppression of pain by genital stimulation in females. *Annual Review of Sex Research, 6,* 151–186.

Kon, I. S. (2004). Russia. In R. T. Francoeur & R. J. Noonan (Eds.), *The Continuum international encyclopedia of sexuality* (pp. 888–908). New York/London: Continuum International.

Kong, S. C. (2004). Kamasutra: A new, complete English translation from the Sanskrit text. *Herisons, 17*(3), 42–43.

Kontula, O., & Haavio-Mannila, E. (2004). Finland. In R. T. Francoeur & R. J. Noonan (Eds.), *The Continuum international encyclopedia of sexuality* (pp. 381–411). New York/London: Continuum International.

Kopelman, L. (1988). The punishment concept of disease. In C. Pierce & D. Vandeveer (Eds.), *AIDS, ethics, and public policy.* Belmont, CA: Wadsworth.

Koropeckyj-Cox, T., Romano, V., & Moras, A. (2007). Through the lenses of gender, race, and class. Students' perceptions of childless/childfree individuals and couples. *Sex Roles, 56,* 415–428.

Korzeniowski, P. (2005). Adult entertainment on a cell phone near you. Retrieved November 5, 2005, from http://www.technewsworld.com/story/41140.html.

Kosfeld, M., Heinrichs, M., Zak, P. J., Fischbacher, U., & Fehr, E. (2005). Oxytocin increases trust in humans. *Nature, 435,* 676–676.

Koskimäki, J., Shiri, R., Tammela, T., Häkkinen, J., Hakama, M., & Auvinen, A. (2008). Regular intercourse protects against erectile dysfunction: Tampere aging male urologic study. *American Journal of Medicine, 121,* 592–596.

Koss, M. P., & Gaines, J. A. (1993). The prediction of sexual aggression by alcohol use, athletic participation and fraternity affiliation. *Journal of Interpersonal Violence, 8*(1), 94–108.

Koster, M., & Price, L. L. (2008). Rwandan female genital modification: Elongation of the labia minora and the use of local botanical species. *Culture, Health and Sexuality, 10,* 19–204.

Kotchick, B. A., Dorsey, S., & Miller, K. S. (1999). Adolescent sexual risk-taking behavior in single-parent ethnic minority families. *Journal of Family Psychology, 13*(1), 93–102.

Koutsky, L. (1997). Epidemiology of genital human papillomavirus infection. *American Journal of Medicine, 102*(Suppl. 5A), 3–8.

Kowal, D. (2004). Coitus interruptus (withdrawal). In R. A. Hatcher et al. (Eds.), *Contraceptive technology* (18th Rev. ed., pp. 311–316). New York: Ardent Media.

Krause, H. (1986). *Family law.* St. Paul, MN: West.

Kreider, R. M. (2005). Number, timing and duration of marriages and divorces: 2001. *Current Population Reports* (P70-97). Washington, DC: U.S. Census Bureau.

Kreinin, T. (2001). Help for the 36 million people with AIDS? *SIECUS Report, 29*(5), 4.

Kresge, K. J. (2008). Balancing AIDS vaccine research. International AIDS Vaccine Initiative, 12. Retrieved September 18, 2008, from http://www.iavireport.org/Issues/Issue12-2/Balance.asp.

Kreuter, M., Dahllof, A. G., Gudjonsson, G., Sullivan, M., & Siosteen, A. (1998). Sexual adjustment and its predictors after traumatic brain injury. *Brain Injury, 12,* 349–368.

Kreuter, M., Siosteen, A., & Biering-Sorensen, F. (2008). Sexuality and sexual life in women with spinal cord injury: A controlled study. *Journal of Rehabilitative Medicine, 40,* 61–69.

Kriebs, J. (2008). Understanding herpes simplex virus: Transmission, diagnosis, and considerations in pregnancy management. *Journal of Midwifery Women's Health, 53,* 202–208.

Krilov, L. (1991). What do you know about genital warts? *Medical Aspects of Human Sexuality, 25,* 39–41.

Kristof, N. (2005, February 16). Bush's sex scandal. Retrieved April 2, 2005, from http://query.nytimes.com/gst/abstract.htm

l?res=F30710FE385E0C758DDDAB0894D D404482.

Kristof, N. D. (1996, February 11). Who needs love! In Japan, many couples don't. *New York Times,* p. A1.

Krone, N., Hanley, N. A., & Arlt, W. (2007). Age-specific changes in sex steroid biosynthesis and sex development. *Best Practice & Research: Clinical Endocrinology Metabolism, 21,* 393–401.

Krstic, Z. D., Smoljanic, Z., Vukanic, D., Varinac, D., & Janiic, G. (2000). True hermaphroditism: 10 years' experience. *Pediatric Surgery International, 16*(8), 580–583.

Krueger, A., & Lau, A. (2008, June 16). For some clergy, topic stirs spiritual struggle. *San Diego Union Tribune.* Retrieved October 2, 2008, from http://www.signonsandiego.com/news/metro/20080616-9999-1n16church.html.

Krüger, T., Schiffer, B., Eikermann, M., Haake, P., Gizewski, E., & Schedlowsk, M. (2006). Serial neurochemical measurement of cerebrospinal fluid during the human sexual response cycle. *European Journal of Neuroscience, 24,* 3445–3452.

Kruks, G. N. (1991). Gay and lesbian homeless/street youth: Special issues and concerns. *Journal of Consulting Clinical Psychology, 62,* 221.

Ku, L., St. Louis, M., Farshy, C., Aral, S. Turner, C., Lindberg, L. D., & Sonenstein, F. (2002). Risk behaviors, medical care, and chlamydial infection among young men in the U.S. *American Journal of Public Health, 92*(7), 1140–1144.

Kuczkowski, K. M. (2006). Labor analgesia for the parturient with lumbar tattoos: What does an obstetrician need to know? *Archives of Gynecology and Obstetrics, 274,* 310–312.

Kuefler, M. (2006). *The Boswell thesis: Essays on Christianity, social tolerance, and homosexuality.* Chicago: University of Chicago Press.

Kuliev, A., & Verlinsky, Y. (2008). Impact of preimplantation genetic diagnosis for chromosomal disorders on reproductive outcome. *Reproductive Biomedical Online, 16,* 9–10.

Kulig, J. (1994). Sexuality beliefs among Cambodians: Implications for health care professionals. *Health Care for Women International, 15*(1), 69–76.

Kunin, C. M. (1997) *Urinary tract infections: Detection, prevention and management.* (5th ed.) Baltimore: Williams & Wilkins.

Kunkel, D., Eyal, K., Finnerty, K., Biely, E., & Donnerstein, E. (2005). Sex on TV4. Retrieved November 9, 2005, from http://www.kff.org/entmedia/upload/Sex-on-TV-4-Full-Report.pdf.

Kupers, T. A. (2001). Psychotherapy with men in prison. In G. R. Brooks & G. E. Good (Eds.), *The new handbook of psychotherapy and counseling with men: A comprehensive guide to settings, problems, and treatment approaches* (pp. 170–184). San Francisco, CA: Jossey-Bass.

Kuppermann, M., Varner, R. E., Summitt, R. L., Learman, L., Ireland, C., Vittinghoff, E., Stewart, A., Lin, F., Richter, H. E., Showstack, J., Hulley, S. B., & Washington, A. E. (2004). Effect of hysterectomy vs. medical treatment on the health-related quality of life and sexual functioning. *Journal of the American Medical Association, 291*(12), 1447–1455.

Kurdek, L. (1995). Lesbian and gay couples. In A.R. D'Augelli & Patterson, C. (Eds.), *Lesbian, gay, and bisexual identities over the lifespan* (pp. 243–261). New York: Oxford University Press.

Kurdek, L. (2004). Are gay and lesbian cohabiting couples really different from heterosexual married couples? *Journal of Marriage and Family, 66,* 880–900.

Kurdek, L. A. (2006). Differences between partners from heterosexual, gay, and lesbian cohabiting couples. *Journal of Marriage and Family, 68,* 509–528.

Kürzinger, M., Pagnier, J., Kahn, J., Hampshire, R., Wakabi, T., Dye, T. (2008). Education status among orphans and non-orphans in communities affected by AIDS in Tanzania and Burkina Faso. *AIDS Care, 20*(6), 726–732.

Kutchinsky, B. (1991). Pornography and rape: Theory and practice? *International Journal of Law and Psychiatry, 14,* 47–64.

Kwan, I., Bhattacharya, S., McNeil, A., & van Rumste, M. (2008). Monitoring of stimulated cycles in assisted reproduction. *Cochrane Database of Systematic Reviews, 16,* CD005289.

Kwee, A. W., Dominguez, A., Ferrell, D. (2007). Sexual addiction and Christian college men: Conceptual, assessment, and treatment challenges. *Journal of Psychology and Christianity. Batavia, 26*(1), 3–14.

Labbate, L. (2008). Psychotropics and sexual dysfunction: The evidence and treatments. *Advances in Psychosomatic Medicine, 29,* 107–130.

LaBrie, J. W., Schiffman, J., & Earleywine, M. (2002). Expectancies specific to condom use mediate the alcohol and sexual risk relationship. *Journal of Sex Research, 39*(2), 145–153.

Lacey, R. S., Reifman, A., Scott, J. P., Harris, S. M., & Fitzpatrick, J. (2004). Sexual-moral attitudes, love styles, and mate selection. *The Journal of Sex Research, 41*(2), 121–129.

Laflamme, D., Pomerleau, A., & Malcuit, G. (2003). A comparison of father's and mother's involvement in childcare and stimulation behaviors during freeplay with their infants at 9 and 15 months. *Sex Roles, 47*(11–12), 507–518.

LaFree, G. (1982). Male power and female victimization. *American Journal of Sociology, 88,* 311–328.

Lahey, K. A. (1991). Pornography and harm—learning to listen to women. *International Journal of Law and Psychiatry, 14,* 117–131.

Lakoff, R. (1975). *Language and woman's place.* New York: Harper.

Lalumière, M. L., & Blanchard, R. (2000). Sexual orientation and handedness in men and women: A meta-analysis. *Psychological Bulletin, 126*(4), 575–593.

Lalumière, M. L., Harris, G. T., Quinsey, V., & Rice, M. E. (2005a). Clinical assessment and treatment of rapists. In M. L. Lalumière & G. Harris (Eds.), *Causes of rape: Understanding individual differences in male propensity for sexual aggression* (pp. 161–181). Washington, DC: American Psychological Association.

Lalumière, M. L., Harris, G. T., Quinsey, V., & Rice, M. E. (2005b). Forced copulation in the animal kingdom. In M. L. Lalumière & G. Harris (Eds.), *Causes of rape: Understanding individual differences in male propensity for sexual aggression* (pp. 31–58). Washington, DC: American Psychological Association.

Lalumière, M. L., Harris, G. T., Quinsey, V., & Rice, M. E. (2005c). Rape across cultures and time. In M. L. Lalumière & G. Harris (Eds.), *Causes of rape: Understanding individual differences in male propensity for sexual aggression* (pp. 9–30). Washington, DC: American Psychological Association.

Lalumière, M. L., Harris, G. T., Quinsey, V., & Rice, M. E. (2005d). Sexual interest in rape. In M. L. Lalumière & G. Harris (Eds.), *Causes of rape: Understanding individual differences in male propensity for sexual aggression* (pp. 105–128). Washington, DC: American Psychological Association.

Lam, A. G., Russell, S. T., Tan, T. C., & Leong, S. J. (2008). Maternal predictors of noncoital sexual behavior: Examining a nationally representative sample of Asian and White American adolescents who have never had sex. *Journal of Youth and Adolescence, 37,* 62–74.

Lambda. (2001). State-by-state map of sodomy laws. Retrieved October 15, 2003, from http://lambdalegal.org/cgi_bin/pages/states/sodomy-map.

Lance, L. M. (2007). College student sexual morality revisited: A consideration of premarital sex, extramarital sex and childlessness between 1940 and 2000–2005. *College Student Journal, 41,* 727–734.

Landau, E. (1987). *On the streets: The lives of adolescent prostitutes.* New York: Julian Messner.

Landau, E. (2008, September 5). When sex becomes an addiction. *CNN.com.* Retrieved October 2, 2008, from http://www.cnn.com/2008/HEALTH/09/05/sex.addiction/.

Landau, J., Garrett, J., Webb, R. (2008). Assisting a concerned person to motivate someone experiencing cybersex into treatment: Application of invitational intervention: The arise model to cybersex. *Journal of Marital and Family Therapy, 34*(4), 498–512.

Landry, T., Bergeron, S., Dupuis, M. J., & Desrochers, G. (2008). The treatment of provoked vestibulodynia: A critical review. *Clinical Journal of Pain, 24,* 155–171.

Lanfranco, F., Kamischke, A., Zitzmann, M., Nieschlag, E. (2004). Klinefelter's syndrome. *The Lancet, 364*(9430), 273–283.

Lang, C., & Kuhnle, U.(2008). Intersexuality and alternative gender categories in nonwestern cultures. *Hormone Research, 69,* 240–250.

Lang, K., & Weiner, D. (2008). Immunotherapy for HCV infection: Next steps. *Expert Reviews in Vaccines, 7,* 915–923.

Lang, R., Flor-Henry, P., & Frenzel, R. (1990). Sex hormone profiles in pedophilic and incestuous men. *Annals of Sex Research, 3,* 59–74.

Langevin, R., & Lang, R. A. (1987). The courtship disorders. In G. D. Wilson (Ed.), *Variant sexuality: Research and theory* (pp. 202–228). Baltimore: Johns Hopkins University Press.

Langevin, R., Langevin, M., & Curnoe, S. (2007). Family size, birth order, and parental age among male paraphilics and sex offenders. *Archives of Sexual Behavior, 36,* 599–609.

Langevin, R., Wortzman, G., Dickey, R., Wright, P., et al. (1988). Neuropsychological impairment in incest offenders. *Annals of Sex Research, 1,* 401–415.

Langstrom, N., Grann, M., & Lindblad, F. (2000). A preliminary typology of young sex offenders. *Journal of Adolescence, 23,* 319–329.

Lanz, M., & Tagliabue, S. (2007). Do I really need someone in order to become an adult? Romantic relationships during emerging adulthood in Italy. *Journal of Adolescent Research, 22,* 531–549.

Laqueur, T. W. (2003). *Solitary sex: A cultural history of masturbation.* Cambridge, MA: Zone Books.

Larkin, M. (1992). Reacting to patients with sexual problems. *Headlines, 3,* 2, 3, 6, 8.

Laroi, V., & Wigglesworth, R. (2007). Norsk Hydro, Orkla rush to add women directors under Norway law. Bloomberg. Retrieved February 22, 2008, from http://www.bloomberg.com/apps/news?pid=20601085&sid=aS.J0gCborKs&refer=europe.

Larsson, I., & Svedin, C. G. (2002). Sexual experiences in childhood: Young adults' recollections. *Archives of Sexual Behavior, 31*(3), 203–273.

LaSala, M. C. (2000). Lesbians, gay men and their parents: Family therapy for the coming out crisis. *Family Process, 39*(2), 257–266.

LaSala, M. C. (2001). The importance of partners to lesbians' intergenerational relationships. *Social Work Research, 25*(1), 27–36.

Lastella, D. D. (2005). Sexual harassment as an interpersonal dynamic: The effect of race, attractiveness, position power and gender on perceptions of sexual harassment. *Dissertation Abstracts International: Section B., #0419–4217.*

Lau, J., Kim, J. H., & Tsui, H. Y. (2005). Prevalence of male and female sexual problems, perceptions related to sex and association with quality of life in a Chinese population. *International Journal of Impotence Research, 17*(6), 494–505.

Laumann, E., & Youm, Y. (2001). Racial/ethnic group differences in the prevalence of STDs in the U.S. In E. O. Laumann & R. T. Michael (Eds.), *Sex, love and health in America* (pp. 327–351). Chicago: University of Chicago Press.

Laumann, E. O., Gagnon, J., Michael, R., & Michaels, S. (1994). *The social organization of sexuality: Sexual practices in the United States.* Chicago: University of Chicago Press.

Laumann, E. O., Masi, C. M., & Zuckerman, E. W. (2000). Circumcision in the United States: Prevalence, prophylactic effects, and sexual practice. In E. O. Laumann and R. T. Michael (Eds.), *Sex, love and health in America: Private choices and public policies.* Chicago: University of Chicago Press.

Laumann, E. O., Paik, A., Glasser, D. B., Kang, J., Wang, T., Levinson, B., et al. (2006). A cross-national study of subjective sexual well-being among older women and men: Findings from the Global Study of Sexual Attitudes and Behaviors. *Archives of Sexual Behavior, 35,* 145–161.

Laumann, E. O., Paik, A., & Rosen, R. (1999). Sexual dysfunction in the United States. *Journal of the American Medical Association, 281,* 537–544.

Laumann, E. O., & Waite, L. J. (2008). Sexual dysfunction among older adults: Prevalence and risk factors from a nationally representative U.S. probability sample of men and women 57–85 years of age. *Journal of Sexual Medicine, 5*(10), 2300–2311.

Laurence, J. (2006). Treating HIV infection with one pill per day. *AIDS Patient Care and STDs, 20,* 601–603.

Laurence, J. (2008). HPV-linked oral cancer: Another argument for universal HPV vaccination of boys and girls. *AIDS Reader, 18,* 345–346.

Lautmann, R., & Starke, K. (2004). Germany. In R. T. Francoeur & R. J. Noonan (Eds.), *The Continuum international encyclopedia of sexuality* (pp. 450–466). New York/London: Continuum International.

Laval, J. D. (2002). Leiomyomata Uteri. Retrieved July 20, 2002, from http://www.medical-library.org/journals/secure/obgyn_review_p/ secure/Leiomyomata%2OU.

Lavee, Y. (1991). Western and non-Western human sexuality: Implications for clinical practice. *Journal of Sex and Marital Therapy, 17,* 203–213.

Lavin, M. (2008). Voyeurism: Psychopathology and theory. In D. Laws & W. O'Donohue (Eds.), *Sexual deviance: Theory, assessment and treatment* (2nd ed., pp. 305–319). New York: Guilford Press.

Lawrence, A. A. (2006). Patient-reported complications and functional outcomes of male and female sex reassignment surgery. *Archives of Sexual Behavior, 35,* 717–727.

Laws, D., & O'Donohue, W. (2008). *Sexual deviance: Theory, assessment, and treatment.* New York: Guilford Press.

Layton-Tholl, D. (1998). Extramarital affairs: The link between thought suppression and level of arousal. *Dissertation Abstracts,* Miami Institute of Psychology of the Caribbean Center for Advanced Studies, #AAT9930425.

Lazarou, S, Morgentaler, A. (2008). The effect of aging on spermatogenesis and pregnancy outcomes. *Urologic Clinics of North America, 35*(2), 331–339.

Lazovich, D., Forster, J., Sorensen, G., Emmons, K., Stryker, J., Demierre, M. F., Hickle, A., & Remba, N. (2004). Characteristics associated with use or intention to use indoor tanning among adolescents. *Archives of Pediatric Adolescent Medicine, 158,* 918–924.

Leaper, C. (2000). The social construction and socialization of gender during development. In P. H. Miller & E. K. Scholnick (Eds.), *Toward a feminist developmental psychology* (pp. 127–152). New York: Routledge.

Leavy, W. (1993). Sex in black America: Reality and myth. *Ebony, 48*(10), 126–130.

Ledger, W. (2004). Implications of an irreversible procedure. *Fertility and Sterility, 82,* 1473.

Lee, G., Lorick, S., Pfoh, E., Kleinman, K., & Fishbein, D. (2008). Adolescent immunizations: Missed opportunities for prevention. *Pediatrics, 122,* 711–717.

Lee, J., Pomeroy, E. C., Yoo, S., & Rheinboldt, K. (2005). Attitudes toward rape: A comparison between Asian and Caucasian college students. *Violence Against Women, 11*(2), 177–196.

Lee, J. A. (1974). The styles of loving. *Psychology Today, 8,* 43–51.

Lee, J. A. (1988). Love-styles. In R. Sternberg & M. Barnes (Eds.), *The Psychology of Love.* New Haven, CT: Yale University Press.

Lee, J. A. (1998). Ideologies of lovestyle and sexstyle. In V. de Munck (Ed.), *Romantic love and sexual behavior* (pp. 33–76). Westport, CT: Praeger.

Lee, M. B., & Rotheram-Borus, M. J. (2002). Parents' disclosure of HIV to their children. *AIDS, 16*(16), 2201–2207.

Lee, S., Liong, M., Yuen, K., Leong, W., Cheah, P., Khan, N., & Krieger, J. (2008). Adverse impact of sexual dysfunction in chronic prostatitis/chronic pelvic pain syndrome. *Urology, 71,* 79–84.

Lee, Y. S., Cheng, A. W., Ahmed, S. F., Shaw, N. J., & Hughes, I. A. (2007). Genital anomalies in Klinefelter's syndrome. *Hormonal Research, 68,* 150–153.

Lehmiller, J. J., & Agnew, C. R. (2007). Perceived marginalization and the prediction of romantic relationship stability. *Journal of Marriage and Family, 9,* 1036–1040.

Leiblum, S. (2007). Persistent genital arousal disorder: Perplexing, distressing, and underrecognized. In S. Leiblum (Ed.). *Principles and Practice of Sex Therapy* (4th Ed., 54–83.), Guilford Press, New York NY.

Leiblum, S., Koochaki, P., Rodenberg, X., Barton, I., & Rosen, R. (2006). Hypoactive sexual desire disorder in postmenopausal women: US results from the women's international study of health and sexuality. *Menopause, 13,* 46–56.

Leibo, S. P. (2008). Cryopreservation of oocytes and embryos: Optimization by theoretical versus empirical analysis. *Theriogenology, 69,* 37–47.

Leichtentritt, R. D., & Arad, B. D. (2005). Young male street workers: Life histories and current experiences. *British Journal of Social Work, 35*(4), 483–509.

Leitenberg, H., & Henning, K. (1995). Sexual fantasy. *Psychological Bulletin, 117*(3), 469–496.

Leo, S., & Sia, A. (2008). Maintaining labour epidural analgesia: What is the best option? *Current Opinions in Anesthesiology, 21,* 263–269.

Leonard, A. S. (2006, September 25). Hong Kong appeals court strikes down differential age of consent law on "buggery." Leonard Link, New York Law School. Retrieved October 2, 2008, from http://newyorklawschool.typepad.com/leonardlink/2006/09/hong_kong_appea.html.

Leonard, K. E. (2005). Editorial: Alcohol and intimate partner violence: When can we say that heavy drinking is a contributing cause of violence? *Addiction, 100*(4), 422–425.

Lerner, H. (1998). *The mother dance: How children change your life.* New York: HarperCollins.

Lerner-Geva, L., Keinan-Boker, L., Blumstein, T., Boyko, V., Olmar, L., Mashiach, S., et al. (2006). Infertility, ovulation induction treatments and the incidence of breast cancer—a historical prospective cohort of Israeli women. *Breast Cancer Research and Treatment, 100,* 201–212.

Leslie, G. R., & Korman, S. K. (1989). *The family in social context.* New York: Oxford University Press.

LeVay, S. (1991). A difference in hypothalamic structure between heterosexual and homosexual men. *Science, 253,* 1034–1037.

Levin, R. J. (2007). Sexual activity, health and well-being—the beneficial roles of coitus and masturbation. *Sexual and Relationship Therapy, 22,* 135–148.

Levine D. (2007). Ectopic pregnancy. *Radiology, 245,* 385–397.

Levine, D. A., & Gemignani, M. L. (2003). Prophylactic surgery in hereditary breast/ovarian cancer syndrome. *Oncology, 17*(7), 932–941.

Levine, J. (1991). Search and find. *Forbes, 148,* 134–135.

Levine, R., Sato, S., & Hashimoto, T. (1995). Love and marriage in eleven cultures. *Journal of Cross-Cultural Psychology, 26*(5), 554–571.

Levine, R. J. (1999). Seasonal variation of semen quality and fertility. *Scandinavian Journal of Work and Environmental Health, 25*(Suppl. 1), 34–37.

Levine, S. B., Risen, C. B., & Althof, S. E. (1990). Essay on the diagnosis and nature of paraphilia. *Journal of Sex and Marital Therapy, 16*(2), 89–102.

Lev-Wiesel, R. (2004). Male university students' attitudes toward rape and rapists. *Child & Adolescent Social Work Journal, 21,* 199.

Lewes, K. (1988). *The psychoanalytic theory of male homosexuality.* New York: Meridian.

Lewin, R. (1988). New views emerge on hunters and gatherers. *Science, 240*(4856), 1146–1148.

Lewis, D. A. (2000). Chancroid: From clinical practice to basic science. *AIDS Patient Care and STDs, 14*(1), 19–36.

Lewis, L., & Kertzner, R. M. (2003). Toward improved interpretation and theory building of African American male sexualities. *Journal of Sex Research, 40*(4), 383–399.

Lewis, M. (1987). Early sex role behavior and school age adjustment. In J. M. Reinish, L. A. Rosenblum, & S. A. Sanders (Eds.), *Masculinity/femininity: Basic perspectives* (pp. 202–226). New York: Oxford University Press.

Lewis, R. J., & Janda, L. H. (1988). The relationship between adult sexual adjustment and childhood experiences regarding exposure to nudity, sleeping in the parental bed, and parental attitudes toward sexuality. *Archives of Sexual Behavior, 17,* 349–362.

Lewis, R. W., Fugl-Meyer, K. S., Bosch, R., Fugl-Meyer, A., Laumann, E. O., Lizza, E., & Martin-Morales, A. (2004). Epidemiology/risk factors of sexual dysfunction. *The Journal of Sexual Medicine, 1*(1), 35.

Lewis, S. E., Agbaje, I., & Alvarez, J. (2008). Sperm DNA tests as useful adjuncts to semen analysis. *Systems Biology in Reproductive Medicine, 54,* 111–125.

Leyendecker, G., Kunz, G., Herbertz, M., Beil, D., Huppert, P., Mall, G., Kissler, S., Noe, M., & Wildt, L. (2004, December). Uterine peristaltic activity and the development of endometriosis. *Annals of the New York Academy of Sciences, 1034,* 338–355.

Leyson, J. F. (2004). Philippines. In R. T. Francoeur & R. J. Noonan (Eds.), *The Continuum international encyclopedia of sexuality* (pp. 825–845). New York/London: Continuum International.

Li, C. I., Malone, K. E., Daling, J. R., Potter, J. D., Bernstein, L., Marchbanks, P. A., et al. (2008). Timing of menarche and first full-term birth in relation to breast cancer risk. *Journal of Epidemiology, 167,* 230–239.

Li, X., Naar-King, S., Barnett, D., Stanton, B., Fang, X., Thurston, C. (2008). A developmental psychopathology framework of the psychosocial needs of children orphaned by HIV. Journal of the Association of Nurses in AIDS Care, 19(2), 147–157.

Liao, C., Wei, J., Li, Q., Li, L., Li, J., & Li, D. (2006). Efficacy and safety of cordocentesis for prenatal diagnosis. *International Journal of Gynecology and Obstetrics, 93,* 13–17.

Liben, L. S., & Bigler, R. S. (2002). The developmental course of gender differentiation. *Monographs of the Society of Research in Child Development, 67*(2), vii–147.

Lie, D. (2000). Contraception update for the primary care physician. Retrieved May 17, 2001, from http://www.medscape.com/medscape/CNO/200/AAFP/AAFP-06.html.

Lie, M. L., Robson, S. C., & May, C. R. (2008). Experiences of abortion: A narrative review of qualitative studies. *BMC Health Services Research, 8,* 150.

Lilley, L. L., & Schaffer, S. (1990). Human papillomavirus: A sexually transmitted disease with carcinogenic potential. *Cancer Nursing, 13,* 366–372.

Lim, A. S., Tsakok, M. F. (1997). Age-related decline in fertility: A link to degenerative oocytes? *Fertility and Sterility, 68*(2), 265–271.

Lim, M.M., Young, L.J. (2006). Neuropeptidergic regulation of affiliative behavior and social bonding in animals. *Hormones and Behavior, 50,* 506–517.

Limanonda, B., Chongvatana, N., Tirasawat, P., Auwanit, W. (1993). *Summary report on the demographic and behavioral study of female commercial sex workers in Thailand.* Bangkok, Thailand: Institute of Population Studies.

Lindau, S., Gavrilova, N., & Anderson, D. (2007). Sexual morbidity in very long term survivors of vaginal and cervical cancer: A comparison to national norms. *Gynecological Oncology, 106,* 413–418.

Lindau, S. T., Schumm, P., Laumann, E. O., Levinson, W., O'Muircheartaigh, C. A., & Waite, L. J. (2007). A study of sexuality and health among older adults in the United States. *Journal of the American Medical Association, 357,* 762–764.

Lindberg, L. D., Jones, R., & Santelli, J. S. (2008, July). Non-coital sexual activities among adolescents. *Journal of Adolescent Health.* Retrieved May 26, 2008, from http://www.guttmacher.org/pubs/JAH_Lindberg.pdf.

Linz, D. (1989). Exposure to sexually explicit materials and attitudes toward rape: A comparison of study results. *The Journal of Sex Research, 26,* 50–84.

Linz, D., & Donnerstein, E. (1992, September 30). Research can help us explain violence and pornography. *The Chronicle of Higher Education,* B3–B4.

Lippa, R. A. (2003). Handedness, sexual orientation, and gender-related personality traits in men and women. *Archives of Sexual Behavior, 32*(2), 103–114.

Lippa, R. A., & Tan, F. P. (2001). Does culture moderate the relationship between sexual orientation and gender-related personality trait? *Journal of Comparative Social Science, 35*(1), 65–87.

Lips, H. (2008). *Sex & gender: An introduction* (6th ed.). New York: McGraw-Hill.

Lipsky, S., Caetono, R., Field, C. A., & Larkin, G. (2005). Psychosocial and substance-use risk factors for intimate partner violence. *Drug & Alcohol Dependence, 78*(1), 39–47.

Lipton, L. (2003). The erotic revolution. In J. Escoffier (Ed.), *Sexual revolution* (pp. 20–30). New York: Thunder's Mouth Press.

Litosseliti, L. (2006). *Gender and language: Theory and practice.* London: Arnold.

Little, A. C., Burt, D. M., & Perrett, D.I. (2006). What is good is beautiful: Face preference reflects desired personality. *Personality and Individual Differences, 41,* 1107–1118.

Littleton, H., Breitkopf, C., & Berenson, A. (2007). Rape scripts of low-income European American and Latina women. *Sex Roles, 56,* 509–516.

Liu, C. (2004). County health officials call for condoms in porn movies. *LA Times.* Retrieved November 15, 2008, from http://articles.latimes.com/2004/oct/08/local/me-porn8.

Lloyd, T., Petit, M. A., Lin, H. M., & Beck, T. J. (2004). Lifestyle factors and the development of bone mass and bone strength in young women. *Journal of Pediatrics, 144*(6), 776–782.

Lo, D., Tsui, N., Chiu, R., Lau, T., Leung, T., Heung, M., et al. (2007). Plasma placental RNA allelic ration permits noninvasive prenatal chromosomal aneuploidy detection. *Nature Medicine, 13,* 218–223.

Lock, J., & Steiner, H. (1999). Gay lesbian and bisexual youth risks for emotional, physical, and social problems: Results from a community-based survey. *Journal of American Academy of Child and Adolescent Psychiatry 38*(3), 297–305.

Locke, B. D., & Mahalik, J. R. (2005). Examining masculinity norms, problem drinking, and athletic involvement as predictors of sexual aggression in college men. *Journal of Counseling Psychology, 52*(3), 279–283.

Lockwood, S. (2008, April 7). Homeless GLBT youths often face violent life on the streets. *Columbia Spectator.* Retrieved October 2, 2008, from http://www.columbiaspectator.com/node/30281.

Long, S., Ullman, S., Long, L., Mason, G., & Starzynski, L. (2007). Women's experiences of male-perpetrated sexual assault by sexual orientation. *Violence and Victims, 22,* 684–701.

Long, V. E. (2003). Contraceptive Choices: New options in the U.S. market. *SIECUS Report, 31*(2), 13–18.

Lonsway, K., Cortina, L., & Magley, V. (2008). Sexual harassment mythology: Definition, conceptualization, and measurement. *Sex Roles, 58,* 599–616.

Lopez, L., Grimes, D. A., Gallo, M., & Schulz, K. (2008). Skin patch and vaginal ring versus combined oral contraceptives for contraception. *Cochrane Database Systems Review, 23,* CD003552.

LoPiccolo, J., & Lobitz, W. C. (1972). The role of masturbation in the treatment of orgasmic dysfunction. *Archives of Sexual Behavior, 2,* 163–171.

LoPiccolo, J., & Stock, W. E. (1986). Treatment of sexual dysfunction. *Journal of Consulting and Clinical Psychology, 54,* 158–167.

Lorio, A. (2004). Assign gender when child can give input, experts say. *Urology Times, 32*(5), 27–30.

Lott, A. J., & Lott, B. E. (1961). Group cohesiveness, communication level, and conformity. *Journal of Abnormal & Social Psychology, 62,* 408–412.

Loucks, A. B., & Nattiv, A. (2005). The female athlete triad. *The Lancet, 366,* s49–s50.

Lovejoy, F. H., & Estridge, D. (Eds.). (1987). *The new child health encyclopedia.* New York: Delacorte Press.

Low, W. Y., Wong, Y. L., Zulkifli, S. W., & Tan, H. (2002). Malaysian cultural differences in knowledge, attitudes and practices related to erectile dysfunction. *International Journal of Impotence Research, 14*(6), 440–445.

Lu, W., Mueser, K., Rosenberg, S., & Jankowski, M. (2008). Correlates of adverse childhood experiences among adults with severe mood disorders. *Psychiatric Services, 59,* 1018–1026.

Lucie-Smith, E. (1991). *Sexuality in western art.* London: Thames & Hudson.

Luckenbill, D. F. (1984). Dynamics of the deviant scale. *Deviant Behavior, 5,* 337–353.

Lue, T. (2000). Erectile dysfunction. *New England Journal of Medicine, 342*(24), 1802–1813.

Lutfey, K. E., Link, C., Rosen, R., Wiegel, M., & McKinlay, J. (2008, January 11). Prevalence and correlates of sexual activity and function in women: Results from the Boston area community health (BACH) survey. *Archives of Sexual Behavior.* Retrieved October 30, 2008, from http://www.springerlink.com/content/f47306253471w048/?p=efd510bd7d9a43c29bd1f1b7ca8b33b3&pi=0.

Lynge, E. (2002). Prostate cancer is not increased in men with vasectomy in Denmark. *Journal of Urology, 168,* 488–490.

Maas, C. P., ter Kuile, M. M., Laan, E., Tuynman, C. C., Weyenborg, P., Trimbos, J. B., & Kenter, G. G. (2004). Objective assessment of sexual arousal in women with a history of hysterectomy. *British Journal of Obstetrics and Gynaecology, 111,* 456–462.

Maas, J. (1998). *Power sleep.* New York: HarperCollins.

Maccoby, E. E. (2002). Gender and group process: A developmental perspective. *Current Directions in Psychological Science, 11*(2), 54–58.

Maccoby, E.E., Jacklin, C.N. (1987). Gender segregation in childhood. In H.W. Reese (Ed.), *Advances in child development and behavior,* (Vol. 20, pp. 239–287). San Diego, CA: Academic Press.

MacDorman, M. F., Mathews, T. J., Martin, J. A., & Malloy, M. H. (2002). Trends and characteristics of induced labour in the U.S., 1989–1998. *Paediatric & Perinatal Epidemiology, 16*(3), 263–274.

Macdowall, W., Wellings, K., Stephenson, J., Glasier, A. (2008). Summer nights; a review of the evidence of seasonal variations in sexual health indicators among young people. *Health Education, 108,* 40.

MacKay, A. P., Berg, C. J., & Atrash, H. K. (2001). Pregnancy-related mortality from preeclampsia and eclampsia. *Obstetrics and Gynecology, 97*(4), 533–538.

Mackay, J. (2000). *The Penguin atlas of human sexual behavior.* New York: Penguin.

Mackesy-Amiti, M., Fendrich, M., & Johnson, T. (2008). Substance-related problems and treatment among men who have sex with men in comparison to other men in Chicago. *Journal of Substance Abuse and Treatment.* Epub ahead of print. Retrieved September 19, 2008, from http://www.ncbi.nlm.nih.gov/pubmed/18715744.

Mackey, R. A., Diemer, M. A., & O'Brien, B. A. (2000). Psychological intimacy in the lasting relationships of heterosexual and same-gender couples. *Sex Roles, 43,* 201–227.

MacKinnon, C. A. (1985, March 26). Pornography: Reality, not fantasy. *The Village Voice.*

MacKinnon, C. A. (1986). Pornography: Not a moral issue. (Special Issue: Women and the law.) *Women's Studies International Forum, 9,* 63–78.

MacKinnon, C. A. (1987). *Feminism unmodified: Discourses on life and law.* Cambridge, MA: Harvard University Press.

MacKinnon, C. A. (1993). *Only words.* Cambridge, MA: Harvard University Press.

Macklon, N., & Fauser, B. (2000). Aspects of ovarian follicle development throughout life. *Hormone Research, 52,* 161–170.

Macneil, S. (2004). It takes two: Modeling the role of sexual self-disclosure in sexual satisfaction. *Dissertation Abstracts International: Section B: The Sciences & Engineering, 65*(1-B), 481. (#0419–4217).

MacNeill, C., & Carey, J. C. (2001). Recurrent vulvovaginal candidiasis. *Current Women's Health Reports, 1*(1), 31–35.

Madigan, N. (2004). Man, 86, convicted under new law against Americans who go abroad to molest minors. Retrieved November 11, 2004, from http://travel2.nytimes.com/2004/11/20/national/20predator.html?ex=1129003200&en=8275e98301fbe992&ei=5070&n=Top%2fFeatures%2fTravel%2fDestinations%2fUnited%20States%2fRegions.

Madigan, N. (2004). Sex-film industry threatened with condom requirement. Retrieved November 8, 2005, from http://www.aegis.com/news/ads/2004/AD041716.html.

Madon, S. (1997). What do people believe about gay males? A study of stereotype content and strength. *Sex Roles, 37*(9–10), 663–686.

Maguire, K. C. (2007). "Will it ever end?": A (re)examination of uncertainty in college student long-distance dating relationships. *Communication Quarterly, 55,* 415–432.

Mah, K., & Binik, Y. (2005). Are orgasms in the mind or the body? Psychosocial versus physiological correlates of orgasmic pleasure and satisfaction. *Journal of Sex & Marital Therapy, 31*(3), 187–200.

Mahabir, S., Spitz, M. R., Barrera, S. L., Dong, Y. Q., Eastham, C., & Forman, M. R. (2008). Dietary boron and hormone replacement therapy as risk factors for lung cancer in women. *American Journal of Epidemiology* (Epub). Retrieved March 18, 2008, from http://www.ncbi.nlm.nih.gov/sites/entrez.

Mahalingam, R. (2007). Beliefs about chastity, machismo, and caste identity: A cultural psychology of gender. *Sex Roles, 56,* 239–249.

Mahay, J., Laumann, E. O., & Michaels, S. (2001). Race, gender, and class in sexual scripts. In E. O. Laumann & S. Michaels (Eds.), *Sex, love, and health in America* (pp. 197–238). Chicago: Chicago University Press.

MaHood, J., & Wenburg, A. R. (1980). *The Mosher survey.* New York: Arno.

Maines, R. (1999). *Hysteria, the vibrator, and women's sexual satisfaction.* Baltimore: The Johns Hopkins University Press.

Maisto, S. A., Carey, M. P., Carey, K. B., Gordon, C. M., Schum, J., & Lynch, K. (2004). The relationship between alcohol and individual differences variables on attitudes and behavioral skills relevant to sexual health among heterosexual young adult men. *Archives of Sexual Behavior, 33*(6), 571–584.

Major, B., Mueller, P., & Hildebrandt, K. (1985). Attributions, expectations, and coping with abortion. *Journal of Personality and Social Psychology, 48,* 585–599.

Makarainen, L., van Beek, A., Tuomivaara, L., Asplund, B., & Coelingh-Bennink, B. (1998). Ovarian function during the use of a single contraceptive implant: Implanon compared with Norplant. *Fertility and Sterility, 69,* 714–721.

Mallon, G. P. (2003). *Gay men choosing parenthood.* New York: Columbia University Press.

Malone, F. D., Canick, J. A., Ball, R. H., Nyberg, D. A., Comstock, C. H., Bukowski, R., Berkowitz, R. L., Gross, S. J., Wolfe, H. M., et al. (2005). First-trimester or second-trimester screening, or both, for Down's syndrome. *The New England Journal of Medicine, 353*(19), 2001–2011.

Maltz, D. W., Borker, R. A. (1982). A cultural approach to male-female communication. In J.J. Gumperz (Ed.), *Language and social identity* (pp. 196–216). New York, NY. Cambridge University Press.

Maltz, W. (1990, December). Adult survivors of incest: How to help them overcome the trauma. *Medical Aspects of Human Sexuality*, 38–43.

Maltz, W. (2002). Treating the sexual intimacy concerns of sexual abuse survivors. *Sexual and Relationship Therapy, 17*(4), 321–327.

Maltz, W., & Boss, S. (2001). *Private thoughts: Exploring the power of women's sexual fantasies.* Novato, CA: New World Library.

Mangan, M. A. (2004). A phenomenology of problematic sexual behavior occurring in sleep. *Archives of Sexual Behavior, 33,* 287–293.

Mannheimer, S., Friedland, G., Matts, J., Child, C., & Chesney, M. (2002). The consistency of adherence to antiretroviral therapy predicts biologic outcome for HIV-infected persons in clinical trials. *Clinical Infectious Disease, 34*(8), 1115–1121.

Manniche, L. (1987). *Sexual life in ancient Egypt.* London: KPI Ltd.

Manning, W. D., Giordano, P. C., & Longmore, M. A. (2006). Hooking up: The relationship contexts of "nonrelationship" sex. *Journal of Adolescent Research, 21,* 459–483.

Manning, W. D., Longmore, M. A., & Giordano, P. C. (2007). The changing institution of marriage: Adolescents' expectations to cohabit and to marry. *Journal of Marriage and Family, 69,* 559–576.

Manson, J. E. (2004, December). Your doctor is in. *Glamour,* p. 104.

Mantica, A. (2005). Better test for a stealthy cancer. *Prevention, 57*(3), 48–51.

Marchbanks, P. A., McDonald, J. A., Wilson, H. G., Folger S. G., Mandel M. G., Daling J. R., et al. (2002). Oral contraceptives and the risk of breast cancer. *New England Journal of Medicine, 346,* 2025–2032.

Margolis, J. (2004). *O: The intimate history of the orgasm.* New York: Grove/Atlantic Press.

Margulies, S. (2003). The psychology of prenuptial agreements. *Journal of Psychiatry & Law, 31*(4), 415–432.

Margulis, L., & Sagan, D. (1991). *Mystery dance: On the evolution of human sexuality.* New York: Summit Books.

Maritz, G. S. (2008). Nicotine and lung development. *Birth Defects Research, Part C. 84,* 45–53.

Mark, K., Wald, A., Magaret, A., Selke, S., Olin, L, Huang, M., & Corey, L. (2008). Rapidly cleared episodes of herpes simplex virus reactivation in immunocompetent adults.

Journal of Infectious Disease. Epub ahead of print. Retrieved September 19, 2008, from http://www.ncbi.nlm.nih.gov/sites/entrez.

Markel, H. (2005). The search for effective HIV vaccines. *The New England Journal of Medicine, 353*(8), 753–757.

Marrazzo, J. (2004). Barriers to infectious disease care among lesbians. *Emerging Infectious Disease, 10,* 1974–1978.

Marrazzo, J., Coffey, P., & Bingham, A. (2005). Sexual practices, risk perception and knowledge of sexually transmitted disease risk among lesbian and bisexual women. *Perspective on Sexual and Reproductive Health, 37,* 6–12.

Marrazzo, J., Cook, R., Wiesenfeld, H., Murray, P., Busse, B., Krohn, M., & Hillier, S. (2007). *Lactobacillus* capsule for the treatment of bacterial vaginosis. *Journal of Women's Health, 15,* 1053–1060.

Marrazzo, J., Koutsky, L., Eshenbach, D., Agnew, K., Stine, K., & Hillier, S. (2002). *Journal of Infectious Disease, 185,* 1307–1313.

Marrazzo, J., Koutsky L., Kiviat, N., Kuypers J., & Stine, K. (2001). Papanicolaou test screening and prevalence of genital human papillomavirus among women who have sex with women. *American Journal of Public Health, 91,* 947–952.

Marrazzo, J., Thomas, K., Fiedler, T., Ringwood, K., & Fredricks, D. (2008). Relationship of specific vaginal bacteria and bacterial vaginosis treatment failure in women who have sex with women. *Annals of Internal Medicine, 149,* 20–28.

Marris, E. (2005). Is tattoo ink safe? Retrieved March 15, 2005, from http://www.nature.com/news/2005/050314/pf/050314-3_pf.html.

Marshall, D., & Suggs, R. (1971). *Human sexual behavior: Variations in the ethnographic spectrum.* Englewood Cliffs, NJ: Prentice Hall.

Marshall, D. S. (1971). Sexual behavior on Mangaia. In D. S. Marshall & R. C. Suggs (Eds.), *Human sexual behavior.* New York: Basic Books.

Marshall, W. L. (1979). Satiation therapy: A procedure for reducing deviant sexual arousal. *Journal of Applied Behavior Analysis, 12*(3), 377–389.

Martin, C., & Théry, I. (2001). The Pacs and marriage and cohabitation in France. *International Journal of Law, Policy and the Family, 15,* 135–158.

Martin, D., Martin, M., & Carvalho, K. (2008). Reading and learning-disabled children:

Understanding the problem. *The Clearing House, 81,* 113–118.

Martin, H. P. (1991). The coming-out process for homosexuals. *Hospital and Community Psychiatry, 42,* 158–162.

Martin, J. (1999, June–July). Nipple piercing: Is it compatible with breastfeeding? *LEAVEN, 35*(3), 64–65.

Martin, J., Puts, D., & Breedlove, S. (2008). Hand asymmetry in heterosexual and homosexual men and women: Relationship to 2D:4D digit ratios and other sexually dimorphic anatomical traits. *Archives of Sexual Behavior, 37,* 119–132.

Martin, J. A., Hamilton, B. E., Sutton, P., Ventura, S., Menacker, F., Kirmeyer, S., & Munson, M. (2007, December 5). Births: Final Data for 2005. *National Vital Statistics Report, 56*(6). Retrieved May 31, 2008, from http://www.cdc.gov/nchs/data/nvsr/nvsr56/nvsr56_06.pdf.

Martin, P. Y., & Hummer, R. A. (1989). Fraternities and rape on campus (Special issue: Violence Against Women). *Gender and Society, 3,* 457–473.

Martin, R. P., Dombrowski, S. C., Mullis, C., Wisenbaker, J., & Huttunen, M. O. (2005, July 7). Smoking during pregnancy: Association with childhood temperament, behavior, and academic performance. *Journal of Pediatric Psychology,* Epub ahead of print. Retrieved July 17, 2005, from http://www.ncbi.nlm.nih.gov/entrez/query.fcgi?cmd=Retrieve&db=pubmed&dopt=Abstract&list_uids=16002482&query_hl=23.

Martin, T. A. (2003). Power and consent: Relation to self—reported sexual assault and acquaintance rape. *Dissertation Abstracts International: Section B: The Sciences & Engineering, 64*(3-B), #0419–4217.

Martin, W. E. (2001). A wink and a smile: How men and women respond to flirting. *Psychology Today, 34*(5), 26–27.

Martinez, G. M., Chandra, A., Abma, J. C., Jones, J., & Mosher, W. D. (2006). Fertility, contraception, and fatherhood: Data on men and women from cycle 6 (2002) of the National Survey of Family Growth. *Vital Health Statistics, 23*(26). Hyattsville, MD: National Center for Health Statistics, Centers for Disease Control.

Martinson, F. M. (1981). Eroticism in infancy and childhood. In L. L. Constantine & F. M. Martinson (Eds.), *Children and sex: New findings, new perspectives* (pp. 23–35). Boston: Little, Brown.

Mason, M. A., Fine, M. A., & Carcochan, S. (2001). Family law in the new millennium:

For whose families? *Journal of Family Issues, 22*(7), 859–882.

Massa, G., Verlinde, F., DeSchepper, J., Thomas, M., Bourguignon, J. P., Craen, M., de Segher, F., Francois, I., Du Caju, M., Maes, M., & Heinrichs, C. (2005). Trends in age at diagnosis of Turner syndrome. *Archives of Disease in Childhood, 90*(3), 267–275.

Masser, B., Viki, T., & Power, C. (2006). Hostile sexism and rape proclivity amongst men. *Sex Roles, 54,* 565–574.

Masters, W. H., & Johnson, V. E. (1966). *Human sexual response.* Boston: Little, Brown.

Masters, W. H., & Johnson, V. E. (1970). *Human sexual inadequacy.* Boston: Little, Brown.

Masters, W. H., & Johnson, V. E. (1979). *Homosexuality in perspective.* Boston: Little, Brown.

Masters, W. H., Johnson, V. E., & Kolodny, R. C. (1982). *Human sexuality.* Boston: Little, Brown.

Masterton, G. (1987). *How to drive your woman wild in bed.* New York: Penguin Books.

Matek, O. (1988). Obscene phone callers. (Special issue: The sexually unusual: Guide to understanding and helping.) *Journal of Social Work and Human Sexuality, 7,* 113–130.

Mathes, E. W. (2005). Relationship between short-term sexual strategies and sexual jealousy. *Psychological Reports, 96*(1), 29–35.

Mathews, F., Johnson, P., & Neil, A. (2008). You are what your mother eats: Evidence for maternal preconception diet influencing foetal sex in humans. *Proceedings of the Royal Society: Biological Sciences, 275,* 1661–1668.

Mathur, S., Greene, M., & Malhotra, A. (2003). *Too young to wed: The lives, rights and health of young married girls.* Washington, DC: International Center for Research on Women.

Maticka-Tyndale, E. T., Herold, E. S., & Mewhinney, D. (1998). Casual sex on spring break: Intentions and behaviors of Canadian students. *Journal of Sex Research, 35*(3), 254–265.

Matsubara, H. (2001, June 20). Sex change no cure for torment. *Japan Times.*

Matsumoto, D. (1996). *Culture and psychology.* Pacific Grove, CA: Brooks/Cole.

Maugh, T. H. (2006, July 14). Rates of prematurity, low birth weight highest ever. *Los Angeles Times.* Retrieved from http://articles.

latimes.com/2006/jul/14/science/sci-children14.

Maunder, R. G., & Hunter, J. J. (2008). Attachment relationships as determinants of physical health. *Journal of the American Academy of Psychoanalysis and Dynamic Psychiatry, 36,* 11–33.

Maurer, T., & Robinson, D. (2008). Effects of attire, alcohol, and gender on perceptions of date rape. *Sex Roles, 58,* 423–435.

Maxmen, J., & Ward, N. (1995). *Essential psychopathology and its treatment* (2nd ed.). New York: Norton.

Mayrand, M., Duarte-Franco, E., Rodrigues, I., Walter, S., Hanley, J., Ferenczy, A., et al. (2007). Human papillomavirus DNA versus Papanicolaou screening tests for cervical cancer. *New England Journal of Medicine, 357,* 1579–1588.

Mays, V. M., Yancy, A. K., Cochran, S. D., Weber, M., & Fielding, J. E. (2002). Heterogeneity of health disparities among African-American, Hispanic and Asian American women. *American Journal of Public Health, 92*(4), 632–640.

Mbügua, K. (2006). Reasons to suggest that the endocrine research on sexual preference is a degenerating research program. *History & Philosophy of the Life Sciences, 28,* 337–358.

McAdams, M. (1996). Gender without bodies. Retrieved September 3, 2005, from http://www.december.com/cmc/mag/1996/mar/mcadams.html

McAndrew, F. T., Bell, E. K., & Garcia, C. M. (2007). Who do we tell and whom do we tell on? Gossip as a strategy for status enhancement. *Journal of Applied Social Psychology, 37,* 1562–1577.

McBride, J. L. (2007). The Family. In *The behavioral sciences and health care* (2nd ed., Section VI, #19). Ashland, OH: Hogrefe & Huber.

McCabe, M., & Wauchope, M. (2005). Behavioral characteristics of men accused of rape: Evidence for different types of rapists. *Archives of Sexual Behavior, 34,* 241–253.

McCabe, M. P. (2002). Relationship functioning among people with MS. *Journal of Sex Research, 39*(4), 302–309.

McCarthy, B. W., & Fucito, L. M. (2005). Integrating medication, realistic expectations, and therapeutic interventions in the treatment of male sexual dysfunction. *Journal of Sex and Marital Therapy, 31*(4), 319–328.

McCarthy, B. W., & Ginsberg, R. L. (2007). Second marriages: Challenges and risks. *Family Journal, 15,* 119.

McCormack, J., Hudson, S. M., & Ward, T. (2002). Sexual offenders' perceptions of their early interpersonal relationships: An attachment perspective. *Journal of Sex Research, 39*(2), 85–93.

McDowell, B. (1986). The Dutch touch. *National Geographic, 170,* 501–525.

McDowell, M., Wang, C., & Kennedy-Stephenson, J. (2008). Breastfeeding in the United States: Findings from the National Health and Nutrition Examination Survey, 1999–2006. *NCHS Data Briefs,* no. 5. Hyattsville, MD: National Center for Health Statistics.

McEnery, R. (2008). AIDS Vaccine Blueprint launched: A challenge to the field. *International AIDS Vaccine Initiative, 12.* Retrieved September 18, 2008, from http://www.iavireport.org/Issues/Issue12-4/VaccineBriefs.asp.

McFadden, D., Loehlin, J.C., Breedlove, S., Lippa, R. A., Manning, J. T., & Rahman, Q. (2005). A reanalysis of five studies on sexual orientation and the relative length of the 2nd and 4th fingers (the 2D:4D). *Archives of Sexual Behavior, 34,* 341–356.

McGrath, R. (1991). Sex offender risk assessment and disposition planning. *International Journal of Offender Treatment and Comparative Criminology, 35*(4), 328–350.

McGuirk, E. M., & Pettijohn, T. F. (2008). Birth order and romantic relationship styles and attitudes in college students. *North American Journal of Psychology, 10,* 37–52.

McKeganey, N., & Bernard, M. (1996). *Sex work on the streets: Prostitutes and their clients.* Philadelphia, PA: Open University Press.

McKenna, K. Y., Green, A. S., & Smith, P. (2001). Demarginalizing the sexual self. *Journal of Sex Research, 38*(4), 302–402.

McKinley, J. (2008, June 17). Same-sex marriages begin in California. *New York Times.* Retrieved June 17, 2008, from http://www.nytimes.com/2008/06/17/us/17weddings.html?th&emc=th.

McLaren, A. (1990). *A history of contraception.* Cambridge, MA: Basil Blackwell.

McLean, L. M., & Gallop, R. (2003). Implications of childhood sexual abuse for adult borderline personality disorder and complex post traumatic stress disorder. *American Journal of Psychiatry, 160*(2), 369–371.

McLusky, D. (2005). Transsexual golfers can play in women's British open. Retrieved March 2, 2005, from http://www.bloomberg.com/apps/news?pid=10000102&sid=aKYeDa2UJ1fE&refer=uk.

McMahon, S. (2004). Student-athletes, rape-supportive culture, and social change. Retrieved October 16, 2005, from http://sexualassault. rutgers.edu/pdfs/student-athletes_rape-supportive_culture_and_social_change.pdf.

McManus, A. J., Hunter, L., & Renan, H. (2006). Lesbian experiences and needs during childbirth: Guidance for health care providers. *Journal of Obstetrics and Gynecology in Neonatal Nursing, 35,* 13–23.

McNally, R. J. (2003). *Remembering trauma.* Cambridge, MA: Belknap Press/Harvard University Press.

McNally, R. J., Clancy, S. A., Barrett, H. M., & Parker, H. A. (2004). Inhibiting retrieval of trauma cues in adults reporting histories of childhood sexual abuse. *Cognition and Emotion, 18*(4), 479–493.

McNally, R. J., Clancy, S. A., Barrett, H. M., & Parker, H. A. (2005). Reality monitoring in adults reporting repressed, recovered, or continuous memories of childhood sexual abuse. *Journal of Abnormal Psychology, 114*(1), 147–152.

McNeely, C., Shew, M., Beuhring, T., Sieving, R., Miller, B., & Blum, R. (2002). Mothers' influence on the timing of first sex among 14- and 15-year olds. *Journal of Adolescent Health, 31*(3), 256–265.

McQuillan, G. M., & Kruszon-Moran, D. (2008). *HIV infection in the United States household population aged 18–49 years: Results from 1999–2006.* NCHS Data Brief No 4. Hyattsville, MD: National Center for Health Statistics.

Mead, M. (1935/1988/2001). *Sex and Temperament in Three Primitive Societies.* New York: William Morrow.

Meadows, S. O., Land, K. C., & Lamb, V. L. (2005). Assessing Gilligan vs. Sommers: Gender-specific trends in child and youth well-being in the United States, 1985–2001. *Social Indicators Research, 70,* 1–52.

MedlinePlus. (2004a). Androgen insensitivity syndrome. Retrieved October 3, 2005, from http://www.nlm.nih.gov/medlineplus/ency/article/001180.htm.

MedlinePlus. (2004b). Congenital adrenal hyperplasia. Retrieved October 1, 2005, from http://www.nlm.nih.gov/medlineplus/ency/article/000411.htm.

Medrano, M. A., Hatch, J. P., & Zule, W. A. (2003). Childhood trauma and adult prostitution behavior in a multiethnic heterosexual drug-using population. *American Journal of Drug and Alcohol Abuse, 29*(20), 463–486.

Medved, M. (1992). *Hollywood vs. America: Popular culture and the war on traditional values.* New York: HarperCollins.

Mehl, M. R., Vazire, S., Ramirez-Esparza, N., Slatcher, R. B., & Pennebaker, J. W. (2007). Are women really more talkative than men? *Science, 317,* 82.

Meier, E. (2002). Child rape in South Africa. *Pediatric Nursing, 28*(5), 532–535.

Meirik, O., Fraser, I., d'Arcangues, C. (2003). Implantable contraceptives for women. *Human Reproduction Update, 9*(1), 49–59.

Melby, T. (2007). Anal sex: An "extraordinary taboo." *Contemporary Sexuality, 41*(1), 4–6.

Menacker, F. (2005). Trends in cesarean rates for first births and repeat cesarean rates for low-risk women: United States, 1990–2003. *National Vital Statistics Reports, 54*(4).

Ménard, K. S., Nagayama Hall, G., Phung, A., Erian Ghebrial, M., Martin, L. (2003). Gender Differences in Sexual Harassment and Coercion in College Students. *Journal of Interpersonal Violence, 18*(10), 1222–1239.

Menon, R. (2008). Spontaneous preterm birth, a clinical dilemma: Etiologic, pathophysiologic and genetic heterogeneities and racial disparity. *Acta Obstetrica Gynecologic Scandinavica, 87,* 590–600.

Merki-Feld, G. S., & Hund, M. (2007). Clinical experience with NuvaRing in daily practice in Switzerland: Cycle control and acceptability among women of all reproductive ages. *European Journal of Contraceptive and Reproductive Health Care, 12,* 240–247.

Merki-Feld, G. S., Seeger, H., & Mueck, A. O. (2008). Comparison of the proliferative effects of ethinylestradiol on human breast cancer cells in an intermittent and a continuous dosing regime. *Hormone and Metabolic Research.* Retrieved March 18, 2008, from http://www.thieme-connect.com/ejournals/abstract/hmr/doi/10.1055/s-2007-1004540.

Mertz, G. (2008). Asymptomatic shedding of herpes simplex virus 1 and 2: Implications for prevention of transmission. *Journal of Infectious Diseases, 198*(8), 1098–1100.

Meschke, L. L., Bartholomae, S., & Zentall, S. R. (2000). Adolescent sexuality and parent–adolescent processes: Promoting healthy teen choices. *Family Relations, 49*(2), 143–155.

Messenger, J. C. (1993). Sex and repression in an Irish folk community. In D. N. Suggs & A. W. Miracle (Eds.), *Culture and human diversity.* Pacific Grove, CA: Brooks/Cole.

Meston, C. M., Hull, E., Levin, R., & Sipski, M. (2004). Disorders of orgasm in women. *Journal of Sexual Medicine, 1,* 66–68.

Meston, C. M., Trapnell, P. D., & Gorzalka, B. B. (1996). Ethnic and gender differences in sexuality: Variations in sexual behavior between Asian and non-Asian university students. *Archives of Sex Behavior, 25*(1), 33–71.

Meston, C. M., & Worcel, M. (2002). The effects of yohimbine plus L–arginine glutamate on sexual arousal in post menopausal women with sexual arousal disorders. *Archives of Sexual Behavior, 31*(4), 323–332.

Metropolitan Community Churches. (2005). About us. Retrieved November 7, 2005, from http://www.mccchurch.org/AM/TextTemplate.cfm?Section=About_Us&Template=/CM/HTMLDisplay.cfm&ContentID=877.

Meyer-Bahlburg, H. F., Dolezal, C., Baker, S. W., & New, M. I. (2008). Sexual orientation in women with classical or non-classical CAH as a function of degree of prenatal androgen excess. *Archives of Sexual Behavior, 37,* 85–99.

Mhloyi, M. M. (1990). Perceptions on communication and sexuality in marriage in Zimbabwe. *Women and Therapy, 10*(3), 61–73.

Michael, R. T., Gagnon, J. H., Laumann, E. O., & Kolata, G. (1994). *Sex in America.* Boston, MA: Little, Brown.

Middlebrook, D. W. (1999). *Suits me: The double life of Billy Tipton.* New York: Houghton Mifflin.

Mihalik, G. (1988). Sexuality and gender: An evolutionary perspective. *Psychiatric Annals, 18,* 40–42.

Mikulincer, M., & Shaver, P. (2005). Attachment theory and emotions in close relationships: Exploring the attachment-related dynamics of emotional reactions to relational events. *Personal Relationships, 12*(2), 149–168.

Miletski, H. (2002). *Understanding bestiality and zoophilia.* Bethesda, MD: East-West.

Milhausen, R. R., & Herold, E. S. (1999). Does the sexual double standard still exist? Perceptions of university women. *Journal of Sex Research, 36*(4), 361–369.

Millburn, M. A., Mather, R., & Conrad, S. D. (2000). The effects of viewing R-rated movie scenes that objectify women on perceptions of date rape. *Sex Roles, 43*(9–10), 645–664.

Miller, G., Tybur, J. M., & Jordan, B. D. (2007). Ovulatory cycle effects on tip earning by lap dancers: Economic evidence for human estrus? *Evolution and Human Behavior, 28,* 375–381.

Miller, J. (1998). A review of sex offender legislation. *Kansas Journal of Law and Public Policy, 7,* 40–67.

Millner, V. S. (2005). Female sexual arousal disorder and counseling deliberations. *Family Journal: Counseling & Therapy for Couples and Families, 13*(1), 95–100.

Mills, J. S., & D'Alfonso, S. R. (2007). Competition and male body image: Increased drive for muscularity following failure to a female. *Journal of Social and Clinical Psychology, 26,* 505–518.

Milner, J., Dopke, C., & Crouch, J. (2008). Paraphilia not otherwise specified. In D. Laws & W. O'Donohue (Eds.), *Sexual deviance: Theory, assessment and treatment* (2nd ed., pp. 384–418). New York: Guilford Press.

Milner, J., & Robertson, K. (1990). Comparison of physical child abusers, intrafamilial sexual child abusers, and child neglecters. *Journal of Interpersonal Violence, 5,* 37–48.

Mindel, A., & Sawleshwarkar, S. (2008). Condoms for sexually transmissible infection prevention: Politics versus science. *Sexual Health, 5,* 1–8.

Miner, M.H., Coleman, E., Center, B., Ross, M., Simon Rosser, B. (2007). The compulsive sexual behavior inventory: Psychometric properties. *Archives of Sexual Behavior, 36*(4), 579–587.

Minervini, A., Ralph, D., & Pryor, J. (2006). Outcome of penile prosthesis implantation for treating erectile dysfunction: Experience with 504 procedures. *British Journal of Urology, 97,* 129–133.

Mishna, F., Newman, P., Daley, A., & Soloman, S. (2008, January 5). Bullying of lesbian and gay youth: A qualitative investigation. *British Journal of Social Work.* Retrieved October 2, 2008, from http://bjsw.oxford-journals.org/cgi/content/abstract/bcm148.

Misri, S., Kostaras, X., Fox, D., & Kostaras, D. (2000). The impact of partner support in the treatment of postpartum depression. *Canadian Journal of Psychiatry, 45*(6), 554–559.

Mitchell, K., Finkelhor, D., Wolak, J. (2003). The exposure of youth to unwanted sexual material on the Internet: A national survey of risk, impact, and prevention. *Youth and Society, 34,* 330–358.

Mitchell, K. J., Wolak, J., & Finkelhor, D. (2005). Police posing as juveniles online to catch sex offenders: Is it working? *Sexual Abuse: A Journal of Research and Treatment, 17*(3), 241–267.

Mittendorf, R., Williams, M. A., Berkey, C. S., & Cotter, P. F. (1990). The length of uncomplicated human gestation. *Obstetrics and Gynecology, 75*(6), 929–932.

Mocarelli, P., Gerthoux, P. M., Patterson, D., Milani, S., Limonta, G., Bertona, M., et al. (2008). Dioxin exposure, from infancy through puberty, produces endocrine disruption and affects human semen quality. *Environmental Health Perspectives, 116,* 70–77.

Mock, S. E., & Cornelius, S. W. (2007). Profiles of interdependence: The retirement planning of married, cohabiting, and lesbian couples. *Sex Roles, 56*(11–12), 793–800.

Modan, B., Hartge, P., Hirsh-Yechezkel, G., Chetrit A., Lubin F., Beller U., et al. (2001). Parity, oral contraceptives, and the risk of ovarian cancer among carriers and noncarriers of a BRCA1 or BRCA2 mutation. *New England Journal of Medicine, 345,* 235–240.

Moen, V., & Irestedt, L. (2008). Neurological complications following central neuraxial blockades in obstetrics. *Current Opinions in Anesthesiology, 21,* 275–280.

Mommers, E., Kersemaekers, J., Kepers, M., Apter, D., Behre, H., Beynon, J., et al. (2008). Male hormonal contraception: A double-blind, placebo-controlled study. *Journal of Clinical Endocrinology and Metabolism, 93,* 2572–2580.

Monasch, R., Boerma, J. (2004). Orphanhood and childcare patterns in sub-Saharan Africa: An analysis of national survey from 40 countries. *AIDS, 18, (suppl 2),* S55–S65.

Monat-Haller, R. K. (1992). *Understanding and experiencing sexuality.* Baltimore: Brookes.

Money, J. (1955). Hermaphroditism, gender, and precocity in hyper-adrenocorticism: Psychologic findings. *Bulletin of the Johns Hopkins Hospital, 96,* 253–254.

Money, J. (1975). Ablatio penis: Normal male infant sex-reassigned as a girl. *Archives of Sexual Behavior, 4*(1), 65–71.

Money, J. (1984). Paraphilias: Phenomenology and classification. *American Journal of Psychotherapy, 38,* 164–179.

Money, J. (1986). *Venuses penuses: Sexology, sexophy, and exigency theory.* Buffalo, NY: Prometheus Books.

Money, J. (1987). Sin, sickness, or status? Homosexual gender identity and psychoneuroendocrinology. *American Psychologist, 42,* 384–399.

Money, J. (1990). Pedophilia: A specific instance of new phylism theory as applied to paraphiliac lovemaps. In J. Feierman (Ed.), *Pedophilia: Biosocial dimensions* (pp. 445–463). New York: Springer-Verlag.

Monroe, L. M., Kinney, L., Weist, M., Dafeamekpor, D., Dantzler, J., & Reynolds, M. (2005). The experience of sexual assault: Findings from a statewide victim needs assessment. *Journal of Interpersonal Violence, 20*(7), 767–776.

Montemurro, B., & McClure, B. (2005). Changing gender norms for alcohol consumption. *Sex Roles, 52,* 279–288.

Montgomery, K. A., Gonzalez, E., & Montgomery, O. (2008). Self-disclosure of sexually transmitted diseases: An integrative review. *Holistic Nursing Practices, 22,* 268–279.

Monto, M. A. (2000). Why men seek out prostitutes. In R. Weitzer (Ed.), *Sex for sale: Prostitution, pornography, and the sex industry* (pp. 67–83). New York: Routledge.

Monto, M. A. (2001). Prostitution and fellatio. *Journal of Sex Research, 38*(2), 140–146.

Monto, M. A., & McRee, N. (2005). A comparison of the male customers of female street prostitutes with national samples of men. *International Journal of Offender Therapy and Comparative Criminology, 49*(5), 505–529.

Mookodi, G., Ntshebe, O., & Taylor, I. (2004). Botswana. In R. T. Francoeur & R. J. Noonan (Eds.), *The Continuum international encyclopedia of sexuality* (pp. 89–97). New York/London: Continuum International.

Moore, M. (1994, October 8). Changing India: Arranged marriages persist with 90s twist. *The Washington Post.*

Moore, S. (1999). Barriers to safer sex: Beliefs and attitudes among male and female adult heterosexuals across four relationship groups. *Journal of Health Psychology, 4*(2), 149–163.

Mor, Z., Kent, C. K., Kohn, R. P., & Klausner, J. D. (2007). Declining rates in male circumcision amidst increasing evidence of its public health benefit. *PLoS ONE, 2*(9). Retrieved April 5, 2008, from http://www.plosone.org/article/info:doi%2F10.1371%2Fjournal.pone.0000861.

Morales, A. (2004). Andropause (or symptomatic late-onset hypogonadism): Facts, fiction and controversies. *Aging Male, 7*(4), 297–304.

Moreno, V., Bosch, F. X., Munoz, N., Meijer C. J., Shah K. V., Walboomers J. M., et al. (2002). Effect of oral contraceptives on risk of cervical cancer in women with human papillomavirus infection: The IARC multicentric case–control study. *Lancet, 359,* 1085–1092.

Moreno-Garcia, M., Fernandez-Martinez, F. J., & Miranda, E. B. (2005). Chromosomal anomalies in patients with short stature. *Pediatric International, 47*(5), 546–549.

Morgan, J. F., Lacey, J. H., & Reid, F. (1999). Anorexia nervosa: Changes in sexuality during weight restoration. *Psychosomatic Medicine, 61,* 541–545.

Morgan, J. F., Murphy, H., Lacey, J. H., & Conway, G. (2005). Long term psychological outcome for women with congenital adrenal hyperplasia: Cross sectional survey. *British Medical Journal, 330*(7487), 340–342.

Morgan, S. P., & Rindfuss, R. (1985). Marital disruption: Structural and temporal dimensions. *American Journal of Sociology, 90*(5), 1055–1077.

Morley, J., & Perry, H. (2000). Androgen deficiency in aging men. *Journal of Laboratory and Clinical Medicine, 135*(5), 370–378.

Morris, B. J. (2007). Why circumcision is a biomedical imperative for the 21st century. *Bioessays, 29,* 1147–1158.

Morris, R. J. (1990). Aikane: Accounts of Hawaiian same-sex relationships in the journals of Captain Cook's third voyage (1776–1780). *Journal of Homosexuality, 19,* 21–54.

Morrison-Beedy, D., Carey, M. P., Cote-Arsenault, D., Seibold-Simpson, S., & Robinson, K. A. (2008). Understanding sexual abstinence in urban adolescent girls. *Journal of Obstetric, Gynecologic, and Neonatal Nursing, 37,* 185.

Morrone, A., Hercogova, J., & Lotti, T. (2002). Stop genital mutilation. *International Journal of Dermatology, 41*(5), 253–263.

Morrow, K. M., & Allsworth, J. E. (2000). Sexual risk in lesbians and bisexual women. *Journal of Gay and Lesbian Medical Association, 4*(4), 159–165.

Morse, E. V., Simon, P. M., Balson, P. M., & Osofsky, H. J. (1992). Sexual behavior patterns of customers of male street prostitutes. *Archives of Sexual Behavior, 21,* 347–357.

Morse, E. V., Simon, P. M., Osotsky, H. J., Balson, P. M., & Gaumer, R. (1991). The male street prostitute. *Social Science Medicine, 32,* 535–539.

Mortenson, S. T. (2002). Sex, communication, values, and cultural values. *Communication Reports, 15*(1), 57–71.

Mosconi, A. M., Roila, F., Gatta, G., & Theodore, C. (2005). Cancer of the penis. *Critical Reviews in Oncology/Hematology, 53*(2), 165–178.

Moseley, D. T., Follingstad, D. R., & Harley, H. (1981). Psychological factors that predict reaction to abortion. *Journal of Clinical Psychology, 37,* 276–279.

Moser, C. (1988). Sadomasochism. Special issue: The sexually unusual: Guide to understanding and helping. *Journal of Social Work and Human Sexuality, 7,* 43–56.

Mosher, C. M. (2001). The social implications of sexual identity formation and the coming-out process: A review of the theoretical and empirical literature. *Family Journal, 9*(20), 164–174.

Mosher, W. D., Martinez, G. M., Chandra, A., Abma, J. C., & Wilson, S. J. (2004). Use of contraception and use of family planning services in the United States: 1982–2002. *Advance Data from Vital and Health Statistics,* no. 350. Retrieved May 27, 2008, from http://www.cdc.gov/nchs/data/ad/ad350.pdf.

Moskowitz, C. (2008, May 16). Same sex couples common in the wild. *LiveScience.* Retrieved October 2, 2008, from http://www.livescience.com/animals/080516-gay-animals.html.

Mueck, A. O., & Seeger, H. (2008). The World Health Organization defines hormone replacement therapy as carcinogenic: Is this implausible? *Gynecological Endocrinology, 24,* 129–132.

Muehlenhard, C. L., & Cook, S. W. (1988). Men's self-reports of unwanted sexual activity. *Journal of Sex Research, 24,* 58–72.

Muehlenhard, C. L., & MacNaughton, J. S. (1988). Women's beliefs about women who "lead men on." *Journal of Social and Clinical Psychology, 7,* 65–79.

Muehlenhard, C. L., & Schrag, J. (1991). Nonviolent sexual coercion. In A. Parrot & L. Beckhofer (Eds.), *Acquaintance rape—The hidden crime* (pp. 115–128). New York: Wiley.

Mueller, P., & Major, B. (1989). Self-blame, self-efficacy, & adjustment of abortion. *Journal of Personality & Social Psychology, 57,* 1059–1068.

Mufti, U., Ghani, K., Samman, R., Virdi, J., & Potluri, B. (2008). Anejaculation as an atypical presentation of prostate cancer: A case report. *Cases Journal, 1,* 81.

Muir, J. G. (1993, March 31). Homosexuals and the 10% fallacy. *The Wall Street Journal,* p. A14.

Mukherjee, B., & Shivakumar, T. (2007). A case of sensorineural deafness following ingestion of sildenafil. *Journal of Laryngology and Otology, 121,* 395–397.

Mulders, T. M., & Dieben, T. (2001). Use of the novel combined contraceptive vaginal ring NuvaRing° for ovulation inhibition. *Fertility and Sterility, 75,* 865–870.

Mulders, T. M., Dieben, T., & Bennick, H. (2002). Ovarian function with a novel combined contraceptive vaginal ring. *Human Reproduction, 17,* 2594–2599.

Mulick, P. S., & Wright, L. W. (2002). Examining the existence of biphobia in the heterosexual and homosexual populations. *Journal of Bisexuality, 2,* 45–65.

Muller, J. E., Mittleman, M. A., Maclure, M., Sherwood, J. B., & Toffer, G. H. (1996). Triggering myocardial infraction by sexual activity. *Journal of the American Medical Association, 275*(18), 1405–1409.

Mulligan, E., & Heath, M. (2007). Seeking open minded doctors. How women who identify as bisexual, queer or lesbian seek quality health care. *Australian Family Physician, 36,* 385–480.

Mulvaney, B. M. (1994). Gender differences in communication: An intercultural experience. Paper prepared by the Department of Communication, Florida Atlantic University.

Munarriz, R., Talakoub, L., & Flaherty, E. (2002). Androgen replacement therapy with dehydroepiandrosterone for androgen insufficiency and female sexual dysfunction: Androgen and questionnaire results. *Journal of Sex & Marital Therapy, 28*(Suppl. 1), 165–173.

Munge, B., Pomerantz, A., Pettibone, J., & Falconer, J. (2007). The influence of length of marriage and fidelity status on perception of marital rape. *Journal of Interpersonal Violence, 22,* 1332–1339.

Munson, M. (1987). How do you do it? *On Our Backs, 4*(1).

Murina F., Bernorio R., Palmiotto, R. (2008). The use of amielle vaginal trainers as adjuvant in the treatment of vestibulodynia: An observational multicentric study. *Medscape Journal of Medicine, 10*(1), 23.

Murnen, S., & Kohlman, M. (2007). Athletic participation, fraternity membership, and sexual aggression among college men: A meta-analysis review. *Sex Roles, 57,* 145–157.

Murnen, S. K., Wright, C., & Kaluzny, G. (2002). If boys will be boys then girls will be victims? A meta-analytic review of the research that relates masculine ideology to sexual aggression. *Sex Roles, 46*(11–12), 359–375.

Murphy, L. R. (1990). Defining the crime against nature: Sodomy in the United

States appeals courts, 1810–1940. *Journal of Homosexuality, 19,* 49–66.

Murphy, W., & Page, J. (2008). Exhibitionism: Psychopathology and theory. In D. Laws & W. O'Donohue (Eds.), *Sexual deviance: Theory, assessment and treatment* (2nd ed., pp. 61–75). New York: Guilford Press.

Murray, J. (2000). Psychological profile of pedophiles and child molesters. *Journal of Psychology, 134*(2), 211–224.

Murray, K. M., Ciarrocchi, J. W., & Murray-Swank, N. A. (2007). Spirituality, religiosity, shame, and guilt as predictors of sexual attitudes and experiences. *Journal of Psychology and Theology, 35,* 222–234.

Murray, S., & Dynes, W. (1999). Latin American gays: Snow Whites and snake charmers. *The Economist, 353*(8150), 82.

Murray-Swank, N. A., Pargament, K., & Mahoney, A. (2005). At the crossroads of sexuality and spirituality: The sanctification of sex by college students. *International Journal of the Psychology of Religion, 15,* 199–219.

Musacchio, N., Hartrich, M., & Garofalo, R. (2006). Erectile dysfunction and Viagra use: What's up with college males? *Journal of Adolescent Health, 39,* 452–454.

Muscarella, F., Fink, B., Grammer, K., Kirk-Smith, M. (2001). Homosexual Orientation in Males: Evolutionary and Ethological Aspects. Neuroendocrinology Letters. Retrieved August 17, 2008, from http://cogprints.org/2163/0/NEL220601R01_Muscarella_.pdf.

Mustanski, B. (2001). Getting wired: Exploiting the internet for the collection of valid sexuality data. *Journal of Sex Research, 38*(4), 292–302.

Myers, D. (2007). *Psychology* (8th ed.). New York: Worth.

Nacci, P. L., & Kane, T. R. (1983). The incidence of sex and sexual aggression in federal prisons. *Federal Probation, 47,* 31–36.

Nadelson, C. C., Notman, M. T., Zackson, H., & Gornick, J. (1982). A follow-up study of rape victims. *American Journal of Psychiatry, 139,* 1266–1270.

Nagel, B., Matsuo, H., McIntyre, K. P., & Morrison, N. (2005). Attitudes toward victims of rape: Effects of gender, race, religion, and social class. *Journal of Interpersonal Violence, 20*(6), 725–737.

Nagel, J. (2003). *Race, ethnicity and sexuality.* New York: Oxford University Press.

Nair, A. R., Klapper, A., Kushnerik, V., Margulis, I., DelPriore, G. (2008). Spinal cord stimulator for the treatment of a woman with vulvovaginal burning and deep pelvic pain. *Obstetrics and Gynecology, 111*(2 Pt 2), 545–547.

Najib, A., Lorberbaum, J. P., Kose, S., Bohning, D. E., & George, M. (2004). Regional brain activity in women grieving a romantic relationship breakup. *American Journal of Psychiatry, 161*(12), 2245–2256.

Najman, J. M., Dunne, M. P., Purdie, D. M., Boyle, F. M., & Coxeter, P. D. (2005). Sexual abuse in childhood and sexual dysfunction in adulthood: An Australian population-based study. *Archives of Sexual Behavior, 34*(5), 517–526.

Nanda, S. (2001). *Gender diversity: Crosscultural variations.* Prospect Heights, IL: Waveland Press.

Nardone, A. (2004, October). Don't sweat it. *Fitness,* p. 78.

Narod, S. A., Dube, M. P., Klijn, J., Lubinski, J., Lynch, H. T., Ghadirian, P., Provencher, D., Heimdal, K., Moller, P., Robson, M., Offit, K., Isaacs, C., Weber, B., Friedman, E., et al. (2002). Oral contraceptives and the risk of breast cancer in BRCA1 and BRCA2 mutation carriers. *Journal of National Cancer Institute, 94*(23), 1773–1779.

Narod, S. A., Sun, P., Ghadirian, P., Lynch, H., Isaacs, C., Garber, J., Weber, B., Karlan, B., Fishman, D., Rosen, B., Tung, N., & Neuhausen, S. L. (2001). Tubal ligation and risk of ovarian cancer in carriers of BRCA1 or BRCA2 mutations: A case-control study. *Lancet, 357*(9267), 843–844.

National Cancer Institute. (2006). Oral contraceptives and cancer risk: Questions and answers. *National Cancer Institute Fact Sheet.* Retrieved October 1, 2008, from http://www.cancer.gov/cancertopics/factsheet/Risk/oral-contraceptives.

National Center for Health Statistics. (2002). *Vital statistics of the U.S., 2000. Vol I: Natality.* Hyattsville, MD: Author.

National Center for Injury Prevention and Control. (2005). Intimate partner violence: Fact sheet. Retrieved October 17, 2005, from http://www. cdc.gov/ncipc/factsheets/ipv-facts.htm.

National Coalition of Anti-Violence Programs. (1998, October 6). Annual report on lesbian, gay, bisexual, and transgender domestic violence. Retrieved May 23, 2003, from http://www.hrc.org/issues/hate_crimes/antiviolence.asp.

National Conference of State Legislatures. (2008, June). *50 state summary of breastfeeding laws.* Retrieved December 19, 2008, from http://www.NCSL.org/programs/health/breast50.htm.

National Institutes of Health. (2008). Studies by topic. Retrieved on January 24, 2008, from http://clinicaltrials.gov/ct2/search/browse.

National Telecommunications and Information Administration and the U.S. Department of Commerce. (1999). Falling through the Net: Defining the digital divide: A report on the telecommunications and information technology gap in America. Retrieved June 1, 2002, from http://www.ntia.doc.gov/ntiahome/fttn99/contents.html.

Naucler, P., Ryd, W., Törnberg, S., Strand, A., Wadell, G, Elfgren, K., et al. (2007). Human papillomavirus and Papanicolaou tests to screen for cervical cancer. *New England Journal of Medicine, 357,* 1589–1597.

Nauru, T., Suleiman, M., Kiwi, A., Anther, M., Wear, S. Q., Irk, S., & Rive, J. (2008). Intracytoplasmic sperm injection outcome using ejaculated sperm and retrieved sperm in azoospermic men. *Urology, 5,* 106–110.

Navarro, M. (2004, November 28). The most private of makeovers. *The New York Times,* Sec. 9, p. 1.

Naz, R. K. (2005). Contraceptive vaccines. *Drugs, 65,* 593–603.

Naziri, D. (2007). Man's involvement in the experience of abortion and the dynamics of the couple's relationship: A clinical study. *European Journal of Contraceptive and Reproductive Health Care, 12,* 168–174.

Neal, J., & Frick-Horbury, D. (2001). The effects of parenting styles and childhood attachment patterns on intimate relationships. *Journal of Instructional Psychology, 28*(3), 178–183.

Nebehay, S. (2004). Cervical cancer epidemic in poor countries. Retrieved December 12, 2004, from http://www.reuters.co.uk/printerFriendlyPopup.jhtml?type=healthNews&storyID=7114888.

Neergaard, L. (2005). Doctors are holding off on surgery for newborns of uncertain gender. Retrieved February 22, 2005, from http://www. cleveland.com/health/plain-dealer/index.ssf?/base/news/110889699317860.xml.

Neff, L., & Karney, B. (2005). To know you is to love you: The implications of global adoration and specific accuracy for marital relationships. *Journal of Personality & Social Psychology, 88*(3), 480–497.

Neisen, J. H. (1990). Heterosexism: Redefining homophobia for the 1990s. *Journal of Gay and Lesbian Psychotherapy, 1,* 21–35.

Nelson, A. L. (2007). Communicating with patients about extended-cycle and continuous use of oral contraceptives. *Journal of Women's Health, 16,* 463–470.

Nelson, C., Ahmed, A., Valenzuela, R., & Melhall, J. (2007). Assessment of penile vibratory stimulation as a management strategy in men with secondary retarded orgasm. *Urology, 69,* 552–555.

Nelson, H. D. (2008). Menopause. *The Lancet, 372,* 760–770.

Nelson, R. (2005). Gottman's sound medical house model. Retrieved September 3, 2005, from http://www.psychpage.com/family/library/gottman.html

Neri, Q., Takeuchi, T., & Palermo, G. (2008). An update of assisted reproductive technologies results in the U.S. *Annals of the New York Academy of Sciences, 1127,* 41–49.

Neruda, B. (2005). Development and current status of combined spinal epidural anaesthesia [article in German]. *Anasthesiol Intensivemed Nofallmed Schmerzther, 40*(8), 4590–460.

New, J. F. H. (1969). *The Renaissance and Reformation: A short history.* New York: Wiley.

Newell, M., Coovadia, H., Cortina-Borja, M., Rollins, N., Gaillard, P., Dabis, F. (2004). Mortality of infected and uninfected infants born to HIV-infected mothers in Africa: A pooled analysis. *The Lancet, 364*(9441), 1236–1243.

Newell, M. L. (2005). Current issues in the prevention of mother-to-child transmission of HIV-1 infection. *Transactions of the Royal Society of Tropical Medicine and Hygiene, 100*(1), 1–5.

Newfield, E., Hart, S., Dibble, S., & Kohler, L. (2006). Female-to-male transgender quality of life. *Quality of Life Research, 15,* 1447–1457.

Newman, L., & Nyce, J. (Eds.). (1985). *Women's medicine: A cross-cultural study of indigenous fertility regulation.* New Brunswick, NJ: Rutgers University Press.

Newport, F. (1998). Americans remain more likely to believe sexual orientation due to environment, not genetics. *The Gallup Poll Monthly, 394*(14–17).

Newring, K., Wheeler, J., & Draper, C. (2008). Transvestic fetishism: Assessment and treatment. In D. Laws & W. O'Donohue (Eds.), *Sexual deviance: Theory, assessment and treatment* (2nd ed., pp. 285–304). New York: Guilford Press.

Ng, E., & Ma, J. L. (2004). Hong Kong. In R. T. Francoeur & R. J. Noonan (Eds.), *The Continuum international encyclopedia of sexuality* (pp. 489–502). New York/London: Continuum International.

Ngai, S. W., Fan, S., Li, S., Cheng, L., Ding, J., Jing, X., Ng, E., & Ho, P. (2004). A randomized trial to compare 24h versus 12h double dose regimen of levonorgestrel for emergency contraception. *Human Reproduction, 20,* 307–311.

Nguyen, M. M., & Ellison, L. M. (2005). Testicular cancer patterns in Asian-American males: An opportunity for public health education to impact outcomes. *Urology, 66*(3), 606–609.

Niccolai, L., Hochberg, A., Ethier, K., Lewis, J., & Ickovics, J. (2007). Burden of recurrent *Chlamydia trachomatis* infections in young women: Further uncovering the "hidden epidemic." *Archives of Pediatric Adolescent Medicine, 161,* 246–251.

Nicholas, D. R. (2000). Men, masculinity and cancer. *Journal of American College Health, 49*(1), 27–33.

Nichols, M. (1990). Lesbian relationships: Implications for the study of sexuality and gender. In D. McWhiter, S. A. Sanders, & J. Reinish (Eds.), *Homosexuality/heterosexuality: Concepts of sexual orientation* (pp. 350–364). The Kinsey Institute Series. New York: Oxford University Press.

Nichols, M. (2004). Lesbian sexuality/female sexuality: Rethinking lesbian bed death. *Sexual and Relationship Therapy, 19*(4), 363–371.

Nichols, S. L. (1999). Gay, lesbian, and bisexual youth: Understanding diversity and promoting tolerance in schools. *The Elementary School Journal, 99*(5), 505.

Nicolaides, K. H., Spencer, K., Avgidou, K., Faiola, S., & Falcon, O. (2005). Multicenter study of first-trimester screening for trisomy 21 in 75,821 pregnancies: Results and estimation of the potential impact of individual risk-orientated two-stage first-trimester screening. *Ultrasound Obstetrics and Gynecology, 25*(3), 221–226.

Nicoll, L. M., & Skupski, D.W. (2008). Venous air embolism after using a birth-training device. *Obstetrics and Gynecology, 111,* 489–491.

Nielsen NetRatings. (2007). Internet users in the Americas. Retrieved February 3, 2008, from http://www.nielsen-netratings.com/.

Nilsson, L. (1990). *A child is born.* New York: Delacorte Press, Bantam Books.

Noack, T. (2001). Cohabitation in Norway: An accepted and gradually more regulated way of living. *International Journal of Law, Policy and the Family, 15,* 102–117.

Noland, V. J., Liller, K. D., McDermott, R. J., Coulter, M. L., & Seraphine, A. E. (2004). Is adolescent sibling violence a precursor to college dating violence? *American Journal of Health Behavior, 28*(Suppl. 1), S13–S23.

Noller, P. (1993, March–June). Gender and emotional communication in marriage: Different cultures or differential social power? *Journal of Language & Social Psychology, 12*(1–2), 132–152.

Nonnemaker, J., McNeely, C., & Blum, R. (2003). Public and private domains of religiosity and adolescent health risk behaviors: Evidence from the National Longitudinal Study of Adolescent Health. *Social Science & Medicine, 57*(11), 2049–2054.

Nordling, N., Sandnabba, N., & Santilla, P., (2000). The prevalence and effects of self-reported childhood sexual abuse among sadomasochistically-oriented males and females. *Journal of Child Sex Abuse, 9,* 53–63.

Nordling, N., Sandnabba, N., Santtila, P., Alison, L. (2006). Differences and similarities between gay and straight individuals involved in the SM subculture. *Journal of Homosexuality, 50*(2–3), 41–67.

Nordtveit, T., Melve, K., Albrechtsen, S., & Skjaerven, R. (2008). Maternal and paternal contribution to intergenerational recurrence of breech delivery: Population based cohort study. *British Medical Journal, 336,* 843–844.

Norton, M. B. (2002). *In the devil's snare: The Salem witchcraft crisis of 1692.* New York: Alfred A. Knopf.

Notman, M. T. (2002). Changes in sexual orientation and object choice in midlife in women. *Psychoanalytic Inquiry, 22,* 182–195.

Nour, N. M. (2004). Female genital cutting: Clinical and cultural guidelines. *Obstetrical & Gynecological Survey, 59*(4), 272–279.

Nour, N. M. (2006). Health consequences of child marriage in Africa. *Emerging Infectious Diseases, 12*(11). Retrieved June 26, 2008, from http://www.cdc.gov/ncidod/EID/vol12no11/06-0510.htm.

Novák, A., de la Loge, C., Abetz, L., & van der Meulen, E. (2003). The combined contraceptive vaginal ring, NuvaRing: An international study of user acceptability. *Contraception, 67,* 187–194.

NuvaRing now available for Australian women. (2007, April 8). *Women's Health Law Weekly.* NewsRX. Retrieved December 19, 2008, from http://www.newsrx.com/article.php?articleID=519768

Nzila, N., Laga, M., Thiam, M., Mayimona, K., et al. (1991). HIV and other sexually transmitted diseases among female prostitutes in Kinshasa. *AIDS, 5,* 715–721.

Obrizzo, L. (2005, March 8). Personal communication.O'Connor, T. G., Thorpe, K., Dunn, J., & Golding, J. (1999). Parental divorce and adjustment in adulthood: Findings from a community sample. *Journal of Child Psychology and Psychiatry, 40,* 777–789.

O'Connell, H. E., & DeLancey, D. O. (2005). Clitoral anatomy in nulliparous, healthy, premenopausal volunteers using enhanced magnetic resonance imaging. *Journal of Urology, 173,* 2060–2063.

Ofman, U. (2004). "… And how are things sexually?": Helping patients adjust to sexual changes before, during, and after cancer treatment. *Supportive Cancer Therapy, 1,* 243–247.

Ogilvie, G., Taylor, D., Trussler, T., Marchand, R., Gilbert, M., Moniruzzaman, A., & Rekart, M. (2008). Seeking sexual partners on the internet: A marker for risky sexual behavior in men who have sex with men. *Canadian Journal of Public Health, 99,* 185–188.

Ogletree, S. M., & Ginsburg, H. J. (2000). Kept under the hood: Neglect of the clitoris in common vernacular. *Sex Roles, 43*(11–12), 917–927.

O'Grady, R. (2001). Eradicating pedophilia toward the humanization of society. *Journal of International Affairs, 55*(1), 123–140.

O'Halloran, R. L., & Dietz, P. E. (1993). Autoerotic fatalities with power hydraulics. *Journal of Forensic Sciences, 38,* 359–364.

O'Hanlan, K. A., & Crum, C. P. (1996). HPV associated cervical intraepithelial neoplastia following lesbian sex. *Obstetrics and Gynecology, 88,* 702–703.

O'Hare, T. (2005). Risky sex and drinking contexts in freshman first offenders. *Addictive Behaviors, 30*(3), 585–588.

Ohl, D., Quallich, S., Sonksen, J., Brackett, N., & Lynne, C. (2008). Anejaculation and retrograde ejaculation. *Urological Clinics of North America, 35,* 211–220.

Okami, P. (1990). Sociopolitical biases in the contemporary scientific literature on adult human sexual behavior with children and adolescents. In J. Feierman (Ed.), *Pedophilia* (pp. 91–121). New York: Springer Verlag.

Okami, P., Olmstead, R., & Abramson, P. R. (1997). Sexual experiences in early childhood: 18-year longitudinal data from the UCLA Family Lifestyles Project. *Journal of Sex Research, 34*(4), 339–347.

Okami, P., Olmstead, R., & Abramson, P. R. (1998). Early childhood exposure to parental nudity and scenes of parental sexuality ("primal scenes"): An 18-year longitudinal study of outcome. *Archives of Sexual Behavior, 27*(4), 361–384.

Okazaki, S. (2002). Influences of culture on Asian Americans' sexuality. *Journal of Sex Research, 39*(1), 34–41.

Oliver, C., Beech, A., Fisher, D., & Beckett, R. (2007). A comparison of rapists and sexual murderers on demographic and selected psychometric measures. *International Journal of Offender Therapy and Comparative Criminology, 51,* 298.

Olsson, S. E., & Möller, A. (2006). Regret after sex reassignment surgery in a male-to-female transsexual: A long-term follow up. *Archives of Sexual Behavior, 35,* 501–506.

O'Neill, N., & O'Neill, G. (1972). *Open marriage: A new life style for couples.* New York: Evans.

Oner, B. (2001). Factors predicting future time orientation for romantic relationships with the opposite sex. *Journal of Psychology: Interdisciplinary & Applied, 135*(4), 430–438.

Ong, K. K., Northstone, K., Wells, J. C., Rubin, C., Neww, A. R., Golding, J., Dunger, D. B. (2007). Earlier mother's age at menarcdhe predicts rapid infancy growth and childhood obesity. *PLoS Medicine, 4*(e132), 737–742. Retrieved March 9, 2008, from http://medicine.plosjournals.org/perlserv/?request=get-document&doi=10.1371%2Fjournal.pmed.0040132.

O'Reilly, S., Knox, D., Zusman, M. (2007). College student attitudes toward pornography use. *College Student Journal, 41*(2), 402–406.

Orenstein, R., & Wong, E. S. (1999, March 1). Urinary tract infections in adults. Retrieved March 22, 2005, from http://www.aafp.org/ afp/990301/1225.html.

Oriel, K. A., & Schrager, S. (1999). Abnormal uterine bleeding. *American Family Physician, 60*(5), 1371–1380.

Orlandi, F., Rossi, C., Orlandi, E., Jakil, M. C., Hallahan, T. W., Macri, V. J., & Krantz, D. A. (2005). First-trimester screening for tisomy-21 using a simplified method to assess the presence or absence of the fetal nasal bone. *American Journal of Obstetrics & Gynecology, 192*(4), 1107–1111.

Orlandi, L. (2008, May 25). Lesbians have a long to-do list after marriage victory. *WomensENews.* Retrieved May 26, 2008, from http://www.womensenews.org/article.cfm?aid=3612.

Ormsby, A. (2007, December 13). Women may get pill without prescription. Reuters UK. Retrieved July 28, 2008, from http://uk.reuters.com/article/domesticNews/idUKL1361800120071213?pageNumber=1&virtualBrandChannel=0.

Ornish, D. (1999). *Love and survival: The scientific basis for the healing power of intimacy.* New York, NY: Harper Paperbacks.

Ortiz, C. A., Freeman, J. L., Kuo, Y. F., & Goodwin, J. S. (2007). The influence of marital status on stage at diagnosis and survival of older persons with melanoma. *Journals of Gerontology, Series A: Biological Sciences and Medical Sciences, 62,* 892–898.

Orzek, A. M. (1988). The lesbian victim of sexual assault: Special considerations for the mental health professional. (Special issue: Lesbianism: Affirming nontraditional roles.) *Women and Therapy, 8,* 107–117.

Ostner, I. (2001). Cohabitation in Germany—Rules, reality and public discourses. *International Journal of Law, Policy and the Family, 15,* 88–101.

O'Sullivan, C. (1991). Acquaintance gang rape on campus. In A. Parrot & L. Bechhofer (Eds.), *Acquaintance rape: The hidden crime* (pp. 140–156). New York: Wiley.

O'Sullivan, L., & Allgeier, E. (1998). Feigning sexual desire: Consenting to unwanted sexual activity in heterosexual dating relationships. *Journal of Sex Research, 35,* 234–243.

Otis, M. D., & Skinner, W. F. (1996). The prevalence of victimization and its effect on mental well-being among lesbian and gay people. *Journal of Homosexuality, 30,* 93–121.

O'Toole, C. J., & Bregante, J. L. (1992). Lesbians with disabilities. *Sexuality and Disability, 10,* 163–172.

Owyang, J. (2008). Social network stats: Facebook, MySpace, Reunion. Retrieved April 27, 2008, from http://www.web-strategist.com/blog/2008/01/09/social-network-stats-facebook-myspace-reunion-jan-2008/.

Ozdemir, O., Simsek, F., Ozkardes, S., Incesu, C., & Karakoc, B. (2008). The unconsummated marriage: Its frequency and clinical characteristics in a sexual dysfunction clinic. *Journal of Sex and Marital Therapy, 34,* 268–279.

Pachankis, J. E., & Goldfried, M. R. (2004). Clinical issues in working with lesbian, gay, and bisexual clients. *Psychotherapy: Theory, Research, Practice, Training, 41,* 227–246.

Padgett, V. R., Brislin-Slutz, J. A., & Neal, J. A. (1989). Pornography, erotica, and attitudes toward women: The effects of repeated exposure. *The Journal of Sex Research, 26,* 479–491.

Palca, J. (1991). Fetal brain signals time for birth. *Science, 253,* 1360.

Palefsky, J. (2008). Human papillomavirus and anal neoplasia. *Current HIV/AIDS Report, 5,* 78–85.

Pamm, C. J. (2001). Effect of attitudes toward women and other attitudinal variables on the formation of rape callousness and sexual misconduct among African, European, and Asian-American college students at a prestigious northeastern university: A longitudinal study. University of Pennsylvania, *Dissertation Abstracts International,* #0-493-257063.

Pandey, M. K., Rani, R., & Agrawal, S. (2005). An update in recurrent spontaneous abortion. *Archives of Gynecology & Obstetrics, 272*(2), 95–108.

Panjari, M., & Davis, S. (2007). DHEA therapy for women: Effect on sexual function and wellbeing. *Human Reproduction Update, 13,* 239–248.

Panzer, C., Wise, S., Fantini, G., Kang, D., Munarriz, R., Guay, A., & Goldstein, I. (2006). Impact of oral contraceptives on sex hormone-binding globulin and androgen levels: A retrospective study in women with sexual dysfunction. *Journal of Sexual Medicine, 3,* 104–113.

Papalia, D. E., Sterns, H. L., Feldman, R., & Camp, C. (2002). *Adult development and aging* (2nd ed.). Boston: McGraw-Hill.

Pappo, I., Lerner-Geva, L., Halevy, A., Olmer, L., Friedler, S., Raziel, A., et al. (2008). The possible association between IVF and breast cancer incidence. *Annals of Surgical Oncology, 15,* 1048–1055.

Pardue, A., & Arrigo, B. (2008). Power, anger, and sadistic rapists: Toward a differentiated model of offender personality. *International Journal of Offender Therapy and Comparative Criminology, 52,* 378–400.

Pardun, C. J., L'Engle, K. L., & Brown, J. D. (2005). Linking exposure to outcomes: Early adolescents' consumption of sexual content in six media. *Mass Communication & Society, 8*(2), 75–1.

Parker, S. K., & Griffin, M. A. (2002). What is so bad about a little name calling? *Journal of Occupational Health Psychology, 7*(3), 195–210.

Parker-Pope, T. (2002, August 6). How eye-rolling destroys a marriage. *Wall Street Journal,* p. D1.

Parkhill, M., & Abbey, A. (2008). Does alcohol contribute to the confluence model of sexual assault perpetration? *Journal of Social and Clinical Psychology, 27,* 529–554.

Parkin, D. M., Bray, F., Ferlay, J., & Pisani, P. (2005). Global cancer statistics, 2002. *CA: A Cancer Journal for Clinicians, 55*(2), 74–108.

Parks, K. A., & Scheidt, D. M. (2000). Male bar drinkers' perspective on female bar drinkers. *Sex Roles, 43*(11/12), 927–935.

Parmer, T., & Gordon, J. J. (2007). Cultural influences on African American sexuality: The role of multiple identities on kinship, power, and ideology. In M. Tepper & A. F. Owens (Eds.), *Sexual health, Vol. 3: Moral and cultural foundations,* (pp. 173–201). Westport, CT: Praeger.

Parrott, D., & Peterson, J. (2008). What motivates hate crimes based on sexual orientation? Mediating effects of anger on antigay aggression. *Aggressive Behavior, 34,* 306–318.

Parry, B. L. (2008). Perimenopausal depression. *American Journal of Psychiatry, 165,* 23–27.

Pasterski, V. L., Brain, C., Geffner, M. E., Hindmarsh, P., Brook, C., & Hines, M. (2005). Prenatal hormones and postnatal socialization by parents as determinants of male-typical toy play in girls with congenital adrenal hyperplasia. *Child Development, 76*(1), 264–279.

Pasterski, V., Hindmarsh, P., Geffnew, M., Brook, C., Brain, C., & Hines, M. (2007). Increased aggression and activity level in 3- to 11-year old girls with congenital adrenal hyperplasia (CAH). *Hormones and Behavior, 52,* 368–374.

Pasupathy, D., & Smith, G. C. (2005). The analysis of factors predicting antepartum stillbirth. *Minerva Ginecology, 57*(4), 397–410.

Patel, R. (2004). Supporting the patient with genital HSV infection. *Herpes, 11*(3), 87–92.

Patil, S., Sultan, A., & Thakar, R. (2007). Bartholin's cysts and abscesses. *Journal of Obstetrics and Gynecology, 27,* 241–245.

Patrick, M. E., & Maggs, J. L. (2007). Reasons to have sex, personal goals, and sexual behavior during the transition to college. *Journal of Sex Research, 44,* 240–249.

Pattatucci, A. M. (1998). Molecular investigations into complex behavior: Lessons from sexual orientation studies. *Human Biology, 70*(2), 367–387.

Patton, G. C., & Viner, R. (2007). Pubertal transitions in health. *The Lancet, 369,* 1130–1139.

Paul, J. P. (1984). The bisexual identity: An idea without social recognition. *Journal of Homosexuality, 9,* 45–63.

Paul, P. (2005). *Pornified: How pornography is transforming our lives, our relationships and our families.* New York: Times Books.

Pawelski, J. G., Perrin, E. C., Foy, J. M., Allen, C. E., Crawford, J. E., Del Monte, M., et al. (2006). The effects of marriage, civil union, and domestic partnership laws on the health and well-being of children. *Pediatrics, 118,* 349–364.

Payer, P. J. (1991). Sex and confession in the thirteenth century. In J. E. Salisbury (Ed.), *Sex in the Middle Ages.* New York: Garland.

Pearson, J., Muller, C., & Wilkinson, L. (2007). Adolescent same-sex attraction and academic outcomes: The role of school attachment and engagement. *Social Problems, 54,* 523–542.

Pearson, J. C., Turner, L. H., & Todd-Mancillas, W. (1991). *Gender and communication* (2nd ed.). Dubuque, IA: William C. Brown.

Pearson, R., & Lewis, M. B. (2005). Fear recognition across the menstrual cycle. *Hormones & Behavior, 47*(3), 267–271.

Peck, S. (1978). *The road less traveled: A new psychology of love, traditional values and spiritual growth.* Oxford, England: Simon & Schuster.

Peele, S., & Brodsky, A. (1991). *Love and addiction.* Jersey City, NJ: Parkwest.

Peeples, E. H., & Scacco, A. M. (1982). The stress impact study technique: A method for evaluating the consequences of male-on-male sexual assault in jails, prisons, and other selected single-sex institutions. In A. M. Scacco (Ed.), *Male rape: A casebook of sexual aggressions* (pp. 241–278). New York: AMS Press.

Peirce, K. (2001). What if the Energizer Bunny were female? Importance in gender perceptions of advertising spokes-character effectiveness. *Sex Roles, 45*(11–12), 845–858.

Pelin, S. T. (1999). The question of virginity testing in Turkey. *Bioethics, 13*(3–4), 256–261.

Penke, L., & Asendorpf, J. B. (2008). Evidence for conditional sex differences in emotional but not in sexual jealousy at the automatic level of cognitive processing. *European Journal of Personality, 22,* 3–30.

Penna-Firme, T., Grinder, R. E., & Linhares-Barreto, M. S. (1991). Adolescent female prostitutes on the streets of Brazil: An exploratory investigation of ontological issues. *Journal of Adolescent Research, 6,* 493–504.

Peplau, L. A., & Conrad, E. (1989). Beyond nonsexist research: The perils of feminist methods in psychology. *Psychology of Women Quarterly, 13,* 381–402.

Peplau, L. A., & Fingerhut, A. (2004). The paradox of the lesbian worker. *Journal of Social Issues, 60*(4), 719–736.

Peplau, L. A., Garnets, L. D., & Spalding, L. R. (1998). A critique of Bem's "Exotic becomes erotic" theory of sexual orientation. *Psychological Review, 105*(2), 387–394.

Peralta, R. L. (2008). "Alcohol allows you to not be yourself": Toward a structured understanding of alcohol use and gender difference among gay, lesbian, and heterosexual youth. *Journal of Drug Issues, 38,* 373–400.

Perelman, M. (2007). Clinical application of CNS-acting agents in FSD. *Journal of Sexual Medicine, 4*(Suppl. 4), 280–290.

Perelman, M., & Rowland, D. (2006). Retarded ejaculation. *World Journal of Urology, 24,* 645–652.

Perkins, R., & Bennett, G. (1985). *Being a prostitute: Prostitute women and prostitute men.* Boston: Allen & Unwin.

Perlman, D. (2007). The best of times, the worst of times: The place of close relationships in psychology and our daily lives. *Canadian Psychology, 48,* 7–24.

Perovic, S. V., & Djordjevic, M. L. (2003). Metoidioplasty: A variant of phalloplasty in female transsexuals. *BJU International, 92,* 981–985.

Perovic, S. V., Stanojevic, D., & Djordjevic, M. (2005). Vaginoplasty in male to female transsexuals using penile skin and urethral flap. *International Journal of Transgenderism, 8,* 43–64.

Perper, T. (1985). *Sex signals: The biology of love.* Philadelphia, PA: ISI Press.

Perrigouard, C., Dreval, A., Cribier, B., & Lipsker, D. (2008). Vulvar vestibulitis syndrome: A clinicopathological study of 14 cases. *Annals of Dermatologie et de Venereologie, 135,* 367–372.

Perrin, E. C. (2002). Technical report: Coparent or second-parent adoption by same-sex parents. *Pediatrics, 109*(2), 341–345.

Perrone, K. M., Webb, L., & Blalock, R. (2005). The effects of role congruence and role conflict on work, marital, and life satisfaction. *Journal of Career Development, 31*(4), 225–238.

Perrow, C., & Guillén, M. F. (1990). *The AIDS disaster.* New Haven, CT: Yale University Press.

Perry, B. (2000). Can some people read minds? *Science World, 57*(1), 16.

Person, E. S., Terestman, N., Myers, W. A., Goldberg, E., et al. (1992). Associations between sexual experiences and fantasies in a nonpatient population. *Journal of American Academy of Psychological Analysis, 20,* 75–90.

Peter, J., & Valkenburg, P. (2007). Adolescents' exposure to a sexualized media environment and their notions of women as sex objects. *Sex Roles, 56,* 381–395.

Peterson, H. B. (2008). Sterilization. *Obstetrics and Gynecology, 111,* 189–203.

Peyton, C. L., Hunt, W. C., Hundley, R. S., Zhao, M., Wheller, C. M., Gravitt, P. E., & Apple, R. J. (2001). Determinants of genital human papillomavirus detection in a U.S. population. *Journal of Infectious Diseases, 183*(11), 1554–1565.

Pfäfflin, F. (2008). Good enough to eat. *Archives of Sexual Behavior, 37,* 286–294.

Pfaus, J., Giuliano, F., & Gelez, H. (2007). Bremelanotide: An overview of preclinical CHS effects of female sexual function. *Journal of Sexual Medicine, 4*(Suppl. 4), 269–279.

Phares, V., Steinberg, A. R., & Thompson, J. K. (2004). Gender differences in peer and parental influences: Body image disturbance, self-worth, and psychological functioning in preadolescent children. *Journal of Youth & Adolescence, 33*(5), 421–430.

Pheterson, G. (1989). *A vindication of the rights of whores.* Seattle: Seal Press.

Philadelphia, D. (2000). Let's remake a deal. *Time, 155*(16), p. 56.

Phillips, J. (2006, September 20). Gay age of consent unfair in Hong Kong. *Pink News.* Retrieved October 3, 2008, from http://www.pinknews.co.uk/news/articles/2005-2523.html.

Phillips, J., & Sweeney, M. (2005). Premarital cohabitation and marital disruption among white, black, and Mexican American women. *Journal of Marriage & Family, 67*(2), 296–314.

Phillips-Green, M. J. (2002). Sibling incest. *The Family Journal, 10*(2), 195–202.

Phipps, M. G., Matteson, K. A., Fernandez, G., Chiaverini, L., & Weitzen, S. (2008, March 19). Characteristics of women who seek emergency contraception and family planning services. *American Journal of Obstetrics and Gynecology, 199*(2), 111 (e1–5).

Phua, V. C., & Kaufman, G. (1999). Using the census to profile same-sex cohabitation: A research note. *Population Research and Policy Review, 18,* 373–386.

Piaget, J. (1951). *Play, dreams, and imitation in children.* New York: Norton.

Pialoux, G., Vimont, S., Moulignier, A., Buteux, M., Abraham, B., & Bonnard, P. (2008). Effect of HIV infection on the course of syphilis. *AIDS Review, 10,* 85–92.

Piccinino, L. J., & Mosher, W. D. (1998). Trends in contraceptive method use in the United States: 1982–1994. *Family Planning Perspectives, 30,* 4–10.

Pierangeli, A., Scagnolari, C., Degener, A., Bucci, M., Ciardi, A., Riva, E., et al. (2008). Type-specific human papillomavirus-DNA load in anal infection in HIV-positive men. *AIDS, 22,* 1929–1935.

Pike, J. J., & Jennings, N. A. (2005). The effects of commercials on children's perceptions of gender appropriate toy use. *Sex Roles, 52,* 83–91.

Pillard, R. C. (1991). Masculinity and femininity in homosexuality: "Inversion" revisited. In J. C. Gonsiorek & J. D. Weinrich (Eds.), *Homosexuality: Research implications for public policy* (pp. 32–43). Newbury Park, CA: Sage.

Pillard, R. C. (1998). Biologic theories of homosexuality. *Journal of Gay and Lesbian Psychotherapy, 2*(4), 75–76.

Pillard, R. C., & Bailey, J. M. (1998). Human sexual orientation has a heritable component. *Human Biology, 70*(2), 347–366.

Ping, W. (2002). *Aching for beauty: Footbinding in China.* New York: Random House.

Pino, N. W., & Meier, R. F. (1999). Gender differences in rape reporting. *Sex Roles, 40*(11–12), 979–990.

Pinquart, M., Stotzka, C., & Silberreisen, R., (2008). Personality and ambivalence in decisions about becoming parents. *Social Behavior and Personality, 36,* 87–96.

Piot, P. (2000). Global AIDS epidemic: Time to turn the tide. *Science, 288*(5474), 2176–2188.

Pipher, M. (1994). *Reviving Ophelia: Saving the selves of adolescent girls.* New York: Ballantine Books.

Pisetsky, E. M., Chao, Y., Dierker, L. C., May, A. M., & Striegel-Moore, R. (2008). Disordered eating and substance use in high-school students: Results from the Youth Risk Behavior Surveillance System. *International Journal of Eating Disorders, 41,* 464.

Pitts, S. A., & Emans, S. J. (2008). Controversies in contraception. *Current Opinions in Pediatrics, 20,* 383–389.

Pivarnik, J. M. (1998). Potential effects of maternal physical activity on birth weight:

Brief review. *Med Science Sports Exercise, 30*(3), 400–406.

Planned Parenthood Federation of America. (2005). Abstinence-only "sex" education. Retrieved May 30, 2005, from http://www.plannedparenthood.org/pp2/portal/medicalinfo/teensexualhealth/fact-abstinence-education.xml.

Planned Parenthood Federation of America. (2008). What to do if you forget to take the pill. Retrieved October 1, 2008, from http://www.plannedparenthood.org/health-topics/birth-control/if-forget-take-pill-19269.htm.

Plante, A. F., & Kamm, M. A. (2008). Life events in patients with vulvodynia. *British Journal of Obstetrics and Gynecology, 115,* 509–514.

Plaud, J. J., Gaither, G. A., Hegstand, H. J., Rowan, L., Devitt, M. K. (1999). Volunteer bias in human psychophysiological sexual arousal research: To whom do our research results apply? *The Journal of Sex Research, 36,* 171–179.

Plaut, A., & Kohn-Speyer, A. C. (1947). The carcinogenic action of smegma. *Science, 105,* 392.

Pleak, R. R., & Meyer-Bahlburg, H. F. (1990). Sexual behavior and AIDS knowledge of young male prostitutes in Manhattan. *Journal of Sex Research, 27,* 557–587.

Plummer, K. (1989). Lesbian and gay youth in England. *Journal of Homosexuality, 17,* 195–223.

Plummer, K. (1991). Understanding childhood sexualities. *Journal of Homosexuality, 20,* 231–249.

Pogatchnik, S. (1995, November 26). Ireland legalized divorce. *Hartford Courant,* p. A1.

Polaris Project. (2005). Testimony of Rosa. Retrieved December 13, 2005, from http://www.humantrafficking.com/humantrafficking/features_ht3/Testimonies/testimonies_mainframe.htm.

Pollock, N. L., & Hashmall, J. M. (1991). The excuses of child molesters. *Behavioral Sciences and the Law, 9,* 53–59.

Polman, R., Kaiseler, M., & Borkoles, E. (2007). Effect of a single bout of exercise on the mood of pregnant women. *Journal of Sports Medicine and Physical Fitness, 47,* 102–111.

Pomeroy, W. B. (1982). *Dr. Kinsey and the Institute for Sex Research.* New Haven, CT: Yale University Press.

Pomeroy, W. C. (1972). *Dr. Kinsey and the Institute for Sex Research.* New York: Harper & Row.

Popovic, M. (2005). Intimacy and its relevance in human functioning. *Sexual and Relationship Therapy, 20*(1), 31–49.

Porter, R. (1982). Mixed feelings: The Enlightenment and sexuality in eighteenth-century Britain. In P.-G. Goucé (Ed.), *Sexuality in eighteenth-century Britain* (pp. 1–27). Manchester, U.K.: Manchester University Press.

Posel, D. (2005). The scandal of manhood: "Baby rape" and the politicization of sexual violence in post-apartheid South Africa. *Culture, Health, & Sexuality, 7*(3), 239–252.

Posner, R. A. (1993). Obsession. *The New Republic, 209,* 31–36.

Posner, R. B. (2006). Early menarche: A review of research on trends in timing, racial differences, etiology and psychosocial consequences. *Sex Roles, 54,* 315.

Pothen, S. (1989). Divorce in Hindu society. *Journal of Comparative Family Studies, 20*(3), 377–392.

Potter, B., Gerofi, J., Pope, M., & Farley, T. (2003). Structural integrity of the polyurethane female condom after multiple cycles of disinfection, washing, drying and relubrication. *Contraception, 67*(1), 65–72.

Potterat, J. J., Rothenberg, R. B., Muth, S. Q., Darrow, W. W., & Phillips-Plummer, L. (1998). Pathways to prostitution: The chronology of sexual and drug abuse milestones. *Journal of Sex Research, 35*(4), 333–340.

Potterat, J. J., Woodhouse, D. E., Muth, J. B., & Muth, S. Q. (1990). Estimating the prevalence and career longevity of prostitute women. *Journal of Sex Research, 27,* 233–243.

Poulson, R. L., Eppler, M. A., Satterwhite, T. N., Wuensch, K. L., & Bass, L. A. (1998). Alcohol consumption, strength of religious beliefs, and risky sexual behavior in college students. *Journal of American College Health, 46*(5), 227–233.

Pozniak, A. (2002). Pink versus blue: The things people do to choose the sex of their baby. Retrieved June 3, 2002, from http://abcnews.go.com/sections/living/DailyNews/choosingbabysex020603.html.

Prause, N., & Graham, C. (2007). Asexuality: Classification and characterization. *Archives of Sexual Behavior, 36,* 341–356.

Predrag, S. (2005). LGBT news and views from around the world. *Lesbian News, 30*(9), 19–21.

Prentice, A. (2001). Endometriosis. *British Medical Journal, 323*(7304), 93–96.

Prentky, R. A., Knight, R. A. (1986). Impulsivity: In The Lifestyle And Criminal Behavior Of Sexual Offenders. *Criminal Justice and Behavior, 13*(2), 141.

Price, M., Kafka, M., Commons, M., Gutheil, T., & Simpson, W. (2002). Telephone scatologia: Comorbidity with other paraphilias and paraphilia-related disorders. *International Journal of Law & Psychiatry, 25*(1), 37–49.

Prinstein, M., Meade, C., & Cohen, G. (2003). Adolescent oral sex, peer popularity, and perceptions of best friends' sexual behavior. *Journal of Pediatric Psychology, 28,* 243–249.

Proto-Campise, L., Belknap, J., & Wooldredge, J. (1998). High school students' adherence to rape myths. *Violence Against Women, 4,* 308–328.

Pryzgoda, J., & Chrisler, J. C. (2000). Definitions of gender and sex: The subtleties of meaning. *Sex Roles, 43*(7–8), 499–528.

Puberty inducer? (2004). *New Scientist, 183,* 5. Retrieved March 20, 2008, from http://space.newscientist.com/article/mg18324540.900-puberty-inducer.html.

Pubic hair transplants are big business in South Korea. (2005). Retrieved March 22, 2005, from http://www.ananova.com/news/story/sm_815503.html?menu=news.quirkies.

Puente, S., & Cohen, D. (2003). Jealousy and the meaning (or nonmeaning) of violence. *Personality and Social Psychology Bulletin, 29*(4), 449–460.

Puentes, J., Knox, D., & Zusman, M. E. (2008). Participants in "friends with benefits" relationships. *College Student Journal, 42,* 176–180.

Pyne, J., Asch, S., Lincourt, K., Kilbourne, A., Bowman, C., Atkinson, H., & Gifford, A. (2008). Quality indicators for depression care in HIV patients. *AIDS Care, 20,* 1075–1083.

Quadagno, D., Sly, D. F., & Harrison, D. F. (1998). Ethnic differences in sexual decisions and sexual behavior. *Archives of Sexual Behavior, 27*(1), 57–75.

Quam, J. K., & Whitford, G. S. (1992). Adaptation and age-related expectations of older gay and lesbian adults. *The Gerontologist, 32*(3), 367–374.

Rabinowitz Greenberg, S. R., Firestone, P., Bradford, J., & Greenberg, D. M. (2002). Prediction of recidivism in exhibitionists: Psychological, phallometric, and offense factors. *Sexual Abuse: Journal of Research & Treatment, 14*(4), 329–347.

Rabkin, J. (2008). HIV and depression: 2008 review and update. *Current HIV/AIDS Reports, 5,* 163–171.

Radestad, I., Olsson, A., Nissen, E., & Rubertsson, C. (2008). Tears in the vagina, perineum, spincter ani, and rectum and first sexual intercourse after childbirth: A nationwide follow up. *Birth, 35,* 98–106.

Radford, B. (2006). Predator panic. *The Skeptical Inquirer, 20,* 20–23.

Rado, S. (1949, rev. 1955). An adaptional view of sexual behavior. *Psychoanalysis of behavior: Collected papers.* New York: Grune & Stratton.

Raffaelli, M., & Green, S. (2003). Parent-adolescent communication about sex; retrospective reports by Latino college students. *Journal of Marriage and the Family, 65,* 474–481.

Rahman, A., Katzive, L., & Henshaw, S. K. (1998). A global review of laws on induced abortion, 1985–1997. *International Family Planning Perspectives, 24*(2), 56–64.

Rahman, Q. (2005). Fluctuating asymmetry, second to fourth finger length ratios and human sexual orientation. *Psychoneuroendocrinology, 30*(4), 382–391.

Rahman, Q., & Koerting, J. (2008). Sexual orientation-related differnces in allocentric spatial memory tasks. *Hippocampus, 18,* 55–63.

Rahman, Q., Kumari, V., & Wilson, G. (2003). Sexual orientation-related differences in prepulse inhibition of the human startle response. *Behavioral Neuroscience, 117,* 1096–1102.

Rahman, Q., & Symeonides, D. (2008). Neurodevelopmental correlates of paraphilic sexual interests in men. *Archives of Sexual Behavior, 37,* 166–171.

Ramchandani, M., Manges, A. R., DebRoy, C., Smith, S. P., Johnson, J. R., & Riley, L. W. (2005). Possible animal origin of human-associated, multidrug-resistant, uropathogenic *Escherichia coli. Clinical Infectious Diseases, 40,* 258–259.

Ramirez, A., & Zhang, S. (2007). When online meets offline: The effect of modality switching on relational communication. *Communication Monographs, 74,* 287.

Rammouz, I., Tahiri, D., Aalouane, R., Kjiri, S., Belhous, A., Ktiouet, J., & Sekkat, F. (2008). Infanticide in the postpartum period: About a clinical case. *Encephale, 34,* 284–288.

Rancour-Laferriere, D. (1985). *Signs of the flesh.* New York: Mouton de Gruyter.

Rand, M., & Catalano, S. (2007, December). *National Crime Victimization Survey: Criminal victimization, 2006.* Bureau of Justice Statistics. Retrieved October 4, 2008, from http://www.ojp.usdoj.gov/bjs/pub/pdf/cv06.pdf.

Rape, Abuse, & Incest National Network. (2008). Frequency of sexual assault. Retrieved November 13, 2008, from http://www.rainn.org/get-information/statistics/frequency-of-sexual-assault.

Rapkin, A. J., & Winer, S. A. (2008). The pharmacologic management of premenstrual dysphoric disorder. *Expert Opinions in Pharmacotherapy, 9,* 429–445.

Raskin, N. J., & Rogers, C. R. (1989). Person-centered therapy. In R. J. Corsini & D. Wedding (Eds.), *Current psychotherapies* (4th ed., pp. 155–196), Pacific Grove, CA: F. E. Peacock.

Rasmussen, P. R. (2005). The sadistic and masochistic prototypes. In P. R. Rasmussen (Ed.), *Personality-guided cognitive-behavioral therapy* (pp. 291–310). Washington, DC: American Psychological Association.

Raspberry, C. N. (2007). A qualitative and quantitative exploration of secondary sexual abstinence among a sample of Texas A&M University undergraduates. Texas A&M University. *Dissertation Abstracts International, Section A: Humanities and Social Sciences, 68*(6-A), 2346.

Rauer, A. J., & Volling, B. L. (2007). Differential parenting and sibling jealousy: Developmental correlates of young adults' romantic relationships. *Personal Relationships, 14,* 495–511.

Ravert, A. A., & Martin, J. (1997). Family stress, perception of pregnancy, and age of first menarche among pregnant adolescents. *Adolescence, 32*(126), 261–269.

Ray, N. (2007). Lesbian, gay, bisexual, and transgendered youth: An epidemic of homelessness. National Gay and Lesbian Task Force Policy Institute. Retrieved October 3, 2008, from http://www.thetaskforce.org/downloads/HomelessYouth.pdf.

Raymond, E., Stewart, F., Weaver, M., Monteith, C., & Van Der Pol, B. (2006). Impact of increased access to emergency contraceptive pills: A randomized controlled trial. *Obstetrics and Gynecology, 108,* 1098–1106.

Raymond, J. G., Hughes, D. M. (2001). Sex trafficking of women in the United States. Retrieved November 16, 2008, from http://www.uri.edu/artsci/wms/hughes/sex_traff_us.pdf.

Reeves, T., & Bennett, C. (2003). The Asian and Pacific Islander population in the United States. Current population report, U. S. Census Bureau. Retrieved August 29, 2003, from http://www.census.gov/prod/2003pubs/p20-540.pdf.

Regan, K. (2005). Mobile industry prepares for cell phone porn. Retrieved November 7, 2005, from http://www.technewsworld.com/story/46206.html.

Regan, P. C. (2006). Love. In R. D. McAnulty & M. M. Burnette (Eds.), *Sex and Sexuality: Sexual Functions and Dysfunctions* (pp. 87–113). Westport, CT: Praeger.

Regnerus, M. D., & Luchies, L. B. (2006). The parent–child relationship and opportunities for adolescents' first sex. *Journal of Family Issues, 27,* 159–183.

Rehman, U. S., & Holtzworth-Munroe, A. (2007). A cross-cultural examination of the relation of marital communication behavior to marital satisfaction. *Journal of Family Psychology, 21,* 759–763.

Reid, R., Bonomi, A., Rivara, F., Anderson, M., Fishman, P., Carrell, D., & Thompson, R. (2008). Intimate partner violence among men: Prevalence, chronicity, and health effects. *American Journal of Preventive Medicine, 34,* 478–485.

Reilly, D. R., Delva, N. J., & Hudson, R. W. (2000). Protocols for the use of cyproterone, medroxyprogesterone, & leuprolide in the treatment of paraphilia. *Canadian Journal of Psychiatry, 45*(6), 559–564.

Reingold, A. L. (1991). Toxic shock syndrome: An update. *American Journal of Obstetrics and Gynecology, 165*(4, Pt. 2), 1236.

Reips, U. D. (2000). The Web experiment method: Advantages, disadvantages, and solutions. In M. H. Birnbaum (Ed.), *Psychological experiments on the Internet* (pp. 89–114). San Diego, CA: Academic Press.

Reips, U. D., & Bachtiger, M. T. (2000). Are all flies drosophilae? Participant selection bias in psychological research. Unpublished manuscript.

Reisenzein, R. (1994). Pleasure-arousal theory and the intensity of emotions. *Journal of Personality and Social Psychology 67*(3), 525–539.

Reiss, I. L. (1982). Trouble in paradise: The current status of sexual science. *Journal of Sex Research, 18,* 97–113.

Reiss, I. L. (1986). *Journey into sexuality: An exploratory voyage.* Englewood Cliffs, NJ: Prentice Hall.

Reiter, E. O. (1986). The neuroendocrine regulation of pubertal onset. In J. B. Lancaster & B. A. Hamburg (Eds.), *School-age pregnancy and parenthood: Biosocial dimensions* (pp. 53–76). New York: Aldine De-Gruyter.

Remafedi, G. (1987). Male homosexuality: The adolescent perspective. *Pediatrics, 79,* 326–330.

Remez, L. (2000, November/December). Oral sex among adolescents: Is it sex or is it abstinence? *Family Planning Perspectives, 32*(6), 298–304.

Rempel, J. K., & Baumgartner, B. (2003). The relationship between attitudes towards menstruation and sexual attitudes, desires, and behavior in women. *Archives of Sexual Behavior, 32*(2), 155–163.

Remsberg, K. E., Demerath, E. W., Schubert, C. M., Chumlea, C., Sun, S. S., & Siervogel, R. M. (2005). Early menarche and the development of cardiovascular disease risk factors in adolescent girls: The Fels longitudinal study. *Journal of Clinical Endocrinology & Metabolism,* published online ahead of print. Retrieved March 22, 2005, from http://jcem.endojournals.org/cgi/content/abstract/jc.2004-1991v1

Renaud, C. A., & Byers, E. S. (1999). Exploring the frequency, diversity, and content of university students' positive and negative sexual cognitions. *Canadian Journal of Human Sexuality, 8*(1), 17–30.

Rennison, C. M. (2001). Criminal victimization, 2000. U.S. Department of Justice, National Crime Victimization Survey. Retrieved November 13, 2008, from http://www.ojp.usdoj.gov/bjs/pub/pdf/cv00.pdf.

Rensberger, B. (1994, July 25). Contraception the natural way: Herbs have played a role from ancient Greece to modern-day Appalachie. *Washington Post,* p. A3.

Renshaw, D. C. (2005). Premature ejaculation-revisted—2005. *Family Journal: Counseling & Therapy for Couples and Families, 13*(2), 150–152.

Resnick, H., Acierno, R., Holmes, M., Kilpatrick, D., & Jager, N. (1999). Prevention of post-rape psychopathology: Preliminary findings of a controlled acute rape treatment study. *Journal of Anxiety Disorders, 13,* 359–370.

Resnick, H., Acierno, R., Kilpatrick, D. G., & Holmes, M. (2005). Description of an early intervention to prevent substance abuse and psychopathology in recent rape victims. *Behavior Modification, 29*(1), 156–188.

Resnick, M. D., Bearman, P. S., Blum, R. W., Bauman, K. E., Harris, K. M., Jones, J., et al. (1997). Protecting adolescents from harm: Findings from the National Longitudinal Study on Adolescent Health. *Journal of the American Medical Association, 278*(10), 823–832.

Revzina, N., & DiClemente, R. (2005). Prevalence and incidence of human papillomavirus infection in women in the USA: A systematic review. *International Journal of STDs and AIDS, 16,* 528–537.

Reynolds, A. L., & Caron, S. L. (2005). How intimate relationships are impacted when heterosexual men cross-dress. *Journal of Psychology & Human Sexuality, 12*(3), 63–77.

Reynolds, H. (1986). *The economics of prostitution.* Springfield, IL: Charles C. Thomas.

Reynolds, T., Vranken, G., Nueten, J. V., & Aldis, J. (2008). Down's syndrome screening: Population statistic dependency of screening performance. *Clinical Chemistry and Laboratory Medicine, 46*(5), 639–647.

Rhoads, J. M., & Boekelheide, P. D. (1985). Female genital exhibitionism. *The Psychiatric Forum,* Winter, 1–6.

Riccio, R. (1992). Street crime strategies: The changing schemata of streetwalkers. *Environment and Behavior, 24,* 555–570.

Rich, A. (1983). Compulsory heterosexuality and lesbian existence. In A. Snitow, C. Stinsell, & S. Thompson (Eds.), *Powers of desire: The politics of sexuality* (pp. 177–205). New York: Monthly Review Press.

Richardson, B. A. (2002). Nonoxynol-9 as a vaginal microbicide for prevention of sexually transmitted infections. *Journal of American Medication Association, 287,* 1171–1172.

Richardson, D., & Campbell, J. L. (1982). The effect of alcohol on attributions of blame for rape. *Personality and Social Psychology Bulletin, 8,* 468–476.

Richardson, D., Nalabanda, A., & Goldmeier, D. (2006). Retarded ejaculation: A review. *International Journal of STDs and AIDS, 17,* 143–150.

Richters, J., Hendry, O., & Kippax, S. (2003). When safe sex isn't safe. *Culture, Health & Sexuality, 5*(1), 37–52.

Rickert, V. I., Sanghvi, R., & Weimann, C. M. (2002). Is lack of sexual assertiveness among adolescent and young adult women a cause for concern? *Perspectives on Sexual and Reproductive Health, 34*(4), 178–183.

Rideout, V., Roberts, D. F., & Foehr, U. G. (2005). Generation M: Media in the lives of 8–18 year-olds. Retrieved November 7, 2005, from http://www.kff.org/entmedia/upload/Executive-Summary-Generation-M-Media-in-the-Lives-of-8-18-Year-olds.pdf.

Ridge, R. D., & Reber, J. S. (2002). "I think she's attracted to me": The effect of men's beliefs on women's behavior in a job interview scenario. *Basic and Applied Social Psychology, 24*(1), 1–14.

Ridley, M. (2003). What makes you who you are: Which is stronger, nature or nurture? *Time Magazine, 161*(22). Retrieved July 4, 2003, from http://www.time.com/time/archive/preview/from_covers/0,10987,1101030602-454451,00.html.

Rieger, G., Chivers, M. L., & Bailey, J. M. (2005). Sexual arousal patterns of gay men. *Psychological Science, 16*(8), 579–584.

Riggs, J. M. (2005). Impressions of mothers and fathers on the periphery of child care. *Psychology of Women Quarterly, 29*(1), 58.

Rio, L. M. (1991). Psychological and sociological research and the decriminalization or legalization of prostitution. *Archives of Sexual Behavior, 20,* 205–218.

Rischer, C.E., Easton, T. (1992). *Focus on Human Biology.* HarperCollins, New York, NY.

Risman, B., & Schwartz, P. (1988). Sociological research on male and female homosexuality. *Annual Review of Sociology, 14,* 125–147.

Rittenhouse, C. A. (1991). The emergence of premenstrual syndrome as a social problem. *Social Problems, 38*(3), 412–425.

Rivers, I., & Noret, N. (2008). Well-being among same-sex- and opposite-sex-attracted youth at school. *School Psychology Review, 37,* 174–187.

Rivers, J., Mason, J., Silvestre, E., Gillespie, S., Mahy, M., Monasch, R. (2008). Impact of orphanhood on underweight prevalence in sub-Saharan Africa. *Food and Nutrition Bulletin, 29*(1), 32–42.

Rizwan, S., Manning, J., & Brabin, B. J. (2007). Maternal smoking during pregnancy and possible effects of in utero testosterone: Evidence from the 2D:4D finger length ratio. *Early Human Development, 83,* 87–90.

Roach, M. K. (2002). *The Salem witch trials.* New York: Cooper Square Press.

Roach, M. K. (2004). *The Salem witch trials: A day-by-day chronicle of a community under siege.* Lanham, MD: Taylor Trade.

Roan, A. (2004, December). Herbs and your sexual health. *Glamour,* p. 108.

Roan, N., & Greene, W. (2007). A seminal finding for understanding HIV transmission. *Cell, 131,* 1044–1046.

Roberts, D. F., Foehr, U. G., & Rideout, V. (2005). Generation M: Media in the lives of 8–18 year-olds. Retrieved November 3, 2005, from http://www.kff.org/entmedia/

upload/Generation-M-Media-in-the-Lives-of-8-18-Year-olds-Report.pdf.

Roberts, J. E., & Oktay, K. (2005). Fertility preservation: A comprehensive approach to the young woman with cancer. *Journal of the National Cancer Institute Monograph, 34,* 57–59.

Robinson, A. (2002). "There's a stranger in this house": African American lesbians and domestic violence. *Women and Therapy, 25,* 125.

Robinson, E. D., & Evans, B. G. I. (1999). Oral sex and HIV transmission. *AIDS, 16*(6), 737–738.

Robinson, J. D. (2001). The thematic content categories of lesbian and bisexual women's sexual fantasies, psychological adjustment, daydreaming variables and relationships functioning. *Dissertation Abstracts,* California School of Professional Psychology–Los Angeles, #0-493-12701-1.

Robinson, J. D., & Parks, C. W. (2003). Lesbian and bisexual women's sexual fantasies, psychological adjustment, and close relationship functioning. *Journal of Psychology & Human Sexuality* 15(4), 85–203.

Robker, R. L. (2008). Evidence that obesity alters the quality of oocytes and embryos. *Pathophysiology,* 15(2):115–121.

Roby, J.L., Shaw, S.A. (2006). The African orphan crisis and international adoption. *Social Work,* 51(3), 199–210.

Rodriguez, I. (2004). Pheromone receptors in mammals. *Hormones & Behavior, 46*(3), 219–230.

Rogers, S. C. (1978). Woman's place: A critical review of anthropological theory. *Comparative Studies in Society and History, 20,* 123–162.

Roisman, G., Clausell, E., Holland, A., Fortuna, K., & Elieff, C. (2008). Adult romantic relationships as contexts of human development: A multimethod comparison of same-sex couples with opposite-sex dating, engaged, and married dyads. *Developmental Psychology, 44,* 91–101.

Rome, E. (1998). Anatomy and physiology of sexuality and reproduction. In The Boston Women's Health Collective (Eds.), *The New Our Bodies, Ourselves* (pp. 241–258). Carmichael, CA: Touchstone Books.

Romenesko, K., & Miller, E. M. (1989). The second step in double jeopardy: Appropriating the labor of female street hustlers. (Special issue: Women and crime.) *Crime and Delinquency, 35,* 109–135.

Romero-Daza, N., Weeks, M., & Singer, M. (2003). "Nobody gives a damn if I live or die": Violence, drugs, and street-level prostitution in inner-city Hartford, Connecticut. *Medical Anthropology, 22*(3), 233–259.

Röndahl, G., Innala, S., & Carlsson, M. (2004). Nurses' attitudes towards lesbians and gay men. *Journal of Advanced Nursing, 47,* 386–392.

Ropelato, J. (2008). Internet pornography statistics. *Top Ten Reviews.* Retrieved October 7, 2008, from http://internet-filter-review.toptenreviews.com/internet-pornography-statistics.html.

Rosario, M., Schrimshaw, E., & Hunter, J. (2004). Predictors of substance use over time among gay, lesbian, and bisexual youths. An examination of three hypotheses. *Addictive Behaviors, 29*(8), 1623–1631.

Rosen, R. C., & Leiblum, S. R. (1987). Current approaches to the evaluation of sexual desire disorders. *Journal of Sex Research, 23,* 141–162.

Rosenbaum, D. E. (2005, October 30). Commissions are fine, but rarely what changes the light bulb. Retrieved November 6, 2005, from http://www.nytimes.com/2005/10/30/weekinreview/30rosenbaum.html?fta=y.

Rosenberg, D. (2007, May 21). (Rethinking) gender. *Time Magazine,* pp. 50–57.

Rosenberg, M. (2004). Top ten spring break locations. Geography About. Retrieved August 10, 2008, from http://geography.about.com/cs/tourismandtravel/qt/spinrgbreak04.htm.

Rosenblatt, P. C., Karis, T. A., & Powell, R. D. (1995). *Multiracial couples.* Thousand Oaks, CA: Sage.

Rosenthal, R., & Rosnow, R. L. (1975). *The volunteer subject.* New York: Wiley.

Rosman, J. P., & Resnick, P. J. (1989). Sexual attraction to corpses: A psychiatric review of necrophilia. *Bulletin of the American Academy of Psychiatry and the Law, 17,* 153–163.

Ross, J. (2001). Pelvic inflammatory disease. *British Medical Journal, 322*(7287), 658–659.

Ross, L. E. (2005). Perinatal mental health in lesbian mothers: A review of potential risk and protective factors. *Women Health, 41*(3), 113–128.

Ross, L. E., Steele, L., & Epstein, R. (2006a). Lesbian and bisexual women's recommendations for improving the provision of assisted reproductive technology services. *Fertility and Sterility, 86,* 735–738.

Ross, L. E., Steele, L. S., & Epstein, R. (2006b). Service use and gaps in services for lesbian and bisexual women during donor insemination, pregnancy, and the postpartum period. *Journal of Obstetrics and Gynecology Canada, 28,* 505–511.

Ross, L. E., Steele, L., Goldfinger, C., & Strike, C. (2007). Perinatal depressive symptomatology among lesbian and bisexual women. *Archives of Women's Mental Health, 10,* 1434–1816.

Ross, L. E., Steele, L., & Sapiro, B. (2005). Perceptions of predisposing and protective factors for perinatal depression in same-sex parents. *Journal of Midwifery Women's Health, 50,* 65–70.

Rossato M., Pagano C., Vettor R. (2008). The cannabinoid system and male reproductive functions. *Journal of Neuroendocrinology, 20*(Suppl 1), 90–93.

Rosser, B. R. (1999). Homophobia: Description, development and dynamic of gay bashing. *Journal of Sex Research, 36*(2), 211.

Rossi, A. S. (1978). The biosocial side of parenthood. *Human Nature, 1,* 72–79.

Rossi, W. A. (1993). *The sex life of the foot and shoe.* Melbourne, FL: Krieger.

Rothman, S. M. (1978). *Woman's proper place.* New York: Basic Books.

Roughgarden, J. (2004). A review of evolution, gender, and rape. *Ethology, 110*(1), 76.

Rowland, D. L., Keeney, C., Slob, A. K. (2004). Sexual response in men with inhibited or retarded ejaculation. *International Journal of Impotence Research, 16*(3), 270–274.

Rozee, P. D. (2005). Rape resistance: Successes and challenges. In A. Barnes (Ed.), *Handbook of women, psychology, and the law* (pp. 265–279). New York: Wiley.

Ruan, F., & Lau, M. P. (2004). China. In R. T. Francoeur & R. J. Noonan (Eds.), *The Continuum international encyclopedia of sexuality* (pp. 182–209). New York/London: Continuum International.

Ruan, F. F., & Tsai, Y. M. (1988). Male homosexuality in contemporary mainland China. *Archives of Sexual Behavior, 17,* 189–199.

Rubin, L. (1990). *Erotic wars.* New York: Farrar, Straus, & Giroux.

Rubin, R. (2008, January 7). Answers prove elusive as C-section rate rises. USAToday, Retrieved October 14, 2008, from http://www.usatoday.com/news/health/2008-01-07-csections_N.htm.

Rubin, R. H. (2001). Alternative lifestyles revisited, or whatever happened to swingers, group marriages, and communes. *Journal of Family Issues, 22*(6), 711–728.

Rubin, Z. (1970). Measurement of romantic love. *Journal of Personality & Social Psychology, 16*(2), 265–273.

Rubin, Z. (1973). *Liking and loving: An invitation to social psychology.* Oxford, England: Holt, Rinehart & Winston.

Rudd, J. M., & Herzberger, S. D. (1999). Brother–sister incest, father–daughter incest: A comparison of characteristics and consequences. *Child Abuse and Neglect, 23*(9), 915–928.

Rudolph, K., Caldwell, M. & Conley, C. (2005). Need for approval and children's well-being. *Child Development, 76*(2), 309–323.

Rudy, K. (2000). Queer theory and feminism. *Women's Studies, 29*(2), 195–217.

Rugh, A. B. (1984). *Family in contemporary Egypt.* Syracuse, NY: Syracuse University Press.

Rule, N.O., Ambady, N. (2008). Brief exposures: Male sexual orientations is accurately perceived at 50 ms. *Journal of Experimental Social Psychology, 44*(4), 1100–1105.

Rupp, J. (2007). The photography of Joseph Rupp: Bound Feet. Retrieved December 19, 2008, from http://www.josephrupp.com/.

Russell, D. E. H. (1984). *Sexual exploitation: Rape, child sexual abuse, and workplace harassment.* Beverly Hills, CA: Sage.

Russell, D. E. H., & Howell, N. (1983). The prevalence of rape in the United States revisited. *Signs: Journal of Women in Culture and Society,* 688–695.

Russell, D. W., & Russell, C. A., & Stern, B. (2006). The soap that can't be dropped: A qualitative inquiry of long-term soap opera viewers. Paper presented at the International Communication Association Annual Meeting, Dresden. Retrieved October 25, 2008, from http://www.allacademic.com/meta/p91524_index.html.

Russell, S. T., Driscoll, A. K., & Truong, N. (2002). Adolescent same-sex romantic attractions and relationships: Implications for substance use and abuse. *American Journal of Public Health, 92,* 198–202.

Russell, S. T., & Joyner, K. (2001). Adolescent sexual orientation and suicide risk: Evidence from a natural study. *American Journal of Public Health, 91*(8), 1276–1282.

Rust, P. C. R. (2000). *Bisexuality in the U.S.* New York: Columbia University Press.

Ryan, C., & Futterman, D. (2001). Social and developmental challenges for lesbian, gay, bisexual youth. *SIECUS Report, 29*(4), 5–18.

Ryan, C. J., & Small, E. J. (2005). Progress in detection and treatment of prostate cancer. *Current Opinion in Oncology, 17*(3), 257–260.

Ryan, S., Franzetta, K., Manlove, J. S., & Schelar, E. (2008). Older sexual partners during adolescence: Links to reproductive health outcomes in young adulthood. *Perspectives on Sexual and Reproductive Health, 40,* 17–26.

Saal, F. E., Johnson, C. B., & Weber, N. (1989). Friendly or sexy? It may depend on who you ask. *Psychology of Women Quarterly, 13,* 263–276.

Sabelli, H., Fink, P., Fawcett, J., & Tom, C. (1996). Sustained antidepressant effect of PEA replacement. *Journal of Neuropsychiatry and Clinical Neuroscience, 8*(2), 168–171.

Sable, M., Danis, F., Mauzy, D., & Gallagher, S. (2006). Barriers to reporting sexual assault for women and men: Perspectives of college students. *Journal of American College Health, 55,* 157–162.

Sabo, D. S., & Runfola, R. (1980). *Jock: Sports and male identity.* New York: Prentice Hall.

Sacks, S. L., Aoki, F., Martel, A., Shafran, S. D., & Lassonde, M. (2005). Clinic-initiated, twice-daily oral famciclovir for treatment of recurrent genital herpes: A randomized, double-blind, controlled trial. *Clinical Infectious Diseases, 41*(8), 1097–1104.

Saewyc, E. M., Bearinger, L. H., Heinz, P. A., Blum, R. W., & Resnick, M. (1998). Gender differences in health and risk behaviors among bisexual and homosexual adolescents. *Journal of Adolescent Health, 23*(2), 181–188.

Safarinejad, M. R. (2008). Evaluation of the safety and efficacy of bremelanotide, a melanocortin receptor agonist, in female subjects with arousal disorder: A double-blind placebo-controlled, fixed dose, randomized study. *Journal of Sexual Medicine, 5,* 887–897.

Safarinejad, M. R., Hosseini, S. Y. (2008). Salvage of sildenafil failures with bremelanotide: A randomized, double-blind, placebo controlled study. *Journal of Urology, 179*(3), 1066–1071.

"Safer sex basics." (2005). Retrieved October 12, 2005, from http://sexuality.about.com/cs/safersex/a/safersexbasics.htm.

Sagarin, B. J., Becker, D., Guadagno, R. E., Nicastle, L. D., & Millevoi, A. (2003). Sex differences (and similarities) in jealousy. The moderating influence of infidelity experience and sexual orientation of the infidelity. *Evolution and Human Behavior, 24*(1), 17–23.

Sakorafas, G. H. (2005). The management of women at high risk for the development of breast cancer: Risk estimation and preventative strategies. *Cancer Treatment Reviews, 29*(2),79–89.

Saleh, F. M., & Berlin, F. (2003). Sex hormones, neurotransmitters, and psychopharmacological treatments in men with paraphilic disorders. *Journal of Child Sexual Abuse, 12,* 233–253.

Salter, D., McMillan, D., Richards, M., Talbot, T., Hodges, J., Bentovim, A., et al. (2003). Development of sexually abusive behavior in sexually victimized males. *Lancet, 361*(9356), 471–476.

Salzmann, Z. (2007). *Language, culture, and society* (4th ed.). Boulder, CO: Westview Press.

Sánchez, J. M., Milam, M. R., Tomlinson, T. M., & Beardslee, M. A. (2008). Cardiac troponin I elevation after orogenital sex during pregnancy. *Obstetrics and Gynecology, 111,* 487–489.

Sanchez, S., Qiu, C., Perales, M., Lam, N., Garcia, P., & Williams, M. (2008). Intimate partner violence and preeclampsia among Peruvian women. *European Journal of Obstetrics, Gynecology, and Reproductive Biology, 137,* 50–55.

Sanday, P. R. (1981). The socio-cultural context of rape: A cross-cultural study. *Journal of Social Issues, 37,* 5–27.

Sanday, P. R. (1990). *Fraternity gang rape: Sex, brotherhood, and privilege on campus.* New York: New York University Press.

Sanders, S. A., & Reinisch, J. M. (1999). Would you say you "had sex" if . . . ? *Journal of the American Medical Association, 281*(3), 275–277.

Sandfort, T. G., Orr, M., Hirsch, J., & Santelli, J. (2008). Long-term health correlates of timing of sexual debut: Results from a national U.S. study. *American Journal of Public Health, 98,* 155–161.

Sandnabba, N., Santilla, P., Alison, L., & Nordling, N. (2002). Demographics, sexual behavior, family background and abuse experiences of practitioners of sadomasochistic sex: A review of recent research. *Sexual and Relationship Therapy, 17,* 39–55.

Sandnabba, N. K., & Ahlberg, C. (1999). Parents' attitudes and expectations about children's cross-gender behavior. *Sex Roles, 40*(3–4), 249–263.

Sandowski, C. L. (1989). *Sexual concerns when illness or disability strikes.* Springfield, IL: Charles C. Thomas.

Sangrador, J. L., & Yela, C. (2000). "What is beautiful is loved": Physical attractiveness in love relationships in a representative sample. *Social Behavior & Personality, 28*(3), 207–218.

Santa Ana, R. (2008, June 30). Watermelon may have Viagra-effect. *Texas A&M Agricultural Communication.* Retrieved August 31, 2008, from http://vfic.tamu.edu/Documents/News/2008/0630%20agnews%20watermelon.pdf.

Santelli, J., DiClemente, R., Miller, K., & Kirby, D. (1999). Sexually transmitted diseases, unintended pregnancy and adolescent health promotion. *Adolescent Medicine: Prevention Issues in Adolescent Health Care, 10,* 87–108.

Santen, R. J. (1995). The testis. In P. Felig, J. D. Baxter, & L. A. Frolman, (Eds.), *Endocrinology and metabolism* (3rd ed.). New York: McGraw-Hill.

Santilla, P., Sandnabba, N., & Nordling, N. (2000). Retrospective perceptions of family interaction in childhood as correlates of current sexual adaptation among sadomasochistic males. *Journal of Psychology and Human Sexuality, 12,* 69–87.

Santos, P., Schinemann, J., Gabarcio, J., & da Graca, G. (2005). New evidence that the MHC influences odor perception in humans: A study with 58 Southern Brazilian students. *Hormones and Behavior, 47*(4), 384–388.

Sarkisian, N., & Gerstel, N. (2008). Till marriage do us part: Adult children's relationships with their parents. *Journal of Marriage and Family, 70,* 360–377.

Sarrel, P., & Masters, W. (1982). Sexual molestation of men by women. *Archives of Sexual Behavior, 11,* 117–131.

Sartorius, A., Ruf, M., Kief, C., & Demirakca, T. (2008). Abnormal amygdala activation profile in pedophilia. *European Archives of Psychiatry and Clinical Neuroscience, 258,* 271–279.

Saslow, B., Boetes, C., Burke, W., Harms, S., Leach, M., Lehman, C., et al. (2007). American Cancer Society guidelines for breast screening with MRI as an adjunct to mammography. *CA Cancer Journal for Clinicians, 57,* 75–89.

Sati, N. (1998). Equivocal lifestyles. The Living Channel. Retrieved July 7, 2003, from http://www.glas.org/ahbab/Articles/arabia1.html.

Sato, S. M., Schulz, K. M., Sisk, C. L., & Wood, R. I. (2008). Adolescents and androgens, receptors and rewards. *Hormones and Behavior 53*(5), 647–658.

Savaya, R., & Cohen, O. (2003). Divorce among Moslem Arabs living in Israel: Comparison for reasons before and after the actualization of the marriage. *Journal of Family Issues, 24*(3), 338–351.

Savic, I., Berglund, H., & Lindström, P. (2005). Brain response to putative pheromones in homosexual men. *Proceedings of the National Academy of Sciences, 102,* 7356–7361.

Savic, I., & Lindström, P. (2008, June 16). PET and MRI show differences in cerebral asymmetry and functional connectivity between homo- and heterosexual subjects. *Proceedings of the National Academy of Sciences.* Retrieved October 3, 2008, from http://www.pnas.org/cgi/content/abstract/0801566105v1.

Savin-Williams, R. C. (2001). *"Mom, Dad. I'm gay." How families negotiate coming out.* Washington, DC: American Psychological Association.

Savin-Williams, R. C., & Diamond, L. M. (2000). Sexual identity trajectories among sexual minority youths: Gender comparisons. *Archives of Sexual Behavior, 29,* 607–627.

Savin-Williams, R. C., & Dube, E. M. (1998). Parental reactions to their child's disclosure of a gay/lesbian identity. *Family Relations, 47,* 7–13.

Savitz, L., & Rosen, L. (1988). The sexuality of prostitutes: Sexual enjoyment reported by "streetwalkers." *Journal of Sex Research, 24,* 200–208.

Sawyer, R. G., Thompson, E. E., & Chicorelli, A. M. (2002). Rape myth acceptance among intercollegiate student athletes. *American Journal of Health Studies, 18*(1), 19–25.

Sayal, K., Heron, J., Golding, J., & Emond, A. (2007). Prenatal alcohol exposure and gender differences in childhood mental health problems: A longitudinal population-based study. *Pediatrics, 119,* 426–434.

Sbarra, D., & Emery, R. (2005). The emotional sequelae of nonmarital relationship dissolution: Analysis of change and intraindividual variability over time. *Personal Relationships, 12*(2), 213–232.

Scarce, M. (1997). *The hidden toll of stigma and shame.* New York: De Capo Press.

Schachter, S., & Singer, J. (1962). Cognitive, social, and physiological determinants of emotional state. *Psychological Review, 69*(5), 379–399.

Schachter, S., & Singer, J. (2001). Cognitive, social, and physiological determinants of emotional state. In W. Parrott (Ed.), *Emotions in social psychology: Essential readings* (pp. 76–93). New York: Psychology Press.

Scheela, R. A. (1995). Remodeling as metaphor: Sex offenders' perceptions of the treatment process. *Issues in Mental Health Nursing, 16,* 493–504.

Schildkraut, J. M., Calingaert, B., Marchbanks, P. A., Moorman, P. G., & Rodriguez, G. C. (2002). Impact of progestin and estrogen potency in oral contraceptives on ovarian cancer risk. *Journal of the National Cancer Institute, 94,* 32–38.

Schlegel, R. (2007, January 17). HPV vaccine. *Washington Post.* Retrieved September 16, 2008, from http://www.washingtonpost.com/wp-dyn/content/discussion/2007/01/16/DI2007011600929.html.

Schlichter, A. (2004). Queer at last? *GLW: A Journal of Lesbian and Gay Studies, 10*(4), 543–565.

Schnarch, D. (1997). *Passionate marriage.* New York: Henry Holt.

Schneider, F., Habel, U., Kessler, C., Salloum, J. B., & Posse, S. (2000). Gender differences in regional cerebral activity during sadness. *Human Brain Mapping, 9*(4), 226–238.

Schneider, J. P. (2000a). Qualitative study of cybersex participants: Gender differences, recovery issues, and implications for therapists. *Sexual Addiction & Compulsivity, 7*(4), 249–278.

Schneider, J. P. (2000b). Effects of cybersex addiction on the family: Results of a survey. *Sexual Addiction & Compulsivity, 7*(1), 31–58.

Schneider, M. (1989). Sappho was a right-on adolescent: Growing up lesbian. *Journal of Homosexuality, 17,* 111–130.

Schoenborn, C. A. (2004). *Marital status and health: United States, 1999–2002.* Advance Data from Vital and Health Statistics, No. 351. Hyattsville, MD: National Center for Health Statistics.

Schone, B. S., & Weinick, R. M. (1998). Health-related behaviors and the benefits of marriage for elderly persons. *The Gerontologist, 38,* 618–627.

Schover, L., & Jensen, S. B. (1988). *Sexuality and chronic illness.* New York: Guilford Press.

Schover, L. R. (2008). Androgen therapy for loss of desire in women: Is the benefit worth the risk? *Fertility and Sterility, 90,* 129–140.

Schulte, J. M., Martich, F. A., & Schmid, G. P. (1992). Chancroid in the United States, 1981–1990: Evidence for underreporting of cases. *Morbidity and Mortality Weekly Report, 992,* 41(no. SS-3), 57–61.

Schultheiss, D. (2008). Urogenital infections and male sexuality: Effects on ejaculation and erection. *Andrologia, 40,* 125–129.

Schützwohl, A. (2008). The intentional object of romantic jealousy. *Evolution and Human Behavior, 29,* 92–99.

Schwartz, I. M. (1999). Sexual activity prior to coitus initiation: A comparison between males and females. *Archives of Sexual Behavior, 28*(1), 63–69.

Schwartz, J. L., Creinen, M. D., & Pymar, H. C. (1999). The trimonthly combination oral contraceptive regimen: Is it cost effective? *Contraception, 60,* 263–267.

Schwartz, J. L., & Gabelnick, H. L. (2002). Current contraceptive research. *Perspectives on Sexual and Reproductive Health, 34*(6), 310–316.

Schwebke, J. R. (2000). Bacterial vaginosis. *Current Infectious Disease Report, 2*(1), 14–17.

Scott, J. E., & Schwalm, L. A. (1988). Rape rates and the circulation rates of adult magazines. *Journal of Sex Research, 24,* 241–250.

Scott, J. R. (2005). Episiotomy and vaginal trauma. *Obstetrics and Gynecology Clinics of North America, 32*(2), 307–321.

Scully, D., & Marolla, J. (1983). *Incarcerated rapists: Exploring a sociological model.* Final Report for Department of Health and Human Services, NIMH.

Scurr, J. (2007). Bras can't support bouncing breasts. British Association of Sport and Exercise Sciences. Retrieved on March 19, 2008, from http://www.port.ac.uk/media/Media,43533,en.pdf.

Sears, B., & Badgett, M. V. (2008). *The impact of extending marriage to same-sex couples on the California budget.* Los Angeles: The Williams Institute. Retrieved June 26, 2008, from http://www.law.ucla.edu/williamsinstitute/publications/EconImpactCAMarriage.pdf.

Sedgh, G., Henshaw, S., Singh, S., Åhman, E., & Shah, I. H. (2007b). Induced abortion: Rates and trends worldwide. *Lancet, 370,* 1338–1345.

Sedgh, G., Hussain, R., Bankole, A., Singh, S. (2007a). Unmet need for contraception in developing countries: Levels and reasons for not using a method. Alan Guttmacher Institute, Occasional Report No. 37. Retrieved July 29, 2008, from http://www.guttmacher.org/pubs/2007/07/09/or37.pdf.

Seeber, B. E., Sammel, M. D., Guo, W., Zhou, L., Hummel, A., Barnhart, K. T. (2006). Application of redefined human chorionic gonadotropin curves for the diagnosis of women at risk for ectopic pregnancy. *Fertility and Sterility, 86*(2):454–459.

Seidman, E. L. (2004). The pornographic retreat: Contemporary patterns of pornography use and the psychodynamic meaning of frequent pornography use for heterosexual men. *Dissertation Abstracts International, 64*(8-B), #0419–4217.

Seidman, S. N. (2007). Androgens and the aging male. *Psychopharmacological Bulletin, 40,* 205–218.

Seidman, S. N., & Rieder, R. O. (1994). A review of sexual behavior in the U.S. *American Journal of Psychiatry, 151,* 330–341.

Seiffge-Krenke, I., Shulman, S., & Klesinger, N. (2001). Adolescent precursors of romantic relationships in young adulthood. *Journal of Social & Personal Relationships, 18*(3), 327–346.

Seki, K., Matsumoto, D., & Imahori, T. T. (2002). The conceptualization and expression of intimacy in Japan and the United States. *Journal of Cross Cultural Psychology, 33,* 303–319.

Seligman, L., & Hardenburg, S. A. (2000). Assessment and treatment of paraphilias. *Journal of Counseling and Development, 78*(1), 107–113.

Sell, R., Wells, J., & Wypij, D. (1995). The prevalence of homosexual behavior and attraction in the U.S., the U.K and France: Results of a national population-based sample. *Archives of Sexual Behavior, 24,* 235–249.

Sellers, J. G., Woolsey, M. D., & Swann, W. B. (2007). Is silence more golden for women than men? Observers derogate effusive women and their quiet partners. *Sex Roles, 57,* 477–482.

Seltzer, J. A. (2000). Families formed outside of marriage. *Journal of Marriage and Family, 62(4),* 1247.

Seng, M. J. (1989). Child sexual abuse and adolescent prostitution: A comparative analysis. *Adolescence, 24,* 665–675.

Sepilian, V., & Wood, E. (2004). Ectopic pregnancy. Retrieved July 19, 2005, from http://www.emedicine.com/med/topic3212.htm.

Seppa, N. (2001). Study reveals male link to preeclampsia. *Science News, 159*(12), 181–182.

Seto, M. (2008). Pedophilia: Psychopathology and theory. In D. Laws & W. O'Donohue (Eds.), *Sexual deviance: Theory, assessment and treatment* (2nd ed., pp. 164–183). New York: Guilford Press.

Seto, M. C. (2004). Pedophilia and sexual offenses against children. *Annual Review of Sex Research, 15,* 321–362.

Sexuality Information and Education Council of the United States. (2004). Guidelines for comprehensive sexuality education (3rd ed.). Retrieved September 22, 2005, from http://www.siecus.org/pubs/guidelines/guidelines.pdf.

Sexwork.com. (1999). The influence of Thai Buddhism on prostitution. Retrieved November 16, 2008, from http://www.sexwork.com/Thailand/buddhism.html.

Seymour, A., Murray, M., Sigmon, J., Hook, M., Edmunds, C., Gaboury, M., et al. (Eds.). (2000). Retrieved May 22, 2003, from http://www.ojp.usdoj.gov/ovc/assist/nvaa2000/academy/welcome.html.

Shabsigh, R., Patrick, D., Rowland, D., Bull, S., Tesfaye, F., & Rothman, M. (2008). Perceived control over ejaculation is central to treatment benefit in men with premature ejaculation: Results from phase III trials with dapoxetine. *BJU International, 102*(7), 824–828.

Shackelford, T. K., & Goetz, A. T. (2007). Adaptation to sperm competition in humans. *Current Directions in Psychological Science, 16,* 47–50.

Shadiack, A., Sharma, S., Earle, D., Spana, C., & Hallam, T. (2007). Melanocortins in the treatment of male and female sexual dysfunction. *Current Topics in Medical Chemistry, 7,* 1137–1144.

Shafaat, A. (2004). Punishment for adultery in Islam: A detailed examination. Retrieved April 10, 2008, from http://www.islamicperspectives.com/Stoning4.htm.

Shafik, A. (1991). Testicular suspension: Effect on testicular function. *Andrologia, 23*(4), 297–301.

Shamloul, R. (2005). Treatment of men complaining of short penis. *Urology, 65*(6), 1183–1185.

Sharma, R. (2001). Condom use seems to be reducing number of new HIV/AIDS cases. *British Medical Journal, 323*(7310), 417–421.

Sharpe, R. M., & Skakkebaek, N. E. (2008). Testicular dysgenesis syndrome: Mechanistic insights and potential new downstream effects. *Fertility and Sterility, 89*(Suppl. 2), e33–38.

Sharpsteen, D. J., & Kirkpatrick, L. A. (1997). Romantic jealousy and adult romantic attachment. *Journal of Personality & Social Psychology, 72*(3), 627–640.

Shaver, F. M. (2005). Sex work research: Methodological and ethical challenges. *Journal of Interpersonal Violence, 20*(3), 296–319.

Shaver, P., & Hazan, C. (1987). Being lonely, falling in love: Perspectives from attachment theory. *Journal of Social Behavior & Personality, 2*(2, Pt 2), 105–124.

Shaver, P. R., Wu, S., & Schwartz, J. C. (1992). Cross-cultural similarities and differences in emotion and its representation: A prototype approach. In M. S. Clark (Ed.), *Emotion* (pp. 175–212). Newbury Park, CA: Sage.

Sheaffer, A. T., Lange, E., & Bondy, C. A. (2008). Sexual function in women with Turner syndrome. *Journal of Women's Health, 17,* 27–33.

Shechory, M., & Idisis, Y. (2006). Rape myths and social distance toward sex offenders and victims among therapists and students. *Sex Roles, 54,* 651–658.

Sheehan, P. (2007). Hyperemesis gravidarum—assessment and management. *Australian Family Physician, 36,* 698–701.

Sheldon, K. M. (2007). Gender differences in preferences for singles ads that proclaim extrinsic versus intrinsic values. *Sex Roles, 57,* 119–130.

Shellenbarger, S. (2008, February 14). Why some single women choose to freeze their eggs. *Wall Street Journal,* p. D1.

Sheppard, C., & Wylie, K. R. (2001). An assessment of sexual difficulties in men after treatment for testicular cancer. *Sexual and Relationship Therapy, 16*(1), 47–58.

Sherfey, J. (1972). *The nature and evolution of female sexuality.* New York: Random House.

Sherif, B. (2004). Egypt. In R. T. Francoeur & R. J. Noonan (Eds.), *The Continuum complete international encyclopedia of sexuality* (pp. 345–358). New York/London: Continuum International.

Sherr, L., Varrall, R., Mueller, J., Richter, L., Wakhweya, A., Adato, M., Belsey, M., Chandan, U., Drimie, S., Haour-Knipe, V., Hosegood, M., Kimou, J., Madhavan, S., Mathambo, V., Desmond, C. (2008). A systematic review on the meaning of the concept 'AIDS orphan': Confusion over definitions and implications for care. *AIDS Care, 20*(5), 527–536.

Shettles, L., & Rorvik, D. (1970). *Your baby's sex: Now you can choose.* New York: Dodd, Mead.

Sheynkin, Y., Jung, M., Yoo, P., Schulsinger, D., & Komaroff, E. (2005). Increase in scrotal temperature in laptop computer users. *Human Reproduction, 20,* 452–455.

Shidlo, A., & Schroeder, M. (2002). Changing sexual orientation: A consumer's report. *Professional Psychology: Research and Practice, 33,* 249–259.

Shifren, J. L., & Avis, N. E. (2007). Surgical menopause: Effects on psychological well-being and sexuality. *Menopause, 14,* 586–591.

Shifren, J. L., Braunstein, G. D., Simon, J. A., Casson, P. R., Buster, J. E., Redmond, G. P., et al. (2000). Transdermal testosterone treatment in women with impaired sexual function after oophorectomy. *New England Journal of Medicine, 343*(10), 682–688.

Shifren, J. L., Monz, B. U., Russo, P., Segreti, A., Johannes, C. (2008). Sexual problems and distress in United States women. *Obstetrics & Gynecology, 112,* 970–978.

Shimanaka, K. (2008, August 8). Ominous rumblings on the love hotel front. *The Tokyo Reporter.* Retrieved August 23, 2008, http://www.tokyoreporter.com/2008/08/11/ominous-rumblings-on-the-love-hotel-front.

Shilts, R. (2000). *And the band played on: Politics, people, and the AIDS epidemic.* New York: St. Martin's Press.

Shindel, A., Nelson, C., & Brandes, S. (2008). Urologist practice patterns in the management of premature ejaculation: A nationwide survey. *Journal of Sexual Medicine, 5,* 199–205.

Shoffman, M. (2006, December 11). Italian politicians attack Vatican's "anti-gay" attitude. *Pink News.* Retrieved July 4, 2008, from http://www.pinknews.co.uk/news/view.php?id=3229.

Shtarkshall, R. A., & Zemach, M. (2004). Israel. In R. T. Francoeur & R. J. Noonan (Eds.), *The Continuum international encyclopedia of sexuality* (pp. 581–619). New York/London: Continuum International.

Shulman, J. L., & Horne, S. G. (2006). Guilty or not? A path model of women's sexual force fantasies. *Journal of Sex Research, 43,* 368–377.

Shutty, M. S., & Leadbetter, R. A. (1993). Case report: Recurrent pseudocyesis in a male patient with psychosis, intermittent hyponatremia, and polydipsia. *Psychosomatic Medicine, 55,* 146–148.

Sidley, P. (2002). Doctor reprimanded for giving antiretroviral drug to baby who was raped. *British Medical Journal, 324*(7331), 191–193.

Sigal, J., Gibbs, M. S., Goodrich, C., Rashid, T., Anjum, A., Hsu, D., Perrino, C., Boratrav, H., Carson-Arenas, A., et al. (2005). Cross-cultural reactions to academic sexual harassment: Effects of individualist vs. collectivist culture and gender of participants. *Sex Roles, 52*(3–4), 201–215.

Siker, J. S. (1994). *Homosexuality in the Church: Both sides of the debate.* Louisville, KY: Westminster John Knox Press.

Silbert, M. (1998). Compounding factors in the rape of street prostitutes. In A. W. Burgess (Ed.), Rape and sexual assault II. London: Taylor & Francis.

Silverman, B., & Gross, T. (1997). Use and effectiveness of condoms during anal intercourse. *Sexually Transmitted Diseases, 24,* 11–17.

Silverstein, C. (1984). The ethical and moral implications of sexual classification: A commentary. *Journal of Homosexuality, 9,* 29–38.

Simmons, M., & Montague, D. (2008). Penile prosthesis implantation: Past, present and future. *International Journal of Impotence Research, 20,* 437–444.

Simon, C. P., & Witt, A., (1982). *Beating the system: The underground economy.* Boston: Auburn House.

Simon, P. M., Morse, E. V., Osofsky, H. J., & Balson, P. M. (1992). Psychological characteristics of a sample of male street prostitutes. *Archives of Sexual Behavior, 21,* 33–44.

Simon, R. W. (2002). Revisiting the relationships among gender, martial status, and mental health. *American Journal of Sociology, 107*(4), 1065–1097.

Simon, R. W., & Marcussen, K. (1999). Marital transitions, marital beliefs, and mental health. *Journal of Health and Social Behavior, 430,* 111–125.

Simons, M. (1996, January 26). African women in France battling polygamy. *New York Times,* p. A1.

Simons, R. L., & Whitbeck, L. B. (1991). Sexual abuse as a precursor to prostitution and victimization among adolescent and adult homeless women. *Journal of Family Issues, 12,* 361–379.

Simpson, G., Tate, R., Ferry, K., Hodgkinson, A., & Blaszczynski, A. (2001). Social, neuroradiologic, medical, and neuropsychologic correlates of sexually aberrant behavior. *Journal of Head Trauma Rehabilitation, 16*(6), 556–572.

Simpson, J. L., & Lamb, D. J. (2001). Genetic effects of intracytoplasmic sperm injection. *Seminars in Reproductive Medicine, 19*(3), 239–249.

Simsir, A., Thorner, K., Waisman, J., & Cangiarella, J. (2001). Endometriosis in abdominal scars. *American Surgeon, 67*(10), 984–987.

Singh, A., Wong, T., & De, P. (2008). Characteristics of primary and late latent syphilis cases which were initially non-reactive with the rapid plasma regain as the screening test. *International Journal of STDs and AIDS, 19,* 464–468.

Singh, D., Vidaurri, M., Zambarano, R. J., & Dabbs, J. M. (1999). Lesbian erotic role identification: Behavioral, morphological, and hormonal correlates. *Journal of Personality and Social Psychology, 76*(6), 1035–1049.

Singh, K., & Ratnam, S. S. (1998). The influence of abortion legislation on maternal mortality. *International Journal of Gynaecology and Obstetrics, 63*(Suppl. 1), S123–129.

Singh, M., Porter, C., & Griffiths, S. (2008). First trimester medical termination of pregnancy: The Nottingham experience. *Journal of Obstetrics and Gynecology, 28,* 315–316.

Sipski, M., Alexander, C., & Gomez-Marin, O. (2006). Effects of level and degree of spinal cord injury on male orgasm. *Spinal Cord, 44,* 798–804.

Skinner, B. F. (1953). *Science and human behavior.* New York: Macmillan.

Skolnick, A. (1992). *The intimate environment: Exploring marriage and the family.* New York: HarperCollins.

Slavney, P. R. (1990). *Perpectives on hysteria.* Baltimore, MD: Johns Hopkins University Press.

Smith, C. J., McMahon, C., & Shabsigh, R. (2005). Peyronie's disease: The epidemiology, aetiology and clinical evaluation of deformity. *British Journal of Urology International, 95*(6), 729–32.

Smith, G. D., Frankel, S., & Yarnell, J. (1997). Sex and death: Are they related? Findings from the Caerphilly cohort study. *British Medical Journal, 315,* 1641–1645.

Smith, J., Green, J., deGonzalez, A., Appleby, P., Peto, J., Plummer, M., Franceschi, S., & Beral, V. (2007). Cervical cancer and use of hormonal contraceptives: A systematic review. *The Lancet, 361,* 1159–1167.

Smith, J., & Robinson, N. (2002). Age-specific prevalence of infection with herpes simplex virus types 2 and 1: A global review. *Journal of Infectious Diseases, 186,* S3–S28.

Smith, K. L., Cornelissen, P. L., & Tovée, M. J. (2007). Color 3D bodies and judgements of human female attractiveness. *Evolution and Behavior, 28,* 48–54.

Smith, K. T. (1971). Homophobia: A tentative personality profile. *Psychological Reports, 29,* 1091–1094.

Smith, M. E. (2005). Female sexual assault: The impact on the male significant other. *Issues in the Mental Health Nursing, 26*(2), 149–167.

Smith, S. A., & Michel, Y. (2006). A pilot study on the effects of aquatic exercises on discomforts of pregnancy. *Journal of Obstetrics and Gynecological Neonatal Nursing, 35,* 315–323.

Smythers, R. (1894). *Instruction and advice for the young bride.* New York: Spiritual Guidance Press.

So, H. W., & Cheung, F. M. (2005). Review of Chinese sex attitudes & applicability of sex therapy for Chinese couples with sexual dysfunction. *Journal of Sex Research, 42*(2), 93–102.

Sobsey, D. (1994). *Violence and abuse in the lives of people with disabilities.* Baltimore, MD: Paul H. Brookes.

Society for the Advancement of Sexual Health. (2008a). Home page. Retrieved November 10, 2008, from http://www.sash.net/.

Society for the Advancement of Sexual Health. (2008b). *Public service announcement: Sexual addiction.* Retrieved October 2, 2008, from http://www.sash.net/.

Soley, L., & Kurzbard, G. (1986). Sex in advertising: A comparison of 1964 and 1984 magazine advertisements. *Journal of Advertising, 15,* 46–54.

Soloman, S. E., Rothblum, D., & Balsam, K. F. (2005). Money, housework, sex, and conflict: Same-sex couples in civil unions, those not in civil unions, and heterosexual married siblings. *Sex Roles, 52,* 561–575.

Sommerfeld, J. (1999). Megan's Law expands to the Internet. Retrieved March 31, 2003, from http://www.msnbc.com/news/297969.asp?cp1=1.

Song, L. M., Gu, Y., Lu, W., Liang, X., & Chen, Z. (2006). A phase II randomized controlled trial of a novel male contraception, an intra-vas device. International *Journal of Andrology, 29,* 489–495.

Sorenson, R. C. (1973). *Adolescent sexuality in contemporary America.* New York: World.

Sorenson, S., & Brown, V. (1990). Interpersonal violence and crisis intervention on the college campus. *New Directions for Student Services, 49,* 57–66.

Sormanti, M., & Shibusawa, T. (2008). Intimate partner violence among midlife and older women: A descriptive analysis of women seeking medical services. *Health and Social Work, 33,* 33–40.

Sortirin, P. (2000). All they do is bitch, bitch, bitch: Political and interactional features of women's office talk. *Women and Language, 23*(2), 19.

South, S. J. (1991). Sociodemographic differentials in mate selection preferences. *Journal of Marriage and the Family, 53,* 928–940.

South, S. J. (1993). Racial and ethnic differences in the desire to marry. *Journal of Marriage and the Family, 55,* 357–370.

Spence, J. T. (1984). Gender identity and its implications for the concepts of masculinity and femininity. In T. B. Sonderegger (Ed.), *Psychology and gender* (pp. 59–95). Lincoln: University of Nebraska Press.

Spira, A., Bajos, N. and the Analyse des Comportements Sexuels en France Investigators. (1993). *Les Comportements Sexuels en France.* Paris: La Documentation Française.

Spolan, S. (1991, March 22). Oh, by the way. *Philadelphia City Paper,* p. 7.

Sprecher, S. (2001). Equity and social exchange in dating couples: Associations with satisfaction, commitment, and stability. *Journal of Marriage and the Family, 63,* 599–613.

Sprecher, S. (2002). Sexual satisfaction in premarital relationships: Associations with satisfaction, love, commitment and stability. *Journal of Sex Research, 39*(3), 190–196.

Sprecher, S., Cate, R., & Levin, L. (1998). Parental divorce and young adults' beliefs about love. *Journal of Divorce & Remarriage, 28*(3–4), 107–120.

Sprecher, S., & Hendrick, S. (2004). Self-disclosure in intimate relationships: Associations with individual and relationship characteristics over time. *Journal of Social and Clinical Psychology, 23*(6), 857–877.

Sprecher, S., & Regan, P. (1996). College virgins: How men and women perceive their sexual status. *Journal of Sex Research, 33*(1), 3–16.

Sprecher, S., & Regan, P. (2002). Liking some things (in some people) more than others: Partner preferences in romantic relationships and friendships. *Journal of Social & Personal Relationships, 19*(4), 463–481.

Sprecher, S., & Toto-Morn, M. (2002). A study of men and women from different sides of earth to determine if men are from Mars and women are from Venus in their beliefs about love and romantic relationships. *Sex Roles, 46*(5–6), 131–147.

Srinivasan, P., & Lee, G. R. (2004). The dowry system in Northern India: Woman's attitudes and social change. *Journal of Marriage and the Family, 66*(5), 1108–1118.

Srivastava, R., Thakar, R., & Sultan, A. (2008). Female sexual dysfunction in obstetrics and gynecology. *Obstetrics and Gynecology Survey, 63,* 527–537.

Stacey, D. (2008). No more periods: The safety of continuous birth control. Retrieved March 18, 2008, from http://contraception.about.com/od/prescriptionoptions/p/MissingPeriods.htm.

Stack, S., & Gundlach, J. H. (1992). Divorce and sex. *Archives of Sexual Behavior, 21*(4), 359–367.

Stadtmauer, L., Oehninger, S. (2005). Management of infertility in women with polycystic ovary syndrome: A practical guide. *Treatments in Endocrinology, 4*(5), 279–292.

Stafford, L., & Reske, J. R. (1990). Idealization and communication in long distance premarital relationships. *Family Relations, 39,* 274–279.

Stahlhut, R. W., vanWijngaarden, E., Dye, T. D., Cook, S., & Swan, S. H. (2007). Concentrations of urinary phthalate metabolites are associated with increased waist circumference and insulin resistance in adult U.S. males. *Environmental Health Perspectives, 115,* 876–882.

Stalking Resource Center. (2000). The extent and nature of the sexual victimization of college women: A national-level analysis. Retrieved October 19, 2005, from http://www.ncvc.org/src/main.aspx?dbID=DB_NCWSV466.

Stanford, E. K. (2002). Premenstrual syndrome. Retrieved July 18, 2002, from http://www.medical-library.org/journals/secure/gynecol/secure/Premenstrual%20syndromes.

Stark, R. (1996). *The rise of Christianity.* Princeton, NJ: Princeton University Press.

Starkman, N., & Rajani, N. (2002). The case for comprehensive sex education. *AIDS Patient Care and STDs, 16*(7), 313–318.

Starling, K. (1999). How to bring the romance back. *Ebony, 54*(4), 136–137.

Starr, B., & Weiner, M. B. (1981). *Sex and sexuality in the mature years.* New York: Stein & Day.

Stayton, W. R. (1996). Sexual and gender identity disorders in a relational perspective. In F. W. Kaslow (Ed.), *Handbook of relational diagnosis and dysfunctional family patterns* (pp. 357–370). New York: Wiley.

Stearns, S. (2001). PMS and PMDD in the domain of mental health nursing. *Journal of Psychosocial Nursing and Mental Health Services, 39*(1), 16–27.

Steel, J., & Herlitz, C. (2007). Risk of sexual dysfunction in a randomly selected nonclinical sample of the Swedish population. *Obstetrics and Gynecology, 109,* 663–668.

Steen, R. (2001). Eradicating chancroid. *Bulletin of the World Health Organization, 79*(9), 818–827.

Steen, S., & Schwartz, P. (1995). Communication, gender, and power: Homosexual couples as a case study. In M. A. Fitzpatrick & A. L. Vangelisti (Eds.), *Explaining family interactions* (pp. 310–343). Thousand Oaks, CA: Sage.

Stein, J. H., & Reiser, L. W. (1994). A study of white, middle-class adolescent boys' responses to 'semenarche'. *Journal of Youth and Adolescence, 23*(3), 373–384.

Stein, R. (2008, May 20). A debunking on teenagers and "technical virginity"; researchers find that oral sex isn't commonplace among young people who avoid intercourse. *The Washington Post.* Retrieved May 29, 2008, from http://www.guttmacher.org/media/nr/nr_euroteens.html.

Steiner, M., Dunn, E., & Born, L. (2003). Hormones and mood: From menarche to menopause and beyond. *Journal of Affective Disorders, 74*(1), 67–83.

Stengers, J., & Van Neck, A. (2001). *Masturbation: The history of a great terror.* New York: Palgrave/St. Martins.

Stephenson, J. M., Imrie, J., Davis, M. M., Mercer, C., Black, S., et al. (2003). Is use of antiretroviral therapy among homosexual men associated with increased risk of transmission of HIV infection? *Sexually Transmitted Diseases, 79*(1), 7–10.

Sterling, T. (2004, March 4). The global view of gay marriage. *CBS News.* Retrieved July 16, 2008, from http://www.cbsnews.com/stories/2004/03/04/world/main604084.shtml.

Sternberg, R. J. (1987). Liking versus loving: A comparative evaluation of theories. *Psychological Bulletin, 102*(3), 331–345.

Sternberg, R. J. (1998). *Cupid's arrow: The course of love through time.* New Haven, CT: Yale University Press.

Sternberg, R. J. (1999). *Love is a story.* New York: Oxford University Press.

Sternberg, S. (2006). Once-a-day drug cocktail—in one pill—wins FDA approval. *USAToday.* Retrieved October 8, 2008, from http://www.usatoday.com/news/health/2006-07-12-hiv-pill_x.htm.

Sternfeld, B., Swindle, R., Chawla, A. Long, S., & Kennedy, S. (2002). Severity of premenstrual symptoms in a health maintenance organization population. *Obstetrics & Gynecology, 99*(6), 1014–1024.

Stevenson, B., & Wolfers, J. (2007). Marriage and divorce: Changes and their driving forces. *Journal of Economic Perspectives, 21*(2), 27–52.

Stevenson, M., & Gajarsky, W. (1992). Unwanted childhood sexual experiences relate to later revictimization and male perpetration. *Journal of Psychology and Human Sexuality, 4,* 57–70.

Stewart, E. A. (2001). Uterine fibroids. *Lancet, 357*(9252), 293–298.

Stewart, F. H., Ellertson, C., & Cates, W. (2004). Abortion. In R. A. Hatcher et al. (Eds.), *Contraceptive technology* (18th Rev. ed., pp. 673–700). New York: Ardent Media.

Stewart, F., & Gabelnick, H. L. (2004). Contraceptive research and development. In R. A. Hatcher et al. (Eds.), *Contraceptive technology* (18th Rev. ed., pp. 601–616). New York: Ardent Media.

Stewart, H. (2005). Senoritas and princesses: The quinceanera as a context for female development. *Dissertation Abstracts, 65*(7-A), 2770, #0419–4209.

Stewart, J. (1990). *The complete manual of sexual positions.* Chatsworth, CA: Media Press.

Stoller, R. J. (1991). The term perversion. In G. I. Fogel & W. A. Myers (Eds.), *Perversions and near-perversions in clinical practice: New psychoanalytic perspectives* (pp. 36–58). New Haven, CT: Yale University Press.

Stoller, R. J. (1996). The gender disorders. In I. Rosen (Ed.), *Sexual deviation* (3rd ed., pp. 111–133). London: Oxford University Press.

Stoller, R. J., & Herdt, G. H. (1985). Theories of origins of male homosexuality. *Archives of General Psychiatry, 42,* 399–404.

Storgaard, L., Bonde, J. P., Ernst, E., Spano, M., Andersen, C. Y., Frydenberg, M., & Olsen, J. (2003). Does smoking during pregnancy affect sons' sperm counts? *Epidemiology, 14*(3), 278–286.

Storms, M. D. (1980). Theories of sexual orientation. *Journal of Personality and Social Psychology, 38,* 783–792.

Storms, M. D. (1981). A theory of erotic orientation development. *Psychological Review, 88,* 340–353.

Strassberg, D. S., & Lockerd, L. K. (1998). Force in women's sexual fantasies. *Archives of Sexual Behavior, 27*(4), 403–415.

Strauss, L. T., Herndon, J., Chang, J., Parker, W., Bowens, S., Zane, S., & Berg, C. J. (2004, November 26). Abortion surveillance—United States, 2001. *MMWR Surveillance Summary, 53,* 1–32.

Strine, T. W., Chapman, D. P., & Ahluwalia, I. B. (2005). Menstrual-related problems and psychological distress among women in the United States. *Journal of Women's Health, 14*(4), 316–323.

Strommen, E. F. (1989). "You're a what?": Family member reactions to the disclosure of homosexuality. *Journal of Homosexuality, 18,* 37–58.

Struckman-Johnson, C., & Struckman-Johnson, D. (1994). Men pressured and forced into sexual experience. *Archives of Sexual Behavior, 23,* 93–115.

Struckman-Johnson, C., & Struckman-Johnson, D. (2002). Sexual coercion reported by women in three midwestern prisons. *Journal of Sex Research, 39*(3), 217–227.

Student Monitor. (2008). What's in on college campuses. Retrieved February 10, 2008, from http://www.studentmonitor.com/whoIsMonitor.php#SlideFrame_9.

Studwell, K. (2004, March). Congressional briefing highlights sexual behavior research. *Psychological Science Agenda, 18*(3). Retrieved February 18, 2005, at http://www.apa.org/science/psa/mar-4briefing.html.

Subramanian, S., Ackerson, L., Subramanyam, M., & Wright, R. (2007). Domestic violence is associated with adult and childhood asthma prevalence in India. *International Journal of Epidemiology, 36,* 569–579.

Sugrue, D. P., & Whipple, B. (2001) The consensus-based classification of female sexual dysfunction: Barriers to universal acceptance. *Journal of Sex and Marital Therapy, 27,* 232.

Sulak, P. J., Kuehl, T. J., Ortiz, M., & Shull, B. L. (2002). Acceptance of altering the standard 21-day/7-day oral contraceptive regimen to delay menses and reduce hormone withdrawal symptoms. *American Journal of Obstetrics and Gynecology, 186*(6), 1142–1149.

Sulak, P. J., Scow, R.D., Preece, C., Riggs, M., Kuehl, T. (2000). Withdrawal Symptoms in Oral Contraceptive Users. *Obstetrics & Gynecology, 95,* 261–266.

Summers, T., Kates, J., & Murphy, G. (2002). The global impact of HIV/AIDS on young people. *SIECUS Report, 31*(1), 14–23.

Suppe, F. (1984). Classifying sexual disorders: The diagnostic and statistical manual of the American Psychiatric Association. *Journal of Homosexuality, 9,* 9–28.

Sussman, N. M., & Tyson, D. H. (2000). Sex and power: Gender differences in computer-mediated interactions. *Computers in Human Behavior, 16*(4), 381–394.

Sutherland, P. (1987). I want sex, just like you. *The Village Voice, 32*(14), 25.

Svoboda, E. (2006, December 5). All the signs of pregnancy except one: A baby. Retrieved from http://www.nytimes.com/2006/12/05/health/05pseud.html.

Swaab, D. F. (2004). Sexual differentiation of the human brain: Relevance for gender identity, transsexualism and sexual orientation. *Gynecological Endocrinology, 19*(6), 201–312.

Swaab, D. F., & Hofman, M. A. (1990). An enlarged suprachiasmatic nucleus in homosexual men. *Brain Research, 537,* 141–148.

Swami, V., & Furnham, A. (2008). *The Psychology of Physical Attraction.* New York: Routledge/Taylor & Francis Group.

Swan, S. (2006). Semen quality in fertile U.S. men in relation to geographical area and pesticide exposure. *International Journal of Andrology, 29,* 62–68.

Swanson, J. M., Dibble, S., & Chapman, L. (1999). Effects of psychoeducational interventions on sexual health risks and psychosocial adaptation in young adults with genital herpes. *Journal of Advanced Nursing, 29*(4), 840–851.

Swartz, J. (2004, March 9). Online porn often leads high-tech way. *USA Today.* Retrieved October 7, 2008, from http://www.usatoday.com/money/industries/technology/2004-03-09-onlineporn_x.htm.

Swearingen, S., & Klausner, J. D. (2005). Sildenafil use, sexual risk behavior, and risk for sexually transmitted diseases, including HIV infection. *American Journal of Medicine, 118,* 571–577.

Szymanski, D. M., Chung, Y., & Balsam, K. (2001). Psychosocial correlates of internalized homophobia in lesbians. *Measurement and Evaluation in Counseling and Development, 34*(1), 27–39.

Tai, Y. C., Domchek, S., Parmigiani, G., & Chen, S. (2007). Breast cancer risk among male BRCA1 and BRCA2 mutation carriers. *Journal of the National Cancer Institute, 99,* 1811–1814.

Taioli, E., Marabelli, R., Scortichini, G., Migliorati, G., Pedotti, P., Cigliano, A., & Caporale, V. (2005). Human exposure to dioxins through diet in Italy. *Chemosphere, 61,* 1672–1676.

Talakoub, L., Munarriz, R., Hoag, L., Gioia, M., Flaherty, E., & Goldstein, I. (2002). Epidemiological characteristics of 250 women with sexual dysfunction who presented for initial evaluation. *Journal of Sex and Marital Therapy, 28* (Suppl. 1), 217–224.

Tannahill, R. (1980). *Sex in history.* New York: Stein & Day.

Tannen, D. (1990). *You just don't understand: Women and men in conversation.* New York: Ballantine Books.

Tanveer, K. (2002, July 7). In Pakistan, gang rape as a tribal punishment. *The Hartford Courant,* A2.

Tao, G. (2008). Sexual orientation and related viral sexually transmitted disease rates among U.S. women aged 15–44 years. *American Journal of Public Health, 98,* 1007–1009.

Tarkovsky, A. (2006). Sperm taste: 10 simple tips for better tasting semen. Ezine articles. Retrieved August 10, 2008, from http://ezinearticles.com/?Sperm-Taste—-10-Simple-Tips-For-Better-Tasting-Semen&id=164106.

Tay, J. I., Moore, J., & Walker, J. J. (2000). Ectopic pregnancy. *British Medical Journal, 320*(7239), 916–920.

Taylor, H. E. (2000). Meeting the needs of lesbian and gay young adults. *The Clearing House, 73*(4), 221.

Taylor, T., Keyse, L., & Bryant, A. (2006). *Contraception and Sexual Health, 2005/2006.* London: Office for National Statistics. Retrieved October 28, 2008, from http://www.statistics.gov.uk/downloads/theme_health/contraception2005-06.pdf.

Taywaditep, K. J., Coleman, E., & Dumronggittigule, P. (2004). Thailand. In R. T. Francoeur & R. J. Noonan (Eds.), *The Continuum complete international encyclopedia of sexuality* (pp. 1021–1053). New York/London: Continuum International.

Teachman, J. (2003). Premarital sex, premarital cohabitation and the risk of subsequent marital dissolution among women. *Journal of Marriage and Family, 65*(2), 444–455.

Teitelman, A. (2004). Adolescent girls' perspectives of family interactions related to menarche and sexual health. *Qualitative Health Research, 14*(9), 1292–1308.

Templeton, A. (1995). Infertility—epidemiology, aetiology and effective management. *Health Bulletin, 53,* 294–298.

Tenore, J.L. (2000). Ectopic pregnancy. *American Family Physician, 61*(4), 1080–1088.

Tepavcevic, D., Kostic, J., Basuroski, I., Stojsavljevic, N., Pekmezovic, T., & Drulovic, J. (2008). The impact of sexual dysfunction on the quality of life measured by MSQoL-54 in patients with multiple sclerosis. *Multiple Sclerosis, 14*(8), 1131–1136.

Terao, T., & Nakamura, J. (2000). Exhibitionism and low-dose trazodone treatment. *Hu-*

man *Psychopharmacology: Clinical & Experimental, 15*(5), 347–349.

Terry, J. (1990). Lesbians under the medical gaze: Scientists search for remarkable differences. *The Journal of Sex Research, 27,* 317–339.

Tesoriero, H. W. (2008, February 19). Infertile couples head overseas for treatments. *Wall Street Journal,* p. D1.

Tew, S., & Wind, R. (2001, November 29). Five-country study points to ways the U.S. could further decrease teenage pregnancy and STD rate [News release]. New York: Alan Guttmacher Institute. Retrieved May 29, 2008, from http://www.guttmacher.org/media/nr/nr_euroteens.html.

Tewksbury, R. (2007). Effects of sexual assaults on men: Physical, mental and sexual consequences. *International Journal of Men's Health, 6,* 22–36.

This, P. (2008). Breast cancer and fertility: Critical review, considerations and perspectives. *Bulletin du Cancer, 95,* 17–25.

This Week in Medicine. (2008). *Lancet, 371,* 871.

Thomas, S. L., & Ellertson, C. (2000). Nuisance or natural and healthy: Should monthly menstruation be optional for women? *Lancet, 355,* 922–924.

Thomasset, C. (1992). The nature of woman. In C. Klapisch-Zuber (Ed.), *A history of women in the West, Volume II: Silences of the Middle Ages* (pp. 43–70). Cambridge, U.K.: Belknap Press.

Thompson, A. P. (1984). Emotional and sexual components of extramarital relations. *Journal of Marriage and the Family, 46,* 35–42.

Thompson, S. J. (2005). Factors associated with trauma symptoms among runaway/homeless adolescents. *Stress, Trauma and Crisis: An International Journal, 8*(2–3), 143–156.

Thomson, R., Finau, S., Finau, E., Ahokovi, L., & Tameifuna, S. (2007). Circumcision of Pacific boys: Tradition at the cutting edge. *Pacific Health Dialogue, 13,* 115–122.

Thorne, N., & Amrein, H. (2003). Vomeronasal organ: Pheromone recognition with a twist. *Current Biology, 13*(6), R220–R222.

Thornhill, R., & Palmer, C. T. (2000). *A natural history of rape: Biological bases of sexual coercion.* Boston: MIT Press.

Thornton, A., & Young-DeMarco, L. (2001). Four decades in attitudes toward family issues in the U.S.: The 1960s to the 1990s. *Journal of Marriage and Family, 63*(4), 1009.

Thorp, J. M., Hartmann, K. E., & Shadigian, E. (2003). Long-term physical and psycho-

logical health consequences of induced abortion: Review of the evidence. *Obstetrical and Gynecological Survey, 58*(1), 67–79.

Thyen, U., Richter-Appelt, H., Wiesemann, C., Holterhus, P. M., & Hiort, O. (2005). Deciding on gender in children with intersex conditions: Considerations and controversies. *Treatments in Endocrinology, 4*(1), 1–8.

Tiefer, L. (1996). The medicalization of sexuality: Conceptual, normative and professional issues. *Annual Review of Sex Research, 7,* 252–282.

Tiefer, L. (2000). A new view of women's sexual problems. *Electronic Journal of Human Sexuality,* (3), 15. Retrieved May 24, 2005, from http://www.ejhs.org/volume3/newview.htm.

Tiefer, L. (2001). A new view of women's sexual problems: Why new? Why now? *Journal of Sex Research, 38*(2), 89–96.

Tiefer, L. (2002). Beyond the medical model of women's sexual problems: A campaign to resist the promotion of "female sexual dysfunction." *Sexual & Relationship Therapy, 17*(2), 127–135.

Tiefer, L. (2004). *Sex Is Not a Natural Act and Other Essays.* Boulder, CO: Westview Press.

Tiefer, L. (2006). Female sexual dysfunction: A case study of disease mongering and activist resistance. PLoS Medicine, 3(4). Retrieved June 19, 2008, from http://medicine.plosjournals.org/perlserv/?request=get-document&doi=10.1371/journal.pmed.0030178&ct=1.

Tietze, C., & Henshaw, S. K. (1986). *Induced abortion: A world review, 1986.* New York: Alan Guttmacher Institute.

Tilley, D. S., & Brackley, M. (2005). Men who batter intimate partners: A grounded theory study of the development of male violence in intimate partner relationships. *Issues in Mental Health Nursing, 26*(3), 281–297.

Timberg, C. (2005, December 2). South Africa's top court blesses gay marriage. *Washington Post.* Retrieved July 13, 2008, from http://www.washingtonpost.com/wp-dyn/content/article/2005/12/01/AR2005120100583.html.

Timmreck, T. C. (1990). Overcoming the loss of love: Presenting love addiction and promoting positive emotional health. *Psychological Reports, 66*(2), 515–528.

Ting-Toomey, S., Gao, G., & Trubisky, P. (1991). Culture, face maintenance, and styles of handling interpersonal conflicts:

A study in five cultures. *International Journal of Conflict Management, 2*(4), 275–296.

Tjaden, P., & Thoennes, N. (1998). *Stalking in America: Findings from the National Violence Against Women Survey.* National Institute of Justice and the Centers for Disease Control and Prevention.

Tjaden, P., & Thoennes, N. (2000). *Extent, nature, and consequences of intimate partner violence: Findings from the National Violence Against Women Survey.* Washington, DC: National Institute of Justice and the Centers for Disease Control and Prevention.

Tjepkema, M. (2008). Health care use among gay, lesbian and bisexual Canadians. *Health Reports, 19,* 53–& Vissers, W. (2008). Scabies outbreaks in nursing homes for the elderly: Recognition, treatment options and control of reinfestation. *Drugs and Aging, 25,* 299–306.

Tobío, C. (2001). Marriage, cohabitation and the residential independence of young people in Spain. *International Journal of Law, Policy and the Family, 15,* 68–87.

Todd, P., Penke, L., Fasolo, B., & Lenton, A. P. (2007). Different cognitive processes underlie human mate choices and mate preferences. *Proceedings of the National Academy of Science, 104,* 15011–15016.

Todosijevic, J., Rothblum, E. D., & Solomon, S. E. (2005). Relationship satisfaction, affectivity, and gay-specific stressors in same-sex couples joined in civil unions. *Psychology of Women Quarterly, 29*(2), 158–166.

Tomaso, B. (2008, July 25). After 40 years, birth control decree still divides American Catholics. *Dallas News.* Retrieved October 28, 2008, from http://religionblog.dallasnews.com/archives/2008/07/after-40-years-birth-control-d.html.

Tonelli, M. (2004). Teens and intimate partner violence. *Journal of Pediatric Adolescent Gynecology, 17,* 421–422.

Toto-Morn, M., & Sprecher, S. (2003). A cross-cultural comparison of mate preferences among university students: The United States vs. the People's Republic of China. *Journal of Comparative Family Studies, 34*(2), 151–170.

Tough, S. C., Newburn-Cook, C., Johnston, D. W., Svenson, L. W., Rose, S., & Belik, J. (2002). Delayed childbearing and its impact on population rate changes in lower birth weight, multiple birth, and preterm delivery. *Pediatrics, 109*(3), 399–403.

Tovar, J., Bazaldua, O., Vargas, L., & Reile, E. (2008). Human papillomavirus, cervical cancer, and the vaccines. *Postgraduate Medicine, 120,* 79–84.

Towne, B., Czerwinski, S. A., Demerath, E. W., Blangero, J., Roche, A. F., & Siervogel, R. M. (2005). Heritability of age at menarche in girls from the Fels longitudinal study. *American Journal of Physical Anthropology,* published online ahead of print. Retrieved March 22, 2005, from http://www.ncbi.nlm.nih.gov/entrez/query.fcgi?cmd=Retrieve&db=pubmed&dopt=Abstract&list_uids=15779076.

Trager, R. S. (2003). Microbicides. Raising new barriers against HIV infection. *Science, 299*(5603), 39.

Treas, J., & Giesen, D. (2000). Sexual infidelity among married and cohabiting Americans. *Journal of Marriage and Family, 62*(1), 48–61.

Trees, D. L., & Morse, S. A. (1995). Chanchroid and *Haemophilus ducreyi:* An update. *Clinical Microbiology Review, 8,* 357–375.

Treloar, S. A., Heath, A. C., & Martin, N. G. (2002). Genetic and environmental influences on premenstrual symptoms in an Australian twin sample. *Psychological Medicine, 32*(1), 25–38.

Tremble, B., Schneider, M., & Appathurai, C. (1989). Growing up gay or lesbian in a multicultural context. In G. Herdt (Ed.), *Gay and lesbian youth* (pp. 253–267). New York: Harrington Park Press.

Trends in HIV/AIDS Diagnoses. (2005, November 18). Trends in HIV/AIDS Diagnoses—33 States, 2001–2004. *Morbidity and Mortality Weekly Report, 54,* 1149–1153.

Trenholm, C., Devaney, B., Fortson, K., Quay, L., Wheeler, J., & Clark, M. (2007). Impact of four Title V, Section 510 Abstinence Education Programs. Princeton, NJ: Mathematic Policy Research. Retrieved on http://www.mathematica-mpr.com/publications/PDFs/impactabstinence.pdf.

Triandis, H. C. (1990). Cross-cultural studies of individualism and collectivism. In J. Berman (Ed.), Nebraska Symposium on Motivation, (pp. 41–133). Lincoln: University of Nebraska Press.

Trieman, K., Liskin, L., Kols, A., Rinehart, W.(1995). IUDs—an update. *Population Reports,* Series B, No. 5. The Johns Hopkins School of Public Health, Population Information Program: Baltimore, MD.

Trigg, B., Kerndt, P., & Aynalem, G. (2008). Sexually transmitted infections and pelvic inflammatory disease in women. *Medical Clinics of North America, 92,* 1083–1113.

Trivits, L. C., & Reppucci, N. D. (2002). Application of Megan's Law to juveniles. *American Psychologist, 57*(9), 690–704.

Troiden, R. R. (1989). The formation of homosexual identities. In G. Herdt (Ed.), *Gay and lesbian youth* (pp. 43–73). New York: Harrington Park Press.

Troncoso, A. P., Romani, A., Carmnze, C. M., Macias, J. R., & Masini, R. (1995). Probable HIV transmission by female homosexuals. *Contact Medicina, 55,* 334–336.

Trost, J. E. (2004). Sweden. In R. T. Francoeur & R. J. Noonan (Eds.), *The Continuum international encyclopedia of sexuality* (pp. 984–994). New York/London: Continuum International.

Trost, J. E., & Bergstrom-Walan, M. (2004). Sweden. In R. T. Francoeur & R. J. Noonan (Eds.), *The Continuum international encyclopedia of sexuality* (pp. 824–845). New York/London: Continuum International.

Trotter, E. C., & Alderson, K. G. (2007). University students' definitions of having sex, sexual partner, and virginity loss: The influence of participant gender, sexual experience, and contextual factors. *Canadian Journal of Human Sexuality, 16,* 11–20.

Trudel, G., & Desjardins, G. (1992). Staff reactions toward the sexual behaviors of people living in institutional settings. *Sexuality and Disability, 10,* 173–188.

Trumbach, R. (1990). Is there a modern sexual culture in the west, or, did England never change between 1500 and 1900? *Journal of the History of Sexuality, 1,* 206–309.

Truscott, P. (1991). S/M: Some questions and a few answers. In M. Thompson (Ed.), *Leatherfolk: Radical sex, people, politics, and practice* (pp. 15–36). Boston: Alyson Publications.

Trussell, J., & Wynn, L.L. (2008). Reducing unintended pregnancy in the U.S. *Contraception, 77,* 1–5.

Tucker, M. B., & Mitchell-Kernan, C. (1995). Trends in African-American family formation: A theoretical and statistical overview. In M. D. Tucker & C. Mitchell-Kernan (Eds.), *The decline of marriage among African- Americans* (pp. 3–26). New York: Russell Sage.

Turner, C. F., Villarroel, M., Chromy, J., Eggleston, E., & Rogers, S. (2005). Same-gender sex among U.S. adults. *Public Opinion Quarterly, 69,* 439–462.

Turner, W. (2000). *A genealogy of queer theory.* Philadelphia: Temple University Press.

TV Turnoff Network. (2005). Facts and figures about our TV habit. Retrieved November 6, 2005, from http://www.tvturnoff.org/images/facts&figs/factsheets/FactsFigs.pdf.

Twenge, J. M., Campbell, W., & Foster, C. (2003). Parenthood and marital satisfaction: A meta-analytic review. *Journal of Marriage & Family, 65*(3), 574–583.

Twiss, J., Wegner, J., Hunter, M., Kelsay, M., Rathe-Hart, M., & Salado, W. (2007). Perimenopause symptoms, quality of life, and health behaviors in users and nonusers of hormone therapy. *Journal of the American Academy of Nurse Practiners, 19,* 602–613.

Tye, M. H. (2006). Social inequality and well-being: Race-related stress, gay-related stress, self-esteem, and life satisfaction among African American gay and bisexual men. *Dissertation Abstracts International: Section B, 67*(4-B), 0419-4217.

Tzeng, O. (1992). Cognitive/comparitive judgment paradigm of love. In O. Tzeng (Ed.), *Theories of love development, maintenance, and dissolution: Octagonal cycle and differential perspectives,* p. 133–149.

Tzortzis, V., Skriapas, K., Hadjigeorgiou, G., Mitsogiannis, I., Aggelakis, K., Gravas, S., et al. (2008). Sexual dysfunction in newly diagnosed multiple sclerosis women. *Multiple Sclerosis, 14,* 561–563.

Uji, M., Shono, M., Shikai, N., & Kitamura, T. (2007). Case illustrations of negative sexual experiences among university women in Japan: Victimization disclosure and reactions of the confidant. *International Journal of Offender Therapy and Comparative Criminology, 51,* 227–242.

Ullman, S., Townsend, S., Filipas, H., & Starzynski, L. (2007). Structural models of the relations of assault severity, social support, avoidance coping, self-blame, and PTSD among sexual assault survivors. *Psychology of Women Quarterly, 31,* 23–37.

UNAIDS. (2005). AIDS Epidemic Update: December, 2005. Retrieved November 22, 2005, from http://www.unaids.org/epi2005/doc/report_pdf.html.

UNAIDS. (2008). 2008: Report on the global AIDS epidemic. UNAIDS Joint United Nations Programme on HIV/AIDS. Retrieved November 3, 2008 from http://www.unaids.org/en/KnowledgeCentre/HIVData/GlobalReport/2008/2008_Global_report.asp.

United National Children's Fund. (2005). *Early marriage: A harmful traditional practice.* Retrieved July 16, 2008, from http://www.unicef.org/publications/files/Early_Marriage_12.lo.pdf.

Upchurch, D. M., Aneshensel, C. S., Mudgal, J., & McNeely, C. S. (2001). Sociocultural contexts of time to first sex among Hispanic adolescents. *Journal of Marriage and Family, 63*(4), 1158.

Upchurch, D. M., Levy-Storms, L., et al. (1998). Gender and ethnic differences in the timing of first sexual intercourse. *Family Planning Perspectives, 30*(3), 121–128.

Update to CDC's STDs Treatment Guidelines, 2006. (2007). Centers for Disease Control and Prevention. *Morbidity and Mortality Weekly Report, 56*, 332–336.

Urbina, I. (2007, May 17). Gay youths find place to call home in specialty shelters. *New York Times.* Retrieved October 3, 2008, from http://www.nytimes.com/2007/05/17/us/17homeless.html?em&ex=1179633600&en=36a511a0fb354001&ei=5087%0A.

Ursus. (2004, December 7). Query: Pubic hair. *Canadian Medical Association Journal, 171*(12), 1569.

U.S. Census Bureau. (1999). *Statistical Abstract of the United States: 1999* (119th ed.). Washington, DC: U.S. Government Printing Office.

U.S. Census Bureau. (2001a). America's families and living arrangements: Population characteristics. Retrieved August 31, 2003, from http://www.census.gov/prod/2001pubs/p20-537.pdf.

U.S. Census Bureau. (2001b). Marital status history for people 15 years old and over by age, sex, race, and ethnicity. Retrieved October 12, 2005, from http://www.census.gov/population/www/socdemo/marr-div/p70-97-tab01.html.

U.S. Census Bureau. (2006, September 21). *Estimated median age at first marriage, by sex—1890 to the present.* Retrieved July 16, 2008, from http://www.census.gov/population/socdemo/hh-fam/ms2.pdf.

U.S. Census Bureau. (2007, September 19). *Most people make only one trip down the aisle, but first marriages shorter, census bureau reports.* Retrieved September 20, 2007, from http://www.census.gov/Press-Release/www/releases/archives/marital_status_living_arrangements/010624.html.

U.S. Department of Health and Human Services. (2004). *Child Health USA.* Rockville, MD: Health Resources and Services Administration, Maternal Child Health Bureau.

U.S. Department of Justice. (2006). Hate crime statistics: Incidents and Offenses. Retrieved October 3, 2008, from http://www.fbi.gov/ucr/hc2006/incidents.html.

U.S. Department of Justice, Federal Bureau of Investigation. (2004). Crime in the United States, 2004: Forcible rape. Retrieved December 3, 2005, from http://www.fbi.gov/ucr/cius_04/offenses_reported/violent_crime/forcible_rape.html.

U.S. Department of Justice, Office on Violence Against Women. (2008). Anonymous reporting and forensic examinations. Retrieved October 25, 2008, from http://www.ovw.usdoj.gov/docs/faq-arfe052308.pdf.

U.S. Department of Justice, Office of Justice Programs. (2002). Rape and sexual assault: Reporting to police and medical attention, 1992–2000. Retrieved October 22, 2005, from http://www.ojp.usdoj.gov/bjs/pub/pdf/rsarp00.pdf.

U.S. Department of Justice, Office of Justice Programs. (2003). Number of victimizations, by type of crime and relationship to offender. Retrieved October 22, 2005, from http://www.ojp.usdoj.gov/bjs/pub/pdf/cvus/current/cv0333.pdf.

U.S. Department of State. (2005). Trafficking in persons report. Retrieved December 12, 2005, from http://www.state.gov/documents/organization/47255.pdf.

U.S. Preventive Services Task Force (USPSTF). (2005). Screening for ovarian cancer: Recommendation statement. *American Family Physician, 71*(4), 759–763.

Vaast, E. (2006). Playing with masks: Fragmentation and continuity in the presentation of self in an occupational online forum. *Information Technology & People, 20*, 334–351.

Valdiserri, R. O. (2002). HIV/AIDS stigma: An impediment to public health. *American Journal of Public Health, 92*(3), 341–343.

Valente, S. M. (2005). Sexual abuse of boys. *Journal of Child and Adolescent Psychiatric Nursing, 18*(1), 10–16.

van Basten, J. P., Van Driel, M. F., Hoekstra, H. J., Sleijfer, D. T., van de Wiel, H. B., Droste, J. H., et al. (1999). Objective and subjective effect of treatment for testicular cancer on sexual function. *British Journal of Urology, 84*(6), 671–678.

Van Berlo, W., & Ensink, B. (2000). Problems with sexuality after sexual assault. *Annual Review of Sex Research, 11*, 235–257.

Van Damme, L., Ramjee, G., Alary, M., Vuylsteke, B., Chandeying, V., Rees, H., et al. (2002). Effectiveness of COL-1492, a N-9 vaginal gel on HIV-transmission in female sex workers. *Lancet, 360*(9338), 971–977.

Van de Ven, P., Campbell, D., & Kippax, S. (1997). Factors associated with unprotected anal intercourse in gay men's casual partnerships in Sydney, Australia. *AIDS Care, 9*(6), 637–649.

Van den Heuvel, M., van Bragt, A., Alnabawy, A., & Kaptein, M. (2005). Comparison of ethinylestradial pharmacokinetics in three hormonal contraceptive formulation: The vaginal ring, the transdermal patch and an oral contraceptive. *Contraception, 72,* 168–174.

van Lankveld, J., Everaerd, W., & Grotjohann, Y. (2001). Cognitive-behavioral bibliotherapy for sexual dysfunctions in heterosexual couples: A randomized waiting-list controlled clinical trial in the Netherlands. *Journal of Sex Research, 38*(1), 51–67.

Van Voorhis, B. J. (2006). Outcomes from assisted reproductive technology. *Obstetrics and Gynecology, 107,* 183–200.

Vanderbilt, H. (1992). Incest: A chilling report. *Lears,* (Feb.), 49–77.

VanderLaan, D., & Vasey, P. (2008). Mate retention behavior of men and women in heterosexual and homosexual relationships. *Archives of Sexual Behavior, 37,* 572–586.

Vanfossen, B. (1996). ITROWs women and expression conference. Institute for Teaching and Research on Women, Towson University, Towson, MD. Retrieved April 15, 2003, from http://www.towson.edu/itrow.

Vardi, Y., McMahon, C., Waldinger, M., Rubio-Aurioles, E., & Rabinowitz, D. (2008). Are premature ejaculation symptoms curable? *Journal of Sexual Medicine, 5,* 1546–1551.

Veenstra, M. Y., Lemmens, P., Friesema, I. H., & Tan, F. (2007). Coping style mediates impact of stress on alcohol use: A prospective population-based study. *Addiction, 102,* 1890–1898.

Venâncio, D. P., Tufik, S., Garbuio, S. A., da Nóbrega, A. C., & de Mello, M. T. (2008). Effects of anabolic androgenic steroids on sleep patterns of individuals practicing resistance exercise. Retrieved April 6, 2008, from http://www.ncbi.nlm.nih.gov/pubmed/18043934?ordinalpos=2&itool=EntrezSystem2.PEntrez.Pubmed.Pubmed_ResultsPanel.Pubmed_RVDocSum.

Vendittelli, F., Riviere, O., Crenn-Hebert, C., Rozan, M., Maria, B., & Jacquetin, B. (2008). Is a breech presentation at term more frequent in women with a history of cesarean delivery? *American Journal of Obstetrics and Gynecology, 198,* 521.

Venkat, P., Masch, R., Ng, E., Cremer, M., Richman, S., & Arslan, A. (2008, May 23). Knowledge and beliefs about contraception in urban Latina women. *Journal of Community Health, 33*(5), 357–362.

Venkatesh, K., Biswas, J., Kumarasamy, N. (2008). Impact of highly active antiretroviral therapy on ophthalmic manifestations in human immunodeficiency virus/acquired immune deficiency syndrome. *Indian Journal of Ophthalmology, 56*(5), 391–393.

Ventura, S., Abma, J., Mosher, W., & Henshaw, S. (2008). Estimated pregnancy rates by outcome for the United States, 1990–2004. *National Vital Statistics Reports, 56* (15). Hyattsville, MD: National Center for Health Statistics.

Ventura, S. J., Abma, J. C., Mosher, W. D., & Henshaw, S. K. (2007). *Recent trends in teenage pregnancy in the United States, 1990–2002.* Hyattsville, MD: National Center for Health Statistics, Centers for Disease Control. Retrieved May 27, 2008, from http://www.cdc.gov/nchs/products/pubs/pubd/hestats/teenpreg1990-2002/teenpreg1990-2002.htm.

Vergnes, J. (2008). Studies suggest an association between maternal periodontal disease and preeclampsia. *Evidence-Based Dentistry, 9,* 46–47.

Verkasalo, P. K., Thomas, H. V., Appleby, P. N., Davey, G. K., & Key, T. J. (2001). Circulating levels of sex hormones and their relation to risk factors for breast cancer: A crosssectional study in 1092 pre- and postmenopausal women. *Cancer Causes and Control, 12*(1), 47–59.

Versfeld, N. J., & Dreschler, W. A. (2002). The relationship between the intelligibility of time-compressed speech and speech-in-noise in young and elderly listeners. *Journal of the Acoustical Society of America, 111,* 401–408.

Verweij, K., Shekar, S., Zietsch, B., Eaves, L., Bailey, J., Boomsma, D., & Martin, N. (2008). Genetic and environmental influences on individual differences in attitudes toward homosexuality: An Australian twin study. *Behavior Genetics, 38,* 257–265.

Vestal, C. (2008, May 16). California gay marriage ruling sparks new debate. *Stateline.* Retrieved from http://www.stateline.org/live/printable/story?contentId=310206.

Vigano, P., Parazzini, F., Somigliana, E., & Vercellini, P. (2004). Endometriosis: Epidemiology and aetiological factors. *Best Practice & Research Clinical Obstetrics & Gynaecology, 18*(2), 177–200.

Vincke, J., & van Heeringen, K. (2002). Confidant support and the mental well-being of lesbian and gay young adults: A longitudinal analysis. *Journal of Community and Applied Social Psychology, 12,* 181–193.

Viswanathan, M., Hartmann, K., McKoy, N., Stuart, G., Rankins, N., Thieda, P., et al. (2007). Management of uterine fibroids: An update on the evidence. *Evidence Report for Technology Assessment, 154,* 1–122.

Voigt, H. (1991). Enriching the sexual experience of couples: The Asian traditions and sexual counseling. *Journal of Sex and Marital Therapy, 17,* 214–219.

Voiland, A. (2008). More problems with plastics: Like BPA, chemical called phthalates raise some concerns. *U.S. News and World Report, 144,* 54.

Volkow, N. D. (2005). Consequences of the abuse of anabolic steroids—before the committee on government reform—U.S. House of Representatives: Statement for the record, May 17, 2005. Bethesda, MD: National Institute on Drug Abuse. Retrieved April 6, 2008, from http://www.nida.nih.gov/testimony/3-17-05Testimony.html.

Von Sydow, K. (2000). Sexuality of older women: The effect of menopause, other physical and social and partner-related factors. *Arztl Fortbild Qualitatssich, 94*(3), 223–229.

Vukovic, L. (1992, November–December). Cold sores and fever blisters. *Natural Health,* 119–120.

Waal, F. B. M. (1995). Bonobo sex and society. *Scientific American,* 82–88. Retrieved July 4, 2003, from http://songweaver.com/info/bonobos.html.

Wacker, J., Parish, S., & Macy, R. (2008). Sexual assault and women with cognitive disabilities: Codifying discrimination in the United States. *Journal of Disability Policy Studies, 19,* 86–95.

Wagner, E. (1991). Campus victims of date rape should consider civil lawsuits as alternatives to criminal charges or colleges' procedures. *The Chronicle of Higher Education,* August 7, B2.

Wakelin, A. (2003). Effects of victim gender and sexuality on attributions of blame to rape victims. *Sex Roles, 49*(9–10), 477–487.

Walboomers, J., Jacobs, M., & Manos, M. (1999). Human papillomavirus is a necessary cause of invasive cervical cancer worldwide. *Journal of Pathology, 189,* 12–19.

Walch, K., Eder, R., Schindler, A., & Feichtinger, W. (2001). The effect of single-dose oxytocin application on time to ejacula-

tion and seminal parameters in men. *Journal of Assisted Reproductive Genetics, 18,* 655–659.

Wald, A. (1999). New therapies and prevention strategies for genital herpes. *Clinical Infectious Diseases, 28* (Suppl. 1), S4–S13.

Wald, A., Zeh, J., Selke, S., Warren, T., Ryncarz, A. J., Ashley, R., et al. (2000). Reactivation of genital herpes simplex virus type-2 infection in asymptomatic seropositive persons. *New England Journal of Medicine, 342*(12), 844–850.

Waldinger, M. (2005). Lifelong premature ejaculation: Definition, serotonergic neurotransmission and drug treatment. *World Journal of Urology, 23,* 102–108.

Waldinger, M., & Schweitzer, D. (2005). Retarded ejaculation in men: An overview of psychological and neurobiological insights. *World Journal of Urology, 23,* 76–81.

Walen, S. R., & Roth, D. (1987). A cognitive approach. In J. H. Geer & W. T. O'Donahue (Eds.), *Theories of human sexuality* (pp. 335–360). New York: Plenum Press.

Walker, J., Archer, J., & Davies, M. (2005). Effects of rape on men: A descriptive analysis. *Archives of Sexual Behavior, 34*(1), 69–80.

Wallerstein, E. (1980). *Circumcision: An American health fallacy.* New York: Springer.

Walsh, N. P. (2002). Barbie is banned in Russia, without love. *The Observer.* Retrieved May 23, 2008, from http://www.guardian.co.uk/world/2002/nov/24/russia.nickpatonwalsh.

Walters, J. (2005, January 2). No sex is safe sex for teens in America. Retrieved October 19, 2005, from http://observer.guardian.co.uk/international/story/0,6903,1382117,00.html.

Wang, H., & Amato, P. R. (2000). Predictors of divorce adjustment: Stressors, resources and definitions. *Journal of Marriage and Family, 62*(3), 655–669.

Wang, J. X., Norman, R. J., & Wilcox, A. J. (2004). Incidence of spontaneous abortion among pregnancies produced by assisted reproductive technology. *Human Reproduction, 19*(2), 272–277.

Wang, S. (2007, November 15). Fertility therapies under the microscope. *Wall Street Journal,* p. D1.

Ward, D., Carter, T., & Perrin, D. (1994). *Social deviance: Being, behaving, and branding.* Boston: Allyn & Bacon.

Wardle, L. D. (1999). Divorce reform at the turn of the millennium: Certainties and possibilities. *Family Law Quarterly, 33,* 783–900.

Wardle, L. D. (2001). Multiply and replenish: Considering same-sex marriage in light of state interests in marital procreation. *Harvard Journal of Law and Public Policy, 24*(3), 771–815.

Warin, J. (2000). The attainment of self-consistency through gender in young children. *Sex Roles, 41,* 209–232.

Warne, G. L., Grover, S., & Zajac, J. D. (2005). Hormonal therapies for individuals with intersex conditions: Protocol for use. *Treatments in Endocrinology, 4*(1), 19–29.

Warner, J. (2005, February 21). Mommy madness. *Newsweek,* pp. 42–49.

Warren, M. P., Brooks-Gunn, J., Fox, R. P., Holderness, C. C., Hyle, E. P., & Hamilton, W. G. (2002). Osteopenia in exercise-associated amenorrhea using ballet dancers as a model: A longitudinal study. *Journal of Clinical Endocrinology Metabolism, 87*(7), 3162–3168.

Warrington, M., & Younger, M. (2000). The other side of the gender gap. *Gender and Education, 12*(4), 493–508.

Wasserman, A. L. (2001). Development of the fetish interest scale: A measure of sexual interest using forced-choice and visual reaction time methodologies. *Dissertation Abstracts International,* Hahnemann University, December, #0419-4217.

Watkins, J. (2003). Insolent and contemptuous carriages. Re-conceptualization of illegitimacy in colonial British America. Retrieved April 10, 2008, from http://etd.fcla.edu/SF/SFE0000137/Thesis.pdf.

Watson, C., Calabretto, H. (2007). Comprehensive review of conventional and non-conventional methods of management of recurrent vulvovaginal candidiasis. *Australian and New Zealand Journal of Obstetrics and Gynaecology, 47*(4), 262–272.

Watson, W., Miller, R., Wax, J., Hansen, W., Yamamura, Y., & Polzin, W. (2008). Sonographic findings of trisomy 18 in the second trimester of pregnancy. *Journal of Ultrasound in Medicine, 27,* 1033–1038.

Watts, D. J. (2003). *Six degrees: The science of a connected age.* New York: Norton.

Waxman, H. (2004). Abstinence-only education. Retrieved September 17, 2005, from http://www.democrats.reform.house.gov/investigations.asp?Issue=Abstinence-Only+Education.

Wdowiak, A., Wdowiak, L., & Wiktor, H. (2007). Evaluation of the effect of using mobile phones on male fertility. *Annals of Agricultural and Environmental Medicine, 14,* 169–172.

Weatherall, A. (2002). *Gender, language and discourse.* London: Hove Routledge.

Weaver, K., Campbell, R., Mermelstein, R., & Wakschlag, L. (2008). Pregnancy smoking in context: The influence of multiple levels of stress. *Nicotine and Tobacco Research, 10,* 1065–1073.

Wechsler, H., & Issac, N. (1992). "Binge" drinkers at Massachusetts colleges. *Journal of the American Medical Association, 267*(21), 2929–2931.

Weed, S. E. (2008). Marginally successful results of abstinence-only program erased by dangerous errors in curriculum. *American Journal of Health Behavior, 32,* 60–73.

Weeks, G., & Hof, L. (1987). *Integrating sex and marital therapy.* New York: Brunner/Mazel.

Wei, E.H. (2000). Teenage fatherhood and pregnancy involvement among urban, adolescent males: Risk factors and consequences. *Dissertation Abstracts International: Section B, 61*(1-B), #0419–4217.

Weigel, D. J. (2007). Parental divorce and the types of commitment-related messages people gain from their families of origin. *Journal of Divorce and Remarriage, 47,* 15.

Weijing H., Neil, S., Kulkarni, H., Wright, E., Agan, B., Marconi, V., et al. (2008). Duffy antigen receptor for chemokines mediates trans-infection of HIV-1 from red blood cells to target cells and affects HIV-AIDS susceptibility. *Cell Host and Microbe, 4,* 52–62.

Weinberg, M. S., Williams, C. J., & Pryor, D. W. (1994). *Dual attraction: Understanding bisexuality.* New York: Oxford University Press.

Weingarten, H. P., & Elston, D. (1991). Food cravings in a college population. *Appetite, 17,* 167–175.

Weinstock, H., Berman, S., & Cates, W. (2004, January/February). Sexually transmitted diseases among American youth: Incidence and prevalence estimates, 2000. *Perspectives on Sexual and Reproductive Health, 36*(1), 6–10. Retrieved October 19, 2005, from http://www.guttmacher.org/pubs/journals/3600604.html.

Weisel, J. J., & King, P. E. (2007). Involvement in a conversation and attributions concerning excessive self-disclosure. *Southern Communication Journal, 72,* 345–354.

Weiss, H. A., Quigley, M. A., & Hayes, R. J. (2000). Male circumcision and risk of HIV infection in sub-Saharan Africa: A systematic review and metaanalysis. *AIDS, 14,* 2361–2370.

Weitzman, G. D. (1999). What psychology professionals should know about polyamory: The lifestyles and mental health concerns of polyamorous individuals. Paper presented at the 8th Annual Diversity Conference. Retrieved June 11, 2005, from http://www.polyamory.org/~joe/polypaper.htm.

Welch, L. (1992). *Complete book of sexual trivia.* New York: Citadel Press.

Wells, J. W. (1970). *Tricks of the trade.* New York: New American Library.

Welty, S. E. (2005). Critical issues with clinical research in children: The example of premature infants. *Toxicology and Applied Pharmacology,* Epub ahead of print. Retrieved July 19, 2005, from http://www.ncbi.nlm.nih.gov/entrez/query.fcgi?cmd=Retrieve&db=pubmed&dopt=Abstract&list_uids=16023161&query_hl=14.

Weng, X., Odouli, R., & Li, D.K. (2008, January 25). Maternal caffeine consumption during pregnancy and the risk of miscarriage: A prospective cohort study. *American Journal of Obstetrics and Gynecology, 198*(3), 279.

Wentworth, A. (2007, September). Beautify your bum: Check out vanity's weird new frontier. *Marie Claire* (14), p. 136.

Wespes, E., & Schulman, C. C. (2002). Male andropause: Myth, reality and treatment. *International Journal of Impotence Research, 14*(Suppl. 1), 593–598.

West, D. J. (1993). *Male prostitution.* Cambridge, U.K.: University of Cambridge Press.

West, L. (1989). Philippine feminist efforts to organize against sexual victimization. *Response to the Victimization of Women and Children, 12,* 11–14.

West, S., D'Aloisio, A., Agans, R., Kalsbeek, W., Borisov, N., & Thorp, J. (2008). Prevalence of low sexual desire and hypoactive sexual desire disorder in a nationally representative sample of U.S. women. *Archives of Internal Medicine, 168,* 1441–1449.

Westefeld, J. S., Buford, B., Taylor, S., & Maples, M. R. (2001). Gay, lesbian and bisexual college students: The relationship between sexual orientation and depression, loneliness, and suicide. *Journal of College Student Psychotherapy, 15*(3), 71–82.

Westermarck, E. (1972). *Marriage ceremonies in Morocco.* London, U.K.: Curzon Press.

Whalen, R. E., Geary, D. C., & Johnson, F. (1990). Models of sexuality. In D. P. McWhirter, S. A. Sanders, & J. M. Reinisch (Eds.), *Homosexuality/heterosexuality:*

Concepts of sexual orientation (pp. 61–70). New York: Oxford University Press.

Whatley, M. A. (2005). The effect of participant sex, victim dress, and traditional attitudes on causal judgments for marital rape victims. *Journal of Family Violence, 20*(3), 191–200.

Wheeler, J., Newring, K., & Draper, C. (2008). Transvestic fetishism: Psychopathology and Theory. In D. Laws & W. O'Donohue (Eds.), *Sexual deviance: Theory, assessment and treatment* (2nd ed., pp. 272–285). New York: Guilford Press.

Whelan, C. I., & Stewart, D. E. (1990). Pseudocyesis: A review and report of six cases. *International Journal of Psychiatry in Medicine, 20,* 97–108.

Whipple, B. (2000). Beyond the G spot. *Scandinavian Journal of Sexology, 3,* 35–42.

Whipple, B., & Brash-McGreer, K. (1997). Management of female sexual dysfunction. In M. L. Sipski & C. Alexander (Eds.), *Maintaining sexuality with disability and chronic illness: A practitioner's guide* (pp. 509–534). Baltimore: Aspen.

Whitam, F. L., Daskalos, C., Sobolewski, C. G., & Padilla, P. (1999). The emergence of lesbian sexuality and identity cross-culturally. *Archives of Sexual Behavior, 27*(1), 31–57.

White, B. H., & Kurpius, S. E. (2002). Effects of victim sex and sexual orientation on perceptions of rape. *Sex Roles, 46*(5–6), 191–200.

White, C. B. (1982). Sexual interest, attitudes, knowledge, and sexual history in relation to sexual behavior in the institutionalized aged. *Archives of Sexual Behavior, 11,* 11–21.

White, S. D., & DeBlassie, R. R. (1992). Adolescent sexual behavior. *Adolescence, 27,* 183–191.

Whitehead, H. (1981). The bow and the burden strap: A new look at institutionalized homosexuality in native North America. In S. Ortner & H. Whitehead (Eds.), *Sexual meanings* (pp. 80–115). Cambridge, U.K.: Cambridge University Press.

Whiting, B., & Edwards, C. P. (1988). A cross-cultural analysis of sex differences in the behavior of children aged 3 through 11. In G. Handel (Ed.), *Childhood socialization* (pp. 281–297). New York: Aldine De Gruyter.

Whiting, B. B., & Whiting, J. W. (1975). *Children of six cultures: A psycho-cultural analysis.* Cambridge, MA: Harvard University Press.

Whitley, R. J., & Roizman, B. (2001). Herpes simplex virus infections. *Lancet, 357*(9267), 1513–1519.

Wiederman, M. W. (1999). Volunteer bias in sexuality research using college student participants. *Journal of Sex Research, 36*(1), 59–66.

Wikan, U. (1977). Man becomes woman: Transsexualism in Oman as a key to gender roles. *Man, 12,* 304–391.

Wilcox, A. J., Weinberg, C. R., & Baird, D. D. (1995). Timing of sexual intercourse in relation to ovulation. Effects on the probability of conception, survival of the pregnancy, and sex of the baby. *New England Journal of Medicine, 333*(23), 1517–1521.

Wilcox, W. B., & Nock, S. L. (2006). What's love got to do with it? Equality, equity, commitment and women's marital quality. *Social Forces, 84,* 1321–1346.

Wilkinson, D., Ramjee, G., Tholandi, M., & Rutherford, G. (2002). Nonoxynol-9 for preventing vaginal acquisition of STIs by women from men. *Cochrane Database System, 4,* CD003939.

Williams, E., Lamson, N., Efem, S., Weir, S., et al. (1992). Implementation of an AIDS prevention program among prostitutes in the Cross River State of Nigeria. *AIDS, 6,* 229–230.

Williams, J. E., & Best, D. L. (1994). Cross-cultural views of women and men. In W. J. Lonner & R. Malpass (Eds.), *Psychology and culture.* Boston: Allyn & Bacon.

Williams, K., & Umberson, D. (2004). Marital status, marital transitions, and health: A gendered life course perspective. *Journal of Health and Social Behavior, 45,* 81–99.

Williams, W. L. (1986). *The spirit and the flesh: Sexual diversity in American Indian culture.* Boston: Beacon Press.

Williams, W. L. (1990). Book review: P. A. Jackson, Male homosexuality in Thailand: An interpretation of contemporary Thai sources. *Journal of Homosexuality, 19,* 126–138.

Wilson, C. A., & Davies, D. C. (2007). The control of sexual differentiation of the reproductive system and brain. *Reproduction, 133,* 331–359.

Wilson, C. (2005). Recurrent vulvovaginitis candidiasis: An overview of traditional and alternative therapies. *Advanced Nurse Practitioner, 13*(2), 24–29.

Wilson, G. D. (1987). An ethological approach to sexual deviation. In G. D. Wilson (Ed.), *Variant sexuality: Research and theory* (pp. 84–115). Baltimore: Johns Hopkins University Press.

Wilson, P. (1994). Forming a partnership between parents and sexuality educators. *SIECUS Report, 22,* 1–5.

Wilson, R. F. (2008). Keeping women in business (and the family). (Washington Lee Legal Studies Paper No. 2008-34.) Retrieved December 18, 2008, from http://ssrn.com/abstract=1115468.

Wimalawansa, S. J. (2008). Nitric oxide: New evidence for novel therapeutic indications. *Expert Opinions in Pharmacotherapy, 9,* 1935–1954.

Wind, R. (2008). Perception that teens frequently substitute oral sex for intercourse a myth. [News release]. New York: Alan Guttmacher Institute. Retrieved September 2, 2008, from http://www.guttmacher.org/media/nr/2008/05/20/index.html.

Wiseman, C., Peltzman, B., Halmi, K. A., & Sunday, S. R. (2004). Risk factors for eating disorders: Surprising similarities between middle school boys and girls. *Eating Disorders: The Journal of Treatment & Prevention, 12*(4), 315–320.

Wiseman, J. (2000). *Jay Wiseman's Erotic Bondage Handbook.* Oakland, CA: Greenery Press.

Wittchen, H. U., Becker, E., Lieb, R., & Krause, P. (2002). Prevalence, incidence and stability of premenstrual dysphoric disorder in the community. *Psychological Medicine, 32*(1), 119–132.

Wiwanitkit, V. (2005). Male rape, some notes on the laboratory investigation. *Sexuality & Disability, 23*(1), 41–46.

Wojnar, D. (2007). Miscarriage experiences of lesbian couples. *Journal of Midwifery Women's Health, 52,* 479–485.

Wolak, J., Finkelhor, D., & Mitchell, K. J. (2005). Child pornography possessors arrested in internet-related crimes: Findings from the National Juvenile Online Victimization Study. Retrieved November 7, 2005, from http://www.missingkids.com/en_US/publications/NC144.pdf.

Wolf, M. (2005, January 3). Married without children: Finding fulfillment with no kids. *Rocky Mountain News.* Retrieved August 6, 2008, from http://www.freerepublic.com/focus/f-news/1312995/posts.

Wolf, N. (1991). *The beauty myth: How images of beauty are used against women.* New York: W. Morris.

Wolfinger, N. H. (2000). Beyond the intergenerational transmission of divorce. *Journal of Family Issues, 21,* 1061–1086.

Wolin, L. D. (2003). Gender issues in advertising an oversight synthesis of research:

1970–2002. *Journal of Advertising Research, 43*(1), 111–129

Wolitski, R. J., Valdiserri, R. O., Denning, P. H., & Levine, W. C. (2001). Are we headed for a resurgence of the HIV epidemic among men who have sex with men? *American Journal of Public Health, 91*(6), 883–888.

Wolpe, J. (1958). *Psychotherapy by reciprocal inhibition.* Stanford, CA: Stanford University Press.

Wonderlich, S. A., Crosby, R. D., Mitchell, J. E., Roberts, J. A., Haseltine, B., DeMuth, G., & Thompson, K. M. (2000). Relationship of childhood sexual abuse and eating disturbance in children. *Journal of the American Academy of Child & Adolescent Psychiatry, 39*(10), 1277–1283.

Wonderlich, S. A., Crosby, R. D., Mitchell, J. E., Thompson, K. M., Redlin, J., Demuth, G., & Smyth, J. (2001). Pathways mediating sexual abuse and eating disturbances in children. *International Journal of Eating Disorders, 29*(3), 270–279.

Woo, J., Fine, P., & Goetzl, L. (2005). Abortion disclosure and the association with domestic violence. *Obstetrics & Gynecology, 105*(6), 1329–1334.

Woo, J. S., & Brotto, L.A. (2008). Age of first sexual intercourse and acculturation: Effects on adult sexual responding. *Journal of Sexual Medicine, 5,* 571–582.

Wood, E., Desmarais, S., & Gugula, S. (2002). The impact of parenting experience on gender stereotyped toy play of children. *Sex Roles, 47*(1–2), 39–49.

Wood, J. (1999). Gendered lives: Communication, gender, and culture. Belmont, CA: Wadsworth.

Wood, K. (2005). Masturbation as a means of achieving sexual health. *Culture, Health & Sexuality, 7*(2), 182–184.

Wood, P. (2008). What your eyes say about you. *Career World, 36,* 5–8.

Woolf, L. M. (2002). Gay and lesbian aging. *SIECUS Report, 30*(2), 16–21.

Wooltorton, E. (2006). Visual loss with erectile dysfunction medications. *Canadian Medical Association Journal, 175,* 355.

World Health Organization. (2001a). Sex and drugs fuel simmering AIDS crisis in Asia and Pacific. *Who News.* Retrieved October 8, 2008, from http://whqlibdoc.who.int/bulletin/2001/issue10/79(10)news_who.pdf.

World Health Organization. (2001b). Technical consultation on nonoxynol-9. Retrieved October 9, 2001, from http://www.conrad.org.

World Health Organization. (2008). *Eliminating female genital mutilation: An interagency statement.* Retrieved March 22, 2008, from http://data.unaids.org/pub/BaseDocument/2008/20080227_interagencystatement_eliminating_fgm_en.pdf.

Wright, K. (1994). The sniff of legend—human pheromones. Chemical sex attractants? A sixth sense organ in the nose? What are we animals? *Discover, 15*(4), 60.

Wright, L., Mulick, P., & Kincaid, S. (2006). Fear of and discrimination against bisexuals, homosexuals, and individuals with AIDS. *Journal of Bisexuality, 6,* 71–84.

Wright, T., Huh, W., Monk, B., Smith, J., Ault, K., & Herzog, T. (2008). Age considerations when vaccinating against HPV. *Gynecological Oncology, 109*(Suppl. 2), S40–S47.

Wright, V. C., Chang, J., Jeng, G., & Macaluso, M. (2008). Assisted reproductive technology surveillance—United States. *Morbidity and Mortality Weekly Report, 57,* 1–23.

Wuthnow, R. (1998). Islam. In *Encyclopedia of politics and religion* (pp. 383–393). Washington, DC: Congressional Quarterly Books.

Wyatt, G. (1998). *Stolen women: Reclaiming our sexuality, taking back our lives.* New York: Wiley.

Wyatt, K. (2008, May 13). Anonymous rape tests are going nationwide. *ABC News.* Retrieved October 7, 2008, from http://abcnews.go.com/Health/Story?id=4847901&page=1.

Wylie, K. R., & Ralph, D. (2005). Premature ejaculation: The current literature. *Current Opinions in Urology, 15*(6), 393–398.

Wysoczanski, M., Rachko, M., & Bergmann, S. R. (2008, April 2). Acute myocardial-infarction in a young man using anabolic-steroids. *Angiology 59*(3), 376–378.

Xu, F., Markowitz, L. E., Sternberg, M. R., & Aral, S. O. (2007). Prevalence of circumcision and herpes simplex virus type 2 infection in men in the United States: the National Health and Nutrition Examination Survey (NHANES), 1999–2004. *Sexually Transmitted Diseases, 34,* 479–484.

Xu, F., Sternberg, M., Kottiri, B., McQuillan, G., Lee, F., Nahmias, A., Berman, S., & Markowitz, L. E. (2006). Trends in herpes simplex virus type 1 and type 2 seroprevalence in the U.S. *Journal of the American Medical Association, 296,* 964–973.

Yalom, M. (1998). *History of the breast.* New York: Ballantine.

Yamawaki, N. (2007). Differences between Japanese and American college students in giving advice about help seeking to rape victims. *Journal of Social Psychology, 147,* 511–530.

Yamawaki, N., & Tschanz, B. T. (2005). Rape perception differences between Japanese and American college students: On the mediating influence of gender role traditionality. *Sex Roles, 52*(5–6), 379–392.

Yancey, G. (2007). Homogamy over the net: Using internet advertisements to discover who interracially dates. *Journal of Social and Personal Relationships, 24,* 913–930.

Yassin, A. A., Saad, F. (2008). Testosterone and sexual dysfunction. *Journal of Andrology, 29*(6), Epub ahead of print. Retrieved October 29, 2008, from http://www.andrologyjournal.org/cgi/content/abstract/29/6/593.

Yates, P., Hucker, S., & Ingston, D. (2008). Sexual Sadism: Psychopathology and Theory. In D. Laws & W. O'Donohue (Eds.), *Sexual deviance: Theory, assessment and treatment* (2nd ed., pp. 213–230). New York: Guilford Press.

Yesalis, C. E., & Bahrke, M. S. (2000). Doping among adolescent athletes. *Best Practice & Research Clinical Endocrinology & Metabolism, 14*(1), 25–35.

Yllo, K., & Finkelhor, D. (1985). Marital rape. In A. W. Burgess (Ed.), *Rape and sexual assault* (pp. 146–158). New York: Garland.

Yoder, V. C., Virden, T. B., & Amin, K. (2005). Internet pornography and loneliness: An association? *Sexual Addiction & Compulsivity, 12*(1), 19–44.

Yonkers, K. A. (1999). Medical management of premenstrual dysphoric disorder. *Journal of Gender-Specific Medicine, 2*(3), 55–60.

Young, K. A., Liu, Y., & Wang, Z. (2008, March 2). The neurobiology of social attachment: A comparative approach to behavioral, neuroanatomical, and neurochemical studies. *Comparative Biochemistry and Physiology: Toxicology and Pharmacology.* Retrieved October 3, 2008, from http://www.ncbi.nlm.nih.gov/pubmed/18417423?ordinalpos=1&itool=EntrezSystem2.PEntrez.Pubmed.Pubmed_ResultsPanel.Pubmed_RVDocSum.

Young, K. S., Griffin-Shelley, E., Cooper, A., O'Mara, J., & Buchanan, J. (2000). Online infidelity. In A. Cooper (Ed.), *Cybersex: The dark side of the force* (pp. 59–74). Philadelphia, PA: Brunner Routledge.

Young, L. J., & Wang, Z. (2004). The neurobiology of pair bonding. *Nature, 7,* 1048–1054.

Youssry, M., Ozmen, B., Zohni, K., Diedrich, K., & Al-Hasani, S. (2008). Current aspects of blastocyst cryopreservation. *Re-*

productive *Biomedicine Online, 16,* 311–320.

Yu, E., & Liu, J. (2007, December 5). Environmental impacts of divorce. *Proceedings of the National Academy of Sciences of the United States of America.* Retrieved December 7, 2008, from http://www.pnas.org/cgi/content/abstract/0707267104v1.

Zacharias, P. (2005). Snap, crackle and profit—the story behind a cereal empire. *The Detroit News.* Retrieved February 5, 2005, from http://info.detnews.com/history/story/index.cfm?id=146&category=business.

Zacur, H. A., Hedon, B., Mansourt, D., Shangold, G. A., Fisher, A. C., & Creasy, G. W. (2002). Integrated summary of Ortho Evra contraceptive patch adhesion in varied climates and conditions. *Fertility and Sterility, 77* (2 Suppl. 2), 532–535.

Zak, A., Collins, C., & Harper, L. (1998). Self-reported control over decision-making and its relationship to intimate relationships. *Psychological Reports, 82*(2), 560–562.

Zanetti-Dallenbach, R. A., Krause, E. M., Lapaire, O., Gueth, U., Holzgreve, W. Wight, E. (2008). Impact of hormone replacement therapy on the histologic subtype of breast cancer. Epub retrieved on March 18, 2008, from http://www.ncbi.nlm.nih.gov/pubmed/

18335229?ordinalpos=1&itool=EntrezSystem2.PEntrez.Pubmed.Pubmed_ResultsPanel.Pubmed_RVDocSum.

Zaslow, J. (2007, August 23). Are we teaching our kids to be fearful of men? *Wall Street Journal.* Retrieved June 10, 2008, from http://online.wsj.com/public/article/SB118782905698506010.html.

Zheng, W., & Hart, R. (2002). The effects of marital and nonmarital union transition on health. *Journal of Marriage and Family, 64*(2), 420–433.

Zieman, M., Guillebaud, J., Weisberg, E., Shangold, G., Fisher, A., & Creasy, G. (2002). Contraceptive efficacy and cycle control with the Ortho Evra transdermal system: The analysis of pooled data. *Fertility and Sterility, 77,* S13–18.

Zimmer-Gembeck, M., & Petherick, J. (2006). Intimacy dating goals and relationship satisfaction during adolescence and emerging adulthood: Identity formation, age and sex as moderators. *International Journal of Behavioral Development, 30,* 167–177.

Zimmer-Gembeck, M. J., & Helfand, M. (2008). Ten years of longitudinal research on U.S. adolescent sexual behavior: Developmental correlates of sexual intercourse, and the importance of age, gender and ethnic background. *Developmental Review, 28,* 153–224.

Zimmerman, F., Christakis, D., & Meltzoff, A. (2007). Television and DVD/Video viewing in children younger than 2 years. *Archives of Pediatrics and Adolescent Medicine, 161,* 473–479.

Zinaman, M. J., Clegg, E. D., Brown, C. C., O'Connor, J., & Selevan, S. G. (1996). Estimates of human fertility and pregnancy loss. *Journal of Fertility and Sterility, 65*(3), 503–509.

Zolese, G., & Blacker, C. V. R. (1992). The psychological complications of therapeutic abortion. *British Journal of Psychiatry, 160,* 742–749.

Zucker, K. J. (1990). Psychosocial and erotic development in cross-gender identified children. *Canadian Journal of Psychiatry, 35,* 487–495.

Zulu, D. (2007). Will sex with a virgin cure HIV/AIDS? *Why Zambian children are being defiled.* The WIP. Retrieved September 19, 2008, from http://www.thewip.net/contributors/2007/07/will_sex_with_a_virgin_cure_hi.html.

Zurbriggen, E. L., & Yost, M. R. (2004). Power, desire, and pleasure in sexual fantasies. *Journal of Sex Research, 41*(3), 288–300.

Zverina, J. (2004). Czech Republic. In R. T. Francoeur & R. J. Noonan (Eds.), *The Continuum international encyclopedia of sexuality* (pp. 320–328). New York/London: Continuum International.

NAME INDEX

SUBJECT INDEX

Bold entries and page references indicate definitions.

premenstrual syndrome (PMS), 132
prenatal development, 85–92
prenatal sex differentiation syndromes, 91
prenuptial agreement, 227
prepuce, 118
presidential commissions, 520
priapism, 158, 401
primary amenorrhea, 131
primary sexual dysfunction, 391
primary voyeurism, 464
prison rape, 493–494
Prison Rape Elimination Act, 493
pro-choice supporter, 378
pro-life supporter, 378
probability sampling, 43
prodromal phase, 433
progesterone, 88, 90
progestin-only birth control method, 366
prolactin, 90, 126
prostaglandin, 381
prostate cancer, 161–162, 411
prostate gland, 152
prostate-specific antigen (PSA), 162
prostatectomy, 411
prosthesis implantation, 401
prostitution
  adolescent, 529–530
  AIDS, 532
  client, 530–531
  defined, 524
  female, 525–538
  law, and, 531
  life after, 533
  male, 528–529
  outside the U.S., 533–535
  pimp, 530
  sociological aspects, 525
  STIs, 532
  types, 527–528
  who becomes one, 525
Protestant Reformation, 14
prurient, 519
PSA, 162
pseudocyesis, 314
pseudofamily, 525
pseudohermaphrodite, 89
psychoanalysis, 31
psychoanalytic theory, 30–31
psychogenic, 400
Psychopathia Sexualis (Kaan), 36
psychosexual develop-ment, 31
psychotropic medications, 390
PT-141, 398
puberty, 127–128, 155
pubic hair, 119
pubic lice, 423
pubococcygeus muscle, 406
pudendum, 116
punishment concept, 420
Puritans, 18

quadriplegia, 412
quadruped, 4
queer theory, 35–36
question statement, 64
questionnaire, 49
quid pro quo harassment, 503

radial prostatectomy, 162
radiation, 162
radical mastectomy, 138
radioimmunoassay (RIA) blood test, 315
random sample, 44
rape, 480
  age of consent, 481
  alcohol, 487–488
  athletes, 488–489
  avoidance strategies, 495
  bisexuals, 491
  characteristics of rapists, 481–482
  college campus, 487
  cross-cultural view, 485–486
  date-rape drugs, 483
  disease model, 482
  ethnic differences, 485
  evolutionary theory, 485
  feminist theory, 483–484
  fraternities, 488
  gender differences, 485
  lesbians, 491
  marital, 491
  men, of, 493–494
  older women, 492
  partner's reaction, 492
  prison rape, 493–494
  prostitutes, 492
  rape trauma syndrome, 489–490
  reporting, 494–495
  silent rape reaction, 491
  sociological theory, 484
  statistics, 480–481
  treating the rapist, 495
  victim precipitation theory, 483
  what to do if raped, 484
  women with disabilities, 492
rape crisis center, 488
rape trauma syndrome (RTS), 489–490
Rapex, 486
rapist psychopathology, 482
Reality Vaginal Pouch, 352
rear-entry position, 270
recidivism, 467
rectal gonorrhea, 426
Reddy, 352
refractory stage, 257
reliability, 48, 53
Renaissance, 14
reparative therapy, 286
repression, 31
research. See sex research
resolution, 252, 256, 257
respiratory illnesses, 411
retarded ejaculation, 402, 405

retrograde ejaculation, 402, 405
revascularization, 401
reverse transcriptase, 438
Rh incompatibility, 332
RhoGAM, 332
rhythm method, 371
rimming, 264, 528
RISUG, 377
Roe v. Wade, 378
role repertoire, 176
romantic love, 168
roseta effect, 166
RTS, 489–490

sadism, 460–462
sadomasochism, 460–462
safe sex, 275
safer sex, 275
safer-sex behaviors, 274, 275
same-sex divorce, 240
same-sex parenting, 238
same-sex relationships, 235–238. *See also* homosexuals
same-sex sexual techniques, 271–272
samples of convenience, 51
satiation therapy, 470, 471
satyriasis, 472
scabies, 423–424
scatolophilia, 463
scatophagia, 461
schema, 98
schizophrenia, 413
scopophilia, 464
scrotoplasty, 104
scrotum, 150
Seasonale, 360
Seasonique, 360
Second Sex, The (de Beauvoir), 23
second-trimester surgical abortion, 380
secondary amenorrhea, 131
secondary sexual characteristics, 89
secondary sexual dysfunction, 391
secure infants, 175
self-actualization, 33
self-disclosure, 72
self-love, 185
semen, 146
semenarche, 196
seminal vesicles, 152
seminiferous tubules, 151
semirigid rod, 401
seniors. See older adults
sensate focus, 400
sequential bisexuality, 303
sequential homosexuality, 291
serial cohabitation, 224
serial divorce, 243
Sex and the City, 511
sex chromosome, 85
sex chromosome disorders, 88–89
sex flush, 254

sex reassignment surgery (SRS), 102
sex research. *See also* theories about sexuality
  Bell/Weinberg, 46
  Bloch, 39
  cross-cultural research, 55
  Davis, 41
  early research, 36–37
  Ellis, 41
  ethical issues, 50
  future directions, 56
  global research, 51–52
  Hirschfeld, 40
  homosexuality, 45–46
  Hooker, 45
  Hunt, 44
  Internet-based research, 54
  Janus Report, 46
  Kinsey, 42–44
  Krafft-Ebing, 40
  Masters & Johnson, 44–45
  methods, 48–50
  Moll, 40
  Mosher, 41
  NHSLS, 46–47
  politics, 38–39
  reliability, 53
  sampling problems, 51–53
  seniors, 47–48
  teens, 47
  volunteer bias, 50–51
sex therapy, 398
sex typing, 98
sexologist, 2, 38
sexology, 22, 34
sexual abuse of children
  characteristics of abusers, 499–500
  development of abuser, 499–500
  effect on children, 497
  incidence, 497
  prevention, 500
  psychological/emotional reactions, 498
  treatment, 500
  victims, 497
sexual addiction, 472–474
sexual arousal and response, 248–276
  ethnicity, 250–252
  foreplay, 263–264
  hormones/neurotransmitters, 250
  manual sex, 264
  masturbation, 261–263
  models of sexual response, 252–259
  older adults, 273–274
  oral sex, 265–266
  safer-sex behaviors, 274, 275
  same-sex sexual techniques, 271–272
  sexual fantasy, 260–261

sexual intercourse, 266–271
sexual arousal disorder, 392, 397–401
sexual assault, 480
sexual aversion, 394
sexual aversion disorder, 392, 396
Sexual Behavior (Hunt), 44
sexual desire disorders, 394–396
sexual dysfunction, 390–407
  categorization, 391
  dyspareunia, 407
  ejaculatory dysfunctions, 404–406
  female orgasmic disorder, 403
  female sexual arousal disorder, 397–399
  hypoactive sexual desire, 394–395
  male erectile disorder, 399–401
  male orgasmic disorder, 404
  orgasmic disorder, 402–406
  overview, 392
  pain disorder, 406–407
  physical factors, 390–391
  premature ejaculation, 404–405
  psychological factors, 390
  sex therapy, 398
  sexual arousal disorders, 397–401
  sexual aversion disorder, 396
  sexual desire disorders, 394–396
  treatment, 393
  vaginismus, 406–407
  vulvodynia, 407
  women, 391
sexual expression. *See* varieties of sexual expression
sexual fantasy, 260–261
sexual harassment, 503–504
sexual images, 510
  advertising, 516–518
  development of pornography, 510
  erotic literature, 511–512
  gender stereotypes on TV and film, 513–514
  historical overview, 510
  minority sexuality, 513
  other media, 518
  pornography. *See* pornography
  sexualization of the media, 515–516
  TV and film, 512–516
  virtual reality, 518
sexual intercourse, 266
  anal intercourse, 270–271
  female-on-top, 269–270
  male-on-top, 267–269